Interdisciplinary Contributions to Archaeology

Series Editor
Jelmer Eerkens, University of California, Davis, CA, USA

Editorial Board Members
Canan Çakırlar, University of Groningen, Groningen, The Netherlands
Fumie Iizuka, University of California, Merced, CA, USA
Krish Seetah, Stanford University, Stanford, CA, USA
Nuria Sugranes, Instituto de Evolución, Ecología Histórica y Ambiente
San Rafael, Mendoza, Argentina
Shannon Tushingham, Washington State University, Pullman, WA, USA
Chris Wilson, Flinders University, Bedford Park, Australia

Archaeology stands alone among the sciences in its attempt to enlighten us about the entire record of humankind. To cover such a broad range of time and space, archaeologists must ensure that their findings are integrated into broader spheres of scientific knowledge. The IDCA series aims to highlight the collaborative and interdisciplinary nature of contemporary archaeological research.

Topics the series has covered include:

- Paleoecology
- Archaeological Landscapes
- Statistical Approaches
- Laboratory Methods
- Human Biological and Cultural Evolution
- Human Nutrition
- Emergence of Agriculture and Pastoralism

For a copy of the proposal form, please contact Christi Lue (christi.lue@springer. com). Initial proposals can be sent to the Series Editor, Jelmer Eerkens (jweerkens@ ucdavis.edu). Proposals should include:

- A short synopsis of the work or the introduction chapter
- The proposed Table of Contents
- The CV of the lead author(s)
- If available: one sample chapter

We aim to make a first decision within 1 month of submission. In case of a positive first decision the work will be provisionally contracted: the final decision about publication will depend upon the result of the anonymous peer review of the complete manuscript. We aim to have the complete work peer-reviewed within 3 months of submission.

This book series is indexed in SCOPUS.

For more information, please contact the Series Editor at (jweerkens@ ucdavis.edu).

Erez Ben-Yosef • Ian W. N. Jones
Editors

"And in Length of Days Understanding" (Job 12:12)

Essays on Archaeology in the Eastern Mediterranean and Beyond in Honor of Thomas E. Levy

Volume 2

Editors
Erez Ben-Yosef (iD)
Department of Archaeology and Ancient
Near Eastern Cultures
Tel Aviv University
Tel Aviv, Israel

Ian W. N. Jones (iD)
Department of Anthropology
University of California, San Diego
La Jolla, CA, USA

ISSN 1568-2722   ISSN 2730-6984   (electronic)
Interdisciplinary Contributions to Archaeology
ISBN 978-3-031-27329-2   ISBN 978-3-031-27330-8   (eBook)
https://doi.org/10.1007/978-3-031-27330-8

© The Editor(s) (if applicable) and The Author(s), under exclusive license to Springer Nature
Switzerland AG 2023, corrected publication 2023
This work is subject to copyright. All rights are solely and exclusively licensed by the Publisher, whether
the whole or part of the material is concerned, specifically the rights of translation, reprinting, reuse of
illustrations, recitation, broadcasting, reproduction on microfilms or in any other physical way, and
transmission or information storage and retrieval, electronic adaptation, computer software, or by similar
or dissimilar methodology now known or hereafter developed.
The use of general descriptive names, registered names, trademarks, service marks, etc. in this publication
does not imply, even in the absence of a specific statement, that such names are exempt from the relevant
protective laws and regulations and therefore free for general use.
The publisher, the authors, and the editors are safe to assume that the advice and information in this book
are believed to be true and accurate at the date of publication. Neither the publisher nor the authors or the
editors give a warranty, expressed or implied, with respect to the material contained herein or for any
errors or omissions that may have been made. The publisher remains neutral with regard to jurisdictional
claims in published maps and institutional affiliations.

Cover illustration: Thomas E. Levy exploring the region of al-Quseir, an Iron Age Edomite stronghold in
southern Jordan (photo by Erez Ben-Yosef, March 2009)

This Springer imprint is published by the registered company Springer Nature Switzerland AG
The registered company address is: Gewerbestrasse 11, 6330 Cham, Switzerland

Introduction: Thomas E. Levy and Archaeology in the Twenty-First Century

No; the two kinds of people on earth I mean,
Are the people who lift, and the people who lean.

— Ella Wheeler Wilcox, *Custer and Other Poems* (1896)

Tom Levy's distinguished career in archaeology is a captivating story of perseverance and significance. He embodies the essence of what Wheeler Wilcox referred to as a "lifter", particularly in his contributions to his students, colleagues, and the scholarly community as a whole.[1] Since earning his PhD from the University of Sheffield in 1981, Tom has remained actively involved in archaeological research, embracing various aspects of the discipline. From leading challenging archaeological expeditions in Israel, Jordan, and Greece to utilizing archaeological sciences and cyber-archaeology for artifact analysis and archaeological information curation, Tom has displayed unwavering dedication. His work consistently demonstrates a deep appreciation for the research community and the responsibilities it entails.

Throughout his illustrious career, Tom has served as a mentor to numerous graduate students, including the editors of this book,[2] and postgraduate researchers. Additionally, he has selflessly assisted colleagues in advancing their own research

---

[1] According to a social network analysis by Steven Edwards of the University of Toronto, based on publications of the American Society of Overseas (previously Schools of Oriental) Research, Tom was found to be "the most connected scholar in the field" (https://socialsciences.ucsd.edu/news/newsletter/2018-tom-levy-most-connected-ASOR-scholar.html; the study was presented at the organization's 2018 Annual Meeting). This observation is yet another testimony to Tom's pivotal role within the research community, often serving as a catalyst to promote collaborations and research.

[2] One of us (EB-Y) commenced working with Tom while still a graduate student at the Hebrew University. This was part of a study focused on the magnetic properties of ancient copper slag, serving as an initial step in the ongoing endeavor to establish a comprehensive reference database for archaeomagnetic dating in the Levant. After a short meeting at the Hebrew Union College in Jerusalem, Tom invited me to join his upcoming expedition to Wadi Faynan, and that is how I found myself trekking through the Jordanian desert in the summer of 2004, looking for a tent camp somewhere on the outskirts of the Bedouin village of Quraiqira. Because of some difficulties descending the cliffs of the Edomite Plateau coming from the village of Shobak, I arrived at the

endeavors. Tom's contagious enthusiasm for archaeology, combined with his willingness to share research access, has had a profound and enduring impact on countless scholars in the field. This festschrift celebrating Tom's remarkable achievements serves as a testament to the magnitude of his influence.

Over 140 of Tom's friends and colleagues have contributed to this book, offering insights that align with his diverse research interests. These range from the late prehistory of the southern Levant to cyber-archaeology and the archaeological sciences. The resulting publication comprises two voluminous books (82 chapters) that make a significant contribution to the study of archaeology in the Eastern Mediterranean and beyond. These volumes also reflect the cutting-edge nature of archaeology in the early twenty-first century, incorporating advancements in methods and theory, many of which Tom has played a role in developing.

For instance, Tom's expedition to Wadi Faynan, conducted in collaboration with Mohammad Najjar, was among the first in the southern Levant to fully embrace digitized recording methods. This pioneering project employed geographic information systems (GIS) to generate daily top plans and final maps. Visitors to the expedition camp in the late 1990s witnessed the practical application of the project's visionary approach. While the team slept in electricity-free tents and showered with cold water, data processing occurred in a nearby Bedouin village. There, a collection of laptops, state-of-the-art photography and documentation instruments, and cutting-edge technology were deployed in a rented house. This expedition, spanning the transition into the third millennium, served as a testing ground for other methodologies that would become integral to twenty-first-century archaeology, including 3D LiDAR documentation, balloon photography, drone-based documentation, and more.

The book covers various themes, including the late prehistory of the southern Levant, biblical archaeology, Wadi Faynan, archaeometallurgy, marine archaeology, cyber-archaeology, archaeological sciences, and anthropological archaeology.

---

camp well past midnight, prompting the Bedouin guard to rouse Tom from his sleep to inquire about the unexpected late-night visitor. During this visit, Tom, his wife Alina, and I spent several days together, exploring various copper smelting sites in this wild and beautiful region. This, for me, was an important benchmark in the long journey of developing a career in research and academia. Tom's mentorship, which started then in the field, amidst millennia-old mounds of industrial waste, has in fact never ceased, and I am most grateful to him for his guidance and friendship. I am also thankful for our mutual love for the desert and archaeology, which brought us together, about 20 years ago. The other (IWNJ) began working with Tom at the beginning of my graduate studies at UC San Diego in 2008. On realizing that my prior excavation experience could be expressed in days, rather than weeks or months, Tom set me up to spend six months of 2009 on various archaeological projects in Israel and Jordan, including his excavations at Khirbat en-Nahas. Although there were occasional setbacks—including Tom having to send a rescue team for Kyle Knabb and myself when the old Land Rover we had been tasked with retrieving from the CBRL in Amman broke down at the Dead Sea, luckily within walking distance of the Mövenpick ice cream counter—this experience established my lasting love of archaeological fieldwork, and of the southern Levant, of course. It was around the same time that Tom encouraged me to consider writing my MA thesis on a small, Islamic period copper smelting site near KEN called Khirbat Nuqayb al-Asaymir, the excavation of which eventually formed the core of my doctoral research. These were pivotal moments in my career, and at this earliest stage of our collaboration, Tom set me down a path that I continue to explore, with his continued mentorship and encouragement, today.

These thematic sections trace the trajectory of Tom's extensive career, from its early days to his most recent endeavors. Although Tom retired from his longstanding academic home at the University of California San Diego in the summer of 2022 and will celebrate his 70th birthday with the publication of this book (late 2023), these milestones merely mark chapters in a continuous journey of exploration. The years ahead undoubtedly hold tremendous potential as Tom leverages his wealth of experience, echoing the sentiment expressed in the Book of Job (12:12, *NKJV*): "Wisdom is with aged men, and with length of days, understanding".

Tom Levy in Wadi Faynan, fall of 2006. (Photo courtesy of Erez Ben-Yosef)

Volume 1: The Southern Levant from Late Prehistory to Biblical Times

This volume is devoted to new research on the two main periods that have been the focus of Tom's archaeological research: late prehistory (from the Neolithic period to the Early Bronze Age) and the Biblical periods (primarily the Iron Age). Tom's research trajectory began in late prehistory with his work on the Late Chalcolithic period in Israel at Shiqmim, Gilat, Abu Hof, and other sites in the northern Negev desert, and he further developed this research when he began working in the Faynan region of Jordan in the late 1990s with excavations at the Pre-Pottery Neolithic site of Tall Tifdan, the Early Bronze Age I site of Wadi Fidan 4, and the EB III–IV site of Khirbat Hamra Ifdan, among others. In the 2000s, his work expanded into the Iron Age with his extensive excavations at the large copper smelting center of Khirbat en-Nahas and smaller smelting sites like Khirbat al-Jariya. While ongoing research on these sites in Jordan is the focus of Part III in Volume 2, Volume 1 instead demonstrates the scope of Tom's influence on research into these periods throughout the southern Levant.

Part I focuses on the late prehistoric archaeology of the southern Levant. It begins with a personal reflection by Simmons on his excavations at the Neolithic site of Ghwair I in the eastern part of the Faynan region at the same time Tom was leading excavations in the western part of the region. Several chapters present regional syntheses of recent research on late prehistory (Finlayson, who also conducted substantial research in Faynan, and Flohr on the Neolithic in the Jordanian *badia*, Rollefson on the Late Neolithic of the eastern *badia*, Shalem and Getzov on the Late Chalcolithic Galilee, and Garfinkel on the Late Chalcolithic Elah Valley), while several others present the results of in-depth research into specific sites (Shooval and colleagues on Tel 'Ein Jezreel, Davidovitch on 'En Gedi and Nahal Mishmar). Others take a more thematic approach, focusing on burials, cemeteries, and analysis of human remains (Milevski; Smith and colleagues; Najjar; Shafiq); botanical (Langgut) and faunal (Namdar and Sapir-Hen; Greenfield and Beller on Shiqmim) remains; specific aspects of material culture (Ilan and Rowan; Rosenberg and colleagues; Freikman and colleagues; Braun; Paz and Walzer); and overarching themes such as urbanism and increasing social complexity (Abadi-Reiss; Getzov and Milevski).

Part II follows Tom's shift in research focus, from late prehistory into the Iron Age and biblical archaeology. It commences with several methodological and theoretical reflections on the present state of biblical archaeology, particularly in light of the "architectural bias" (Ben-Yosef 2019, *Vetus Testamentum* 69(3)), a novel understanding of the significance of nomads during this transformative era, as emphasized by Levy's research in Edom. These reflections include Ben-Yosef and Thomas' extended critique of how social complexity has been deduced from the archaeological record in the Levant, presenting the case for a radical shift in methodology; Malena's examination of the challenges posed by the Iron Age as a historical period in regions with limited or absent written sources; and Thomas' investigation into the implications of the nomenclature employed for Iron Age archaeology in the Levant.

Several contributions take a wide view, focusing on specific themes in the Late Bronze and Iron Age archaeology of the Levant (Maeir; Wolff; Halpern) and Egypt (Bányai; Schneider), while others present thematic regional syntheses (Ben Dor Evian and Martin on Philistine burials; Hardin on social transformation in the Hesi region; Gadot and colleagues on interactions between Jerusalem and Samaria; Gibson and colleagues on the economy of the Buqei'a Plateau; Daviau on decorated Moabite ceramics). Many of the contributions explore themes central to Tom's research—such as chronology and dating methods (radiocarbon dating, archaeomagnetic dating), trade and the economy, religion, and the relationship between archaeology and historical texts—through new analyses of the material culture of specific sites (Ben-Shlomo; Maher and Nahshoni; Shai; Ortiz; Finkelstein; Vaknin and colleagues; Bruins; Roddy and colleagues; Younker; Bárta; and Fischer). Noteworthy is the wide range of scholars, spanning various—and at times opposing—approaches to biblical archaeology. This is a testimony to Tom's extensive impact, and his role in promoting a wider discussion and bridging gaps.

Volume 2: From Archaeological Sciences to Archaeological Theory

This volume celebrates Tom's substantial work in the Wadi Faynan region of southern Jordan, his contributions to the development of several important subdisciplines of archaeology, notably archaeometallurgy, marine archaeology, cyber-archaeology, and archaeological sciences, and the impacts these have had on anthropological archaeology as a field.

Part III is focused on the Faynan copper ore district of southern Jordan, where from 1997 to 2015 Tom conducted research on the role of copper mining and metallurgy in sociopolitical change as co-director of the UC San Diego Edom Lowlands Regional Archaeology Project (ELRAP). This section contains contributions from many of Tom's current and former students and collaborators at UCSD, as well as colleagues inspired by Tom's research to explore Faynan's connections to the southern Levant and other parts of West Asia. Gidding opens this section with an analysis of changes in the organization of copper production during the Early Bronze Age based on Levy's excavations at Khirbat Hamra Ifdan, which is followed by several contributions (Howland and Liss, Stroth and colleagues, and Beherec) using Levy's excavations at Khirbat en-Nahas and Khirbat al-Jariya to explore several aspects of Iron Age copper production. This is followed by several chapters (Yahalom-Mack and colleagues, Klassen and Danielson, and Ben-David) that consider the implications of Levy's work in Faynan for our understanding of the copper trade during the Iron Age and later periods. Finally, Jones explores the potential religious and socioeconomic implications of a surprising sherd found during Levy's excavations at Khirbat Faynan (Biblical Punon and Roman Phaino).

Part IV expands on Part III, recognizing the contributions of Tom's early work on Chalcolithic copper metallurgy in the Negev and later work with ELRAP in southern Jordan to wider discussions in archaeometallurgy. The contributions in this volume expand many of the conversations started by Tom, notably his focus on the social, economic, and political impacts of metallurgy, to other periods and regions of the world. Erel considers how lead concentrations in human remains can be used to understand fluctuations in the intensity of lead production, comparing individuals buried in Rome and the Levant. Eshel and colleagues address the question of the source of silver and lead circulating in the Levant during the Hellenistic period. Several contributions (Knapp, Kassianidou, and Papasavvas) consider questions related to the archaeometallurgy of Bronze Age Cyprus, at scales ranging from regional to microscopic. Lehner and colleagues engage Levy's work through a comparative study of Iron Age copper production in southeast Arabia. Schultze and Stanish, likewise, provide a comparative case study in copper production, which takes the form of a synthetic overview of the development of copper metallurgy in the Andes. Finally, Eliyahu-Behar explores the potential of experimental archaeo-metallurgy for understanding Levantine iron production.

In recent years, Tom's expansive scholarly interests have taken him from the desert to the Mediterranean coast. In **Part V**, Tom's recent work in marine archaeology is celebrated by scholars working in the eastern Mediterranean and beyond. Many of the contributions in this section approach marine archaeology from the perspective of theoretical and methodological approaches Tom developed over the course of his career, including craft production and spatial analysis. Tsiafaki bridges the gap between this section and Part IV by exploring the evidence for crafting activities at an Archaic period harbor site in northern Greece. Shtienberg and Cantu use coring to address the question of a possible inland anchorage at Tel Dor, Israel, the site of Levy's recent research. Demesticha and Polidorou consider the interpretation of "stray" finds in harbors through an analysis of a "stray" pottery assemblage found off the southeastern coast of Cyprus. Gambash considers the implications of changes in shipbuilding technologies in the southern Levant during the first millennium CE. Finally, Byrd and Brandy provide a thematic transition between this and the next section by using Geographic Information Systems (GIS) to explore the choices made by Indigenous groups living around what is today the San Francisco Bay between maritime and overland transport routes.

Part VI includes contributions on the topics of cyber-archaeology, an exciting field that Tom often defines as "the marriage of archaeology, computer science, engineering, and the natural sciences", and archaeological sciences. Throughout his career, Tom made many important contributions to these fields, beginning with his early adoption of digital recording technologies in the field for his excavations in Jordan in the late 1990s and continuing to today through experimentation with new developments in underwater photogrammetry and scanning. The contributions in this chapter celebrate this ongoing legacy and showcase the latest developments in these dynamic, diverse, and constantly evolving fields, with chapters exploring topics ranging from archaeogaming and virtual storytelling to erosion modeling and archaeomagnetism. Avni and colleagues address this at a large scale through a discussion of the system used by the Israel Antiquities Authority (IAA) to digitize and publish the data from the hundreds of excavations and surveys it conducts. Ridder and colleagues return to the theme of GIS modeling, in this case to analyze the erosion and deposition of sediments at a Bronze Age site in central Cyprus. Pavlidis bridges the gap between past, present, and future by exploring both present 3D-documentation technologies and possible future uses of Artificial Intelligence (AI) in archaeology. Smith considers the potential of video game technologies to allow archaeologists to visualize digitized versions of excavations in real time. Vincent considers the potential of digital documentation to help recover heritage post-conflict, using work conducted at the Mosul Cultural Museum as a case study, while Richard and Clark consider the potential of technology to aid in community archaeology during periods when travel is difficult, using their own work conducted early in the Covid-19 pandemic as a test case. Sobieralski engages Levy's work on both cyber-archaeology and copper production through the creation of a 3D game allowing users to simulate the experience of smelting copper firsthand. Tauxe and colleagues explore the same relationship with a very different technology, instead exploring archaeomagnetic research conducted on archaeological materials, including copper slag from Levy's excavations in Faynan.

The final part of the book, **Part VII**, expands the focus of the volume to anthropological archaeology as a whole. It begins with chapters exploring theoretical issues Tom addressed throughout his career, including archaeological interpretation, pragmatism (a body of theory that formed the basis of a volume Tom edited in 2010), state formation, ancient economies, and ethnic identity. It ends with several chapters exploring the recent historical archaeology and history of archaeology in the southern Levant. Greenberg commences by addressing theory directly, considering the questions of how archaeological interpretation happens and, at some level, what archaeology is. Dever builds on Levy's explorations of pragmatism in the last decade to consider the limitations and "ends" of archaeological theory. LaBianca returns to a theme that loomed large not only in Tom's work, but twentieth century anthropological archaeology more generally: the issue of state formation, in this case focusing on the southern Levant. Braswell expands this into the political-economic dimension by considering markets and the origins of money in early states. Ji addresses a related theme by considering the expansion of the Nabataean kingdom into central Jordan from the third century BCE to the first century CE. Arbel explores the question of religious imagery and religious identification, considering a surprising use of the hexagram symbol in Late Ottoman period Jaffa. Killebrew and Skinner use a combination of archival and archaeological research to investigate contradictory claims about Napoleon's presence (or not) at the site of Tel 'Akko. Finally, Cline uses archival research to investigate a mysterious potential conflict between William F. Albright and the University of Chicago excavations at Megiddo, providing a unique look into many key archaeological figures of the early twentieth century.

It would be difficult—indeed, perhaps impossible—for any book to fully encompass the breadth of Tom's contributions to archaeology over his long and distinguished career. Nonetheless, the wide scope of topics covered by these two volumes demonstrate the extensive impact Tom has had on the archaeology of the Eastern Mediterranean and beyond, in addition to providing a useful introduction to the current state-of-the-art in these subfields. We hope Tom will find it a fitting tribute.

Acknowledgments

This book represents the culmination of several years of hard work involving numerous individuals. We would like to express our gratitude to the authors for their dedication and patience, as well as the publisher's production team for their accommodating and efficient workflow. We extend our thanks to Myrna Polak for her English editing of several chapters in the book, which greatly improved its quality. Her contributions were invaluable. We are also grateful for the support received to produce this book. We acknowledge the partial funding provided by the Israel Science Foundation grant #408/22 (to E.B.-Y.) and the contributions from the Koret Foundation and the Murray Galinson San Diego-Israel Initiative (MGSDII). Furthermore, we would like to thank Susan and Bob Lapidus, Alina Levy, Paul and Maggie Meyer, and Stacy and Don Rosenberg for their generous contributions, which played a significant role in making this book possible.

Erez Ben-Yosef

Ian W.N. Jones

Levy in Paradise: From Israel to San Diego

A Tribute

Every now and then a scholar comes along who is more than just good. This magical scholar doesn't merely play the game well. He or she changes the very nature of the enterprise. I'm talking about Thomas Levy. With this *Festschrift* we honor him, true, but really he honors us, the contributors and readers of this collection. Tom had done significant work before he joined the faculty of the University of California in San Diego, but it seems fair to say that the symbiosis between Tom and UCSD produced a plethora of innovation. Two things in particular that that institution had to offer to Tom were capable of providing significant potential development, and in his willing hands they blossomed. The first was a group of colleagues with well-known records in biblical research. Not only the permanent UC faculty: Freedman, Friedman, Propp, and Goodblatt, but also a host of eminent guests who came as visiting faculty, guest lecturers, and participants in a long chain of international conferences: Frank Cross, Moshe Weinfeld, Baruch Halpern, Jo Ann Hackett, Alan Cooper, Moshe Greenberg, Jacob Milgrom, Menahem Haran, Arnaldo Momigliano, Moshe Goshen-Gottstein, Randy Garr, Ronald Hendel, Tomoo Ishida, Hugh Williamson, John Emerton, Shalom Paul, Carol Meyers – and that is just a sample. Levy interacted with all the guests, and he became a true friend to all of the permanent colleagues. When Tom first arrived in La Jolla, his interests were largely too early for exchange with most of us. As far as I could tell, for any period when people knew how to write, Tom lost interest. In a way, it served us right. For so long we had chuckled at classicists and others who were latecomers from our point of view as scholars of the Hebrew Bible and the ancient Near East. So now we got a much-needed lesson in relativity of time from a colleague to whom we were the Johnny-come-latelies in human development. So now Tom and we mutually profited from expansion of our horizons of time and civilization.

The second thing that UCSD had to offer Professor Levy was its special character as an advanced institution in the natural sciences. During Levy's years in the field, archaeology has gone from washing pots to radiocarbon dating to awesome three-dimensional virtual reality visualizations of sites within buildings on his campus to visualizing sites beneath the surface before excavating to sea-level change to the strength of the earth's magnetic field and its implications for dating Pre-Pottery to Pottery Neolithic sites. UCSD's advanced status in technology and engineering enabled him to do pretty much anything he wanted to do in this new state of the field. And its top-ranking Scripps School of Oceanography was in driving distance of his house—just as underwater archeology was offering a *tehom* of new discoveries. Fearless in the face of each new opportunity, Tom had to pass a swimming endurance test that was more suited to a young Olympic athlete than to a senior professor.

It's almost as if archaeology was waiting for this convergence: the arrival of new tools at a quantum leap higher than ever before and the right person who would know how to put all this to use. He not only mastered the new tech himself; he was a prime mover in the field, attracting others to the new archaeology as well.

It was there from the beginning. After years in Israel, Levy was interested in returning to the United States, preferably back to California, where he had grown up. And just then San Diego had moved to the forefront of research in the Hebrew Bible and was ready for an archaeologist. The job was advertised at a level that was below Levy's professional status at the time, but he applied anyway. When I asked a colleague what he thought about this, he answered: "If you can get Tom Levy at this level you'll be getting the bargain of the century." And we did. And Tom moved at warp speed through the ranks to full professor and eventually to an endowed chair. In his first year in La Jolla, he proposed an international conference that would bring together a tremendous who's who of archaeologists. He found the funding for it himself (another of his gifts) and published a substantial book of the fruits of that gathering. More conferences and more volumes followed.

He attracted students as well, both to his courses and to his excavations in Israel and Jordan. And several of his fine graduate students have gone on to careers in the field.

In all, I can't think of a scholar more deserving of a *Festschrift* than Professor Thomas Levy. From all of us: לחיים Tom. עד מאה ועשרים

Ann & Jay Davis Professor
of Jewish Studies Emeritus
University of Georgia
Athens, GA, USA

Richard Elliott Friedman

Katzin Professor of Jewish Civilization Emeritus
University of California, San Diego
La Jolla, CA, USA

Contents of Volume 2

Volume 2: From Archaeological Sciences to Archaeological Theory

Part III   New Research on the Archaeology of Faynan, Southern Jordan

Organizing Principles in Early Bronze Age Copper Manufacturing.... 1087
Aaron Gidding

Maps and Models: Applications of GIS and Image-Based Modeling to Field Archaeology in Faynan, Jordan 1107
Matthew D. Howland and Brady Liss

Archaeological Evidence of Casual Snacking and Resource Provisioning at Khirbat al-Jariya (ca. Eleventh to Tenth Centuries BCE), an Iron-Age Copper Production Site 1133
Luke Stroth, Arianna Garvin Suero, Brady Liss, Matthew D. Howland, and Jade D'Alpoim Guedes

City of Copper, Ruin of Copper: Rethinking Nelson Glueck's Identifications of Ir Nahash and Ge Harashim 1155
Marc A. Beherec

Assessing the Circulation of Arabah Copper (Timna vs. Faynan) from the End of the Late Bronze and Iron Age in the Southern Levant by Combining Lead Isotopic Ratios with Lead Concentrations 1181
Naama Yahalom-Mack, Daniel M. Finn, and Yigal Erel

Copper Trade Networks from the Arabah: Re-assessing the Impact on Early Iron Age Moab................... 1201
Stanley Klassen and Andrew J. Danielson

The Negev Highlands — A Corridor for the Copper
and Incense Trade during Nonconsecutive Periods
between the Chalcolithic and Roman Periods 1227
Chaim Ben David

Fragments of an Archaeology of Late Roman Religion at Phaino
(Khirbat Faynān, Southern Jordan) 1255
Ian W. N. Jones

Part IV Archaeometallurgy Beyond Faynan

Lead in Human Bones and Teeth Reflecting Historical
Changes in Lead Production: Rome and the Levant................. 1275
Yigal Erel

The Source of Southern Levantine Hellenistic Silver and Lead........ 1287
Tzilla Eshel, Gideon Hadas, Asaf Oron, Irina Segal, Ofir Tirosh,
and Yehiel Zelinger

A Social Archaeometallurgy of Bronze Age Cyprus 1303
A. Bernard Knapp

Early Types of Cypriot Bronze Age Metal Ingots 1323
Vasiliki Kassianidou

A Change in Attitude: X-Ray Images of the Ingot
God from Enkomi 1355
George Papasavvas

Iron Age Copper Metallurgy in Southeast Arabia: A Comparative
Perspective.. 1391
Joseph W. Lehner, Ioana A. Dumitru, Abigail Buffington, Eli Dollarhide,
Smiti Nathan, Paige Paulsen, Mary L. Young, Alexander J. Sivitskis,
Frances Wiig, and Michael J. Harrower

Copper Metallurgy in the Andes 1419
Carol Schultze and Charles Stanish

Experimental Bloomery Iron Smelting in the Study
of Iron Technology in the Southern Levant 1449
Adi Eliyahu Behar

Part V Marine Archaeology and Maritime Trade
         in the Eastern Mediterranean and Beyond

Unearthing Craft Activities in the North Aegean:
The Karabournaki Settlement................................... 1469
Despoina Tsiafaki

Contents of Volume 2

**The Inland Late Bronze – Iron Age Anchorage of Dor:
Ancient Reality or Fantasy?** 1493
Gilad Shtienberg and Katrina Cantu

**Stray Finds in the Periphery of Harbours:
The Case of Paralimni- *Louma*, Famagusta Bay, Cyprus** 1507
Stella Demesticha and Miltiadis Polidorou

**The Shell and the Skeleton: The Circumstances
for the Transition in Shipbuilding Technologies
in the Late-Antique Southern Levant** 1539
Gil Gambash

**By Boat or by Land – GIS Least-Cost Modeling
of Indigenous Native American Transportation Choices
in the San Francisco Bay Area** 1553
Brian F. Byrd and Paul Brandy

**Part VI Cyber-Archaeology and Archaeological Science:
The Future of the Past**

**From the Field to the Web: Towards an Integrative Approach
in Data Processing from Excavations and Surveys
into Quantitative Digital Archaeology – The Israeli Case Study** 1581
Gideon Avni, Avraham S. Tendler, and Liat Weinblum

**Photogrammetric and GIS-Based Modeling of Rapid
Sediment Erosion and Deposition on the Taskscape
of Bronze Age Politiko-*Troullia*, Cyprus** 1603
Elizabeth Ridder, Patricia L. Fall, and Steven E. Falconer

**From Digital Recording to Advanced AI Applications
in Archaeology and Cultural Heritage** 1627
George Pavlidis

New Approaches to Real-Time Rendering in Cyber-Archaeology 1657
Neil G. Smith

**Preservation of the Memory of Lost Cultural Heritage
in Post-conflict Communities** 1683
Matthew Vincent

**Local Voices, Storytelling, and Virtual Reality:
Fostering Community Archaeology and Preserving
Cultural Heritage in a COVID Lockdown** 1701
Suzanne Richard and Douglas R. Clark

xviii   Contents of Volume 2

**"Cult and Copper": A VR Game Exploring
the Intangible Heritage of Copper Smelting** 1723
Casondra Sobieralski

**Uncertainties in Archaeointensity Research:
Implications for the Levantine Archaeomagnetic Curve.** 1753
Lisa Tauxe, Ron Shaar, Brendan Cych, and Erez Ben-Yosef

**Part VII   Anthropological Archaeology in the Southern
Levant and Beyond**

More than Antiquity: How Archaeologists See 1777
Raphael Greenberg

Pragmatism in Archaeology: The End of Theory? 1789
William G. Dever

**Polycentrism and the Rise of Secondary States
in the Eastern Mediterranean: Aspects of a Southern
Levantine Cultural Paradigm** 1801
Øystein S. LaBianca

**Markets, Barter, and the Origins of Money: How Archaic States
and Empires Organized Their Economies** 1823
Geoffrey E. Braswell

**Making Peoples: The Nabatean Settlement
of the Dhiban Plateau and Beyond** 1855
Chang-ho Ji

The Hexagram Graves: Symbols and Identity in Ottoman Jaffa. 1889
Yoav Arbel

"Napoleon's Hill" and the 1799 Siege of Acre/Akko, Israel 1911
Ann E. Killebrew and Jane C. Skinner

**The Curious Case of Albright at Megiddo
(aka "A Mysterious Affair at Armageddon").** 1933
Eric H. Cline

Correction to: "And in Length of Days Understanding" (Job 12:12) ... C1
Erez Ben-Yosef and Ian W. N. Jones

Index. 1953

Contents of Volume 1

Volume 1: The Southern Levant from Late Prehistory to Biblical Times

Part I   The Later Prehistory of the Southern Levant

Tom Levy and "Deep Time": Forays into the Neolithic 3
Alan H. Simmons

The Neolithic of the Jordanian *Badia* 7
Bill Finlayson and Pascal Flohr

**The Emergence of Fruit Tree Horticulture
in Chalcolithic Southern Levant** 39
Dafna Langgut and Arik Sasi

**Animal Economy in the Chalcolithic of the Southern Levant:
From Meat Source to Marketable Commodity** 59
Linoy Namdar and Lidar Sapir-Hen

**Butchering Patterns and Technology in a Chalcolithic Settlement:
Analysis of the Butchered Fauna from Shiqmim, Israel** 83
Haskel J. Greenfield and Jeremy A. Beller

**The Concept of Burial Modes as a Research Tool
in the Late Prehistory of the Southern Levant** 113
Ianir Milevski

**Home on the Range: Late Neolithic Architecture
and Subsistence in Jordan's Black Desert** 147
Gary Rollefson

**Tel 'Ein Jezreel in the Neolithic and Chalcolithic Periods:
New Finds, New Insights** 173
Tamar Shooval, Ian Cipin, Sonia Pinsky, Jennie Ebeling,
Norma Franklin, and Danny Rosenberg

Interpreting the Chalcolithic Steles of the Southern Levant 191
David Ilan and Yorke Rowan

The En Gedi Shrine and the Cave of the Treasure:
Disentangling the Entangled 205
Uri Davidovich

The Ghassulian Galilean Sub-Culture
in the Late Chalcolithic Period 219
Dina Shalem and Nimrod Getzov

The Late Chalcolithic in the Valley of Elah, Israel 245
Yosef Garfinkel

Cultural, Socio-economic and Environmental Influences
on Health Status of Chalcolithic Populations
in the Northern Negev. 267
Patricia Smith, Marina Faerman, and Liora Kolska Horwitz

Socio-economic Complexity in Chalcolithic Villages:
A Re-evaluation in Light of New Excavations 295
Yael Abadi-Reiss

Perforated and Unperforated Flint Discs
from Late Chalcolithic Fazael: A Note on Their Characteristics
and Possible Implications. 323
Danny Rosenberg, Sonia Pinsky, and Shay Bar

V-Shaped Bowls and Feasting Ceremonies
in the Late Chalcolithic Period in the Southern Levant:
The Case Study of Neve Ur 343
Michael Freikman, David Ben-Shlomo, Jacob Damm,
and Oren Gutfeld

Pottery Production in Late Phases of Early Bronze 1
in the Southern Levant. 359
Eliot Braun

The Outline and Design of Fortified Cities
of the Early Bronze IB and II 389
Nimrod Getzov and Ianir Milevski

An-Naqʻ and Fifa in the Southern Ghor, Jordan:
A Tale of Two Cemeteries. 411
Mohammad Najjar

A Note on the Earliest Appearance of the Hand-Made,
Straight-Sided Cooking Pot in the Southern Levant. 443
Yitzhak Paz and Naama Walzer

Contents of Volume 1 xxi

**Can DISH Be a Marker for Greater Social Stratification:
Jericho's Early Bronze IV and Tell Atchana, Alalakh** 453
Rula Shafiq

Part II New Directions in Biblical Archaeology

**Theoretical and Methodological Comments on Social Complexity
and State Formation in Biblical Archaeology** 471
Erez Ben-Yosef and Zachary Thomas

**History Without Texts: Interdisciplinary Interpretive
Methods for Understanding the Early Iron Age** 535
Sarah Malena

**What Is the Name of Our Discipline? Or, the Onomastic Stew
That Is Archaeology in the Southern Levant** 555
Zachary Thomas

**"Their Voice Carries Throughout the Earth, Their Words
to the End of the World" (Ps 19, 5): Thoughts on Long-Range
Trade in Organics in the Bronze and Iron Age Levant** 573
Aren M. Maeir

**The Site of Khirbet 'Aujah el-Foqa:
Identifying Its Iron Age Architecture** 601
David Ben-Shlomo

Die Like an Egyptian: Burial Customs in Iron Age I Philistia 625
Shirly Ben Dor Evian and Mario A. S. Martin

**Philistine Rural Temple Economy: The Early Iron Age Fauna
from Nahal Patish** 639
Edward F. Maher and Pirhiya Nahshoni

**The Hesi Region: A Regional Perspective on Interaction
and Integration Processes During the Iron I/II Transition** 681
James W. Hardin

**Agricultural and Economic Change in the Iron
II Judean Shephelah as a Result of Geopolitical Shifts:
A View from Tel Burna** 711
Itzhaq Shai

Gezer Destructions: A Case Study of a Border City 723
Steven M. Ortiz

Jerusalem's Settlement History: Rejoinders and Updates 753
Israel Finkelstein

The Interconnections Between Jerusalem and Samaria
in the Ninth to Eighth Centuries BCE: Material Culture,
Connectivity and Politics 771
Yuval Gadot, Assaf Kleiman, and Joe Uziel

Tel Beth-Shean in the Tenth–Ninth Centuries BCE:
A Chronological Query and Its Possible
Archaeomagnetic Resolution 787
Yoav Vaknin, Amihai Mazar, Ron Shaar, and Erez Ben-Yosef

Time and Paradigm at Tel Megiddo: David, Shoshenq I,
Hazael and Radiocarbon Dating 811
Hendrik J. Bruins

The Buqeiʿa Plateau of the Judean Desert in the Southern
Levant During the Seventh to Early Sixth Centuries BCE:
Iron Age Run-off Farmland or a Pastoralist Rangeland? 839
Shimon Gibson, Rafael Y. Lewis, and Joan E. Taylor

Recognizing Ceramic Traditions: Moabite Painted
and Decorated Wares 899
P. M. Michèle Daviau

The Qasr at Baluʿa 923
Kent Bramlett, Monique Roddy, Craig Tyson, and Friedbert Ninow

The Case for Jalul as Biblical Bezer 943
Randall W. Younker

Remarks on the Typology and Chronology of Iron Age
and Persian Period Winepresses 961
Samuel Richard Wolff

My Heart Is To …: Some Cruxes in Identity Formation
in Iron I Israel? 977
Baruch Halpern

Merenptah and Amenmesse – Egyptian Rumors
Concerning the Exodus. 1013
Michael Bányai

Moses the Egyptian? A Reassessment of the Etymology
of the Name "Moses" 1047
Thomas Schneider

Heraclitus' Law and the Late Period Shaft Tombs of Abusir 1057
Miroslav Bárta

Hala Sultan Tekke, Cyprus. Trade with Egypt in the Bronze Age 1069
Peter M. Fischer

Contributors

Yael Abadi-Reiss Israel Antiquities Authority, Jerusalem, Israel

Yoav Arbel Israel Antiquities Authority, Jerusalem, Israel

Gideon Avni Israel Antiquities Authority, Jerusalem, Israel

Michael Bányai Independent Scholar, Stuttgart, Germany

Shay Bar University of Haifa, Haifa, Israel

Miroslav Bárta Charles University, Prague, Czechia

Marc A. Beherec Independent Scholar, Los Angeles, CA, USA
Michael Baker International, Los Angeles, CA, USA

Jeremy A. Beller Simon Fraser University, Burnaby, BC, Canada

Chaim Ben-David Kinneret College on the Sea of Galilee, Zemach, Israel

Shirly Ben Dor Evian University of Haifa, Haifa, Israel

David Ben-Shlomo Ariel University, Ariel, Israel

Erez Ben-Yosef Tel Aviv University, Tel Aviv, Israel

Kent Bramlett La Sierra University, Riverside, CA, USA

Paul Brandy Far Western Anthropological Research Group, Davis, CA, USA

Geoffrey E. Braswell University of California, San Diego, La Jolla, CA, USA

Eliot Braun W.F. Albright Institute of Archaeological Research, Jerusalem, Israel

Hendrik J. Bruins Ben-Gurion University of the Negev, Beer-Sheva, Israel

Abigail Buffington College of William and Mary, Williamsburg, VA, USA

Brian Byrd Far Western Anthropological Research Group, Davis, CA, USA

Katrina Cantu University of California, San Diego, La Jolla, CA, USA

Ian Cipin University of Haifa, Haifa, Israel

Douglas R. Clark La Sierra University, Riverside, CA, USA

Eric H. Cline George Washington University, Washington, DC, USA

Brendan Cych Scripps Institution of Oceanography, La Jolla, CA, USA
University of Liverpool, Liverpool, UK

Jade D'Alpoim Guedes University of California, San Diego, La Jolla, CA, USA

Jacob Damm Cornell University, Ithaca, NY, USA

Andrew J. Danielson University of British Columbia, Vancouver, BC, Canada

P. M. Michèle Daviau Wilfrid Laurier University, Waterloo, ON, Canada

Uri Davidovich The Hebrew University of Jerusalem, Jerusalem, Israel

Stella Demesticha University of Cyprus, Nicosia, Cyprus

William G. Dever Lycoming College, Williamsport, PA, USA
University of Arizona, Tucson, AZ, USA

Eli N. Dollarhide New York University Abu Dhabi, Abu Dhabi, UAE

Ioana A. Dumitru Aarhus University, Aarhus, Denmark

Jennie Ebeling University of Evansville, Evansville, IN, USA

Adi Eliyahu-Behar Ariel University, Ariel, Israel

Yigal Erel The Hebrew University of Jerusalem, Jerusalem, Israel

Tzilla Eshel University of Haifa, Haifa, Israel

Marina Faerman The Hebrew University of Jerusalem, Jerusalem, Israel

Steven E. Falconer University of North Carolina at Charlotte, Charlotte, NC, USA

Patricia L. Fall University of North Carolina at Charlotte, Charlotte, NC, USA

Israel Finkelstein Tel Aviv University, Tel Aviv, Israel
University of Haifa, Haifa, Israel

Bill Finlayson University of Oxford, Oxford, UK

Daniel M. Finn The Hebrew University of Jerusalem, Jerusalem, Israel

Peter M. Fischer University of Gothenburg, Gothenburg, Sweden

Pascal Flohr University of Kiel, Kiel, Germany
University of Oxford, Oxford, UK

Norma Franklin University of Haifa, Haifa, Israel

Michael Freikman The Hebrew University of Jerusalem, Jerusalem, Israel

Richard Elliott Friedman University of Georgia, Athens, GA, USA

Yuval Gadot Tel Aviv University, Tel Aviv, Israel

Gil Gambash University of Haifa, Haifa, Israel

Yosef Garfinkel The Hebrew University of Jerusalem, Jerusalem, Israel

Arianna Garvin Suero University of California, San Diego, La Jolla, CA, USA

Nimrod Getzov Israel Antiquities Authority, Jerusalem, Israel

Shimon Gibson University of North Carolina at Charlotte, Charlotte, NC, USA

Aaron D. Gidding University of California, Santa Barbara, Santa Barbara, CA, USA

Raphael Greenberg Tel Aviv University, Tel Aviv, Israel

Haskel J. Greenfield University of Manitoba, Winnipeg, MB, Canada

Oren Gutfeld The Hebrew University of Jerusalem, Jerusalem, Israel

Gideon Hadas Dead Sea and Arava Science Center, Jerusalem, Israel

Baruch Halpern University of Georgia, Athens, GA, USA

James W. Hardin Mississippi State University, Mississippi State, MS, USA

Michael J. Harrower Johns Hopkins University, Baltimore, MD, USA

Liora Kolska Horwitz The Hebrew University of Jerusalem, Jerusalem, Israel

Matthew D. Howland University of Georgia, Athens, GA, USA

David Ilan Hebrew Union College, Jerusalem, Israel

Chang-ho Ji La Sierra University, Riverside, CA, USA

Ian W. N. Jones University of California, San Diego, La Jolla, CA, USA

Vasiliki Kassianidou University of Cyprus, Nicosia, Cyprus

Ann E. Killebrew The Pennsylvania State University, University Park, PA, USA

Stanley Klassen University of Toronto, Toronto, ON, Canada

Assaf Kleiman Ben-Gurion University of the Negev, Beer-Sheva, Israel

A. Bernard Knapp University of Glasgow, Glasgow, Scotland, UK
Cyprus American Archaeological Research Institute, Nicosia, Cyprus

Øystein LaBianca Andrews University, MI, USA

Dafna Langgut Tel Aviv University, Tel Aviv, Israel

Joseph W. Lehner University of Sydney, Sydney, NSW, Australia

Rafael Y. Lewis Ashkelon Academic College, Ashkelon, Israel
University of Haifa, Haifa, Israel

Brady Liss University of California, San Diego, La Jolla, CA, USA

Aren M. Maeir Bar-Ilan University, Ramat Gan, Israel

Edward F. Maher Northeastern Illinois University, Chicago, IL, USA

Sarah Malena St. Mary's College of Maryland, MD, USA

Mario A. S. Martin University of Innsbruck, Innsbruck, Austria

Amihai Mazar The Hebrew University of Jerusalem, Jerusalem, Israel

Ianir Milevski Israel Antiquities Authority, Jerusalem, Israel
National Scientific and Technical Research Council, Buenos Aires, Argentina

Pirhiya Nahshoni Independent Scholar, Beer-Sheva, Israel

Mohammad Najjar Independent Scholar, Amman, Jordan

Linoy Namdar Tel Aviv University, Tel Aviv, Israel

Smiti Nathan Anthico LLC, Baltimore, MD, USA

Friedbert Ninow La Sierra University, Riverside, CA, USA
Theologische Hochschule Friedensau, Möckern, Germany

Asaf Oron Tel Aviv Museum of Art, Tel Aviv, Israel

Steven M. Ortiz Lipscomb University, Nashville, TN, USA

George Papasavvas University of Cyprus, Nicosia, Cyprus

Page E. Paulsen Johns Hopkins University, Baltimore, MD, USA

George Pavlidis Athena Research Center, Xanthi, Greece

Yitzhak Paz Israel Antiquities Authority, Jerusalem, Israel

Sonia Pinsky University of Haifa, Haifa, Israel

Miltiadis Polidorou National and Kapodistrian University of Athens, Athens, Greece

Suzanne Richard Gannon University, Erie, PA, USA

Elizabeth Ridder California State University, San Marcos, San Marcos, CA, USA

Monique Roddy La Sierra University, Riverside, CA, USA
Walla Walla University, WA, USA

Gary Rollefson Whitman College, Walla Walla, WA, USA

Danny Rosenberg University of Haifa, Haifa, Israel

Contributors

Yorke Rowan University of Chicago, Chicago, IL, USA

Lidar Sapir-Hen Tel Aviv University, Tel Aviv, Israel

Arik Sasi Tel Aviv University, Tel Aviv, Israel

Thomas Schneider University of British Columbia, Vancouver, BC, Canada

Carol A. Schultze WestLand Engineering & Environmental Services, Seattle, WA, USA

Irina Segal Geological Survey of Israel, Jerusalem, Israel

Ron Shaar The Hebrew University of Jerusalem, Jerusalem, Israel

Rula Shafiq Yeditepe University, Istanbul, Turkey

Itzhaq Shai Ariel University, Ariel, Israel

Dina Shalem Israel Antiquities Authority, Jerusalem, Israel
Kinneret College on the Sea of Galilee, Zemach, Israel

Tamar Shooval University of Haifa, Haifa, Israel

Gilad Shtienberg University of California, San Diego, La Jolla, CA, USA

Alan H. Simmons University of Nevada, Las Vegas, Paradise, NV, USA
Desert Research Institute, Reno, NV, USA

Alexander J. Sivitskis Teton Science Schools, Jackson, WY, USA

Jane C. Skinner The Pennsylvania State University, University Park, PA, USA

Neil G. Smith University of California, San Diego, La Jolla, CA, USA

Patricia Smith The Hebrew University of Jerusalem, Jerusalem, Israel

Casondra Sobieralski University of California, Santa Cruz, Santa Cruz, CA, USA

Charles Stanish University of South Florida, Tampa, FL, USA

Luke Stroth University of California, San Diego, La Jolla, CA, USA

Lisa Tauxe Scripps Institution of Oceanography, La Jolla, CA, USA

Joan E. Taylor King's College London, London, UK

Avraham Tendler Israel Antiquities Authority, Jerusalem, Israel

Zachary Thomas Tel Aviv University, Tel Aviv, Israel

Ofir Tirosh The Hebrew University of Jerusalem, Jerusalem, Israel

Despoina Tsiafaki Athena Research Center, Xanthi, Greece

Craig Tyson D'Youville University, Buffalo, NY, USA

Joe Uziel Israel Antiquities Authority, Jerusalem, Israel

Yoav Vaknin Tel Aviv University, Tel Aviv, Israel
The Hebrew University of Jerusalem, Jerusalem, Israel

Matthew Vincent American Center of Research, Amman, Jordan

Naama Walzer Tel Aviv University, Tel Aviv, Israel

Liat Weinblum Israel Antiquities Authority, Jerusalem, Israel

Frances Wiig University of New South Wales, Sydney, NSW, Australia

Samuel R. Wolff W.F. Albright Institute of Archaeological Research, Jerusalem, Israel

Naama Yahalom-Mack The Hebrew University of Jerusalem, Jerusalem, Israel

Mary L. Young College of William and Mary, Williamsburg, VA, USA

Randall W. Younker Andrews University, MI, USA

Yehiel Zelinger Israel Antiquities Authority, Jerusalem, Israel

Part III
New Research on the Archaeology of Faynan, Southern Jordan

Excavating a deep probe into one of the largest slag mounds at Khirbat en-Nahas, Faynan (Area M). Part of the 2006 field season of the Edom Lowlands Regional Archaeological Project (ELRAP) led by Thomas E. Levy and Mohammad Najjar. (Photo courtesy of Erez Ben-Yosef)

Organizing Principles in Early Bronze Age Copper Manufacturing

Aaron Gidding

Abstract Metals played an important role in the maintenance of elite structures as an item of "wealth finance" in ancient societies. The affordance structure that supported the production of metals in particular provides an important mechanism to describe the organization of the elite structures that relied on metals. In one of his earlier works, Thomas E. Levy created a "metallurgical chain" for copper production at Khirbat Hamra Ifdan in the region of Faynan in southern Jordan. I further develop his model with additional data on the *chaîne opératoire* of production within the site. The application of Behavioral Archaeology in Schiffer's idea of the performance matrix is utilized to show changes in copper production in the region of Faynan over time in relation to broader socio-political changes in the broader southern Levant.

Keywords Chaîne opératoire · Early Bronze Age · Faynan · Copper · Archaeometallurgy · Performance matrix

1 Introduction

The Early Bronze Age in the southern Levant (3500 BCE–2000 BCE) is noted for the development of a variety of features associated with urbanism. Especially in the fertile zones, there are notable changes to settlement structures and features that have been implicated with the development of social hierarchies (de Miroschedji, 2018; Greenberg, 2019; Greenberg et al., 2012; Sapir-Hen et al., 2022). In the southern arid regions, the dynamics of settlement are different and only one settlement, Arad, developed structural features of associated cities: walls and temples (Amiran, 1978). Nevertheless, radiocarbon data indicates changes in settlement

---

A. Gidding (✉)
University of California, Santa Barbara, Santa Barbara, CA, USA
e-mail: agidding@gmail.com

© The Author(s), under exclusive license to Springer Nature Switzerland AG 2023
E. Ben-Yosef, I. W. N. Jones (eds.), *"And in Length of Days Understanding" (Job 12:12): Essays on Archaeology in the Eastern Mediterranean and Beyond in Honor of Thomas E. Levy*, Interdisciplinary Contributions to Archaeology,
https://doi.org/10.1007/978-3-031-27330-8_46

activity that broadly mirror changes in settlement patterns in the fertile zones (Avner & Carmi, 2001). However, the ephemeral nature of most sites in the arid periphery from the Early Bronze Age makes qualification of socio-political organization more challenging based only on structural features.

Rather than studying the physical features of sites, changes in technology offer a useful alternative to resolve changes in social structure. This is especially important for modern discussions of the Early Bronze Age where the problematic assumptions of correlating changes in site structure with social structure have been raised (Chesson, 2003; Chesson & Philip, 2003; Joffe, 2013; Paz & Greenberg, 2016). As a direct imprint of group decision-making processes the interrelation of changes in the application of technology over time and patterned social relations indicate changes in social structures (Lemonnier, 1986). Further, approaches that build on this data to offer important opportunities resolve the contexts of decision-making as it applies to technological change (Schiffer, 2005).

More recent work in the southern arid periphery has begun to focus on different aspects of technological change and exchange to better understand social networks and implicit socio-political organization. This is the underlying premise of the alternative chronological terminology that has been applied to sites in the arid zone, based on their alternative economic trajectory (Rosen, 2011a; Rothenberg & Glass, 1992). Examples of important exports from this region include groundstone and stone tools (Abadi-Reiss & Schneider, 2006; Fujii, 2011; Rosen, 2011b, 2020). The data from the exchanges of these materials highlights how inhabitants of the largely pastoral arid areas interacted with their urban neighbors to the north. The changes in demand for these products was tied to a variety of causal factors such as increased settlement density and other technological developments. For instance, changes in stone tool manufacturing techniques and applications can be related to the social contexts for the adoption and practical use of copper tools during and beyond the Early Bronze Age (Manclossi et al., 2019). Of the different products that originate in the arid periphery, changes in the organization of production of copper offers a useful lens to study concurrent social change. The introduction of metallurgy is often thought to be a component in early urbanism due to the fungible quality of metals and the implicit potential of metals for facilitating long-distance exchange. It is for this reason that the role of copper trade during the Early Bronze Age has been an important point of discussion.

This paper seeks to contribute to this discussion by building on the work of Thomas E. Levy and colleagues in the region of (Levy et al., 2002). The technical aspects of copper production in this region have been comprehensively studied in previous research and highlight specific changes in smelting techniques over the course of the Early Bronze Age (Hauptmann, 2007). Instead, the application of theoretical considerations of both the social contexts of copper production and changes in the performance characteristics of copper production installations will be used to highlight nuances in the socio-political organization of copper producers through the Early Bronze Age (Fig. 1).

Organizing Principles in Early Bronze Age Copper Manufacturing

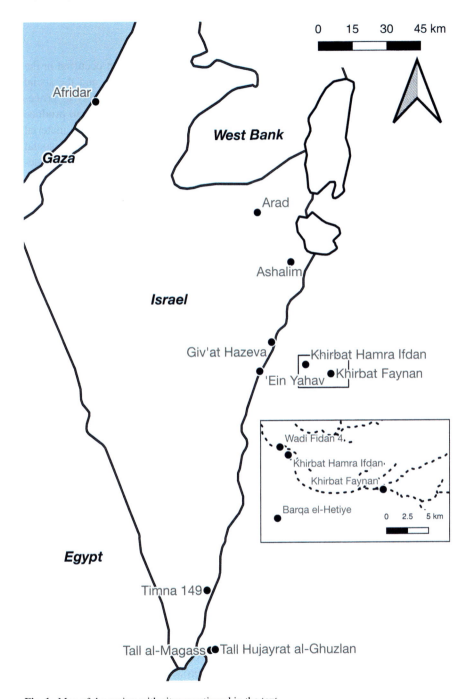

Fig. 1 Map of the region with sites mentioned in the text

2 Archaeology of Socio-technical Processes

There are two components to the study of technical processes that occurred in the past: the actual technology that was employed to produce objects and the social framework of production. Studies of ancient technologies use a variety of procedures to either recreate or parse the skills necessary for ancient people to produce different materials and artifacts. Such studies are important to frame the material constraints and intentional technical decisions of ancient producers. The social framework of production establishes the ideational qualities that led to the production of a given artifact. This is informed by institutional requirements that establish the rationale for why and how different artifacts would have been produced. In reality, these components are inseparable when considering the decision-making processes of ancient craftspeople, which has influenced modern theoretical approaches to production as a socio-technical system.

Chaîne opératoire is one theoretical approach to the study of production that focuses on the chain of actions or operations that lead to the production of a final product. Derived from Mauss' (1990) approach to research of total social phenomenon that surrounded the process of gift giving, *chaîne opératoire* focuses on the social gestures that surround production (Leroi-Gourhan, 1943, 1973). The practitioners of the *chaîne opératoire* seek to trace the steps of production in order to detect social residues implicit in the choices made during the production sequence that would be unique to different societies. While a production process in broad terms could be seen as homologous, the identification of unique aspects of the production process for any given society could be used to explain social institutional distinctions. Within this framework, the actions required to produce a given artifact would be guided by institutional structures implicit within the society that produces that artifact as a part of a larger socio-technical system (Pfaffenberger, 1998). *Chaîne opératoire* was initially used to describe the process of lithic production but the approach was expanded upon by Lemonnier (1986) and the associated work of Pfaffenberger (1988, 1992) popularized the approach in the English language literature. The most important aspect of *chaîne opératoire* as an approach is the explication of the social gestures of production in order to map the organization of the production system as a means to infer the sociopolitical contexts of production (Dobres, 1999: 124). As such, qualitative judgments about choices in the production process are not made as part of the analysis. It is acknowledged that different contexts of production might lead to intentionally inefficient production practices. In such analysis, it is important to identify specific processes involved in production that are comparable, in order to resolve how institutional differences alter the circumstances of production.

A similar, but independent theoretical model for understanding the implications of different production processes is derived from broader ideas found in Behavioral Archaeology (Schiffer, 2010). Schiffer's (1975) behavior chain analysis is a part of the larger suite of Behavioral Archaeology. It was independently developed and very similar to this approach albeit with a more diachronic focus (Bar-Yosef & van

Peer, 2009: 105). Unlike the *chaîne opératoire* method, which was developed with socio-cultural anthropological models in mind, behavioral archaeology focused specifically on archaeological applications and the results that are specifically applicable to archaeological research interests. For instance, behavior chain analysis identifies the expected depositional results of different actions that are part of a productive sequence (Schiffer, 1975). Another important method related to understanding ancient production from Behavioral Archaeology is the performance matrix which is used to understand the structure of technological choices over time. "A performance matrix is a list of the performative characteristics thought to be relevant to all activities of each artifact's life history, from procurement through use and maintenance. For each characteristic, one estimates its performance value…one can identify patterns of compromise in performance characteristics that can be related through correlates, to extratechnological factors" (Schiffer & Skibo, 1987: 601). The estimate of the performance value is an important distinction from what is achieved through *chaîne opératoire*, which tries to remove such value judgments from the analysis. However, in order to consider why choices were made by societies over time, it is especially useful to evaluate changes in performance of different tasks within a system in order to better understand change.

Already different models have been presented to contextualize the implications of different chains of operations for copper production during the Early Bronze Age. In order to understand the implications of the changes over time in copper production I will elaborate on those models and present them within a performance matrix. For the main phase of occupation, the *chaîne opératoire* at Khirbat Hamra Ifdan will be examined in detail to highlight how activity areas within the site illuminate the complexity of copper production during the Early Bronze Age.

3 Regional Perspectives on Socio-technical Processes of Early Bronze Age Copper Production Over Time

The regional mechanisms of copper production during the Early Bronze Age are derived from four key sources: the mines, smelting locations, object production sites and sites with copper tools. The context of actions related to mining, smelting and object production clearly provides specific details about socio-technical processes related to production. Sites that have copper tools but have no evidence of production, are useful for understanding the economic and social connections of copper producers as they relate to the other three sources. For each of those loci, different technical processes took place that required unique tools, technical knowledge and operational capacity. The specific steps of production include extractive mining activities, smelting in wind powered furnaces, transportation of prills and metal containing components to processing sites, crushing those components with stone tools, remelting metals in crucibles, casting into molds, removal of molds with stone tools, and a final shaping and polishing of objects (Levy et al., 2002).

Understanding whether those different operations occurred in a single location, or were spread out across the landscape, can be used to develop our knowledge of control and the operational capacity of metalworkers at different times. The variability seen in these factors can be used to understand how different priorities were met to manage issues of efficiency to meet internal and external pressures and demands.

Broadly speaking, during the Early Bronze Age the ore deposits in the region of Faynan were the point of origin for the majority of copper that moved through the Negev Desert to other locations. This fact has been supported by lead isotope analysis of objects found primarily in the southern areas of Israel that date to the later part of the Early Bronze Age (Hauptmann et al., 1999, 2015; Hauptmann & Schmitt-Strecker, 2011; Yahalom-Mack et al., 2014). Petrographic data from sites in the Negev region that also date to the later part of the Early Bronze Age showed high levels of interconnectivity with sites in Faynan (Goren, 1996). But most of this work has focused on later transit of finished goods, not the issue of production.

Rothenberg and Glass (1992) offered the first socio-technical model that focused on those producing copper during the Early Bronze Age. Their work did not include data from Faynan, as that area had not yet been comprehensively explored, but instead focused on copper mines in southern Sinai and the Timna Valley. They argued that copper production in this region could be best understood to be autochthonous. Changes in the technology of copper production were used to create three phases: Early, Middle and Late. These phases broadly correspond respectively to the Chalcolithic/EBI transition, Arad Stratum I-III and the end of the Early Bronze Age. The defining characteristics of each phase were changes in the technology used for production that led to increased specialization, performance characteristics and the disassociation of production from habitation sites. The relationship between different aspects of production relative to habitation sites provides a means to track changes in the socio-technical system associated with Early Bronze Age copper production using the newest data from Faynan (Table 1).

For the present discussion of the location of different copper production processes across the landscape during the Early Bronze Age, the aforementioned phase system will be used with the addition of a fourth phase between the Middle and

Table 1 Performance matrix for copper production at Early Bronze Age sites

Performance characteristics	Early phase	Middle phase	Middle-Late phase	Late phase
Smelting				
Smelting close to ore sources	−	+	+	−
Smelting near habitation sites	+	+	−	−
Smelting independent of habitation	−	+	+	+
Object production				
Occurs in conjunction with smelting	+	+	−	?
Distinct operation from smelting	−	+	+	?

Late Phases, a Middle-Late Phase. Rothenberg and Glass (1992) in their phasing leave a large temporal gap between the collapse of Arad and the end of the Early Bronze Age, during which time copper production in Faynan takes off (Levy et al., 2002). It is important to note that the four phases approach describe here does not correlate to the recently updated chronology for the four phases of the Early Bronze Age: EBI, EBII, EBIII, and EBIV/IBA (Regev et al., 2012). Instead, the phased approach to describe technological change at sites in the southern arid periphery more closely follows alternative chronological phasing based on lithic tools that identify this period, the "Timnian" (Rosen, 2011a). The early phase broadly matches the end of the Chalcolithic and the EBI in the new chronology, roughly 3700 BCE–3000 BCE. For the Middle Phase, a reexamination of the data from Arad suggests that dating of Strata I-III should no longer be constrained to the EBII, but likely also include the beginning of the EBIII, roughly 3000 BCE–2600 BCE (Finkelstein et al., 2018; Gidding, 2016; Gidding & Levy, 2020). The Middle-Late Phase correlates to Stratum III at Khirbat Hamra Ifdan, which is roughly 2600 BCE–2300 BCE, straddling the EBIII to EBIV divide (Levy et al., 2002). Finally, the Late Phase corresponds to the final phases of the EBIV, which is noted by the adoption of the wavy comb pattern on jars at a number of sites in the southern Levant (D'Andrea, 2012; Rothenberg & Glass, 1992).

At the start of the Early Bronze Age, during the Early Phase, there is evidence of copper production at a number of sites near the Timna and Faynan ore sources in addition to other areas away from the mines. In the region of Timna, about 24 km from the Timna ore sources, the sites Tall Hujayrat al-Ghuzlan and Tall al-Magass were first occupied during the Late Chalcolithic and continued into the beginning of the Early Bronze Age (Khalil & Schmidt, 2009). Both sites combined evidence for habitation and copper operations, and included the full array of copper production operations from smelting through final production of ingots, which suggests large scale production for export to Egypt (Klimscha, 2013; Pfeiffer, 2009; Rehren et al., 1997). In the Faynan region the first site with evidence of copper production was Wadi Fidan 4. Wadi Fidan 4, 10 km from the ore sources, has material culture indicating an occupation similar to Tall Hujayrat al-Ghuzlan and Tall al-Magass (Adams, 1999: 53). Unlike the Timna sources, copper production at Wadi Fidan 4 was considered a cottage industry, integrated within a habitation site (Adams & Genz, 1995). Copper production at Wadi Fidan 4, Hujayrat al-Ghuzlan and Tall al-Magass ended midway through the EBI. Copper smelting and the production of finished artifacts continued at other sites outside of the mining regions away from the mines, including Halif and Tell esh-Shuna (Pfeiffer, 2009; Rehren et al., 1997; Shalev, 1994). One of the best known is Afridar, near Ashkelon, on the Levantine coast (Shalev, 2003). At the end of the EBI, Egypt exerted direct influence over the area of southwestern Israel and engaged directly with the inhabitants of sites in the Negev Highlands (Yekutieli, 2004). The fact that Afridar seems to sustain a position as a locus of copper production through the EBI has been suggested to be due to the site's importance as a hub of trade with Egypt and the northern Levant (Golani, 2004, 2014; Gophna & Liphschitz, 1996). All of the aforementioned sites show the full *chaîne opératoire* of copper production at habitation sites. After the EBI, Egypt was less involved in the southern Levant, but trade with the region continued to be important.

The important change from the EBI to the EBII was the reconfiguration of the Levantine settlement pattern, with large, independent "urban" settlements appearing including in the arid, northern Negev. Starting in this period a feature of Levantine trade in the settled areas is increased consumption of copper products, but evidence for production is largely absent within habitation sites (Greenberg, 2002: 117–121). At sites associated with the Middle Phase more sophisticated smelting technology was adopted to match this change in copper consumption (Rothenberg & Glass, 1992). Of the large EBII sites Arad, in the northern Negev, showed the greatest density, with 212 copper objects including axes, one adze, chisels, and pins/awls that have been universally sourced to Faynan or Timna (Amiran, 1986; Hauptmann et al., 1999). Pins/awls make up 73% of the assemblage and the objects are widely distributed leading to the conclusion that they were part of regular activity, and not necessarily elite tools (Ilan & Sebbane, 1989). Provenience studies of copper objects from areas north of the Negev, at sites such as Kfar Monash and Pella, indicate that the objects originated both from Faynan and Anatolia (Hauptmann & Schmitt-Strecker, 2011; Phillip et al., 2003). The provenience data reinforces the regional distinctions between the northern and southern areas of the southern Levant but highlights the different interaction spheres. During this time the majority of sites that are associated with different aspects of production, both smelting and the production of objects, are found near the copper sources.

During the Middle Phase in Faynan there is evidence of smelting using wind-blown furnaces both in association with habitation areas and outside of habitation areas. Although many locations have been identified in the Faynan area for smelting during the EBII, there is only one very small habitation site, Barqa el-Hetiye, that has been identified where the full *chaîne opératoire* would have taken place (Hauptmann, 2007; Adams, 2003; Fritz, 1994). The excavations at Khirbat Hamra Ifdan revealed evidence of occupation during this phase, but no evidence of intensive copper production (Levy et al., 2002). Recent excavations at the large site of Khirbet Faynan revealed an occupation that dates to this this phase as well with a single casting mold, but no evidence of smelting (Levy et al., 2012). In addition to the aforementioned sites, it is during the Middle Phase that the first smelting sites appear without directly associated habitations. One of the sites, Faynan 9, near the mines with wind-blown furnaces, includes a radiocarbon date that likely places activity at the end of the Middle Phase (Hauptmann, 2007). Another site, Ashalim, about 50 km away from Faynan, on the way to Arad, has evidence for smelting associated with ritual masseboth (Ben-Yosef et al., 2016). Ashalim might be an anomalous instance of copper smelting that was not close to the ore sources, with the ritual installations being tied to the act of smelting for those trading copper out of the Araba Valley. For different reasons each of the aforementioned sites is thought to have interacted with Arad and supplied the finished copper goods found at the site.

One of the other key regions that is often associated with Arad copper production during the EBII in the southern Levant is the Sinai Peninsula. In Sinai a number of sites appear near the copper mines in the south. Based on ceramic petrographic studies it is suggested that there is a connection between the Sinai sites and Arad which has led some to call the occupation of southern Sinai "Canaanite." However there is some conflict about the direction of influence with the opposite possibility, that the settlement in Arad had its origins in Sinai via the Negev (Finkelstein & Perevolotsky, 1990; Finkelstein, 1990). The work of Beit-Arieh in southern Sinai revealed metallurgical installations for finished products created on a small-scale, including casting molds made of sandstone (Beit-Arieh, 2003). However, the analysis of the copper objects from Arad indicates that most of the copper found there did not originate in Sinai (Hauptmann et al., 1999). The disconnect between the copper and ceramic data might indicate that while the sites in each area were inhabited by groups within the same sphere of interaction, the flow of copper from Sinai was not to Arad but to Egypt. Khirbat Hamra Ifdan was first occupied during the EBII but large-scale production of copper did not begin until the following period.

Regional copper shifted into what could be described as a vertically integrated system during the Middle-Late Phase. The only sites with evidence for the smelting of ores are in the direct vicinity of the ore sources (Hauptmann, 2007). The copper from those smelting installations was then brought to Khirbat Hamra Ifdan, a habitation site with extensive workshop space, where there is ample evidence for remelting and casting the copper into both ingots and final products (Levy et al., 2002). Similar ingots to those identified at Khirbat Hamra Ifdan have been found at a number of sites in the Negev Highlands, and the copper in the Negev Highlands ingots originated at Faynan (Hauptmann et al., 2015). Early research on the Negev Highlands sites used the co-presence of hammerstones and the ingots to suggest that in the absence of local pastoral production the Negev sites were stations on a copper transportation network that ended in Egypt (Haiman, 1996). However, more recent excavations have questioned that conclusion noting that there is little evidence of metal working residues within the structures (Dunseth et al., 2018). The *chaîne opératoire* of copper production during this phase within Khirbat Hamra Ifdan highlights localized socio-technical complexity that is distinct from the copper production in the previous and following phases, and will be discussed in the following section.

During the Late Phase wind-blown furnaces continued to be used away from habitation sites and also farther away from the ore sources. Each of these sites has been identified on small hillocks where exposure to prevailing winds would have the copper smelting. One example near the ore sources comes from the Timna Valley, Site 149, where late EBIV sherds were found in association with windblown furnaces and a small workshop for removing copper from slag (Rothenberg & Shaw, 1990). Other sites have been identified up the Wadi Araba, about 30 km from the Faynan ore sources. 'Ein Yahav is small slag mound where ceramics and a radiocarbon date suggest a date at the very end of the Early Bronze Age (Yekutieli et al., 2005). Here too there is evidence of the local crushing of slag to yield the copper prills (Vardi et al., 2008). It is notable however that the workshop for crushing slag at Site 149 in Timna appears to have been more organized with well-defined anvils, compared to 'Ein Yahav where XRF was required to verify their use. Finally, archaeomagnetic dating of the slags has estimated Giv'at Hazeva, a site near 'Ein

Yahav, to be a relative contemporary of the Late Phase sites (Ben-Yosef et al., 2016). In total during the Late Phase the majority of evidence for copper production comes from small smelting sites that were away from the mines; suggesting a change in the socio-techincal system from the Middle-Late Phase.

Based on the data from the excavations at 'Ein Yahav, Yekutieli et al. (2005) proposed a model for copper production during the Late Phase that suggests a step-wise system of production by pastoralists. 'Ein Yahav was interpreted to be a part of a tiered system of copper production and object manufacture that saw different zones of activity the further the agro-pastoralists got from the ore sources. The proposed steps, in order, start with mining at the ore source, followed by smelting at the next step, annealing and production of objects and finally distribution through the aforementioned network of agro-pastoralists in Sinai and beyond. The model for the EBIV as described by Yekutieli broadly mirrors the core steps in the *chaîne opératoire* outlined for copper production generally above, but spread out across the landscape. In such a system the pastoralists take advantage of various natural and geographic features as they traverse the landscape, partaking in copper production opportunistically where water was readily available and natural topography offered a good location for a wind-blown furnace. In this model it is assumed that the large sites in the Negev Highlands were copper processing sites based on Haiman's (1996) observations of the material assemblages being comprised of many hammerstones. However, as mentioned above, those conclusions have been debated recently (Dunseth et al., 2018). As a result, other than the small smelting installations mentioned above, during the Late Phase there is no direct evidence so far for other parts of the *chaîne opératoire*.

4 Perspectives on Socio-technical Processes of Early Bronze Age Copper Production Over Time at Khirbat Hamra Ifdan

It was during the Late-Middle Phase that the intensity of copper production in Faynan increased beyond simple cottage level production with the smelting process clearly disarticulated from the process of producing objects for trade. Based on current knowledge, it was only during this period that smelting occurred adjacent to the mines and large-scale production of artifacts was centralized to a single site, Khirbat Hamra Ifdan (Adams, 2002; Levy et al., 2002). That change signifies an important shift in the overall organization of production that was likely driven by the need for more efficient transportation of material in conjunction with the increase in production.

The excavations at Khirbat Hamra Ifdan revealed a well-preserved manufacturing center with significant quantities of material for the creation of copper objects. The site was first excavated by Russell Adams and published as a part of his dissertation (Adams, 2000). He later collaborated with Thomas E. Levy and Mohammad

Najjar to expand the excavations for two seasons, which revealed most of the data to be discussed (Levy et al., 2002). Finally, two more seasons were supervised by T. Levy and M. Najjar to clarify questions about the stratigraphy of the site (Levy et al., 2012). T. Levy supervised two dissertations on different aspects of the material culture at Khirbat Hamra Ifdan, which will be used to elaborate on the *chaîne opératoire* at the site (Gidding, 2016; Muniz, 2008).

The shift in the socio-technical system between the Middle and the Middle-Late Phase signified an important change in the organization of copper production. This change has been likened to industrialization, with a presumed external source of power managing production (Adams, 2002). In the previous phases copper production occurred on the household level with evidence of the full process from primary smelting to the finished product occurring on a household level. With the separation of smelting from habitation sites and the development of a well-defined manufactory a new socio-technical system developed to facilitate the increased production capacity that can be plainly observed by the large quantity of metallurgical remains from this phase, not seen during the previous or subsequent phases (Levy et al., 2002). Importantly, the excavations at Khirbat Hamra Ifdan showed material for each step of the *chaîne opératoire* after the primary smelt.

The distribution of artifacts related to copper production at Khirbat Hamra Ifdan reflects a differentiated production system according to different tasks. While a detailed examination of the metallurgical remains, in total, has not been carried out differential activity areas within the site are obvious (Fig. 2). The central action at Khirbat Hamra Ifdan was the remelting of copper to make various objects. That action is represented by the presence of the copper molds highly concentrated in different rooms across the site. Groundstone tools would have been used both before and after casting of copper objects. These tools can be found with some frequency in the vicinity of the areas where casting molds were also found. However, the majority of groundstone tools are found separate from the molds in the northern area of the excavated site. This data suggests that different areas of the site were used for different processes. Rather than simply amplifying the processes seen in the cottage industry of previous phases the *chaîne opératoire* evolved after the Middle Phase to differentiate the tasks of metal production within the site.

Other data from the site can be used to elaborate on how the community dynamics interplayed with the changes in the organization of production. Broadly speaking the ceramic and faunal data also suggest clearly distinct activity areas within the site. Certain ceramic types were distributed widely across the site; lamps and very large vats for storing liquids are found in many rooms across the site. However, cooking vessels and large storage jars are found predominantly in only a few rooms (Gidding, 2016: 318). These rooms are spread across the site, so it is not assumed that the specialized function of rooms was part of exclusion of access according to social hierarchies within the site. The faunal data revealed that three rooms within the workshop areas contained the most bones and that the majority of bones identified were meat bearing bones, from the limbs (Muniz, 2008: 174–251). By comparison axial and cranial bones were identified in three different rooms, suggesting that there was a distinction between areas of consumption and butchering. The ceramics

Fig. 2 Map of Khirbat Hamra Ifdan highlighting the distribution of molds and ceramics as identified in the field. The data in this map is incomplete because more material has been found at a later date and certainly some material was misidentified, but nevertheless the figure provides a good, general picture of the estimated distribution of different artifact types

associated with food preparation were concentrated in the rooms with axial and cranial bones supporting centralized food processing. In most cases, when bones were identified in other parts of the site, they were limb bones. The wide distribution of limb bones does not suggest differential access according to social hierarchies. The association of specific bone types with function of ceramics within the site reinforces an interpretation of the ceramic assemblage that there is a clear division of activity within the rooms at Khirbat Hamra Ifdan.

Finally, variability in the distribution of copper objects that were produced at Khirbat Hamra Ifdan reinforces the lack of strong centralized control within the site. A study of the different ingots that were produced at Khirbat Hamra Ifdan shows broad, but not precise formal consistency and modest metrological similarity (Gidding & Levy, 2021). The common bar shaped ingot, which has been identified at many sites in the Negev Highlands, was made at Khirbat Hamra Ifdan with a broad pattern for shape, but differences in specific aspects of the form, especially the distal phlanges. Among the ingots found at the site there are features that are metrologically consistent for ingots found within caches, but not between caches within Khirbat Hamra Ifdan. This has been interpreted to imply that while there was a consensus regarding the overall form of the ingots, there was no universal standard imposed for all ingots created at the site. In fact, the differences might signify different internal factions among the copper producers at Khirbat Hamra Ifdan. Given that there does not appear to be singular control of storage or foodstuffs, this supports a decentralized pattern of multiple groups working simultaneously using a commonly understood division of labor within the site.

5   Discussion and Conclusions

The changes in the context of copper production through the Early Bronze Age highlight a series of decisions made by copper producers to alter production strategies according to a variety of external factors. When considering the performance matrix, important changes occur over time regarding the locations of different parts of the copper production sequence (Table 1). From a broad landscape perspective many of these changes can be understood through the broad rubric of change of efficiency. In order to maximize production during the Middle-Late Phase the smelting of copper ores moved close to mines. However, during the other phases the location of production sites is not designed to maximize production as much as fit other socio-political needs of the copper producers.

As a limited resource, the geographical relationship between the different parts of copper processing is an important reference to describe the investment in production. The most important factor for determining the importance of site location is the distance between primary smelting sites and ore sources. In the Early Bronze Age, the location of copper production as a commodity was limited by a number of technological factors, most important of which was transportation, which for intense production logically places all aspects of production as close to the mines as possible. It is expected that that when planning to produce large quantities metal smelting will occur near the mines due to the mass of ore compared to the final product. Due to the labor investment of moving ore, if primary smelting occurs farther from the site of the mines the scale of production will often be less. The other constraint for copper production is the availability of resources necessary for smelting, especially charcoal. It has been estimated that the amount of charcoal to ore charge using ancient techniques is 20/40 to 1 (Horne, 1982: 12). If the estimates for copper production at smelting pits in the region of Faynan during the Early Bronze Age were an estimate between 9000 tons and 15,000 tons of charcoal would have been needed (Hauptmann, 2007: Fig. 5.3). While there is good evidence of local availability of trees, it has also been suggested that they were being exploited significantly around the time of the Third Millennium (Hunt et al., 2007: 1323). The acquisition of charcoal would have been a significant step in the production process that would have required considerable time harvesting trees nearby. Plainly, for each of the major processes in the production of copper there are important associated practical constraints. The nature of the constraints implicate different significances for the location of each step in the production process. In combination the processes within a place implies the affordance structure of that place in the total system.

When we consider the nature of production at sites during the Early Phase, the integration of production with habitation sites is an important distinguishing feature. A number of factors likely influenced this process when copper production moved near to mining zones for the first time. The metallurgical technology used for smelting for this phase was still similar to the "slagless" techniques used during the Chalcolithic, which would not have been aided by natural wind flows as the wind-blown furnaces in later phases (Hauptmann, 2007; Pfeiffer, 2009). Domestication of the donkey was in its early stages at this time. This might have limited its use for long distance transportation (Rossel et al., 2008) and would further explain why the habitation sites were located closer to the mines.

During the Middle Phase the organization of production seems to be in transition. This is noted by the presence of all characteristics identified in the performance matrix (Table 1). The sites identified with copper production in Faynan tend to be small and are associated with Arad based on ceramic correlations, petrographic data and lead-isotope analysis (Adams, 2003; Fritz, 1994; Hauptmann et al., 1999; Levy et al., 2012; Porat, 1989). It is during this phase that regional interconnections between the Negev Highlands and Faynan become more important. The small smelting/ritual site Ashalim, situated between Faynan and Arad with associated masseboth, might indicate the changing role of mobile pastoralists in the production of copper (Ben-Yosef et al., 2016). It is notable that the first wind-blown furnaces near the copper mines appear at the end of this phase. The changes in settlement patterning implicate the intensification of production during the following phase, which was likely driven by the increased interaction with neighboring regions that is also clear during this phase.

It is during the Middle-Late Phase that the locations of production reflect an expected pattern for maximum efficiency of production utilizing Early Bronze Age technology. The smelting of ores occurs adjacent to the mines and the resulting copper material is what is transported for the production of copper objects elsewhere. This enabled the copper workers to take advantage of the different technical needs for each part of the operational chain from smelting to object production. The closer analysis of the organization of production within Khirbat Hamra Ifdan indicates elements of coordination and distinction. The specialized nature of sites during this phase is matched within the site, where different areas of the site are utilized for specific tasks, not within households as in previous phases but across the whole site. Even so, that differentiation occurs in clusters within the site that precludes the assumption of top-down, centralized control of copper production. The combination of features that enhance efficiency while maintaining distinct groups of operators within the copper production system is surprising. I have suggested elsewhere that the design choices in ingot manufacture represent a signaling mechanism for the origin of copper from Faynan as part of what was likely a disjointed trading mechanism (Gidding & Levy, 2021). Not all of the changes that occur during this phase lead to what might be considered a fully optimized product; instead, there is evidence for differentiation in the production process that is reflected in the various kinds of clustering seen in the material record from Khirbat Hamra Ifdan. Within these clusters there is clear evidence for the specialization of specific kinds of operations related to copper production that were not observed in earlier phases when operated as a cottage industry. The internal distinctions reflected in the operations within Khirbat Hamra Ifdan are further implicated in the following phase, when clearly the demand for copper disappears.

During the Late Phase copper production continues to occur at specialized facilities, which are no longer adjacent to the mines. The absence of clear workshops for the production of objects is also notable; regionally this period lacks many significant urban centers. Yekutieli et al. (2005) presented a model for the activity during this phase that breaks down the production processes into a four-part division of labor: smelting, tool production and a buffer zone before hitting "foreign markets," That division of labor would have occurred across the landscape, with pastoralists taking advantage of geographic features to enact the *chaîne opératoire* in locations best suited for the needs of pastoral production and copper production. Within such a system less copper would have been produced than in the previous phase, and this likely represents that change in demand and the adoption of metal production within a mobile pastoralist subsistence strategy.

The broad changes that are observed using the performance matrix highlight that over the four phases of copper production, site activities shifted from the early development of surpluses to the adoption of new strategies that maximized productive potential. The constellation of where different steps in the chain of production occurred on the landscape developed in conjunction with external socio-political factors. The choice of site locations was taken to leverage new sources of labor, specifically the donkey as a beast of burden, and to increase the availability of resources necessary for copper production in an otherwise inhospitable environment. Even when the demand for copper decreased regionally, the people that engaged in copper production actively adapted their strategy to the location of different parts of the *chaîne opératoire*. It is notable that during the Late Phase copper producers maintained elements of the specialized production strategy from the previous phase but now dispersed production across the landscape.

Acknowledgments I wish to thank Prof. Tom Levy, who has had a great influence on my work, especially regarding the application of specific anthropological ideas connecting technology and culture. He introduced me to the ideas of Schiffer, behavioral archaeology, and the *chaîne opératoire* methods. It is my honor to dedicate this article to him.

References

Abadi-Reiss, Y., & Schneider, J. S. (2006). Design theory and milling stone production and consumption in the Highland Negev Early Bronze Age. In S. A. Rosen & V. Roux (Eds.), *Memoires et Travaux du Centre de Recherche Francais a Jerusalem* (pp. 81–98). De Boccard.

Adams, R. B. (1999). The Development of copper metallurgy during the Early Bronze Age of the southern levant: Evidence from the Faynan region, southern Jordan. In PhD Dissertation, University of Sheffield.

Adams, R. B. (2000). The Early Bronze Age III–IV transition in southern Jordan: Evidence from Khirbet Hamra Ifdan. In G. Philip & D. Baird (Eds.), *Ceramics and change in the Early Bronze Age of the southern Levant* (pp. 379–402). Sheffield Academic Press.

Adams, R. B. (2002). From farms to factories: The development of copper production at Faynan, southern Jordan, during the Early Bronze Age. In B. S. Ottaway & E. C. Wager (Eds.), *Metals and society* (pp. 21–32). Archaeopress.

Adams, R. B. (2003). External influences at Faynan during the Early Bronze Age: A re-analysis of building 1 at Barqa el-Hetiye, Jordan. *Palestine Exploration Quarterly, 135*(1), 6–21.

Adams, R. B., & Genz, H. (1995). Excavations at Wadi Fidan 4: A Chalcolithic village complex in the copper Ore District of feinan, southern Jordan. *Palestine Exploration Quarterly, 127*, 8–20.

Amiran, R. (1978). *Early Arad I: The chalcolithic settlement and Early Bronze City* (Judean Desert studies). Israel Exploration Society.

Amiran, R. (1986). The fall of the Early Bronze Age-Ii City-of-Arad. *Israel Exploration Journal, 36*(1–2), 74–76.

Avner, U., & Carmi, I. (2001). Settlement patterns in the southern Levant deserts during the 6th–3rd Millenia BC: A revision based on 14C dating. *Radiocarbon, 43*(3), 1203–1216.

Bar-Yosef, O., & van Peer, P. (2009). The chaîne opératoire approach in Middle Paleolithic archaeology. *Current Anthropology, 50*(1), 103–131. https://doi.org/10.1086/592234

Beit-Arieh, I. (2003). *Archaeology of Sinai: the Ophir expedition*. Tel Aviv: Tel Aviv University, Sonia and Marco Nadler Institute of Archaeology.

Ben-Yosef, E., Gidding, A., Tauxe, L., Davidovich, U., Najjar, M., & Levy, T. E. (2016). Early Bronze Age copper production systems in the northern Arabah Valley: New insights from archaeomagnetic study of slag deposits in Jordan and Israel. *Journal of Archaeological Science, 72*, 71–84. https://doi.org/10.1016/j.jas.2016.05.010

Chesson, M. S. (2003). Households, houses, neighborhoods and corporate villages: Modeling the Early Bronze Age as a house society. *Journal of Mediterranean Archaeology, 16*(1), 79–102.

Chesson, M. S., & Philip, G. (2003). Tales of the city? "Urbanism" in the Early Bronze Age Levant from Mediterranean and Levantine perspectives. *Journal of Mediterranean Archaeology, 16*(1), 3–16.

de Miroschedji, P. (2018). The urbanization of the southern Levant in its near eastern setting. *Origini, XLII*(2), 109–148.

D'Andrea, M. (2012). The Early Bronze IV period in south-central Transjordan: Reconsidering chronology through ceramic technology. *Levant, 44*(1), 17–50. https://doi.org/10.117 9/175638012x13285409187838

Dobres, M. A. (1999). Technology's links and chaines: The processual unfolding of technique and technician. In M. A. Dobres & C. R. Hoffman (Eds.), *The social dynamics of technology, practice, politics, and world views* (pp. 124–146). Smithsonian Institution Press.

Dunseth, Z. C., Finkelstein, I., & Shahack-Gross, R. (2018). Intermediate Bronze Age subsistence practices in the Negev Highlands, Israel: Macro- and microarchaeological results from the sites of Ein Ziq and Nahal Boqer 66. *Journal of Archaeological Science: Reports, 19*. https://doi. org/10.1016/j.jasrep.2018.03.025

Finkelstein, I. (1990). Early Arad —Urbanism of the Nomads. *Zeitschrift Des Deutschen Palästina-Vereins, 106*, 34–50

Finkelstein, I., & Perevolotsky, A. (1990). Processes of sedentarization and nomadization in the History of Sinai and the Negev. *Bulletin of the American Schools of Oriental Research, 279*, 67–88. https://doi.org/10.2307/1357210

Finkelstein, I., Adams, M. J., Dunseth, Z. C., & Shahack-Gross, R. (2018). The archaeology and history of the Negev and neighbouring areas in the third millennium BCE: A new paradigm. *Tel Aviv, 45*(1), 63–88. https://doi.org/10.1080/03344355.2018.1412054

Fritz, V. V. (1994). Vorbecht über die Grabungen in Barqa el-Hetiye im Gebiet von Fenan, Wadi el-Araba (Jordanien) 1990. *Zeitschrift Des Deutschen Palastina-Vereins, 110*, 125–150.

Fujii, S. (2011). "Lost property" at Wadi Qusayr 173: Evidence for the transportation of tabular scrapers in the Jafr Basin, southern Jordan. *Levant, 43*(1), 1–14. https://doi.org/10.117 9/007589111x12966443320738

Gidding, A. (2016). *Approaches to production and distribution in anthropological archaeology: Views from the Early Bronze Age of Jordan and Israel*. University of California.

Gidding, A., & Levy, T. E. (2020). Manufacturing copper in the periphery: Radiocarbon and the question of urbanism during the Early Bronze Age III-IV transition. In S. Richard (Ed.), *New horizons in the study of the Early Bronze III and Early Bronze IV of the Levant*. Eisenbrauns.

Gidding, A., & Levy, T. E. (2021). The political economy of Early Bronze Age copper production at Khirbat Hamra Ifdan (Jordan): Implications for southern Levantine urbanism. In *Transitions, urbanism, and collapse in the Bronze Age – Essays in Honor of Suzanne Richard*. Equinox eBooks Publishing. https://doi.org/10.1558/equinox.37727

Goren, Y. (1996). The southern Levant in the Early Bronze Age IV: The petrographic perspective. *Bulletin of the American Schools of Oriental Research, 303*, 33–72.

Greenberg, R. (2019). *The archaeology of the Bronze Age Levant. The archaeology of the Bronze Age Levant*. Cambridge University Press. https://doi.org/10.1017/9781316275993

Greenberg, R., Paz, S., Wengrow, D., & Iserlis, M. (2012). Tel Bet Yerah: Hub of the Early Bronze Age Levant. *Near Eastern Archaeology, 75*(2), 88–107.

Golani, A. (2004). Salvage excavations at the Early Bronze Age Site of Ashqelon, *Afridar—Area E. 'Atiqot, 45*, 9–62.

Golani, A. (2014). Ashqelon during the EB I period – a centre for copper processing and trade. In A. Mączyńska (Ed.), *The Nile Delta as a centre of cultural interactions between Upper Egypt and the Southern Levant in the 4th millennium BC* (Issue 13). Poznan Archaeological Museum

Gophna, R., & Liphschitz, N. (1996). The Ashkelon trough settlements in the Early Bronze Age I: New evidence of maritime trade. *Tel Aviv, 23*, 143–153.

Greenberg, R. (2002). *Early urbanizations in the Levant: A Regional Narrative*. Leicester University Press.

Haiman, M. (1996). Early Bronze Age IV settlement pattern of the Negev and Sinai deserts: View from small marginal temporary sites. *Bulletin of the American Schools of Oriental Research, 303*, 1–32. http://www.jstor.org.ezp-prod1.hul.harvard.edu/stable/pdfplus/1357468.pdf

Hauptmann, A. (2007). The archaeometallurgy of copper: Evidence from Faynan, Jordan. In B. Herrmann & G. A. Wagner (Eds.), *Natural science in archaeology*. Springer.

Hauptmann, A., & Schmitt-Strecker, S. (2011). Bronze Age Kfar Monash, Palestine — A chemical and lead isotope study into the provenance of its copper. *Paleorient, 37*(2), 65–78.

Hauptmann, A., Begemann, F., & Schmitt-Strecker, S. (1999). Copper objects from Arad: Their composition and provenance. *Bulletin of the American Schools of Oriental Research, 314*, 1–17. https://doi.org/10.2307/1357449

Hauptmann, A., Schmitt-Strecker, S., Levy, T. E., & Begemann, F. (2015). On Early Bronze Age copper bar ingots from the southern Levant. *Bulletin of the American Schools of Oriental Research, 373*, 1–24.

Horne, L. (1982). Fuel for the metal worker. *Expedition Magazine, Penn Museum, 25*(1), 6–13. http://www.penn.museum/sites/expedition/?p=5281

Hunt, C. O., Gilbertson, D. D., & El-Rishi, H. A. (2007). An 8000-year history of landscape, climate, and copper exploitation in the Middle East: The Wadi Faynan and the Wadi Dana National Reserve in southern Jordan. *Journal of Archaeological Science, 34*, 1306–1338. https://doi.org/10.1016/j.jas.2006.10.022

Ilan, O., & Sebbane, M. (1989). Metallurgy, trade, and the urbanization of southern Canaan in the chalcolithic and Early Bronze Age. In P. de Miroschedji (Ed.), *L'urbansation de la Palestine à l'âge du Bronze ancien: Bilan et perspectives des Recherches actuelles: Acts du Colloque D'Emmaüs*. British Archaeological Reports International Series.

Joffe, A. H. (2013). Review. *Bulletin of the American Schools of Oriental Research, 370*, 230–234. https://doi.org/10.5615/bullamerschoorie.370.0230

Khalil, L., & Schmidt, K. (2009). *Prehistoric Aqaba. Orient-Archaologie*. Verlag Marie Leidorf.

Klimscha, F. (2013). Innovations in chalcolithic metallurgy in the southern Levant during the 5th and 4th millennium BC. Copper-production at Tall Hujayrāt al-Ghuzlān and Tall al-Magaşş, Äqaba area, Jordan. In S. Burmeister, S. Hansen, M. Kunst, & N. Müller-Scheeßel (Eds.), *Metal matters: Innovative technologies and social change in prehistory and antiquity* (pp. 31–63). Verlag Marie Leidorf.

Lemonnier, P. (1986). The study of material culture today: Toward an anthropology of technical systems. *Journal of Anthropological Archaeology, 5*, 147–186.

Leroi-Gourhan, A. (1943). *Evolution et Techniques: L'apos; Homme et la Matière*. Albin Michel.

Leroi-Gourhan, A. (1973). *Evolution et Techniques: Milieu et Techniques* (2nd ed.). Albin Michel.

Levy, T. E., Adams, R. B., Hauptmann, A., Prange, M., Schmitt-Strecker, S., & Najjar, M. (2002). Early Bronze Age metallurgy: A newly discovered copper manufactory in southern Jordan. *Antiquity, 76*, 425–437.

Levy, T. E., Najjar, M., Gidding, A., Jones, I. W. N., Knabb, K., Bennallack, K., et al. (2012). The 2011 Edom Lowlands Regional Archaeology Project (ELRAP): Excavations and surveys in the Faynan Copper Ore District, Jordan. *Annual of the Department of Antiquities of Jordan, 56*, 423–445.

Manclossi, F., Rosen, S. A., & Boëda, E. (2019). From stone to metal: The dynamics of techno-logical change in the decline of chipped stone tool production. A case study from the southern Levant (5th–1st millennia BCE). *Journal of Archaeological Method and Theory*. https://doi.org/10.1007/s10816-019-09412-2

Mauss, M. (1990). *The gift*. Norton.

Muniz, A. (2008). *Feeding the periphery: Modeling early Bronze Age economies and the cultural landscape of the faynan district, southern Jordan*. Anthropology, University of California.

Paz, S., & Greenberg, R. (2016). Conceiving the city: Streets and incipient urbanism at Early Bronze Age Bet Yerah. *Journal of Mediterranean Archaeology, 29*(2), 197–233. https://doi.org/10.1558/jmea.v29i2.32572

Pfaffenberger, B. (1988). Fetishised objects and humanised nature: Towards an anthropology of technology. *Man, 23*(2), 236–252. http://www.jstor.org/stable/2802804

Pfaffenberger, B. (1992). Social anthropology of technology. *Annual Review of Anthropology, 21*, 491–516. http://www.jstor.org/stable/2155997

Pfaffenberger, B. (1998). Mining communities, chaînes opératoires and sociotechnical systems. In E. W. Herbert, A. B. Knapp, & V. C. Pigott (Eds.), *Social approaches to an industrial past:*

The archaeology and anthropology of mining (pp. 307–316). Routledge. https://doi.org/10.432 4/9780203068922-27

Pfeiffer, K. (2009). The technical ceramic for metallurgical activities from Hujayrat al-Ghuzlan and comparable sites in the southern Levant. In L. Khalil & K. Schmidt (Eds.), *Prehistoric Aqaba I* (pp. 305–338). Marie Leidorf.

Phillip, G., Clogg, P. W., & Dungworth, D. (2003). Copper metallurgy in the Jordan Valley from the third to the first millenia BC: Chemical metallographic and lead isotope analyses of artefacts from Pella. *Levant, 35*, 71–100.

Porat, N. (1989). Petrography of pottery from southern Israel and Sinai. In P. de Miroschedji (Ed.), *L'urbansation de la Palestine à l'âge du Bronze ancien: Bilan et perspectives des Recherches actuelles: Acts du Colloque D'Emmaüs* (Vol. Internatio, pp. 169–188). British Archaeological Reports.

Regev, J., de Miroschedji, P., Greenberg, R., Braun, E., Greenhut, Z., & Boaretto, E. (2012). Chronology of the Early Bronze Age in the southern Levant: New analysis for a high chronology. *Radiocarbon, 54*(3–4), 525–566.

Rehren, T., Hess, K., & Philip, G. (1997). Fourth millennium BC copper metallurgy in northern Jordan: The evidence from Tell esh-Shuna. In H. G. K. Gebel, Z. Kafafi, & G. O. Rollefson (Eds.), *The prehistory of Jordan, II: Perspectives from 1997* (pp. 625–640). Ex Oriente.

Rosen, S. A. (2011a). Desert chronologies and periodization systems. In J. L. Lovell & Y. M. Rowan (Eds.), *Culture, chronology and the chalcolithic: Theory and transition* (pp. 71–84). Oxbow.

Rosen, S. A. (2011b). *An investigation into early desert pastoralism: Excavations at the Camel Site, Negev* (UCLA Cotsen Institute of Archaeology Press Monographs, Vol. Monograph). Cotsen Institute of Archaeology Press. http://hollis.harvard.edu/?itemid=%7Clibrary/m/aleph%7C013109404

Rosen, S. A. (2020). Exchange of tabular scrapers as an indicator of complexity of pastoral barter systems in the Late Prehistoric Periods. In Y. Abadi, D. Varga, & G. Lehmann (Eds.), *Desert Archaeology, Proceedings of the 16th Annual Southern Conference* (pp. 115–126). Israel Antiquities Authority.

Rossel, S., Marshall, F., Peters, J., Pilgram, T., Adams, M. D., & O'Connor, D. (2008). Domestication of the donkey: Timing, processes, and indicators. *Proceedings of the National Academy of Sciences of the United States of America, 105*(10), 3715–3720. https://doi.org/10.1073/pnas.0709692105

Rothenberg, B., & Glass, J. (1992). The beginnings and the development of early metallurgy and the settlement and chronology of the Western Arabah, from the Chalcolithic Period to the Early Bronze Age IV. *Levant, 24*, 141–157.

Rothenberg, B., & Shaw, C. T. (1990). The discovery of a copper mine and smelter from the end of the Early Bronze Age (EB IV) in the Timna Valley. *Institute for Archaeo-Metallurgical Studies, 15*(16), 1–8.

Sapir-Hen, L., Fulton, D. N., Adams, M. J., & Finkelstein, I. (2022). The temple and the town at Early Bronze Age I Megiddo: Faunal evidence for the emergence of complexity. *Bulletin of the American Society of Overseas Research, 387*(May). https://doi.org/10.1086/718777

Schiffer, M. B. (1975). Behavioral chain analysis: Activities, organization, and the use of space. *Fieldiana. Anthropology, 65*, 103–119. http://www.jstor.org/stable/29782476

Schiffer, M. B. (2005). The electric lighthouse in the nineteenth century: Aid to navigation and political technology. *Technology and Culture, 45*, 275–305. http://media.proquest.com.ezp-prod1.hul.harvard.edu/media/pq/classic/doc/866573331/fmt/pi/rep/NONE?hl=&cit%3Aauth=Schiffer%2C+Michael+Brian&cit%3Atitle=The+Electric+Lighthouse+in+the+Nineteenth+Century&cit%3Apub=Technology+and+Culture&cit%3Avol=46&cit%3Ai

Schiffer, M. B. (2010). *Behavioral archaeology: Principals and practice. Equinox handbooks in anthropological archaeology.* Equinox.

Schiffer, M. B., & Skibo, J. M. (1987). Theory and experiment in the study of technological change. *Current Anthropology, 28*, 595–622. http://www.jstor.org.ezp-prod1.hul.harvard.edu/stable/pdfplus/2743357.pdf

Shalev, S. (1994). The change in metal production from the Chalcolithic period to the Early Bronze Age in Israel and Jordan. *Antiquity, 68,* 630–637.

Shalev, S. (2003). Early Bronze Age I copper production on the coast of Israel: Archaeomatellurgical analysis of finds from Ashkelon-Afridar. In T. Potts, M. Roaf, & D. Stein(Eds.), *Cuture through objects: Ancient near eastern studies in honour of P.R.S. moorey* (pp. 313–324). Griffith Institute Oxford.

Vardi, J., Shilstein, S., Shalev, S., & Yekutieli, Y. (2008). The Early Bronze Age IV chipped and ground stone assemblage of 'En Yahav and its relation to copper smelting activities. *Journal of the Israel Prehistoric Society, 38,* 1–20.

Yahalom-Mack, N., Galili, E., Segal, I., Eliyahu-Behar, A., Boaretto, E., Shilstein, S., & Finkelstein, I. (2014). New insights into Levantine copper trade: Analysis of ingots from the Bronze and Iron Ages in Israel. *Journal of Archaeological Science, 45*(0), 159–177. https://doi.org/10.1016/j.jas.2014.02.004

Yekutieli, Y. (2004). The Desert, The Sown and The Egyptian Colony. *Ägypten Und Levante/Egypt and the Levant, 14,* 163–171. https://doi.org/10.2307/23788141

Yekutieli, Y., Shilstein, S., & Shalev, S. (2005). 'En Yahav: A copper smelting site in the 'Arava. *Bulletin of the American Schools of Oriental Research, 340,* 1–21. http://www.jstor.org/stable/25066912

Maps and Models: Applications of GIS and Image-Based Modeling to Field Archaeology in Faynan, Jordan

Matthew D. Howland ⓘ **and Brady Liss**

Abstract At the turn of the twenty-first century, project directors Tom Levy and Mohammad Najjar made the decision to move the Edom Lowlands Regional Archaeology Project (ELRAP) fully into the digital realm. Since then, the project has been on the forefront applying digital technologies to archaeological research. Levy's advocacy for the use of interdisciplinary approaches in the field has resulted in many studies and publications pushing the boundaries of original research in the Southern Levant. Most notably, Levy's "cyber-archaeology" has broken new ground in the integration of methods from diverse fields to bring new perspectives to the study of ancient society. This paper provides three new case studies based on original research in Faynan, Jordan, inspired by Levy's significant contributions to cyber-archaeology: integrated use of 3-D modeling to record excavations, use of aerial photography and image-based modeling for site mapping, and the application of GIS for spatial analysis of archaeological landscapes.

Keywords GIS · Photogrammetry · Cyber-archaeology · 3D

1 Introduction: "From Camels to Computers"

In 1995, Tom Levy appropriately claimed that the integration of the computer would "dwarf" all other recent changes to archaeological methods at the time. In his review, Levy (1995) mapped the development and trajectory of archaeological methods and techniques "from camels to computers" emphasizing how new and powerful tools

---

M. D. Howland (✉)
Laboratory of Archaeology, University of Georgia, Athens, GA, USA
e-mail: mdh5169@gmail.com

B. Liss
University of California, San Diego, La Jolla, CA, USA
e-mail: bliss@ucsd.edu

© The Author(s), under exclusive license to Springer Nature Switzerland AG 2023
E. Ben-Yosef, I. W. N. Jones (eds.), *"And in Length of Days Understanding" (Job 12:12): Essays on Archaeology in the Eastern Mediterranean and Beyond in Honor of Thomas E. Levy*, Interdisciplinary Contributions to Archaeology,
https://doi.org/10.1007/978-3-031-27330-8_47

like geographic information systems and global positioning systems were replacing more antiquated and romanticized methods done "perched on the hump of a camel". Within 5 years, Levy's excavations used entirely digital recording strategies (see below), and his projects were at the forefront of a new approach toward archaeology: "cyber-archaeology" (Levy et al., 2012). Cyber-archaeology, "the melding of the latest developments in computer science, engineering and hard science with archaeology," was the culmination of Levy's claim in 1995—an archaeology founded on computers and digital methods (Levy et al., 2012; Levy & Liss, 2020; c.f. Forte, 2010, 2011). Levy's dedication to and advancement of cyber-archaeological methods are clear in his more than 20 years of research in Faynan, Jordan.

The Faynan region is located about 30 km south of the Dead Sea in the deserts of Jordan, and it is one of the largest copper ore resource zones in the southern Levant. Exploitation of these abundant ores throughout antiquity (intermittently between roughly the Chalcolithic/Early Bronze Age and Islamic Periods) resulted in a rich archaeological record characterized by copper smelting centers and mining sites. Since 1997, the relationship between periods of intense copper production and social complexity in Faynan, particularly during the Early Iron Age, has been a major focus of the Edom Lowlands Regional Archaeology Project (ELRAP), a collaborative research project between the University of California San Diego and the Department of Antiquities Jordan, directed by Levy and Mohammad Najjar. Through surveys and excavations, ELRAP provided new insights on the industrial landscape of Iron Age Faynan (Levy et al., 2014; Fig. 1). The combination of stratigraphic excavation and rigorous collection of radiocarbon samples facilitated a re-dating of industrial scale copper smelting in Faynan to the Early Iron Age, ca. 1200–800 BCE (previously dated to the Late Iron Age based on excavations on the Edomite Plateau) (Levy et al., 2008; c.f., Bienkowski, 1990).

Along with standard archaeological methods, ELRAP embraced the latest advancements in digital methods under Levy's direction. In 1999, Levy made the decision to make ELRAP excavations entirely paperless relying on a combination of digital platforms including computers, tablets, and eventually even iPods with custom software packages to handle all archaeological recording with exclusively digital methods and platforms (Levy et al., 2012; Levy, 2013, 2015, 2017). In addition, advanced technologies were integrated into his "cyber-archaeology" workflow including (but not limited to) using geographic information systems (GIS), aerial photography, photogrammetry, 3-D scanners, laser-scanning, and geophysical surveying (Levy et al., 2012). Critically, paperless methods and digital datasets allowed the entire excavation data collection to be easily moved to the research lab on computers and portable harddrives. These data continue to be used by Levy's lab providing the foundations for publications and dissertations making important contributions to the archaeology of Faynan.

Here, we present three original case studies based on research in Faynan and utilizing the cyber-archaeological methods endorsed by Levy. First, applying photogrammetry to archived excavation photographs is tested using the 2006 excavations of the Area M slag mound at Khirbat en-Nahas in Faynan to generate a 3-D model of the since-collapsed excavation. Second, aerial photography and image-based modeling are combined with GIS to produce a new highly-detailed map of Khirbat en-Nahas and to evaluate the site as at-risk cultural heritage. Finally, using

Maps and Models: Applications of GIS and Image-Based Modeling to Field... 1109

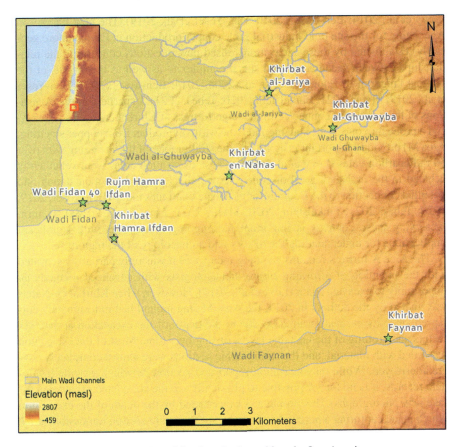

Fig. 1 Map of the Faynan region of Southern Jordan, with major Iron Age sites

GIS, hydrology tools are applied to the industrial landscape of Iron Age Faynan to investigate the strategic locations of smelting sites along access routes to the copper mines. Together, these studies apply cutting-edge digital methods to examine Iron Age society in Faynan, in the tradition of Levy's cyber-archaeology.

2 Bringing "The Past Forward": Using Archived Photography to 3-D Model Previous Excavations in Faynan

2.1 Introduction

The ELRAP excavations at Khirbat en-Nahas, the largest Iron Age copper smelting center in the region, were critical in establishing a secure chronology for copper production in Faynan and for examining the development of social complexity

(Levy et al., 2014; Ben-Yosef, 2010; Ben-Yosef et al., 2019). The new Early Iron Age dating for the site (and industrial scale copper production in Faynan more generally) established by these excavations raised new questions concerning the relationships between sedentarism and social complexity as well as the origins of the biblical kingdom of Edom (Levy et al., 2008, 2014; Ben-Yosef, 2021; Ben-Yosef et al., 2019; Maeir, 2021; Finkelstein, 2020; Tebes, 2021). In particular, the excavations of the gatehouse connected to the large fortress at Khirbat en-Nahas (Area A) and a probe into one of the slag mounds (the waste byproduct from copper smelting, Area M) provided important insights into the stratigraphy of the site along with over 50 radiocarbon dates (Levy et al., 2014). These excavation areas were vehemently debated in the archaeological discourse, especially in regards to their dating and potential connection to the Edomites; this debate continues today (Ben-Yosef, 2019, 2020; Tebes, 2021; Finkelstein, 2020; Maeir, 2021; Levy et al., 2018a). In turn, preserving these contexts is important for ongoing discussions with significant implications for understanding the history and archaeology of the region.

The Area A fortress remains standing today, and it was only partially excavated with the intention of affording future archaeologists with advanced methods an opportunity to excavate again (Levy et al., 2014). However, when Khirbat en-Nahas was visited by the authors in 2014, the Area M slag mound had unfortunately collapsed since its excavation in 2006 due to the depth of the excavation at over six meters and eroding of the unstable layers of slag over time. Most of the excavation was filled with material, and the stratigraphic sections were almost completely covered/destroyed. While the excavation report and section drawings provide invaluable records, it is no longer possible to physically see the completed excavation (or take new photographs).This problem is exacerbated by the depth of the excavation which made capturing a perpendicular image of the entire section impossible at the time. Thus, the excavation photos are mostly from above and oblique to the sections, making the drawings the only available orthographic record of the area's stratigraphy.

Fortunately, as part of Levy's commitment to digital methods, the entire excavation process was rigorously documented with a digital camera in 2006. The images provide a unique opportunity to attempt to create a 3-D model of the excavation using image-based modeling (IBM)—generating a 3-D model from a collection of 2-D images using principles of digital photogrammetry. The advent of IBM and its integration into archaeological research has introduced new opportunities for creating and sharing 3-D models of archaeological sites, excavations, and even individual artifacts (De Reu et al., 2014; Howland, 2018; Howland et al., 2014; Olson et al., 2013; Levy & Liss, 2020). In addition, 3-D models allow for preservation of the archaeological record (discussed further below); every scale of an excavation or historical site can be recorded and preserved with a photorealistic 3-D model (Levy et al., 2020; Lercari et al., 2016; Levy & Liss, 2020; Olson et al., 2013; Garstki, 2017). Generating 3-D models of excavations using these methods is now a common practice on many modern archaeological projects (see Magnani et al., 2020 and Marín-Buzón et al., 2021 for overviews of the increasing use of photogrammetry in archaeology).

While not originally intended for photogrammetry, the excavation photographs from Area M can still provide a valuable basis for modeling. Critically, the excavators captured many photographs at the completion of the excavation, both focused within the slag mound to capture the bottommost layers and from above using a boom system to record the entire area. By taking photographs from several angles around the probe, the excavators unwittingly managed to create the overlap between many of the images that is necessary for IBM. Given the coverage provided by the images, we tested the possibility of using them to produce a 3-D model of Area M. We also attempted to combine the produced model with a site-wide model of Khirbat en-Nahas (constructed based on aerial photography captured in 2014, discussed further below) to contextualize the Area M excavation in 3-D (Howland et al., 2020). Finally, the model could also be used to generate orthophotographs (typically an aerial image that has been geometrically corrected to remove distortion and create uniform scale) of the stratigraphic sections. While orthophotos are often used to provide a top-down perspective of a site or excavation square/area for mapping purposes, they have also been used for generating images of sections for record keeping or as a basis for section drawing (Vincent et al., 2015). An orthophoto could provide a complete, perpendicular image of the Area M sections for the first time. In doing so, the results could essentially reconstruct the Area M slag mound excavations, bringing "the past forward" (Levy, 2015).

2.2 Methods and Workflow

Returning to the digital excavation records on the lab server, there were 251 photographs of the completed Area M excavation from various angles, heights, and perspectives. As we wanted the model to capture the entire excavation probe, only these photographs were included, and any images of the excavation process (e.g., the initial layers of the excavation) were intentionally excluded. The main concern was ensuring maximum coverage and overlap between the photographs to facilitate generating the model which relies on points of similarities between images. As such, the entire collection of 251 photographs was used in producing a model. Many of the images included artifact tags, measuring tapes, and even occasionally a member of the excavation team, but these were not edited/masked out given the limited number of photographs. All the digital photographs were copied, and converted into a TIFF format for upload into photogrammetry software.

For producing 3-D models through IBM, the UCSD Levantine and Cyber-Archaeology Lab uses Agisoft Metashape, a standalone software for photogrammetric processing of digital images. Agisoft is commonly used by archaeological projects for its intuitive interface with a straightforward workflow and its georeferencing capabilities which is critical for generating orthophotos used for top plans and site maps (see below). Simply put, Agisoft begins constructing a 3-D model from a collection of digital images by aligning the photographs to find points of similarity and generating an initial point cloud. From this sparse point cloud, a dense point cloud and a mesh, which is essentially the 3-D topography of the model, are produced. Finally, the original photographs are used to create a "texture" which gives the mesh its photorealistic appearance (see Howland et al., 2014 for a detailed overview of the entire process using Agisoft Metashape). The 251 photographs of Area M were uploaded into Agisoft, and the model was generated (as a .obj file) using this process.

The produced model could then be used to create orthophotos of the stratigraphic sections. In order to see the section and orient it correctly, unneeded portions of the model were first removed; the rest of the model was simply highlighted and deleted leaving only the section of interest. The remaining model could then be oriented for a perpendicular perspective, providing an ideal view of the stratigraphy. The ortho-photo was produced using Agisoft's functionality. To test this approach, orthopho-tos were generated for the eastern and southern sections of the Area M excavation as samples of slag and charcoal were collected from these sections for more detailed analysis (Ben-Yosef, 2010; Ben-Yosef et al., 2019). There were some noticeable inconsistencies in the lighting and focus of the produced images; these were corrected using Image Assignment in Agisoft. This tool allows the user to highlight problematic areas within the orthophoto (or 3-D model) and see the specific original photos used in texturing that part of the model. Any images that are not in focus or have incorrect lighting can be removed and replaced with more desirable photos to improve the overall quality.

Finally, the produced Area M model was combined with the site-wide 3-D model of Khirbat en-Nahas. When the site model was produced in 2014, it inherently included the collapsed Area M. While this is an important record of the site at this time, we also wanted to produce an archaeologically-focused version that included the original Area M excavation. To do so, both models were uploaded into the Blender software, a free graphics software for editing 3-D datasets among other functionalities. Both models could be viewed simultaneously in the Blender work-space, and the Area M model could be manually positioned in the correct location within the site model. The two models were aligned using primarily the edges of the excavation pit and also the walls of the adjacent excavated structure.[1] Then, the col-lapsed Area M was simply removed from the site model using Blender to select and delete polygons from the mesh, in turn, revealing the new Area M model. The inter-sections between the two models were smoothed by adjusting the polygons of the mesh to fill any gaps from deleted polygons or to reduce any unnatural edges. The file was then saved as a single model.

---

[1] This alignment process could be automated with higher accuracy if both models are georefer-enced, but this data was not available for the Area M excavation. A georeferenced model would also allow for including other geospatial data such as artifact locations.

2.3 Results and Discussion

The excavation photographs collected in 2006 proved to be an excellent dataset for producing a 3-D model of Area M, despite not being intended for this purpose (Fig. 2). The created model is almost complete, with only a small portion missing where one of the excavators was standing in many of the original photographs. Critically, the entire slag mound probe is visible in the model down to the bedrock, and the archaeologically significant stratigraphic sections are almost completely intact. This photorealistic model now provides the best visual record of the completed excavation, and it is also a proof of concept for using archived excavation photographs for photogrammetry. Because the model was near-perfect, it could also be used to produce the orthophotos of the stratigraphy (Fig. 3). The orthophotos were able to capture the entire stratigraphic section from surface to bedrock in a single image with a perpendicular perspective despite the depth of the excavation. These images can be used in tandem with the section drawings to see the stratigraphic layers identified during the excavation and to contextualize the samples collected during the process, particularly the radiocarbon and slag samples (Levy et al., 2008, 2014; Ben-Yosef, 2010; Ben-Yosef et al., 2019). Finally, the combination of Agisoft Metashape and Blender proved to be a viable workflow for integrating multiple 3-D models (Fig. 4). The manual alignment and adjustment of

Fig. 2 3-D model of the Area M slag mound excavation at Khirbat en-Nahas produced from archived excavation photographs

Fig. 3 Orthophotographs of the south (left) and east (right) sections of the Area M slag mound excavation at Khirbat en-Nahas. The white lines are measuring tapes from the original excavation photos. The shifts in the measuring tapes and lighting in the southern section are due to the step that was left unexcavated (see Fig. 2)

Fig. 4 Before (left) and after (right) the Area M model was integrated into the site-wide 3-D model of Khirbat en-Nahas to replace the collapsed excavation as captured in 2014

individual polygons created some distortion from reality, but this does not significantly impact the archaeological record as it is along the surface edges. There are also some lighting differences between Area M and the rest of the site (which potentially could be corrected using photography software); however, this also creates a clear distinction between the two models, allowing users to immediately identify the parts that have been manually manipulated. In general, the combined model provides a unique opportunity to explore the Area M excavation as one component of the entire site, providing its full context, in comparison to the stand-alone model.

Taken together, these 3-D datasets can now be used to "revisit" the excavation and can be referenced in ongoing discussions concerning the history and archaeology of Faynan. For example, the stratigraphy and dating of Area M specifically have recently been emphasized/evaluated by Ben-Yosef (2019) and Tebes (2021), reiterating the importance of creating a digital record of this excavation. Additionally, these 3-D models provide new avenues for data sharing and outreach with scholars and the general public alike (Howland et al., 2020 and citations therein). With this in mind, the Area M and Khirbat en-Nahas models can be freely viewed at https://sketchfab.com/ELRAP.

3 "The Future of the Past" and At-Risk Cultural Heritage: Modeling and Mapping Khirbat en-Nahas

3.1 Introduction

The application of cyber-archaeology methods to record and preserve at-risk cultural heritage has been one of the central goals of Levy's lab and fieldwork (Lercari et al., 2016; Levy et al., 2018b, 2020; Pavlidis et al., 2017; Savage et al., 2017; Sideris et al., 2017). The implementation of fully-digital field recording results in a "data avalanche" (Levy et al., 2010) that can be a boon for future scholars looking to reinterpret and re-examine an excavation, as seen above. In addition to their analytical utility, the digital datasets produced through these methods document the conditions of a site at the moment of recording and even the choices made by archaeologists during fieldwork (Roosevelt et al., 2015). Such datasets are especially useful in the case of destruction of an archaeological site via excavation, environmental degradation, or anthropogenic causes.

On the ELRAP, digital field recording takes place at multiple scales ranging from artifact to locus to area to site (Levy et al., 2010; Howland et al., 2014; Smith et al., 2015). At the sitewide scale, combined methods of low-altitude aerial photography (LAAP) and image-based modeling (IBM) have been effective in producing 3-D models of entire sites, with GIS-based mapping techniques allowing for highly-comprehensive and accurate vectorization of archaeological features (Howland et al., 2014; Howland et al., 2015). More specifically, ELRAP has applied balloon photography in order to take hundreds of high-resolution photographs of archaeological sites across the Faynan region. These images, when processed through Agisoft Metashape, are sufficient for the production of 3-D models of entire sites, which provide an excellent basis for GIS datasets, such as digital elevation models (DEMs) and orthophotos. In turn, DEMs and orthophotos facilitate intra-site mapping and modeling (Howland et al., 2015; Hill & Rowan, 2017; Liss et al., 2020; Magnani & Schroder, 2015; Quartermaine et al., 2014). The ELRAP project has applied these approaches to many sites in the Faynan region, providing a diachronic record of architectural and metallurgical remains from across the Faynan region.

As the largest copper producing site in the region, Khirbat en-Nahas has a particularly long history of being subject to mapping and modeling efforts. The site has been mapped several times over the past century using traditional methods, with varying degrees of coverage, quality, and accuracy (Frank, 1934: Plan 16; Glueck, 1935: Pl. 4; MacDonald 1992: 73–77, Fig. 15; Levy et al., 2003: Fig. 12; Hauptmann, 2007: Fig. 5.33b; Fig. 5). Khirbat en-Nahas has also been recorded using a terrestrial laser scanning system as part of ELRAP, producing a point cloud that served as the basis for display and overlay of other digital datasets from the site (Levy et al., 2010; Petrovic et al., 2011). However, despite the high resolution of this dataset, it lacks the comprehensivity needed for mapping of the entire site and its environs. Thus, LAAP-IBM methods were used in 2014 to build on previous efforts for documenting the site.

3.2 Methods

The renewed mapping campaign at Khirbat en-Nahas applied the ELRAP LAAP platform, which consists of a Kingfisher Aerostat K9U balloon tethered to a reel carried by an operator. A Canon EOS 50D DSLR camera equipped with an 18 mm lens was suspended from the balloon on a custom frame. The balloon was flown in transects across the site at an elevation of ca. 75–150 meters to capture overlapping photographs using an intervalometer to automatically take pictures during flight (described in greater detail in Howland et al., 2014). Over the course of two flights taking place over the course of one total hour, the site was subject to 700 balloon photographs covering its entire extent and the surrounding environs. Using the methods described above, Agisoft Metashape was used to generate a 3-D model of the site, and it was georeferenced based on key architectural features that were spatially-recorded during previous excavations at the site and visible in many of the balloon images.A georeferenced orthophoto was then produced from the model to provide a base for vectorization and map making in GIS.

3.3 Results and Discussion

The 3-D model and two-dimensional spatial datasets from Khirbat en-Nahas have facilitated the remapping of the site with increased comprehensivity and precision (Fig. 6). The new map places an emphasis on mapping architecture as visible on the surface rather than on hypothesized structure plans as seen in previous maps. More importantly, the new map provides a more detailed and nuanced reflection of the distribution of copper slag at the site than prior mapping efforts. For the first time, concentrations of crushed slag at the site are mapped with high level of detail (cf. Hauptmann 2007: Fig. 5.33b, in which crushed slag is mapped at coarser resolution), facilitated by their clear visibility on the IBM-LAAP produced orthophoto

Fig. 5 Original ELRAP map of Khirbat en-Nahas produced using terrestrial survey and total station in 2002. (Levy et al., 2003)

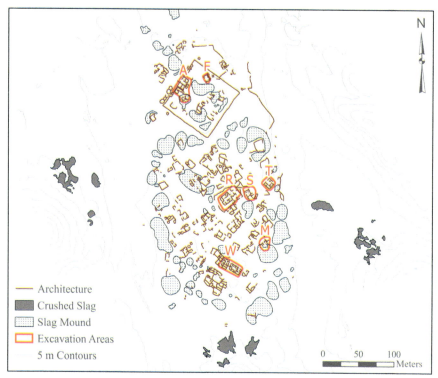

Map created by Matthew D. Howland and Brady Liss
Vectorization Assistance by Tyler Tucker

Project Directors: Thomas E. Levy and Mohammad Najjar

Fig. 6 New ELRAP map of Khirbat en-Nahas produced using low-altitude aerial photography and Image-Based Modeling in 2014. Note the increased detail in slag mounds at the site, including crushed slag mounds. An interactive, online version of this map is available at https://bit.ly/KENOnline

and ground-truthing. The spatial distribution of this type of metallurgical byproduct at the site provides important context to the study of this archaeologically significant material, which has also been mapped at the contemporaneous site of Khirbat al-Jariya (Liss et al., 2020), providing an important link between the two sites.

The value of this high-resolution documentation of site conditions was unfortunately demonstrated in July 2019, when KEN was damaged by a large vehicle driving through the center of the site (Fig. 7). This damage, passing between excavation Areas S and T and continuing into the center of the site, disturbed several of the slag mounds that provide an invaluable source of evidence of metallurgical activity in Faynan during the Iron Age. This destruction can be situated against plans to renew

Maps and Models: Applications of GIS and Image-Based Modeling to Field... 1119

Fig. 7 Image of recent (ca. July 2019) destruction at Khirbat en-Nahas, when a large vehicle drove through the site, disturbing slag mounds and architectural remains. The destruction is at the bottom-left (northeast) part of the site. Photo credit: APAAME, APAAME_20211022_DS-0159

copper mining within the Dana Biosphere Reserve in which the archaeological sites of the Faynan region are located, posing additional threats to these sites (ICOMOS, 2021; Uddin, 2021). Economic development projects, such as mining operations for example, are a well-known threat to archaeological heritage (Petzet et al. 2000; Zaina, 2019). In general, the economic benefit derived from these projects should be balanced against the risk to heritage sites through sustainable development (Petzet et al., 2000). Finding this balance is beyond the scope of this paper.

However, digital recording techniques, when applied to at-risk archaeological sites, can mitigate the effects of the damage caused to these sites by economic development or post-excavation site degradation, as seen above (for more on cultural heritage risk in Faynan: https://bit.ly/KENDamage). Three-dimensional recording, in particular, can play a key role in digital preservation of cultural heritage (Lercari et al., 2016; Stylianidis & Remondino, 2016). In addition, digital datasets can be shared publicly, on platforms such as SketchFab for 3-D datasets or ArcGIS Online, a for-profit web-mapping platform (Baione et al., 2018; Means, 2015; Scopigno et al., 2017; Smith, 2016). The publication of spatial datasets online can be a valuable tool for teaching and public outreach and scholarly publishing (Cannon et al., 2021; Howry, 2017; Malinverni et al., 2019; von Schwerin, 2013). As discussed above, making 3-D models of sites publicly and freely available can complement ongoing debate about the role of Khirbat en-Nahas during the Iron Age and serve as a public record of the condition of the site when it was recorded in 2014 prior to being damaged in 2019. The same research and documentation benefits hold true for publishing the site orthophoto and derivative vectorization of key features at the site, many of which were irreversibly altered by the damage to the site. The 3-D model recorded through the LAAP-IBM methods and combined with the post-excavation model of Area M is published on Sketchfab at https://skfb.ly/ozZ6p. Also, the model-derived orthophoto of Khirbat en-Nahas is available with vectorized architecture and slag mounds at https://bit.ly/KENOnline. By publishing these datasets in open access formats online, we aim to publicly preserve the condition of Khirbat en-Nahas prior to the recent damages, as well as facilitating scholarly and public engagement with the site and its remains.

Despite the advantages of digital recording and publication, caution is warranted when these datasets are produced with the intent of preservation. It is important to note that 3-D models are not objective records of their subject, but rather a subjective depiction, which, like a photograph, brings in the bias of its author (Garstki, 2017). Indeed the tools used to create the model influence the questions being asked of the archaeological remains (Zubrow, 2006). A digital model of a site also provides a limited perspective on the remains at the site. Understanding the remains at Khirbat en-Nahas still depends on physical investigation of the material culture at the site, allowing archaeologists to make observations and develop skills (Caraher, 2016; Kersel, 2016). Thus, a digital record of the original appearance of the site is necessarily limited in its usefulness. Moreover, digital preservations and reconstructions must reckon with the ownership of cultural heritage and the implications of publishing in certain ways (Thompson, 2017). These are challenging issues that apply to many digital archaeology projects. However, these can be mitigated by community engagement and multivocality in the presentation of archaeological data (Morgan & Eve, 2012; Richardson, 2018).

Overall, cyber-archaeological recording facilitates the digital preservation of at-risk cultural heritage sites, but 3-D models and 2-D maps are not objective records of archaeological remains, nor do they rectify the damage done to sites, limiting the potential for future research. However, these models do retain information about the original appearance of the site, which can facilitate future reinterpretations as well as serve as the basis for public archaeology projects—the "future of the past" (Levy, 2017).

4 "Rivers in the Desert": Applying Hydrology Tools in GIS to Understand Site Location

4.1 Introduction

A growing body of evidence points to the significance of an industrial landscape in Iron Age Faynan, Jordan, in which the natural resources across the entire region were leveraged for the production of copper by a complex society. The distribution of sites across the region has been examined by a number of surveys (Barker et al., 2007; Knabb et al. 2014; Levy et al., 2001, 2003; MacDonald 1988, 1992; MacDonald et al., 2004). However, understanding the specific reasons why these Iron Age copper production sites are located where they are has not been comprehensively addressed, beyond a general understanding of their proximity to the copper resources of the region.

Addressing the reasons behind site location in detail requires a holistic perspective on the landscape and movement. Such analysis, conducted in the arid regions of the Southern Levant, must contend with the central importance of wadi channels to ancient life. This is demonstrated nowhere more vividly than in Levy's work (with David Alon; Alon & Levy, 1980; Levy, 1984; Levy & Alon, 1983) surveying the Nahal Besor and Nahal Be'er Sheva, illustrating the Chalcolithic population expansion that developed in tandem with exploitation of the hydrological potential of wadis. In short, this is *How Ancient Man First Utilized the Rivers in the Desert* (Levy, 1990; cf. Glueck, 1959). Levy's surveys illustrate the importance of physical presence in the landscape for understanding the patterns of ancient life. Yet, his more recent work also demonstrates the power of technology in providing insight into the past—3-D modeling and GIS have been central components of the ELRAP field methodology for decades (Levy et al., 2001). GIS in particular is a tool well-suited to address settlement patterns across the ancient landscape.

Sophisticated GIS modeling of the landscape must take into account the human experience in the landscape (Tilley, 1994). Such an approach can be termed "situated subjectivity" (Lock et al., 2014) which is lacking in many early GIS studies of site location, in which predictive models attempt to explain site locations in terms of environmental variables (Kvamme, 2005; Wescott & Brandon, 2003). This essentially functional and environmentally deterministic approach often fails to factor in social or political variables that are frequently primary variables in site location decisions (Gaffney & Van Leusen, 1995; Kvamme, 2005). Thus, approaches that consider human interaction with their surroundings are preferable (Wheatley, 2004). Cost-path analysis and visibility studies are two common approaches in this avenue (Verhagen, 2018). In recent years, scholars have used increasingly sophisticated forms of these approaches to unlock the potential of GIS for understanding social factors behind site location decisions (Earley-Spadoni, 2015; Frachetti et al., 2017; Howey, 2007; Howey & Brouwer Burg, 2017; Murrieta-Flores, 2012; Verhagen et al., 2019). More specifically, the use of hydrological tools in GIS, which generally model the flow of water across a surface, can be useful for understanding natural movement corridors across the landscape. In particular, the *Flow Accumulation* tool offered by ArcGIS has been used to identify potential ancient movement networks (Fábrega Álvarez, 2006; Frachetti, 2006; Frachetti et al., 2017; Llobera et al., 2011; Whitley & Hicks, 2003). This tool produces a raster dataset where each pixel represents the accumulation of water based on the direction of flow on a raster surface, thereby identifying stream channels. The tool can also be adjusted using a weight raster, typically to reflect different rates of rainfall across the landscape (Esri, 2021). However, it can also be used to model the movement of humans, therefore allowing for a more nuanced understanding of site location (Fábrega Álvarez,

2006; Frachetti, 2006; Frachetti et al., 2017; Llobera et al., 2011; Whitley & Hicks, 2003). These studies conceptually relate to analysis of optimal routes through least cost-paths (e.g., Lucero et al., 2021; Rosenswig & Martínez Tuñón, 2020; Taliaferro et al., 2010). However, flow accumulation-based approaches differ in that their analyses are somewhat more open-ended and can be used to study general patterns of movement rather than specific paths from one site to another (Llobera et al., 2011). As such, this approach can be useful for examining the distribution of sites in a region in comparison to social variables.

Iron Age Faynan can be described as an "industrial landscape" (Liss et al. 2020). Largely occupied by pastoral nomads, the degree of sedentism represented by major copper smelting sites in the region such as Khirbat en-Nahas and Khirbat al-Jariya can be explained by the exploitation of the plentiful copper resources in the wadis of Faynan. However, proximity to copper ores is not the only factor that explains the location of these sites. It is also likely that the locations of these sites were selected based on the availability of water and food resources to provision workers involved in copper mining and smelting as well as strategic considerations involving protecting copper from potential enemies. The latter consideration is suggested by the presence of a large, 75 m × 75 m fortress at Khirbat en-Nahas (Levy et al., 2014) on the bank of the wadi that provides an access route to the copper mines in the area. The hypothesis that key sites in Iron Age Faynan were carefully located with an eye toward protecting copper resources can be examined through the study of potential movement patterns in the landscape using hydrological tools in GIS.

4.2 Methods

In order to understand the extent to which wadis in the Faynan region are central to movement patterns, we applied a number of hydrological tools to an ASTER GDEM elevation dataset. First, in order to prepare the 30 m DEM for hydrological modeling, we filled sinks (minor depressions in an elevation dataset that disrupt flow modeling) in the dataset using the *Fill* tool in ArcGIS Pro in order to ensure that flow across the landscape would be appropriately modeled. Second, the *Flow Direction* tool was applied to the filled DEM which maps the flow of water based on elevation. Ordinarily, when applying hydrological tools to the movement of people across the landscape, a cost distance tool may be applied to reflect the practicality of movement in various directions, including uphill. However, in this case, copper ore mined in the region was largely moved downhill to smelting sites and likely distributed westward. Moreover, wadi channels would have been the only viable routes for the transport of copper and ore. Thus, the flow of water downhill (modeled using the *Flow Direction* tool) and through the wadis provides a useful hypothesis for how copper was transported from mines to smelting sites and subsequently traded. However, a key conceptual difference comes in the application of *Flow Accumulation*. In applying this tool, we have introduced the locations of copper mines across the Faynan region as a *Weight* for the tool, with each mine assigned a value of 1 given

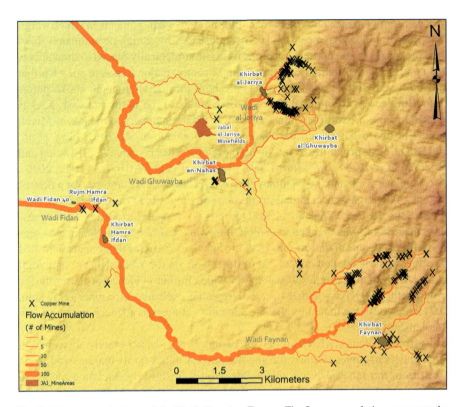

Fig. 8 Flow accumulation model of Early Iron Age Faynan. The flow accumulation represents the movement of copper from mines in the region to copper smelting sites, and westward to the Wadi Arabah

the uncertainty in evaluating how much copper ore was recovered from each mine. In effect, the results of the *Flow Accumulation* tool therefore model the "flow" of copper from the mines, through the natural transportation corridors of the wadis in the region, and into the Wadi Arabah. These results (Fig. 8) provide a useful analytical frame to determine which sites in the Faynan region are optimally positioned to control the movement and distribution of copper from mines to eventual trade destinations.

4.3 Results and Discussion

Results of this analysis point toward the significance of the Wadi Fidan, Wadi Faynan, Wadi al-Ghuwayba, and Wadi al-Jariya, to the copper resources of the Faynan region. The accumulated flow modeled by the hydrological tools described above, though a crude estimate of the amount of copper potentially moving through these strategic channels, provides a quantifiable estimate of the relative prominence of each location in the wadis of Faynan. Proximity to wadi segments in which a high flow rate of copper has been modeled (represented by a high accumulated flow) therefore suggests the optimal locations for a site strategically placed to limit access and control the distribution of copper. Significantly, major Iron Age sites Khirbat en-Nahas and Khirbat al-Jariya (KAJ) are both located at strategic choke points controlling access to mines further up these wadis to the north and east. KAJ is located in close proximity to mines (the Wadi al-Jariya mines and the Ras al-Miyah mines) in two tributaries to the Wadi al-Jariya (Knabb et al., 2014; Levy et al., 2003). The clear proximity of the site to these mines has been previously noted and proposed as a *raison d'être* for the site (Ben-Yosef et al., 2010; Liss et al., 2020). The 38 mines north and the 28 mines east of KAJ "flow" and combine (for a flow of 66, one of the highest accumulations in proximity to a site in the entire region) just south of the site in the Wadi al-Jariya. This modeling appears to corroborate suggestions that the site was founded to exploit these mines. However, modeling also suggests that occupants of the site may have mediated access to the mines and controlled the movement of smelted copper out of the region via the Wadi al-Jariya and Wadi Fidan. Analysis of ceramics at the site provides further evidence of the exclusive control elites at KAJ wielded over interregional exchange of copper (Howland, 2021), a process facilitated by the site's location at a key bottleneck in the narrow Wadi al-Jariya.

Khirbat en-Nahas (KEN), on the other hand, is not located exactly adjacent to a large cluster of mines. Rather, the site has several mines on its margins and is ca. 1 km from the Jabal al-Jariya minefields. However, flow accumulation modeling provides another hypothesis for the site's location. Khirbat en-Nahas is located at a strategic narrowing of the Wadi al-Ghuwayba downstream from an accumulated 95 copper mines according to the modeling presented here. This includes all of the mines from the Wadi al-Jariya and Ras al-Miyah complexes, as well as the mines on the margins of the site. Thus, the large fortress at the north end of the site directly overlooks the key passage to about half of the ancient copper mines in the Faynan region. This flow accumulation model helps us to understand that the fortress at KEN and the site itself occupy key strategic positions in the industrial landscape allowing elites at this site to control and manage access to copper resources and its distribution via trade.

These two sites are the most strategically placed Iron Age sites with regard to the copper resources of northern Faynan. However, study of other contemporaneous sites also provides relevant observations. Three important Early Iron Age sites are also located alongside an area of significant flow at the mouth of the Wadi Fidan: Rujm Hamra Ifdan, Wadi Fidan 40, and Khirbat Hamra Ifdan, a watchtower, a cemetery, and a copper smelting site, respectively. An accumulated flow of over 90 passes these sites, largely from mines located in tributaries of the Wadi Faynan, north of Khirbat Faynan. Though these sites are located over 6 km away from the southern mine district in the Wadi Faynan, the flow accumulation model still helps to indicate the strategic location of these sites at one of the key entrances to the Faynan region. This interpretation meshes with previous viewshed analysis of Rujm Hamra Ifdan, which has demonstrated the site's advantageous position for surveying access routes to the Wadi al-Ghuwayba and KEN from the Wadi Arabah (Smith et al., 2014). The location of these sites should therefore be interpreted as part of an overall landscape approach to controlling and limiting access to copper resources in the region.

Finally, one significant Early Iron Age site in the region, Khirbat al-Ghuwayba, is not located adjacent to any accumulated flow of copper due to its location in the Wadi al-Ghuwayba east of any copper mines. This seemingly inauspicious location, however, can be explained by the site's position straddling the 'Ain al-Ghuwayba, a perennial spring that may have provided much of the water used by the inhabitants of Faynan during the Early Iron Age (Liss et al., 2020). Thus, the actual flow of water provides a likely explanation for the location of this site. Taken as a whole, most of the Early Iron Age sites in the Faynan region seem to be strategically positioned to limit access to and control the distribution of the two most valuable resources in the region—water and copper.

Despite the utility of the flow accumulation model for modeling the movement of copper across the Iron Age landscape, some observations based on the data show the limitations of this approach. First, as noted above, the Jabal al-Jariya minefields are located ca. 1 km from KEN. This distance is well within the sphere of influence of the site; however, the flow accumulation model does not reflect KEN's influence over the copper resources from these fields due to the nature of the watersheds in the region. Thus, it is likely that the model actually substantially underestimates the degree to which occupants of KEN exercised control over the copper resources in the region. The Jabal al-Jariya (JAJ) minefields also provide another example of another major caveat to this analysis—the difficulty of quantifying the copper ores exploited from each mine. Each ancient mine identified through the various surveys in the region has been given an equal weight for considering its relative role in the exploitation of copper in the region, despite the certainty that mines varied in their productivity. However, calculating the amount of copper exploited from each mine is an impossible task, and therefore this simplifying assumption was necessary. In the case of the JAJ minefields, which contain hundreds of pit mines located to exploit the copper resources of the colluvium/alluvium deposits (Ben-Yosef et al., 2009), the distribution of individual mines has not been mapped at high-resolution. With only a few mines to represent the overall copper exploited in this specific area, the accumulated flow from these minefields is not proportional to copper resources mined here. Finally, all of this analysis relies on the assumption that copper mined in Faynan moved primarily from mines, down wadis to copper production sites, and from copper production sites westward to the Negev and beyond. This general scheme is consistent with existing reconstructions of the Early Iron Age copper trade (Ben Dor Evian, 2017; Howland, 2021; Martin & Finkelstein, 2013). However, other proposals for the movement of copper—including northward through Moab—have been suggested, though without the same degree of corroborating evidence (Finkelstein & Lipschits, 2011). As such, this model is largely appropriate for considering the paradigm of westward exchange of copper.

In sum, the flow accumulation model described here serves as a useful analytical tool for considering how movement of key resources across the landscape can be controlled and restricted by elites at strategically located settlements such as KEN and KAJ, whose excavation by ELRAP under the direction of Levy and Najjar provides the basis of this study. This work also serves as a foundation for future, more sophisticated analyses of movement and exchange that go further in factoring in the situated subjectivity of the human experience in moving across the landscape.

5 Conclusions

As predicted by Levy in 1995 and as evidenced by his cyber-archaeology approach on the ELRAP project, the development of digital methods within archaeology has been revolutionary for the discipline. The case studies presented here provide three examples of how the combination of traditional methods of field excavation and digital methods can open new avenues in our approach toward the archaeological record. These approaches apply equally to data acquisition, curation, analysis, and dissemination, the four components of Levy's cyber-archaeology (Levy, 2017). Each of the three case studies presented here builds on cutting-edge digital data acquisition techniques, including GIS-based survey and IBM. The curation of legacy datasets such as digital site photographs is critical, as demonstrated in the first case study, for the preservation of the fragile archaeological record. Moreover, the flow accumulation model presented in the third case study provides an example of how digital techniques can serve as the basis for hypothesis generation for archaeological analysis. Finally, the first two case studies also serve as an example of the dissemination of data in digital environments, facilitating future reuse and reinterpretation. Thus, these case studies aim to model the full potential of cyber-archaeology as applied to datasets derived from archaeological fieldwork.

Acknowledgments A special thanks to Tom Levy for making this research possible. Thanks also to Mohammad Najjar. We would like to thank Erez Ben-Yosef and Ian W.N. Jones for the opportunity to contribute to this volume. Thanks also to members of the communities of Faynan and Qirayqira for their hospitality and assistance in the fieldwork described here. Finally, thanks to Scott McAvoy and Anthony Tamberino for all their help with the 3-D modelling components of this research, and Tyler Tucker for his work on the Khirbat en-Nahas map.

References

Aerial Photographic Archive of Archaeology in the Middle East (APAAME), archive accessible from: www.humanities.uwa.edu.au/research/cah/aerial-archaeology

Alon, D., & Levy, T. E. (1980). Preliminary note on the distribution of Chalcolithic sites on the Wadi Beer-Sheba—Lower Wadi Besor drainage system. *Israel Exploration Journal*, 140–147.

Baione, C., Johnson, T. D., & Megale, C. (2018, July). Communicating archaeology at Poggio del Molino. 3D virtualization and the visitor experience on and off site. In *International and interdisciplinary conference on digital environments for education, arts and heritage* (pp. 681–690). Springer.

Barker, G., Gilbertson, D. D., & Mattingly, D. J. (2007). *Archaeology and desertification: The Wadi Faynan Landscape Survey, Southern Jordan*. Oxbow Books.

Ben-Dor Evian, S. (2017). *Follow the negebite Ware road* (pp. 19–27). Studies in the History and Archaeology of Ancient Israel in Honor of Israel Finkelstein.

Ben-Yosef, E. (2010). *Technology and social process: Oscillations in Iron Age copper production and power in Southern Jordan* (Publication No. BenYosef_ucsd_0033-D_11379) [Doctoral dissertation, University of California San Diego]. ProQuest Dissertations Publishing.

Ben-Yosef, E. (2019). The architectural bias in current biblical archaeology. *Vestus Testamentum, 69*(3), 361–387.

Ben-Yosef, E. (2020). And yet, a nomadic error: A reply to Israel Finkelstein. *Antiguo Oriente, 18*, 33–60.

Ben-Yosef, E. (2021). Rethinking the social complexity of early Iron Age nomads. *Jerusalem Journal of Archaeology, 1*, 155–179.

Ben-Yosef, E., Levy, T., & Najjar, M. (2009). New Iron Age copper-mine fields discovered in southern Jordan. *Near Eastern Archaeology, 72*, 98–101.

Ben-Yosef, E., Levy, T. E., Higham, T., Najjar, M., & Tauxe, L. (2010). The beginning of Iron Age copper production in the southern Levant: New evidence from Khirbat al-Jariya, Faynan. *Jordan. Antiquity, 84*(325), 724–746.

Ben-Yosef, E., Liss, B., Yagel, O. A., Tirosh, O., Najjar, M., & Levy, T. E. (2019). Ancient technology and punctuated change: Detecting the emergence of the Edomite Kingdom in the Southern Levant. *PLoS One, 14*(9), e0221967.

Bienkowski, P. (1990). Umm el-Biyara, Tawilan and Buseirah in Retrospect. *Levant, 22*, 91–109.

Cannon, M. B., Cohen, A. S., & Jimenez, K. N. (2021). Connecting native students to STEM research using virtual archaeology: A case study from the water heritage anthropological project. *Advances in Archaeological Practice, 9*(2), 175–185.

Caraher, W. (2016). Slow archaeology: Technology, efficiency, and archaeological work. In E. W. Averett, J. M. Gordon, & D. B. Counts (Eds.), *Mobilizing the past for a digital future: The potential of digital archaeology* (pp. 421–442). The Digital Press at the University of North Dakota.

De Reu, J., De Smedt, P., Herremans, D., Van Meirvenne, M., Laloo, P., & De Clercq, W. (2014). On introducing an image-based 3-D reconstruction method in archaeological excavation practice. *Journal of Archaeological Science, 41*, 251–262.

Earley-Spadoni, T. (2015). Landscapes of warfare: Intervisibility analysis of Early Iron and Urartian fire beacon stations (Armenia). *Journal of Archaeological Science: Reports, 3*, 22–30.

Esri. (2021). *Flow accumulation function*. Flow Accumulation function-ArcGIS Pro | Documentation. Retrieved November 8, 2021, from https://pro.arcgis.com/en/pro-app/latest/help/analysis/raster-functions/flow-accumulation-raster-function.htm.

Fábrega-Álvarez, P. (2006). Moving without destination: A theoretical, GIS based determination of routes (optimal accumulation model of movement from a given origin). *Archaeological Computing Newsletter, 64*, 7–11.

Finkelstein, I. (2020). The Arabah copper polity and the rise of Iron Age Edom: A bias in biblical archaeology? *Antiguo Oriente, 18*, 11–32.

Finkelstein, I., & Lipschits, O. (2011). The genesis of Moab: A proposal. *Levant, 43*(2), 139–152.

Forte, M. (2010). *Cyber-archaeology* (BAR international series) (Vol. 2177). Archaeopress.

Forte, M. (2011). Cyber-archaeology: Notes on the simulation of the past. *Virtual Archaeology Review, 2*, 7–18.

Frachetti, M. (2006). Digital archaeology and the scalar structure of pastoral landscapes. In T. Evans & P. Daly (Eds.), *Digital archaeology: Bridging method and theory* (pp. 113–132). Routledge.

Frachetti, M. D., Smith, C. E., Traub, C. M., & Williams, T. (2017). Nomadic ecology shaped the highland geography of Asia's silk roads. *Nature, 543*(7644), 193–198. https://doi.org/10.1038/nature21696

Frank, F. (1934). Aus der 'Araba I. Reiseberichte. *Zeitschrift des Deutschen Palästina-Vereins, 57*(3/4), 191–280.

Gaffney, V., & Van Leusen, M. (1995). Postscript-GIS, environmental determinism and archaeology: A parallel text. In G. Stancic & Z. Stančič (Eds.), *Archaeology and geographical information systems: A European perspective* (pp. 367–382).

Garstki, K. (2017). Virtual representation: The production of 3-D digital artifacts. *Journal of Archaeological Method and Theory, 24*(3), 726–750.

Glueck, N. (1935). Explorations in eastern Palestine, II. *Annual of the ASOR, 15*, 1–288.

Glueck, N. (1959). *Rivers in the desert*. Farrar, Straus and Cudahy.

Hammer, E., & Ur, J. (2019). Near eastern landscapes and declassified U2 aerial imagery. *Advances in Archaeological Practice, 7*(2), 107–126.

Hauptmann, A. (2007). *The Archaeometallurgy of copper: Evidence from Faynan, Jordan*. Springer.

Hill, A. C., & Rowan, Y. (2017). Droning on in the badia: UAVs and site documentation at Wadi al-Qattafi. *Near Eastern Archaeology, 80*(2), 114–123.

Howey, M. C. L. (2007). Using multi-criteria cost surface analysis to explore past regional landscapes: A case study of ritual activity and social interaction in Michigan, AD 1200–1600. *Journal of Archaeological Science, 34*(11), 1830–1846.

Howey, M. C. L., & Brouwer Burg, M. (2017). Assessing the state of archaeological GIS research: Unbinding analyses of past landscapes. *Journal of Archaeological Science, 84*, 1–9.

Howland, M. D. (2018). 3-D recording in the field: Style without substance? In I. W. N. Jones & T. E. Levy (Eds.), *Cyber-archaeology and grand narratives: Digital technology and deep-time perspectives on culture change in the middle east* (pp. 19–33). Springer.

Howland, M. D. (2021). *Long-distance trade and social complexity in Iron Age Faynan, Jordan*. [Doctoral dissertation, University of California San Diego]. ProQuest Dissertations Publishing.

Howland, M. D., Kuester, F., & Levy, T. E. (2014). Structure from motion: Twenty-first century field recording with 3-D technology. *Near Eastern Archaeology, 77*, 187–191.

Howland, M. D., Liss, B., Najjar, M., & Levy, T. E. (2015). GIS-based mapping of archaeological sites with low-altitude aerial photography and structure from Motion: A case study from Southern Jordan. In *In 2015 Digital Heritage* (Vol. 1, pp. 91–94). IEEE.

Howland, M. D., Liss, B., Levy, T. E., & Najjar, M. (2020). Integrating digital datasets into public engagement through ArcGIS StoryMaps. *Advances in Archaeological Practice, 8*(4), 351–360.

Howry, J. C. (2017). Publishing landscape archaeology in the digital world. *Journal of Landscape Ecology, 10*(3), 213–229.

ICOMOS. (2021). *Dana Biosphere Reserve: An international call for protection*. https://icomosjordan.org/dana-biosphere-reserve-an-international-call-for-protection/. Accessed 23 Nov 2021.

Kersel, M. M. (2016). Response: Living a semi-digital Kinda life. In E. W. Averett, J. M. Gordon, & D. B. Counts (Eds.), *Mobilizing the past for a digital future: The potential of digital archaeology* (pp. 474–492). The Digital Press at the University of North Dakota.

Knabb, K., Jones, I. W. N., Levy, T. E., & Najjar, M. (2014). Patterns of Iron Age mining and settlement in Jordan's Faynan district: the Wadi al-Jariya survey in context. In T. E. Levy, M. Najjar, & E. Ben-Yosef (Eds.), *New Insights into the Iron Age Archaeology of Edom, Southern Jordan* (pp. 557–625). The Cotsen Institute of Archaeology Press.

Kvamme, K. L. (2005). There and back again: Revisiting archaeological locational modeling. In M. W. Mehrer & K. L. Wescott (Eds.), *GIS and archaeological site location modeling* (pp. 3–38). Taylor and Francis.

Lercari, N., Schulze, J. P., Wendrich, W., Porter, B., Burton, M., & Levy, T. E. (2016). 3-D digital preservation of at-risk global cultural heritage. In C. E. Catalano & L. De Luca (Eds.), *Proceedings of Eurographics Workshop on Graphics and Cultural Heritage (GCH), Genova, Italy, Oct 5–7* (pp. 123–126) The Eurographics Association.

Levy, T. E. (1984). *Chalcolithic settlement and subsistence in the Northern Negev Desert Israel*. [Doctoral dissertation, University of Sheffield].

Levy, T. E. (1990). How ancient man first utilized rivers in the desert. *The Biblical Archaeology Review, 16*(6), 20–31.

Levy, T. E. (1995). From camels to computers: A short history of archaeological method. *The Biblical Archaeology Review, 21*(4), 44–51.

Levy, T. E. (2013). Cyber-archaeology and world cultural heritage: Insights from the Holy Land. *Bulletin of the American Academy of Arts and Sciences, 66*, 26–33.

Levy, T. E. (2015). The past forward. *Biblical Archaeology Review Special Issue: "40 Futures: Experts Predict What's Next for Biblical Archaeology"*, 81–87.

Levy, T. E. (2017). The future of the past: At-risk world heritage, cyber-archaeology, and transdisciplinary research. In O. Lipschits, Y. Gadot, & M. J. Adams (Eds.), *Rethinking Israel: Studies in the history and archaeology of ancient Israel in honor of Israel Finkelstein* (pp. 221–232). Eisenbrauns.

Levy, T. E., & Alon, D. (1983). Chalcolithic settlement patterns in the northern Negev desert. *Current Anthropology, 24*(1), 105–107.

Levy, T. E., & Liss, B. (2020). Cyber-archaeology. In C. Smith (Ed.), *Encyclopedia of global archaeology*. Springer.

Levy, T. E., Adams, R. B., Witten, A. J., Anderson, J. D., Arbel, Y., Kuah, S., Moreno, J., Lo, A., & Wagonner, M. (2001). Early metallurgy, interaction, and social change: The Jabal Hamrat Fidan (Jordan) research design and 1998 archaeological survey: Preliminary report. *Annual of the Department of Antiquities of Jordan, 45*, 159–187.

Levy, T. E., Adams, R. B., Anderson, J. D., Najjar, M., Smith, N., Arbel, Y., Soderbaum, L., & Muniz, A. (2003). An Iron Age Landscape in the Edomite Lowlands: Archaeological Surveys Along the Wadi al-Guwayb and Wadi al-Jariya, Jabal Hamrat Fidan, Jordan, 2002. *Annual of the Department of Antiquities of Jordan, 47*, 247–277.

Levy, T. E., Higham, T., Bronk Ramsey, C., Smith, N. G., Ben-Yosef, E., Robinson, M., Munger, S., Knabb, K., Schulze, J. P., Najjar, M., & Tauxe, L. (2008). High-precision radiocarbon dating and historical biblical archaeology in southern Jordan. *Proceedings of the National Academy of Science, 105*, 16460–16465.

Levy, T. E., Petrovic, V., Wypych, W., Gidding, A., Knabb, K., Hernandez, D., Smith, N. G., Schulz, J. P., Savage, S. H., Kuester, F., Ben-Yosef, E., Buitenhuys, V., Barret, C. J., Najjar, M., & DeFanti, T. (2010). On-site digital archaeology 3.0 and cyber-archaeology: Into the future of the past – New developments, delivery and the creation of a data avalanche. In M. Forte (Ed.), *Cyber-archaeology* (BAR international series) (Vol. 2177, pp. 135–153). Archaeopress.

Levy, T. E., Smith, N. G., Najjar, M., DeFanti, T. A., Lin, A. Y.-M., & Kuester, F. (2012). *Cyber-archaeology in the Holy Land: The future of the past*. The Biblical Archaeology Society.

Levy, T. E., Najjar, M., & Ben-Yosef, E. (Eds.). (2014). *New Insights in the Iron Age Archaeology of Edom, Southern Jordan*. UCLA Cotsen Institute of Archaeology Press.

Levy, T. E., Ben-Yosef, E., & Najjar, M. (2018a). Intensive surveys, large-scale excavation strategies and Iron Age industrial metallurgy in Faynan, Jordan; fairy tales don't come true. In E. Ben-Yosef (Ed.), *Mining for ancient copper: Essays in memory of Beno Rothenberg* (pp. 245–258). Eisenbrauns and Emery and Claire Yass Publications in Archaeology.

Levy, T. E., Sideris, T., Howland, M., Liss, B., Tsokas, G., Stambolidis, A., Fikos, E., Vargemezis, G., Tsourlos, P., Georgopoulos, A., Papatheodorou, G., Garaga, M., Christodoulou, D., Norris, R., Rivera-Collazo, I., & Liritzis, I. (2018b). At-risk world heritage, cyber, and marine archaeology: The Kastrouli–Antikyra Bay land and sea project, Phokis, Greece. In T. E. Levy & I. W. N. Jones (Eds.), *Cyber-archaeology and grand narratives* (pp. 143–234). Springer.

Levy, T. E., Smith, C., Agcaoili, K., Kannan, A., Goren, A., Schulze, J. P., & Yago, G. (2020). At-risk world heritage and virtual reality visualization for cyber-archaeology. In M. Forte & H. Murteira (Eds.), *Digital cities: Between history and archaeology* (pp. 151–171). Oxford University Press.

Liss, B., Howland, M. D., Lorentzen, B., Smitheram, C., Najjar, M., & Levy, T. E. (2020). Up the Wadi: Development of an Iron Age Industrial Landscape in Faynan, Jordan. *Journal of Field Archaeology, 45*(6), 413–427.

Llobera, M., Fábrega-Álvarez, P., & Parcero-Oubiña, C. (2011). Order in movement: A GIS approach to accessibility. *Journal of Archaeological Science, 38*(4), 843–851.

Lock, G., Kormann, M., & Pouncett, J. (2014). Visibility and movement: Towards a GIS-based integrated approach. In S. Polla & P. Verhagen (Eds.), *Computational approaches to the study of movement in archaeology. Theory, practice and interpretation of factors and effects of long term landscape formation and transformation* (pp. 23–42). De Gruyter.

Lucero, G. F., Castro, S. C., & Cortegoso, V. (2021). GIS modeling of lithic procurement in highlands: Archaeological and actualistic approach in the Andes. *Journal of Archaeological Science: Reports, 38*, 103026.

MacDonald, B. (1988). *The Wadi el-Hasa archaeological survey 1979–1983, West-Central Jordan.* Wilfrid Laurier University Press.

MacDonald, B. (1992). *The Southern Ghors and northeast 'Araba archaeological survey.* J. R. Collis.

MacDonald, B., Herr, L. G., Neely, M. P., Gagos, T., Moumani, K., & Rockman, M. (2004). *The Tafila-Busayra archaeological survey 1999–2001, West-Central Jordan.* American Schools of Oriental Research.

Maeir, A. M. (2021). Identity creation and resource controlling strategies: Thoughts on Edomite Ethnogenesis and development. *Bulletin of ASOR, 386.*

Magnani, M., & Schroder, W. (2015). New approaches to modeling the volume of earthen archaeological features: A case-study from the Hopewell culture mounds. *Journal of Archaeological Science, 64*, 12–21.

Magnani, M., Douglass, M., Schroder, W., Reeves, J., & Braun, D. R. (2020). The digital revolution to come: Photogrammetry in archaeological practice. *American Antiquity, 85*(4), 737–760.

Malinverni, E. S., Pierdicca, R., Colosi, F., & Orazi, R. (2019). Dissemination in archaeology: A GIS-based StoryMap for Chan Chan. *Journal of Cultural Heritage Management and Sustainable Development, 9*(4), 500–519.

Marín-Buzón, C., Pérez-Romero, A., López-Castro, J. L., Jerbania, I. B., & Manzano-Agugliaro, F. (2021). Photogrammetry as a new scientific tool in archaeology: Worldwide research trends. *Sustainability, 13*, 5319.

Martin, M. A. S., & Finkelstein, I. (2013). Iron IIA pottery from the Negev Highlands: Petrographic investigation and historical implications. *Tel Aviv, 40*(1), 6–45.

Means, B. K. (2015). Promoting a more interactive public archaeology: Archaeological visualization and reflexivity through virtual artifact curation. *Advances in Archaeological Practice, 3*(3), 235–248.

Morgan, C., & Eve, S. (2012). DIY and digital archaeology: What are you doing to participate? *World Archaeology, 44*(4), 521–537.

Murrieta-Flores, P. (2012). Understanding movement during late prehistory through spatial technologies: The role of natural areas of transit in south-western Iberia. *Trabajos de Prehistoria, 69*, 114–133.

Olson, B. R., Placchetti, R. A., Quartermaine, J., & Killebrew, A. E. (2013). The Tel Akko Total Archaeology Project (Akko, Israel): Assessing the suitability of multi-scale 3-D field recording in archaeology. *Journal of Field Archaeology, 38*(3), 244–262.

Pavlidis, G., Liritzis, I., & Levy, T. E. (2017). Pedagogy and engagement in at-risk world heritage initiatives. In M. L. Vincent, V. M. López-Menchero Bendicho, M. Ioannides, & T. E. Levy (Eds.), *Heritage and archaeology in the digital age: Acquisition, curation, and dissemination of spatial cultural heritage data* (pp. 167–183). Springer.

Petrovic, V., Gidding, A., Wypych, T., Kuester, F., DeFanti, T., & Levy, T. E. (2011). Dealing with archaeology's data avalanche. *Computer, 44*(7), 56–60.

Petzet, M., Burke, S., & Bumbaru, D. (2000). *ICOMOS world report 2000 on monuments and sites in danger.*

Quartermaine, J., Olson, B. R., & Killebrew, A. E. (2014). Image-based modeling approaches to 2D and 3D digital drafting in archaeology at Tel Akko and Qasrin: Two case studies. *Journal of Eastern Mediterranean Archaeology and Heritage Studies, 2*(2), 110–127.

Richardson, L. J. (2018). Ethical challenges in digital public archaeology. *Journal of Computer Applications in Archaeology, 1*(1), 64–73.

Roosevelt, C. H., Cobb, P., Moss, E., Olson, B. R., & Ünlüsoy, S. (2015). Excavation is destruction digitization: Advances in archaeological practice. *Journal of Field Archaeology, 40*(3), 325–346.

Rosenswig, R. M., & Martínez Tuñón, A. (2020). Changing Olmec trade routes understood through Least Cost Path analysis. *Journal of Archaeological Science, 118*, 105146.

Savage, S. H., Johnson, A., & Levy, T. E. (2017). Terrawatchers, crowdsourcing, and at-risk world heritage in the Middle East. In M. L. Vincent, V. M. López-Menchero Bendicho, M. Ioannides, & T. E. Levy (Eds.), *Heritage and archaeology in the digital age: Acquisition, curation, and dissemination of spatial cultural heritage data* (pp. 67–77). Springer.

Scopigno, R., Callieri, M., Dellepiane, M., Ponchio, F., & Potenziani, M. (2017). Delivering and using 3D models on the web: Are we ready? *Virtual Archaeology Review, 8*(17), 1–9.

Sideris, A., Liritzis, I., Liss, B., Howland, M. D., & Levy, T. E. (2017). At-risk cultural heritage: New excavations and finds from the Mycenaean site of Kastrouli, Phokis, Greece. *Mediterranean Archaeology & Archaeometry, 17*(1), 271–185.

Smith, D. A. (2016). Online interactive thematic mapping: Applications and techniques for socioeconomic research. *Computers, Environment and Urban Systems, 57*, 106–117.

Smith, N. G., Najjar, M., & Levy, T. E. (2014). A picture of the early and Late Iron Age II in the lowlands. In T. E. Levy, M. Najjar, & E. Ben-Yosef (Eds.), *New Insights into the Iron Age Archaeology of Edom, Southern Jordan* (pp. 723–739). The Cotsen Institute of Archaeology Press.

Smith, N. G., Howland, M., & Levy, T. E. (2015, September). Digital archaeology field recording in the 4th dimension: ArchField C++ a 4D GIS for digital field work. In *2015 Digital Heritage* (Vol. 2, pp. 251–258). IEEE.

Stylianidis, E., & Remondino, F. (Eds.). (2016). *3D recording, documentation and management of cultural heritage*. Whittles Publishing.

Taliaferro, M. S., Schriever, B. A., & Shackley, M. S. (2010). Obsidian procurement, least cost path analysis, and social interaction in the Mimbres area of southwestern New Mexico. *Journal of Archaeological Science, 37*(3), 536–548.

Tebes, J. M. (2021). A reassessment of the Chronology of the Iron Age Site of Khirbet en-Nahas, Southern Jordan. *Palestine Exploration Quarterly*.

Thompson, E. L. (2017). Legal and ethical considerations for digital recreations of cultural heritage. *Chapman Law Review, 20*(1), 153–176.

Tilley, C. (1994). *A phenomenology of landscape: Places, paths, and monuments*. Berg.

Uddin, R. (2021, August 20). Jordan to open copper mine in country's largest nature reserve. *Middle East Eye*. https://www.middleeasteye.net/news/jordan-dana-nature-reserve-open-copper-mine.

Verhagen, P. (2018). Spatial analysis in archaeology: Moving into new territories. In C. Siart, M. Forbriger, & O. Bubenzer (Eds.), *Digital geoarchaeology. Natural science in archaeology*. Springer. https://doi.org/10.1007/978-3-319-25316-9_2

Verhagen, P., Nuninger, L., & Groenhuijzen, M. R. (2019). Modelling of pathways and movement networks in archaeology: An overview of current approaches. In P. Verhagen, J. Joyce, & M. R. Groenhuijzen (Eds.), *Finding the limits of the limes: Modelling demography, economy and transport on the edge of the Roman empire* (pp. 217–249). Springer.

Vincent, M., Vincent, M. L., & Logee, J. R. (2015). Balking at balks: New approaches to section drawings. Poster. *American Schools of Oriental Research Annual Meeting*.

von Schwerin, J., Richards-Rissetto, H., Remondino, F., Agugiaro, G., & Girardi, G. (2013). The MayaArch3-D project: A 3-D WebGIS for analyzing ancient architecture and landscapes. *Literary and Linguistic Computing, 28*(4), 736–753.

Wescott, K. L., & Brandon, R. J. (Eds.). (2003). *Practical applications of GIS for archaeologists: A predictive modelling toolkit*. CRC Press.

Wheatley, D. (2004). Making space for an archaeology of place. *Internet Archaeology, 15*.

Whitley, T. G., & Hicks, L. M. (2003). A geographic information systems approach to understanding potential prehistoric and historic travel corridors. *Southeastern Archaeology, 22*, 77–91.

Zaina, F. (2019). A risk assessment for cultural heritage in southern Iraq: Framing drivers, threats and actions affecting archaeological sites. *Conservation and Management of Archaeological Sites, 21*(3), 184–206.

Zubrow, E. (2006). Digital archaeology: A historical context. In T. Evans & P. Daly (Eds.), *Digital archaeology: Bridging method and theory* (pp. 10–31). Routledge.

Archaeological Evidence of Casual Snacking and Resource Provisioning at Khirbat al-Jariya (ca. Eleventh to Tenth Centuries BCE), an Iron-Age Copper Production Site

Luke Stroth, Arianna Garvin Suero, Brady Liss, Matthew D. Howland ⓘ, **and Jade D'Alpoim Guedes**

Abstract In this chapter we present the results of a paleobotanical analysis of Khirbat al-Jariya, an Iron-Age (ca. eleventh to tenth centuries BCE) copper smelting workshop in Faynan, Jordan. The macrobotanical collection was dominated by easily procured fruits and nuts that required little preparation, such as dates (*Phoenix dactylifera*), grapes (*Vitis* sp.) and figs (*Ficus* sp.) which we characterize as likely "snack foods." Evidence for grain processing, in terms of cleaning and removal of chaff, is largely absent, and there is no meaningful spatial patterning to the discard of food debris. This suggests that food consumption was a casual process at Khirbat al-Jariya and that food products requiring preparation were processed elsewhere. Comparing this data to that of contemporary sites indicates that this dominance of snack foods is particular to the Faynan region. It is possible that Khirbat al-Jariya was only seasonally occupied, under which circumstances a practice of casual snacking supplemented by prepared foods from elsewhere was sustainable. This complicates the typical binary of "consumer" and "producer," and we argue that such distinctions may be as much a result of sampling strategies and spatial patterning. We also evaluate how sampling strategies played a role in interpreting the data from Khirbat al-Jariya, which may represent the casual snacking behavior associated with an itinerant industrial community rather than the full spectrum of subsis-

---

Supplementary Information The online version contains supplementary material available at https://doi.org/10.1007/978-3-031-27330-8_48.

L. Stroth (✉) · A. Garvin Suero · B. Liss · J. D'Alpoim Guedes
University of California, San Diego, La Jolla, CA, USA
e-mail: lstroth@ucsd.edu; agarvin@ucsd.edu; bliss@ucsd.edu; jguedes@ucsd.edu

M. D. Howland
Laboratory of Archaeology, University of Georgia, Athens, GA, USA
e-mail: mdh5169@gmail.com

© The Author(s), under exclusive license to Springer Nature Switzerland AG 2023
E. Ben-Yosef, I. W. N. Jones (eds.), *"And in Length of Days Understanding" (Job 12:12): Essays on Archaeology in the Eastern Mediterranean and Beyond in Honor of Thomas E. Levy*, Interdisciplinary Contributions to Archaeology,
https://doi.org/10.1007/978-3-031-27330-8_48

tence during the Iron Age of the Wadi Faynan. Although all societies are some combination of producer and consumer, we argue that the inhabitants of Khirbat al-Jariya were much closer to the consumer end of the spectrum based on both positive evidence for the dominance of snack foods and the negative evidence for food preparation. Their diet consisted of convenient, although seasonal, snack foods, for which the archaeological signal is high, and prepared foods that have not preserved, for which the archaeological signature for local production is almost negligible.

Keywords Paleobotany · Snacking behavior · Paleobotanical sampling · Wadi Faynan · Iron Age archaeology · Consumer-producer spectrum

1 Introduction

Archaeologists have applied a useful, but necessarily simplified, producer-consumer spectrum to describe the suite of food acquisition practices in use at a particular site (e.g., Clark, 1996; Costin, 2001). Comparative ratios of wild to domestic taxa have been used to determine if the inhabitants of certain sites were primary agricultural producers or received cleaned grain from elsewhere (e.g., Fuller & Stevens, 2009). This does assume that there is a clear archaeological signature of a platonic producer and consumer site which may overlook connections or seasonal movement of people between different sites. Very few analyses, however, have looked at the proportions of foods that are transportable and "snackable" foods, such as dates (*Phoenix dactylifera*) or figs (*Ficus* sp.), to foods that require milling or other preparation, such as wheat (*Triticum* sp.) or barley (*Hordeum* sp.). We explore these issues at Khirbat al-Jariya (KAJ), an Iron-Age (ca. eleventh to tenth centuries) copper smelting site in the Faynan region of southern Jordan and propose that high signal of snacking foods can be added to the archaeological correlates of itinerant metallurgists (Ben-Yosef, 2019:362).

In this chapter, we report on the results of a macrobotanical analysis conducted on samples from the 2014 excavation at the site. These samples were collected from a stone structure (Building 2/Area B; Liss et al., 2020) and an industrial slag mound (Area C; Liss et al., 2020). We ask: how did the Iron-Age metalworkers feed themselves? Did they produce their own food, or did they acquire prepared foods through trade or a local sponsor? To what extent did they incorporate convenient "snackable" foods that required no processing? These questions are particularly significant given the desert environment of Faynan (Palmer et al., 2007). We began our analysis with the expectation that the collection would not show evidence for on-site food production given the desert context of the site. If KAJ residents were dependent on a local supplier for their survival, it may suggest that the occupants of KAJ were attached specialists embedded in the economies of the larger region (Clark, 1996; Costin, 2001). This interpretation is supported by recent data indicating that the origins of KAJ were closely tied to the rapid development of the copper-producing industry in the region (Ben-Yosef et al., 2010; Levy et al., 2016), potentially spurred by contact with or emulation of external imperial influences (Ben-Yosef, 2019:364; Ben-Yosef, 2021:162).

Our analysis revealed an overall dominance of fruit and nut taxa that could be sourced locally from nearby sites such as Khirbat al-Ghuwayba, which saddles a perennial spring that feeds local orchards. Other foods that require preparation, such as wheat and barley grains which must be milled into flour to make bread, appear commonly in archaeobotanical assemblages across the region yet are not well represented at Khirbat al-Jariya (Table 1; Supplemental Table 1). The content of the KAJ paleobotanical collection is compared to other sites in the region, which overall demonstrated greater dependence on prepared cereals and less frequent exploitation of fruits, nuts, and other "snack" foods. Our results are consistent with observations from other metalworking sites, such as Timna Valley Site 30 (David et al., 2022). We consider the role that spatial bias may play in the interpretation of this data and discuss the archaeological correlates to casual snacking behavior. We argue that the workers' diets at this site focused on the transport of foods that were either fully prepared, such as baked bread (which leaves little trace in the archaeobotanical record), or on dried/pickled/preserved fruit and nut-based snack foods. This supports prior interpretations that KAJ was occupied by itinerant-worker communities, perhaps supported by the nearby Khirbat en-Nahas. This paper serves as a contribution to Iron-Age paleobotany, a literature for which the "relative dearth of paleoethnobotanical studies" has been noted (Farahani et al., 2016:28). This is the first report of a paleobotanical sample from a metal-working context recovered through systematic flotation (but see David et al., 2022).

2 Archaeological Background to the Faynan Region

The Faynan region of southern Jordan is a small, arid box-canyon rich in copper ores approximately 30 kilometers south of the Dead Sea. Faynan is located in the Saharo-Arabian desert, characterized by a hot and arid climate. The average annual rainfall in Faynan today is only 50–60 millimeters and is highly variable (Palmer et al., 2007). Despite this desert environment, the archaeological record shows that the abundant copper ores of Faynan were exploited since as early as the ninth millennium BCE and intermittently mined into the Islamic period (Ben-Yosef et al., 2010). In the Iron Age (ca. twelfth–ninth centuries BCE), copper production in Faynan reached its industrial peak when the region was characterized by large smelting centers and mining camps (Fig. 1a; Ben-Yosef et al., 2010; Ben-Yosef et al., 2019; Hauptmann, 2007; Levy et al., 2014). Excavations at copper smelting sites in Faynan offer comprehensive records on the timing, scale, and management of copper production during the Early Iron Age, potentially connected to the Biblical Kingdom of Edom (Ben-Yosef, 2010; Ben-Yosef et al., 2019; Levy et al., 2014).

The archaeological and archaeometallurgical findings at Khirbat en-Nahas, Khirbat al-Jariya, and Khirbat al-Ghuwayba, three Iron-Age smelting sites,

Table 1 Total counts and weights of taxa from KAJ

Taxa	Common name	Organ	Condition[a]	Total (count)	Total (weight)
Grains					
Avena/Secale sp.	Oat/Rye	Seed	W	3	0.0077
Cerealia		Seed	W	12	0.044
cf. Cerealia		Seed	W	21	0.1509
Hordeum vulgare	Barley	Grain	W	18	0.1172
Hordeum vulgare	Barley	Grain	F	14	0.0777
Hordeum vulgare	Barley (two-row)	Rachis	W	3	<0.0001
Hordeum vulgare	Barley (hulled)	Grain	W	10	0.0612
Hordeum vulgare	Barley (hulled)	Grain	F	1	0.007
Panicoideae		Seed	W	1	<0.0001
Triticum sp.	Wheat	Grain	W	9	0.0691
Triticum aestivum	Wheat (rachis)	Rachis	W	1	<0.0001
Triticum/Hordeum sp.	Wheat/Barley (seed)	Grain	W	4	0.1095
Triticum/Hordeum sp.	Wheat/Barley	Rachis	F	20	0.0031
Pulses					
Cicer sp.	Chickpea	Seed	W	1	0.1112
cf. *Cicer* sp.	cf. Chickpea	Seed	W	2	0.0975
Fabaceae		Seed	F	17	0.0261
Lens culinaris	Lentil	Seed	W	133	0.6527
Lens culinaris	Lentil	Seed	F	2	<0.0001
Lens/Pisum sp.	Lentil/Pea	Seed	W	35	0.1139
cf. *Lens* sp., cooked	Lentil	Seed	W	4	0.0045
Pisum sativum	Pea	Seed	W	14	0.2299
Pisum sativum	Pea	Seed	F	7	0.0423
Fabaceae	Unidentified domesticated Fabaceae	Seed	W	2	0.0287
Fabaceae	Unidentified wild Fabaceae	Seed	W	2	<0.0001
cf. *Vicia faba*	Faba bean	Seed	W	2	0.0136
Vicia sp.	Vetch	Seed	W	9	0.0502
Fruits					
cf. *Ficus* sp.	cf. Fig	Seed	W	1080	0.2584
Ficus sp.	Fig	Fruit	F	2	0.0206
Phoenix dactylifera	Date palm	Pit	W	135	12.6425
Phoenix dactylifera	Date palm	Pit	F	380	11.9723
Phoenix dactylifera	Date palm	Fruit	W	1	0.4225
Phoenix dactylifera	Date palm	Fruit and Pit	F	3	0.3653
cf. *Pistacia* sp.	cf. Pistachio	Seed	W	8	0.0151
Punica		Seed	W	1	0.0453

(continued)

Archaeological Evidence of Casual Snacking and Resource Provisioning at Khirbat... 1137

Table 1 (continued)

Taxa	Common name	Organ	Condition[a]	Total (count)	Total (weight)
cf. *Rubus* spp.	Rose	Seed	W	1	<0.0001
Vitis sp.	Grapevine	Seed	W	110	1.1797
Vitis sp.	Grapevine	Seed	F	98	0.2379
	Unidentified Fruit	Seed	W	1	0.0035
	Unidentified Fruit	Skin	F	2	0.0113
	Unidentified endocarp	Endocarp	F	3	0.0569
Fiber					
cf. *Linum* sp.	cf. Flax	Seed	F	4	0.0037
Linum usitatissimum	Flax	Seed	F	17	0.025
Weeds/ Wild					
Amaranthaceae	Amaranth	Seed	W	1	<0.0001
Boraginaceae	Borage	Seed	W	8	0.0123
Coix sp.	Job's Tears	Seed	W	1	0.0025
Cyperaceae		Seed	W	7	<0.0001
Chenopodium sp.	Goosefoot	Seed	W	2	<0.0001
Galium sp.	Bedstraw	Seed	W	7	0.0124
cf. *Juniperus* sp.	cf. Juniper	Seed	W	2	0.0203
Poaceae		Seed	W	3	0.0085
Poaceae	Wild Poaceae	Seed	W	20	0.0206
cf. Malvaceae	Mallows	Seed	W	2	0.0004
cf. *Tribulus/Juniperus* sp.		Seed	W	1	0.0038
cf. Solanaceae	cf. Nightshades	Seed	W	1	0.0785

[a]*W* whole specimen, *F* fragment

complement each other to provide insight into Iron-Age industry (Ben-Yosef et al., 2010). Khirbat en-Nahas, which translates to "ruins of copper" in Arabic, was occupied from the twelfth- to ninth-century BCE (Levy et al., 2014; Levy et al., 2016). Khirbat en-Nahas has been subject to significant archaeological attention, being both the largest Iron-Age, copper-smelting site and the center of the copper industry in Faynan during this period (Levy et al., 2014), with the most significant production dating to the early tenth- to ninth-century BCE (Ben-Yosef et al., 2010; Levy et al., 2014). The size of the fortress, containing over 100 architectural structures and 50–60,000 tons of slag, attest to the scale of the industry at this site (Hauptmann, 2007; Levy et al., 2014).

Khirbat al-Jariya (Fig. 1b), another Iron-Age, copper-smelting site and the focus of this analysis, is located approximately 2 kilometers north-east from Khirbat en-Nahas (Levy et al., 2018). The site was dated to the eleventh–tenth centuries BCE and includes an estimated 15–20,000 tons of copper slag (Hauptmann, 2007; Liss et al., 2020).

Finally, Khirbat al-Ghuwayba was a smaller-scale, copper-smelting site located about 2.5 kilometers southeast of Khirbat al-Jariya and adjacent to a perennial spring, Ain al-Ghuwayba. This spring provides enough water for modern fruit orchards, and it was likely an important resource in the Iron Age (Ben-Yosef, 2010; Liss et al., 2020). Excavations dated the site to eleventh–tenth centuries BCE based on radiocarbon samples, and this dating is supported by the similarity to archaeometallurgical material at Khirbat al-Jariya (Ben-Yosef, 2010). Based on excavations at these sites (and others in the region), Early Iron-Age settlement in Faynan is represented by an "industrial landscape" in the region focused primarily on mining and smelting copper (Ben-Yosef et al., 2010; Ben-Yosef et al., 2019; Liss et al., 2020). Copper production was centered at Khirbat en-Nahas, and Khirbat al-Jariya likely was occupied as an organized expansion of production during the mid-eleventh century BCE (Liss et al., 2020). Khirbat al-Ghuwayba played a smaller role in copper production but could have controlled the spring as an important water source.

2.1 Khirbat al-Jariya

In 2006, the Edom Lowlands Regional Archaeology Project (ELRAP), directed by Thomas E. Levy and Mohammad Najjar, excavated at Khirbat al-Jariya for the first time under the field supervision of Dr. Erez Ben-Yosef (Ben-Yosef et al., 2010). ELRAP developed the stratigraphy in Area A (A1-A6) based on the excavation of a small structure and a slag mound probe (Ben-Yosef et al., 2010). Radiocarbon dating along with geomagnetic archaeointensity connected the area's stratigraphy to the stratigraphy at Khirbat en-Nahas, establishing the contemporaneity of the two sites during the Iron Age. To expand on the 2006 results and to develop a more profound understanding of how Khirbat al-Jariya was situated in the culture of Iron-Age copper production in the Faynan region, ELRAP returned to the site in 2014 and excavated two contexts, Area B/Building 2 (Fig. 2a) and Area C (Fig. 2b). Area B/Building 2 is the largest extant architectural structure (ca. 7.5 × 7.5 m) at Khirbat al-Jariya and was likely first occupied in the mid-11th BCE (Liss et al., 2020). The building, which includes four to seven rooms, was potentially an elite residence or served administrative purposes with connections to an industrial function (Liss et al., 2020). Area C was a 1 × 1 meter probe into a large slag mound on the southeastern edge of the site (Liss et al., 2020). The sounding was excavated to bedrock at a depth of about 1.75 meters,

Of the 3292 charcoal fragments recovered from dry screens from excavations in Areas B and C, 90% were identified to 22 taxa by visual identification using stereo and polarizing microscopes (Liss et al., 2020). Sixty-four specimens were analyzed using a scanning electron microscope to identify the presence or absence of fungal hyphae, filamentous structures that grow in deadwood. The most abundant taxa, which appeared in all loci, were tamarisk (*Tamarix* sp.) and white broom (*Retana raetam*). These taxa, along with acacia (*Acacia tortilis*), which appears in at least half of the samples, are local to the region, growing in the wadis and interfluvial zones of the dry Faynan box canyon (Levy et al., 2018).

Fig. 1 (**a**) Major Iron Age sites within the Faynan copper ore district; (**b**) Khirbat al-Jariya looking roughly North. Map and photograph by Brady Liss

Fig. 2 (**a**) Aerial image of completed Area B excavation; (**b**) photograph of completed probe in Area C slag mound. Photographs from the UC San Diego Levantine and Cyber-Archaeology Laboratory

Study of fuelwood from Wadi Arabah likewise showed a preference for local taxa (Engel, 1993). Wood from date palm (*Phoenix dactylifera*) and olive trees (*Olea europaea*) appear in at least half of the samples, and wood from fig (*Ficus* sp.), and grape (*Vitis vinifera*) appear in fewer than that. *Phoenix dactylifera* does grow locally, although is limited in distribution to the perennial spring-fed oases (Levy et al., 2018). Grape vines would have had to have been imported from a region with a less arid climate. Ben-Yosef et al. (Ben-Yosef et al., 2017) speculate that they could have been imported from the highlands of Edom. The presence of wood remains from fruit-producing trees suggest that at least one important source of firewood for the inhabitants of KAJ was the cuttings removed during the mainte-nance of orchards (Liss et al., 2020:8). This material may have been acquired from Khirbat al-Ghuwayba if that site did indeed mediate access to the perennial spring and associated resources, or from the Mediterranean climatic strip around the Edomite Plateau (Ben-Yosef, 2019:369; Ben-Yosef, 2023:247). A similar sustain-able model of fuelwood coming from deadwood and coppicing has been described elsewhere (Levy et al., 2018). As an interesting comparison point, study of the fuel-woods from Megiddo showed an overall increase in reliance on fruit woods at the expense of wild timber species, particularly olive (*Olea* sp.), during the Iron Age, suggesting a shift in landscape ecology driven by horticulture (Benzaquen et al., 2019).

3 Methods

In 2014, ELRAP collected a total of 57 sediment samples (1023.5 liters) from all KAJ loci, except from loci within structural features (i.e., architectural fill) (Hoshino, 2014). This systematic sampling avoids issues associated with opportunistic sam-pling (Lennstrom & Hastorf, 1995), which we note has been cited as a concern with legacy datasets in the region (Farahani et al., 2016:28). The samples were floated in a froth flotation machine that recirculated water using a gas pump. The light frac-tion, consisting of 54 samples, was recovered with a 0.25 mm mesh and dried indoors, out of direct sunlight. These samples were exported to the United States and analyzed at the University of California, San Diego, under the supervision of Dr. Jade d'Alpoim Guedes. The samples were filtered through geological sieves (4 mm, 2 mm, 1 mm, 0.5 mm, and 0.25 mm fraction). Macrobotanical material was extracted from all sample fractions, although wood charcoal fragments were only extracted from the 1 mm fraction and above. All archaeobotanical material was counted and weighed, a total of 4793 whole and fragmentary carbonized specimens. In 2014, Dr. Brita Lorentzen analyzed the wood charcoal from the site (Lorentzon 2017; Liss et al., 2020: Table 3).

Identifications were based on comparative collections from the d'Alpoim Guedes lab and reference books, including *Digital Atlas of Economic Plants in Archaeology* (Neef et al., 2012) and *Identification of Cereal Remains from Archaeological Sites* (Jacomet, 2006). In addition to wood charcoal (n = 30,579), the remains were sorted into 31 taxa, 21 at the genus/species level (n = 1924) and 10 at the family level (n = 87). There were also 31 unidentified categories (n = 113), fruit and nut epicarps (n = 7), and an unidentified fruit (n = 1). Some (n = 2545) specimens were not identifiable due to small size or poor preservation. Table 1 presents the full weight and count data for identifiable taxa, aggregated from the entire site. Counts and weights by context are presented in Supplemental Table 1.

4 Results

Fruits, particularly the date palm (*Phoenix dactylifera*), consistently dominate the samples through all time periods (Fig. 3). Other fruit and nut taxa included figs (*Ficus* sp.), pistachio (*Pistacia* sp.), grapes (*Vitis* sp.), and pomegranates (*Punica* sp.) (Table 1). The samples mostly consist of easily obtainable, local fruit taxa that require little preparation and could be preserved through drying or pickling. These high-calorie snacks would have been a nutritious treat for a working population, similar to those enjoyed at the ore-processing sites within the Timna Valley (David et al., 2022:244). At Khirbat al-Jariya, these fruit taxa are particularly abundant in the Area B building. Although figs (*Ficus* sp.) dominate the standardized count by density, dates become the most abundant fruit when the counts are standardized by the average number of seeds per fruit (Table 2). There is no meaningful pattern of fruit distribution as aggregate, but Rooms 4 and 6 exhibited the largest concentration of date palm pits (Fig. 4).

Figure 5 shows the proportion of foods requiring preparation (all pulses, all grains, *Vicia* sp.; "prep") to those which do not (all fruits, all nuts; "snacks") in different combinations. The first two bars show Prep vs Grapes, Figs, Dates, Nuts (*Pistacia* sp., cf. *Pistacia* sp., Nutshell/Endocarp) and Other Fruits (*Punica* A, *Punica* B, *Rubus* sp., Undet Fruit 1) with density calculated two ways, using both counts and weights divided by the sum of the volume of all soil samples collected from a particular context. Importantly, none of the following figures include Basket 10,684 EDM 561, for which the sample number and soil volume were not recorded on the original package and density could not be calculated. The second two bars show the same density by count and mass, but all "snack" foods are amalgamated in a single category.

The next most abundant taxa in terms of counts are pulses, including lentil (*Lens* sp.), pea (*Pisum* sp.) and chickpea (*Cicer* sp.) (Table 1 **and** Fig. 3). The lentil proportions were far greater than the pea and chickpea proportions. A few of these lentil specimens appear to have been cooked. Following pulses, wheat and barley represent the next most abundant category by count. It is possible that these pulses were transported uncooked to the site to be prepared into soups or dips.

Several different types of wheat and barley were recovered (Table 1). A total of 9 grains of poorly preserved wheat (*Triticum* sp.) and one bread wheat (*Triticum aestivum*) rachis was found in our samples. Several well-preserved grains and fragments of barley (*Hordeum vulgare*) were also found in our samples. Three rachises of two-row barley were found, which might suggest that barley was present

Archaeological Evidence of Casual Snacking and Resource Provisioning at Khirbat...

Fig. 3 Ratio of grains to pulses to weeds to particular fruits, by stratum and area, standardized by counts per volume and weights per volume, including both whole and fragmented specimens

primarily in two-row form. In addition, several fragments of hulled barley and 3 grains of poorly preserved specimens of either oat or rye were also recovered. A number of very poorly preserved grains that were only identified to the Cerealia level, but were likely wheat or barley, were retrieved. Only a small number of rachis bases and spikelet forks, which are common indicators of crop processing, were present. These were concentrated primarily in Area C, a likely midden. Other economic taxa unearthed at the site include flax seeds (*Linum usitatissimum*).

Table 2 Estimated number of fruits corresponding to low and high estimates based on the total number of recovered seeds

Taxa	Count (seeds)	No. fruits, low estimate	No. fruits, high estimate
Ficus sp.	1082	0.67625	36.06667
Phoenix dactylifera	518	518	518
Vitis sp.	208	52	104

High estimates per fruit are 2 seeds per Vitis sp., 30 seeds per Ficus sp., and 1 seed per Phoenix dactylifera. Low estimates per fruit are 4 seeds per Vitis sp., 1600 seeds per Ficus sp., and 1 seed per Phoenix dactylifera

Wild taxa were dominated by various wild grasses (Poaceae). Other taxa included bedstraw (*Galium* sp.), *Coix* sp., and members of the sedge (Cyperaceae) family, *Chenopodium* sp., Malvaceae family, and Boraginaceae family, as well as a single fruit of the nightshade family (Solanaceae) and several juniper fruits.

The comparisons of taxa by room (Fig. 4) show that rooms 2, 3, 4 and 6 are dominated by date palms (*Phoenix dactylifera*). Room 2 has the largest specimen count (n = 120), and although dominated by date palms, it also includes pulses, grains, weeds, grapes (*Vitus* sp.) and pistachios (cf. *Pistacia* sp.). The samples from Rooms 2 and 6 do contain grains, including the only evidence of chaff that could have been removed during food preparation. Room 1 (n = 3) and room 5 (n = 0) contain too little material to make meaningful conclusions.

It is clear that foodstuffs coded as "snack" foods dominate the collection, particularly when considering the site in aggregate (Fig. 5). To assess how the distribution of food remains was concentrated, a discriminant analysis was performed in which the density of Prep, *Phoenix* sp., *Vitis* sp., *Ficus* sp., Other Fruit and Nut from each sample were coded by context (Room 1, 2, 3, 4, 5, 6, Area C, in a second analysis by Strata, and in the third by exterior/interior). If there was a meaningful pattern of a particular taxa being deposited in specific locations, we would expect clustering by context. The discriminant analysis was run twice using density by count and mass, each time yielding a misclassification rate of 44/53, just over 75%. In other words, the relative proportion of snack to prep food showed no meaningful patterning throughout the excavated contexts. It is unlikely that activity areas were demarcated in a way that produced patterned deposition of the macrobotanical remains, either between Areas B and C, or within the different rooms of Area B. There was likewise no statistically significant pattern to the distribution of plant remains by strata or by room (d'Alpoim Guedes et al., 2019a, b). It is unlikely that food-processing and consuming and discarding activities occurred within specific areas of the site because the discard of plant remains was not structured in a way that suggests particular rooms had particular culinary functions. This makes intuitive sense for a practice of convenient snacking that took place throughout all the spaces of the site.

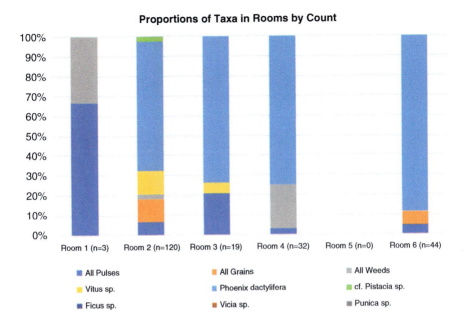

Fig. 4 Ratio of grains to pulses to weeds to particular fruits, by room, standardized by counts per volume and weights per volume, including both whole and fragmented specimens. "N" represents the total number of specimens per room

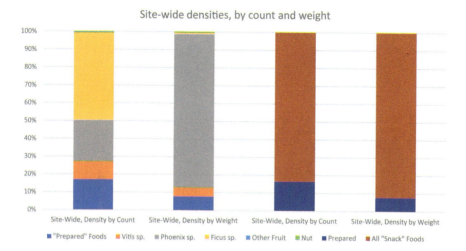

Fig. 5 Site-wide densities of prepared foods to snack foods by count and weight. The category "Prep" refers to those foods that requiring processing (all pulses, all grains, *Vicia* sp.) whereas those foods that do not (Grapes, Figs, Dates, *Pistacia* sp., cf. *Pistacia* sp., Nutshell/Endocarp, *Punica* A, *Punica* B, *Rubus* sp., and Undet Fruit 1) are included in the category "Snack"

5 Discussion

We compared our results to data from other nearby or contemporary sites for which comparative data are available: the Wadi Faynan survey (Austin, 2007; Kennedy, 2007), Wadi Arabah (David et al., 2022; Engel, 1993), Tel Meggido (Benzaquen et al., 2019), Khirbat al-Mudayna al-'Aliya (Farahani et al., 2016), Tall Dhirbat (Fatkin et al., 2011), Tel Batash (Kislev et al., 2006), and Tall al-'Umayri (Ramsay & Mueller, 2016). Raw counts were only available for Tall al-'Umayri, Mudayna al-'Aliya, Meggido, and the Wadi Faynan survey, although only nine contexts that exhibited the most specimens were reported for Tall al-'Umayri. We compared counts - which were more commonly reported than weights - of taxa associated with prepared foods and those labeled as "snack" foods, to that of Khirbat al-Jariya (Fig. 6).

The sites outside of the Wadi Faynan region show a greater reliance on cultivated cereals, whereas samples taken from the trenches of the Wadi Faynan survey show a degree of exploitation of convenient plant foods similar to that present at Khirbat al-Jariya. These samples were recovered from the 1998 survey of WF16, a Pre-Pottery Neolithic A site, the majority from midden contexts (Kennedy, 2007:425). Although considerably predating the later Iron-Age settlements, it indicates a long history of exploiting local plant foods within the Wadi Faynan. More contemporary paleobotanical studies show that local resources tend to dominate the subsistence base of various Bronze- and Iron-Age settlements (Benzaquen et al. 2019; Engel, 1993; Farahani et al., 2016; Fatkin et al., 2011; Ramsay & Mueller, 2016). Cereal agriculture was complemented by arboriculture and orchard vine crops (Benzaquen

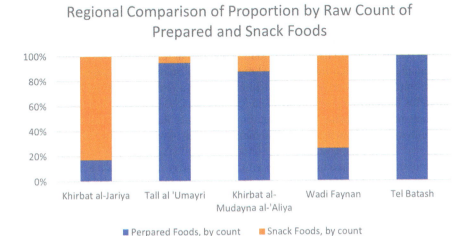

Fig. 6 Regional comparison of proportion (by raw count) of prepared and snack foods. Volumes of samples were only reported for Khirbat al-Mudayna al-'Aliya and Wadi Faynan, so comparison by count density was not possible for all sites but produced an overall similar pattern. It is not clear how the macrobotanical remains were collected from Tel Batash (Kislev et al., 2006), by hand or by flotation, so some sample bias may be present towards larger, more easily recognizable specimens

et al., 2019; Knabb et al., 2016; Ramsay & Mueller, 2016). Samples documenting the transition from the Late Bronze Age to Iron Age I from Tall al-'Umayri exhibited "no evidence of long-distance exchange or redistribution of surplus by elites[,]" with local plant husbandry "dominated by domesticated subsistence crops such as wheat, barley, legumes, grapes, figs, and nuts." (Ramsay & Mueller, 2016:16) During this time, based on "the material culture recovered[,]" the authors indicate that long-distance trade declines (Ramsay & Mueller, 2016:16).

That is not to say that nonlocal resources were absent from Iron-Age subsistence. It is worth noting that during the Iron Age, Tel Meggido began making greater use of nonlocal fuelwoods and the wood of imported arboriculture species, such as almond (*Amygdalus communis*) and Persian walnut (*Juglans regia*; Benzaquen et al., 2019:52). The exploitation of local resources is coupled with local processing, which took place in dedicated areas often separate from storage of grain ready for human consumption and/or animal fodder. This is typically characterized in the archaeological record by high frequencies but low ubiquities of glumes and rachises of cereals (Farahani et al., 2016; Kennedy, 2007; Ramsay & Mueller, 2016). This stands in contrast to the high frequency and high ubiquity of fruit taxa exhibited at Khirbat al-Jariya.

Another metal-working context, Site 30 in the Timna Valley, Israel, demonstrates a similar dominance of fruit and nut taxa, particularly dates, grapes, and the Atlantic pistachio (David et al., 2022: Supplemental Table 1). Despite differences in recovery techniques and predating Khirbat al-Jariya by a few centuries, the data is similar enough to support the general assertion that these likely nomadic-working camps, likely embedded within larger political and economic entities (Ben-Yosef, 2019; Ben-Yosef, 2021; David et al., 2022:235), were fed through locally acquired (and easily preserved) snack foods, with processed foods prepared elsewhere.

The results reported here appear to indicate that–at least at Khirbat al-Jariya–the inhabitants of the Wadi Faynan relied more heavily on readily available foodstuffs, likely employing arboriculture. At Khirbat al-Jariya and the Wadi Faynan survey, the ratios of chaff to grain, chaff including rachises, glumes, and non-useful plant products removed during processing, are much lower than that of Tall al-'Umayri, although only moderately lower than that of Khirbat al-Mudayna al-'Aliya (Fig. 7). The lower the ratio, the greater the proportion of end-stage food materials ready for consumption, whereas a higher proportion of chaff may indicate on-site production. Consumption and production represent a spectrum of behavior, rather than a binary (Stevens, 2003), and so it could be argued that Khirbat al-Jariya and Tel Batash are closer to the consumer side of the spectrum, relying on trade with or direct support from other polities – in the case of Khirbat al-Jariya, potentially support from Khirbat en-Nahas, which may have controlled the exchange of copper, supplemented further by locally available convenient snack foods.

It is important to consider how sample bias may influence the chaff:grain ratio, and accordingly how we interpret the consumption-production spectrum. Tel Batash offers an example of how the spatial patterning of paleobotanical material, and sampling methodology, may influence the interpretation of data. The paleobotanical material from Tel Batash was dominated by a single storage jar full of wheat grains (Locus 437, n > 147,000). That, combined with the apparent lack of flotation (no

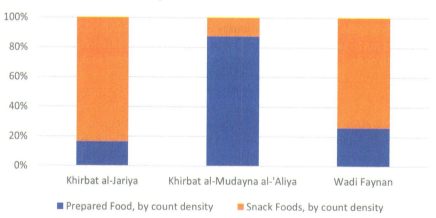

Fig. 7 Site-wide proportions by raw count of grain to chaff. The Wadi Faynan survey reported chaff present only in a fragment of mudbrick that contained impressions of chaff fragments in four samples, but these were not identified (Kennedy, 2007:424). The macrobotanical remains from Tel Batash were dominated by a single storage jar full of wheat grains (Locus 437, n = 147,000), but the ratio is not remarkably changed when this context is removed

such recovery technique was described by the authors), could lead to underrepresentation of chaff and grain from other excavated contexts, and potentially misrepresent a site as a "consumer" site. Similarly when discussing the Timna Valley material, whereas we emphasize the strong positive signal of snack food recovered from Site 30, due to the lack of systematic flotation (David et al., 2022:231) we cannot be as confident in the lack of evidence for processing.

Processing, discard of chaff, and storage are also often spatially organized behaviors. The case study from Khirbat al-Mudayna al-'Aliya (Farahani et al., 2016:55) shows how room function can be inferred from the paleobotanical record, identifying different stages of processing within a single site. It is likely all sites employed some combination of processing and storage. In the case of Khirbat al-Jariya, the systematic sampling and flotation recovery allows us to say that there is less evidence for on-site processing and further evidence for the reliance on convenient, locally available foodstuffs. In other words, there is both positive evidence for this snacking behavior and negative evidence for food preparation, despite the systematic flotation used during the 2014 ELRAP field season. The population of Khirbat al-Jariya likely worked within the site and lived, perhaps cooked, outside of the excavated portion of the site. We emphasize the positive evidence (high frequency and ubiquity) of casual snacking behavior and comparison to the archaeological signal of these same snack/prep taxa at other sites, particularly the results of the Wadi Faynan survey. Future excavations may reveal evidence of crop processing at a different location within Khirbat-al-Jariya for it is unlikely that smelting and dwelling areas directly overlapped (Ben-Yosef, 2019:366; Ben-Yosef, 2023:238). Focus on stone architecture and other highly visible features may prevent us from fully describing food preparation practices of seasonal nomads (Ben-Yosef, 2021:162–163). Therefore we emphasize the positive archaeological evidence for the casual snacking behavior practiced within the working environment of Khirbat al-Jariya and specific correlates of that behavior, including the lack of spatial organization of discarded foodstuffs and higher signal of snack foods compared to prepared foods as compared to other contemporary, permanent settlements.

6 Conclusion

The presence of glume bases, rachises, and culms, which are removed in the early stages of cereal processing, has been attributed to "producer" sites that process the grain, whereas higher ratios of seeds to chaff may represent "consumer" sites (Jones, 1985; Stevens, 2003). This model has been criticized as oversimplifying the complex dynamics of supplying sites across a landscape but provides a useful starting point for interpreting archaeobotanical assemblages. Although producer/consumer is a spectrum, not a binary, in this case, we have neither an abundance of chaff nor seeds. There is no evidence of the full spectrum of food harvesting and preparation, from cutting to threshing, sieving, and grinding, nor of storage of large quantities of grains onsite. If food made from cereal was present, it was introduced to the site in

Fig. 8 Domestic taxa recovered from Khirbat al-Jariya. (**a**) *Triticum* sp.; (**b**) *Hordeum vulgare* (hulled); (**c**) cf. *Avena/ Secale* sp.; (**d**) *Hordeum vulgare* rachis (two row); (**e**) *Linum* sp.; (**f**) *Lens culinaris* (cooked); (**g**) cf. *Vicia faba*; (**h**) *Vitis* sp. (**i**) *Ficus* sp. (fruit and seeds); (**j**) *Punica* sp.; (**k**) *Phoenix dactylifera*; (**l**) *Cicer* sp.; (**m**) *Pisum sativum*

a form that is not represented by the paleobotanical assemblage, such as pre-processed flour or breads. Instead, our macrobotanical analysis suggests that the inhabitants of Khirbat al-Jariya were favoring locally available, easily preparable foods (Figs. 8 and 9), although these were likely only seasonally available (Levy et al., 2018). If these were the primary food resources on which the inhabitants of Khirbat al-Jariya relied, then the site may have only been seasonally occupied.

The inhabitants of Khirbat al-Jariya did have access to non-local, pre-processed foodstuffs - a cup-spouted jar likely used for olive oil was recovered from Area B. Nevertheless, the primary source of food appears to have been convenient "snack foods" focused on dried, pickled, or raw fruits and nuts, and potentially the transport of processed foods like bread or flour. It is likely that Khirbat en-Nahas, the center of the copper industry in Faynan, mediated access to additional foodstuffs, and horticultural products may have been supplied by the perennial springs near Khirbat al-Ghuwayba. The population of Khirbat al-Jariya was an itinerant one, taking advantage of local resources but not establishing a permanent living space.

Acknowledgments The authors would like to thank Drs. Thomas E. Levy and Mohammad Najjar and the UCSD Levantine and Cyber-Archaeology Laboratory for providing access to the collection. Special thanks to Dr. Neil G. Smith, Craig Smitheram, Rosemary Y. Hoshino, Marc Wallace, and the local Bedouin of Qirayqira and Faynan for their assistance in the field and the lab. Also, thanks to Dr. Barbara Porter of the American Center of Oriental Research (ACOR) in Amman and Dr. M. Jamhawi, former Director General of the Department of Antiquities of Jordan. Thank you to the students in Dr. d'Alpoim Guedes's 2018 Introduction to Paleoethnobotany course for assisting in the analysis: Katrina Cantu, Clara Dawson, Shelby Jones-Cervantes, Brandon Gay, Isabel Hermsmeyer, Xiyuan Huang, Bridget C. Lawrence, Sunyoung Park, Eric Rodriguez, Julianna Santillan-Goode, Sarah Sheridan, Fabian Humberto Toro, Isabel Villasana, Emma Villegas, and Zhen Yu.

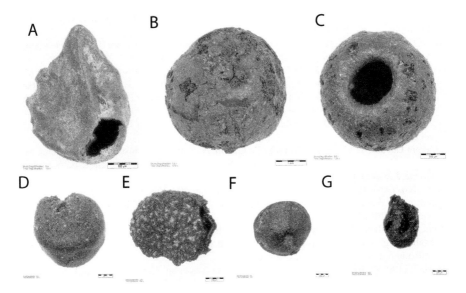

Fig. 9 Wild taxa recovered from Khirbat al-Jariya. (**a**) Boraginceae; (**b**) *Juniperus* sp.; (**c**) *Galium* sp.; (**d**) Malvaceae; (**e**) Solanaceae; (**f**) *Chenopodium* sp.; (**g**) Cyperaceae

References

Austin, P. (2007). The wood charcoal macroremains. In B. Finlayson & S. Mithen (Eds.), *The Early Prehistory of Wadi Faynan, Southern Jordan: Archaeological survey of Wadis Faynan, Ghuwayr and Al Bustan and the Evaluation of the Pre-Pottery Neolithic A Site of WF16* (pp. 408–419). Oxbow Books.

Ben-Yosef, E. (2010). *Technology and social process: Oscillations in Iron Age copper production and power in Southern Jordan* (Publication No. BenYosef_ucsd_0033-D_11379) [Doctoral dissertation, University of California San Diego]. ProQuest Dissertations Publishing.

Ben-Yosef, E. (2019). The architectural bias in current biblical archaeology. *Vetus Testamentum, 69*, 361–387.

Ben-Yosef, E. (2021). Rethinking the social complexity of Early Iron Age nomads. *Jerusalem Journal of Archaeology, 1*, 155–179.

Ben-Yosef, E. (2023) A false contrast? On the possibility of an Early Iron Age nomadic monarchy in the Arabah (early Edom) and its implications to the study of ancient Israel. In O. Lipschits, O. Sergi, and I. Koch (Eds.), *From nomadism to monarchy? "The archaeology of the settlement period" thirty years Later* (pp. 235–262), University Park.

Ben-Yosef, E., Levy, T. E., Higham, T., Najjar, M., & Tauxe, L. (2010). The beginning of Iron Age copper production in the southern Levant: New evidence from Khirbat al-Jariya, Faynan, Jordan. *Antiquity, 84*, 724–746.

Ben-Yosef, E., Langgut, D., & Sapir-Hen, L. (2017). Beyond smelting: New insights on Iron Age (10th c. BCE) metalworkers community from excavations at a gatehouse and associated livestock pens in Timna, Israel. *Journal of Archaeological Science: Reports, 11*, 411–426.

Ben-Yosef, E., Liss, B., Yagel, O. A., Tirosh, O., Najjar, M., & Levy, T. E. (2019). Ancient technology and punctuated change: Detecting the emergence of the Edomite Kingdom in the Southern Levant. *PLoS One, 14*(9), e0221967. https://doi.org/10.1371/journal.pone.0221967

Benzaquen, M., Finkelstein, I., & Langgut, D. (2019). Vegetation history and human impact on the environs of Tel Megiddo in the Bronze and Iron Ages: A dendrochronological analysis. *Tel Aviv, 46*, 42–64.

Clark, J. E. (1996). Craft specialization as an archaeological category. *Research in Economic Anthropology, 16*, 267–294.

Costin, C. L. (2001). Craft production systems. In G. M. Feinman & T. D. Price (Eds.), *Archaeology at the millennium: A sourcebook* (pp. 273–327). Springer Press.

d'Alpoim Guedes, J., Cantu, K., Dawson, C., Garvin, A., Gay, B., Hermsmeyer, I., Howland, M., Huang, X., Jones-Cervantes, S., Lawrence, B., Liss, B., Park, S., Rodriguez, E., Santillan-Goode, J., Sheridan, S., Stroth, L., Tamberino, A.T., Toro-Uribe, F., Villasana, I., Villegas, I., Yu, Z., & Levy, T.E. (2019a) *The archaeobotany of an early copper production site in Faynan, Jordan.* Poster presented at the 42nd conference of the Society of Ethnobiology, Vancouver, B.C., May 8–11.

d'Alpoim Guedes, J., Cantu, K., Dawson, C., Garvin, A., Gay, B., Hermsmeyer, I., Howland, M., Huang, X., Jones-Cervantes, S., Lawrence, B., Liss, B., Park, S., Rodriguez, E., Santillan-Goode, J., Stroth, L., Tamberino, A.T., Toro-Uribe, F., Villasana, I., Yu, Z., & Levy, T.E. (2019b) *Analysis of the Paleobotanical Collection from Khirbat al-Jariya, an Early Copper Production Site in the Faynan, Jordan.* Poster presented at the 2019 ASOR Meeting, San Diego, CA, November 20–23.

David, M., Kislev, M., Melamed, Y., Ben-Yosef, E., & Weiss, E. (2022). Plant remains from Rothenberg's excavations in Timna: Smelter's food and cultic offerings at the turn of the first Millenium BCE. *TEL AVIV, 49*, 230–249.

Engel, T. (1993). Charcoal remains from an Iron Age copper smelting slag heap at Feinan, Wadi Arabah (Jordan). *Vegetation History and Archaeobotany, 2*, 205–211.

Farahani, A., Porter, B. W., Huynh, H., & Routledge, B. (2016). Crop Storage and Animal Husbandry at Early Iron Age Khirbat al-Mudayna al-'Aliya (Jordan): A Paleoethnobotanical Approach. In K. M. McGeough (Ed.), *The archaeology of agro-pastoralist economies in Jordan* (Vol. 69, pp. 27–89). The Annual of the American Schools of Oriental Research.

Fatkin, D. S., Adelsberger, K., Farahani, A., Fischer, A., Kansa, S. W., Lev-Tov, J., Morgan, C., Porter, B. W., Routledge, B. E., & Wilson, A. T. (2011). Digging deeper: Technical reports from the Dhiban excavation and development project (2004-2009). *Annual of the Department of Antiquities of Jordan, 55*, 249–266.

Fuller, D., & Stevens, C. J. (2009). Agriculture and the development of complex societies: An Archaeobotanical agenda. In A. Fairbairn & E. Weiss (Eds.), *From foragers to farmers: Papers in honour of Gordon Hillman* (pp. 37–57). Oxbow Books.

Hauptmann, A. (2007). *The Archaeometallurgy of copper: Evidence from Faynan, Jordan.* Springer.

Hoshino, R. (2014). *Preliminary results from the ELRAP 2014 environmental sampling and flotation program.* Unpublished site report.

Jacomet, S. (2006). *Identification of cereal remains from archaeological sites.* IPAS, Basel University.

Jones, M. (1985). Archaeobotany beyond subsistence reconstruction. In G. Barker & C. Gamble (Eds.), *Beyond domestication in prehistoric Europe.* Academic.

Kennedy, A. (2007). The plant macrofossils. In B. Finlayson & S. Mithen (Eds.), *The early prehistory of Wadi Faynan, southern Jordan: Archaeological survey of Wadis Faynan, Ghuwayr and Al Bustan and the evaluation of the pre-pottery Neolithic a site of WF16* (pp. 420–428). Oxbow Books.

Kislev, M. E., Melamed, Y., & Langsam, Y. (2006). Plant remains from Tel Batash. In N. Panitz-Cohen & A. Mazar (Eds.), *Timnah (Tel Batash) III: The finds from the second millennium BCE* (Monographs of the Institute of Archaeology Vol. 45) (pp. 295–310). The Hebrew University of Jerusalem.

Knabb, K. A., Erel, Y., Tirosh, O., Rittenour, T., Laparidou, S., Najjar, M., & Levy, T. E. (2016). Environmental impacts of ancient copper mining and metallurgy: Multi-proxy investigation of human-landscape dynamics in the Faynan valley, southern Jordan. *Journal of Archaeological Science, 74*, 85–101.

Lennstrom, H. A., & Hastorf, C. A. (1995). Interpretation in context: Sampling and analysis in paleoethnobotany. *American Antiquity, 60,* 701–721.

Levy, T. E., Najjar, M., & Ben-Yosef, E. (Eds.). (2014). *New insights in the Iron Age archaeology of Edom, southern Jordan.* UCLA Cotsen Institute of Archaeology Press.

Levy, T. E., Bettilyon, M., & Burton, M. M. (2016). The Iron Age copper industrial complex: A preliminary study of the role of ground stone tools at Khirbat en-Nahas, Jordan. *Journal of Lithic Studies, 3.* https://doi.org/10.2218/jls.v3i3.1648

Levy, T. E., Ben-Yosef, E., & Najjar, M. (2018). Intensive surveys, large-scale extraction strategies and Iron Age industrial metallurgy in Faynan, Jordan: Fairy tales don't come true. In E. Ben-Yosef (Ed.), *Mining for ancient copper: Essays in memory of Beno Rothenberg* (Sonia and Marco Nadler Institute of Archaeology monograph 37) (pp. 245–258). Tel Aviv University.

Liss, B., Howland, M. D., Lorentzen, B., Smitheram, C., Najjar, M., & Levy, T. E. (2020). Up the Wadi: Development of an Iron Age Industrial landscape in Faynan, Jordan. *Journal of Field Archaeology,* 1–15.

Lorentzon, B. (2017). *Analysis of wood charcoal remains from ELRAP excavations at Khirbat al-Jariya, Jordan.* Cornell Tree-Ring Laboratory.

Neef, R., Cappers, R. T. J., Bekker, R. M., Boulos, L., Dinies, M., Ertuğ, Z. F., Keller, N., Lahitte, M., Meulenbeld, G. J., & Zhu, Y. P. (2012). Digital atlas of economic plants in archaeology. *Groningen Archaeological Studies, No. 17.*

Palmer, C., Gilbertson, D., El-Rishi, H., Hunt, C., Grattan, J., McLaren, S., & Pyatt, B. (2007). The Wadi Faynan today: Landscape, environment, people. In G. Barker & D. Gilbertson (Eds.), *Archaeology and desertification: The Wadi Faynan landscape survey, southern Jordan* (pp. 27–57). Oxbow Books.

Ramsay, J., & Mueller, N. (2016). Telling seeds: Archaeobotanical investigations at Tall al-'Umayri, Jordan. In K. M. McGeough (Ed.), *The archaeology of agro-pastoralist economies in Jordan* (Vol. 69, pp. 1–25). The Annual of the American Schools of Oriental Research.

Stevens, C. (2003). An investigation of agricultural consumption and production models for prehistoric and Roman Britain. *Environmental Archaeology, 8,* 61–76.

City of Copper, Ruin of Copper: Rethinking Nelson Glueck's Identifications of Ir Nahash and Ge Harashim

Marc A. Beherec

Abstract One of the important Jordanian sites Tom Levy excavated is Khirbat en-Nahas, "The Ruin of Copper." Khirbat en-Nahas is the largest copper production site in the southern Levant. In 1940, Tom's predecessor to the site, American archaeologist Nelson Glueck, proposed the identification of "The Biblical City of Copper" with Khirbat en-Nahas and "the Valley of Smiths," Ge Harashim, with the Wadi Arabah. This paper reconsiders Glueck's identifications and ultimately rejects both those identifications. Earlier identifications of Deir Nakhkhas with Ir Nahash and Sarafand el-Kharab with Ge Harashim are more likely given the available biblical and other textual evidence. Felix-Marie Abel's identification of the site with the Edomite Daidan is also rejected. The ancient name of Khirbat en-Nahas is unfortunately lost to time.

Keywords Deir Nakhkhas · Ge Harashim · Ir Nahash · Khirbat en-Nahas · Nelson Glueck · Sarafand el-Kharab Wadi Arabah

1 Introduction

Among Tom's many accomplishments is leading a series of excavations at the largest Iron Age copper-smelting site in the southern Levant, Khirbat en-Nahas (Fig. 1). His excavations resulted in numerous scholarly articles and his two-volume *New Insights into the Iron Age Archaeology of Edom, Southern Jordan*. I had the privilege of working for Tom as an area supervisor during two field seasons at Khirbat

M. A. Beherec (✉)
Independent Scholar, Los Angeles, CA, USA

Michael Baker International, Los Angeles, CA, USA
e-mail: marc.beherec@mbakerintl.com

© The Author(s), under exclusive license to Springer Nature Switzerland AG 2023
E. Ben-Yosef, I. W. N. Jones (eds.), *"And in Length of Days Understanding" (Job 12:12): Essays on Archaeology in the Eastern Mediterranean and Beyond in Honor of Thomas E. Levy*, Interdisciplinary Contributions to Archaeology,
https://doi.org/10.1007/978-3-031-27330-8_49

Fig. 1 Principal sites mentioned in the text

en-Nahas, at Area M in 2006 and at Area R in 2009, experiences I found very enriching.

One of Tom's predecessors to Khirbat en-Nahas was the American archaeologist Nelson Glueck. Glueck visited the site in the 1930s his surveys in the Negev and the Emirate of Transjordan—what he called his Explorations in Eastern Palestine.

Glueck was not the first to visit the site, but he was the first archaeologist to correctly date the site to the Iron Age. He made much of fact that the site dated to the United Monarchy and would have been exploited by King Solomon himself. In 1940 Glueck reported the results of his surveys in a popular book, *The Other Side of the Jordan*. In that book Glueck proposed a biblical identification for Khirbat en-Nahas. He argued, "the *City of Copper* mentioned in connection with the *Valley of Smiths* is to be identified with the large Iron Age mining and smelting site of Khirbet Nahas (the Copper Ruin)" (Glueck, 1940b:83). Glueck identified Ge Harashim, what he called the Valley of Smiths, with the Wadi Arabah. Glueck called Solomon a "copper king" (Glueck, 1940b:99) and likened the Wadi Arabah to a vast copper-working factory akin to the American rustbelt with its center at Tell el-Khalifieh, "the Pittsburgh of Palestine" (Glueck, 1940b:94).

These two identifications, and particularly Glueck's association of Khirbat en-Nahas with a biblical "City of Copper," remain compelling and have been accepted by many scholars. But Glueck was mistaken in his identifications of Ir Nahash and the Ge Harashim. The Bible and other available texts suggest both sites are located in biblical Judah, and in the years before Glueck wrote historical geographers had already associated them more accurately with different archaeological sites. Ir Nahash is Deir Nakhkhas in the Shephelah, and Ge Harashim is most likely in the vicinity of Sarafand el-Kharab. The name by which Khirbat en-Nahas was known to the ancient Israelites and Edomites is sadly lost, and barring new archaeological discoveries, is unknowable.

2 Nelson Glueck in Edom

In the spring and summer of 1934, Nelson Glueck conducted his second series of archaeological surveys in the Emirate of Transjordan and the Negev. Glueck's mission was to visit and document archaeological sites of all ages in the understudied territory. His first field season focused on ancient Moab. In the 1934 field season he traversed biblical Edom. Perhaps seeing his work as a continuation of the Palestine Exploration Fund's Survey of Western Palestine, Glueck called the expeditions the Survey of Eastern Palestine. The survey was a joint expedition of the American School of Oriental Research, Baghdad (ASOR, of which Glueck was Annual Professor) and Hebrew Union College (with which Glueck was affiliated and which he would later lead as President), as well as the American Council of Learned Societies and the Transjordan Department of Antiquities. Because of civil unrest in Iraq, for the 1934 season Glueck was also able to appropriate ASOR's staff and budget originally intended for excavations at Tell Billa and Tepe Gawra (Gordon, 2000:44). On his trip to the Arabah Glueck was accompanied by Inspector of Antiquities Robert G. Head; Antiquities Guard Ali Abu Ghosh; ASOR Fellows Cyrus Gordon and Percy B. Upchurch; guide Hasan Safi; and Sheikh Audeh ibn Ahmed el-Asfar of the Beni Atiyeh and three of his tribesmen, Salim ibn Mes'ad, `Audeh ibn `Id, and Ifrij ibn Sabbah. But Glueck ensured he would control the data and his would be the only voice for the expedition. When Gordon, an expert epigrapher, asked for the right to publish any inscriptions that might be found in exchange for his assistance, Glueck refused to allow him even to coauthor any of the expeditions' publications (Gordon, 2000:44). Head and the expedition's other members were not writers, and Gordon would only describe the expedition decades later in his memoirs (Gordon, 1957, 2000). As a result, the expedition's voice was limited to Glueck's. Its scope was defined by his abilities, but also circumscribed by his limitations.

One of the expedition's goals was to visit Khirbat en-Nahas, a large but mysterious site visited by only a few westerners. Czech theologian Alois Musil was perhaps the first European to visit the site, on May 5, 1898, but he devoted only one paragraph to the site in his multivolume geographical work on Moab and Edom (Musil, 1907: II (1):298). More recently Fritz Frank visited the site on November 10 through 11, 1932, and described his experience (Frank, 1934:218). Major Sir Alec Kirkbride, George I. Horsfield, and R. G. Head also all visited the site, and Head made ceramic collections there (Glueck, 1935:29), but Kirkbride and Head published nothing about the site. Horsfield does not even mention the site in his comprehensive article on Edom (Horsfield & Conway, 1930).

Glueck's party reached Khirbat en-Nahas on the Wadi al-Ghuweiba on March 24, 1934. After a brief examination they left the large and complex site to visit other locations (Glueck, 1935:22). They returned on March 25 and devoted most of the day to studying the site. They camped at the site overnight and left on March 26, 1934 (Glueck, 1935:26–30). The three-day visit was apparently the only time Glueck ever visited the site. After 1948 he would be prevented from traveling to the other side of the Jordan ever again (Brown & Kutler, 2005).

Glueck was the first to correctly date Khirbat en-Nahas to the Iron Age on the basis of ceramic evidence. Frank observed "the ceramics are not Roman, but seem much older" (Frank, 1934:218), but was unable to say more about the site's age. L.-H. Vincent and William Foxwell Albright erroneously dated the site to the Bronze Age (Albright, 1934:16), but they never visited the site and based their date on Vincent's reading of pottery Head collected at a different site and mislabeled as from Khirbat en-Nahas (Glueck, 1935:7). It took Glueck's skill to correctly identify the coarse Iron Age wares.

Glueck also documented the site's ruined buildings. He described the site's fortress and many slag heaps. He erroneously identified some buildings as smelters. Probably influenced the monumental structures of twentieth century American metallurgy that he would have seen growing up in his native Cleveland, Glueck looked for tall buildings he assumed were foundries. At Khirbat en-Nahas, Glueck identified two copper smelters, one rectangular and one circular. The circular structure is not illustrated in Glueck's published material, but the rectangular building appears in photographs (Glueck, 1935:27, fig. 12, 1940b:59, fig. 26). Beyond looking vaguely smokestack-like and having "two compartments one above the other" (Glueck, 1935: 27), there is nothing to link it to metallurgy any more than any other building at the site. By contrast, when Gordon finally wrote about his experiences, he said that the team observed "hundreds of stone furnaces" (Gordon, 1957: 22) at

Khirbat en-Nahas rather than Glueck's two. Neither man explained their methodology for identifying an Iron Age smelter, because in 1934 no one knew what an Iron Age smelter looked like. At other sites he visited over the course of the survey, Glueck similarly erroneously identified other ruins as smelters. He also associated several sites with biblical locations.

Glueck also attempted to associate the sites he visited with biblical locations. He identified Tawilan with Teman, and Umm el-Biyarah with Sela. Glueck went on to excavate Tell El-Khalifieh, which he believed to be the biblical Ezion-geber. He identified a large building with wall openings that he believed to be flues designed to take advantage of the region's winds in order to refine copper. The site was "an elaborate complex of industrial plants," Glueck declared; "Ezion-geber was the Pittsburgh of Palestine, in addition to being its most important port" (Glueck, 1940b:94).

In the decades following Glueck's Explorations in Eastern Palestine, contributions by other scholars forced Glueck to abandon or at least walk back many of his conclusions. By the time *The Other Side of the Jordan* was reprinted in 1970, he knew Umm el-Biyarah was not Sela, and admitted, "I had once thought that Tawilan is to be equated with Biblical Teman, but doubt now whether that is correct" (Glueck, 1970:32). The photograph that had been captioned "Smelting furnace at Khirbat Nahas" (Glueck, 1940b:59) in the book's first edition was captioned "A small ruined structure at Khirbet Nahas" (Glueck, 1970:70) in the second. In 1970, Glueck was forced to admit, "We do not yet understand the nature and purpose of numerous small structures" (Glueck, 1970:69) at Khirbat en-Nahas, including the buildings he once confidently described as smelters. He was forced to acknowledge that the buildings at Tell El-Khalifieh, which he had identified as a massive smelting factory at the center of Solomon's metal working operations, were not an industrial complex at all. By that time Beno Rothenberg's excavations at Timna had shown the world that an Iron Age copper smelter was a small clay semi-subterranean structure rather than a large building (e.g., Rothenberg, 1962, 1972, 1990). However, Glueck's major contribution—literally putting so many archaeological sites on the map and accurately dating them with ceramic evidence—remains.

Glueck's identification of the largest copper smelting site in the ancient Levant, as a biblical City of Copper remains compelling. Many scholars accept Glueck's identification (e.g., Aharoni, 1979:378; Kallai, 1986:117; Miller, 2021:95; Myers, 1965a:29; Rainey & Notley, 2006:152). Khirbat en-Nahas is given as a probable location of Ir Nahash in the *Anchor Bible Dictionary's* entry on "Irnahash" (Seely, 1992b: vol. 3, pg. 462). In the final monumental report for Tom's excavations at Khirbat en-Nahas, even Erez Ben-Yosef, Thomas Levy, and Mohammad Najjar note, "The first to correctly date these sites to the Iron Age and to identify Khirbat en-Nahas with biblical `Ir-Nahas ... was the American archaeologist Nelson Glueck" (Ben-Yosef et al., 2014:500), without critically assessing Glueck's association of Khirbat en-Nahas with Ir Nahash. But do Glueck's two identifications have any merit?

3 Ir Nahash

Glueck made no attempt to identify the ancient name of Khirbat en-Nahas in "Explorations in Eastern Palestine." However, in *The Other Side of the Jordan,* he argued "the *City of Copper* mentioned in connection with the *Valley of Smiths* is to be identified with the large Iron Age mining and smelting site of Khirbet Nahas (the Copper Ruin)" (Glueck, 1940b:83). He would make the same claim, though somewhat more tentatively, in his scholarly article "Kenites and Kenizzites" (Glueck, 1940a) and his much later book *Rivers in the Desert* (Glueck, 1959:156). Unlike many of his other biblical identifications, Glueck never retracted his identifications of Khirbat en-Nahas with Ir Nahash and the Wadi Arabah with the Valley of Smiths. When the revised edition of *The Other Side of the Jordan* published, the year before Glueck's 1971 death, most of the biblical identifications he made were rescinded or walked-back. But his arguments identifying Ir Nahash and the Valley of Smiths remained just as vigorous as they were in 1940 (Glueck, 1970:98).

Ir Nahash is mentioned only once in the Bible, in genealogical lists in I Chronicles (I Chronicles 4:12). Ge Harashim is mentioned twice. The name first appears in the genealogical lists of I Chronicles (I Chronicles 4:14). A Ge Harashim, almost certainly the same place, is also mentioned in the narrative describing the resettlement of the land found in the Book of Nehemiah (Nehemiah 11:35). Both Books of Chronicles, the Book of Ezra, and the Book of Nehemiah all date to the Persian Period or later. The books are so similar in style, date, and outlook that they are often ascribed to a single individual or at least a single workshop, known as the Chronicler (Albright, 1921; Myers, 1965a, b; Noth, 1987). If I Chronicles and Nehemiah were written and curated by the same person or group of persons, who shared a similar knowledge of and approach to sacred geography, they most likely both discussing the same Ge Harashim. The argument that all these books can be ascribed to a single individual or group has been challenged. While the argument still has its advocates, scholars generally no longer proceed from an a priori assumption of single authorship (Klein, 1992; Knoppers, 2003:74–75). But even if I Chronicles and Nehemiah were written by different individuals or groups, Ge Harashim most likely appears in both works because it was a place name that the author or authors knew would be widely recognizable to readers.

The term *ir* (עִיר) is usually translated city, and it is natural to assume that Ir Nahash would be a large site with an urban character. It would seem to be an appropriate name for the largest copper smelting site in the Levant. But the term is also applied to much smaller settlements. The Chronicler most often uses the word in the name of Ir David, that part of Jerusalem David is said to have conquered and where the tombs of the kings were later located. Elsewhere, however, the Chronicler applies the term to any settlement (Ezra 10:14; Nehemiah 11:1) and even to satellite settlements around what itself is a relatively small town (I Chronicles 6:45). Ir Nahash may have been a hamlet rather than an urban center, and the fact that it is mentioned only once, among a list of other settlements, many of which never appear again in the Bible, suggests it was a small and relatively unimportant settlement.

The word Nahash (נָחָשׁ) means snake. The same word is used in Genesis 3. Ir Nahash literally means City of Snake, and is an appropriate name for a place inhabited by serpents, just as Jericho is also known as the City of Palm Trees (Deuteronomy 34:3).

But as Glueck suggested, Ir Nahash may have meant Copper City (Glueck, 1940b:83, 1970:98). Nahash, shares its root with nahoset (נְחֹשֶׁת), copper or bronze. A play on words between the words for serpent and copper is important in the story of the brazen serpent (נְחַשׁ נְחֹשֶׁת) Moses made near Punon in Edom (Numbers 21:9). According to Judges, Moses married a Kenite woman, and there are linguistic associations tying together the legendary first blacksmith Tubal-Cain, the Kenites, metal working, and the brazen serpent (Halpern, 1992). Although Moses is said to have constructed his brazen serpent in Faynan, worship of the copper snake was not limited to that region. The bronze serpent or Nehushtan (נְחֻשְׁתָּן) destroyed by Hezekiah, which was said to be the same one crafted by Moses, appears to have been worshiped somewhere in Hezekiah's Kingdom of Judah (II Kings 18:4). The name Ir Nahash may have carried multiple connotations associated with serpents, copper metallurgy, and possibly a snake god or totem.

Nahash is also a man's name; for example, the Chronicler mentions an Ammonite king named Nahash (I Chronicles 19:1), who is unconnected to Ir Nahash. A place called Ir Nahash could be named after a lineage's apical ancestor. Ir Nahash appears in I Chronicles as though it is a man's name, and is mentioned in a short list of the descendants of an individual named Kelub (I Chronicles 4:11–12). The list is appended to a genealogy of Judah, but Kelub's ancestry is not traced back to Judah. Kelub's genealogy appears in this part of Chronicles because the individuals listed in Kelub's genealogy are generally considered to be Calebites. The Calebite clans are somehow associated with Caleb son of Jephunneh, a Kenizzite spy sent by Moses into the land of Israel representing the tribe of Judah and whose people settled in Hebron (Joshua 14:13–14; Numbers 13) (Fretz & Panitz, 1992). The genealogical lists are grouped together both by geographical proximity and by ties of fictive kinship.

4 Ge Harashim

Ge (גִּיא) Harashim (חֲרָשִׁים) means Valley of Craftsmen. The Craftsmen are not necessarily smiths, as Glueck states. The noun harash is applied to engravers of jewels (Exodus 28:11), carpenters (I Chronicles 14:1), stone masons (I Chronicles 22:15), those who cast idols from molten metal (Isaiah 40:19), and both bronzeworkers and iron workers (II Chronicles 24:12). Even wizards (Isaiah 3:3) and men skilled in destruction (Ezekiel 21:31) might be called harashim, at least poetically. The term harashim is applied to artisans or craftsmen in almost any medium, including destruction; the term is not specifically to metal workers and is never applied to those who smelt metal in the Bible.

If the term harashim is meant to apply to metal workers there is still no reason to assume that these artisans smelt their own metal. Where the biblical authors use the term to refer to metal workers, they refer to those who shape metal into a final product, not those who mine metal or smelt metal ore. Nor is it necessary that these metal craftsmen would work at a metal source. The most famous metalworker in the Bible is Hiram of Tyre, the son of a widow of Naphtali, who we are told crafted the bronze or copper vessels for the Solomonic Temple. The Bible does not say he smelted ore, and he did not do his work at a mining area. Hiram cast the vessels in molds, and did so not in the Wadi Arabah, but in the plain of the Jordan between Succoth and Zarethan (I Kings 7:46). When Solomon recalled Hiram to Israel he went to the allotment his mother's people, Naphtali, and did his work in a place where he could obtain clay for molds. If the biblical narrative is to be believed, an abundant source of clay and a labor force with family ties were more important to Hiram than a nearby source of copper ore.

In its appearance in I Chronicles, Ge Harashim appears in a genealogical list that enumerates the descendants of Kenaz (I Chronicles 4:13–14). This list is similar to, and immediately follows, the list of the descendants of Kelub. But it is also a floating genealogy, which is directly tied neither to the list of the descendants of Kelub nor to that of Judah. It is included in this place because Kenaz was understood to somehow be related to Caleb son of Jephunneh. There are several ways Jephunneh was understood to be related to Kenaz, despite the fact that he served as Moses' representative for the tribe of Judah. Jephunneh was said to be a Kenezite (Numbers 32:12; Joshua 14:6). Another tradition held that Caleb's younger brother was called Kenaz (Joshua 15:17; Judges 1:13). Finally, a third tradition claimed that Kenaz was Caleb's grandson (I Chronicles 4:15). A man named Othniel is similarly described as a son of Kenaz (Joshua 15:17; Judges 1:13) and a cousin of Ge Harahsim (I Chronicles 4:13). The Kenizzites are generally considered to be a non-Israelite ethnic group from somewhere in the Negev, part of which was adopted into the tribe of Judah through ties of fictive kinship (Kuntz, 1992). Another faction of the Kenizzites may have been adopted into Edom through similar processes (Genesis 36:15; I Chronicles 1:53). But the lands of the Kenites and Kenizzites, like those of many other peoples, were included in the territories promised to Abraham (Genesis 15:19).

Glueck's assumption that the craftsmen of Ge Harashim were metal workers rather than artisans in some other medium is based on a series of deductions. The term harash does appear numerous times in relation to metal work. It is also assumed that the genealogy that includes Ir Nahash is linked to the genealogy that includes Ge Harashim, even though these two scraps of genealogical material are never explicitly linked to a single apical ancestor. Glueck assumes that Ir Nahash means Copper City, rather than Snaketown, and infers that the craftsmen of Ge Harashim are therefore copper workers. Glueck assumes that the linguistic evidence and legend of Tubal-Cain tying Kenites to metallurgy, and the biblical passages linking Kenites and Kenizzites, indicate that the Kenizzites were also metal workers (Glueck, 1940a).

5 Placing Ir Nahash and Ge Harashim

Although the documents preserved in I Chronicles 4 are presented as genealogical lists, most of the names appear to be of geographical locations. Names such as Penuel, Bethlehem, and Tekoa, which are included in the genealogies as though they are the names of people are readily recognizable place names. In order to avoid disputed identifications, one may identify thirteen place names in I Chronicles 4 using only those places identified in the *Oxford Bible Atlas* (Curtis, 2007; Table 1). When charted on a map, they are located predominantly in the Shephelah, and within the traditional allotment granted to Judah (Fig. 2). This is where one would expect to find the lands granted to Caleb's descendants, who are said to have been given the land around Hebron (I Chronicles 6:41). Every one of these identifiable place names is located very far from Khirbat en-Nahas.

Unfortunately, the genealogical fragments documented in I Chronicles 4 that include Ir Nahash and Ge Harashim include only one easily identifiable place name, that of Ophrah. Ophrah is listed as one of the great-grandsons of Kenaz through his son Othniel. Ge Harashim, who is described as a great-grandson of Kenaz through

Table 1 Identifiable place names in I Chronicles 4

I Chronicles 4, verse	Biblical place name	Modern place name (Curtis, 2007)	Location
2	Jezreel	Khirbet Terrama?	31.480833, 35.0325
	Etam	Khirbet el-Khokh	31.684780, 35.178840
4	Penuel	Tulul edh-Dhabab	32.18575, 35.68667
	Gedor	Khirbat Jedur	31.632629, 35.092145
	Bethlehem	Bethlehem	31.7054, 35.2024
5	Tekoa	Khirbat al-Tuqu`	31.636389, 35.214444
14	Ophrah	Taybeh	31.954444, 35.300278
17	Eshtemoa	Es-Samu`	31.400833, 35.067222
18	Soco	Khirbat Shuweikeh	31.682108, 34.973866
	Zanoah	Khirbat Zanu`	31.732222, 34.999167
19	Keilah	Khirbet Qila	31.6119, 35.0025
	Eshtemoa	Es-Samu'	31.400833, 35.067222
21	Mareshah	Tel Sandahannah	31.593056, 34.898333

Fig. 2 Identified sites mentioned in in I Chronicles 4

another son, Seraiah, is therefore a third cousin of Ophrah. Ophrah is identified with Taybeh, a village 12 kilometers northeast of Ramallah (Fig. 2). One would expect Ge Harashim to be somewhere in the vicinity of modern Taybeh.

It is possible that the reason the Chronicler included the Ge Harashim genealogy in I Chronicles is because the site was important in his narrative in Nehemiah 11:31–35. This segment of the Book of Nehemiah describes the resettling of the land after the Exile. In this second appearance of the name Ge Harashim, the term is unambiguously a place name. Ge Harashim is specifically included in a list of places resettled by Benjaminites from Geba. Of the sixteen places listed, ten are securely identified (Table 2). When charted on a map, they form two clusters, one in the vicinity of Ramallah and the other around Lod (Fig. 3). These Benjaminites settled in the area of their ancient tribal allotment, spilling over into the lands of neighboring tribes, including the land of Judah. There is no reason to believe that these returning Bejaminites would settle in the Wadi Arabah, and none of the ten identifiable sites are located in the Wadi Arabah.

Ge Harashim is specifically listed in connection to Lod and Ono. The three names are so closely associated in this verse that the early Rabbis of the Mishnah spoke of them as though they were a single place (Schwartz, 1991:39). Lod has returned to its ancient Hebrew name, although it was known for centuries as Lydda. Ono is generally believed to be Kafr Ana.

Ram Gophna, Itamar Taxel, and Amir Feldstein argue that Kafr Juna, located approximately one kilometer northeast of Kafr Ana, is a more likely candidate for the biblical Ono. Unlike Kafr Ana, Kafr Juna has yielded archaeological evidence from all the time periods for which we also have documentary evidence, ranging from the Late Bronze Age through the Early Islamic Period. Also, in the Byzantine period, when Ono was a Jewish Center, Kafr Ana was inhabited by Christians, while Kafr Juna was a Jewish site. Gophna and his associates suggest that Ono was originally applied only to the site now known as Kafr Juna and was later applied to both Kafr Juna and Kafr Ana (after the latter was founded during the Byzantine period), and that finally, in the early Islamic period, Kafr Juna was abandoned and only the space now occupied by Kafr Ana was known as Ono (Gophna et al., 2005).

Table 2 Identified places mentioned in Nehemiah 11:31–35

Nehemiah 11, verse	Biblical place name	Modern name (Curtis, 2007)	Location
31	Geba	Jeba`	31.8575, 35.261111
	Michmash	Mukhmas	31.872778, 35.276944
	Bethel	Beitin	31.928333, 35.238333
32	Anathoth	Ras el-Kharrubeh	31.801667, 35.253333
33	Ramah	Er-Ram	31.853611, 35.233333
	Gittaim	Tell Ras Abu Hamid	31.903020, 34.889940
34	Hadid	Tel Hadid	31.9677, 34.933597
	Neballat	Beit Nabala	31.985556, 34.956667
35	Lod	Lydda	31.951944, 34.888056
	Ono	Kafr Ana	32.024444, 34.868611

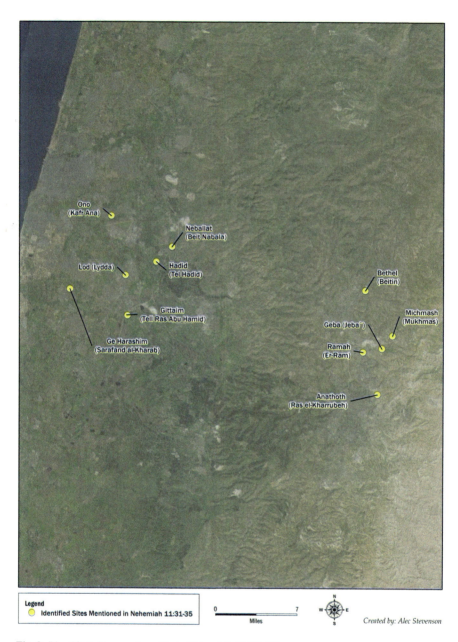

Fig. 3 Identified sites mentioned in in Nehemiah 11:31–35

City of Copper, Ruin of Copper: Rethinking Nelson Glueck's Identifications of Ir...   1167

Nevertheless, whether Kafr Ana or Kafr Juna is ancient Ono, Ono is known from both the Bible and other documents to have been in the vicinity of Lod. Both Kafr Ana and Kafr Juna are in the Lod Valley. Nehemiah gives us no indication that we should look for Ge Harashim in the Negev or the Wadi Arabah. The most reasonable deduction is that Ge Harashim should be sought in the vicinity of Lod.

6 A Site with Three Names

Glueck never set out criteria for evaluating his association of Khirbat en-Nahas with Ir Nahash, but he implied that the name of the ancient city survived in the name of the modern ruin. Name survival would seem to be one of the strongest arguments in favor of Khirbat en-Nahas being the Biblical Ir Nahash. Jozef Milik, who disagreed with the equation of Khirbat en-Nahas and Ir Nahash, admitted the identification is "linguistically irreproachable" (Milik, 1961:127). John R. Bartlett also explicitly points out the close parallel between the two names (Bartlett, 2006:153). The name Khirbat en-Nahas would appear to be an obvious survival of Ir Nahash, and it is compelling to believe that the site retained that name through the millennia. However, the site had three names in the early twentieth century, all of them descriptive, and it is unlikely that any of them were ancient survivals.

Glueck implies in both "Explorations in Eastern Palestine" and *The Other Side of the Jordan* that the name Khirbat en-Nahas was an ancient survival, and that the modern Bedouin were ignorant of why the site had such a name. Glueck repeatedly states that the local Bedouin all knew the site as the Ruin of Copper, but did not know that copper was to be found in the vicinity (Glueck, 1935:29, 1940b:57). Glueck never explicitly states that the name has survived the ages, but states, "Repeated questions elicited no sensible replies from our Arab guides as to why the site was called by that particular name. They were well aware of [the site's] presence … but had no idea whatsoever with regard to the origin of the name, except to repeat over and over again that it had been called so by their fathers" (Glueck, 1940b:57). The obvious implication if the Bedouin did not know why the site was called Ruin of Copper is that they were simply passing down a name from antiquity.

But Glueck does not point out in any of his publications that earlier publications indicated that the Bedouin gave Khirbat en-Nahas three different names, all of them descriptive. Musil calls the site "Khirbat en-Nahas or also as it has come to be called Rujim el-'Atik" (Musil, 1907: II (1): 298). Musil records the site not only as the Ruin of Copper, but also as the Old Rock Pile. In the solitary instance when he chooses to use a single name he uses the name h. en-Nahas, suggesting that name has primacy.

Frank introduces another name, and appears to give it precedence over Khirbat en-Nahas. Frank calls the site "*chirbat es-samra* or *chrēbet en-naḥās* (I heard both names for this location)" (Frank, 1934:216). Chirbat es-Samra means Dark Ruin, and is an appropriately descriptive name for a site covered in piles of black copper slag. When Frank uses a single name for the site, he always chooses Chirbat es-Samra. His map (Plan 16) uses the name Chirbet es-Samra, with Chrebet en-Nahas appearing only in parentheses, and in the caption to his photograph of the site—the first photograph ever published of Khirbat en-Nahas—Frank calls the site Chirbet es-Samra (Frank, 1934:Tafel 30 B). When Frank uses the name Khirbat en-Nahas, it may be simply to differentiate it from other sites called Khirbat es-Samra, like the Khirbat es-Samra located higher on the Edom plateau (Philby, 1925). Samra is common in place names across the Arabic-speaking world. Frank thought of the site primarily as Chirbet es-Samra, Dark Ruin.

Had Glueck not made his explorations at the time he did, immediately after Frank published his observations, Tom might have made his excavations at Khirbat es-Samra instead of Khirbat en-Nahas. Thanks to Frank, Khirbat es-Samra was already beginning to enter the scholarly literature the same year that Glueck published his initial description of the site. Albrecht Alt, who erroneously assumed the fortress at Khirbat en-Nahas was Roman, adopted the name Khirbat es-Samra in his article on Roman streets and fortresses (Alt, 1935:4). It is logical to conclude that other scholars would have also naturally adopted Frank's preferred name as they discussed the site in the scholarly literature, if Glueck had not published his own description of the site, in English and with dates derived from ceramic data, immediately after Frank.

Musil and Frank, like Glueck, relied upon local inhabitants for their information, and both Musil and Frank came away with multiple names for the site. All three names for the site are descriptive. Both Ruin of Copper (Khirbat en-Nahas) and Dark Ruin (Khirbat es-Samra) are apt names for a site covered in black slag mounds. It is likely that, as Glueck says, Sheikh Audeh of the Beni Atiyeh and his four compatriots who joined the expedition did not know that copper could be mined around Khirbat en-Nahas. But over the millennia that Khirbat en-Nahas sat in ruins, other Arabs could have easily recognized the rich green ore eroding out of the Nubian sandstone. Copper smelting has never been a lost art, and anyone who had seen copper slag would recognize it in the ubiquitous slag heaps of Khirbat en-Nahas. Khirbat en-Nahas is a descriptive place name, worthy of such a large metal working site, and it could have been applied to the archaeological site at any time after it fell into ruins. Old Rock Pile (Rujim el Atik) is a similarly apt descriptive name for the site with its many building ruins laying in piles on the surface. The very fact that all three names are so descriptive suggest that they could have been applied to the site after it was already a ruin.

7 Evidence from the Roman Period

If the name Ir Nahash survived into the twentieth century, one would expect it would appear in documents in the intervening years. Historical evidence from the Roman period supports the related contentions that Ir Nahash was located in the Shephelah and that no name survived for Khirbat en-Nahas. Our sources for this period are Bishop Eusebius Pamphilias of Caesarea (ca. 263–339?) and the fragmentary archives of Simon Bar Kohkba. Eusebius was well acquainted with the Faynan region and identifies several places there as biblical sites, but never mentions Ir Nahash. Meanwhile, documents from the Second Jewish Revolt discovered during Glueck's lifetime suggest a place known as Ir Nahash lay in the domain of Bar Kokhba, on the edge of the Judean hill country. None of these documents mention Ge Harashim.

Eusebius Pamphilias compiled his *Onomasticon* in order to record the locations of biblical places. Although he was a Caesarean, Eusebius was very familiar with the Faynan region. Eusebius lived through the Diocletian persecutions, during which many Christians were sent to work in the empire's mines, including the copper mines at Faynan. Eusebius survived the persecutions and lived to be honored as a bishop and have Christianity raised to the state religion. In his writings, including his *Ecclesiastical History*, Eusebius documents the sufferings of some of those who suffered in the mines. Eusebius was an individual who was very interested in, and knowledgeable about, biblical historical geography in general and the specific geography of the Faynan region in particular.

While Eusebius never mentions Ir Nahash in the *Onomasticon*, he does ascribe biblical identities to sites in the Faynan region. Eusebius correctly identifies Faynan—the Phaeno of his own day—with the Punon of the Bible. He also identifies the Edomite Daidan. Most scholars equate the Edomite Daidan mentioned in God's message in Jeremiah 49:8 with the Arabian Dedan. The Arabian Dedan was a Lihyanite state with its capital at the oasis of Al-'Ula, and it is also mentioned by Jeremiah (Jeremiah 25:23; Graf, 1992). Eusebius, however, understood the Edomite Daidan to be a different place, in Edom itself, just as Jeremiah 49 describes it. Euseubius even spells the two place names differently. The Edomite place he calls Daidan ($\Delta\alpha\iota\delta\alpha\nu$) and the Arabian place he calls Dadan ($\Delta\alpha\delta\alpha\nu$). Eusebius places the Edomite Daidan "in Phainon [Feinan], about 4 milestones north" (80; Freeman-Grenville, 2003: 48).

Abel was familiar with Glueck's latest work and integrated the results of his "Explorations in Eastern Palestine" (Glueck, 1935) into the second volume of his *Géographie de la Palestine*. Examining Glueck's maps, Abel claimed that Khirbat en-Nahas is "without doubt" (Abel, 1933–1938: Volume II, pg. 304) the site Eusebius calls Daidan. In his "Annotated Index to Eusebius' *Onomasticon*," Rupert L. Chapman III accepts this designation (Chapman, 2003:125). But Abel's claims do not fit the topography well. It is unlikely that Eusebius would measure the distance from Faynan to Khirbat en-Nahas in milestones, given the broken nature of the landscape between the two sites. Yoel Elitzur proposes a more likely placement for Eusebius' Daidan, modern Dana, about twelve kilometers northeast of Faynan (Elitzur, 2004:239–245). Because Faynan lies in a bend of the Wadi Fayan, the track twists upstream towards Dana. Elitzur solves the apparent problem of the distance between Faynan and Dana by noting that Eusebius' measurements by milestones would have been the distance traveled along the main highway to the turn-off to Daidan, not the total distance traveled from Faynan to Daidan. By this measurement, Eusebius reports the distance between Faynan and Dana accurately. But regardless of the correct identification of the Edomite Daidan, the fact that Eusebius does not identify Ir Nahash with a place in the Faynan region suggests that in the Roman period no place in the Faynan region was called Ir Nahash.

There is evidence from the Bar Kohkba archives that earlier in the Roman period a place named Ir Nahash was well known in the Judean hill country. Among the papyrus legal documents from the Second Jewish Revolt recovered from the caves of Wadi Murabba'at (Nahal Darga) are a series of agricultural land leases. These leases are made out between Hillel ben Garis, who was one of Bar Kokhba's representatives, and various farmers. The leases are for agricultural land in Ir Nahash, and indicate that an agricultural settlement known as Ir Nahash existed securely within Bar Kokhba's domain (Milik, 1961:122–132). The Ir Nahash mentioned in these documents was therefore almost certainly within the Judean hill country.

8   Deir Nakhkhas as Ir Nahash

The strongest argument that Khirbat en-Nahas is not Ir Nahash is the fact that another site, Deir Nakhkhas (دير النقّاس), is a stronger contender for the name. In 1858, C.W.M. Van De Velde published a map of the Holy Land based on his surveys of 1851 and 1852. He included "a village with ancient remains" he called Deir Nakhas or Deir Nakhaz, which he suggested was the biblical Ir Nahas (Van De Velde, 1858:322). Van De Velde may have been the first in modern times to make the association.

Between 1872 and 1877 the Palestine Exploration Fund conducted its Survey of Western Palestine and in the process documented Deir Nakhkhas. They encountered "A very small village perched on a high, steep hill looking down the valley to the north" (Conder & Kitchener, 1881–1883: vol. III, pg. 258). They noted its archaeological remains consisted of "A ruined birkeh and a cave with 250 niches" (Conder & Kitchener 1881–1883: vol. III, pg. 275). The Fund translated the name "The monastery of the cattle drover" (Palmer, 1881:367). Expedition leaders Claude Conder and Horatio Kitchener suggested, "This is possibly Ir-Nahash" (Conder & Kitchener 1881–1883: vol. III, pg. 258; cf. Armstrong et al., 1908:92).

Prior to Glueck's survey, the identification of Deir Nakhkhas as the biblical Ir Nahash went unchallenged, and even after Glueck wrote it was still widely accepted. The identification was accepted by Abel (Abel, 1933–1938: Vol. II, 351) and Jan Jozef Simons (Simons, 1959: 156). Simons lumped Deir Nakhkhas together with the other towns in the Shephelah which "are more or less manifestly recognizable as being topographical names or at least as *nomina gentilicia* derived from such names" (Simons, 1959: 154). Glueck makes no attempt to refute this identification; instead, on this point he simply ignores the scholarly work of his predecessors.

The place can be traced under the name Deir Nakhkhas or a similar name for centuries. I Chronicles and the Bar Kokhba archive both suggest that Ir Nahash was in the Judean hill country. In the twelfth century Deir Nakhkhas was a casale or hamlet known as Deir Nachar, ruled by the Knights Hospitallers (Conder, 1890:31). In a 1596 Ottoman census Deir Nakhkhas appears as an agricultural settlement of

13 families (Hütteroth & Abdulfattah, 1977:123). In Glueck's time Deir Nakhkhas was a small village on a hilltop overlooking Wadi Bayt Jibrin approximately 20 kilometers northwest of Hebron. The agricultural village consisted of 86 houses in 1931. According to Palestinian historian Walid Khalidi, "Dayr Nahkhkas was located in an area rich in archaeological sites. In the nearly 15,000 dunums that belonged to the village there were some fifteen sites, including the village itself (which was built over an archaeological site)" (Khalidi, 1992:217). The hamlet was depopulated in 1948.

Archaeological evidence indicates that Deir Nakhkhas was an important place during the Second Jewish Revolt, which therefore also supports the identification of Deir Nakhkhas with Bar Kokhba's Ir Nahash. Milik notes that sites in the vicinity of Deir Nakhkhas exhibited evidence of destruction at the end of the revolt, suggesting the region was Bar Kokhba's heartland (Milik, 1961:127). Subsequent excavations have identified numerous artificial caves in Bar Kokhba's kingdom that were used by the rebels (Zissu & Kloner, 2014). One of the hiding complexes, excavated by Amos Kloner, was at Deir Nakhkhas. A coin minted by Bar Kohkba coin was found in the hiding place (Zissu & Eshel, 2002:159). Deir Nakhkhas was one of Bar Kokhba's settlements and was important enough to have an artificial cave hiding complex. The preponderance of the evidence indicates that Deir Nakhkhas was the place known as Ir Nahash to both Bar Kokhba and the Chronicler.

9 Sarafand el-Kharab, Wadi Arabah, and Ge Harashim

Ge Harashim was also associated with a more appropriate geographical area shortly before Glueck suggested the valley was identical to the Wadi Arabah. In a list of ancient place names and their modern associations, Abel noted, "The Valley of Artisans, mentioned in company with Lod and Ono, is possibly Sarafand el-Kharab, situated in a meandering tributary of Nahr Rubin. The Arabic Sarafand disguises the old word of Sarpeta [*sic*], which signifies a foundry" (Abel, 1933–1938: Vol. I, pg. 405). Another village similarly displays the transformation of Sarepta, "smelting place," into the Arabic Sarafand (الصرفند). Today's Al-Sarafand near Haifa was known to the Crusaders as Sarepta Yudee (Ben-Ze'ev & Aburaiya, 2004). Sarafand is thus an appropriate Arabization Sarepta, which in turn is likely derived from Harashim.

Sarafand el-Kharab lies on the coastal plain, approximately seven kilometers west of Ramla (Fig. 1). About five kilometers northeast of Sarafand el-Kharab is Sarafand al-Amar (Populated Sarafand), also known as Sarafand al-Kubra (Bigger Sarafand). Abel focused on Sarafand el-Kharab simply because it was the Sarafand in ruins at the time. The villages are somewhat to the north of the clusters of sites mentioned in I Chronicles, but it is no further north than Ophrah, the only securely identified site that is included in the same genealogy of Kenaz that lists Ge Harashim (Fig. 2). Sarafand el-Kharab's relative proximity to Lod is in conformity with its being among the sites listed in Nehemiah 11:35 (Fig. 3). The twin villages named

Sarafand are approximately where one would expect Ge Harashim to be located in the context of I Chronicles 4 and Nehemiah 11.

In a study of Ge Harashim, Menashe Har-El notes that Ge Harashim may be Sarafand el-Kharab or one of the valleys in the vicinity, and that craftsmen would have been drawn to the region by the firewood necessary for metalworking which he argues would have grown in abundance near Sarafand. Sarafand is near or within the ancient Philistine territories, and Har-El argues that the name does not commemorate Solomon as a copper king but rather is a memory of the reputation of Philistines as smiths (I Samuel 13:19; Har-El, 1977).

The name Sarafand can be traced through time at least as far as the sixteenth century. Sarafand el-Kubra is mentioned as an agricultural village of 48 households in Ottoman tax records in 1596 (Hütteroth & Abdulfattah, 1977:152). The fact that it is called el-Kubra suggests that its sister settlement also already existed and therefore the name was probably already of some antiquity. The Sufi traveler Mustafa al-Dumyuti al-Luqaymi visited a shrine in Sarafand al-Amar in the eighteenth century (Khalidi, 1992:411). Robinson mentions both Sarafands, and believed that one of them was the same city that appears in records of the year 796 as Sariphaea (Robinson & Smith, 1856: vol. 3, pg. 45). The Survey of Western Palestine describes rock cut tombs at Sarafand (Condner & Kitchener, 1881: vol. 2, pg. 33). Unlike Khirbat en-Nahas, Sarafand is indisputably an old name, and is not simply descriptive of its modern state.

Meanwhile, the biblical authors simply do not use the phrase Ge Harashim when they describe the Wadi Arabah. If Glueck's thesis were correct that the Wadi Arabah was known as Ge Harashim, and particularly if that part of the Wadi Arabah linking Khirbat en-Nahas and Tell el-Kheleifeh were known as Ge Harashim, then we would expect the term to be applied to the road there. Instead, the biblical author calls the road the Israelites took from Elat and Ezion-Geber the Arabah Road (Deuteronomy 2:8). No instance can be cited where the biblical authors use the term Ge Harashim to describe that geographical area which Glueck claims was the Valley of Smiths (Seely, 1992a). The evidence indicates that Ge Harashim was a small, relatively unimportant valley in the area settled by the Benjaminites after the Exile. Sarafand el-Kharab and Sarafand al-Amar most likely preserve an ancient memory of foundries in the vicinity, and these sites are within a location which, geographically, is a more reasonable location to find Ge Harashim than the Wadi Arabah.

Glueck's identification of the Wadi Arabah as a Valley of Smiths is due more to his archaeological interpretation of the region than his interpretation of historical documents. Glueck was born in 1900 in Cincinnati, Ohio, on the edge of the America's steel producing area. At the time cities like Cleveland and Pittsburgh were metallurgical and commercial centers. Beginning in the middle nineteenth century, steel companies that controlled every aspect of metal production from the mine to the final mold shipped many tons of iron ore and coal to these cities by rail and canal. Enormous foundries and industrial complexes in the cities smelted the ore into iron or steel, formed it into transportable units and an array of final products, and shipped it via water to market (Lamoreaux, 2000:430–431). All work was

City of Copper, Ruin of Copper: Rethinking Nelson Glueck's Identifications of Ir... 1173

under the control of companies like US Steel, directed by industrial and shipping magnates like US Steel President James J. Hill.

Glueck envisioned the Wadi Arabah as a vast metallurgical workshop, in which the entire region was integrated into the manufacture of the copper product. Different parts of the Wadi Arabah were involved in different components of the copper production. In Glueck's reconstruction, copper was mined at Faynan and Timna. Quantities were smelted in stone smelters at sites like Khirbat en-Nahas, but most of the ore was preliminarily roasted, and then shipped to Ezion-Geber, where it was smelted in a vast industrial complex that Glueck excavated. Thus, Glueck's Wadi Arabah was one vast industrial complex, working in unison to manufacture and ship copper under the direction of the wise King Solomon, who was "a copper king, a shipping magnate, a merchant prince, and a great builder" (Glueck, 1940b:99) reminiscent of an American steel tycoon. Such a cohesive unit would aptly be called a Valley of Craftsmen.

Subsequent research by scholars including Rothenberg, Andreas Hauptmann, Gary Pratico, and more recently Tom Levy, Mohammad Najjar, and Erez Ben-Yosef, among others, has largely disproven Glueck's model (Hauptmann, 2006, 2007; Levy et al., 2014; Pratico, 1993; Rothenberg, 1962, 1972, 1990). Copper deposits are not uniformly distributed across the Wadi Arabah; rather, the ore was mined in two main locations, Timna and Faynan, where the copper is exposed in uplifted Cambrian rocks within tributaries to the Arabah. These two discrete locations are separated by approximately 100 kilometers due to tectonic action. The ore was smelted at these locations in relatively small, saucer-shaped smelting ovens. The ore was not taken to Tell el-Khalifieh, which was not an industrial center and was probably not a port. Rather than one vast integrated valley of smiths, the Wadi Arabah was a large and diverse area with two important copper production areas located in widely separated tributaries. Valley of Smiths would not be an appropriate term for the Wadi Arabah from the south end of the Dead Sea to the Red Sea, or even from Wadi Faynan to the Red Sea.

10 Summary and Conclusions

In the 1930s, Nelson Glueck conducted his pioneering surveys in what is today Southern Israel and Jordan. His work was revolutionary, not only because he documented many archaeological sites that were previously unknown to scholars, but even more because he brought a level of sophistication to the ceramic dating of both previously documented and newly discovered sites in Transjordan. Glueck was the only voice for the expedition, and published his data quickly, first in the *Annual of the American Schools for Oriental Research* and the *Bulletin of the American Schools for Oriental Research* and later in popular form, in *The Other Side of the Jordan* and other books. Like the work of any early scientific pioneer, Glueck's findings needed refinement, and he made mistakes. At times he was unaware of and even ignored past scholarship. But as a responsible scholar, Glueck ultimately acknowledged when other scholars came forth with data that contradicted his interpretations. This included not only when he misidentified biblical sites (and most of identifications were quickly refuted following his initial publications), but even when theories in which he was heavily invested, like the purpose and function of the buildings at Tell el-*Kheleifeh*, were disproven.

Glueck never recanted two of his identifications of biblical sites, his association of Khirbat en-Nahas with Ir Nahash and his identification of the Wadi Arabah as Ge Harashim. Many scholars have adopted these identifications, and Glueck's theories have made their way into standard reference texts. However, in making these identifications Glueck ignored existing, better identifications for both sites.

Glueck reported only one of at least three Bedouin names for the site that has come to be known as Khirbat en-Nahas. He presents the name as though it were mysterious in origin and handed down since time unknown. The six Transjordanian nationals who joined Glueck's expedition may have only known the name Khirbat en-Nahas and not known its origin. But other names also had local currency, and two additional names, Khirbat es-Samra and Rujim el-'Atik, had already entered the scholarly literature. All three names are descriptive of an old pile of stones covered in dark copper slag. It required no special knowledge of the site's ancient name to apply any of these three adjectival names to the site. Glueck's scholarship helped fix the name Khirbat en-Nahas to the site. Frank preferred the name Khirbat es-Samra, and the latter name might have been fixed in the scholarly literature had Glueck not written so soon after Frank.

Deir Nakhkhas is almost certainly the site of ancient Ir Nahash. Mentioned only once in the Bible, in genealogical lists for clans adopted into the tribe of Judah, Ir Nahash the biblical context indicates that Ir Nahash was located in the Judean hill country. Surviving leases from the Bar Kokhba revolt confirm that a site known as Ir Nahash existed in Bar Kokhba's domain, which was centered in the Shephelah. The name Deir Nakhkhas is not a descriptive name that could have been recently applied to the site; rather, the village appears in sixteenth century Ottoman documents as Deir Nakhkhas and in twelfth century Crusader documents as Deir Nachar. The historical silence is punctuated regularly with a name resembling Ir Nahash in this location. The identification of Ir Nahash with Deir Nakhkhas was made by some of the region's earliest historical geographers, including the Survey of Western Palestine. Glueck ignores rather than rebuts these earlier scholars.

Glueck similarly does not contend with earlier identifications of Ge Harashim. Ge Harashim is the Valley of Craftsmen, not necessarily the Valley of Smiths. In those places where the Wadi Arabah is obviously mentioned in the Bible, the term Ge Harashim is not used. Like Ir Nahash it appears in a genealogy of a clan adopted into Judah, but it also appears in a list of sites settled by Benjaminites. One would expect to find such a place in the allotments of Judah or Benjamin, not in Edom, and most likely near Lod and Ono, with which it is linked. Abel proposed that Sarafand el-Kharab is Ge Harashim. Sarafand el-Kharab is located in the general vicinity of the identified sites of I Chronicles and Nehemiah and therefore where one would expect Ge Harashim. Abel also argued that Sarafand is a corruption of Sarepta, the Arabic word for foundry, an appropriate allusion to metal craftsmen. If Sarafand el-Kharab is not Ge Harashim, it may lie in a region once known as Ge Harashim that includes modern Sarafand el-Kharab and Sarafand al-Amar.

Accepting either of Glueck's identifications has much broader implications than simply mapping an erroneous name onto an archaeological site. As Zecharia Kallai points out, "If Ir-nahash has been correctly identified [with Khirbat en-Nahas], then the connection to this area is reflected in the genealogical lists of Judah" (Kallai, 1986:117). Kallai then argues that biblical allotment of the tribe of Judah consisted of hundreds of square kilometers more territory than is generally believed, and even annexed parts of the land of Edom. Some scholars offhandedly refer to "the Edomite Ir Nahash" (Aharoni, 1979:36; Rainey & Notley, 2006:152). But neither the Bible nor any other ancient document mentions an Ir Nahash in Edom.

Moreover, the misidentification of these sites prevents us from answering important research questions. There is much speculation as to who the Kenites were, where they came from, what economic pursuits they engaged in, and how their religion interplayed with that of ancient Israel. The Kenites' very name is linguistically associated with metallurgy. Were the Kenites and Kennizites trade guilds, as I. Mendelsohn suggested (Mendelsohn, 1940), or ethnicities? The Biblical narrative indicates associations between the Kenites and early Israelite religious practices. How did they impact the beginnings of Israelite religion? These lines of questioning also apply to related groups, such as the mysterious Rechabites of Jeremiah 35, the subjects of much speculation, who are associated with Ir Nahash in the genealogical lists of I Chronicles 4. Were these Rechabites a clan, a metallurgical guild, a military league, a cult that maintained an alleged "nomadic ideal," all of these or none of these (Frick, 1971, 1992)? Questions of economics and ethnicity are exactly the kinds of research questions archaeology can help answer when textual analysis has reached its limits. The Kenites are associated with the Negev and Edom, and there has been some attempt to identify a Kenite signature at Timna, particularly in the gilded brazen serpent found in the temple at Timna Site 200 (Rothenberg, 1972:183–184, 1988). But the Bible tells us the specific names of towns in which to look for Kenites and Kennizites in Judah. Any archaeological signature that might be associated with these peoples needs to first be sought in the specific places where they are known to have lived.

No major archaeological remains from either the early Second Temple period (when the Chronicler wrote about Ir Nahash and Ge Harashim) or the Late Bronze period (when the Kenites might have been expected to be an identifiable people interacting with proto-Israelites) have been reported at either Deir Nakhkhas or the two Sarafands. Ir Nahash and Ge Harashim were so unimportant that they only appear in minor lists, and little in the way of archaeological remains might be expected from these minor hamlets. However, a careful analysis of Late Bronze and Early Iron remains at these sites and others figuring into the genealogical lists may yield material data about these still shadowy peoples.

The ancient name of Khirbat en-Nahas remains unknown and, at this late date, is probably unknowable. To the early biblical authors the site lay in the foreign land of Edom. If it was not in enemy territory then it was at least not located in the land that most interested them and with which they were most familiar. Unlike Deir Nakhkhas, which either survived continuously or was repeatedly resettled up to the present day, and unlike Faynan, which was also important in later periods, Khirbat en-Nahas was abandoned in the Iron Age and never resettled. The Bedouin who tended their flocks in the shadows of its fortress had names for the site, but these names were based on the site's physical characteristics and could have been given to it by the Bedouin or travelers in the desert at any time in the past three thousand years. New archaeological evidence in the form of inscriptions, properly interpreted, may give us back this site's ancient name. Nelson Glueck's surveys, and Tom Levy's excavations, have reawakened the memory of the ancient copper workers of the Wadi al-Ghuweiba. But now the name by which the Iron Age kings and copper craftsmen called this once-great factory as forgotten as the flowers of the field of three millennia past.

Acknowledgments I would like to express my gratitude to the many people who contributed to the production of this essay. First, I would like to thank Tom Levy, my graduate adviser and dissertation supervisor. I am grateful to him for his advice first as an undergraduate taking his field school and then throughout my graduate career. I am thankful for the encouragement and opportunities he gave me during that period. My academic career was shaped by his influence, and I am appreciative for it.

I would also like to thank Erez Ben-Yosef and Ian Jones for their efforts editing this volume and for inviting me to publish this paper, and to Alec Stevenson for taking time out of a successful commercial archaeological career to make the maps. Thanks also to the anonymous reviewer, whose comments improved the manuscript.

This paper began its existence as a seminar paper, delivered first to the University of California, San Diego (UCSD) Judaic Studies Graduate Seminar and then at the Society for Biblical Literature Annual Meeting, Boston, 2008. Tom organized that session and encouraged all his graduate students to contribute, for which I am grateful. I am thankful to the Seminar professors, Tom, David Noel Freedman, William H.C. Propp, Richard Elliott Friedman, and David Goodblatt, as well as to Mohammad Najjar and my additional Committee members, Robert McCormick Adams, Anatoli Khazanov, and Guillermo Algaze. In those days giants walked UCSD, and I appreciated their efforts to form a naive but eager young graduate student in their midst. I am also thankful to my fellow graduate students in both Judaic Studies and the Levantine Archaeology Laboratory. They include Erez, Ian, Kyle Knabb, Elizabeth Monroe, Kathleen Bennallack, Aaron Gidding, Neil Smith, Adolfo Muniz, Yoav Arbel, Sarah Malena, Bradley Root, Brian Kelly, Elizabeth Goldstein, Guinevere Thomas, Annabelle Teng, *Micah Glass-Siegel,* and Daniel Freese. I apologize to the many others I am sure I am forgetting who contributed to my intellectual life at UCSD and my thinking in the creation of this paper. Naturally its final form and conclusions, complete with any errors, remain my own.

References

Abel, F.-M. (1933–1938). *Géographie de la Palestine* (Vol. 2 vols). Librairie Lecoffre.
Aharoni, Y. (1979). *The land of the Bible: A historical geography.* Westminster Press.
Albright, W. F. (1921). The date and personality of the chronicler. *Journal of Biblical Literature, 40*(3/4), 104–124.
Albright, W. F. (1934). Soundings at Ader, A Bronze Age City of Moab. *Bulletin of the American Schools of Oriental Research, 53,* 13–18.
Alt, A. (1935). Aus der 'Araba. II. Römische Kastelle und Straßen. *Zeitschrift des Deutschen Palästina-Vereins, 58,* 1–59.

Armstrong, G., Wilson, C. W., & Conder, C. R. (1908). *Names and places in the old and new Testament and Apocrypha*. The Committee of the Palestine Exploration Fund.

Bartlett, J. R. (2006). The Wadi Arabah in the Hebrew scriptures. In P. Bienkowski & K. Galor (Eds.), *Crossing the rift: Resources, routes, settlement patterns, and interaction in the Wadi Arabah* (pp. 151–156). Oxbow Books.

Ben-Ze'ev, E., & Aburaiya, I. (2004). "Middle-ground" politics and the re-Palestinization of places in Israel. *International Journal of Middle East Studies, 36*(4), 639–655.

Ben-Yosef, E., Mohammad, N., & Levy, T. E. (2014). Local iron age trade routes in northern Edom. In T. E. Levy, M. Najjar, & E. Ben-Yosef (Eds.), *New insights into the iron age archaeology of Edom, Southern Jordan* (Vol. 2, pp. 493–575). The Cotsen Institute of Archaeology Press.

Brown, J. M., & Kutler, L. (2005). *Nelson Glueck: Biblical archaeologist and president of Hebrew Union College-Jewish Institute of Religion*. Hebrew Union College Press.

Chapman, R. L., III. (2003). Annotated index to Eusebius' Onomasticon. In *The Onomasticon* (Eusebius of Caesarea, translated by G. S. P. Freeman-Grenville) (pp. 99–184). Jerusalem, Carta.

Conder, C. R. (1890). Norman Palestine. *Palestine Exploration Quarterly, 22*(1), 29–37.

Conder, C. R., & Kitchener, H. H. (1881–1883). *Survey of Western Palestine*. Committee of the Palestine Exploration Fund.

Curtis, A. (2007). *Oxford Bible atlas, fourth edition*. Oxford University Press.

Elitzur, Y. (2004). *Ancient place names in the Holy Land: Preservation and history*. Hebrew University Magnes Press and Eisenbrauns.

Frank, F. (1934). Aus der 'Araba. I. Reiseberichte. *Zeitschrift des Deutschen Palästina-Vereins, 57*, 191–280.

Freeman-Grenville, G.S.P. (2003). Translator. *The Onomasticon, by Eusebius of Caesarea*. Carta.

Fretz, M. J., & Panitz, R. I. (1992). Caleb. In D. N. Freedman (Ed.), *The anchor Bible dictionary* (Vol. I, pp. 808–810). Doubleday.

Frick, F. S. (1971). The Rechabites reconsidered. *Journal of Biblical Literature, 90*(3), 279–287.

Frick, F. S. (1992). Recab. In D. N. Freedman (Ed.), *The anchor Bible dictionary* (Vol. V, pp. 630–632). Doubleday.

Glueck, N. (1935). Explorations in Eastern Palestine, II. *The Annual of the American Schools of Oriental Research, 15*: ix, 1–149, 151–161, 163–202.

Glueck, N. (1940a). Kenites and Kenizzites. *Palestine Exploration Quarterly, 72*, 22–24.

Glueck, N. (1940b). *The other side of the Jordan*. American Schools of Oriental Research.

Glueck, N. (1959). *Rivers in the desert: A history of the Negev*. W. W. Norton & Company.

Glueck, N. (1970). *The other side of the Jordan*. American Schools of Oriental Research.

Gophna, R., Taxel, I., & Feldstein, A. (2005). A new identification of ancient Ono. *Bulletin of the Ango-Israel Archaeological Society, 23*, 167–176.

Gordon, C. H. (1957). *Adventures in the nearest east*. Essential Books.

Gordon, C. H. (2000). *A Scholar's odyssey*. Society of Biblical Literature.

Graf, D. F. (1992). Dedan. In D. N. Freedman (Ed.), *The anchor Bible dictionary* (Vol. II, pp. 121–123). Doubleday.

Har-El, M. (1977). Valley of the craftsmen (Ge' Haharasim). *Palestine Exploration Quarterly, 109*(2), 75–86.

Halpern, B. (1992). Kenites. In D. N. Freedman (Ed.), *The anchor Bible dictionary* (Vol. IV, pp. 17–22). Doubleday.

Hauptmann, A. (2006). Mining archaeology and Archaeometallurgy in the Wadi Arabah: The mining districts of Faynan and Timna. In P. Bienkowski & K. Galor (Eds.), *Crossing the rift: Resources, routes, settlement patterns, and interaction in the Wadi Arabah* (pp. 125–134). Oxbow Books.

Hauptmann, A. (2007). *The Archaeometallurgy of Copper—Evidence from Faynan, Jordan*. Springer.

Horsfield, G., & Conway, A. (1930). Historical and topographical notes on Edom: With an account of the first excavations at Petra. *The Geographical Journal, 76*(5), 369–388.

Hütteroth, W.-D., & Abdulfattah, K. (1977). *Historical geography of Palestine, Transjordan and southern Syria in the late 16th century*. Vorstand der Fränkischen Geographischen Gesellschaft.

Kallai, Z. (1986). *Historical geography of the Bible: The tribal territories of Israel*. The Magnes Press.

Khalidi, W. (Ed.). (1992). *All that remains: The Palestinian villages occupied and depopulated by Israel in 1948*. Institute for Palestine Studies.

Klein, R. W. (1992). Chronicles, book of 1-2. In D. N. Freedman (Ed.), *The anchor Bible dictionary* (Vol. I, pp. 992–1002). Doubleday.

Knoppers, G. N. (2003). *I chronicles 1–9: A new translation with introduction and commentary* (The anchor Bible) (Vol. 12). Doubleday & Company.

Kuntz, J. K. (1992). Kenaz. In D. N. Freedman (Ed.), *The anchor Bible dictionary* (Vol. IV, p. 17). Doubleday.

Lamoreaux, N. R. (2000). Entrepreneurship, business organization, and economic concentration. In S. L. Engerman & R. E. Gallman (Eds.), *The Cambridge economic history of the United States, volume 2: The long nineteenth century* (pp. 403–434). Cambridge University Press.

Levy, T. E., Najjar, M., & Ben-Yosef, E. (Eds.). (2014). *New insights into the Iron Age archaeology of Edom, Southern Jordan* (2 volumes). The Cotsen Institute of Archaeology Press.

Mendelsohn, I. (1940). Guilds in Ancient Palestine. *Bulletin of the American Schools of Oriental Research, 80*, 17–21.

Milik, J. T. (1961). Textes Hébreaux et Araméens. In B. P. Benoit, J. T. Milik, & R. de Vaux (Eds.), *Les Grottes de Murabba'ât* (Discoveries in the Judean Desert II) (Vol. I, pp. 67–205). Clarendon Press.

Miller, R. D., II. (2021). *Yahweh: Origin of a desert god*. Vandenhoeck & Ruprecht Verlag.

Musil, A. (1907). Arabia Petraea. 3 vols. Vienna. In *Kommission bei Alfred Hölder*.

Myers, J. M. (1965a). *I chronicles: A new translation with commentary and notes* (The anchor Bible) (Vol. 12). Doubleday & Company.

Myers, J. M. (1965b). *Ezra-Nehemiah: A new translation with commentary and notes* (The anchor Bible) (Vol. 14). Doubleday & Company.

Noth, M. (1987). *The Chronicler's history*. Sheffield University Press.

Palmer, D. H. (1881). *The survey of Western Palestine Arabic and English name lists*. Committee for the Palestine Exploration Fund.

Philby, H. S., & J.B. (1925). The Dead Sea to 'Aqaba. *The Geographical Journal, 66*(2), 134–155.

Pratico, G. D. (1993). *Nelson Glueck's 1938–1940 excavations at Tell el-Kheleifeh: A reappraisal*. Scholar's Press.

Rainey, A. F., & Notley, R. S. (2006). *The sacred bridge: Carta's atlas of the biblical world*. Carta Jerusalem.

Robinson, E., & Smith, E. (1856). *Biblical researches in Palestine, 1838–52. A journal of travels in the year 1838* (Vol. 2 vols). Crocker and Brewster.

Rothenberg, B. (1962). Ancient Copper Industries in the Western Arabah. *Palestine Exploration Quarterly, 94*, 44–56.

Rothenberg, B. (1972). *Were these king Solomon's mines? Excavations in the Timna Valley*. Stein and Day Publishers.

Rothenberg, B. (1988). *The Egyptian mining Temple at Timna*. Institute for Archaeo-Metallurgical Studies.

Rothenberg, B. (1990). In B. Rothenberg (Ed.), *The ancient metallurgy of copper: Archaeology – Experiment – Theory*. Institute for Archaeo-Metallurgical Studies.

Schwartz, J. J. (1991). *Lod (Lydda), Israel: From its origins through the Byzantine period, 5600 B.C.E.—640 C.E* (BAR international series 571). Tempvs Reparatvm.

Seely, D. (1992a). Arabah. In D. N. Freedman (Ed.), *The anchor Bible dictionary* (Vol. I, pp. 321–327). Doubleday.

Seely, J. A. H. (1992b). Irnahash. In D. N. Freedman (Ed.), *The anchor Bible dictionary* (Vol. III, p. 462). Doubleday.

Simons, J. (1959). *The geographical and topographical texts of the old testament: A concise commentary in XXXII chapters*. E. J. Brill.

Van De Velde, C. W. M. (1858). *Memoir to accompany the map of the Holy Land constructed by C.W.M. Van De Velde*. Justus Perthes.

Zissu, B., & Eshel, H. (2002). The geographical distributions of coins from the Bar Kokhba war. *Israel Numismatic Journal, 14*, 157–167.

Zissu, B., & Kloner, A. (2014). Rock-cut hiding complexes from the Roman period in Israel. *Der Erdstall, Beitraege zur Erforschung kuenstlicher Hoehlen, 40*, 96–119.

Assessing the Circulation of Arabah Copper (Timna vs. Faynan) from the End of the Late Bronze and Iron Age in the Southern Levant by Combining Lead Isotopic Ratios with Lead Concentrations

Naama Yahalom-Mack, Daniel M. Finn, and Yigal Erel ⓘD

Abstract Faynan is one of the most extraordinary copper production sites in the Near East. Recent excavations by Tom Levy and colleagues highlighted the peak of the activities at the site during Iron Age I and IIA. Most influential were the advanced methodologies which Levy employed during surveys and excavations in the region and the vast radiocarbon dating project which established extensive use of the area between the eleventh and ninth centuries BCE. The overlap which exists in lead isotopic values between ores from Timna and Faynan has prevented discerning between the two, however the use of lead concentrations in conjunction with the isotopic values provides additional insight regarding the use of Arabah copper in the Levant. In this study we examine the chemical and isotopic composition of 81 artefacts originating in well-dated contexts from 11 sites in the southern Levant. All the studied samples can be divided into three categories: (1) Samples that plot within the range of one or more of the expected ore sources (i.e., Faynan DLS, Timna Amir and Avrona, and Cyprus). Some of these can also be interpreted as mixing; (2) Samples that plot outside these ranges and can be accounted for by mixing of either Faynan DLS or Timna with a geologically younger copper ore; (3) Samples that require the addition of a third source (most likely a lead rather than a Pb-rich copper ore). In LBIII the vast majority of the samples are either from Timna or are mixtures of Sardinian lead with lead-poor copper with an Aegean/Anatolian origin. Only one sample might originate from Faynan. During Iron I most of the samples are consistent with Timna and Faynan (32/39). Six Iron I samples can be attributed to mixing between Arabah and Aegean/Anatolian sources, while a single object is inconsistent with ores from the Arabah. All Iron IIA samples (n = 9) are consistent with the

---

N. Yahalom-Mack (✉) · D. M. Finn · Y. Erel
Hebrew University, Jerusalem, Israel
e-mail: naama.yahalom@mail.huji.ac.il; daniel.finn@mail.huji.ac.il;
yigal.erel@mail.huji.ac.il

© The Author(s), under exclusive license to Springer Nature Switzerland AG 2023
E. Ben-Yosef, I. W. N. Jones (eds.), *"And in Length of Days Understanding" (Job 12:12): Essays on Archaeology in the Eastern Mediterranean and Beyond in Honor of Thomas E. Levy*, Interdisciplinary Contributions to Archaeology,
https://doi.org/10.1007/978-3-031-27330-8_50

Arabah ores. Iron IIB samples (n = 16), except for a single object are inconsistent with the Arabah copper sources. Thus, this study reinforces the chronological framework provided by the radiocarbon dates from the mining regions and suggests that Faynan copper was not in circulation before the late twelfth century BCE or during the eighth century BCE.

Keywords Lead isotopes · Copper · Timna · Faynan · Late Bronze Age · Iron Age · Ancient trade · Archaeometallurgy

1 Introduction

The Faynan mining district is located in the Wadi Arabah approximately 80 km south of the Dead Sea and 120 km north of Eilat. Wadi Faynan is created from the intersection of three wadis (the Dana, Ghuwayr, and Shayqar), and transitions further downstream into Wadi Fidan. The region has a rich history of archaeological research. The first description of the Faynan area stems from surveys conducted in the early twentieth century (Musil, 1907; Blanckenhorn, 1912) and later during the 1930's (Frank, 1934; Glueck, 1935, 1940). Archaeological work accelerated here during the second half of the twentieth century. In the 1960's, Faynan was highlighted in the reporting of the German Geological Mission (Kind, 1965). Geological work was conducted by Bender, who first addressed ancient mining practices (Bender, 1968). Raikes (1980) and MacDonald (1992) completed extensive surveys of the area, and from 1983–1993, surveys and excavations were carried about in the region by the Deutsches Bergbau-Museum Bochum, with subsequent cooperation with the Department of Antiquities in Jordan (Hauptmann, 2007). Together, researchers documented and dated prominent sites such as Khirbat Faynan, Wadi Fidan 4, Khirbat Hamra Ifdan, and Khirbat en-Nahas, as well as recorded hundreds of mines. Beginning in 1995, The Wadi Faynan Land Survey began to explore the Wadi Faynan area primarily focused on investigating the relationship between environmental change and human history within arid zones (Barker et al., 2007).

Since the 1990s, further evidence of Faynan's history of exploitation has come to light. During 1989–1992, the Wadi Fidan Project initiated excavations in the western Faynan region focused on Neolithic and Early Bronze Age settlements (Adams, 1991, 1992, 1998). Subsequent excavations by the Jabal Hamrat Fidan Archaeological Project revealed a large Early Bronze Age metalworking industry and settlements including Khirbat Hamra Ifdan (Adams, 2000) and Wadi Fidan 4 (Adams & Genz, 1995), as well as the initial dating results of Wadi Fidan 40 (Levy et al., 1999, 2001, 2002). Notably, excavations at Khirbat Hamra Ifdan unearthed significant Early Bronze Age remains, including a copper workshop containing crucible fragments, copper ingots, lumps of copper, prills, slags, and copper tools (Levy et al., 2002).

Beginning in 2002, large-scale surveys were undertaken by the Edom Lowlands Regional Archaeology Project (ELRAP), a derivation of the Jabal Hamrat Fidan

Assessing the Circulation of Arabah Copper (Timna vs. Faynan) from the End of...

project (Levy et al., 2014a: 69). Excavations, headed by Tom Levy, commenced at Khirbat Faynan (Novo et al., 2012); Khirbat al-Jariya (Levy et al., 2003; Ben-Yosef et al., 2010; Liss et al., 2020); Khirbat Nuqayb al-Asaymir (Jones et al., 2012) and Wadi Fidan 40 (Beherec et al., 2014). Most important were the excavations at the exceptional site of Khirbet en-Nahas, the largest copper smelting site in the Southern Levant, which uncovered a four-chambered gatehouse and fortress, elite residences, and clusters of structures (Levy et al., 2014b). The major contribution of the study to the region's history was the incorporation of cutting edge recording methods (e.g., Levy et al., 2014a: 31–66; Smith & Levy, 2014; Howland et al., 2015, 2018, 2020; Liss et al., 2017) and an extensive radiocarbon dating project, which exposed together with the excavations results, the true scale of the robust and unprecedent copper production activities at Faynan during the early Iron Age (Levy et al., 2004, 2008, 2014b; Ben-Yosef et al., 2010).

Geologically, Faynan and Timna copper ores were formed by processes associated with the termination of the Arabian-Nubian Precambrian magmatism. At that stage, they were located adjacent to one another. It was proposed that weathering of the igneous Arabian-Nubian magmatic rocks followed by subsurface mobilization provided sedimentary copper and other metals into the Timna and Faynan basins (Wurzburger, 1967; Beyth, 1987; Segev et al., 1992). According to Asael et al. (2012) copper sulphide formation in the Cambrian dolomite, together with partial oxidation of these sulphides to malachite, occurred during early diagenesis under lagoonal marine conditions (Shlomovitch et al., 1999; Asael et al., 2007), after which some of the copper minerals were deposited within Lower Cambrian sandstones (Asael et al., 2012). These processes placed the copper-rich minerals chiefly in the Timna formation in Timna, and the Burj dolomite-shale (also called DLS – Dolomite-Limestone-Shale) in Faynan. More than 400 Mya lapsed until significant remobilization of copper into Lower Cretaceous rocks in Timna (Amir and Avrona formations) and other Cambrian rocks in Faynan (Umm Ishrin; MBS – Massive Brown Sand) took place, involving reactions of copper-bearing solutions with iron sulphides and direct precipitation of Cu-sulphides from solutions to form secondary Cu ores. This secondary mineralization event might have been triggered in the Miocene by the strike-slip movement of the Dead Sea Transform, pushing the Arabian plate northward relative to the Sinai sub-plate, placing Faynan in its current position approximately 105 km north of Timna. As a result, the main units that host Cu-rich minerals are the Cambrian Timna and the Burj dolomite-shale and Umm Ishrin formations in Faynan, and the Lower Cretaceous Amir and Avrona formations in Timna (Segev et al., 1992). In Faynan, the DLS was the major unit exploited for copper in most periods, while the MBS was of lesser importance, mostly mined during the Chalcolithic and the Roman periods (Hauptmann, 2007: 146, Fig. 5.46). In Timna, Amir and Avrona formations were the major source of copper mining in most periods (see Hauptmann, 2007: 66; Ben-Yosef, 2010: 96–104 and references therein).

Multiple radiocarbon dates retrieved during the excavations of Khirbet al-Jariya and Khirbet en-Nahas indicate that copper extraction during the Iron Age was performed mainly during the eleventh–ninth centuries BCE (IA I – IA IIa). However, there are several second millennium radiocarbon dates from Faynan which predate the Iron Age, although these are not indicative of systematic production activities at the site. One sample, from a backfill in Mine 42 at Wadi Khalid, is dated to the fifteenth century. Another, from a waste dump in Mine 13 at Wadi Dana, has a very wide range spanning the thirteenth–eleventh centuries BCE, as do other samples from the fortress at KEN and from Khirbet Faynan (Ben-Yosef et al., 2010: 727–730, Table 1). A single date, from the deepest sounding in Area M at Khirbet en-Nahas, produced a date in the thirteenth century BCE (Layer M5b) and another in the first half of the twelfth century BCE (Layer M5a) (Levy et al., 2014b: 150–151). Additional twelfth century dates were retrieved from Khirbet al-Jariya, but modelled in the eleventh century BCE (Ben-Yosef et al., 2010: 742, Fig. 9).

The chrono-historical framework differs from that in the Timna Valley, as in the latter, copper mining and smelting activities took place during the Late Bronze Age (Rothenberg, 1988, 1990; Ben-Yosef et al., 2012; Yagel et al., 2016). There is clear evidence for the presence of 19th and 20th Dynasty Egyptians in Timna, as the names of pharaohs from these dynasties (Seti I – Ramesses IV) were inscribed on finds recovered from the Hathor Temple (Site 200). However, it has been convincingly shown by Avner (2014) that the Egyptians took over existing copper production activity. In Faynan, there is no evidence for the presence of the New Kingdom Egyptians nor for copper production by indigenous population during this time. The earliest radiocarbon dates which are few, indicate that copper production was resumed there, towards the end of the Egyptian involvement in Canaan. However, while radiocarbon may be used to establish the date for the beginning of copper production at Faynan during the Late Bronze/Iron Age transition, provenancing copper-based objects from well-dated contexts may be used to establish when either Faynan or Timna copper was traded in the southern Levant.

2   Materials and Methods

This paper attempts to frame the use of Faynan and/or Timna copper using lead isotopic ratios and lead concentrations of well-dated copper-based objects from the LB/Iron Age transition (denoted here 'LBIII'),[1] and Iron I-IIB contexts in the southern Levant. For this purpose, we incorporate here relevant artifacts which were previously analysed (see Table 1). Lead isotopic ratios and chemical composition from Hazor, Megiddo and Tel Beer Sheba that are forthcoming, are presented in Table 2.

---

[1] This period is also denoted 'Iron 1a' (see summary in Mazar, 2005) and recently 'LB/Iron Age Overlap period' (Bunimovitz, 2019) and refers to the period of the 20th Egyptian dynasty domination of Canaan, until the Egyptian withdrawal during the time of Ramessess VI, 1140/1130 BCE.

Assessing the Circulation of Arabah Copper (Timna vs. Faynan) from the End of...

Table 1 Analysed Late Bronze Age III and Iron Age I-IIB objects from southern Levant sites included in the study

Period	Site	Reference	Selected samples
LBIII	Tel Beth Shean	Yahalom-Mack and Segal (2018)	Str. S-4: BS-11; BS-12 Str. S-3a: BS-1; BS-5; BS-8; BS-9; BS-20
	Tel Dan		Str. VIIA1/VI: Dan-3 Str. VI: Dan-12
	Tel Rehov	Yahalom-Mack and Segal (2020)	Str. D-7a: METB05; METB11 Str. D-6b: Re 1
	Megiddo	Yahalom-Mack et al., (forthcoming)	Str. K-6 (=VIIA): Meg 3; meg 6
Iron I	Pella	Philip et al. (2003)	PE100201; PE100222
	Tel Beth Shean	Yahalom-Mack and Segal (2018)	Str. S-2: BS-7 Str. S-2/S-1b: BS-4; BS-10
	Tel Dan		Str. IV: Dan-6 Str. IVB: Dan-4; Dan-7; Dan-8; Dan-11; Dan-15
	Tel Dor		Str. G-10: Dor-1; Dor-3; Dor-4; Dor-7; Dor-9
	Giloh		BS-3 (dagger)
	Tell Jatt	Stos-Gale (2006)	Hoard: J-15; J-16; J-17; J-19; J-22; J-30; J-33; J-46; J-48; J-52; J-53
	Tel Rehov	Yahalom-Mack and Segal (2020)	Str. D-5: METB7 Str. C-3: Re 3
	Tell es-Safi	Yahalom-Mack et al., (forthcoming)	Str. A-5: Saf 5
	Megiddo		Str. Q-7 (=VIA): Meg-1; meg-2; meg-8 Str. K-4 (=VIA): Meg-5 Str. H-9 (=VIA): Meg-7
	Khirbet Qeiyafa		Qe-1; Qe-2; Qe-3; Qe-4; Qe-5
Iron IIA	Tel Rehov	Yahalom-Mack and Segal (2020)	Str. G-2a (=VI): METB01 Str. C-1a (=IV) re 4; re 5 Str. E-1-a-b (=V-IV): METB02; re 2;
	Tell es-Safi	Yahalom-Mack et al., (forthcoming)	Str. A-3: Saf-3; Saf-4
	Tel beer Sheba		Str. VII: METB87 Str. IV: METB85
Iron IIB	Tell es-Safi	Eliyahu-Behar and Yahalom-Mack (forthcoming)	Str. F-7: Saf 1
	Tel Rehov	Yahalom-Mack and Segal (2020)	Str. J-3-4 (=III): METB04
	Tel beer Sheba	Forthcoming	Str. III: METB81; METB84 Str. II-III: METB82; METB83 Str. II: METB86
	Hazor		Str. VIII-VII: METB15 Str. VIIB: HA 1 Str. VIIA: HA 2; METB06 Str. VI: HA 3 Str. VC: HA 4 Str. VB: HA 5; HA 15 Str. V: HA 14

Table 2 Estimated isotopic and lead concentration ranges from Faynan, Timna, Cyprus, and Aegean/Anatolian ores used in Fig. 2

Ore fields	Type	Pb Min-Max (%)	206Pb/204Pb	Source
Faynan DLS	Ores	0.05–5.30	17.906–18.019	Hauptmann (2007: Tables A.1a and A.2)
	Bar ingots	0.23–2.96	17.852–18.020	Hauptmann (2015: 11–12: Table 4)
Timna Amir Avrona	Ores	0.002–0.50	17.852–18.289	Leese et al., (1986: Table 1) and Hauptmann (2007: Table A.3)
Cyprus	Ores	0.0001–0.005	18.404–19.002	Hauptmann (2007: 201) following Stos-Gale and Gale (1994), OXALID (http://oxalid.arch.ox.ac.uk/; Stos-Gale & Gale, 2009).
Aegean/ Anatolia	Ores	0.01–0.20	18.700–19.020	Gale and Stos-Gale (1982), Seeliger et al. (1985), Wagner et al. (1985, 1986), Yener et al. (1991), Begemann et al. (2003), OXALID (http://oxalid.arch.ox.ac.uk/; Stos-Gale & Gale, 2009).

3 Lead Isotope Analysis

Lead isotope analysis (LIA), a method used to provenance copper artefacts, is based on lead isotopic ratios which are determined by the age and geological history of the ore and do not significantly alter in the process of smelting. Thus, this method allows for a comparison of the isotopic ratios of lead or lead-containing end products to those of potential ores (as lead is present in varying amounts in copper-ore forming minerals). In the case of bronze objects, if lead was intentionally added, the isotopic ratios likely reflect those of the added lead, rather than those of the lead which is naturally present in the copper in small amounts. If copper from more than one source is used in the production, for example, as a result of recycling, then the isotopic ratios should reflect a mixture between these ore sources. For a recent discussion of the method and its limitations, see Pernicka, 2014 and bibliography therein.

One of the major problems with LIA is the overlap between different ore sources. Such an overlap occurs in the Arabah where the Faynan DLS ores overlap some of those from the Amir and Avrona formations in Timna (see above), which have a much wider distribution. Our attempt to frame the use of Faynan copper during the Iron Age raised the question of whether the two sources can be discerned from one another. In the following study, we try to determine which samples plot against both Faynan DLS and Timna (Amir and Avrona formations), and which plot outside the Faynan DLS limited Pb isotopic range. We consider only these specific formations because it was previously shown that they were the main formations utilized during these periods. In Faynan, the highly radiogenic Middle Brown Sandstone formation was utilized mainly during the Chalcolithic and Roman periods (Hauptmann, 2007:

146, Fig. 5.46), while in Timna, only few outcrops of the rich Cambrian Timna formation occur and there is no evidence for their exploitation during the Iron Age (see Discussion in Ben-Yosef, 2010: 99–100). Lead isotopic values of ores from the Amir and Avrona formations are thus used to delineate the Timna range, while for Faynan DLS we used both the analyses of ores from this formation, which are few (Hauptmann et al., 1992), and Intermediate Bronze Age bar ingots (Hauptmann et al., 2015). Some of the latter were found at Khirbet Hamrat Ifdan, a production site in the Faynan region (Levy et al., 2002). Others were found in the Hebron hills and the Negev highland sites and are derived from Faynan with high certainty (Hauptmann et al., 2015). We thus use both in Fig. 2, although mark differently the group that was actually found at Faynan.

In order to better discern between these sources, Pb concentrations are used in conjunction with the Pb isotopic values (for discussion on lead differences in ore deposits, see Hauptmann, 2007: 201). This is based on the observations that Faynan DLS ores have higher Pb concentrations measuring up to 5.3% in the ores (Hauptmann et al., 1992: Table 1b), up to 3% in the bar ingots from the Negev Highlands, and up to 1.5% in bar ingots found in the Faynan region itself, at Khirbet Hamrat Ifdan (ibid.). A potential problem with using the concentration of Pb in the bar ingots as proxy for the concentration of Pb in metallic copper from Faynan is that these are unrefined products (Hauptmann et al., 2015; Yahalom-Mack et al., 2014). The low melting and evaporation temperatures of Pb (327.5 °C and 1749 °C, respectively; Lide, 2005) would cause at least some of it to evaporate during the remelting process, and thus, remelting practices would affect the Pb concentration of the resulting metal. For this reason, metallic copper objects with low Pb concentrations cannot be assigned to either mining region with certainty and only samples with Pb concentrations exceeding the reported highest Pb concentration from Timna ores can be considered to have been derived from Faynan ores.

The Pb concentrations in sandstone copper ores from the Amir and Avrona formations in Timna is 0.33% (median) and thus do not exceed 0.7% Pb (Hauptmann et al., 1992: Table 2), and this is the maximum value that is used in Fig. 2. However, Pb concentrations in the metallic products may be in fact lower. At Faynan, metallic ingots contain up to 3.0% Pb, which is about 40% less than in the ores (see above). Using the same logic, the metal produced from the Timna sandstones would contain approximately 0.4% Pb. In addition, of almost 300 copper-based objects found in Site 200 (The Hathor Temple) in the Timna Valley, 70% have Pb below 0.4% and 90% have Pb below 0.54% Pb (Craddock, 1988). Assuming that most of these objects were produced from local copper, this fits nicely with the above estimate. Nevertheless, as some of the objects may have been extraneous or mixed, we use here the value calculated from the ores (0.7% Pb), although it may be higher in reality than the actual Pb concentrations in the metal. Lead isotope and Pb concentration ranges for selected Mediterranean ores are summarized in Table 2.

Lead isotopic ratios in conjunction with Pb concentrations were used here also to reveal possible mixing trajectories (for the use of such methodology in archaeology, see for example: Pollard & Bray, 2015; Beherec et al., 2016; Eshel et al., 2021). Mixing calculations were conducted in order to account for the samples plotted outside the range of Pb isotopic composition and Pb concentrations of the expected ore sources. The latter include Faynan DLS, the Amir and Avrona formations in Timna and Cyprus, which is the closest and richest ore source (e.g. Knapp, 1986; Muhly, 1989; Stos-Gale et al., 1997; Kassianidou, 2013). Additional potential ore sources (Wadi Amram and several ore sources in the Sinai) are not well characterized archaeologically and/or geochemically and thus remain to be discussed in future studies (Abdel-Motelib et al., 2012; Avner et al., 2018; Ketelaer & Hauptmann, 2016).

We calculated a mixing of two copper-ore endmembers ('a' and 'b') using three equations, where x and y are the fractions of 'a' and 'b' endmember in the sample, respectively. [Pb] is the concentration of lead, and [^{206}Pb] is the concentration of isotope ^{206}Pb.

1. $[Pb]sample = x*[Pb]a + y*[Pb]b$
2. $[^{206}Pb]sample = x*[^{206}Pb]a + y*[^{206}Pb]b$; where $[^{206}Pb]a = [Pb]a * (^{206}Pb^{204}Pb)a/(^{206}Pb^{204}Pb + ^{207}Pb^{204}Pb + ^{208}Pb^{204}Pb + 1)a$, and $[^{206}Pb]b$ is calculated similarly $[^{204}Pb]sample = x*[^{204}Pb]a + y*[^{204}Pb]b$; where $[^{204}Pb]a = [Pb]a * 1/(^{206}Pb^{204}Pb + ^{207}Pb^{204}Pb + ^{208}Pb^{204}Pb + 1)a$, and $[^{204}Pb]b$ is calculated similarly. Once both [^{206}Pb] and [^{204}Pb] are calculated, they are divided to obtain $^{206}Pb/^{204}Pb$.
3. $x + y = 1$

We use the maximum and the minimum Pb concentrations and Pb isotopic values of the assumed endmembers to calculate the expected Pb isotopic ratios and Pb concentrations of the samples created by mixing these endmembers. The choice of the endmembers was determined based on archaeological and historical-geographical considerations and a few alternatives were tested (see results below).

In addition to the exclusion of relevant ore sources because the nature of the available data, we also take into consideration the possibility of outliers, such as the occasional use of ores from other formations (likelier in Faynan than in Timna) and isolated Pb-rich ores from Timna, none of which were systematically reported. We thus propose that our conclusions should be taken with the necessary caution.

Lastly, as this paper deals with the use of Faynan versus Timna copper, we do not systematically identify here and discuss additional ore sources that are indicated by the results (particularly geologically young sources, see below), but rather focus on indicating whether samples from each period are consistent or inconsistent with one or more of the Arabah copper deposits and whether a mixing line between the Arabah sources and other sources outside the region, is indicated by the results.

4 Results

The results are shown in Figs. 1 and 2. Figure 1 shows $^{206}Pb/^{204}Pb$ against $^{207}Pb/^{204}Pb$ of the sampled objects according to period, plotted against two-stage Pb-Pb age model (Stacey & Kramers, 1975), and $^{206}Pb/^{204}Pb$ against $^{208}Pb/^{204}Pb$. Figure 2 shows $^{206}Pb/^{204}Pb$ against Pb concentrations, indicating possible mixing of Faynan DLS

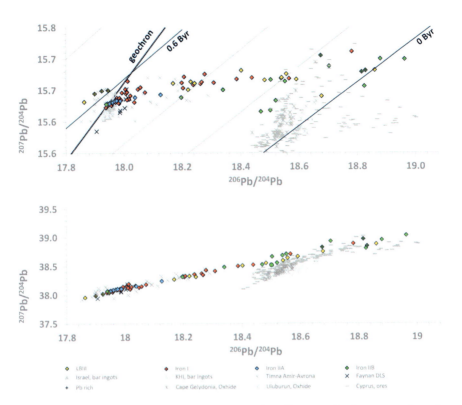

Fig. 1 Lead isotope ratios of objects from the southern Levant and relevant ores from the Mediterranean region (Seeliger et al., 1985; Wagner et al., 1985, 1986; Yener et al., 1991; Begemann et al., 2003; Gale et al., 1990; Hauptmann et al., 1992; Hauptmann, 2007; OXALID: http://oxalid.arch.ox.ac.uk/). $^{206}Pb/^{204}Pb$ vs $^{207}Pb/^{204}Pb$ values are also plotted against plotted against two-stage Pb-Pb age model (Stacey & Kramers, 1975)

and Timna Amir and Avrona mixed with geologically younger ores (Aegean/Anatolian?). All the studied samples can be divided into three categories: (1) Samples that plot within the range of one or more of the expected ore sources (i.e., Faynan DLS, Timna Amir and Avrona, and Cyprus). Some of these can also be interpreted as mixing; (2) Samples that plot outside these ranges and can be accounted for by mixing of either Faynan DLS or Timna with geologically younger copper ore; (3) samples that require the addition of a third source (most likely a lead rather than a Pb-rich copper ore).

Combining Pb isotopic ratios with Pb concentrations shows that of the 15 LBIII samples, only one is consistent with Faynan DLS ores (BS-5 from Tel Beth Shean). Two samples (BS-11 from Tel Beth Shean and METB05 from Tel Rehov) are consistent isotopically with Faynan DLS (and Timna), but have Pb concentrations of ca. 20%, which reflect a lead rather than a copper source. As lead does not occur in the Arabah nor in Sinai, it must be traced to one of the geologically old Pb sources in the western Mediterranean, such as Iglesiente, Sardinia. BS-5, mentioned above,

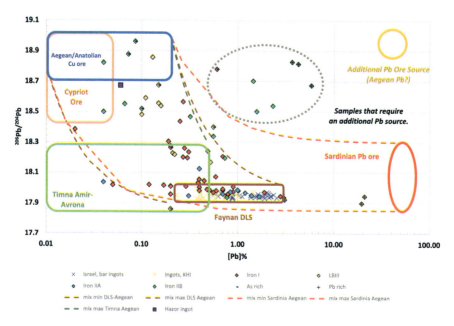

Fig. 2 $^{206}Pb/^{204}Pb$ values of objects included in this study are plotted against lead concentrations on a logarithmic scale. Faynan DLS values are based on analysis of ores and bar ingots. Also plotted are bar ingots from Israel and Jordan (Hauptmann et al., 2015); Pb-rich objects with lead contents over 3%; As-rich objects with arsenic values over 0.5%; and a single copper ingot from Hazor (Yahalom-Mack et al., 2014, METB-55). For isotopic and lead concentration ranges, see Table 2. Faynan DLS ranges are based on bar ingots. The maximum value of Cypriot lead concentration is estimated at 0.5% based on Oxhide ingots (Muhly et al., 1977: Table 2; Hauptmann et al., 2002; Yahalom-Mack et al., 2014: Table 3)

has 3.09% Pb. It is roughly consistent with the highest Pb concentration reported for the bar ingots (2.96% Pb, See Hauptmann et al., 2015: 11–12), or could be alternatively explained as a mixture between the Iglesiente source and a geologically younger copper source.

Five of the 15 LBIII samples (one third) are consistent with Timna ores both isotopically and in terms of their Pb concentrations. Four samples are isotopically consistent with Cypriot ores (BS-1, BS-20, Meg-6 and Dan-10, see Fig. 1), but have Pb concentrations which are significantly higher than those that are characteristic of Cypriot copper (Fig. 2), which according to data available for oxhide ingots do not exceed 0.05%. These samples are either derived from an alternative source of copper, or are the product of mixing, as are the six remaining samples.

Iron I samples are mostly consistent with Timna Amir and Avrona and/or Faynan DLS (32/39). Figure 2 shows that 14 can be clearly attributed to the Faynan DLS source, rather than Timna, based on their relatively high Pb concentrations. Four samples are consistent with both sources, while samples that are consistent only with Timna (n = 14) can also be explained as mixing the Faynan source with another geologically younger copper source, not necessarily the one used during LBIII. None of the samples are consistent with Cypriot ores. Six of the seven remaining samples fall within a mixing line between Faynan and a geologically younger Cu source (Aegean/Anatolia?). Finally, one sample is clustered together with higher leaded objects produced with younger ores, possibly a mix between a geologically younger Cu source and Pb source.

Iron IIA samples (n = 9) are fully consistent with the Arabah ores. Based on the isotopic ratios and the Pb concentrations, 6 out of 9 are consistent exclusively with only Faynan DLS ores. Two samples are consistent with Timna, or alternatively are mixed between Faynan DLS and some other ore source. The remaining sample is consistent with both Faynan DLS and Timna Amir and Avrona formations.

Iron IIB samples (n = 16), except for a single object (METB82, a fibula from Tel Beer-Sheba), are inconsistent with the Arabah copper sources. Two objects (METB83 and METB86 from Tel Beer-Sheba) are consistent with Cypriot ores both in their Pb isotopic ratios and Pb concentrations. Figure 2 shows that 10/16 (including the above-mentioned three) may be mixed between a geologically old Cu source and a geologically young one (Anatolian/Aegean?). The remaining six samples, all from Hazor, are plotted outside the mixing range having high Pb concentrations and intermediate to high $^{206}Pb/^{204}Pb$ values that require contribution from an additional Pb source/s.

5 Discussion

The results show that the majority of the Iron I-IIA samples are consistent with the Arabah ores, while most of the LBIII and Iron IIB samples, are not. This picture fits nicely with the main periods of Iron Age copper production activity in Timna and Faynan, as are known from radiocarbon dates from these regions, namely between the eleventh and ninth centuries BCE (Levy et al., 2004, 2008, 2014b; Ben-Yosef, 2016; Ben-Yosef et al., 2010).

Five LBIII objects are consistent with the Amir and Avrona ore formations from Timna. This corroborates evidence of an 20th Dynasty presence at the site (Rothenberg, 1987, 1988, 1990; Yagel et al., 2016). The objects originate from Tel Dan, Megiddo and Tel Beth Shean, the latter of which was occupied at the time by an Egyptian Garrison (Panitz-Cohen & Mazar, 2009), suggesting that Timna copper circulated throughout the region and was directed at least partly to the Egyptian activities there.

One of the 15 LBIII objects, a stick pin (BS-5) from Tel Beth Shean is consistent isotopically with both Timna Amir and Avrona and Faynan DLS, however, based on the relatively high lead concentration (3.09% Pb), it is either compatible with a Faynan origin, or has a contribution of lead from a geologically old Pb source, as clearly shown for two other contemporary objects (METB05 and BS-11), likely from the Iglesiente ores in southwestern Sardinia. It has been shown that lead from this source was extensively used around the Mediterranean at the end of the Late Bronze, ca. thirteenth- early twelfth centuries BCE (Stos-Gale & Gale, 1994; Gale & Stos-Gale, 2010; Yahalom-Mack et al., 2022). Even if BS-5, dated to the later part of the LBIII, Str. S-3a in Tel Beth Shean, is fact made of Faynan copper, further sampling is required in order to indicate the circulation of Faynan copper during the time of the 20th Egyptian Dynasty.

One significant assemblage certainly related to the question of whether Faynan was active during the LB-Iron Age transition, is that from the underwater cargo of Neve Yam, composed of 86 copper ingots (for an updated discussion see Galili et al., forthcoming). These ingots are consistent in terms of their Pb concentrations, Pb isotopic composition and general chemical composition with Faynan DLS ores (Yahalom-Mack et al., 2014). If these are indeed made of Faynan copper, they provide invaluable illustration of Faynan's final products – plano-convex ingots weighing 1.4–4.4 kg. The date of the cargo is unknown but attributed based on various considerations to the twelfth century BCE (Galili et al., forthcoming). Furthermore, several ingots from Nuraghe Arrubio in Sardinia are comparable, according to Montero-Ruiz (2018), to the Neve Yam ingots, in shape, chemical and lead isotopic composition.[2] The date of the latter group ranges between the fourteenth and the twelfth centuries BCE (ibid.). Since some of the Sardinian ores, both Pb and Cu, are as geologically old as the Faynan ones, a major difficulty arises in differentiating isotopically between metal from the two regions. Theoretically, Sardinian copper or copper with Sardinian lead would be isotopically indistinguishable from Faynan copper, with its naturally relatively high Pb contents.

This becomes a major issue since lead ingots made of Sardinian Iglesiente lead likely dating to the thirteenth–twelfth centuries BCE were found along the coast of Israel (Yahalom-Mack et al., 2022) and since Sardinian silver was identified in Iron IIA silver hoards (Eshel et al., 2019), meaning that contact between the regions is not beyond reason in certain parts of the LB-Iron Age sequence. When copper objects contain Pb above the characteristic values of Faynan (ca. 3%, see above) with Faynan's isotopic values, the possible contribution of Sardinian lead is more plausible, as suggested above for some of the LBIII samples. However, when Pb is slightly below this value, it remains to be determined whether the Pb is extraneous or inherent. Logic says that copper objects found in the southern Levant with lower than 3% Pb, consistent with isotopic values of Arabah ores, contain Pb which is more likely inherent to the copper, rather than added deliberately. There was certainly no reason to add 1–3% Pb to ingots such as those Neve Yam, and thus we can safely conclude that their origin is likely from Faynan. The date of the cargo remains however inconclusive. If it is indeed dated to the LBIII or earlier, then systematic production in Faynan would be earlier than thought. The current study, based on the composition of objects from the southern Levant, does not support systematic

---

[2] A slightly lower Pb concentration in the Arrubio ingots may be related to the analytical method used (XRF).

copper production prior to the Iron I (late twelfth century BCE), and supports a late twelfth century date at the earliest for the Neve Yam assemblage.

Iron I-IIA artefacts (late twelfth–ninth century BCE) are partly consistent with Timna Amir-Avrona ores, partly with Faynan DLS ores and partly with both. A possible mixing line between Faynan and a geologically younger copper source is apparent more for the Iron I samples, but this could be related to the number of samples available from each period. Faynan copper was certainly in circulation in the southern Levant during this time, and it has been suggested that both mining regions were part of the same socio-political system and operated in conjunction to one another (Ben-Yosef, 2010; Levy et al., 2014a). Analysis of several Ushabti figurines indicated that copper from one or both sources was used by the Egyptians during the time of Pharaoh Psusennes I (second half of the eleventh century BCE), indicating that Egypt was a consumer of Arabah copper at least during part of the Third Intermediate Period (Ben-Dor Evian et al., 2021; Vaelske et al., 2019).

Arabah copper appears to have been used on the Greek mainland for the production of bronze cauldrons (Kiderlen et al., 2016). Lead concentrations in the cauldrons indicate Faynan as the likelier copper source than Timna (ibid.: 309). It remains to be explained how the use of copper from Faynan in Olympia postdates the copper production activities in Faynan, which ceased during the ninth century BCE (see below). The possibility that the copper was traded through Phoenician hands is reinforced by the analysis of copper from Sidon in Vaelske and Bode' s preliminary study (2018–2019). However, Bienkowski (2021) rightly argues that objects provenanced to Faynan are likelier to show the extent of the local market than the geo-political entity or entities that were involved in its trade. Further sampling is no doubt required in order to fully illustrate the distribution of Arabah copper during the Iron IIA, in the southern Levant and beyond.

Artefacts dated to the Iron IIB clearly show that Arabah copper was no longer used in the southern Levant at this time. Even though some of the Iron IIB samples are plotted along the mixing range of the Arabah with a younger copper source, as there are almost no samples with Arabah values, another geologically old copper source may be sought. Alternatively, these samples can be explained by mixing a Sardinian-like Pb source with an Aegean-like copper source (Fig. 2). A major shift in Pb ore sources during the Iron IIB is evidenced by a group of Pb-rich samples from Hazor that must have an additional contribution from a geologically relatively young lead source.

The scarcity of samples with Arabah values from this period validates the general lack of Iron IIB copper mining and smelting activities in Faynan (see above). A possible shift to Cypriot copper, which is suggested by textual sources from as early as the time of Tukulti-Ninurta II (889–884 BC) (Kassianidou, 2012; after Zaccagnini, 1990) is only partially supported by the results of this study, which admittedly is based on a small number of samples. A single unrefined ingot from Hazor (METB55), isotopically consistent with Cypriot ores, was broadly dated to the ninth century BCE based on radiocarbon dating of charcoal embedded in its surface (Yahalom-Mack et al., 2014). The ingot contains 0.06% Pb, a value similar to that measured in Cypriot oxhide ingots (Muhly et al., 1977: Table 2; Hauptmann et al.,

2002; Yahalom-Mack et al., 2014: Table 3), and thus is generally consistent with a Cypriot origin, perhaps with small amounts of added lead. Further analyses are required in order to better understand the shift from Arabah to Cypriot sources during this time.

References

Abdel-Motelib, A., Bode, M., Hartmann, R., Hartung, U., Hauptmann, A., & Pfeiffer, K. (2012). Archaeometallurgical expeditions to the Sinai Peninsula and the Eastern Desert of Egypt (2006, 2008). *Meta, 19*, 3–59.

Adams, R. B. (1991). The Wadi Fidan project, Jordan, 1989. *Levant, 23*(1), 181–182.

Adams, R. B. (1992). Romancing the stones: New light on Glueck's 1934 survey of Eastern Palestine as a result of recent work by the Wadi Fidan project. In P. Bienkowski (Ed.), *Early Edom and Moab. The beginning of the iron age in Southern Jordan* (pp. 177–186). John Collis Publications.

Adams, R. B. (1998). *The development of copper metallurgy during the Early Bronze Age of the Southern Levant: Evidence from the Feinan Region, Southern Jordan.* Dissertation, University of Sheffield.

Adams, R. B. (2000). The Early Bronze Age III-IV transition in Southern Jordan: Evidence from Khirbet Hamra Ifdan. In G. Philip & D. Baird (Eds.), *Ceramics and change in the early Bronze Age of the Southern Levant* (pp. 379–402). Sheffield Academic Press.

Adams, R. B., & Genz, H. (1995). Excavations at Wadi Fidan 4: A Chalcolithic Village complex in the copper Ore District of Feinan, Southern Jordan. *Palestine Exploration Quarterly, 127*(1), 8–20.

Asael, D., Matthews, A., Bar-Matthews, M., & Halicz, L. (2007). Copper isotope fractionation in sedimentary copper mineralization (Timna Valley, Israel). *Chemical Geology, 243*, 238–254.

Asael, D., Matthews, A., Bar-Matthews, M., Harlavan, Y., & Segal, I. (2012). Tracking redox controls and sources of sedimentary mineralization using copper and lead isotopes. *Chemical Geology, 310–311*, 23–35.

Avner, U. (2014). Egyptian Timna – Reconsidered. In J. M. Tebes (Ed.), *Unearthing the wilderness: Studies on the history and archaeology of the Negev and Edom in the Iron Age* (Ancient near studies, supplement 45) (pp. 103–162). Peeters.

Avner, U., Ginat, H., Shalev, S., Shilstein, S., Langford, B., Frumkin, A., et al. (2018). Ancient copper mining at Nahal Amram, Southern Araba: A new research. In E. Ben-Yosef (Ed.), *Mining for ancient copper, essays in memory of Beno Rothenberg* (pp. 147–177). Eisenbrauns.

Barker, G., Gilbertson, D., & Mattingly, D. (2007). *Archaeology and desertification: The Wadi Faynan landscape survey, Southern Jordan.* Oxford Books.

Begemann, F., Schmitt-Strecker, S., & Pernicka, E. (2003). On the composition and provenance of metal finds from Beşiktepe (Troia). In A. Wagner, E. Pernicka, & H.-P. Uerpmann (Eds.), *Troia and the troad* (pp. 173–201). Springer.

Beherec, M. A., Najjar, M., & Levy, T. E. (2014). Wadi Fidan 40 and mortuary archaeology in the Edom Lowlands. New Insights into the Iron Age Archaeology of Edom, Southern Jordan: Surveys, Excavations and Research from the University of California, San Diego & Department of Antiquities of Jordan, Edom Lowlands Regional Archaeology Project (ELRAP). In T. E. Levy, M. Najjar, & E. Ben-Yosef (Eds.), *New insights into the Iron Age Archaeology of Edom, Southern Jordan* (pp. 665–722). Cotsen Institute of Archaeology Press, University of California.

Beherec, M. A., Levy, T. E., Tirosh, O., Najjar, M., Knabb, K. A., & Erel, Y. (2016). Iron Age Nomads and their relation to copper smelting in Faynan (Jordan): Trace metal and Pb and Sr isotopic measurements from the Wadi Fidan 40 cemetery. *Journal of Archaeological Science, 65*, 70–83. https://doi.org/10.1016/j.jas.2015.10.006

Bender, F. (1968). Geologie Von Jordanien. Beitraege Zur Regionalen Geologie. *Regionalen Geologie der Erde, 7.*

Ben-Dor Evian, S., Yagel, O., Harlavan, Y., Seri, H., Lewinsky, J., & Ben-Yosef, E. (2021). Pharaoh's copper: The provenance of copper in bronze artifacts from post-imperial Egypt at the end of the second millennium BCE. *Journal of Archaeological Science: Reports, 38.*

Ben-Yosef, E. (2010). *Technology and social process: Oscillations in Iron Age copper production and power in Southern Jordan.* Dissertation, University of California.

Ben-Yosef, E. (2016). Back to Solomon's era: Results of the first excavations at "slaves' hill" (site 34, Timna, Israel). *BASOR, 376*(1), 169–198.

Ben-Yosef, E., Levy, T. E., Higham, T., Najjar, M., & Tauxe, L. (2010). The beginning of Iron Age copper production in the Southern Levant: New evidence from Khirbat al-Jariya, Faynan, Jordan. *Antiquity, 84*(325), 724–746.

Ben-Yosef, E., Shaar, R., Tauxe, L., & Ron, H. (2012). A new chronological framework for Iron Age copper production at Timna (Israel). *Bulletin of the American Schools of Oriental Research, 367*, 31–71.

Beyth, M. (1987). Precambrian magmatic rocks of Timna Valley, southern Israel. *Precambrian Research, 36*, 21–38.

Bienkowski, P. (2021). The end of Arabah copper production and the destruction of Gath: A critique and an alternative interpretation. *Palestine Exploration Quarterly*, 1–14.

Blanckenhorn, M. L. P. (1912). *Naturwissenschaftliche Studien Am Toten Meer Und Im Jordental: Bericht Über Eine Im Jahre 1908 (Im Auftrage SM Des Sultans Der Türkei Abdul Hamid II. Und Mit Unterstützung Der Berliner Jagor-Stiftung) Unternommene Forschungsreise in Palästina.* R. Friedländer & Sohn.

Bunimovitz, S. (2019). The late Bronze Age. In A. Faust & H. Katz (Eds.), *Introduction to the archaeology of the land of Israel from the Neolithic to Alexander's conquests.* The Open University of Israel (In Hebrew).

Craddock, P. (1988). The composition of the metal finds. In B. Rothenberg (Ed.), *The Egyptian mining Temple at Timna: Ressearches in the Arabah 1959–1984* (Vol. 1). Institute for Archaeo-Metallurgical Studies, Institute of Archaeology, University College of London.

Eliyahu-Behar, A., & Yahalom-Mack, N. (forthcoming). Copper objects and their provenance. In I. Shai, H. J. Greenfield, & A. M. Maeir (Eds.), *Tell es-Safi/Gath III: The Early Bronze Age, Part 1* (Ägypten und Altes Testament 105). Zaphon Verlag.

Eshel, T., Erel, Y., Yahalom-Mack, N., Tirosh, O., & Gilboa, A. (2019). Lead isotopes in silver reveal earliest Phoenician quest for metals in the west Mediterranean Significance. *Proceedings of the National Academy of Sciences, 116*(13), 6007–6012. https://doi.org/10.1073/pnas.1817951116

Eshel, T., Gilboa, A., Yahalom-Mack, N., Tirosh, O., & Erel, Y. (2021). Debasement of silver throughout the Late Bronze – Iron Age transition in the Southern Levant: Analytical and cultural implications. *Journal of Archaeological Science, 125*, 105268. https://doi.org/10.1016/j.jas.2020.105268

Frank, F. (1934). Aus Der'Arabah. I. Reiseberichte. *Zeitschrift Des Deutschen Palästina-Vereins (1878–1945), 57*(3/4), 191–280.

Gale, N. H., & Stos-Gale, Z. A. (1982). Bronze Age copper sources in the Mediterranean: A new approach. *Science, 216*(4541), 11–19.

Gale, N. H., & Stos-Gale, Z. A. (2010). Bronze Age metal artefacts found on Cyprus – Metal from Anatolia and the Western Mediterranean. *Trabajos de Prehistoria, 67*(2), 389–403. https://doi.org/10.3989/tp.2010.10046

Gale, N. H., Bachmann, H. G., Rothenberg, B., Stos-Gale, Z. A., & Tylecote, R. F. (1990). The adventitious production of iron in the smelting of copper. In B. Rothenberg (Ed.), *The ancient metallurgy of copper* (pp. 182–190). Institute of Archae-Metallurgical Studies.

Galili, E., Langgut, D., Arkin Shalev, E., Rosen, B., Yahalom-Mack, N., Ogloblin, I., et al. (forthcoming). A Late Bronze/Early Iron Age Shipwreck assemblage containing copper ingots from neve yam, Israel. In A. Yasur-Landau, G. Gambash, & T. E. Levy (Eds.), *Mediterranean resilience: Collapse and adaptation in antique maritime societies.* Equinox Publishing.

Glueck, N. (1935). Explorations in Eastern Palestine, II. *Annual of the American schools of oriental research 15.* American Schools of Oriental Research.

Glueck, N. (1940). *The other side of the Jordan.* American Schools of Oriental Research.

Hauptmann, A. (2007). *The Archaeometallurgy of copper: Evidence from Faynan, Jordan.* Springer.

Hauptmann, A., Begemann, F., Heitkemper, E., Pernicka, E., & Schmitt-Strecker, S. (1992). Early copper produced at Feinan, Wadi Arabah, Jordan: The composition of ores and copper. *Archeomaterials, 6,* 1–33.

Hauptmann, A., Maddin, R., & Prange, M. (2002). On the structure and composition of copper and tin ingots excavated from the shipwreck of Uluburun. *Bulletin of the American Schools of Oriental Research, 328*(1), 1–30.

Hauptmann, A., Schmitt-Strecker, S., Levy, T. E., & Begemann, F. (2015). On Early Bronze Age copper bar ingots from the southern Levant. *Bulletin of the American Schools of Oriental Research, 373*(1), 1–24.

Howland, M. D., Liss, B., Najjar, M., & Levy, T. E. (2015). GIS-based mapping of archaeological sites with low-altitude aerial photography and structure from Motion: A case study from Southern Jordan. *2015 Digital Heritage, Grenada,* 91–94.

Howland, M. D., Jones, I. W., Najjar, M., & Levy, T. E. (2018). Quantifying the effects of erosion on archaeological sites with low-altitude aerial photography, structure from motion, and GIS: A case study from southern Jordan. *Journal of Archaeological Science, 90,* 62–70.

Howland, M. D., Liss, B., Levy, T. E., & Najjar, M. (2020). Integrating digital datasets into public engagement through ArcGIS StoryMaps. *Advances in Archaeological Practice, 8*(4), 351–360.

Jones, I. W., Levy, T. E., & Najjar, M. (2012). Khirbat Nuqayb al-Asaymir and Middle Islamic Metallurgy in Faynan: Surveys of Wadi al-Ghuwayb and Wadi al-Jariya in Faynan, Southern Jordan. *Bulletin of the American Schools of Oriental Research, 368*(1), 67–102.

Kassianidou, V. (2012). The origin and use of metals in Iron Age Cyprus. In M. Iacovou (Ed.), *Cyprus and the Aegean in the Early Iron Age: The Legacy of Nicolas Coldstream* (pp. 229–226). Bank of Cyprus Cultural Foundation.

Kassianidou, V. (2013). The production and trade of Cypriot copper in the Late Bronze Age. An analysis of the evidence. *Pasiphae, 7,* 133–146.

Ketelaer, A., & Hauptmann, A. (2016). In the Shadow of Timna? The mining region of Wadi Amram new analytical and archaeological aspects. *Meta, 22*(2), 169–183.

Kiderlen, M., Bode, M., Hauptmann, A., & Bassiakos, Y. (2016). Tripod cauldrons produced at Olympia give evidence for trade with copper from Faynan (Jordan) to South West Greece, c. 950–750 BCE. *JAS Reports, 8,* 303–313.

Kind, H. D. (1965). Antike Kupfergewinnung zwischen Rotem und Totem Meer. *Zeitschrift Des Deutschen Palästina-Vereins (1953-), 81*(1), 56–73. http://www.jstor.org/stable/27930730

Knapp, A. B. (1986). *Copper production and divine protection: Archaeology, ideology and social complexity on Bronze Age Cyprus.* Paul Åströms Förlag.

Leese, M. N., Craddock, P. T., Freestone, I. C., & Rothenberg, B. (1986). The composition of ores and metal objects from Timna, Israel. *Wiener Berichte über Naturwissenschaft in der Kunst, 2,* 90–120.

Levy, T. E., Adams, R. B., & Shafiq, R. (1999). The Jabal Hamrat Fidan project: Excavations at the Wadi Fidan 40 cemetery, Jordan (1997). *Levant, 31*(1), 293–308.

Levy, T. E., Adams, R. B., Witten, A. J., Anderson, J., Arbel, Y., Kuah, S., et al. (2001). Early metallurgy, interaction, and social change: The Jabal Ḥamrat Fidan (Jordan) research design and 1998 archaeological survey. Preliminary report. *Annual of the Department of Antiquities of Jordan, 45,* 159–187.

Levy, T. E., Adams, R. B., Hauptmann, A., Prange, M., Schmitt-Strecker, S., & Najjar, M. (2002). Early bronze age metallurgy: A newly discovered copper manufactory in Southern Jordan. *Antiquity, 76*(292), 425–437.

Levy, T. E., Adams, R. B., Anderson, J. D., Najjar, M., Smith, N., Arbel, Y., et al. (2003). An iron age landscape in the Edomite lowlands: Archaeological surveys along Wadi al-Ghuwayb and Wadi al-Jariya, Jabal Ḥamrat Fidan, Jordan, 2002. *Annual of the Department of Antiquities of Jordan, 47,* 247–277.

Levy, T. E., Adams, R. B., Najjar, M., Hauptmann, A., Anderson, J. D., Brandl, B., Robinson, M. A., & Higham, T. (2004). Reassessing the chronology of Biblical Edom: new excavations and 14 C dates from Khirbat en-Nahas (Jordan). *Antiquity, 78*(302), 865–879. https://doi.org/10.1017/S0003598X0011350X

Levy, T. E., Higham, T., Bronk Ramsey, C., Smith, N. G., Ben-Yosef, E., Robinson, M., Münger, S., Knabb, K., Schulze, J. P., Najjar, M., & Tauxe, L. (2008). High-precision radiocarbon dating and historical biblical archaeology in southern Jordan. *Proceedings of the National Academy of Sciences, 105*(43), 16460–16465. https://doi.org/10.1073/pnas.0804950105

Levy, T. E., Najjar, M., & Ben-Yosef, E. (2014a). *New insights into the Iron Age archaeology of Edom, Southern Jordan*. Cotsen Institute of Archaeology Press, University of California.

Levy, T. E., Najjar, M., Higham, T., Arbel, Y., Muniz, A., Ben-Yosef, E., et al. (2014b). Excavations at Khirbet en-Nahas 2002–2009: An Iron Age copper production Center in the Lowlands of Edom. In T. E. Levy, M. Najjar, & E. Ben-Yosef (Eds.), *New insights into the Iron Age archaeology of Edom, Southern Jordan* (Vol. 1, pp. 89–245). Cotsen Institute of Archaeology Press, University of California.

Lide, D. R. (2005). *CRC handbook of chemistry and physics* (86th ed.). CRC Press.

Liss, B., Howland, M. D., & Levy, T. E. (2017). Testing Google earth engine for the automatic identification and vectorization of archaeological features: A case study from Faynan, Jordan. *Journal of Archaeological Science: Reports, 15*, 299–304.

Liss, B., Howland, M. D., Lorentzen, B., Smitheram, C., Najjar, M., & Levy, T. E. (2020). Up the Wadi: Development of an Iron Age industrial landscape in Faynan, Jordan. *Journal of Field Archaeology, 45*(6), 413–427.

MacDonald, B. (1992). *The Southern Ghors and Northeast Arabah archaeological survey* (Vol. 5). J.R. Collis Publications.

Mazar, A. (2005). The debate over the chronology of the Iron Age in the southern Levant: Its history, the current situation and a suggested resolution. In T. E. Levy & T. Higham (Eds.), *The bible and radiocarbon dating: Archaeology, text and science* (pp. 15–30). Equinox.

Montero-Ruiz, I. (2018). Copper ingots from the Nuraghe Arrubiu at orroli. In A. Giumlia-Mair & F. Lo Schiavo (Eds.), *Bronze Age metallurgy on Mediterranean Islands* (pp. 165–175). Editions Mergoil.

Muhly, J. D. (1989). The organization of the copper industry in Late Bronze Age Cyprus. In E. Peltenburg (Ed.), *Early society in Cyprus* (pp. 298–314). Edinburgh University.

Muhly, J. D., Wheeler, T. S., & Maddin, R. (1977). The Cape Gelidonya shipwreck and the Bronze Age metals trade in the eastern Mediterranean. *Journal of Field Archaeology, 4*(3), 353–362.

Musil, A. (1907). *Arabia Petraea, II. Edom*. Topographischer Reisebericht.

Novo, A., Vincent, M. L., & Levy, T. E. (2012). Geophysical surveys at Khirbat Faynan, an ancient mound site in southern Jordan. *International Journal of Geophysics, 2012*(432823), 1–8.

Panitz-Cohen, N., & Mazar, A. (2009). *Excavations at Tel Beth-Shean 1989–1996: The 13th–11th century BCE strata in areas N and S*. Israel Exploration Society.

Pernicka, E. (2014). Provenance determination of archaeological metal objects. In B. W. Roberts & C. P. Thornton (Eds.), *Archaeometallurgy in global perspective: Methods and syntheses* (pp. 239–268). Springer.

Philip, G., Clogg, P. W., Dungworth, D., & Stos, S. (2003). Copper metallurgy in the Jordan Valley from the third to the first millennia BC: Chemical, metallographic and Lead isotope analyses of artefacts from Pella. *Levant, 35*(1), 71–100.

Pollard, A. M., & Bray, P. J. (2015). A new method for combining lead isotope and lead abundance data to characterize archaeological copper alloys. *Archaeometry, 57*(6), 996–1008. https://doi.org/10.1111/arcm.v57.610.1111/arcm.12145

Raikes, T. D. (1980). Notes on some Neolithic and later sites in Wadi Araba and the Dead Sea Valley. *Levant, 12*(1), 40–60.

Rothenberg, B. (1987). Pharaonic copper mines in Southern Sinai. *Institute for Archaeo-Metallurgical Studies (IAMS) Newsletter, 10*(11), 1–7.

Rothenberg, B. (1988). *The Egyptian mining Temple at Timna. Researches in the Arabah 1959–1984* (Vol. 1). Institute for Archaeo-Metallurgical Studies, Institute of Archaeology, University College London.

Rothenberg, B. (1990). *The ancient metallurgy of copper, researches in the Arabah 1959–1984* (Vol. II). Institute for Archaeo-Metallurgical Studies, Institute of Archaeology, University College London.

Seeliger, T. C., Pernicka, E., Wagner, G. A., Begemann, F., Schmitt-Strecker, S., Eibner, C., et al. (1985). Archäometallurgische Untersuchungen in Nord- und Ostanatolien. *Jahrbuch des Römisch-Germanischen Zentralmuseums Mainz, 32*, 597–659.

Segev, A., Beyth, M., & Bar-Matthews, M. (1992). The geology of the Timna Valley with emphasis on copper and manganese mineralization – Updating and correlation with the eastern margins of the dead sea rift. *Geological Survey Israel Rep No GSI, 14*, 1–31.

Shlomovitch, N., Bar-Matthews, M., & Matthews, A. (1999). Sedimentary and epigenetic copper mineral assemblages in the Cambrian Timna Formation, southern Israel. *Israel Journal of Earth Sciences, 48*, 195–208.

Smith, N. G., & Levy, T. E. (2014). ArchField in Jordan: Real-time GIS data recording for archaeological excavations. *Near Eastern Archaeology, 77*(3), 166–170.

Stacey, J. S., & Kramers, J. D. (1975). Approximation of terrestrial lead isotope evolution by a two-stage model. *Earth and Planetary Science Letters, 26*, 207–221. https://doi.org/10.1016/0012-821X(75)90088-6

Stos-Gale, Z. A. (2006). Provenance of metals from Tel Jatt based on their Lead isotope analyses. In M. Artzy (Ed.), *The Jatt Metal Hoard in Northern Canaanite/Phoenician and Cypriote context* (pp. 115–120). Laboratorio de Arqueología, Universidad Pompeu Fabra de Barcelona.

Stos-Gale, Z. A., & Gale, N. H. (1994). The origin of metals excavated on Cyprus. In A. B. Knapp & J. Cherry (Eds.), *Provenience studies and Bronze Age Cyprus: Production exchange and politico-economic change* (pp. 92–122). Prehistoric Press.

Stos-Gale, Z. A., & Gale, N. H. (2009). Metal provenancing using isotopes and the Oxford archaeological lead isotope database (OXALID). *Archaeological and Anthropological Sciences, 1*(3), 195–213.

Stos-Gale, Z. A., Maliotis, G., Gale, N. H., & Annetts, N. (1997). Lead isotope characteristics of the Cyprus copper ore deposits applied to provenance studies of copper Oxhide ingots. *Archaeometry, 39*(1), 83–123.

Vaelske, V., & Bode, M. (2018–2019). Early Iron Age copper trails: First results of a pilot-study at Sidon. *Archaeology & History in Lebanon, 48–49*, 130–133.

Vaelske, V., Bode, M., & Loeben, C. E. (2019). Early Iron Age Copper Trail between Wadi Arabah and Egypt during the 21st dynasty: First results from Tanis, ca. 1000BC. *Zeitschrift für Orient-Archäologie, 12*, 184–203.

Wagner, G. A., Pernicka, E., Seeliger, T. C., Öztunali, Ö., Baranyi, I., Begemann, F., et al. (1985). Geologische untersuchungen zur frühen metallurgie in NW-Anatolien. *Bulletin of the Mineral Research and Exploration Institute of Turkey, 101*(102), 45–81.

Wagner, G. A., Pernicka, E., Seeliger, T. C., Lorenz, I. B., & Begemann, F. (1986). Geochemische und isotopische charakteristika früher rohstoffquellen für kupfer, blei, silber und gold in der Türkei. *Jahrbuch des Römisch-Germanischen Zentralmuseums Mainz, 33*(2), 723–752.

Wurzburger, U. S. (1967). *The occurrence of sulfides in the Timna massif and secondary copper minerals in the Timna copper deposit, Negev (southern Israel)*. M.Sc. thesis unpublished, Imperial College of Science and Technology.

Yagel, O. A., Ben-Yosef, E., & Craddock, A. P. T. (2016). Late Bronze Age copper production in Timna: New evidence from site 3. *Levant, 48*(1), 33–51.

Yahalom-Mack, N., & Segal, I. (2018). The origin of the copper used in Canaan during the Late Bronze – Iron Age transition. In E. Ben-Yosef (Ed.), *Mining for Ancient Copper; essays in memory of Beno Rothenberg* (pp. 313–331). Tel Aviv University, Sonia and Marco Nadler Institute of Archaeology.

Yahalom-Mack, N., & Segal, I. (2020). Chemical and lead isotope analysis of copper-based and Lead objects. In A. Mazar & N. Panitz-Cohen (Eds.), *Tel Reḥov, a Bronze and Iron Age City in the Beth-Shean Valley* (Various objects and natural-science studies) (Vol. V). The Institute of Archaeology, The Hebrew University of Jerusalem.

Yahalom-Mack, N., Galili, E., Segal, I., Eliyahu-Behar, A., Boaretto, E., Shilstein, S., et al. (2014). New insights into Levantine copper trade: Ingots from the Bronze and Iron Ages in Israel. *Journal of Archaeological Science, 45*, 159–177.

Yahalom-Mack, N., Finn, D. M., Erel, Y., Tirosh, O., Galili, E., & Yasur-Landau, A. (2022). Incised Late Bronze Age lead ingots from the southern anchorage of Caesarea. *Journal of Archaeological Science: Reports, 41*, 103321.

Yener, K. A., Sayre, E. V., Joel, E. C., Özbal, H., Barnes, I. L., & Brill, R. H. (1991). Stable lead isotope studies of Central Taurus ore sources and related artifacts from Eastern Mediterranean Chalcolithic and Bronze Age sites. *Journal of Archaeological Science, 18*(5), 541–577.

Zaccagnini, C. (1990). The transition from Bronze to Iron in the Near East and in the Levant: Marginal notes. *Journal of the American Oriental Society, 110*, 493–502.

Copper Trade Networks from the Arabah: Re-assessing the Impact on Early Iron Age Moab

Stanley Klassen and Andrew J. Danielson

Abstract Substantial archaeological research has identified the significance and wide-ranging implications of large-scale copper extraction and refining in the Arabah region of the southern Levant between the thirteen and ninth centuries B.C.E. Concomitant with these metallurgical developments is the necessity of understanding the way in which these resources reached subsidiary markets, both through trade networks and intermediary social or political agents. While research continues to identify the importance of a western trade route through the Negev and southern Shephelah to the southern Coastal Plain, the possibility of an eastern route that travels north through the highlands of Edom and Moab has also been raised. In particular, these suggestions have at times linked the purported eastern trade in copper to developments in the socio-political complexity of Moab during the late Iron I/early Iron IIA period (eleventh–tenth centuries). This paper assesses the scope and nature of settlement patterns along with recent archaeological data of the region to evaluate the potential of major trade activity through central Transjordan during this period. Ultimately, it argues against a strong association of the copper trade to central Transjordan, unlike the exchange network and established infrastructure along the major trade route identified westward from the Arabah.

Keywords Moab · Transjordan · Iron Age I · Iron Age II · King's highway · Copper production · Trade routes

---

S. Klassen (✉)
University of Toronto, Toronto, ON, Canada
e-mail: stanley.klassen@utoronto.ca

A. J. Danielson
University of British Columbia, Vancouver, BC, Canada
e-mail: danielson.a.j@gmail.com

© The Author(s), under exclusive license to Springer Nature Switzerland AG 2023
E. Ben-Yosef, I. W. N. Jones (eds.), *"And in Length of Days Understanding" (Job 12:12): Essays on Archaeology in the Eastern Mediterranean and Beyond in Honor of Thomas E. Levy*, Interdisciplinary Contributions to Archaeology,
https://doi.org/10.1007/978-3-031-27330-8_51

1 Introduction

This volume is dedicated to Thomas Levy who in many ways has fundamentally changed our understanding of the archaeology of the southern Levant. One of his central contributions has been the excavations in the Faynan region of southern Jordan that have revised our chronological and technological understanding of copper production in the region. In myriad ways the results of this work continue to reverberate through our understanding of the agents, institutions, and networks that link the Arabah with its surrounding regions, affecting developments there. It is along one of these related avenues that this contribution seeks to provide a re-evaluation, namely in examining the relation of copper production and trade from the Arabah with early Iron Age Moab.

The excavations of the Edomite Lowlands Regional Archaeological Project (ELRAP) have articulated the long-term trajectory of copper production in the Faynan region of the Wadi Arabah in the southern Levant (Levy et al., 2014b). The subsequent excavations of the Central Timna Valley Project (CTV) have revealed largely contemporaneous activity to that of Faynan, evidencing that copper production was not restricted to one locale, but was part of a broader enterprise within the Arabah (Ben-Yosef et al., 2012; Ben-Yosef, 2016, 2018). Excavations in both regions have established copper production in the thirteen through ninth centuries BCE, with a peak in both production and technological development in late tenth century BCE (Ben-Yosef et al., 2019), prior to its eventual abandonment in the mid to late ninth century BCE (Ben-Yosef & Sergi, 2018). This copper production has been attributed to the mobile, non-sedentary groups present within the region, who have been identified as early Edom (Ben-Yosef, 2019).[1] In relation to these centuries of copper production, it is necessary to explore the destinations of the copper produced and also the routes by which this trade was facilitated. In the southern Levant, two major trade networks have been proposed: one that travelled westward towards the Coastal Plain and another that travelled to the north and east through the region of Moab. This paper will analyze the potentiality of this northeastern route through Moab in the eleventh and tenth century BCE using settlement and ceramic data to ultimately argue against a strong relation of interregional trade to this region, and against its role as an impetus for rising sociopolitical complexity.

2 History of Trade in the Region: Lessons from the Late Bronze Age

Prior to examining the sociopolitical and economic realia of west-central Jordan during the eleventh and tenth century BCE, it is of value to establish what existed immediately prior, during the Late Bronze Age. In doing so, we can gain a broader

---

[1] For critique and alternative identifications, see Bienkowski (2022) and Finkelstein (2020); but also Ben-Yosef (2020).

Copper Trade Networks from the Arabah: Re-assessing the Impact on Early Iron Age... 1203

sense of what economic enterprise looked like in a better documented period and the extent to which it related to Transjordan.

2.1 Trade and the Amarna Letters

Our understanding of trade in the Late Bronze Age is enriched by the textual detail provided in the Amarna Letters of the fourteenth century BCE. Within the corpus, the primary context in which trade is mentioned is in relation to instances where it has been disrupted or threatened. Concern over caravan security was paramount and fear over safe passage for trade was directed toward both state- and non-state sanctioned actors alike (e.g., EA 8; EA 16; EA 200; EA 287; Moran, 1992, pp. 16, 39, 277, 328). For example, in one letter, EA 7, Burna-Buriash II, the ruler of Karduniash complains that his caravans—en route to Egypt—were being raided by Egypt's own vassal governors in the Levant (EA 7; Moran, 1992, p. 14).[2] In other instances, we see that upon entering a new territory, caravans were not allowed to pass or were turned back (EA 149; Moran, 1992, p. 236). For such reasons, we see that assurances of safe passage by the rulers of regions through which the trade travelled or to where it was destined was a major concern and was frequently negotiated within the letters (in the form of taxes, tariffs, or "gifts"; EA 39; Moran, 1992, p. 112). As a result, state-sanctioned security escorts were often provided in addition to a caravan's own guards (EA 199; EA 255 Moran, 1992, pp. 276, 308). In all, the letters outline the risk involved in caravan trade, the vulnerability of caravans while on the road, and the need for physical protection and ensured safe passage through diverse regions.[3]

Subtextually, the Amarna Letters also provide a window into the routes taken by different caravans as the locality of writing is often referenced. Many of the letters reference caravans originating from far-off destinations such as Karduniash, Hanigalbat or Qatna on their way to Egypt (EA 52, 255; Moran, 1992, pp. 123, 308). The most logical routes for such caravans in crossing the southern Levant would have been the regions of Cisjordan, travelling along major routes near or

---

[2] There is a detailed account of a raid led by the governor of Suḫu and Mari on the Euphrates on a wealthy caravan from Arabia during the eighth century BCE—on "the people of Tayma and Saba' whose own country is far away," capturing purple cloth, wool, precious stones, and iron (Byrne, 2003, p. 15). The account highlights the need for guards and the negotiation of safe passage (taxes/bribes). See Bienkowski and Van der Steen for similar circumstances along the *hajj* routes through the Sinai and Negev in the nineteenth century CE (2001, p. 33), and dating back to the second through seventh centuries CE (2001, pp. 34–35).

[3] Note also similar examples of Middle Assyrian trade agreements with the local rulers whose lands were traversed by caravans en route to Kanesh from Ashur (Larsen, 2015, p. 176). Larsen argues for the necessity of a "stable and well-organized political system" for long-term trade stability (1967, p. 5). Routes outside of the negotiated safe passage (smuggling) were devoid of security (Larsen, 2015, p. 179). Lastly, note the general tone of anxiety in the texts regarding safety as evidenced in ritual measures to protect against danger (Larsen, 2015, p. 177).

along the coast, and through centers (ostensibly) under the rule of the Egyptian Empire. Other letters written from southern Levantine locales likewise indicate Cisjordanian roads by virtue of their origins at locales such as Jerusalem, Gezer, Yurza, Sidon or Akko, outlining many of major centers linked within existing trade networks (EA 8, EA 149, EA 264, EA 287, EA 295; Moran, 1992, pp. 16, 236, 313, 328, 337).

Within the Amarna Letters there is little if any indication that caravans would have travelled through central or southern Transjordan. References are made only to sites within the Jordan Valley or northern Transjordan, the latter of which appears to hold stronger connections to the north and west than to the south (Kitchen, 1992, p. 26). This is not to say that west-central Jordan—a region already known as Moab—was terra incognita for those involved in inter-regional exchange as it was the recipient of at least one instance of Egyptian aggression (Routledge, 2004, pp. 58–60). Rather, in Egyptian texts, the region appears as described as a land occupied by the Shasu mobile non-sedentary groups, and existing on the periphery of Egyptian interaction and knowledge, and broader transregional economic endeavors.

An informative example of this situation can be found in the case of the Amman Airport Structure (henceforth AAS). Dated to the Late Bronze IIA through the Late Bronze IIB or perhaps early Iron Age I, the site is located on the outskirts of Amman in north-central Transjordan. The AAS has often been used as evidence for north-south trade through Transjordan with Arabia due to the presence of Qurayyah Painted Ware (QPW) at the site that indicates contact with the Hejaz. While the sherds certainly indicate connection with Arabia, when fully contextualized, the imports from the AAS reveal a different story. Notably the QPW corpus accounts for only 0.4 percent (n = 9) of the overall assemblage, a quantity that stands in stark contrast to other imports, particularly Mycenean wares (19 percent; n = 452+); Egyptian items (9 percent; n = 225) and other Mediterranean types (e.g., Cypriot wares at 2 percent; n = 58; Mumford, 2015, pp. 99, 186–187).[4] Such quantities reveal that while indeed there were contacts with the Hejaz, they were rather minimal, particularly when contrasted with the Mediterranean and Egyptian wares that demonstrate far stronger east-west connections between Cisjordan and north/central Transjordan, than north-south movement within Transjordan itself. Such a pattern indeed appears to play out on a grander scale within northern Transjordan when Mediterranean imports are considered (Leonard, 1987). This is certainly reflected in the Aegean and Cypriot imports evident at Late Bronze Age II sites in the Jordan valley (i.e., Tall Abu Kharaz, Sahem tombs, Deir ʿAlla, Pella, Tall es-Saʿidiyeh, Beth Shean, the Baqah Valley), and the northern Madaba Plain (ʿUmayri, Sahab, and Madaba; see Leonard, 1987; Strange, 2008). In summary, the cumulative data from the Late Bronze Age appears to position central Transjordan as a peripheral region in the broader Levant, with northern Transjordan exhibiting stronger east-

---

[4] From the overall assemblage of the AAS, 64 percent (n = 1534) of the sherds and other items were categorized as "local wares" (Mumford, 2015, p. 99).

west connections than formalized north-south routes that would have traversed Moab. As a working hypothesis, barring any substantive data to the contrary, it ought to be assumed that previously established roads and trade patterns would continue in use from the Late Bronze to the Iron Age.

3 Arabah Copper Production and Potential Trade Routes in the Iron I – Early Iron IIA Periods

During the early Iron Age, the massive scale of copper production in the Arabah indicates its participation within a much larger trade and consumption system that would have been achieved via equid and camel caravans (Grigson, 2012). To reach such external contexts, two major roads through the Levant have been proposed, a western trade route leading toward the Coastal Plain of the Mediterranean, and a northeastern route through Transjordan.

3.1 The Western Trade Route(s)

Detailed chemical and lead isotopic analyses supporting the movement of copper along trade routes westward from the Arabah has accumulated in recent years. These analyses have sourced copper objects in Egypt and identified the Arabah as initially one of a number of copper sources for Egypt already in the thirteenth century BCE (Rademakers et al., 2017), and have identified that the Arabah was the main source for Egyptian copper by the late eleventh and tenth centuries BCE (21st Dynasty; Vaelske et al., 2019; Ben-Dor Evian et al., 2021). Beyond Egypt, chemical and lead isotopic analyses of copper from shipwrecks off the Carmel coast (Yahalom-Mack et al., 2014) demonstrate significant consumption of Arabah copper in maritime contexts, indicating broader Mediterranean involvement.

To reach such consumers, copper from the Arabah would have moved westward along several identified routes (see Fig. 1). A route through the central Negev has been identified in part in relation to the settlement system associated with Kadesh Barnea (Ben-Dor Evian, 2017), and in ceramic petrographic data that has established links between the central Negev and the Arabah (Martin & Finkelstein, 2013).[5] Likewise, long-argued as a factor within the Arabah trade network, evidence from Tel Masos and the western Negev has identified the significance of the Beersheba-Arad Valley in connecting the Arabah to the Coastal Plain and Mediterranean ports (Holladay, 1995; Tebes, 2003; Fantalkin & Finkelstein, 2006;

---

[5] Note also the presence of additional roads through the northern Sinai, and along the Darb al-Ghazza, both of which would have been significant in relation to Timna in particular (Somaglino and Tallet, 2013).

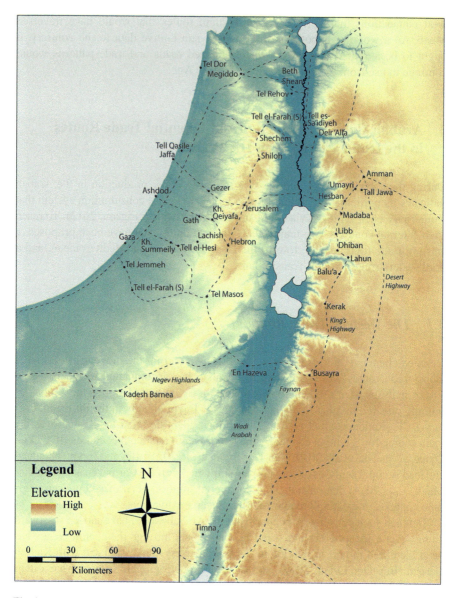

Fig. 1 Map of the southern Levant with major sites and routes identified. Routes inferred from: Ben-Yosef et al. 2014, p. Fig. 6.39; Dearman 1997; Dolan and Edwards 2020, p. Figure 2; Dorsey 1991; Hardin and Blakely 2019, p. Fig. 12. (Figure by A. Danielson and A. Karoll)

Grigson, 2012; Holladay & Klassen, 2014; Yahalom-Mack, 2017, pp. 455–456; Ben-Yosef & Sergi, 2018; Hardin & Blakely, 2019).[6]

---

[6] Such a pattern of western movement is similarly well attested in subsequent periods (Danielson, 2022a, 2021).

3.2 The Northeastern Trade Route

Similar routes to the northeast have also been hypothesized. These would have crossed the Transjordanian highlands via the famed King's Highway, a roadway system that is well known in later contexts (see Fig. 1; Mattingly, 1996, 2009; Dearman, 1997). Levied in support of such a route are lead isotope analyses of copper objects excavated at Beth-Shean and Tel Dan that identify the Arabah as the most likely source and posit a Transjordanian route as the means of access to copper (Yahalom-Mack, 2017, pp. 454–455). Such chemical analyses are combined with biblical traditions of copper working and casting in the Jordan Valley whose narrative settings are situated in the tenth century BCE (e.g., 1 Kings 7:46), and archaeological discoveries in the Jordan Valley that appear to evidence activity related to metal casting (Mazar, 2018; Mazar & Kourou, 2019). It should be noted, however, that none of the above destinations necessitate a route through Transjordan.

Lastly, and central among such discussions are certain (mis)understandings of the nature of settlement systems of west-central Jordan. Notably, these include arguments for a coherent, and integrated socio-political entity in Moab, or an "early" Moabite Kingdom—sedentary or nomadic—that is viewed as integrally associated with Arabah copper production and especially trade (Finkelstein & Lipschits, 2011; Ben-Yosef, 2021, pp. 166–170). In fact, the assumption of a functioning route through this region at this early stage, in whatever form of distribution and exchange, has been largely assumed in much recent literature (Artzy, 1994; Mattingly, 1996; Tebes, 2007; Yahalom-Mack, 2017; Amzallag, 2021; Singer-Avitz, 2021).

Regarding this potential trade, there are generally two major hypothesized north-south routes. The first and most significant was the so-called King's Highway that crosses the central highlands and intersects with many of the major Iron Age II settlements of Transjordan (see Fig. 2). A second north-south route, the Desert Highway, ran to the east on the fringe of the settled region and east of the major sedentary centers of the Iron Age II. Associated with this route and the King's Highway especially, were a series of secondary roadways linking settlements and importantly aiding in access across the major landscape barriers of the Wadi al-Hasa and the Wadi al-Mujib (Dearman, 1997; Kloner & Ben-David, 2003; Ninow, 2009; Ben-Yosef et al., 2014; Dolan & Edwards, 2020).

It is worth emphasizing the inherent challenges in this landscape that are not made readily apparent on two-dimensional maps, namely the significant barriers presented by the Wadi al-Hasa, and the Wadi al-Mujib to the northeast of the Arabah. Beyond the physical toll of traversing these wadis in a semi-arid climate, the varied landscape renders visibility as quite poor, accentuating concerns over safety (Maraqten, 1996), a fact that is well captured within recent memory.[7] The need to ensure the safety for caravans and stability of routes was paramount, a situation that, as discussed above, was achieved by bringing protection, and from consistent assurances from local leaders. In evaluating such a situation for early Iron Age Moab, in

---

[7] See discussion in Ben-Yosef et al. (2014, p. 504).

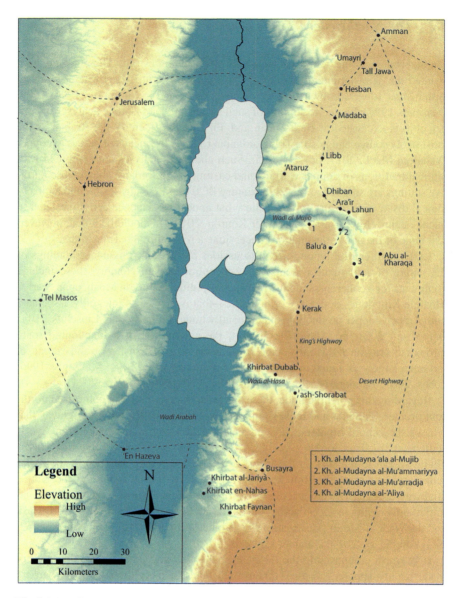

Fig. 2 Map of Moab within its regional context. Routes inferred from: Ben-Yosef et al. 2014, p. Fig. 6.39; Dearman 1997; Dolan and Edwards 2020, p. Figure 2; Dorsey 1991; Hardin and Blakely 2019, p. Fig. 12. (Figure by A. Danielson and A. Karoll)

the absence of texts that describe the region, we must rely on the proxy evidence of settlement patterns to inform our understanding of regional stability, and material culture remains as potential evidence for interregional connections.

4 Iron I and Iron IIA Central and Southern Transjordan: Settlement Patterns and Mobile Communities

Beginning in southern Transjordan, while surveys of the low-lying northern Arabah region have identified significant activity in association with copper production (MacDonald, 1992, pp. 73–82; Levy et al., 2014a, Knabb et al., 2014), the same cannot be said for the highlands of Edom to the east. Here, a series of surveys have revealed a near total absence of contemporaneous sedentary settlement. Such a portrait characterizes the Late Bronze Age and continues into the early Iron Age (Iron I and IIA). The few early Iron Age sites that have been identified—and that initially only gradually increase in the Iron Age—consist of small agricultural villages or hamlets, farmsteads, and some potential watchtowers, with a focus along the western edge of the highlands near the Arabah. It is not until later within the Iron II, during the ninth and especially the eighth century BCE, that there is a robust increase in identifiable sedentary sites (Bienkowski & van der Steen, 2001; MacDonald, 2015, pp. 24–41, 96). These patterns are consistent in southern Transjordan in the numerous surveys conducted in the region (MacDonald, 2004, pp. 56–58, 2012, pp. 421, 431; Smith et al., 2014b; MacDonald et al., 2016, pp. 482–489). The resultant regional portrait appears to be characteristic of a landscape largely comprised of more mobile, non-sedentary groups, consistent with Late Bronze Age Egyptian descriptions of the region as comprised of Shasu communities (Crowell, 2021, pp. 359–366).

From the Wadi al-Hasa adjacent the northern Arabah, there is a slightly stronger signal for sedentary activity in the Late Bronze through Iron I and IIA, though still on a low-intensity, decentralized scale (MacDonald, 1988, pp. 171–189), and appearing in part to reflect communities focussed on local subsistence (MacDonald, 2015, pp. 27–28). Notably, we must also contend with the fact that some sites identified in survey as dating to the Late Bronze and early Iron Age have, upon excavation, only presented secure later Iron II contexts (ash-Shorabat) or Iron II material culture in even later contexts (Khirbat Dubab; see Bienkowski et al., 1997; Bienkowski & Adams, 1999).[8]

In fact, such a challenge in understanding settlement patterns is accentuated to the north, in the Kerak and Dhiban plateaus that formed the heart of the region of Moab. Here, while Miller's survey of the Kerak plateau appeared to identify a strong signal for Late Bronze Age sites (Miller, 1991, pp. 308–309), upon further investigation it has been determined that many of the sherds that formed the basis for a Late Bronze Age designation ought to be assigned to the Iron I, Iron II or even later

---

[8] There are challenges in dating these sites on the basis of fragmentary ceramic remains. There is a notable absence of occupied sites that present a sufficient stratified ceramic sequence. As a result, the dominance of "Iron II" sites dated predominantly to the eighth through sixth centuries BCE, may in fact skew our perception and evidence settlement activity both earlier in the Iron Age and later into the Achaemenid period. Regardless, the general pattern of a significant increase in settlement during the late Iron Age is undeniable (Bienkowski, 2008; Danielson, 2020, pp. 84–89).

contexts (Finkelstein, 1998, p. 125; Routledge, 2004, pp. 78–82). Rather, when a stricter criterion for identifying Late Bronze Age occupation is used (i.e., five or more (ostensibly) Late Bronze sherds to qualify as a "site"), it appears that occupation during this period was either in isolated settlements, or in small settlement clusters focused in the northwest or southwestern regions of Moab, areas of greater agricultural stability (Routledge, 2004, pp. 80–81; Herr, 2009). More recent excavation at Baluʿa has now confirmed an Iron I occupation phase with the possibility of earlier Late Bronze Age occupation, although the extent of either phase is still unknown (Bramlett et al., 2018). Overall, there is little evidence from the Late Bronze Age of intensive sedentary occupation on the Kerak plateau, nor indicators of greater regional integration. Beyond the scattered sedentary sites, the region would appear to support the idea of mobile, non-sedentary Shasu groups as described in New Kingdom Egyptian texts (Routledge, 2004, pp. 77–78; Strange, 2008).

This pattern continues in the Iron I, with settlements significantly focussed to the north on the Madaba plateau at site sites such as Hesban, Madaba, Jalul, ʿUmayri, Tall Jawa, Sahab, and Khirbat Safra (Herr, 2012; Foran & Klassen, 2013; Rivas, 2020; Herr, 2006; Daviau, 2003; Ibrahim, 1978; Gregor et al., 2018), and subsequently increasing to the south on the Dhiban plateau (Dhiban, Lahun, Araʿir; Winnett and Reed, 1964; Swinnen, 2009; Olávarri, 1965) and Kerak plateaus (see below). However, the most striking feature of the increasing number of settlements that appear to the south especially in the eleventh century BCE, is their focus along the edges of major wadi systems, particularly the Wadi al-Mujib and its tributary the Wadi al-Nukhayla (Porter, 2014). While some interpretations suggest they form a ring projecting outward from a central location in the Kerak plateau—ostensibly Baluʿa (Finkelstein & Lipschits, 2011), it appears rather that their raison d'être is the inverse. Rather than projecting from the plateau, the focus of these sites appears to be on the wadi's themselves. These fortified sites (Khirbat al-Mudayna al-ʿAliya, Khirbat al-Mudayna al-Muʿarradja, Khirbat al-Mudayna al-Muʿammariyya, Khirbat al-Mudayna ʿala al-Mujib, Lahun, and Araʿir) take advantage of the local topography in their establishment atop promontories surrounded by steep cliffs, in locations that provided access to perennial water sources, and the opportunity for a subsistence regime based on agropastoral extensification (Porter et al., 2014).

Recent studies have identified increasing aridity at the termination of the Late Bronze Age influencing settlement patterns and subsistence regimes (Langgut et al., 2015), particularly as the Kerak plateau is located within the 200–300 mm rainfall isohyet, where an increase in aridity would create higher risk for crop failures (Ababsa, 2013, p. Fig. I.12; Langgut et al., 2015, p. Figure 1).[9] While extensification and the wadi riparian zones potentially mitigate aspects of a drier climate—or create alternative opportunities for exploitation in moister decades—considerations must also include the active choices of the communities involved in these regions and the

---

[9] See Porter's discussion on the challenge of identifying the specific climatic context of the early Iron Age in the Mujib region (2014, pp. 142–147).

manner in which they are constituted (Porter, 2013; Porter et al., 2014, pp. 141–143, 146).

The best documented of these sites, Khirbat al-Mudayna al-ʿAliya (henceforth KMA), presents important detail on the nature of settlement at these locations. First, the fortifications of KMA indicate that substantial labor was invested in providing security for the site and its inhabitants, with its single-event construction likely necessitating the entirety of the population and perhaps even contributions from neighboring communities, and suggesting a degree of regional volatility (Routledge, 2004, pp. 100–101; Porter, 2013, pp. 78–82). The faunal and botanical data reveals primarily low-intensity agropastoral subsistence focussed on both the riparian zones of the wadi bed and the surrounding plateau (Lev-Tov et al., 2011; Porter et al., 2014).

There is little to no evidence for public structures or evidence of external forms of administration. Within the site itself, however, there is limited evidence for small-scale internal hierarchies. These appear to be indicated by slightly larger, and other domestic structures that appear dedicated to food storage with restricted access, suggesting intra-site differences in household wealth, and by extension, influence (Porter, 2013, pp. 74–78, 91–96; Porter et al., 2014, p. 138). The material culture identified within the structures appears focussed on subsistence from local resources with an absence of evidence for interregional exchange, particularly notable in the small number of metal objects excavated (Porter et al., 2014, p. 144). Lastly, it is necessary to emphasize the short-term nature of the settlement, constructed sometime within the eleventh century BCE and abandoned gradually in the tenth century BCE (Porter, 2013, pp. 66, 129; Routledge et al., 2014, pp. 65, 82). Therefore, rather than integrated within a broader settlement hierarchy, the indicators from KMA, and by extension, the surrounding sites, appear to demonstrate independent communities focussed on localized, low-intensity agropastoral subsistence and on security and household mobility (Porter, 2013; Routledge, 2008, p. 170).

In general then, during the Iron I in the region of Moab there appears to be a number of shifts in both settlement foundations, abandonments, and in regions inhabited (Miller, 1991, pp. 308–309; Porter et al., 2014, pp. 142–143). While the survey data appears to present an increase in sedentary occupation during the Iron I, the dating of such settlement patterns from surveys tends to homogenize and present as contemporary what are potentially rather sequential occupations. More detailed data from excavated sites reveals a volatile period of short-lived occupations, abandonments and destructions (Routledge, 2004, pp. 92–93). In all, these sites fail to present evidence of settlement hierarchies that would be expected in an early kingdom (sedentary or nomadic), or forms of specialization with the goal of broader inter-regional exchange that would be expected were this region integrated within a network associated with the Arabah copper production and exchange (Routledge, 2008; Porter, 2013, 2014, p. 139; Porter et al., 2014).

In the subsequent Iron IIA period, many of the aforementioned sites are abandoned and sedentary settlements in this region are difficult to identify. This situation only changes later in the ninth century BCE (Iron IIB) when public building projects are identifiable together with inscriptional rhetoric (Mesha Inscription) that describes the integration of diverse settlements and regions into the nascent kingdom of Moab (Routledge, 2004, pp. 131–168; Harrison & Barlow, 2005; Routledge, 2008, pp. 170–172, 2016, p. 83; Danielson & Foran, 2021, pp. 108–109). From the Mesha Inscription it is clear that Mesha is integrating settlements and social groups already in existence that appear to have lacked prior unification as well as to a degree, archaeological visibility (Routledge, 2000; Harrison & Barlow, 2005). By the time of Mesha and the Iron IIB however, copper production and exchange from the Arabah had ceased, indicating that the real presence of a kingdom or "state" in Moab is only really well attested at the close of copper production.

5 The Ceramic Perspective

Essential to our current analysis is the recognition of the movement of goods along potential trade routes utilizing the various exchange networks, highlighting both inter- and intra-regional distribution. Although evidence pertaining to the influence of groups such as nomads along and within close proximity to these routes may not be tangible on the ground (Ben-Yosef, 2019, 2020, 2021), for our immediate purposes, beyond direct evidence of copper manufacturing, the most ubiquitous artifact indicating interactive relationships and communication between groups is the occurrence of ceramics with provenance identified outside of the regions from which they were excavated. Archaeometric analysis of pottery in the form of both mineralogical and chemical analyses has been instrumental in the identification of the movement of these goods during the Iron I–IIA period. Following, is a brief summary of the evidence (based on both petrographic and macroscopic analysis) which potentially highlights the directional flow of pottery pertaining both to the copper industry and potential extra-mural interaction throughout the region.

5.1 Midianite Pottery, "Qurayyah Painted Ware"

The appearance of Qurayyah Painted Ware (QPW) at various sites in the southern Levant has long highlighted connections with the Hejaz region of northwest Arabia. Tebes' (2007) overview of this pottery suggests a greater chronological range than was first suggested which tied it to the late fourteenth to mid-twelfth centuries BCE.[10] However, based on evidence from the production sites of Tayma and Qurayyah, and the distribution of QPW in the southern Levant, an end date of the production of QPW has been proposed to the mid-eleventh century BCE (Singer-

---

[10] See also Singer-Avitz (2019, p. 388) for a list of scholars suggesting a later date falling in the Iron IIA and IIB periods.

Avitz, 2019, p. 389). Distribution of QPW is clearly focused northwards into the Arabah, as well as westward through the Beer Sheva basin continuing north to a limited number of sites in the Shephelah (Tebes, 2007, Fig. 3, Table 1). As described in Sect. 2.1 above, QPW imports are restricted to central Transjordan with only a few sherds occurring at the Amman Airport Structure and one sherd from the Amman Citadel excavations (Kalsbeek & London, 1978), suggesting that west central Transjordan (Moab) was less well integrated into the broader trade networks of these imports from the Hejaz.

Table 1 Petrographic groups of the Arabah (ELRAP); bold indicates dominant local fabric and temper. (Table by S. Klassen)

Sites	Publication	F/PG	Group	Description	Phase	Vessel type
KEN, RHI sounding A	Smith et al. (2014a)	PG1A	A1	**Lower cretaceous shale (LCS)**		bwls, jgs, jrs, jgt, krs, pyx
			A1b	**LCS** – highly fired gray fabric	e. 10th–e. 9th	bwls, jgs, jgt
			A1c	**LCS** – fine ware	e. 10th–e. 9th	bwls
			A2	**LCS – slag** inclusions	e. 10th–e. 9th	st. jrs
			A2b	**LCS – coarse slag** incl.	e. 10th–e. 9th	bwl, st. jr
			A3	**LCS – basalt** incl.	e. 10th–e. 9th	bwls, jg,
			A4	**LCS** – calcite rich	e. 10th–e. 9th	bwls
			A5	**LCS** – fossiliferous limestone	e. 10th–e. 9th	jr
			A6	**LCS** – cooking pot fabric	e. 10th–e. 9th	ck pts., jg
			A6b	**LCS** – cooking pot fabric – **slag** incl.	e. 10th–e. 9th	ck pts
KEN		PG2	A7	**(LC) Arkose,** med.-fine ware	e. 10th	bwls, ck pot, jg, kr, st. jr
			A8	**LC Arkose**	e. 10th	bwl
KEN		PG3	A9	**LC Disi formation sandstone**	?	bwl, jgs, jr, jgt, kr, st. jr
KEN		PG4		Paleozoic micaceous clay	l. 10th–e. 9th	bwls
KEN		PG5		Loess soil	10th	bwls
KEN		PG6		LC with micaceous clay	10th	QPW
KEN		PG7		Moza dolomite clay	l. 10th–e. 9th	jgts
KEN		PG8		Cypriote Aegean	9th	jgts
KEN		PG9		Syro-Lebanese coast—Neogene clay with amphiroa fossils	10th	jrs
KEN		PG10		Greek transport	l. 10th–e. 9th	amph

(continued)

Table 1 (continued)

Sites	Publication	F/PG Group		Description	Phase	Vessel type
KAJ	Howland (2021)	PG1	1A	**LCS** – fabrics with quartz and calcareous sand incl.	m. 11th–m. 10th	krs, jrs, jg
			1B	**LCS** – with quartz and calcareous sand incl., **slag**	m. 11th–m. 10th	jr
			1C	**LCS** – cooking pot fabrics	m. 11th–m. 10th	ck jg
			1D	**LCS** – fabrics with sandstone incl.	m. 11th–m. 10th	kr, hm jr
			1E	**LCS** – calcareous fabric with ooids	m. 11th–m. 10th	kr
			1F	**LCS** – rich fabric, grog	m. 11th–m. 10th	bases
		PG2		**LC Disi formation sandstone**	m. 11th–m. 10th	kr, bwl
		PG3		Loess soil	m. 11th–m. 10th	jr, bwls

5.2 Pottery from the Arabah

The most recent and extensive petrographic analysis of pottery from the Faynan region was conducted as part of ELRAP. From the analysis of approximately 170 samples analyzed from Khirbat en-Nahas (KEN) and Rujm Hamrat Ifdan Sounding A (RHI-A; Smith et al., 2014a),[11] as well as over 20 additional samples from Khirbat al-Jariya (KAJ) by Matthew Howland (2021), numerous petrographic groups and sub-groups were identified (see Table 1). For both projects, local Lower Cretaceous Shale (LCS) rich clays dominate the local petrographic groups. At KEN/RHI-A, PG1A accounts for 70 percent of the samples (see Smith et al., 2014a, Table 5.9) and of these, over 40 percent are tempered with slag inclusions indicating a local technological style. Although KAJ also has fabrics predominately from LCS clays (PG1) at 79 percent of the sampled sherds (Howland, 2021, p. 262), only one sample (PG1B) is tempered with slag indicating a clear difference in production technique as opposed to KEN/RHI-A.[12] Differences in calcareous sands used as temper within these groups are also noticeable between sites suggesting the use of local wadi sands as temper (Howland, 2021, p. 266). Although local clays attributed to the LC Disi Sandstone Formation appear at both sites (KAJ – PG2 and KEN/RHI-A – A9), the use of LC Arkose clays (PG2) are unique to KEN/RHI-A. What is clear from these two analyses is that similar local clays accessible to potters from

---

[11] Only samples attributed to strata dated to the Iron I and IIA from KEN and RHI Sounding A are considered here. Of the 306 samples analyzed, 136 belong to PG1-B which date to Iron IIB period and are not factored into our assessment; see Smith et al. (2014a, Table 5.9).

[12] This was also determined by Smith et al. (2014a, p. 483) where none of the seven samples they analyzed from KAJ were slag tempered.

Copper Trade Networks from the Arabah: Re-assessing the Impact on Early Iron Age...   1215

both regions were used to produce most of the pottery at these sites. However, the types of temper utilized was not a shared technique between production centers.

Common to both assessments are clearly attested western fabrics derived from loess soils attributed to the northern Negev or southern Shephelah (KAJ – PG3 and KEN/RHI-A – PG5) along with wheel made red-slipped wares common to that region. Southern imports appear at KEN/RHI-A in the form of QPW (PG6), along with other petrographic groups from the central hill country (PG7), Cyprus (PG8), Lebanon (PG9), and the Aegean (PG10).

Macroscopic analysis of the pottery from the various surveys conducted by MacDonald (2004, 2012) and colleagues (MacDonald, 1992; MacDonald et al., 2016), show little in the way of pottery that could be attributed to ware groups from further west as at KEN/RHI-A and KAJ suggesting minimal regional trade to sites in this region. Of the pottery published from these surveys, only a few examples of what is now known to be locally produced Arabah Hand Made Ware (AHMW) are evident, with some dated to earlier periods (i.e., MacDonald 1992, p. 184, Pl. 6),[13] whereas others are attributed to Iron II sites (Macdonald et al., 2016, pp. 165, 198–99, 400–401). Seven of the ten wheel-made sherds dating to the Iron I Site #159 (KEN; MacDonald, 1992, p. 208, Pl. 18) have inclusions identified as basalt. After considering the petrographic assessment by Smith et al. (2014a), it is likely that these inclusions are slag.

Overall, the pottery from the Arabah indicates diversity in the local production of pottery with varied technological styles in the form of tempering locally accessible clays. Albeit minimal, 11 percent of the petrographic groups analyzed from KEN/RHI-A clearly demonstrate strong connections to the west along the established western trade route to the Coastal Plain, with 3 percent appearing through trade with the Hejaz.

5.3   Pottery Along the Western Trade Route(s)

The sites attributed to the Western Trade routes are largely those situated in the Negevite Highlands. Recent petrographic analysis (Martin & Finkelstein, 2013) has added immensely to the many archaeometric studies so far conducted on pottery from the area (see Martin and Finkelstein (2013, pp. 12–13) for a review of previous analyses). The primary goal of these earlier investigations was the enhancement of our understanding of the production of "Negevite Ware" that is so apparent throughout the region. As this type of pottery occurs in multiple chronological contexts, it is difficult to date due to its continued production between the late LB II through the

---

[13] Four hand-made sherds from Site 29 are dated to the Neolithic-Chalcolithic period. However, Site 29 has a high percentage of pottery dating to the Iron II period (MacDonald, 1992, Pl. 6). We would suggest these sherds may represent AHMW as they fit closely with other Iron Age examples see Martin and Finkelstein (2013, Fig. 4) and should be dated to this later phase of occupation.

Table 2 Petrographic groups of the Negev Highlands; bold indicates dominant fabric and temper associated with the Arabah. (Table by S. Klassen)

Sites	Publication	F/PG Group	Description	Phase	Vessel type
Negev Highland sites	Martin and Finkelstein (2013)	PG1	**LCS – slag** tempered clays	Ir IIA	bwls, lmp, ck krs,
		PG2	Igneous-rock tempered clays (**Arkose**)	Ir IIA	krs, ck pts., pith
		PG3	**LC clays** – de-dolomitic iron oxides in silt fraction (**argillaceous shales**)	Ir IIA	bwls, krs, jgs, jgt, st. jr, pith, ck krs
		PG4	Loess clays	Ir IIA	bwls, krs, ck pts., jgs, st. jr
			Terra rossa wares	Ir IIA	ck pt., st. jr
			Taqiyeh marls	Ir IIA	Wheel made vessels
			Chalk, limestone and olivine basalts	Ir IIA	jgts
			Moza wares	Ir IIA	?

Iron IIC period (Martin & Finkelstein, 2013, p. 12).[14] Martin and Finkelstein (2013) focus on the Iron IIA contexts and convincingly argue that the provenance of this material was the Arabah and aptly (re)named this unique pottery as Arabah Hand Made Ware (AHMW). They identify seven petrographic groups (Table 2) from the pottery analyzed with the first three attributed to the Arabah (PG1–PG3). Slag tempering is common in PG1 and is found at all sites (Martin & Finkelstein, 2013, Fig. 6) highlighting the specific connection with the region involved in copper production to the east. Arabah fabrics are not specific to hand-made pottery as wheelmade vessels are also sourced to the Arabah. Soil derived loess clays are predominate at the sites and were utilized exclusively for wheel-made vessels. These clays are widespread through the region from the northern Negev to the southern Coastal Plain indicating movement of these vessels from production centres situated north and northwest of the Negev Highlands. Other petrographic groups suggest further connections with the central hill country and the northern valleys of Cisjordan. What is evident from the Negev Highlands study is the fluid nature of the western trade route in multiple directions, with a focus on the copper producing regions of the Arabah towards the Coastal Plain as well as to the northwest.

5.4   Pottery Along the Northeast Trade Route

The pottery assessed in this section is ascribed to sites that fall along the proposed northeast route through Transjordan north of the Edomite highlands towards the Madaba plateau. For ease of description and to highlight diversity in production, we

---

[14] See also Martin and Finkelstein (2013, p. 11, n. 10) on references to similar pottery occurring during the Early Bronze Age and early Islamic period.

have divided this route into three separate sections: the Wadi al-Hasa region, the Kerak and Dhiban plateaus, and the Madaba plateau.

As discussed above (see Sect. 4), the Wadi-al-Hasa region shows a slight increase in small scale sedentary sites as opposed to the northern Arabah to the south. However, unlike the northern Arabah surveyed sites, the pottery collected in Macdonald's survey (1988) does not indicate a connection to the ware groups typical of the Arabah. Nor is there any evidence of pottery that would suggest interaction with sites along the western trade route or beyond.

Miller's survey of the Kerak plateau identified sherds that are dated to the Iron I and early Iron IIA periods (Brown, 1991) although some of this material has been questioned (Bienkowski & Adams, 1999; Herr, 2009, p. 558; Routledge, 2004, p. 79). It is possible that the sherds identified with red slip (Brown, 1991, pp. 255–257) could possibly date to the Iron II period as suggested by Herr (2009, p. 558). No obvious characteristics in Brown's fabric descriptions identify ware groups from outside the region and the mention of organic tempering as "occasional" (Brown, 1991, p. 193) fits well with the technological style applied at other sites to the north (see below).

Other sites on the Kerak plateau do have more detailed assessment of fabric groups that are more informative. At the site of Khirbat al-Mudayna al-ᶜAliya (KMA), six local petrofabric groups (Table 3) were identified (Routledge et al., 2014; Klassen & Routledge, 2021). Two groups (KMA 1 and 5) are produced with LCS rich clays exposed to the north and west of the site whereas Groups 2, 3 and 6 are harvested in closer proximity in the wadis nearby, while KMA 4 is composed of the Red Mediterranean Soils (RMS) from the plateau. Common to all groups, other than KMA 4, are basalt inclusions exposed in the immediate vicinity of the site (Table 3). Although not analyzed by means of petrography, Khirbat al-Mudayna al-Muᶜarradja (KMM) fabrics show similarities to those at KMA. Groups 1 and 2 show a strong resemblance to the majority of KMA petrofabrics with the identification of black inclusions—potentially basalt. The Group 3 cooking pots are also made with RMS tempered with calcite, and pink inclusions occurring in Group 6, potentially shale, are likely attributed to LCS clays (see Olàvarri, 1983). However, until more thorough analysis is conducted, these suggestions remain speculative.

On the northern ridge of the Wadi Mujib at the site of Lehun, Steiner and Jacobs (2008) have identified three fabric groups all showing evidence of shale rich clays of the LC period exposed in the Wadi Mujib below the site (Table 3). Fabrics A and C[15] have basalt inclusions much like the Karak plateau sites, however, the Lahun groups differ in that groups A and B have percentages of organic and dung temper unseen at the southern sites.

Moving north to the Madaba plateau, similar diversity in the ceramic industry of the period exists (Table 4). Pottery production at these sites predominately use local calcareous clays tempered with grog, chert, and limestone for most vessels, and RMS tempered with crystalline calcite for cooking pots (London et al., 1991;

---

[15] Lahun Group C cooking pot fabric strongly resembles the cooking pots belonging to KMA 5.

Table 3 Fabric and Petrographic groups of the Dhiban and Kerak plateaus; bold indicates dominant local fabric and temper; > = high percentage, < = low percentage. (Table by S. Klassen)

Sites	Publication	F/PG group	Description	Phase	Vessel type
Lahun	Steiner and Jacobs (2008)	A	>c. **ferrug.Rock (basalt)**, iron oxides, <limestone, mudstone, some flint, quartz, siltstone, **shale**, fine **organic/dung** incl.	LB/Ir I	l. st. jrs, m. to l. bwls
		B	Moderately sorted, >**mudstone**, limestone, calcite and **shales**, <**organic**	LB/Ir I	Mainly krs
		C	>c. inclusions **calcite temper**, >**ferrug. Rock (basalt)**, <oxides, **mud/siltstone** and quartz	LB/Ir I	ck pts
KMA	Routledge et al. (2014); Klassen and Routledge (2021)	KMA 1	**LCS clays** - > **basalt**, >**limestone**, <fine quartz, <**shale** and clay nodules, <chert and opaques	Ir IB	bwls, lmp, jrs, jg, jgt, ck pt., krs
		KMA 2	**Calcareous** - > **basalt**, >limestone, >f. quartz and oxides, <**f. dolomite**	Ir IB	bwls, jrs
		KMA 3	**Calcareous** - > **basalt**, >limestone, <clay nodules, f. quartz and chert	Ir IB	bwls
		KMA 4	RMS - > c. calcite, <limestone, >f. quartz, <oxides, clay nodules and chert	Ir IB	ck pts
		KMA 5	**RMS/LCS clays** - > m.-c. calcite and limestone, >f. quartz, <oxides, **basalt**, **shale** and clay nodules	Ir IB	ck pts
		KMA 6	**Fossiliferous** - > m.-c. **basalt** and limestone, <oxides, f. quartz, and clay nodules	Ir IB	bwls, jr
KMM	Olàvarri (1983)	1a	White fabric with **black incl.**	Ir IB	car. bowl
		1b	Whitish fabric with **black incl.**	Ir IB	car. bowl
		2	Red fabric with **black incl.**	Ir IB	car. bowl
		3	Reddish fabric with calcite	Ir IB	ck pts
		4	Ochre fabric with incl.	Ir IB	bwl
		5a	Red fabric with incl.	Ir IB	pith, krs
		5b	Red fabric with abundant incl.	Ir IB	pith, krs
		6a	Red fabric with **pink incl.**	Ir IB	pith
		6b	Red fabric with abundant **pink incl.**	Ir IB	pith, kr

Copper Trade Networks from the Arabah: Re-assessing the Impact on Early Iron Age...   1219

Table 4 Petrographic groups of the Madaba plateau; bold indicates dominant local fabric and temper; > = high percentage, < = low percentage. (Table by S. Klassen)

Sites	Publication	F/PG group	Description	Phase	Vessel type
Tall al-'Umayri	London et al. (1991)	1	**Fossiliferous clay** with oolites	Ir I	coll. pith
		3	**RMS – crystalline calcite, f.** quartz, feldspar, oxides	Ir I	ck pt
Hesban	London (2012)	1	**Quartz** prime inclusion >75% of non-plastics	Ir IC	ck pt
		4	**Grog** prime inclusion >60% of non-plastics	Ir IB	bwl
		6	**Limestone** prime inclusion >60% of non-plastics	LB/Ir I, Ir IA, Ir IB, Ir IC	coll. pith, pith, jg, jgt, jr
		7	**Limestone** rich 50–59% of non-plastics	LB/Ir I, Ir IA, Ir IB, Ir IC	coll. pith, jg
		8	Mixed non-plastics with calcite, no single dominant inclusion	Ir IB, Ir IC	kr, bwl
		9	Mixed non-plastics with no calcite, no single dominant inclusion	LB/Ir I, Ir IA, Ir IB, Ir IC	coll. pith, bwl, jr, jg
		10acp	**Calcite** prime or rich	Ir IA, Ir IB, Ir IC	ck pt
		12cpc	**Basalt** with **calcite** dominant	Ir IA, Ir IB, Ir IC	ck pt
Tall Jawa	Klassen (2019)	Jawa A	**LCS/calcareous** > **chert temper,** med. c. Limestone, <med. Oxides and clay nodules <**organic** < fine quartz	Ir IB	coll. pith
		Jawa B	**LCS/calcareous,** >m. - c. **chert and limestone,** <oxides and **organic,** trace fine quartz	Ir IB	coll. pith
		Jawa C	**LCS/calcareous** > **chert temper,** <m.- c. limestone, <**shale,** <f. quartz, oxides, **organic**	Ir IB	coll. pith
		Jawa D	**RMS,** >**crystalline calcite,** f. quartz, carbonates, and oxides	Ir IB	ck pt
Tall Madaba	Klassen (2012)	Madaba A	**Calcareous slightly fossiliferous clay,** >f. quartz and opaque, **limestone temper,** >organics.	LB/Ir I	coll. pith
		Madaba B	**Calcareous clay** - > limestone, f. **dolomite rhombs,** >quartz, chaff	LB/Ir I	coll. pith
		Madaba C	**Calcareous** clay - > f. quartz <m. **chert,** trace **siltstone**	LB/Ir I	coll. pith
		Madaba D	**RMS** - > m. – c. **crystalline calcite,** f. quartz, carbonates, oxides	LB/Ir I	ck pts

Klassen, 2012; London, 2012). Tall Jawa is unique in the region utilizing mixed LCS fabrics for collared pithoi exclusively tempered with chert (Klassen, 2019). Adding organic temper is also a common technique utilized at sites on the Madaba plateau. Neutron activation analysis (Porter, 2007; London, 2012) reinforces the suggestion that early Iron Age ceramic vessel production in west-central Jordan was unspecialized and reliant on local clay sources and a common production technology, with the possible exception of cooking pots and collared pithoi, particularly on the Madaba plateau.

From this brief overview, it is apparent that pottery from outside the region did not move through central Transjordan as it did along the western trade routes outlined above. Archaeometric analysis of pottery from sites along this northeast trade route supports the notion that pottery production on the 'Moabite' and northern plateaus during this period emphasizes local production, as well as communication and interaction with other settlements in the region. However, this interaction does not take the form of integrated systems of production and exchange as evidenced in the south and along the western trade route.

6 Conclusion

The above data strongly indicate that the region of Moab was not highly integrated into the interregional systems of exchange originating in the Arabah during the Iron I–IIA periods, and extensive trade activity related to the Arabah copper industry along the King's Highway as proposed, is not convincing. Thus, we would suggest that this industry does not appear to have had an influence on rising sociopolitical complexity on the Moabite plateaus, as in the region of Faynan (Ben-Yosef et al., 2019). That is **not** to say there was no trade or interregional movement in Moab at all, but rather that what existed would have been low-intensity and limited. When we consider the scale of the Arabah copper production during the eleventh–ninth centuries BCE, and patterns of trade seen in the preceding Late Bronze Age, it becomes evident that the contextual indicators of a stable route (e.g., sociopolitical stability and continuity) are not present, with the region rather indicating volatility as seen in short-lived occupation, abandonment and destruction. Evidence for rising sociopolitical complexity—whether sedentary or nomadic—does not appear to be present, with the settlements of the region appearing to rather evidence small communities focussed on low-intensity agropastoral subsistence, security, and household mobility, with little evidence for participation in broader interregional exchange. Such a pattern for central and southern Transjordan may be contrasted with the later Iron II period (Danielson, 2022b).

This interpretation is especially evident in the ceramic data, particularly on the Kerak and Madaba plateaus, where pottery production is relatively unspecialized with a focus on local resources to produce a variety of vessel forms with regional technological styles evident. This is also true of pottery production in the Arabah where similar local resources were utilized at varying sites, but with differing emphasis on the use of unique tempers highlighting the diversity in the potting industry during this period. However, unlike the northern plateaus, stronger inter-regional relations are clearly evident in the movement of pottery along the east-west trade route between the Arabah and the Coastal Plain. The development and economic benefit of these western trade routes related to Arabah copper production and the potentially expanding South Arabian trade, is also emphasized by the contrast in the settlement expansion, development of administrative centres, and opportunism occurring in the northern Negev and southern Shephelah during the late Iron I–early Iron Age IIA period (Holladay & Klassen, 2014; Hardin & Blakely, 2019), as opposed to the primary focus on low intensity agropastoral subsistence in central Moab. As in the region of Faynan, here too the evidence suggests increasing social complexity and budding statehood unlike that in late Iron I Moab.

Although our knowledge of the Iron I–IIA period in central Jordan still relies heavily on survey and settlement data, recent and renewed excavations are expanding our understanding of this region during its formative years in the early Iron Age. The increased application of archaeometric analyses of pottery and local resources, faunal, and paleobotanical research, enable us to focus on the relationships of inhabitants within and between communities (sometimes at great distances) utilizing these resources, and interpret how these groups interacted with and adapted to their environment. Our inspiration for this paper is heavily influenced by the work of Thomas Levy and ELRAP, and we hope that by highlighting the benefits of reviewing larger datasets, we as archaeologists will increasingly rely less on singular evidence such as architectural morphological checklists, in this case, the occurrence of "fortified sites" along a potential trade route through central Transjordan, and focus more on holistic approaches to create more nuanced historical reconstructions.

References

Ababsa, M. (Ed.). (2013). *Atlas of Jordan: History, territories and society.* Institut Français du Proche-Orient.

Amzallag, N. (2021). A metallurgical perspective on the birth of ancient Israel. *Entangled Religions, 12*(2), 1–32.

Artzy, M. (1994). Incense, camels and collared rim jars: Desert trade routes and maritime outlets in the second millennium. *Oxford Journal of Archaeology, 13*(2), 121–147.

Ben-Dor Evian, S. (2017). Follow the Negebite Ware road. In O. Lipschits, Y. Gadot, & M. J. Adams (Eds.), *Rethinking Israel: Studies in the history and archaeology of ancient Israel in honor of Israel Finkelstein* (pp. 19–28). Eisenbrauns.

Ben-Dor Evian, S., Yagel, O., Harlavan, Y., Seri, H., Lewinsky, J., & Ben-Yosef, E. (2021). Pharaoh's copper: The provenance of copper in bronze artifacts from post-imperial Egypt at the end of the second millennium BCE. *Journal of Archaeological Science: Reports, 38*, 1–13.

Ben-Yosef, E. (2016). Back to Solomon's Era: Results of the first excavations at "Slaves' Hill" (Site 34, Timna, Israel). *Bulletin of the American Schools of Oriental Research, 376*, 169–198.

Ben-Yosef, E. (2018). The Central Timna Valley project: Research design and preliminary results. In E. Ben-Yosef (Ed.), *Mining for ancient copper: Essays in memory of Beno Rothenberg* (pp. 28–63). Sonia and Marco Nadler Institute of Archaeology, Tel Aviv University.

Ben-Yosef, E. (2019). The architectural bias in current biblical archaeology. *Vetus Testamentum, 69*, 361–387.

Ben-Yosef, E. (2020). And yet, a nomadic error: A reply to Israel Finkelstein. *Antiguo Oriente, 18*, 33–60.

Ben-Yosef, E. (2021). Rethinking the social complexity of early Iron Age nomads. *Jerusalem Journal of Archaeology, 1*, 155–179.

Ben-Yosef, E., & Sergi, O. (2018). The destruction of Gath by Hazael and the Arabah copper industry: A reassessment. In I. Shai, J. Chadwick, L. Hitchcock, A. Dagan, C. McKinny, & J. Uziel (Eds.), *Tell it in Gath: Essays in honor of Aren M. Maeir on the occasion of his sixtieth birthday* (pp. 461–480). Münster.

Ben-Yosef, E., Shaar, R., Tauxe, L., & Ron, H. (2012). A new chronological framework for Iron Age copper production at Timna (Israel). *Bulletin of the American Schools of Oriental Research, 367*, 31–71.

Ben-Yosef, E., Najjar, M., & Levy, T. (2014). Local Iron Age trade routes in Northern Edom: From the Faynan copper ore district to the highlands. In T. Levy, M. Najjar, & E. Ben-Yosef (Eds.), *New insights into the Iron Age archaeology of Edom, Southern Jordan* (pp. 493–576). Cotsen Institute of Archaeology.

Ben-Yosef, E., Liss, B., Yagel, O., Tirosh, O., Najjar, M., & Levy, T. (2019). Ancient technology and punctuated change: Detecting the emergence of the Edomite kingdom in the Southern Levant. *PLoS One, 14*(9), 1–16.

Bienkowski, P. (2008). The Persian Period. In R. Adams (Ed.), *Jordan: An archaeological reader* (pp. 335–353). Equinox.

Bienkowski, P. (2022). The formation of Edom: An archaeological critique of the "early Edom" hypothesis. *Bulletin of the American Schools of Oriental Research, 338*, 113–132.

Bienkowski, P., & Adams, R. (1999). Soundings at Ash-Shorabat and Khirbat Dubab in the Wadi Hasa, Jordan: The pottery. *Levant, 31*, 149–172.

Bienkowski, P., & van der Steen, E. (2001). Tribes, trade, and towns: A new framework for the late Iron Age in Southern Jordan and the Negev. *Bulletin of the American Schools of Oriental Research, 323*, 21–47.

Bienkowski, P., Adams, R., Philpott, R. A., & Sedman, L. (1997). Soundings at Ash-Shorabat and Khirbat Dubab in the Wadi Hasa, Jordan: The stratigraphy. *Levant, 29*, 41–70.

Bramlett, K., Vincent, M., & Ninow, F. (2018). Baluʿa 2017. *The Institute of Archaeology Siegfried H. Horn Museum Newsletter, 39*(1), 1–3.

Brown, R. (1991). Ceramics from the Kerak plateau. In M. Miller (Ed.), *Archaeological survey of the Kerak plateau* (pp. 169–279). Scholars Press.

Byrne, R. (2003). Early Assyrian contacts with Arabs and the impact on Levantine vassal tribute. *Bulletin of the American Schools of Oriental Research, 331*, 11–25.

Crowell, B. (2021). *Edom at the edge of empire: A social and political history*. Society of Biblical Literature.

Danielson, A. (2020). *Edom in Judah: An archaeological investigation of identity, interaction, and social entanglement in the Negev during the late Iron Age (8th–6th Centuries BCE)*. Unpublished PhD dissertation. University of California, Los Angeles.

Danielson, A. (2021). Culinary traditions in the borderlands of Judah and Edom in the late Iron Age. *Tel Aviv, 48*, 87–111.

Danielson, A. (2022a). Edom in Judah: identity and entanglement in the late Iron Age Negev. In B. Hensel, D. Edelman, & E. Ben Zvi (Eds.), *About Idumea and Edom: Recent research and approaches from archaeology, Hebrew bible studies and ancient Near East studies* (pp. 117–150). Equinox.

Danielson, A. (2022b). Trade, kingdom, and empire: Edom and the south Arabian trade. *Journal of Ancient Near Eastern History, 0*, 1–37.

Danielson, A., & Foran, D. (2021). Iron Age Nebo: Preliminary investigations at Khirbat al-Mukhayyat and Rujm al-Mukhayyat. *Palestine Exploration Quarterly, 153*(2), 83–112.

Daviau, P. M. M. (2003). *Excavations at Tall Jawa, Jordan. Volume 1: The Iron Age town*. Brill.

Dearman, A. (1997). Roads and settlements in Moab. *The Biblical Archaeologist, 60*(4), 205–213.

Dolan, A., & Edwards, S. (2020). Preference for periphery? Cultural interchange and trade routes along the boundaries of late Iron Age Moab. *Palestine Exploration Quarterly, 152*(1), 53–72.

Dorsey, D. A. (1991). *The roads and highways of ancient Israel*. Johns Hopkins University.

Fantalkin, A., & Finkelstein, I. (2006). The Sheshonq I campaign and the 8th-century BCE earthquake-more on the archaeology and history of the south in the Iron I–IIa. *Tel Aviv, 33*, 18–42.

Finkelstein, I. (1998). From sherds to history: A review article. *Israel Exploration Journal, 48*, 120–131.

Finkelstein, I., & Lipschits, O. (2011). The genesis of Moab: A proposal. *Levant, 43*(2), 139–152.

Finkelstein, I. (2020) The Arabah copper polity and the rise of Iron Age Edom: A bias in biblical archaeology? *Antiguo Oriente, 18*, 11–32.

Foran, D., & Klassen, S. (2013). Madaba before Mesha: The earliest settlements on the city's west acropolis. *Studies in the History and Archaeology of Jordan, 11*, 211–219.

Gregor, P., Ray, P., Grace, C., Broy, T., & Moody, J. (2018). Khirbet Safra 2018. *The Institute of Archaeology Siegfried H. Horn Museum Newsletter, 39*(3), 1–3.

Grigson, C. (2012). Camels, copper and donkeys in the early Iron Age of the Southern Levant: Timna revisited. *Levant, 44*(1), 82–100.

Hardin, J., & Blakely, J. (2019). Land use, regional integration, and political complexity: Understanding the Hesi region as pasturage during Iron Age IIA. *Strata: Bulletin of the Anglo-Israel Archaeological Society, 37*, 61–94.

Harrison, T., & Barlow, C. (2005). Mesha, the Mishor, and the chronology of Iron Age Madaba. In T. Levy & T. Higham (Eds.), *The bible and radiocarbon dating* (pp. 179–190). Equinox.

Herr, L. (2006). An early Iron Age I house with a cultic corner at Tall al-ʿUmayri, Jordan. In S. Gitin, J. E. Wright, & J. P. Dessel (Eds.), *Confronting the past: Archaeological and historical essays on ancient Israel in honor of William G. Dever* (pp. 61–73). Winona Lake..

Herr, L. (2009). Jordan in the Iron I period. *Studies in the History and Archaeology of Jordan, 10*, 549–562.

Herr, L. (2012). The Iron Age. In J. Sauer & L. Herr (Eds.), *Hesban 11: Ceramic finds, typological and technological studies of the pottery remains from Tell Hesban and vicinity* (pp. 9–172). Andrews University.

Holladay, J. S. Jr. (1995). The kingdoms of Israel and Judah: Political and economic centralization in the Iron IIA-B (ca. 1000–750 BCE). In T. Levy (Ed.), *The archaeology of society in the Holy Land* (pp. 368–398). Facts on File.

Holladay, J. S. Jr., & Klassen, S. (2014). From bandit to king: David's time in the Negev and the transformation of a tribal entity into a nation state. In J. M. Tebes (Ed.), *Unearthing the wilderness: Studies on the history and archaeology of the Negev and Edom in the Iron Age* (pp. 31–46). Peeters.

Howland, M. (2021). *Long-distance trade and social complexity in Iron Age Faynan, Jordan* (unpublished PhD. Dissertation). University of California, San Diego.

Ibrahim, M. (1978). The collared-rim jar of the early Iron Age. In R. Moorey & P. Parr (Eds.), *Archaeology in the Levant: Essays for Kathleen Kenyon* (pp. 116–126). Aris & Phillips.

Kalsbeek, J., & London, G. (1978). A late second millennium B.C. potting puzzle. *Bulletin of the American Schools of Oriental Research, 232*, 47–56.

Kitchen, K. (1992). The Egyptian evidence on ancient Jordan. In P. Bienkowski (Ed.), *Early Edom and Moab: The beginning of the Iron Age in Southern Jordan* (pp. 21–34). J.R. Collis.

Klassen, S. (2012). *Iron Age I collared Pithoi in central Jordan: Modes of production and technical style*. Paper presented at the ASOR Annual Meeting Chicago.

Klassen, S. (2019). Petrographic analysis of Iron I pottery. In M. Daviau (Ed.), *Excavations at Tall Jawa, Jordan. Volume 3: The Iron Age pottery* (pp. 305–317). Brill.

Klassen, S., & Routledge, B. (2021). *Pottery production and human interaction with the landscape: Evidence from the late Iron Age I site of Khirbat al-Mudayna al-ʿAliya, Jordan*. Presented at the ASOR Annual Meeting.

Kloner, A., & Ben-David, C. (2003). *Mesillot* on the Arnon: An Iron Age (pre-Roman) road in Moab. *Bulletin of the American Schools of Oriental Research, 330*, 65–81.

Knabb, K., Jones, I., Najjar, M., & Levy, T. (2014). Patterns of Iron Age mining and settlement in Jordan's Faynan District: The Wadi al-Jariya survey in context. In T. Levy, M. Najjar, & E. Ben-Yosef (Eds.), *New insights into the Iron Age archaeology of Edom, southern Jordan* (pp. 577–626). Cotsen Institute of Archaeology.

Langgut, D., Finkelstein, I., Litt, T., Neumann, F., & Stern, M. (2015). Vegetation and climate changes during the Bronze and Iron Ages (~3600–600 BCE) in the Southern Levant based on palynological records. *Radiocarbon, 57*(2), 217–235.

Larsen, M. T. (1967). *Old Assyrian caravan procedures.* Nederlands Historisch-Archaeologisch Instituut in het Nabije Oosten.

Larsen, M. T. (2015). *Ancient Kanesh: A merchant colony in Bronze Age Anatolia.* Cambridge University Press.

Leonard, A. (1987). The significance of the Mycenean pottery found East of the Jordan River. *Studies in the History and Archaeology of Jordan, 3*, 261–266.

Lev-Tov, J., Porter, B., & Routledge, B. (2011). Measuring local diversity in early Iron Age animal economies: A view from Khirbat al-Mudayna al-ʿAliya (Jordan). *Bulletin of the American Schools of Oriental Research, 361*, 67–93.

Levy, T., Najjar, M., & Ben-Yosef, E. (2014a). Conclusion. In T. Levy, M. Najjar, & E. Ben-Yosef (Eds.), *New insights into the Iron Age archaeology of Edom, Southern Jordan* (pp. 977–1001). Cotsen Institute of Archaeology.

Levy, T., Najjar, M., Ben-Yosef, E., & Smith, N. (2014b). *New insights into the Iron Age archaeology of Edom, Southern Jordan.* Cotsen Institute of Archaeology.

London, G. (2012). Ceramic Technology at Hisban. In J. Sauer & L. Herr (Eds.), *Hesban 11* (pp. 597–763). Andrews University.

London, G., Plint, H., & Smith, J. (1991). Preliminary petrographic analysis of pottery from Tell el-ʿUmeiri and hinterland sites, 1987. In L. Geraty, L. Herr, Ø. LaBianca, & R. Younker (Eds.), *Madaba Plains project 2: The 1987 season at Tell el-ʿUmeiri and vicinity and subsequent studies* (pp. 429–439). Andrews University Press.

MacDonald, B. (1988). *The Wadi el-Ḥasā archaeological survey, 1979–1983, West-Central Jordan.* Wilfrid Laurier University Press.

MacDonald, B. (2004). *The Tafila-Busayra archaeological survey 1999–2001, West-Central Jordan.* American Schools of Oriental Research.

MacDonald, B. (2012). *The Ayl to Ras an-Naqab archaeological survey, Southern Jordan (2005–2007).* American Schools of Oriental Research.

MacDonald, B. (2015). *The Southern Transjordan Edomite plateau and the Dead Sea Rift Valley.* Oxbow Books.

MacDonald, B. (1992). *The Southern Ghors and Northeast ʿArabah archaeological survey.* Collis.

MacDonald, B., Clark, G., Herr, L., Quaintance, D., Hayajneh, H., & Eggler, J. (2016). *The Shammakh to Ayl archaeological survey, Southern Jordan (2010–2012).* American Schools of Oriental Research.

Maraqten, M. (1996). Dangerous trade routes: On the plundering of caravans in the pre-Islamic Near East. *ARAM, 8*, 213–236.

Martin, M., & Finkelstein, I. (2013). Iron IIA pottery from the Negev highlands: Petrographic investigation and historical implications. *Tel Aviv, 40*(1), 6–45.

Mattingly, G. (1996). The King's Highway, the Desert Highway, and Central Jordan's Kerak plateau. *ARAM, 8*, 89–99.

Mattingly, G. (2009). Literary and archaeological evidence of trade and travel on the Karak plateau. *Studies in the History and Archaeology of Jordan, 10*, 467–472.

Mazar, A. (2018). The Iron Age apiary at Tel Rehov, Israel. In F. Hatjina, G. Mavrofridis, & R. Jones (Eds.), *Beekeeping in the Mediterranean – from antiquity to the present* (pp. 40–49). Nea Moudania..

Mazar, A., & Kourou, N. (2019). Greece and the Levant in the 10th–9th centuries BC. A view from Tel Rehov. *Opuscula, 12*, 369–392.

Miller, J. M. (1991). *Archaeological survey of the Kerak plateau*. Scholars Press.

Moran, W. L. (1992). *The Amarna Letters*. Johns Hopkins University.

Mumford, G. (2015). The Amman Airport Structure: A re-assessment of its date-range, function and overall role in the Levant. In T. Harrison, E. Banning, & S. Klassen (Eds.), *Walls of the prince: Egyptian interactions with Southwest Asia in antiquity* (pp. 89–198). Brill.

Ninow, F. (2009). Crossroads and sites at the northern edge of the Central Moabite plateau. *Studies in the History and Archaeology of Jordan, 10*, 633–640.

Olàvarri, E. (1965). Sondages a ʿAroʿer sur l'Arnon. *Revue Biblique, 72*(1), 77–94.

Olàvarri, E. (1983). La campagne de fouilles 1982 à Khirbet Medeinet al-Muʿarradjeh près de Smakieh (Kerak). *Annual of the Department of Antiquities of Jordan, 27*, 165–178.

Porter, B. (2007). *The archaeology of community in Iron I Central Jordan* (unpublished PhD. Dissertation). University of Pennsylvania, Philadelphia.

Porter, B. (2013). *Complex communities: The archaeology of early Iron Age West-Central Jordan*. University of Arizona Press.

Porter, B. (2014). Toward a socionatural reconstruction of the early Iron Age settlement system in Jordan's Wadi al-Mujib canyon. In E. Gubel & I. Swinnen (Eds.), *From Gilead to Edom: Studies in the archaeology of Jordan in honor of Denyse Homès-Fredericq* (pp. 133–150). Akkadica Supplementum 12.

Porter, B., Routledge, B., Simmons, E., & Lev-Tov, J. (2014). Extensification in a Mediterranean semi-arid marginal zone: An archaeological case study from early Iron Age Jordan's Eastern Karak Plateau. *Journal of Arid Environments, 104*, 132–148.

Rademakers, F., Rehren, T., & Pernicka, E. (2017). Copper for the Pharaoh: Identifying multiple metal sources for Ramesses' workshops from bronze and crucible remains. *Journal of Archaeological Science, 80*, 50–73.

Rivas, A. (2020). *From the Iron Age to the Persian period: The chronological development of Tall Jalul Field G*. Presented at the ASOR Annual Meeting, Virtual.

Routledge, B. (2000). The politics of Mesha: Segmented identities and state formation in Iron Age Moab. *Journal of the Economic and Social History of the Orient, 43*(3), 221–256.

Routledge, B. (2004). *Moab in the Iron Age: Hegemony, polity, archaeology*. University of Pennsylvania Press.

Routledge, B. (2008). Thinking "globally" and analysing "locally": South-Central Jordan in transition. *In Israel in transition: From LB II-Iron IIB* (pp. 144–176). T & T Clark.

Routledge, B. (2016). Conditions of state formation at the edges of empires: The case of Iron Age Moab. In R. Kessler, W. Sommerfeld, & L. Tramontini (Eds.), *State formation and state decline in the Near and Middle East* (pp. 77–97). Harrassowitz Verlag.

Routledge, B., Smith, S., Mullan, A., Porter, B., & Klassen, S. (2014). A late Iron Age I ceramic assemblage from Central Jordan: Integrating form, technology and distribution. In E. van der Steen, J. Boertien, & N. Mulder-Hymans (Eds.), *Exploring the narrative. Jerusalem and Jordan in the Bronze and Iron Ages (Papers in Honour of Margreet Steiner)* (pp. 82–107). Bloomsbury T & T Clark.

Singer-Avitz, L. (2019). Epilogue: The dating of Qurayyah Painted Ware in the Southern Levant. In S. Gitin (Ed.), *The ancient pottery of Israel and its neighbors from the Middle Bronze Age through the Late Bronze Age* (pp. 388–399). Israel Exploration Society.

Singer-Avitz, L. (2021). Yotvata in the Southern Negev and its association with copper mining and trade in the Early Iron Age. *Near Eastern Archaeology, 84*(2), 100–109.

Smith, N., Goren, Y., & Levy, T. (2014a). The petrography of Iron Age Edom: From the lowlands to the highlands. In T. Levy, M. Najjar, & E. Ben-Yosef (Eds.), *New insights into the Iron Age archaeology of Edom, Southern Jordan* (pp. 461–491). Cotsen Institute of Archaeology.

Smith, N., Najjar, M., & Levy, T. (2014b). New perspectives on the Iron Age Edom steppe and highlands: Khirbat al-Malayqtah, Khirbat al-Kur, Khirbat al-Iraq Shmaliya, and Tawilan. In

T. Levy, M. Najjar, & E. Ben-Yosef (Eds.), *New insights into the Iron Age archaeology of Edom, Southern Jordan* (pp. 247–296). Cotsen Institute of Archaeology.

Somaglino, C., & Tallet, P. (2013). A road to the Arabian Peninsula in the reign of Ramesses III. In F. Förster & H. Reimer (Eds.), *Desert road archaeology in ancient Egypt and beyond* (pp. 511–520). Heinrich Barth Institut.

Steiner, M., & Jacobs, L. (2008). The Iron Age pottery of al-Lehun: Fabrics and technology. *Leiden Journal of Pottery Studies, 24*, 133–140.

Strange, J. (2008). The Late Bronze Age. In B. MacDonald, R. B. Adams, & P. Bienkowski (Eds.), *The archaeology of Jordan* (pp. 271–289). Sheffield Academic.

Swinnen, I. (2009). The Iron Age I settlement and its residential houses at al-Lahun in Moab, Jordan. *Bulletin of the American Schools of Oriental Research, 354*, 29–53.

Tebes, J. M. (2003). A new analysis of the Iron Age "chiefdom" of Tel Masos (Beersheba Valley). *Aula Orientalis, 21*, 63–78.

Tebes, J. M. (2007). Pottery makers and premodern exchange in the fringes of Egypt: An approximation to the distribution of Iron Age Midianite pottery. *Buried History, 43*, 11–26.

Vaelske, V., Bode, M., & Loeben, C. (2019). Early Iron Age Copper Trail between Wadi Arabah and Egypt during the 21st dynasty: First results from Tanis, ca. 1000 BC. *Zeitschrift für Orient-Archäologie, 12*, 184–203.

Winnett, F., & Reed, W. (1964). *The excavations at Dibon (Dhiban) in Moab*. American Schools of Oriental Research.

Yahalom-Mack, N. (2017). Metal production and trade at the turn of the first millennium BCE: Some answers, new questions. In O. Lipschits, Y. Gadot, & M. Adams (Eds.), *Rethinking Israel: Studies in the history and archaeology of ancient Israel in honor of Israel Finkelstein* (pp. 451–461). Eisenbrauns.

Yahalom-Mack, N., Galili, E., Segal, I., Eliyahu-Behar, A., Boaretto, E., Shilstein, S., & Finkelstein, I. (2014). New insights into Levantine copper trade: Analysis of ingots from the Bronze and Iron Ages in Israel. *Journal of Archaeological Science, 45*, 159–177.

The Negev Highlands — A Corridor for the Copper and Incense Trade during Nonconsecutive Periods between the Chalcolithic and Roman Periods

Chaim Ben David

Abstract The Negev Highlands, unlike the coastal road, the Darb Ghaza or even the Wadi Arabah, is a difficult, unnatural trade corridor. Traversing it is bleak and uninviting and indeed, for long periods, it was off the beaten track of main south Levantine trade routes.

The copper and incense trade altered this situation, albeit not for all periods. If the destination of the mined copper was Be'er Sheva or ports of call in the north, there was no need to cross the Negev Highlands except on its most northeastern flank, the Scorpions' Ascent. However, if the destination was Egypt (in the EB IB and Iron Age) crossing the Negev Highlands was more tempting and even necessary.

During the approximately 1500 years of the incense trade, the Gaza Port was apparently a major terminus. Yet when the main stations in the Edomite territory were Tell el-Kheleifeh, Busseira and 'Ein Ḥusub, those who plied this route preferred to bypass the heart of the Negev Highlands by traveling either via the Darb Ghaza, coming from Tell el-Kheleifeh, or via the Scorpions' or Amiaz Ascents.

Only when Petra became the Nabatean hub and subsequently its capital, did the incense trade routes between Petra and Gaza cross the Negev Highlands directly.

Keywords Negev · Copper route · Incense route · Ancient roads · Long distance trade · Donkey caravans · Peutinger map

1 Introduction

As noted by scholars in recent decades, the history of the Negev Highlands is characterized by sharp settlement oscillations (Finkelstein et al., 2018; Ben-Yosef et al., 2021). Several periods featured robust human activity with remains of hundreds of

---

C. B. David (✉)
Kinneret College on the Sea of Galilee, Zemach, Israel
e-mail: bendavidhm@gmail.com

© The Author(s), under exclusive license to Springer Nature Switzerland AG 2023
E. Ben-Yosef, I. W. N. Jones (eds.), *"And in Length of Days Understanding" (Job 12:12): Essays on Archaeology in the Eastern Mediterranean and Beyond in Honor of Thomas E. Levy*, Interdisciplinary Contributions to Archaeology, https://doi.org/10.1007/978-3-031-27330-8_52

sites with stone-built enclosures and structures, while other periods left no evidence of such features behind.

One of the models explaining this phenomenon is the two-phase, long-distance trade route model, stating that the peaks of settlement activity in the Negev Highlands corresponded to copper exploitation in the Arabah during earlier periods and their transport to Egypt in the first phase. A correlation can be seen between the main copper-production periods in Faynan and the waves of major human activity in the Negev Highlands. Later on, the peaks of settlement activity corresponded to the incense trade from Petra to Gaza.

The article deals with the main copper routes passing through the Negev Highlands on the way from Faynan to Be'er Sheva'and Arad in the Chalcolithic period and the Early Bronze Age, and the routes from Faynan to Egypt via the Negev Highlands and Sinai in the Intermediate Bronze and Iron Ages. The Arabian incense trade apparently bypassed the main Negev Highlands in the late Iron Age but in the Hellenistic and Roman periods, it passed through the Negev Highlands and once again brought flourishing settlement activity to the area.

Most of the Hebrew and Arabic names in the article are transliterated according to the Israel Hebrew Language Academy. When discussing Nineteenth- and early twentieth-century scholars we use the Arabic names they used. Identification of biblical sites such as Kadesh Barnea', Scorpions' Ascent (Ma'ale 'Aqrabim) and Tamar is beyond the scope of this article.

2   Geographical Setting of the Negev Highlands

The Negev Highlands refers mainly to the four geological anticlines south of Be'er Sheva'and the Dead Sea Area and to the 'Avdat Plateau (Fig. 1). The four anticlines all lie southwest to northeast, and range in altitude from 500 to 1000 m asl. The Negev Highlands as a unit constitute an east–west topographical challenge for traffic going north to south (Fig. 2). Two major north–south routes can bypass the Negev Highlands: from the west is the Darb Ghaza route (Meshel, 2000: 99–117) and from the east the Wadi Arabah route (Avner, 2016). While the western bypass could avoid the Negev Highlands, the eastern bypass eventually must climb up and out of the Wadi Arabah either via the Scorpions' Ascent on the southeastern-most Hatzera anticline or via the Ami'az or Zohar Ascents in the Judean Desert. The latter have been suggested as the leading candidates for the biblical Road of Edom (Cohen-Sasson et al., 2021).

As for water sources, it should be noted that the Negev Highlands is a relatively short leg along the trade routes that crossed the Sinai or Arabian deserts. Small but perennial water sources along the Arabah east of the Negev Highlands (Fig. 1), from south to north are: Moyet 'Awad, 'Ein Rahel, 'Ein Wuibeh and Ein Husub. In the Negev Highlands the following sources should be mentioned: 'Ein Saharonim,'Ein Ziq, 'Ein Zin and 'Ein Ma'rif (Shertzer et al., 2021: 71–80).

Fig. 1 The Negev Highland ridges and water sources. (Map prepared by Amir Eidelman, Lior Enmar and Vered Shatil with additions made by Dina Shalem)

3   The 19th and Early Twentieth-Century Negev Highlands Road Network

The 19th and early twentieth-century travelers and scholars in the Negev area dealt mainly with the biblical "Exodus route" from Sinai to Canaan. The combined data from these travelers and scholars, like Robinson, Palmer, Musil, Woolley and Lawrence, and from the very important cartographic work of Newcomb (Fig. 3) lead to the following findings:

The main route connecting southern Palestine and Wadi Arabah is Darb es-Sultan, which crossed the Boker Ridge via Naḥal Ha-Besor, descending by the easy Naqb Gharib pass to the Zin Valley (Wadi Fukra) and then crossing the low ridge of the western flank of the Ramon anticline and reaching the springs of 'Ein Haruf ('Ein Raḥel) and 'Ein Wuibeh in Wadi Arabah. Two major routes marked by Newcomb as roads passable by light-wheeled traffic were: 1. Be'er sheva'–Kurnub–Naqb Sfai–'Ein Ḥusub, (the steep Naqb Sfai itself was marked as passable by fully laden camels); 2. Naqb Gharib–Wadi Fukra–'Ein Ḥusub. Roads passable by fully laden camels were 1. 'Uja el-Ḥafir–Bir Ḥafir–Abdeh; 2. Abdeh–Nafakh–Naqb Saḥli–Wadi Raman–Wadi Sik–Kh. Umm Keseir–Moyat 'Awad; 3. Abdeh–Bir Ḥafir–el-Kossaime. The later-discovered Nabataean incense route in the section between Abdeh and the Grafon area was not marked on the map, and the segment descending into Maktesh Ramon via Naqb el-Ḥamla is marked on the map as a regular trail.

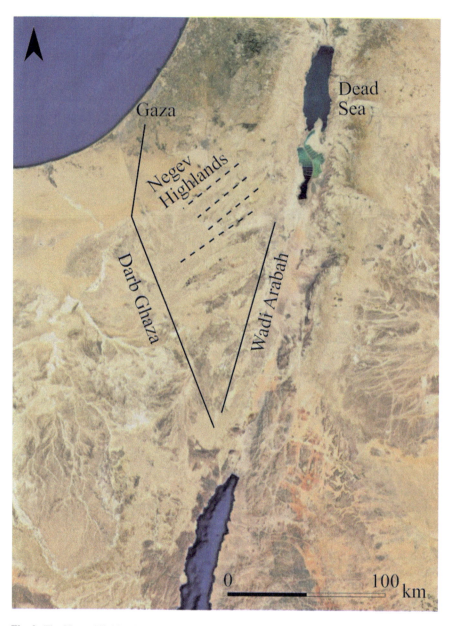

Fig. 2 The Negev Highlands and the two major north–south routes can bypass them. (Map prepared by Dina Shalem on Google Earth satellite map)

The Negev Highlands -- A Corridor for the Copper and Incense Trade...

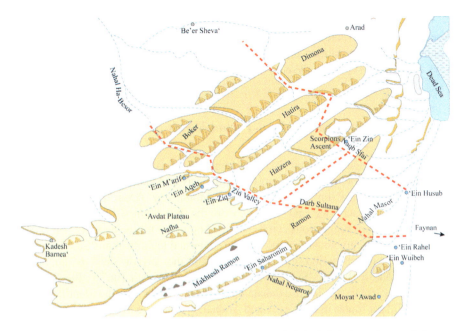

Fig. 3 The main route connecting southern Palestine and Wadi Arabah in the early twentieth century. (Map prepared by Amir Eidelman, Lior Enmar and Vered Shatil with additions made by Dina Shalem)

4 Defining Ancient Routes from the Bronze Age and the Iron Age

Unlike the relatively easy task of defining the Roman imperial network (Kolb, 2019), defining the Bronze and Iron Age routes, especially detecting the archaeological remains, is quite frustrating.. The main problems and methods of dating roads is in regard to pre-Roman periods, as summed up well by Ben-Yosef (Ben-Yosef et al., 2014: 511). Remains of ancient roads in desert areas seem to be a bit easier to detect, as noted by some scholars in recent decades, in studies of the Judean Desert (Yekutieli, 2006), the Egyptian Sahara (Förster & Riemer, 2013) and southern Jordan (Ben David, 2010; Ben-Yosef et al., 2014).

I find it more appropriate to refer to a corridor of potential routes than one or two specific routes when dealing with the copper or incense routes in the Negev Highlands,. I find the words of Manfred Linder (Lindner et al. 2000: 538), who researched the routes of the Petra area for almost 30 years, significant: "One is at a loss to define any one of the enumerated passages as 'the road between Petra and Umm Ratam.' At different times with different animals, different loads, different people, in different seasons, clandestine smuggling or openly trading one or another passage may have been chosen."

We shall describe the use of the following sources and methods of analysis in the research of ancient routes in the Negev Highlands: historical sources, the origin and destination of major stations, topographic insights, road-related structures, field surveys and least-cost path analysis.

4.1 The Debate over Biblical-Period Roads in the Negev

According to various scholars, six roads named in the Bible were identified in the Negev area: "the way to Shur" (Gen. 16:7) "the way of Atharim" (Num. 21:1), "the way to the Red Sea" (Num. 21:4), "the way of Mount Seir" (Deut. 1:2), "the way of the Arabah" (Deut. 2:8), and "the way to the hill-country of the Amorites" (Deut.1:19). These suggestions can be summed up in the following table (Table 1).

There is basic agreement that most of the suggested identifications functioned as roads in the biblical period, and agreement that "the way of Shur" is the Be'er Sheva'or Kadesh Barnea'–Sinai route and "the way of Atharim" is the Kadesh Barnea'–Arad route. Yet intense debate has ensued over the specific identifications of the other four routes in the Negev and Arabah. It should be noted that most of the suggestions are not based on archaeological remains of the road itself or remains of road-related structures dated to the Iron Age but on fragmentary and at times contradictory descriptions found in biblical accounts, and on geographical considerations.

Table 1 Biblical roads in the Negev

Name of Scholar	Shur	Atarim	Arabah	Mount Seir	Red Sea	Amorites
Aharoni (1967: 40, 53–54)	Kadesh Barnea'–Sinai	Kadesh Barnea'–Arad	Faynan–Kadesh Barnea'	Darb el-Hajj–Aqaba–Egypt	Wadi Arabah	Kadesh Barnea'–Darb el-Ghaza–Yotvata
Rothenberg (1967: 161)	Kadesh Barnea'–Sinai	Kadesh Barnea'–Be'er Sheva'or Kadesh Barnea'–Arad	Faynan–Kadesh Barnea'	Kadesh Barnea'–Zin Valley–Dead Sea	Kadesh Barnea'–Darb el-Ghaza–Eilat	?
Meshel (1979: 299)	Be'er Sheva'–Sinai	Kadesh Barnea'–Arad	Wadi Arabah	Darb el-Ghaza–Eastern Central Sinai	Southern section of Darb el-Ghaza	Northern section of Darb el-Ghaza

5 Road-Related Structures in the Negev Highlands from the Bronze Age

5.1 Stone-Heap Road Markers

Woolley and Lawrence (1914–1915) described 12 types of stone monuments in the Negev Highlands, three of which seem to be along routes: memorial heaps, ritual heaps and roadside heaps (Woolley & Lawrence, 1914–1915: 28).

In 1984 Uzi Avner published his first article on cultic sites in the Negev and Sinai Deserts. He noted that most of the cultic structures were found along ancient routes (Avner, 1984: 116 Map 1). Apart from *masseboth* and open sanctuaries, he defined heaps of small stones placed alongside each other in a row as "cairn lines" (Avner, 1984: 126–127) and suggested a cultic interpretation. In the Negev Highlands he marked (from north to south) concentrations of the cairn lines along four main east–west routes: the Scorpions' Ascent, Darb es-Sultan, Moyat 'Awad, the Sha'ar Ramon route and the Wadi Paran route (Fig. 4). The author wrote that he himself had encountered more than 80 cairn lines in the southern Negev and Sinai. Israel and Nahlileli (1991: 84–85) called these heaps of stones "crenellations" (in Hebrew,

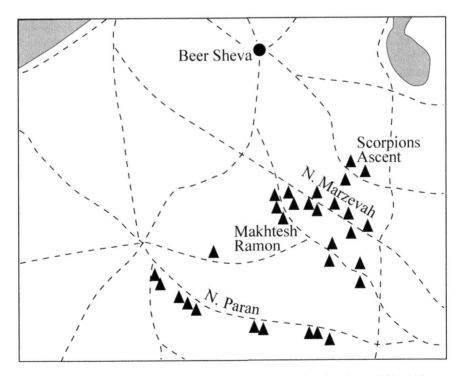

Fig. 4 Cairn lines along the east–west Negev Highlands routes based on Avner. (1984: 116, map 1) (map prepared by Dina Shalem)

shiniyot). They noted that they were erected along ancient roads and at both major and secondary junctions. They surveyed 26 systems of these stone heaps along the Sha'ar Ramon–Moyat 'Awad route and noted others along the Darb es-Sultan, Naḥal Masor, and Scorpions' Ascent routes.

Haiman (1996) preferred the road marker theory over the cultic explanation. Erickson-Gini et al. (in press) deemed them "navigation lines." The various scholars who have studied this phenomenon tend to date them to the Intermediate Bronze Age. Amichai Sadeh (in preparation) is conducting a GIS-based survey and study of these stone-heap road markers.

5.2 Rectangular "Navigation Platforms"

Haiman (1996) was the first to suggest that Intermediate Bronze Age (EB IV in his terminology) stone structures in the Negev Highlands are connected to the copper trade between Faynan and Egypt via the Negev Highlands. These unique stone structures in the past were called tumuli; Haiman called them "rectangular platforms." These platforms are 15 to 30 m long, 3 to 7 m wide, and up to 1 m high. The frame of the platform was made of large stones and filled with earth and small stones. The distribution of platforms is connected to that of temporary sites. Only a few platforms of this kind were found near the permanent settlements. Haiman (1996: 13, Fig. 12) marked these platforms in the Negev Highlands, a cluster east of Wadi Arabah, north of the Faynan area and in Gebel Maghara in central Sinai. These three clusters form a corridor from the Faynan area to central Sinai via the Negev Highlands.

Based on her excavation at Rosh Ma'ale Zadok of three rectangular platforms, Erickson-Gini (2014, in press) suggested dating them to the EB II–III and identified them as "navigation platforms." Although in the past the platforms were generally described as cairns or rectangular tumuli, their distribution pattern supports Haiman's contention that they were constructed to serve as road markers. Their position along well-traveled desert tracks made them useful for burials, but as noted by Haiman, not every navigation platform was used for burial (Haiman, 2006: 46).

Erickson-Gini notes that these platforms are not known from the Eilat and southern Negev areas and not from the Judean Desert. The navigation platforms have been recorded as far west as central North Sinai in the area of Ain Muweilleh (Woolley & Lawrence, 1914–1915: 44, Fig. 2) and in the area of Gebel Maghara, at Wadi Lagama, Bir Umm Werib, Wadi Mushabi and Wadi Malḥi (Clamer & Sass, 1977: 246–248, Fig. 113: C, Pl. 117:3–4) and as far east as a ridge overlooking Wadi Ifdan near Khirbet Ḥamra-Ifdan.

According to Erickson-Gini the navigation platforms at Rosh Ma'ale Zadok appear to mark the southern-most track between the Western Border and the Faynan region by way of Makhtesh Ramon and Naḥal Neqarot (Fig. 5). The presence of

The Negev Highlands — A Corridor for the Copper and Incense Trade...

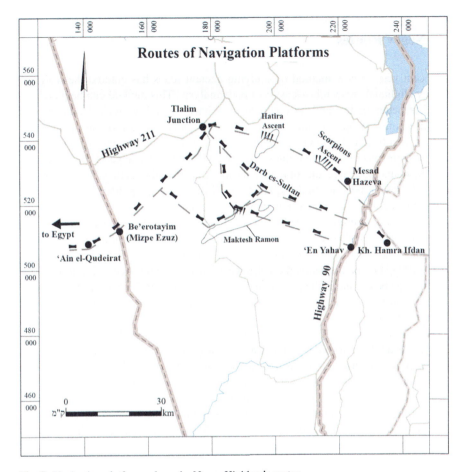

Fig. 5 Navigation platforms along the Negev Highlands routes

multiple platforms leading up to major descents has been observed personally by the excavators near the head of the northern-most track at Maʻale Ḥatira, where it leads down into Makhtesh Ha-Gadol (Makhtesh Ḥatira) and further southeast along the same route in Mishor Ha-Yamim, at the top of Scorpions' Ascent. Multiple platforms were also recorded between the western border and Mizpe 'Ezuz/Be'erotayim (Erickson-Gini, 2014). Erickson-Gini notes that in spite of the secondary use of the platforms for mortuary purposes, their primary purpose was to be visible against the desert landscape as an aid in navigating desert tracks, presumably by long-distance caravans between Egypt and the Faynan region. She notes that the platforms were constructed in the same manner deep in the Sinai Peninsula, in the west and in Wadi Arabah and in the Faynan region in the east. The amount of work required in their construction suggests the involvement of a central authority (Egyptian?) underwriting and directing work crews.

6 Least-Cost Path Analysis in the Study of Ancient Negev Routes

In recent years a new method of studying ancient roads has entered the realm of Negev Highlands research—least-cost path analysis. This method can help archaeologists better understand how people may have moved across a landscape. Its premise is that people decide how to move geospatially in a rational manner and rely on their thorough knowledge of the landscape, and thus attempt to minimize the cost of their travel from one point to another. The main advantage of this method is that the mathematical results of the ideal route challenge the facts on the ground and compels researchers to find explanations (historical? geopolitical?) as to why ancient travelers preferred a route other than the ideal one.

Cohen-Sasson used this method in his dissertation research regarding the route from the centers of Lower and Upper Egypt to the copper production site in Timna (Cohen-Sasson, 2017: 60–74). In an appendix to his dissertation (Cohen-Sasson, 2017: 192–211), he discusses the Petra–Gaza incense route. According to his conclusion, the best route is the Scorpions' Ascent–Kurnub–Be'er Sheva'–Gaza route. The second-best is the Darb es-Sultan route and the third is the Moyat 'Awad–Ramon–Oboda route.

Moti Zohar and Tali Erickson-Gini (2019) checked the Darb es-Sultan and the Moyat 'Awad–Oboda route, concluding that slope and distance to water resources are dominant factors in reconstructing the accurate path of the incense route. According to their calculations, Darb es-Sultan is preferable to the Maḥmal Pass.

Ziv Shertzer (2021: 213) used this method during his discovery of the new segment of the Roman road along the incense route in the Grafon area. Schwimer and Yekutieli (2021: 238) used this method in their study of the Intermediate Bronze Age copper trade routes between Faynan and Be'er Milka on the northern Sinai route to Egypt.

7 Copper Trade Routes During the Chalcolithic Period and the Bronze and Iron Age

7.1 Chalcolithic Period

Following the discovery of copper production sites in the Be'er Sheva'Valley, it became clear that the copper itself did not originate in the Be'er Sheva'area, and in recent decades there have been several indications that the copper derived from Faynan (Shugar, 2018; Ackerfeld et al., 2020).

In Nelson Glueck's book, *Rivers in the Desert* (1959: 89), the author suggested that copper from the Faynan area came to Be'er Sheva' via 'Ein Ḥusub and the Scorpions' Ascent. Yet in another article (Glueck, 1960: 8) he wrote: "The Darb es-Sultaneh is one of the major roads used in the Chalcolithic period to bring chunks

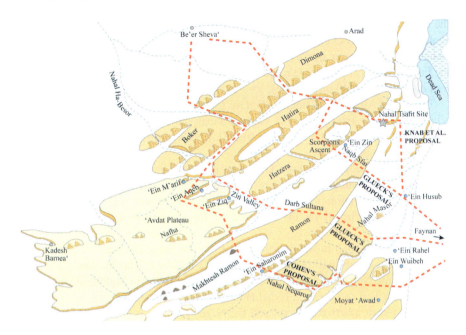

Fig. 6 The potential routes from Faynan to Be'er Sheva in the Chalcolithic Period. (Map prepared by Amir Eidelman, Lior Enmar and Vered Shatil with additions made by Dina Shalem)

of raw copper from the Wadi Feinan to Tell Abu Matar on the outskirts of Be'er Sheva'".

Based on Chalcolithic sites at Har Masa, Naḥal Neqarot and Ramat Saharonim (Cohen, 1999: 21–29) all along the later Nabataean incense route, Cohen suggested that copper from Faynan and/or Timna may also have been transported to the Be'er Sheva'Valley along this route.

Following an excavation at Naḥal Tsafit, Knab et al. (2018), entitled their article "A Middle Timnian Nomadic Encampment on the Faynan-Be'er Sheva' Road." Although no evidence of copper trade was found on the site itself, the authors claim that the petrography of the ceramics at the site indicates origins in Faynan (Knab et al. 2018: 28). Thus, from the topographical point of view all these routes (Fig. 6) could have served as copper trade routes, yet apart from the ceramic petrographic data found at the Naḥal Tsafit site none of the suggestions are based on findings of copper or other signs of trade along them.

7.2 Early Bronze Age

Unlike in the Chalcolithic period, when the copper ore was brought to Be'er Sheva'for smelting, in the Early Bronze Age smelting was done in the Faynan area, at Khirbat Hamra Ifdan, a large (ca. 1.5 ha.) metal-refining and casting workshop at the time (Levy et al., 2002), as well as sites along the Arabah: Ein Yahav (Yekuteli et al., 2005; Ben-Yosef et al., 2016); Giv'at Hazeva (Ben-Yosef et al., 2016: 45) and Ashalim (Ben-Yosef et al., 2016). The Ashalim site seems to have been situated on the Faynan–Arad copper trade route that ascended to Arad by an Early Bronze Age trail discovered by Yekuteli (2006).

The site of Afridar in Ashqelon (Golani, 2014) provides significant evidence for relations between Faynan and the Mediterranean during the Early Bronze I A (ca. 3500–3300 BCE). The shortest route from Faynan to Afridar was probably via the Scorpions' Ascent.

As mentioned above, Erickson-Gini dates the "navigation platforms" to the Early Bronze Age and suggests that they all lead to Sinai and Egypt via the Negev Highlands. Connection between Egypt and Early Bronze sites in the Negev Highlands is confirmed by the presence of Egyptian-made ceramics at Negev Highland sites.

Cohen, on his map presenting the data from the Early Bronze Age (1999: 38, Map 3), marks an ancient route from Faynan via the site of Har Mathhsa, which is situated on the Nabatean-period incense route at that time via Makhtesh Ramon to the Nafha Plateau and then via Nahal Ha-Besor to the western Negev.

The connection between Egypt and the Negev Highlands is also noted through the Egyptian pottery found in the Negev. Petrographic analysis of the pottery of the Early Bronze age site in Mizpe Sede Hafir in the Western Negev showed that 40% of the pottery comes from Egypt and Jordan, 22% and 18% respectively (Atkins & Yekutieli, 2022: 39*). The researchers of the site note the probability that the site is connected to the copper trade (ibid: 43*).

7.3 *Intermediate Bronze Age*

Copper ingots were found in five major Intermediate Bronze Age settlements in the Negev Highlands — 'En Ziq, Mashabe Sadeh, Be'er Resisim, Har Tsayad and Har Yeroham (Cohen, 1999: 262). Mollusk shells that originated in the Nile have been found in three of the above-mentioned sites (Bar-Yosef, 1999).

Cohen (1999: 85, Map 4) marks a route from Faynan to 'En Ziq, the largest known Intermediate Bronze Age site in the Negev Highlands and then via the Oboda area to Be'er Resisim and on to Kadesh Barnea'in Sinai.

Stone-heap road markers suggested to date to the Intermediate Bronze Age were found mainly along the east–west routes potentially connecting the Faynan area and Sinai–Scorpions' Ascent road, Nahal Masor, Darb es-Sultan and the Moyat 'Awad–Ramon route.

Based on a uniquely widespread type of petroglyph depicting human figures with crescent-shaped headgear found in the Negev Highlands, Schwimer and Yekutieli (2021) marked two Intermediate Bronze Age copper trade routes from Faynan to the coastal road to Egypt near El Arish in Sinai via the Negev Highlands (Fig. 7). The northern route, via Darb es-Sultan–'En Ziq–Matred Plateau and the southern route,

The Negev Highlands -- A Corridor for the Copper and Incense Trade...

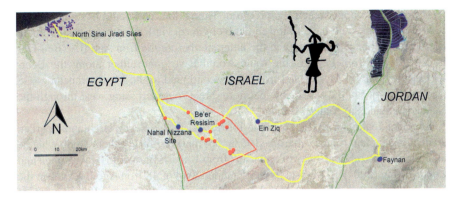

Fig. 7 Two Intermediate Bronze Age copper trade routes from Faynan to the coastal road to Egypt near El Arish in Sinai via the Negev Highlands. (Map prepared by Lior Schwimer and Yuval Yekutieli)

passing south of Har Nafha, converge at two places—5 km east of Be'er Resisim and again near Be'er Milka. According to the authors, "most of the panel sites are found adjacent to features resembling ancient paths that pass through the main valleys or cross the low-rising ridges that separate them" (Schwimer & Yekutieli, 2021: 238). However, the authors did not provide firm evidence of this important claim.

7.4 Iron Age

Iron Age copper production in Faynan lasted from the eleventh century BCE until the end of the Iron Age IIA. Our understanding of the Iron Age "Israelite fortresses" in the Negev has completely changed in recent years, due to the clear connection between them and the copper industry in Faynan. Bits of copper slag from Faynan (and perhaps also from Timna) were found in simple handmade pottery known as Negebite Pottery (Martin & Finkelstein, 2013).

The composition of the bronze chisel found at Horvat Haluqim in the Negev Highlands dated to the twelfth century BCE, shows that the copper ore originated in Faynan (Bruins et al., 2018), and as the excavators at the site noted, trade relations probably existed in the eleventh century BCE between Horvat Haluqim and the Faynan area. The Zin Canyon with its springs is a convenient, natural east–west route that connects the Faynan area with Horvat Haluqim.

A study of the provenance of copper used in artifacts from Egypt during the 21st Dynasty (which ruled Lower Egypt for about 100 years, from 1070 to ca. 950 BCE) strongly suggests that the copper of these artifacts originated in the Arabah mines (Ben-Dor Evian et al., 2021). The analysis in this study cannot conclusively distinguish between the two main Arabah mining sites of Timna and Faynan, nor can the archaeological evidence support a distinction, as both regions were active at the end of the eleventh century BCE.

How did the copper reach Egypt? From Timna, the road could have passed via central Sinai or would have followed Darb el-Ghaza via Kadesh Barneaʻ, but there is no clear evidence for activity at the latter site before the Iron Age IIA (Ben-Dor Evian, 2017). From Faynan, the route would have gone either along the Beer-sheba Valley via Tel Masos, and from there, continued to the Mediterranean coast, reaching Egypt via the sea, or by the more direct route, crossing west through the Negev Highlands to Kadesh Barneaʻ.

Scholars dealing with the "Israelite fortresses" in the Negev Highlands marked them along ancient routes. Aharoni (1963a: 56) marked most of them along what he identified as the biblical "way of Atharim" from Kadesh Barneaʻ to Arad. Cohen and Cohen-Amin (2004: 10 Map 1) in their detailed map of 48 Iron Age IIA sites in the Negev Highlands, marked most of these sites along ancient routes. Indeed many of the Negev Highland fortresses (Fig. 8) are along a potential route between Kadesh Barneaʻ and the northeastern Negev Highlands. The northeastern-most Negev Highland fortress along this route is Ḥorbat Raḥba (no. 1 on the map) near the modern Dimona road junction leading northwest to Arad or Beʼer Shevaʻ, or southeast to Wadi Arabah via the Scorpions' Ascent. Unlike Aharoni, who suggested that the Negev Highland fortresses are along the road leading to Arad, Glueck (1956: 29), in discussing Horbat Rahba, suggested that the site protected the ancient route coming from Wadi Arabah to Mamshit (the Scorpions' Ascent route) and then southwest toward Kadesh Barneaʻ or northwest to Beʼer Shevaʻ. What we now know about the

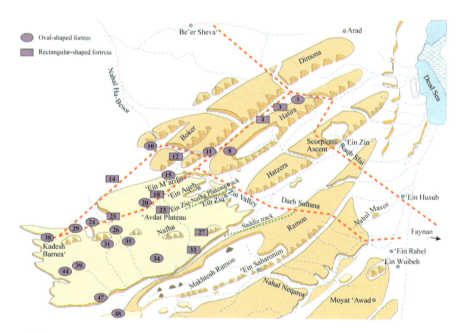

Fig. 8 The routes from Faynan to Egypt via Kadeh Barnea and the Negev Highlands in the Iron Age. The numbers on the fortresses are according to Cohen and Cohen-Amin 2004 publication. (Map prepared by Eidelman, Lior Enmar and Vered Shatil with additions made by Dina Shalem)

Negebite pottery connection with Wadi Arabah copper slag, and that Iron Age copper from the Arabah reached Egypt, seem to support Glueck's proposal that many of the Negev Highlands fortresses are along a route from Wadi Arabah to Kadesh Barnea'(Cohen and Cohen-Amin [2004: 10 Map 1] in their detailed map of 48 Iron Age IIA sites in the Negev Highlands marked most of the sites along ancient routes).

As can be seen on the map (Fig. 8), the Negev Highlands Iron Age fortresses are situated on the 'Avdat Plateau and the Ḥatira and Ḥaluqim-Boker anticlines. Yet none were found along the two main routes from Wadi Arabah to Ma'ale 'Aqrabim (Scorpions' Ascent) or along Darb es-Sultan. What do we know of the use of these routes in the Iron Age? As for the Scorpions' Ascent road, it should be noted that two neighboring ancient ascents share the name Ma'ale 'Aqrabim — the Scorpions' Ascent. The western one — the Roman Scorpions' Ascent — is called Naqb Sfar in Arabic, where the Late Roman fortified structures of Ḥorvat Ẓafir, Mezad Zafir and Rogem Zafir are located. The eastern one is called Naqb Sfai in Arabic, where the modern road was built above the ancient Roman ascent. On his way from Kurnub and el-Ḥusub, Nelson Glueck (1935: 115) noted a site he called "Rujm Sfei," which he described as "several small, completely ruined towers and houses built on a flat topped elevation." From there he continued to Qasr Sfar "a small rectangular structure measuring 7.5 meters square, overlooking the precipitous descant of Naqb Sfar." Today this site is named Ḥorvat Zafir (Cohen, 1993: 1143). The former site, which Glueck called Rujm Sfei is not known today in the field or on current maps. In 1937 George Kirk (1938) visited the upper sites of the two *naqbs*, Sfar and Sfai, and noted two towers near the vehicle road from Kurnub to Wadi Arabah — one north of the road (Naqb Sfai) and one south of the road (Naqb Sfar). Apparently the tower north of the road is Glueck's Rujm Sfei, which Kirk called "Qasr" in his sketch in the files of the Archive of the Department of Antiquity in Mandatory Palestine and the southern one is Qasr Sfai, modern Ḥorvat Zafir. Near one of the buildings north of Qasr Sfai, two pottery rims from the Iron Age II were collected.

Rothenberg (1967: 164–165) claimed that Naqb Sfai was in use in the Iron Age while Naqb Sfar saw use only in the Byzantine period. He noted many structures at the head of Naqb Sfai including a site he called Rujm Sfai. Rothenberg collected Iron Age pottery in some of the structures and noted that during the construction of the road in 1950 all the remains were destroyed (ibid: 273 note 272). As for the western ascent, Naqb Sfar, Aharoni (1963b: 33) noted Iron Age pottery along it; Iron Age pottery was later detected in the vicinity of Ḥorvat Zafir (Cohen, 1993: 1144), in an encampment site along Naḥal Ma'ale about 3 km north of Metsad Ẓafir. According to the surveyors of this encampment site, Negebite pottery was detected among the Iron Age pottery (n.a., 1977: 70).

In Glueck's description of Darb es-Sultan (1960: 8) he noted: "We came across some very extensive MB I and Iron II sites along the Darb es-Sultan or close to it along one or the other sides of the Wadi Murrah and the Wadi Marzeva." In two sites at Wadi Marzeva (the lower part of Darb es-Sultan) that Glueck defined as caravan sites, he noted numerous Iron II pottery (Glueck, 1960: 11).

In recent years, two paths passable for donkeys have been identified that potentially connect Darb es-Sultan and the 'Avdat Plateau (Fig. 8) . Itay Lubel (2014) a high school student in the Environmental High School in Sde Boker in the Negev documented what he called "the saddle track" between 'En Orḥot on Darb es-Sultan and the area of Grafon. Ziv Shertzer from the Sde Boker Field School found a path connecting 'En Ziq in the Zin Valley and the Nafḥa Plateau not far from 'Avdat. Along some sections small retaining walls were found. Although no research was conducted to date them in my view they were not erected by the local Bedouins in the last centuries. These two paths enable connection between the Darb es-Sultan and the 'Avdat Plateau, potentially leading then to Kadesh Barnea'. They could be part of the Negev Highlands copper routes of the EB IB and the Iron Age. Further high resolution field research is needed to check these and other paths in the Negev Highlands and to check if other Negev Highlands Iron Age fortresses are indeed situated along other ancient routes connecting Faynan and Kadesh Barnea' (Fig. 8).

8 The Arabian Incense Trade in the Iron Age

Trade with southern Arabia created one of the main commercial routes in the ancient Near East. A debate has gone on for decades over the beginnings of this trade. Some date the trade to as early as the end of the Late Bronze (Jasmin, 2006) or the Early Iron Age (Finkelstein, 1988). Albright pointed out that the conveyance of goods across the Arabian desert would have been impossible without camels. In his opinion, camels were domesticated only toward the end of the twelfth century BCE (Albright, 1960: 206–207), and below we will suggest that donkey caravans could have crossed the Arabian desert before the domestication of the camel.

As for the Negev, Erickson-Gini (pers. comm.) dates the first clues of Arabian trade to the lowest dated phase at 'Ein Ḥusub — the mid-eleventh century BCE— an incense burner, an alabaster handle and a few fragments of Qurayyah Painted Ware. More data concerning Arabian trade from 'Ein Husub comes from later phases of the Iron Age.

From 'Ein Ḥusub toward Be'er Sheva' and further north or west, the Scorpions' Ascent seems to be the best candidate. As mentioned above, Iron Age pottery was found at two sites above the Naqb. Another option from 'Ein Husub is that the route headed north to the Amiaz or Zohar ascents in the Judean Desert, which are suggested as the leading candidates for the biblical "Road of Edom" (Cohen-Sasson et al., 2021).

How did the Arabian trade in the Iron Age reach 'Ein Ḥusub? Tebes (2007), and Finkelstein and Piasetzky (2008: 182) suggested two alternative routes, both of them bypassing the heart of the Negev Highlands. One comes from the west via the Darb Ghaza from Tell el-Kheleifeh via Ajrud and Kadesh Barnea' to Gaza, and the other climbs from Tell el-Kheleifeh to the Edom Highlands and then descends from Buseirah to 'Ein Ḥusub and via the Scorpions' Ascent to the Be'er Sheva'Valley and Gaza.).

As for the suggestion of a route climbing from Tell el-Kheleifeh to the Edom Highlands and then descending from Buseirah to 'Ein Ḥusub, it should be noted that there seems to be no reason to climb 1500 m to the Edomite Highlands and then descend again to Ein Ḥusub at 200 m below sea level. Apparently, the authors favored Rothenberg's claim that in antiquity there was no major traffic route in Wadi Arabah. Avner (2016), however, has convincingly shown that this idea is completely wrong. Moreover, the main Arabian trade route in the Iron Age could come from inland Arabia to the Edomite Highlands without going down to the head of the Red Sea as it did during later periods.

In any case, descending from Buseira to 'Ein Ḥusub was via the very convenient Naqb Daḥal, which has an Iron Age road station along the route (Ben-Yosef et al., 2014: 532–533).

9 Donkeys as the Main Pack Animals in Leading the Copper Trade and the Early Arabian Trade

Apparently, donkeys transported all the copper along the copper trade routes from Faynan via the Negev Highlands toward Be'er Sheva'or Sinai and Egypt. The ability of donkeys to make long trans-desert journeys, including crossing the Sahara, is well documented as early as the Early Bronze Age in Egypt (Riemer, 2013; Kopp, 2013: 105–106; Hendrickx et al., 2013).

As noted by Power (2004: 131), "The donkey is perhaps one of the most important, albeit neglected and misrepresented animals in history. Indeed, it may be said that everything that early man needed to take them from hunter-gatherers to settlements, and to great and complex civilizations, was carried on the backs of donkeys. Despite all the evidence, be it archaeological, ethnographical, or ecological, this animal's relentless work and almost explicable endurance over possibly 6000 years of domestication is overshadowed by one of the worst reputations in the animal world,"

According to Förster et al. (2013: 195) donkeys require less water than other domesticated animals, except of course the camel. Although it is recommended that donkeys be offered water at least once a day, they can go without water for up to 3 days. This is possible because the donkey can tolerate losing water up to 30% of its body weight — the same ratio as the camel. To restore such a deficit, a dehydrated donkey can drink 24–30 liters of water within 2–5 min.

Could donkeys have led the Arabian trade? A few scholars have suggested that before the domestication of the camel, the Arabian trade was led by donkeys (Zarins & Hauser, 2014: 33–36). This suggestion was reinforced by the discovery of a rock inscription with cartouches of Ramesses III near Taymā᾽ in northwestern Saudi Arabia (Sperveslage & Eichmann, 2012). As camel bone finds from Taymā᾽ correspond to the generally accepted thesis concerning the first appearance and exploitation of the domestic dromedary not before 1000 BCE (Prust & Hausleiter, 2020) the Egyptian caravan that reached Taymā᾽ during the reign of Ramsses III, must have done so with donkeys.

Based on the Ramesses III rock inscriptions in western Sinai, the Eilat and Timna region and Taymā', Somaglino and Tallet (2013: 511–518) suggested an inland trade route between Egypt and Taymā'.

Taymā' is one of the great oases along the Arabian trade route in the driest area of the entire incense route. Reaching Taymā' from Egypt by donkey, a mission no more complicated than crossing the Sahara, facilitates a connection to southern Arabia as well. Hopefully future data from southern Arabia will shed light on the possibility of donkey caravans leading the Arabian trade before the domestication of the camel.

10   The Incense Route in the Negev Highlands in the Persian Period

Gaza in the Persian period was the main port shifting the Arabian trade overseas. After Alexander the Great conquered Gaza in 332 BCE, Plutarch notes that Alexander "…took the city. Moreover, as he was dispatching great quantities of the spoils home to Olympias and Cleopatra and his friends, he sent also to Leonidas his tutor five hundred talents' weight of frankincense and a hundred of myrrh, in remembrance of the hope with which that teacher had inspired his boyhood. It would seem, namely, that Leonidas, as Alexander was one day sacrificing and taking incense with both hands to throw upon the altar-fire, said to him: 'Alexander, when thou hast conquered the spice-bearing regions thou canst be thus lavish with thine incense; now, however, use sparingly what thou hast.' Accordingly, Alexander now wrote him: 'I have sent thee myrrh and frankincense in abundance, that thou mayest stop dealing parsimoniously with the gods.'" Thus, we see that in the Persian period Gaza was already the main port by which the incense was shipped overseas.

Based only on a few Persian-period fortified sites in the Negev Highlands and the Persian period phases in the sites of Tell el-Kheleifeh and Kadesh Barnea'Meshel (2009) proposed that during this period the incense trade came from Tell el-Kheleifeh via Darb Ghaza to Kadesh Barnea'and then via the Persian period sites of Be'erotaim, Qasr Ruḥeiba and Ḥorvat Rotem toward Naḥal Ha-Besor to Gaza. According to Meshel, the sites in the Sde Boker area — Ḥorvat Masora and Ḥorvat Retema — may hint to the use of the Petra–Darb es-Sultan–Gaza route; however, no Persian-period remains were found along the Darb es-Sultan route.

Evidence of the Arabian trade passing through the Negev Highlands comes from a unique burial site excavated in 2021 near the Tellalim Junction (Pasternak & Erikson-Gini, 2022. According to the preliminary report, the burial site is situated on an ancient road junction, dated to the Iron and Persian periods. The main evidence of Arabian trade comes from beehive-shaped alabaster perfume vessels, incense burners, and some jewelry, all of which have a south Arabian origin. Other objects in the burial have a Phoenician origin and the burial site seems to belong to long-distance traders.

11 History of Research of the Nabataean Incense Route from Petra to Gaza along the Negev Highlands

Palmer (1871: 535) noted remains of a road southeast of Oboda and identified it as the "Roman road to Petra" yet he did not mention a connection to the incense trade.

Thomsen (1917: 85) presented two main roads crossing the Negev Highlands. One from Be'er Sheva'to Ayla via Oboda and western Negev Highlands, his interpretation to the Peutinger map (see below) and the other road following the description of Palmer from Oboda to Petra via Makhtesh Ramon.

The German scholar Fritz Frank visited Wadi Arabah and the Negev and was the first scholar to investigate and publish parts of the Negev Highlands incense route. Frank (1934: 270–276) identified sections of a wide road, milestones, and road-related structures like Mezad Neqarot (Qasr Wadi Sik) and Ḥorvat Qazra (Qasr al-'Abd). He suggested that most of these elements should be identified as a Roman fortification system along the road.

Albrecht Alt (1935) never visited the area, but studied Frank's data. He made an architectural analysis of the forts, suggesting that they were part of a Late Roman defense system along the road from Be'er Sheva', Elusa and Oboda to Petra.

In 1937 and 1938, George Kirk (1938: 231–234), visited the sites that Frank had discovered. He collected more sherds and concluded that all the sites dated only from the Nabatean period.

In 1952, Nelson Glueck visited the site of Qasr Wadi es-Sik (Metsad Neqarot) and noted that the built roofed cistern was Nabatean (Glueck, 1953: 13). As for the milestones and paved sections in the Makhtesh Ramon, Glueck attributed them to a Roman road leading from Be'er Sheva'to Ayla (Glueck, 1959: 228).

Avraham Negev (1966) traveled the road between Ma'ale Mahmal and Moyat 'Awad and examined the pottery at the sites along this section. He concluded that the road and its use were solely Nabataean. In the 1960s, Zeev Meshel and Yoram Tsafrir (1974, 1975) conducted a wide-ranging survey along the built sections between 'Avdat (Oboda) and Sha'ar Ramon and proposed that the sections and the milestones they observed were Nabataean and part of the Petra-Gaza trade route.

Rudolph Cohen (1982), after undertaking excavations at several sites along the incense route, was the first to state that use of the road did not cease in 106 CE as Negev, Meshel and Tsafrir had surmised, but continued in use during the second and even the third centuries CE. However, Cohen did not contradict the basic hypothesis that the road was originally constructed by the Nabataeans. Cohen was also the first to suggest an alternative Nabatean incense route in the Negev Highlands. Following his excavations in the Hellenistic period fortified structures in Moyat 'Awad (Cohen, 1993: 1137–1140) 'Ein Haruf ('En Rahel) (Cohen, 1993: 1143) and 'En Ziq (Cohen, 1991:43). Rudolph Cohen suggested that in the second century BCE there were two routes from Petra to Gaza crossing the Negev Highlands, one via Darb es-Sultan from 'En Rahel to 'En Ziq and Nahal Ha-Besor and the other, which until then was the only route to which scholars referred as leading from Petra to Gaza, from Moyat

'Awad via Maktesh Ramon and Oboda. Erickson-Gini (2006, 2021) suggested that in the Hellenistic period the incense route to Gaza passed only via Darb es-Sultan. Based also on her interpretation of Meshel and Cohen's excavation in Metsad Magora, where she noted a Judean-Hasmonean fort built on a former second-century BCE Nabatean caravanserai, she argued that this Nabatean incense route was blocked by the Hasmonean King Alexander Jannaeus. Only later, in the first century CE, did the main incense route shift to Makhtesh Ramon–Oboda and then the caravanserais of Moyat 'Awad and Sha'ar Ramon were erected. The route continued as mentioned above after 106 CE and then ceased to exist sometime following 222 CE (Fig. 9).

Ben David (2012) argued that the paved sections and milestones were not Nabataean but were rather erected as part of Roman military activity in the Negev. Erickson-Gini and Israel (2013, 29–30) suggested that the paved road and milestones were erected by the Roman army in the Severan and Diocletianic periods. They also noted that in the second half of the second century a new type of fort was constructed along the incense road in the Negev and suggested that "their construction may have taken place during the reign of Septimius Severus (193–211 CE). This Roman emperor who took the title Arabicus following his first war with Parthia (194–195 CE|) later traveled through Arabia on his way to Egypt (Ben David, 2012: 42). The option of dating the milestones to the Diocletianic period was based upon the date of the construction of the Roman army camp at Oboda (Erickson-Gini,

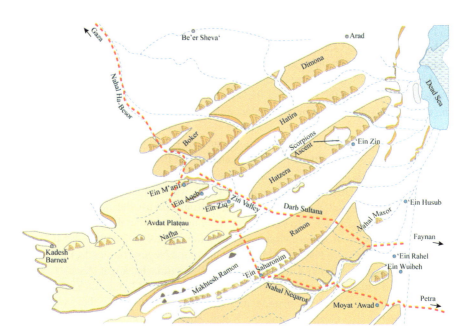

Fig. 9 The incense routes in the Negev Highlands in the Hellenistic and Roman periods. (Map prepared by Amir Eidelman, Lior Enmar and Vered Shatil with additions made by Dina Shalem)

2002, 2010: 17–19, 88–91) and the reoccupation of some of the forts along the route in the late third century.

In 2018 a new segment along the incense route between Oboda and Sha'ar Ramon was identified west of the route known until then. In this segment, seven new milestone stations were found. On two of the milestones, the inscriptions mention the Roman emperors Parthinax and Severus, and the *caput via* was Elusa (Ben David & Isaac, 2020; Shertzer, 2021).

12 The Negev Highlands Road on the Roman-Period Peutinger Map

Apart from the archaeological research regarding the incense route, many studies that deal with routes across the Negev Highlands in the Roman period refer to the Peutinger Map.

The Peutinger Table or Map is a road map of the Roman Empire that apparently represents the 3rd–fourth centuries CE (Talbert, 2010; Rathmann, 2016). As in most parts of the empire, the map presents only part of the Imperial Roman roads that were constructed in the Roman provinces of Judea/Palaestina and Arabia mainly in the 2nd–third centuries CE. In the Negev area only one road is marked in a general north–south direction: the road from Jerusalem to Ayla on the shore of the Red Sea (Fig. 10). The map marked the following stations and distances: Elusa, 71 miles; Oboda, 24 miles; Lysa, 47 miles; Gypsaria, 27 miles; Rasa, 16 miles; Ad-Dianam, 16 miles; and Ayla, 16 miles. In the northern part of the route, Elusa and Oboda are well identified and the distance between them is close to the actual distance. In the southern section, Ayla is of course identified, as Eilat, and most scholars suggest that Ad-Dianam is 'Ein Ghadiyan, modern Yotvata, although the accurate distance from Ayla is almost two times the distance marked on the map.

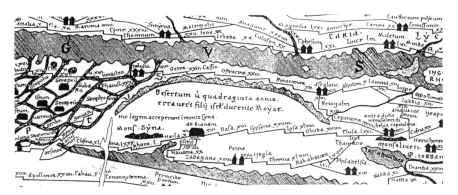

Fig. 10 The Roman road from Jerusalem to Ayla in the Peutinger map

The main research debate concerns the stations between Oboda and Ad-Dianam the stations of Lysa, Gypsaria and Rasa. These three stations are also recorded in the second-century Ptolmaeus geographic list of the cities of Arabia. In any case, this route connecting Oboda and Ayla must have crossed the Negev Highlands.

Following Robinson's (1841: 276–277) and Palmer's (1871: 347–348) identification of Lysa in Wadi Lusan southwest of Makhtesh Ramon most scholars of the Negev route in the Peutinger Map trace the road between Oboda and Ayla in the western Negev and along parts of Darb Ghaza (Thomsen, 1917: 85, Aharoni (1954), Schmitt, 1995: 232–233, Paprocki, 2019: 123–127). After Frank discovered the fortified sites along the Oboda–Makhtesh Ramon–Wadi Arabah route, Alt (1935: 53–58) suggested that they be understood as stations along the route drawn in the Peutinger Map between Oboda and Ayla. However, Rothenberg (1967: 167–171) and Meshel and Tsafrir (1975: 19–21) rejected his proposal on the basis of their understanding that the incense route between Petra and Gaza in the Negev Highlands ceased to exist after 106 CE, so the route could not have appeared on a 2nd–third century document. Cohen (2000: 64–65), who noted that the sites related to the Negev Highlands incense route[that?] continued in existence during the 2nd–third centuries CE, returned to Alt's proposal that the route in the Peutinger Map should be identified with the incense route from Oboda to Wadi Arabah and thence to Ayla.

In 2018 a new segment along the incense route between Oboda and Sha'ar Ramon was identified west of a route known till then (Shertzer, 2021). On this segment, seven new milestone stations were found. On two of the milestones, the inscriptions indicate that they were installed during the reign of the Roman emperors Parthinax and Severus, and the *caput via* was Elusa (Ben David & Isaac, 2020), thus emphasizing that this was the Roman road route marked on the Peutinger Map leading from Elusa to Oboda and from there to Ayla (Fig. 11). There is no logic in reaching the road that passed above Makhtesh Ramon and then heading westward toward Darb Ghaza. Furthermore, by now firm evidence of a Roman road and road related-structures dated to the 2nd–third centuries CE have been detected along the Negev Highlands incense route between Oboda and Wadi Arabah.

13 Summary

The Negev Highlands, unlike the coastal road, the Darb Ghaza or even the Wadi Arabah, is a difficult, unnatural trade corridor. Traversing it is bleak and uninviting and indeed, for long periods, it was off the beaten track of main south Levantine trade routes.

The copper and incense trade altered this situation, albeit not for all periods. If the destination of the mined copper was Be'er Sheva or ports of call in the north, there was no need to cross the Negev Highlands except on its most northeastern

The Negev Highlands -- A Corridor for the Copper and Incense Trade...

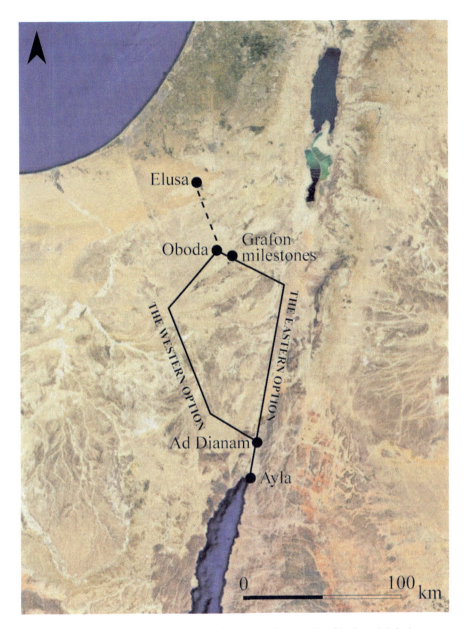

Fig. 11 The two options of the route of the Roman road connecting Oboda and Ayla (map prepared by Dina Shalem on Google Earth satellite map)

flank, the Scorpions' Ascent. However, if the destination was Egypt (in the EB IB and Iron Age) crossing the Negev Highlands was more tempting and even necessary.

During the approximately 1500 years of the incense trade, the Gaza Port was apparently a major terminus. Yet when the main stations in the Edomite territory were Tell el-Kheleifeh, Busseira and 'Ein Ḥusub, those who plied this route preferred to bypass the heart of the Negev Highlands by traveling either via the Darb Ghaza, coming from Tell el-Kheleifeh, or via the Scorpions' or Amiaz Ascents.

Only when Petra became the Nabatean hub and subsequently its capital, did the incense trade routes between Petra and Gaza cross the Negev Highlands directly.

References

Ackerfeld, D., Abadi-Reiss, Y., Yagel, O., Harlavan, Y., Abulafia, T., Yegorov, D., et al. (2020). Firing up the furnace: New insights on metallurgical practices in the Chalcolithic Southern Levant from a recently discovered copper-smelting workshop at Horvat Beter (Israel). *Journal of Archeological Science: Reports, 33*, 102578.

Aharoni, Y. (1954). The Roman road to Aila. *Israel Exploration Journal, 4*, 9–16.

Aharoni, Y. (1963a). *Eilath and the Negev roads in the biblical period*. In Y. Aviram (Ed.), *Elath: The 18th archaeological convention* (pp. 54–73). Israel exploration society. (Hebrew).

Aharoni, Y. (1963b). Tamar and the roads to Elath. *Israel Exploration Journal, 13*, 30–42.

Aharoni, Y. (1967). *The land of the bible a historical geography*. Burns & Oates.

Albright, W. F. (1960). *The archaeology of Palestine*. Penguin Books.

Alt, A. (1935). Aus der 'Araba II: Romische Kastellen und Strassen. *Zeitschrift des Deutschen Palastina-Vereins, 58*, 1–78.

Atkins, S., & Yekutieli, Y. (2022). Correlating Egyptian-Levantine connectivity in ceramic assemblage profiles: Between Tel 'Erani and Mizpe Sede Ḥafir. *Archaeological excavations and research studies in Southern Israel collected papers, 5*, 29–48.

Avner, U. (1984). Ancient cult sites in the Negev and Sinai deserts. *Tel Aviv, 11*(2), 115–131.

Avner, U. (2016). Ancient roads in the 'Arabah Valley' Negev. *Dead Sea and Arava Studies, 8*(1), 25–44. (Hebrew).

Bar-Yosef, D. (1999). Shells from three middle Bronze Age I sites in the Negev highlands. In R. Cohen (Ed.), *Ancient settlement of the Central Negev, Vol. I: The chalcolithic period, the early Bronze Age and the middle Bronze Age I* (IAA Reports No. 6) (pp. 322–326). Israel antiquities authority.

Ben David, C. (2010). Iron Age roads in Moab and Edom: The archaeological evidence. *Studies in the history and archaeology of Jordan, X*, 723–729.

Ben David, C. (2012). Nabataean or late Roman? Reconsidering the date of the paved sections and milestones along the Petra–Gaza road. In L. Nehme & L. Wadeson (Eds.), *The Nabataeans in focus: Current archaeological research at Petra* (pp. 17–25). Archaeopress.

Ben David, C., & Isaac, B. (2020). Six milestone stations and new inscriptions discovered in the Negev along the Petra-Gaza incense route. *Palestine Exploration Quarterly, 152*, 234–247.

Ben-Dor, E. S. (2017). Follow the Negebite-ware road. In O. Lipschits, Y. Gadot, & J. M. Adams (Eds.), *Rethinking Israel — Studies in the history and archaeology of ancient Israel in honor of Israel Finkelstein* (pp. 19–27). Eisenbrauns.

Ben-Dor, E. S., Yagel, O., Harlavan, Y., Seri, H., Lewinsky, J., et al. (2021). Pharaoh's copper: The provenance of copper in bronze artifacts from post-imperial Egypt at the end of the second millennium BCE. *Journal of Archaeological Science: Reports, 38*, 103025.

Ben-Yosef, E., Najjar, M., & Levy, T. E. (2014). Local Iron Age trade routes in Northern Edom. In T. E. Levy, M. Najjar, & E. Ben-Yosef (Eds.), *New insights into the Iron Age archaeology of Edom, Southern Jordan* (pp. 493–575). Cotsen Institute of Archaeology Press.

Ben-Yosef, E., Gidding, A., Tauxe, L., Davidovich, U., Najjar, M., & Levy, T. E. (2016). Early Bronze Age copper production systems in the northern Arabah Valley: New insights from archaeomagnetic study of slag deposits in Jordan and Israel. *Journal of Archaeological Science, 72*, 71–84.

Ben-Yosef, E., Beeri, R., & Davidovich, U. (2021). *Ancient copper exploitation in the Arabah Valley and the archaeology of the Negev highlands: The Bronze and Iron Age sites around Yeruham. Israel geological society field trip guide* (pp. 3–54). Israel Geological Society (Hebrew).

Bruins, H. J., Segal, I., & Van der Plicht, J. (2018). Bronze chisel at Horvat Haluqim (central Negev highlands) in a sequence of radiocarbon dated late bronze to iron I layers. In E. Ben-Yosef (Ed.), *Mining for Ancient Copper, essays in memory of Beno Rothenberg* (Tel Aviv University Monograph Series 37). Tel Aviv University Sonia and Marco Nadler Institute of Archaeology.

Clamer C., & Sass B. (1977). Chapter IX: Middle Bronze I. In E. Bar-Yosef & J. L. Philips (Eds.), *Prehistoric investigations in Gebel Maghara in Northern Sinai* (pp. 245–254) (Qedem 7). Jerusalem: The Hebrew University of Jerusalem Institute of Archaeology.

Cohen, R. (1982). New light on the date of the Petra-Gaza road. *Biblical Archaeologist, 45*, 240–247.

Cohen, R. (1991). The ancient roads from Petra to Gaza in light of new discoveries, the incense routes. In E. Orion & J. Eini (Eds.), *The incense routes* (pp. 28–77). Midreshet Sde Boker (Hebrew).

Cohen, R. (1993). Hellenistic, Roman and Byzantine sites in the Negev Hills. In *New encyclopedia of archaeological excavations in the Holy Land* (Vol. 3, pp. 1135–1145). Jerusalem.

Cohen, R. (1999). *Ancient settlement of the central Negev, the chalcolithic period, the early Bronze Age and middle Bronze Age I (IAA reports 6).* Israel Antiquities Authority.

Cohen, R. (2000). The ancient roads from Petra to Gaza in light of new discoveries, the incense routes. In E. Orion & A. Goren (Eds.), *The incense routes* (pp. 54–113). Midreshet Sde Boker (Hebrew).

Cohen, R., & Cohen-Amin, R. (2004). Ancient settlement of the Negev highlands. Volume II: The Iron Age and the Persian period (Israel Antiquities Authority Reports No. 20). Jerusalem.

Cohen-Sasson E. (2017). A renewed examination of the Egyptian mining operation in Timna Valley: The social aspects of the copper production organization during the new-kingdom. PhD. dissertation. Ben-Gurion University of the Negev, Beersheba.

Cohen-Sasson, E., Varoner, O., Friedman, E., & Herriott, C. (2021). Gorer tower and the biblical Edom road. *Palestine Exploration Fund Quarterly, 153*, 113–128.

Erickson-Gini, T. (2002). Nabataean or Roman? Reconsidering the date of the camp at Avdat in light of recent excavations. In N. P. Freeman, J. Bennett, Z. T. Fiema, & B. Hofmann (Eds.), *Limes XVIII. The proceedings of the XVIIIth international congress of Roman frontier studies held in Amman, Jordan (September 2000)* (BAR International Series 1082, I) (pp. 113–130). Archaeopress.

Erickson-Gini, T. (2006). 'Down to the sea' Nabataean colonization in the Negev highlands. In P. Bienkowski & K. Galor (Eds.), *Crossing the rift — Resources, routes, settlement patterns and interaction in the Wadi Arabah* (pp. 157–166). CBRL & Oxbow.

Erickson-Gini, T. (2014). Mizpe 'Ezuz, Survey (ESI 126). https://www.hadashot-esi.org.il/report_detail_eng.aspx?id=6466&mag_id=121

Erickson-Gini, T. (2021). The Hellenistic period incense route and the erection of the Hasmonaean fort in Magora. In C. B. David & D. Perry (Eds.), *The incense routes 2020* (pp. 151–158). n.p. (Hebrew).

Erickson-Gini, T., & Israel, Y. (2013). Excavating the Nabataean incense road. *Journal of Eastern Mediterranean Archaeology and Heritage Studies, 1*(1), 24–53.

Erickson-Gini, T., Vardi, J., & Darby, E. (In press). Rosh Ma'ale Ẓadok, Excavations at the Head of an Early Ascent on the Edge of Makhtesh Ramon.

Finkelstein, I. (1988). Arabian trade and socio-political conditions in the Negev in twelfth-eleventh centuries B.C.E. *Journal of the Near Eastern Studies, 47*(4), 241–252.

Finkelstein, I., & Piasetzky, E. (2008). The date of Kuntillet'Ajrud: The 14C perspective. *Tel Aviv, 35*(2), 175–185.

Finkelstein, I., Adams, M. J., Dunseth, Z. C., & Shahack-Gross, R. (2018). The archaeology and history of the Negev and neighboring areas in the third millennium BCE: a new paradigm. *Tel Aviv, 45*(1), 63–88.

Förster, F., & Riemer, H. (Eds.). (2013). *Desert road archaeology in ancient Egypt and beyond.* Heinrich-Barth-Institut.

Förster, F., Riemer, H., & Mahir, M. (2013). Donkeys to El-Fasher or how the present informs the past. In F. Förster & H. Riemer (Eds.), *Desert road archaeology in ancient Egypt and beyond* (Africa Praehistorica 27) (pp. 193–218). Heinrich-Barth-Institut.

Frank, F. (1934). Aus der Araba. *Zeitschrift des Deutschen Palastina-Vereins, 57*, 191–280.

Glueck, N. (1935). *Explorations in Eastern Palestine, II* (Annual of the American Schools of Oriental Research 15). American Schools of Oriental Research.

Glueck, N. (1953). Explorations in Western Palestine. *Bulletin of the American Schools of Oriental Research, 131*, 6–15.

Glueck, N. (1956). The fourth season of exploration in the Negeb. *Bulletin of the American Schools of Oriental Research, 142*, 17–25.

Glueck, N. (1959). *Rivers in the desert: A history of the Negev*. Farrar, Straus & Cudahy.

Glueck, N. (1960). Archaeological exploration in the Negev in 1959. *Bulletin of the American Schools of Oriental Research, 159*, 3–14.

Golani, A. (2014). Ashqelon during the EB I period — A centre for copper processing and trade. In A. Mączyńska (Ed.), *The Nile delta as a centre of cultural interactions between upper Egypt and the southern Levant in the 4th Millennium BC* (Proceedings of the Conference Held in the Poznań Archaeological Museum, Poznań, Poland 21–22 June 2012) (pp. 119–137). Studies in African Archaeology 13.

Haiman, M. (2006). The archaeological surveys in the Arabah reconsidered: Data and metadata. In P. Bienkowski & K. Galor (Eds.), *Crossing the rift — Resources, routes, settlement patterns and interaction in the Wadi Arabah* (pp. 45–50). CBRL & Oxbow.

Hendrickx, S., Förster, F., & Eyckerman, M. (2013). The pharaonic pottery of the Abu Ballas Trail: Filling stations' along a desert highway in southwestern Egypt. In F. Förster & H. Riemer (Eds.), *Desert road archaeology in ancient Egypt and beyond* (Africa Praehistorica 27) (pp. 339–379). Heinrich-Barth-Institut.

Israel, Y., & Nahlieli, D. (1991). Campsites, religion and worship sites along desert routes. In E. Orion & Y. Eini (Eds.), *The incense routes* (pp. 80–87). Midreshet Sde Boker.

Jasmin, M. (2006). The emergence and first development of the Arabian trade across the Wadi Arabah. In P. Bienkowski & K. Galor (Eds.), *Crossing the rift — Resources, routes, settlement patterns and interaction in the Wadi Arabah* (pp. 143–150). CBRL & Oxbow.

Kirk, G. E. (1938). Archaeological exploration in the Southern Desert. *Palestine Exploration Quarterly, 70*, 211–235.

Knab, K., Rosen, S. A., Hermon, S., Vardi, J., Horwitz, L. K., & Goren, Y. (2018). A middle Timnian nomadic encampment on the Faynan-Beersheba road: Excavations and survey at Nahal Tsafit (late 5th/early 4th millennia B.C.E.). *Bulletin of the American Schools of Oriental Research, 380*, 27–60.

Kolb, A. (Ed.). (2019). *Roman roads new evidence — New perspectives*. De Gruyter.

Kopp, H. (2013). Desert travel and transport in ancient Egypt, an overview based on epigraphic, pictorial and archaeological evidence. In F. Förster & H. Riemer (Eds.), *Desert road archaeology in ancient Egypt and beyond* (Africa Praehistorica 27) (pp. 107–132). Heinrich-Barth-Institut.

Levy, T. E., Adams, R. B., Hauptmann, A., Prange, M., Schmitt-Strecker, S., & Najjar, M. (2002). Early Bronze Age metallurgy: A newly discovered copper manufactory in Southern Jordan. *Antiquity, 76*(292), 425–437.

Lindner, M., Hubner, U., & Hubl, J. (2000). Nabataen and Roman presence between Petra and Wadi Arabah survey exepedition 1997/98: Umm Ratam. *Annual of the Department of Antiquities of Jordan, 44*, 535–567.

Lubel, I. (2014). *The Ein Hava–Abu Treifa Valley, ancient route in the Negev*. Environmental High School in Sdeh Boker (Hebrew).

Martin, M. A. S., & Finkelstein, I. (2013). Iron IIA pottery from the Negev highlands: Petrographic investigation and historical implications. *Tel Aviv, 40*, 6–45.

Meshel, Z. (1979). A history of the roads in the Negev. In A. Shmueli & Y. Grados (Eds.), *The land of the Negev, man and desert* (pp. 297–307). Ministry of Defense.

Meshel, Z. (2000). *Sinai excavations and studies* (BAR International Series 876). Archaeopress.

Meshel, Z. (2009). *The Persian period road system in the Negev* (Eretz-Israel 29) (pp. 298–309). Israel exploration society (Hebrew with English abstract).

Meshel, Z., & Tsafrir, Y. (1974). The Nabataean road from 'Avdat to Sha'ar-Ramon. Part I. the survey of the road. *Palestine Exploration Quarterly, 106*, 103–118.

Meshel, Z., & Tsafrir, Y. (1975). The Nabataean road from 'Avdat to Sha'ar-Ramon (concluded). Part II. The features of the road. *Palestine Exploration Quarterly, 107*, 3–21.

n.a. (1977). *Survey, Har zin – Hazeva region* (Hadashot Arjheologiyot 63–64: 69–70). Israel Antiquities Authority.

Negev, A. (1966). The date of the Petra-Gaza road. *Palestine Exploration Quarterly, 88*, 89–98.

Palmer, E. H. (1871). The desert of the exodus: Journeys on foot in the wilderness of the forty years' wanderings. *Deighton: Bell, 3, 21*, 107.

Paprocki, M. (2019). *Roads in the deserts of Roman Egypt*. Oxbow.

Pasternak, M. D., & Erikson-Gini, T. (2022). The secret in the desert: Preliminary conclusions from the excavation of a unique funerary compound in the Negev highlands. *Archaeological excavations and research studies in southern Israel collected papers, 5*, 7–26. (Hebrew).

Power, R. (2004). Deconstructing, deciphering and dating the donkey in old kingdom Wall paintings and relief. *Bulletin of the Australian Center for Egyptology, 15*, 131–151.

Poznań Archaeo Haiman, M. (1996). Early Bronze Age IV settlement pattern of the Negev and Sinai Desert: View from small marginal temporary sites. *Bulletin of the American Schools of Oriental Research, 303*, 1–32.

Prust, A., & Hausleiter, A. (2020). Camel exploitation in the oasis of Taymā'— Caravan or consumption? In D. Agut-Labrodere & B. Redon (Eds.), *Les vaisseaux du desert et des steppes, Les camélidés dans l'Antiquité* (Camelus dromedarius et Camelus bactrianus) (pp. 95–121). MOM editions.

Rathmann, M. (2016). *Tabula Peutingeriana: Die einzige Weltkarte aus der Anike*. Philipp von Zabern.

Riemer, H. (2013). Lessons in landscape learning: The dawn of long-distance travel and navigation in Egypt's Western Desert from prehistoric to old kingdom times. In I., F. Förster & H. Riemer (Eds.), *Desert road archaeology in ancient Egypt and beyond* (Africa Praehistorica 27) (pp. 77–106). Heinrich-Barth-Institut.

Robinson, E. (1841). Biblical researches in Palestine. In *Mount Sinai and Arabia Petraea*. Murray.

Rothenberg, B. (1967). *Negev, archaeology in the Negev and the Arabah*. Ramat Gan (Hebrew).

Sadeh, A. (In preparation). *"Navigation lines" along ancient roads in the Negev, analysis through applications of GIS*. University of Haifa.

Schmitt, G. (1995). *Siedlungen Palastinas in griechisch-romischer Zeit*. Reichert.

Schwimer, L., & Yekutieli, Y. (2021). Intermediate Bronze Age crescent-headed figures in the Negev highlands. *Bulletin of the American Society of Oriental Research, 385*, 219–243. https://doi.org/10.1086/712920

Shertzer, Z. (2021). The discovery of the new section and milestones in the Grafon area. In C. B. David & D. Perry (Eds.), *The incense routes 2020* (pp. 207–220). n.p. (Hebrew).

Shertzer, Z., Avni, Y., & Ginat, H. (2021). The importance of water sources along the incense route. In C. B. David & D. Perry (Eds.), *The incense routes 2020* (pp. 63–80). n.p. (Hebrew).

Shugar, A. N. (2018). Extractive metallurgy in the chalcolithic southern Levant: Assessment of copper ores from Abu Matar. In E. Ben-Yosef (Ed.), *Mining for ancient copper: Essays in memory of Beno Rothenberg* (pp. 276–296). The Institute of Archaeology of Tel Aviv University.

Somaglino, C., & Tallet, P. (2013). A road to the Arabian peninsula in the reign of Ramesses III. In F. Förster & H. Riemer (Eds.), *Desert road archaeology in ancient Egypt and beyond* (Africa Praehistorica 27) (pp. 511–520). Heinrich-Barth-Institut.

Sperveslage, G., & Eichmann, R. (2012). Egyptian cultural impact on North-West Arabia in the second and first millennium BC. *Proceedings of the Seminar for Arabian Studies, 42*, 371–383.

Talbert, R. (2010). *Rome's world: The Peutinger map reconsidered.* Cambridge University.

Thomsen, P. (1917). Die romischen Meilensteine der Provinzen Syria, Arabia, und Palastina. *Zeitchrift des Deutschen Palastina-Vereins, 40*, 1–103.

Woolley C.E. & Lawrence T. E. (1914–1915). The wilderness of zin. : Palestine Exploration Fund.

Yekutieli, Y. (2006). Is somebody watching you? Ancient surveillance systems in the southern Judean Desert. *Journal of Mediterranean Archaeology, 19*(1), 65–89.

Yekutieli, Y., Shalev, S., & Shilstien, S. (2005). En Yahav — A copper smelting site in the Arava. *Bulletin of the American Schools of Oriental Research, 340*, 35–55.

Zarins, J., & Hauser, R. (2014). *The domestication of equidae in third-millennium BCE Mesopotamia* (Vol. 24). Cornell University Studies in Assyriology and Sumerology.

Zohar, M., & Erickson-Gini, T. (2019). The 'incense road' from Petra to Gaza: An analysis using GIS and cost functions. *International Journal of Geographical Information Science., 34*, 292–310. https://doi.org/10.1080/13658816.2019.1669795

Fragments of an Archaeology of Late Roman Religion at Phaino (Khirbat Faynān, Southern Jordan)

Ian W. N. Jones ⓘ

Abstract This chapter presents the discovery of a remarkable sherd from a Late Roman period application-decorated bowl unearthed in the 2012 excavations at Khirbat Faynān, carried out by the Edom Lowlands Regional Archaeology Project, co-directed by Thomas E. Levy and Mohammad Najjar. Prior to the identification of this sherd in the Khirbat Faynān assemblage, the known distribution of this type was limited to a ca. 35 km radius around Jerusalem, its production center. This find extends distribution of the type an additional 100 km southeast. The chapter opens with an overview of the type and the context of the find. It then considers several explanations for the unexpected presence of the sherd at the site. While the evidence remains patchy and inconclusive, the sherd may hint at the presence of metallurgical laborers from the Jerusalem region at Khirbat Faynān, as well as possibly providing a glimpse into worship of Dionysus or Qos during the Late Roman period in Area 16 of the excavations.

Keywords Phaino · Khirbat Faynan · Late Roman · Dionysus · Qos

1 Introduction

Over the course of his long and distinguished career, Tom Levy has investigated a wide range of social, economic, and political transformations in the archaeology of the southern Levant. While his work on the role of metallurgy in socio-political change is best known, Tom has also used archaeology to consider questions related to religion (e.g., Levy, 2006) and identity (e.g., Levy, 2008), and he has advocated for a "pragmatic" approach to Levantine archaeology, integrating archaeological and historical evidence with anthropological theory and up-to-date field and

---

I. W. N. Jones (✉)
Department of Anthropology, University of California, San Diego, La Jolla, CA, USA
e-mail: ijones@ucsd.edu

© The Author(s), under exclusive license to Springer Nature Switzerland AG 2023
E. Ben-Yosef, I. W. N. Jones (eds.), *"And in Length of Days Understanding" (Job 12:12): Essays on Archaeology in the Eastern Mediterranean and Beyond in Honor of Thomas E. Levy*, Interdisciplinary Contributions to Archaeology,
https://doi.org/10.1007/978-3-031-27330-8_53

laboratory methods (Levy, 2010). This chapter addresses similar questions of religion and identity in Late Roman Faynān, using the admittedly scanty evidence from Khirbat Faynān. While certainly not based on the sort of "robust dataset" Tom envisions as part of his "New Pragmatism" (Levy, 2010: 11), the analysis presented here nonetheless draws on a range of archaeological, historical, and theoretical evidence in an attempt to explain a surprising ceramic sherd found at Khirbat Faynān.

2 The Site

Khirbat Faynān (Fig. 1), located in the eastern portion of Wādī Faynān, in southern Jordan (Fig. 2), is the Roman town and *metallum* of Phaino and likely the station of Punon mentioned in Numbers 33:42–43. Archaeological investigation has been conducted at the site for more than a century, but the most intensive research was conducted at the site in the early twenty-first century, beginning with detailed survey work by the Council for British Research in the Levant's (CBRL) Wādī Faynān Landscape Survey (WFLS) (Barker et al., 2007) and continuing with two seasons of excavation by the Edom Lowlands Regional Archaeology Project (ELRAP), directed by Tom Levy and Mohammad Najjar, in 2011 and 2012. While one of the primary goals of the latter excavations was to investigate the Iron Age settlement at the site (Levy et al., 2012: 423), the project was cut short after only two seasons, and although residual Iron Age material was found, no stratified Iron Age contexts were excavated. Instead, the excavations primarily revealed evidence of settlement during the Early Bronze Age and the Nabataean through Islamic periods. The majority of this material came from the third–sixth century CE (i.e., the Late Roman–Byzantine periods) occupation of the site, as perhaps should be expected given that the site's appearance in historical sources is essentially limited to the same period.

The ELRAP excavations focused primarily on a part of the mound's western slope designated Area 16 (Fig. 3). Two additional areas—a Middle Islamic period slag mound in Area 15 adjacent to a Late Byzantine structure tentatively identified as a monastery in Area 8, and a Late Byzantine–Early Islamic cistern complex on the site's northern slope in Area 18—were opened in 2012, but Area 16 was the only area excavated during both seasons. During the 2011 season, the team opened a 5 × 40 m step trench (half of squares 16.54, 16.55, 16.56, and 16.57) intended to establish a stratigraphic profile for the site (Fig. 4). Unfortunately, the area was not

Fig. 1 Panoramic view of Khirbat Faynān, looking north over Wādī Faynān. (Photo: Craig Smitheram/UC San Diego Levantine Archaeology Laboratory)

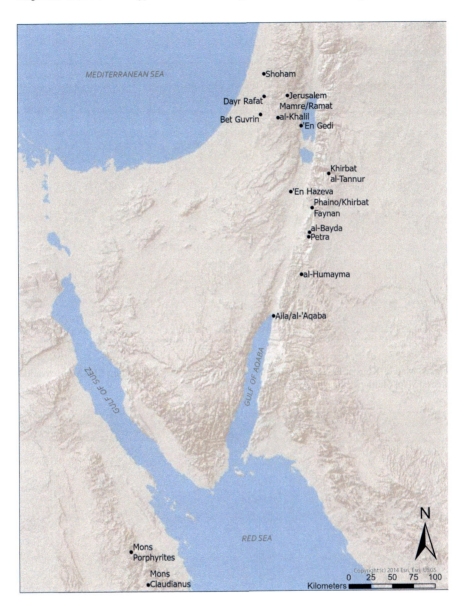

Fig. 2 Map of the southern Levant and eastern Egypt, showing the location of sites mentioned in the text. (Basemap: © Esri)

well-stratified and was horizontally heterogeneous, essentially divided into four terraces. The lowest of these, Terrace 1/Sq. 54, consisted primarily of mixed material washed down from the higher parts of the site, and no architecture was identified. The next, Terrace 2/Sq. 55, contained a structure built some time during the Roman period and destroyed in the late sixth century, with some evidence of reoccupation

Khirbat Faynan, Jordan
2011
Grid System: 100 meter

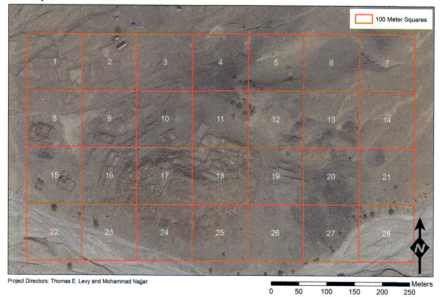

Fig. 3 Map of Khirbat Faynān showing the 100 m grid squares designating ELRAP excavation areas. (Map: Matthew Vincent/UCSD LAL)

Fig. 4 Aerial photograph of 2011 Khirbat Faynān Area 16 excavations in progress prior to the excavation of the Early Bronze Age structures in Terrace 4, with terraces labeled. (Photo: Craig Smitheram/UCSD LAL)

during the Early Islamic period. The highest, Terrace 4/Sq. 57, was perhaps the most surprising, containing an Early Bronze Age structure just below topsoil in its eastern portion and a Roman period fill reinforcing the terrace wall, Wall 1049, in its western portion. The most relevant to the present chapter, however, is Terrace 3, which contained Sq. 56 in the 2011 season and was expanded into Squares 27 and 37 during the 2012 season. Here excavations revealed a probable domestic complex dating to the second–fourth century CE, which was destroyed in the mid-fourth century, probably by the earthquake of 363, and reoccupied in the Early Byzantine period. The phasing and the nature of the complex were most clear from the 2011 excavations, while the extension in 2012 was excavated primarily in a pathway or courtyard between two structures and was cut short midway through the season for reasons beyond the excavators' control (Fig. 5). Nonetheless, the material from both seasons provides insight into the occupation of the site during the peak of copper production in the Roman and Early Byzantine periods.

Final analysis and publication of the material from these excavation seasons are underway, but an observation can be made here about the general nature of the assemblage. The majority of the Nabataean–Byzantine ceramics from Khirbat Faynān belong to what Gerber (2016: 130) calls the southern Jordanian "ceramic *koine*," and Petraean forms and fabrics are particularly common. This is, of course, unsurprising given the site's proximity to Petra, but it is nonetheless worth noting that, despite the presence of a small number of atypical and in some cases extraordinary imports, the assemblage as a whole is fairly typical for a site of this period in southern Jordan. In terms of understanding the economy of the site as a whole, the general character of the assemblage must be kept in mind, but, as Stern (2014) has demonstrated for the Late Islamic period, there are also insights to be gained through the analysis of rare, statistically insignificant imports. With this is mind, I will now zoom in and focus on the conclusions that can be drawn from a unique Late Roman sherd excavated in Area 16 at Khirbat Faynān during the 2012 excavations.

3   The Sherd and Its Context

The sherd under discussion here, R. 31048 (Fig. 6b), was found during the 2012 excavations in Area 16, Locus 104. Locus 104 was assigned to Stratum T3-1, dating to the Islamic period. The latest material in the locus were sherds of African Red Slip Ware Hayes Form 107, dating to the early seventh century CE (Hayes: 170–171), Late Roman D Hayes Form 9 (probably Form 9b), dating to the late sixth–seventh century CE (Hayes, 1972: 379–382), and Magness Cooking Pot Form 4C, dating to the sixth–early eighth century CE (Magness, 1993: 219–220), but residual sherds of the Early Bronze Age, Iron Age, and Nabataean–Byzantine period were also common. Like most Stratum T3-1 contexts, L. 104 is not far below topsoil and is a mixed fill without associated architecture. Its contents, therefore, likely include material washed down from higher parts of the site, and caution should be exercised in its interpretation.

At a general level, R. 31048 belongs to Magness's Jerusalem Rouletted Bowls Form 1 (Magness, 1993: 185–187). In her revised doctoral dissertation, Magness (1993: 185) dated this form to the late third/early fourth–fifth century CE. In her analysis of the ceramics from the Jerusalem Convention Center/Binyanei HaUma

Fig. 5 Aerial photograph of the 2012 excavations in Area 16 in progress. (Photo and map: Matthew D. Howland/UCSD LAL)

excavations, however, she revised the dating of the emergence of the form to the turn of the third century at the latest, concluding that the type emerged as a local interpretation of African Red Slip Ware Hayes (1972: 32–35) Form 8A, dating to the late first–mid-second century CE; although rare in most of the southern Levant, local versions of ARS Form 8A were produced by Roman legionary potters at the

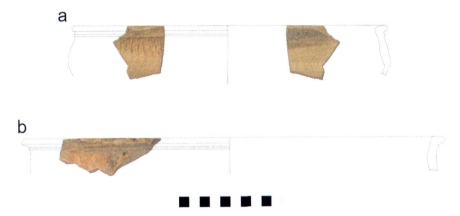

Fig. 6 Illustrations of (**a**) Jerusalem Rouletted Bowl Form 1 (R. 8720) and (**b**) application-decorated bowl (R. 31048) found in Khirbat Faynān Area 16. Note traces of applied roundel on left side of photo in (**b**)

Binyanei HaUma site (Magness, 2005: 72, 105). More recent work, for example Rapuano's (2013: 63; Spivak, 2013) analysis of the ceramics from the site of al-Khirba in Shoham, ca. 35 km northwest of Jerusalem, has pushed the emergence of the form back to the late first or early second century CE, although it is most common in the third–fifth century. As the name used here suggests, this type was produced in or around Jerusalem of clay from the Moza formation (Cohen-Weinberger et al., 2020: 55), and it is most commonly found in this region. It is rare in the south, and in her discussion of its distribution, the southernmost site at which Magness (1993: 153–156) identifies its presence is 'En Gedi, although it has since also been found in mid-fourth century contexts at 'En Hazeva, ca. 30 km northwest of Khirbat Faynān (Erickson-Gini, 2010: 130, 134, Fig. 4.6, 293, Fig. 4). It is rare at Khirbat Faynān, but two additional examples (one of which is illustrated in Fig. 6a) were found during the 2011 excavations in Area 16 Stratum T3-2b (pre-363, second–fourth century CE).

The presence of Jerusalem rouletted bowls at Khirbat Faynān is interesting due to their rarity in the south, but their presence is not unprecedented in the region, as the discussion above indicates. While the examples from Stratum T3-2b are rather typical of the type, however, R. 31048 is not. Instead, R. 31048 belongs to a related group, the application-decorated bowls, which lack the typical rouletted design and are instead decorated with a row or several rows of applied clay disks bearing human, vegetal, or geometric motifs. Magness (2005: 107) notes that "their profiles resemble the Jerusalem rouletted bowls," they date to essentially the same period (the second or early third–fifth century CE), and they were probably inspired by local versions of western terra sigillata forms produced at the Binyanei HaUma site in much the same way the Jerusalem rouletted bowls were inspired by locally produced ARS Form 8A vessels. Taxel (2007: 179), reviewing the evidence for the type, notes that the appearance of the type in the second or early third century is easier to date than its disappearance, as examples dated to the Late Byzantine period generally come from poorly dated or mixed contexts. R. 31048, unfortunately, does not help to resolve this problem, as L. 104 is certainly a mixed context, but the bulk of the evidence does point to a similar date to the Form 1 Jerusalem rouletted bowls.

More interesting for the present discussion is the distribution of the type. In reviewing the published evidence for these vessels, Taxel (2007: 180) notes that, while examples of Form 1 rouletted bowls have been found relatively far from Jerusalem, the distribution of the application-decorated bowls is much more restricted. At the time of his writing, Taxel (2007: 180) identified ca. 30 published sherds of this type, with the most distant examples from their production center found at Bet Guvrin, Dayr Rafāt, and Rāmat al-Khalīl/Mamre, all within 35 km of Jerusalem. This makes Khirbat Faynān, ca. 130 km southeast of Jerusalem, the most distant site from Jerusalem at which a sherd of an application-decorated bowl has been found, and R. 31048 the only example of the type currently known outside of southern Syria Palaestina/Palaestina Prima.

4 A Religious Significance?

Taxel (2007: 182–183), observing that the highest concentration of this type was found at Rāmat al-Khalīl/Mamre, suggested that, given the site's religious significance (notably as the place where Abraham and Sarah receive the prediction of Isaac's birth in Genesis 18), these vessels might have been connected to religious practice, probably as kraters, or vessels for mixing wine with water. Specifically, noting the presence of a small altar with an inscription containing the name of the Edomite god, Qos,[1] and a fragment of a statue of Dionysus, he suggests that these vessels may have been associated with practices associated with these gods, although he is careful to point out that because little is known about the religious practices associated with Qos, it is not possible to associate these vessels directly with Idumaean religious practice, and indeed, their distribution seems to indicate associations with both pagan and Christian religious practices (Taxel, 2007: 183). Taxel (2007: 183) ultimately concludes that the limited distribution of application-decorated bowls is due primarily to ceramic regionalism but points out that the small number of these bowls found within their area of distribution does suggest a specialized function, probably related to religious practices involving the mixing of wine.

These suggestions deserve further consideration in light of the presence of an application-decorated bowl at Khirbat Faynān, well outside of the previously known distribution of the type. Although Qos was an important Idumaean god, worship of Qos is also attested in Nabataea, perhaps most notably in the Qos stele from Khirbat al-Tannūr, probably dating to the first century BCE, where Qos is identified as the

---

[1]Qos is often thought of as being the Edomite "national god" during the late Iron Age, but Bienkowski (2013: 791) argues that the evidence is insufficient to identify Qos as the primary Edomite god, rather than simply one of several gods worshipped by the Edomites.

god of Ḥūrawā or Ḥawarawā, potentially identifiable with Ḥawara, the ancient name of al-Ḥumayma (Healey, 2013: 51–54). Wenning (2007: 27) points out that it is uncertain whether this indicates continuity of Edomite worship of Qos among the Nabataeans or Idumaean influence rather than strict continuity, and Tebes (2020: 342), following an earlier argument by Roche, notes that these two possibilities are not mutually exclusive, and Nabataean kings may have drawn on Edomite traditions as part of a "political strategy" aimed at Idumaeans living in Nabataea. Erickson-Gini (2015: 309, 314) suggests that the name of the head of the Nabataean pantheon, Dushara ("the one from Shara"), "probably reflects continuity in the worship of Qos," and further notes that Dushara was identified with Dionysus, although, as Patrich (2005: 97–98) notes, the key source for this identification is rather late, dating to the late fifth–sixth century CE. Worship of Dionysus is evident in the Petra region, for example in the Dionysian hall identified at al-Bayḍā' (Bikai et al., 2008), however, Wenning (2016: 199–200) argues that this likely demonstrates worship of both Dionysus and Dushara, rather than equation of the two.

5 Religion at Late Roman Khirbat Faynān

Three and a half decades ago, Knauf and Lenzen (1987: 83) lamented that the historical evidence for copper production in the Faynān region was limited to accounts of the third–fourth century, and came primarily from Christian authors—notably Eusebius of Caesarea and his translator, St. Jerome—concerned with martyrs who had been sentenced to *damnatio ad metallum*, or condemnation to the mines (see also Friedman, 2008: 283–284; Najjar & Levy, 2011). Considering this, it is perhaps surprising how little we know about religious practices at the site during this period.

The best-documented period for religious practice at the site is the later Byzantine period. As Schick (2001: 583) notes, Khirbat Faynān has five churches (Fig. 7), including the structure in Area 8 commonly identified as a monastery, the construction or reconstruction of which can be dated to 587–588 CE on the basis of a foundation inscription mentioning a Bishop Theodore that was surface collected in the building (Alt, 1935: 65; Sartre, 1993: 146). We can say with some certainty that Phaino was a bishopric during the fifth and sixth centuries, as bishops of Phaino are attested at the Council of Ephesus in 431, the Second Council of Ephesus in 449, and synods in Jerusalem in 518 and 536 (Jobling, 1996: 71). Considering the dating of the application-decorated bowls, it is possible that R. 31048 arrived at Phaino after the town had attained importance as a Christian religious site, and perhaps a pilgrimage center, due to its association with Christians who had been martyred in the mines in the late third and early fourth centuries. Considering that the only sherds of Jerusalem Rouletted Bowl Form 1 found at the site came from contexts predating the earthquake of 363, however, it is perhaps more likely that R. 31048

Fig. 7 Satellite image of Khirbat Faynān with churches and other features mentioned in the text labeled. (Basemap: © Esri, Maxar, Earthstar Geographics, USDA FSA, USGS, Aerogrid, IGN, IGP, and the GIS User Community)

should be associated with this earlier period, although certainly ceramics continued to be imported to the site in the fifth century and later.

Evidence for religion at the site is much more difficult to identify during the second–fourth century. In reviewing the archaeological evidence for Nabataean "cultic/mortuary" sites outside of Petra, Tebes (2020: 335, 337) identified a "big cluster" in the Faynān region, but he does not elaborate on the practices that would have taken place at these sites, beyond noting revisitation and reuse of the early Neolithic cemetery at Wādī Faynān 16. The WFLS identified little specific evidence that could be associated with religious practice, although Mattingly et al. (2007b: 294) caution that the nearby site of Tall al-Miraḍ, which they suggest served a military function potentially related to surveillance, might also have been a Nabataean religious site. At Khirbat Faynān itself, no structures can necessarily be related to religious practices during this period, and Kind et al. (2005: 169) list temples among the public buildings and amenities the site does not seem to have. It must be noted, however, that the summit of the site, with its large central building and surrounding structures, has not been excavated and is still poorly understood (Mattingly et al., 2007a: 315). Ward (2016) has argued that, in southern Jordan, the earthquake of 363 marks the end of "public paganism" through the destruction of many temples that were never rebuilt, particularly in Petra, and this process may be relevant to the chronology of the Christianization of Phaino, as well. Phaino was certainly affected by the earthquake of 363, which probably caused the Stratum T3-2b destruction in Area 16, but it is not clear, as the discussion above indicates, that "public paganism" was ever part of the religious life of the town. Comparison to the Roman imperial quarries at Mons Porphyrites and Mons Claudianus in Egypt (e.g., Kaper, 1998: 146; Peacock & Maxfield, 2001: 11–12; van der Veen, 1998: 115), however, would suggest that temples might also be present at Phaino, although the sites are certainly not identical, and this comparison should be taken with caution given both regional differences and differences in the nature of the three *metalla*.

Beyond the ambiguous archaeological evidence, the writings of Eusebius of Caesarea provide glimpses into Christian religious activity at the site during this period. According to *Martyrs of Palestine* 13.1–4, in 310 CE, the seventh year of the Great Persecution, a Christian community was practicing their religion and had built "houses for church assemblies" at Phaino, but after Roman authorities discovered this, the members of the community were sent to perform forced labor in a number of other places and the "four who seemed most like their leaders" were killed (Eusebius of Caesarea, 1927: 395–397; see also Friedman, 2008: 38). It is interesting to consider whether these houses might be archaeologically identifiable, as in the case of the possible early fourth century church at Aila/al-'Aqaba (Parker, 1998), but in either case, the account provides little concrete insight into the nature of religious practices at the site in the Late Roman period. As the discussion above indicates, our understanding of religion at Late Roman Phaino is fragmentary, and as such, even small insights have the potential to be important.

6 Interpreting the Application-Decorated Bowl at Phaino

Several possible explanations, not all of which are necessarily mutually exclusive, can be suggested to explain the presence of an application-decorated bowl at Phaino. On one level, this explanation must concern distribution, as it is clear that Phaino is well outside of the usual area of distribution for these vessels. If these vessels did serve a religious function, it is possible that a resident of the site traveled to Jerusalem to procure the vessel to which R. 31048 belonged. As Taxel (2007: 183) suggests, however, the distribution of application-decorated bowls seems to be related to ceramic regionalism, and their absence outside of the Jerusalem region is likely not due to the lack of demand for kraters, but rather the fact that other types filled this role. As such, it is more likely that the vessel arrived at the site as part of a personal ceramic inventory. Whether the person who brought this vessel to Phaino was Idumaean is impossible to say, but certainly it is likely that they had previously been a resident of the Jerusalem region.

This raises the question of the workforce and population at Phaino. While Eusebius of Caesarea describes a workforce of Christians sent from various regions of the Roman Empire to perform forced labor at Phaino, it is important to remember that this account covers a very limited span of time—primarily the first decade of the fourth century CE—and was likely "[f]ar from … typical of the normal operation of the mining region" (Mattingly et al., 2007a: 333). As Mattingly et al. (2007a: 334) argue, comparison to the better-documented case of Mons Claudianus would suggest that free labor made up a substantial component of the workforce and the events of the early fourth century may paint a quite atypical picture of labor at Phaino. Indeed, at Mons Claudianus forced labor is not mentioned at all in the large corpus of ostraca, and while this is an argument from absence of evidence, Bülow-Jacobsen (2009: 2) argues, "Seeing how everything else was counted and accounted for, I find it well nigh inconceivable that we should not have found accounts of prisoners, had there been any."

Free laborers, of course, may also have migrated to Phaino from elsewhere—and this may especially be the case for the skilled metallurgical laborers the site would have required—and it is possible R. 31048 may have arrived at the site with such a laborer. Strontium stable isotope analysis of 31 individuals buried in the Faynān South Cemetery/WF3 indicated that the vast majority had strontium isotope ratios typical of the region, with only one individual, buried in Grave 102, having values outside of the local range (Perry et al., 2009, 2011). The dating of the South Cemetery, however, is not entirely secure. While the excavators suggest a date in the Late Roman–Early Byzantine period, they also note that most of the evidence places the use of the cemetery in the late fifth–sixth century (Findlater et al., 1998: 82). Indeed, all 10 published tombstones from the South Cemetery date to the fifth–sixth century, and three of these date to the last decade of the sixth century (Meimaris & Kritikakou-Nikolaropoulou, 2008: 147–158). As such, the South Cemetery may be more typical of the site's population after copper production had scaled down or ended, and the isotopic data should not be taken as secure evidence that the majority of the workforce during the second–fourth century was local. R. 31048 can, perhaps, be taken as limited evidence that some of the workforce during this period was not.

A second question concerns the use and original context of the application-decorated bowl. As discussed above, a religious function seems likely, although as Taxel (2007: 179, 183) points out, they are perhaps associated with both pagan and Christian ceremonies, and the latest secure example comes from a Christian monastery. Given that R. 31048 comes from a relatively late mixed context, the possibility should be considered that it is relatively late and associated with one of Phaino's five churches. This is unlikely, however, as none of the churches is located in a part of the site where erosion into Area 16 is possible (see Fig. 7), although certainly the sherd could have been intentionally moved for disposal after the vessel broke.

As discussed above, only two sherds of Jerusalem Rouletted Bowls Form 1 were found in Area 16 Stratum T3-2b during the 2011 excavation season. If the hypothesis above is correct and R. 31048 arrived at Phaino as part of a personal ceramic inventory, it is possible that these bowls arrived with the same person, and it is worth considering other relevant evidence from Terrace 3 here. While a bread oven associated with a Stratum T3-2b floor in Terrace 3 Room 3 indicates domestic use of this structure, other finds hint at possible religious functions. A bronze bell (R. 8426, Fig. 8), although lacking an attachment for a clapper, was also found in Stratum

Fig. 8 A bronze bell, R. 8426, found in Area 16 Stratum T3-2b. (Photo: Aaron Gidding/ UCSD LAL)

Fig. 9 Architectural fragment or ceramic sherd with applied grape decoration, R. 8948, found in Area 16 Stratum T3-2a. (Photo: Aaron Gidding/ UCSD LAL)

T3-2b. Bells and bell-shaped objects have been found associated with Nabataean tombs in and around Petra, although they seem to have served a variety of functions, with some used as bells and others perhaps as small cups; nonetheless, their association with tombs seems to indicate a possible religious function (Perry, 2016: 395–396). More broadly, bells served a variety of functions and, intriguingly, were "used in connection with the Dionysian cult" (Waner, 2014: 282), as, perhaps, were the application-decorated bowls. In light of this, it is also interesting to consider an architectural fragment or ceramic sherd found in Stratum T3-2a, the post-363 phase, decorated with an applied motif probably representing grapes (R. 8948, Fig. 9), which are also associated with Dionysus; given the small size of this fragment, it is possibly residual from Stratum T3-2b.

7 Conclusion

As the title of this chapter suggests, our understanding of Late Roman religion at Phaino, and indeed, of Late Roman Phaino more generally, is quite fragmentary. While the fragments presented here certainly do not add up to a clear picture, they do point in several interesting directions. If nothing else, R. 31048 is currently the only example of an application-decorated bowl found more than 35 km from Jerusalem, and, as such, presents a challenge to current understandings of the type. While the vessel could have traveled from Jerusalem to Phaino in a number of ways, the most likely explanation for its presence, given the otherwise very limited distribution of the type, seems to be that it traveled as part of a personal ceramic inventory, possibly with a laborer from the Jerusalem region. Although the evidence from Area 16 Terrace 3 is quite limited, the presence of R. 31048, in combination with a handful of other artifacts, may suggest worship of Dionysus (or, perhaps, Qos) at Phaino. While much work remains to be done, Tom Levy's excavations at Khirbat Faynān have provided an important window into a relatively obscure period at this unique site.

Acknowledgments I should first thank Tom Levy for inspiring this chapter and, of course, for his mentoring and encouragement throughout my career. I thank Tom and Mohammad Najjar, co-directors of the Edom Lowlands Regional Archaeology Project, for allowing me to discuss the material from the Khirbat Faynān excavations here. I also acknowledge the Department of Antiquities of Jordan, particularly current Director General Fadi Balawi, and Ziad al-Saaʿd and Faris al-Hmoud, Directors General during the fieldwork reported here, for their support of the project. I also thank the ELRAP field staff, particularly Aaron Gidding, Area 16 supervisor in 2011 and 2012, Kathleen Bennallack, Area 16 assistant supervisor in 2011, and Ashley Richter, Area 16 assistant supervisor in 2012, as well as the student volunteers and workers from Faynān and al-Qurayqira, who made these excavations possible.

References

Alt, A. (1935). Aus der ʿAraba. II. Römische Kastelle und Straßen. *Zeitschrift des Deutschen Palästina-Vereins, 58*(1/2), 1–78.

Barker, G., Gilberston, D., & Mattingly, D. (2007). *Archaeology and desertification: The Wadi Faynan Landscape Survey, Southern Jordan*. Oxbow.

Bienkowski, P. (2013). Edom during the Iron Age II period. In A. E. Killebrew & M. Steiner (Eds.), *The Oxford handbook of the archaeology of the Levant* (pp. 782–794). Oxford University Press. https://doi.org/10.1093/oxfordhb/9780199212972.013.052

Bikai, P. M., Kanellopoulos, C., & Saunders, S. L. (2008). Beidha in Jordan: A Dionysian hall in a Nabataean landscape. *American Journal of Archaeology, 112*(3), 465–507. https://doi.org/10.3764/aja.112.3.465

Bülow-Jacobsen, A. (2009). *Mons Claudianus ostraca graeca et latina IV: The Quarry-Texts O. Claud. 632–896*. Institute français d'archéologie orientale.

Cohen-Weinberger, A., Levi, D., & Beʾeri, R. (2020). On the raw materials in the ceramic workshops of Jerusalem, before and after 70 C.E. *Bulletin of the American Schools of Oriental Research, 383*, 33–59. https://doi.org/10.1086/707611

Erickson-Gini, T. (2010). *Nabataean settlement and self-organized economy in the Central Negev: Crisis and renewal*. Archaeopress.

Erickson-Gini, T. (2015). Piecing together the religion of the Nabataeans. *Religion Compass, 9*(10), 309–326. https://doi.org/10.1111/rec3.12148

Eusebius of Caesarea. (1927). *The ecclesiastical history and the Martyrs of Palestine*. (H. J. Lawlor & J. E. L. Oulton, Trans.) (Vol. 1). Society for Promoting Christian Knowledge.

Findlater, G., El-Najjar, M., Al-Shiyab, A.-H., O'Hea, M., & Easthaugh, E. (1998). The Wadi Faynan Project: The South Cemetery excavation, Jordan 1996: A preliminary report. *Levant, 30*(1), 69–83.

Friedman, H. A. (2008). *Industry and empire: Administration of the Roman and Byzantine Faynan*. PhD thesis, University of Leicester.

Gerber, Y. (2016). The Jabal Hārūn ceramics: Typology and chronology. In Z. T. Fiema, J. Frösén, & M. Holappa (Eds.), *Petra—The Mountain of Aaron: The Finnish archaeological project in Jordan, volume II: The Nabataean Sanctuary and the Byzantine Monastery* (pp. 128–201). Societas Scientiarum Fennica.

Hayes, J. W. (1972). *Late Roman pottery*. British School at Rome.

Healey, J. F. (2013). The Nabataean inscriptions. In J. S. McKenzie, J. A. Greene, A. T. Reyes, C. S. Alexander, D. G. Barrett, B. Gilmour, et al. (Eds.), *The Nabataean Temple at Khirbet et-Tannur, Jordan, volume 2—Cultic offerings, vessels, and other specialist reports: Final report on Nelson Glueck's 1937 excavation* (pp. 47–56). American Schools of Oriental Research.

Jobling, W. J. (1996). New evidence for the history of indigenous Aramaic Christianity in southern Jordan. In L. Olson (Ed.), *Religious change, conversion and culture* (pp. 62–73). Sydney Association for Studies in Society and Culture.

Kaper, O. E. (1998). Temple building in the Egyptian deserts during the Roman period. In O. E. Kaper (Ed.), *Life on the Fringe: Living in the Southern Egyptian deserts during the Roman and Early-Byzantine periods: Proceedings of a Colloquium held on the occasion of the 25th anniversary of the Netherlands Institute of Archaeology and Arabic Studies in Cairo, 9–12 December 1996* (pp. 139–158). Research School CNWS, School of Asian, African, and Amerindian Studies.

Kind, H. D., Gilles, K. J., Hauptmann, A., & Weisgerber, G. (2005). Coins from Faynan, Jordan. *Levant, 37*, 169–195.

Knauf, E. A., & Lenzen, C. J. (1987). Edomite copper industry. In A. Hadidi (Ed.), *Studies in the history and archaeology of Jordan III* (pp. 83–88). Department of Antiquities of Jordan.

Levy, T. E. (2006). *Anthropology, archaeology and cult: The Sanctuary at Gilat, Israel*. Equinox.

Levy, T. E. (2008). "You shall make for yourself no molten gods": Some thoughts on Archaeology and Edomite Ethnic Identity. In S. Dolansky (Ed.), *Sacred history, sacred literature: Essays on ancient Israel, the Bible, and Religion in Honor of R.E. Friedman on his sixtieth birthday* (pp. 239–255). Eisenbrauns.

Levy, T. E. (2010). The new pragmatism: Integrating anthropological, digital, and historical Biblical archaeologies. In T. E. Levy (Ed.), *Historical Biblical archaeology and the future: The new pragmatism* (pp. 3–42). Equinox.

Levy, T. E., Najjar, M., Gidding, A. D., Jones, I. W. N., Knabb, K. A., Bennallack, K., et al. (2012). The 2011 Edom Lowlands Regional Archaeology Project (ELRAP): Excavations and surveys in the Faynān Copper Ore District, Jordan. *Annual of the Department of Antiquities of Jordan, 56*, 423–445.

Magness, J. (1993). *Jerusalem ceramic chronology: Circa 200–800 CE*. JSOT Press.

Magness, J. (2005). The Roman legionary pottery. In B. Arubas & H. Goldfus (Eds.), *Excavations on the site of the Jerusalem International Convention Center (Binyanei Ha'Uma): A settlement of the Late First to Second Temple Period, The Tenth Legion's Kilnworks, and a Byzantine Monastic Complex: The pottery and other small finds* (pp. 69–191). Journal of Roman Archaeology.

Mattingly, D., Newson, P., Creighton, O., Tomber, R., Grattan, J., Hunt, C., et al. (2007a). A landscape of imperial power: Roman and Byzantine *Phaino*. In G. Barker, D. Gilbertson, &

D. Mattingly (Eds.), *Archaeology and desertification: The Wadi Faynan Landscape Survey, southern Jordan* (pp. 305–348). Oxbow.

Mattingly, D., Newson, P., Grattan, J., Tomber, R., Barker, G., Gilbertson, D., & Hunt, C. (2007b). The making of early states: The Iron Age and Nabataean periods. In G. Barker, D. Gilberston, & D. Mattingly (Eds.), *Archaeology and desertification: The Wadi Faynan Landscape Survey, southern Jordan* (pp. 271–303). Oxbow.

Meimaris, Y. E., & Kritikakou-Nikolaropoulou, K. I. (2008). *Inscriptions from Palaestina Tertia, vol. Ib: The Greek Inscriptions from Ghor es-Safi (Byzantine Zoora)* (Supplement), *Khirbet Qazone and Feinan*. National Hellenic Research Foundation, Research Centre for Greek and Roman Antiquity.

Najjar, M., & Levy, T. E. (2011). Condemned to the mines: Copper production & Christian persecution. *Biblical Archaeology Review, 37*(6), 30–39, 71.

Parker, S. T. (1998). An early church, perhaps the oldest in the world, found at Aqaba. *Near Eastern Archaeology, 61*(4), 254.

Patrich, J. (2005). Was Dionysos, the Wine God, venerated by the Nabataeans? *ARAM Periodical, 17*, 95–113. https://doi.org/10.2143/ARAM.17.0.583323

Peacock, D., & Maxfield, V. (2001). The central complex. In V. Maxfield & D. Peacock (Eds.), *The Roman imperial quarries: Survey and excavation at Mons Porphyrites, 1994–1998, volume 1: Topography and quarries* (pp. 11–56). Egypt Exploration Society.

Perry, M. A. (2016). New light on Nabataean mortuary rituals in Petra. In M. Jamhawi (Ed.), *Studies in the history and archaeology of Jordan XII: Transparent borders* (pp. 385–398). Department of Antiquities of Jordan.

Perry, M. A., Coleman, D. S., Dettman, D. L., & Al-Shiyab, A. H. (2009). An isotopic perspective on the transport of Byzantine mining camp laborers into southwestern Jordan. *American Journal of Physical Anthropology, 140*(3), 429–441. https://doi.org/10.1002/ajpa.21085

Perry, M. A., Coleman, D. S., Dettman, D. L., Grattan, J. P., & Al-Shiyab, A. H. (2011). Condemned to *metallum*? The origin and role of 4th–6th century A.D. *Phaeno* mining camp residents using multiple chemical techniques. *Journal of Archaeological Science, 38*(3), 558–569. https://doi.org/10.1016/j.jas.2010.10.010

Rapuano, Y. (2013). The Pottery of Judea between the First and Second Jewish Revolts. *STRATA: Bulletin of the Anglo-Israel Archaeological Society, 31*, 57–102.

Sartre, M. (1993). *Inscriptions de la Jordanie, Tome IV: Pétra et la Nabatène Méridionale du wadi al-Hasa au golfe de 'Aqaba*. Librairie Orientaliste Paul Geuthner.

Schick, R. (2001). Christianity in southern Jordan in the Byzantine and Early Islamic periods. In K. 'Amr (Ed.), *Studies in the history and archaeology of Jordan VII: Jordan by the Millenia* (pp. 581–584). Department of Antiquities of Jordan.

Spivak, P. (2013). Shoham (Hill 10). *Hadashot Arkheologiyot—Excavations and Surveys in Israel, 125*. https://www.hadashot-esi.org.il/report_detail_eng.aspx?id=2263&mag_id=120

Stern, E. J. (2014). Imported pottery from the Late Mamluk and Ottoman periods at the al-Waṭa Quarter, Safed (Ẓefat). *'Atiqot, 78*, 143–151.

Taxel, I. (2007). Application-decorated bowls: A cultural characterisation of the Pagan and Christian population of Jerusalem in the Late Roman and Byzantine periods. *Israel Exploration Journal, 57*(2), 170–186.

Tebes, J. M. (2020). Beyond Petra: Nabataean cultic and mortuary practices and the cultural heritage of the Negev and Edom. *Jordan Journal for History and Archaeology, 14*(4), 333–347.

van der Veen, M. (1998). A life of luxury in the desert? The food and fodder supply to Mons Claudianus. *Journal of Roman Archaeology, 11*, 101–116.

Waner, M. (2014). Aspects of music culture in the Land of Israel during the Hellenistic, Roman and Byzantine periods: Sepphoris as a case study. In J. Goodnick Westenholz, Y. Maurey, & E. Seroussi (Eds.), *Music in antiquity: The near East and the Mediterranean* (pp. 273–297). De Gruyter. https://doi.org/10.1515/9783110340297.273

Ward, W. D. (2016). The 363 earthquake and the end of public paganism in the Southern Transjordan. *Journal of Late Antiquity, 9*(1), 132–170.

Wenning, R. (2007). The Nabataeans in history. In K. D. Politis (Ed.), *The world of the Nabataeans: Volume 2 of the international conference The World of the Herods and the Nabataeans held at the British Museum, 17–19 April 2001* (pp. 25–44). Franz Steiner Verlag.

Wenning, R. (2016). The many faces of Dushara—A critical review of the evidence. In M. Jamhawi (Ed.), *Studies in the history and archaeology of Jordan XII: Transparent borders* (pp. 189–209). Department of Antiquities of Jordan.

Part IV
Archaeometallurgy Beyond Faynan

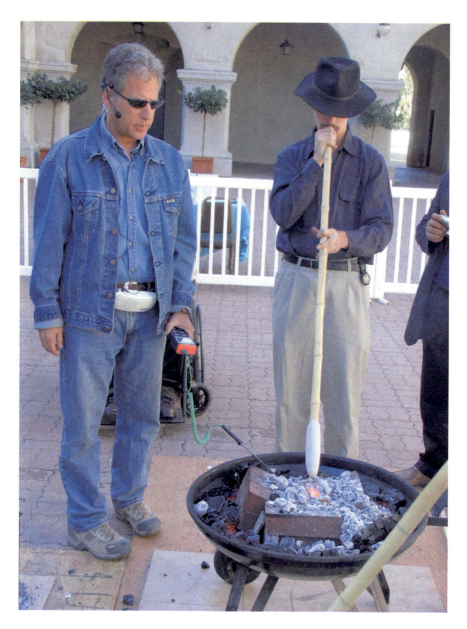

Tom Levy conducting copper smelting experiments using Chalcolithic technologies. Museum of Man, San Diego, 2007. (Photo courtesy of Erez Ben-Yosef)

Lead in Human Bones and Teeth Reflecting Historical Changes in Lead Production: Rome and the Levant

Yigal Erel

Abstract This paper marks the culmination of two research journeys, one that began 35 years ago while I was studying with Clair C. Patterson at Caltech, and the other prompted by my friend Tom Levy, that started 16 years ago. It follows a paper I co-authored recently, demonstrating that the rates of worldwide lead production since the discovery of cupellation, some 5000 years ago (first outlined by Patterson and co-workers) are chronicled in the Pb/Ca of humans buried in Rome. In the current work, the Roman Pb/Ca record is compared with that found in individuals from the Levant (initially determined with Tom). The Pb/Ca records from both locations are then compared with Co/Ca, Cu/Ca, Ba/Ca and Zn/Ca. It emerges that, whereas Ba/Ca and Zn/Ca are not affected by metal mining, production and use, and reflect homeostatic processes and the addition of Ba to many samples after burial, Pb/Ca and to a lesser extent Co/Ca do offer evidence of these metal-related activities. Cu/Ca values display an equivocal record. The use of a Ba/Ca threshold to detect the post-mortem addition of Ba and Pb allows me to construct a clearer record of Pb/Ca in both locations. The central position of Rome, especially during the Roman period, is revealed in a pronounced difference in Pb/Ca records, where the Roman values are two to three orders of magnitude higher than the Levantine values. This highlights the close association between lead production rates and human pollution, and leads me to reiterate the warning that the expected escalation in the worldwide production of lead and other metals may well jeopardize human health in the near future.

Keywords Lead · Pollution · Teeth · Petrous bones

Y. Erel (✉)
The Hebrew University of Jerusalem, Jerusalem, Israel
e-mail: yigal.erel@mail.huji.ac.il

© The Author(s), under exclusive license to Springer Nature Switzerland AG 2023
E. Ben-Yosef, I. W. N. Jones (eds.), *"And in Length of Days Understanding" (Job 12:12): Essays on Archaeology in the Eastern Mediterranean and Beyond in Honor of Thomas E. Levy*, Interdisciplinary Contributions to Archaeology, https://doi.org/10.1007/978-3-031-27330-8_54

1 Introduction

Changes in the production and emission of lead and other metals over millennia feature in many scholastic discussions (Settle & Patterson, 1980; Hong et al., 1994, 1996; Renberg et al., 1994; Nriagu, 1996; Rosman et al., 1997; Shotyk et al., 1998; Martínez Cortizas et al., 2002; Longman et al., 2018; McConnell et al., 2018). It has been demonstrated that anthropogenic lead production and emissions led to higher concentrations of lead in polar ice and sediments of lakes and peat bogs (Murozumi et al., 1969; Hong et al., 1994; Renberg et al., 1994; Rosman et al., 1997; Shotyk et al., 1998; Alfonso et al., 2001; Martínez Cortizas et al., 2002; Mighall et al., 2002; Borsos et al., 2003; Le-Roux et al., 2003, 2004; Durali-Müller, 2005; Delile et al., 2017; Longman et al., 2018; McConnell et al., 2018). Lead production, as first noted by Settle and Patterson (1980), began approximately 5000 years ago, coinciding with the invention of cupellation (Wagner et al., 1979; Hess et al., 1998; Pernicka et al., 1998; Momenzadeh & Nezafati, 2000; Nokandeh & Nezafati, 2003). It then developed slowly through the Bronze and Iron Ages. The introduction of coins at the end of the Iron Age saw its acceleration, reaching a peak in production (and emission and use) during the Roman period. Following Rome's decline, lead production slumped, a trend that continued through the early and mid-Middle Ages. Around the eleventh century CE, it picked up again, driven by silver mining in Germany, followed by the New World exploitation. From the onset of the Industrial Revolution, lead production surged, reaching unprecedented levels in the early twentieth century with the introduction of alkyl-lead additives to gasoline. This brief summary shows that for millennia lead production was largely a by-product of silver mining, and only in the wake of the Industrial Revolution did lead find its own spotlight, primarily motivated by a host of new lead-based applications (Patterson, 1972; Nriagu, 1996).

The production, emission and use of lead over time manifested in the concentrations of this metal in human bones and teeth (Ericson et al., 1979; Nriagu, 1983; Patterson et al., 1987, 1991; Aufderheide et al., 1988; Manea-Krichten et al., 1991; Oakberg et al., 2000; Pyatt et al., 2002, 2005; Sponheimer & Lee-Thorp, 2006; Grattan et al., 2007; Beherec et al., 2016; Kamenov et al., 2018; Longman et al., 2018; Eshel et al., 2020; Erel et al., 2021). Lead concentrations and ratios of lead to calcium (the major element in tooth and bone apatite – Pb/Ca) have been used as proxies to assess the extent of lead pollution, as well as informing on lead production and use (Ericson et al., 1979; Patterson et al., 1987, 1991; Aufderheide et al., 1988; Manea-Krichten et al., 1991; Oakberg et al., 2000; Pyatt et al., 2002, 2005; Sponheimer & Lee-Thorp, 2006; Grattan et al., 2007; Beherec et al., 2016; Kamenov et al., 2018; Eshel et al., 2020; Erel et al., 2021).

It was further demonstrated that measured concentrations of lead (and other metals) in bones and teeth could be affected by post-mortem diagenetic processes and that the resulting additions differently impact various types of bones and teeth

(Ericson et al., 1979; Schoeninger et al., 1989; Patterson et al., 1991; Kamenov et al., 2018; Harkness & Darrah, 2019; Erel et al., 2021). Following Patterson and his co-workers, we found that comparing Pb/Ca with barium-to-calcium (Ba/Ca) ratios is a reliable method to detect the diagenetic addition of lead to bones and teeth (Ericson et al., 1979; Patterson et al., 1987, 1991; Beherec et al., 2016; Eshel et al., 2020; Erel et al., 2021). The Patterson team established that Ba and Pb have similar tendencies to be incorporated into bone or tooth apatite and argued that anthropogenic Ba emissions are insignificant relative to natural, rock-derived background Ba fluxes (Ericson et al., 1979; Patterson et al., 1987, 1991). This implies that elevated Ba concentrations exceeding the in-vivo threshold of Ba/Ca in tooth enamel (5E-6 mole/mole; Ericson et al., 1979; Patterson et al., 1987, 1991; Eshel et al., 2020) indicate that at least some Ba, and probably also Pb, were absorbed by the tooth after burial. Lately, we have applied the same methodology to lead and barium in petrous bones, demonstrating a tenfold higher Ba/Ca threshold than in tooth enamel (Erel et al., 2021).

Lately, it was confirmed that lead concentrations in petrous bones of people buried in and around Rome reflect the historical developments in lead production outlined above (Erel et al., 2021). In the current study, I combine the Rome record (Erel et al., 2021) with records from the Levant (Beherec et al., 2016; Eshel et al., 2020). I use these published values, which reveal Pb/Ca, Ba/Ca, Zn/Ca, Cu/Ca, Co/Ca in tooth enamel and petrous bones, and add to them unpublished data of the same elemental ratios in tooth enamel from the Levant. I then compare the data obtained from 132 individuals buried in Rome (127) and Sardinia (5) with 235 samples from the southern Levant. The comparison reveals a disparity in pollution, as recorded by lead and cobalt in a major urban center (Rome) versus rural sites in the Levant.

2 Materials and Methods

The 64 tooth samples analyzed in this study and their burial sites and elemental concentrations are provided in Table 1. Tooth preparation closely followed the methodology of Patterson and co-workers and Eshel et al. (2020). Briefly, it involved mechanical enamel separation from dentin followed by several steps of enamel pre-cleaning with various reagents, and then dissolution using distilled concentrated HNO_3 (Ericson et al., 1979; Manea-Krichten et al., 1991; Patterson et al., 1991; Eshel et al., 2020). After sample dissolution, the concentrations of trace metals (Pb, Zn, Cu, and Co) and diagenetic-control barium (Ba) were measured by ICP-MS (Agilent 7500cx), as detailed in Eshel et al. (2020). Calcium was measured with ICP-OES (Analytic Jena PlasmaQuant PQ9000 Elite). The precision and accuracy of the ICP-MS and ICP-OES were ±5% for most samples.

Table 1 Samples' locations, age and Ba/Ca, Pb/Ca, Co/Ca, Cu/Ca and Zn/Ca values

Site	Period – archaeological context	BP age	Ba/Ca	Pb/Ca	Co/Ca	Cu/Ca	Zn/Ca
			mole/mole				
Shikmim	Chalcolithic	−6000	7.9E-04	1.1E-06	2.0E-06	1.2E-05	1.1E-04
		−6000	1.9E-04	6.2E-07	1.2E-06	1.1E-05	1.5E-04
		−6000	2.5E-04	1.2E-06	1.7E-06	2.6E-05	1.1E-04
		−6000	1.1E-04	2.5E-06	2.7E-06	1.2E-05	8.9E-05
Pekiin		−6000	7.0E-06	1.9E-08	3.4E-08	1.9E-07	1.3E-04
		−6000	1.1E-05	3.1E-08	4.7E-08	3.2E-07	1.4E-04
		−6000	4.1E-06	3.9E-08	4.6E-08	8.6E-08	1.2E-04
		−6000	2.2E-05	3.6E-08	4.2E-08	2.1E-07	1.9E-04
		−6000	3.4E-04		4.6E-08	5.6E-07	1.5E-04
		−6000	2.0E-05	3.1E-08	3.6E-08	8.4E-08	1.5E-04
		−6000	1.1E-05	4.1E-07	6.0E-08	7.0E-08	1.0E-04
		−6000	2.5E-05	5.2E-08	4.6E-08	2.8E-07	1.4E-04
		−6000	3.5E-06	8.4E-08	4.2E-08	1.4E-07	1.9E-04
		−6000	5.4E-05	1.1E-07	4.1E-08	7.3E-07	1.4E-04
		−6000	7.8E-05	6.9E-08	3.7E-08	5.9E-07	1.1E-04
Wadi Fidan 1, 4	Neolithic	−10,000	5.8E-06	9.2E-07	5.7E-08	9.5E-08	1.2E-04
	Iron Age	−3000				1.6E-06	5.8E-05
		−3000	3.5E-07	9.9E-08	3.3E-08	1.8E-06	6.2E-05
		−3000	2.8E-06	2.2E-07	3.7E-08	1.0E-05	1.8E-04
		−3000	3.6E-06	5.2E-07	4.5E-08	8.4E-06	1.2E-04
		−3000	4.8E-06	4.8E-07	4.7E-08	1.9E-05	1.1E-04
		−3000		4.6E-08	8.0E-08	3.9E-07	1.1E-04
Megiddo	Middle Bronze Age/ Late Bronze Age	−3500	2.7E-06	1.7E-07	2.6E-07	8.6E-07	1.4E-04
		−3500	4.7E-06	3.2E-08	6.1E-08	3.8E-08	1.7E-04
		−3500	6.1E-06	3.2E-08	2.0E-07	3.6E-07	1.7E-04
		−3500	7.3E-06	2.6E-08	5.5E-08	5.1E-08	1.7E-04
		−3500	4.4E-06	3.3E-08	6.9E-08	1.6E-07	1.5E-04
		−3500	5.8E-06	1.5E-08	6.8E-08		1.5E-04
		−3500	2.9E-06	4.4E-09	4.7E-08	5.6E-07	1.5E-04
		−3500	7.4E-06	1.8E-08	1.7E-07	4.1E-07	9.9E-05
		−3500	2.0E-06	2.5E-08	5.8E-08	3.6E-08	1.1E-04
	Middle Bronze Age	−4000	8.2E-06	5.6E-08	1.3E-07	1.3E-07	1.1E-04
	Middle Bronze Age/ Late Bronze Age	−3500	6.9E-06	9.8E-08	1.0E-07	2.3E-06	1.4E-04
		−3500	4.1E-06	1.4E-07	1.6E-07	2.0E-07	1.2E-04
Timna	Iron Age	−3000	8.6E-07	3.3E-07	1.1E-07	4.3E-07	1.0E-04

(continued)

Table 1 (continued)

Site	Period – archaeological context	BP age	Ba/Ca mole/mole	Pb/Ca	Co/Ca	Cu/Ca	Zn/Ca
Wallage – Jerusalem	Roman	−2000	3.4E-06	1.4E-07			
		−2000	2.9E-06	2.5E-06			1.4E-04
		−2000	1.6E-07	1.0E-06			
		−2000	2.2E-06	4.7E-06			2.3E-04
		−2000	4.6E-06	2.7E-07		2.3E-07	5.3E-05
		−2000	1.2E-06	7.6E-07			
		−2000	2.7E-07	2.1E-07			
		−2000	2.2E-06	3.3E-07			7.7E-05
		−2000	5.9E-07	2.4E-07			1.3E-05
Ein Gedi		−2000	2.1E-06	4.5E-07		3.0E-07	1.2E-04
		−2000	1.4E-06	4.8E-07			1.2E-04
Jerusalem		−2000	2.8E-06	1.4E-07	5.6E-08	3.1E-07	1.3E-04
		−2000	2.7E-06	1.8E-07	7.1E-08		1.7E-04
		−2000	3.0E-06	3.5E-07	7.2E-08		1.8E-04
		−2000	1.2E-06	1.2E-07			2.0E-04
		−2000	5.5E-06	1.1E-06	6.8E-08		1.4E-04
		−2000	6.7E-06	3.8E-07	6.6E-08		1.4E-04
		−2000	3.2E-06	1.8E-06	3.5E-08		1.4E-04
		−2000	4.5E-06	2.4E-07	7.0E-08		1.4E-04
		−2000	8.0E-06	4.1E-07	8.4E-08	2.0E-07	1.4E-04
		−2000	2.2E-06	9.7E-07	7.9E-08		1.5E-04
Lahav	Islamic	−1000	4.0E-06	3.7E-06	6.3E-08	1.8E-07	2.1E-04
		−1000	6.7E-06	4.7E-07	6.0E-08	1.6E-07	1.8E-04
		−1000	1.7E-06	1.6E-07	9.3E-08	2.6E-07	2.3E-04
		−1000	6.1E-06	6.4E-07		2.8E-06	7.7E-04
		−1000	1.3E-06	9.9E-07	7.9E-08	1.5E-07	1.6E-04
		−1000	1.8E-06	2.4E-06	7.4E-08	2.1E-07	2.0E-04
		−1000	6.5E-06	7.0E-08	4.9E-08	4.6E-08	1.9E-04
		−1000	3.4E-06	9.3E-07	3.1E-08	1.2E-07	1.7E-04

3 Results and Discussion

The elemental ratios of Pb, Ba, Zn, Cu and Co with Ca in 132 petrous bone samples and 235 enamel tooth samples are plotted as a function of time in Fig. 1. The petrous bones were measured in people buried in Rome while the tooth enamel samples were measured in people buried in the Levant. As the main goal of this study is to compare the extent of metal uptake between these regions, one must first compare the difference in metal uptake by petrous bone versus tooth enamel of the same individuals. This task was undertaken by Erel et al. (2021) and the results of the six studied elements are presented in Table 2 and Fig. 1. Three of the studied elements (Pb/Ca, Zn/Ca, Co/Ca) yield ratios with similar values in petrous bones and tooth

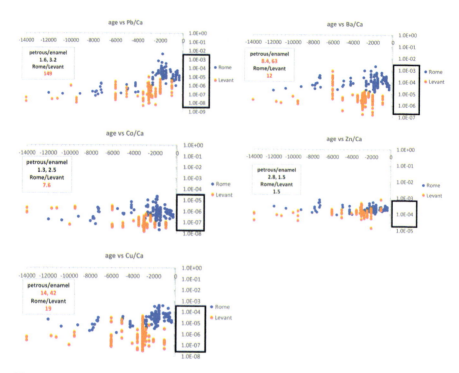

Fig. 1 Lead/Ca, Co/CA, Cu/Ca, Ba/Ca, and Zn/Ca (mole/mole) in petrous bones of individuals from Rome and Sardinia and in tooth enamel of individuals from the Levant ranging in age from approximately 12,000 BCE (14,000 BP) to circa 1650 CE

enamel (less than a threefold difference), while Ba/Ca and Cu/Ca have approximately an order of magnitude higher values in petrous bones compared with tooth enamel (Table 2).

Two of the studied metals (Ba and Zn) are expected to be regulated by homeostatic processes and possibly by a diagenetic addition, but should not be affected by metal production (Ericson et al., 1979; Patterson et al., 1987, 1991; Harkness & Darrah, 2019). Indeed, neither ratio displays time-dependent changes, but whereas Ba/Ca has a wide range of values, Zn/Ca does not (Fig. 1). Also, the Roman average Ba/Ca is approximately 10 times higher than the Levant average, quite like the difference between Ba/Ca values in petrous versus tooth enamel (Fig. 1). On the other hand, Zn/Ca values of Roman and Levant samples are similar (Fig. 1). Furthermore, the average value of Zn (85 ppm) is close to the range of Zn concentrations in modern human bones and teeth, whereas that of Ba/Ca is substantially higher than modern values (Fig. 1; Kamenov et al., 2018; Harkness & Darrah, 2019). This suggests that while Zn remained relatively intact in the buried bones and teeth, substantial amounts of Ba were absorbed by many bones and teeth after burial. The behavior of Ba will be further elaborated when lead is discussed.

Table 2 Elemental ratios of petrous bones (multiple analyses) and tooth enamel of two individuals

Individual	Type	Sub-type	Molar ratios				
			Pb/Ca	Ba/Ca	Cu/Ca	Zn/Ca	Co/Ca
Ind #1	Enamel	?	2.1E-07	3.3E-06	1.08E-06	1.71E-04	3.44E-07
	Petrous	Right petrous	1.8E-07	2.7E-05	1.23E-05	4.14E-04	3.85E-07
			6.1E-07	2.4E-05	1.55E-05	5.18E-04	5.06E-07
			2.3E-07	3.3E-05	1.76E-05	5.04E-04	4.15E-07
		Average	3.4E-07	2.8E-05	1.5E-05	4.8E-04	4.4E-07
		Stdev	2.4E-07	4.6E-06	2.7E-06	5.6E-05	6.3E-08
		RSD (%)	70	16	18	12	14
	Petrous/enamel		**1.6**	**8.4**	**14**	**2.8**	**1.3**
Ind #2	Enamel	2nd MLL	1.2E-07	1.0E-05	1.5E-06	1.91E-04	5.38E-07
	Petrous	Right petrous	3.5E-07	5.4E-04	6.78E-05	2.67E-04	1.3E-06
			3.2E-07	5.0E-04	7.68E-05	2.61E-04	1.22E-06
			4.0E-07	6.3E-04	5.08E-05	2.56E-04	1.17E-06
			5.9E-07	9.5E-04	8.41E-05	3.73E-04	1.61E-06
			2.6E-07	6.2E-04	3.55E-05	2.41E-04	1.53E-06
		Average	3.8E-07	6.5E-04	6.3E-05	2.8E-04	1.4E-06
		Stdev	1.3E-07	1.8E-04	2.0E-05	5.3E-05	2.0E-07
		RSD (%)	33	27	31	19	14
	Petrous/enamel		**3.2**	**63**	**42**	**1.5**	**2.5**

Three of the studied metals (Cu, Co and Pb) are expected to be affected by anthropogenic additions caused by mining, production and use (Settle & Patterson, 1980; Yaffe et al., 1983; Filippelli et al., 2005; Petit et al., 2015). None of them displays a pronounced increase in a metal/Ca ratio with time in the Levant samples (Pb/Ca has one jump in values at about ~6000 BP, that, as will be discussed later, can be ignored), but they all display an increase in values in the Roman samples (with one jump at ~7000 years BP, that, as will be discussed, can also be ignored; Fig. 1). All three ratios are substantially higher in the Roman samples than in those from the Levant (Fig. 1). The behavior of Cu is difficult to interpret since the Roman samples have higher Cu/Ca values than the Levant samples, roughly resembling the petrous/enamel ratio (Table 2 and Fig. 1). In addition, the increase in Cu/Ca in the Roman samples during the Roman period is on the order of tenfold, while that of Co/Ca is 100-fold and that of Pb/Ca is ~1000-fold (Fig. 1). This implies that Cu/Ca values cannot be used to trace metal pollution. Co/Ca and, more so, Pb/Ca ratios depict two pollution-related trends. They both have higher values in the Roman samples (though there was no difference in petrous versus tooth enamel values), and they show a clear increase in values in those samples with time, reaching a peak during the Roman period, as expected (Settle & Patterson, 1980). Pb/Ca is the best indicator for metal pollution, as evident from its pronounced increase in values with time and especially when considering only the Pb/Ca of samples screened based on their Ba/Ca values (Fig. 2).

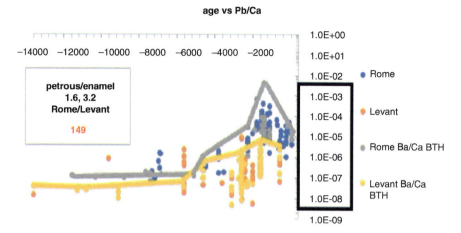

Fig. 2 Lead/Ca (mole/mole) in petrous bones of individuals from Rome and Sardinia and in tooth enamel of individuals from the Levant ranging in age from approximately 12,000 BCE to circa 1650 CE. The lines connect the highest Pb/Ca values of same-age samples with Ba/Ca below/equal to the threshold (BTH)

Following Eshel et al. (2020) and Erel et al. (2021), Ba/Ca thresholds for determining post-mortem diagenetic additions to tooth enamel and petrous bones are used. The threshold is 5E-5 (mole/mole) for petrous bones, which is a factor of 10 higher than the Ba/Ca threshold for tooth enamel (Ericson et al., 1979; Patterson et al., 1987, 1991; Eshel et al., 2020; Erel et al., 2021). Considering only samples from both Rome and the Levant that have Ba/Ca values below their respective thresholds, several interesting observations can be made (Fig. 2). First, in both regions there was a gradual increase in Pb/Ca values with time in the last 5000 years; second, in both regions, there is no clear trend with time in samples older than 5000 years; and third, the Roman values are fivefold higher than the Levant Pb/Ca values during the Epipaleolithic-Neolithic, but are two to three orders of magnitude higher during the Roman period. We suspect that during the Epipaleolithic-Neolithic, pre-metallic period, the Pb/Ca values in humans reflect lead uptake regulated by inputs from the country rock through water, food and atmospheric dust (Settle & Patterson, 1980). In the Levant sites sampled by us, carbonate rocks predominate, while in Rome numerous volcanic rocks are exposed as well (Periferia, 2008). These rocks have approximately 10-times higher concentrations of lead than carbonates (Taylor & McLennan, 1985).

As presented in Erel et al. (2021), Pb/Ca in the Ba/Ca-corrected Roman samples follow Settle and Patterson's (1980) record of lead production over time (Fig. 2). There is a clear rise in Pb/Ca values 5000 years ago, when cupellation was first used (Wagner et al., 1979; Hess et al., 1998; Pernicka et al., 1998; Momenzadeh & Nezafati, 2000; Nokandeh & Nezafati, 2003). In Rome, Pb/Ca levels then remain constant until the Bronze Age, when they start to slowly rise until the Iron Age (Fig. 2). From the Iron Age on, a sharper increase is observed, peaking during the

Roman period, followed by lower, but still high, Pb/Ca values during the decline of the Roman Empire and again in the late Medieval period. In the Levant, the increase is much less pronounced and the difference between the two regions widens, reaching the maximum disparity during the Roman period (Fig. 2). In both records, the apparent increases at ~7000 BP in Rome and ~ 6000 BP in the Levant can be ignored, as all these samples contain significant additions of post-mortem barium and lead.

According to Settle and Patterson (1980), there are roughly four orders of magnitude increase in lead production between the discovery of cupellation and the height of the Roman Empire. Erel et al. (2021) reported an approximately 4000-fold increase in the Pb/Ca ratio in petrous bones from Rome during the same period, maintaining that the Roman Pb/Ca record reveals how lead pollution in humans has reflected past lead production in a major urban center. The difference between Rome and the Levant, especially at the height of the Roman Empire, further validates the sensitivity of lead pollution as affected by lead production, trade and use.

Following the cautionary call of Erel et al. (2021), this paper reiterates that the past provides us with clues as to what awaits us in the future with respect to metal pollution near mining, recycling and manufacturing sites, especially in less-than-optimally regulated regions (e.g., Gäbler et al., 2011; Bleischwitz et al., 2012; UNEP and GRID-Arendal, 2020). This forecast highlights the impact of socio-economic status on the likelihood of metal pollution in humans, and is highly relevant in light of the mounting global need for metals for the construction of solar panels, wind turbines and electronic devices which have their advantages in our world today – but the dark side of which cannot be ignored (Robinson, 2009; Baldé et al., 2015, 2017; Drexhage et al., 2017; Hsu et al., 2019).

Acknowledgments The author wishes to thank Ofir Tirosh for his craftsmanship in performing the chemical analysis, and Renana Oz and Adi Ticher for their assistance in the lab. He also deeply thanks all the archaeologists who provided the 64 tooth samples (Tom Levy, UCSD – Shikmim and Wadi Fidan 1, 4; Israel Hershkovitz, Tel Aviv University – Pekiin; Israel Finkelstein, Tel Aviv University – Megiddo; Erez Ben-Yosef, Tel Aviv University – Timna; Yossi Nagar, the Israel Antiquities Authority – Wallage, Ein Gedi, Jerusalem; Gideon Avni, the Israel Antiquities Authority – Lahav). He also thanks the Hebrew University for a generous internal grant.

References

Alfonso, S., Grousset, F., Masse, L., & Tastet, J.-P. (2001). European lead isotope signal recorded from 6000 to 300 years BP in coastal marshes (SW France). *Atmospheric Environment, 35,* 3595–3605.

Aufderheide, A. C., Wittmers, L. E., Jr., Rapp, G., Jr., & Wallgren, J. (1988). Anthropological applications of skeletal lead analysis. *American Anthropologist, 90,* 931–936.

Baldé, C. P., Wang, F., Kuehr, R., & Huisman, J. (2015). *The global e-waste monitor – 2014.* United Nations University, IAS – SCYCLE.

Baldé, C. P., Forti, V., Gray, V., Kuehr, R., & Stegmann, P. (2017). *The global e-waste monitor – 2017.* United Nations University, IAS – SCYCLE.

Beherec, M. A., Levy, T. E., Tirosh, O., Najjar, M., Knabb, K. A., & Erel, Y. (2016). Iron Age Nomads and their relation to copper smelting in Faynan (Jordan): Trace metal and Pb and Sr isotopic measurements from the Wadi Fidan 40 cemetery. *Journal of Archaeological Science, 65*, 70–83.

Bleischwitz, R., Dittrich, M., & Pierdicca, C. (2012). Coltan from Central Africa, international trade and implications for any certification. *Resources Policy, 37*, 19–29.

Borsos, E., Makra, L., Beczi, R., Vitanyi, B., & Szentpeteri, M. (2003). Anthropogenic air pollution in the ancient times. *Acta Climatologica et Chorologica, 36*, 5–15.

Delile, H., Keenan-Jones, D., Blichert-Toft, J., Goiran, J.-P., Arnaud-Godet, F., & AlbarÃ¨de, F. (2017). Rome's urban history inferred from Pb-contaminated waters trapped in its ancient harbor basins. *Proceedings of the National Academy of Sciences, 114*, 10059–10064.

Drexhage, J., Porta, D. L., Hund, K., McCormick, M., & Ningthoujam, J. (2017). *The growing role of minerals and metals for a low carbon future*. International Bank for Reconstruction and Development/The World Bank.

Durali-Müller, S. (2005). *Roman lead and copper mining in Germany their origin and development through time, deduced from lead and copper isotope provenance studies*. Unpublished PhD, Johann Wolfgang Goethe-Universität, Frankfurt am Main.

Erel, Y., Pinhasi, R., Coppa, A., Ticher, A., Tirosh, O., & Carmel, L. (2021). Lead in archeological human bones reflecting historical changes in lead production. *Environmental Science and Technology, 55*, 14407–14413.

Ericson, J. E., Shirahata, H., & Patterson, C. C. (1979). Skeletal concentrations of lead in ancient Peruvians. *The New England Journal of Medicine, 300*, 946–951.

Eshel, T., Yahalom-Mack, N., Tirosh, O., Maeir, A. M., Harlavan, Y., Gilboa, A., & Erel, Y. (2020). Pollution and human mobility in the southern Levant during the Iron Age using chemical and isotopic analysis of human tooth enamel. *Journal of Archaeological Science, 124*, 105262. https://doi.org/10.1016/j.jas.2020.105262

Filippelli, G. M., Laidlaw, M. A. S., Latimer, J. C., & Raftis, R. (2005). Urban lead poisoning and medical geology: An unfinished story. *GSA Today, 15*, 4–11.

Gäbler, H. E., Melcher, F., Graupner, T., Bahr, A., Sitnikova, M. A., Henjes-Kunst, F., et al. (2011). Speeding up the analytical workflow for Coltan fingerprinting by an integrated mineral liberation analysis/LA-ICP-MS approach. *Geostandards and Geoanalytical Research, 35*, 431–448.

Grattan, J. P., Gilbertson, D. D., & Hunt, C. O. (2007). The local and global dimensions of metalliferous pollution derived from a reconstruction of an eight-thousand-year record of copper smelting and mining at a desert-mountain frontier in southern Jordan. *Journal of Archaeological Science, 34*(1), 83–110.

Harkness, J. S., & Darrah, T. H. (2019). From the crust to the cortical: The geochemistry of trace elements in human bone. *Geochimica et Cosmochimica Acta, 249*, 76–94.

Hess, K., Hauptmann, A., Wright, R., & Whallon, R. (1998). Evidence of fourth millennium B.C. silver production at Fatmalı-Kalecik, East Anatolia. In A. H. T. Rehren & D. J. Muhly (Eds.), *Metallurgica Antiqua* (pp. 123–134). Der Anschnitt Beiheft 8.

Hong, S., Candelone, J.-P., Patterson, C. C., & Boutron, C. F. (1994). Greenland ice evidence of hemispheric lead pollution two millennia ago by Greek and Roman civilizations. *Science, 265*, 1841–1843.

Hong, S., Candelone, J. P., Patterson, C. C., & Boutron, C. F. (1996). History of ancient copper smelting pollution during Roman and medieval times recorded in Greenland ice. *Science, 272*, 246–249.

Hsu, E., Barmak, K., Westa, A. C., & Park, A. A. (2019). Advancements in the treatment and processing of electronic waste with sustainability: A review of metal extraction and recovery technologies. *Green Chemistry, 21*, 919–936. https://doi.org/10.1039/c1038gc03688h

Kamenov, G. D., Lofaro, E. M., Goad, G., & Krigbaum, J. (2018). Trace elements in modern and archaeological human teeth: Implications for human metal exposure and enamel diagenetic changes. *Journal of Archaeological Science, 99*, 27–34.

Le-Roux, G., Weiss, D., Cheburkin, A., Rausch, N., Grattan, J., Kober, B., et al. (2003). Heavy metals, especially lead, deposition recorded in an ombrotrophic peat bog near Manchester, United Kingdom. *Journal de Physique, 107*, 739–742.

Le-Roux, G., Weiss, D., Grattan, J. P., Givelet, N., Krachler, M., Cherburkin, A., et al. (2004). Identifying the sources and timing of ancient and medieval atmospheric metal pollution in England by a peat profile. *Journal of Environmental Monitoring, 6*, 502–510.

Longman, J., Veres, D., Finsinger, W., & Ersek, V. (2018). Exceptionally high levels of lead pollution in the Balkans from the Early Bronze Age to the industrial revolution. *Proceedings of the National Academy of Sciences of the United States of America, 115*, E5661–E5668. https://doi.org/10.1073/pnas.1721546115

Manea-Krichten, M., Patterson, C., Miller, G., Settle, D., & Erel, Y. (1991). Comparative increases of lead and barium with age in human tooth enamel, rib and ulna. *The Science of the Total Environment, 107*, 179–203.

Martínez Cortizas, A., García-Rodeja, E., Pombal, X. P., Muñoz, J. C. N., Weiss, D., & Cheburkin, A. (2002). Atmospheric Pb deposition in Spain during the last 4600 years recorded by two ombrotrophic peat bogs and implications for the use of peat as archive. *Science of the Total Environment, 292*, 33–44.

McConnell, J. R., Wilson, A. I., Stohl, A., Arienzo, M. M., Chellman, N. J., Eckhardt, S., Thompson, E. M., Pollard, A. M., & Steffensen, J. P. (2018). Lead pollution recorded in Greenland ice indicates European emissions tracked plagues, wars, & imperial expansion during antiquity. *Proceedings of the National Academy of Sciences of the United States of America, 115*, 5726–5731. https://doi.org/10.1073/pnas.1721818115

Mighall, T. M., Abrahams, P., Grattan, J. P., Hayes, D., Timberlake, S., & Forsyth, S. (2002). Geochemical evidence for atmospheric pollution derived from prehistoric copper mining at Copa Hill, Cwm Ystwyth, Mid-Wales, UK. *The Science of the Total Environment, 292*, 69–80.

Momenzadeh, M., & Nezafati, N. (2000). Sources of ores and minerals used in Arisman: A preliminary study. In N. N. Chegini, M. Momenzadeh, H. Parzinger, E. Pernicka, T. Stöllner, R. Vatandoust, G. Weisgerber, N. Boroffka, A. Chaichi, D. Hasanalian, Z. Hezarkhani, M. M. Eskandari, & N. Nezafati (Eds.), *Preliminary report on archaeometallurgical investigations around the prehistoric site of Arisman near Kashan, Western Central Iran*. Dietrich Reimer Verlag GmbH.

Murozumi, M., Chow, T. J., & Patterson, C. (1969). Chemical concentrations of pollutant lead aerosols, terrestrial dusts and sea salts in Greenland and Antarctic snow strata. *Geochimica et Cosmochimica Acta, 33*, 1247–1294.

Nokandeh, J., & Nezafati, N. (2003). *The Silversmiths of Sialk: Evidence of the precious metals' metallurgy at the southern mound of Sialk*.

Nriagu, J. O. (1983). *Lead and lead poisoning in antiquity*. Wiley.

Nriagu, J. O. (1996). A history of global metal pollution. *Science, 272*, 223–224.

Oakberg, K., Levy, T., & Smith, P. (2000). A method for skeletal arsenic analysis, applied to the Chalcolithic copper smelting site of Shiqmim, Israel. *Journal of Archaeological Science, 27*(10), 895–901.

Patterson, C. C. (1972). Silver stocks and losses in ancient and medieval times. *The Economic History Review, 25*, 205–235.

Patterson, C. C., Shirahata, H., & Ericson, J. E. (1987). Lead in ancient human bones and its relevance to historical developments of social problems with lead. *The Science of the Total Environment, 61*, 167–200.

Patterson, C. C., Ericson, J., Manea-Krichten, M., & Shirahata, H. (1991). Natural skeletal levels of lead in Homo sapiens uncontaminated by technological lead. *Science of the Total Environment, 107*, 205–236.

Periferia, A. (2008). *The geology of Rome. From the historical center to the outskirts*. Tech. Periodicals, Memorie Descrittive della Carta geologica d'Italia, 80/2008. ISBN:978-88-240-2893-6.

Pernicka, E., Rehren, T., & Schmitt-Strecker, S. (1998). Late Uruk silver production by cupellation at Habuba Kabira, Syria. In T. Rehren, A. Hauptmann, & D. J. Muhly (Eds.), *Metallurgica Antiqua* (pp. 123–134). Der Anschnitt Beiheft 8.

Petit, D., Veron, A., Flament, P., Deboudt, K., & Poirier, A. (2015). Review of pollutant lead decline in urban air and human blood: A case study from northwestern Europe. *Comptes Rendus Geoscience, 347*, 247–256.

Pyatt, F. B., Amos, D., Grattan, J. P., Pyatt, A. J., & Terrell-Nield, C. E. (2002). Invertebrates of ancient heavy metal spoil and smelting tip sites in southern Jordan: Their distribution and use as bioindicators of metalliferous pollution derived from ancient sources. *Journal of Arid Environments, 52*, 53–62.

Pyatt, F. B., Pyatt, A. J., Walker, C., Sheen, T., & Grattan, J. P. (2005). The heavy metal content of skeletons from an ancient metalliferous polluted area in southern Jordan with particular reference to bioaccumulation and human health. *Ecotoxicology and Environmental Safety, 60*(3), 295–300.

Renberg, I., Persson, M. W., & Emteryd, O. (1994). Pre-industrial atmospheric lead contamination detected in Swedish lake sediments. *Nature, 368*, 323–326.

Robinson, B. H. (2009). E-waste: An assessment of global production and environmental impacts. *Science of the Total Environment, 408*, 183–191.

Rosman, K. J., Chisholm, W., Hong, S., Candelone, J.-P., & Boutron, C. F. (1997). Lead from Carthaginian and Roman Spanish mines isotopically identified in Greenland ice dated from 600 B.C. to 300 A.D. *Environmental Science & Technology, 31*, 3413–3416.

Schoeninger, M. J., Moore, K. M., Murray, M. L., & Kingston, J. D. (1989). Detection of bone preservation in archaeological and fossil samples. *Applied Geochemistry, 4*(3), 281–292.

Settle, D. M., & Patterson, C. C. (1980). Lead in albacore: Guide to lead pollution in Americans. *Science, 207*, 1167–1176.

Shotyk, W., Weiss, D., Appleby, P. G., Cheburkin, A. K., Frei, R., Gloor, M., et al. (1998). History of atmospheric lead deposition since 12,370 14C yr BP from a peat bog, Jura Mountains, Switzerland. *Science, 281*, 1635–1640.

Sponheimer, M., & Lee-Thorp, J. A. (2006). Enamel diagenesis at South African Australopith sites: Implications for paleoecological reconstruction with trace elements. *Geochimica et Cosmochimica Acta, 70*, 1644–1654.

Taylor, S. R., & McLennan, S. M. (1985). *The continental crust: Its composition and evolution.* Blackwell Scientific Publications.

UNEP and GRID-Arendal. (2020). *The illegal trade in chemicals.*

Wagner, G. A., Gentner, W., & Gropengiesser, H. (1979). Evidence for third millennium lead-silver mining on Siphnos Island (Cyclades). *Naturwissenschaften, 66*, 157–158.

Yaffe, Y., Flessel, C. P., Wesolowski, J. J., del Rosario, A., Guirguis, G. N., Matias, V., et al. (1983). Identification of lead sources in California children using the stable isotope ratio technique. *Archives of Environmental and Occupational Health, 38*, 237–245.

The Source of Southern Levantine Hellenistic Silver and Lead

Tzilla Eshel ⓘ, Gideon Hadas, Asaf Oron, Irina Segal, Ofir Tirosh, and Yehiel Zelinger

Abstract A silver bowl, which dates to the early second century BCE, and eight samples of leaded bronzes dating to early first century BCE, were analyzed for chemical and lead-isotopic analysis. Results suggest that the metals originated from various Aegean ores, including Laurion and Chalkidiki and/or Thasos. The results therefore suggest that multiple Greek ores supplied silver and lead to the southern Levant throughout the Hellenistic period (second and early first centuries BCE). It is further suggested that Laurion was a significant source of lead to the southern Levant in the early first century BCE. A larger database is needed to further establish these suggestions.

Keywords Silver · Leaded bronze · Wine-drinking set · Hellenistic period · Levant · Laurion

---

T. Eshel (✉)
Department of Archaeology, Zinman Institute of Archaeology, University of Haifa, Haifa, Israel
e-mail: tzillaeshel@gmail.com

G. Hadas
Dead Sea and Arava Science Center; ʿEin Gedi Oasis Excavations, Jerusalem, Israel
e-mail: gideonhadas@gmail.com

A. Oron
Department of Conservation, Tel Aviv Museum of Art, Tel Aviv, Israel
e-mail: asaforo@gmail.com

I. Segal
Geological Survey of Israel, Jerusalem, Israel
e-mail: idsegal@gmail.com

O. Tirosh
The Fredy and Nadine Herrmann Institute of Earth Sciences,
The Hebrew University of Jerusale, Jerusalem, Israel
e-mail: ofirtirosh@gmail.com

Y. Zelinger
Israel Antiquities Authority, Jerusalem, Israel
e-mail: yehiel@israntique.org.il

© The Author(s), under exclusive license to Springer Nature Switzerland AG 2023
E. Ben-Yosef, I. W. N. Jones (eds.), *"And in Length of Days Understanding" (Job 12:12): Essays on Archaeology in the Eastern Mediterranean and Beyond in Honor of Thomas E. Levy*, Interdisciplinary Contributions to Archaeology,
https://doi.org/10.1007/978-3-031-27330-8_55

1 Introduction

Silver was produced in antiquity from silver-rich lead ores in a two-step process, named cupellation. First, the lead-rich ore was smelted, and a lead-silver alloy was formed and separated from the rest of the ore. Then, the lead-silver alloy was heated again with hot air in a clay conical vessel, named a cupel. The heated air oxidized the lead (forming a by-product named litharge), allowing for the easy removal of the silver (e.g., Pernicka & Bachmann, 1983; Pernicka et al., 1998; Pollard & Heron, 2008). The origin of silver is often traced using chemical and Lead Isotope Analysis (LIA).

Silver and lead do not occur naturally in the Levant; therefore, their appearances are often prime indicators of long-distance maritime trade. Historically, Laurion, located in Attica (Fig. 1; mainland Greece), was known to be a major silver-producing deposit, heavily exploited throughout antiquity (Gale & Stos-Gale, 1981; Stos-Gale et al., 1996; Stos-Gale & Gale, 1982). The production of silver at Laurion, however, was not continuous, and was affected by historical events. Former isotopic studies have shown that Laurion was the main supplier of silver to the Levant at the end of the Iron Age (seventh and early sixth centuries BCE; Stos-Gale, 2001; Thompson, 2007; Eshel et al., 2022). Silver production at Laurion was probably at

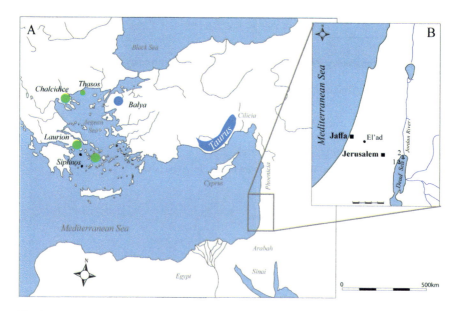

Fig. 1 (a) The East Mediterranean and lead ore sources associated with silver production, referenced in the text. Color code for ores: green, the Aegean; blue, Anatolia. (b) Location of sites where metals were found: Dead Sea anchorages of Khirbet Mazin (#1) and Maʿagenat Ha-Melah (#2), and the site of Elʿad. (Illustrator: Svetlana Matskevich)

its height in the fifth century BCE followed by a decrease in metal output suspended by intermittent periods of growth in the mid-fourth century BCE and again after the Roman closure of Macedonian and Thracian mines after the Battle of Pydna (168 BCE; e.g., Meier, 1990; Crawford, 1977; Davis, 2014). According to Herodotus, Chalkidiki and the nearby island of Thasos were also of major importance for ancient silver production in the north Aegean (Herodotus 7.44). Archaeological and geological studies also confirm that the Chalkidiki Peninsula had a leading role in silver production during the fifth–second centuries BCE (Fig. 1; Gale et al., 1980; Wagner et al., 1986; Kuleff et al., 2006; Tselekas, 2010; Birch et al., 2020; Vaxevanopoulos et al., 2022). Numerous ancient galleries and shafts were found at the Peninsula, suggesting that the scale of the mining there was comparable with that of Laurion (Wagner et al., 1986; Tselekas, 2010). Silver production has been attested at Thasos, and at the Rhodope Mountains including Mt. Pangaion as well (Fig. 1; Pernicka et al., 1981; Gale & Stos-Gale, 2014). The island group of the Cyclades also hosts several occurrences of argentiferous ores; only Siphnos, however, is proven to have been an important source of silver in ancient times (Fig. 1; Gale & Stos-Gale, 1981; Pernicka, 1987). It is generally assumed that Aegean ores, e.g., Thasos and Chalkidiki compensated for Laurion's periodical declines in silver production (Birch et al., 2020).

Further to the east were the silver-bearing ores in Balya, located in the Biga Peninsula in northwestern Anatolia (Fig. 1; Pernicka et al., 1984, 2003), Taurus Mountains in southern Turkey (Sayre et al., 2001) and Naklak, Iran (Nezafati & Pernicka, 2012). The Phoenicians exploited silver in Sardinia and Iberia in the Western Mediterranean during the Iron Age (Eshel et al., 2019, 2022). There was also mining in Roman times in the south of France in Massif Central (Baron et al., 2006).

Lead isotope compositions of 160 Archaic Greek coins dated to sixth–fifth centuries BCE, suggests that the majority of the silver was from Laurion, Chalkidiki and the deposits in the Rhodope Mountains. Small quantities of silver in these coins seem to have originated from Siphnos, Thasos, the West Mediterranean and perhaps the Carpathians (Stos-Gale & Davis, 2020). Twenty Athenian-style tetradrachms dated from the mid-fifth to the mid-fourth centuries BCE, found in several excavations in the southern Levant show a similar distribution. Most of the coins were struck of silver from Laurion, while others may have originated from Chalikidiki (Gitler et al., 2009; Ponting et al., 2011). The origin of Levantine silver from later periods has seldom been studied.

Lead was the main byproduct of silver production, therefore the origin of lead, which can also be traced based on LIA can often serve as a good indicator of silver sources of the period. Nevertheless, there are only a few isotopic analysis of lead artifacts of the Hellenistic period in the southern Levant. Sling bullets from Seleucid Tell Iẓṭabba, dating to the second half of the 2nd century BCE, originate from Laurion (Klein et al., 2022). In this study, the origin of silver and lead found in the southern Levant and dating to the early second and early first centuries BCE, is studied.

Fig. 2 (a) Restored and (b) unrestored bowl fragments from Elʿad. (Photographs: Clara Amit, courtesy of the Israel Antiquities Authority)

2 Materials

Three bowl fragments (Fig. 2), which are part of a mid-second century BCE Hellenistic wine-drinking silver set from a farmstead located in the modern city of Elʿad (near ancient Lydda) were subjected to chemical and isotopic analysis.

In addition, eight Pb-isotope and chemical analyses of first century leaded-bronze sculpture fragments, seven from Khirbet Mazin (Fig. 3) and one from Maʿagenat Ha-Melah ("the salt harbor"; Fig. 4), both located on the northern shores of the Dead Sea, were obtained in 2010 are published here for the first time (see site locations in Fig. 1).[1]

3 Methods and Methodology

3.1 Silver Bowl Fragments from Elʿad

Three unrestored bowl fragments (Fig. 2) were subjected to detailed chemical and Pb-isotopic analysis, in order to determine the source of the silver. As the fragments were too thin to sample by drilling, a drill was used to scrape both sides of the fragments' surfaces. This process determined that the fragments contained silver that

---

[1] Twenty-four artifacts were analyzed by Irina Segal in 2010, including eight coins from ʿEin Gedi, eight coins from Khirbet Mazin, seven bronze fragments from Khirbet Mazin, and a bronze object from Maʿagenat Ha-Melah. The coins were subjected to a Laser Ablation (LA) system LSX-213 (Cetac Technologies) coupled with an MC-ICP-MS for lead isotope ratio determination. Standard $^{204}Pb/^{206}Pb$ ratio errors reported in this method were high, and therefore the coins were excluded from this study.

Fig. 3 Leaded-bronze sculpture fragments from Kh. Mazin, at the Dead Sea. (Photograph: Gideon Hadas)

was not corroded. The silver core of the fragments was crushed into powder, and samples of 30–50 mg of metal were obtained. The samples were dissolved in nitric acid and diluted for analysis. Remaining residue was dissolved in aqua regia. For LIA, aliquots containing 100 ng of Pb from the samples were processed through ion exchange columns (Dowex 1X8 resin).

Sample dissolution was performed in the laboratory of Adi Eliyahu of Ariel University. Additional sample preparation for analysis and measurements were performed by Ofir Tirosh, at the laboratory at the Institute of Earth Sciences at the Hebrew University of Jerusalem. Chemical composition was determined using a quadrupole Inductively Coupled Plasma – Mass Spectrometer (ICP-MS, Agilent 7500cx). The precision and accuracy of the ICP-MS were ± 5%. Isotopic measurements were performed with a MC- ICP-MS (Thermo Neptune Plus). The full protocol is described in Eshel et al., 2019. Replicate measurements of National Institute of Standards and Technology (NIST) SRM-981 standards yielded mean values of $^{206}Pb/^{204}Pb = 16.930 \pm 0.006$, $^{207}Pb/^{204}Pb = 15.484 \pm 0.005$, and $^{208}Pb/^{204}Pb = 36.673 \pm 0.013$ (2σ, $n = 3$).

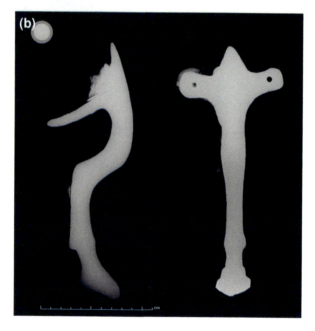

Fig. 4 (**a**) Bronze leg from Ma'agenat Ha-Melah (photograph: Gideon Hadas). (**b**) X-ray photographs of the bronze leg, showing coins attached to the leg. (Photograph: Asaf Oron)

3.2 Bronze Fragments from the Dead Sea

Seven objects from Kh. Mazin (Fig. 3) and a single object from Ma'agenat Ha-Melah (Fig. 4) were analyzed in the laboratory of the Geological Survey of Israel. They were cleaned and drilled and the drillings were dissolved in aqua regia. The solution was used for bulk chemical and for Pb isotope analysis. Chemical composition was

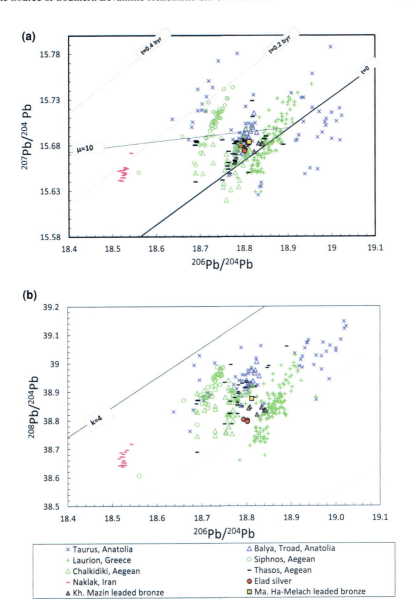

Fig. 5 (a) $^{207}Pb/^{204}Pb$ vs. $^{206}Pb/^{204}Pb$ and (b) $^{208}Pb/^{204}Pb$ vs. $^{206}Pb/^{204}Pb$ of the silver from Elʿad and leaded bronzes from Dead Sea. The results plotted on the two-stage geological model (Stacey & Kramers, 1975), alongside major Aegean silver-bearing Pb ores: Laurion, Mainland Greece and Siphnos, Aegean (Gale & Stos-Gale, 1981; Stos-Gale & Gale, 1982; Vaxevanopoulos et al., 2022), Balya in NW Anatolia, Chalkidiki in northern Greece, Thasos and Rhodope Mountains in the Aegean (Gale & Stos-Gale, 1981; Pernicka et al., 1981; Wagner et al., 1986; Begemann, Schmitt-Strecker and Pernicka 2003; Pernicka et al., 2003; Gale & Stos-Gale, 2014); and ores from Naklak, Iran (Nezafati & Pernicka, 2012), the Apuseni and Baia Mare in the Carpathians (Marcoux et al., 2002), and Almeria in Iberia (Gale & Stos-Gale, 2014)

defined by ICP-OES (Optima 3300, Perkin Elmer). Scandium in final concentration of 5 mg L-1 (internal standard) was added to all samples and standard solutions. Pb isotope ratios were determined from the aliquots of same solution by MC-ICP-MS (NU Instrument, Wrexham, UK). Tl was added to standard NIST SRM 981 and to sample solutions. Full analysis procedure was described in Segal and Halich (2005). The precision (RSD) of the lead isotope measurements for the samples using MC-ICP-MS was reported to be 0.01–0.02% for $^{206}Pb/^{204}Pb$ and $^{207}Pb/^{204}Pb$, and 0.01% for $^{208}Pb/^{204}Pb$.

3.3 *Methodology*

The results of both assemblages are plotted here against the two-stage geological model (Stacy & Kramers, 1975). For a full explanation of the significance of the geological model for the provenance of metals see Eshel et al. (2019). In addition, the results were compared to Pb-isotopic ratios of ores, based on Euclidian distances (for an explanation of the method see Birch et al., 2020).

4 Results

Results are presented in Table 1. Chemical concentrations indicate that the silver core in all three silver bowl fragments from El'ad contained pure silver (Ag wt.% > 95). The bronze fragments from Kh. Mazin and Ma'agenat Ha-Melah contain 73–91 wt.% copper (Cu), 7–12 wt.% tin (Sn) and 1.2–8 wt.% lead (Pb). The relatively high Pb concentrations suggest that these are leaded bronzes, namely that lead was alloyed with copper and tin.

The results show that the three silver bowl fragments from El'ad have very similar chemical and Pb-isotopic compositions, suggesting that the fragments originated from a single bowl. The results do not overlap isotopically with any specific ore, yet they fall between the Pb-isotopic ratios of several well-exploited ores in the Aegean, including the silver-rich lead ores in Chalkidiki in northern Greece, on the island of Thasos in the Aegean and farther south in Laurion in Attica (Fig. 5).

Five of the seven leaded-bronze sculpture fragments from Kh. Mazin are isotopically consistent with the Laurion mines, while the isotopic results of two additional fragments from Kh. Mazin and the leg-fragment from Ma'agenat Ha-Melah fall between several ores, including Laurion, Thasos, Chalkidiki and Balya in Western Anatolia (Fig. 5).

The Pb-isotopic compositions of the samples from El'ad and the Dead Sea are inconsistent with most silver and lead sources from eastern and central Anatolia, which have elevated $^{208}Pb/^{204}Pb$ ratios compared to the silver from El'ad (for some Anatolian ores see Fig. 5b). The results are also inconsistent with silver and lead sources from Iberia which were exploited by the Romans from the second century

Table 1 Detailed chemical compositions and lead isotope ratios and of three silver bowl fragments from El^{c}ad and seven Pb-rich bronze fragments from Kh. Mazin and Ma^{c}agenat Ha-Melah. The chemical compositions are presented in ppm, unless stated otherwise

Sample	Au	Al	Fe	Ni	Co	Cu wt.%	Zn	As	Sn wt.%	Sb	Pb wt.%	^{206}Pb/^{204}Pb	2σ	^{207}Pb/^{204}Pb	2σ	^{208}Pb/^{204}Pb	2σ
El 'ad 1	11	189	175	6		1.35	n.d.	n.d.			0.20	18.802	0.003	15,674	0.003	38.800	0.007
El 'ad 2	9	115	101	31		1.35	n.d.	n.d.			0.20	18.802	0.006	15,674	0.006	38.795	0.011
El 'ad 3^a	7	n.d.	32	15		1.37	n d	n.d.			0.20	18.793	0.002	15,679	0.005	38.803	0.011
Kh. Mazin 1			525	505	445	84.1	228	2530	10.0	290	5.3	18.841	0.003	15,682	0.003	38.837	0.003
Kh. Mazin 2			519	505	455	85.5	176	2461	9.4	253	4.6	18.840	0.002	15,681	0.002	38.835	0.002
Kh. Mazin 3			1083	325	623	80.0	121	2414	10.9	428	8.4	18.834	0.002	15,682	0.002	38.844	0.003
Kh. Mazin 4			972	689	432	82.5	119	4487	12.5	475	4.2	18.843	0.003	15,681	0.003	38.835	0.004
Kh. Mazin 5			2291	540	1361	88.5	195	3029	7.6	497	3.1	18.808	0.002	15,683	0.002	38.848	0.002
Kh. Mazin 6			1123	344	716	90.7	99	2200	7.5	425	1.2	18.823	0.003	15,673	0.003	38.821	0.004
Kh. Mazin 7			1872	528	1231	83.4	152	3699	9.3	618	6.4	18.805	0.002	15,680	0.003	38.842	0.003
Ma. Ha-Melah 1			1775	1.1 wt.%	473	85.2	47	1420	6.7	947	6.5	18.812	0.002	15,684	0.003	38.875	0.003

^{a}Element concentrations were normalized based on the sum of elemental concentrations including Ag (not displayed)

BCE onwards (Birch et al., 2020). The lead sources and silver-rich jarosites there are of much older geological ages (~400 Myr, out of the range of the graphs in Fig. 5).

Gold (Au) concentrations are often used as an additional method to distinguish between different silver-bearing lead deposits (e.g., Meyers, 2003). Au contents ranging between 200–500 ppm has been typically associated with silver from Laurion (Gale et al., 1980; Gale & Stos-Gale, 1981: 175; Ponting et al., 2011: 123). However, such Au contents are not restricted to presumed Laurion silver: In North and Central Anatolia, Au in silver is lower, but is still expected to reach up to 500 ppm and in the Taurus mountains, Au in silver usually does not exceed 300 ppm (Sayre et al., 2001). In the Chalkidiki ores, Au concentrations in silver typically range between a few ppm up to 50 ppm (Wagner et al., 1986). Silver from Thasos is exceptionally low in Au and is not expected to contain more than a few ppm of Au (Pernicka et al., 1981).

Au concentrations in the sampled silver bowls from Elʿad are very low (7–11 ppm; Table 1). Therefore, they probably do not originate from Laurion, and are more similar in this sense to silver from Thasos and Chalkidiki.

Most other element concentrations in silver (e.g., Cu, Sn, Sb, Bi and As) are not indicative of the ore source, but rather of the production process, or of alloying with other metals (e.g., Eshel et al., 2019, forthcoming; L'Héritier et al., 2015; Pernicka & Bachmann, 1983).

5 Discussion and Conclusions

The farmstead of Elʿad (Fig. 6) was built in the late third century BCE (~220 BCE), and conquered and occupied by the Hasmoneans, ca. 145–142 BCE. The silver set was hoarded just before the Hasmonean conquest of the farmstead. It may have been in use in the last decades before the Hasmonean occupation, and therefore should be dated to the early second century BCE; Eshel forthcoming; Rozenberg forthcoming; Zelinger, 2021).

Kh. Mazin was an active anchorage during the Hasmonean period, as part of a central policy of ruling the shores of the Dead Sea (Bar-Adon, 1989: 5). The finds from Khirbet Mazin were sculpture fragments (Fig. 3) collected by the late Prof. Hirschfeld, who surveyed the Dead Sea coastline in 2002. They were found alongside thousands of small bronze coins of Alexander Jannaeus (minted 84/83–80/79 BCE) in an area which in the past was the sea bottom of Kh. Mazin anchorage, not far from the dock (Fig. 7; Hirschfeld & Ariel, 2005; Hadas, 2008: 36, note 1).

Alexander Jannaeus' small coins circulated in Judean markets, alongside other coins, till as late as the subjugation of the Jewish revolt against the Romans in 70 CE (e.g., Hadas, 2006). However, the fact that out of thousands of coins uncovered at Kh. Mazin, nearly all of the coins date to the last years of the 80 s BCE (84/83 BCE), and a single later coin in the assemblage dates to 80/79 BCE (Hirschfeld & Ariel, 2005: 85), makes it likely that the anchorage was active in the Hasmonean period and not later.

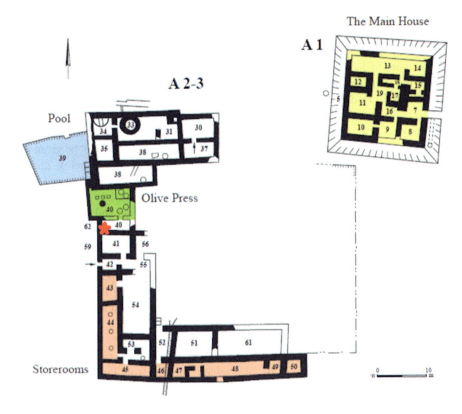

Fig. 6 Plan of the Hellenistic farmstead of Elʿad. The silver-set was unearthed in Room 40, south of the oil press. (Illustrator: Dov Protzki, Israel Antiquities Authority)

Fig. 7 Proposal for the reconstruction of Khirbet Mazin, based on the archaeological evidence. (Illustrator: Roi Elbag)

The fragment from Maʿagenat Ha-Melah is a bronze animal-leg, possibly of a brazier (Fig. 4a; 20 cm long and 1.4 kg weight). It was found ca. one km south of the site, by the team of Dead Sea Coast Archaeological Survey, alongside small bronze coins of Jannaeus, with a few coins attached to the leg, as seen in the X-ray photo (Fig. 4b). This anchorage, too, was active in the days of Alexander Jannaeus (103–76 BCE; Hadas, 2011).

The large assemblage of coins and sculpture fragments from Kh. Mazin was suggested by some scholars to be the place where coins were thrown to the Dead Sea according to a Jewish law (halakhah), in which objects which could not be given to the Temple, were "nullified" by being thrown into the Dead Sea (Eshel & Zissu, 2003: 96). Alternatively, it was suggested that this was a shipwreck cargo, and that the bronze sculpture fragments were intended for recycling (Hirschfeld & Ariel, 2005: 72). Regardless of the circumstances in which the coins and bronzes were brought to the Dead Sea, the bronzes should probably be dated to late in the reign of Alexander Jannaeus, at which time the coins found with the bronzes were minted, namely, the early first century BCE.

The production of leaded-bronzes is typical of the Hellenistic period (e.g., Klein & Hauptman, 1999: 1097; Craddock, 1977: 107). As a result, the Pb-isotope ratios are expected to be consistent with the source of the Pb rather than the Cu.

The Pb-isotopic ratios of the drinking bowls from Elʿad (ca. 145 BCE) fall between several Aegean silver-bearing lead ores from Greece and the Aegean (Thasos, Chalkidiki and Laurion), while the lead added to the bronzes from the Dead Sea anchorages (ca. 84–79 BCE) originates mostly from Laurion ($n = 5/8$), with some contributions from additional Greek ores ($n = 3/8$). Since the Pb originates from the Ag-rich ores of Laurion, it is probably the by-product of silver production, indicating that Laurion was actively producing silver and lead at this period.

The results, although few and preliminary, suggest that throughout the second and early first centuries BCE, Greece was the main supplier of silver and lead to the southern Levant. The metals were produced from more than one ore source. In this sense, the results are comparable to Pb-isotopic studies of Greek silver coins from the sixth–third centuries BCE in Greece and the Aegean Islands (Gale et al., 1988; Birch et al., 2020; Stos-Gale & Davis, 2020), and of 20 Athenian-style tetradrachms dated from the mid-fifth to the mid-fourth centuries BCE, found in several excavations in the southern Levant (Gitler et al., 2009; Ponting et al., 2011). The above studies suggest a multiple origin of the silver, in which Greek coins were not struck of silver from a single origin, but rather contained silver from mixed origins, including Laurion, Thasos/Chalkidiki (which overlap), and Rhodopes (the two latter located in northern Greece).

The fact that the Pb-isotope ratios of the silver bowl do not directly correlate to any ore field, raises the possibility that silver from several sources was mixed, possibly due to silver recycling. Recycling may also lower the concentration of the additional elements in the silver, and may explain low Pb concentrations in the silver (Table 1).

The Source of Southern Levantine Hellenistic Silver and Lead

Based on our limited sample set and a previous publication (Klein et al., 2022), we carefully suggest that Laurion was a significant source of lead to the southern Levant throughout the second half of the second century and early first century BCE. This is observed in the early first century bronzes found in the Dead Sea (current study) and in the analysis of lead sling bullets from Tell Iẓṭabba, dating to the second half of the 2nd century BCE (Klein et al., 2022). Additional analyses, however, of well-stratified second and first century BCE silver and lead metal artifacts are needed to further establish the results, and to determine whether silver and lead indeed originated from the same sources.

Acknowledgments We wish to thank Adi Eliyahu of Ariel University, and Yigal Erel of the Institute of Earth Sciences at the Hebrew University of Jerusalem, for dissolution, measurements and analyses of the silver objects. We are also grateful to Donald T. Ariel of the Israel Antiquities Authority and Sylvia Rozenberg of the Israel Museum for their assistance and advice. Finally, we thank Roi Elbag for allowing us to publish Fig. 7 and Or Roz of the Israel Antiquities Authority who assisted with the graphics.

References

Bar-Adon, P. (1989). *Excavations in the Judean Desert.* 'Atiqot, Hebrew series 9. (Hebrew).

Baron, S., Carignan, J., Laurent, S., & Ploquin, A. (2006). Medieval lead making on Mont-Lozère Massif (Cévennes-France): Tracing ore sources using Pb isotopes. *Applied Geochemistry, 21*(2), 241–252.

Birch, T., Westner, K. J., Kemmers, F., Klein, S., Höfer, H. E., & Seitz, H. M. (2020). Retracing magna Graecia's silver: Coupling lead isotopes with a multi-standard trace element procedure. *Archaeometry, 62*(1), 81–108.

Craddock, P. T. (1977). The composition of the copper alloys used by the Greek, Etruscan and Roman civilizations. *Journal of Archaeological Science, 4*, 103–123.

Crawford, M. H. (1977). Rome and the Greek world: Economic relationships. *The Economic History Review New Series, 30*(1), 42–52.

Davis, G. (2014). Mining money in late Archaic Athens. *Historia: Zeitschrift für Alte Geschichte, 63*(3), 257–277.

Eshel, T. (forthcoming). Chemical and lead isotope analysis of Hellenistic (2nd century BCE) silver drinking bowls from El'ad. In D. Amit, Y. Zelinger, D. T. Ariel, & I. Zilberbod (Eds.), *Hellenistic farms at El'ad.* Journal of Hellenistic Pottery and Material Culture (JHP) Supplement.

Eshel, H., & Zissu, B. (2003). A note on the Rabbinic phrase: 'Cast them into the Dead Sea'. *Judea and Samaria Research Studies, 12*, 91–96.

Eshel, T., Erel, Y., Yahalom-Mack, N., Tirosh, O., & Gilboa, A. (2019). Lead isotopes in silver reveal earliest Phoenician quest for metals in the West Mediterranean. *Proceedings of the National Academy of Sciences, 116*(13), 6007–6012.

Eshel, T., Erel, Y., Yahalom-Mack, N., Tirosh, O., & Gilboa, A. (2022). From Iberia to Laurion: Interpreting changes in silver supply to the Levant in the late Iron Age based on Pb-isotope analysis.

Eshel, T., Erel, Y., Yahalom-Mack, N., & Gilboa, A. (forthcoming). *One thousand years of mediterranean silver trade to the levant: A review and synthesis of analytical studies.*

Gale, N. H., & Stos-Gale, Z. (1981). Cycladic lead and silver metallurgy. *Annual of the British School at Athens, 76*, 169–224.

Gale, N. H., & Stos-Gale, A. Z. (2014). *OXALID Database*. https://oxalid.arch.ox.ac.uk/

Gale, N. H., Gentner, W., & Wagner, G. A. (1980). Mineralogical and geographical silver sources of Archaic Greek coinage. In D. M. Metcalf & W. A. Oddy (Eds.), *Metallurgy in Numismatics I* (pp. 3–49).

Gale, N. H., Picard, O., & Barrandon, J. N. (1988). The archaic Thasian silver coinage. In G. A. Wagner & G. Weisgerber (Eds.), *Antike Edel-und Buntmetallgewinnung auf Thasos (Vol. 6)* (pp. 212–223). Selbstverlag des Deutschen Bergbau-Museums.

Gitler, H., Ponting, M., & Tal, O. (2009). Athenian tetradrachms from Tel Mikhal (Israel): A metallurgical perspective. *American Journal of Numismatics, AJN2, 21*, 29–49.

Hadas, G. (2006). ʿEn Gedi. Hadashot Archeologiot 118.

Hadas, G. (2008). Dead Sea sailing routes during the Herodian period. *Bulletin of the Anglo-Israel Archaeological Society, 26*, 31–36.

Hadas, G. (2011). Dead Sea anchorages. *Revue Biblique, 118*(2), 161–179.

Hirschfeld, Y., & Ariel, D. T. (2005). A coin assemblage from the reign of Alexander Jannaeus found on the shore of the Dead Sea. *Israel Exploration Journal, 55*, 66–89.

Klein, S., & Hauptman, A. (1999). Iron age leaded tin bronzes from Khirbet Edh-Dharih, Jordan. *Journal of Archaeological Science, 26*(8), 1075–1082.

Klein, S., Jansen, M., Lichtenberger, A., & Tal, O. (2022). Archaeometallurgical analysis of lead weights and Sling Bullets from Seleucid Tell Iẓṭabba: More on lead origin in Seleucid Palestine. *Tel Aviv, 49*(2), 267–292.

Kuleff, I., Iliev, I., Pernicka, E., & Gergova, D. (2006). Chemical and lead isotope compositions of lead artefacts from ancient Thracia (Bulgaria). *Journal of Cultural Heritage, 7*(4), 244–256.

L'Héritier, M., Baron, S., Cassayre, L., & Téreygeol, F. (2015). Bismuth behaviour during ancient processes of silver–lead production. *Journal of Archaeological Science, 57*, 56–68.

Marcoux, E., Grancea, L., Lupulescu, M., & Milési, J. (2002). Lead isotope signatures of epithermal and porphyry-type ore deposits from the Romanian Carpathian Mountains. *Mineralium Deposita, 37*(2), 173–184.

Meier, S. (1990). Bleibergbau in der Antike. In *Lagerstätten, Bergbau, Aufbereitung, Verhüttung, Licentiate thesis*. Universität Zürich.

Meyers, P. (2003). Production of silver in antiquity: Ore types identified based upon elemental compositions of ancient silver artifacts. In L. V. Zelst (Ed.), *Patterns and process: A festschrift in honor of Dr. Edward V. Sayre* (pp. 271–288).

Nezafati, N., & Pernicka, E. (2012). Early silver production in Iran. *Iranian Archaeology, 3*, 38–45.

Pernicka, E. (1987). Erzlagerstätten in der Ägäis und ihre Ausbeutung im Altertum: geochemische Untersuchungen zur Herkunftsbestimmung archäologischer Metallobjekte. *Jahrbuch des Römisch-Germanischen Zentralmuseums Mainz, 34*(2), 607–714.

Pernicka, E., & Bachmann, H. G. (1983). Archäometallurgische Untersuchungen zur Antiken Silbergewinnung in Laurion. *Erzmelall, 36*, 592–597.

Pernicka, E., Gentner, W., Wagner, G., Vavelidis, M., & Gale, N. H. (1981). Ancient lead and silver production on Thasos (Greece). *ArchéoSciences, revue d'Archéométrie, 1*(1), 227–237.

Pernicka, E., Seeliger, T. C., Wagner, G. A., Begemann, F., Schmitt-Strecker, S., Eibner, C., Oztunali, O., & Baranyi, I. (1984). Archaometallurgische untersuchungen in Nordwestanatolien. *Jahrbuch des Romische-Germanischen Zentralmuseums, 31*, 533–599.

Pernicka, E., Rehren, T., & Schmitt-Strecker, S. (1998). Late Uruk silver production by cupellation at Habuba Kabira, Syria, in Rehren, T., Hauptmann, A., Muhly, J.D. (Eds.), *Metallurgica Antiqua, der Anschnitt. Honour of Hans Gert Bachmann and Robert Maddin, Deutsches Bergbau Museum* (pp. 123–134), Bochum.

Pernicka, E., Eibner, C., Öztunalı, O., & Wagner, G. A. (2003). Early Bronze Age metallurgy in the North-East Aegean. In G. A. Wagner, E. Pernicka, & H. P. Uerpmann (Eds.), *Troia and the Troad* (pp. 143–172). Springer.

Pollard, A. M., & Heron, C. (2008). *Archaeological chemistry* (2nd ed.). Royal Society of Chemistry.

Ponting, M., Gitler, H., & Tal, O. (2011). Who minted those owls? Metallurgical analyses of Athenian-styled tetradrachms found in Israel. *Revue Belge de Numismatique et de Sigillographie, 157*, 117–134.

Rozenberg, S. (forthcoming). Chapter 8: Hellenistic silver objects from farm A. In D. Amit, Y. Zelinger, D. T. Ariel, & I. Zilberbod (Eds.), *Hellenistic farms at El'ad*. Journal of Hellenistic Pottery and Material Culture (JHP) Supplement.

Sayre, E. V., Joel, E. C., Blackman, M. J., Yener, K. A., & Ozbal, H. (2001). Stable lead isotope studies of Black Sea Anatolian ore sources and related Bronze Age and Phrygian artefacts from nearby archaeological sites. Appendix: New central Taurus ore data. *Archaeometry, 43*(1), 77–115.

Segal, I., & Halicz, L. (2005). Provenance studies in archaeometallurgy using lead isotope ratios determination by Q-ICP-MS and MC-ICP-MS. *Israel Journal of Earth Sciences, 54*(2), 87–96.

Stacey, J., & Kramers, J. (1975). Approximation of terrestrial lead isotope evolution by a two-stage model. *Earth and Planetary Science Letters, 26*, 207–221.

Stos-Gale, Z. A. (2001). The impact of the natural sciences on studies of Hacksilber and early silver coinage. In M. S. Balmuth (Ed.), *Hacksilber to coinage: New insights into the monetary history of the Near East and Greece: A Collection of Eight Papers Presented at the 99th Annual Meeting of the Archaeological Institute of America* (pp. 53–76). American Numismatic Society.

Stos-Gale, Z., & Gale, N. H. (1982). The sources of Mycenaean silver and lead. *Journal of Field Archaeology, 9*(4), 467–485.

Stos-Gale, Z. A., Gale, N. H., & Annetts, N. (1996). Lead isotope data from the Isotrace laboratory, Oxford: Archaeometry data base 3, ores from the Aegean, part 1. *Archaeometry, 38*(2), 381–390.

Stos-Gale, Z. A., & Davis, G. (2020). The minting/mining nexus: New understandings of Archaic Greek silver coinage fromlead isotope analysis. In *Metallurgy, 87* (pp. 87–100).

Thompson, C. M. (2007). *Silver in the age of iron and the Orientalizing economics of archaic Greece*. University of California.

Tselekas, P. (2010). Observations on the silver coin production and use in the Chalkidike during the 5th century BC. In T. Faucher, M. C. Marcellesi, & O. Picard (Eds.), *Nomisma* (pp. 169–184). La circulation monétaire dans le monde grec antique, Bulletin de Correspondance Hellénique Supplément 53 (2011).

Vaxevanopoulos, M., Blichert-Toft, J., Davis, G., & Albarède, F. (2022). New findings of ancient Greek silver sources. *Journal of Archaeological Science, 137*, 105474.

Wagner, G., Pernicka, E., Seeliger, T. C., Lorenz, I., Begemann, F., Schmitt-Strecker, S., & Oztunali, O. (1986). Geochemische und isotopische charakteristika früher rohstoffquellen für kupfer, blei, silber und gold in der Türkei. In *Jahrbuch des römisch-germanischen Zentralmuseums Mainz* (Vol. 33, pp. 723–752).

Zelinger, Y. (2021). Go West: Archaeological evidence for Hasmonean expansion toward the Mediterranean coast. In A. Berlin & P. J. Kosmin (Eds.), *The middle Maccabees: Archaeology, history, and the rise of the Hasmonean Kingdom* (pp. 107–122). Archaeology and Biblical Studies.

A Social Archaeometallurgy of Bronze Age Cyprus

A. Bernard Knapp ⓘ

Abstract As a major producer of copper throughout the Bronze Age (ca. 2400–1100 BC), the island of Cyprus assumed a key role in the social and economic networks within and beyond the eastern Mediterranean. Consequently, research into mining and metallurgy on the island during the Bronze Age was undertaken early and by the 1980s had become an integral part of the archaeology of Cyprus. While archaeometallurgical research on Cyprus has been and continues to be prolific and informative, its focus is by and large technological and 'scientific' in nature. When it comes to the Late Bronze Age (after ca. 1600 BC) especially, other issues also come to the fore—e.g., modes of production and exchange, historical and political links to other polities near and far. Less well considered are the social and material factors of Cypriot metallurgy, namely the prehistoric landscapes of mining and metallurgical production, the mining communities, hoarding practices, the social aspects of producing and exchanging copper, and the networks—terrestrial and maritime—that facilitated the entire system. This paper focuses on these social aspects of metallurgical production and exchange and considers the impact of metals and metallurgy on the Bronze Age inhabitants of Cyprus.

Keywords Cyprus · Eastern Mediterranean · Bronze Age · Social archaeology · Archaeometallurgy · Mining · Copper production · Trade/exchange networks · Mining communities · Mining landscapes · Hoards

---

A. B. Knapp (✉)
Archaeology, Department of Humanities, University of Glasgow, Glasgow, Scotland, UK

Cyprus American Archaeological Research Institute, Nicosia, Cyprus
e-mail: bernard.knapp@glasgow.ac.uk

© The Author(s), under exclusive license to Springer Nature Switzerland AG 2023
E. Ben-Yosef, I. W. N. Jones (eds.), *"And in Length of Days Understanding" (Job 12:12): Essays on Archaeology in the Eastern Mediterranean and Beyond in Honor of Thomas E. Levy*, Interdisciplinary Contributions to Archaeology, https://doi.org/10.1007/978-3-031-27330-8_56

1 Introduction

> Numerous projects over the last half-century have applied science-based approaches to the study of metalwork to address archaeological questions of alloy selection, development, distribution, and provenance, the latter long considered the 'Holy Grail' of the discipline.
> (Radivojević et al., 2019: 165)

Along with other science-based treatments of metals and the remains of metallurgical production, the 'holy grail' of provenance studies has long formed a key part of the archaeometallurgy of Cyprus, and lead isotope analysis (LIA)—whatever its potential or pitfalls—has enjoyed particular prominence (e.g., Gale & Stos-Gale, 1986, 1987, 2012; cf. Muhly, 1995, 2003; Knapp, 2000, 2002). In a steady stream of articles, Kassianidou has presented an array of archaeometallurgical studies on Cypriot ores, slags, ingots, metals and mines (e.g., 2004, 2009a, 2012, 2013, 2018a; Karageorghis & Kassianidou, 1999); our work on the mining and smelting site of Politiko *Phorades* has also been published in a preliminary manner (Knapp & Kassianidou, 2008; see also Knapp, 2003). More pertinent to the present study, however, was our co-authored paper on Mediterranean archaeometallurgy writ large, an initial attempt to consider some of the social aspects of the mining, technology and trade in metals (Kassianidou & Knapp, 2005). In that study, we discussed the production and use of specific metals throughout the Mediterranean, and attempted to assess some of the relevant metallurgical data with respect to mining and metallurgical landscapes, mining communities and the impact of metals and metallurgy on Mediterranean production, exchange and consumption.

On Cyprus, the known Middle or Late Bronze Age copper production sites—Ambelikou *Aletri*, Politiko *Phorades*, Apliki *Karamallos*—were all located in the igneous zone within the foothills of the (northern) Troodos mountains, in close proximity to ore deposits (Fig. 1). These sites were thus relatively isolated from the island's main population centres, which at least in the Late Bronze Age (LBA) were often located on or near the seacoast (e.g., Enkomi, Kition, Hala Sultan Tekke, Maroni, Kalavasos). Innovations in technology not only impacted the environment around these production sites but also would have altered the social practices of those who mined and produced metals, particularly in cases where more extensive mining operations and more intensified production were involved (Stöllner, 2003: 430–432).

The technological advances associated with intensified production also necessitated a sophisticated communication network, the systematic organisation of copper mining and distribution, and a maritime shipping capacity to meet overseas demand. Moreover, various 'paraphernalia of power' (bronze statuettes and stands, miniature ingots, ingot representations on pottery, stands and seals) associated with the technology of smelting sulphide ores not only symbolised socioeconomic aspirations but also served ideological functions, and helped to legitimise the authority and bolster the social position of those who organised metallurgical production (Knapp, 1988a: 144–146; Papasavvas, 2011). During the LBA, increased copper production

A Social Archaeometallurgy of Bronze Age Cyprus

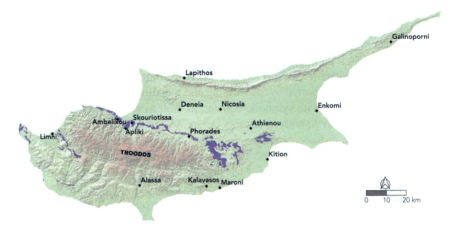

Fig. 1 Map of Cyprus, indicating all sites and locations mentioned in the text, with Upper Pillows Lavas shown in purple. (Prepared by Nathan Meyer. Geology adapted from the Cyprus Geological Survey map portal at: https://arcg.is/0qeDPD)

ultimately led to the widespread availability of Cypriot copper throughout the Near East and the Mediterranean (Muhly et al., 1988: 287–288; Knapp, 2012: 17–18).

In this study, dedicated to a scholar who has long been involved in matters archaeometallurgical (e.g., Levy & Shalev, 1989; Levy et al., 2002, 2012, 2018), my aim is to reconsider some of the social changes associated with developments in extractive and metallurgical technologies on Bronze Age Cyprus, and with the intensified production, distribution and consumption of metals and metal objects during that era.

2 Social Archaeometallurgy

Archaeometallurgical analyses and related research play a fundamental role in interpreting multiple aspects of prehistoric cultures: chronology, subsistence and economy, ritual and ideology, craft specialisation, production and exchange, connectivity and mobility, and the myriad manifestations of identity. Yet as Radivojević et al. (2019: 131) point out, the focus of archaeometallurgical research tends to fall on determining the geological origin of metals, especially copper and tin, and how metals and ores might have moved from production sites to consumption centres. The impact, or not, of recycling on the composition of the circulating metals has also attracted much attention (most recently, Sainsbury et al., 2021). In addition, debates over the value and/or perception of metals, whether as finished objects or hoarded material, continue to generate scholarly discussion (e.g., Renfrew, 2012; Iacono, 2016: 110–113; Erb-Satullo, 2019: 563–566; Radivojević et al., 2019).

Once metal is obtained from ores, it is invested with multiple and changing social and politico-economic meanings. Metals and metal artifacts may take on material and symbolic expressions of wealth/status, identity, fertility or other 'life changes', as well as religious or ideological affiliation (Childs & Killick, 1993: 330–332). Even in the preindustrial world, metals were valuable commodities, and their value was enhanced when transported by sea. Mining and metallurgy in preindustrial contexts were often imbued with symbolic content, as well as various other aspects of culture that have little to do with metallurgy *per se*. Material remains and analytical results are the stock-in-trade of archaeologists and archaeometallurgists, who are often able not only to reconstruct metallurgical installations with an extraordinary degree of detail but also to postulate if not demonstrate some of the social aspects of prehistoric mining and metallurgy. The material record of mining sites, rural or agricultural villages, production centres and distribution points is well suited to a study of archaeological variability from a broad comparative and chronological perspective.

The relationship between mining, settlement and landscape varies according to the scale and organisational level of production (Raber, 1987: 301–302; Erb-Satullo, 2022). For example, the intermittent small-scale, localised production of the medieval era on Cyprus contrasts significantly with the larger scale industries and major labour forces typical of the Imperial Roman period (Kassianidou, 2000). From Galen's well-known account of his second century AD visit to the mines near Soli and Skouriotissa on Cyprus (Kassianidou et al., 2021), to the tales and rituals associated with the supernatural powers who 'owned' the hills worked by Bolivian tin miners (e.g., Godoy, 1991; Nash, 1993), to the rich ethnographic accounts of 'ancestors' who developed and passed along to their kin the knowledge of metal smelting processes in pre-colonial Africa (Childs & Killick, 1993), mining and extractive metallurgy are activities with dynamic social and intellectual implications that impacted significantly on the social and natural order of things.

Next to the often rich and extensive documentation of metals and the metals' trade in Bronze Age documentary sources (e.g., for Anatolia, Larsen, 2015; for the Levant, Monroe, 2009; Bell, 2012; for Egypt, Moran, 1992; for Cyprus, Knapp, 2008: 307–316; Kassianidou, 2009b), the actual numbers of metals and metal objects in the archaeological record are comparatively limited. This situation may suggest that managers or elites in the urban centres of these areas valued metals so highly that there was only a limited deposition of metals and/or high rates of re-melting and recycling (Radivojević et al., 2019: 155).

With respect to Cyprus specifically, a social archaeometallurgical approach should also consider what motivated the export of copper (oxhide ingots) to areas like Sardinia or the eastern Balkans, themselves rich in copper ore deposits. Were such exchanges directed and carried out solely by Cypriot agents, or were they the outcome of initiatives based on social or economic factors embedded in the interaction spheres of those regions? I consider both questions in further detail below.

3 Metallurgy and Society on Bronze Age Cyprus

3.1 Mining Landscapes: Material and Social Context

Despite over a half-century of archaeological survey in the Mediterranean, and the wealth of historical documentation available on mining, deforestation, overgrazing, manuring and other agricultural practices, we still understand all too little about the complex relationship between land use, resource exploitation and landscape change in the Mediterranean basin (Walsh, 2014). Throughout the Mediterranean, islands of volcanic origin and mainland zones of mineral wealth often enjoyed special prominence because of their raw materials. Such places often retained their status long after demand for certain resources dried up, or when the focus and direction of regional trade shifted. In turn, long distance contacts often resulted in outside interference if not domination, as well as the relentless exploitation of both insular and mainland resources. Such overexploitation of metals and other minerals particularly affected Mediterranean islands, whether large or small.

In order to understand the configuration of ancient metallurgical landscapes, one has to consider how the physical makeup of the land conditioned the location of mines, ore beneficiation installations, primary and secondary smelting sites, and distribution centres (Erb-Satullo, 2022). In addition, one needs to evaluate how mining or other archaeometallurgical enterprises transformed natural features into an industrial landscape.

The material culture of the mining enterprise impacts heavily on the configuration of industrial landscapes. Because unprocessed ores are by nature both bulky and weighty, metals were almost always produced near the ore deposits. Basal geology is thus a key factor in selecting such a deposit for exploitation and mining. Other factors affect social production and economic demand: the nature of the labour force (free or servile), the availability of water (for energy or drinking), the difficulties in exploiting ore sources and transporting the end product, and the micro-environments where ores were refined and smelted. On Cyprus, Constantinou (1992: 56–57, 60–61) pointed out that other 'natural' features—for example the bright gossan 'cap' that distinguishes many copper ore deposits, or a specific type of vegetation (e.g., *pinus Brutia*; see Griggs et al., 2014) associated with certain ore bodies—would have been well known to prospectors and miners.

Still other factors influence where ores were prepared for smelting or refining. If, for example, washing ores forms part of the beneficiation process, then either a fresh water source must be nearby, or water must be collected from elsewhere and stored for use, or the ores must be transported to a water source. In some cases, the primary stages in smelting ores take place in the immediate vicinity of a mine; in other cases, the determining factor may be the availability of fuel. Because certain metals are also highly valued commodities, production sites or workshops tend to be established in secure and easily defensible places, especially when economic organisation is lax or political unity is lacking. Two of the best examples of such prehistoric industrial landscapes are the intensively studied and excavated areas around Faynan in Jordan and Timna in the Negev, which include mines, shafts and adits, copper smelting installations, habitational remains, a 'sanctuary', and more (most recently, see Ben-Yosef, 2016; Yagel et al., 2016; Levy et al., 2018).

The smelting of copper required significant amounts of wood or charcoal. Based on a more recent Mediterranean analogy (the island of Elba), Weisgerber (1982: 28) argued that deforestation for fuel so completely denuded primary copper production areas on Cyprus that evidence of prehistoric metallurgical activities would only be found buried deep beneath alluvial deposits triggered by widespread erosion. The discovery and excavation of a LBA smelting site at Politiko *Phorades* (Knapp & Kassianidou, 2008), however, indicates that prehistoric metallurgical sites on Cyprus are not all buried deep under alluvial soils.

Although Cyprus never had truly palatial economies like those that characterised contemporary communities in the Aegean or the Levant, once some person or group managed to organise all the factors involved in producing, transporting and distributing the island's copper resources, and in meeting the subsistence needs of miners and metalsmiths, Cyprus rapidly assumed a prominent economic and political position in what was to become a Mediterranean-wide trade in metals and other luxury goods in demand. In social terms, whereas the intensified production of copper employing an advanced technology did not preclude a strong sense of local community, such factors served to increase social distinctions between those at the top of the control structure and those at the bottom (Hardesty, 1988: 102, 116; Knapp, 2003).

Colourful gossans and sparkling ores, along with fluxes like manganese oxide, haematite and silica (used to lower the melting point and viscosity of the gangue during smelting) were amongst the most obvious features of the ancient mining landscape. The deep brown layers of umber and the black nodules of manganese concretions take on further significance in a mining landscape. Mining galleries usually require pit-props, and smelting needs fuel: the production of metal, in other words, requires forests, not just trees. Beyond various species of pine, hardwoods like olive, oak and hawthorn were also common in the Mediterranean forests of antiquity: because they produce a long, hot burn and could be coppiced easily, they are ideally suited as a fuel source for roasting and as charcoal for smelting. On Cyprus, the denuded landscape of many areas close to the copper-ore-bearing Pillow Lavas of the Troodos Mountains (see Fig. 1, above), must have resulted at least in part from 4000 years of copper mining on the island (Kassianidou et al., 2021).

Whenever the production of copper exceeded the local or regional scale, mining communities became linked into interregional, national or global networks of communication and exchange. Invariably this development impacted on the mining landscape in the form of imports, migrant labour, possibly even new settlements in the face of other socio-structural changes.

People use the landscape for everything from producing food to expressing formal design (e.g., in buildings) to making social statements. Ethnographic and historical evidence shows that mining can be a very significant factor in this relationship between people and their environment: e.g., the huge modern spoil heap of Kokkinopezoula within the Cypriot village of Mitsero (Fig. 2) stands as a

Fig. 2 Photo of *Kokkinopezoula* modern mining spoil heap, Mitsero village, Cyprus. (Photograph by A.B. Knapp)

monumental example of how human modification of the landscape can define a village, give its inhabitants a sense of identity and provide an economic basis that ensures their survival.

3.2 Mining Communities

During the Middle Bronze Age on Cyprus, current evidence suggests that, for the first time in the island's history, intensified copper production and the manufacture of metal goods led to the practice of locating sites in or near the cupriferous zone. As Stech (1985: 102–103) pointed out long ago, transport and logistical factors dictated that the primary smelting of copper ores ideally would be conducted in close proximity to the mines. Moreover, the exploitation of sulphide ores within the Pillow Lavas of the northern foothills of the Troodos provided a catalyst for the development of inter-island relations and interregional if not external trade (Knapp, 1990: 159–160; Webb & Knapp, 2021: 217–218, 235).

The site of Ambelikou *Aletri* (Middle Cypriot I-II, ca. 1950–1850 BC) has revealed residues of what was likely a mining community (Webb & Frankel, 2013), one linked to other communities on the island (e.g., Lapithos on the north coast, Deneia and Nicosia on the central plain—Webb & Knapp, 2021: 223). A three-ha-site situated within 150 m of a small ore body, Ambelikou was first excavated in 1942. Merrillees (1984: 3–4, and figs. 2–4) reported on two partially excavated areas as well as ten restricted trial trenches that produced some fragmentary wall sections and a number of incomplete adjacent units. Area 1 contained indisputable evidence for metalworking: a hearth for melting and casting, work platforms, pits, an ingot mould, a tuyère, mortars, and many crushing and grinding stone tools (Webb & Frankel, 2013: 206–213; Webb, 2015) (Fig. 3). Ground stone tools and (Red Polished III) pottery sherds were recovered deep within modern mining shafts—approximately 19 m deep inside the Stoa 2 shaft and 2 m deep inside the Kekleimenou 1 shaft. Although no formal excavations were carried out in these shafts, the artefacts were clearly *in situ*, and there was some evidence for 'ancient workings' (Webb & Frankel, 2013: 29, fig. 3.2).

All this material evidence suggests that marketable seams of quality ore were available deep inside the mines, and Webb and Frankel (2013: 206–213) maintain that the mining, smelting and casting of ingots were carried out at Ambelikou. In addition, Area 2 housed a pottery workshop, complete with a kiln, wasters, blocks of unfired clay, and 39 jugs, perhaps the final kiln load (Webb & Frankel, 2013: 213–219). Although the finds from Ambelikou are limited, they nonetheless reveal a few structures that served either to facilitate the production of ores or to shelter those working inside the mining shafts. Whilst Areas 1 and 2 demonstrate a focus on industrial activities, the wider array of material from Ambelikou indicates that the site was also used for domestic and agricultural purposes.

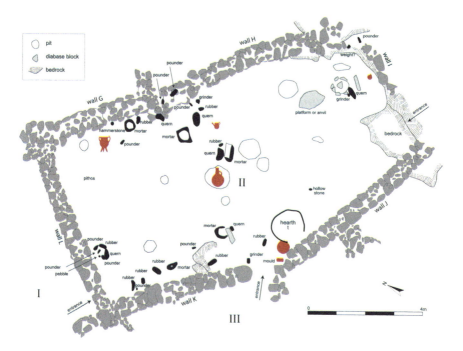

Fig. 3 Plan of metallurgical workshop at Ambelikou *Aletri*, showing features, ground stone objects and pottery *in situ*. (Courtesy of Jennifer Webb)

A Social Archaeometallurgy of Bronze Age Cyprus

On LBA Cyprus, smelting sites like Politiko *Phorades* (Late Cypriot 1, ca. 1600–1500 BC) and mining villages like Apliki *Karamallos* (Late Cypriot 2, ca. 1300–1200 BC) were also situated in close proximity to the rich copper ore deposits in the northern Troodos foothills (see Fig. 1, above). Whereas the remains at *Phorades* indicate an industrial site where copper was produced for local use or before shipment elsewhere, most likely to coastal centres (Knapp & Kassianidou, 2008), Apliki more likely represents a community where those who produced copper actually lived (Kling & Muhly, 2007).

House A at Apliki—the only one of several structures to be fully excavated—was built about 1300 BC and destroyed approximately one century later (Manning and Kuniholm, in Kling & Muhly, 2007: 328). The many spindle whorls and loom weights recovered in House A suggest spinning and weaving practices (Smith, in Kling & Muhly, 2007: 233). Although diverse metal objects were found at Apliki (e.g., bronze drills, awls, a knife and chisel, some bronze leaf, two lead objects, a gold earring—du Plat Taylor, 1952: 152; Kling & Muhly, 2007: 311–313), the excavations uncovered no physical evidence for ore dressing activities (Kassianidou, in Kling & Muhly, 2007: 283; see also du Plat Taylor, 1952: 150). Some of the faunal remains (sheep, goat, ox), however, were stained green, which suggests they were impregnated with copper or iron 'salts' (Croft, in Kling & Muhly, 2007: 321). Moreover, there are other indicators of metallurgical activities in House A: Kassianidou's study (in Kling & Muhly, 2007: 277) of the ground stone tools (pestles, rubbers, querns) led her to suggest that Apliki was both an industrial site where copper was extracted from sulphide ores and a settlement that contained storage facilities for goods used or consumed by the workforce.

The site at *Karamallos* is situated about two miles from the ore body at Apliki, and it is widely agreed that it was a miners' community, one that reveals many of the accoutrements of daily life and likely provided living space for the miners who worked the ore body (cf. du Plat Taylor, 1952: 150, 164). Muhly (1989: 306–307, fig. 35.1), for example, maintained that the large blocks of black ropy slag, present in many of the rooms in House A, along with the massive tuyères found at the site, confirmed that '… extensive mining and smelting operations were carried out at Apliki during the 13th and 12th centuries BC' (but cf. du Plat Taylor, 1952: 142). Moreover, explorations by the Cyprus Mines Corporation found discarded furnace remnants at the 'North Hill' of Apliki, at the time covered in slag heaps (du Plat Taylor, 1952: 152). All this, along with the presence of flat, round-sectioned and 'elbow' tuyères (House A, a pit in trench B), as well as fragments of crucibles, stone hammers and the quantities of slag, suggests that those who dwelt at *Karamallos* were intimately involved in preparing and processing copper ores.

Of the three Cypriot Bronze Age sites directly associated with metallurgy, only Politiko *Phorades* served primarily industrial functions. Excavations at *Phorades* indicated that river channel deposits were used to construct an artificial working platform on which the metalworkers operated smelting furnaces (Knapp & Kassianidou, 2008: 138). A stone-lined cavity found on this artificial bank contained several tuyère fragments, and several almost complete tuyères lay just outside the cavity: this installation may have served as a tapping pit associated with smelting. A small slag heap that resulted from smelting was piled against the bank of the creek. Along with the large quantity of slag, the concentrations of broken tuyères (cylindrical, double-walled, elbow) and furnace fragments indicate that copper (sulphide) ores were smelted at the site. Other finds such as pottery, chipped stone and ground stone tools were limited. The pottery sherds, recovered almost exclusively within the metalworking levels, could be dated closely to Late Cypriot I– early Late Cypriot II (sixteenth–fifteenth centuries BC); this dating was confirmed by AMS radiocarbon analyses on charcoal found within the furnace walls and slag (Knapp & Kassianidou, 2008: 139–140, fig. 6).

The rich archaeometallurgical remains from *Phorades* comprise over 6000 fragments of furnace rims, walls and bases, 50 almost complete tuyères and nearly 600 tuyère fragments. The furnaces and tuyères were manufactured from local clays that the metalworkers seem to have chosen specifically because their inclusions enabled the installations to withstand temperatures up to 1200 °C (Hein & Kilikoglou, 2007; Hein et al., 2007). The 3.5 tons of slag fragments, mainly represented by large plano-concave cakes weighing about 20 kg, contained copper averaging 2.7%; the slag from *Phorades* differs in type and shape from all other known Late Bronze slags excavated on the island.

We have argued that the metal produced at *Phorades* was matte, based on the presence of matte prills within the slag matrix, and the discovery of a small piece of silver-blue matte that consisted of 73.5% copper, 2.6% iron and 23.9% sulphur (Knapp & Kassianidou, 2008: 143–144, fig. 16; Knapp, 2012: 18–19, fig. 3.8). Rarely found in excavations, matte is an intermediate product in the production of copper metal, and its presence at the site signals yet again that *Phorades* was a primary smelting workshop, one that served this function exclusively: once the site was abandoned, the remains had no further use to the metalworkers.

The smelting site at *Phorades* formed part of a nested, regional community with a distinct social organisation and communication networks linked to other regional if not supra-regional polities (Knapp, 2003; Kassianidou, 2022). The social and spatial relationships between a smelting site like *Phorades*, its agricultural catchment area, other industrial sites in the near vicinity, and the wider regional, human community vary with respect to the organisational level and scale of production. Industrial sites like *Phorades* fulfilled some of the basic needs for raw materials and perhaps even certain finished products within the regional community. In turn, however, during successive phases of Cyprus's Late Bronze Age, as external demand accelerated the production of copper beyond local or regional capacities, at least some if not the majority of industrial sites and their community networks would have become integrated into supra-regional exchange networks. Such developments brought migrant labour and new ideologies, and in certain places exotic goods, into the mining region, all of which would have led to new social uses of space as well as changes in the social structure of the regional community. All these factors led to unprecedented technological and social developments: Cyprus became not only a major purveyor of copper to the Bronze Age Mediterranean world but also an urbanised, state-level power.

A Social Archaeometallurgy of Bronze Age Cyprus

3.3 Production and Exchange Networks

One of the key indicators of maritime movement within the Mediterranean during the LBA was the widespread distribution of oxhide ingots (e.g., Muhly et al., 1988; Gale, 1991; Lo Schiavo et al., 2009; Lehner et al., 2020). Many authors regard oxhide ingots—wherever they were produced and in whatever direction they may have moved—to represent the output of Cypriot productive activity and the prerogative of Cypriot (or Aegean) agents. Sabatini (2016a: 34), for example, regards the presence of oxhide ingots or depictions of oxhide ingots in continental Europe as the result of Cypriot market expansion strategies. In her view, Cyprus profited from a high demand for metal in second millennium BC Europe, and the oxhide ingots represent a 'brand' of commodity in 'a strategy to guarantee specific economies (such as fourteenth and thirteenth century BC Cyprus) consistent slices of the market' (Sabatini, 2016a: 41; see also Sabatini, 2016b: 46–47). Athanassov et al. (2020: 337-38), however, interpret the whole or fragmented oxhide ingots found in the eastern Balkans (and in Oberwilflingen, Germany) not as Cypriot exports, but as European imports, results of different local, regional and transregional factors that have nothing to do with Cypriot entrepreneurs or Cypriot market strategies.

Most oxhide ingots analysed using LIA, however, are at least consistent with production from Cypriot ores (see, e.g., Budd et al., 1995; Stos-Gale et al., 1997; Gale, 1989; Hauptmann et al., 2002; Graziadio, 2014). They were transported within and beyond the Mediterranean by maritime merchants—not necessarily Cypriots—who must have been familiar with the languages, social conventions, exchange networks and economic infrastructures of the wider Mediterranean world, from Egypt and the Levant in the east to Sicily, Sardinia, Corsica and France in the west. Such socio-economic and maritime links presume not just foreign demand and a surplus of copper or metal goods, but also exchange networks and communal alliances if not kin-based relations (Kassianidou & Knapp, 2005: 215; Knapp et al., 2022).

Even so, no single explanation can account for this widespread distribution of Cypriot oxhide ingots within and beyond the Mediterranean. As Athanassov et al. (2020: 338) argue, we should move beyond simplistic 'external' explanations such as Sabatini's and instead consider how imports such as oxhide ingots '… were translated and incorporated into local social and economic realities … the driving powers of European long-distance exchange'. In turn, as Radivojević et al. (2019) maintain in their recent reassessment of the circulation of metals in the European Bronze Age, we should investigate the objects, minerals or metals in question as well as the nature, scale and significance of human contacts by attempting to determine the motives for exchange, the 'translated' meanings ascribed to the objects or metals by the people involved, as well as the consequences of the exchange.

In his study of the appropriation and translation of amber objects in Mycenaean Greece, Maran (2013: 147, 149) defines 'translation' in the sense of negotiating the fluid meanings of external goods and objects '… through their integration into social practice and discourses within constantly re-assembled networks comprising human and non-human actants'. Indirect exchange—or a combination of diverse types of exchange—between different regions was facilitated through a chain of interlocking (maritime) networks, where the direct presence of Aegean (or Cypriot or Sardinian) traders was not essential for the implementation of all the trading ventures that must have existed in the vast expanse of territory between Gibraltar and the Levant. Indeed, Knapp et al. (2022) have recently challenged the allegedly direct trade route between Sardinia and Cyprus during the Late Bronze–early Iron Ages. They suggest instead a network that hinges on multiply connected nodes, where a variety of social actors were involved in creating and maintaining long-distance maritime connections (Fig. 4). Simply asserting the dominance of Aegean, Cypriot or Sardinian mariners fails to explain the complex material evidence and at the same time eschews possible social interpretations: maritime connectivity is an inherently social activity, and the culturally diverse LBA Mediterranean was obviously connected by multiple interlocking and overlapping networks.

The models and mechanisms developed to explore the nature of these exchange networks should consider not only the extent to which people and ideas moved with metals (or other commodities) but also the types of goods that may have been exchanged for ores, ingots or finished metal products (Radivojević et al., 2019: 163). The extensive network(s) involved in the spread of oxhide ingots, for example, brought foreign objects and raw materials to Cyprus (and to Sardinia for that matter), and all such foreign objects must have been exchanged for something in return. Such models also require some archaeological 'imagination', and should engage the evidence for spice, drugs, grain and grog, not to mention livestock and labour (Knapp, 1991; Pérez-Jordà et al., 2021). Equally relevant are the liminal and symbolic aspects of maritime space, the real or imaginary experiences and the 'common sense geography' of mariners and seafarers (Monroe, 2011; Geus & Thiering,

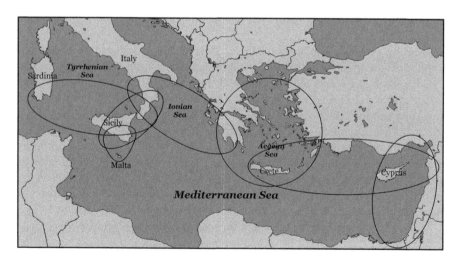

Fig. 4 Suggested network of overlapping regional interaction spheres in the Late Bronze Age Mediterranean. (Prepared by Anthony Russell)

A Social Archaeometallurgy of Bronze Age Cyprus

2014). Finally, the mechanics involved in networks of Mediterranean exchange involved not only economic factors such as the nature and amount of goods traded, but also social factors such as cooperation, competition and status amongst merchants, mariners and consumers, as well as the ideologies of exchange (Kassianidou & Knapp, 2005: 237). Closer to the core of such extensive systems that linked traded goods and economic or political status were the managers or other representatives of elites who would have interacted in diverse ways with miners and metalworkers.

3.4 Metal Hoards

In an early study of Late Cypriot and Aegean hoards, Knapp et al. (1988) categorised them as representing either utilitarian (hidden by merchants or metalworkers with the intention of recovery) or non-utilitarian deposits (votive or building deposits never intended for retrieval); Kassianidou (2018b) reassesses and corrects the contents of some of these hoards. Swiny (2020: 312–313) maintains that all but one of the twelve hoards from Enkomi may be classified as a 'founder's hoard' (i.e., utilitarian); in his view, the 'weapon hoard' is actually a concentration of metal debris from a destruction level (IIIA) at the site. Since the original publication by Knapp et al. (1988), only one further 'hoard'—all weapons, no scrap metal—has been published, from a Late Cypriot IIIA deposit at Alassa *Pano Mandilares* (Hadjisavvas, 2011: 23–24; cf. Bartelheim et al., 2008 on a LBA hoard from the locality *Vasili*, near Galinoporni, illegally excavated in the Turkish-occupied north of the island, and thus not considered further here).

Like most of the other hoards in question, the one from Alassa also appears to be associated with a metallurgical workshop; as Swiny (2020: 314) notes, there is obviously a link between scrap metal, utilitarian hoarding and metalworking on a practical level. Blackwell's (2018) recent re-assessment of broadly contemporary Aegean hoards, which contained a range of complete and broken items but most importantly a broadly common grouping of tools, suggests a similar link but one that may have been controlled by the Mycenaean state (either as stock or the remnants of metal provided to a smith). In their recent study of European Bronze Age hoards, Radivojević et al. (2019: 162) point out that standardised ingots and hack-bronze objects tend to occur in mutually exclusive deposits, which may support their notion that they represent two different, pre-monetary 'currency' systems. In their view, hoarding practice is at least partially embedded in local cultural and political developments linked to increasing social inequality and the accumulation of wealth. Paraphrasing the distinction already made between utilitarian and non-utilitarian deposits, Radivojević et al. (2019: 164–165) suggest that the hoarding of metals indicates at least two, often entangled motivations: (1) curation of direct benefit for the living and (2) offerings to gods or ancestors of indirect benefit (see also Osborne, 2004; Wengrow, 2011).

On Cyprus, there has been little in-depth consideration of the possible social meanings of hoards or the intentions of those who deposited them, whether as utilitarian or votive deposits (cf. Swiny, 2020). One striking aspect of these Cypriot metal deposits, however, is that virtually all of them belong to a narrow window of time (thirteenth–twelfth centuries BC) and that the majority have been found within a restricted, 70 by 30 km corridor in southeastern Cyprus. Even if it were allowed that this (artificial) 'corridor' somehow represented a distinctive region, the majority stem from Enkomi, well known for its role as a centre for copper production (smelting) and distribution (e.g., Muhly, 1989; Crewe, 2007: 17–18, 156–157). Moreover, only three deposits can be defined as 'votive' in nature (Kition 'Temple' 4; Enkomi 'Horned God'; Enkomi 'Maison des Bronzes'). Because these three votive deposits contain a total of 12 objects (bronze stands, metal figurines, miniature ingots, some scrap—i.e., mostly paraphernalia of power, long used in Cyprus before their final, twelfth century BC deposition), it is difficult without further, focused research to ascertain anything meaningful about their contents vis-à-vis the contents of utilitarian hoards.

In sum, we can only speculate on the extent to which the social value of copper might be reflected in the selective deposition of certain kinds of metal artifacts or ingots as votive or utilitarian hoards. Radivojević et al. (2019: 167) suggest that the material as well as the social value of copper may be related to factors associated with interregional and long-distance trade of metal as part of a wider Bronze Age economic setting. On Cyprus, the study of hoards suggests a similar phenomenon, but one that was may have been linked to the unsettled conditions in the eastern Mediterranean during the century between ca. 1250–1150 BC (Knapp, 1988b; Meyer & Knapp, 2021).

4 Discussion and Conclusions

The mining of ores and the production of metals had profound social implications that structured and altered people's lives. Within the isolated settings of Cyprus's mining communities (what Douglass [1998] termed a 'community without a locus'), miners and metalworkers—whose living space and subsistence base may have been situated elsewhere in the wider regional territory—typically had a social organisation that was expedient and perhaps seasonal in nature, as mining often alternated with agricultural demands (Knapp, 2003).

Most primary copper smelting was conducted within the mining region itself, and the economic aspects of copper mining meant that most copper produced was intended for exchange, with little set aside to meet the needs of industrial communities such as Ambelikou *Aletri* or Apliki *Karamallos*. Limited growing conditions within such communities, located in igneous zones or in semi-montane regions, meant that they were at least partially reliant on other communities devoted to agricultural activities. Some primary smelting and certainly secondary smelting were carried out in communities situated some distance from the ore sources, e.g., at

Enkomi, Hala Sultan Tekke, Athienou or Kalavasos *Ayios Dhimitrios*. Although such towns would have benefitted from higher returns on their labour by engaging in agricultural or other exchange activities, they too may have used some of their production for exchange purposes.

Supra-regional and state-level politico-economic power on LBA Cyprus was based in part on convertible resources such as copper ingots and metal goods, in part on the people who were able to organise production (and the labour involved) and who were capable of establishing or co-ordinating the exchange networks that moved such materials within and beyond the island. In turn, such movement was propelled by consumer (or supplier) demand and, importantly for external exchange, by maritime technology, which also allowed not just goods but ideas to move between different people, communities and polities.

In the wider Mediterranean world of the LBA, several social changes were associated with developments in extractive and metallurgical technologies, and with the intensified production and distribution of metals and metal objects (Kassianidou & Knapp, 2005: 239). Such changes included the emergence of town centres; an expansion in interregional trade; the increasing use of sailing ships; the growth of palatial regimes and other coastal polities; the elaboration of mortuary practices with large quantities of precious metal goods. In the eastern Mediterranean, other, related changes included the emergence of writing systems (used at least in part to record economic transactions); the frequent occurrence of metal hoards on Cyprus and in the Aegean; a trade in recycled and scrap metal; the development of craft specialisation; and the spread of an iconographic koine. The circulation of minerals, ores and metal goods across maritime and terrestrial space and through diverse economic systems represents a social transaction that entangled producers, distributors and consumers in broader yet closer relations of alliance and dependence.

As Kunze and Pernicka (2020: 67) recently argued, technological innovations associated with the production of copper precipitated certain changes that promoted the hierarchical organisation of societies. The growing demand for metals (copper in particular) and a 'clearly segmented chain of production'—from mining to ore processing to the transfer and exchange of ingots or finished metal products—led to new modes of interaction between producers and consumers and necessitated close communications and more intimate social relations within and between communities.

From the early third millennium BC onward in the increasingly interconnected Mediterranean world, the interplay of social and economic forces with resource diversity helped to shape the entire history of shipping and commerce, the emergence and divergence of political regimes, the configuration of ideologies, the implementation and spread of religious doctrines, and the ever-changing face of the landscape. The diverse *mentalités* of ancient miners, metalsmiths, merchants, entrepreneurs and traders set the stage for individual exchanges, community relations, social alliances, regional polities, interregional systems of production and exchange, and imperial regimes of exploitation and consumption. The knowledge of and control over metal and mineral resources, the circulation of valued goods (metals in particular) in demand, expertise in navigation and maritime technology, and the impact of distance and the exotic on local people and ideologies served to shape and continually to reform economic connections, power relations and social conventions. Such factors all combine to provide the framework—the sources and outcomes—for a social archaeometallurgy.

Acknowledgments My thanks to Jennifer Webb for reading and providing helpful comments on an earlier draft of this study. I also thank her for providing Fig. 3 (Ambelikou *Aletri* metallurgical workshop). Special thanks to Nathan Meyer for preparing Fig. 1 and to Anthony Russell for producing Fig. 4 (an earlier version of which appeared in Knapp et al., 2022: fig. 3).

References

Athanassov, B., Chernakov, D., Krauß, R., Dimitrov, K., Popov, H., Schwab, R., et al. (2020). A new look at the Late Bronze Age oxhide ingots from the eastern Balkans. In J. Maran, R. Băjenaru, S.-C. Ailincăi, A.-D. Popescu, & S. Hansen (Eds.), *Objects, ideas and travelers. Contacts between the Balkans, the Aegean and western Anatolia during the Bronze and Early Iron Age* (Universitätsforschungen zur prähistorischen Archäologie 350) (pp. 299–356). Verlag Dr. Rudolf Habelt.

Bartelheim, M., Kizilduman, B., Müller, U., Pernicka, E., & Tekel, H. (2008). The Late Bronze Age hoard of Kaleburnu/Galinoporni on Cyprus. *Památky Archeologické, 99*, 161–188.

Bell, C. (2012). The merchants of Ugarit: oligarchs of the Late Bronze Age trade in metals? In V. Kassianidou & G. Papasavvas (Eds.), *Eastern Mediterranean metallurgy and metalwork in the second millennium BC* (pp. 180–187). Oxbow.

Ben-Yosef, E. (2016). Back to Solomon's era: Results of the first excavations at "Slaves' Hill" (Site 34, Timna, Israel). *Bulletin of the American Schools of Oriental Research, 376*, 169–198.

Blackwell, N. G. (2018). Contextualizing Mycenaean hoards: Metal control on the Greek mainland at the end of the Bronze Age. *American Journal of Archaeology, 122*(4), 509–539.

Budd, P., Pollard, A. M., Scaife, B., & Thomas, A. M. (1995). Oxhide ingots, recycling and the Mediterranean metals trade. *Journal of Mediterranean Archaeology, 8*(1), 1–32.

Childs, S. T., & Killick, D. (1993). Indigenous African metallurgy: Nature and culture. *Annual Review of Anthropology, 22*, 317–337.

Constantinou, G. (1992). Ancient copper mining in Cyprus. In A. Marangou & K. Psillides (Eds.), *Cyprus, copper and the sea* (pp. 43–74). Government of Cyprus.

Crewe, L. (2007). *Early Enkomi. Regionalism, trade and society at the beginning of the Late Bronze Age on Cyprus* (British Archaeological Reports, International Series 1706). Archaeopress.

Douglass, W. A. (1998). The mining camp as community. In A. B. Knapp, V. C. Pigott, & E. Herbert (Eds.), *Social approaches to an industrial past: The archaeology and anthropology of mining* (pp. 97–108). Routledge.

du Plat Taylor, J. (1952). A Late Bronze Age settlement at Apliki, Cyprus. *Antiquaries Journal, 32*, 133–167.

Erb-Satullo, N. L. (2019). The innovation and adoption of iron in the ancient Near East. *Journal of Archaeological Research, 27*(4), 557–607.

Erb-Satullo, N. L. (2022). Towards a spatial archaeology of crafting landscapes. *Cambridge Archaeological Journal, 32*(4), 567–583.

Gale, N. H. (1989). Archaeometallurgical studies of Late Bronze Age copper oxhide ingots from the Mediterranean region. In A. Hauptmann, E. Pernicka, & G. A. Wagner (Eds.), *Old World archaeometallurgy* (Der Anschnitt 7) (pp. 247–268). Deutsches Bergbau-Museums.

Gale, N. H. (1991). Copper oxhide ingots and their relation to Bronze Age metals trade. In N. H. Gale (Ed.), *Bronze Age trade in the Mediterranean* (Studies in Mediterranean Archaeology 90) (pp. 197–239). P. Åström's Förlag.

Gale, N. H., & Stos-Gale, Z. A. (1986). Oxhide copper ingots in Crete and Cyprus and the Bronze Age metals trade. *Annual of the British School at Athens, 81*, 81–100.

Gale, N. H., & Stos-Gale, Z. A. (1987). Oxhide ingots from Sardinia, Crete and Cyprus and the Bronze Age copper trade: New scientific evidence. In M. S. Balmuth (Ed.), *Studies in Sardinian archaeology 3. Nuragic Sardinia and the Mycenaean world* (British Archaeological Reports, International Series 387) (pp. 135–178). British Archaeological Reports.

Gale, N. H., & Stos-Gale, Z. A. (2012). The role of the Apliki mine in the post c. 1400 BC copper production and trade networks in Cyprus and in the wider Mediterranean. In V. Kassianidou & G. Papasavvas (Eds.), *Eastern Mediterranean metallurgy and metalwork in the second millennium BC* (pp. 70–82). Oxbow.

Geus, K., & Thiering, M. (Eds.). (2014). *Features of common sense geography: Implicit knowledge structures in ancient geographical texts* (Antike Kultur und Geschichte 16). LIT Verlag.

Godoy, R. (1991). *Mining and agriculture in highland Bolivia: Ecology, history and commerce among the Jukumanis*. University of Arizona Press.

Graziadio, G. (2014). The oxhide ingots production in the eastern Mediterranean. *Egitto e Vicono Oriente, 37*, 5–25.

Griggs, C., Pearson, C., Manning, S. W., & Lorenzen, B. (2014). A 250-year annual precipitation reconstruction and drought assessment for Cyprus from Pinus brutia Ten. tree-rings. *International Journal of Climatology, 34*(8), 2702–2714.

Hadjisavvas, S. (2011). Broken symbols: Aspects of metallurgy at Alassa. In P. P. Betancourt & S. C. Ferrence (Eds.), *Metallurgy: Understanding how, learning why. Studies in honor of James D. Muhly* (pp. 21–27). Institute for Aegean Prehistory Press.

Hardesty, D. L. (1988). *The archaeology of mining and miners: A view from the silver state* (Society for Historical Archaeology, Special Publication 6). Society for Historical Archaeology.

Hauptmann, A., Maddin, R., & Prange, M. (2002). On the structure and composition of copper and tin ingots excavated from the shipwreck of Uluburun. *Bulletin of the American Schools of Oriental Research, 328*, 1–30.

Hein, A., & Kilikoglou, V. (2007). Modeling of thermal behavior of ancient metallurgical ceramics. *Journal of the American Ceramic Society, 90*(3), 878–884.

Hein, A., Kilikoglou, V., & Kassianidou, V. (2007). Chemical and mineralogical examination of metallurgical ceramics from a Late Bronze Age copper smelting site in Cyprus. *Journal of Archaeological Science, 34*(1), 141–154.

Iacono, F. (2016). Value, power, and encounter between the eastern and Central Mediterranean during the Late Bronze Age. *Studi Micenei ed Egeo-Anatolici n.s., 2*, 101–118.

Karageorghis, V., & Kassianidou, V. (1999). Metalworking and recycling in late bronze age Cyprus—The evidence from Kition. *Oxford Journal of Archaeology, 18*(2), 171–188.

Kassianidou, V. (2000). Hellenistic and Roman mining on Cyprus. In G. C. Ioannides & S. A. Hadjistellis (Eds.), *Acts of the third international congress of Cypriot studies* (pp. 745–756). Society of Cypriot Studies.

Kassianidou, V. (2004). 'And at Tamassos there are important mines of copper' (Strabo, Geograpy 14.6.5). *Cahier du Centre d'Études Chypriotes, 34*, 33–46.

Kassianidou, V. (2009a). Oxhide ingots in Cyprus. In F. Lo Schiavo, J. D. Muhly, R. Maddin, & A. Giumlia Mair (Eds.), *Oxhide ingots in the Central Mediterranean* (pp. 41–81). Leventis Foundation, INSTAP and Consiglio Nazionale delle Ricerche.

Kassianidou, V. (2009b). 'May he send me silver in very great quantities': EA 35. In D. Michaelides, V. Kassianidou, & R. Merrillees (Eds.), *Egypt and Cyprus in antiquity* (pp. 48–57). Oxbow.

Kassianidou, V. (2012). Metallurgy and metalwork in Enkomi: The early phases. In V. Kassianidou & G. Papasavvas (Eds.), *Eastern Mediterranean metallurgy and metalwork in the second millennium BC* (pp. 94–106). Oxbow.

Kassianidou, V. (2013). Mining landscapes of prehistoric Cyprus. *Metalla, 20*(2), 36–45.

Kassianidou, V. (2018a). Ancient copper mining, oxhide ingots and a hoard—New data on Mathiatis from the state archives of Cyprus. In A. Giumlia-Mair & F. L. Schiavo (Eds.), *Bronze Age metallurgy in the Mediterranean Islands. In honour of Robert Maddin and Vassos Karageorghis* (Monographies Instrumentum 56) (pp. 578–598). Editions Mergoil.

Kassianidou, V. (2018b). Late Bronze Age Cypriot hoards and modern collections. In L. Hulin, L. Crewe, & J. M. Webb (Eds.), *Structures of inequality on Bronze Age Cyprus. Studies in honour of Alison K. South* (Studies in Mediterranean Archaeology PB 187) (pp. 211–226). Åström Editions.

Kassianidou, V. (2022). Placing Politiko *Phorades* in the historiography and evolution of Late Cypriot metallurgy. In S. W. Manning (Ed.), *Critical approaches to Cypriot and wider Mediterranean archaeology* (Monographs in Mediterranean Archaeology 16) (pp. 87–107). Equinox.

Kassianidou, V., & Knapp, A. B. (2005). Archaeometallurgy in the Mediterranean: The social context of mining, technology and trade. In E. Blake & A. B. Knapp (Eds.), *The archaeology of Mediterranean prehistory* (pp. 215–251). Blackwell.

Kassianidou, V., Agapiou, A., & Manning, S. W. (2021). Reconstructing an ancient mining landscape: A multidisciplinary approach to copper mining at Skouriotissa, Cyprus. *Antiquity, 95*(382), 986–1004.

Kling, B., & Muhly, J. D. (2007). *Joan du Plat Taylor's excavations at the Late Bronze Age mining settlement at Apliki Karamallos, Cyprus* (Studies in Mediterranean Archaeology 134.1). P. Åström's Förlag.

Knapp, A. B. (1988a). Ideology, archaeology and polity. *Man, 23*(1), 133–163.

Knapp, A. B. (1988b). Hoards d'oeuvres: Of metals and men on Bronze Age Cyprus. *Oxford Journal of Archaeology, 7*(2), 147–176.

Knapp, A. B. (1990). Production, location and integration in Bronze Age Cyprus. *Current Anthropology, 31*(2), 147–176.

Knapp, A. B. (1991). Spice, drugs, grain and grog: Organic goods in Bronze Age eastern Mediterranean trade. In N. H. Gale (Ed.), *Bronze Age trade in the Mediterranean* (Studies in Mediterranean Archaeology 90) (pp. 21–68). P. Åström's Förlag.

Knapp, A. B. (2000). Archaeology, science-based archaeology and the Mediterranean Bronze Age metals trade. *European Journal of Archaeology, 3*(1), 31–56.

Knapp, A. B. (2002). Disciplinary fault lines: Science and social archaeology. *Mediterranean Archaeology and Archaeometry, 2*(1), 37–44.

Knapp, A. B. (2003). The archaeology of community on Bronze Age Cyprus: Politiko *Phorades* in context. *American Journal of Archaeology, 107*(4), 559–580.

Knapp, A. B. (2008). *Prehistoric and protohistoric Cyprus: Identity, insularity and connectivity.* Oxford University Press.

Knapp, A. B. (2012). Metallurgical production and trade on Bronze Age Cyprus: Views and variations. In V. Kassianidou & G. Papasavvas (Eds.), *Eastern Mediterranean metallurgy and metalwork in the second millennium BC* (pp. 14–25). Oxbow.

Knapp, A. B., & Kassianidou, V. (2008). The archaeology of Late Bronze Age copper production: Politiko *Phorades* on Cyprus. In Ü. Yalçin (Ed.), *Anatolian Metal IV: Frühe Rohstoffgewinnung in Anatolien und seinen Nachbarländern* (Die Anschnitt, Beiheft 21; Veröffentlichungen aus dem Deutschen Bergbau-Museum 157) (pp. 135–147). Deutsches Bergbau-Museum.

Knapp, A. B., Muhly J. D., & Muhly P. M. (1988). To hoard is human: The metal deposits of LC IIC-LC III. *Report of the Department of Antiquities, Cyprus,* 233–262.

Knapp, A. B., Russell, A., & van Dommelen, P. (2022). Cyprus, Sardinia and Sicily: A maritime perspective on interaction, connectivity and imagination in Mediterranean prehistory. *Cambridge Archaeological Journal, 32*(1), 79–97.

Kunze, R., & Pernicka, E. (2020). The beginning of copper and gold metallurgy in the old world. In R. Krauss, E. Pernicka, R. Kunze, K. Dimitrov, & P. Leshtakov (Eds.), *Prehistoric mining and metallurgy at the southeast Bulgarian Black Sea coast* (Ressourcekulturen 12) (pp. 67–86). Tübingen University Press.

Larsen, M. T. (2015). *Ancient Kanesh: A Merchant Colony in Bronze Age Anatolia*. Cambridge University Press.

Lehner, J. W., Kuruçayırlı, E., & Hirschfeld, N. (2020). Oxhides, buns, bits, and pieces: Analyzing the ingot cargo of the Cape Gelidonya shipwreck. In A. Gilboa & A. Yasur-Landau (Eds.), *Nomads of the Mediterranean: Trade and contact in the Bronze and Iron Ages. Studies in honor of Michal Artzy* (pp. 161–176). Brill.

Levy, T. E., & Shalev, S. (1989). Prehistoric metalworking in the southern Levant: Archaeometallurgical and social perspectives. *World Archaeology, 20*(3), 352–372.

Levy, T. E., Adams, R. B., Hauptmann, A., Prange, M., & Schmitt- Strecker, S. & Najjar, M. (2002). Early Bronze Age metallurgy: A newly discovered copper manufactory in southern Jordan. *Antiquity, 76*(292), 425–437.

Levy, T. E., Ben-Yosef, E., & Najjar, M. (2012). New perspectives on Iron Age copper production and society in Faynan region, Jordan. In V. Kassianidou & G. Papasavvas (Eds.), *Eastern Mediterranean metallurgy and metalwork in the second millennium BC* (pp. 197–214). Oxbow.

Levy, T. E., Ben-Yosef, E., & Najjar, M. (2018). Intensive surveys, large-scale excavation strategies and Iron Age industrial metallurgy in Faynan, Jordan: Fairy tales don't come true. In E. Ben-Yosef (Ed.), *Mining for ancient copper: Essays in memory of Beno Rothenberg* (Sonia and Marco Nadler Institute of Archaeology Monograph Series 37) (pp. 245–258). Nadler Institute of Archaeology, Tel-Aviv University.

Lo Schiavo, F., Muhly, J. D., Maddin, R., & Guimlia-Mair, A. (Eds.). (2009). *Oxhide ingots in the Central Mediterranean*. Istituto di Studi sulle Civiltà dell'Egeo e del Vicino Oriente del Consiglio Nazionale delle Ricerche.

Maran, J. (2013). Bright as the sun: The appropriation of amber objects in Mycenaean Greece. In H. P. Hahn & H. Weiss (Eds.), *Mobility, meaning and the transformations of things* (pp. 147–169). Oxbow

Merrillees, R. S. (1984). Ambelikou-*Aletri*: A preliminary report. *Report of the Department of Antiquities, Cyprus*, 1–13.

Meyer, N., & Knapp, A. B. (2021). Resilient social actors in the transition from the Late Bronze to the Early Iron Age on Cyprus. *Journal of World Prehistory, 34*(4), 433–487.

Monroe, C. M. (2009). *Scales of fate: Trade, tradition, and transformation in the eastern Mediterranean* (Alter Orient und Altes Testament 357). Ugarit-Verlag.

Monroe, C. (2011). 'From luxuries to anxieties': A liminal view of the Late Bronze Age world-system. In T. C. Wilkinson, S. Sherratt, & J. Bennett (Eds.), *Interweaving worlds: Systemic interactions in Eurasia, 7th to the 1st millennia BC* (pp. 87–99). Oxbow.

Moran, W. L. (1992). *The Amarna letters*. Johns Hopkins University Press.

Muhly, J. D. (1989). The organisation of the copper industry in Late Bronze Age Cyprus. In E. J. Peltenburg (Ed.), *Early society in Cyprus* (pp. 298–314). Edinburgh University Press.

Muhly, J. D. (1995). Lead isotope analysis and the archaeologist. *Journal of Mediterranean Archaeology, 8*(1), 54–58.

Muhly, J. D. (2003). Trade in metals in the Late Bronze Age and Iron Age. In N. C. Stampolidis & V. Karageorghis (Eds.), *Ploes.. sea Routes...: Interconnections in the Mediterranean, 16th–6th c. BC* (pp. 141–150). University of Crete, Leventis Foundation.

Muhly, J. D., Maddin, R., & Stech, T. (1988). Cyprus, Crete and Sardinia: Copper oxhide ingots and the metals trade. *Report of the Department of Antiquities, Cyprus, 281–298*.

Nash, J. (1993). *We eat the mines and the mines eat us: Dependency and exploitation in Bolivian tin mines* (2nd ed.). Columbia University Press.

Osborne, R. (2004). Hoards, votives, offerings: The archaeology of the dedicated object. *World Archaeology, 36*(1), 1–10.

Papasavvas, G. (2011). From smiting into smithing: The transformation of a Cypriot god. In P. P. Betancourt & S. C. Ferrence (Eds.), *Metallurgy: Understanding how, learning why. Studies in honor of James D. Muhly* (pp. 59–66). Institute for Aegean Prehistory Press.

Pérez-Jordà, G., Peña-Chocarro, L., & Pardo-Gordó, S. (2021). Fruits arriving to the west. Introduction of cultivated fruits in the Iberian Peninsula. *Journal of Archaeological Science, Reports, 35*, article 102683. https://doi.org/10.1016/j.jasrep.2020.102683

Raber, P. A. (1987). Early copper production in the Polis region, western Cyprus. *Journal of Field Archaeology, 14*(3), 297–312.

Radivojević, M., Roberts, B. W., Pernicka, E., Stos-Gale, Z., Martinón-Torres, M., Rehren, T., Bray, P., Brandherm, D., Ling, J., Mei, J., Vandkilde, H., Kristiansen, K., Shennan, S. J., & Broodbank, C. (2019). The provenance, use, and circulation of metals in the European Bronze Age: The state of debate. *Journal of Archaeological Research, 27*(2), 131–185.

Renfrew, A. C. (2012). Systems of value among material things: The nexus of fungibility and measure. In J. K. Papadopoulos & G. Urton (Eds.), *The construction of value in the ancient world* (Cotsen Advanced Seminar Series 5) (pp. 249–260). Cotsen Institute of Archaeology, UCLA.

Sabatini, S. (2016a). Late Bronze Age oxhide and oxhide-like ingots from areas other than the Mediterranean: Problems and challenge. *Oxford Journal of Archaeology, 35*(1), 29–45.

Sabatini, S. (2016b). Revisiting Late Bronze Age oxhide ingots: Meanings, questions and perspectives. In O. C. Aslaksen (Ed.), *Local and global perspectives on mobility in the eastern Mediterranean* (Papers and Monographs from the Norwegian Institute at Athens 5) (pp. 15–62). Norwegian Institute.

Sainsbury, V. A., Bray, P., Gosden, C., & Pollard, M. (2021). Mutable objects, places and chronologies. *Antiquity, 95*(379), 215–227.

Stech, T. (1985). Copper and society in Late Bronze Age Cyprus. In A. B. Knapp & T. Stech (Eds.), *Prehistoric production and exchange: The Aegean and East Mediterranean* (UCLA Institute of Archaeology, Monograph 25) (pp. 100–105). UCLA Institute of Archaeology.

Stöllner, T. (2003). Mining and economy: A discussion of spatial organisations and structures of early raw material exploitation. In T. Stöllner, G. Körlin, G. Steffens, & J. Cierny (Eds.), *Man and mining-Mensch und Bergbau. Studies in honour of Gerd Weisgerber on occasion of his 65th birthday* (Die Anschnitt, Beiheft 16) (pp. 415–446). Deutsches Bergbau-Museum.

Stos-Gale, Z. A., Maliotis, G., Gale, N. H., & Annetts, N. (1997). Lead isotope characteristics of the Cyprus copper ore deposits applied to provenance studies of copper oxhide ingots. *Archaeometry, 39*(1), 83–123.

Swiny, S. (2020). The rag-and-bone trade at Enkomi: Late Cypriot scrap metal and the bronze industry. In A. Gilboa & A. Yasur-Landau (Eds.), *Nomads of the Mediterranean: Trade and contact in the Bronze and Iron Ages. Studies in honor of Michal Artzy* (pp. 300–317). Brill.

Walsh, K. (2014). *The archaeology of Mediterranean landscapes: Human-environment interaction from the Neolithic to the Roman period.* Cambridge University Press.

Webb, J. M. (2015). Identifying stone tools used in mining, smelting, and casting in Middle Bronze Age Cyprus. *Journal of Field Archaeology, 40*(1), 22–36.

Webb, J. M., & Frankel, D. (2013). *Ambelikou Aletri: Metallurgy and pottery production in Middle Bronze Age Cyprus* (Studies in Mediterranean Archaeology 138). Åström's Förlag.

Webb, J. M., & Knapp, A. B. (2021). Rethinking Middle Bronze Age communities on Cyprus: 'Egalitarian' and isolated or complex and interconnected? *Journal of Archaeological Research, 29*(2), 203–253.

Weisgerber, G. (1982). Towards a history of copper mining in Cyprus and the Near East: Possibilities of mining archaeology. In J. D. Muhly, R. Maddin, & V. Karageorghis (Eds.), *Early metallurgy in Cyprus, 4000–500 BC* (pp. 25–32). Pierides Foundation.

Wengrow, D. (2011). 'Archival' and 'sacrificial' economies in bronze age Eurasia: An interactionist approach to the hoarding of metals. In T. C. Wilkinson, S. Sherratt, & J. Bennett (Eds.), *Interweaving worlds: Systemic interactions in Eurasia, 7th to the 1st millennia BC* (pp. 135–144). Oxbow.

Yagel, O. A., Ben-Yosef, E., & Craddock, P. T. (2016). Late Bronze Age copper production in Timna: New evidence from Site 3. *Levant, 48*(1), 33–51.

Early Types of Cypriot Bronze Age Metal Ingots

Vasiliki Kassianidou 🔟

Abstract It is now well known, thanks to Lead Isotope Analysis, that in the Late Bronze Age Cypriot copper was traded in the form of oxhide and discoid, plano-convex/bun ingots. Both types were used at the same time as indicated by their presence in the Uluburun, the Cape Gelidonya and now the Antalya Kumluca shipwreck. According to ancient sources, however, Cypriot copper was traded to the East already since the nineteenth century BC: in texts dating to the Old Babylonian period and found at Mari, Babylon and Alalakh there are several mentions to copper from Alashiya, the name by which Cyprus was known to her neighbours. The texts show that metal from the island was traded all the way to Babylon. It was probably exchanged for gold, tin, silver and lead which were not locally available but are found in tombs of this period. In what form, however, was Cypriot copper traded in the earlier phases of the Bronze Age? The aim of this paper is to discuss Cypriot ingots and especially the early forms of metal ingots produced on the island.

Keywords Cyprus · Bronze Age · Ingot · Copper · Tin · Trade · Oxhide ingot

1 Introduction

According to the online version of the Merriam Webster Dictionary an ingot is "a mass of metal that has been cast into a size and shape (such as a bar, plate, or sheet) that is convenient to store, transport, and work into a semi-finished or finished product" (https://www.merriam-webster.com/dictionary/ingot). Already since the Late Bronze Age, glass was also traded in the form of ingots for the same reasons. This

---

V. Kassianidou (✉)
Archaeological Research Unit, Department of History and Archaeology,
University of Cyprus, Nicosia, Cyprus
e-mail: v.kassianidou@ucy.ac.cy

© The Author(s), under exclusive license to Springer Nature Switzerland AG 2023
E. Ben-Yosef, I. W. N. Jones (eds.), *"And in Length of Days Understanding" (Job 12:12): Essays on Archaeology in the Eastern Mediterranean and Beyond in Honor of Thomas E. Levy*, Interdisciplinary Contributions to Archaeology,
https://doi.org/10.1007/978-3-031-27330-8_57

was revealed by the discovery of the Uluburun shipwreck which was carrying glass ingots in the shape of truncated cones in four different colours (Pulak, 2008).

One may thus argue that ingots are an essential part of trade. Ingots are necessary for the exchange, under regulated conditions, of manufactured raw materials such as metals or glass. What these materials have in common is that they can be melted and cast into moulds, so that ingots of a certain shape and most importantly a specific weight can be created. It is thus not surprising that in Southern Levant copper ingots appear already in the Late Chalcolithic, namely the time when the trade of copper begins (Hauptmann et al., 2015).

2 Discoid, Plano-Convex/Bun Ingots and Oxhide Ingots

Different ingot shapes were used in Antiquity as highlighted by Hauptmann et al. (2015). A variety of shapes, sometimes even for the same metal, were used in the same period, as indicated by the Uluburun shipwreck which carried an assortment of copper and tin ingots (Pulak, 2000, 2008, 2009).

I would like to initially focus on two ingot shapes – one because it is so basic and simple and because it was used from the earliest phases of the Bronze Age to the later historical periods, the other, because it was exclusively used in the Late Bronze Age.

2.1 Discoid, Plano-Convex/Bun Ingots

The first is the discoid, plano-convex or bun ingot, which was most probably produced by pouring metal in small pits or sand moulds (Hauptmann et al., 2015). The shape appears already from the earliest phases of the Bronze Age, when it weighed only a few kilos. It continues all the way down to the Roman period, during which ingots with weights ranging between 20 kilos and all the way up to 97 kg were produced (Bode et al., 2018; Tylecote, 1992). This type of ingot not only has a wide geographical, as well as chronological span, but it was also used for the trade of different metals. From the second millennium BC there are copper bun ingots (e.g. from Crete and elsewhere in the Aegean (Mangou & Ioannou, 2000), from Cape Gelidonya (Bass, 1967; Lehner et al., 2020), from Uluburun (Pulak, 2000, 2008), from Antalya (Öniz, 2019, 2020), from Sardinia (Begemann et al., 2001; Lo Schiavo et al., 2005, 2009), from Bulgaria (Athanassov et al., 2020) and from Devon (Wang et al., 2018)). From the same period, there are tin bun ingots (e.g., from Uluburun (Pulak, 2000, 2008, 2009); from shipwrecks off the coast of Israel (Galili et al., 2013, 6–8) and from Devon (Wang et al., 2016)), as well as lead bun ingots (e.g., from several shipwrecks off the coast of Israel (Galili et al., 2013; Yahalom Mack et al., 2022)).

2.2 Oxhide Ingots

The second type I would like to discuss is the oxhide ingot, which is the largest and heaviest type of the Bronze Age as examples weigh from 20.2 kg to 39 kg. Many of them weigh around 29 kg, the equivalent of a talent (Buchholz, 1959; Pulak, 2000; Rice Jones, 2007) and have an average length of about forty centimetres and a thickness of about four centimetres (Bass, 1967) (Fig. 1). Papasavvas (2018) has recently discussed the value of copper in the Late Bronze Age and what could be produced with just one oxhide ingot (Papasavvas, 2021). The numbers he presents are impressive. One oxhide ingot would have produced 88 swords of the Late Minoan II type or 65 Naue II swords, 225 chisels such as the one found on the Uluburun shipwreck, or 86 double adzes such as an example from Enkomi (Papasavvas, 2021).

Buchholz (1959: 7) was the first to suggest a typology of oxhide ingots, later refined by Bass (1967). The earliest type is pillow-shaped without extremities and is known from Crete, from a shipwreck off the coast of Kyme on the island of Euboea (Buchholz, 1959), and now from Antalya (see below). In later examples the

Fig. 1 Oxhide ingot (Inv. 1939/VI-20/4). Perhaps from Enkomi. (Photograph by the Department of Antiquities of Cyprus and drawing by Clara Vasitsek)

corners are protruding to form four extremities or handles. One surface, the top one, is rough, while the other which is where the metal was in contact with the mould, is smooth but bears many small air holes and is often outlined by a raised rim (Bass, 1967).

The rough surface, as well as the resemblance of the shape to hides of oxen depicted in Egyptian wall paintings led archaeologists to use the term "oxhide" to describe them (Bass, 1967). In 1924 in his book entitled *Athens, its History and Coinage before the Persian Invasion,* Charles Seltman (1924) suggested that since the ox used to have monetary value in Antiquity, each ingot would have had the value of an ox and, therefore, it was an early type of currency in this pre-monetary society. Muhly (2009) explains that, in what he calls the early "numismatic phase" of oxhide ingot studies, this idea seemed to be further supported because the weight of an ingot was the equivalent of a talent. This proposition by Seltman, however, was strongly opposed by many, including Buchholz (1959). Bass (1967) showed that the weight of the ingots is not always the same, while their fragments are never accurate fractions of the whole. Furthermore, Buchholz's (1959) typological study showed that the earlier ingots are almost rectangular, and it is latter examples that have four well defined handles which make them resemble hides. He argued that the shape changed, to facilitate carrying and transport (Buchholz, 1959). Moreover, it has been argued that the rough top surface of the ingots is a result of the casting conditions and the use of an open mould (Tylecote, 1982).This has now been demonstrated experimentally (Hauptmann et al., 2016). In other words, the resemblance to the shape of a stretched hide is accidental and not deliberate, while the whole idea of the value of an ingot in relation to an ox cannot be supported. Hence, this idea of oxhide ingots being early forms of currency is no longer accepted (for a detailed discussion see Muhly, 2009). More recently it was argued that the shape was chosen to facilitate casting: experimental casting showed that to produce such as size of ingot copper would have been melted in four different crucibles and poured in the mould through the four corners (Hauptmann et al., 2016).

2.2.1 Copper Oxhide Ingots

Many scholars believe that the oxhide ingot may well have been the trademark of Cypriot copper (Papasavvas, 2009; Stos-Gale, 2011), as provenance studies have shown that all oxhide ingots dating after 1400 BC and some which date even earlier (1500–1450 BC) are consistent with the Apliki ore deposit on the island (Gale, 1999, 2011). All new finds which have been analysed, for example those that have been found at sites in the Balkans (Athanassov et al., 2020), or in Israel (Galili et al., 2011; Yahalom Mack et al., 2014), are also consistent with a Cypriot provenance.

Furthermore, in Cyprus the oxhide ingot appears regularly in the iconographic repertoire of works of art, such as the well-known four-sided stands, the two figurines standing on ingots, the cylinder seals and the miniature ingots (Papasavvas, 2009). The cylinder seals are particularly important as the oxhide ingot shape appears in some of the earliest Cypriot seals which date to the beginning of the Late

Cypriot (Graziadio, 2003), a period during which no oxhide ingots have been found on the island (Kassianidou, 2009). Nevertheless, the depictions of ingots are contemporary with the earliest oxhide ingots which have been found on Crete in contexts dating to Late Minoan IB (LMIB), namely ca 1500–1450 BC (Hakulin, 2004; Kassianidou, 2014). Cylinder seals are objects which relate to trade, and it is not surprising that they first begin to be manufactured on the island in the beginning of the Late Bronze Age (Webb & Weingarten, 2012). This is the time when Cyprus started to act as a central node in the international trading networks which circulated metals around the Eastern Mediterranean and beyond.

Lead Isotope Analysis has found that most of the early ingots from Crete are not consistent with a Cypriot provenance; in fact, their provenance remains obscure (Stos Gale, 2011). But some of the early oxhide ingots found in Crete, such as four of the six complete ingots from Zakros, are consistent with the Solea axis ore deposits and, therefore, are believed to have been made with Cypriot copper (Stos Gale, 2011). A new shipwreck loaded with copper oxhide ingots, as well as discoid, plano-convex/bun ingots, that was recently discovered off the coast of Antalya, at the site of Kumluca, promises to enhance our understanding of the metals' trade in this early phase of the LBA. Because the ingots resemble the LMIB ingots from Crete, it has been argued that the shipwreck, most probably dates to the sixteenth–fifteenth centuries BC (Öniz, 2019). During the last season of excavation in 2019, 94 oxhide ingots and five bun ingots were recorded on the surface of the seabed; more may be lying below them (Öniz, 2020). A few examples were lifted and upon conservation an inscribed sign was revealed on one of the oxhide ingots. We eagerly await the interdisciplinary study of this assemblage and the results of Lead Isotope Analysis which hopefully will allow us to understand where such ingots were produced in the beginning of the Late Bronze Age.

In 1991, Gale estimated that 130 copper oxhide ingots had been found in archaeological sites anywhere on land (Gale, 1991). Since then, there have been several more discoveries, that have not only increased this number, but also stretched the geographical distribution of these finds, to the west and to the north (for recent reviews and distribution maps see Sabatini, 2016a, 2016b). The results of Lead Isotope Analysis shows that all these oxhide ingots, whether they have been found in archaeological sites on land and under the sea in the Aegean, the Balkans, Sardinia, Germany, Egypt, Anatolia or Israel are all consistent with a Cypriot provenance (Gale, 1999, 2005; Hauptmann, 2009; Gale & Stos Gale, 2005, 2011; Stos Gale, 2009; Yahalom Mack et al., 2014).

2.2.2 Tin Oxhide Ingots

Although we tend to relate the oxhide ingot shape with copper, it was suspected from early on that, other metals were also traded in this form. This is because Egyptian wall paintings such as those in the Tomb of Rekh-mi-re depicted oxhide ingots of two different colours—red and grey—and those were interpreted as ingots of copper and of tin or lead respectively (Bass, 1967; Papasavvas, 2009). The discovery of tin oxhide ingots in the cargo of the Uluburun shipwreck showed that this was indeed the case. In fact, the tin oxhide ingots offer yet another argument against the idea that the value of oxhide ingots was equivalent to that of an ox: since tin was much more expensive than copper, a tin oxhide ingot would certainly have had a higher value (Bass, 1990). If we accept that the oxhide ingot shape is the trademark of Cypriot copper, then we should contemplate what it may mean that some of the tin ingots on the Uluburun ship are also cast in the shape of an oxhide. I have argued elsewhere that the fact that some of the tin ingots (not only oxhide, but also other types) bear Cypro-Minoan signs, a specifically Cypriot practice, implies that the ingots had either been routed via Cyprus or handled by people familiar with the Cypriot marking system (Kassianidou, 2003). This, in other words, suggests that Cyprus played a significant role in the trade of tin from the Syro-Palestinian coast, where it arrived from overland routes to reach areas across the sea, such as the Aegean. It has recently been argued that the same is true for the trade of lead (Yahalom Mack et al., 2022).

3 Late Bronze Age Copper Ingots from Cyprus

Shipwrecks especially the three well preserved ones found off the coast of Turkey, namely Cape Gelidonya, Uluburun, and now Antalya Kumluca show that different types of copper ingots, were used at the same time. As already mentioned, the Antalya Kumluca ship carried oxhide and bun ingots (Öniz, 2019, 2020). The Uluburun ship carried ten tons of copper in the form of discoid, plano- convex/bun ingots, oval shaped bun ingots, oxhide ingots, oxhide ingots with two handles instead of four, two smaller oxhide ingots with a shape similar to the older types, and a unique example which has four protrusions but is thick and squat in shape (Pulak, 2000, 2008). The Cape Gelidonya ship carried just over one ton of copper in the form of oxhide and discoid, plano-convex/bun ingots, as well as twenty slab ingots (Bass, 1967; Lehner et al., 2020). Interestingly, chemical analysis showed that some of these slab ingots are made of bronze rather than pure copper. As pointed out by Lehner et al. (2020) this, namely the production of ingots of alloyed metal, is not a common practice. Furthermore, unlike the cargo of Uluburun, the cargo of Cape Gelidonya included a significant quantity of fragmented ingots of both types (Bass, 1967; Lehner et al., 2020).

As already mentioned, lead isotope analysis of oxhide and bun ingots from Uluburun (Gale, 1999; Gale and Stos Gale, 2005) and Cape Gelidonya (Stos Gale, 2009) shipwrecks revealed that both oxhide ingots and discoid, plano-convex/bun ingots from both shipwrecks are consistent with a Cypriot provenance, and more specifically with the ore deposits of the Solea mining district, which includes the ore deposits of Apliki, Skouriotissa, Ambelikou and Mavrovouni. Chemical analysis also shows that they have a similar chemical composition. This means that the main difference between the two, apart from the shape of course, is the weight. The bun ingots are much smaller. Based on published data, those from Uluburun

Early Types of Cypriot Bronze Age Metal Ingots

weigh between 3 kg and 9 kg (Pulak, 2000), while those from Cape Gelidonya have a weight that ranges between 1.35 kg and 5.5 kg. On the other hand, as noted previously, oxhide ingots range from 20.2 to 39 kg (Buchholz, 1959; Pulak, 2000). The heaviest example is one of the three found in Cyprus and currently in the Cyprus Museum (Inv. 1939/VI-20/4) (Fig. 1). Unfortunately, it comes from the Antiquities market and its archaeological context remains uncertain. The man who gifted it to the Cyprus Museum declared that the ingot was found together with others at Enkomi (for the history and analysis of this object see Kassianidou, 2009, 2018a, b).

It is not clear why Cypriot copper was traded in two different forms at the same time: the oxhide and discoid, plano-convex/bun ingots were used simultaneously in the fourteenth century BC, as shown by the Uluburun shipwreck and in the thirteenth century BC as shown by the Cape Gelidonya shipwreck. The reason is not that the two different types were produced in two different mining regions, as the lead isotope analysis has found both types to be consistent with the same mining district – that of the Solea axis. Several proposed models regarding the organization of the copper industry in Cyprus suggest that, although copper ores would have been smelted near the ore deposit, where fuel was abundant and readily available, secondary processes such as matte smelting and the refining of black copper would have taken place in the workshops within the urban centres, the most important of which are on the coast (Keswani, 1993; Knapp, 1997, 2008). Extensive workshops have been found at Enkomi on the east coast of the island (Kassianidou, 2012, 2016; Muhly, 1989), but a rich archaeometallurgical assemblage has been recovered from many more Late Bronze Age urban centres such Kalavasos *Agios Dhimitrios* (South, 2012; Van Brempt & Kassianidou, 2016), Alassa *Pano Pandilaris* (Hadjisavvas, 2011; Van Brempt & Kassianidou, 2017), Athienou (Maddin et al., 1983), Hala Sultan Tekke (Fischer, 2018), and most importantly at Apliki *Karamallos,* where in 1938 the remains of a miners' settlement came to light (Du Plat Taylor, 1952; Kassianidou, 2018c; Kling & Muhly, 2007) (Fig. 2). This may explain the surprising result of Lead Isotope Analysis of copper slag from Kalavasos, which suggests that it is consistent with the ore deposit at Apliki in the Solea Axis (Gale & Stos Gale, 2012). This ore deposit lies 50 km to the northwest (as the crow flies) or almost 100 km if using a route that circumvents the Troodos mountains from the site of Kalavasos *Agios Dhimitrios*. Does this mean that copper discoid, plano-convex/bun ingots were produced in some sites while copper oxhide ingots were produced in others? As no moulds have been found for either of the types (the current view is that they both would have been produced in sand moulds which leave no traces behind (see Hauptmann et al., 2016)), this remains an open question.

Alternatively, the smaller discoid, plano-convex/bun ingots were produced in the same workshops but for a different use. Being significantly smaller, they would have been cheaper and therefore more accessible to a larger number of smiths/customers. According to Pulak (2000): "The two main ingot shapes, therefore, do not seem to reflect differing copper compositions or purity; they may be attributable, instead, to different production techniques or areas, or *to the need of smaller units of copper*" (emphasis mine). As pointed out by Papasavvas (2021) the Pylos Jn

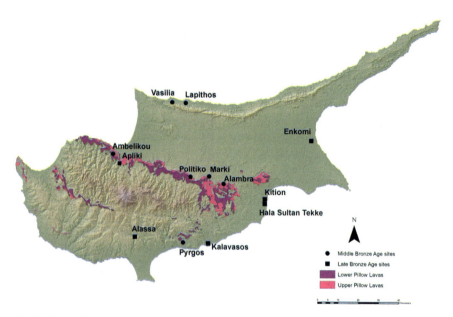

Fig. 2 Map of Cyprus showing the pillow lava geological formation where copper ore deposits are located, and sites mentioned in the text. (Produced by V. Kassianidou with digital geological data provided by the Cyprus Geological Survey)

series of tablets which record the allocation of metal to smiths (for a discussion of the tablets see Ventris & Chadwick, 1956; Smith, 1993; Dialismas, 2001; Blackwell, 2018), each smith received on average 3.5 kg of copper or bronze on a certain allotment. This, he argues, means that a single oxhide ingot would have had to be fragmented and rationed to as many as eight craftsmen (Papasavvas, 2021). On the other hand, each smith could have been given a single discoid, plano- convex/bun ingot for the same purpose! Their transport would also have been easier. The bun ingots of the Cape Gelidonya ship were stored in baskets together with other metal artefacts and ingot fragments (Bass, 1967). In the scene depicting the casting of bronze doors from the Tomb of Rekh-mi-re, apart from a copper oxhide ingot carried by a man on his shoulder, small oval shaped grey ingots, most probably of tin, are shown being brought in baskets on the shoulders of two men (Wainright, 1944; Bass, 1967).

According to Zaccagnini (1986), in the letters from Alashiya found in the archive of Amarna, there are two different terms used to describe the shipment of copper sent from Alashiya to Egypt (for a discussion of the letters from Alashiya in the Amarna archive see Muhly, 1972; Knapp, 1996, 2011). There are "(ingots) of copper" and there are "talents of copper" and in the case of letter EA33 both terms are used (Moran, 1992: 104). Although Graziadio (2014) rejects the idea that reference is actually made to oxhide ingots, I wonder whether we may suppose one term refers to oxhide ingots, which weigh one talent, and the other to bun ingots? Does this explain why in letter EA 35 (Moran, 1992: 107–108), the king of Alashiya apologizes to the Pharaoh for sending only 500 ingots of copper? If we use 6.2 kg for the weight of a bun ingot, as this is the published calculated mean weight of bun ingots on board the Uluburun shipwreck (Pulak, 2000), then the amount sent would have been 3100 kg namely a tenth of the cargo of Uluburun. If the 500 ingots where oxhide ingots, using again the mean ingot weight from Uluburun which is 23.9 kg (Pulak, 2000) then the amount of copper sent is 11,600 kg or if we use the weight of a talent which is roughly 28 Kg the amount is 14,000 kg. This is a staggering amount of metal which does not merit an apology on behalf of the king of Alashiya. On the other hand, the Uluburun ship has shown that such shipments were real!

4   Cypriot Copper Ingots Dating to the Earlier Phases of the Bronze Age

What do we know about Cypriot copper ingots which date to the earlier phases of the Bronze Age, and what can they tell us about the trade of copper in the second half of the third millennium (roughly corresponding to the Early Bronze Age or Early Cypriot (EC)) and the first half of the second millennium (roughly corresponding to the Middle Bronze Age or Middle Cypriot (MC))? This is the period to which one can trace the roots of copper production on the island (Kassianidou, 2008; Knapp, 2012).

4.1   Ingots from the Philia Facies and the Early Bronze Age/ Early Cypriot

The transition from the Chalcolithic to the Bronze Age came with major cultural changes in all features of material culture (architecture, pottery, metalwork etc), and all other aspects of life (changes in animal husbandry with the reintroduction of cattle and the introduction of donkeys, the revolution of secondary products) and death (new burial customs and tomb types) (Knapp, 2013). The most important changes related to the topic of this paper are those regarding metallurgy. The earliest part of the Bronze Age is defined as the Philia Facies (named after the archaeological site near the modern village of Philia, excavated by P. Dikaios), which dates from c. 2500/2400–2200 BC (Manning, 2014). This cultural phase is known only from a few sites most of which are cemeteries (Webb & Frankel, 1999). In the Philia Facies there is a sharp increase in metal artefacts, which are cast in moulds and belong to new types, including weapons, previously not found on the island (Webb & Frankel, 1999). It is therefore believed that the smelting of local ores had started by then, even though no smelting workshop or even waste from such processes (namely slag or metallurgical ceramics) dating to this period have yet been found (Kassianidou, 2008; Knapp, 2013). The indirect evidence for the local production of copper metal is provided by Lead Isotope Analysis of a group of Philia Facies and

Early Cypriot objects, which showed that the majority were made of metal consistent with a Cypriot provenance. Others were made of metal imported from Anatolia and others of copper imported from the Cyclades (Webb et al., 2006). Some of this imported metal came in the form of finished objects: two objects, a spearhead and sword, that were found to be isotopically consistent with an Anatolian source, are of Anatolian types (Webb et al., 2006).

Most importantly, it is this early phase of the Bronze Age that has delivered the earliest evidence for the production of ingots. A stone mould (Inv. S850), used to produce a perforated axe was found incorporated in a Philia Facies wall at the site of Marki *Alonia* (Frankel & Webb, 2001, 2006; Fasnacht & Künzler Wagner, 2001) (Fig. 3). The volume of the cavity is estimated at 140 cm^3 which would correspond to 1250 g of copper (Frankel & Webb, 2006). It has been argued that these perforated axes were an early form of ingot, and that the perforation was used to hang the axes on a string for easy transport (Fasnacht & Künzler Wagner, 2001). Chemical analysis of such axes from different sites on the island showed that they are often made of unalloyed copper (Weinstein Balthazar, 1990). This conforms with the idea that they may have been used as ingots. But there are exceptions as will be shown below.

It is remarkable that, although dating to a period before the introduction of writing into Cyprus, two axes dating to the Philia Facies, namely the earliest phase of the Early Bronze Age, bear the same inscribed linear sign, recalling the linear signs found on the ingots of different shapes and metals dating to the Late Bronze Age. Both are in the metal collection of the Cyprus Museum. One, (Inv. 1959/IV-20/3), is a perforated example weighing 626.4 g (Karageorghis, 1960; Webb et al., 2006), while the other (Inv. 1938/I-27/1), weighing 680.6 g, is not (Dikaios, 1939) (Fig. 4). Although their provenance is unknown it is believed that the perforated one came from the site of Vasilia (Karageorghis, 1960).

With permission from the Department of Antiquities, we were able to chemically analyse these two artefacts using a Hand Held Portable X-Ray Fluorescence Spectrometer (HHpXRF). The analysis was carried out by Dr. Andreas Charalambous using an Innov-X Delta (now Olympus) instrument equipped with a 4 W, 50 kV tantalum anode X-Ray tube and a high-performance Silicon Drift Detector (SDD) with a resolution of 155 eV (Mo-Kα). The diameter of the collimated X-Ray beam was 3 mm and the measurement time for each spot analysis was 70 s. The analytical mode of the instrument employed for the analyses was 'Alloy Plus'. Three certified reference materials were used for testing the accuracy and the consistency of the measurements of the applied analytical mode. The detection limits of the applied instrument for elements usually present in copper-based artefacts are 0.1 wt% Ni, 0.2 wt% Zn, 0.1 wt% Sn, 0.2 wt% As, 0.1 wt% Sb, 0.2 wt% S and 0.1 wt% Pb. The average errors for the elements' measurements are 5% for Sn, 6% for As and Pb and 7% for Zn and S (Charalambous et al., 2014; Charalambous et al., 2021; Charalambous & Webb, 2020). The results are presented in Table 1. The analysis revealed that one of the inscribed axes (Inv. 1938/ I-27/1) was made of unalloyed copper, while the other, the perforated one (Inv. 1959/IV-20/3), was made of bronze. This is an interesting result as it is means that this is now among one of the earliest

Early Types of Cypriot Bronze Age Metal Ingots

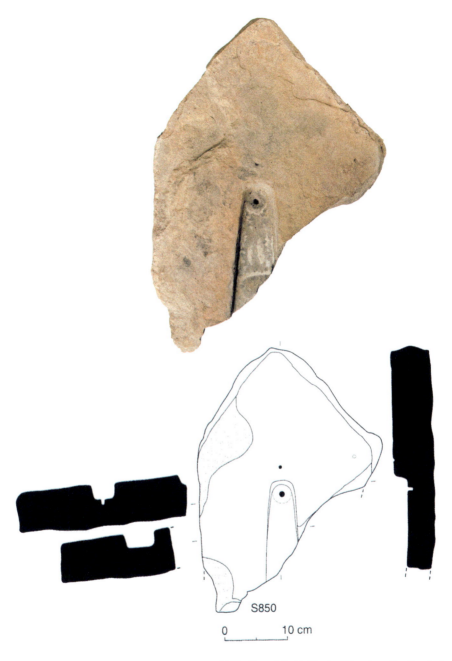

Fig. 3 Stone mould for a perforated axe (Inv. S850). From Marki *Alonia*. (Drawing after Frankel & Webb, 2001; photograph Department of Antiquities, Cyprus)

Fig. 4 Perforated axe with inscribed sign (Inv. 1959/IV-20/3). Perhaps from Vasilia. Axe with the same sign (Inv. 1938/I-27/1). Unknown provenance. (Photograph Department of Antiquities, Cyprus)

bronze objects on the island (see Charalambous & Webb, 2020; Webb et al., 2006). Since it is a local type, it shows that it was locally produced and was not imported as a finished object. The tin was clearly imported. The provenance of the copper has not been determined. Another perforated axe, now in the collection the University of New England Museum of Antiquities (Inv. UNEMA 74/6/3), dating to the Philia Facies and weighing 592.3 g, perhaps from the site of Vasilia, was also made of unalloyed copper. According to Lead Isotope Analysis it is consistent with a Cycladic provenance (Webb et al., 2006). The shape is a local one. This indicates that in this earliest phase of the Bronze Age copper imported to Cyprus from the

Early Types of Cypriot Bronze Age Metal Ingots

Table 1 Chemical composition of Philia Facies axes and ring ingot and ingots from Alambra *Mouttes* in weight %

a/a	Inv. No	Type	Weight (g)	Chemical composition (wt% ± std)						Material
				Cu	As	Sn	Pb	Fe	S	
1	1938/I-27/1	Axe	680.6	97.9 ± 0.3	n.d	n.d	0.2 ± 0.02	n.d	1.9 ± 0.1	Unalloyed copper
2	1959/IV-20/1	Ring ingot	452.3	96.4 ± 0.4	n.d	n.d	1.0 ± 0.1	1.1 ± 0.1	1.5 ± 0.1	Arsenical copper
3	1959/IV-20/3	'Axe' ingot	626.4	86.0 ± 0.7	10.8 ± 0.4	0.6 ± 0.05	0.5 ± 0.05	0.3 ± 0.03	1.8 ± 0.1	Bronze
4	M5 (CM0026)	Ingot	163	98.3 ± 0.2	0.3 ± 0.03	n.d	Traces (< 0.1 wt%)	1.3 ± 0.05	n.d	Unalloyed copper
5	M6 (CM0027)	Ingot	166	97.8 ± 0.2	0.3 ± 0.03	n.d	Traces (< 0.1 wt%)	1.8 ± 0.1	n.d	Unalloyed copper

Aegean (in an unknown form) was also cast in the form of perforated axes, in moulds such as the one found in Marki *Alonia*.

The excavations at Marki *Alonia* brought to light two other moulds which were clearly used to cast ingots (Inv. S744 and Inv. S745). The moulds were found among other stones of a collapsed wall, and they are chronologically placed within the ECI or ECII (Frankel and Webb 2006) (according to Manning 2004 the EC dates from 2200–2100/2050 BC). Both have clear evidence of having been used (Fasnacht & Künzler Wagner, 2001). S744 was used to cast boat shaped ingots (Fig. 5). One cavity is completely preserved and has volume of approximately 52 cm^3 which corresponds to around 460 g of copper, while the second partially preserved cavity would have had a larger volume that would have corresponded to approximately 500 g of copper (Fasnacht & Künzler Wagner, 2001; Frankel & Webb, 2006). The state of the mould indicates that it had been used several times (Frankel & Webb, 2006). S745 includes three cavities of two different shapes (Fig. 6). One cavity would have been used to cast narrower "tongue" shaped ingots the weight of which is estimated at 220 g (Fasnacht & Künzler Wagner, 2001; Frankel & Webb, 2006). The other cavity is deeper so it would have been used to cast a larger object. A third cavity, similar in shape to the larger example, is found on the other side of the mould (Fasnacht & Künzler Wagner, 2001; Frankel & Webb, 2006).

The two moulds, with several cavities of different volume, show that in the Early Bronze Age, just like in the Late Bronze Age, there were several types of copper ingots in circulation at the same time. Some would have weighed around 200 g while others would have weighed around 500 g. The latter are significantly heavier that the Early Bronze Age III (2700–2200 BC) crescent shaped bar ingots from the Levant, such as the ones produced at the site of Khirbat Hamra Ifdan excavated by Tom Levy (Levy et al., 2002). Those ingots weigh around 100–300 g (Hauptmann et al., 2015).

Fig. 5 Stone mould to cast boat shaped ingots (Inv. S744). From Marki *Alonia*. (Photograph Department of Antiquities, Cyprus)

Fig. 6 Stone mould to cast tongue shaped ingots (Inv. S745). From Marki *Alonia*. (Photograph Department of Antiquities, Cyprus)

In this earliest phase of the Bronze Age ring ingots may additionally have been used. Five such examples are known from the Early Bronze Age (Webb et al., 2006). Three were found in a deposit in the dromos of Tomb 1 excavated at the site of Vasilia (Hennesy et al., 1988). They are currently in the Cypriot collection of the Ashmolean Museum in Oxford (Inv.: AN1957.23, AN1957.24 and AN1957.25). The other two are thought to also have come from Vasilia, although they were acquired from the antiquities market (from the same antiques dealer, Petros Colocassides). One is in the Cyprus Museum (Inv. 1959/ IV-20/1) (Fig. 7) (Karageorghis, 1960; Webb et al., 2006), the other is in the collection of the University of New England Museum of Antiquities (Inv. UNEMA 74/5/1) (Webb et al., 2006). In earlier publications these artefacts are identified as bracelets or armbands. Their small diameter of about 8 cm and their weight, which in the case of the example now in the University of New England Museum of Antiquities is 444 g and the case of the one in the collection of the Cyprus Museum is 452.3 g, has been used to argue that they were actually ingots (Webb et al., 2006).

The two from the excavations at site of Vasilia now in the Ashmolean, which have been analysed, were found to be made of unalloyed copper (Weinstein Balthasar, 1990). The one in the University of New England Museum of Antiquities was made of copper with a low percentage of lead (1.47%) (Webb et al., 2006). Here we report on the analysis of a fourth ring-ingot, the one in the Cyprus Museum (Inv. 1959/ IV-20/1), which was found to have 1.1% arsenic (Table 1). Lead Isotope Analysis of the example in the University of New England Museum of Antiquities collection, found it to be consistent with copper from the Cyclades (Webb et al.,

Fig. 7 Ring ingot or bracelet (Inv. 1959/ IV-20/1). Perhaps from Vasilia. (Photograph Department of Antiquities, Cyprus)

2006; Stos Gale & Gale, 2010), while one of the ring ingots in the Ashmolean Museum (Inv. AN1957.24), was found to be consistent with copper from the Taurus Mountains (Stos Gale & Gale, 2010). In other words, the chemical analysis and the lead isotope analysis reveal that copper from different regions and with different chemical composition was transformed into ring ingots which were similar but not identical in shape. New provenance analysis is needed to investigate whether Cypriot copper was also circulated in the form of ring ingots in the EC period.

To conclude, in the earliest phase of the Bronze Age copper from Cyprus but also copper imported from the Cyclades and Anatolia circulated on the island in a variety of ingot shapes which were locally produced. There were boat and tongue shaped ingots, ring ingots and perforated axes which perhaps were also used as ingots. There does not seem to have been a standard weight for these ingots, as the sighted examples have a weight ranging from 200 g to 500 g. Furthermore, the ingots were not all made of pure copper. In some lead or arsenic are present as minor elements, perhaps reflecting the original ore source, while one of the perforated axes was found to have been made of bronze.

4.2 Ingots from the Middle Bronze Age/Middle Cypriot

The MC (c. 2100/2050–1690/1650 cal BC (Manning, 2014)), which roughly corresponds to the first half of the second millennium BC (for a recent discussion of the MC see Webb & Knapp, 2021), is the period during which the earliest clear evidence for underground mining has been found. This comes from the ore deposit of Ambelikou, in the Solea axis mining district. Modern miners while working underground discovered pottery and stone tools inside ancient shafts (Dikaios, 1946; Merrillees, 1984; Webb & Frankel, 2013). The sherds come from Red Polished III pithoi and jugs, of the MC I period, which dates to the nineteenth century BC. In the same year, the Department of Antiquities conducted rescue excavations at a contemporary nearby settlement, Ambelikou *Aletri,* which must have been associated with the mine (Dikaios, 1946; Merrillees, 1984; Webb & Frankel, 2013). There, among other finds, such as stone tools, that were shown to have been used for ore beneficiation (Webb, 2015), pieces of ore were collected as well as a well preserved crucible and a ceramic blow pipe (Georgakopoulou & Rehren, 2013; Webb & Frankel, 2013; Zwicker, 1982). Among the finds was a double-sided ceramic mould used to cast axes (excavation catalogue number 50) which may have been the form in which the local copper was exported in this period, just as in the period before (Fig. 8). One should bear in mind that the mould is heavily reconstructed and that the shape may have actually been longer and larger and more similar to contemporary moulds from other sites discussed below.

The most abundant evidence for Middle Bronze Age copper smelting was brought to light during the excavation of Pyrgos *Mavrorakhi,* where a complex of structures has been excavated, including a large building which, according to the excavator, was dedicated to the production of olive oil, perfumed oils, textiles and copper (Belgiorno, 2004). The building was destroyed by an earthquake which accounts for the high number of finds at the site. The archaeometallurgical assemblage is rich and has been the topic of the PhD thesis of Marco Romeo Pitone (2022). The presence of significant amounts of slag throughout the excavated area and metallurgical ceramics, including a complete crucible deposited in a tomb that

Fig. 8 Heavily restored double-sided ceramic mould for an axe (Inv. 50). From Ambelikou *Aletri*. (Photo Department of Antiquities, Cyprus)

was identified as the tomb of a metalsmith (Belgiorno, 1997), evidently shows that smelting and metalworking was taking place at the site (Belgiorno, 2004; Romeo Pitone, 2022). Scientific analysis of the slag shows that the ore smelted was a copper sulphide (Giardino, 2000; Romeo Pitone, 2022). Among the finds are two well preserved ceramic moulds for the casting of perforated axes (Inv. 351 and Inv. 352) (Belgiorno et al., 2012) (Fig. 9). Mould 351 has a preserved length of 23 cm while Mould 352 has a preserved length of 19 cm (information kindly provided by the excavator Maria Rosaria Belgiorgo). Both have double perforations which have yet to be observed in contemporary axes (see Catling, 1964; Weinstein Balthazar, 1990). Could this be the form in which copper from Pyrgos was traded? The volume of the cavities has not been calculated but there is an axe of similar length which can indicate the weight of the artefacts produced in these moulds. A perforated axe, perhaps from Deneia and dating to ECIII-MCI-II (2100/2050–1800/1750 BC (Manning, 2014)), with a length of 18.5 cm weighs 945.7 g (Webb et al., 2006). It is made of arsenical copper (As content 3.16%). Lead Isotope Analysis found it to be

Early Types of Cypriot Bronze Age Metal Ingots 1341

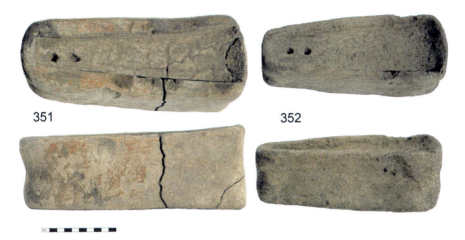

Fig. 9 Two ceramic moulds for perforated axes (Inv. 351 and Inv. 352). From Pyrgos *Mavrorakhi*. (Photograph by Antonio de Strobel courtesy of Maria Rosaria Belgiorno)

consistent with a Cypriot provenance and specifically with the ore deposits of either Mathiatis or Laxia tou Mavrou (Webb et al., 2006).

But there were also definite ingots in circulation in the MC. The excavations at the site of Alambra *Mouttes* brought to light two fragmentary ceramic moulds (Inv. A10 and Inv. A11), which would have been used to produce small bar-shaped ingots (Gale et al., 1996a) (Fig. 10). According to radiocarbon dating, the site was occupied between 1900 and 1800 B.C. (Coleman et al., 1996). Among the finds from the settlement were pieces of slag indicating that the copper, which would have been cast in those moulds, was locally produced most probably by smelting ores collected in the nearby ore deposits of Mathiati or Sha (Gale et al., 1996b).

Excavations at the site of Alambra *Mouttes* were resumed in recent years by a team led by Andrew Sneddon (2016, 2022). The new excavations made an extraordinary discovery. The excavation of a house which had been destroyed by fire, revealed the burial of a gracile individual (perhaps female although it is not certain) (Sneddon, 2019, 2022). The deceased's body was adorned with a copper alloy pin, a fragmentary lead ring (or possibly earring) and at least 237 faience beads (presumably originally part of a necklace or perhaps a bracelet). The surprise comes from the fact that two small bar copper ingots, cast in an open mould, had been placed on the deceased's chest. The ingots (Inv. M5 and Inv. M6) are 10 cm long, 2.5 cm wide, and weigh 165.41 grams and 168.23 grams respectively (Fig. 11). They are similar but they are not identical (Fig. 12). This means they are not mould – siblings: namely they have not been cast in the same mould or at least the same cavity). Astonishingly the excavations uncovered a stone mould with two cavities, one on each side, that could have been used to produce such small bar ingots (Inv. S62) (Sneddon et al., 2022) (Fig. 13). Both cavities are longer than the two ingots which have been recovered from the site which means that this is not the mould that was used to produce them (Kassianidou & Charalambous, 2022).

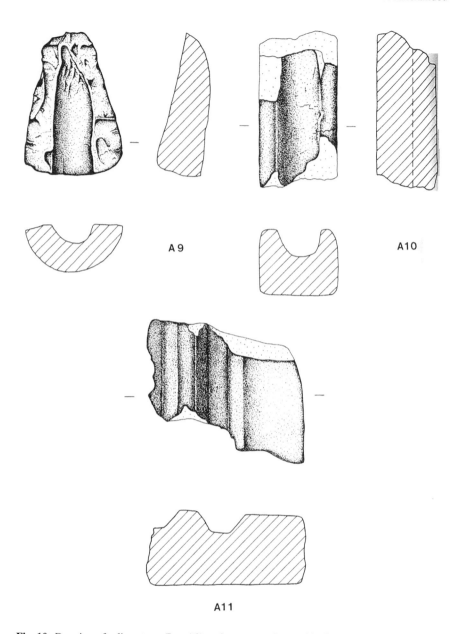

Fig. 10 Drawing of a limestone (Inv. A9) and two ceramic moulds (Inv. A10 and Inv. A11) for casting bar ingots. From Alambra *Mouttes*. (After Coleman et al., 1996)

With permission from the excavator, we had the opportunity to analyse the two ingots using the HHpXRF of the Archaeological Research Unit of the University of Cyprus (Kassianidou & Charalambous, 2022). The results are presented in Table 1. The ingots are made of pure copper with a small amount of iron (probably

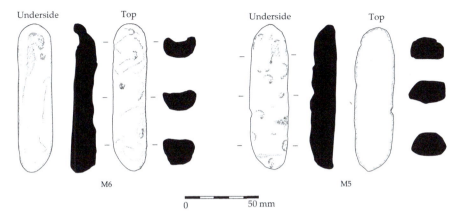

Fig. 11 Drawing of two bar ingots (Inv. M5 and Inv. M6). From Alambra *Mouttes*. (Drawing by G. Deftereos, courtesy of Andrew Sneddon)

Fig. 12 Photograph of two bar ingots (Inv. M5 and Inv. M6). From Alambra *Mouttes*. (Photograph V. Kassianidou)

present because of the smelting of sulphide ores) and traces of arsenic. These results are important as they indicate that copper (at least the one produced at Alambra probably from the nearby ore deposits of Mathiatis and/or Sha) was traded as a pure metal in this period, as it was in the Late Bronze Age.

One must consider what this means for the circulation of copper in Cyprus during the Middle Cypriot. Chemical analysis shows that the arsenical copper used to produce the majority of metal artefacts dating to this period (Weinstein Balthasar,

Fig. 13 Double sided stone mould for casting bar ingots (Inv. S62). From Alambra *Mouttes*. (Photograph V. Kassianidou)

1990; Charalambous & Webb, 2020). The vast majority of the analysed objects has an arsenic content that ranges between 0.1 and 2.8% (according to Weinstein Balthazar, 1990) or 0.25 and 2.5% according to Charalambous & Webb, 2020). The presence of even 1–2% of arsenic in the Cypriot metal artefacts indicates the intentional preparation of an arsenical copper alloy: Cypriot copper sulphide ores have a rather simple chemical composition and other metals such as arsenic, antimony or even lead are only present as trace elements (Charalambous & Webb, 2020; Constantinou, 1992). For arsenical copper to be produced, other minerals, such as the complex polymetallic ores of the Limassol Forest which include arsenides (Thalhammer et al., 1986), would have had to be deliberately added either to the smelting charge or to the molten copper. The debate about the way arsenical copper is formed is on-going among scholars working in the Old and the New World: some believe that ores rich in arsenic would have been added to the smelting charge, thus the alloy was a product of co-smelted ores. Others believe that arsenic rich minerals were added to molten copper and as a result some of the arsenic was absorbed by cementation (Craddock, 1995). The discovery of ingots made of pure copper at Alambra *Mouttes* indicates that at least in this part of Cyprus (and probably everywhere else as well) arsenical copper was not produced by *smelting* arsenic rich minerals together with copper minerals but rather arsenical rich minerals or speiss were added to pure copper in a crucible probably just prior to casting. This is further supported by the fact that arsenic had not been detected in prills entrapped in the slag recovered from Alambra *Mouttes* (Gale et al., 1996b) or Pyrgos *Mavrorakhi* (Giardino, 2000; Romeo Pitone, 2022).

These two ingots are extremely important finds. They are obviously unique, and their archaeological context is intriguing. Dating to the same period there is the example of the burial of metalsmith together with his (hers?) tools (Belgiorno, 1997). The tool kit includes a complete crucible, a whetstone, perforated stone hammers, and a perforated copper alloy axe, which may or may not have been a form of ingot. In Alambra we have for the first time ever on the island, the burial of an individual with two copper ingots. And this individual is most probably a woman. According to the excavator: "Their presence in the burial at Alambra reflects the considerable metal-working activities there towards the end of the settlement's occupation (Coleman et al., 1996). They may also indicate changing attitudes to portable wealth towards the end of the prehistoric Bronze Age, with the value of metal being embodied in the raw product (the ingots) rather than in the finished product alone (e.g., jewellery and weaponry)" (Sneddon, 2019).

Cuneiform documents from Mari, Babylon, and Alalakh, all dated from c. 1900 BC onward, reveal that Alashiya, the name by which Cyprus was known to her eastern neighbours, had started to provide copper to the Levant and the Near East (Knapp, 1996, 2008; Muhly, 1972). Thanks to the work of colleagues in Israel we now have finds that show one of the forms Cypriot copper was exported at this time. A small plano-convex (Inv. METB54) ingot weighing 285 g was found at the site of Hazor and dating to the seventeenth–sixteenth centuries BC, thus towards the end of the Middle Bronze Age, was found to be consistent with the ore deposit of Ambelikou, as was another one which dates to the same phase (Yahalom Mack et al., 2014). Also consistent with the same ore deposit was another ingot found in the same levels in Hazor, that is shaped like a ring and weighs 87 g. Chemical analysis showed that this was made of black unrefined copper. Perhaps these small plano-convex ingots form the bridge for the trade of Cypriot copper in the Middle Bronze Age and the trade of Cypriot copper in the Late Bronze Age.

5 Discussion

This review of the evidence for ingots dating to the earliest phases of the Bronze Age leads to some interesting observations. Throughout this period, namely from the Early Cypriot/Philia Facies up to the Middle Cypriot II which Knapp (2013) has defined as the Prehistoric Bronze Age (ca 2400–1700 BC) Cypriot copper was circulating in a great variety of shapes and sizes such as perforated axes, boat and tongue-shaped ingots, bar ingots and ring ingots. The weights of ingots found on Cyprus dating to this phase of the Bronze Age range from 165 g (the examples from Alambra) to almost 1 kg (the perforated axe from Deneia or the axes that would have been cast in the larger mould from Pyrgos). In the Early Bronze Age, the artefacts which have been identified as possible ingots have a range of compositions (pure copper, arsenical copper and bronze). There does not seem to exist any form of standardization either in size and shape or in weight. In the Middle Bronze Age, the two definite examples of ingots are made of pure copper with some impurities, such as iron. This suggests that arsenical copper, the most common copper alloy used at this time, was not produced during the smelting of sulphidic copper ores but rather in a second, separate stage, where metallic copper was mixed with arsenic rich minerals or speiss. Cypriot ingots found in Hazor and dating to the end of the Middle Bronze Age have a plano-convex shape which will continue in the Late Bronze Age but are significantly smaller than their later counteparts. The size of the ingots indicates that copper was traded in batches which were large enough to produce one large artefact (such as an axe or dagger) or several small ones (such as pins or needles).

In the Late Bronze Age Cypriot copper was traded in two shapes – the discoid, plano-convex/bun ingot which weighed around 6 kg and the oxhide ingot, the trademark of Cypriot metal which weighed around 29 kg. Both, but especially the oxhide ingot, were substantially larger than their earlier counterparts. What does this mean about the Cypriot copper industry of the second half of the second millennium BC? I would like to argue that it shows that copper production on the island had reached a technologically more advanced level. I have argued elsewhere (Kassianidou, 2011, 2013), that the big technological innovation which came with the transition to the Late Bronze Age was the use of a system of bellows and tuyères in the smelting furnaces. By raising the temperature to a higher level, they made the smelting process more efficient and reduced the loss of metal in the slag. Large quantities of copper could thus easily be produced from the sulphidic ores of the Troodos foothills. The oxhide ingots also show the ability of Late Bronze Age smiths to handle larger amounts of molten metal in better designed crucibles and to produce large casts most probably in sand moulds.

Known examples of ingots that belong to one or the other type exhibit only slight differences in the shape and the weight is more or less standardized. Furthermore, both oxhide and discoid, plano-convex/bun ingots are always made of copper metal and not of different copper base alloys. This shows significant control over the production and the trade of copper, a control which would have had to have been centralized. I would argue that even a single oxhide ingot would most probably have been beyond the economic reach of a simple metal smith or an individual merchant and suggest that these ingots may have been purposely produced for bulk trade in metal that was state-controlled. This is similar to the idea of Rehren and Pusch (2012) who suggested that oxhide ingots were part of a system of bulk copper exchange which was meant for special projects. In other words, a more complicated system of exchange was put in place in the Late Bronze Age, through which very large amounts of metal would and could move around at the same time. This idea is of course also supported by the written sources such as the Amarna letters and the evidence from the Uluburun shipwreck.

6 Conclusion

There is still a lot to learn about the production and trade of Cypriot copper in the earliest phases of the Bronze Age. Ideally what we would like to find is a site like the one excavated so masterfully by Tom Levy at Khirbat Hamra Ifdan (Levy et al., 2002), where the whole chaine opératoire of copper production was so well preserved. Until then we need to content ourselves with the scraps of information that is available from different sites and different archaeological contexts, in this case ingots of various shapes and sizes. What they reveal is an interesting picture of an industry that slowly transforms and becomes highly standardized and regulated.

Acknowledgments I would like to express my gratitude to Andrew Sneddon for granting me permission to study and analyse the ingots and ingot mould from his excavation at Alambra *Mouttes* and Maria Rosaria Belgiorno for providing information and the permission to publish photographs of the two moulds from her excavations at Pyrgos *Mavrorakhi*. My sincere thanks to the Director of the Department of Antiquities of Cyprus, Dr. Marina Solomidou-Ieronymidou and Curator of Antiquities Eutuchia Zaxariou for granting me permission to study and analyse the axes and ring ingot perhaps from Vasilia and now in the metal collection of the Cyprus Museum and to archaeological officer Aspasia Georgiades who helped me acquire new photographs of these objects. I am deeply grateful to Andreas Charalambous for carrying out the chemical analysis of objects reported here. Valuable feedback was provided by my husband George Papasavvas and Jennifer Webb both of whom I would like to sincerely thank.

Above all I would like to sincerely thank Erez Ben-Yosef and Ian Jones for inviting me to be a part of this tribute to Tom Levy and to congratulate them for bringing so many friends and colleagues together in what promises to be an excellent volume worthy of the person we have gathered to honour. I met Tom in 2000 during a conference organised by CBRL in Amman and then Faynan. In Faynan we were guided in the excavated sites, including, Khirbat Hamra Ifdan, and were introduced to the cutting-edge excavation methodology and pioneering use of digital archaeology, that Tom was developing and using in his projects. It was many years after that that we had a chance to work together, this time here in Cyprus on the project entitled "The Cyprus Archaeomagnetic Project (CAMP): high resolution dating, magnetic characterization and archaeointensity correlation of major slag deposits in Cyprus and the Eastern Mediterranean" with a team consisting of Tom Levy, Lisa Tauxe, Erez Ben-Yosef, Ron Shaar and myself. The collaboration was the beginning of friendships which I cherish to this day. My wish to Tom is that he continues to lead the way, to continue to mentor younger colleagues and to form valuable partnerships all around the world.

References

Athanassov, B., Chernakov, D., Dimitrov, K., Krauss, R., Popov, H., Schwab, R., Slavchev, V., & Pernicka, E. (2020). A new look at the Late Bronze age oxhide ingots from the eastern Balkans. In J. Maran, R. Băjenaru, S.-C. Ailincăi, A.-D. Popescu, & S. Hansen (Eds.), *Objects, ideas and travelers contacts between the Balkans, the Aegean and Western Anatolia during the Bronze and Early Iron Age. Volume to the memory of Alexandru Vulpe (Universitätsforschungen zur Prähistorischen Archäologie Band 350)* (pp. 299–356). Verlag Dr. Rudolf Habelt GmbH.

Bass, G. F. (1967). Cape Gelidonya: A Bronze Age Shipwreck. *Transactions of the American Philosophical Society, 57*, 8.

Bass, G. F. (1990). Evidence of trade from Bronze Age shipwrecks. In N. H. Gale (Ed.), *Bronze age trade in the Mediterranean, studies in Mediterranean archaeology 90* (pp. 69–82). Paul Åströms Förlag.

Begemann, F., Schmitt-Strecker, S., Pernicka, E., & Schiavo, F. L. (2001). Chemical composition and Lead isotopy of copper and bronze from Nuragic Sardinia. *European Journal of Archaeology, 4*(1), 43–85.

Belgiorno, M. R. (1997). *A coppersmith tomb of Early-Middle Bronze Age in Pyrgos (Limassol)* (pp. 119–146). Report of the Department of Antiquities.

Belgiorno, M. R. (2004). *Pyrgos-Mavroraki: Advanced technology in Bronze Age Cyprus*. CNR-ITABC and Archaeological Mission at Pyrgos.

Belgiorno, M. R., Ferro, D., & Loepp, D. R. (2012). Pyrgos-Mavrorachi in Cypriot metallurgy. In V. Kassianidou & G. Papasavvas (Eds.), *Eastern Mediterranean metallurgy and metalwork in the second millennium BC* (pp. 26–34). Oxbow Books.

Blackwell, N. G. (2018). Contextualizing Mycenaean hoards: Metal control on the Greek mainland at the end of the Bronze Age. *American Journal of Archaeology, 122*(4), 509–539.

Bode, M., Rothenhoefer, P., & Batanero, D. G. (2018). Lost in the South: A Roman copper ingot from the area of Tarragona in the Baetica. *Onoba. Revista de Arqueología y Antigüedad, 6*, 243–248.

Buchholz, H. G. (1959). Keftiubarren und Erzhandel in zweiten vorchristlichen Jahrtausend. *Praehistorische Zeitschrift, 37*, 1–40.

Charalambous, A., & Webb, J. M. (2020). Metal procurement, artefact manufacture and the use of imported Tin Bronze in Middle Bronze Age Cyprus. *Journal of Archaeological Science, 113*, Article 105047. https://doi.org/10.1016/j.jas.2019.105047

Charalambous, A., Kassianidou, V., & Papasavvas, G. (2014). A compositional study of Cypriot bronzes dating to the Early Iron Age using portable X-ray fluorescence spectrometry (pXRF). *Journal of Archaeological Science, 46*, 205–216. https://doi.org/10.1016/j.jas.2014.03.006

Charalambous, A., Papasavvas, G., & Kassianidou, V. (2021). Enkomi (Cyprus): Using pXRF spectroscopy to identify LBA copper alloys. *Journal of Archaeological Science: Reports, 35*, 102726. https://doi.org/10.1016/j.jasrep.2020.102726

Coleman, J. E., Barlow, J. A., Mogelonsky, M. K., & Schaar, K. W. (1996). *Alambra, A Middle Bronze Age settlement in Cyprus. Archaeological investigations by Cornell University 1974–1985*. Studies in Mediterranean Archaeology 118. Paul Åströms Förlag.

Constantinou, G. (1992). The mining industry of Cyprus in modern times. In A. Marangou & K. Psillides (Eds.), *Cyprus copper and the sea* (pp. 328–367). The Government of Cyprus.

Craddock, P. T. (1995). *Early metal mining and production*. Edinburgh University Press.

Catling, H. W. (1964). *Cypriot bronzework in the mycenaean world*. Clarendon Press.

Dialismas, A. (2001). Metal artefacts as recorded in the linear B tablets. In A. Michailidou (Ed.), *Manufacture and measurement. Counting, measuring and recording. Craft items in early Aegean societies, Μελετήματα Κέντρου Ελληνικής και Ρωμαϊκής Αρχαιότητος 33* (pp. 120–143). National Research Centre.

Dikaios, P. (1939). Principal acquisitions of the Cyprus museum, *report of the Department of Antiquities, Cyprus* (1937–39), 199–202.

Dikaios, P. (1946). A new chapter in the long history of Cyprus: Wartime discoveries of the earliest Copper Age. *Illustrated London News, 208*(5576), 244–245.

Du Plat Taylor, J. (1952). A Late Bronze Age settlement at Apliki, Cyprus. *The Antiquaries Journal, 32*, 133–167.

Fasnacht, W., & Künzler Wagner, N. (2001). Stone casting moulds from Marki-Alonia. *Report of the Department of Antiquities, Cyprus, 2001*, 38–41.

Fischer, P. M. (2018). Notes on metal production in CQ1 and CQ2. In P. M. Fischer & T. Bürge (Eds.), *Two late Cypriot City quarters at Hala Sultan Tekke*. The Soderberg Expedition 2010–2017, Studies in Mediterranean Archaeology 147. Astrom Editions.

Frankel, D., & Webb, J. M. (2001). *Excavations at Marki-Alonia, 2000* (pp. 15–43). Report of the Department of Antiquities.

Gale, N. H. (1991). Copper Oxhide ingots: Their origin and their place in the Bronze Age metals trade. In N. H. Gale (Ed.), *Bronze Age Trade in the Mediterranean, studies in Mediterranean archaeology 10* (pp. 197–239). Paul Åströms Förlag.

Gale, N. H. (1999). Lead isotope characterization of the ore deposits of Cyprus and Sardinia and its application to the discovery of the sources of copper for Late Bronze Age Oxhide Ingots. In S. M. M. Young, A. M. Pollard, P. Budd, & R. A. Ixer (Eds.), *Metals in Antiquity, British Archaeological Reports-International Series 792* (pp. 100–221). Archaeopress.

Gale, N. H. (2005). Die Kupferbarren aus von Uluburun. Teil 2: Bleiisotopenanalysen von Bohrkernen aus den Barren. In Ü. Yalçin, C. Pulak, & R. Slota (Eds.), *Das Schiff von Uluburun – Welthandel vor 3000 Jahren* (pp. 141–148). Deutsches Bergbau Museum.

Gale, N. H. (2011). Copper Oxhide ingots and Lead isotope Provenancing. In P. P. Betancourt & S. C. Ferrence (Eds.), *Metallurgy: Understanding how, learning why. Studies in honor of James D. Muhly, prehistory monographs 29* (pp. 213–220). Instap Academic Press.

Gale, N.-H., & Stos-Gale, Z. A. (2005). Zur Herkunft der Kupferbarren aus dem Schiffswrack von Uluburun und der spätbronzezeitliche Metallhandel im Mittelmeerraum. In Ü. Yalçin, C. Pulak, & R. Slota (Eds.), *Das Schiff von Uluburun – Welthandel vor 3000 Jahren* (pp. 117–132). Deutsches Bergbau Museum.

Gale, N. H., & Stos-Gale, Z. A. (2012). The role of the Apliki mine region in the post c. 1400 BC copper production and trade networks in Cyprus and the wider Mediterranean. In V. Kassianidou & G. Papasavvas (Eds.), *Eastern mediterranean metallurgy and metalwork in the second millennium BC* (pp. 70–83). A conference in honour of James D. Muhly. Nicosia 10th–11th October 2009. Oxbow Books.

Gale, N., Stos-Gale, Z., & Fasnacht, W. (1996a). Metal and metalworking. In J. E. Coleman, J. A. Barlow, M. K. Mogelonsky, & K. W. Schaar (Eds.), *Alambra, a Middle Bronze Age settlement in Cyprus. Archaeological investigations by Cornell University 1974–1985* (pp. 129–142). Paul Åströms Förlag.

Gale, N., Stos-Gale, Z., & Fasnacht, W. (1996b). Appendix 2. Copper and copper working at Alambra. In J. E. Coleman, J. A. Barlow, M. K. Mogelonsky, & K. W. Schaar (Eds.), *Alambra, a Middle Bronze Age settlement in Cyprus. Archaeological investigations by Cornell University 1974–1985* (pp. 359–426). Paul Åströms Förlag.

Galili, E., Gale, N., & Rosen, B. (2011). Bronze age metal cargoes off the Israeli coast. *Skyllis, 11*, 64–73.

Galili, E., Gale, N., & Rosen, B. (2013). A late bronze age shipwreck with a metal cargo from Hishuley Carmel, Israel. *International Journal of Nautical Archaeology, 42*(1), 422–423.

Georgakopoulou, M., & Rehren, T. (2013). Report on the analyses of metallurgical samples from Ambelikou Aletri. In J. Webb & D. Frankel (Eds.), *Ambelikou Aletri metallurgy and pottery production in Middle Bronze Age Cyprus, studies in Mediterranean archaeology 138* (pp. 197–199). Åströms Förlag.

Giardino, C. (2000). *Prehistoric copper activity at Pyrgos* (pp. 19–32). Report of the Department of Antiquities.

Graziadio, G. (2003). I lingotti Oxhide Nella Glittica Cipriota. *Studi Micenei ed Egeo-Anatolici, 45*, 27–69.

Graziadio, G. (2014). The Oxhide ingots production in the Eastern Mediterranean. *Egitto e Vicino Oriente, 37,* 5–25. https://doi.org/10.12871/97888674150141

Hadjisavvas, S. (2011). Broken symbols: Aspects of metallurgy at Alassa. In P. P. Betancourt & S. C. Ferrence (Eds.), *Metallurgy: Understanding how, learning whY. Studies in honor of James D. Muhly* (pp. 2–27). Instap Academic Press.

Hakulin, L. (2004). *Bronzeworking on late Minoan Crete. A diachronic study (BAR International Series 1245).* Archaeopress.

Hauptmann, A. (2009). Lead isotope analysis and the origin of Sardinian metal objects. In F. Lo Schiavo, J. D. Muhly, J. D. Maddin R, & A. Giumlia Mair (Eds.), *Oxhide ingots in the Central Mediterranean* (pp. 499–514). A.G. Leventis Foundation and CNR – Istituto di Studi Sulle Civiltà Dell'Egeo e Del Vicino Oriente.

Hauptmann, A., Schmitt-Strecker, S., Levy, T. E., & Begemann, F. (2015). On Early Bronze Age copper bar ingots from the Southern Levant. *Bulletin of the American Schools of Oriental Research, 373,* 1–24. https://doi.org/10.5615/bullamerschoorie.373.0001

Hauptmann, A., Laschimke, R., & Burger, M. (2016). On the making of copper oxhide ingots: Evidence from metallography and casting experiments. *Archaeological and Anthropological Sciences, 8,* 751–761. https://doi.org/10.1007/s12520-015-0255-2

Henessy, J. B., Eriksson, K. O., & Kehrberg, I. C. (1988). Ayia Paraskevi and Vasilia. Excavations by J. R. B. Stewart. In *Studies in Mediterranean archaeology 82.* Åströms Förlag.

Karageorghis, V. (1960). Chronique des fouilles et découvertes archéologiques à Chypre en 1959. *Bulletin de Correspondance Hellénique, 84,* 242–299.

Kassianidou, V. (2003). The trade of tin and the Island of copper. In A. Giumlia Mair & F. Lo Schiavo (Eds.), *Le problème de l'étain à l'origine de la métallurgie/the problem of early tin, BAR International Series 1199* (pp. 109–119). Archaeopress.

Kassianidou, V. (2008). The formative years of the Cypriot copper industry. In I. Tzachilli (Ed.), *Aegean metallurgy in the Bronze Age. Proceedings of an International Symposium held at the University of Crete Rethymnon, Greece, on November 19–21, 2004* (pp. 249–267). Ta Pragmata Publications.

Kassianidou, V. (2009). Oxhide ingots in Cyprus. In F. Lo Schiavo, J. D. Muhly, R. Maddin, & A. Giumlia Mair (Eds.), *Oxhide ingots in the Central Mediterranean* (pp. 41–81). A.G. Leventis Foundation and CNR – Istituto di Studi Sulle Civiltà Dell'Egeo e Del Vicino Oriente.

Kassianidou, V. (2011). Blowing the wind of change: The introduction of bellows in Late Bronze Age Cyprus. In P. P. Betancourt & S. C. Ferrence (Eds.), *Metallurgy: Understanding how, learning why. Studies in honor of James D. Muhly, prehistory monographs 29* (pp. 41–48). Instap Academic Press.

Kassianidou, V. (2012). Metallurgy and metalwork in Enkomi: The early phases. In V. Kassianidou & G. Papasavvas (Eds.), *Eastern Mediterranean metallurgy and metalwork in the second millennium BC. A conference in honour of James D. Muhly. Nicosia 10th–11th October 2009* (pp. 94–106). Oxbow Books.

Kassianidou, V. (2013). The production and trade of Cypriot copper in the Late Bronze Age. An analysis of the evidence. *Pasiphae. Rivista di Filologia a Antichità Egee, 7,* 133–146.

Kassianidou, V. (2014). Appendix II. Oxhide ingots made of Cypriote copper found in Crete. In V. Karageorghis, A. Kanta, N. Chr. Stambolidis, & Y. Sakellarakis (Eds.), *Kypriaka in Crete from the bronze age to the end of the archaic period* (pp. 307–311).

Kassianidou, V. (2016). Metallurgy and metalwork in Enkomi – Revisiting Porphyrios Dikaios' excavations. In G. Bourogiannis & C. Muhlenbock (Eds.), *Ancient Cyprus today: Museum collections and new research, studies in Mediterranean archaeology-pocketbook 184* (pp. 79–90). Astrom Editions.

Kassianidou, V. (2018a). Late Bronze Age Cypriot hoards and modern collections. In L. Hulin, L. Crewe, & J. M. Webb (Eds.), *Structures of inequality on bronze age Cyprus: Studies in honour of Alison K. South. Studies in Mediterranean archaeology pocketbook 187* (pp. 211–226). Astrom Editions.

Kassianidou, V. (2018b). Ancient copper mining, oxhide ingots and a hoard—New data on Mathiatis from the state archives of Cyprus. In A. Giumlia-Mair & F. L. Schiavo (Eds.), *Bronze age metallurgy in the Mediterranean Islands. In honour of Robert Maddin and Vassos Karageorghis, monographies Instrumentum 56* (pp. 578–598). Editions Mergoil.

Kassianidou, V. (2018c). Apliki *Karamallos* on Cyprus: The 13th century BCE miners' settlement in context. In E. Ben Yosef (Ed.), *Mining for ancient copper. Essays in memory of Beno Rothenberg, Tel Aviv University – Sonia and Marco Nadler Institute of Archaeology Monograph Series 37* (pp. 345–356). Emery and Claire Yass Publications in Archaeology and Eisenbrauns.

Kassianidou, V., & Charalambous, A. (2022). 10. Chemical analysis of metal artefacts. In A. Sneddon, L. Graham, T. Rymer, & G. Defteros (Eds.), *The Middle Bronze Age settlement at Alambra in Cyprus, 2012–2016, Studies in Mediterranean archaeology 153* (pp. 95–97). Astrom Editions.

Keswani, P. S. (1993). Models of local exchange in Late Bronze Age Cyprus. *Bulletin of the American School of Oriental Research, 292*, 73–83. https://doi.org/10.2307/1357249

Kling, B., & Muhly, J. D. (2007). Joan du Plat Taylor's excavations at the Late Bronze Age mining settlement at Apliki Karamallos, Cyprus. *Studies in Mediterranean Archaeology, 94*(1). Paul Åströms Förlag.

Knapp, A. B. (1996). Sources for the history of Cyprus. *Volume II near eastern and Aegean texts from the third to the first millennia BC*. Cyprus Research Centre

Knapp, A. B. (1997). The archaeology of Late Bronze Age Cypriot society: The study of settlement, survey and landscape. In *Department of archaeology, University of Glasgow, occasional paper 4*. University of Glasgow.

Knapp, A. B. (2008). *Prehistoric and protohistoric Cyprus: Identity, insularity, and connectivity*. Oxford University Press.

Knapp, A. B. (2011). Cyprus, copper and Alashiya. In P. P. Betancourt & S. C. Ferrence (Eds.), *Metallurgy: Understanding how, learning why. Studies in honor of James D. Muhly, prehistory monographs 29* (pp. 249–254). Instap Academic Press.

Knapp, A. B. (2012). Metallurgical production and trade on Bronze Age Cyprus: Views and variations. In V. Kassianidou & G. Papasavvas (Eds.), *Eastern Mediterranean metallurgy and metalwork in the second millennium BC. A conference in honour of James D. Muhly. Nicosia 10th–11th October 2009* (pp. 14–25). Oxbow Books.

Knapp, A. B. (2013). *The archaeology of Cyprus. From Earliest Prehistory through the Bronze Age*. University of Cambridge Press.

Lehner, J. W., Kuruçayırlı, E., & Hirschfeld, N. (2020). Oxhides, buns, bits, and pieces: Analyzing the ingot cargo of the cape Gelidonya shipwreck. In A. Gilboa & A. Yasur-Landau (Eds.), *Nomads of the Mediterranean: Trade and contact in the Bronze and Iron Ages. Studies in honour of Michal Artzy* (pp. 161–176). Brill.

Levy, T. E., Adams, R. B., Hauptmann, A., Prange, M., Schmitt-Strecker, S., & Najjar, M. (2002). Early Bronze Age metallurgy: A newly discovered copper manufactory in southern Jordan. *Antiquity, 76*, 425–437. https://doi.org/10.1017/S0003598X00090530

Lo Schiavo, F., Giumlia-Mair, A., Sanna, U., & Valera, R. (2005). *Archaeometallurgy in Sardinia from the origin to the Early Iron Age*. Monique Mergoil.

Lo Schiavo, F., Muhly, J. D., Maddin, R., & Giumlia Mair, A. (2009). *Oxhide ingots in the Central Mediterranean*. A.G. Leventis Foundation and CNR – Istituto di Studi Sulle Civiltà Dell'Egeo e Del Vicino Oriente.

Maddin, R., Muhly, J. D., & Stech Wheeler, T. (1983). Metal working. In T. Dothan & A. Ben-Tor (Eds.), *Excavations at Athienou Cyprus 1971–72, QEDEM 16* (pp. 132–138). Israel Museum.

Mangou, H., & Ioannou, P. V. (2000). Studies of the Late Bronze Age copper-based ingots found in Greece 1. *Annual of the British School at Athens, 95*, 207–217.

Manning, S. W. (2014). A radiocarbon-based chronology for the chalcolithic through Middle Bronze Age of Cyprus (as of AD 2012). In F. Höflmayer & R. Eichmann (Eds.), *Egypt and the southern Levant in the early bronze age, orient-Archäologie 31* (pp. 207–240). Verlag Marie Leidorf.

Merrillees, R. S. (1984). *Ambelikou-Aletri: A preliminary report, Report of the Department of Antiquities* (pp. 1–14).

Moran, W. L. (1992). *The Amarna letters.* Johns Hopkins University Press.

Muhly, J. D. (1972). The land of Alashiya: References to Alashiya in the texts of the second millennium B.C. and the history of Cyprus in the Late Bronze Age. In V. Karageorghis & A. Christodoulou (Eds.), *Acts of the First International Congress of Cyprological Studies.* (pp. 201–219). Etairia Kypriakon Spoudon.

Muhly, J. D. (1989). The organisation of the copper industry in Late Bronze Age Cyprus. In E. Peltenburg (Ed.), *Early Society in Cyprus.* (pp. 298–314). Edinburgh University Press.

Muhly, J. D. (2009). Oxhide ingots in the Aegean and Egypt. In F. Lo Schiavo, J. D. Muhly, R. Maddin, & A. G. Mair (Eds.), *Oxhide Ingots in the Central Mediterranean* (pp. 17–39). A.G. Leventis Foundation, and CNR-Instituto di Study Sulle Civilta' Dell'Egeo e Del Vicino Oriente.

Öniz, H. (2019). A New Bronze Age shipwreck with ingots in the West of Antalya—Preliminary results. *Palestine Exploration Quarterly, 151,* 3–14. https://doi.org/10.1080/0031032 8.2019.1579467

Öniz, H. (2020). Antalya-Kumluca Bronze Age shipwreck 2019 studies – First analyses. *Palestine Exploration Quarterly, 151,* 172–183. https://doi.org/10.1080/00310328.2019.1700640

Papasavvas, G. (2009). The iconography of Oxhide ingots. In F. Lo Schiavo, J. D. Muhly, R. Maddin, & A. Giumlia Mair (Eds.), *Oxhide ingots in the Central Mediterranean.* (pp. 83–132). A.G. Leventis Foundation and CNR – Istituto di Studi Sulle Città Dell'Egeo e Del Vicino Oriente.

Papasavvas, G. (2018). Values, weights and equivalences of metals in the Late Bronze Age Eastern Mediterranean, or what could a copper oxhide ingot "buy"? In A. Giumlia-Mair & F. Lo Schiavo (Eds.), *Bronze Age Metallurgy on Mediterranean Islands. Volume in honour of Robert Maddin and Vassos Karageorghis, monographies Instrumentum 56* (pp. 600–629). Editions Mergoil.

Papasavvas, G. (2021). What could a copper oxhide ingot 'buy' in the Markets of the Late Bronze Age Eastern Mediterranean? In M. Perra & F. Lo Schiavo (Eds.), *Cultural concacts and trade in Nuragic Sardinia: The southern route (Sardinia, Sicily, Crete and Cyprus). Proceedings of the Fourth Festival of the Nuragic Civilization (Orroli, Cagliari), Gagliari 2021* (pp. 127–150). Arkadia Editore.

Pulak, C. (2000). The copper and tin ingots from the Late Bronze Age shipwreck at Uluburun. In Ü. Yalçin (Ed.), *Anatolian Metal I, Der Anschnitt. Beiheft 13* (pp. 137–157). Deutsches Bergbau Museum.

Pulak, C. (2008). The Uluburun shipwreck and Late Bronze Age trade. In J. Aruz, K. Benzel, & J. M. Evans (Eds.), *Beyond Babylon. Art, trade and diplomacy in the second millennium B.C* (pp. 289–385). The Metropolitan Museum of Art.

Pulak, C. (2009). The Uluburun tin ingots and the shipment of tin by sea in the Late Bronze Age Mediterranean. *Tuba-Ar-Turkish Academy of Sciences Journal of Archaeology, 12,* 189–207.

Rehren, T., & Pusch, E. B. (2012). Alloying and resource management in New Kingdom Egypt: The bronze industry at Qantir – Pi-Ramesse and its relationship to Egyptian copper sources. In V. Kassianidou & G. Papasavvas (Eds.), *Eastern Mediterranean metallurgy and metalwork in the second millennium BC. A conference in honour of James D. Muhly. Nicosia 10th–11th October 2009* (pp. 215–221). Oxbow Books.

Rice Jones, M. (2007). *Oxhide ingots, copper production, and the Mediterranean trade in copper and other metals in the bronze age.* Master Thesis submitted to Texas A & M University.

Romeo Pitone, M. (2022). *Reconstructing early Cypriot Metallurgy: The Case of Pyrgos-Mavroraki.* PhD Thesis, Newcastle University.

Sabatini, S. (2016a). Late Bronze Age Oxhide and Oxhide-like ingots from areas other than the Mediterranean: Problems and challenges. *Oxford Journal of Archaeology, 35*(1), 29–45. https://doi.org/10.1111/ojoa.12077

Sabatini, S. (2016b). Revisiting Late Bronze Age copper Oxhide ingots: Meanings, questions and perspectives. In O. C. Aslaksen (Ed.), *Local and global perspectives on mobility in the eastern Mediterranean, papers and monographs from the Norwegian Institute at Athens, volume 5* (pp. 15–62). The Norwegian Institute at Athens.

Seltman, C. (1924). *Athens, its History and Coinage before the Persian invasion*. Cambridge University Press.

Smith, J. (1993). The Pylos Jn series. *Minos, 27-28*, 167–259.

Sneddon, A. (2016). Revisiting Alambra Mouttes: Defining the spatial configuration and social relations of a prehistoric Bronze Age settlement in Cyprus. *Journal of Mediterranean Archaeology, 28*(2), 141–170. https://doi.org/10.1558/jmea.v28i2.29529

Sneddon, A. (2019). An analog from the prehistoric Bronze Age site of Alambra *Mouttes* (Cyprus) for adornments on the enigmatic "Vounous bowl". *Bulletin of the American School of Oriental Research, 382*, 2–15. https://doi.org/10.1086/705485

Sneddon, A., Graham, L., Rymer, T., & Deftereos, G. (2022). *The middle bronze age settlement at Alambra in Cyprus, 2012–2016, studies in Mediterranean archaeology 153*. Astrom Editions.

South, A. (2012). Tinker, tailor, farmer, miner: Metals in the Late Bronze Age economy at Kalavasos. In V. Kassianidou & G. Papasavvas (Eds.), *Eastern Mediterranean metallurgy and metalwork in the second millennium BC. A conference in honour of James D. Muhly. Nicosia 10th–11th October 2009*. (pp. 35–47). Oxbow Books.

Stos, Z. A. (2009). Across the Wine Dark Seas… Sailor Tinkers and Royal Cargoes in the Late Bronze Age Eastern Mediterranean. In A. J. Shortland, I. C. Freestone, & T. Rehren (Eds.), *From mine to microscope: Advances in the study of ancient technology* (pp. 163–180). Oxbow Books.

Stos, Z. A. (2011). "Biscuits with ears": A search for the origin of the earliest Oxhide ingots. In P. P. Betancourt & S. C. Ferrence (Eds.), *Metallurgy: Understanding how, learning WhY. Studies in honor of James D. Muhly, prehistory monographs 29*. (pp. 221–229) Instap Academic Press.

Stos-Gale, Z. A., & Gale, N. H. (2010). Bronze Age metal artefacts found on Cyprus – Metal from Anatolia and the Western Mediterranean. *Trabajos de Prehistoria, 67*(2), 389–403. https://doi.org/10.3989/tp.2010.10046

Thalhammer, O., Stumpfl, E. F., & Panayiotou, A. (1986). Postmagmatic, hydrothermal origin of sulfide and arsenide mineralizations at Limassol forest, Cyprus. *Mineralium Deposita, 21*, 95–105.

Tylecote, R. F. (1982). The ancient slags of Cyprus. In J. D. Muhly, R. Maddin, & V. Karageorghis (Eds.), *Early metallurgy in Cyprus 4000–500 BC* (pp. 81–100). The Pierides Foundation.

Tylecote, R. F. (1992). *A history of metallurgy* (2nd ed.). Maney for the Institute of Metals.

Van Brempt, L., & Kassianidou, V. (2016). Facing the complexity of copper-sulphide ore smelting and assessing the role of copper in south-central Cyprus: A comparative study of the slag assemblage from Late Bronze Age Kalavasos-*Ayios Dhimitrios*. *Journal of Archaeological Science: Reports, 7*, 539–553. https://doi.org/10.1016/j.jasrep.2015.08.022

Van Brempt, L., & Kassianidou, V. (2017). Appendix II the study of the metallurgical remains from Alassa *Pano Mantilaris* and *Paliotaverna*. In S. Hadjisavvas (Ed.), *Alassa. Excavations at the Late Bronze Age sites of Pano Mantilaris and Paliotaverna 1984–2000* (pp. 479–485). Department of Antiquities.

Ventris, M., & Chadwick, J. (1956). *Documents in Mycenaean Greek: Three hundred selected tablets from Knossos, Pylos and Mycenae with commentary and vocabulary*. Cambridge University Press.

Wainwright, G. A. (1944). Rekhmirê's metal-workers. *Man, 44*, 94–98.

Wang, Q., Strekopytov, S., Roberts, B. W., & Wilkin, N. (2016). Tin ingots from a probable Bronze Age shipwreck off the coast of Salcombe, Devon: Composition and microstructure. *Journal of Archaeological Science, 67*, 80–92. https://doi.org/10.1016/j.jas.2016.01.018

Wang, Q., Strekopytov, S., & Roberts, B. W. (2018). Copper ingots from a probable bronze age shipwreck off the coast of Salcombe, Devon: Composition and microstructure. *Journal of Archaeological Science, 97*, 102–117. https://doi.org/10.1016/j.jas.2018.07.002

Webb, J. M. (2015). Identifying stone tools used in mining, smelting, and casting in Middle Bronze Age Cyprus. *Journal of Field Archaeology, 40*(1), 22–36. https://doi.org/10.117 9/0093469014Z.000000000108

Webb, J. M., & Frankel, D. (1999). Characterising the Philia facies. Material culture, chronology and the origin of the Bronze Age in Cyprus. *American Journal of Archaeology, 103*, 3–43.

Webb, J. M., & Frankel, D. (2013). *Ambelikou Aletri metallurgy and pottery production in Middle Bronze Age Cyprus, Studies in Mediterranean Archaeology 138.* Åströms Förlag.

Webb, J. M., & Knapp, A. B. (2021). Rethinking Middle Bronze Age communities on Cyprus: "Egalitarian" and isolated or complex and interconnected? *Journal of Archaeological Research, 29*(2), 203–253. https://doi.org/10.1007/s10814-020-09148-8

Webb, J. M., & Weingarten, J. (2012). Seals and seal use: Markers of social, political and economic transformations on two islands. In G. Cadogan, M. Iacovou, K. Kopaka, & J. Whitley (Eds.), *Parallel lives. Ancient Island societies in Crete and Cyprus.* (pp. 85–104). British School at Athens Studies 20. https://www.jstor.org/stable/23541203

Webb, J. M., Frankel, D., Stos, Z. A., & Gale, N. (2006). Early Bronze Age metal trade in the eastern Mediterranean: New compositional and Lead isotope evidence from Cyprus. *Oxford Journal of Archaeology, 25*, 261–288. https://doi.org/10.1111/j.1468-0092.2006.00261.x

Weinstein Balthazar, J. (1990). *Copper and bronze working in early through middle Bronze Age Cyprus, Studies in Mediterranean Archaeology Pocket-book 84.* Paul Åströms Förlag.

Yahalom-Mack, N., Galili, E., Segal, I., Eliyahu-Behar, A., Boaretto, E., Shilstein, S., & Finkelstein, I. (2014). New insights into Levantine copper trade: Analysis of ingots from the bronze and iron ages in Israel. *Journal of Archaeological Science, 45*, 159–177. https://doi.org/10.1016/j.jas.2014.02.004

Yahalom-Mack, N., Finn, D. M., Erel, Y., Tirosh, O., Galili, E., & Yasur-Landau, A. (2022). Incised Late Bronze Age lead ingots from the southern anchorage of Caesarea. *Journal of Archaeological Science: Reports, 41*, 103321. https://doi.org/10.1016/j.jasrep.2021.103321

Zaccagnini, C. (1986). Aspects of copper trade in the Eastern Mediterranean during the Late Bronze Age. In M. Marazzi, S. Tusa, & L. Vagnetti (Eds.), *Traffici micenei nel Mediterraneo: Problemi storici e documentazione archeologica.* (pp. 413–424). Istituto per la Storia e l'Archeologia della Magna Grecia.

Zwicker, U. (1982). Bronze Age metallurgy at Ambelikou – *Aletri* and arsenical copper in a crucible from Episkopi – *Phaneromeni.* In J. D. Muhly, R. Maddin, & V. Karageorghis (Eds.), *Early metallurgy in Cyprus, 4000–500 B.C.* (pp. 63–68). The Pierides Foundation.

A Change in Attitude: X-Ray Images of the Ingot God from Enkomi

George Papasavvas

Abstract The bronze statuette of the Ingot God from Enkomi, showing a warrior with a helmet, spear and shield, and standing on a base in the shape of an oxhide ingot, is one of the best-known Late Bronze Age works of the Eastern Mediterranean. The eclecticism discernible in the choice of his iconographic features, which fuse the traditional type of a Smiting God with the exceptional presence of the ingot as a support or base, indicates that an established Near Eastern perception of the divine and a long-standing iconographic concept for godly representations had been adapted to create a novel image of a local deity that expressed the concerns and interests of Cypriots in this period.

In a previous work I suggested that the Ingot God was initially much closer to the image of a Smiting God than its present appearance suggests. This initial image lacked the denominating feature of the statuette, i.e., the oxhide ingot, which was added to it at a later stage. This proposition was based on close visual examination of the lower part of the figure, which is covered by a distinct layer of metal, previously misidentified as a pair of greaves, but actually added when the striding posture was replaced by a different one. This double life of the Ingot God, initially as a Smiting God and later as a still smiting deity but with some additional association to metallurgy, as epitomized by the ingot, can now for the first time be confirmed through a look under the metallic surface. That the pose of the figure, indeed its whole lower part, was altered to conform to the addition of a support in the shape of an oxhide ingot, is clearly disclosed in some old, but unknown, X-Ray images of the statuette, executed in the 1970s in the Römisch-Germanisches Zentalmuseum in Mainz, Germany, where it was taken for restoration. The confirmation of the initial hypothesis about the change effected on an older image allows us to discuss the significance of ancient alterations, changing meanings and extended lifespans of ancient works.

G. Papasavvas (✉)
University of Cyprus, Nicosia, Cyprus
e-mail: georgep@ucy.ac.cy

© The Author(s), under exclusive license to Springer Nature Switzerland AG 2023
E. Ben-Yosef, I. W. N. Jones (eds.), *"And in Length of Days Understanding" (Job 12:12): Essays on Archaeology in the Eastern Mediterranean and Beyond in Honor of Thomas E. Levy*, Interdisciplinary Contributions to Archaeology,
https://doi.org/10.1007/978-3-031-27330-8_58

Keywords Ingot God · X-ray · Casting-on · Enkomi · Smiting God · Bronze casting · Image alteration

Tradition and innovation are two essential concepts in the study of ancient cultures of the Eastern Mediterranean, often examined in juxtaposition to each other, as they are thought to describe the dynamic tension between continuity and change. This paper, which discusses the Ingot God, a Late Cypriot bronze statuette from Enkomi that exhibits both traditional and innovative aspects in its iconography and technology, is presented here in appreciation of the work of Thomas Levy, who has devoted much of his life to describing and interpreting tradition (e.g., Levy et al., 2008), and studying, as well as, embracing and implementing, innovation (Levy et al., 2012, 2014).

1 The Ingot God

1.1 Context and Date

The Ingot God is one of the most remarkable examples of Late Bronze Age statuary in the Eastern Mediterranean (Figs. 1, 2 and 3). Since its publication (Schaeffer, 1965, 1971), this work has been extensively discussed in relation to its date, style, context, and identity, and has featured prominently in deliberations on a possible association between cult, economy and metallurgy (e.g., Catling, 1971; Kassianidou, 2005; Knapp, 1986; Lagarce & Lagarce, 1986; Muhly, 1988; Peltenburg, 2007; Spigelmann, 2012; Webb, 1999); in fact, it has been the principal advocate for such an association.

The statuette was found in a small room in the northeast corner of a building that was identified as a sanctuary because of its spatial arrangement and the abundant ritual paraphernalia it contained, such as bucrania, kernoi, and various terracottas, which gave it the fitting name 'Sanctuary of the Ingot God' (Courtois, 1971, 1986; Webb, 1999, 2001). It was discovered in an upright position on a floor designated by the excavators as *Sol III*, within a compact mudbrick fill sealed by *Sol II*, which was thought to present signs of continued occupation. The excavators concluded that the statuette was deliberately cached between the two floors and kept out of sight, while cult activities continued in the building for some time (Courtois, 1971; Schaeffer, 1971). This reconstruction is in need of some re-evaluation, as it is reminiscent of similar, more or less synchronous behavioral patterns in other areas of Enkomi, particularly in the Sanctuary of the Horned God, where the homonymous bronze statuette was also believed to have been cached between two floors, some time before the abandonment of its sacred space (Dikaios, 1969–1971; Webb, 1999). This latter conclusion can be contested on grounds of some stratigraphic observations, and the same is probably true for the Sanctuary of the Ingot God (Papasavvas, 2014, in preparation).

A Change in Attitude: X-Ray Images of the Ingot God from Enkomi

Fig. 1 The Ingot God from Enkomi; Cyprus Museum, F.E. 63/16.15. (Image: Department of Antiquities, Cyprus)

The circumstances that led to the deposition of the Ingot God and to the abandonment not only of the respective sanctuary but also of Enkomi, have been the subject of some discussion (Iacovou, 1988, 1991; Kling, 1989; Mountjoy, 2005, 2017, 2018; Papasavvas, 2011; Webb, 1999, 2001). The date of this process depends on the classification of the ceramics from the latest deposits not only from this building itself but also from the entire site. The main phase of use of the Sanctuary of the Ingot God and its abandonment all fall within *Sols III-I*, which have provided a wide range of Proto-White Painted Ware, and were accordingly assigned to the Late Cypriot IIIB period, dated from the late twelfth to the mid-eleventh cenuries BCE. According to Iacovou (1988), nothing comparable appears among the

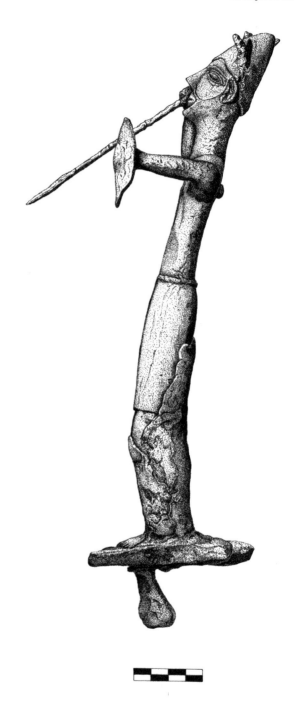

Fig. 2 The Ingot God, seen from the left; drawing by Clara Vasitsek

A Change in Attitude: X-Ray Images of the Ingot God from Enkomi

Fig. 3 The Ingot God, seen from the rear. (Image: Römisch-Germanisches Zentralmuseum Mainz/ photographer: F. Hummel)

published material from other sectors of Enkomi, which would suggest that the sanctuary continued to be used at a time when all other areas had been deserted. On the other hand, Kling (1989), and recently also Mountjoy (2005, 2017, 2018), assert that parallels of the wares from sanctuary's *Sols III-I* do exist elsewhere in the town, and suggest that its use overlapped with the final occupation of at least some parts of Enkomi. Webb (2001) reckons that the site was abandoned rather gradually, and that parts of it may have been inhabited as long as the Sanctuary of the Ingot God was still functioning, while others were deserted. Recent research has shown that, although the termination of both sanctuaries at Enkomi is clearly associated with gradual abandonment processes and, specifically, with closure rituals, these do not seem to have involved the caching of statuettes, or the continuation of sacred spaces beyond the time of the statuettes' final deposition (Papasavvas, 2011, 2014, in preparation).

It is erroneous, even if often inevitable, to rely excessively on ceramics to date so exceptional a metal find as the statuette of the Ingot God (cf. Muhly, 1980). The find context of metal statuettes is often secondary, as they tended to endure over long periods and to be placed in the service of long-lasting cults. Thus, they may have been manufactured long before they came to be deposited in their find spot (Moorey & Fleming, 1984; Ornan, 2011a, b). The Ingot God, in particular, most certainly had such an extended life, as it was associated with a change in its original appearance and two distinct iconographies: Initially, it was only a warrior, which was at some point transformed into the Ingot God now before us (Papasavvas, 2011; see below). Therefore, an earlier date than its context suggests is a reasonable assumption (Carless Hulin, 1989; Knapp, 1986; Muhly, 1980), even if we cannot be more precise, as close stylistic parallels are lacking on Cyprus and elsewhere. This means that *Sol III* which yielded the Ingot God together with Late Cypriot IIIB pottery, is relevant only for the final stage in the statuette's life and use, not for its manufacture or transformation. In fact, an earlier building, only partially excavated and very briefly reported, but possibly also serving cult purposes and ruined during the twelfth century BCE was found underlying the Sanctuary of the Ingot God (Courtois, 1971; Schaeffer, 1971; Webb, 1999, 2001). Its occupation floors, *Sols IV-V* were assigned by the excavator to Late Cypriot IIC (Courtois, 1971; *Sol V* in particular is associated with Late Cypriot IIIA in Kling, 1989). This is where the earlier vases that were found together with the Ingot God (Iacovou, 1988), possibly originated. Late Cypriot IIC can thus be taken as the latest possible date for the inception of the Ingot God at Enkomi, although at that stage it was probably not an Ingot God at all, but a Smiting God, distinguished from its Near Eastern counterparts only by an imposing height of 35 cm. This size is unusual for bronze statuary of the second, as well as of the early first, millennium BCE, which tended to produce much smaller figures, usually below 10–15 cm (for some other, rare cases of comparable, tall bronze figures, see Schorsch & Wypyski, 2009; Ornan, 2011a, 2012). Nine other bronze examples of this Smiting type (none with an ingot) have been excavated on Cyprus (Webb, 1999), none, however, attained the iconographic complexity, size or quality of the Ingot God.

1.2 Iconography

The Ingot God is a heavily armed warrior, with a horned helmet, a small, round shield in his bent left arm, and a spear in his raised right. The warlike pose follows the iconography of the Smiting God, commonly shown in the arts of the Near East, Anatolia, and Egypt (Fulco, 1976; Negbi, 1976; Muhly, 1980; Seeden, 1980; Cornelius, 1994; Lipinski, 2009; Munnich, 2013). There are many variations that fall under this general nomenclature and they present difficulties in the classification and identification of these representations. The variations pertain mainly to the types of weapons and headdresses shown, and even in the gender of the figures. Even the efficacy of the broad term "Smiting Gods" has been questioned and substituted by that of "Menacing Gods," with the argument that no enemy to be smitten is present (Cornelius, 1994). In any case, the association with weapons is a conventional feature of the Ingot God, which appears regularly in the bronze statuary of the Mediterranean and the Near East. On the contrary, the denominating feature under the figure's feet, that is, the miniaturized oxhide ingot, is a most eccentric, close to unique, element, so far uknown outside Cyprus.

Although strongly recalling the Oriental Smiting Gods, the Ingot God diverts in many ways from this general type. Despite the apparent resemblance in posture and the overall belligerent iconography, this bronze from Enkomi does not strictly conform to the genre of Near Eastern armed figurines and cannot be conveniently classified as such (cf. Webb, 1999). Its sleeved, V-necked garment is completely different from the short kilt worn by the majority of these statuettes (Seeden, 1980). Its shield is also a rather rare, even if not unknown, attribute among the armed bronze figurines (Seeden, 1980; Cornelius, 1994). More importantly, the fact that the Ingot God stands on a base, cast in one piece with the figure (or so it seems, see below) is most atypical for this group (Papasavvas, 2009, 2011).

1.3 The Ingot

Although some reservations have been expressed in the past (Balmuth, 1994; Masson, 1992), there is no doubt that the element serving as a base or support for the figure replicates the shape of an oxhide ingot in a miniature form (Figs. 1, 2, 3 and 4). An ingot is not a justifiable selection for a base of anything, not only because it does not offer more support than any plain orthogonal base would, but mainly because there is certainly more to it than a purely practical function. The choice of the smith to give the Ingot God a base at all, in one piece with the figure itself, is also unexpected. Statuettes of this and later periods were normally equipped with pegs extending down from one or both feet and inserted into a support made of some other material, such as wood or stone (Negbi, 1976; Seeden, 1980). Even the Horned God from Enkomi, larger by 20 cm than the Ingot God and much heavier (Dikaios, 1969–1971), did not require an integral base. The separate base and the possibility

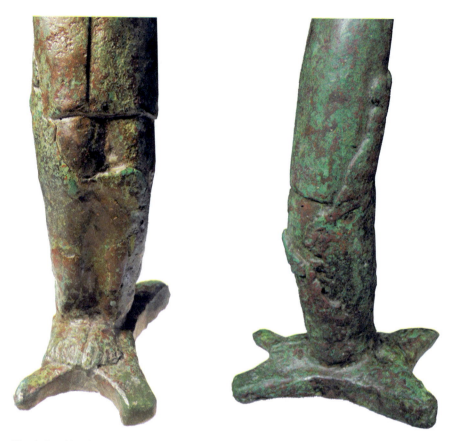

Fig. 4 Details of the lower part of the Ingot God, from the front (left), and left profile (right). (Photos by the author, by permission of the Department of Antiquities, Cyprus)

it offered of detaching the figure from its support, has in fact been associated with ritual practices, namely with the idea that they may have been temporarily removed from their standpoints and exhibited in processions (Hill, 2004; Maran, 2011; Schorsch, 2019). A small base would not need to be detached for such a purpose, but if statuettes were instead set on larger and permanent, or semi-permanent fixtures, such as stone altars or benches and wooden tables, this concept gains in perspective. In any case, the Ingot God itself is equipped with a substantial, flattened peg, projecting from underneath the ingot (Schaeffer, 1971) (Figs. 1, 2, and 4). It was meant to be inserted into a separate, now missing, support, whereas a dowel projecting from its back, now broken (Buchholz, 1979), was possibly meant to secure the statuette against a vertical surface. In other words, the ingot itself, not just the statuette, rested on a base from which it could have been detached, if needed.

These observations make it clear that the ingot is, strictly speaking, not a base at all. It is not, that is, a structural element meant to support the figure and keep it upright, as this was accomplished by a separate, missing base. It seems, thus, that the ingot was not a support for the male figure, or, at least, not a functional one; rather, it was more of an attribute, that fulfilled some iconographic, i.e., ideological, needs, and was an integral part of the figure's appearance and identity, probably reflecting the significance of the full-sized oxhide ingots. This identity must accordingly have been related both to weapons and to something different, alluded to by the ingot. Anything that found a place in the representation of such an imposing figure must have been telling for its nature, as in the case of male and female figures standing on lions and other animals (Collon, 1972; Cornelius, 1994), which also do not serve merely as bases, as they are themselves equipped with pegs for insertion into other supports.

2 Technology and Iconography

2.1 Evidence of the Alteration of an Image

A further striking difference between the Ingot God and the armed figures of the Near East is the positioning of its legs on top of the ingot. Near Eastern and Egyptian Smiting Gods are typified by a forceful striding, part of an aggressive movement that is justified by the use of their weapons The Ingot God, on the contrary, keeps his legs and feet side by side in a very tight position, resulting in a static posture, that contrasts with the impression conveyed by the upper body of a warrior.

From the time it was first presented, it was thought that the weaponry of the Ingot God included a pair of greaves (Schaeffer, 1965, 1971), the warrior's accessory that appeared in the Eastern Mediterranean in the thirteenth century BCE (Fortenberry, 1991; Molloy, 2013). This belief, however, is a fallacy (Papasavvas, 2011, 2013; cf. Buchholz, 1979; Lagarce & Lagarce, 1986; Balmuth, 1994). A closer look, even with the unaided eye, reveals that, what was misjudged as greaves, is a thick layer of metal wrapped around the lower part of the figure, starting just below the knees and completely covering the legs from this point downwards (Figs. 1, 2 and 3). This positioning partly accounts for the misunderstanding, despite the fact that this layer has a very irregular outline and no consistent shape or form, as it is placed rather diagonally in the front, while at the back it rises up to the thighs – not a reasonable place for greaves, either. Nor is the lower edge of the putative greaves indicated above the feet in any way, whether at the front or at the back. Moreover, this metal coating completely hides the hemline of the kilt in the rear, although it distinctly appears in the front – and this should have sufficed to show the mistake. It also reaches down to the feet and the ingot, and, in fact, it is there *because* of the ingot.

I have elsewhere argued that the Ingot God was initially more compatible with the image of a Smiting God than its present appearance suggests (Papasavvas, 2011). In this reconstruction (Fig. 6), the original work lacked the name-giving feature of the statuette, the ingot, which was added to it at a later stage. The metal layer is the result of this addition, which was designed to alter the appearance of the figure, without eliminating its association with weapons. To that effect, the Cypriot smith used a particular bronze casting technique on the lower part of an already cast statuette. This technique is called *casting-on*, and the added metal layer is an unmistakable sign of its application.

2.2 The Casting-on Technique

This technique involves the direct casting of a bronze part on top of another, previously cast, item. It was used either for manufacture, that is, for permanently joining two parts of the same object with each other, or as a repair method, for adding missing parts on damaged bronze objects or miscasts (Armbruster, 2003; Drescher, 1958; Willer, 2016). As it operates along the principles of the lost wax method, this technique entailed the preparation of a wax model of a specific part of a bronze object, most of which had been cast beforehand. This wax model was invested in clay to form a mold, wax was liquefied by heat and molten metal was poured in; upon cooling, the mold was broken to reveal the complete bronze artifact. Clay molds did not just contain the wax and then the liquid bronze, but also kept the spot free of oxygen, as oxidization would prevent the joining of the two different metallic parts. The technique is best exemplified in its use for casting the hilts of swords directly *on* their blades in Central, Northern and Western Europe of the Urnfield period (Armbruster, 2000; Wüstemann, 2004), although it has recently been argued, that it was not used for this purpose as often as previously thought (Bunnenfeld, 2015, 2016).

Casting-on produced strong and durable joins, but, despite the fact that it involves molten metal, it is, strictly speaking, a method for mechanical, not metallurgical, joins (Drescher, 1958; Bunnenfeld & Schwenzer, 2011; Willer, 2016). Surface features, such as a rough texture may improve adhesion and joining, but temperatures were not high enough to achieve any actual fusion of the metal, and the cast-on metal would only envelop the areas around the join (Schorsch, 1988). Apart from riveting, this technique was the only one that could produce strong, efficient joins in the Bronze Age, and for a large part of the Iron Age, as well. Hard soldering, based on solders with a high melting point, that could deliver durable joins on bronzes, was not fully mastered before the sixth century BCE, as it required the application of controlled, high temperatures on fine joins over prolonged periods. Soft soldering, on the other hand, based on alloys of tin and lead and operating at much lower temperatures, was already practiced in the Bronze Age, but could not provide any really strong joins (Armbruster, 2000; Willer, 2016; Willer & Meijers, 2014).

In the East, one of the earliest manifestations of the casting-on technique is found on the remarkable, Middle Elamite bronze statue of Queen Napir-Asu of the late fourteenth century BCE from Susa, which, although fragmentary, still measures 1.29 m in height and weighs an impressive 1750 kg. It consists of two bronze layers, made of different alloys, the outer one with 1% tin, and the inner one with 11%, cast one upon the other with a process that remains obscure (Meyers, 2002). In Egypt, casting-on appeared in the New Kingdom and continued in later periods. Some old but recently published finds from Qubbet el-Hawa (in the cliffs opposite Aswan), offer important evidence for the potential and variations of this technique. These finds certainly originated in a bronze workshop, but were recovered in an Old Kingdom tomb that was reused by the local Elephantine priesthood in the sixth–fifth centuries BCE, contained in a jar and in an enigmatic association with a burial of the latter period. They are the remnants of various stages of casting processes, ranging from the manufacture of the wax models, represented by wooden and stone molds and actual wax models, to several unbroken, clay molds, made for casting or recasting failed casts, or for rejoining fragmented bronze statuettes (see the collection of papers in Fitzenreiter et al., 2016).

This most important material was recently studied in an exemplary way with the use of a wide range of advanced analytical and imaging techniques, such as Energy Dispersive X-Ray Fluoresence (ED-XRF), Raman-Spectroscopy, and, in particular, Micro-Computed Tomography (μCT). The latter produced digital images with the highest possible resolution and provided an unprecedented high degree of accuracy and precision. The examination has shown that some of the clay molds still contain multiple or single figures made up of wax, which were never cast. Others still hold figures partly composed of wax models, attached to previously cast, bronze parts, and still others encase failed casts that were never revealed. Some molds were meant for a single figure, others for up to five in the same cast, whereas a single one contains 34 small statuettes, in a casting that failed, filling the mold only partly with bronze (Auenmüller, 2017).

The bronze parts in some of these molds are either remnants of failed casts, or fragments of once complete bronze statuettes. One of the moulds contained four separate fragments of the bronze feet of an equal number of Osiris figures, whose bodies were covered with wax, in an effort to recreate and recast the miscast statuettes. In one of these bronze fragments, CT scans revealed clear breaks, indicating that it belonged to a broken statuette, not a miscast. The high potential of CT scans in archaeological investigations is further demonstrated by their ability to detect the presence, on the same fragment, still within the mold, of a tiny fragment of gold leaf that covered the bronze figurine when complete. A further clay mold contained fragments from more than one broken, bronze statuette, assembled together to form a new figure. In fact, these fragments originated from different statuettes, as indicated by differences in technique and proportions. Furthermore, before it was invested in clay, this mélange was entirely coated with a 1.5 mm thick layer of wax, so as to produce a thin bronze layer all around after casting (Auenmüller, 2014; Auenmüller & Fitzenreiter, 2014; Meinel & Willer, 2016).

This evidence demonstrates not only the complexity of the processes and the ingenuity of ancient smiths in finding solutions to casting problems but also the many variations and the wide range of applications of the casting-on technique, both for manufacture and for repairs. It was a practical and efficient method used in different ways and for different purposes, in different areas and times. In fact, the technique used to join the separately cast parts in Greek bronze statuary since Archaic times, or to repair some casting flaws on their surface with cast-in patches, is a variation of this technique (Formigli, 1999). These variations explain the diversity of the terms used to describe the technique: *Überfangguss, Anguss, Nachguss, Gussverband, Vergiessen,* in German, or *casting-on* and *casting-in* in English (Armbruster, 2003; Hill & Schorsch, 2005).

2.3 Casting-on and the Ingot God: Upgrading a Smiting God

As casting-on was used for different purposes, its use on the Ingot God needs some discussion. There are three possibilities for this incident: Either there was a casting problem on the figurine's bottom part, such as a miscast of the legs, which the smith chose to repair by casting-on the missing parts; or this same part was damaged in some way and had to be restored at a later date; and third, as the cast-on metal layer is closely linked to the ingot, which diverges from the usual iconography of the Smiting Gods, the use of this technique here may be related precisely to the presence of the ingot.

To start, the cast-on metal does not appear to have been the work of the same craftsman who cast the figure. The fine modeling of the face stands in sharp contrast with the sloppy work done on the cast-on part, or on the feet of the figure, that seem to have been shaped in a hasty, clumsy way (Figs. 1, 2, 4 and 5). This inconsistency in quality and execution suggests that the casting-on technique was not used to correct a casting problem, as in this case, the craftsman would presumably have corrected the mistake immediately, soon after breaking the clay mold to reveal the statuette. Furthermore, the fact that the cast-on layer reaches up to an unnecessarily higher level in the rear than in the front of the figure, indicates that this was not meant to repair damage on its lower part. This extent of the cast-on layer was meant to secure a strong hold between the two parts it envelops, i.e., the lower body of the figure and the ingot. The conclusion is that the casting-on technique was applied on the Ingot God by a different smith, and that it was all about the ingot.

The ingot itself appears to have acquired its present form after two distinct casting operations. Its outline, thickness, width and texture are different from the upper and side parts and from the front to its rear. The latter is wider and thicker, and has a more uneven surface and less sharply defined contours than the front. Two successive, horizontal layers of metal are discernible on the rear part of the ingot from the side seen on the left of the figure, the upper one thinner and rougher than the lower. In addition, the apices of the ingot on this same side, seem to protrude from a surrounding, thicker mass, which clearly represents the cast-on metal (Figs. 4, 5). These observations, which are confirmed by a radiographic examination (see below), imply that not only was the ingot added to the figurine with the casting-on technique, but also that, an already cast, miniature ingot was used for this addition (for the miniature ingots, Papasavvas, 2009; Giumlia Mair et al., 2011; Meneghetti, 2022). The added, cast-on metal presents, in fact, a very clear outline at the back, left corner of the ingot. This peculiarity explains why the cast-on layer had to reach all the way up to the thighs at the back; it had to secure an effective, primarily

Fig. 5 Lower part of the Ingot God with the ingot, side view of the right profile (left; photo by the author, by permission of the department of antiquities, Cyprus); the image to the right shows the ingot's underside. (Image: Römisch-Germanisches Zentralmuseum Mainz/photographer: F. Hummel)

mechanical join of two bronze parts, the statuette and the ingot, the former being relatively heavy. It also explains the awkward position of the figure in relation to the ingot, which is completely off-center in relation to the vertical axis and of the figure (Fig. 3). It should be noted here that this was the work of a craftsman who had little appreciation for stylistic and aesthetic norms (Papasavvas, 2011). Furthermore, the large peg underneath the ingot, which once held the statuette on its base, would also have been added during this secondary casting operation. The ingot as an independent unit would not have needed such a feature, and it certainly does not belong to the original statuette of the Smiting God, not only because it is not placed on the same vertical axis, or because of the intervention of the ingot, but also because this original figurine would have had its own dowels for insertion in a base under its feet. The addition of the ingot necessitated the removal of these dowels. That the peg under the ingot was cast-on is also indicated by the distinct join between them (which, however, could have been produced by lost wax casting), but mainly by a thin, metal layer adhering to the bottom surface of the ingot.

What this reconstruction proposes, is that an older, bronze figurine of a Smiting God acquired a new appearance, dominated by the ingot as much as by the weapons. This is an iconographic twist that gave new meaning to a figure with a pronounced martial character, hinting at a new identity not hitherto indicated by the weapons. The dual life of the Ingot God, initially as a Smiting God and later as a still smiting one, but with some additional flair, i.e.. an association with copper production as epitomized by the ingot (Figs. 1 and 6), has already been deduced from a visual, macroscopic inspection, that disclosed both the use of the casting-on technique and the addition of this particular iconographic feature (Papasavvas, 2011, 2013). This suggestion can now be confirmed by a radiographic examination of the statuette God, which enables the eye to penetrate through the metal volume.

Fig. 6 Hypothetical, digital reconstruction of the Ingot God in his original guise as a Smiting God; based on the Ingot God as shown in Fig. 1, and the lower legs of an Egyptian, bronze figure of Seth, as shown in Schorsch and Wypyski (2009)

3 Radiography

3.1 X-Ray Imaging

Röntgen's discovery of radiography was placed at the service of archaeology soon after its first presentation at the end of the nineteenth century (Middleton & Lang, 2005). It is an imaging technique based on electromagnetic radiation that can penetrate matter, thereby revealing variations in the internal structure of the examined subjects or objects. These variations reflect differences in the chemical composition and density of materials, which result in varying degrees of absorption of X-Ray radiation, themselves recorded on films as different radiopacities (Schorsch, 1988, 2014a; Schreiner et al., 2004). The degree of penetration depends on the mass of the analyzed object, as well as on the power and intensity of the electric energy used, that is, the settings of voltage, amperage, exposure time, and the distances and view angles from X-Ray source to target to film (Lang, 2005).

Bronze objects have attracted much attention in radiographic examinations, as they are able to retrieve information on technological features that are hidden from the eye. The principles of visualization through X-Rays are simple: Materials of greater thickness or density, that is, of a higher atomic mass, are more radiopaque and will better resist penetration, meaning that they will appear in white tones on the radiograph; those with a lighter atomic weight or volume, are more radiotransparent and will appear in gray or black shades. In bronze statues and statuettes, in particular, the range of radiopacity is in direct relation to their mass and volume. Solid sections are more radiopaque, appearing white, whereas dark areas correspond to internal voids, indicating hollow castings (Schorsch, 2014a). Any lead-tin solders used for joints will be evident against the less opaque surroundings, because of the higher density of lead that makes it almost opaque to X-Rays. The technique is fairly sensitive, to the point that it can reveal incised inscriptions that are hidden under corrosion layers, due to differences in metal thickness (Hill & Schorsch, 2005; Lang, 2005; Schorsch & Wypyski, 2009). Common problems in the X-Radiography of metal statuary include the overlap of some parts when seen from certain angles, which produces some confusion when transferred into the 2-Dimensional radiographic images, as well as the thickness and density of some solid cast figures that resist penetration (Lang, 2005; Middleton & Lang, 2005). Recording the objects with multiple exposures and from different angles may partially solve these problems, but the best choice, when available, is the use of more sophisticated imaging techniques.

Recent advances in digital capture technology have revolutionized the study of archaeological materials. Not only can conventional X-Ray images be scanned and visually enhanced for study (see, for instance, the high quality X-Rays in Hemingway & Stone, 2017), but also new techniques, such as Computer Tomography (CT), referred to above, and Gamma Radiography, provide far more sophisticated, 3-Dimensional information and much sharper images that can be analyzed in a series of cross sections, eliminating the distortion of overlapping parts (Applbaum & Applbaum, 2005; Berg & Berg, 2010; Casali, 2006; Meinel & Willer, 2016; Schorsch et al., 2019). The possibility to look into the hermetically sealed clay molds from Qubbet el-Hawa presented above, and to acquire important information without any physical intervention on them, was offered not by conventional radiography but by Computer Tomography (compare the conventional radiographs with the CT scans shown in Auenmüller, 2014). These new techniques, however, require far more expensive and not easily accessible equipment.

In sum, radiography and digital imaging provide remarkable insights into the internal structure of ancient objects, which explains why they are being increasingly used in archaeological projects. Radiographic studies of metal statues and statuettes, in particular, offer invaluable information on a large variety of archaeological questions that is difficult to attain with any other technique: Details of manufacture and types of materials used, evidence for repairs, alterations and restorations, ancient as well as modern ones, and documentation of an artifact's state of preservation (Giannoulaki et al., 2006; Schorsch, 2014a). X-Ray imaging can show beyond any doubt whether a statue or statuette is hollow or solid, whether it was cast in one piece or assembled from different parts, and the method and position of joins, whether metallurgical, with solders, or mechanical, with internal mortises and tenons. It can also reveal details, such as the position and direction of the casting gates, and whether any cores and core supports, or any internal armature, are present. Furthermore, it can identify casting problems and expose the quality of casting, as manifested in the thickness of the bronze walls, the presence of any internal or external spilling of metal, and the extent of porosity in the metal, which, in its turn, provides further information on the alloy composition. Even conventional radiography has the capacity to capture extremely fine details, for instance, to detect whether the long-gone wax models were free-hand modeled or made in bivalve molds, judging from seam-like, almost invisible lines in the X-Ray images of bronze figurines (Gehrig, 1979). These findings are, in addition, very useful in tackling issues of authenticity (Becker et al., 1994; Hill & Schorsch, 2005; Schorsch, 1988; Schorsch & Wypyski, 2009), as well as essential in planning conservation strategies (Hemingway & Stone, 2017; Lang & Middleton, 2005; Plattner et al., 2017; Schorsch, 2014a, b, 2019; Schorsch & Frantz, 1997; Schreiner et al., 2004). Overall, radiographic examinations of ancient artifacts offer views of features that are hidden from the eye, credibility and clarity to inferences from visual examination, and valuable information on ancient metalworking technology.

3.2 Some X-Rays from 1975: Looking Through the Ingot God

I have elsewhere suggested that the Ingot God should be examined with radiography to cast light on the structure beneath the cast-on metal (Papasavvas, 2011). This enterprise proved to be logistically difficult, as the Cyprus Museum does not possess such equipment. A different approach to the problem was to perform an elemental analysis on the statuette with XRF, in order to establish whether more than one alloy was present in different parts, reflecting different casting operations, one for the statuette of the Smiting God, the other for the addition of the ingot. Such an analysis has been undertaken by the present author and Dr. A. Charalambous, and the data will be processed and presented elsewhere; it should be noted here, however, that, contrary to a previous understanding of mine, which was based on an earlier, unquantified analysis, the Ingot God was not made of pure copper, but is, in fact, a tin bronze.

Although it was known that an X-Ray investigation was carried out in the Römisch-Germanisches Zentralmuseum in Mainz, Germany (hereafter RGZM) in the mid-1970s, where the Ingot God was taken for restoration, these X-Ray images were never published and have remained largely unknown, with some exceptions of very short notes and a photograph (Buchholz, 1979; Lagarce & Lagarce, 1986; Zwicker & Breme, 1988, Fig. 92b). Nine X-Ray images from this investigation are kept, now digitized, in the RGZM Bildarchiv, bearing the numbers R-1975_00289–00297. A short report on the chemical composition of some samples taken from the statuette and analyzed with XRF had been prepared at the request of Cl. Schaeffer, but it, too, remains unpublished, and will be presented together with the recent XRF analyses mentioned above. These radiogrsphic images will be presented here for the first time, thanks to the good will and assistance of colleagues from the RGZM (see Acknowledgments). Although these almost 50-year-old X-Ray images are not up to today's standards, they do confirm beyond any doubt that the attitude of the Ingot God was indeed altered at some point to conform to the addition of the oxhide ingot.

The RGZM radiographs of the Ingot God were taken in 1975 by a team led by the chemist D. Ankner, and by the photographer F. Hummel. A Seifert Eresco 300 X-Ray generator was used, placed at a distance of 90 cm from the film. Several gradations of voltage and exposure time were employed for different views and parts of the statuette, ranging from 190 to 230 KV, and from 10 to 18 min.; amperage remained stable at 5 mA. Results varied considerably depending on these variants, producing images of unequal quality. Images taken at 190 KV, even if in longer periods of exposure, reaching up to 18 min., have produced very poor results (such as R_1975_00295, showing the head in right profile). R_1975_00296 (Fig. 7), an image of the exact same view, gave better, but not sufficient, results, even if taken again at 190KV/5 mA, with the exposure time reduced at 10 min., and perhaps from a different angle. As expected, even small elevations in voltage had an effect on the images: Two radiographs of the exact same view, the left side of the statuette from the waist downwards, one taken at 210 KV, the other at 230 KV (R_1975_00291 and 00293 respectively), illustrate this difference, with the details appearing sharper in the latter image (Fig. 8). Modern standards for X-Ray imaging of ancient artefacts require an X-ray Unit operating in at least 300 KV and at 3 mA, for much shorter periods, of 1–3 min., although occasionally employing lower or higher charges, depending on the mass of the examined objects. Increase of the X-Ray energy reveals fine details, but in the case of smaller objects, this may lead to overexposed areas and blurry outlines that merge into the background (Mechling et al., 2018; Middleton & Lang, 2005). X-Ray images R_1975_00289 (rear view of the statuette), R_1975_00291 (left profile of the lower part), R_1975_00294 (left forearm with the shield), and R_1975_00295 (head in right profile) are not depicted here, because of their lesser quality.

The most illuminating of the RGZM X-Ray images is one showing the left side view of the statuette, from the waist down to the ingot (R_1975_00293; Figs. 8 and 9, left) – unfortunately, none was taken of the right side. This enables the eye to penetrate into the lower body of the Ingot God and see hidden parts of the original statuette, in its Smiting God guise. The X-Ray clearly shows how the cast-on metal

Fig. 7 Head and neck of the Ingot God, right profile. (R_1975_00296; Image: Römisch-Germanisches Zentralmuseum Mainz/photographer: F. Hummel)

encases the legs of the figure, starting from the surface of the ingot and rising up to the thighs in the back and to the knees in the front. This course and outline were already clear in the exterior of the statuette (Figs. 1, 2, 3 and 4), but the X-Ray reveals the situation beneath, showing the cast-on metal completely filling in the space around the legs and acquiring different thicknesses as it follows their contours. What is more important, the figure's right leg conspicuously appears inside the cast-on metal. Even the foot is clearly discernible in profile, resting on the ingot and completely encased by the cast-on mass. There is absolutely no sign of this leg and foot on the exterior of the statuette. This means that the feet, which are visible side by side on top of the ingot in the exterior (Fig. 4), are in fact not organically connected to the figure, but were added there by the craftsman who was responsible for the addition of the ingot to the statuette, as part of the casting-on process. These "new" feet are so thin that they are completely radiotransparent in the radiograph. In fact, it seems that the smith planned to use the cast-on metal layer as a proxy for a long garment, with the feet emerging from underneath, even if the hem of the figure's skirt was still discernible just above the knees (Figs. 1, 2 and 4) – so much for his/her artistic perception. Furthermore, although this X-Ray image (Fig. 8) shows that the original statuette of a Smiting God is preserved in its entire height, it appears that

A Change in Attitude: X-Ray Images of the Ingot God from Enkomi

Fig. 8 Print of an X-Ray image (R_1975_00293) showing the lower part of the Ingot God in left profile. (Image: Römisch-Germanisches Zentralmuseum Mainz/photographer: F. Hummel)

the lower part of the figure is disproportionally short in relation to the slender upper body. This is actually the result of the addition of the cast-on layer, which made this section thicker and distorted the statuette's proportions.

Equally, if not more, important is the opportunity to inspect the figure's left leg in this same image. Given the indications for the alteration at the lower part of the figure, it is not surprising that this leg is broken just below the knee. The lower left leg is thus altogether missing, whereas its place is completely taken up by the cast-on metal. The break itself is also hidden within the added metal but is unmistakenly shown in the X-Ray. It is very irregular, suggesting that it was affected with a forceful blow (Figs. 8 and 9, left). What remains, that is, the thigh and knee, leaves no doubt that the leg was slightly advanced, in a short stride movement. Although the right knee may appear at first to be very slightly advanced, it is the left leg that is brought forward, even if the difference is very small at this height. As no movement is discernible at the height of the hips, the legs would have started to slightly deviate from each other at a lower point, just below the knees, meaning that the stride must have been rather reserved (Fig. 9, right). It is of course no coincidence that most Near Eastern and Egyptian Smiting Gods advance their left leg, too (Negbi, 1976; Seeden, 1980), and although this is not a broad step, it shows how close the original figure was to this type.

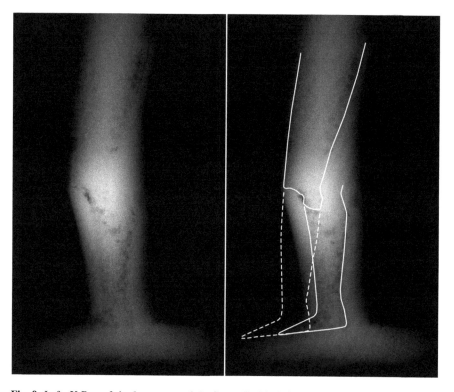

Fig. 9 Left: X-Ray of the lower part of the Ingot God in left profile (R_1975_00293; Image: Römisch-Germanisches Zentralmuseum Mainz/photographer: F. Hummel); Right: Reconstruction of the legs of the statuette within the cast-on metal, in its original guise as a Smiting God; the continuous white line shows the right leg, and the broken left leg (closer to the viewer) of the Smiting God; the dashed white line reconstructs the missing part of the left leg

It was exactly this movement of the left leg that compelled the smith responsible for the casting-on and the modification of the original statuette of a Smiting God, to cut-off the leg at the point it was extending forwards – or else, the statuette would have required a larger surface to stand on, which in this case would mean a longer ingot. Considering, as argued above, that a bronze miniature ingot was used for this purpose, this was clearly not an option, all the more so because its concave sides reduce its surface and would also not provide enough space for the" new" feet noted above (Figs. 4 and 5). The latter is actually confirmed by three RGZM radiographs, R_1975_00290 (Fig. 10), R_1975_00291 and R_1975_00293 (Figs. 8 and 9): Most of the ingot is radiopaque, but the apices, which in visual examination appear to stick out from within a thicker metal mass, are more radiotransparent, indicating two different casting alloys. The awkward backward tilt of the vertical axis of the figure (Fig. 2) is to be explained in the same way, as it seems that the removal of the advanced leg had distorted the original vertical alignment and standpoint. This is why in the reconstructions published here, approximate postures are corrected with a more vertical alignment (from 3° to 5° forward).

Visual examination has shown that the shield is attached to a deficiently shaped hand in a rather sloppy way, with a misshapen feast inserted in a shallow depression, itself outlined by a ruffled ridge (Fig. 11, left). I have elsewhere suggested (Papasavvas, 2011) that the shield was also added to the figure with the casting-on technique. This may have happened, either because the iconography of this statuette initially did not include any shield, but perhaps a different weapon, such as a sword or a dagger, as seems to be the case, for instance, of a bronze Smiting God found near the Sanctuary of the Ingot God (Schaeffer, 1971). Alternatively, casting may have failed here, especially since the angle and position of the shield at the end of the arm, which runs at right angles away from the vertical axis of the body, would have hindered the flow of the metal. For this reason, Near Eastern and Egyptian statuettes often had one or both arms separately cast and added with tenons to the body (e.g., Ornan, 2011b, 2012; Schorsch & Wypyski, 2009). For similar technological reasons, the spear (Figs. 1 and 2) must also have been prepared separately and attached to the right hand, definitely at the time of the original cast.

That the shield was added at a later stage can be confirmed by RGZM X-Rays R_1975_00292 (Fig. 11, right) and 00294 (the latter of insufficient quality), showing the left forearm with the shield. A thin (radiotransparent) void is clearly visible between the figure's feast and the weapon, rather than a continuous metallic mass. This is a clear indication of the casting-on technique, with a wax model of a shield being added to the bronze feast, then invested in clay and cast in place; the temperature was not high enough to produce a fusion between the two surfaces. When exactly the shield was added to the figure cannot be established, but it is very probable that this was done at the same time as the addition of the ingot. In these X-Rays, the central part of the left forearm appears in a slightly different shade of white (i.e., less radiopaque) than the surrounding parts. This might be due to casting problems referred to above, or to the processes of adding the shield. However, because of the mediocre quality of these particular radiographs, this will have to be further examined in the future, perhaps with some new X-Ray images or XRF analysis.

Fig. 10 X-Ray image of the Ingot God in left profile (R_1975_00290; Image: Römisch-Germanisches Zentralmuseum Mainz/ photographer: F. Hummel)

A Change in Attitude: X-Ray Images of the Ingot God from Enkomi

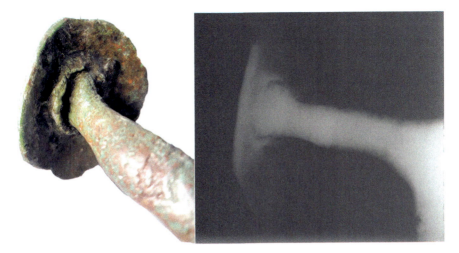

Fig. 11 Left: Photo of the left arm with the shield as seen from the back (photo by the author, by permission of the Department of Antiquities, Cyprus); Right: X-Ray of the forearm and the shield (R_1975_00292; Image: Römisch-Germanisches Zentralmuseum Mainz/photographer: F. Hummel)

RGZM images R_1975_00291 and 00293 (Figs. 8 and 9), showing the lower half of the statuette in its left profile, R_1975_00296, head in right profile (Fig. 7), and R_1975_00297, taken from the back (Fig. 12), allow some comments on the casting quality of the Ingot God. As expected, they reveal that this is a solid cast. They also show a high porosity all over, obvious in radiotransparent spots that correspond to small voids in the metal, caused by air bubbles trapped in the mold during casting. There is perhaps a concentration of these voids in the figure's surviving leg (R_1975_00293; Fig. 8), indicating that it was cast upside down, as not uncommon for anthropomorphic statuettes – although the head's X-Ray (R_1975_00296; Fig. 7) also shows porosity at the back and chin. On the contrary, the cast-on layer on the ingot and around the legs is far more radiopaque and homogenous than the metal it envelops, and shows no porosity (Figs. 8 and 9). This is not unexpected, since these parts represent two distinct casting operations, even separated in time and agents, but whether this is due to the composition of the respective alloys, perhaps with more lead present in the more radiopaque mass, or if it was the result of a more even distribution of the metal due to its smaller volume, will be shown by an elemental analysis. The rather low voltage (190 KV) may be responsible for some other irregularities observed in image R_1975_00296 (Fig. 7), such as the concentration of porous contours at the chin and the back of the head in right profile as opposed to the more radiopaque area in between, probably resulting from differences in the volume of the respective areas.

A further point for discussion is the assertion of Buchholz (1979), and Zwicker and Breme (1988), who were informed by D. Ankner on the existence of the RGZM X-Ray images, that the beard of the Ingot God was added to the face at a later stage. Visual inspection of the area and the very fine beard (Figs. 1 and 2), however, does

Fig. 12 X-Ray image of the rear view of the Ingot God (R_1975_00297; Image: Römisch-Germanisches Zentralmuseum Mainz/ photographer: F. Hummel)

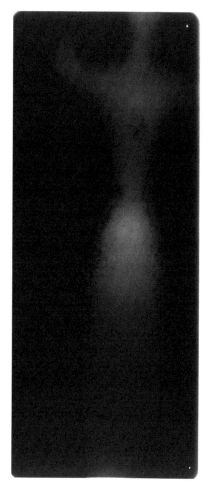

not show any signs of such an intervention. In fact, the modeling of the face, including the beard, is very delicate and precise, with very defined outlines, clearly not a match for the clumsy work of the cast-on metal on the legs. This false claim may have arisen from the fact that radiograph R_1975_00290 (Fig. 10) does show a more radiopaque mass exactly in the area of the beard. However, as there is no physical indication for any added metal on the face, this difference in radiopacity is probably due to a coincidence and the difficulty noted above in transposing 3-Dimensional works into 2-Dimensional images: When seen from the side and from this particular angle, the beard exactly overlaps with the feast of the raised hand holding the spear on the other side. This overlap created a succession of two metallic volumes, and this combination may have resisted penetration of the X-Rays to a greater extent than the surrounding parts, producing this radiopaque area and giving the

A Change in Attitude: X-Ray Images of the Ingot God from Enkomi   1379

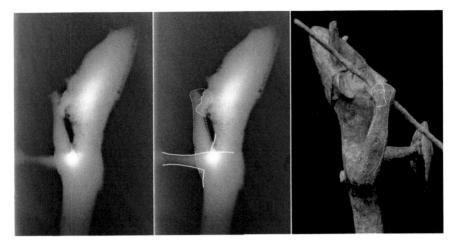

Fig. 13 Left: Detail of X-Ray R_1975_00290, as shown in Fig. 10 (Image: Römisch-Germanisches Zentralmuseum Mainz/photographer: F. Hummel); Middle: the same, with added lines, the dashed one for the outline of the raised, right arm, the continuous one for the left arm and neck; Right: Photo (by the author, by permission of the Department of Antiquities, Cyprus), projecting the contours of the right arm on this side, to show the overlap with the beard; slight deviations are due to slightly different angles

impression of an added metal layer. In fact, the outline of the beard does coincide exactly with that of the hand holding the spear (Fig. 13). A similar situation is observed in the same radiograph, in the area where the left elbow, the upper part of the chest and the right forearm overlap with each other. Needless to say, Computer Tomography, with its ability to eliminate the problems of superposition, would have never caused such confusion in the interpretation of the images.

In sum, at some point in the life of this figure from Enkomi, a smith was assigned with the transformation of an existing bronze statuette of a Smiting God, shown in a usual, striding posture (albeit in a slight one; Fig. 6). This was achieved with the introduction of a new iconographic feature, i.e., the ingot, placed under the figure's feet. The only other possible way to link a male figure with an ingot was that of an ingot bearer, as on some Late Cypriot bronze, four-sided stands (Papasavvas, 2012, 2013). These, however, make a completely different impression and convey a different message as to the identity of the associated figure and the purpose of the ingot. In order to adjust the positioning of the figure on the ingot, this smith had to cut off the statuette's left leg, and recreate its lower part with the casting-on technique, making use of an already cast, miniature bronze ingot (Figs. 4, 8, and 9). This technique had actually been applied on some other Late Cypriot bronzes, such as on four-sided stands and rod tripods, as well as on the cast rims of bronze amphoroid craters, although in those cases it was used for repairs of miscasts or damages (Papasavvas, 2003; Schorsch & Hendrix, 2003; Scorsch, 2014a).

4 The Transformation of the Ingot God

4.1 Ancient Alterations on Bronze Statuettes

The confirmation of the initial hypothesis about the modification of the Ingot God offers the opportunity to discuss the significance of ancient, purposeful alterations of older works that gave them new meanings and uses. It was not uncommon for Egyptian and Near Eastern divine and royal statuary to exhibit particularly long lives, and to be used in different contexts over several generations, occasionally demonstrating significant iconographic and other changes (Charloux et al., 2017; Schorsch, 2019). Recent radiographic and art historical examinations of Egyptian bronze statuettes, in particular, have revealed much evidence for extensive, often politically motivated alterations in their iconography and epigraphy, meant to obliterate the signs and attributes of previous owners and to reintegrate them into new contexts. Such alterations include the introduction of new inscriptions, or the erasure and replacement of older ones, the addition or elimination of royal insignia, such as uraei or headdresses, re-carvings of faces and other features, even the removal of legs and arms and their repositioning to show a different posture, all intended to associate the figure to a different person than the one originally depicted. This phenomenon is commonly connected to the usurpation of older monuments, which took immense dimensions in certain periods and under certain rulers, such as Ramesses II (Hill, 2015; Schorsch, 2019). It is also common in small-scale bronze statuary of the first millennium BCE, as in an Egyptian bronze statuette in the National Archaeological Museum in Athens (Inv. No. 6241) that may have served cult purposes through the reigns of at least four kings in a row, but only after its regalia and inscriptions, identifying the represented persons, were changed (Hill, 2004; Schorsch, 2019). Further examples include a large bronze figure of Seth in the Ny Carlsberg Glyptotek, that was later changed into Amun (Schorsch & Wypyski, 2009), a figure of Nefertem in Leiden that was modified through the alteration of specific attributes to show Montu (Schorsch, 2019), and some Kushite royal figures in bronze, usurped and reused by their Saite successors, after they were defaced, and their regalia and inscriptions changed (Hill, 2004). Recording these alterations allows the reconstruction of the appearance of the statuettes before they were changed, as well as the evaluation of the visual impact of these works in various stages of their lifetimes, and of their respective social meanings (Hill & Schorsch, 2005; Schorsch, 2019).

4.2 A Change of Identity

In the absence of relevant information, such as exclusive attributes or inscriptions, any discussion of ancient bronze statuettes faces two challenges, that is, distinguishing mortals from gods, and giving them names. It is of course impossible to establish any universal criteria for such distinctions, and only a context-specific approach to each case can be constructive in that respect (Moorey & Fleming, 1984; Muhly, 1980). This is a far-reaching discussion, and only a few thoughts will be offered here, focusing on the purpose of the alterations on the Ingot God and the allocation of a new, or an additional, identity to this figure.

The identity of the Ingot God, its divine nature, and, above all, the implications of the ingot, have been extensively discussed (e.g. Carless Hulin, 1989; Catling, 1971; Courtois, 1986; Lagarce & Lagarce, 1986; Schaeffer, 1971; Webb, 1999). The statuette may be assumed to depict the deity worshipped in the homonymous sanctuary. The context of the statuette is certainly suggestive of a deity (Courtois, 1971, 1986), while its recovery within a corner, small room of a monumental building, even qualifies it as a cult statue (Webb, 1999, 2001). Above all, the Ingot God's claim of divine status is sustained through the eccentric presence of the ingot under his feet, which must be informative of his character. Although he is thought to be related to metallurgy, as a protector or benefactor of this industry (Catling, 1971), his identity, let alone his name, elude us, as evident by his descriptive appellation. That the ingot was added at a later stage cannot be doubted, but the reason for this amplification is less obvious. Since we know much about oxhide ingots, and a few things about Smiting Gods, this should have been an informative combination. However, in the absence of contemporary, readable textual evidence from the island, we remain in the dark about Late Cypriot religion in general and the character of the Ingot God in particular, in any of his guises, whether as a Smiting God, or in his second life, as an Ingot God.

The metal figurines of warriors in a smiting pose from the Bronze Age Eastern Mediterranean are often interpreted as representations of a Syrian god, either Baal or Reshef, or the latter's Mesopotamian divine counterpart, Nergal, all of whom had clear military connotations. The latter deity has been linked to Cyprus through one of the Amarna Letters, sent by the king of Alashiya to the Pharaoh, in an explicit reference to copper production, although this association is not as straightforward as once thought (Kassianidou, 2005). These menacing deities are represented in similar poses and with similar attributes throughout the Late Bronze and Early Iron Age Ages, although there are some variations in the attributes and functions (Fulco, 1976; Lipinski, 2009; Munnich, 2013). According to Cornelius (1994), Reshef is distinguished as a protector by his shield, which is not found in representations of Baal, whereas the horned helmet is more common for Baal. Thus, although the Ingot God apparently is a local divine epiphany, whose name could only be revealed by contemporary, local texts, his image eclectically incorporates attributes of different deities, and combines foreign with indigenous elements – the ingot is certainly an indigenous feature. Isolating specific foreign elements from one or the other direction and imposing names taken from abroad on this Cypriot deity, has even led some scholars to turn to the Aegean and to suggest an unsubstantiated identification with Hephaistos or Ares (Catling, 1971; see the criticisms of Carless Hulin, 1989), on the basis of the metallurgical aspect (the ingot) and by association with another, related find (see below). It should be noted in that respect, however, that the main argument for an association with the Aegean world relied on the hypothetical greaves (Catling, 1971), meaning that any claims for an Aegean influence on this work must be downplayed (Knapp, 2012; Papasavvas, 2011; Webb, 1999).

The peculiarity of an oxhide ingot under the feet of an anthropomorphic figure is repeated in an unprovenanced, bronze statuette of a much smaller size (about 10 cm), showing a nude female, the so-called Bomford Goddess, stylistically dated to the Late Cypriot period (Catling, 1971). The ingot of this figurine was an original feature, that is, it was not added later, as it was on the Ingot God. It is clear in any case, that this was not an eccentricity of a smith, but something with a deeper significance for Late Cypriot society, or a part of it. It represents a novelty, that was combined with the traditional types of a nude female figure with pronounced sexual attributes, as known from the indigenous coroplastic art (Catling, 1971), and of a Near Eastern Smiting God (Webb, 1999). In both cases, the ingot must have added a new layer of meaning to a pre-existing one, this time associated, in some elusive way, with copper and metallurgy. How was this new meaning related to the martial character of the Ingot God? What ideological background allowed the infusion of a metallurgical quality in the pronounced female nature of the Bomford statuette? Was the ingot intended to attach a metallurgical notion to the aspect of control or protection, if this is what the warlike attitude means, or to the concept of productiveness and well-being, thought to be expressed by nude, female figurines? What are the names of these figures and how are they related to each other? In what way were the disparate concepts of war, female nudity, and metallurgy linked to each other? These questions will be discussed elsewhere, but what can perhaps be claimed at this juncture, is that the decision of the worshipping group of Enkomi that was using the Sanctuary of the Ingot God, to revise an existing statuette of a warrior and create a new divine identity, with an emphasis on a metallurgical aspect, is perhaps indicative of a time of change, even of crisis. This may be related to the gradual abandonment of Enkomi, which coincides with closure rituals and the termination of sacred spaces, including those of the Ingot God and the Horned God, as mentioned above (Papasavvas, 2011, 2014, in preparation; Webb, 1999, 2001). This timing could perhaps be held responsible for the poor quality of the work done for this transformation. According to Muhly (1985), the metallurgical workshops in the vicinity of the Sanctuary of the Ingot God were not in use since Late Cypriot IIIA.

Furthermore, the simultaneous operation of these two important sanctuaries a short distance from each other, together with some other signs, such as the wide distribution of copper working residues across Enkomi rather than in a limited area of the town, may reflect the decline of a centralized authority and the activities of competing social groups (Pickles & Peltenburg, 1998; Webb, 2001). Such factions would have set up not only independent metalworking facilities but perhaps also separate cult places in adjacent sectors of the town. The diverse character of the divinities, with an emphasis on weaponry first and metallurgy later for the Ingot God, and the absence of any of these elements (with the exception of the horned helmet) for the Horned God, could also hint at different social groups that were perhaps appealing to different deities or each chose to emphasize different aspects of divine benevolence. One of these groups may have instigated a novel idea and a new image, by promoting a Smiting God into an Ingot God, associating an established deity with copper, and perhaps advertising closer connections to its production for its benefit (Papasavvas, 2011; Webb, 2001). The importance of this reinterpretation of a traditional deity was lost when the community that introduced the Ingot God eventually had to abandon the town. The statuette was left behind, and so was its new identity.

No novel gods had to be created for this assignment. It was, instead, conferred to some old ones who, however, did not have to dispose of their other, established attributes and roles. Both could still be represented without the ingot, with the emphasis placed accordingly on their other attributes. Not every bronze smiting figure from Cyprus had to stand on an ingot; in fact, a small bronze statuette of this type, without any base, was found in the vicinity of the Sanctuary of the Ingot God (Schaeffer, 1971, 510–513). Likewise, none of the terracottas, or some related bronze figurines, that are typologically associated with the Bomford statuette (Karageorghis, 2002) present such a feature. The inception of the ingot in the Cypriot divine iconography is, thus, not indicative of the arrival of new gods on the island.

Irrespective of the exact identity and name of the Ingot God or the Bomford figurine, there is a very important conclusion to be drawn: If two different deities, a male and a female, with age-old identities suddenly appear with such an expressive, innovative feature, that is alien in their proper spheres of interaction or their established iconography, this can only mean that the ingot was invested with the power of a symbol, which could signal the inclusion of copper business in divine affairs. As oxhide ingots certainly refer to copper, and hence to an economic basis that was apparently a matter of great concern to ancient Cypriots, the implication is that this symbolic representation must also be connected to a similar concept. Ingots, after all, are nothing if not a mark of Cypriot economic activities, beyond their plain association with metallurgy. In fact, they appear frequently in Late Cypriot iconography, and despite the rather limited pictorial tradition of the island in this period, no other place in the Mediterranean or the Near East has produced such an extensive and consistent "ingot iconography" (Papasavvas, 2009). This evidence implies that Cypriots of the Late Bronze Age had gone all the way to accept that a deity, which was known in a different capacity, could also be associated with a metallurgical, or rather economic, aspect. Since no iconographic type for a deity associated with copper existed on the island or in the arts of the Near, Cypriots of the Late Bronze Age merged an Oriental iconographic type, that of the warrior god, as well as the type of the naked female, which had a long tradition on the island, with a local symbol in a direct reference to their concerns in life (Papasavvas, 2011).

Whether the original statue of the Smiting God was cast on the island or was imported from the Near East, where a much larger number of statuettes of this type have been found, is a question that cannot be resolved. The statuette from Enkomi is as unique in style and size as it would have been on the opposite coast, had it been found there. However, that Cypriots were capable of producing "whatever caught their fancy" by mixing tradition with innovation and local with foreign elements (Muhly, 1988), and hence a bronze of such exceptional quality and originality is demonstrated by the abundance of some other outstanding, locally produced bronze artifacts, such as the four-sided stands or the Horned God (Papasavvas, 2013).

The eclecticism discernible in the choice of the iconographic and stylistic features of the Ingot God, and the exceptional presence of the ingot, indicate that a Near Eastern concept for divine representations had been adapted to create an image of a local deity. In a world that so excessively depended on metal production and circulation, some benevolent, age-old gods could be assigned new responsibilities, associated in this case with the economy of metal. Such a duality in one and the same deity is also exemplified in the case of Hathor, who, apart from her other established roles, was christened the protector of the copper mines at Timna (for the site see Ben-Yosef et al., 2012; cf. Kassianidou, 2005; Peltenburg, 2007). This, however, did not make her an exclusive or universal patron deity of copper mines. Nor did she acquire a distinct iconography, related specifically to metallurgy. Nergal and other Mesopotamian gods have also been occasionally associated, at least for the Neo-Assyrian period, with metalworking activities as patron deities (Dalley, 1988; but see Lambert, 1991). These inferences, however, are primarily based on some ambiguous, textual evidence, and nowhere is there any iconographic attestation of such a divine quality as unequivocal as it appears on the Ingot God from Enkomi. Cypriots of the Late Bronze Age, that is, certainly went a step further, when they created a new iconographic type for this divine aspect. Above all, the evocation of warfare and female nudity under the common denominator of the ingot seems to illustrate the prominence of copper in Cypriot affairs.

Acknowledgments I would like to thank Erez Ben-Yosef and Ian Jones for the invitation to participate in this volume honoring the inspiring work of Thomas Levy in the Eastern Mediterranean and beyond. I am also very grateful to Prof. Dr. Markus Egg, former director of the Conservation Labs of the Römisch-Germanisches Zentalmuseum in Mainz, Ute Klatt and Mag. Dominik Kimmel, former and present persons in charge of this Museum's Photo Archives, and Stephan Patscher, conservator in the same Museum, for digitizing the X-Ray images and providing permissions for publication and important information on this material in a very efficient and collegial way. This paper would not have been possible without their help. Many thanks are also due to Victor Klinkenberg and Holly Kunst for their work on some of the digital images published here.

References

Applbaum, N., & Applbaum, Y. (2005). The use of medical computed tomography (CT) imaging in the study of ceramic and clay archaeological artifacts from the ancient near east. In M. Uda, G. Demortier, & I. Nakai (Eds.), *X-rays for archaeology* (pp. 231–245). Springer. https://doi.org/10.1007/1-4020-3581-0_17

Armbruster, B. R. (2000). Goldschmiedekunst und Bronzetechnik. In *Studien zum Metallhandwerk Atlantischen Bronzezeit auf der Iberischen Halbinsel. Monographies instrumentum 15.* Éditions Mergoil.

Armbruster, B. R. (2003). Vor- und frühgeschichtlicher Guss von Gold und Bronze. *Ferrum: Nachrichten aus der Eisenbibliothek (Technikgeschichtliche Tagung der Eisenbibliothek 2002), 75,* 24–32. https://www.e-periodica.ch/digbib/view?pid=fer-002:2003:75::34#35

Auenmüller, J. (2014). Die Ergebnisse der bildgebenden Verfahren. In M. Fitzenreiter, C. E. Loeben, D. Raue, & U. Wallenstein (Eds.), *Gegossene Götter: Metallhandwerk und Massenproduktion im Alten Ägypten* (pp. 113–126). Marie Leidorf.

A Change in Attitude: X-Ray Images of the Ingot God from Enkomi 1385

Auenmüller, J. (2017). The Qubbet el-Hawa casting moulds – Late Period bronze working at the First Cataract. In G. Rosati & M. C. Guidotti (Eds.), *Proceedings of the XI International Congress of Egyptologists. Florence, 23–30 August 2015, Museo Egizio Firenze. Archaeopress Egyptology 19* (pp. 19–25). Archaeopress.

Auenmüller, J., & Fitzenreiter, M. (2014). Eine Gusswerkstatt auf der Qubbet el-Hawa? In M. Fitzenreiter, C. E. Loeben, D. Raue, & U. Wallenstein (Eds.), *Gegossene Götter: Metallhandwerk und Massenproduktion im Alten Ägypten* (pp. 101–106). Marie Leidorf.

Balmuth, M. (1994). Reconsideration of the Bronze "Ingot God" from Enkomi. *American Journal of Archaeology, 98*(2), 289–343. https://doi.org/10.2307/506639

Becker, L., Pilosi, L., & Schorsch, D. (1994). An Egyptian silver statuette of the Saite period: A technical study. *Metropolitan Museum Journal, 29*, 37–56. https://doi.org/10.2307/1512958

Ben-Yosef, E., Shaar, R., Tauxe, L., & Ron, H. (2012). A new chronological framework for Iron Age copper production in Timna (Israel). *Bulletin of the American Schools of Oriental Research, 367*, 31–71. https://doi.org/10.5615/bullamerschoorie.367.0031

Berg, K.U. & Berg, H.W. (2010). *Radiographie–Radioskopie–Computertomographie: Vergleichende Darstellungen an Kunstobjekten zur Beurteilung bei Fälschungen und unter restauratorischen Aspekten im Spiegel des Kunstrechts. Deutsche Gesellschaft für Zerstörungsfreie Prüfung – Jahrestagung 2010* (pp. 1–9). BMB Gessellschaft für Materialprüfung. https://www.ndt.net/search/docs.php3?id=10113

Buchholz, H. G. (1979). Beobachtungen zum prähistorischen Bronzeguss in Zypern und der Ägäis. In V. Karageorghis (Ed.), *Acts of the International Symposium "The Relations between Cyprus and Crete, ca. 200–500 B.C."* (pp. 76–86). Department of Antiquities.

Bunnefeld, J.-H. (2015). Bronzezeitliche Schwerter in Westfalen. *Ausgrabungen und Funde in Westfalen-Lippe, 12*, 5–58. https://doi.org/10.11588/afwl.2015.0.26259

Bunnefeld, J.-H., & Schwenzer, S. (2011). Traditionen, Innovationen und Technologietransfer – zur Herstellungstechnik und Funktion älterbronzezeitlicher Schwerter in Niedersachsen. *Prähistorische Zeitschrift, 86*, 207–253. https://doi.org/10.1515/pz.2011.012

Bunnenfeld, J.-H. (2016). *Älterbronzezeitliche Vollgriffschwerter in Dänemark und Schleswig-Holstein. Studien zu Form, Verzierung, Technik und Funktion. Studien zur nordeuropäischen Bronzezeit 3.* Wachholtz Verlag.

Carless Hulin, L. (1989). The identification of Cypriot cult figures through cross-cultural comparison: Some problems. In E. Peltenburg (Ed.), *Early Society in Cyprus* (pp. 127–139). Edinburg University Press.

Casali, F. (2006). X-ray and neutron digital radiography and computed tomography for cultural heritage. In D. Bradley & D. Creagh (Eds.), *Physical techniques in the study of art, archaeology and cultural heritage* (Vol. 1, pp. 41–123). Elsevier. https://doi.org/10.1016/S1871-1731(06)80003-5

Catling, H. W. (1971). A cypriot bronze statuette in the Bomford collection. In C. F. A. Schaeffer, M. Aitken, P. Åström, P. Ducos, H. W. Catling, J.-C. Courtois, J. Bouzek, H. Hadjioannou, H.-J. Hundt, R. W. Hutchinson, W. Johnstone, V. Karageorghis, J. Lagarce, O. Masson, E. Masson, & A. H. S. Megaw (Eds.), *Alasia: Première Série. Mission Archéologique d'Alasia IV* (pp. 15–32). Mission Archéologique d' Alasia.

Charloux, G., Thiers, C., Abd Al-Aziz, M., Ali Abady Mahmoud, M., Boulet, S., Bourse, C., Guadagnini, K., Laroye, J., & Sayed Elnasseh, A. M. (2017). The afterlife of Egyptian statues: a cache of religious objects in the temple of Ptah at Karnak. *Antiquity, 91*(359), 1189–1204. Cambridge University Press. https://doi.org/10.15184/aqy.2017.137

Collon, D. (1972). The smiting God: A study of a bronze in the Pomerance collection in New York. *Levant, 4*, 111–134. https://doi.org/10.1179/lev.1972.4.1.111

Cornelius, I. (1994). *The iconography of the Canaanite gods Reshef and Ba'al: Late Bronze and Iron Age I periods (c 1500–1000 BCE). Orbis biblicus et orientalis 140.* University Press.

Courtois, J.-C. (1971). Le sanctuaire du Dieu au Lingot d'Enkomi-Alasia. In C. F. A. Schaeffer, M. Aitken, P. Åström, P. Ducos, H. W. Catling, J.-C. Courtois, J. Bouzek, H. Hadjioannou, H.-J. Hundt, R. W. Hutchinson, W. Johnstone, V. Karageorghis, J. Lagarce, O. Masson, E. Masson, & A. H. S. Megaw (Eds.), *Alasia: Première Série. Mission Archéologique d'Alasia IV* (pp. 151–162). Mission Archéologique d' Alasia.

Courtois, J.-C. (1986). Bref historique des recherches archéologiques à Enkomi. In J. C. Courtois, J. Lagarce, & E. Lagarce, Enkomi et le Bronze Récent à Chypre (pp. 1–50). : The A. G. Leventis Foundation.

Dalley, S. (1988). Neo-Assyrian textual evidence for Bronzeworking Centres. In J. Curtis (Ed.), *Bronzeworking Centres of Western Asia c. 1000–539 B.C* (pp. 97–110). Kegan Paul International.

Dikaios, P. (1969–1971). *Enkomi, excavations 1948–1958 Vols. I-IIIb.* Philip von Zabern.

Drescher, H. (1958). *Der Überfangguss. Ein Beitrag zur vorgeschichtlichen Metalltechnik.* Verlag des Römisch-Germanischen Zentralmuseums.

Fitzenreiter, M., Willer, F., & Auenmüller, J. (2016). *Materialien einer Gusswerkstatt von der Qubbet el-Hawa. Bonner Aegyptiaca.* EB Verlag Dr. Brandt. https://www.iak.uni-bonn.de/de/abteilungen/aegyptologie/aegyptologie/aktuelle-publikationen/ebook_gusswerkstatt_ebverlag

Formigli, E. (1999). Resoconto degli esperimenti di saldatura per colarta e di rifiniturea a freddo sui grandi bronzi antichi. In E. Formigli (Ed.), *I Grandi Bronzi Antichi. Le fonderie e le techniche di lavorazione dall'età arcaica al Rinscimento. Atti del seminari di studi ed esperimenti, Murlo 1993 e 1 1995* (pp. 317–334). Nuova Immagine.

Fortenberry, D. (1991). Single greaves in the Late Helladic Period. *American Journal of Archaeology, 95*(4), 623–627. https://doi.org/10.2307/505895

Fulco, W. J. (1976). *The Canaanite God Rešep. American Oriental Series: Essay 8.* American Oriental Society.

Gehrig, U. (1979). Frühe griechische Bronzegusstechniken. *Archäologischer Anzeiger,* 547–558.

Giannoulaki, M., Argyropoulos, V., Panou, T. H., Moundrea-Agrafioti, A., & Themelis, P. (2006). The feasibility of using portable X-Ray radiography for the examination of the technology and the condition of a metals collection housed in the Museum of Ancient Messene, Greece. *e-Journal of Science & Technology (e-JST),* 48–63. http://ejst.uniwa.gr/issues/issue_2_2006/giannoulaki.pdf

Giumlia Mair, A., Kassianidou, V., & Papasavvas, G. (2011). Miniature ingots from Cyprus. In P. Betancourt & S. Ferrence (Eds.), *Metallurgy: Understanding how, learning why. Studies in honour of James D. Muhly* (pp. 11–19). INSTAP Press, Prehistory Monographs 29.

Hemingway, S. & Stone, R. (2017). The New York sleeping Eros: A hellenistic statue and its ancient restoration. *Technè: La science au service de l'histoire de l'art et de la préservation des biens culturels 45: Bronzes grecs et romains: études récentes sur la statuaire antique,* 47–63. http://journals.openedition.org/techne/1266

Hill, M. (2004). *Royal Bronze statuary from ancient Egypt, with special attention to the kneeling pose. Egyptological Memoirs 3.* Brill.

Hill, M. (2015). The later life of Middle Kingdom monuments: Interrogating Tanis. In A. Oppenheim, D. Arnold, D. Arnold, & K. Yamamoto (Eds.), *Ancient Egypt transformed* (pp. 294–299). Metropolitan Museum of Art.

Hill, M., & Schorsch, D. (2005). The Gulbenkian torso of King Pedubaste: Investigations into Egyptian large bronze statuary. *Metropolitan Museum Journal, 40,* 163–195. https://doi.org/10.1086/met.40.20320651

Iacovou, M. (1988). The pictorial Pottery of Eleventh Century b.c. In *Cyprus. Studies in Mediterranean Archaeology LXXIX.* Paul Åströms Förlag.

Iacovou, M. (1991). Proto white painted pottery: A classification of the ware. In J. Barlow, D. Bolger, & B. Kling (Eds.), *Cypriot ceramics. Reading the prehistoric record. University Museum Monograph 74* (pp. 199–205). University of Pennsylvania Press.

Karageorghis, V. (2002). *Early Cyprus: Crossroads of the Mediterranean.* The J. Paul Getty Museum.

Kassianidou, V. (2005). Was copper production under divine protection in Late Bronze Age cyprus? Some thoughts on an old question. In V. Karageorghis, H. Matthäus, & S. Rogge (Eds.), *Cyprus: Religion and Society from the Late Bronze Age to the end of the Archaic Period. Proceedings of an International Symposium on Cypriote Archaeology, Erlangen, 23–24 July 2004* (pp. 127–141). Bibliopolis.

Kling, B. (1989). *Mycenaean IIIC:1b and related pottery in Cyprus.* SIMA LXXXVII.

Knapp, A. B. (1986). *Copper production and divine protection: Archaeology, ideology and social complexity on Bronze Age Cyprus, Studies in Mediterranean Archaeology pocket-book 42.* Paul Åströms Förlag.

Knapp, A. B. (2012). Matter of fact: Transcultural contacts in the Late Bronze Age Eastern Mediterranean. In J. Maran & P. W. Stockhammer (Eds.), *Materiality and social practice: Transformative capacities of intercultural encounters* (pp. 32–50). Oxbow Books.

Lagarce, J. & Lagarce, E. (1986). La métallurgie. In J-C. Courtois, J. Lagarce, & E. Lagarce, Enkomi et le Bronze Récent à Chypre (pp. 60–99). : The A. G. Leventis Foundation.

Lambert, W. G. (1991). Metal-working and its patron deities in the early Levant. *Levant, 23*(1), 183–186. https://doi.org/10.1179/lev.1991.23.1.183

Lang, J. (2005). Metals. In J. Lang & A. Middleton (Eds.), *Radiography of cultural material* (2nd ed., pp. 49–75). Elsevier and Butterworth-Heinemann.

Lang, J., & Middleton, A. (2005). *Radiography of cultural material* (2nd ed.). Elsevier and Butterworth-Heinemann.

Levy, T. E., Levy, A. M., Radhakrishna Sthapathy, R., Srikanda Sthapathy, D., & Swaminatha Sthapathy, W. (2008). *Masters of fire: Hereditary Bronze Casters of South India. Veröffentlichungen aus dem Deutschen Bergbau-Museum Nr. 162.* Deutsches Bergbau-Museum.

Levy, Th. E, Smith, N., Najjar, M., Defanti, TH., Yu, A., Lin, M., & Kuester, F. (2012). *Cyber-archaeology in the holy land: The future of the past.* Biblical Archaeology Review (eBook). https://www.researchgate.net/publication/233955406_Cyber-Archaeology_in_the_Holy_Land_The_Future_of_the_Past

Levy, T. E., Najjar, M., & Ben-Yosef, E. (Eds.). (2014). *New insights into the Iron Age archaeology of Edom, southern Jordan – Surveys, excavations and research from the Edom Lowlands Regional Archaeology Project (ELRAP).* Cotsen Institute of Archaeology. https://escholarship.org/uc/item/7s92w18w

Lipiński, E. (2009). *Resheph: A Syro-Canaanite deity. Orientalia Lovaniensia Analecta 181, Studia Phoenicia XIX.* Peeters Publishers.

Maran, J. (2011). Evidence for Levantine religious practice in the Late Bronze Age sanctuary of Phylakopi on Melos? *Eretz-Israel, 30,* 65–73.

Masson, E. (1992). Le Dieu Guerrier d' Enkomi: est-il debout sur un lingot? In G. K. Ioannidis (Ed.), *Studies in honour of Vassos Karageorghis* (pp. 155–156). Society of Cypriot Studies.

Mechling, M., Vincent, B., Baptiste, P., & Bourgarit, D. (2018). The Indonesian bronze-casting tradition: Technical investigations on thirty-nine Indonesian bronze statues (7th–11th c.) from the Musée National des Arts Asiatiques–Guimet, Paris. *Bulletin de l'Ecole française d'Extrême-Orient, 104,* 63–139. https://doi.org/10.3406/befeo.2018.6270

Meinel, D., & Willer, F. (2016). Röntgen-Mikro-Computertomographie (μCT): Virtuelle Freilegung innenliegender Strukturen. In M. Fitzenreiter, F. Willer, & J. Auenmüller (Eds.), *Materialien einer Gusswerkstatt von der Qubbet el-Hawa. Bonner Aegyptiaca* (pp. 82–117). EB Verlag Dr. Brandt. https://www.iak.uni-bonn.de/de/abteilungen/aegyptologie/aegyptologie/aktuelle-publikationen/ebook_gusswerkstatt_ebverlag

Meneghetti, F. (2022). *Miniature oxhide ingots from Late Bronze Age Cyprus. An update on the material. Frankfurter Archäologische Schriften.* Habelt Verlag.

Meyers, P. (2002). The casting process of the statue of Queen Napir-Asu in the Louvre. In C.C. Mattusch, A. Brauer, & S. Knudsen (Eds.), *From the Parts to the Whole: Acta of the 13th International Bronze Congress, held at Cambridge, Massachusetts, 1996. Journal of Roman Archaeology, Supplementary Series, 39,* 1–18.

Middleton, A., & Lang, J. (2005). Radiography: Theory. In J. Lang & A. Middleton (Eds.), *Radiography of cultural material* (2nd ed., pp. 1–19). Elsevier and Butterworth-Heinemann.

Molloy, B. (2013). The Origins of Plate Armour in the Aegean and Europe. In A. Papadopoulos (Ed.), *Recent research and perspectives on the Late Bronze Age Eastern Mediterranean. Talanta. Proceedings of the Dutch Archaeological and Historical Society,* 2012, Vol. XLIV, 273–294. http://www.talanta.nl/wp-content/uploads/2015/02/TAL-44-NAHG-H14.pdf

Moorey, P. R. S., & Fleming, S. (1984). Problems in the study of the anthropomorphic metal statuary from Syro-Palestine before 330 B.C. *Levant, 16*(1), 67–90. https://doi.org/10.1179/007589184790586283

Moran, W. (1992). *The Amarna letters*. The Johns Hopkins University Press.

Mountjoy, P. A. (2005). The end of the Bronze Age at Enkomi, Cyprus: The problem of level III B. *The Annual of the British School at Athens, 100*, 125–214. http://www.jstor.org/stable/30073227

Mountjoy, P.A. (2017). Enkomi Levell IIB: Floor II and Sol III. The deposition of the gods. *Report of the Department of Antquities, Cyprus* 2011–2012, 393–414.

Mountjoy, P.A. (2018). *Decorated Pottery in Cyprus and Philistia in the 12th Century BC, Cypriot IIIC and Philistine IIIC, Vols. I–II. Contributions to the Chronology of the Eastern Mediterranean* 36. Verlag der Österreichischen Akademie der Wissenschaften,

Muhly, J. D. (1980). Bronze figurines and near eastern metalwork. *Israel Exploration Journal, 30*, 148–161. http://www.jstor.org/stable/27925754

Muhly, J. D. (1985). The Late Bronze Age in Cyprus: A 25 years retrospect. In V. Karageorghis (Ed.), *Archaeology in Cyprus 1960–1985* (pp. 20–46). The A. G. Leventis Foundation.

Muhly, J. D. (1988). Concluding remarks. In J. Curtis (Ed.), *Bronzeworking Centres of Western Asia, c. 1000–539 B.C* (pp. 329–342). Kegan Paul International.

Münnich, M. M. (2013). The god Resheph in the ancient near east. In *Orientalische Religionen in der Antike 11*. Mohr Siebeck.

Negbi, O. (1976). *Canaanite Gods in Metal: An Archaeological Study of Ancient Syro-Palestinian Figurines. Publications of the Institute of Archaeology, Tel Aviv University* No. 5. Tel Aviv: Institute of Archaeology.

Ornan, T. (2011a). Let Ba'al be enthroned: The date, identification and function of a bronze statue from Hazor. *Journal of Near Eastern Studies, 70*(2), 253–280. https://doi.org/10.1086/661261

Ornan, T. (2011b). The long life of a dead king: A bronze statue from Hazor in its ancient Near Eastern context. *Bulletin of the American Schools of Oriental Research, 366*(1), 1–23. https://doi.org/10.5615/bullamerschoorie.366.0001

Ornan, T. (2012). The role of gold in royal representation: The case of a bronze statue from Hazor. In R. Matthews & J. Curtis (Eds.), *Proceedings of the 7th International Congress on the Archaeology of the Ancient Near East, 12 April – 16 April 2010, the British Museum and UCL, Vol. 2: Ancient & Modern Issues in Cultural Heritage, Colour & Light in Architecture, Art & Material Culture, Islamic Archaeology* (pp. 445–458). Harrassowitz Verlag.

Papasavvas, G. (2003). *Cypriot casting technology I: The stands* (pp. 23–52). Report of the Department of Antiquities, Cyprus.

Papasavvas, G. (2009). The iconography of the oxhide ingots. In F. Lo Schiavo, J. D. Muhly, R. Maddin, & A. Giumlia-Mair (Eds.), *Oxhide ingots in the Central Mediterranean. Biblioteca di Antichità Cipriote 8* (pp. 83–132). The A. G. Leventis Foundation and CNR – Istituto di studi sulle civiltà dell'Egeo e del Vicino Oriente.

Papasavvas, G. (2011). From smiting to Smithing: The transformation of a Cypriot God. In P. Betancourt & S. Ferrence (Eds.), *Metallurgy: Understanding how, learning why. Studies in honor of James D. Muhly* (pp. 59–66). INSTAP Press, Prehistory Monographs 29.

Papasavvas, G. (2012). Pictorial narrative on Cypriot metalwork (pp. 55–84). *Cyprus Numismatic Society, Numismatic Report XXXIX–XLII.*

Papasavvas, G. (2013). Cypriot metalwork of the Late Bronze Age. *PASIPHAE. Rivista de Filologia e Antichità Egee, VII*, 169–178.

Papasavvas, G. (2014). Feasting, deposition and abandonment in the Sanctuary of the Horned God at Enkomi. In J. M. Webb (Ed.), *Structure, measurement and meaning. Studies on prehistoric Cyprus in honour of David Frankel. Studies in Mediterranean Archaeology CXLIII* (pp. 245–260). Paul Åströms Förlag.

Papasavvas, G. (in preparation). *Closure Rituals, abandonment, and destruction at Enkomi: Stratigraphies and formation processes of the archaeological record.*

Peltenburg, E. (2007). Hathor, faience and copper on Late Bronze Age Cyprus. *Cahiers du Centre d'Etudes Chypriotes* 37. Hommage à Annie Caubet, 375–394. https://doi.org/10.3406/cchyp.2007.1514

Pickles, S. & Peltenburg, E. (1998). Metallurgy, Society and the Bronze/Iron Transition in the East Mediterranean and the Near East. *Report of the Department of Antiquities, Cyprus*, 67–100.

Plattner, G. A., Gschwantler, K., & Vak, B. (2017). The bronze athlete from Ephesos. In J. M. Daehner, K. Lapatin, & A. Spinelli (Eds.), *Artistry in bronze. The Greeks and their legacy. XIXth International Congress on Ancient Bronzes* (pp. 6–20). The J. Paul Getty Museum and the Getty Conservation Institute.

Schaeffer, C. F. A. (1965). An Ingot God from Cyprus. *Antiquity XXXIX, 39*, 56–57.

Schaeffer, C. F. A. (1971). Les Peuples de la Mer et leur sanctuaires à Enkomi-Alasia aux 12e-11e s. av.n.è. In C.F.A. Schaeffer, M. Aitken, P. Åström, P. Ducos, H.W. Catling, J.-C. Courtois, J. Bouzek, H. Hadjioannou, H.-J. Hundt, R.W. Hutchinson, W. Johnstone, V. Karageorghis, J. Lagarce, O. Masson, E. Masson, A.H.S. Megaw (Eds.), *Alasia: Première Série. Mission Archéologique d'Alasia* IV (pp. 505–566). Mission Archéologique d' Alasia.

Schorsch, D. (1988). Technical examination of ancient Egyptian Theriomorphic hollow cast bronzes. In S. C. Watkins & C. E. Brown (Eds.), *Conservation of ancient Egyptian materials: Preprints of a conference organised by the United Kingdom Institute for Conservation, Archaeology Section, Bristol 1988* (pp. 41–50). Institute of Archaeology Publications.

Schorsch, D. (2014a). A conservator's perspective. In B. W. Roberts & C. P. Thornton (Eds.), *Archaeometallurgy in global perspective: Methods and syntheses* (pp. 269–301). Springer. https://www.researchgate.net/publication/288241857_A_Conservator's_Perspective_on_Ancient_Metallurgy

Schorsch, D. (2014b). Lebanese mountain figures: Advances in the study of Levantine anthropomorphic metal statuary. In *Metropolitan museum studies in art, science and technology 2* (pp. 115–155). The Metropolitan Museum of Art.

Schorsch, D. (2019). Ritual metal statuary in ancient Egypt: A long life and a great good old age. In A. Masson-Berghoff (Ed.), *Statues in context: Production, meaning and (re)uses* (pp. 252–255). Peeters Publishers. https://www.researchgate.net/publication/341565047_Ritual_metal_statuary_in_ancient_Egypt_'A_long_life_and_a_great_and_good_old_age

Schorsch, D., & Frantz, J. H. (1997). A tale of two kitties. *The Metropolitan Museum of Art Bulletin, 55*(3), 16–29.

Schorsch, D., & Hendrix, E. (2003). *Ambition and competence in Late Bronze Age Cyprus* (pp. 53–77). Report of the Department of Antiquities.

Schorsch, D., & Wypyski, M. T. (2009). Seth, 'figure of mystery'. *Journal of the American Research Center in Egypt, 45*, 177–200. https://www.jstor.org/stable/25735453

Schorsch, D., Lawrence, B., & Carò, F. (2019). Enlightened technology: Casting divinity in the Gupta Age. *Arts of Asia, 49*(2), 131–143. https://www.researchgate.net/publication/331573831_Enlightened_Technology_Casting_Divinity_in_the_Gupta_Age

Schreiner, M., Frühmann, B., Jembrih-Simbürger, D., & Linke, R. (2004). X-rays in art and archaeology: An overview. *Powder Diffraction, 19*(1), 3–11. https://doi.org/10.1154/1.1649963

Seeden, H. (1980). *The standing armed figurines in the Levant. Prähistorische Bronzefunde I(1).* C.H. Beck.

Spigelmann, M. (2012). Copper and cult in Bronze Age Cyprus. In A. Geoergiou (Ed.), *Cyprus: An Island culture: Society and social relations from the Bronze Age to the Venetian period* (pp. 133–152). Oxbow Books.

Webb, J. M. (1999). *Ritual architecture, iconography and practice in late Cypriot Bronze Age, Studies in Mediterranean archaeology pocket-book 75.* Paul Åströms Förlag.

Webb, J. M. (2001). The sanctuary of the Ingot God at Enkomi. A new Reading of its construction, use and abandonment. In P. M. Fischer (Ed.), *Contributions to the archaeology and history of the bronze and iron ages in the Eastern Mediterranean. Studies in honour of Paul Aström. Österreichisches Archäologisches Institut Sonderschriften 39* (pp. 69–82). Österreichisches Archäologisches Institut.

Willer, F. (2016). Exkurs: Zur antiken Übergang- bzw. Angusstechnik. In I. M. Fitzenreiter, F. Willer, & J. Auenmüller (Eds.), *Materialien einer Gusswerkstatt von der Qubbet el-Hawa. Bonner Aegyptiaca* (pp. 139–142). EB Verlag Dr. Brandt. https://www.iak.uni-bonn.de/de/abteilungen/aegyptologie/aegyptologie/aktuelle-publikationen/ebook_gusswerkstatt_ebverlag

Willer, F., & Meijers, R. (2014). Hightech trifft Antike. Römischen Bronzegießern auf der Spur. In G. Uelsberg, J. Heiligmann, & M. Brouwer (Eds.), *Gebrochener Glanz. Römischer Grossbronzen am UNESCO Welterbe Limes* (pp. 166–179). Landesmuseum. https://landesmuseum-bonn.lvr.de/media/lmb/forschung/bilder_4/restaurierung/Meijers_R._Willer_F._High_Tech_trifft_Antike_2015.pdf

Wüstemann, H. (2004). *Die Schwerter in Ostdeutschland. Prähistorische Bronzefunde IV(15)*. Franz Steiner..

Zwicker, U., & Breme, J. (1988). *Kupfer und Kupferlegierungen in der Vor- und Frühgeschichte. Teil 2 (Kupferlegierungen)*. Institut für Werkstoffwissenschaften.

Iron Age Copper Metallurgy in Southeast Arabia: A Comparative Perspective

Joseph W. Lehner ⓘ**, Ioana A. Dumitru** ⓘ**, Abigail Buffington** ⓘ**, Eli Dollarhide** ⓘ**, Smiti Nathan** ⓘ**, Paige Paulsen** ⓘ**, Mary L. Young** ⓘ**, Alexander J. Sivitskis, Frances Wiig** ⓘ**, and Michael J. Harrower** ⓘ

Abstract From the southern Levant to southeast Arabia, new technologies and social networks shaped metal production and trade in a variety of important ways. In this paper, we review the development of copper metallurgy in Early Iron Age Oman ca. 1300–800 BCE and compare it with development in the southern Levant. Settlement intensification, innovations in irrigation technologies, dromedary domestication, and the emergence of industrial copper sulfide smelting played major roles in shaping southeast Arabian societies during the late second to early first millennium BCE. Although there are similarities in the scale of copper production between the southern Levant and southeast Arabia during this period, key differences in resources impacted how societies adopted and organized metal technologies. Based on recent surveys and excavations, we discuss evidence for large-scale copper sulfide smelting at Wadi al-Raki, one of the largest copper-producing areas in Oman, and findings at 'Uqdat al-Bakrah, where hundreds of pits and more than 600 copper-based artifacts have been recovered.

J. W. Lehner (✉)
Department of Archaeology, The University of Sydney, Sydney, Australia
e-mail: joseph.lehner@sydney.edu.au

I. A. Dumitru
Centre for Urban Network Evolutions (UrbNet), Aarhus University, Aarhus, Denmark
e-mail: ioana.dumitru@sydney.edu.au

A. Buffington · M. L. Young
Department of Archaeology, College of William and Mary, Williamsburg, VA, USA
e-mail: afbuffington@wm.edu; mlyoung@email.wm.edu

E. Dollarhide
New York University Abu Dhabi, Abu Dhabi, UAE
e-mail: eli.dollarhide@nyu.edu

S. Nathan
Anthico LLC, Baltimore, MD, USA
e-mail: smiti.nathan@anthico.com

© The Author(s), under exclusive license to Springer Nature Switzerland AG 2023
E. Ben-Yosef, I. W. N. Jones (eds.), *"And in Length of Days Understanding" (Job 12:12): Essays on Archaeology in the Eastern Mediterranean and Beyond in Honor of Thomas E. Levy*, Interdisciplinary Contributions to Archaeology,
https://doi.org/10.1007/978-3-031-27330-8_59

Keywords Iron Age · Arabia · Metallurgy · Copper · Social organisation · Hierarchy · Mobility

1 Introduction

How metallurgy originated in Arabia, its causes and consequences, remains a major issue in archaeology. The Arabian Peninsula and adjacent regions of the southern Levant and Iran provide some of the earliest evidence of metal production in the world. Even so, the diversity of technological lineages from the southern Levant/ Sinai to southeast Arabia demonstrates certain discontinuities. Primary copper smelting sites currently dating as early as the mid- to late fifth millennium BCE in the southern Levant (Ackerfeld et al., 2020; Golden 2010; Hauptmann, 2007; Klimscha, 2013) and the late fourth millennium BCE in Oman (Giardino, 2017; Schmidt & Döpper, 2019), show similarities, yet it is unclear how these regions interrelated, if at all, in the innovation and adoption of metallurgy. Perhaps one of the most astounding parallels is the mutual rise of large-scale industrial copper production in the Wadi Arabah and in Oman during the thirteenth century BCE, with some waste heaps amounting to tens of thousands of tons of serially produced slag that accumulated over the course of five to six centuries.

During a period of intense productivity ca. 1300–800 BCE, bracketed in time by periods of relatively less production, both regions also experienced major social and cultural changes that are highly visible archaeologically. Yet how the social and cultural traditions are expressed in these copper-producing regions are profoundly diverse. In this contribution we examine how these differences are evidenced archaeologically. This comparative approach offers insight into the social capital and capacities of Iron Age communities in Arabia, and how differing political economies can manifest large-scale, high intensity and serialized production. We provide an argument here that the political economy in Iron Age southeast Arabia contrasts with the southern Levant in terms of archaeologically visible or historically attested social stratification and elite administration. We suggest that there is little evidence that supports an overarching direct elite control of industrial copper smelting in southeast Arabia, and that copper materials were rather exchanged in a

---

P. Paulsen · M. J. Harrower
Department of Near Eastern Studies, Johns Hopkins University, Baltimore, MD, USA
e-mail: ppaulse2@jhu.edu; mharrower@jhu.edu

A. J. Sivitskis
Teton Science Schools, Jackson, WY, USA
e-mail: alex.sivitskis@tetonscience.org

F. Wiig
School of Civil and Environmental Engineering, University of New South Wales, Sydney, NSW, Australia
e-mail: frances.wiig@environment.nsw.gov.au

highly regionalized and internal exchange system that fostered social cohesion through ritual consumption, intentional deposition and decommissioning of wealth. These two divergent networks of copper exploitation highlight how emergent and established industries can take on a variety of organizational systems and are not necessarily contingent on the sponsorship or control of elites and their legitimation.

2 The Rise of Extractive Metallurgy in Arabia

Our knowledge of Arabian metallurgical technologies, their evolution over time, and the societies associated with them is largely limited to the southern Levant due in large part to decades of careful and focused research. Archaeometallurgical investigations in this region, as argued by many authors (e.g., Ben-Yosef & Shalev, 2018; Golden, 2010; Hauptmann, 2007; Levy & Shalev, 1989; Rothenberg, 1990), establish clearly that metals and metal production are important markers for technological histories and sociocultural processes in the region, and more broadly, the kinds of long distance relationships that developed with the craft.

One of the emergent themes of this uneven attention, due in part to historical circumstances, is that the development of metallurgy and how it interfaced with society in the southern Levant has in some cases been used to describe analogous developments elsewhere in West Asia. As summarized by Thornton (2009), models of metal technology and its development in the Levant, in particular copper smelting technologies, influenced how scholars understood copper production in other regions in Anatolia, the Caucasus, Iran and Oman, despite the fact that data from these regions are not entirely consistent with how early metal production developed in the southern Levant. Most recently, the work by Radivojević et al. (2021) provides convincing evidence that metallurgical technologies in the Balkans exhibit early convergence and independent innovation through pathways that are potentially distinct from neighboring regions. While these studies principally deal with the earliest phases of copper smelting during the early fifth to fourth millennia BCE, their cautious criticism urges us to be careful when applying our understanding of the innovation and adoption of metallurgy in all time periods.

The Arabian Peninsula as a whole, extending from the southern portions of modern Iraq and Jordan to Yemen, the Sultanate of Oman and the Persian Gulf, occupies an immense region rich with metal deposits (Figs. 1 and 2), yet empirical data concerning metal industries, in particular primary copper smelting, is poorly known outside of the Levant. Precambrian basement rocks, which extend as part of the Arabian-Nubian shield from the Sinai through the Hijaz and Yemen, host numerous major deposits of copper, gold, silver, lead and iron that have archaeological significance (Hassan Ahmed, 2022a). Associated with these sources in western Arabia are expansive industrial landscapes, including mining settlements and copper smelting sites, though concrete evidence providing dates earlier than the Early Islamic period is rare (Al-Zahrani, 2014; de Jesus, 1982; Hassan Ahmed, 2022b; Hester et al., 1983; Kisnawi et al., 1983), a fact owing to the dearth of available evidence and

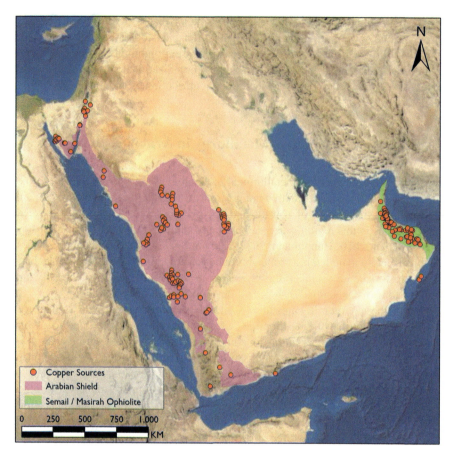

Fig. 1 Major copper deposits in the Arabian Peninsula. (Data Source for Geologic Provinces: (Pollastro, 1998). Copper localities after ArWHO survey and Hauptmann, 2007: 41; Hassan Ahmed, 2022: 464; Hauptmann, 1985: 116; Levy et al., 2014: 18; Pugachevsky et al., 2009; Roberts, 1975: 46. Basemap Credits: Earthstar Geographics; Esri, USGS; World Hillshade)

targeted research. Historic gold and silver processing in Yemen has been documented through some materials analysis, brief survey reconnaissance and remote sensing (Deroin et al., 2012; Mallory-Greenough et al., 2000; Merkel et al., 2016), and local second millennium BCE copper production in southwest Arabia has been inferred on the basis of lead isotope analysis of finished copper-alloy objects alone (Weeks et al., 2009).

Our understanding of the traditions of extractive metallurgy in southeast Arabia is substantially improved due primarily to geological and archaeometallurgical surveys and small-scale excavations in Oman conducted primarily during the 1970s and 80s. Extending along the piedmont of the Hajar Mountains of Oman, one of the world's best-preserved exposures of ophiolite attracted prospectors because of its rich association of volcanogenic massive sulfide (VMS) bodies rich in copper and other metals like gold, nickel, cobalt, and arsenic (Coleman et al., 1979). Similar to

Iron Age Copper Metallurgy in Southeast Arabia: A Comparative Perspective

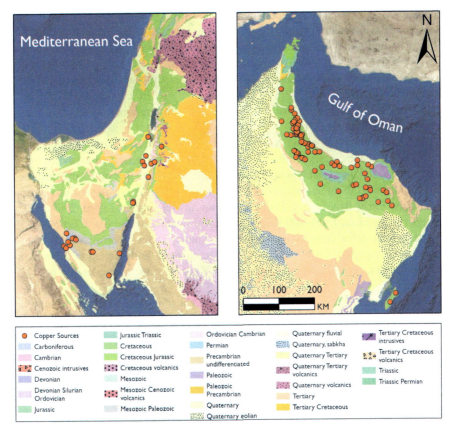

Fig. 2 Major copper deposits in the Arabian Peninsula: close-up of the Levant and the Sinai Peninsula (left) and southeastern Arabia (right). Data source for bedrock geology: Pollastro, 1998. Copper localities after ArWHO survey and Hauptmann, 1985: 116; Levy et al., 2014: 18. Basemap Credits: Earthstar Geographics; Esri, USGS; World Hillshade

the ores associated with the Troodos ophiolite in Cyprus, many of the copper deposits are near the surface and immediately identifiable by iron-rich gossan caps. While there is important variation in the VMS deposits in terms of general composition and stratigraphic placement geologically (Belgrano et al., 2019), most available copper ore used by past communities would have interfaced quickly with a range of copper mineral types, from leached, weathered, and oxidised ores to deeper massive sulfides.

After brief recording of significant production sites by archaeologists working closely with geologists mapping the region for major minerals (Berthoud et al., 1978; Carney & Welland, 1974; Goettler et al., 1976), the first focused research targeting the deep history of mining and metallurgy in Oman was conducted by Gerd Weisgerber and Andreas Hauptmann with the support of the Deutsches Bergbau Museum (DBM). This extensive fieldwork developed along the same lines of inquiry as the same team's fieldwork in Faynan in Jordan, and it led to the documentation of over 100 copper smelting sites located within the vicinity of copper sources associated with the Semail ophiolite exposed along the piedmont of the Hajar Mountains and further copper producing sites on Masirah Island (Weisgerber, 1977, 1978, 1980, 1987; Weisgerber & Al-Shanfari, 2013). This ground-breaking work also included physical analyses of copper ores and slags (Hauptmann, 1985; Hauptmann & Weisgerber, 1981), extensive analyses of copper metal (Prange, 2001) and chemical fingerprinting of ores collected through the course of their surveys (Begemann et al., 2010).

One of the most important results of these early investigations is evidence for cycles of intensive copper production. Rough dating of slag heaps based on associated pottery, and more rarely with radiocarbon, demonstrate that most smelting sites can be attributed to three major periods of intensity, including bursts of production during the Early Bronze Age Hafit and Umm an-Nar periods (3200–2000 BCE), Early Iron Age (ca. 1300–800 BCE), and Early Islamic period (ca. CE 650–900). While evidence for copper consumption is known in the interim periods, these multi-century gaps of little to no copper production are likely linked to a combination of factors, from fuel depletion to major shifts in trade networks and political economy.

Current data demonstrate that the earliest evidence of copper metal consumption in southeast Arabia dates to as early as ca 4200 BCE. Small tools and fragments of smelted copper from small coastal Late Neolithic settlements, including Wadi Shab and Ras al-Hamra, provide concrete evidence of copper consumption (Giardino, 2017: 33–39). These earliest examples display variations in elemental concentration, many with significant and anomalous quantities of silver (>8.0 wt.%). While it remains untested whether this copper was locally produced or imported from other regions in Iran or beyond, current data are nevertheless consistent with locally available copper ores. Contrary to so-called natural alloys, these types of alloys may have been intentionally produced through mixed smelting as is evidenced by more complex copper alloys in Anatolia (Dardeniz, 2020; Lehner & Yener, 2014; Yener, 2000), the Caucasus (Courcier, 2014), and Balkans (Radivojević et al., 2013).

The best-documented evidence for the earliest copper smelting in southeast Arabia is from the Hafit period site of al-Khashbah in central Oman. Dating to as early as 3200 BCE, small fragments of copper slag, prills, and thousands of furnace and crucible fragments, were recorded in abundance and associated with settlement activities and monumental architecture (Schmidt & Döpper, 2019, 2020). Marking an important transition in southeast Arabia, al-Khashbah provides key data on a Bronze Age cultural horizon that develops regionally through to the end of the third millennium BCE. This and earlier work have helped build the case that the copper sources in southeast Arabia were linked with third millennium BCE attestations of Magan in Mesopotamian texts (Desch, 1929; Hauptmann & Weisgerber, 1981; Laursen & Steinkeller, 2017; Peake, 1928; Weeks, 2004; Weisgerber, 1983, 1984).

Analysis of slags from Maysar-1 by A. Hauptmann (1985), dating roughly to the late third millennium BCE, demonstrates a sequence of possible crucible and furnace smelting and selective ore choice. Some slags show undeveloped microstructures and pronounced concentrations of copper up to 30 wt.%, due to significant inclusions of copper prills, cuprite, and Cu-Fe oxides. Slightly later slags and copper ingots from the site demonstrate a different technology including use of furnaces and tapping of a more developed slag. Clear indications of direct smelting of mixed copper oxide and sulfide ores together with iron oxide/hydroxide fluxes at this site reveal an advanced smelting technology that resembles evidence from roughly contemporary sites in Iran, including Shahr-i Sokhta (Artioli et al., 2005). Planoconvex ingots and slags with bottom circular impressions in these cases show smelters were able to achieve a highly efficient separation of copper from the slag.

The intensity of copper production declined during the beginning of the second millennium BCE (known from distinct material traditions during the Wadi Suq 2000–1600 BCE and Late Bronze Age 1600–1300 BCE), which accompanies a regional transformation that sees novel mortuary traditions, shifts towards increased mobility patterns and pastoralism. S. Döpper (2021) recently summarized likely causes, including environmental degradation, resistance against social hierarchies, reorganization of long-distance trade networks, and challenges around the mobilization of labor in settlements. This provides for intriguing comparison with the Late Bronze Age/Early Iron Age transition in the Mediterranean region, which also gave rise to new cultural traditions that dramatically altered political and economic landscapes.

3 Iron Age Copper Industries in Southeast Arabia

The Iron Age of both southwest and southeast Arabia is a period of pronounced transformation and one that witnesses numerous technological and social innovations (Magee, 2014; McCorriston, 2011, 2013). A resurgence in settlement intensification is associated with novel environmental niches associated with new irrigation technologies. This is coupled with the rapid adoption of the domestic camel for transportation. Long-distance trade, ritual spaces associated with monumental architecture, fortified settlements, new types of mortuary structures, and ritual elaboration associated with several types of sites mark an Iron Age phenomenon in southeast Arabia that is defined also by a distinctly shared material culture.

Another distinct innovation during the Iron Age is the sudden appearance of industrial scale copper production likely linked to copper sulphide smelting (Weeks et al., 2016). Scores of Iron Age copper smelting sites across southeast Arabia attest to this dramatic change, many of which are multiperiod occupations (Yule et al., 2021). According to the DBM surveys, there is a range in size of smelting sites, from sites with just 100 tons to 1000 tons; however one site, Raki 2, has up to 45,000 tons (Fig. 3) (Hauptmann, 1985). This transformation represents at least an order of magnitude greater intensity of copper production than the first burst of productivity during the third millennium BCE and spans a broad period of time ca. 1300–800 BCE or 500 years of activity.

Raki 2 is located within the Wadi al-Raki drainage ca. 10 km northeast of modern Yanqul in al-Dhahirah governate (Fig. 4). Wadi al-Raki is known variously in

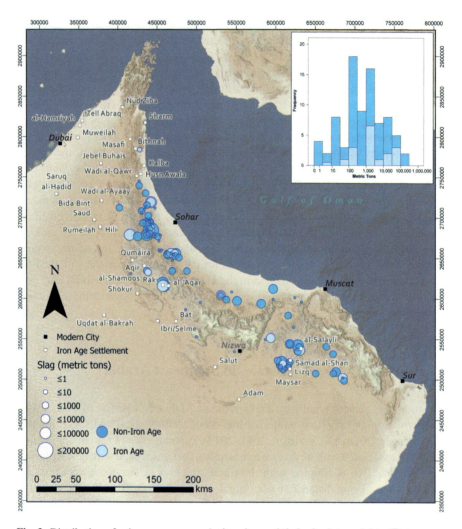

Fig. 3 Distribution of primary copper producing sites and their absolute weights. (Data source Hauptmann, 1985. Basemap Credits: ESRI World Hillshade)

the geological literature and maps as Wadi Rakah. The wadi develops around and erodes the edges of significant exposures of upper and lower extrusives of the volcanic sequence of the Semail ophiolite, including several areas of copper-bearing pillow lavas. There are at least three major VMS deposits in this zone, including al-Bishara, Hayl al-Safil, Raki, and and smaller deposit at Tawi Raki (also modern al-Bukhaira). Of these, modern open cast mining operations extracted copper and gold from the weathered gossan caps of the al-Bishara and Raki sulfide bodies from 1994 to 2005.

First recorded in the 1970s by Prospection (Oman) Limited (Prospect Nos. 29–30), and soon after by the United States Geological Survey (Coleman & Bailey,

Fig. 4 Distribution of smelting sites in Wadi al-Raki, Yanqul, Ad-Dhahirah Governorate, Oman. (Basemap Credits: Earthstar Geographics; Esri, USGS; World Hillshade)

1981), the archaeological significance of Raki was quickly apparent. Raki was subsequently discussed by Goettler et al. (1976) and Berthould et al. (1978). G. Weisgerber conducted two seasons (1995–96) of survey and excavations in Wadi al-Raki, focusing efforts on the early Iron Age settlement and slag heaps at Raki 2 (Weisgerber & Yule, 1999; Yule & Weisgerber, 1996). The Archaeological Water Histories of Oman (ArWHO) Project renewed investigations of the Raki sites starting in 2019 (Harrower et al., 2021; Sivitskis et al., 2019).

Weisgerber's investigations at Raki 2 found convincing evidence for the serial production of copper and mining associated with an agglutinated village that is dispersed over an approximately 12 ha area. Radiocarbon determinations place this activity between 1200–800 cal BCE. Slag heaps are composed of crushed and fragmented tap and furnace slags and significant quantities of ceramic furnace lining. The deepest accumulations of slag (ca. 6.5 m) occur at the western edge of the site (Fig. 5).

Evidence from Raki 2 is consistent with smelting practices reconstructed for Iron Age sites in southeast Arabia involving one-off furnace smelting producing ca. 4–8 kgs of slag with characteristic flow patterns and preserved furnace bottoms with planoconvex impressions where copper or matte separated (Fig. 6). Presently, there is no evidence for use of tuyères or bellows, since fragments of these have yet to be documented. Further, given the morphological uniformity of the slags at Raki, it appears that the production sequence maintained a certain degree of standardization, though there is little overarching material evidence for elite administration and control, such as administrative technologies or specialized architecture.

Fig. 5 Excavations of the largest slag heap (ca. 6.5 m deep) at Raki 2 in 2019. (Credit: Archaeological Water Histories of Oman Project)

4 Copper, Complexity, and the Iron Age Transformation in Arabia

The transition between the Late Bronze Age (LBA) and the Early Iron Age (EIA) is accompanied by a shift in the sociopolitical and cultural landscape of the Aegean, Eastern Mediterranean, and Southwest Asia. Earlier reconstructions of this period theorized societal collapse (Cline, 2014; Drews, 1993; Muhly, 1980) engendered by population migration and foreign invasion (Albright, 1939; Lapp, 1967; Redford, 1992, 2000; Stager, 1995). Recent reinterpretations are more nuanced, both in terms of motivating factors and scale of transformation, highlighting one or a combination of catalysts including mounting internal social tensions (Magee, 2014; Zuckerman, 2007), natural disasters (Nur & Cline, 2000), and large-scale, drought-induced famine brought about by rapid climate change (Cunliffe, 2005; Drake, 2012; Langgut et al., 2013; Singer, 2007). Instead of outright collapse, such theories see this transition as characterized by a decline in political centralization and palace economies, where present, and a renegotiation of internal social structures.

Beginning in this period, the balance of power gradually shifted in favor of previously marginal social actors, with the rise of historically attested groups of Arameans, Phoenicians, Philistines, Chaldaeans, Hebrews, Edomites, Ammonites, Moabites, Arabs, Iranians, Urartians, Phrygians, Medes, and Ionians. In contrast to

Fig. 6 Typical example of a larger copper slag from Raki 2. Examples like this are preserved because they were selected for architectural building materials and were not crushed down further. (Credit: Archaeological Water Histories of Oman Project)

earlier periods, community and social organization during the EIA were deeply ideologically connected to notions of family ties and alliances between kin-based or nomadic groups (Porter, 2013). This transition altered regional geopolitics as an increasing strain was placed on old empires in Egypt, Anatolia, Assyria, and Babylonia. What emerged was a period characterized by elements of continuity amid considerable change, cultural and technological synergies, and sundry new or reinforced expressions of socio-cultural identity (Cline, 2014; Mazzoni, 2010).

The break-up of the Bronze Age system in the Levant system left a vacuum of power that generated the conditions for the rise in prominence of different locally organized groups that arguably embraced opportunities towards some level of economic, socio-political, and cultural self-determination. In the southern Levant, LBA copper production within the Timna Valley was controlled by the Egyptian Nineteenth Dynasty (Rothenberg, 1972; Rothenberg & Bachmann, 1988; Sapir-Hen & Ben-Yosef, 2014; Ventura, 1974; Yagel et al., 2016). By the Twentieth Dynasty, evidence is consistent with a shift in control from the Egyptians, and subsequent EIA production demonstrates a move towards local control by nomadic groups (Ben-Yosef, 2010; Ben-Yosef et al., 2012). In the Arabah, the Negev, and the Edomite Plateau, the emerging model of social organization was one of elite control and legitimization through copper production (Ben-Yosef, 2010, 2021; Howland, 2021). Among the elite were arguably the craft producers themselves (Howland, 2021), nomads who transitioned polymorphous nomadic societies into politically resilient polities (Ben-Yosef, 2010, 2021).

Interpretations of the southeast Arabian LBA variously identify either external geopolitical dynamics or internal restructurings as catalysts for the transition into the distinct EIA cultural horizon. Where external factors are concerned, scholars have pointed to the political changes that took place in Mesopotamia, southern Iran, and the Indus Valley (Crawford, 1996; Crawford, 1998). Others propose a Marxian model intent on highlighting the impact of local developments (Azzarà & De Rorre, 2018). This model affirms that some changes within southeast Arabia predate the period of political breakdowns in Mesopotamia (Sallaberger & Schrakamp, 2015) and the Indus Valley (Kenoyer, 1998; Kenoyer, 2008) and suggest that socio-political reorganization developed as a response aimed at curbing rising wealth inequality in the southern Gulf (Magee, 2014: 124–125). Both models iterate the importance of seeing southeast Arabia as embedded in and entangled with social groups across southwest Asia (Magee, 2005).

The narrative reconstructed for LBA southeast Arabia (1600–1300 BCE) includes lower densities in settlement pattern and increased economic dependence on pastoralism (Cleuziou & Tosi, 2007: 258; Magee, 2014: 188). This was accompanied by a notable shift away from monumental architecture. The so-called towers of the Bronze Age seem to enter into disuse at the end of the third millennium BCE. Similarly, above-ground stone cairns gave way to a new form of mortuary expression, including semi-subterranean collective tombs (Magee, 2014: 189; Laursen & Steinkeller, 2017: 66). Where copper production was concerned, southeast Arabia experienced a transition in copper consumption and production (Weisgerber, 2007). Evidence of LBA metallurgy is limited, consisting principally of objects uncovered in mortuary contexts (Weeks, 1997; Nasser S. Al-Jahwari et al., 2021). A significant decrease in long-distance exchange is also associated with this period. Except for a small number of texts that mention commercial contacts with Dilmun, the rest of the southern Gulf is scarcely mentioned in the cuneiform record from this period (Potts, 2001). When exchange is recorded, it seems to indicate that the export of Omani copper to Mesopotamia was mediated by the communities from Dilmun of the Upper Gulf (Begemann et al., 2010: 160–161; Laursen & Steinkeller, 2017: 68; Frenez, 2019: 29–31).

5 Factors Linked to Transformation in Early Iron Age Southeast Arabia

Socio-political, economic, environmental, and climatic conditions and changes across the eastern Mediterranean and southwest Asia led to a diverse array of local adaptations including contrasting trajectories in southeast Arabia and the southern Levant. In both regions, changes occurred amidst considerable continuity in material culture, social structure, and composition (Gregoricka & Sheridan, 2017) and were marked both by transformations (Avanzini & Phillips, 2010) and by a reinforcement of elements of Bronze Age cultural expression (Frenez et al., 2021). As for the broad trajectory of the EIA, the southern Levant saw the development of centralized polities born out of polymorphous societies which are defined as comprising fluctuating proportions of nomadic and settled populations (Ben-Yosef, 2019; Ben-Yosef, 2021). In contrast, a centralized polity did not develop in southeast Arabia, where elements of social stratification are either negligible or do not adhere to our expectations of material culture correlates (Cleuziou & Tosi, 2007; Magee, 2014).

The southeast Arabian early Iron Age is commonly associated with settlement expansion, economic intensification, and population growth (Boucharlat, 1984: 190; Schreiber, 2007: 272–273; Al-Tikriti, 2002: 150; Nasser Said Ali Al-Jahwari, 2013: 168; Yule, 2014; Magee, 2005, 2014: 214). Two major autochthonous changes – appearance of falaj irrigation technologies and the use of domesticated dromedary camels for transportation – facilitated and encouraged major socio-political and socio-economic changes (Magee, 2005). These internal catalysts contravene the notion that powerful regional neighbors (like Mesopotamia) had an outsized and fundamental impact on changes in southeast Arabian societies. Instead, major social changes EIA southeast Arabia appear to have been part of eminently indigenous shifts in cultural expression.

Falaj (pl. aflaj) irrigation systems, involving underground infiltration galleries that tap aquifers, are found at Iron Age settlements along the piedmont flanks of the al-Hajar Mountains. This technological innovation led to an expansion of irrigated lands and facilitated permanent settlements in previously marginal ecological zones (Magee, 2000: 33, Magee, 2014: 214, 258; Häser, 2010). This led to an unprecedented increase in the number of settlements, and most Iron Age oases are associated with evidence of falaj irrigation (Häser, 2010).

Another major push factor is represented by the domestication of dromedary camels (*Camelus dromedaries*) in southeast Arabia. While exclusively used for meat over the previous millennia (Curci et al., 2014; Magee, 2015: 271–272), dromedaries began to be used for transport and as pack animals during the Iron Age. This change in human-animal relationships generated a network of terrestrial trade routes that expanded and invigorated long-distance trade crisscrossing the Peninsula (Loreto, 2021; Magee, 2014).

The Iron Age in the southern Levant is similarly characterized by settlement and population growth. In contrast to southeast Arabia, socio-political changes in the southern Levant involve gradual centralization under local, nomadic groups that culminated in kingdoms (LaBianca & Younker, 1995). This process is closely entwined with control over copper production and trade, particularly where evidence from copper-producing sites in the Faynan and Timna districts is concerned. Recent models connecting evidence from sites like Khirbat en-Nahas (KEN) to the kingdom of Edom have proposed an EIA date for this state (Ben-Yosef, 2019, 2021; Levy et al., 2005, 2007, 2014; Levy & Najjar, 2014; Smith & Levy, 2008). This contrasts with earlier interpretations which argued that Edom developed largely as a result of interactions with the Assyrian empire beginning in the eighth century BCE (Bienkowski, 1990). Initial challenges to this model (Finkelstein, 2005; Finkelstein & Singer-Avitz, 2008, 2009; van der Steen & Bienkowski, 2006) have largely been resolved (Ben-Yosef, 2020; Higham et al., 2005; Levy et al., 2005; Levy & Najjar, 2014).

Patterns evident in the southern Levant also highlight indigenous processes and dynamics amid active involvement of Egyptian agency at the time of the 22nd Dynasty. Despite losing control over the Levant during the Twentieth Dynasty (Bietak, 2007; Martin, 2011; Stager, 1995), the Egyptians appear to have maintained economic relations with this locally-controlled enterprise (Ben-Dor Evian et al., 2021). As a primary importer, they had a vested interest in streamlining copper production and decreasing operating costs and did so primarily by disseminating technological knowledge to the Edomites (Ben-Yosef et al., 2019; Sapir-Hen & Ben-Yosef, 2013; Ben-Yosef, 2021) who had stepped into the vacuum of power. Consolidating control of the immensely lucrative copper industry, the same nomadic group likely occupied the contemporaneous producing regions in Timna and the Faynan (Ben-Yosef, 2016; Ben-Yosef et al., 2019).

6 Community Life

Evidence pertinent to reconstructing public life during the EIA can be retrieved by evaluating settlements patterns, public or communal architectural forms, and the scale and degree of unity within the material culture record. In southeast Arabia, examination of Iron Age settlements (Benoist, 2001; Boucharlat, 1984; Boucharlat & Lombard, 1985; Córdoba, 2010; Magee, 1998; Potts, 1990) have enhanced our understanding of socio-political organization and social life. Instead of a centralized polity, a set of village communities emerged to form a network of settlements that were connected by the circulation of commodities, people, and ideas. With some important local differences, as represented by divergent trajectories in material culture between central Oman and the UAE (Phillips, 2010; Schreiber, 2010), expressions of cultural unity characterize southeast Arabia, as indicated by commonly intelligible social and ritual practices (Benoist, 2010a). Although influenced by interactions with long-distance trade partners, this was a broadly indigenous cultural patterning (Magee, 2005). This network demonstrates the development and sharing of collective resources, technologies, beliefs, and norms. In contrast to the Levantine example, there is an absence of evidence of social stratification both among and within settlements (Benoist, 2010a; Córdoba, 2010).

Over the years, different properties have been variously selected to develop a settlement model according to environment (Boucharlat, 1984; Boucharlat & Lombard, 1985), geography (Potts, 1990), innovations in hydraulic technologies (Magee, 1998), developments in social-organization of water management (Benoist, 2001), and activities associated with production and trade (Córdoba, 2010). These properties converge to reveal a network of coastal settlements (with differences between sites of the al-Batinah coast and sites of the western littoral of the Arabian Gulf), oasis settlements of the interior, mountain villages, and fortified sites.

To the extent that this is understood, the layout of Iron Age settlements and public architecture associated with defense, public gatherings, meetings, festivities, religious life, and cultic practices reveal aspects of community life and social organization that further delineate a society with little evidence of coercion and elite control and a flexible approach to adherence to norms and rules (Benoist, 2010a).

As public works, fortified sites are expressions of large-scale cooperation and community defense over settlements, structures, resources, economic activities, etc. These have been found in different locations across southeast Arabia and demonstrate variation in layout or construction methods (Benoist, 2010a). The extent to which these structures, together with the large assemblages of Iron Age metallic weaponry, emerged as a response to perceived or actualized threats, is a topic of ongoing debate (Aksoy, 2018; Potts, 1998; Yule, 2014).

Community building was also structured around collective events that occurred at cultic and gathering sites. Despite a lack of standardization in religious architecture in southeast Arabia (Benoist, 2010a: 118), material culture associated with cultic sites demonstrates some degree of homogeneity, as represented by the ubiquity of snake symbols among a characteristic assemblage with ritual associations (Condoluci & Esposti, 2018).

Collective events also occurred in so-called columned or pillared buildings (Benoist, 2010a; Condoluci & Esposti, 2018), where communal gatherings involved ritual consumption of food and drink. The co-occurrence of ritual paraphernalia with items associated with feasting (drinking vessels, carinated cups, long-handled bowls, bridge-spouted jars, bronze ladles, etc.) evokes communal gatherings where cultic activities took place alongside feasting and banqueting (Condoluci & Esposti, 2018; Benoist, 2010b; a; Benoist et al., 2015). A model that emerges is one where feasts and festivities are understood as ways of reifying social cohesion and negotiating aspects of community life. An association with ritual or religious practices would have arguably legitimized these social events (Benoist, 2010a).

Examples of social architecture generally appear to be spatially distinct from private residences. This provides further support that an elite class with structural power had not emerged in the southeast Arabian EIA. Instead, this infrastructure suggests the existence of a society that valued community building activities, one in which the group was arguably the smallest unit of control (Avanzini & Phillips, 2010; Benoist, 2010a). In addition to serving cultic and ceremonial functions, columned buildings have also been interpreted as administrative centers (Boucharlat & Lombard, 2001; Magee, 2003), loci that facilitated discussions around shared community issues, such as the collective management of common strategic resources including water (Al-Tikriti, 2002; Benoist, 2000; Boucharlat & Lombard, 2001).

In contrast to southeast Arabia, where the role of nomads in the development of EIA society is less understood, EIA nomadic groups of the southern Levant were arguably the prime movers in Iron Age state formation (Ben-Yosef, 2019, 2021). A fundamental part of the southern Levantine social matrix, nomadic groups established political institutions and centralized polities in ancient Israel (Finkelstein, 1994; Rainey, 2007), Ammon, Moab, and Edom (LaBianca & Younker, 1995).

Iron Age social organization departs from the traditional ethnographic model. Based on observations of twentieth-century Bedouin societies, the ethnographic model describes a society with a dimorphic structure (Rowton, 1976), made up of both a settled and an enclosed nomadic component (Lattimore, 1962; Rowton, 1974), wherein nomads existed in a state of dependency in relation to settled populations that wielded disproportionate political power. Diverging from this model, scholars of Iron Age southern Levant have recently argued that nomadic groups, like the Edomites, developed a socially stratified society that built political institutions and controlled the Iron Age copper industry. Rather than existing in a subordinate social position, nomads represented the core of the emerging polity, driving socio-political processes both for themselves and arguably for the settled populations within their sphere of influence. What emerges is a model of enclosing nomadism (Abbas Alizadeh, 2010; Ben-Yosef, 2021), based on a polymorphous society (Lemche, 1985) whose population existed on a continuum between nomadic and settled.

In addition to an overreliance on analogies with the Bedouin model and the ancient Near Eastern textual record (Rowton, 1974), the reluctance to associate state formation with mobile populations results from the flawed expectation that sedentism necessarily precedes states. A reticence to accept the political importance of nomadic groups is also owing to the characteristically ephemeral nature of the material culture associated with mobile populations. The nomads of the southern Levantine EIA, however, are exceptionally visible within the archaeological record due to their command of a large-scale copper industry with a rich assemblage (Ben-Yosef, 2021).

Indeed, the development of social hierarchy within the southern Levant's Arabah valley is tied to control of copper exploitation, production, and trade (Ben-Yosef, 2021; Howland, 2021). A process of political consolidation in this region appears to have occurred soon after the departure of Egyptian forces from the Timna Valley in the twelfth century BCE (Ben-Yosef et al., 2019). Adapting models and technologies from the Egyptians, the nomadic population took charge of copper production in the Arabah, defended regional copper trade networks, and maintained stability over their territory (Ben-Yosef, 2021). Both the geographical extent of the Edomite polity and the broader structure of the economy are difficult to ascertain by virtue of the characteristically muted material signature of mobile populations.

7 Power, Ritual and Cooperation

In addition to being a traded commodity, copper in the southern Levant also retained symbolic associations and was arguably central to an ideology of elite legitimization (Howland, 2021). Imbuing metal objects with symbolism is a recognized phenomenon (Arnold, 1987; Budd & Taylor, 1995; Helms, 1993; Inomata, 2001). By extension, those involved in copper production are often marked with the same connotations. In the southern Levant, this model relies on the discovery of evidence of smelting within elite domestic contexts (Howland, 2021). An alternate scenario in which smelters are non-elite individuals attached to elite circles is also possible (Costin, 2005); however, a current model convincingly argues that copper smelters themselves, possessed highly specialized knowledge, traded on the positive association that their contemporaries had with copper production to legitimize their status in society (Sapir-Hen & Ben-Yosef, 2014). What emerged was a social class with enduring structural power in Levantine society (Howland, 2021). Whether this was power to coerce or merely logistical power over production and trade has yet to be established (Levy et al., 2014).

In southeast Arabia, smelting and metal objects were similarly imbued with ritual and symbolic connotations having been found in funerary contexts, hoards, cultic, or ceremonial spaces (Nashef, 2010; Goy et al., 2013; Benoist et al., 2015; Weeks et al., 2017; Rodrigo et al., 2017; Karacic et al., 2017; Frenez et al., 2021; Nasser S. Al-Jahwari et al., 2021). Hoards rich with finished metal objects, ingots, and slags are known also at settlements with ritual deposits at Masafi 1 in Fujairah (Benoist et al., 2012), and at Mudhmar East in central Oman where scores of copper alloy weapons, including facsimiles of quivers produced of copper alloy, were discovered in the floors of a prominent building (Gernez & Giraud, 2019; Jean et al., 2021).

Further evidence linking copper production, consumption and ritual has also been identified in the far reaches of the Rub al-Khali desert. Extensive evidence from three stratigraphic horizons spanning ca. 1300–800 BCE at Saruq al-Hadid in the UAE link ritualized deposits of high-quality status objects produced of a wide variety of metals and shapes, including exotic iron weapons, in association with copper smelting slags and feasting events (James Roberts et al., 2018; Weeks et al., 2019; Stepanov et al., 2019b; Stepanov et al., 2019a). The diversity expressed within the material culture at Saruq al-Hadid, connecting cultural spheres from Egypt to Iran, demonstrates profound connectivity in a limiting geography.

The site of Uqdat al-Bakrah, located in Oman ca. 100 km southeast of Saruq al-Hadid, is a comparable site with ritual significance. Similarly associated with a landscape of hundreds of circular pits of presumably different functions all linked to pyrotechnological practice, hundreds of copper-alloy objects and a smaller amount of fragmentary iron weaponry were discovered deposited over the surface of the desert floor. Objects include a wide range of types, including mostly heavy agricultural implements, vessels, and weapons. The first excavators of the site interpreted the location to be a metal workshop deep in the desert (Yule & Gernez, 2018), however, the data are also consistent with ritual deposition and decommissioning. Unlike at Saruq al-Hadid, very few slags or technical ceramics were recovered at the site.

In contrast to developments in the southern Levant, engaging in copper metallurgy and trade did not catalyse the development of social stratification and inequality in southeast Arabia. Rather, evidence is most consistent with an internal trade system of copper where, unlike the previous period during the Bronze Age, copper and copper-related materials were used in part to promote social cohesion. Primary production sites, such as at Raki 2, show very little evidence of elite administration and rather supplied localized networks of interaction to produce a wide range of objects that were consumed regionally. In some cases, evidence from sites located at the edge of the Rub al-Khali dune fields like Saruq al-Hadid and 'Uqdat al-Bakrah support the hypothesis that finished objects and bulk materials were provisioned, deposited or decommissioned in locations that were not necessarily tied to regional centers. The overarching pattern in southeast Arabia is one where industrial production may not have been driven by a need of elites to legitimize their own position in society or produce power through access to scarce materials, but rather materials like copper and its alloys were fed into a sector of society where power was generated through ritual. This stark contrast with other regions in southwest Asia, like the southern Levant, provides an important comparative perspective that highlights how industry need not center on social hierarchies and power imbalances to thrive.

Acknowledgments We would like to acknowledge the Ministry of Heritage and Tourism of the Sultanate of Oman, including Sultan Al-Bakri, Khamis Al-Asmi and Suleiman Al-Jabri, for their collaboration and permission to conduct fieldwork in Oman. We thank the communities in Wadi al-Raki, Yanqul and Dhahir al-Fawaris for welcoming us through the course of our fieldwork in the region. We are grateful to the editors of this volume for their patience and feedback. This research was supported by grants from National Aeronautics and Space Administration (ROSES) Research Opportunities in Space and Earth Sciences (#NNX13AO48G), Australian Research Council Discovery Early Career Award DE180101288, Johns Hopkins University Catalyst and Space@ Hopkins grants, and Danish National Research Foundation under grant DNRF119 – Centre of Excellence for Urban Network Evolutions (UrbNet). Finally, we thank Tom Levy, whose research has transformed our understanding ancient society in West Asia, especially in the southern Levant, and inspired many aspects of our own work in Oman.

References

Abbas Alizadeh. (2010). The Rise of the Highland Elamite State in Southwestern Iran: "Enclosed" or Enclosing Nomadism? *Current Anthropology, 51*(3), 353–383. https://doi.org/10.1086/652437

Ackerfeld, D., Abadi-Reiss, Y., Yagel, O., Harlavan, Y., Abulafia, T., Yegorov, D., & Ben-Yosef, E. (2020) Firing up the furnace: New insights on metallurgical practices in the Chalcolithic Southern Levant from a recently discovered copper-smelting workshop at Horvat Beter (Israel). *Journal of Archaeological Science: Reports, 33*, 102578. https://doi.org/10.1016/j.jasrep.2020.102578

Aksoy, Ö. C. (2018). Functions and uses of metallic axe-heads and arrowheads from Safah, Oman: An analysis of metalwork wear and weapon design. *Journal of Archaeological Science: Reports, 19*, 727–752. https://doi.org/10.1016/j.jasrep.2018.03.023

Al-Jahwari, N. S., Yule, P., Douglas, K. A., Pracejus, B., Al-Belushi, M., & El-Mahi, A. T. (Eds.). (2021). *The Early Iron Age Metal Hoard from the Al Khawd Area (Sultan Qaboos University), Sultanate of Oman.* Archaeopress.

Al-Jahwari, N. S. A. (2013). *Settlement patterns, development and cultural change in northern Oman Peninsula: A multi-tiered approach to the analysis of long-term settlement trends.* Archaeopress.

Al-Tikriti, W. Y. (2002). The south-east Arabian origin of the falaj system. *Proceedings of the Seminar for Arabian Studies, 32*, 117–138. http://www.jstor.org/stable/41223728

Al-Zahrani, A. A. A. (2014). *Mining in al-Baha Region, southwestern Saudi Arabia in Islamic Era: The Archaeology of Asham.* Unpublished PhD dissertation,. University of York.

Albright, W. F. (1939). The Israelite conquest of Canaan in the light of archaeology. *Bulletin of the American Schools of Oriental Research, 74*, 11–23. https://doi.org/10.2307/3218878

Arnold, J. E. (1987). *Craft specialization in the prehistoric Channel Islands, California.* University of California Press.

Artioli, G., Giardino, C., Guida, G., Lazzari, A., & Vidale, M. (2005). On the exploitation of copper ores at Shahr-i Sokhta (Sistan, Iran) in the 3rd millennium BC. In U. Franke-Vogt & H.-J. Weisshaar (Eds.), *South Asian archaeology 2003* (pp. 179–184). Verlag Linden Soft.

Avanzini, A., & Phillips, C. (2010). An outline of recent discoveries at Salut in the Sultanate of Oman. In A. Avanzini (Ed.), *Eastern Arabia in the first millennium BC* (pp. 93–108). L'Erma di Bretschneider.

Azzarà, V. M., & De Rorre, A. P. (2018). Socio-cultural innovations of the Final Umm an-Nar period (c.2100–2000 BCE) in the Oman peninsula: New insights from Ra's al-Jinz RJ-2. *Arabian Archaeology and Epigraphy, 29*(1), 10–26. https://doi.org/10.1111/aae.12095

Begemann, F., Hauptmann, A., Schmitt-Strecker, S., & Weisgerber, G. (2010). Lead isotope and chemical signature of copper from Oman and its occurrence in Mesopotamia and sites on the Arabian coast. *Arabian Archaeology and Epigraphy, 21*(2), 135–169. https://doi.org/10.1111/j.1600-0471.2010.00327.x

Belgrano, T. M., Diamond, L. W., Vogt, Y., Biedermann, A. R., Gilgen, S. A., & Al-Tobi, K. (2019). A revised map of volcanic units in the Oman ophiolite: Insights into the architecture of an oceanic proto-arc volcanic sequence. *Solid Earth, 10*(4), 1181–1217. https://doi.org/10.5194/se-10-1181-2019

Ben-Yosef, E. (2010). *Technology and social process: Oscillations in Iron Age copper production and power in southern Jordan.* Unpublished PhD dissertation, University of California, San Diego.

Ben-Yosef, E. (2016). Back to Solomon's Era: Results of the First Excavations at "Slaves' Hill" (Site 34, Timna, Israel). *Bulletin of the American Schools of Oriental Research, 376*, 169–198. https://doi.org/10.5615/bullamerschoorie.376.0169

Ben-Yosef, E. (2019). The architectural bias in current biblical archaeology. *Vetus Testamentum, 69*(3), 361–387. https://doi.org/10.1163/15685330-12341370

Ben-Yosef, E. (2020). And yet, a nomadic error: A reply to Israel Finkelstein. *Antiguo Oriente, 18*, 33–60.

Ben-Yosef, E. (2021). Rethinking the social complexity of Early Iron Age nomads. *Jerusalem Journal of Archaeology, 1*, 155–179. https://doi.org/10.52486/01.00001.6

Ben-Yosef, E., Liss, B., Yagel, O. A., Tirosh, O., Najjar, M., & Levy, T. E. (2019). Ancient technology and punctuated change: Detecting the emergence of the Edomite Kingdom in the Southern Levant. *PLoS One, 14*(9), e0221967. https://doi.org/10.1371/journal.pone.0221967

Ben-Yosef, E., Shaar, R., Tauxe, L., & Ron, H. (2012). A new chronological framework for Iron Age copper production at Timna (Israel). *Bulletin of the American Schools of Oriental Research, 367*, 31–71. https://doi.org/10.5615/bullamerschoorie.367.0031

Ben-Yosef, E., & Shalev, S. (2018). Social archaeology in the Levant through the lens of archaeometallurgy. In A. Yassur-Landau, E. Cline, & Y. M. Rowen (Eds.), *The social archaeology of the Levant: From prehistory to the present* (pp. 536–550). Cambridge University Press. https://doi.org/10.1017/9781316661468.031

Benoist, A. (2000). *La céramique de l'Age du Fer en Péninsule d'Oman (1350–300 av. J. -C.).* Unpublished PhD thesis, University of Paris.

Benoist, A. (2001). Quelques réflexions à propos de l'utilisation des céramiques dans la péninsule d'Oman au cours de l'Âge du Fer (1350-300 av. J.C.). *Paléorient, 27*(1), 45–67. https://www.persee.fr/doc/paleo_0153-9345_2001_num_27_1_4719

Benoist, A. (2010a). Authority and religion in South East Arabia during the Iron Age: A review of architecture and material from columned halls and cultic sites. In A. Avanzini (Ed.), *Eastern Arabia in the first millennium BC* (pp. 109–141). di Bretschneider.

Benoist, A. (2010b). Fouilles à Masāfī-3 en 2009 (Émirat de Fujayrah, Émirats Arabes Unis): premières observations à propos d'un espace cultuel de l'Âge du Fer nouvellement découvert en Arabie orientale. *Proceedings of the Seminar for Arabian Studies, 40*, 119–130.

Benoist, A., Bernard, V., Ohnenstetter, M., Ploquin, A., Saint-Gernez, F., & Schiettecatte, J. (2012). Une occupation de l'âge du fer à Masafi. Travaux récents de la Mission archéologique française aux E.A.U. dans l'émirat de Fujairah (Émirats Arabes Unis). *Chroniques Yéménites, 17*. https://doi.org/10.4000/cy.1803

Benoist, A., de Veslud, C. L. C., Goy, J., Degli Eposti, M., Armbruster, B., & Attaelmanan, A. G. (2015). Snake, copper and water in south-eastern Arabian religion during the Iron Age: The Bithnah and Masāfi evidence. In M. Arbach & J. Schiettecatte (Eds.), *Pre-Islamic South Arabia and its neighbours: New developments of research* (pp. 21–36). Archaeopress.

Ben-Dor Evian, S., Yagel, O., Harlavan, Y., Seri, H., Lewinsky, J., & Ben-Yosef, E. (2021). Pharaoh's copper: The provenance of copper in bronze artifacts from post-imperial Egypt at the end of the second millennium BCE. *Journal of Archaeological Science: Reports, 38*, 103025. https://doi.org/10.1016/j.jasrep.2021.103025

Berthoud, T., Besenval, R., Cleuziou, S., & Drin, N. (1978). *Les anciennes mines de cuivre de Sultanat d'Oman.* Université Pierre et Marie Curie.

Bienkowski, P. (1990). Umm el-Biyara, Tawilan and Buseirah in retrospect. *Levant, 22*(1), 91–109. https://doi.org/10.1179/lev.1990.22.1.91

Bietak, M. (2007). Egypt and the Levant. In T. Wilkinson (Ed.), *The Egyptian world* (pp. 417–448). Routledge.

Boucharlat, R. (1984). Les périodes pré-islamiques récentes aux Emirates Arabes Unis. In R. Boucharlat (Ed.), *Arabie orientale, Mésopotamie et Iran méridonal de l'âge du fer au début de la période islamique* (pp. 189–199). Editions Recherche sur les civilisations.

Boucharlat, R., & Lombard, P. (1985). The Oasis of Al-Ain in the Iron Age. Excavations at Rumeilah (1981–83). Survey at Hili 14. In *Archaeology in the United Arab Emirates* (pp. 44–73). Department of Antiquities and Tourism Al-Ain.

Boucharlat, R., & Lombard, P. (2001). Le Bâtiment G de Rumeilah (oasis d'Al Ain). Remarques sur les salles à poteaux de l'âge du Fer en Péninsule d'Oman. *Iranica Antiqua, 36*, 213–238. https://doi.org/10.2143/IA.36.0.107

Budd, P., & Taylor, T. (1995). The faerie Smith meets the bronze industry: Magic versus science in the interpretation of prehistoric metal-making. *World Archaeology, 27*(1, Symbolic Aspects of Early Technologies), 133–143. https://doi.org/10.1080/00438243.1995.9980297.

Carney, J. N., & Welland, M. J. P. (1974) *Geology and mineral resources of the Oman Mountains.* Institute of Geological Sciences Overseas Division Report No. 27.

Cleuziou, S., & Tosi, M. (2007). Collapse and transformation: The Wadi Suq period. In S. Cleuziou & M. Tosi (Eds.), *In the shadow of the ancestors: The prehistoric foundations of the early Arabian civilization in Oman* (pp. 257–276). Ministry of Heritage and Culture.

Cline, E. H. (2014). *1177 B.C. the year civilization collapsed.* Princeton University Press.

Coleman, R. G., & Bailey, E. H. (1981) '*Mineral deposits and geology of northern Oman as of 1974' – USGS Open-File Report 81–452 [Report].* Available at: http://pubs.er.usgs.gov/publication/ofr81452

Coleman, R. G., Bailey, E. H., Huston, C. C., El-Boushi, I. M., & Al-Hinai, K. M. (1979). The Semail ophiolite and associated massive sulfide deposits, Sultanate of Oman. In A. M. S. Al-Shanti (Ed.), *Evolution and mineralization of the Arabian–Nubian Shield* (pp. 179–192). Pergamon. https://doi.org/10.1016/B978-0-08-024467-9.50021-6

Condoluci, C., & Esposti, M. D. (2018). The function of the site. In A. Avanzini & M. Degli Eposti (Eds.), *Husn Salut and the Iron Age of South East Arabia* (pp. 363–370). L'Erma Di Bretschneider.

Córdoba, J. M. (2010). L'architecture domestique de l'Age du Fer (1300-300 a. C.) dans la péninsule d'Oman: quelques documents sur les villages et la culture des oasis. In A. Avanzini (Ed.), *Eastern Arabia in the first millennium BC* (pp. 143–157). di Bretschneider.

Costin, C. L. (2005). Craft production. In H. D. G. Maschner & C. Chippindale (Eds.), *Handbook of methods in archaeology* (pp. 1032–1105). AltaMira Press.

Courcier, A. (2014). Ancient metallurgy in the Caucasus from the sixth to the third millennium BCE. In B. W. Roberts & C. P. Thornton (Eds.), *Archaeometallurgy in global perspective: Methods and syntheses* (pp. 579–664). Springer. https://doi.org/10.1007/978-1-4614-9017-3_22

Crawford, H. (1996). Dilmun, victim of world recession. *Proceedings of the Seminar for Arabian Studies, 26,* 13–22. http://www.jstor.org/stable/41223567

Crawford, H. (1998). *Dilmun and its Gulf neighbours.* Cambridge University Press.

Cunliffe, B. (2005). *Iron Age communities in Britain: An account of England, Scotland and Wales from the seventh century BC until the Roman conquest.* Routledge. https://doi.org/10.4324/9780203326053

Curci, A., Carletti, M., & Tosi, M. (2014). The camel remains from site HD-6 (Ra's al-Hadd, Sultanate of Oman): An opportunity for a critical review of dromedary findings in eastern Arabia. *Anthropozoologica, 49*(2), 207–222.

Dardeniz, G. (2020). Why did the use of antimony-bearing alloys in Bronze Age Anatolia fall dormant after the Early Bronze Age?: A Case from Resuloğlu (Çorum, Turkey). *PLoS One, 15*(7), e0234563. https://doi.org/10.1371/journal.pone.0234563

de Jesus, P. S. (1982). Preliminary report of mining survey, 1981 (1401). *Atlal: The Journal of Saudi Arabian Archaeology, 6,* 63–79.

Deroin, J.-P., Téreygeol, F., & Heckes, J. (2012). Remote sensing study of the ancient Jabali silver mines (Yemen): From past to present. In R. Lasaponara & N. Masini (Eds.), *Satellite remote sensing: A new tool for archaeology* (pp. 231–245). Springer. https://doi.org/10.1007/978-90-481-8801-7_10

Desch, C. H. (1929). Sumerian Copper. *Report of the 96th Meeting of the British Association for the Advancement of Science,* 437–441.

Döpper, S. (2021). The middle and Late Bronze Age in Central Oman: New insights from Tawi Said, Al-Mudhairib and the Wilayat al-Mudhaybi. *Arabian Archaeology and Epigraphy,* 1–15. https://doi.org/10.1111/aae.12181

Drake, B. L. (2012). The influence of climatic change on the Late Bronze Age collapse and the Greek Dark Ages. *Journal of Archaeological Science, 39*(6), 1862–1870. https://doi.org/10.1016/j.jas.2012.01.029

Drews, R. (1993). *The end of the Bronze Age: Changes in warfare and the catastrophe ca. 1200 B.C.* Princeton University Press. 10.12987/9780691209975.

Finkelstein, I. (1994). The emergence of Israel: A phase in the cyclic history of Canaan in the third and second millennia BCE. In I. Finkelstein & N. Na'aman (Eds.), *From nomadism to monarchy: Archaeological and historical aspects of early Israel* (pp. 150–178). Israel Exploration Society.

Finkelstein, I. (2005). Khirbet en-Nahas, Edom and biblical history. *Tel Aviv, 32*(1), 119–125. https://doi.org/10.1179/tav.2005.2005.1.119

Finkelstein, I., & Singer-Avitz, L. (2008). The pottery of Edom: A correction. *Antiguo Oriente, 6*, 13–24.

Finkelstein, I., & Singer-Avitz, L. (2009). The pottery of Khirbet en-Nahas: A rejoinder. *Palestine Exploration Quarterly, 141*(3), 207–218. https://doi.org/10.1179/003103 209X12483454548202

Frenez, D. (2019). Cross-cultural trade and socio-technical developments in the Oman Peninsula during the Bronze Age, ca. 3200 to 1600 BC. *OCNUS, 27*, 9–49.

Frenez, D., Genchi, F., David-Cuny, H., & Al-Bakri, S. (2021). The Early Iron Age collective tomb LCG-1 at Dibbā al-Bayah, Oman: Long-distance exchange and cross-cultural interaction. *Antiquity, 95*(379), 104–124. https://doi.org/10.15184/aqy.2020.224

Gernez, G., & Giraud, J. (Eds.). (2019). *Taming the Great Desert: Adam in the prehistory of Oman.* Archaeopress.

Giardino, C. (2017). *Magan – The Land of copper: Prehistoric metallurgy of Oman.* Ministry of Heritage and Culture, Sultanate of Oman.

Goettler, G. W., Firth, N., & Huston, C. C. (1976). A preliminary discussion of ancient mining in the Sultanate of Oman. *Journal of Oman Studies, 2*, 43–56.

Golden, J. M. (2010). *Dawn of the metal age: Technology and society during the Levantine Chalcolithic.* Equinox.

Goy, J., Carlier, L., de Veslud, C., Degli Eposti, M., & Attaelmanan, A. G. (2013). Archaeometallurgical survey in the area of Masafi (Fujairah, UAE): Preliminary data from an integrated programme of survey, excavation, and physicochemical analyses. *Proceedings of the Seminar for Arabian Studies, 2013*, 127–143.

Gregoricka, L. A., & Sheridan, S. G. (2017). Continuity or conquest? A multi-isotope approach to investigating identity in the Early Iron Age of the Southern Levant. *American Journal of Physical Anthropology, 162*(1), 73–89. https://doi.org/10.1002/ajpa.23086

Harrower, M., Nathan, S., Dumitru, I. A., Lehner, J. W., Paulsen, P., Dollarhide, E. N., et al. (2021). From the Paleolithic to the Islamic Era in Wilayah Yanqul: The Archaeological Water Histories of Oman (ArWHO) Project Survey 2011-2018. *Journal of Oman Studies 22*, 1–21.

Häser, J. (2010). Continuity and change: Iron Age oasis settlements in Oman. In A. Avanzini (Ed.), *Eastern Arabia in the first millennium BC* (pp. 159–180). di Bretschneider.

Hassan Ahmed, A. (2022a). Classification and general distribution of mineral deposits in the Arabian–Nubian Shield: A review. In *Mineral deposits and occurrences in the Arabian–Nubian Shield* (pp. 69–87). Springer. https://doi.org/10.1007/978-3-030-96443-6_2

Hassan Ahmed, A. (2022b). Mining history of the Arabian–Nubian Shield. In *Mineral deposits and occurrences in the Arabian–Nubian Shield* (pp. 447–521). Springer International Publishing. https://doi.org/10.1007/978-3-030-96443-6_8

Hauptmann, A. (1985). *5000 Jahre Kupfer in Oman. Bd. 1: Die Entwicklung der Kupfermetallurgie vom 3. Jahrtausend bis zum Neuzeit.* Deutsches Bergbau-Musum.

Hauptmann, A. (2007). *The archaeometallurgy of copper.* Springer. https://doi.org/10.1007/978-3-540-72238-0

Hauptmann, A., & Weisgerber, G. (1981). Third millennium BC copper production in Oman. *Revue d'Archéométrie, 1*(1), 131–138.

Helms, M. W. (1993). *Craft and the kingly ideal: Art, trade, and power.* University of Texas Press. https://doi.org/10.7560/730748

Hester, J., Hamilton, R., Rahbini, A., Eskoubi, K. M., & Khan, M. (1983). Preliminary report on the third phase of ancient mining survey Southwestern Province – 1403 A.H. 1983. *Atlal: The Journal of Saudi Arabian Archaeology, 8*, 115–141.

Higham, T., van der Plicht, J., Ramsey, C. B., Bruins, H. J., Robinson, M., & Levy, T. E. (2005). Radiocarbon dating of the Khirbat-en Nahas site (Jordan) and Bayesian modeling of the results. In T. E. Levy & T. Higham (Eds.), *The Bible and radiocarbon dating: Archaeology, text and science* (pp. 164–178). Equinox.

Howland, M. D. (2021). *Long-distance trade and social complexity in Iron Age Faynan, Jordan.* Unpublished PhD dissertation, University of California, San Diego.

Inomata, T. (2001). The power and ideology of artistic creation. *Current Anthropology, 42*(3), 321–349. https://doi.org/10.1086/320475

Jean, M., Pellegrino, M. P., Bigot, L., Pinot, J., de Castéja, V., & Gernez, G. (2021). The Archaeological Site of Mudhmar East (Adam, Ad-Dakhiliyah, Oman): Results from the 2019 Excavations. *Journal of Oman Studies, 22*, 158–185.

Karacic, S., Boraik, M., Qandil, H., & David-Cuny, H. (2017). Snake decorations on the Iron Age pottery from Sarūq al-Ḥadīd: A possible ritual centre? *Proceedings of the Seminar for Arabian Studies, 47*, 139–150. http://www.jstor.org/stable/45163456

Kenoyer, J. M. (1998). *Ancient Cities of the Indus Valley Civilization.* Oxford University Press.

Kenoyer, J. M. (2008). Indus civilization. In D. M. Pearsall (Ed.), *Encyclopedia of archaeology* (pp. 715–733). Elsevier.

Kisnawi, A., de Jesus, P. S., & Rihani, B. (1983). Preliminary report on the mining survey, northwest Hijaz, 1982. *Atlal: The Journal of Saudi Arabian Archaeology, 7*, 76–83.

Klimscha, F. (2013). Innovations in Chalcolithic metallurgy in the Southern Levant during the 5th and 4th millennium BC. Copper-production at Tall Hujayrat al-Ghuzlan and Tall al-Magass, Aqaba Area, Jordan. In S. Burmeister, S. Hansen, M. Kunst, & N. Müller-Scheeßel (Eds.), *Metal matters. Innovative technologies and social change in prehistory and antiquity* (pp. 31–64). Leidorf.

LaBianca, Ø. S., & Younker, R. W. (1995). The Kingdoms of Ammon, Moab and Edom: The archaeology of Society in Late Bronze/Iron Age Transjordan (ca. 1400-500 BCE). In T. E. Levy (Ed.), *The archaeology of society in the Holy Land* (pp. 399–415). NY Facts on File.

Langgut, D., Finkelstein, I., & Litt, T. (2013). Climate and the Late Bronze collapse: New evidence from the southern Levant. *Tel Aviv, 40*(2), 149–175. https://doi.org/10.117 9/033443513X13753505864205

Lapp, P. W. (1967). *The conquest of Palestine in the light of archaeology.* Concordia Theological Monthly.

Lattimore, O. (1962). *Studies in frontier history: Collected papers, 1928–1958.* Oxford University Press.

Laursen, S., & Steinkeller, P. (2017). *Babylonia, the Gulf region, and the Indus: Archaeological and textual evidence for contact in the third and early second millennia B.C.* Eisenbrauns.

Lehner, J. W., & Yener, K. A. (2014). Organization and specialization of early mining and metal technologies in Anatolia. In B. W. Roberts & C. P. Thornton (Eds.), *Archaeometallurgy in global perspective* (pp. 529–557). Springer Verlag. https://doi.org/10.1007/978-1-4614-9017-3_20

Lemche, N. P. (1985). *Early Israel: Anthropological and historical studies on the Israelite society before the monarchy.* Brill.

Levy, T. E., & Najjar, M. (2014). Some thoughts on Khirbet En-Nahas, Edom, Biblical history and anthropology: A response to Israel Finkelstein. *Tel Aviv, 33*(1), 3–17. https://doi.org/10.1179/tav.2006.2006.1.3

Levy, T. E., Najjar, M., & Ben-Yosef, E. (Eds.). (2014). *New insights into the Iron Age archaeology of Edom, southern Jordan.* Cotsen Institute of Archaeology Press. https://escholarship.org/uc/item/7s92w18w

Levy, T. E., Najjar, M., & Higham, C. (2007). Iron Age complex societies, radiocarbon dates and Edom: Working with the data and debates. *Antiguo Oriente, 5*, 13–34.

Levy, T. E., Najjar, M., van der Plicht, J., Smith, N., Bruins, H. J., & Higham, C. (2005). Lowland Edom and the high and low chronologies: Edomite state formation, the Bible and recent archaeological research in southern Jordan. In T. E. Levy & C. Higham (Eds.), *The Bible and radiocarbon dating: Archaeology, text and science* (pp. 129–163). Routledge.

Levy, T. E., & Shalev, S. (1989). Prehistoric metalworking in the southern Levant: Archaeometallurgical and social perspectives. *World Archaeology, 20*(3), 352–372. https://doi.org/10.1080/00438243.1989.9980078

Loreto, R. (2021). The Role of Adummatu among the Early Arabian Trade Routes at the Dawn of the Southern Arabian Cultures. In G. Hatke & R. Ruzicka (Eds.), *South Arabian long-distance trade in antiquity: "Out of Arabia"* (pp. 66–110). Cambridge Scholars Publishing.

Magee, P. (1998). Settlement patterns, polities and regional complexity in the Southeast Arabian Iron Age. *Paléorient, 24*(2), 49–60. http://www.jstor.org/stable/41492711

Magee, P. (2000). Patterns of settlement in the southeast Arabian Iron Age. *Adumatu, 1*, 29–39.

Magee, P. (2003). Columned halls, power and legitimisation in the southeast Arabian Iron Age. In D. Potts, H. Al-Naboodah, & P. Hellyer (Eds.), Archaeology of the United Arab Emirates, Proceedings of the First International Conference on the Archaeology of the UAE (pp. 182–191). : Trident Press.

Magee, P. (2005). Cultural interaction and social complexity in the southeast Arabian Iron Age. *Iranica Antiqua, 33*(1), 135–142. https://doi.org/10.2143/IA.33.0.519127

Magee, P. (2014). *The archaeology of prehistoric Arabia: Adaptation and social formation from the Neolithic to the Iron Age.* Cambridge University Press. https://doi.org/10.1017/CBO9781139016667

Magee, P. (2015). When was the dromedary domesticated in the ancient Near East? *Zeitschrift für Orient-Archaeologie, 8*, 252–277.

Mallory-Greenough, L., Greenough, J. D., & Fipke, C. (2000). Iron Age gold mining: A preliminary report on camps in the Al Maraziq Region, Yemen. *Arabian Archaeology and Epigraphy, 11*(2), 223–236. https://doi.org/10.1111/j.1600-0471.2000.aae110207.x

Martin, M. (2011). *Egyptian-type pottery in the Late Bronze Age southern Levant.* Verlag der Österreichischen Akademie der Wissenschaften.

Mazzoni, S. (2010). Arabia in the first millennium BC: The Near Eastern background. In A. Avanzini (Ed.), *Eastern Arabia in the first millennium BC* (pp. 17–27). di Bretschneider.

McCorriston, J. (2011). *Pilgrimage and household in the ancient near east.* Cambridge University Press.

McCorriston, J. (2013). Pastoralism and pilgrimage: Ibn Khaldūn's Bayt-state model and the rise of Arabian Kingdoms. *Current Anthropology, 54*(5), 607–641. https://doi.org/10.1086/671818

Merkel, S., Hauptmann, A., Kirnbauer, T., & Téreygeol, F. (2016). Silver production at al-Radrad: Archaeometallurgical analysis of ore, slag and technical ceramics from early medieval Yemen. *Arabian Archaeology and Epigraphy, 27*(1), 107–126. https://doi.org/10.1111/aae.12070

Muhly, J. D. (1980). Bronze figurines and near eastern metalwork (review article). *Israel Exploration Journal, 30*(3/4), 148–161. http://www.jstor.org/stable/27925754

Nashef, K. (2010). Saruq al-Hadid: An industrial complex of the Iron Age II period. In A. Avanzini (Ed.), *Eastern Arabia in the first millennium BC* (pp. 213–226). di Bretschneider.

Nur, A., & Cline, E. H. (2000). Poseidon's horses: Plate tectonics and earthquake storms in the Late Bronze Age Aegean and eastern Mediterranean. *Journal of Archaeological Science, 27*(1), 43–63. https://doi.org/10.1006/jasc.1999.0431

Peake, H. (1928). The Copper Mountain of Magan. *Antiquity, 2*(8), 452–457. https://doi.org/10.1017/S0003598X00002520

Phillips, C. (2010). Iron Age chronology in south east Arabia and new data from Salut, Sultanate of Oman. In A. Avanzini (Ed.), *Eastern Arabia in the first millennium BC* (pp. 71–79). di Bretschneider.

Pollastro, R. M. (1998). *Geological provinces of the Arabian Peninsula and adjacent areas, 2000 (prv2bg).* U.S. Geological Survey, Central Energy Resource Team.

Porter, B. W. (2013). *Complex communities: The archaeology of Early Iron Age west-central Jordan*. University of Arizona Press.

Potts, D. T. (1990). *The Arabian Gulf in antiquity: From prehistory to the fall of the Achaemenid Empire*. Clarendon Press.

Potts, D. T. (1998). Some issues in the study of the pre-Islamic weaponry of southeastern Arabia. *Arabian Archaeology and Epigraphy, 9*(2), 182–208.

Potts, D. T. (2001). Before the Emirates: An archaeological and historical account of developments in the region ca. 5000 BCE to 676 CE. In A. Abed & P. Hellyer (Eds.), *United Arab Emirates: A new perspective* (pp. 28–69). Trident Press.

Prange, M. K. (2001). *5000 Jahre Kupfer im Oman: Bd. II Vergleichende Untersuchungen zur Charakterisierung des omanischen Kupfers mittels chemischer und isotopoischer Analysenmethoden*. Deutsches Bergbau-Museum.

Pugachevsky, A., Land, B., Cole-Baker, J., Cosi, M., & Thompson, H. (2009). *'Yemen mineral sector review report no. 47985-YE' G. Oil, mining policy division, oil, gas, mining and chemicals department, Middle East and North Africa region*. World Bank.

Radivojević, M., Rehren, T., Kuzmanović-Cvetković, J., Jovanović, M., & Northover, J. P. (2013). Tainted ores and the rise of tin bronzes in Eurasia, *c.* 6500 years ago. *Antiquity, 87*(338), 1030–1045. https://doi.org/10.1017/S0003598X0004984X

Radivojević, M., Roberts, B. W., Marić, M., Cvetković, J. K., & Rehren, T. (Eds.). (2021). *The rise of metallurgy in Eurasia: Evolution, organisation and consumption of early metal in the Balkans*. Archaeopress. https://doi.org/10.32028/9781803270425

Rainey, A. F. (2007). Whence came the Israelites and their language? *Israel Exploration Journal, 57*(1), 41–64.

Redford, D. B. (1992). *Egypt, Canaan, and Israel in ancient times*. Princeton University Press.

Redford, D. B. (2000). Egypt and Western Asia in the Late New Kingdom: An overview. In E. D. Oren (Ed.), *The sea peoples and their world: A reassessment* (pp. 1–20). University of Pennsylvania Press. https://doi.org/10.9783/9781934536438.1

Roberts, J., Weeks, L., Cable, C., Fillios, M., Aali, Y. Y. A., Radwan, M. B., et al. (2018). The role of wild terrestrial animals in late prehistoric societies of South-Eastern Arabia: New insights from Saruq al-Hadid. *Arabian Archaeology and Epigraphy, 29*(2), 115–134. https://doi.org/10.1111/aae.12112

Roberts, R. J., Greenwood, W. R., Worl, D. G., Dodge, F. C. W., & Kiilsgaard, T. H. (1975). *Mineral deposits in western Saudi Arabia*. DGMR.

Rodrigo, F. C., Vila, B., Albarracín, P., Bukhash, R. M., Abbar, S. O. A., Karim, M. B. R., et al. (2017). Excavations in Area 2A at Sarūq al-Ḥadīd: Iron Age II evidence of copper production and ceremonial activities. *Proceedings of the Seminar for Arabian Studies, 47*, 57–66. http://www.jstor.org/stable/45163449

Rothenberg, B. (1972). *Timna: Valley of biblical copper mines*. Thames and Hudson.

Rothenberg, B. (Ed.). (1990). *The ancient metallurgy of copper*. Institute for Archaeo-Metalurgical Studies.

Rothenberg, B., & Bachmann, H.-G. (1988). *The Egyptian mining temple at Timna*. Institute for Archaeo-Metallurgical Studies.

Rowton, M. B. (1974). Enclosed nomadism. *Journal of the Economic and Social History of the Orient, 17*, 1–30.

Rowton, M. B. (1976). *Dimorphic structure and the tribal elite*. Verlag des Anthropos Instituts.

Sallaberger, W., & Schrakamp, I. (2015). Philological data for a historical chronology of Mesopotamia in the 3rd millennium. In W. Sallaberger & I. Schrakamp (Eds.), *ARCANE III* (pp. 1–136). Brepols.

Sapir-Hen, L., & Ben-Yosef, E. (2013). The introduction of domestic camels to the southern Levant: Evidence from the Aravah Valley. *Tel Aviv, 40*(2), 277–285. https://doi.org/10.1179/033443513X13753505864089

Sapir-Hen, L., & Ben-Yosef, E. (2014). The socioeconomic status of Iron Age metalworkers: Animal economy in the 'Slaves' Hill', Timna, Israel. *Antiquity, 88*(341), 775–790. https://doi.org/10.1017/S0003598X00050687

Schmidt, C., & Döpper, S. (2019). The Hafit period at Al-Khashbah, Sultanate of Oman: Results of four years of excavations and material studies. *Proceedings of the Seminar for Arabian Studies, 29*, 265–274.

Schmidt, C., & Döpper, S. (2020). Die Anfänge der Kupferproduktion in Oman und ihre Verbindung zu den archaischen Texten aus Uruk. In J. Baldwin & J. Matuszak (Eds.), *mu-zu an-za₃-še₃ kur-ur₂-še₃ ḫe₂-ğal₂: Altorientalistische Studien zu Ehren von Konrad Volk* (pp. 433–443). Zaphon.

Schreiber, J. (2007). *Transformationsprozesse in Oasensiedlungen Omans. Die vorislamische Zeit am Beispiel von Izki, Nizwa und dem Jebel Akhdar.* Unpublished PhD Thesis,. Ludwig Maximilian University.

Schreiber, J. (2010). The Iron I-period in South-Eastern Arabia-a view from Central Oman. In A. Avanzini (Ed.), *Eastern Arabia in the first millennium BC* (pp. 81–90). di Bretschneider.

Singer, A. (2007). *The soils of Israel.* Springer. https://doi.org/10.1007/978-3-540-71734-8

Sivitskis, A. J., Lehner, J. W., Harrower, M. J., Dumitru, I. A., Paulsen, P. E., Nathan, S., et al. (2019). Detecting and mapping slag heaps at ancient copper production sites in Oman. *Remote Sensing, 11*(24), 3014. https://doi.org/10.3390/rs11243014

Smith, N. G., & Levy, T. E. (2008). The Iron Age pottery from Khirbat en-Nahas, Jordan: A preliminary study. *Bulletin of the American Schools of Oriental Research, 352*, 41–91. https://doi.org/10.1086/BASOR25609301

Stager, L. E. (1995). The impact of the Sea Peoples in Canaan (1185–1050 BCE). In T. E. Levy (Ed.), *The archaeology of society in the Holy Land* (pp. 332–348). Facts on File.

Stepanov, I., Weeks, L., Franke, K., Rodemann, T., Salvemini, F., Cable, C., et al. (2019a). Scrapping ritual: Iron Age metal recycling at the site of Saruq al-Hadid (U.A.E.). *Journal of Archaeological Science, 101*, 72–88. https://doi.org/10.1016/j.jas.2018.11.003

Stepanov, I., Weeks, L., Salvemini, F., Al Ali, Y., Radwan, M. B., Zein, H., et al. (2019b). Early Iron Age ferrous artefacts from southeastern Arabia: Investigating fabrication techniques using neutron tomography, optical microscopy, and SEM-EDS. *Archaeological and Anthropological Sciences, 11*(6), 2971–2988. https://doi.org/10.1007/s12520-018-0730-7

Thornton, C. P. (2009). The emergence of complex metallurgy on the Iranian plateau: Escaping the Levantine paradigm. *Journal of World Prehistory, 22*(3), 301–327. https://doi.org/10.1007/s10963-009-9019-1

van der Steen, E., & Bienkowski, P. (2006). How old is the kingdom of Edom?: A review of new evidence and recent discussion. *Antiguo Oriente, 4*, 160–179.

Ventura, R. (1974). An Egyptian rock stela in Timna. *Tel Aviv, 1*(3), 60–63. https://doi.org/10.1179/033443574788593421

Weeks, L. (1997). Prehistoric metallurgy at Tell Abraq, UAE. *Arabian Archaeology and Epigraphy, 8*(1), 11–85.

Weeks, L. (2004). *Early metallurgy of the Persian Gulf.* Brill. https://doi.org/10.1163/9789004495449

Weeks, L., Cable, C., Franke, K., Newton, C., Karacic, S., Roberts, J., et al. (2017). Recent archaeological research at Saruq al-Hadid, Dubai, UAE. *Arabian Archaeology and Epigraphy, 28*(1), 31–60. https://doi.org/10.1111/aae.12082

Weeks, L., Cable, C., Karacic, S., Franke, K. A., Price, D. M., Newton, C., et al. (2019). Dating persistent short-term human activity in a complex depositional environment: Late prehistoric occupation at Saruq al-Hadid, Dubai. *Radiocarbon, 61*, 1041–1075. https://doi.org/10.1017/RDC.2019.39

Weeks, L., Franke, K., & Cable, C. M. (2016). Investigating an enigmatic Iron Age metallurgical site in southeastern Arabia. *The Crucible, 8–9.*

Weeks, L., Keall, E., Pashley, V., Evans, J., & Stock, S. (2009). Lead isotope analysis of Bronze Age copper-based Artifacts from al-Midamman, Yemen: Towards the identification of an indigenous metal production and exchange system in the southern red sea region. *Archaeometry, 51*(4), 576–597. https://doi.org/10.1111/j.1475-4754.2008.00429.x

Weisgerber, G. (1977). Beobachten zum alten Kupfergebau in Sultanat Oman. *Der Anschnitt, 29,* 189–211.

Weisgerber, G. (1978). Evidence of ancient mining sites in Oman: A preliminary report. *The Journal of Oman Studies, 4,* 15–28.

Weisgerber, G. (1980). Patterns of early Islamic metallurgy in Oman. *Proceedings of the Seminar for Arabian Studies, 10,* 115–129.

Weisgerber, G. (1983). Copper production during the third millennium B.C. in Oman and the question of Makkan. *Journal of Oman Studies, 6*(2), 269–276.

Weisgerber, G. (1984). Makkan and Meluhha: Third millennium B.C. Copper production in Oman and the evidence of contact with the Indus Valley. In B. Allchin (Ed.), *South Asian archaeology 1981* (pp. 196–201). Cambridge University Press.

Weisgerber, G. (1987). Archaeological evidence of copper exploitation at 'Arja. *The Journal of Oman Studies, 9,* 145–172.

Weisgerber, G. (2007). Copper from Magan for Mesopotamian cities. In S. Cleuziou & M. Tosi (Eds.), *In the shadow of the ancestors: The prehistoric foundations of the early Arabian civilization in Oman* (pp. 195–303). Ministry of Heritage and Culture.

Weisgerber, G., & Al-Shanfari, A. A. B. (2013). *Archaeology in the Arabian Sea: Masirah and Al Hallaniyyat Islands, Sultanate of Oman.* Ministry of Heritage and Culture, Sultanate of Oman.

Weisgerber, G., & Yule, P. (1999). Preliminary report of the 1996 season of excavation in the Sultanate of Oman. In P. Yule (Ed.), *Studies in the archaeology of the Sultanate of Oman* (pp. 97–117). Verlag Marie Leidorf.

Yagel, O., Ben-Yosef, E., & Craddock, P. T. (2016). Late Bronze Age copper production in Timna: New evidence from Site 3. *Levant, 48*(1), 33–51. https://doi.org/10.1080/0075891 4.2016.1145943

Yener, K. A. (2000). *The domestication of metals: The rise of complex metal Industries in Anatolia.* Brill. https://doi.org/10.1163/9789004496934

Yule, P. (2014). *Cross-roads: Early and Late Iron Age south-eastern Arabia.* Harrassowitz Verlag.

Yule, P., & Gernez, G. (Eds.). (2018). *Early Iron Age metal-working workshop in the empty quarter, al-Ẓāhira province, Sultanate of Oman.* Habelt-Verlag.

Yule, P., Gaudiello, M., & Lehner, J. W. (2021). Al-Ṣalaylī valley in eastern Oman, Early Iron Age burial and multi-period copper production. *Zeitschrift für Orient-Archäologie, 14,* 276–317.

Yule, P., & Weisgerber, G. (1996). Die 14. Deutsche Archäologische Oman-Expedition 1995. *Mitteilungen der Deutschen Oreint-Gesellschaft, 128,* 135–155.

Zuckerman, S. (2007). Anatomy of a destruction: Crisis architecture, termination rituals and the fall of Canaanite Hazor. *Journal of Mediterranean Archaeology, 20*(1), 3–32. https://doi.org/10.1558//jmea.2007.v20i1.3

Copper Metallurgy in the Andes

Carol Schultze ⓘ **and Charles Stanish** ⓘ

Abstract Like the Eastern Hemisphere, the cultures of the Americas developed a rich tradition of metallurgy millennia ago. The Andes were an independent center of innovation, arriving at the similar technologies and end products in the absence of direct or indirect contact. It is fascinating that human ingenuity and experimentation arrived at similar industrial processes in at least two areas of the world. In this paper we review the great metallurgy traditions in the Pre-Columbian Andes with an emphasis on copper.

Keywords Andes · Metallurgy · Cultural evolution · Pyrotechnology · Copper

1 Introduction

The Andean mountain chain and corresponding culture region is very large, spanning no less than 8900 km from north to south (5000 km from Medellín, Colombia to Santiago, Chile), and ranging between 250 and 700 km from east to west (Fig. 1). Humans have occupied this region an estimated 16,000 years (Brandini et al., 2018; Prates et al., 2020) and have been engaged in copperworking since the Initial Period, circa 1800 BC. While there are commonalities to the technology and ideology surrounding metalworking across these zones, any general discussion must account for a multitude of local subregional cultures with independent (though intertwined) trajectories of metallurgical development.

C. Schultze (✉)
WestLand Engineering & Environmental Services, Seattle, WA, USA
e-mail: cschultze@westlandresources.com

C. Stanish
Institute for Advanced Studies in Culture and Environment, University of South Florida,
Tampa, FL, USA
e-mail: stanish.charles@gmail.com

© The Author(s), under exclusive license to Springer Nature Switzerland AG 2023
E. Ben-Yosef, I. W. N. Jones (eds.), *"And in Length of Days Understanding" (Job 12:12): Essays on Archaeology in the Eastern Mediterranean and Beyond in Honor of Thomas E. Levy*, Interdisciplinary Contributions to Archaeology,
https://doi.org/10.1007/978-3-031-27330-8_60

Fig. 1 The Andes

We define the major mineral and metalworking zones in the Andes as Colombia-Ecuador, North-Central Peru, Peruvian and Bolivian Altiplano, North Chile and Argentina, and South Coast Peru (Fig. 2). We will also distinguish between the pre-Inca and Inca period approaches to copper working. People arrived as transhumant hunter-fisher-gatherers before the Holocene. Over the millennia, people developed an amazingly rich array of cultures and societies of varying levels of complexity. The first complex societies in the region emerged in the late 4th millennium BC at sites in the Casma and Supe valleys (Stanish, 2020), culminating in the empire of the Inca in the fifteenth century of the common era (Table 1).

Copper Metallurgy in the Andes

Fig. 2 Locations mentioned in text

The earliest evidence for metal working in the Andes at present comes from a site in the high altiplano regions of southern Peru. Excavations at the site of Jiskairumoko discovered a 4000-year-old neckless with native gold and sodalite beads (Aldenderfer

Table 1 Chronology in the central Andes

Period	Date range
Late period	AD 1400–1532
Late intermediate period	AD 1100–1400
Middle horizon	AD 600–1100
Early intermediate period	100 BC – AD 600
Early horizon	800–100 BC
Initial period	1800–800 BC
Late archaic	3200–1800 BC
Middle archaic	6000–3200 BC
Early archaic	12,000–6000 BC

et al., 2008). The pre-Inca cultures pioneered most of the techniques that characterize Andean metalwork, however a broad distinction can be made between pre-Inca and Inca approaches. This is not a difference of kind, but of scale. While coastal Chimú (AD 900–1450) and Sicán (AD 750–1350) cultures as well as highland Wari and Tiwanaku ones utilized specialized labor, established outposts to control raw materials and labor, and controlled the distribution of finished products, the Inca scaled this up in a meaningful way (at least as can be viewed in the archaeological record). To a greater extent than before, the Inca structured expansionary activities toward the pursuit, processing, and socially stratified distribution of metals (Fig. 3).

A quick caveat should be put forward regarding the isolation of copper working for study in the Andean context. As we will see, copper occurs in a variety of locations alongside many other precious metals, semi-precious stones, and utilitarian minerals. Each of these had applications and people experimented with all the materials available in their environment. Further, the most common metal 'stock' used in the Andes was *tumbaga,* an alloy combining varying parts copper, silver, and gold. Surface treatments were used to bring out the color and luster needed for any particular crafted object, and many of the items reported by Spaniards as 'gold and silver' would have been made of these *tumbaga* alloys.

Copper working must be viewed as part of an evolving pyrotechnological and metallurgical complex that took place in the context of multi-crafting that included more than just precious metals and firing ceramics (Schultze, 2013). Sites such as Punanave in Puno, Peru show a range of craft industries including lithic tool production, high temperature smelting, fiber processing (spindle whorls), and shell bead manufacture. This site was occupied from at least AD 1000 to the Spanish Colonial Period beginning in 1532. Trace metal and isotopic analyses corroborate these archaeological data, as the sediment cores found evidence for metallurgy as early as the Tiwanaku state circa AD 500–1000 (Guédron et al., 2021). Smelting crucibles and adhered slag were recorded at this site, along with bits of unprocessed red ochre (hematite) and copper ores. These categories of artifacts co-occur in a ridgeline workshop location whose use-life spans all ceramic periods (Schultze, 2008: 143–145, 189, 488). Copper may be the basis of central Andean metallurgy, as argued by Lleras (2013: 42), but it was not pursued as an isolated industry (until

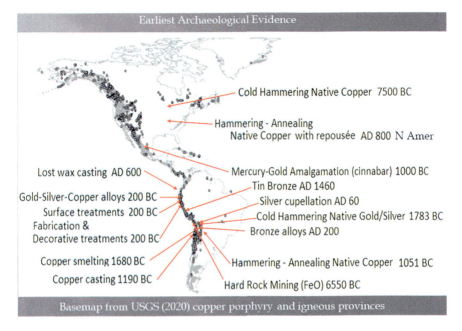

Fig. 3 Chronology of metallurgical developments across the Americas

perhaps the Inca period). Therefore, the following sections discusses metals and metallic ores as a group.

2 Metal Artifacts in the Prehistoric Andes

Exquisitely crafted items have been collected from all along the length of the Andes (Emmerich, 1965; McEwan, 2000). There was an emphasis on ornamentation in silver and gold, but copper and bronze were favored for utilitarian goods and weaponry. There was an emphasis on the cultic and political uses of crafted metals. Specific items that require definition are *Tumis*, aka ceremonial knives, and *Keros* which are drinking tumblers with a slightly concave form. *Tupus* are a pin-like clothing fastener that is preferentially made out of metal and *naipes* are rectangular standardized copper sheets that are used for interregional exchange (Fig. 4).

Metal goods held in museums, regional bank, and private collections include *tumi* ceremonial knives, plaques, beads, burial masks; rings, pectorals, backflaps, earspools, nose ornaments, crowns and drinking vessels (King, 2000; Larco de Alvarez-Calderón, 2000). Sumptuary utilitarian items include gold tweezers, lime bottles, and spatulas for coca-chewing, as well as elaborately decorated tools that would not have been functional.

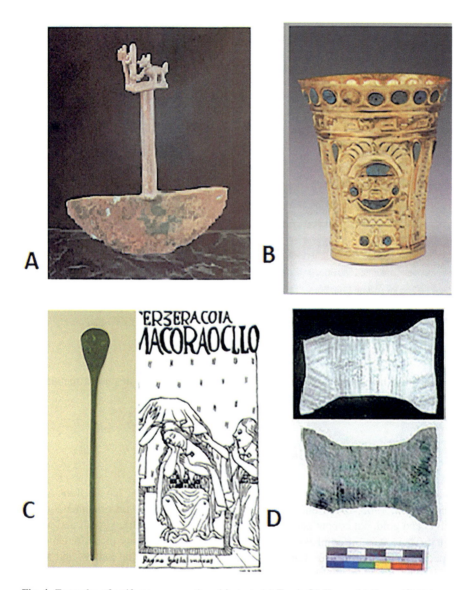

Fig. 4 Examples of artifact types mentioned in text: (**a**) Tumi, (**b**) Keros, (**c**) Tupu, (**d**) Naipes. (Reproduced from Carcedo, 1998; Göransson & Carcedo de Mufarech, 2011; Metropolitan Museum of Art open source collection with tupu use illustrated by Guaman Poma de Ayala 1613; Shimada & Merkel, 2021)

The Inca Empire reserved the use of gold and silver to elite classes and made it a high priority to control the mining and production of metals (Lechtman, 1996). The great Andean chroniclers and historians describe the use of silver and gold in the great temple district of Cuzco, including delicately fabricated figurines displaying the plants, animal, life-size people, and customs of the realm, as well as wall

Copper Metallurgy in the Andes

coverings of hammered gold or silver (as corresponded to the deities of the sun and moon). De la Vega details five fountains which were fed from different sources using pipes of solid gold. In the Inca capitol, even, "modest utensils used in the temple, such as pots and pans, or pitchers, were also made of the precious metals" (de la Vega, 1979 [1608]: 120). He identifies this as an element of Inca statecraft, and that each provincial capital (e.g. Tumbez) was also equipped with gold and silver covered temples for the worship of the sun and for the housing of the 'chosen women' (de la Vega, 1979 [1608]: 372). The quantities of gold, silver, and precious stone were so great that by the time the Spanish Conquistadors had looted their way to Cuzco and the massive hoard of treasures therein, Cieza de Leon reports, "It irritated them to see so much gold. Many left it, scoffing at it, not wanting to take more than some delicate and fine little jewels for their Indian women.... When they attacked villages, they found large amounts of silver. They brought some to the mound (in Cuzco) and left a great deal ..." (Cieza de León, 1998 [1553]: 319).

Figurines are a high-status item associated with ritual offerings (Dransart, 2000: 79 figs. 4.1, 4.3; Reinhard, 1992: 131 fig. 14). Three-dimensional human figures, often clothed in textiles and feathers, were constructed of dozens of intricately interwoven hammered sheets of *tumbaga,* gold, silver or bronze. Reinhard found a garbed silver figurine at a high-altitude ceremonial platform on the volcano Copiapó in Chile. Figurines, both human and llama, made of high-valued Spondylus shell were also recovered. The Inca in particular crafted gold and silver anthropomorphic and zoomorphic figurines that were left at offering sites along thousands of kilometers of pilgrimage routes (Bauer & Stanish, 2001).

Finds on sunken ridgelines adjacent to the shores on the Island of the Sun in Lake Titicaca demonstrated that both the Tiwanaku (ca. AD 400–1100) and Inca cultures made offerings of precious metal artifacts at areas on the water's edge (Delaere et al., 2019; Pareja, 1992). Hundreds of ritual offerings were recovered in two separate underwater expeditions lead by Reinhard in 1989 and 1990 followed by Delaere a generation later. The objects were placed inside carved andesite stone boxes and submerged (Delaere, 2017). The Middle Horizon metal artifacts included several Tiwanaku puma incensarios, gold keros, a gold plaque engraved with the front-face deity, a gold beaker, gold foil, spondylus, lapidary objects, stone anchors, and camelid offerings (Delaere et al., 2019: 8237).

High status tombs of the Moche Lord of Sipán (AD 50–300) and Middle Sicán Huaca Loro (AD 900–1100) have yielded vast quantities of exquisitely crafted metal artifacts (Alva & Donnan, 1993; Shimada et al., 2000). Some of the gold and silver objects including headdresses; eye, nose, and chin ornaments; earspools; necklaces; ceremonial knives; backflaps; and bells. Copper was used to created pellets inside of rattles, beads of human heads, peanuts, and other ornaments.

Hammered gold, silver, and copper alloy plaques which date to the Early Horizon Siguas culture (200 BC–AD 100) found in the Sihuas Valley of Northern Peru (McEwan & Haeberli, 2000). These are *tumi*-shaped and decorated with repoussé of anthropomorphic designs. Some of the imagery is that of a front facing deity common at this time in the Andes. Metal plaques and textiles, decorated with ideological content, may have covered the highly visible stone panel façades on the terraces of the Akapana pyramid at Tiwanaku (Kolata, 2003: 183). It is possible that repoussé and engraved metal plaques covered public buildings with official histories or other materialized content of value to the state during Tiwanaku and Inca periods.

A hammered gold burial mask was recovered from an elite burial at the Putuni palace at the site of Tiwanaku (Couture & Sampeck, 2003: 253, fig. 9.41; Kolata, 1993). A silver tube containing pigment was also recovered, along with a polished copper mirror and smaller finds. Hammered and repoussé gold burial masks held in private collections are also published in the Sanchez-Young volume.

Tiwanaku-style cast gold pieces are naturalistic bird and animal figurines (Young-Sánchez, 2004: figs.2.39, 2.38). The plaques are decorated with engraving and rocker- stamping, and one has red pigment-filled incisions, depicting the front face deity (Young-Sánchez, 2004: fig. 2.41). Others are engraved and stamped plaques that depict llamas and serpents.

The sites of Tulán 54 and Tulán 85 in Atacama, northern Chile, yielded burials with hammered gold and copper artifacts. Sites are dated between 1130 and 890 BC. It is argued that herders that lived in the region in small dwellings around 1200 BC used native gold and copper, which was quite abundant in the area.

Gold hammer-repoussé portrait keros, some rubbed with red ochre, were recovered from Atacama sites Callejon Larrache – Conde Duque and Casa Parroquial dating from AD 500–900. They are housed at the Museo Arqueológico Gustavo Le Paige in San Pedro de Atacama, Chile.

Skill in metalwork appears to be one avenue through which status was achieved. At Dos Cabezas in the Jequetepeque Valley near Trujillo in northern Peru, a Moche I burial of a 20-year-old male, dating to circa 200 BC., was wrapped in extremely finely made copper headbands. This individual also had several metal shields, mace heads, atl-atl launchers, metal chisels, metal axes, and darts. Insignia of rank included metal earspools, several elaborate nose ornaments, and a bronze mummy mask. In his hand, he held small metal-working chisels (Donnan, 2001). This suggests that the individual was both a warrior and a metallurgist.

Tupu pins were used for fastening clothing and were made of bronzes and tumbaga alloys (Vetter & Guerra, 2017). There was no coinage in the ancient Andes. However, rectangular copper sheets from the far northern coast, called *naipes*, could have served as a kind of currency. These standardized metal objects of various sizes and weights, also called axes and llamitas, have properties suggestive of media of exchange (Shimada & Merkel, 2021). Specifically, they are portable, recognizable, consistent in shape, and are found in bundles, implying increased value in quantity. They range in size from about 4–10 cm in length. They are reported from Lambayeque, Vicus and Piura regions of northern Peru (Hosler et al., 1990: 19). Caches of naipes have been found in elite tombs at sites such as Huaca Menor, where a stack of 500 arsenical bronze specimens of the same size and form were found. Elite tombs at Huaca Loro had caches of *tumbaga* scrap (up to 300 g.) along with the finer finished objects. The massed produced copper or bronze axes for export (Shimada & Szumilewicz, 2019) most likely also served as a medium of exchange on the coast.

Copper and bronze alloys were more commonly those used toward utilitarian ends, including stoneworking chisels, tweezers, needles, awls, axes, fishhooks and mace- and axe-heads. Undated finds from the Diaguita area of Chile show a military emphasis and include, star-shaped mace heads, wrist guards for archery, rectangular knife blades, axes with flaring wigs, disks with a flat handles and wire earrings, along with chisels and tweezers (Burger, 1995; Lothrop, 1946).

Mirrors were made of polished gold, silver, obsidian, anthracite coal ($C_{15}H_{11}O$), bronze, pyrite (FeS_2), and polished volcanic stone. Precious metal, though valued, was only one of several materials that could be used in sacred and high-status contexts. Semi-precious gemstone, spondylus, feathers, finely woven cloth were esteemed as highly as precious metals.

Lead artifacts have been reported from pre-Hispanic contexts. There are Inca period lead bola projectiles reported from Mantaro Valley (Howe & Petersen, 1994) and described by the traveler von Tschudi (1865: 219). Further, an analysis of funerary lots from the Casma polity circa AD 700 to 1400 identified an unexpectedly large quantity of lead objects including a spindle whorl and lead scrap, alongside copper lead alloys (Vogel et al., 2015). Copper mines were identified within 4 km of the site.

Lead isotopes can be used to identify ore sources and efforts are underway to identify patterns of lead isotope distribution across the Andes. Studies have found that ore bodies can be differentiated east to west, and that bronzes from the Altiplano region can be distinguished from those in the Central Andes (Macfarlane & Lechtman, 2016).

This is in no way an exhaustive list of Andean metal artifact types and assemblages, however it presents a general picture of the uses of metal in the pre-Columbian period, as well as the ideological importance of metalworking. In addition to these major finds, smaller fragments of worked metal are described in most archaeological reports in the Andes. Metal in some quantity is found at nearly every sizable archaeological site in the area.

3 Ores and Ore Processing

Like other global centers of metallurgical innovation, the Andes have abundant deposits of copper polymetallic ores (Radivojević & Roberts, 2021: 5). The Andes are the highest mountains peaks to be found outside of the Himalayas. They were formed by the convergence and subduction of the Nazca Plate beneath the South American continent, a process that continues to this day (Kay et al., 2005).

Metallic ores can be formed by a variety of igneous, hydrothermal, and even sedimentary processes (Robb, 2005). The common factors that contribute to the formation and precipitation of metals include extreme pressure, rapidly changing geological conditions (e.g., lateral slip faults), and hydrothermal action. These complex processes have been creating metals and ores since the beginning of geologic time – thousands of millions of years – and have left large and small mineral ore deposits pocketed about the earth's surface (Rassmussen, 2012).

The uplift of the Andean mountains creates perfect conditions for formation of all types of minerals (Tassara & Echaurren, 2012). Among these, molten thermal deposits at convergence zones in the sea floor, forming metallic deposits that are incorporated into volcanic magma that uplifted into significant gold, silver, and copper deposits in the highest altitudes (Petersen, 2010: 41–45). Copper additionally forms via copper porphyry deposits, and forms as a precipitate in sedimentary deposits.

The locations of any given mineral resource – e.g., copper, gold, silver, hematite, cinnabar, fine grain basalts, rose quartz, opal, onyx, topaz, slate, even nitrates, and a myriad of others – are unpredictable, but not inherently rare. There are economically important mineral resources in all zones throughout the western coast of South America.

Copper (Cu) is found in porphyry copper deposits and volcanic deposits (Ozdemir & Sahinoglu, 2018). Copper mineral ores are classified as sulfide, oxide and native (Hofman, 2015). Smelting temperatures and techniques vary for each of these ore types. An analogous classification can be made for silver and gold, into sulfide and native (Palyanova, 2020). Galena (PbS) is the most common sulfide ore in which silver and gold are found as impurities. The noble metals (silver, gold) are the least reactive and thus do not form stable oxide ores (Perroud, 2021). Any oxides that may form as precipitate will quickly degrade under normal conditions.

Copper sulfide ores, from a metallurgical perspective, consist of CuS and FeS with 'gangue' impurities such as Ni or As. Some examples of sulfide ores are covellite (CuS), chalcocite (Cu_2S), enargite ($3Cu_2S \cdot As_2S_5$), chrysocolla [$Cu_2H_2Si_2O_5(OH)_4$], and chalcopyrite ($Cu_2S.Fe_2S_3$ or $CuFeS_2$). Examples of oxide ores are cuprite (Cu_2O), malachite [$CuCO_3 \cdot Cu(OH)$], azurite [$2CuCO_3 \cdot Cu(OH)_2$], chrysocolla ($CuSiO_3$ + $2H_2O$), and atacamite [$CuCl_2 \cdot 3Cu(OH)_2$ or $Cu(OH,Cl)_2 \cdot 3H_2O$]. Native copper can be very pure containing 99.92% Cu with minor impurities such as Ag, Au, Fe, Ni, or As.

The sulfide ores chrysocolla, azurite, or malachite were preferred types of raw materials. These were available in outcrops in both mountain and coastal regions, weathering providing the mechanism by which the lower oxidizing zones were exposed. There is also evidence for access to the deeper chalcocite, covellite, and chalcopyrite enrichment zone deposits below the water table, specifically, "vein occurrences ... from the weathering zone where transformation to oxides was not complete" (Petersen, 2010: 50; Carcedo, 1998).

Copper ores were first collected as semiprecious stones for inlay and adornments in the Andes. In North and Central America, this continued as a principal use of copper ores into the later periods. Copper was found in rocks of a variety of colors, frequently with a blue or green color, and was often mixed with silver and gold. Sepúlveda et al. (2014, 2021) discuss the widespread use of use of copper mineral pigments in the Atacama desert. Mining was a simple matter of following pure copper with intermittent pockets of pure metallic gold or silver. Silver mixed in the copper vein was found by 'trial and error' search through copper veins to depths where the mineralizing fluids deposited richer metal. Mining of these sorts of pure metal deposits was reported from the Lipéz region of Bolivia, near San Pedro de Atacama (Petersen, 2010: 36).

Gold (Au) was most commonly collected in alluvial deposits. Also silver and mercury could be retrieved from placers that are located near up-slope vein deposits. Gold was primarily harvested from placer deposits, so winnowing/washing and annealing was usually sufficient. Electrum was used in its unrefined state and no attempt was made to separate the gold from silver. The presence of mercury in many of the ore bodies would have lent itself to the discovery of amalgamation processing of both gold and silver (Brooks et al., 2013).

Silver (Ag) was commonly available in gossan deposits. A gossan is an extremely oxidized, decomposed and/or weathered rock. This is typically the upper and exposed part of a mineral vein or ore deposit. In an ideal gossan or 'iron cap' all that remains are iron oxides and quartz often in the form of boxworks (irregular, honeycomb patterns). It is also possible for quartz (SiO_2) and iron oxides, limonite ($FeO(OH) \cdot H_2 0$), goethite (ferrous quartz), and jarosite [$K_2Fe{+}{+}6(SO_4)4(OH)_{12}$]to exist as pseudomorphs that have replaced pyrite (FeS_2)and primary ore minerals. It is most common for gossan to appear as a red stain against the background rock due to the quantity of oxidized iron. It also tends to be a high spot on the rock because of the erosion resistant quartz and iron oxides. Most gossans are red, yellow, or orange, but black gossans also result from manganese oxides that form at the oxidized portion of the mineral deposits. Miners and prospectors use gossans as guides to buried ore deposits.

Lead (Pb) and platinum (Pb) were also available and worked on some occasions (Scott & Bray, 1994). Lead functions as a collector for silver in the cupellation refining process. Galena (PbS) was used as a collector for silver during smelting. Argentiferous galena is an important silver ore in the Andes. The Quechua term for galena is, *Sorojche*, same term as altitude sickness, translated as "that which runs with silver during smelting," (Petersen, 2010: 6).

Mercury (Hg) was a source of vibrant red pigment and is also useful as a collector for silver and gold in a refining processed known as 'amalgamation' processing. Gabriel Prieto et al. (2016) report that cinnabar (HgS) was used since at least the middle of the second millennium BC. One known source of cinnabar is located near the highland town of Huancavelica, which became the primary source of mercury for amalgamation of silver during the Colonial period. Documentary information (Garcilaso de la Vega in the seventeenth century) indicates that the toxic properties of mercury were understood, and that mercury was retorted from cinnabar in the Inca period (Arriaza et al., 2018; Burger & Leikin, 2018).

Iron (Fe) is present in the ores of the Andes, for example iron oxide (ochres). These were used as pigments ranging from red to black and even purple. Additionally, iron appears as a remnant impurity in Moche copper artifacts that have been analyzed (Friedman et al., 1972). However, there is no evidence for iron smelting emerging as an industry in the Andes. The high temperatures (circa 1550 °C) required to forge iron (Carcedo, 1998: 67) and the minimal contribution that iron could make to the prestige economy likely combined to dis-incentivize experimentation. Additionally, there are superior sources of iron (banded iron formations) in Brazil which is currently a leading world exporter of iron. That would be the location to look for any pre-Columbian experimentation in iron working, rather than the Andes. The Andes are more noted for copper porphyry deposits.

Mining practices in the pre-Columbian period included placer, open pit, and underground mines. Gold was acquired through placer mining of golden sand and nuggets running down from the high-altitude erosional vein deposits. Gold panning can be an individual or household level activity, although the Inca instituted large scale placer mining using hydraulic engineering to extract gold- bearing mud from galleries, pits and gold-bearing mud from caves and tunnels along the sides of the ravine (Berthelot, 1986: 78).

Silver was largely hewn from gossan deposits. A Colonial period (1540–1577) report from North Chile and Argentina indicates that silver miners at Huantajaya, Chile, "simply gouged out chunks of native silver from the conspicuous surface outcrops. Some bonanzas of nearly pure silver weighed as much as one hundred pounds" (Brown & Craig, 1994: 311). For copper and gold, pits were rarely excavated to depths below sunlight. Miners commonly opened several shallow adits in softer alluvial deposits, instead of digging deep adits or attempting to chisel into harder metamorphic or igneous stone (Carcedo, 1998).

Significant ancient mining districts have been recorded in the copper-rich Atacama Desert, Northern Chile (Figueroa et al., 2013). Beads, pigments, and copper objects circulated from here throughout the southern Andes beginning in the earliest ceramic periods. Figueroa and colleagues summarize an assemblage of some 650 archaeological objects related to mining production and seven mummified human remains of miners from cave-in contexts, including the famous Copper Man (Bird, 1979). The arid Atacama Desert provided remarkable preservation of these assemblages, which have been radiocarbon dated to a range cal AD 291 (1804 ± 48 BP) to cal AD 1242 (Figueroa et al., 2013: 8). They describe an extended tool kit that includes stone hammers and digging tools hafted on algarrobo (*Prosopis chilensis*) handles using llama sinew attachments. In addition to the mining tools, the complete toolkit accounts for transportation of the ore in baskets on llama caravans, and personal items including clothing, foodstuffs, and coca leaves.

All types of ores were refined into pure metal. The refining process involved several steps. First ores were crushed, for example with *quimbaletes* (large rocker stones attached to wooden poles). More than a thousand *quimbaletes* were reported from the Cochasayhause site in the Apurimac district west of Cusco, North-Central Peru. Additional large reported prehispanic smelter operations in North-Central Peru were at Chan Chan near Trujillo, and Batan Grande in Lambayeque (Shimada, 2009), with a major copper processing sector found at Cerro Songoy spanning 90 BC to AD 970 (Sharp, 2009: 66). Beneficiation is the crushing and sorting of metal-bearing mineral ore. Smaller quality ore pieces were then selected and crushed in a mortar (Lechtman, 1976).

With sulfide ores, low temperature roasting can be used to drive off the sulfur. In twentieth century experiments, finely powdered copper sulfide ore begins roasting at 200 °C, with staged reactions taking place at 330 °C, 550 °C and 1069 °C. In order to drive off all the sulfur, the roasting must be slow enough to consume all the products at each of these temperature levels (Vetter Parodi, 2008). Annealing requires temperatures as low as 350–400 °C (Domanski & Webb, 2007).

For comparison, kiln firing of earthenware pottery requires temperatures in the range of 600–800 °C (Maggetti et al., 2010). The control of oxidizing and reducing atmospheres been mastered in ceramic firing kilns by Early Horizon cultures, for example Chavín, Chimú, and Qeya (Formative Tiwanaku) who produced fine polished blackware ceramics for elite consumption and export.

These experiments led to the development of higher temperature smelting operations. The crushed ore was mixed with charcoal and fired. During combustion, the charcoal reacted with oxygen and resulted in a pure metal which separated from the slag by gravity during cooling. Pure copper has a melting point of 1085 °C. Gold's melting point is 1064 °C. The melting point of Cu_2S is 1130 °C. Although in replication experiments, it was necessary to attain temperature of 1300 °C for 1 h to extract copper from local ores (Donnan, 1973). The ideal temperature for annealing copper-arsenic and gold alloys is approximately 300–400 °C. (Shimada et al., 2007). Gossan deposits of argentiferous Galena (AgPbS) are the most commonly reported ore sources for silver. Galena has a melting point of 1114 5 °C, although lead melts at 327.5 °C, and silver at 961.8 °C (Hofman, 2015: 69). The addition of copper to silver lowers their respective melting points from 1083 °C and 961.8 °C to 779 °C for the combined silver-copper alloy (Shimada, 1998: 48).

On the north coast of Peru, blow furnaces were used requiring several workers to stoke the fires to a sufficient heat for smelting. An excellent illustration of this is found sculptured on a Moche ceramic piece which shows four (possible five) workers stoking a circular furnace with *tumi* knives and other metal objects in the center (Donnan, 1998: 10, 11). This method uses either an above or belowground furnace, stoked by a number of people blowing on the fire through copper or reed tubes (Donnan, 1973: 293).

In the Southern Andes, the preferred smelting furnace was the wind-driven *wayra* or *huayrachina* (van Buren & Mills, 2005; Vetter Parodi, 2008). The *wayra* is an upright ceramic construction, with vent holes along the side. It is placed along ridgelines to take advantage of strong winds. Crucibles full of crushed ore, flux and reducing agents are placed inside and the fire is heated by the action of the wind. Camelid dung, called *taquia*, was the main fuel available in the high-altitude mining districts (Fig. 5).

To extract pure silver requires an additional oxidizing step (called cupellation). Lead functions as a collector for silver. As such, smelting argentiferous galena with a charcoal reducing agent will result in a button of purified lead-silver bullion. To separate these two metals, a reverberatory or draft furnace (called a *tocochimbo* in the Andes) is used to oxidize the lead, leaving the noble metal silver behind in its metallic state. The lead forms lead-oxide (litharge) which can be mechanically separated from the pure silver metal. The litharge can be smelted directly into lead metal, or recycled back to the *wayra* furnace to serve as a collector for additional silver smelts (Xie & Rehren, 2009).

Fig. 5 Example of production steps mentioned in text: (**a**) Quimbalete, (**b**) Tuyeres, (**c**) Wayra. (Reproduced from Florsch et al., 2015; GEF, 2022; Maldonado, 2006; Téreygeol & Cruz, 2014)

Replication studies have detailed the mechanics of the *wayra* furnace (Téreygeol & Cruz, 2014) as well as the reverberatory furnace both of which were independently innovated in the Andes (Peele Jr, 1893; Angiorama & Becerra, 2017; Téreygeol et al., 2020). After some experimentation, the Spaniards returned to the use of *wayras*, as bellows-driven furnaces failed in the high altitude, low-fuel, environment (Craig, 1994: 271).

4 Chronology of Metallurgical Innovations

The earliest hard rock mining was for pigments, specifically iron oxides, dating to the Archaic period – potentially as early as circa 8500 BP (Salazar et al., 2013: 139). As mentioned above, the oldest evidence for metalworking in the Andes consists of several laminated native gold sheets shaped as beads from the northern Titicaca Basin site of Jiskairumoko. These objects were dated to 3733 ± 43 14C years BP. The objects were most likely manufactured with cold hammering of relatively pure naturally occurring gold nuggets. Placer sources are found in the Carabaya region to the east. Current excavation data indicate that metals do not enter the archaeological record of the altiplano prior to the Late Archaic period (Randall Haas pers comm, 2021).

The earliest currently known worked native copper is a funerary mask found in Argentina associated with a child burial dated to 3001 ± 45 cal years BP (Cortés & Scattolin, 2017). A pendant was also found. Elemental analysis showed pure copper. No tin or arsenic alloys were detected. The techniques used were energy-dispersive

Copper Metallurgy in the Andes

X-ray spectroscopy (EDS), wavelength-dispersive X-ray spectroscopy (WDS) and X-ray fluorescence (XRF). (Cortés & Scattolin, 2017: 691–692).

Additional early finds of hammered metalwork have been found at Mina Perdida, central coast Peru, circa 25 km south of Lima (Burger & Gordon, 1998). Fragments of laminated copper are associated with radiocarbon dates of 3120 ± 130 and 3020 ± 100 14C years BP (Burger & Gordon, 1998). Mina Perdida is the largest of six monumental U-shaped ceremonial centers in the Lurín Valley dating to Initial Period, circa 2000–900 BC. These objects are associated with the Cupisnique culture. Hammered copper and gold artifacts were found in association with a C-14 date of circa 1410–1090 BC. The artifacts were gold foil attached to copper, copper foil, and four copper artifacts (including one with traces of gold). The metal was found in ceremonial areas atop the monuments, indicating ritual. The copper foil is in a very pure form, and excavators suspect it was fashioned of native copper. Microscopic analysis confirmed that the very thin (0.1–0.05 mm) foils were cold hammered, and possibly annealed.

An early cold-hammer metalworking toolkit comes from Waywaka, a small village in the Andahuaylas region of the south-central highlands, circa 200 km west of Cuzco. There were two burials, one with a set of nine gold leaves and the other with 25 leaves and the tools of a metal smith inside a stone jar (Lleras, 2013). Several pieces of gold foil were found in a burial along with a simple toolkit for cold hammering small pieces of metal foil. The tools were hand sized 'mushroom-shaped' anvil and hammerstone set of fine-grained volcanic stone green porphyry and a series of three small, polished stone hammers. Newer dates published by Grossman (2013) suggest the earliest date of this tool kit to be around 1680 BC.

Reindel et al. (2013) describe the mining and metallurgical sequence in the Nasca valley, which began with gold adornments in the Early Horizon. In the mining district of Palpa, gold and copper gemstone beads predominated until a shift to copper metallurgy in the Middle Horizon (Stöllner et al., 2013). Vaughn et al., 2013 describe the hematite mine site of Mina Primavera in the Nasca region on the southern coast of Peru. This Early Intermediate period mine was a small cave carved into the side of a quebrada (arroyo). The cave had hematite deposits along with hammerstones and mortars.

Experimentation with kiln-firing pottery manufacture was underway by 3830± 50 ^{14}C years BP (Cortés & Scattolin, 2017). This experience with controlling firing temperatures and oxygen availability, particularly the inclusion of mineral tempers, would have naturally lent to experimentation in mineral smelting. Cortés and Scattolin (2017: 695) report copper smelting slag from the site of Wankarani in the Bolivian Altiplano. This slag dated to between 3160 ± 110 (calibrated 1680–1124 calibrated BC) and 2200 ± 80 14C years BP (Ponce Sanginés, 1970: table 2, fig. 35).

In northern Chile site of Tulán 55, there is recorded smelted and hammered copper sheets along with ground copper ore. Radiocarbon dates from this site are 3010 ± 40 and 2700± 100 14C years BP (Cortés & Scattolin, 2017). In northern Chile, copper casting is found along with mining and metallurgical debris are associated with the Tilocalar Phase (3140 ± 80 14C years BP to 2380± 70 14C years

BP),[1] Núñez et al. (2006: table 2), based on the presence of a stone masher, mining hammerstones, cast copper, and abundant milled copper ore (Cortés & Scattolin, 2017: 695).

Evidence for smelting copper ores dated to 2040 14C years BP (calibrated 50 BC) comes from the Atacama region of northern Chile at the Late Archaic village site, Ramaditas. This occurs within a household or small-scale context. Ramaditas was a typical residential village of the period, and not an industrial center or trade hub. Excavations revealed crushed copper sulfate ore, slag, and furnace remains. These artisans were working with the semiprecious varieties copper minerals that also had lapidary uses, reported as brochantite [$Cu_4(SO_4)(OH)_6$], cuprite, malachite, and chrysocolla (Graffam et al., 1996: 106).

Ice core data provide support that this was a region wide phenomenon. Cores from the peaks of Mt. Illimani preserve a record of the volatilized by-products from copper and silver production. This indirect evidence of copper smelting becomes recordable at the circa 3000 BP (1000 BC) range, concomitant with early social complexity (Eichler et al., 2017).

Gold, silver and copper objects are additionally reported from the site of Salango in the Central coast of Ecuador that was radiocarbon dated to 1500 BC. Copper slag is reported from the lower levels of the capital of Tiwanaku circa 1000 BC, as well as Chiripa and Pucara (Lleras, 2013). Circa 890 BC, there is a reported burial of a metal smith from Los Cerritos, Ecuador that included metallurgy tools. At the site of Putushio in the South Sierra of Ecuador gold furnaces were found dating to circa AD 180 to AD 1515 (Rehren & Temme, 1994).

Early evidence for silver cupellation (a complex, multi-stage purification technology requiring precise control over firing temperatures and oxygen availability), comes from the Peruvian and Bolivian Altiplano site of Huajje in Puno, Peru. Workshop debris indicative of the reprocessing of matte to recover pure silver-lead bullion was found associated with radiocarbon dates circa 1900 BP (2-sigma calibrated range from AD 60 to 120) with similar materials continuing through to the Inca and Colonial period (Schultze et al., 2009, 2012). Silver-lead cupellation debris has also found dating to AD 600 at the North-Central Peru site of Ancón (Lechtman, 1976).

Lake sediment profiles from Lake Taypi Chaka in Bolivia registered an increase in sedimentary lead levels interpreted as an indirect byproduct of silver production, circa AD 400, (Cooke et al., 2008). This comports with the ice core evidence from Illimani which indicate experimentation in silver smelting and continued steady production of copper during the Middle Horizon early states circa AD 500–1100. Both copper and silver production show evidence of collapse in the Late Intermediate Period circa 1100–1450 in the Illimani data corresponding to the collapse of the early state societies (Eichler et al., 2017: 5).

The Altiplano data (from Lake Taypi Chaka and Mt. Illimani) contrast with lake sediment samples from northern and southern Andean lakes, Morococha (Cooke

---

[1] 1611–1205 calBC; − 766-236 CalBC; 95.4%; IntCal 20.

et al., 2007) and Cerro Rico de Potosí (Abbott & Wolfe, 2003) respectively, where lead deposition significantly increases only after circa AD 1000. These data suggest the Peruvian and Bolivian Altiplano zone as an early center of innovation for silver smelting, but that centers of production shifted dramatically with the collapse of the Middle Horizon states.

The Illimani ice core data show a spike in the level of silver output during the Inca period and a dramatic increase in volatized by products of both copper and silver production into the Republican and modern periods (Eichler et al., 2015, 2017: 5).

5 Alloys and Fabrication Techniques

5.1 Alloys

Alloys were an important area of experimentation and innovation in Andean metalworking. Tumbaga was the principal alloy in the Andes. These included binary or tertiary blends of silver or gold, with copper provided the basic stock material for fine metalwork (e.g. Scott, 1995; Hörz & Kallfass, 2000). Differing proportions of copper, gold, and/or silver were utilized according to the intended use and regional preference (Guevara-Duque, 2018). The Colombia-Ecuador zone also utilized a gold-copper *tumbaga* with copper content as high as 60% which facilitated casting by decreasing the melting point over unalloyed gold (La Niece & Meeks, 2000).

Chemical analyses of artifacts confirm the use of arsenical and tin bronzes, both along the north coast and in the altiplano (Bennett, 1946; Lechtman, 1996; Merkel et al., 1994). North-Central Peru, Middle Horizon bronzes are generally arsenical. Items personal adornment assayed from the Wari site of Pikillacta were exclusively arsenical bronze or unalloyed copper (Lechtman, 2005: 146). However, in the contemporary Peruvian and Bolivian Altiplano site of Tiwanaku, analysis of bronzes discovered uncommon bronze alloys including nickel (Lechtman, 2003; Uhland et al., 2001). Another significant technological finding from the Tiwanaku bronzes was the process of casting bronze into rods prior to hammering. "The use of cast as opposed to hammered stock represents a major difference between central and south-central Andean metalworking traditions (Lechtman, 2003: 410). These findings identify the site of Tiwanaku as a locus of an independent trajectory of metallurgical technology in the altiplano.

Nickel and tin bronzes are also found in burials with Tiwanaku style snuff tablets at San Pedro de Atacama. Quantities of nickel and arsenic rise in equal proportion to one another, suggesting that nickel arsenide (NiAs) was added to molten copper (Lechtman, 2003). An interesting copper-arsenic-zinc alloy is used locally in northwest Argentina, in the Catamarca Province (González, 1979). It has been postulated as San Pedro de Atacama was the primary extraction and processing location for Tiwanaku coppers (Núñez, 1987) as long-distance transport was involved in its acquisition. More traditional *tumbagas* are also found in the Altiplano regions, such as a silvered copper ring from Lukurmata.

Bronze alloy composition changes in the samples from the site of Tiwanaku. During the Late Formative 2 through Late Tiwanaku IV periods, artifacts included uncommon alloys, including a tertiary nickel bronze (CuAsNi) alloy. Tin was also included in the nickel bronze, and sulfur is sometimes present as well. By the transition to Tiwanaku V, roughly a third of the analyzed sample was tin bronze (Lechtman, 2003). The Bolivian Andes is known for cassiterite (SnO_2) deposits, located principally in Central Andean Tin Belt encompassing the Japo, Santa Fe, and Morocala districts in the Eastern Bolivian Cordilleras (Jiménez-Franco et al., 2018).

As the Inca expanded south into these tin-rich zones, their alloy compositions followed suit. Excavations of household groups at Mantaro Valley sites, over the Late Intermediate (Wanka II) and Late Horizon (Wanka III/local Inca) periods, recovered unusually high quantities of copper-based metals (along with silver and lead). These finds show a trajectory from native copper in Wanka I, to arsenical bronze in Wanka II, followed by tin bronze in the Late Horizon Wanka III period (Howe & Petersen, 1994).

5.2 Fabrication Techniques

There was an explosion of metalworking innovation during the Early Intermediate period in North-Central Peru. With the exception of tin bronze, all the major developments in Andean metalworking, including the principal alloying, gilding and joining technologies, were in use by Moche artisans (Jones, 2005). Documented metalworking technologies among the Moche include smelting, alloying, annealing, cold-hammering, casting, block-twisting, strip-twisting, clinching (or stapling), welding, soldering, openwork, wire, filigree, false-filigree, repoussé, inlay, rocker-stamping, and incision/engraving. Surface treatments included burnishing, overlay coating, gold foil joining, and other methods for gilding or silvering.

Hammered sheet metal was the primary technology across all the Andean metalworking zones. Thinness of sheets, alloying, and control of surface color were important areas of experimentation. For example, artifacts from the royal tombs at Sipán were mostly made of exceedingly thin sheet metal ranging in thickness from 1 mm to <0.1 mm (Hörz & Kallfass, 2000). There are multiple hammered metal finds from the Initial Period and Early Horizon sites, including from Kotosh, Chavin de Huantar, Supe, Lurín Valley, and Chogoyape in Lambayeque Valley (Lechtman, 1980). Several fine hammered gold crowns and items of personal adornment are published from the Early Horizon site of Kuntur Wasi. These are decorated in repoussé relief to depict chavinoid figures and trophy head motifs. Chongoyape, North Sierra of Peru Initial Period -goes along with Chavín probably before 700 BC. These last ones are quite complex because they combine hammering and welding (Lleras, 2013).

Along the coast there is evidence of cold-hammering of metal sheets, that were then cut into shapes, embossed using a chisel on a leather anvil, or decorated in repoussé using carved molds. Repoussé decoration used the plasticity of the metal by impressing the hammered sheet from the interior with a mold or tool (McEwan & Haeberli, 2000: 17). Such carved molds could have been made of stone and would probably also have been covered with leather to prevent damage to the sheet metal. Additional decoration of sheet metal was executed through cutting, embossing, punching, and chasing. Hammer-annealing later became the most common method for creating thin sheets, which could then be decorated by punching, stamping, engraving or repoussé work. Sheets were sometimes cast in the northern zones by the Muisca using lost wax casting. A Sicán (circa 850–1050) silver tumi knife was found to have been cast to a remarkable thickness of 0.13 mm (Scott, 1996).

An example of repoussé technique is provided by Pillsbury and Mackey's (2020) detailed description of two Lambayeque silver vessels from Chicama/Piura Valleys of northern Peru in the AD 700–1300 period. The hammered and annealed sheet is covered in four distinct registers of complex repoussé illustration with a procession theme. One specimen is a double wall hammered sheet artifacts comprised of 90.4% silver, 7.4% copper and 1.9% lead 0.2% bismuth, and 0.1% gold. The second is a single walled hammered silver sheet comprised of 92.4% silver, 5.9% copper, traces of bismuth 0.2%, gold 0.1% This contrast with a Chimú alloy comprised of 89% silver, 10.5% copper with traces of lead 0.25% gold .1%, arsenic 0.04%, nickel 0.03%.

This iconography is complex, and while it can directly reflect the dominant ideological canons of each period, there is also room for whimsical expressions of both daily life and local myth. There is a great potential for ideological content to be conveyed through repoussé on hammered sheet metal.

A richly illustrated volume on Tiwanaku material culture (Young-Sánchez, 2004) includes several hammered gold and silver plaques, keros (drinking tumblers with a slightly concave form) and cast gold figures. From the collection of the Metropolitan Museum of Art is one of the earliest goldwork artifacts surviving from the south-central Andes (Young-Sánchez, 2004: 95 fig. 3.28). It was collected from the department of Cuzco (Rowe, 1977) and shows Pucara or early Tiwanaku characteristics (circa 200 BC – AD 400). It is a hammered gold headdress ornament, incised with a front-facing supernatural feline, informally placed above several human and animal figures.

One major regional metalworking center is found in the Colombia-Ecuador zone at La Tolita-Tumaco where metallurgical innovation began during the Early Horizon (Martinon-Torres et al., 2017). This region is known for lost wax casting of gold alloys, and the production of small personal ornaments of impressive complexity (Shimada, 1994).

Artisans from Ecuador-Colombia and North Coast Peru made use of thin strands of metal wire as structural and decorative elements. These were used to suspend and hold together other decorative elements, or simply formed into stand-alone figures or designs (e.g. Lleras-Pérez, 2000: fig. 6.6). They were also used for filigree decoration and to sculpt openwork pendants and designs, for example mesh wire gold and silver ear spools from Chancay, Peru (La Niece & Meeks, 2000: fig. 11.8). They could also be cut into smaller droplets for granulation, the placement of small spheres of metal in rows or patterns, such as has been found in La Tolita, Vicús, Lambayeque and Chimú goldwork.

Wire was primarily made by hand working, although hammered and cast wire has been found in Rio Cauca (Meeks, 2001). Additionally, evidence for annealing, block- twisting and strip twisting of gold alloy wire is found from La Tolita-Tumaca region, circa 325 BC (Scott, 1991). In the areas that used lost-wax casting, false fili-gree and other elements were modeled in wax and assembled before casting. Great skill is shown in the assembly of the small wax molds and in controlling the flow of the molten metal to assure complete replacement of the wax (La Niece & Meeks, 2000).

There were several methods employed to join hammered sheets (Donnan, 1976: 292). Clinching, or stapling, is a process of folding and fitting the edges of the two pieces together. There is also a very direct form of welding, in which the edges to be joined are simply heated and hammered together. The third is a soldering technique, achieved by mixing a copper salt powered with a gum and applying this to the surfaces to be joined. The application of heat reduced the copper slats to metallic form and fused the edges. Another form of soldering from La Tolita involved joining delicate pieces of metal with drops of molten alloy of 42% gold, 48% copper, and 10% silver (Scott, 1990; Scott & Doehne, 1990).

5.3 Surface Treatments

Many methods of gilding and silvering were used. The simplest is the mechanical approach in which a thin sheet of gold or silver foil was hammered out and wrapped around a copper artifact and burnished into place. Copper nose-rings from Central America have been found gilded with foil in this manner (Bray, 1993).

Diffusion-bond gilding takes this process a step further by heating the wrapped artifact to below the melting point. This creates a better bond through limited solid-state diffusion. This process has been found at the La Campañía site in Ecuador. Fusion gilding requires the gilding layer to be molten and has been found at La Tolita, and Dept. of Nariño in Colombia (Scott, 1986a, b).

Multiple mechanisms of fusion gilding have been documented. The base metal object could be dipped into a coating alloy, as was found for a silver nose-ring (Scott, 1986a), or the gold mixture could be let to run over the surface. However, there is difficulty in controlling the spread and ensuring complete coverage using these methods. A more controlled method would be to spread the gold alloy in a paste with flux and then heat it until gilding melted into place. In the Old World, amalgam (fire, or mercury) gilding used mercury as the flux to paint gilding onto a surface or portions of the surface. When heated, it forms a strong bond onto the base metal and does not flake of peel as is common with other methods. There is currently no evidence of amalgam gilding in the Americas, possibly because the popularity of *tumbagas* led to greater experimentation in depletion gilding than in additive gilding processes (La Niece & Meeks, 2000).

Depletion (or *mise en couleur*) gilding works by removing the base metal from the surface of gold alloy object and then burnishing to affect the surface appearance of pure gold. The simplest method is to heat a gold-copper *tumbaga* in an open hearth until the copper oxidizes. The blackened oxide can then be dissolved in a solution of salt with acid, postulated to be extracts of plants of the genus *Oxalis* (Scott, 1983) or an acidic compound of iron sulfate minerals (Petersen, 2010: 8; Carcedo, 1998: 175), then burnished to create a golden surface. The heating and pickling process creates a porous and pock- marked surface that can be seen at high magnification. The procedure can be repeated to make a deeper finish up 3–10 microns thick. It is more difficult to de-silver gold. However, replication studies have produced similar results to that seen on a silver-gold Chimú mask (Lechtman, 1997).

Another ingenious method that has been replicated from Vicús and Moche period artifacts is that of electrochemical replacement gilding. Although they did not work with electric current, the electrochemical reaction of heating ions in solution, with the copper sheet, was sufficient to drive the plating reaction. The process involved heating gold in solution with salt, saltpeter, and potash alum gently for 2–5 days until it was dissolved. This acidic solution was neutralized with sodium bicarbonate and then heated to boiling point. Submerged copper objects were plated with a very thin and irregular gold lens of some 1.5 micrometers.

6 Inca

The Inca empire was vast stretching some 4000 km north to south. The Inca state set up mining and smelting facilities throughout the Andes. The Inca used the same technologies as earlier cultures, but at a greater intensity and organization in their core territories and strategically important valleys. Technologically, they invented tin bronze, arsenic capture, but their main innovation was organizationally and structurally. They elevated production levels and established military outposts and invested in production centers and labor.

Tin bronze was the imperial metal of the Inca (Garrido & Plaza, 2020). The Inca took advantage of the tin-rich casserite mineral deposits that were made available by their expansion into the southern Andes to expand the use of this alloy. There is evidence that the Inca were concerned about the ill health effects of arsenical bronze production – just as they were aware of the hazards of decorative cinnabar used for personal adornment. Tin bronze was an entirely suitable replacement that did not carry the same toxic exposure hazard. It became the imperial bronze and may have eventually replaced arsenical bronze throughout the Andes had the Inca continued in power.

In the Tarapacá valley in northern Chile, the Inca built a small town of Tarapacá Vieja that was ringed with 26 silver smelting sites with wind-driven furnaces. The investigators found abundant debris including slag, vitrified ceramics, crucibles, and unused fuel (Zori, 2011, 2019). The Tarapacá Vieja settlement was a major, formal one which incorporated earlier copper mining and expanded processing activities to include purification of silver galena ores from the nearby Huantajaya mine (Zori & Tropper, 2013). Tarapaca Vieja represents a massive investment in metallurgical production an order of magnitude larger than seen in other areas in northern Chile. It appears that people would independently bring ore to the town and they were repaid with food, drink, textiles and most likely pottery.

In the Elqui Valley of Chile the Diaguita developed bronze and copper working. Analysis of artifacts from San Pedro de Atacama by Salazar et al. (2011), Maldonado et al. (2013) and Horta Tricallotis and Faundes Catalán (2018) indicate substantial production of copper objects and other metals during Tiwanaku times circa AD 600–900. The Inca targeted this locale for intensification of copper/bronze production (Cantarutti, 2013).

In Nazca Valley, South Coast Peru, the Inca period saw a distinct shift toward valley-scale administration of mineral resources, concomitant with restriction of access to sumptuary goods (e.g. metals, coca leaves) to the elite classes within an increasingly centralized prestige economy (Van Gijseghem et al., 2013).

Metal smelting sites are generally located near an ore source, such as the Inca period sites of Quillay Wayras in Catamarca, NW Argentina (Hein et al., 2018), or Viña del Cerro in Copiapó, N Chile, (Niemeyer et al., 1983). However, this is not always the case. Ancón is a monumental site near Lima with occupations that began in the Preceramic period (Lechtman, 1976: 34–37). This site is not located near a metal ore source. It may have been located here because of consistently windy conditions. Many of the smelting areas are located atop ridges that would facilitate wind-driven smelters.

Salazar (2008) describes an Inca copper mining complex in the Atacama region of northern Chile. The area also contained chrysocolla, turquoise, silver, and gold. This complex was composed of buildings, mines, production areas, roads, and storehouses. The empire established a formal settlement system to extract minerals, principally copper on a scale not documented in the Andes before.

Outside of the core provincial territories, Inca organization was more informal as Garrido and Plaza (2020) demonstrate for a valley in north central Chile called Copiapó (and see Garrido Escobar, 2015; Campbell et al., 2018). María Teresa Plaza Calonge et al. (2021) and her colleagues demonstrated how a metallurgical technique invented in NW Argentina was imported to an Inca installation in central Chile.

Another metalworking site is Curamba, located on an Inca road, in the puna zone due west of Cusco. This regional center has a stepped- pyramid and was an Inca period regional silver smelting facility. As Curamba is not located near a silver source, the ores had to have been transported to it for processing. These sites are evidence for modular integration of metalwork under Inca and Wari administration. Spanish chroniclers suggest that "near industrial" levels of production were attained by the Inca (Lechtman, 1976: 28). There is evidence that the Chimú may also have practiced a modular organization of metalworking. Copper smelting was carried out in the Batán Grande region, with evidence for finishing work found at Chotuna (Donnan, 1981), and Chan Chan (Topic, 1990).

7 Summary

Like the Eastern Hemisphere (Kaufman, 2011, 2013), gold, silver, and copper were the key metals exploited to make artisan ritual objects and personal adornments. It is always important to recall that all of the developments in the Americas were completely independent of the Eastern Hemisphere.

Acknowledgments The authors thank the editors of this volume for inviting us to contribute this article. Schultze thanks Wm Randy Haas, Luis-Flores Blanco, and Kayeleigh Sharp for generously contributed their time in discussion of these topics. Stanish expresses his deep affection and respect for Tom and Alina Levy, colleagues and friends for many years.

References

Abbott, M., & Wolfe, A. (2003). Intensive pre-Incan metallurgy recorded by lake sediments from the Bolivian Andes. *Science, 26*, 1893–1895.

Aldenderfer, M., Craig, N. M., Speakman, R. J., & Popelka-Filcoff, R. (2008). Four-thousand-year-old gold artifacts from the Lake Titicaca basin, Southern Peru. *Proceedings of the National Academy of Sciences, 105*(13), 5002–5005.

Alva, W., & Donnan, C. B. (1993). *Royal tombs of Sipán*. Fowler Museum of Cultural History, University of California.

Angiorama, C. I., & Becerra, M. F. (2017). Reverberatory furnaces in the Puna of Jujuy, Argentina, during colonial times (from the end of the 16th to the beginning of the 19th century AD). *Journal of Anthropological Archaeology, 48*, 181–192.

Arriaza, B., Ogalde, J. P., Campos, M., Paipa, C., Leyton, P., & Lara, N. (2018). Toxic pigment in a Capacocha burial: Instrumental identification of cinnabar in Inca human remains from Iquique, Chile. *Archaeometry, 60*(6), 1324–1333.

Bauer, B. S., & Stanish, C. (2001). *Ritual and pilgrimage in the ancient Andes: The Islands of the Sun and the Moon*. University of Texas Press.

Bennett, W. (1946). The Andean highlands: An introduction. In J. H. Steward (Ed.), *Handbook of South American Indians Vol. 2 Andean civilization* (Smithsonian Institution Bureau of American Ethnology Bulletin 143) (pp. 1–60). US Government Printing Office.

Berthelot, J. (1986). The extraction of precious metals at the time of the Inka. In J. Murra, N. Wachtel, & J. Revel (Eds.), *Anthropological history of Andean polities* (pp. 69–88). Cambridge University Press.

Bird, J. (1979). The "copper man": A prehistoric miner and his tools from northern Chile. In E. P. Benson (Ed.), *Pre-columbian metallurgy of South America*. Dumbarton Oaks Research Library and Collections.

Brandini, S., Bergamaschi, P., Cerna, M. F., Gandini, F., Bastaroli, F., Bertolini, E., Cereda, C., Ferretti, L., Gómez-Carballa, A., Battaglia, V., & Salas, A. (2018). The Paleo-Indian entry into South America according to mitogenomes. *Molecular Biology and Evolution, 35*(2), 299–311.

Bray, W. (1993). Techniques of gilding and surface-enrichment in pre-Hispanic American metallurgy. In *Metal plating and patination* (pp. 182–192). Butterworth-Heinemann.

Brooks, W. E., Schwörbel, G., & Castillo, L. E. (2013). Amalgamation and small-scale gold mining in the ancient Andes. In N. Tripcevich & K. J. Vaughn (Eds.), *Mining and quarrying in the Ancient Andes* (pp. 213–229). Springer.

Brown, K., & Craig, A. (1994). Silver mining at Huantajaya, viceroyalty of Peru. In A. K. Craig & R. C. West (Eds.), *Quest of mineral wealth. Aboriginal and colonial mining and metallurgy in Spanish America* (GeoScience and Man 33) (pp. 303–328). Louisiana State University.

Burger, R. (1995). *Chavín and the origins of Andean civilization*. Thames and Hudson.

Burger, R. L., & Gordon, R. B. (1998). Early central Andean metalworking from Mina Perdida, Peru. *Science, 282*(5391), 1108–1111.

Burger, R. L., & Leikin, J. B. (2018). Cinnabar use in prehispanic Peru and its possible health consequences. *Journal of Archaeological Science: Reports, 17*, 730–734.

Campbell, R., Carrión, H., Figueroa, V., Peñaloza, Á., Plaza, M. T., & Stern, C. (2018). Obsidianas, turquesas y metales en el Sur de Chile. *Chungará (Arica), 50*(2), 217–234.

Cantarutti, G. E. (2013). Mining under Inca rule in North-Central Chile: The Los Infieles mining complex. In N. Tripcevich & K. J. Vaughn (Eds.), *Mining and quarrying in the Ancient Andes* (pp. 185–211). Springer.

Carcedo, M. P. (1998). *Cobre del Antiguo Perú*. In J. A. de Lavelle (Ed.), *Cobre del Antiguo Perú*. AFP Integra, Lavalle Editores S.R. L.

Cieza de León, P. (1613 [1998]). *The discovery and conquest of Peru: Chronicles of the New World encounter*. Duke University Press.

Cooke, C., Abbott, M., Wolfe, A., & Kittleson, J. (2007). A millennium of metallurgy recorded by lake sediments from Morococha, Peruvian Andes. *Environmental Science & Technology, 41*, 3469–3474.

Cooke, C., Abbott, M., & Wolfe, A. (2008). Late Holocene atmospheric lead deposition in the Peruvian and Bolivian Andes. *Holocene, 18*(2), 353–359.

Cortés, L. I., & Scattolin, M. C. (2017). Ancient metalworking in South America: A 3000-year-old copper mask from the Argentinian Andes. *Antiquity, 91*(357), 688–700.

Couture, N. C., & Sampeck, K. (2003). Putuni: A history of palace architecture at Tiwanaku. In A. Kolata (Ed.), *Tiwanaku and its hinterland: Archaeology and paleoecology of an Andean civilization, 2* (pp. 226–263). Smithsonian Institution/Combined Academic.

Craig, A. K. (1994). Spanish colonial silver beneficiation at Potosí. In A. K. Craig & R. C. West (Eds.), *Quest of mineral wealth: Aboriginal and colonial mining and metallurgy in Spanish America, Geoscience and man* (Vol. 33, pp. 271–285). Louisiana State University.

de la Vega, G. (1633 [1979]) *The Incas: The Royal Commentaries of the Inca.* (M. Jolas, Trans.). Editorial Alfa.

Delaere, C. (2017). The location of Lake Titicaca's coastal area during the Tiwanaku and Inca periods: Methodology and strategies of underwater archaeology. *Journal of Maritime Archaeology, 12*(3), 223–238.

Delaere, C., Capriles, J. M., & Stanish, C. (2019). Underwater ritual offerings in the Island of the Sun and the formation of the Tiwanaku state. *Proceedings of the National Academy of Sciences, 116*(17), 8233–8238.

Domanski, M., & Webb, J. (2007). A review of heat treatment research. *Lithic Technology, 32*(2), 153–194.

Donnan, C. (1973). A pre-Columbian smelter from northern Peru. *Archaeology, 26*(4), 289–297. New York.

Donnan, C. (1976). *Moche art and iconography*. Latin American Center Publications, University of California.

Donnan, C. (1981). Proyecto Chotuna-Chornancap: 1980 season. *Willay, 8*, 3. Princeton.

Donnan, C. (1998). Un ceramio Moche y la fundición prehispánica de metales. *Boletín, Museo Chileno de Arte Precolombino, 7*, 9–18. Santiago, Chile.

Donnan, C. (2001, March). Moche burials uncovered. *National Geographic, 199*, 58–73.

Dransart, P. (2000). Clothed metal and the iconography of human form among the Incas. In C. McEwan (Ed.), *Precolumbian gold: Technology, style, and iconography* (pp. 76–91). Fitzroy Dearborn Publishers.

Eichler, A., Gramlich, G., Kellerhals, T., Tobler, L., & Schwikowski, M. (2015). Pb pollution from leaded gasoline in South America in the context of a 2000-year metallurgical history. *Science Advances, 1*, e1400196.

Eichler, A., Gramlich, G., & Kellerhals, T. (2017). Ice-core evidence of earliest extensive copper metallurgy in the Andes 2700 years ago. *Scientific Reports, 7*, 41855. https://doi.org/10.1038/srep41855

Emmerich, A. (1965). *Sweat of the Sun and tears of the Moon: Gold and Silver in Pre-Columbian art*. University of Washington Press.

Figueroa, V., Salazar, D., Salinas, H., Núñez-Regueiro, P., & Manríquez, G. (2013). Ergología minera prehispánica del Norte de Chile: una perspectiva arqueológica. *Chungará (Arica), 45*(1), 61–81.

Florsch, N., Téreygeol, F., & Cruz, P. J. (2015). The ore-dressing grindstone called a 'Quimbalete': A mechanics-based approach. *Archaeometry, 58*(6), 881–898. https://doi.org/10.1111/arcm.12203

Friedman, A. M., Olsen, E., & Bird, J. B. (1972). Moche copper analyses: Early New World metal technology. *American Antiquity, 37*(2), 254–258.

Garrido Escobar, F. J. (2015). *Mining and the Inca Road in the Prehistoric Atacama Desert, Chile*. Dissertation for the University of Pittsburgh Dietrich School of Arts and Science.

Garrido, F., & Plaza, M. T. (2020). Provincial Inca metallurgy in northern Chile: New data for the Viña del Cerro smelting site. *Journal of Archaeological Science: Reports, 33*, 102556.

GEF -Global Environment Facility. (2022). *Quimbalete use, Electronic document*. https://www.thegef.org/news/making-mercury-history-artisanal-small-scale-gold-mining-sector. Accessed 20 Mar 2022.

González, A. R. (1979). Pre-Columbian metallurgy of NW Argentina: Historical development and cultural process. In E. P. Benson (Ed.), *Pre-Columbian metallurgy of South America*. Dumbarton Oaks Museum.

Göransson, K., & Carcedo de Mufarech, P. (2011). *Inca Gold Treasure in the Skeppsholmen Caverns*. Catalogue of the Varaldskulturmuseern National Museum of World Culture Exhibit Stockholm.

Graffam, G., Rivera, M., & Carević, A. (1996). Ancient metallurgy in the Atacama: Evidence for copper smelting during Chile's early ceramic period. *Latin American Antiquity, 7*(2), 101–113.

Grossman, J. W. (2013). The Waywaka gold: New chronometric evidence. *Andean Past, 11*(1), 13.

Guédron, S., Tolu, J., Delaere, C., Sabatier, P., Barré, J., Heredia, C., Brisset, E., Campillo, S., Bindler, R., Fritz, S. C., Baker, P. A., & Amouroux, D. (2021). Reconstructing two millennia of copper and silver metallurgy in the Lake Titicaca region (Bolivia/Peru) using trace metals and lead isotopic composition. *Anthropocene, 34*, 100288. https://doi.org/10.1016/j.ancene.2021.100288

Guevara-Duque, M. I. (2018). *Between metals and treads: An archaeometric approach to metallic artefacts from Yaguachi chiefdom burials (Guayas Basin, Ecuador)*. Doctoral dissertation, Universidade de Evora (Portugal).

Hein, A., Gluzman, G., & Kilikoglou, V. (2018). Pre-Columbian metallurgy – Evidence of pytotechnical ceramics from Rincón Chico, northwestern Argentina. *Journal of Archaeological Science Reports, 21*, 1163–1170.

Hofman, H. (2015). *Metallurgy of copper*. Arkose Press. (1924) 2nd edition. McGraw-Hill Books.

Horta Tricallotis, H., & Faundes Catalán, W. (2018). Manufactura de cuentas de mineral de cobre en Atacama (Chile) durante el período medio (ca. 400-1.000 dc): nuevas evidencias contextuales y aportes desde la experimentación arqueológica. *Chungará (Arica), 50*(3), 397–422.

Hörz, G., & Kallfass, M. (2000). The treasure of gold and silver artifacts from the Royal Tombs of Sipán, Peru—A study on the Moche metalworking techniques. *Materials Characterization, 45*(4–5), 391–419.

Hosler, D., Lechtman, H., & Holm, O. (1990). *Axe-monies and their relatives (Studies in Precolumbian art & archaeology 30)*. Dumbarton Oaks Research Library and Collection.

Howe, E. G., & Petersen, U. (1994). Silver and lead in the late prehistory of the Mantaro Valley, Peru. In D. A. Scott & P. Meyers (Eds.), *Archaeometry of Pre-Columbian sites and artifacts* (pp. 183–198). Getty Conservation Institute.

Jiménez-Franco, A., Alfonso Abella, M. P., Canet Miquel, C., & Trujillo, J. E. (2018). Mineral chemistry of In-bearing minerals in the Santa Fe mining district, Bolivia. *Andean Geology, 45*(3), 410–432. https://doi.org/10.5027/andgeoV45n3-3052

Jones, J. (2005). Innovation and resplendence: Metalwork for Moche Lords. In J. Pillsbury (Ed.), *Moche Art and Archaeology in Ancient Peru* (Studies in the History of Art 63, first issued 2001). National Gallery of Art.

Kaufman, B. (2011). Metallurgy and ecological change in the ancient Near East. *Backdirt, Annual Review of the Cotsen Institute of Archaeology, 2011*, 86–92.

Kaufman, B. (2013). Copper alloys from the 'Enot Shuni cemetery and the origins of bronze metallurgy in the EB IV–MB II Levant. *Archaeometry, 55*(4), 663–690.

Kay, S., Mpodozis, C., & Ramos, V. (2005). Andes. In *Encyclopedia of geology*. Elsevier Academic Press.

King, H. (2000). *Rain of the moon: Silver in ancient Peru*. The Metropolitan Museum of Art.

Kolata, A. (1993). *The Tiwanaku: Portrait of an Andean civilization*. Wiley.

Kolata, A. (2003). The social production of Tiwanaku: Political economy and Authority in a Native Andean State. In A. L. Kolata (Ed.), *Tiwanaku and its hinterland Vol. 2*. Smithsonian Institution Press.

La Niece, S., & Meeks, N. (2000). Diversity of goldsmithing traditions in the Americas and the Old World. In *Precolumbian gold, technology, style and iconography* (pp. 220–239). British Museum Press.

Larco de Alvarez-Calderón, I. (2000). *La Ceremonia del Sacrificio: Batallas y Muete en el Arte Mochica*. Museo Arqueológico Rafael Larco Herrera.

Lechtman, H. (1976). A metallurgical site survey in the Peruvian Andes. *Journal of Field Archaeology, 3*(1), 1–42.

Lechtman, H. (1980). *The Central Andes, metallurgy without iron*. Yale University Press.

Lechtman, H. (1996). Arsenic Bronze: Dirty copper or chosen alloy? A view from the Americas. *Journal of Field Archaeology, 23*(4), 477–514.

Lechtman, H. (1997). Arsenic bronze and the middle horizon. In G. Varon & J. Flores (Eds.), *Arqueología, Antropolgía e Historia en los Andes: Homenaje a Maria Rostworowski* (pp. 153–186). Instituto de Estudios Peruanos, Lima.

Lechtman, H. (2003). Tiwanaku period (middle horizon) Bronze Metallurgy in the Lake Titicaca Basin: A preliminary assessment. In A. L. Kolata (Ed.), *Tiwanaku and its hinterland: Urban and rural archaeology vol. 2* (Smithsonian Series in Archaeological Inquiry). Smithsonian Institution Press.

Lechtman, H. (2005). Arsenic bronze at Pikillacta. In G. McEwan (Ed.), *Pikillacta: The Wari empire in Cuzco*. University of Iowa Press.

Lleras, R. (2013). *Metallurgy in the prehistory of America: A synthetic overview*. Paper presented at the Quaternary and Prehistory at the Universita degli Studi di Ferrara. https://www.academia.edu/21969273/

Lleras-Pérez, R. (2000). The iconography and symbolism of metallic votive offerings in the eastern cordillera, Colombia. In D. A. Scott & P. Meyers (Eds.), *Archaeometry of Precolumbian sites and artifacts*. Proceedings of the Getty Conservation Institute.

Lothrop, S. (1946). Diaguita of Chile. In J. H. Steward (Ed.), *Handbook of South American Indians Vol 2 Andean civilization* (Smithsonian Institution Bureau of American Ethnology Bulletin 143) (pp. 633–636). US Government Printing Office.

Macfarlane, A. W., & Lechtman, H. N. (2016). Andean ores, bronze artifacts, and lead isotopes: Constraints on metal sources in their geological context. *Journal of Archaeological Method and Theory, 23*(1), 1–72.

Maggetti, M., Neururer, C., & Ramseyer, D. (2010). Temperature evolution inside a pot during experimental surface (bonfire) firing. *Applied Clay Science, 9*(13), 500–508. https://doi.org/10.1016/j.clay.2010.09.013, https://core.ac.uk/download/pdf/205548754.pdf

Maldonado, B., Rehren, T., Pernicka, E., Núñez, L., & Leibbrandt, A. (2013). Early copper metallurgy in Northern Chile. *Open Journal of Archaeometry, 1*(1), e26–e26.

Martinon-Torres, M., Uribe-Villegas, M. A., Saenz-Samper, J., & Lobo Guerrero Arenas, J. (2017). Archaeometallurgy in Colombia: Recent developments. *Archaeology International, 20*, 80–84.

McEwan, C. (2000). *Pre-Columbian gold: Technology, style, iconography*. Fitzroy Dearborn Publishers.

McEwan, G., & Haeberli, J. (2000). Ancestors past but present: Gold diadems from the far south coast of Peru. In C. McEwan (Ed.), *Precolumbian gold: Technology, style, and iconography* (pp. 16–27). British Museum, London Press.

Meeks, N. (2001). Pre-hispanic goldwork in the British museum: Some recent technological studies. Boletín de Museo de Oro.

Merkel, J. F., Shimada, I., Swann, C. P., & Doonan, R. (1994, October). Pre-Hispanic copper alloy production at Batan Grande, Peru: Interpretation of the analytical data for ore samples. In *Archaeometry of pre-Columbian sites and artifacts: proceedings of a symposium organized by the UCLA Institute of Archaeology and the Getty Conservation Institute, Los Angeles, California, March 23–27, 1992* (pp. 199–227).

Metropolitan Museum of Art. (2021). *Open source catalog*. https://www.metmuseum.org/art/collection/search/309105. Accessed Dec 2021.

Niemeyer, H., Cervellino, M., & Muñoz, E. (1983). Viña del Cerro, expresión metalúrgica inca en el valle de Copiapó. *Creces, 4*(4), 50–57.

Núñez, A. L. (1987). Tráfico de metales en el área centro-sur andina: factos y expectativas. *Cuadernos del Instituto Nacional de Antropología y Pensamiento Latinoamericano, 12*(1), 73–105.

Núñez, L., Cartajena, I., Carrasco, C., de Souza, P., & Grosjean, M. (2006). Emergencia de Comunidades Pastoralistas Formativas en el Sureste de la Puna de Atacama. *Estudio Atacameños, 32*, 93–117. https://doi.org/10.4067/s0718-10432006000200008

Ozdemir, A., & Sahinoglu, A. (2018). Importance of gossans in mineral exploration: A case study in Northern Turkey. *International Journal of Earth Science and Geophysics, 4*(1), 1–20.

Palyanova, G. A. (2020). Gold and silver minerals in sulfide ore. *Geology of Ore Deposits, 62*(5), 383–406.

Pareja, S. E. (1992). *Descripción y conservación de piezas arqueológicas*. Exploraciones arqueológicas subacuáticas en el Lago Titikaka: Informe científico (La Palabra Producciones, La Paz, Bolivia), pp. 583–706.

Peele, R., Jr. (1893). A primitive smelting furnace. *School of Mines Quarterly, 15*, 8–10.

Perroud, P. (2021). *Athena mineralogy online database hosted by Université de Genève*. https://athena.unige.ch/athena/index.html

Petersen, G. (2010/1970). *Mining and metallurgy in ancient Perú, Special Paper 467* (W. E. Brooks, Trans.). The Geological Society of America.

Pillsbury, J., & Mackey, C. J. (2020). Lambayeque silver beakers: Further considerations. *Ñawpa Pacha, 40*(2), 223–247.

Plaza Calonge, M. T., Pavlovic, D., & Martinón-Torres, M. (2021). Crisoles y moldes en Los Nogales: Estudio tecnológico de cerámicas metalúrgicas del Período Tardío en el valle del Aconcagua, Chile Central. *Estudios Atacameños, 67*, 1–43.

Ponce Sanginés, C. (1970). Wankarani y Chiripa y su relación con Tiwanaku. Academia Nacional de Ciencias de Bolivia.

Prates, L., Politis, G. G., & Perez, S. I. (2020). Rapid radiation of humans in South America after the last glacial maximum: A radiocarbon-based study. *PLoS One, 15*(7), e0236023. https://doi.org/10.1371/journal.pone.0236023

Prieto, G., Wright, V., Burger, R. L., Cooke, C. A., Zeballos-Velasquez, E. L., Watanave, A., Suchomel, M. R., & Suescun, L. (2016). The source, processing and use of red pigment based on hematite and cinnabar at Gramalote, an early Initial Period (1500–1200 cal. BC) maritime community, north coast of Peru. *Journal of Archaeological Science: Reports, 5*, 45–60.

Radivojević, M., & Roberts, B. (2021). Early Balkan metallurgy: Origins, evolution and society, 6200-3700 BC. *Journal of World Prehistory, 34*, 195–278. https://doi.org/10.1007/s10963-021-09155-7

Rassmussen, J. (2012). *Geologic history of Arizona, rocks & minerals* 87(1): 56–63. Taylor & Frances. https://doi.org/10.1080/00357529.2012.639192.

Rehren, T., & Temme, M. (1994). Pre-Columbian gold processing at Putushio, South Ecuador: The archaeolmetallurgical evidence. In D. A. Scott & P. Meyers (Eds.), *Archaeometry of Pre-Columbian sites and artifacts* (pp. 267–284). Getty Conservation Institute.

Reindel, M., Stöllner, T. R., & Gräfingholt, B. (2013). Mining archaeology in the Nasca and Palpa region, south coast of Peru. In N. Tripcevich & K. J. Vaughn (Eds.), *Mining and quarrying in the ancient Andes* (pp. 299–322). Springer.

Reinhard, J. (1992). Underwater archaeological research in Lake Titicaca, Bolivia. In *Contributions to New World archaeology* (pp. 117–143). Oxbow Books.

Robb, L. (2005). *Introduction to ore-forming processes*. Blackwell.

Rowe, J. (1977). El arte religioso del Cuzco en el Horizonte Temprano. *Ñawpa Pacha, 14*, 1–20.

Salazar, D. (2008). "La produccion minera en San Jose del Abradurante el periodo Tardio Atacameno" [Mining production in San Jose del Abra during the Late period]. *Estudios Atacamenos, 36*, 46–72.

Salazar, D., Figueroa, V., Morata, D., Mille, B., Manriquez, G., & Cifuentes, A. (2011). Metalurgia en San Pedro de Atacama durante el Período Medio: Nuevos datos, nuevas preguntas. *Revista Chilena de Antropología, 13*, 123–148.

Salazar, D., Salinas, H., Guendon, J. L., Jackson, D., & Figueroa, V. (2013). Hunter–gatherer–fisher mining during the archaic period in coastal northern Chile. In N. Tripcevich & K. J. Vaughn (Eds.), *Mining and Quarrying in the Ancient Andes* (pp. 137–156). Springer.

Schultze, C. (2008). *The role of silver ore reduction in Tiwanaku state expansion into Puno Bay, Peru*. Dissertation, University of California, Los Angeles.

Schultze, C. A. (2013). Silver mines of the Northern Lake Titicaca Basin. In N. Tripcevich & K. J. Vaughn (Eds.), *Mining and quarrying in the Ancient Andes: Sociopolitical, economic, and symbolic dimensions* (pp. 231–249). Springer.

Schultze, C. A., Stanish, C., Scott, D. A., Rehren, T., Kuehner, S., & Feathers, J. K. (2009). Direct evidence of 1,900 years of indigenous silver production in the Lake Titicaca Basin of Southern Peru. *Proceedings of the National Academy of Sciences, 106*(41), 17280–17283.

Schultze, C., de la Vega, E., & Chávez, C. (2012). La ocupación Tiwanaku en la Bahía de Puno: tradición metalúrgica. In L. Flores Blanco & H. Tantaleán (Eds.), *Arqueología de la Cuenca del Titicaca, Perú* (pp. 261–294). Instituto Francés de Estudios Andinos.

Scott, D. (1983). Depletion gilding and surface treatment of gold alloys from the Nariño area of ancient Colombia. *Journal of the Historical Metallurgy Society, 17*(2), 99–115.

Scott, D. (1986a). Fusion gilding and foil gilding in pre-Hispanic Colombia and Ecuador. In P. de Nieto (Ed.), *Metalurgia de América Precolombina*. Banco de la República.

Scott, D. (1986b). Gold and silver alloy coatings over copper: And examination of some artifacts from Ecuador and Colombia. *Archaeometry, 28*(1), 33–50.

Scott, D. (1990). Soldering with gold alloys in ancient South America: Examination of two Small gold studs from Ecuador. *Archaeometry, 32*(2), 183–190.

Scott, D. (1991). Technical examination of some gold wire from pre-hispanic South America. *Studies in Conservation, 36*, 35–75.

Scott, D. (1995). Goldwork of Pre-Columbian Costa Rica and Panama: A technical study. *Materials Research Society Symposium Proceedings, 352*, 499–525.

Scott, D. (1996). Technical study of a ceremonial Sicán Tumi figurine. *Archaeometry, 38*(2), 305–311.

Scott, David and Warwick Bray. (1994). Pre-Hispanic platinum alloys: Their composition and use in Ecuador and Colombia. In Scott and Meyers, eds. pp. 285–322. Archaeometry of Precolumbian sites and artifacts. Proceedings of the Getty Conservation Institute, .

Scott, D., & Doehne, E. (1990). Soldering of gold alloys in ancient South America: Examination of two small gold studs from Ecuador. *Archaeometry, 32*(2), 183–190.

Sepúlveda, M., Figueroa, V., & Cárcamo, J. (2014). Pigmentos y pinturas de mineral de cobre en la región de Tarapacá, Norte de Chile: Nuevos datos para una tecnología pigmentaria prehispánica. *Estudios Atacameños, 48*, 23–37.

Sepúlveda, M., Urzúa, C. L., Cárcamo-Vega, J., Casanova-Gónzalez, E., Gutiérrez, S., Maynez-Rojas, M. Á., et al. (2021). Colors and dyes of archaeological textiles from Tarapacá in the Atacama Desert (South Central Andes). *Heritage Science, 9*(1), 1–21.

Sharp, K. (2009). *Rethinking the Gallinazo: A northern perspective form the mid-Zaña Valley, Peru.* Dissertation, Southern Illinois University Carbondale Department of Anthropology.

Shimada, I. (1994). *Pampa Grande and the Mochica culture.* University of Texas Press.

Shimada, I. (1998). Prólogo. Hacia una Veradera Apreciación de Cobre en el Antiguo Perú. In J. A. de Lavelle (Ed.), *Cobre del Antiguo Perú.* AFP Integra, Lavalle Editores S.R. L.

Shimada, I. (2009). Introduction. Who were the Sicán? Their development, characteristics and legacies. In *The Golden Capital of Sicán exhibit catalog.* Tokyo Broadcasting System.

Shimada, I., & Merkel, J. F. (2021). *Naipes*: Functions and significance of Middle Sicán standardized Sheetmetal artifacts. *Ñawpa Pacha, 41*(2), 211–249.

Shimada, I, & Szumilewicz, A. (2019). *Large-scale craft production and the Andean religious center: A reconsideration.* Contributing paper presented at the 84th SAA annual meeting, Albuquerque, NM.

Shimada, I., Griffin, J. A., & Gordus, A. (2000). *The technology, iconography and social significance of metals: A multi-dimensional analysis of Middle Sican objects.* British Museum.

Shimada, I., Goldstein, D. J., Wagner, U., & Bezúr, A. (2007). Pre-hispanic sicán furnaces and metalworking: Toward a holistic understanding. In R. L. Pérez (Ed.), *Metalurgía en la América Antigua: Teoría, Arqueología, Simbología y Tecnología de los Metales Prehispánicos* (pp. 337–361). Instituto Francés de Estudios Andinos (IFEA). https://doi.org/10.4000/BOOKS. IFEA.5888

Stanish, C. (2020). The evolution of social institutions in the Central Andes. In D. M. Bondarenko, S. A. Kowalewski, & D. B. Small (Eds.), *The evolution of social institutions. World-systems evolution and global futures* (pp. 555–576). Springer.

Stöllner, T., Reindel, M., Gassman, G., Gráfingholt, B., & Cuadrado, J. I. (2013). Precolumbian raw-material exploitation in southern Peru – structures and perspectives. *Chungara, Revista de Antropología Chilena, 45*(1), 105–129.

Tassara, A., & Echaurren, A. (2012). Anatomy of the Andean subduction zone: Three-dimensional density model upgraded and compared against global-scale models. *Geophysical Journal International, 189*(1), 161–168. https://doi.org/10.1111/j.1365-246X.2012.05397.x

Téreygeol, F., & Cruz, P. (2014). Metal del Viento. Aproximación experimental para la comprensión del funcionamiento de las Wayras Andinas. *Estudios Atacameños, 48*, 39–54. https://www.researchgate.net/publication/269035777

Téreygeol, F., Cruz, P., & Méaudre, J. C. (2020). The reverberatory furnace for ore smelting: An experiment on a south American innovation. *Journal of Archaeological Science: Reports, 33*, 102580. https://doi.org/10.1016/j.jasrep.2020.102580

Topic, J. (1990). Craft production in the Kingdom of Chimor. *The Northern Dynasties: Kingship and Statecraft in Chimor.* A symposium at Dumbarton Oaks 12th and 13th October 1985.

Uhland, S., Lechtman, H., & Kaufman, L. (2001). Assessment of the As-Cu-Ni system: An example from archaeology. *Calphad, 25*(1), 109–124.

van Buren, M., & Mills, B. (2005). Huayrachinas and Tocochimbos: Traditional smelting technology of the Southern Andes. *Latin American Antiquity, 16*(1), 3–25. https://doi.org/10.2307/30042484

Van Gijseghem, H., Vaughn, K. J., Whalen, V. H., Linares Grados, M., & Olano Canales, J. (2013). Economic, social, and ritual aspects of copper mining in ancient Peru: An Upper Ica Valley case study. In N. Tripcevich & K. J. Vaughn (Eds.), *Mining and quarrying in the ancient Andes: Sociopolitical, economic, and symbolic dimensions* (pp. 275–298). Springer.

Vaughn, K. J., Van Gijseghem, H., Whalen, V. H., Eerkens, J. W., & Grados, M. L. (2013). The organization of mining in Nasca during the early intermediate period: Recent evidence from Mina Primavera. In N. Tripcevich & K. J. Vaughn (Eds.), *Mining and quarrying in the Ancient Andes* (pp. 157–182). Springer.

Vetter Parodi, L., & Guerra, M. F. (2017). Los tupus y esatuillas de Plata Inka: una aproximación a sus aleaciones. *Bulletin de l'institute Francais d'Etudes Andines, 46*(1), 171–192. https://doi.org/10.4000/bifea.8397

Vetter Parodi, L. M. (2008). *Platero indígenas en el Virreinato del Perú: Siglos XVI y XVII*. Fondo Ediorial de la Universidad Nacional Mayor de San Marcos.

Vogel, M., Fowler, J., Drake, L., & Brooks, W. E. (2015). Geochemical evidence for the use of lead in Prehispanic metallurgy at El Purgatorio, Casma Valley, Peru. *Journal of Archaeological Science: Reports, 4*, 326–335.

von Tschudi, J. J. (1865). *Travels in Peru: On the coast, in the sierra, across the cordilleras and the Andes, into the Primeval Forests*. AS Barnes & Company.

Xie, P., & Rehren, T. (2009). Scientific analysis of lead-silver smelting slag from two sites in China. In *Metallurgy and civilisation: Eurasia and beyond, Archetype in Association with the University of Science and Technology Beijing and the Institute for Archaeo-metallurgical Studies* (pp. 177–183). Archetype.

Young-Sánchez, M. (Ed.). (2004). *Tiwanaku: Ancestors of the Inca*. University of Nebraska Press.

Zori, C. (2011). *Metals for the Inka: Craft production and empire in the Quebrada de Tarapacá, Northern Chile*. Dissertation, University of California, Los Angeles.

Zori, C. (2019). Extracting insights from prehistoric Andean metallurgy: Political organization, interregional connections, and ritual meanings. *Journal of Archaeological Research, 27*, 501–556.

Zori, C., & Tropper, P. (2013). Silver lining: Evidence for Inka silver refining in northern Chile. *Journal of Archaeological Science, 40*(8), 3282–3292.

Experimental Bloomery Iron Smelting in the Study of Iron Technology in the Southern Levant

Adi Eliyahu Behar (iD)

Abstract Iron production is often considered one of humankind's most significant technological advances. While the identification of ironworking remains has improved our understanding of this practice in the early Iron Age in the southern Levant, several major technological and sociopolitical aspects remain unanswered. Particularly significant is the source of the raw material. Several geological iron-rich ore deposits are known in the southern Levant. However, archaeological evidence for exploitation in antiquity derives solely from the Mugharet el-Wardeh ore deposit in modern Jordan. To identify the use of other ore sources, a reliable provenancing method for ferrous metals is required.

This paper describes the use of experimental bloomery iron smelting in order to investigate some of the technological aspects of iron production, particularly the role of raw materials and provenance. A series of systematic smelting experiments were conducted under carefully controlled scientific conditions. Several aims were put forward for the experiments, the main one being to establish a provenancing method for archaeological iron based on osmium isotopic analysis. The experiments were run by professional and experienced iron smelters, utilizing ore deposits from the Negev region in southern Israel in two types of furnaces: the shaft-tapping furnace and the bowl furnace.

I share some of the decisions made while planning and conducting the experiments and their implications for the results obtained. I then summarize several significant contributions of the experiments to interpreting the archaeological record, as gleaned from previous field and analytical observations.

Keywords Bloomery iron smelting · Experimental archaeology · Provenance · Iron Age · Chaîne Opératoire · Southern Levant

---

A. E. Behar (✉)
The Department of Archaeology and the Land of Israel Studies and The Department of Chemical Sciences, Ariel University, Ariel, Israel
e-mail: adieli@ariel.ac.il

© The Author(s), under exclusive license to Springer Nature Switzerland AG 2023
E. Ben-Yosef, I. W. N. Jones (eds.), *"And in Length of Days Understanding" (Job 12:12): Essays on Archaeology in the Eastern Mediterranean and Beyond in Honor of Thomas E. Levy*, Interdisciplinary Contributions to Archaeology, https://doi.org/10.1007/978-3-031-27330-8_61

1 Introduction

Experimental archaeology studies past behavioral processes through experimental reconstruction under carefully controlled scientific conditions (Outram, 2008; Renfrew & Bahn, 2004: 578). Modern experiments utilizing various techniques in different fields have proven vital in understanding the archaeological record. Moreover, experimental archaeology has often helped to predict the sorts of artifacts and debris we should be looking for in the course of an excavation or even to "fill the gaps" though cautiously, in cases where the archaeological record is partial or even completely absent. Archaeological experiments were successfully applied to various research questions, from site-formation processes, use-wear analysis, technological processes, and the spread or spatial distribution of manufacturing debris (e.g., Banerjea, 2008; Dolfini, 2011; Gur-Arieh et al., 2012).

Technological and pyro-technological experiments are often used alongside archaeological materials in an attempt to replicate specific practices or to corroborate evidence, while others are motivated by the effort to reconstruct the *chaîne opératoire* of such activities (Hodgkinson & Bertram, 2020; Juleff, 1996; S. Merkel & Rehren, 2007; Paynter, 2008). The technology of metal production and the field of Archaeometallurgy are eminently suitable for this research method.

Archaeometallurgists are particularly interested in the procurement and mining of raw materials, smelting of the ores and the various processes and techniques involved in manufacturing and working of raw metals into final objects. Another equally important aim is to identify the origin of metal artifacts, i.e., to provenance raw materials used for their production. These topics are essential for understanding early socio-economic structures and the interactions between social groups and regions.

Experimental studies in the field of Archaeometallurgy are abundant. However, research in the southern Levant predominantly focused on copper metallurgy. Attention was placed on the early mining and smelting of copper in the Timna Valley in the Arabah (Merkel, 1985, 1990). In 1997, more than 30 years after the discovery of the hoard at Nahal Mishmar in the Judean Desert, Tom Levy was invited by *National Geographic* to lead an experimental archaeological expedition focusing on fifth-millennium BCE methods of copper mining, transport, and smelting. Supported by a group of international scholars, Levy set out on a 10-day donkey caravan journey from the copper mining district of Faynan to the Beer-Sheba Valley, where copper smelting experiments were performed using the ores collected from the mines. Other experiments, to name just two, including the reconstruction of the elaborate Nahal Mishmar casting techniques, using the help of sculptures and foundry craftsman from the UK (Shalev, 1999) and the reconstruction of the copper smelting and melting processes at Abu Matar (Shugar, 2001).

In addition to the contribution of experimental archaeology, important information can be gathered from ethnographic studies, which provide critical insights for reconstructing ancient technologies, particularly regarding metallurgical practices. One example is Levy's work in India with his wife Alina, which involved ethnoarchaeology and experimentation. In their seminal book, *Masters of Fire* (Levy et al.,

2008), the Levys researched the bronze icon industry of Tamil Nadu, one of India's unique and beautiful traditional crafts. Working from an anthropological and archaeological perspective, Levy used traditional craftsmanship in India to shed light on his archaeological research interests, focusing on the material culture and the role of metal production in the social context of the southern Levant. From his perspective, the "living traditional metal craft industries of India could provide a unique opportunity to help us understand prehistoric and historic metal production found at sites [he] had excavated in the Holy Land—Israel and Jordan" (Levy et al., 2008: 10).

Significant insights were gained from this work concerning the organization of the metal craft, the relationship between production and ritual, the complete *chaîne opératoire* of metal production in general, and that of the "lost wax" method in particular. The latter was achieved through an experiment in which Levy asked the bronze caster of the Sthapathy family to reconstruct the "Double Headed Ibex" copper mace head, one of the most elaborate and spectacular objects from the abovementioned Nahal Mishmar hoard.

Levy's work in Jordan, Israel, and India constitutes a landmark and a source of inspiration for me. The idea of using experimental archaeology to develop methodological applications for provenance while shedding light on metallurgical practices was an invaluable insight. In 2009, shortly after I received my doctorate,[1] I realized that to answer one of the more fundamental questions regarding the advent of iron into the southern Levant, the provenance issue must be resolved, and an experimental approach should be applied. Although it took another ten years for the seeds to ripen, the experiments finally materialized into reality, as I describe below.

1.1   Iron Production in the Southern Levant

Archaeological evidence for iron production via the bloomery process has accumulated in recent years, and understanding regarding the invention and innovation of iron production, and use was dramatically improved. Iron production was identified at major Iron Age sites in the southern Levant (Fig. 1), for example, at Hazor, Megiddo, Tel Rehov, Ashkelon, Tel Beth-Shemesh and Tell es-Safi-Gath in Israel and Tell Hammeh in Jordan (Eliyahu-Behar et al., 2012, 2013; Erb-Satullo & Walton, 2017; Veldhuijzen & Rehren, 2007; Workman et al., 2020; Yahalom-Mack et al., 2014, 2017). Production remains attest to a wide range of activities and hint at varying forms of technological practices, reflected by varying waste products. The metallurgical activity at all of these sites was dated no earlier than the Iron Age IIA, tenth–ninth centuries BCE, and was often associated with administrative buildings, suggesting that it had been controlled by a central authority (Yahalom-Mack & Eliyahu-Behar, 2015).

---

[1] When joining the European Research Council (ERC) sponsored program entitled "Reconstructing Ancient Israel – The Exact and Life Sciences Perspective" (2009–2014) granted to Israel Finkelstein (Tel Aviv University) and Steve Weiner (Weizmann Institute of Science).

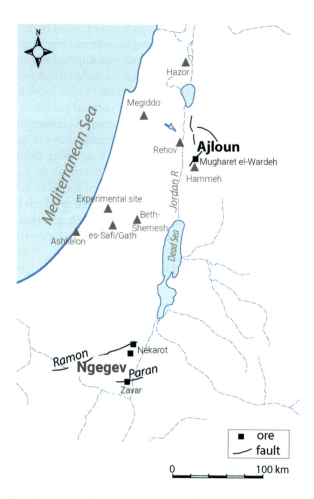

Fig. 1 Map of southern Levant. Showing the location of the three epigenetic hydrothermal iron ores used for the experimental smelting (Nekarot and Zavar), and the location of the Mugharet el-Wrdeh ore deposit of the Ajloun region. (Modified from Brauns et al., 2020). Also shown are some Iron Age archaeological sites mentioned in the text, and the experimental site

One of the first discoveries that fundamentally affected my perspective regarding iron production in the southern Levant was an *in-situ* bronze and iron smithy unearthed at Tell es-Safi/Gath. In the summer of 2010, after a bronze crucible was identified in the field, Naama Yahalom-Mack and I received an invitation from the excavation director, Aren Maeir, to excavate the particular context of the find, located in Area A, the site's acropolis and assigned to Stratum A4, the late tenth-early ninth centuries BCE. The context was excavated slowly and meticulously, using archaeometallurgical methodologies, with frequently repeated sampling and analysis of sediments and other collected materials. As the excavation proceeded, two pit-like features, differing considerably from one another in color, texture, and content, were identified. Adhering to one of the pits was solidified iron slag, unique in its appearance, which through chemical and microstructure analysis, was identified as a "furnace bottom" smelting slag (Eliyahu-Behar et al., 2012).

This was the first time I proposed that iron ores were brought to the site from a currently unknown ore source and that the complete *chaîne opératoire* of iron production was performed on-site, in the midst of an urban center. Subsequently, this idea was further strengthened based on microstructure and chemical analysis of production debris, mainly slag cakes and bloom fragments, from Hazor, Tel Beer-Sheba, and Tel Rehov (Eliyahu-Behar et al., 2013).

Although this claim remains debatable, it raised intriguing questions regarding the available technologies during this early stage of iron production. Based on the apparent variability in production debris, I suggested that three different smelting technologies were simultaneously in use; pit smelting resulting in molten slag (Tell es-Safi/Gath), pit smelting(?) resulting in slag cakes (e.g., at Hazor, Tel Beer-Sheba, Tel Rehov, and possibly Megiddo), and the use of tapping furnaces yielding tapping slag (at Tell Hammeh, Jordan).

The choice of furnace type and the technology used was likely related to the available knowledge, as well as the amount and type of ore processed, which in turn would determine the type of slag formed. Thus, identifying the ore sources has become a primary research question. Which iron ore deposits were exploited? Were there one or more available sources? Can we correlate the range and types of smelting slag to different smelting technologies and/or the use of different ore sources?

To date, the only known archaeological evidence of iron ore exploitation within the southern Levant derives from Tell Hammeh, the only site directly connected to an iron ore source, being located ca. 2.5 km from the Mugharet el-Wardeh ore deposit of the Ajloun region in modern Jordan (Al-Amri & Hauptmann, 2008; Dill et al., 2010; Veldhuijzen & Rehren, 2007). However, a range of smaller deposits, geologically and mineralogically similar to the Wardeh ores, exists in the broader region, notably in the Negev desert (Fig. 1).

Thus, it became clear that as a means to verify the on-site smelting hypothesis, the ore sources of the southern Levant must be identified. Furthermore, provenancing archaeological iron would, in turn, shed light on geopolitical, economic, and social factors of a period in which iron becomes prevalent in daily use. In the southern Levant, this change occurred in the early first millennium BCE, with the rise of Iron Age kingdoms, such as Judah and Israel (Bunimovitz & Lederman, 2012; Yahalom-Mack & Eliyahu-Behar, 2015). The control of iron sources likely became a strategic military and economic advantage at that time.

1.2 Iron Provenancing

The provenancing of metals relies heavily on applying geochemical and analytical techniques accompanied by the compilation of a database of geological ore sources. While chemical and lead isotope analyses (LIA) are routinely used for the provenancing of lead, silver, and copper-based alloys (Pernicka, 2014; Stos-Gale & Gale, 2009), the provenancing of iron has remained limited due to the currently available methodologies which are almost exclusively focused on correlating major, minor, and trace element concentrations of slag inclusions with those of the ore and smelting slag (Blakelock et al., 2009; Buchwald & Wivel, 1998; Charlton et al., 2012; Coustures et al., 2014; Desaulty et al., 2008, 2009; Dillmann & L'Héritier, 2007; Leroy et al., 2012). In addition to the destructive nature of these analyses, one major disadvantage is that it relies on the fact that the relevant ore sources are known and can be used for comparison. As ore sources of the southern Levant are yet unknown (apart from the Mugharet el-Wardeh deposit, see below), this has been a significant obstacle, and the ability to provenance iron objects has remained a major challenge

In 2013, Brauns et al. (2013) suggested using osmium isotopic analysis as a method for the provenancing of ferrous metals. Based on a small set of samples, they reached the important conclusion that the $^{187}Os/^{188}Os$ ratio does not alter during smelting (similar to provenancing by LIA) – a necessary supposition that allows the association of geological iron ore resources with the archaeological metal. However, substantial development and testing were still required.

2 Bloomery Iron Smelting Experiments

To provide some answers to the above questions, I initiated a series of bloomery iron smelting experiments using locally available iron ores. Almost ten years after first conceiving this idea, the experiments finally became a reality[2]. The experiments were conducted over two sessions, during February 2019 and February 2020, at Mesheq Hanan, Kidron Village, Israel. The farm (which belongs to a close friend who is also a blacksmith) is situated in the Shephelah, less than 20 km northwest of the Tell es-Safi/Gath. It is thus characterized by similar geology and, specifically, similar clays. This was most advantageous as we used local mud/clay material to construct of the technical ceramics for some of the experiments (see below).

The value of experimental smelting strongly depends on its purpose and aims. The experiments conducted in this project were designed with three goals in mind:

(1) to examine the compatibility of local iron ores for smelting in a bloomery furnace;
(2) to produce end-products, including metal bloom and bar, and by-products (slag), in a closed and well-documented system that would be used to affirm the potential of osmium isotope analysis as a means to provenance iron; and
(3) to replicate the metallurgical debris which is unearthed during archaeological excavation and to reconstruct the metallurgical practices involved.

---

[2] This was made possible with the support of the Israel Science Foundation.

Based on the successful iron smelting experiments Jane Humphris conducted in Meroe, Sudan, just a few years earlier (Humphris et al., 2018), and the very warm recommendations I received from her, I was lucky to assemble an international team headed by two experienced, professional smelters, Jake Keen (UK) and Lee Sauder (US).

Jake founded and directed The Ancient Technology Centre, devoted to Experimental Archaeology at Cranborne, UK, in 1985. Since then, he has been involved in various projects, specializing in iron smelting in recent years. Lee is a professional blacksmith and sculptor. For the last 20 years, a central focus of his work has been independent research into the practical techniques of bloomery smelting and forging. Based on many years of experimental trials and investigations, he has perfected a smelting technique that utilizes a shaft furnace with slag tapping, operated at moderately reducing conditions, yielding a well-consolidated, forgeable bloom of iron (Sauder, 2013; Sauder & Williams, 2002).

Bloomery iron smelting is a complicated technology involving multiple steps which can be roughly divided into three main stages: the smelting (reduction) of the ores to produce a bloom (a spongy mass that is a mixture of metal and slag), the refining of the bloom (primary smithing) to produce a more compacted metal (a bar ingot), and the forging of the final product—an iron tool/object (secondary smithing). Apart from these stages, the *chaîne opératoire* of iron production requires many processes and decisions dealing with the procurement and preparation of raw materials, the technical design and construction of the furnace, and the smelting protocol itself with its many (dependent and independent) variables. Each objective in our experimental trials influenced the decisions and choices made for each of these stages.

The choice of iron ore was dictated by their availability and accessibility in the local geology. Based on previous geological surveys, and following crucible smelting experiments under laboratory conditions conducted a year earlier (Stepanov et al., 2020), three deposits in the Negev region were selected. These are epigenetic, hydrothermal ores that appear as veins and lenses along major trending faults related to the Dead Sea Transform (DST) in Israel and Jordan (Ilani Ilani, 1989). Chemical and mineralogical analysis of the ores showed common mineralogical and geochemical properties, similar to the Mugharet el-Wardeh ore deposit (Jordan) for which evidence for ancient exploitation is known (Al-Amri & Hauptmann, 2008; Dill et al., 2010; Veldhuijzen & Rehren, 2007, Fig. 1). Predominantly the ores are composed of goethite and hematite (Fe_2O_3, 70–80 wt%), associated with quartz (as chert), calcite, and evaporite minerals such as gypsum and barite (for detailed analysis of the ores, see Stepanov et al., 2020). Being exposed on the surface, these ores were easily accessible, and after receiving the necessary permits (the ores are located within a national park reserve), we set out to collect a large amount for our experiments. Within an hour or two, and using only hand hammers, we collected about 100 kg of ore from each deposit.

Before smelting, ores were beneficiated and prepared by crudely crushing the iron-rich chunks and roasting in a wood fire for several hours. After roasting, ores were crushed into "pea-sized" pieces, 1–2 cm in size. Commercially available charcoal (imported from Colombia) was used as fuel.

Two main types of smelting furnaces were used for the experiments, designed to achieve the aims specified above: a slag tapping shaft furnace and various designs of a bowl/hearth furnace (Fig. 2). The shaft furnace was used to investigate the potential of the local ores and to conduct the complete iron production sequence to obtain the necessary materials, products, and by-products in order to develop the provenance methodology for osmium isotope analysis. The shaft furnace was chosen to assure the best results, i.e., to have a successful smelt, resulting in a well-consolidated bloom that can easily be forged into a bar. As this was the study's

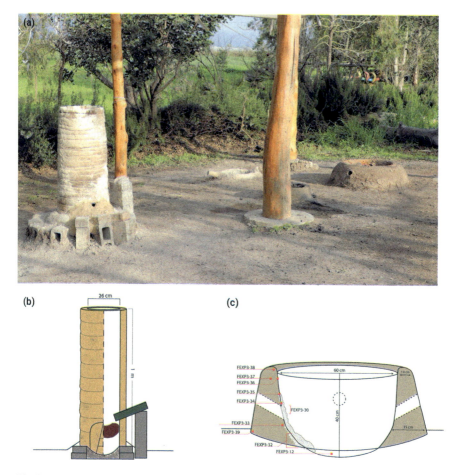

Fig. 2 The smelting furnace. (**a**) Picture was taken at the end of the 2019 season showing several of the bowl furnace installations used during the experiments and the shaft furnace (left). (**b**) scheme of the shaft furnace (taken from Stepanov et al., 2022) and (**c**) bowl furnace used for experiment 3, showing locations of sampled materials studied and analysed by Workman V. (taken from Workman et al., 2021). Plans credit: V. Workman (not to scale)

primary aim, it affected many of the decisions made and parameters used during smelting and thus the general "nature" of the experiments (described below).

It should be emphasized that this decision was based on practical reasons rather than archaeological incentives. In contrast, the bowl-furnace installations were designed with the archaeological findings and production debris in mind, especially molten slag and slag cakes, to better understand or simulate production practices that led to the formation of these debris. For this purpose, a combination of more authentic materials and techniques were used alongside modern ones. Below is a brief description of the experiments conducted and a summary of the results obtained.

2.1 Smelting Experiments via Shaft Furnace and Slag Tapping

Both the design of the smelting furnace and the smelting protocol were largely dictated by our major goal—to produce a well-consolidated, forgeable bloom of soft iron that would allow the completion of the entire *chaîne opératoire* from smelting the ore to the forging of a final object of a bar (including production debris). This assured that we would obtain all the necessary samples for developing the osmium isotopic analysis provenance method. Hence, parameters related to the design of the smelting furnace and its operation protocol were solely the choice of Sauder based on his vast experience gathered over many years of experimentation. His methodology is widely known and has become a common practice in contemporary bloomery smelting experiments all over the world (e.g., Benvenuti et al., 2016; Humphris et al., 2018) and was used in several smelts conducted during the *Woodford Furnace Festival* in 2018–2020.

Sauder's furnace design is a simple, relatively small, cylindrical shaft furnace, ca. 1 m high and 26 cm inner diameter, operated with forced air (Fig. 2). This design enables the smelter to achieve a well-compacted, moderately sized bloom that could be easily refined using hand hammers. Kaolinite commercial clay mixed with building sand and shredded straw was used to build the furnace walls. The clay structure was built against a round column of bamboo. Prior to operation, the furnace was dried out with a fire set in its interior, burning the bamboo inner structure. The choice of a refractory clay mixture was made to ensure minimum melting of the furnace walls, thus enabling multiple reuses of the structure, and limiting the contamination of the osmium isotopic signal of the ore and products.

During smelting, air was supplied via an electric blower and a copper tuyère to ensure a stable and constant airflow which is important for the success of the smelt. This system was used instead of a more authentic hand-operated bellows due to the lack of skills needed to maintain a consistent supply of air over the duration of several hours, in keeping with the initial aim of these experiments.

Bloom forging was conducted in a small hearth, specifically built for this purpose using the above-described clay mixture. Forging consisted of re-heating and

Fig. 3 Various stages of field smelting experiments. (**a–c**) ores collected in the field, inspected, and, prepared for roasting in an open fire by Jake Keen, (**d**) Lee Sauder is loading the furnace during smelting and the team measuring the temperature using thermocouples, (**e**) removing the bloom when red hot, (**f**) cutting the bloom while still red hot (**g**) smithing a quarter of bloom into a bar on an iron anvil. (Modified from Brauns et al., 2020)

hammering quarters of the blooms from each conducted experiment into bars (Fig. 3).

Initially, three smelting experiments were successfully conducted under similar conditions, using roughly the same parameters of air flow, temperature, ore to fuel ratio, and charging rates, but each using a different ore deposit. A fourth experiment was conducted in the following year (2020), in which some of the operating parameters were slightly tweaked to investigate their effect on the physical properties of the produced bloom and the overall outcome of the experiment.

Using the three ore deposits from the Negev region, we were able to obtain metallic iron in the form of a bloom which was then hammered and forged into iron bars

Fig. 4 Bloom and bars from the experiments. (**a**) One quarter of the bloom prior to smithing (**b**) Red hot bar, (**c**) A quarter of the bloom sectioned in the lab (**d**) bar sectioned for analysis

(Fig. 4), thus confirming the suitability of these ores to be reduced in a bloomery smelting and to produce metallic iron. Detailed description and documentation of all four experiments, the various operation parameters, total yields, durations, and comprehensive analysis of the metal and slag produced were recently summarized by Ivan Stepanov as part of his post-doctorate studies (Stepanov et al., 2022). Stepanov rigorously analysed all the products of the smelting process using various analytical techniques, including pXRF, optical and electron microscopy, metallography, and hardness tests. This enabled us to investigate the effect of decisions and choices made during smelting, by a skilful iron smelter, on the physical properties of the final products, iron metal, and slag. This also gave us the opportunity to understand skills and techniques which are usually invisible in the archaeological record and are impossible to directly deduce from the analysis of slag and other materials.

For example, the results show that after the first smelt, the smelter learned how to optimize the smelting protocol to account for the characteristics of the new, unfamiliar iron ore. These fine adjustments were, in turn, reflected in the chemical composition and physical properties of the final products (iron and slag), as well as the practical yield which was the lowest in the first smelt (for detailed results, see Stepanov et al., 2022).

A separate study was dedicated to the major aim of this project—the development of a robust tool that will enable identifying the ore sources of the southern Levant by correlating archaeological iron objects with known geological iron ore deposits using osmium isotopic composition analysis. To accomplish this, all materials used during smelting—ores, charcoal, and furnace clay—and all the smelting products and by-products—iron metal (blooms and bars) and tap slag—were subjected to Os isotopic analysis. Analyses were conducted by our colleague and friend, Michael Brauns (Curt-Engelhorn-Zentrum Archaometrie, Mannheim, Germany). Results, which were recently published (Brauns et al., 2020), confirm that the $^{187}Os/^{188}Os$ isotopic ratio is maintained from ore to metal, with no significant isotopic fractionation—a necessary requirement without which the method cannot be applied. In addition, enrichment and depletion of osmium content were observed in the transition from ore to metal and from ore to slag respectively. This observation has potential significance for our ability to differentiate between the various process stages of iron production and sheds light on the suitability of various production remains for this method. Moreover, it can serve as another discriminating factor between iron ores with similar $^{187}Os/^{188}Os$ isotopic ratios but varying Os content. Thus, we were able to demonstrate the high potential the Os isotopic analysis has to offer for the provenancing of archaeological ferrous metals. However, for this method to be successfully applied, a large database of iron ore deposits for the region in question, in our case, the southern Levant and neighboring regions, need to be systemically created. This is the aim for the years to come.

2.2 Smelting Experiments via Bowl Furnace with No Slag Tapping

The third goal set within the framework of this project was to suggest a more realistic reconstruction of the archaeological evidence. What were the known parameters we could introduce to these experiments? The ore source was unknown. Unfortunately, the Mugharet el-Wardeh ore deposit was not accessible for these experiments. What did we know about installations and other technical ceramics involved in the process?

While the conclusion that smelting was performed in settlement sites was based on the analysis of slag cakes and other debris, it lacked support from built installations and/or furnace remains. Regrettably, evidence for a smelting furnace/installation that would enable a full reconstruction of its shape and the choice of smelting technique (pit/shaft/tapping furnace) was not preserved in any of the abovementioned sites. Evidence does appear in the form of some vitrified ceramic fragments, some small, localized patterns of heated sediments associated with iron debris, and the plastered pit with no superstructure identified at Tell es-Safi/Gath. Tuyères in various forms, notably ones with a square profile and differing in their vitrification degree, were also found at most sites, suggesting that some air-blowing system was used, likely built of perishable materials. Reasons for the infrequent preservation of such installation structures may be diverse but can also be inherent to the process as such installations were often dismantled at the end of the smelting process to remove the bloom (based on ethnographic examples and modern smelting experiments).

Thus, there was not much archaeological evidence to work with apart from the size and general appearance of the dense molten slag from Tell es-Safi/Gath and slag cakes typically found at other sites, previously identified as smelting slag. Following consultation with our professional smelters, it was proposed that the slag cakes might have been produced within a small, pit-like hearth or a bowl furnace. The bowl furnace is a simple pit dug into the ground with a superstructure of a low dome or straight clay walls. This furnace type was suggested for the earliest phases of iron production in diverse chronological and geographical settings. However, it is considered enigmatic and highly debated (for discussions on its validity and use in Europe, see Dungworth, 2014; Rondelez, 2017 and references therein). Also, the bowl-furnace design implies smelting without tapping.

Several smelting attempts were conducted in various designs of bowl furnaces but all shared a similar basic structure designed by Jake Keen. Local mud (sandy clay) available at the farm, mixed with chaff to improve structural integrity and resistance to thermal shock, was used for construction. Structures were built on top of a small pit, dug below ground level. Tuyères made from the same clay recipe were utilized in these experiments. Smelting was operated by several types of air-blowing systems. In some, one to three alternating commercial hairdryers were used to regulate the airflow, while other attempts were made using various types of hand-operated bellows. Temperatures in the range of 1000–1300°C were generated (recorded using thermocouples). Slag was not tapped during the smelt; instead, we attempted to create a bloom and a pool of slag at the bottom of the hearth. Each attempt was performed in a different way, with no clear or strict protocol. Ideas were proposed and tried, with some more successful than others, and some complete failures.

All these attempts were unsuccessful in the sense that a consolidated iron bloom did not form. Instead, generally loose pieces and larger chunks of partially reacted ore with some molten slag were found at the end of the smelt with the occasional formation of a more dense, blocky slag sharing some similar characteristics to the archaeological evidence. Materials obtained from these experiments still await analysis, and future work might shed some light on the possible faults and mistakes of these attempts. It should, however, be highlighted that none of the participants in these smelting experiments, including the professional smelters, had substantial previous experience with bowl-furnace bloomery smelting.

Nevertheless, some interesting insights were gained from the bowl-furnace experiments, which were recently summarized by Workman et al. (2021). In this study, we used the archaeological experiments to investigate and interpret an assemblage of vitrified technical ceramics found in an early Iron Age metal workshop in the lower city of Tell es-Safi/Gath. Specifically, emphasis was given to the deformations and vitrification of the experimental installations through the smelting process, and the implication this has for understanding the lack of preservation of such installations in the archaeological record.

For example, we were able to show that even though the experimental bowl-furnace installation underwent severe vitrification (and melting) of the inner walls, especially in regions below or adjacent to protruding tuyères due to the very high temperatures achieved during smelting, the outside clay walls showed no signs of alteration due to heat (based on FTIR analysis; for details see Workman et al., 2021). This inevitably means that even after high-temperature firing, over time, these unaltered clay walls would essentially disintegrate, leaving only the thin vitrified inner surface (ca. 3–4 cm thick, Fig. 5a–b) of the construction. Similar vitrified clay fragments were previously unearthed, for example, at Tell es-Safi/Gath, associated with other iron production debris, but their interpretation was based on assumptions alone. Here, we were able to produce the evidence directly, leaving no room for speculation. In other words, the remains from the bowl-furnace experiments match the vitrified archaeological remains identified at Tell es-Safi/Gath both visually and chemically, corroborating the association of the latter to iron production, and possibly hinting at the use of similar installations for the activity (see Fig. 5).

An explanation can now be given for the relatively better preservation of the orange-colored pit feature identified in the upper city of Tell es-Safi/Gath, mentioned at the beginning of this article. It was made using a purposeful mixture of clay and calcite (Eliyahu-Behar et al., 2012). Upon heating, this mixture hardened

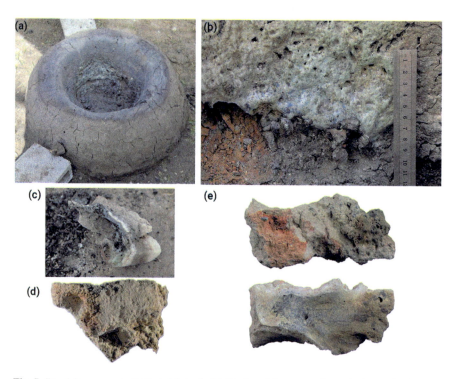

Fig. 5 Bowl furnace and vitrified debris. (**a, b**) The bowl furnace at the end of a smelt, showing the vitrification of the inner walls and the underneath reddish clay layer (in-close up). (**c**) a fragment of experimental tuyere vitrified to the furnace clay. (**d, e**) Similar archaeological debris unearthed at Tell es-Safi/Gath; (**d**) vitrified tuyere from the acropolis (Area A), and (**e**) vitrified clay fragment from the lower city (Area D). (Not to scale)

to become a plaster-like material that was clearly different from the surrounding sediments, and thus was easier to identify during excavation.

3 Conclusions and Ruminations

Experimental archaeology in iron smelting experiments proved invaluable in providing answers for some of the main aims set forward, i.e. establishing osmium isotopic analysis is a viable tool for provenancing archaeological ferrous metals. No doubt, the success of the experiments lies in their coherence. When the aim of the experiment was firmly set, results were clear and coherent, and vice versa; when the aim was very general, and many unknown variables were involved, the results were inconclusive. Nevertheless, all experiments introduced insightful observations and useful data for the interpretation of the archaeological record, and for future research and experiments. For developing the provenancing method we worked with a well-known system, managed by an experienced professional smelter, who had all the empirical means needed in order to determine the right ore- to- fuel ratio, charging rate, air flow rate, and temperature control. Each of these parameters, affecting the others in the system, was closely monitored by means of pure experience and "feel" of the system behavior. Certainly, similar skills were required in ancient times.

This made it possible to hold all but one variable constant (the ore deposit), thus creating a protocol that was as close as possible to a controlled, scientific experiment. In contrast, the bowl-furnace experiments involved experimenting with many different variables at a time, resulting in less definitive outcomes.

Success of the shaft furnace experiments enabled us to obtain two of our main objectives: to demonstrate the potential of the local iron ores of the Negev for smelting in antiquity, and to produce good, consolidated metal (bloom and bar) with corresponding slag which allowed the provenancing method to be tested. However, if we were to consider only the results of the bowl-furnace experiments, it may have been concluded that the ores are not good enough for bloomery smelting, that smelting is impossible in the designed bowl furnace used, and that a smelting slag cake cannot be produced in such a furnace. This would negate our smelting hypothesis and the interpretation of the archaeological record. Clearly, this would be wrong and even misleading.

One conclusion that can be drawn from the bowl-furnace experiments is that skilled artisans are a significant advantage when reconstructions of ancient technologies are sought. Recently, experimental archaeology has become more prevalent, yet some of the experiments are problematic. Using non-professional artisans adds extraneous variables; these are extra factors that may influence the outcome of an experiment, even though they are not the focus of the experiment, and thus can lead to a bias. with appropriately formulated research questions and a strategy for monitoring the influence of each variable should be established. Clearly, if aspects of bowl-furnace smelting are to be further researched, more experiments should be undertaken, leaving time for improvement, learning from mistakes, and conducting analysis, to allow better reconstruction of the archaeological record.

Despite these caveats, it is obvious that such experiments can generate many new ideas that can guide future excavation strategies, help formulate research questions and, above all, encourage a certain humility about what we can discern from archaeological remains.

Acknowledgments This research and the ability to carry out the experiments were made possible by the support of the Israel Science Foundation research grant awarded to the author (grant no.1047/17, titled "Early Iron (Iron Age I-IIA) Smelting in the Southern Levant; Technological Aspects), for which I am sincerely thankful.

I would like to thank Prof. Tom Levy (UCSD) for his initial inspiration and long-distance support over the years, and Dr. Jane Humphris for introducing me to the magnificent Jake Keen and Lee Sauder without whom none of this would have been so productive, fun, and pleasant. Many people contributed to the research and subsequent analysis, in particular Dr. Ivan Stepanov, Dr. Michael Brauns, Dr. Naama Yahalom-Mack, and Vanessa Workman. I am also grateful to Maria Eniukhina and Lina Maria Campos Quintero for their valuable help in sampling, documentation, and photography during experiments, and to Yoav and Tamar Hanan for providing their backyard and iron workshop for the smelting experiments, and for their hospitality during these two seasons. A special and warm-hearted thanks are due to my private blacksmith and enthusiastic partner, Etay Spector, who was there to enjoy the charm of smelting and support me when needed. Thanks also goes to Brady Liss for his valuable comments and suggestions for improvements in this manuscript. Finally, I would like to add a special acknowledgment to my dear friend and colleague, Dr. Naama Yahalom-Mack for walking along with me for more than 20 years in the fields of archaeometallurgy, providing inspiration, endless hours of brainstorming, guidance, and fruitful discussions.

References

Al-Amri, Y., & Hauptmann, A. (2008). The Iron Ore Mine of Mugharat el-Wardeh/Jordan in Southern Bilad al-Sham: Excavation and new dating. In Ü. Yalçin, H. Özbal, & A. G. Paşamehmetoğlu (Eds.), *Ancient mining in Turkey and The Eastern Mediterranean* (pp. 415–434). Atilim University.

Banerjea, R. Y. (2008). Experimental geochemistry: A multi-elemental characterization of known activity areas. *Antiquity, 82,* 318.

Benvenuti, M., Orlando, A., Borrini, D., Chiarantini, L., Costagliola, P., Mazzotta, C., & Rimondi, V. (2016). Experimental smelting of iron ores from Elba Island (Tuscany, Italy): Results and implications for the reconstruction of ancient metallurgical processes and iron provenance. *Journal of Archaeological Science, 70,* 1–14.

Blakelock, E., Martinon-Torres, M., Veldhuijzen, H. A., & Young, T. (2009). Slag inclusions in iron objects and the quest for provenance: An experiment and a case study. *Journal of Archaeological Science, 36*(8), 1745–1757.

Brauns, M., Schwab, R., Gassmann, G., Wieland, G., & Pernicka, E. (2013). Provenance of Iron Age iron in southern Germany: A new approach. *Journal of Archaeological Science, 40*(2), 841–849.

Brauns, M., Yahalom-Mack, N., Stepanov, I., Sauder, L., Keen, J., & Eliyahu-Behar, A. (2020). Osmium isotope analysis as an innovative tool for provenancing ancient iron: A systematic approach. *Plos one, 15*(3), e0229623.

Experimental Bloomery Iron Smelting in the Study of Iron Technology in the Southern... 1465

Buchwald, V. F., & Wivel, H. (1998). Slag analysis as a method for the characterization and provenancing of ancient iron objects. *Materials Characterization, 40*(2), 73–96.

Bunimovitz, S., & Lederman, Z. (2012). Iron Age iron: From invention to innovation. In J. M. Webb & D. Frankel (Eds.), *Studies in Mediterranean Archaeology*: Fifty years on (pp. 103–112).

Charlton, M. F., Blakelock, E., Martinón-Torres, M., & Young, T. (2012). Investigating the production provenance of iron artifacts with multivariate methods. *Journal of Archaeological Science, 39*(7), 2280–2293.

Coustures, M. P., Dieudonné-Glad, N., Dillmann, P., & Béziat, D. (2014). Tentative chemical characterization of a Roman smelting workshop (Oulches, France): From the ore to the finished product. *Early Iron in Europe, Montagnac, Editions Monique-Mergoil, coll.«Monographies Instrumentum, 50*, 93–115.

Desaulty, A.-M., Mariet, C., Dillmann, P., Joron, J. L., & Fluzin, P. (2008). The study of provenance of iron objects by ICP-MS multi-elemental analysis. *Spectrochimica Acta Part B, 63*, 1253–1262.

Desaulty, A.-M., Dillmann, P., L'Héritiera, M., Mariet, C., Gratuze, B., Joron, J.-L., & Fluzin, P. (2009). Does it come from the Pays de Bray? Examination of an origin hypothesis for the ferrous reinforcements used in French medieval churches using major and trace element analyses. *Journal of Archaeological Science, 36*(10), 2445–2462.

Dill, H. G., Botz, R., Berner, Z., Abdullah, M. B., & Hamad, A. (2010). The origin of pre-and synrift, hypogene Fe-P mineralization during the Cenozoic along the Dead Sea transform fault, Northwest Jordan. *Economic Geology, 105*(7), 1301–1319.

Dillmann, P., & L'Héritier, M. (2007). Slag inclusion analyses for studying ferrous alloys employed in French medieval buildings: Supply of materials and diffusion of smelting processes. *Journal of Archaeological Science, 34*(11), 1810–1823.

Dolfini, A. (2011). The function of Chalcolithic metalwork in Italy: An assessment based on use-wear analysis. *Journal of Archaeological Science, 38*(5), 1037–1049.

Dungworth, D. (2014). Who's afraid of the bowl furnace? *Historical Metallurgy, 48*(1 & 2), 1–7.

Eliyahu-Behar, A., Yahalom-Mack, N., Shilstein, S., Zukerman, A., Shafer-Elliott, C., Maeir, A. M., et al. (2012). Iron and bronze production in Iron Age IIA Philistia: New evidence from Tell es-Safi/Gath, Israel. *Journal of Archaeological Science, 39*(2), 255–267.

Eliyahu-Behar, A., Yahalom-Mack, N., Gadot, Y., & Finkelstein, I. (2013). Iron smelting and smithing in major urban centers in Israel during the Iron Age. *Journal of Archaeological Science, 40*, 4319–4330.

Erb-Satullo, N. L., & Walton, J. T. (2017). Iron and copper production at Iron Age Ashkelon: Implications for the organization of Levantine metal production. *Journal of Archaeological Science: Reports, 15*, 8–19.

Gur-Arieh, S., Boaretto, E., Maeir, A., & Shahack-Gross, R. (2012). Formation processes in Philistine hearths from Tell es-Safi/Gath (Israel): An experimental approach. *Journal of Field Archaeology, 37*(2), 121–131.

Hodgkinson, A. K., & Bertram, M. (2020). Working with fire: Making glass beads at Amarna using methods from metallurgical scenes. *Journal of Archaeological Science: Reports, 33*, 102488.

Humphris, J., Charlton, M. F., Keen, J., Sauder, L., & Alshishani, F. (2018). Iron smelting in Sudan: Experimental archaeology at the Royal City of Meroe. *Journal of Field Archaeology, 43*(5), 399–416.

Ilani, S. (1989). Epigenetic metallic mineralization along tectonic elements in Israel. Israel Geological Survey Report No. GSI/12/89.

Juleff, G. (1996). An ancient wind-powered iron smelting technology in Sri Lanka. *Nature, 379*(6560), 60–63.

Leroy, S., Cohen, S. X., Verna, C., Gratuze, B., Téreygeol, F., Fluzin, P., et al. (2012). The medieval iron market in Ariège (France). Multidisciplinary analytical approach and multivariate analyses. *Journal of Archaeological Science, 39*(4), 1080–1093.

Levy, T. E., Levy, A. M., Sthapathy, D. R., Sthapathy, D. S., & Sthapathy, D. S. (2008). *Masters of fire. Hereditary Bronze Casters of South India.*

Merkel, J. (1985). Ore beneficiation during the late Bronze/early Iron age at Timna, Israel. *MASCA Journal, 3*(5), 164–169.

Merkel, J. F. (1990). Experimental reconstruction of Bronze Age copper smelting based on archaeological evidence from Timna. *The Ancient Metallurgy of Copper, 2*, 78–122.

Merkel, S., & Rehren, T. (2007). *Parting layers, ash trays and Ramesside glassmaking: An experimental study.* Verlag Gebrüder Gerstenberg.

Outram, A. K. (2008). Introduction to experimental archaeology. *World Archaeology, 40*(1), 1–6.

Paynter, S. (2008). Experiments in the reconstruction of Roman wood-fired glassworking furnaces: Waste products and their formation processes. *Journal of Glass Studies, 50*, 271–290.

Pernicka, E. (2014). Provenance determination of archaeological metal objects. In B. W. Roberts & C. P. Thornton (Eds.), *Archaeometallurgy in global perspective: Methods and syntheses* (pp. 239–268). Springer.

Renfrew, C., & Bahn, P. G. (2004). *Archaeology: Theories, methods and practice.*

Rondelez, P. (2017). The Irish bowl furnace: Origin, history and demise. *The Journal of Irish Archaeology, 26*, 101–116.

Sauder, L. (2013). An American bloomery in Sussex. In *Accidental and experimental archaeometallurgy* (pp. 69–74). The Historical Metallurgy Society.

Sauder, L., & Williams, S. (2002). A practical treatise on the smelting and smithing of bloomery iron. *Historical Metallurgy, 36*(2), 122–131.

Stepanov, I., Borodianskiy, K., & Eliyahu-Behar, A. (2020). Assessing the quality of iron ores for bloomery smelting: Laboratory experiments. *Minerals, 10*(1), 33.

Stepanov, I. S., Sauder, L., Keen, J., Workman, V., & Eliyahu-Behar, A. (2022). By the hand of the smelter: Tracing the impact of decision making in bloomery iron smelting. *Journal of Archaeological and Anthropological Sciences.*

Stos-Gale, Z. A., & Gale, N. H. (2009). Metal provenancing using isotopes and the Oxford archaeological lead isotope database (OXALID). *Archaeological and Anthropological Sciences, 1*(3), 195–213.

Shalev, S. (1999). *Recasting the Nahal Mishmar hoard: Experimental acheology and metallurgy.*

Shugar, A. N. (2001). *Archaeometrical investigation of the Chalcolithic site of Abu Matar, Israel: A re-assessment of technology and its implications for the Ghassulian culture.* University of London, University College London (United Kingdom).

Veldhuijzen, H. A., & Rehren, T. (2007). Slags and the city: Early iron production at Tell Hammeh, Jordan, and Tel Beth-Shemesh, Israel. In S. La Niece, D. R. Hook, & P. T. Craddock (Eds.), *Metals and mines: Studies in archaeometallurgy* (pp. 189–201). London.

Workman, V., Maeir, A. M., Dagan, A., Regev, J., Boaretto, E., & Eliyahu-Behar, A. (2020). An Iron IIA Iron and Bronze Workshop in the Lower City of Tell es-Safi/Gath. *Tel Aviv, 47*(2), 208–236.

Workman, V., Maeir, A. M., & Eliyahu-Behar, A. (2021). In search of the invisible hearth: An experimental perspective on early Levantine iron production. *Journal of Archaeological Science: Reports, 36*, 102803.

Yahalom-Mack, N., & Eliyahu-Behar, A. (2015). The transition from bronze to iron in Canaan: Chronology, technology, and context. *Radiocarbon, 57*(2), 285–305.

Yahalom-Mack, N., Gadot, Y., Eliyahu-Behar, A., Bechar, S., Shilstein, S., & Finkelstein, I. (2014). Metalworking at Hazor: A long-term perspective. *Oxford Journal of Archaeology, 33*(1), 19–45.

Yahalom-Mack, N., Eliyahu-Behar, A., Kleiman, A., Shahack-Gross, R., Homsher, R. D., Gadot, Y., & Finkelstein, I. (2017). Metalworking at Megiddo during the Late Bronze and Iron Ages. *Journal of Near Eastern Studies, 76*, 53–74.

Part V
Marine Archaeology and Maritime Trade in the Eastern Mediterranean and Beyond

Tom Levy conducting an underwater archaeological survey near Tel Dor, Israel. (Photo courtesy of Marko Runjajic)

Unearthing Craft Activities in the North Aegean: The Karabournaki Settlement

Despoina Tsiafaki

Abstract The North Aegean was a region densely inhabited already in the Iron Age. Archaeological research has brought to light an abundance of material remains and information that enable us to picture glimpses of the life there and of the inhabitants. The agropastoral economies appear to have had dominant roles within the settlements, many of which begun to florish from the Archaic period onwards. Trade or other activities can be traced among the findings from different sites. Closely related to primary occupations are the development and employment of technological expertise in order to serve and fulfill the daily needs of the residents.

The focus of this paper is the Archaic settlement of Karabournaki, which is located on the Thermaic Gulf, and it is identified with the harbor of ancient Therme. Based on the up-to-date archaeological data, the settlement had a strong commercial character developing at the same time significant skills and expertise in certain domains. The location of at least one pottery workshop, which produced its own types of vessels among other products, and of at least one metalworkshop, which produced iron and bronze objects, provide important evidence for the technologies used at the site and the occupations of its inhabitants.

Keywords North Aegean · Iron Age · Karabournaki · Settlement · Crafts · Pottery production · Metalworking

---

A great number of the published archaeological research regarding several sites of the Thermaic Gulf, can be found at the digital repository ARENA: http://arena.athenarc.gr/

D. Tsiafaki (✉)
Culture & Creative Industries Department, Athena Research Center, Xanthi Division, Xanthi, Greece
e-mail: tsiafaki@athenarc.gr

© The Author(s), under exclusive license to Springer Nature Switzerland AG 2023
E. Ben-Yosef, I. W. N. Jones (eds.), *"And in Length of Days Understanding" (Job 12:12): Essays on Archaeology in the Eastern Mediterranean and Beyond in Honor of Thomas E. Levy*, Interdisciplinary Contributions to Archaeology, https://doi.org/10.1007/978-3-031-27330-8_62

1 Introduction

The North Aegean was a region well populated throughout Antiquity with Iron Age and Archaic periods being no exception. Despite the scarcity of literary sources regarding the area before the Classical and mostly Hellenistic times, the archaeological research has brought to light significant information and material remains dated from Prehistory down to the Roman times (Vlachopoulos & Tsiafaki, 2017). Among the areas of the North Aegean that enjoyed a significant development and attracted people and trade networks was Thermaic Gulf, which appears to have been densely inhabited throughout all these periods based particularly on the material remains and secondarily on the written sources (Soueref, 2011; Tiverios, 2008; Tsiafaki, 2020, 2021). Even though not fully excavated yet, in their majority the ancient sites unearthed in the Thermaic Gulf area follow the typical organization of the region, and they are placed on the top of manmade mounds (*toumba*) or flatter hills (table or *trapeza*) with continuous habitation for long periods. A region abundant in resources, timber, harbors, rivers and access to Aegean and inland, the Thermaic Gulf attracted Greek settlers from various places, with the established *apoikiae* that played an important role in the urbanization of the area and its incorporation to various commercial, political and other networks (Archibald, 2013; Tiverios, 2008; Tiverios, 2017; Tsiafaki, 2020, 2021). Furthermore, this landscape and resources contributed to the formation of the character, the societies and their economy(ies). Despite their major agropastoral role, the communities of the Thermaic Gulf maintained a long technological tradition apparent in a variety of fields (e.g. pottery, metalworking, textiles) and extended from Prehistory down to the Historical times (Andreou, 2019; Tsiafaki, 2021). The numerous metal and ceramic remains throughout the entire region, provide indisputable proofs of it, while there is solid evidence for the operation of various workshops and consequently skilled artisans at least from the Late Bronze Age. The distribution of their products in other, often neighboring sites, suggests that their clientele was not limited within the borders of their own community; rather it was expanded at a regional level (Tsiafaki, 2022).

Methone forms a good example of a well-organized settlement with established artisanal character already in the Early Iron Age (Besios, 2017; Besios et al., 2012). An Eretrian *apoikia* founded in the eighth century BC, it developed soon to the most important urban center in the Thermaic Gulf at least until the Archaic period (Tsiafaki, 2020). Large-scale craft production of an artisanal character is reflected through the findings of the subterranean space (*Ypogeio*), which has brought to light numerous types of artefacts (metal objects, clay and glass vessels, faience pendants, ivory, bone, and deer horns) linked with extensive workshop activities (Besios et al., 2012). It is possible that their products covered local and regional needs and they might even have supplied communities in the Balkans. At the Archaic levels of the site a building complex has been unearthed that was part of a greater area with public and artisanal activities, and it has been identified as market (*Agora*). Remains of two pottery kilns and pits with parts of melted copper, clay crucibles and stone

Unearthing Craft Activities in the North Aegean: The Karabournaki Settlement

molds for metal objects show that pottery and metal workshops were active within this building complex. The ivory waste located also in the greater area is indicative of further operating workshops.

A number of those communities (*komes*) formed probably the reputation known from the literary sources of ancient Therme (*Θέρμη*), a 'town in clusters' (Flensted-Jensen, 2004; Rhomaios, 1940; Tiverios, 2009). Taking into account that among the earlier inhabitants there were Thracians, it is possible that it was named Therme by the Greeks replacing the Thracian name Tindi (*Τίνδη*), which means hot, warm. The name recalls thermal springs existing in the area and the Thermaic Gulf was named after this site, an indication of its importance (Nigdelis, 1995; Tiverios, 1997). Therme was a town (*polis*) of Greek Thracians according to Hekataios (FGrHist 1, F 163) from Miletus, who is the earliest preserved literary source to mention the population of the area and Therme (Xydopoulos, 2007). Based on Herodotos (7.121.123.127.128.183), Therme was the place where Xerxes camped with his army and navy on his way to South Greece in the early fifth century BC. The settlement located at nowadays Toumba (Andreou, 2001; Chavela, 2018, 2021; Soueref, 2011) played an important role in the earlier phases of Therme, functioning perhaps as its nucleus, with the harbor of the city probably located in Karabournaki to have a significant position from the Archaic times onwards, if not somewhat earlier. It was here where Xerxes most likely camped during the Persian Wars (490–479 BC), because Therme was the safest harbor.

The latter, namely the settlement in Karabournaki, is the focus of this paper. Based on the archaeological data, it will explore its position and its role in the region of the Thermaic Gulf, especially during the Archaic times. Taken into consideration its major commercial character, which apparently had its impact on the incorporation of the settlement within the surrounding area, it will present the growth of significant skills and expertise in certain domains that there were developed there. The location of at least one pottery workshop in Karabournaki, which produced its own types of vessels among other products, and of at least one metalworkshop for the production of iron and bronze objects, will be examined as important evidence for the technologies employed at the site and the occupation of its inhabitants.

2 The Ancient Settlement at Karabournaki

Located at the edge of the promontory at the center of the East part of the Thermaic Gulf, nearby Thessaloniki, the settlement at Karabournaki was inhabited from Late Bronze Age until the Roman period (Manakidou & Tsiafaki, 2017; Soueref, 2021; Tsiafaki & Manakidou, 2021). It occupies a flatter hill (table or *trapeza*), situated next to the natural harbor, which probably determined the establishment of the settlement and was essential for its existence, longevity, and development (Fig. 1). The revealed parts of this community show that the cemeteries extended to the area that surrounds the bottom of this hill, which is reached by the Thermaic Gulf (Gardner & Casson, 1918–1919; Ignatiadou et al., 2008; Pandermali & Trakosopoulou, 1994,

Fig. 1 Aerial view of the archaeological site at Karabournaki

1995; Rey, 1927, 1928, 1932). The excavated burials date from the Iron Age until the Classical times, with several of them containing rich burial offerings (Panti & Vasileiou, 2018; Tsimbidou-Avloniti, 1999). Moreover, the remains of the ancient harbor are still distinguishable under the water in the zone of the modern *Kyverneion* (*Palataki*).

Functioning as a hub for receiving and distributing goods, the harbor and the settlement linked to it, enjoyed a prosperity, which reached its peak undoubtedly in the Archaic and Classical times (7th–4th century BC). It is possible, however, that this flourishing period had begun already in the Geometric/Iron Age times. Karabournaki was one of the 26 settlements, which participated in the foundation of Thessaloniki by the Macedonian king Kassandros in the late fifth century BC (Strabo VII, frg. 21). Other communities, such as Apollonia, Chalastra, Aineia, Kissos, Polichni, Toumba and modern Therme-Sedes, probably participated also in the establishment of Thessaloniki (Lioutas, 2021). Unlike other settlements, however, the Karabournaki site continued to be inhabited during the next centuries, perhaps due to the significance of its harbor. Moreover, Pliny (*NH* IV.10) mentions that Thessaloniki and Therme co-existed at his time (first century AD).

The site has been identified with the harbor of ancient Therme (Hammond, 1972; Tiverios, 1997), and it apparently acted as a major coastal center for trading activities (*emporion*), which was organically linked with its hinterland. It is possible that it was depended on inland resources for minerals and timber, as well as various construction materials and domestic transport. However, a parallel dependency should be observed in the inland communities, which were in turn dependent on the harbor for the supply of materials and goods they were lacking. Furthermore, the harbor (Karabournaki) would be the export point for their surplus and the products they meant to trade within the Aegean and elsewhere, possibly following the exchange of goods in trading networks and routes as far as the Levant (Rollinger,

Unearthing Craft Activities in the North Aegean: The Karabournaki Settlement

2020; Van Alfen, 2016). The Carian inscriptions found in Karabournaki and Polichni (Adiego et al., 2012; Tzanavari & Christidis, 1995) are indicative for the long-distance trade that took place here.

The archaeological data accumulated through the Aristotle University excavations during the past 25 years[1] reveal a settlement with permanent character and installations at least during the Archaic times, when most of the recent finds are dated (Tiverios et al., 2003, 2016; Tsiafakis, 2010). The long-term recent occupation of the site by the army resulted in serious disturbance of the ancient remains. For the same reason, however, the site was saved from contemporary building constructions that might have caused even serious damage. Moreover, horse burials took place throughout the settlement during the twentieth century also affecting the antiquities. These contemporary disturbances led to the horizontal excavation of the site, which revealed a great extent parts of the Archaic phase, although earlier and later remains have been detected sporadically. Their presence is good evidence for the existence and the use of the settlement for a long period. Through those sporadic findings from the current excavations, the best documented periods -apart from the Archaic- are the eighth century BC and the Classical times (Chatzis, 2012; Manakidou, 2019; Tiverios et al., 2003). Moreover, the habitation of the site for the period 800 to fifth century BC is well documented also from the necropoleis with the burials dated during this time (Pandermali & Trakosopoulou, 1994, 1995; Panti & Vasileiou, 2018; Rey, 1927, 1928, 1932; Tsimbidou-Avloniti, 1999).

The settlement preserves architectural remains, which show a permanent character without however, a pre-conceived plan, something common in multi-phased settlements (Tsiafakis, 2010). The role of the settlement as a trading center might have had a significant impact on its development and spatial organization (Fig. 2). Therefore, it wouldn't be a surprise to find a multifunctional character of buildings or individual rooms as it is suggested by the current excavated architectural remains, which seem to accommodate shops, workshops and residential needs in the same area (Tsiafaki, 2021).

The preserved structures appear to be rectilinear buildings constructed of stone foundations laid in two or three rows (Fig. 3). With a few exceptions, rubble masonry was employed for the foundations, while the superstructure was made by sun-dried mud brick (adobe). The thickness of the walls, which ranges between 0,30 and 0,50 m. suggests that they could support a second story in case there was one. Their floors were usually made of beaten earth and the roofs were covered with roof tiles mostly of Laconian types as show the numerous examples revealed in the settlement. Some of the structures may also have included a courtyard, occasionally paved with stones laid in a circular shape. They may be processing areas related to household and broader activities, or they could be used as foundations of granaries (Tsiafaki, 2021). The structures appear to follow a common orientation from

---

[1] The Aristotle University of Thessaloniki conducts since 1994, the excavations of the settlement on the top of the flatter hill and the archaeological research takes place in collaboration with the Athena Research Center, which is also in charge for the digital part. http://culturalheritage.ceti.gr/en/karabournaki-2

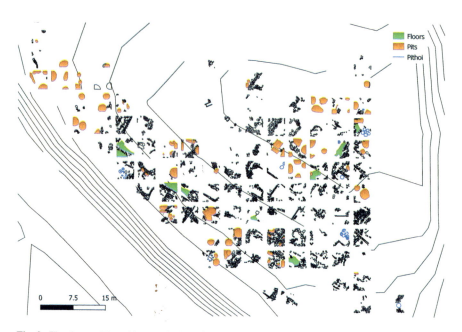

Fig. 2 Karabournaki: architectural plan of the excavated are in the ancient settlement

Fig. 3 Architectural remains of the ancient settlement

Northwest to Southeast, with the long walls to preserve a North to South direction, while the narrow walls have an East-West way. This orientation coincides with Xenophon's description about ancient Greek houses. According to Xenophon (*Memorabilia* 3.8.9, *Oeconomicus* 9.4), the most often used rooms faced south in order to gain sun during the winter and to be shaded from the higher sun during the summer.

The rooms are placed next to one another (*paratactically*), without, however, being clear whether the constructions belong to a single-room or multi-room buildings, due to the contemporary disturbance of the site. Hearths (mostly parts of them) have been found sporadically in various trenches, denoting the residential character along with various movable objects (e.g., kitchenware, loom weights). Ground stone mortars and pestles were found in several places used for household and workshop activities. Clay flat-bottomed mortars were also popular at the site for grinding and pounding raw substances (Manakidou, 2014). A great number of them are of Cypro-Phoinicean origin, like examples found in Naukratis, East Greek and Levantine sites (Spataro & Villing, 2009). Their usefulness to accomodate housing and workshop needs and activities explains their popularity at the settlement.

Storerooms with pithoi (*pitheones*) are common on the site (Tsiafaki, 2021; Tsiafakis, 2010). Based on the tentative multifunctional role of many buildings or certain rooms within them, it is possible that at least some of those *pitheones* belong to shops and not to individual households. Due to the contemporary disturbance, it is not possible to calculate the exact number of the pithoi in each storeroom, but it seems that there were over 10. The pithoi were usually half-buried in the ground, occasionally below the level of the foundation walls. According to Xenophon (*Oeconomicus* 9.2–11), the storeroom with the pithoi should be a semisubterranean, cool space in order to be suitable for the grain and wine storage. A schist plaque covered most of the Karabournaki pithoi and occasionally trade amphorae were placed next to them.

Widespread on the top of the flatter hill are various shaped and types of dugouts. A great number of them are typical trash pits for disposal of waste. Therefore, their shape and placement does not follow a particular pattern. Some others, however, are beehive-shaped semi-subterranean structures (*yposkapta*), which share certain characteristics and form one group (Tsiafakis, 2013). (Fig. 4) The type is not unique in Karabournaki but similar dugouts are known from other sites in the area, such as Nea Kallikrateia, Toumba, and Pieria.

As regards the Karabournaki examples, they are found in certain areas of the settlement and in some cases are located below the foundation walls of the buildings and/or incorporated within the Archaic structures. Even though, their study is still in progress, the general impression so far is that at least in their majority they precede the stone buildings and belong to earlier phases of the settlement. It is not known if they were all constructed simultaneously, but based on the up-to-date archaeological data, a possible date of them is the 7th or even the eighth century BC as those unearthed in neighboring Toumba and they are interpreted as storage spaces (Chavela, 2021). Noteworthy is that they were still in use during the Archaic times when they were probably integrated and adapted in secondary use. Their initial

Fig. 4 Beehive semi-subterranean structures in pairs

function is not clear yet, but according to the known contexts it appears that they had auxiliary roles and they serviced household and storage needs as well as workshop and craft activities. The placement of some of them in areas related to pottery and metalworkshops, as it will be discussed below, is indicative of their role in the craft production on the site.

3 Craft Production in the Karabournaki Community

The recently unearthed archaeological material in Karabournaki provides adequate information for various activities that took place within the settlement (Tsiafaki, 2021). Its commercial character is well documented through its geographical position as well as the movable findings, in particular ceramics. Numerous imports of the best known centers in mainland Greece, Aegean, Asia Minor and beyond, have been unearthed throughout the settlement. Fine pottery and trade amphorae are among the most popular imports. (Filis, 2012; Manakidou, 2010a).

At the same time, however, the inhabitants of the site developed their own technologies and produced various goods in situ (Tsiafaki, 2021). Craft activities have been identified in different parts of the settlement. Their products to exceeded household needs and covered the entire settlement, possibly extended beyond that. Among them there are two crafts at the site considered to be in close connection in general (Segbers, 2018). This refers to pottery production and metalworking with the identification of related workshops within the settlement. They are the most characteristic examples of craftsmanship at the site, and they will be discussed below.

3.1 Pottery Workshop

The large quantities of a certain type of vases, conventionally called eggshell pottery due to their very thin walls, which were unearthed in Karabournaki led to the first assumptions by M. Tiverios that it was produced in situ (Tiverios, 1995–2000). The type was widespread in the vicinity of the Thermaic Gulf with examples to be found in neighboring to Karabournaki communities, such as modern Therme-Sedes, Neo Rhysio, Toumba, Sindos, Polichni, Nea Philadelphia (Skarlatidou, 2007; Panti, 2008, 2012b; Adam-Veleni et al., 2013; Chavela, 2018; Manoledakis, forthcoming). The waste remains of a pottery workshop located at Karabournaki proved the site was at least one of the production centers (Manakidou, 2010a; Panti, 2008; Tiverios et al., 2001; Tiverios et al., 2003).

The excavations held in 2001 revealed a beehive semi-subterranean dugout (*yposkapton*) such the ones described earlier, which was filled with pottery waste (Fig. 5). More specifically, it contained a large quantity of lumps of clay, misfired vases, fragments fired in low temperature (less than 500 °C), and sun-dried cup handles (Tiverios et al., 2001; Tsiafaki & Manakidou, 2013) (Fig. 6). Their presence demonstrates the activity of a pottery workshop located in this area. The

Fig. 5 Beehive semi-subterranean structure in trench 27-79d with pottery waste

Fig. 6 Pottery waste from the workshop at Karabournaki

Fig. 7 Eggshell pottery from Karabournaki

macroscopic examination of the material recognized them as the eggshell type of pottery, widespread at the site and the Thermaic. Through the clay analysis and the relation of the ceramic composition to the local geology, we were able to assign the specific types of pottery to local manufacture (Tsiafaki & Manakidou, 2013; Tsiafaki & Tsirliganis, 2008). Through the scientific examination it was shown that the eggshell vases were fired at around 800 °C in a reducing atmosphere (Vivtenko, 2008).

The waste included all the major shapes of the type along with some cups with more intense paint and a ladle (Tsiafaki & Manakidou, 2013) (Fig. 7). The latter is a rare shape not known so far elsewhere, although recent excavations in the nearby site at Neo Rhysio brought to light some types of ladle shape vessels related to local monochrome and eggshell pottery (Manoledakis, forthcoming). This particular finding appears to be related with the waste of a certain production lot that took place in the sixth century BC. The activity of the workshop, however, can be dated at least from the seventh century BC onwards.

The numerous examples and fragments of the eggshell category unearthed throughout the entire site, indicate that the group included small size vessels with its most common shapes being the monochrome red or brown and black-brown glazed footless cups, one handled bowls with or without spout, mugs and small jugs. Occasionally the cups might be decorated with a reserved band. Their clay was particularly fine with little mica and a considerable amount of iron oxide. The eggshell pottery is related to another popular ceramic in the Thermaic category, the monochrome with thick walls, which was produced in the area during the eighth century BC (Havela, 2012; Saripanidi, 2013; Tsiafaki, 2019).

The production of the workshopwas not limited to the eggshell type, however, or exclusively to sympotic shapes. Based for the moment, on the macroscopical examination of the clay and technological similarities, it is almost certain that other kind of vessels were made here as well. Thus, several types recognized earlier as 'local' manufactures with the term to refer generally in the entire vicinity of the Thermaic Gulf, get now at least one production center (Adam-Veleni et al., 2013; Havela, 2012; Manakidou, 2017; Saripanidi, 2013; Tsiafaki, 2019). Among this broad geographically 'local' production is included wheel made and handmade pottery.

The products of the workshop include various types of oinochoae, which were used for purposes other than the obvious (drinking water or communal wine drinking). The remains for example of the numerous seashells, which were probably contained inside the broken large local oinochoae found together in a kitchen related area (*optanion*), indicate the multipurpose function of the vessels (Tiverios et al., 2013). In this case the oinochoae were used as temporary storage to keep fresh cockles within seawater.

The handmade vases hold a prominent position in Karabournaki retaining a tradition that continues down to the Archaic and possibly Classical times. Apart from a few exceptions, it makes sense that most were made in situ. Coarse cooking ware, such as *chytrae* and baking pans, unearthed throughout the settlement (Manakidou, 2014), could also have been among the products of the workshops operating in the site as well as building materials, loom weights, lamps and other categories of ceramic utensils. As has been already demonstrated through other examples in the area, pottery workshops weren't necessary specialized in specific types, rather they had a great variation of ceramic products (Adam-Veleni et al., 2013; Tsiafaki, 2019). The eighth century BC kiln found in Torone (Chalcidice) for example, which collapsed during the firing process, shows that wheel- and hand-made pottery as well as vases, loom weights and other clay products were made here (Papadopoulos, 2013). A similar picture presents the late Archaic workshop at Phari on Thasos island (Perreault et al., 2013).

The consumption of the pottery workshop products was not limited within the settlement. The monochrome eggshell vases found in some of the tombs were probably also made by the local workshop(s), and the other types of local pottery used as burial offerings. Worth noting is that *symposion related* vessels hold a distinctive role among the grave offerings of the contemporary necropolis, following perhaps a more general trend (Panti & Vasileiou, 2018). The Karabournaki vases may identified another clientele for the consumption of the local pottery products.

Pots related to (communal) drinking or *symposion type* activities, comprise a primary production category of the local workshop(s) and they are suggestive for the position of the ceremonial drinking in this particular society. Their presence in the residential areas and the necropoleis, namely in life and death, indicates a culture-oriented character in this communal or ceremonial drinking. The numerous grape pips (*Vitis vinifera*) among the archaeobotanical remains of the site, along with the many trade amphorae unearthed throughout the settlement, show extensive consumption of wine as well as the important role of wine in the community (Tsiafaki, 2021).

The unearthed beehive dugout with the pottery waste was located to the west side of the settlement (trench 27-79d), within an area that does not preserve any other constructions except for various pits and beehive dugouts (Fig. 8). Even though the

Fig. 8 Architectural plan of the pottery waste and workshop area

beehive dugout retains only waste, it cannot be placed far away from the manufacture installations. An open-air space could be appropriate for the location of this and other workshops. The molds for metal objects and the slag unearthed in this part of the site are indicative of workshop activities that maybe took place here (Tsiafaki & Manakidou, 2013).

The current findings do not allow a reconstruction of the organization of the workshop. The remains of the Phari workshop, however, in Thasos, which preserves an installation with all the needed infrastructures, show the existence of well-organized units in the region at least from the sixth century BC, when the Karabournaki workshop was also in use.

The location of the workshop within the premises of the settlement is not unusual (Kourou, 2004) and seems to be common in Karabournaki. The metal workshop, which will be presented next, is also near the buildings of the community.

3.2 Metal Workshop(s)

Mining and metal working have long traditions in the region and in Northern Greece in general, that goes back to the prehistoric times, with the archaeological findings related to metal extraction to document an indigenous metal tradition (Archibald, 2013; Koukouli-Chrysanthaki & Bassiakos, 2002; Nerantzis, 2015). As an area rich in metals, such as gold, silver, bronze and iron (Herod. 3.63, 4.46–47, 7.12; Strabo 7.34), it naturally not only attracted the interest of various external people to trade and acquire them but to develop skills in the production of metal objects. The local inhabitants had the authority and the rights to the mining (Herod. 7.112), and their expertise was the reason that Peisistratos might have brought Thracians to work in the silver mines at Laurion, in the sixth century BC. (Triantafyllos, 2000). The abundance of metal artifacts, weapon and tools found in the entire region is an indisputable proof for the knowledge of the inhabitants in metalworking as well, a skill mentioned by Herodotos (7.119) when he states that for the symposia offered to Xerxes, the local people manufactured gold and silver drinking vessels, kraters, and tableware.

Metalworking has a long tradition in Macedonia that goes back at least to the late Bronze Age (Descamps-Lequime & Charatzopoulou, 2011) with the Thermaic Gulf being no exception. Bronze and gold smithing has been recognized in Toumba during the Bronze Age with continuation in the Iron Age (Mavroeidi et al., 2004). The gold bearing sands of river Echedorus (contemporary Gallikos) in Mydgonia where Toumba and Karabournaki belonged, may have been exploited already in the eighth century BC, a period when metallurgy flourished in the region. From the eighth century BC onwards and with the data provided by the established colonies, such as Methone, it appears that the production of metal objects (iron, bronze, gold) played a distinctive role in the societies of the Thermaic Gulf supported by the abundance of metals in the area (Soueref, 2021). The burial offerings rich in metal occur in various cemeteries (e.g. Archontiko, Sindos, Agia Paraskevi, Therme-Sedes) and include weapons and armory, jewelry, vessels, miniature objects (e.g. furniture, carts) as well as golden masks and strips of gold leaf, often lozenge-shaped, to cover the mouth or the eyes (Chrysostomou & Chrysostomou, 2012; Despini, 2016a, b; Despini et al., 2009; Manakidou, 2010b; Panti, 2012a; Skarlatidou, 2007; Vlachopoulos & Tsiafaki, 2017), all evidence of the longstanding tradition and sophistication in metalworking. This local cultural tradition established in the seventh or even the eighth century BC, accounts for the abundant unearthed bronze jewelry with the most popular artefacts being earrings, pendants, beads, pins, fibulae, bracelets, and finger rings (Misailidou-Despotidou, 2011).

Based on the archaeological findings of the site, it appears that the settlement in Karabournaki followed this trend of the time and the region. Molds for metal objects and clay crucibles found dispersed within the settlement are witness of the metalworking taking place here (Tsiafaki, 2021). (Fig. 9) For example, a clay mold like that for metal jewelry found in the settlement, could have been used by the local workshop to produce bronze spectacle fibulae such as the ones found in the cemetery (Panti & Vasileiou, 2018, fig. 87).

In addition to the sporadic indications for metalworking on the site, we have found the location of a metal workshop, active at least in the seventh century BC (Tiverios et al., 2007, 2008; Tsiafakis, 2010, Tsiafaki, 2021). Given the contemporary disturbance at the settlement and the scarcity of metal objects, and the fact that traces of metalworking are not as common as the pottery production in the Greek world (Lehoërff, 2004), this discovery has a special importance. Its working space was located on the south side of the flatter hill and its study is in progress. Remains

Fig. 9 Molds for metal objects

of the workshop such as few pits, a certain amount of slag and clay vessels with metal residue on the bottom, have been identified so far within two trenches (23-12c and 23-12d) (Fig. 10a, b). It is possible that the installation was extended in the two trenches to the north (23-12a and 23-12b), but it is still under consideration if the east remains (trenches E, 23-13a, 23-13b and 23-13c) are somehow related to the workshop and its activities (Fig. 11). It is noteworthy that its location is within the settlement, something not unusual at the time as it is shown in other places such as Thasos and Argilos for example (Perrault & Bonias, 2021; Sanidas, 2013).

The analysis of the slag and other metallurgical waste indicates the existence of more than one workshop active at the site (Sanidas et al., 2015). Iron appears to be the primary material worked at this particular workshop, even though copper working waste has been also traced. Of particular importance is the cooking vessel used for metallurgical procedures as it is shown by the metal residue on its bottom (Fig. 12). It is a rare discovery, not known from elsewhere in Greece and the earliest compared to others found in Europe (Sanidas et al., 2015).

This workshop(s) dealt primary with iron forging and the shaping of ready to use metallic objects. The production based on the in situ remains (Sanidas et al., 2015; Tiverios et al., 2007), included small objects such as daggers, spearheads, arrowheads, pins, fibulae, tools, utensils, metal fittings, nails and mirrors. Taken into consideration, the extended exploitation of the marine fauna by the inhabitants of the

Fig. 10 (**a**) Remains of the metal workshop in trench 23-12c. (**b**) Remains of the metal workshop in trench 23-12d

Fig. 10 (continued)

site (Tiverios et al., 2013; Tsiafaki, 2021), tools related to fishing activities such as hooks, could be also made here. Among the plentiful ceramic vessels found in the settlement, there is a great number preserving repairing holes. As it is known metallic pins or staples were common for the repairs of broken vases (Bentz et al., 2010; Elston, 1990), and the local workshops (pottery and/or metal) could have undertaken this activity as well, perhaps even in collaboration. Nevertheless, a close connection between the two crafts at the site is indisputable since they were interrelated in terms of equipment, technology, and manufacture (cf. Segbers, 2018). Worth of note are the iron and copper filings and hammerscales found among the waste of the pottery workshop presented above (Tsiafaki & Manakidou, 2013); a suggestion for shared activities in a common area.

Examples of the types of the iron daggers produced in the site are perhaps the burial offerings found in the cemetery (Panti & Vasileiou, 2018, figs. 43, 67, 74). The dating of the latter in the eighth or seventh century BC (Bräuning & Kilian-Dirlmeier, 2013; Chrysostomou, 2000), is in agreement with the active period of the metal workshop located at the settlement. Iron and bronze objects (e.g. daggers, strigils, spearheads), placed as burial offerings within the graves of the settlement could have been produced locally by the metal workshops of the community. Although, there has been no analysis of them or a detailed examination to check whether they were used or new, it is possible that part of the production of the local workshops was meant also for burial use. The bronze jewelry for example, found in

Unearthing Craft Activities in the North Aegean: The Karabournaki Settlement 1485

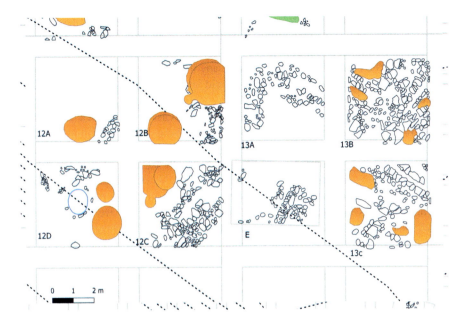

Fig. 11 Architectural plan of the metalworking area

Fig. 12 Handmade vessel with metallurgical residue from the metal workshop

the Iron Age cemetery (Panti & Vasileiou, 2018) might have been made here as well as the bronze and iron exaleiptron found in an early fifth century BC grave (Descamps-Lequime, 2002, 2009).

Although the current data do not provide any information regarding the production of gold smithing, the few examples of gold jewelry found in the settlement and the cemeteries (Manakidou & Tsiafaki, 2017; Panti & Vasileiou, 2018), could have been locally made. Their simplicity would support this assumption since they do not reflect high specialization and artistic skills. Nevertheless, gold smithing has been recognized at the neighboring community located in Toumba (Mavroeidi et al., 2004), a settlement presenting several similarities with Karabournaki and probably in close relation with it as being both parts of ancient Therme. Therefore, it cannot be excluded that gold jewelry in Karabournaki was brought from Toumba.

Thus, it seems that workshops for pottery and metal objects were active at the site at least from the seventh century onwards, if not earlier. However, what it is not clear yet is whether they were totally separate installations or if and how they might have been related. A certain level of specialization and skills can be seen through their products, and a tentative connection between potters and metalworkers can be made. What it is not clear yet is if they were the same artisans or not.

4 Conclusions

The Karabournaki community was well integrated within its region and the similarities with other settlements in the vicinity of the Thermaic Gulf (Tsiafaki, 2021) indicate that it was in close contact with them, especially as a number of those formed ancient Therme. Apart from the material remains coming from the habitation areas, the revealed part of the Iron Age necropolis at Karabournaki, is in correlation with other cemeteries placed at the seashore of this side of the Thermaic, such as in modern Therme-Sedes, Toumba, Polichni, Nea Eukarpia, Oraiokastro (Panti & Vasileiou, 2018).

The settlement in Karabournaki played a crucial role within the maritime and landward networks operating in the Thermaic Gulf. Placed on the promontory in the center of the gulf, it was seen by any boat and its harbor accessible for exchanges as well as for any other needs (accommodations, repairs, supplies etc.). Following Methone, which was probably the most important harbor of the region, the harbor in Karabournaki, had its share in the economic wellbeing of the region and functioned as a hub for interchanges between coastal and inland areas. The archaeological data could provide a baseline for future comparative studies that may help to illuminate connections between sites and local diachronic development of ceramic technology and metalworking.

The recognition of at least one active pottery workshop and possibly more than one metalworkshop at the site during the seventh and sixth century BC, is of great importance for the knowledge of the community, the activities of the inhabitants as well as its economy. It places the settlement within the framework of the societies

Unearthing Craft Activities in the North Aegean: The Karabournaki Settlement

living in the Thermaic Gulf and it is indicative for their interregional relations and activities. The identification of a significant range of ceramic goods produced in Karabournaki also eliminates the broad term 'local' for at least one specific production center. The diffusion of the eggshell pottery within the Thermaic, regardless of how many of them were manufactured in Karabournaki, shows a common cultural feature and taste.

All the above may be used for understanding socio-economic organization of the settlement. The architectural remains indicate that the site was inhabited all year round and maintained workshops with skilled specialized artisans, even if theirs was not necessarily a full-time occupation. The workshops functioned beyond the household production. They covered the community needs as well as the requirements of the temporary visitors at the harbor (sailors, merchants, local products suppliers etc). Moreover, they could be involved in the interregional trade and distribute their ceramic and metal objects within the Thermaic Gulf vicinity. All these are indicators of specialized production despite its seasonal or yearly character and whether it was exclusive or supplementary occupation of the craftsmen (cf. Lewis, 2020).

The architectural remains of the settlement located in Karabournaki, along with the movable findings scattered among and within them, indicate an interrelation of the living quarters with the working spaces and the workshops. Worthy of note is that even though productions such as pottery manufacturing and metalworking, get a large scale and possible an artisanal character, they take place within the residential contexts. Moreover, the presence of their or similar products throughout the vicinity of the Thermaic, is suggestive for the relations and the contacts of those neighboring communities. In any case they provide a good picture for the organization of the settlements in the Thermaic Gulf, before the flourishing of the Macedonian kingdom.

Acknowledgments I would like to thank Prof. E. Ben-Yosef and Dr. I. Jones for their kind invitation to participate in the volume and their patience. The maps and architectural plans are done in the AeGIS Athena (http://aegis.athenarc.gr) by Dr. V. Evangelidis and Dr. Y. Mourthos; I thank them both. I am grateful to Dr. Marion True for the improvement of the English and the language editing. A significant number of the bibliographical references were found through the ARENA repository (http://arena.athenarc.gr).

References

Adam-Veleni, P., Kefalidou, E., & Tsiafaki, D. (Eds.). (2013). *Pottery workshops in Northeastern Aegean (8th-early 5th c. BC), scientific meeting AMTh 2010.* Archaeological Museum of Thessaloniki & Athena Research Center.

Adiego, I. X., Tiverios, M., Manakidou, E., & Tsiafakis, D. (2012). Two Carian inscriptions from Karabournaki/Thessaloniki, Greece. In K. Konuk (Ed.), *"Stephanèphoros". De l'économie antique à l'Asie Mineure. Hommages à Raymond Descat* (pp. 195–202). Ausonius.

Andreou, S. (2001). Exploring the patterns of power in the Bronze Age settlements of Northern Greece. In K. Branigan (Ed.), *Urbanism in the Aegean Bronze Age* (pp. 160–173). Sheffield Academic Press.

Andreou, S. (2019). The Thermaic gulf. In I. S. Lemos & A. Kotsonas (Eds.), *A companion to the archaeology of early Greece and the Mediterranean* (Vol. 2, pp. 913–938). Wiley-Blackwell.

Archibald, Z. H. (2013). *Ancient economies of the Northern Aegean. Fifth to First Centuries BC*. Oxford University Press.

Bentz, M., Geominy, W. A., & Müller, J. M. (Eds.). (2010). *Tonart: Virtuosität antiker Töpfertechnik*. Universität Bonn. Akademisches Kunstmuseum.

Besios, M. (2017). Μεθώνη. In Vlachopoulos & Tsiafaki 2017, pp. 162–165.

Besios, M., Tzifopoulos, G. Z., & Kotsonas, A. (2012). Μεθώνη Πιερίας I: Επιγραφές, χαράγματα και εμπορικά σύμβολα στη γεωμετρική και αρχαϊκή κεραμική από το 'Υπόγειο' της Μεθώνης Πιερίας στη Μακεδονία. Centre for the Greek Language.

Bräuning, A., & Kilian-Dirlmeier, I. (2013). *Die eisenzeitlichen Grabhügel von Vergina. Die Ausgrabungen von Photios Petsas 1960–1961*. Verlag.

Chatzis, N. (2012). Η παρουσία της πρωτογεωμετρικής και γεωμετρικής αττικίζουσας κεραμικής στο Βόρειο Αιγαίο. Δύο ενδιαφέροντα παραδείγματα από το Καραμπουρνάκι. In E. Kefalidou & D. Tsiafaki (Eds.), *Kerameos Paides. Studies offered to professor Michalis Tiverios by his students* (pp. 239–246). Etaireia Andrion Epistimonon.

Chavela, K. (2018). Transformations and formations around the Thermaic Gulf in the Late Bronze Age and early Iron Age: The evidence of burial practices. In S. Gimatzidis, M. Pieniazek, & S. Mangaloglu-Votruba (Eds.), *Archaeology across Frontiers and borderlands. Fragmentation and connectivity in the North Aegean and the Central Balkans from the Bronze Age to the Iron Age* (pp. 159–186). Verlag der Österreichischen Akademie der Wissenschaften.

Chavela, K. (2021). Ο οικισμός και το νεκροταφείο της Τούμπας Θεσσαλονίκης. In A. Lioutas & Y. Karliambas (Eds.), *Κώμες και πολίσματα στον μυχό του Θερμαϊκού κόλπου* (pp. 52–60). Greek Ministry of Culture & Ephorate of Antiquities of Thessaloniki City.

Chrysostomou, A. (2000). Βόρεια Βοττιαία και Αλμωπία στην εποχή του Σιδήρου και τα αρχαϊκά χρόνια. In P. Adam-Veleni (Ed.), *Μύρτος. Μνήμη Ιουλίας Βοκοτοπούλου* (pp. 229–242). Ministry of Culture & Aristotle University of Thessaloniki.

Chrysostomou, A., & Chrysostomou, P. (2012). The Gold Wearing Archaic Macedonians from the Western Cemetery of Archontiko, Pella. In M. Tiverios, P. Nidgelis, & P. Adam-Veleni (Eds.), *Threpteria. Studies on ancient Macedonia* (pp. 490–516). AUTH Press.

Descamps-Lequime, S. (2002). Un exaleiptron en fer et en bronze de la nécropole macédonienne de Karabournaki, dans les collections du Musée du Louvre. In A. Giumlia-Mair (Ed.), *I Bronzi Antichi: Produzione e tecnologia. Atti del XV Congresso Internazionale sui Bronzi Antichi, organizzato dall' Università di Udine, sede di Gorizia Grado-Aquileia, 22–26 maggio 2001* (pp. 108–115). Montagnac.

Descamps-Lequime, S. (2009). Σιδερένια αντικείμενα της Βόρειας Ελλάδας στις συλλογές του Μουσείου του Λούβρου. In D. Ignatiadou (Ed.), *Σίδηρος. Ημερίδα συντήρησης Αρχαιολογικού Μουσείου Θεσσαλονίκης* (pp. 133–142). Archaeological Museum of Thessaloniki.

Descamps-Lequime, S., & Charatzopoulou, K. (2011). Les nécropoles de Mikra Karaburun (actuelle Karabournaki) et de Zeitenlik (actuelle Stavroupolis). Huit pesons & Karabournaki. In S. Descamps-Lequime & K. Charatzopoulou (Eds.), *Au royaume d'Alexandre le Grand. La Macédoine antique, Catalogue d'exposition, Paris, musée du Louvre, 13 octobre 2011–16 janvier 2012* (pp. 105–132, 387, 669). Louvre Éditions.

Despini, A. (2016a). *Σίνδος II. Το νεκροταφείο Ανασκαφικές έρευνες 1980–1982. Πήλινα, γυάλινα και φαγεντιανά αγγεία, πήλινοι λύχνοι, μεταλλικά αγγεία, πήλινα ειδώλια και πλαστικά αγγεία, νομίσματα*. The Archaeological Society at Athens.

Despini, A. (2016b). *Σίνδος III. Το νεκροταφείο Ανασκαφικές έρευνες 1980–1982. Μάσκες και χρυσά ελάσματα, κοσμήματα, μικροαντικείμενα και στλεγγίδες, είδη οπλισμού*. The Archaeological Society at Athens.

Despini, A., Schürmann, W., & Gisler, J.-R. (2009). Gold funerary masks. *Antike Kunst, 52,* 20–65. http://www.jstor.org/stable/23296850

Elston, M. (1990). Ancient repairs of Greek vases in the J. Paul Getty museum. *The J. Paul Getty Museum Journal, 18,* 53–68. http://www.jstor.org/stable/4166600

Filis, K. (2012). Εμπορικοί αμφορείς από το Καραμπουρνάκι. In E. Kefalidou & D. Tsiafaki (Eds.), *Kerameos Paides. Studies offered to professor Michalis Tiverios by his students* (pp. 309–320). Etaireia Andrion Epistimonon.

Flensted-Jensen, P. (2004). Thrace from Axios to Strymon. In M. H. Hansen & T. H. Nielsen (Eds.), *An inventory of archaic and classical poleis* (pp. 810–853). Oxford University Press.

Gardner, E. A., & Casson, S. (1918–1919). Antiquities found in the British Zone. *BSA, 23,* 10–39.

Hammond, N. (1972). *A history of Macedonia I.* The Clarendon Press.

Havela, K. (2012). Τοπικά κεραμικά εργαστήρια του 8ου αι. π.Χ. περιμετρικά του Θερμαϊκού κόλπου. In E. Kefalidou & D. Tsiafaki (Eds.), *Kerameos Paides. Studies offered to professor Michalis Tiverios by his students* (pp. 247–256). Etaireia Andrion Epistimonon.

Ignatiadou, D., Descamps, S., Kefalidou, E., & Boucher, A. (2008). Mikra Karaburun 1917: ανακτώντας αρχαιολογικά συμφραζόμενα. *Το Αρχαιολογικό Έργο στη Μακεδονία και στη Θράκη, 22,* 335–342.

Koukouli-Chrysanthaki, C., & Bassiakos, I. (2002). Nonslagging copper production of 5th millennium: The evidence from the Neolithic settlement of Promachon-Topolnica (Eastern Macedonia, Greece). In *8th EAA annual meeting, 24–29 September 2002* (pp. 193–194). Thessaloniki Hellas. Abstracts book.

Kourou, N. (2004). Οι οικισμοί των σκοτεινών χρόνων. In A. F. Lagopoulos (Ed.), *Η ιστορία της αρχαίας ελληνικής πόλης* (pp. 147–162). Athens.

Lehoërff, A. (2004). Sources et méthodes pour l'étude de l'artisanat métallurgique dans les sociétés anciennes de la péninsule italienne. L'idéal du métallurgiste et la réalité archéologique. In A. Lehoërff (Ed.), *L'artisanat métallurgique dans les sociétés anciennes en Méditerranée occidentale. Techniques, lieux et formes de production, Actes du colloque de Ravello, Mai 2000* (pp. 161–169). École française de Rome.

Lewis, D. M. (2020). Labour specialization in the Athenian economy: Occupational hazards. In E. Stewart, E. Harris, & D. Lewis (Eds.), *Skilled labour and professionalism in ancient Greece and Rome* (pp. 129–174). Cambridge University Press. https://doi.org/10.1017/9781108878135.005

Lioutas, A. (2021). Οι 26 (ή 54;) κώμες και πολίσματα του κασσάνδρειου οικισμού. In A. Lioutas & Y. Karliambas (Eds.), *Κώμες και πολίσματα στον μυχό του Θερμαϊκού κόλπου* (pp. 31–39). Greek Ministry of Culture & Ephorate of Antiquities of Thessaloniki City.

Manakidou, E. (2010a). Céramiques indigènes de l'époque géométrique et archaïque du site de Karabournaki en Macédoine et leur relation avec les céramiques importées. In H. Tréziny (Ed.), *Grecs et Indigènes de la Catalogne à la Mer Noire. Actes des rencontres du programme européen Ramses2 (2006–2008)* (pp. 463–470). Publications du Centre Camille Jullian. Available at https://books.openedition.org/pccj/646. Last visit 28/2/2022.

Manakidou, E. (2010b). Παραστάσεις και ομοιώματα αμαξών στα αρχαϊκά και κλασικά χρόνια: χρήσεις και συμβολισμοί. In D. Triantafyllos & D. Terzopoulou (Eds.), *Αλογα και άμαξες στον αρχαίο κόσμο* (pp. 177–197). Ministry of Culture and Tourism.

Manakidou, E. (2014). Kitchenware from the settlement at Karabournaki/Thessaloniki in the Archaic Period. In P. Bádenas de la Peña, P. Cabrera Bonet, M. Moreno Conde, A. Ruiz Rodrνguez, C. Sánchez Fernández, & T. Tortosa Rocamora (Eds.), *Homenaje a Ricardo Olmos. Per speculum in aenigmate. Miradas sobre la Antigüedad* (pp. 116–121). Asociación Cultural Hispano-Helénica.

Manakidou, E. (2017). New perspectives in the study of pottery assemblages from settlements and their cemeteries in Central Macedonia during the Archaic Period. In D. Rodríguez Pérez (Ed.), *Greek art in context. Archaeological and art historical perspectives* (pp. 42–53). Routledge.

Manakidou, E. (2019). Αττικά μελαμβαφή και ερυθρόμορφα αγγεία στο Καραμπουρνάκι. In E. Manakidou & A. Avramidou (Eds.), *Η κεραμική της κλασικής εποχής στο Βόρειο Αιγαίο* και την περιφέρειά του (480–323/300 π.Χ.). πρακτικά του διεθνούς αρχαιολογικού συνεδρίου, Θεσσαλονίκη 17–20 Μαΐου 2017 (pp. 339–351). University Studio Press.

Manakidou, E., & Tsiafaki, D. (2017). Καραμπουρνάκι Θεσσαλονίκης. In Vlachopoulos & Tsiafaki 2017, 336–337.

Manoledakis, M. (forthcoming). Ανασκαφή του Διεθνούς Πανεπιστημίου της Ελλάδος στην Τράπεζα Νέου Ρυσίου – Καρδίας, 2018–2019. Το Αρχαιολογικό Έργο στη Μακεδονία και στη Θράκη 33 (2019–2020).

Mavroeidi, I., Andreou, S., & Vavelidis, M. (2004). Μεταλλικά αντικείμενα και μεταλλοτεχνικές δραστηριότητες κατά την Εποχή του Χαλκού στην Τούμπα Θεσσαλονίκης. Το Αρχαιολογικό Έργο στη Μακεδονία και στη Θράκη, 18, 315–328.

Misailidou-Despotidou, V. (2011). Χάλκινα κοσμήματα αρχαϊκών χρόνων από τη Μακεδονία. Archaeological Institute of Macedonian and Thracian Studies.

Nerantzis, N. (2015). Rhesos' Gold, Heracles' Iron: The archaeology of metals exploration in Northeast Greece. Potingair Press.

Nigdelis, P. (1995). Η οικογένεια των Ιταλικών Aulii Avii στη Θεσσαλονίκη: με αφορμή μια δίγλωσση αναθηματική επιγραφή. Τεκμήρια, 1, 47–65.

Pandermali, E., & Trakosopoulou, E. (1994). Καραμπουρνάκι 1994. Η ανασκαφή της ΙΣΤ' ΕΠΚΑ. Το Αρχαιολογικό Έργο στη Μακεδονία και στη Θράκη, 8, 203–215.

Pandermali, E., & Trakosopoulou, E. (1995). Καραμπουρνάκι 1995. Η ανασκαφή της ΙΣΤ' ΕΠΚΑ. Το Αρχαιολογικό Έργο στη Μακεδονία και στη Θράκη, 9, 283–292.

Panti, A. (2008). Τοπική κεραμική από τη Χαλκιδική και το μυχό του Θερμαϊκού κόλπου (Άκανθος, Καραμπουρνάκι, Σίνδος). City Publish.

Panti, A. (2012a). Burial customs in the Thermaic gulf and Chalcidice in the archaic period. In M. Tiverios, P. Nidgelis, & P. Adam-Veleni (Eds.), Threpteria. Studies on ancient Macedonia (pp. 466–489). AUTH Press.

Panti, A. (2012b). Νέα στοιχεία για την ωοκέλυφη κεραμική. In E. Kefalidou & D. Tsiafaki (Eds.), Kerameos Paides. Studies offered to professor Michalis Tiverios by his students (pp. 257–264). Etaireia Andrion Epistimonon.

Panti, A., & Vasileiou, S. (2018). Το νεκροταφείο της ΠΕΣ στην οδό Θ. Σοφούλη στο Καραμπουρνάκι Θεσσαλονίκης. Archaeologikon Deltion 69–70, A (2014–2015), 83–144.

Papadopoulos, J. K. (2013). Some further thoughts on the Early Iron Age Potter's Kiln at Torone. In Adam-Veleni et al. 2013, pp. 39–50.

Perrault, J., & Bonias, Z. (2021). Argilos: The booming economy of a silent city. In M. Gleba, B. Marín-Aguilera, & B. Dimova (Eds.), Making cities. Economies of production and urbanization in Mediterranean Europe, 1000–500 BC (pp. 9–20). Cambridge University Library.

Perreault, J., Blondé, F., & Peristeri, K. (2013). The Pottery Workshop at Phari, Thasos. In Adam-Veleni et al., pp. 27–38.

Rey, L. (1927). La Nécropole de Mikra-Karaburun près de Salonique. Albania, 2, 48–57.

Rey, L. (1928). La Nécropole de Mikra-Karaburun près de Salonique. Albania, 3, 60–66.

Rey, L. (1932). La nécropole de Mikra-Karaburun près de Salonique. Albania, 4, 67–76.

Rhomaios, K. (1940). Που έκειτο η αρχαία Θέρμη. Μακεδονικά, 1, 1–7.

Rollinger, R. (2020). Neo-Assyrian through Persian empires. In F. De Angelis (Ed.), A companion to Greeks across the ancient world (pp. 173–198). Wiley-Blackwell.

Sanidas, G. (2013). La production artisanale en Grèce Une approche spatiale et topographique à partir des exemples de l'Attique et du Péloponnèse du viie au ier siècles avant J.-C. CTHS.

Sanidas, G., Georgakopoulou, M., Jagou, B., Tiverios, M., Manakidou, E., & Tsiafaki, D. (2015). Επεξεργασία σιδήρου στο Καραμπουρνάκι κατά την αρχαϊκή περίοδο. Το Αρχαιολογικό Έργο στη Μακεδονία και στη Θράκη, 29, 267–273.

Saripanidi, V. (2013). Αντιπροσωπευτικές κεραμικές κατηγορίες του Βορειοελλαδικού χώρου (Πρώιμη Εποχή Σιδήρου - πρώιμος 5ος αι. π.Χ.), Appendix B. In Adam-Veleni et al. 2013, pp. 245–254.

Segbers, A. (2018). A smith in the pottery workshop – Evidence of a close connection between two crafts. In M. Bentz & T. Helms (Eds.), *Craft production systems in a cross-cultural perspective* (pp. 113–118). Verlag.

Skarlatidou, E. (2007). *Thermi. The Ancient Cemetery beneath the Modern Town*. Municipality of Thermi and 16th Ephorate of Antiquities of Thessaloniki.

Soueref, K. (2011). *Τοπογραφικά και αρχαιολογικά κεντρικής Μακεδονίας*. University Studio Press.

Soueref, K. (2021). Ο μυχός του Θερμαϊκού κόλπου – Ιστορικό και γεωγραφικό περιβάλλον. In A. Lioutas & Y. Karliambas (Eds.), *Κώμες και πολίσματα στον μυχό του Θερμαϊκού κόλπου* (pp. 20–30). Greek Ministry of Culture & Ephorate of Antiquities of Thessaloniki City.

Spataro, M., & Villing, A. (2009). Scientific investigation of pottery grinding bowls from the Archaic and Classical Eastern Mediterranean. *The British Museum Technical Research Bulletin, 3*, 89–100.

Tiverios, M. (1995–2000). Έξι χρόνια πανεπιστημιακών ανασκαφών στο Καραμπουρνάκι Θεσσαλονίκης (1994–1999). *Εγνατία, 5*, 297–321.

Tiverios, M. (1997). Οι ιστορικοί χρόνοι στην περιοχή της Θεσσαλονίκης πριν από την ίδρυσή της. In I. K. Chasiotis (Ed.), *ΤΟΙΣ ΑΓΑΘΟΙΣ ΒΑΣΙΛΕΥΟΥΣΑ. Θεσσαλονίκη. Ιστορία και Πολιτισμός* (Vol. 1, pp. 78–87). Paratiritis.

Tiverios, M. (2008). Greek colonisation of the northern Aegean. In G. Tsetskhlatdze (Ed.), *Greek colonisation. An account of Greek colonies and other settlements overseas* (Vol. v. 2, pp. 1–154). Brill.

Tiverios, M. (2009). Η πανεπιστημιακή ανασκαφή στο Καραμπουρνάκι Θεσσαλονίκης. In P. Adam-Veleni & K. Tzanavari (Eds.), *Το Αρχαιολογικό Έργο στη Μακεδονία και στη Θράκη 20 Χρόνια* (pp. 385–396). Ministry of Culture and Tourism & Aristotle University of Thessaloniki.

Tiverios, M. (2017). Μακεδονία. Εποχή του Σιδήρου (1050-480 π.Χ.). In Vlachopoulos & Tsiafaki 2017, 46–55.

Tiverios, M., Manakidou, E., & Tsiafaki, D. (2001). Ανασκαφικές έρευνες στο Καραμπουρνάκι κατά το 2001: Ο αρχαίος οικισμός. *Το Αρχαιολογικό Έργο στη Μακεδονία και στη Θράκη, 15*, 255–270.

Tiverios, M., Manakidou, E., & Tsiafaki, D. (2003). Πανεπιστημιακές ανασκαφές στο Καραμπουρνάκι Θεσσαλονίκης (2000-2002). *Εγνατία, 7*, 327–351.

Tiverios, M., Manakidou, E., & Tsiafaki, D. (2007). Ανασκαφικές έρευνες στο Καραμπουρνάκι κατά το 2007: ο αρχαίος οικισμός. *Το Αρχαιολογικό Έργο στη Μακεδονία και στη Θράκη, 21*, 263–268.

Tiverios, M., Manakidou, E., & Tsiafaki, D. (2008). Ανασκαφικές έρευνες στο Καραμπουρνάκι κατά το 2008: ο αρχαίος οικισμός. *Το Αρχαιολογικό Έργο στη Μακεδονία και στη Θράκη, 22*, 329–334.

Tiverios, M., Manakidou, E., Tsiafakis, D., Valamoti, S. M., Theodoropoulou, T., & Gatzogia, E. (2013). Cooking in an Iron Age pit at Karabournaki. An interdisciplinary approach. In S. Voutsaki & S. M. Valamoti (Eds.), *Diet, economy and Society in the Ancient Greek World. Towards a better integration of archaeology and science, Proceedings of the international conference, Netherlands Institute at Athens, 22–24 March 2010* (pp. 205–214). Peeters.

Tiverios, M., Manakidou, E., & Tsiafaki, D. (2016). 23 χρόνια πανεπιστημιακών αρχαιολογικών ερευνών στο Καραμπουρνάκι: αποκαλύψεις, διαπιστώσεις, προοπτικές. *Το Αρχαιολογικό Έργο στη Μακεδονία και στη Θράκη, 30*, 291–300.

Triantafyllos, D. (2000). Ancient Thrace. In *Thrace* (pp. 35–97). General Secretariat of the Region of East Macedonia and Thrace.

Tsiafaki, D. (2019). Archaic pottery workshops in northern Greece. In M. Denti & M. Villette (Eds.), *Archéologie des espaces artisanaux. Fouiller et comprendre les gestes des potiers, Rennes 27-28/11/2014* (pp. 99–110). UMR 5140 du CNRS.

Tsiafaki, D. (2020). The Northern Aegean. In F. De Angelis (Ed.), *A companion to Greeks across the ancient world* (pp. 409–430). Wiley-Blackwell.

Tsiafaki, D. (2021). Regional economies and productions in the area of the Thermaic gulf. In M. Gleba, B. Marín-Aguilera, & B. Dimova (Eds.), *Making cities. Economies of production and urbanization in Mediterranean Europe, 1000–500 BC* (pp. 21–38).

Tsiafaki, D. (2022). Crafts and craftsmanship within the societies of Northern Greece in Archaic times. In M. Bentz & M. Heinzelmann (Eds.), *Sessions 2 – 3, Single Contributions. Archaeology and Economy in the Ancient World 53* (Heidelberg, Propylaeum 2022) (pp. 91–101). https://doi.org/10.11588/propylaeum.999.c13347

Tsiafaki, D., & Manakidou, E. (2013). Ένα εργαστήριο αρχαϊκής κεραμικής στο Καραμπουρνάκι. In Adam-Veleni et al. 2013, pp. 73–88.

Tsiafaki, D., & Manakidou, E. (2021). Ο οικισμός στο Καραμπουρνάκι. In A. Lioutas & Y. Karliambas (Eds.), *Κώμες και πολίσματα στον μυχό του Θερμαϊκού κόλπου* (pp. 61–68). Greek Ministry of Culture & Ephorate of Antiquities of Thessaloniki City.

Tsiafaki, D., & Tsirliganis, N. (2008). Ανασκαφή στο Καραμπουρνάκι: χημική ανάλυση κεραμικών οστράκων με φασματοσκοπία ατομικής απορρόφησης και φλογοφωτομετρία. Appendix C. In Panti 2008, pp. 265–273.

Tsiafakis, D. (2010). Domestic architecture in the Northern Aegean: The evidence from the ancient settlement of Karabournaki. In H. Tréziny, (ed.), *Grecs et Indigènes de la Catalogne à la Mer Noire. Actes des rencontres du programme européen Ramses2 (2006-2008)*, (pp. 379–388). Publications du Centre Camille Jullian. Available at https://books.openedition.org/pccj/594. Last visit 28/2/2022.

Tsiafakis, D. (2013). Architectural similarities(?) between Black Sea and North Aegean settlements. In G. Tsetskhladze, S. Atasoy, A. Avram, Ş. Dönmez, & J. Hargrave (Eds.), *The Bosporus: Gateway between the Ancient West and East (1st millennium BC-5th century AD), Proceedings of the fourth international congress on Black Sea antiquities, Istanbul, 14th–18th September 2009* (pp. 61–68) BAR International Series.

Tsimbidou-Avloniti, M. (1999). Καλαμαριά. *Archaeologikon Deltion, 54*, 531–532.

Tzanavari, K., & Christidis, A. P. (1995). A Carian Graffito from the Lebet Table Thessaloniki. *Kadmos, 34*, 13–17.

Van Alfen, P. (2016). Aegean-Levantine Trade, 600–300 BCE. Commodities, consumers, and the problem of Autarkeia. In E. M. Harris, D. M. Lewis, & M. Woolmer (Eds.), *The ancient Greek economy markets, households and City-states* (pp. 277–298). Cambridge University Press. https://doi.org/10.1017/CBO9781139565530.013

Vivtenko, S. (2008). Μικροσκοπική μελέτη δειγμάτων κεραμικής από το Καραμπουρνάκι. Appendix B. In Panti 2008, pp. 264–265.

Vlachopoulos, A. & Tsiafaki, D. (Eds.), (2017). Αρχαιολογία. Μακεδονία και Θράκη. .

Xydopoulos, I. (2007). *Η εικόνα των Θρακών στην κλασική ιστοριογραφία*. Kyriakidis Bros.

The Inland Late Bronze – Iron Age Anchorage of Dor: Ancient Reality or Fantasy?

Gilad Shtienberg and Katrina Cantu

Abstract Around the Levantine coast, ancient anchorages facilitated urban center establishment by enabling travel that connected between sites and civilizations, leading to expanding trade network possibilities. Various scholars previously hypothesized that this growing maritime economic prosperity was permitted along the Israeli coast in Yaffo, Dor, Tel Naami, Tel Akko, and Tel Achziv due to a natural process in the marine-terrestrial interface subsequent development of lagoonal systems. Once formed, these natural, brackish, protected aquatic systems were postulated to have been utilized by the coastal inhabitants as inland harbors constructed adjacent to the settlement. Here the complex long-term relationships between sea-level rise, sedimentation variation, and resulting coastal morphogenesis are examined in the area of tel-Dor. This investigation relies on a high-resolution spatial and temporal paleoenvironmental record combining dated terrestrial and shallow marine sediment cores with sedimentological and faunal analysis as well as seismic profiles collected from the shallow marine south bay of Dor. The current stratigraphic framework indicates that the coast of Dor has undergone morphological changes over the Holocene. These consist of a brackish wetland environment (ca. 9000–7000 years ago) that then changed to a high energy beach (ca. 7000–4000 years ago) to finally settle as a backshore influenced by anthropogenic activity of the coastal inhabitants (4000 years ago–present). The time constraint stratigraphy, the surface elevation of each lithological unit, and association to sea level variation over the last 9000 years rule the existence of a lagoon out. As a result, it is unlikely that the area facilitated an inland anchorage, making previous hypotheses on this matter unplausible. The holistic approach utilized in Dor provides a unique opportunity for studying ancient coastal processes, which are essential for properly understanding the interplay between the varying environment and coastal settlers.

G. Shtienberg (✉) · K. Cantu
University of California, San Diego, La Jolla, CA, USA
e-mail: gshtienberg@ucsd.com; kcantu@ucsd.edu

© The Author(s), under exclusive license to Springer Nature Switzerland AG 2023
E. Ben-Yosef, I. W. N. Jones (eds.), *"And in Length of Days Understanding" (Job 12:12): Essays on Archaeology in the Eastern Mediterranean and Beyond in Honor of Thomas E. Levy*, Interdisciplinary Contributions to Archaeology, https://doi.org/10.1007/978-3-031-27330-8_63

Keywords Landscape reconstruction · Environmental change · Sea level rise · Inland anchorage · Tel-Dor · Middle-bronze age · Coastal habitation patterns · Lagoon

1 Introduction

The ancient coast of Israel (Fig. 1a) has a long history of maritime connectivity, with several ancient port cities such as Jaffa, tel Dor, tel Nami, tel Abu-Hawam, tel Akko, and tel Achziv located along the central to north coast of Israel (Fig. 1; Giaime et al., 2018; Zviely et al., 2006). The environmental setting of these cities is often of great interest to historians and archaeologists as the modern coastline may not be ideal or even compatible with the needs of a port – mainly, that the harbor must be deep enough to accommodate ships, be safely accessible from the sea, and be protected against wave action (Burke et al., 2017; Marriner & Morhange, 2007; Marriner et al., 2012). One such city, Akko, on the north end of Haifa Bay in Northern Israel, was a regionally significant port beginning in the Middle Bronze age. Historical texts and archaeological evidence attested to the presence of a port, but the ancient settlement on the tel is located several hundred meters landward from the modern shoreline. Sediment coring revealed that the tel had once been located adjacent to a lagoon, which over time filled with fluvial and later Nile sand deposits (Giaime et al., 2021; Morhange et al., 2016). Similarly, the anchorage at Jaffa, near Tel Aviv, has long been considered problematic and even dangerous for ships to sail and dock in, and the city's function as a port was somewhat puzzling.

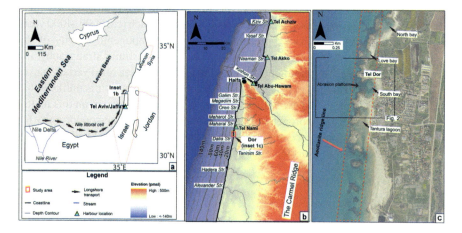

Fig. 1 Locality maps. (**a**) The direction of longshore transport along the eastern Mediterranean shown by black arrows. Dashed blue line represents the Nile; dashed red lines represent approximate international borders. Outlined rectangle shows location of inset (**b**), which illustrates the area of investigate in North-central coast of Israel and (**c**) the coast of Dor annotating its geomorphological properties

The Inland Late Bronze – Iron Age Anchorage of Dor: Ancient Reality or Fantasy?

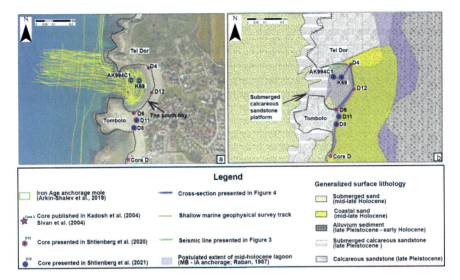

Fig. 2 Maps representing coring and sampling locations of the south bay of Dor and its pocket beach (see Fig. 1 for inset locations). (**a**) Aerial photographs with drilling locations and seismic profiles discussed in the current paper and seismic section location presented in Fig. 3 (**b**) surface lithologies, archeological remains of the MB Anchorage, and location of cross-section presented in Fig. 4

Investigation of historical maps, topography, and sediment cores suggests that the anchorage was, prior to the Classical period, located in an inland body of water to the east of the tel which has since filled in with sediment (Burke et al., 2017). With these examples in mind, we turn to the ancient port city of tel Dor, on the Carmel Coast of Northern Israel (Fig. 2).

In his 1987 article, "The Harbor of the Sea Peoples at Dor", Avner Raban posited that during the Late Bronze Age to Iron age Dor's South Harbor was connected to the sea by a long, North-South oriented lagoon stretching approximately one mile south of the tel (proposed location of the Dor's lagoon is presented in Fig. 2b). According to Raban, this body of water also wrapped around the east side of the tel, creating a "haven" for ships after entering the lagoon and sailing north toward the settlement. This hypothesis was based on Raban's understanding of the coastal sedimentary profile of Dor as well as the assumption that sea level was approximately a half-meter lower than today's, too low to allow access to the harbor from the Mediterranean due to an aeolianite ridge blocking its western side. While this ridge has an opening wide enough for boats to pass through today, Raban suggested that it would have been much less eroded in the thirteenth century BCE, thereby closing off the west side of the harbor. A recent geophysical investigation of the area found evidence of an ancient channel connecting Tantura Lagoon to Dor's South Harbor through what is now a tombolo (Figs. 1c and 2), seemingly supporting Raban's hypothesis (Lazar et al., 2021).

Was the lagoonal harbor proposed by Raban a reality? If not, what did the landscape surrounding ancient Dor look like? To answer these questions, we present several lines of stratigraphic evidence from seismic profiles conducted in the shallow south bay of Dor along with seven sediment cores collected in the vicinity of the South Harbor (Fig. 2) and examine the Carmel coast relative sea level curve that has been largely constructed after the publication of Raban's, 1987 paper with correlative chronostratigraphic data of Dor.

2 Regional Setting

In general terms, the morphology of the narrow, 3 km wide Carmel coast – from east to west – consists of alluvial plain, embayments and sand beaches separated by aeolianite ridges which trend parallel-subparallel to the current coastline (Fig. 1c; Gvirtzman et al., 1983 among others). The late Pleistocene to Holocene unconsolidated sedimentary sequences of the Carmel coast accumulated in a terrestrial–coastal environment composing of alternating aeolianites and red-brown sandy-loam paleosols. In the lowlands between the ridges, the paleosols are covered by a dark silty clay unit, rich in organic material (Shtienberg et al., 2017). As sea level rose during the late Pleistocene-Holocene transition (15,000–12,000 years ago; Rohling et al., 2014), the shoreline migrated eastwards, flooding the shallow shelf around 9000 years ago (depth shallower than −20 m; Sivan et al., 2004a). Archaeological observations from the coast (Sivan et al., 2001; Galili et al., 2019) confirm that sea level continued to rise during the early stages of the Holocene until ca. 6000 to 7000 years ago, when transgression slowed considerably. As sea level and the coastline neared their present elevation and location ca. 6000 to 4000 years ago (Sivan et al., 2001) the volume of windblown sand which accumulated along the coast increased (Roskin et al., 2015; Shtienberg et al., 2016, 2017). Although sea level was believed to have been relatively stable from ca. 3000 years ago to present, some archaeological coastal structures and their base elevation and location compared to the present shoreline point toward lower levels of up to 2.5 meters compared to present (Anzidei et al., 2011; Galili et al., 1993; Yasur-Landau et al., 2021). Based on these anthropogenic constraints sea level finally reached its current elevation, fluctuating in magnitudes lower than ±0.5 ca. 2000 years ago (Toker et al., 2012).

The ancient city of Dor is located in the Carmel coast (Fig. 1) 21 km south of present-day Haifa, and 50 km north of Tel Aviv and presents an ideal location for studying long term dynamics between natural – human interactions since the prehistory. The sedimentological, geomorphological, and historical characteristics of this location include a shallow lagoon (Tantura lagoon) and three low-energy embayments located adjacent to the site (Fig. 1c). From north to south, these are the North Bay, the Love Bay, and the south bay with the latter located immediately south of the tel Dor. The Tantura lagoon and the three bays have an extensive and detailed evidence of human remains (Arkin Shalev et al., 2019a; Arkin Shalev et al., 2019b; Yasur-Landau et al., 2021 and reference therein) and sedimentary deposits (Kadosh

The Inland Late Bronze – Iron Age Anchorage of Dor: Ancient Reality or Fantasy? 1497

et al., 2004; Shtienberg et al., 2020, 2021; Sivan et al., 2004b) covering most of the Holocene period. In the past, the bays served as anchorages which can be directly linked to Dor as a successful port with long-term continuous occupation and includes structures on land (Raban, 1995; Marriner et al., 2014) and underwater (Gilboa & Sharon, 2008).

Occupation at tel Dor (Fig. 2) began in the Middle Bronze Age II (3900–3500 years ago) and the settlement continued to grow and develop throughout the Roman (2000–1700 years ago), Byzantine (1700–1400 years ago), and Crusader (1100–750 years ago) periods (e.g., Stern, 1994; Raban, 1995; Gilboa & Sharon, 2008; Nitschke et al., 2011). On the seashore an immense record of maritime constructions was previously identified. These include massive coastal fortifications dated to the Iron 1b period (3100 years ago; Gilboa & Sharon, 2008; Sharon & Gilboa, 2013) and an artificial mole, currently covered by a biogenic rock, serving as the main harbor installation of the city (Arkin et al., 2019a; Raban, 1995). In the ninth century BCE maritime activity continued in Dor and by the seventh century BCE it became a maritime center under the Assyrian empire with a sea-gate and fortifications (Arkin et al., 2019a). During the Hellenistic period (2300–2100 years ago) it seems that Dor continued to be a sturdy coastal city, fortified with defense structures (Nitschke et al., 2011) guarding the entrance to the bay. These structures were identified in underwater excavations and coastal geophysical surveys at the southern edge of the south bay of Dor (Lazar et al., 2021). The rich settlement history of Dor and its long-lasting existence as a coastal port site make it an ideal case for examining the possible usage of the natural coastal characteristics of Dor for establishing a Bronze Age inland harbor.

3 The Holocene Coastal Stratigraphy of Dor

In order to test Rabans' hypothesis (Raban, 1987) regarding the possible existence of an inland harbor (Figs. 1c and 2), a multidisciplinary approach was applied incorporating interpreted shallow marine geophysical profiles (Figs. 2 and 3), sedimentological, bio-stratigraphical, and chronological results previously published in Kadosh et al. (2004); and Shtienberg et al. (2020, 2021) (Figs. 4 and 5). The correlation between the previously dated sequences of Dor, identification of their depositional environment and association with the Carmel coast relative sea level curve (Galili et al., 2019; Sivan et al., 2001, 2004a; Yasur-Landau et al., 2021) enabled us to determine whether an inland lagoon existed in the area from the Late Bronze to Iron age during occupation of the tel.

Based on this integration (Fig. 5), the coastal zone sequence of the area consisted of two main units (F4; F5) that comprise of loam and quartz sand: at the base of the sequence, a 9200–7000 years ago (pre-pottery Neolithic LB-C to Pottery Neolithic) dark grey – dark brown homogenous silty loam sediment containing shallow shelf and fresh-brackish ostracods, gastropod shells, foraminifera, and sea urchin spine remains. The surface elevations of this unit range from -2.2 to -3.2 relative to

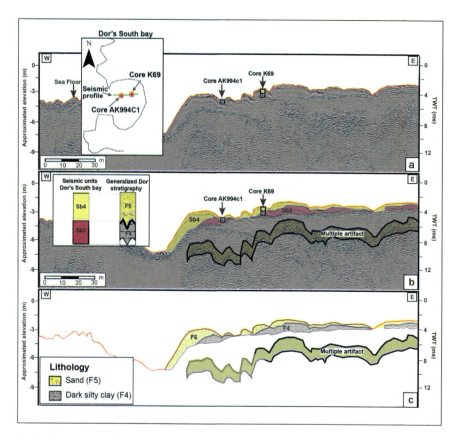

Fig. 3 Results from the geophysical survey (modified after Shtienberg et al., 2021): (**a**) Shore-perpendicular seismic section from the south bay of Dor; (**b**) the interpretation of the seismic section (**c**) transformation from acoustic units to lithologies was achieved based on boreholes AK994C1, K69 as well as surface lithologies identified on the shallow seabed of the south bay. The locations of the seismic section and boreholes are displayed in Fig. 2b

mean sea level (msl) with thickness of ~1 m. Relying on the sedimentological properties of the unit and its skeletal assemblage, unit F4 was interpreted as a brackish wetland deposit.

Covering the brackish wetland, a 2 to 6-meter-thick quartz rich sand unit was identified throughout the study area. This unit, which was chronologically constraint from 7000 years ago to present, has been broken down into three sub-units, and is described here from bottom to top:

Sub-unit F5a (Fig. 2) comprises of surface elevations ranging from −3.5 to −0.5 m relative to msl, and thicknesses of up to 2.5 m. The deposit consists of sub-rounded, course to medium grained, light brown to yellow sand. Glycymeris shells, unidentifiable gastropod and bivalve shells and abraded shallow shelf foraminifera were evident all through the sub-unit with abundance and size increasing upward. The chronostratigraphic correlation of the core data (Fig. 4b) constrains the beach

The Inland Late Bronze – Iron Age Anchorage of Dor: Ancient Reality or Fantasy? 1499

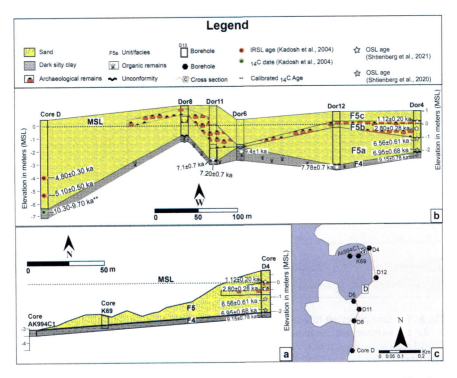

Fig. 4 Fence diagram presenting the chronostratigraphy of the South Bay coastal zone. The chronostratigraphic correlation based on the cores D4, D12, D6, D11, D8, AK994C1, K69 previously published in Shtienberg et al. (2020, 2021) of the (**a**) terrestrial – shallow offshore; (**b**) shoreline. The annotated ages are listed in ka (thousand years ago). Follow the cross-section in space in (**c**)

sand deposit, typically found in an area with high depositional energies, from 7000 to 4500 years ago (Chalcolithic – Middle Bronze age).

Overlying the beach sand deposit sub-unit F5b was identified with surface elevations of 0 to 0.3 m relative to msl, and a thickness of 0.4 m to 1 m (Figs. 4 and 5). The sub-unit is characterized by a light gray to light yellow medium-coarse grain sand abundant with Glycymeris shells, aeolianite fragments, chert and limestone pebbles. F5b also contains cultural material such as pottery sherds, pieces of iron, and charcoal fragments. OSL results from the base and upper portions of this anthropogenic rich deposit produced an age constraint of 2.8 to 1100 years ago, associating it with the Bronze Age–Crusader settlement at Tel-Dor.

F5c is the uppermost facies identified in the south bay of Dor with surface elevations of 1 to 1.5 m above msl and a thickness of 0.5 to 1 m (Fig. 5). This deposit is light gray to light brown with medium – fine grain sand littered with modern anthropogenic remains in its upper 0.3 m. Relying on the accompanying contemporary features and its base limiting age constraint of 1100 years sub-unit F5c is interpreted as an aeolian deposit which started to accumulate once the tel was deserted and continued until the modern settlement of Israel.

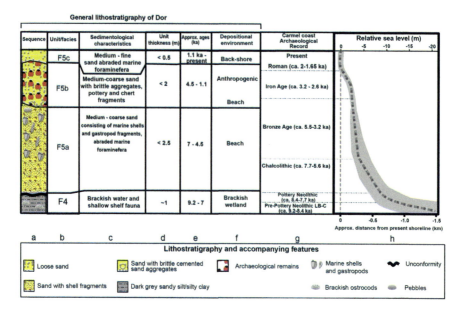

Fig. 5 The time constraint lithostratigraphy of Dor (a, b); with sedimentological characteristics (c, d); approximate age constraints (e); associated depositional environments (f); correlative Carmel coast archeological period. The annotated ages are listed in ka (thousand years ago) (g) and associated relative sea level based on Galili et al. (2019), Sivan et al. (2001, 2004b) and Yasur-Landau et al. (2021) (h). This generalization is based on the results presented in Figs. 3 and 4

4 The Coastal Evolution of Dor and Associated Shoreline Location

The temporal constraint of the sequence enables us to reconstruct the coastal evolution of Dor and link these geomorphic changes with the Holocene sea level rise to the cultural periods of the site (Fig. 5). Coastal wetlands of brackish salinity (Sivan et al., 2011, 2004b; Shtienberg et al., 2021) developed in the depressions of the south bay of Dor reflecting the wet climate conditions (Bar-Matthews et al., 2003; Grant et al., 2016) of the African Humid Period (ca. 15,000–8000 years ago; Natufian to Pottery Neolithic period). Relying on the youngest age constraint of the wetland surface (ca. 7200 years ago; Fig. 5) and initial deposition of the overlying coastal sand at 7100 years ago; the south bay bathymetry of the wetland surface (presented in Shtienberg et al., 2021) which was around 3 to 1 meter lower then present, relative msl (Galili et al., 2019; Sivan et al., 2004b) and the submerged rectangular building associated with a Pottery Neolithic settlement (Shtienberg et al., 2020) we postulate that during this time the entire south bay of Dor was a terrestrial environment. The ages from the surface of the wetland and overlying coastal sand confine the termination of wetland deposition to ca. 7000 years ago. This suggests that the environmental transition from a wetland to a coastal site is linked to

The advancing shoreline which deposited and buried the wetland surface under increasing volumes of coastal sand (Shtienberg et al., 2017).

A 2 m-thick bioclastic sand facies (F5a; Fig. 5) found in the current study area was dated between 7000 and 4500 years ago (Chalcolithic Period to Middle Bronze age). Based on its location, elevation range of 1.5 to −0.5 relative to msl, bathymetric data, relative sea level elevation of −5 to −2.5 (compared to present sea level) and the high percentage of the worn marine fauna, it seems that during this period the shoreline was still a few hundred to tens of meters west of its current location (Fig. 6a). Overlying the coastal sand facies (F5a), sub-unit 5b consists of poorly sorted, medium-coarse grain sand that was found to be rich with marine gastropod and bivalve fragments as well as archaeological remains. These sedimentological characteristics, the two late Holocene ages (2800 and 1100 years ago), and correlation with the relative sea-level curve of the Israeli coast, indicate that sub-unit F5b was deposited in a coastal environment when sea level was nearing its present elevation (Yasur-Landau et al., 2021) while the archeological remains (sherds, iron fragments) are the result of extensive human habitation from at least since Middle Bronze Age II and into the Roman period (Stern, 1994; Raban, 1995; Shahack-Gross et al., 2005; Sharon et al., 2005; Gilboa & Sharon, 2008). Unit F5 is topped by facies F5c which is a ∼ 0.5 m thick deposit, comprised of a medium- to fine-grained sand distributed with abraded shell material. Given that the seasonal beach profile changes of the Carmel coast can fluctuate between 1–1.5 m (Shtienberg et al., 2014) and the presence of glass and other recent artifacts, this facies is interpreted as modern pocket-beach sands. In the next section we use this chronostratigraphical data to evaluate the possible existence of an inland anchorage during the Late Bronze – Iron Age as well as test possible sailing routs for reaching the south bay anchorage of Dor.

5 Evaluation of the Possible Late Bronze – Iron Age Anchorage of Dor and Summary

In order for an inland anchorage to have existed during the Late Bronze – Iron Age (3500–2600 years before present), the elevation of the area around Dor's South Harbor would need to be deep enough to allow ships to enter. Comparing the dated sediment units from the cores collected around the harbor and the temporal correlation with the local sea level curve shows that not only were the evaluated locations not deep enough for ships to pass, but they were already above msl and likely tens to hundreds of meters from shore during the Chalcolithic and up to the middle Bronze Age, from circa 6500 to 4500 years before present (see Fig. 6). The characteristics of the sediment support this interpretation, as the coarse sand and poorly preserved marine fauna are consistent with a beach environment. As sea level continued to rise through the Late Bronze to Iron Ages before largely stabilizing during the Roman Period, the sediments continue to reflect a beach depositional

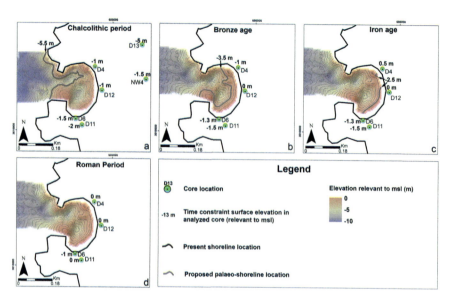

Fig. 6 Time constraint surface maps of Dor's shallow marine-terrestrial coastal side for the following periods: Chalcolithic period (7700–5600 years ago); Bronze Age (5500–3200 years ago); Iron age (3200–2600 years ago); Roman (2000–1600 years ago). The green dots illustrate core location with their surface elevation relative to modern mean sea level for each time constraint map while the thick grey contour line annotated the proposed shoreline location

environment, with the addition of anthropogenic materials. This stratigraphy is consistent across the examined cores which surround south bay of Dor demonstrating that there was no channel across the tombolo on the south side of the bay as Lazar et al. (2021) proposed, nor did a harbor extend inland to the eastern side of the tel (see Figs. 2b and 4). If Dor's harbor was not connected to the Mediterranean via a channel through the tombolo, then boats must have entered the western entrance to south bay. The bathymetric and sub-bottom survey results discussed in Shtienberg et al. (2021) show a 5-m deep west-east trending channel (relevant to msl) cutting across the aeolianite platform found in at the entrance of the south bay of Dor (Fig. 6). Subtracting two meters in consideration of the lower sea level during the middle to late Bronze Age (Galili et al., 2019; Sivan et al., 2004b; Yasur-Landau et al., 2021) still yields a depth of approximately 3 meters, likely deep enough for many ancient ships that possessed shallow keels (Polzer, 2011; Wachsmann, 2009).

Raban (1987) suggested that the submerged aeolianite ridge blocking much of the entrance to the south bay of Dor was higher during the Bronze Age, because it has been eroded in the intervening time. However, it seems that the aeolianites found around the entrance of the bay were only subjected to wave erosion for a period of 1000 years, during this time when the shoreline was situated right against the entrance of the bay. This is based on sea level rise (Fig. 5), the resulting shoreline transgression (Fig. 6) during most of the Chalcolithic (7000–6000 years before present), and erosional rate constraints of calcareous sandstones evaluated at 0.02–0.91 mm/year (Flemming, 2011). Taking these factors into account, it seems

The Inland Late Bronze – Iron Age Anchorage of Dor: Ancient Reality or Fantasy? 1503

that the submerged aeolianite platform could have been eroded up to a magnitude of 1 meter, which still allows the channel to be suitable for sailing during the Late Bronze – Iron Age.

The evidence presented in this analysis shows that Raban's vision of an inland harbor was not possible during the Late Bronze and Iron Ages, and that the south bay of Dor was surrounded on three sides by a beach environment rather than a lagoon. This further demonstrates that the western entrance to south bay of Dor was the only way for ships to access the port.

References

Anzidei, M., Antonioli, F., Benini, A., Lambeck, K., Sivan, D., Serpelloni, E., & Stocchi, P. (2011). Sea level change and vertical land movements since the last two millennia along the coasts of southwestern Turkey and Israel. *Quaternary International, 232*, 13–20. https://doi.org/10.1016/j.quaint.2010.05.005

Arkin Shalev, E., Gilboa, A., & Yasur-Landau, A. (2019a). The Iron Age Maritime Interface at the South Bay of Tel Dor: Results from the 2016 and 2017 excavation seasons. *International Journal of Nautical Archaeology, 48*, 439–452. https://doi.org/10.1111/1095-9270.12360

Arkin Shalev, E., Gambash, G., & Yasur-Landau, A. (2019b). Disheveled tenacity: The North Bay of Roman and Byzantine Dor. *Journal of Maritime Archaeology, 14*, 205–237. https://doi.org/10.1007/s11457-019-09235-y

Bar-Matthews, M., Ayalon, A., Gilmour, M., Matthews, A., & Hawkesworth, C. J. (2003). Sea–land oxygen isotopic relationships from planktonic foraminifera and speleothems in the Eastern Mediterranean region and their implication for paleorainfall during interglacial intervals. *Geochimica et Cosmochimica Acta, 67*, 3181–3199. https://doi.org/10.1016/S0016-7037(02)01031-1

Burke, A. A., Peilstöcker, M., & Burke, K. S. (Eds.). (2017). The history and archaeology of Jaffa 2. *Cotsen Institute of Archaeology Press at UCLA*. https://doi.org/10.2307/j.ctvdmwwr7

Flemming, B. W. (2011). Geology, morphology, and sedimentology of estuaries and coasts. In E. Wolanski & M. L. DS (Eds.), *Treatise on estuarine and coastal science* (Vol. 3, pp. 7–38). Academic.

Galili, E., Dahari, U., & Sharvit, J. (1993). Underwater surveys and rescue excavations along the Israeli coast. *The International Journal of Nautical Archaeology, 22*(1), 61–77.

Galili, E., Benjamin, J., Eshed, V., Rosen, B., McCarthy, J., & Kolska Horwitz, L. (2019). A submerged 7000-year-old village and seawall demonstrate earliest known coastal defense against sea-level rise. *PLoS One, 14*, e0222560. https://doi.org/10.1371/journal.pone.0222560

Giaime, M., Morhange, C., Marriner, N., López-Cadavid, G. I., & Artzy, M. (2018). Geoarchaeological investigations at Akko, Israel: New insights into landscape changes and related anchorage locations since the Bronze Age. *Geoarchaeology, 33*, 641–660. https://doi.org/10.1002/gea.21683

Giaime, M., Jol, H. M., Salmon, Y., López, G. I., Hamid, A. A., Bergevin, L., Bauman, P., McClymont, A., Sailer-Haugland, E., & Artzy, M. (2021). Using a multi-proxy approach to locate the elusive Phoenician/Persian anchorage of Tel Akko (Israel). *Quaternary International, 602*, 66–81. https://doi.org/10.1016/j.quaint.2021.06.008

Gilboa, A., & Sharon, I. (2008). Between the Carmel and the sea: Tel Dor's iron age reconsidered. *Near Eastern Archaeology., 71*, 146–170.

Grant, K. M., Grimm, R., Mikolajewicz, U., Marino, G., Ziegler, M., & Rohling, E. J. (2016). The timing of Mediterranean sapropel deposition relative to insolation, sea-level and African monsoon changes. *Quaternary Science Reviews, 140*, 125–141. https://doi.org/10.1016/j.quascirev.2016.03.026

Gvirtzman, G., Shachnai, E., Bakler, N., & Ilani, S. (1983). *Stratigraphy of the Kukar group (Quaternary) of the coastal Palin of Israel* (pp. 70–82). Geological Survey of Israel.

Kadosh, D., Sivan, D., Kutiel, H., & Weinstein-Evron, M. (2004). A late quaternary paleoenvironmental sequence from Dor, Carmel coastal plain, Israel. *Palynology, 28*, 143–157. https://doi.org/10.1080/01916122.2004.9989595

Lazar, M., Basson, U., Himmelstein, A. G., Levy, T. E., Arkin Shalev, E., & Yasur-Landau, A. (2021). The door to Dor: Tracing unseen anthropogenic impact in an ancient port. *Geoarchaeology, 36*(2), 203–212. https://doi.org/10.1002/gea.21825

Marriner, N., & Morhange, C. (2007). Geoscience of ancient Mediterranean harbours. *Earth-Science Reviews, 80*(3–4), 137–194. https://doi.org/10.1016/j.earscirev.2006.10.003

Marriner, N., Goiran, J. P., Geyer, B., Matoïan, V., al-Maqdissi, M., Leconte, M., & Carbonel, P. (2012). Ancient harbors and Holocene morphogenesis of the Ras Ibn Hani peninsula (Syria). *Quaternary Research, 78*(1), 35–49. https://doi.org/10.1016/j.yqres.2012.03.005

Marriner, N., Morhange, C., Kaniewski, D., & Carayon, N. (2014). Ancient harbour infrastructure in the Levant: Tracking the birth and rise of new forms of anthropogenic pressure. *Scientific Reports, 4*(1), 1–11. https://doi.org/10.1038/srep05554

Morhange, C., Giaime, M., Marriner, N., Hamid, A. A., Bruneton, H., Honnorat, A., Kaniewski, D., Magnin, F., Porotov, A. V., Wante, J., Zviely, D., & Artzy, M. (2016). Geoarchaeological evolution of Tel Akko's ancient harbour (Israel). *Journal of Archaeological Science: Reports, 7*, 71–81. https://doi.org/10.1016/j.jasrep.2016.03.046

Nitschke, J. L., Martin, S. R., & Shalev, Y. (2011). Between Carmel and the sea: Tel Dor: The Late Periods. *Near Eastern Archaeology, 74*, 132–154. https://doi.org/10.5615/neareastarch.74.3.0132

Polzer, M. E. (2011). Early eastern Mediterranean ship construction (Ch. 16). In A. Catsambis, B. L. Ford, & D. L. Hamilton (Eds.), *The Oxford handbook of maritime archaeology* (pp. 349–378). Oxford University Press.

Raban, A. (1987). The harbor of the sea peoples at Dor. *The Biblical archaeologist, 50*, 118–126.

Raban, A. (1995). *Dor-Yam: Marine and coastal installations at Dor in their geomorphological and stratigraphic context* (pp. 286–354). Final Report. Institute of Archaeology, Hebrew University of Jerusalem.

Rohling, E. J., Foster, G. L., Grant, K. M., Marino, G., Roberts, A. P., Tamisiea, M. E., & Williams, F. (2014). Sea-level and deep-sea-temperature variability over the past 5.3 million years. *Nature, 508*, 477–482. https://doi.org/10.1038/nature13230

Roskin, J., Sivan, D., Shtienberg, G., Roskin, E., Porat, N., & Bookman, R. (2015). Natural and human controls of the Holocene evolution of the beach, Aeolian sand and dunes of Caesarea (Israel). *Aeolian Research, 19*, 65–85.

Shahack-Gross, R., Albert, R.-M., Gilboa, A., Nagar-Hilman, O., Sharon, I., & Weiner, S. B. (2005). Geoarchaeology in an urban context: The uses of space in a Phoenician monumental building at Tel Dor (Israel). *Journal of Archaeological Science, 32*, 1417–1431. https://doi.org/10.1016/j.aeolia.2015.09.007

Sharon, I., & Gilboa, A. (2013). The SKL Town: Dor in the Early Iron Age. In A. E. Killebrew & G. Lehmann (Eds.), *The philistines and other "sea peoples" in text and archaeology* (pp. 393–468). Society of Biblical Literature. Available: http://www.jstor.org/stable/j.ctt46n483

Sharon, I., Gilboa, A., Boaretto, E., & Jull, & A.J.T. (2005). The early Iron Age dating project: introduction, methodology, progress report and an update on the Tel Dor radiometric dates. In T. Levy & T. Higham (Eds.), *The Bible and radiocarbon dating: Archaeology, text and science* (pp. 65–92). Acumen Publishing Ltd..

Shtienberg, G., Zviely, D., Sivan, D., & Lazar, M. (2014). Two centuries of coastal change at Caesarea, Israel: Natural processes vs. human intervention. *Geo-Marine Letters, 34*, 365–379. https://doi.org/10.1007/s00367-014-0355-5

Shtienberg, G., Dix, J., Waldmann, N., Makovsky, Y., Golan, A., & Sivan, D. (2016). Late-Pleistocene evolution of the continental shelf of Central Israel, a case study from Hadera. *Geomorphology, 261*, 200–211. https://doi.org/10.1016/j.geomorph.2016.03.008

Shtienberg, G., Dix, J. K., Roskin, J., Waldmann, N., Bookman, R., Bialik, O. M., Porat, N., Taha, N., & Sivan, D. (2017). New perspectives on coastal landscape reconstruction during the Late Quaternary: A test case from Central Israel. *Palaeogeography, Palaeoclimatology, Palaeoecology, 468*, 503–519. https://doi.org/10.1016/j.palaeo.2016.12.045

Shtienberg, G., Yasur-Landau, A., Norris, R. D., Lazar, M., Rittenour, T. M., Tamberino, A., Gadol, O., Cantu, K., Arkin-Shalev, E., Ward, S. N., & Levy, T. E. (2020). A Neolithic mega-tsunami event in the eastern Mediterranean: Prehistoric settlement vulnerability along the Carmel coast, Israel. *Plos one, 15*(12), e0243619. https://doi.org/10.1371/journal.pone.0243619

Shtienberg, G., Gadol, O., Levy, T. E., Norris, R. D., Rittenour, T. M., Yasur-Landau, A., Tamberino, A., & Lazar, M. (2021). Changing environments and human interaction during the Pleistocene – Early Holocene from the shallow coastal area of Dor, Israel. *Quaternary Research, 105*, 64–81. https://doi.org/10.1017/qua.2021.30

Sivan, D., Widowinski, S., Lambeck, K., Galili, E., & Raban, A. (2001). Holocene sea-level changes based on archeological sites off northen Israel. *Palaeogeography, Palaeoclimatology, Palaeoecology, 167*, 101–117.

Sivan, D., Eliyahu, D., & Raban, A. (2004a). Late Pleistocene to Holocene wetlands now covered by sand, along the Carmel Coast of Israel, and their relation to human settlement: An example from the coastal site of Dor. *Journal of Coastal Research, 204*, 1035–1048. https://doi.org/10.2112/03503A.1

Sivan, D., Lambeck, K., Toueg, R., Raban, A., Porath, Y., & Shirman, B. (2004b). Ancient coastal wells of Caesarea Maritima, Israel, an indicator for relative sea level changes during the last 2000 years. *Earth and Planetary Science Letters, 222*, 315–330. https://doi.org/10.1016/j.epsl.2004.02.007

Sivan, D., Greenbaum, N., Cohen-Seffer, R., Sisma-Ventura, G., & Almogi-Labin, A. (2011). The origin and disappearance of the late Pleistocene–early Holocene short-lived coastal wetlands along the Carmel coast, Israel. *Quaternary Research, 76*, 83–92. https://doi.org/10.1016/j.yqres.2011.04.006

Stern, E. (1994). *Dor Ruler of the Seas* (p. 348). Israel Exploration Society.

Toker, E., Sivan, D., Stern, E., Shirman, B., Tsimplis, M., Spada, G. (2012). Evidence for centennial-scale sea level variability during the Medieval Climate Optimum (Crusader Period) in Israel, eastern Mediterranean. *Earth and Planetary Science Letters, 315–316*, 51–61.

Wachsmann, S. (2009). *Seagoing ships & seamanship in the Bronze Age Levant*. Texas A & M University Press.

Yasur-Landau, A., Shtienberg, G., Gambash, G., Spada, G., Melini, D., Arkin-Shalev, E., Tamberino, A., Reece, J., Levy, T., & Sivan, D. (2021). New relative sea-level (RSL) indications from the Eastern Mediterranean: Middle Bronze Age to the Roman period (~ 3800–1800 y BP) archaeological constructions at Dor, the Carmel coast, Israel. *PloS one, 16*(6), e0251870. https://doi.org/10.1371/journal.pone.0251870

Zviely, D., Sivan, D., Ecker, A., Bakler, N., Rohrlich, V., Galili, E., Boarreto, E., Klein, M., & Kit, E. (2006). Holocene evolution of the Haifa Bay area, Israel, and its influence on ancient tell settlements. *The Holocene, 16*, 849–861. https://doi.org/10.1191/0959683606hol977rp

Stray Finds in the Periphery of Harbours: The Case of Paralimni- *Louma*, Famagusta Bay, Cyprus

Stella Demesticha and Miltiadis Polidorou

Abstract In 2017, a team from the University of Cyprus was invited by the Cypriot Department of Antiquities to conduct an underwater archaeological assessment at the location Paralimni *Louma*, Famagusta Bay, prior to the extension of a modern marina. An enigmatic assemblage of stray pottery finds was located outside the marina, with no direct association with anchorage activities. A geoarchaeological survey was deemed necessary to document possible palaeogeographic changes of the coastal topography, in order to exclude any possibility that a buried archaeological site might be at risk. According to the results, no significant coastal changes can be suggested, whereas it was clear that the seabed stratigraphy was disturbed. This led to the conclusion that the pottery assemblage at the entrance of the cove might be "seafaring debris" from the periphery zone of the Salamis harbour, moved to *Louma* by fishing activities, in antiquity or the recent past. Taking one step beyond the pronounced emphasis on trade in the archaeological discourse, this paper discusses the secondary contexts of stray underwater finds, as these found at Louma, and attempts an interpretative approach to the formation processes that have affected their life in the dynamic zone of shallow waters, from antiquity to the recent past. In this respect it is argued that fishing with nets, a maritime activity with a very long history in the Mediterranean waters, can act as a repetitive 'scrambling' process that reshuffles stray finds on the seabed.

Keywords Underwater archaeology · Ancient anchorages · Marine geoarchaeology · Underwater pottery assemblages · Cypriot archaeology · Harbours · Anchorages · Marine geomorphology · Coastal changes · Site formation processes

---

S. Demesticha (✉)
Archaeological Research Unit, University of Cyprus, Nicosia, Cyprus
e-mail: demesticha.stella@ucy.ac.cy

M. Polidorou
Faculty of Geology and Geoenvironment, National and Kapodistrian University of Athens, Athens, Greece
e-mail: mpolidorou@geol.uoa.gr

© The Author(s), under exclusive license to Springer Nature Switzerland AG 2023
E. Ben-Yosef, I. W. N. Jones (eds.), *"And in Length of Days Understanding" (Job 12:12): Essays on Archaeology in the Eastern Mediterranean and Beyond in Honor of Thomas E. Levy*, Interdisciplinary Contributions to Archaeology,
https://doi.org/10.1007/978-3-031-27330-8_64

1 Introduction

Underwater pottery assemblages that do not belong to shipwrecks are often difficult to interpret and contextualise. At bays and coves that provide shelter from the waves and winds, their presence could be related to land and sea communications, agricultural or manufacturing industries, fishing, trade and exchange, to mention only some of the maritime landscape components, associated with harbours' hinterlands and forelands (Houston, 1988: 562–564; Karmon, 1985; Westerdahl, 2011). Pottery assemblages found off capes and promontories are linked with shipwreck episodes and mark sea routes as well as navigational hazards (Leidwanger, 2013a: 180–181). As Muckelroy (1978: 146) remarked, however: *'Without the presence of anchors or other indications of an anchorage, the evidence of stray finds on the seabed is unsatisfactory, since so many other explanations for their presence are possible alongside that of an anchorage jetsam'*. Stray finds may indicate possible cargo jettisons from merchantmen transporting containers during their prime use, and/or episodes of on-board ceramics' dumping, during anchorage. In deep waters they have been convincingly interpreted as 'debris trails' of random jettison episodes, that highlight busy searoutes over long periods of time (Foley & Ballard, 2004).

Maarleveld (2010: 257), building on the work of Schiffer (1972, 1987), warned us that 'what happened *originally* is only partly responsible for what we know'. What happened *in the meantime* is another filter because 'it encompasses a whole body of processes affecting the integrity of the original deposit' (Maarleveld, 2010: 260). What Schiffer (1987) called Cultural (C-) transforms affect drastically site formation processes, on land or on the seabed. Formation processes of shipwreck sites have been discussed at length (Muckelroy, 1978; see also Keith, 2016) but other maritime activities, especially in the dynamic shallow zone, have attracted less scholarly attention. Oleson and Hohlfelder (2011: 823–824) discussed challenges presented by the archaeology of drowned sites, i.e. underwater sites of long and varied existence; artefact drifting and lack of stratigraphy coupled with the broad chronological range and uncertain provenance of the finds, cannot be easily linked to specific maritime activities. Apart from such difficulties, though, the presence of pottery sherds in shallow waters also affords opportunities for new insights into local maritime histories. For example, 'debris trails' of stray pottery finds can be formed on busy seascapes in shallow waters, especially when they are in proximity to urban harbours and are part of the networks of sea routes that are built around them. Such 'pottery debris' trails are rarely recorded systematically because they lay outside the context of specific sites and are perennially disturbed by coastal maritime activities that reshuffled the underwater archaeological record randomly. Nonetheless, ignoring them can deprive the archaeological record of a material testimony of maritime activity over long periods of time, especially in cases where systematic archaeological research of harbour sites is difficult. With the above ideas in mind, this paper discusses the results of a brief interdisciplinary survey at Paralimni *Louma*, an underwater site at the eastern coasts of Famagusta Bay, Cyprus, and attempts an interpretation of an enigmatic pottery assemblage that was recorded in the shallow waters.

2 The Site of Paralimni *Louma*

Between the years 2015 and 2018, a small team from the University of Cyprus conducted an extensive survey at the location Paralimni-*Louma*, along the coast of Protaras, after an invitation from the Department of Antiquities of Cyprus. The aim of the survey was the archaeological assessment of the site, prior to a planned extension of the modern marina, recently named *Agios Nikolaos* (or *Golden Coast*) (Fig. 1). No survey was attempted inside the harbour basin because of the low visibility and the fact that the site had already been highly disturbed by modern use. A reconnaissance survey over a zone of 150–250 m off the modern marina yielded a few scattered finds (Cat. Nos 29, 31 and 36). Right outside the basin, however, north of the harbour entrance, a concentration of pottery finds, dated to various periods, was located by the survey team, over an area of approximately 90 sq m, on a sandy bottom with rocky outcrops, at a depth of 3–5 m. To the west, the site is demarcated by a shallow rocky formation, the upper part of which is now at a depth of 1.5–2 m and its bottom at −5 m. It runs parallel to the coastline in a south- north orientation and seems to be the underwater section of a coastal promontory, on which the modern north mole was founded.

Fig. 1 Map of the survey area at Paralimni *Louma*, with the locations of the cores (green dots), the geological formations and features (red dots), the scattered archaeological finds outside the main concentration (white dots) and the main pottery assemblage (red lined squares). (Map: Miltiadis Polidorou)

Aerial photographs of the year 1963 (Land and survey Department) show the coastal relief at Paralimni *Louma* before the construction of the modern marina of Agios Nikolaos, in 1982. The original toponym *Louma* (*washing* in Greek) was common at certain localities on the island, where sheep were led to be washed in sea water before shearing in the spring, usually after Easter (Ionas, 2001: 127). The necessary affordances of a stretch of coast suitable for this procedure were safe access to the sea and a depth sufficient to force the animals to swim. *Louma* is situated directly south of Mena (or Serena) Bay. It was first surveyed by Leonard (2005: 380–381) who reported 'a cove surrounded by an erosional scarp and a nearby *villa rustica*' with no further details. The coastline, as documented from the aerial photographs of 1963, shows no harbouring activity at *Louma* during the recent past, but there is no way to know if there were any underwater remains in the cove, because no archaeological survey had taken place before 1982. As winds and waves characterise specific sea places and were crucial dynamics for the selection of ports and anchorages (Safadi, 2016: 349), it is important to mention that *Louma* offers no protection from the strongest prevailing winds that blow from the N-NE and are the ones that create significant waves in the area. Temporary shelter, however, could be offered from winds that blow less frequently from the S-SE.

Given the lack of evidence for anchoring activity at *Louma*, the interpretation of the pottery assemblage outside the main cove is problematic. It is rather improbable that their current location is the result of recent erosion episodes in the immediate vicinity (for eroding archaeological sites on the south coast of Cyprus see Andreou, 2018). The date of the pottery is very diverse and the damaged surfaces of many of the pottery fragments are indicative of exposure to the impact of sea environment dynamics in shallow waters, over long periods of time; for instance, the three fragments of the cooking dish (Cat no 2), which were found scattered in Area 1, have damaged edges and bear different marine encrustations on their surface (Fig. 2). Moreover, some of the artefacts were found conglomerated among the rocky outcrops or Areas 1 and 2 (Fig. 3). Given the uncertain character of the pottery assemblage, decision was made to allow the development plans for the extension of the marina. It was also deemed necessary, however, to recover all surface finds and document possible palaeogeographic changes, in order to exclude any possibility that a buried archaeological site might be at risk or that the coastal topography has undergone major changes.

The coastal zone at the wider Paralimni and Protaras area consists mainly of rocky Pleistocene calcarenaites. These formations belong to the Pleistocene Marine terraces sequence and can be observed along most coastal sites around Cyprus (Zomeni, 2012). Stratigraphically, the calcarenites are part of the circum-Troodos sedimentary deposits (Lagroix & Borradaile, 2000). Although their composition might change in certain places, they are generally very well cemented, they consist of coarse-grained calcarenitic material (Pettijohn, 1975) and appear with cross bedded lamination, in several occurrences. Along the stretch of coast at Paralimni *Protaras,* i.e. from the Green line to Cape Greco, a low frequency of large rivers is observed, which is responsible for the low supply of sediments to the coastal areas.

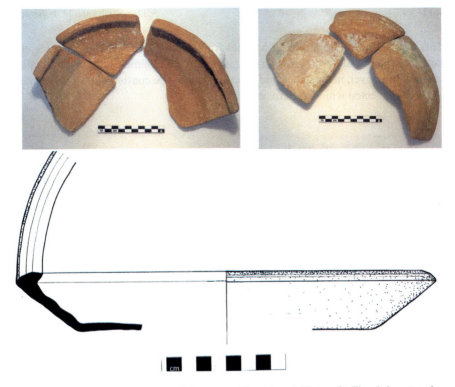

Fig. 2 Three fragments of a cooking dish recovered from Area 1 (Cat. no 2). They belong together but they were found scattered, with eroded edges and different marine encrustations of their surface. (Photographs and drawing: Stella Demesticha)

Fig. 3 Divers recovering a conglomerated pottery fragment from Area 1 (Cat. no 29). (Photograph: Andreas Kazamias, MARELab UCy)

This resulted in the formation of beaches from erosional material of the calcarenites, and the coastline presents an asymmetrical development due to differential erosion. Moreover, in the wider study area, platform type coasts are observed, which are also connected with wave erosion.

3 The Geomorphological Survey

The study area was investigated and documented both landward and seaward (Fig. 1). Geomorphological mapping and field survey were conducted with the use of topographic maps at a scale of 1:5000 (Table 1). Aerial photographs and satellite images (Land and Survey Department, 2022: Quickbird 2003, 2008, 2009, 2010, and 2011) were introduced and analysed in a GIS environment. For the evaluation of the geomorphological evolution of the studied area five shallow sediment cores, approximately 1 m long each, were retrieved. The shallower core was located at -3, 6 m and the deeper at -5.4 m (Fig. 1).

The cores were extracted manually, using 2 inch diameter plastic PVC tubes inserted into a metal tube housing, with a drilling head. Their locations were strategically selected in order to identify the environment and the rate of sedimentation. The positions of the cores were measured with a Spectra SP80 differential GPS/GNSS system receiver with vertical and horizontal accuracy less than 2 cm. The stratigraphic analysis of the cores was accomplished by studying sedimentary sequences through visual inspection of the sediments. Detailed granulometric analysis (sieves diameter from 10 mm to 0.053 mm, according to CYSEN 933-1:2012) were carried out on the cores. For the determination of grain size, 20 samples were analysed and classified based on Folk's (1954) nomenclature. The sedimentological statistical parameters such as mean, sorting, skewness, and kurtosis were calculated using Gradistat V.4 software and they appear at Table 2 (Blott & Pye, 2001).

Table 1 Geological description of coastal formation at the study area

Geological stop	Easting	Northing	Description
1	5,94,533	3,878,026	Yellow-brown calcareous sandstone and man-made steps
2	594,505	3,878,014	Calcartenite with cracks filled with syntectonic orange calcareous sandstone
3	594,480	3,878,017	Coarse grained fossilferous calcarenite presence of cracks filled with syntectonic orange calcareous sandstone and white angular centimetric lithoclasts
4	594,421	3,878,018	Yellow medium grained calcarenite
5	594,416	3,877,863	Excavation for construction, at -10 m. Havarised calcarenite, two layers of brown paleo-sol, khaki silt, layer of reef limestone aggregates (fill), sandy silty clay (fill), silty sand (fill)

Stray Finds in the Periphery of Harbours: The Case of Paralimni- *Louma*...

Table 2 Classification and sedimentological statistical parameters of core sediments

Sample no	Textural group	Mean	Sorting	Skewness	Kurtosis
3122	Gravelly sand	Coarse sand	Poorly sorted	Fine skewed	Mesokurtic
3123	Gravelly sand	Coarse sand	Poorly sorted	Fine skewed	Leptokurtic
3124	Sandy gravel	Very fine gravel	Moderately sorted	Very fine skewed	Very platykurtic
3125	Sandy gravel	Very coarse sand	Poorly sorted	Fine skewed	Platykurtic
3126	Sandy gravel	Very fine gravel	Poorly sorted	Very fine skewed	Leptokurtic
3127	Slightly gravelly sand	Fine sand	Moderately well-sorted	Symmetrical	Leptokurtic
3128	Slightly gravelly sand	Fine sand	Well-sorted	Fine skewed	Mesokurtic
3129	Slightly gravelly sand	Medium sand	Moderately sorted	Symmetrical	Mesokurtic
3130	Slightly gravelly sand	Medium sand	Moderately well-sorted	Symmetrical	Platykurtic
3131	Slightly gravelly sand	Fine sand	Moderately well-sorted	Symmetrical	Leptokurtic
3132	Slightly gravelly sand	Medium sand	Poorly sorted	Symmetrical	Platykurtic
3133	Gravelly sand	Coarse sand	Moderately sorted	Symmetrical	Mesokurtic
3134	Gravelly sand	Very coarse sand	Moderately sorted	Fine skewed	Mesokurtic
3135	Sandy gravel	Very coarse sand	Poorly sorted	Symmetrical	Mesokurtic
3136	Sandy gravel	Very fine gravel	Poorly sorted	Very fine skewed	Very platykurtic
3137	Gravelly sand	Coarse sand	Poorly sorted	Symmetrical	Platykurtic
3138	Gravelly sand	Coarse sand	Poorly sorted	Symmetrical	Platykurtic
3139	Gravelly sand	Very coarse sand	Poorly sorted	Symmetrical	Mesokurtic
3140	Slightly gravelly sand	Fine sand	Moderately well-sorted	Symmetrical	Leptokurtic
3141	Slightly gravelly sand	Medium sand	Moderately well-sorted	Coarse skewed	Mesokurtic

Downcore relative elemental composition (Mg; Al; Si; P; S; K; Rb; Ca; Sr; Ti; V; Cr; Mn; Fe; Co; Ni; Cu; Zn; As; Se; Y; Zr; Nb; Mo; Ag; Cd; Sn; Sb; W; Au; Hg; Pb; Bi; Th and U) of sediment cores were analysed using an Olympus Vanta handheld XRF scanner, equipped with the Olympus "Geochem" Suite (Table 3). Analysis of the elemental composition was performed using an X-ray source with the voltage set to 8–40 kV, which enabled measurements of major and minor elements (Rothwell & Croudace, 2015). The XRF data acquired reported as elemental ratios (Brunović et al., 2020; Emmanouilidis et al., 2018; Haenssler et al., 2014; Katrantsiotis et al., 2018; Polidorou et al., 2021b).

Table 3 Relative elemental composition of the retrieved cores

No	Borehole	Mg	Al	Si	P	S	K	Ca	Ti	V	Cr	Mn	Fe
3122	BH1	2674	1060	3769	96	456	362	210238	964	34	549	272	5490
3123	BH1	3393	1915	16935	111	243	2303	120662	1021	40	190	342	11366
3124	BH1	3004	1359	3997	101	97	733	189733	853	30	163	617	19173
3125	BH1	9831	3720	16687	135	540	4376	68976	3026	43	201	275	25047
3126	BH1	5144	6174	32179	138	153	4584	60387	3321	53	105	177	34838
3127	BH2	3863	1966	22779	116	92	2815	100759	1678	39	205	359	10602
3128	BH2	3367	6398	56953	105	175	3673	104811	1601	49	401	389	13400
3129	BH3	3179	1443	16477	108	111	2215	121457	1522	28	273	345	9959
3130	BH3	2657	2735	31083	97	444	2060	149803	1304	40	120	296	9177
3131	BH3	3431	2189	18284	115	116	2537	104273	1382	45	121	345	10024
3132	BH4	2797	1404	10896	101	159	2308	143806	959	56	366	274	7079
3133	BH4	2338	1136	2916	92	206	117	212618	582	49	115	325	4564
3134	BH4	2609	3542	34838	96	530	1937	170352	1578	25	846	363	10755
3135	BH4	2819	3468	37793	99	466	1830	153439	1265	36	392	444	11165
3136	BH4	2798	3693	40949	98	673	1990	154563	1542	46	892	326	9800
3137	BH4	6283	11044	74872	140	105	7409	28936	3579	35	216	224	38387
3138	BH4	6441	12122	68988	146	108	7568	30959	4046	46	374	211	38782
3139	BH4	5008	8693	43430	133	162	5249	50540	3255	27	176	1175	39994
3140	BH5	3612	2343	15648	120	107	2266	99388	1867	45	292	298	10832
3141	BH5	4560	2780	22831	133	66	3348	69533	3130	57	227	489	21012

No	Borehole	Co	Ni	Cu	Zn	As	Se	Rb	Sr	Y	Z	Nb
3122	BH1	16	24	11	85	24	1	5	1343	12	28	2
3123	BH1	20	23	12	63	25	1	22	1040	15	36	1
3124	BH1	29	14	9	22	23	1	5	1100	14	18	2
3125	BH1	28	34	26	53	15	0	31	961	15	66	3
3126	BH1	34	57	37	118	9	1	36	570	15	96	8
3127	BH2	19	23	11	39	22	1	23	905	12	35	1
3128	BH2	21	30	8	62	21	1	24	765	13	43	1
3129	BH3	18	29	10	29	24	1	20	1117	12	33	1
3130	BH3	18	27	11	35	25	1	24	1277	13	41	1
3131	BH3	18	30	10	50	22	1	23	956	12	48	1
3132	BH4	16	24	12	123	23	1	20	1319	11	30	1
3133	BH4	14	21	8	51	30	1	3	1837	13	24	2
3134	BH4	21	19	14	61	23	1	18	1330	15	42	2
3135	BH4	21	22	19	40	26	1	19	1284	14	44	2
3136	BH4	20	17	11	43	24	1	19	1284	15	32	2
3137	BH4	35	55	153	111	14	0	54	447	19	104	14
3138	BH4	36	51	149	100	17	0	53	376	20	103	14
3139	BH4	35	51	126	114	12	0	40	490	19	77	6
3140	BH5	19	29	8	41	20	1	20	878	11	43	1
3141	BH5	26	42	11	62	16	1	20	533	20	55	4

(continued)

Table 3 (continued)

No	Borehole	Mo	Ag	Cd	Sn	Sb	W	Au	Hg	Pb	Bi	Th	U
3122	BH1	2	9	10	15	19	8	39	4	4	6	6	4
3123	BH1	2	7	8	12	16	6	32	4	4	10	4	3
3124	BH1	2	9	10	15	18	7	38	4	3	6	5	4
3125	BH1	2	7	8	11	14	6	29	3	9	5	4	3
3126	BH1	2	7	8	11	14	6	28	3	10	10	4	3
3127	BH2	2	7	8	12	16	6	32	3	5	5	4	3
3128	BH2	2	8	8	13	16	6	31	3	6	5	4	3
3129	BH3	2	7	8	12	16	6	31	4	5	9	4	3
3130	BH3	2	8	9	13	16	7	34	4	4	5	5	3
3131	BH3	2	7	8	12	15	6	31	3	5	9	4	3
3132	BH4	2	8	8	13	16	7	34	4	7	5	5	3
3133	BH4	2	8	9	14	18	7	38	5	2	6	6	4
3134	BH4	2	8	9	13	17	7	34	4	8	6	5	4
3135	BH4	2	8	9	13	17	7	35	4	6	6	5	4
3136	BH4	2	8	9	14	17	7	36	4	4	6	5	4
3137	BH4	2	7	7	11	13	6	27	3	12	4	4	2
3138	BH4	2	6	7	10	13	6	27	3	12	4	4	2
3139	BH4	2	6	7	10	13	5	25	3	11	4	4	2
3140	BH5	2	7	8	12	15	6	31	3	5	5	4	3
3141	BH5	2	7	8	12	15	6	29	4	8	4	4	3

Geochronological studies with AMS radiocarbon dating were applied into one sample which was extracted from the cores, by Beta Analytics Laboratory (Miami. Florida). Radiocarbon age was calibrated through the online software Calib 7.10 (Stuiver et al., 2017), using the MARINE13 curve for marine samples (Reimer et al., 2013) with a DR value of −149/±62 estimated for the Eastern Mediterranean (Reimer & McCormac, 2002).

For the evaluation of the coastal erosion rates, remote sensing techniques were used including Drone recording of the study area, satellite and aerial photographs GIS software (ArcGis 10.8) and Digital Shoreline Analysis System (DSAS) software (USGS). DSAS allows the statistical calculation of the shoreline displacement rate (forward/backward) using historical shorelines in the form of vector data (Thieler et al., 2009). To calculate shoreline displacement, DSAS generates transects along the shoreline and perpendicular to a baseline. The statistics are calculated for each cross-sectional line and stored in a data table. Each method used to calculate the shoreline displacement rate is based on the measured differences between shoreline locations over time. The resulting values are expressed as measures of displacement of the shoreline position along the intersection lines per year (Thieler et al., 2009). Negative values indicate a reversal of the coastline, while positive values indicate an advance of the coastline (Fig. 4).

Fig. 4 DSAS Model of the study area. (Map created by Miltiadis Polidorou and Apostolia Komi)

3.1 Results

The coast of *Louma* is composed of calcarenite deposits covered by Aeolian deposits of medium to fine sand. The stratigraphic succession appears to be in normal order and represents the upper part of a marine terrace sequences. According to the granulometric analyses and the petrographic elements of the sediments obtained from the cores, most of the sediments can be described as monotropic (unimodal) sandy, fine-grained to mesococcal (Table 2). This type of sediment is an indicator of the dynamics of the study area, in terms of wave action and coastal currents (longshore drift). More specifically, a concentration of fine-grained material is observed in the study area, with good statistical distributions and normal stratigraphy. The deposition of fine-grained material indicates a medium to low energy sedimentation environment, which refers to a typical semi-protected beach environment (pocket beach).

The study of sediments with the method of X-ray diffraction (XRF) provides the ratio of specific chemical elements, which act as indicators of the palaeo-environment and confirmed the moderate to low energy that prevailed in the study area in the past. More specifically, for the geochemical analysis of the area, the proportions of chemical elements were selected, which determine the following paleo-environmental conditions:

1. Sulfur (S): Indicates increased marine activity.
2. Strontium/Calcium (Sr/Ca): Autogenous calcium production/deposition.
3. Aluminum/Silicon (Al/Si): Chemical corrosion.
4. Titanium/Calcium (Ti/Ca): alternating river/marine influence.

The projections of the above chemical proportions and elements in a Cartesian axis system, give an area of change of environment, which is located at a depth of approximately 25–30 cm. The increase of S at this depth indicates the increased marine influence, which is probably due to a differentiation of the beach relief caused by tectonic phenomena or anthropogenic actions. Then it seems that the balance inside the beach is restored. The Strontium/Calcium ratio follows the Sulphur pattern, with an increase in depth of 25–30 cm and then a gradual decrease, with which it returns to normal levels. The increase in the Strontium/Calcium ratio is likely to be associated with a temporary natural dredging of the area due to tectonic forces and/or anthropogenic factors. Accordingly, the differentiation of the environment is located at the same point at all of the retrieved cores, with small differences due to the morphology of the seabed.

Although the stratigraphic sequence and the typology and petrography of the sediments appear normal, there is strong evidence of major anthropogenic influence at the study area. The development of the modern marina affected the dynamics of the studied coastal area and most probably created a re-deposition of sediments around the depth of 25–30 cm and above. This also can be suggested by the geochronological studies with AMS radiocarbon dating which reviled the age of the anomaly at 1917calAD (67.6%).

For the calculation of the shoreline displacement in the study area, the respective shorelines were digitized from orthophoto maps of 1963, 1993 and 2014. The DSAS created 84 intersection lines at intervals of 20 m along the coastline and extend 50 m from the reference line to the sea. The statistical method used through the DSAS 4.3 tool was the LRR (Linear Regression rate). As shown on the map (Fig. 4), most of the coastline is characterized by a displacement rate between −0.04 and 0.25 m/year. The outlined areas are man-made and the rate of displacement corresponding to these areas is not taken into account. In the SE part of the area there is a setback of the coastline from 1963 to 2014, with a displacement rate between −0.3 and −0.2 m/year. According to the DSAS calculations the general geomorphological features of the study area and the proposed sea level curves for Cyprus (Polidorou et al., 2021a), it is suggested that the archaeological landscape and the morphology of the seabed suffered minimal changes regarding the time duration from antiquity to the present day.

4 The Pottery Finds

Our knowledge about the pottery record in the district of Famagusta Bay, from the late Iron Age until the recent past, can be considered fragmented, at best. The war of 1974 interrupted archaeological research in the area, so the publications of Hellenistic and Roman pottery from the French excavations at Salamis (Calvet, 1972, 1978; Diedrichs, 1980) and the pottery assemblages excavated from the Necropoleis of Salamis (Karageorghis, 1967, 1970, 1973/1974) remain the main source of information for household and transport vessels over a long period of time in the region. During the survey at *Louma*, 230 pottery fragments were recovered from the seabed, of which only 45 were diagnostic (see Sect. 4.1 Catalogue of Finds, below). The diagnostic finds date to various periods, from Classical to Medieval, and many remain unidentified. They belong to coarse ware classes, commonly attested at underwater sites (Leidwanger, 2020: 163), i.e. transport containers, tiles, utility and table wares; for similar assemblages see the pottery finds from the urban harbour of Dor in Israel (Kingsley & Raveh, 1996: 42–54) or the natural shelter of Lara in Cyprus (Giangrande et al., 1987).

Very few of the utility wares (cooking pots and basins) recovered from *Louma* (Cat. nos 1–7) could be identified (Figs. 5 and 6). A few table wares and tiles were also recovered (Cat. nos 8–17), dating from the Roman to Medieval periods. The majority (28 of 45) belong to transport containers of well-attested types in the Cypriot archaeological record. The two Phoenician amphorae (Cat. nos 19 and 22) are common Levantine imports to Cyprus during the Classical period. Similarly, amphorae from North Aegean, like Chios and Thasos (Cat. nos 17 and 21) (Fig. 7), are also predominant Aegean imports to Cyprus (Lawall, 2013: 58–59), whereas Rhodian amphorae of the Hellenistic period (Cat. no 24) have been found in abundant quantities on the island (Barker, 2013; Dobosz, 2013; Lund, 2015: 192–194), often together with other southern Aegean types, like Koan (Cat. no 23). Some of

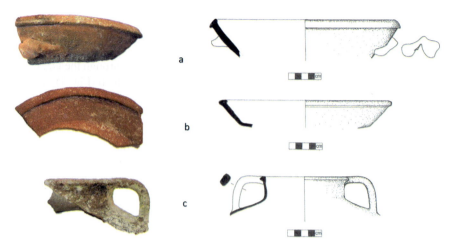

Fig. 5 Cooking ware types found at Paralimni *Louma*: (**a**). Casserole with traces of glaze (Cat. no 1); (**b**). Cooking dish (Cat. no 4); (**c**). Cooking pot (Cat. no 5). (Photographs and drawings: Stella Demesticha)

Fig. 6 Basin (Cat. no 6). (Photograph and drawing: Stella Demesticha)

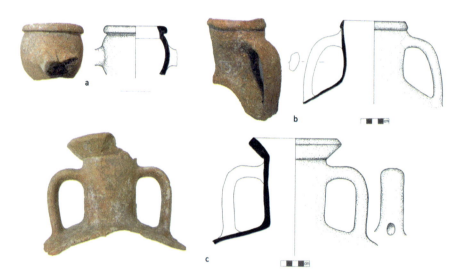

Fig. 7 Transport amphorae of Classical to Hellenistic period: (**a**). Chian amphora (Cat. no 17); (**b**). Possibly a variant of the Cypriot 'Kouriaka' group (Cat. no 25); (**c**). Possibly an Aegean import (Cat. no 26). (Photographs and drawings: Stella Demesticha)

the Louma assemblage types are less common, such as a possible variant of the local 'Kouriaka' group (Cat. no 26) (see Kaldeli, 2013 with bibliography) or the unidentified neck Cat. no 26 (Fig. 7c).

The amphorae known as Mid Roman 4 (Riley, 1979: 186–187), Agora G199 (Robinson, 1959: 43) or 'pinched handled' (Leonard 195: 144–145) (nos 29, 30) are common in the eastern Mediterranean (Reynolds, 2005: 564; Bezeczky, 2013: 83–84) and have been attested in several Roman Cypriot sites (for a general discussion, see Lund, 2015: 172–174). North African imports during the Roman period are not unknown (Kaldeli, 2008: 119–120), but they become rare during the Late Roman period (at Louma, Cat. no 32; for a possible example from Akamas, see Lund, 2007: 788).

Late Roman 1 amphorae (LRA1) are the most numerous groups of transport containers (nos 34–44). This is one of the predominant amphora types in Cyprus and the entire eastern Mediterranean during the Late Roman period (Riley, 1979: 212–216; Piéri, 2005: 69–85; Reynolds, 2005: 565–567; for a recent overview, see Demesticha, 2013) (Fig. 10). The provenance of the types spreads over a wide geographical zone, which includes north Syria, Cilicia and Cyprus, as well the Aegean, Egypt and the Black Sea (Empereur & Picon, 1989; Yangaki, 2005; Burragato et al., 2007; Kassab Tezgör, 2009; Autret et al., 2010; Diamanti, 2010; Dixneuf, 2011; Şenol & Alkaç, 2017). The ten necks recovered at *Louma* belong to several variants, both Cypriot and imported (for the morphological features of Cypriot production see Demesticha, 2014).

4.1 Catalogue of Pottery Finds

Diagnostic Pottery fragments too eroded to be identified: 16 (12 amphorae, 4 table ware).

Total number of non-diagnostic sherds: 169. Area 1: 50; Area 1b: 24; Area 2: 53; Area 3: 66.

<u>Kitchen and Cooking ware</u>

1. [MP01] Area 1. Body fragment of a baking dish that preserves one horizontal ledge handle and a thickened rim, bevelled on the outside. Traces of glaze on the interior and the exterior. A burnt zone on along the broken edge, on the exterior. The type belongs to the Beirut Cooking Ware series, dated to the thirteenth c AD (Stern, 2012: 41-44, pl. 4.14). External rim diameter = 28.8 cm (Fig. 5a).

2. [MP02; MP38; MP78] Three body fragments of a carinated basin or cooking dish. The rim is inverted, with parallel incisions on its upper face. External rim diameter = 28.2 cm (Fig. 2).

3. [MΠ03] (Area 1b): Basin with a flat base and a thickened rim, square in section. Rim D. = 36 cm, H. = 10.7 cm. A similar vessel with flat base was found at a possible anchorage (site 10), at Cape Andreas (Green, 1970: 19, fig. 7.7) (Fig. 6).

4. [MΠ77] Area 1b. Rim and body of a basin or cooking dish. Rim D. = 26 cm (Fig. 5b).
5. [MP83] Area 1b. Upper part of a thin-walled cooking pot with a collar neck and a ring rim. Rim diameter = 12.8 cm. Possibly of a Late Hellenistic or Early Roman date (for a similar one from Panayia Ematousa, see Wriedt Sørensen & Winther Jacobsen, 2006: 239–240, CW14; see also a similar example form Hazor, in Lehmann, 1996: 453–454, Type 458 Pl 87) (Fig. 5c).
6. [MP89] Area 1b. Fragmented upper part of a cooking pot that preserves one strap handle with a central shallow groove along the exterior. The rim is vertical, with no neck. Possibly Late Hellenistic (for an illustrated example, see Catling, 1972: fig. 17 no P385).
7. [MP85] Area 2a. Handle of a cooking pot, of unidentified type.

Table Wares

8. [MP14] Area 1b. Neck of a jug, with trefoil rim.
9. [MP18]. Area 1b. Upper part of a neck of a closed vessel.
10. [MP22]. Area 1b. Neck of a closed vessel that preserves a strainer at the bottom.
11. [MP64] Area 1a. Neck of a closed vessel (gargoulette?) that preserves one handle and a strainer at the bottom (possibly the same type as MP22).
12. [MP43] Area 1a Lower part of a closed vessel with flat disc-base.
13. [MP81]. Area 1b. Plate fragment, possibly with relief decoration on the interior (very eroded surfaces).
14. [MP56] Area 2a. Fragment of a medieval bowl (thirteenth c AD), with traces of glaze and decoration on the interior. Possibly from Paphos (Papanikola-Bakirtzis, 1996: 58–60, Pl. II).

Roof Tiles

15. MP39 [Area 1a]. Tile fragment of Corinthian type.
16. MP82. [Area 1b] Fragment of a roof tile.

Transport Amphorae

17. [MP13] Area 1a. Upper part of a bulging Chian amphora neck. Type Lawall C/2 ('bobbin neck' type), 480–440 BC (Lawall, 1995: 90–92, 1998). In Cyprus, the type is common in Marion (Gjerstad, 1948, pl. LVIII.4, Plain White VI Ware). Other examples have been published from the area of Kition (Johnston, 1981: 40, nos 30–33; Cannavò et al., 2018: 372, Tombe MLA 2073; Wriedt Sørensen & Winther Jacobsen, 2006: 311–312, for Panayia Ematousa) (Fig. 7a).
18. [MP19]. Area 1a. Lower amphora body of Aegean provenance. The base ends to a hollowed knob toe, with a convex outer surface and a marked transition to the stem.

Fig. 8 Phoenician amphorae found at Paralimni *Louma*: (**a**). Cat. no 19; (**b**). Cat. no 20. (Photographs and drawings: Stella Demesticha)

19. [MP23] (Area 1b). Almost intact Phoenician amphora. It belongs to the carinated-shoulder group, Sagona (1982: 81–82) Type 6a/6c*; Lehmann (1996: 437–438, pl. 74) Type 394; Bettles (2003: 108) Type A1, dated to the fifth to fourth centuries BC. Only three examples of this type are known from the necropolis of Salamis (Karageorghis, 1967–1978, vol II: Pl. CXXVIII, Tombs 51.39 and 90.2; Karageorghis, 1970, vol II, Pl. CCXXII), Tomb 27.a) but it had a wide distribution on the rest of the island: Amathous (Bikai, 1987, Tomb 130.85), Kourion *Bamboula* (Benson, 1956, pl 34), Marion *Kaparka* (Gjerstad et al., 1935, Tomb 20.2, pl XLI), Vouni *Korakas* (Gjerstad et al., 1937, Tombs 1.11 and 2.7, pl XCIX). The most numerous examples have been excavated at Kition, mostly in tombs; see for example 16 containers from the necropolis of Agios Georgios (Hadjisavvas, 2012, Tombs 1.1, 3.8, 11.27, 15.1, 22.18, 23.2, 24.3, 29.1, 31.2, 33.6, 37.1, 44.1, 51.14 and 23, 57.1 and 3) (Fig. 8a).
20. [MP27] Area 1b. Partly preserved Phoenician amphora, Sagona (1982: 81–82) Type 7c, Aznar (2005: 69) Type 9D, Lehmann (1996: 436, pl. 74) Type 392. The type is dated from the seventh to the fifth centuries BC. Fourteen examples have been found in the necropolis of Salamis (Karageorghis, 1967–1978, Tombs 12.2, 15.1, 20.19, 20.31, 21.9, 23.38, 30.5, 64.5, 79. 592, 716, 812, 813, and 933, 82.7), but the bulk of the imported exampled to Cyprus were excavated at Kition and its periphery: Agios Georghios (Hadjisavvas, 2012, Tomb 5.1, 51.1, 52.17, 52.28) and Kition Perivolia (Cannavò et al., 2018, MLA1884. 1, Tomb 398. KEF-1351, Tomb 379. KEF-1262, Tomb MLA 2069. 5, 6 and 23) (Fig. 8b).
21. [MP24] Area 1b. Partly preserved Thasian amphora handle with a stamp, possibly depicting the end of a ladle (Tzochev, 2016).
22. [MP36] Area 1a. Lower body of n amphora, possibly Koan or a Nikandros Group type (first century BC?) (Empereur & Hesnard, 1987: fig. 20. Lawall, 2004: 179). For similar types in Paphos see Dobosz, 2020: 331–332.

23. [MP86] Area 2a. A stamped Rhodian amphora handle. The stamp is heavily eroded with no details preserved.
24. [MP72] Area 2a Base of a Phoenician amphora of unidentified type.
25. [MP76] Area 1b. Half part of a neck, possibly of a local amphora of the 'Kouriaka' group (Deshayes, 1963, Type A2) (Fig. 7).
26. [MP12] Area 1b. Amphora neck with a high everted rim, possibly of Aegean origin (Fig. 7c).
27. [MP08] Half of an amphora neck with a thick rim, round in section.
28. [MP28] Area 1a. Upper part of amphora, that preserves the neck and two handles. The neck is slightly conical and the rim has a stepped profile.
29. [MP29]. Found 150–200 m off the modern marina (Section C). Upper part of a Mid Roman 4 amphora (Riley, 1979: 186–187) Short, cylindrical neck, rim and two angular, grooved handles pinched in from the sides. Date: Second to fourth centuries AD.
30. [MP92] Area 1a. Upper part of a small Mid Roman 4 amphora (for the type, see Cat. no 28).
31. [MP31] Found 150–200 m off the modern marina (Section C). Upper part of a Dressel 2–4 amphora. Tall neck, ring rim and two opposite bifid handles. A horizontal groove runs around the base of the neck and three more at the lower part of the shoulder. A similar amphora is published from Karpasia, Agios Philon, possibly dated to the second century AD (Du Plat Taylor, 1980, 210, fig. 35 no 305) (Fig. 9).

Fig. 9 Dressel 2-4 amphora (Cat. no 31). (Photographs and drawings: Stella Demesticha)

Fig. 10 LR1 amphora (Cat. no 34). (Photographs and drawings: Stella Demesticha)

32. [MP05] Area 1a. Upper part (neck and both handles) of a North African (Tunisian) Keay (1984) Type 8B/Bonifay (2004: 132) Type 38, dated to the late fifth to sixth centuries AD.
33. [MP21] Area 1a. Handle of a Late Roman 5 amphora (Riley, 1979: 224).
34. [MP09]. Area 1a. LR1 amphora neck that preserves one handle with a flattened groove along the outer side. Early variant, possibly fourth century AD (for the type, see Williams, 1987: 237) (Fig. 10).
35. [MP16] Area 1a. Type same as Cat no 33.
36. MP30 Found outside the main site (Section C). Upper part of a LR1 amphora that preserves both handles. Possibly sixth century AD (for the type, see Demesticha, 2013: 176, fig. 3a).
37. [MP40] Area 1a. Heavily eroded neck and one handle, possibly of a LR1 amphora (for the type, see Cat no 33, above).
38. [MP70] Area 1a. Handle of an amphora, of the same type, as Cat no 33, above.
39. [MP71] Area 2b. Eroded neck of a LR1 amphora. Possibly sixth century AD (for an illustrated example of the type, see Leidwanger, 2013a: 186, Fig. 12).
40. [MP73] Area 2a Part of a LR1 amphora neck, missing the rim.
41. [MP06] Area 1a Two large fragments of a LR1 amphora lower body. Pitch remains on the interior.
42. [MP07] Area 1a. Base of a LR1 amphora. Pitch remains on the interior. Possibly of Cilician fabric.
43. [MP11]: Area 1a. Half neck of a LR1 amphora, that preserves one handle. Possibly Aegean fabric (for an illustrated example of the type, see Leidwanger, 2013a: 183, fig. 4).
44. [MP74] Area 2a. Neck that preserves the beginning of both handles of a LR1 amphora for an illustrated example of the type, see (Demesticha, 2013: 176, fig. 3c). Possibly of non-Cypriot fabric.
45. [MP91] Area 1b. Neck and one handle of a LR1 amphora, of a type similar to Cat no 43 above.
46. [MP41] Area 1b. Upper part of an amphora that preserves both handles. Unidentified type.

5 The Maritime Capacity of Famagusta Bay

Famagusta Bay, on the east coast of Cyprus is one of the most hospitable maritime places of the island. In the summer, 25% of the winds blow from the east and 17% from the SW (Sailing Directions, 2017: 71). The location of Salamis and Famagusta, at the head of the bay, is naturally protected from the prevailing west and north winds, whereas the nearby sandy beach has always provided a very advantageous natural harbouring affordance. Salamis was established in the eleventh century BC (Yon, 1999) and was the first fully urbanised city-harbour of the island (Iacovou, 2013: 36, 2018). It held a central role in the maritime connections of Cyprus throughout antiquity (Karageorghis, 1969: 23–24), with trade networks to the Levant during the Iron Age (Georgiadou, 2017; Waiman-Barak et al., 2021).

Although little is known about its port facilities, Isocrates (*Evagoras,* 47) and Diodorus Siculus (*Bibliotheca Historica* XV, 2.4) wrote about Evagoras's investment to make the city a naval power and to enlarge its harbour facilities during the fourth c BC. The actual harbourworks remain elusive, although remains have been located during diverse survey investigations (Flemming, 1974: 163–164; Raban, 1995: 163–4; Davies, 2012). Arsinoe- Ammochostos, founded by Prolemy, possibly declined by the second century BC, when the capital of the island was transferred from Salamis to Paphos. The city's main harbour must have suffered from siltation, but new ones may have been used further to the north, close to some monumental Hellenistic buildings, like the Gymnasium (Karageorghis, 1969: 167). Despite the vicissitudes of its harbour facilities, the city of Salamis kept its central place in Roman Cyprus and had all of the key structural elements of a centralized port city (Leonard, 2005: 148; Mitford, 1980: 1322; Gordon, 2019), serving intermittently as administrative capital of the island during the second and third centuries AD (Papacostas, 2001: 108).

After the catastrophic earthquakes of the mid fourth century AD, the city was reconstructed as Salamis-Constantia and flourished as the provincial capital of the island and as an important node of interaction within regional and long-distance trade networks with the rest of the Mediterranean (Papageorghiou, 1993: 31). There is not enough evidence about the maritime activity at the harbour of Salamis after the seventh century AD but the city kept its urban character and importance, during a period of decline for the entire island (Metcalf, 2009: 276–281; Zavagno, 2017: 144–147). During the Frankish period, and especially following the fall of Acre in 1291, it served as a naval base and developed into an important node in the eastern Mediterranean trade networks (Jacoby, 2020). In the fifteenth century, it was 'the only harbour in Cyprus worthy of its name' and the Venetian administration undertook extensive maintenance works in order to link it to Venice's system of international trade (Arbel, 2014: 96). During the Ottoman period, only small vessels could use the silted harbour of the city (Bonato, 2019), which was reconstructed and extended under the British Rule (Tozan, 2019).

The rich maritime history of Salamis and Famagusta had an impact on the maritime landscape of the entire Famagusta Bay. On the northern part of the bay, no diagnostic pottery was reported at the anchor-site of Khelones (Green, 1973), whereas it is uncertain if a concentration of opus sectile tiles and five stone anchors located at KTU2, Cilaes island, belong to a harbour assemblage (Harpster, 2010). The south-eastern section of Famagusta Bay is the most sinuous stretch of coastline of all southern Cyprus, replete with small coves that would have been suitable in antiquity for sheltering small vessels (Leonard, 2005: 373–4). Nowadays, a series of small coves have been turned into modern marinas (e.g. Ayia Triada, Agios Nikolaos, Nissia, and Konnos Bay). Before the touristic development that followed the war of 1974, however, there were no coastal settlements along this stretch of coast (see the 1814 account by McDonald Kinneir, in Martin, 1998: 147, and Kitchener's map of 1882). Underwater archaeological assemblages have been located at Nissia Cove and Konnos Bay (or *Green Bay*) (Leonard, 2005: 383–384; Leidwanger, 2018: 635). Two land excavations have brought to light a Neolithic settlement at Nissia (Flourentzos, 2008) and a Roman tomb at Sykia tou Protara (Georgiou, 2011).

The south-eastern part of the bay, which is protected from the prevailing westerlies, was on the sea route that connected Salamis with the other city harbours of the south coast, namely Kition, Amathus, Kourion and Paphos. A series of shipwrecks along the coast are indicative of the busy maritime activity in the area: two Roman shipwrecks dated to the second to third centuries AD (for the FigTree site, see Leidwanger, 2013b: 203–204; for a recent discovery (2019) of second shipwreck, still unpublished, see: http://www.mcw.gov.cy/mcw/da/da.nsf/DMLnews_en/DMLnews_en?OpenDocument), a Late Roman wreck site (Ausiayevich, 2019) and an unpublished one of the Ottoman period, both off Paralimni *Nissia* (https://www.ucy.ac.cy/marelab/en/research/nissia-shipwreck).

6   Fishing Nets as Dynamic Scrambling Devices

Fishing is one of the longest maritime engagements in history that link people and coasts. Many recent studies focus on different aspects of it, such as catching methods, fish species, fish processing and the trade of fish products (Bekker-Nielsen & Bernal Casasola, 2010; Marzano, 2013; Mylona & Nicholson, 2018; for a recent overview, see Leidwanger, 2020: 93–98; for Cyprus see Mavromichalou & Michael, 2020). Fishing with nets is a common catching method practiced in the Mediterranean, at least since the first century BC (Bekker-Nielsen, 2010: 86), and as such it has been discussed in the archaeological literature. The impact of modern fishing nets as 'scrambling devices' at shipwreck sites (Muckelroy, 1978) has been acknowledged regarding trawlers and their catastrophic effects (Maarleveld et al., 2013: 267–271). But the impact of fishing nets as *diachronic* 'scrambling devices' of the underwater archaeological record has escaped scholarly attention.

Mediterranean fishermen have been recovering artifacts with their nets for centuries. Some of these finds are reported to the authorities, as is the case, for example, with the pronounced pieces of ancient art exhibited in the National Museum of Athens (Agourides, 1997). Endless fragments of pottery, however, have been caught by fishing nets but have never been reported or systematically recorded. More importantly for this discussion, there is no way to record such fragments that were regarded as 'debris' or 'useless catch', and were dumped back in the water, most likely not at their original find spot. Artefacts removed accidentally from shipwrecks are thrown back to the sea at random places, and from there they could have been removed again several times. The same could be true for stray artefacts jettisoned *en route* from merchantmen that were sailing from and to harbours and anchorages in antiquity. In this respect, fishing nets have acted as scrambling devices on the seabed for centuries.

Boats that approached small coves, like Paralimni *Louma*, could not have been engaged in long distance endeavours (Marzano, 2013: 80–88). Ethnographic reports mention fishermen that used to spend the night in their boats, somewhere by the coast, close to the place they had cast their nets late in the night; they would go back to collect them very early in the following morning and started removing the fish from the nets on the way to the coast (Ionas, 2001: 220–221). The three artefacts recovered outside the main concentration at *Louma*, only a small sample of hundreds of stray finds that lie on the seabed of Protaras, in a zone of approximately 200 m off the coast, could be fishing debris that gets reshuffled almost daily. The pottery assemblage of the remaining 232 pieces found right outside the cove, could also be the material evidence of fishing activity in the vicinity. In this respect, their archaeological value does not lie in their accurate position but in the fact that they mark the spatial range of fishing activity in the region and they attest to maritime activities within the impact zone of the harbour of Salamis, a central place in the maritime foreland of the bay.

7 The Diverse Contexts of Paralimni *Louma*

Given that thorough archaeological investigation of the landward section of the *Louma* cove was hindered, any evidence that the site was used as an anchorage in antiquity is still lacking or has been destroyed forever. Thus, the poor anchoring affordances of the *Louma* cove and the absence of anchors do not negate the hypothesis that the concentration of the recorded pottery finds represent the remnants of a harbour that was destroyed by the construction of the modern marina. Its topography and the toponym *Louma* provide indications that it could have been used occasionally as a landing site, as Ilves (2011: 3) defined it, i.e. as 'a site in between water and land that people have launched from and reached with different kinds of watercrafts and where they have performed activities associated with this' (see also Leidwanger, 2020: 165). The geomorphological survey at the site has demonstrated that modern disturbance has caused changes in the stratigraphy of the seabed but it has also provided evidence that the morphology of the cove has not undergone significant changes since antiquity.

Natural events such as currents and wave action, as well as local hydrodynamic conditions, can also play an important role for the redeposition of finds on the sea bottom. Ward et al. (2022) demonstrated the complexity of such parameters, regarding an assemblage of lithic scatters in Australia (on the same subject but different case study, see also Menzela et al., 2018). Although no such study was conducted at

Louma, based on archaeological and geomorphological observations we argue that movement of much larger objects, like the pottery finds discussed in this paper, along significant distances, i.e. not within the *Louma* cove, is highly improbable. First, some of the finds have complex geometrical shapes and preserved their angular features (see especially Cat. nos 3, 19, 20 and 31), with no traces of friction that would be expected if large objects had been drifted on the seabed by currents. Moreover, such movement would require strong currents, something that has not been reported in the area (Garzanti et al., 2000; Department of Fisheries and Marine Research, 2012). On top of the above, the action of strong local currents would have caused sediment movements which should have buried the pottery. Most of the pottery scatters at *Louma*, however, were found on top of the disturbed seafloor, not buried or half-buried. Another indication that the deposition occurred locally comes from the fact that three different fragments of the same dish were collected from Area 1 (Cat. no 2). Thus, it is plausible to suggest that the pottery fragments of *Louma* were deposited at their recorded location either during or after the construction of the modern marina. If the original archaeological context of the pottery assemblage was associated with 'anchorage-debris' deposited at a natural harbour inside the cove, then its current location is a result of disturbance because of the marina construction. Another possibility is that the pottery assemblage was the result of 'fishing debris', i.e. the vessels were accidentally caught in fishing nets and were dumped outside the cove during the process of untangling the fish from the nets, by ancient or modern fishermen.

The seabed of Protaras is riddled with stray pottery finds that mark a diachronic maritime route to and from the harbour of Salamis, which is situated less than 7 miles further north of *Louma*. Without a systematic recording of these finds, it is impossible to determine the size of the Salamis harbour impact-zone. If the shipwrecks discussed above can be used as indicators, then this zone may have extended all along the Protaras coast. The pottery finds at *Louma* are by no means representative of the long and multiscalar maritime activity at Salamis, but they are indicative of it; they belong to diverse types, common on the island, which cover a long period, from the fifth century BC to the pre-modern period. Their recorded location at *Louma* may mark only the latest of the many different places on the seafloor of Famagusta, where they have been moved by fishermen, throughout a long period of maritime interactions, from antiquity to the recent past. In this respect, the archaeological value of this assemblage lies exactly in its dynamic contexts, within the impact zone of main harbours.

An interesting parallel from the Cypriot archaeological record can be found with the pottery assemblages recovered off the west coast of Akrotiri, Cyprus (Leidwanger, 2020: 178–179). Just off a series of coves open to the prevailing strong westerlies, where no anchors were found, transport amphorae, cooking pots and common ware were recovered and have been interpreted as 'the remains of occasional dumping of pots broken either *en route* or else during loading and unloading' (Leidwanger, 2013c: 227–228). The interpretation of the coves as 'opportunistic ports' remains uncertain, but there is little doubt that these stray finds were found within the 'impact zone' of the two neighbouring main harbours, namely Kourion and Akrotiri-Dreamer's Bay (James et al., 2021).

8 Conclusions

As Maarleveld (2010: 262) argued, 'it is not enough that a site in which archaeological objects and information are contained is exposed. It is equally essential that traces or artefacts are recognized as of potential interest, that they are appreciated as significant enough to be inscribed in the "record", through a reporting system or otherwise. We only see when we look and we only look for what we want, or expect, to see.' The interdisciplinary investigation triggered by the enigmatic pottery assemblage of Paralimni *Louma* demonstrates that underwater stray finds can provide rich archaeological information, if they are recorded systematically and placed in the diverse cultural and natural maritime processes associated with them. Maritime activities, such as landing, harbouring and transport, are the primary context of most isolated pottery vessels that end up in the water.

The "pottery debris" of ancient seafaring may be found in dense concentrations within the periphery of urban harbours with long histories, such as Salamis-Famagusta. Once these pottery fragments lose their primary spatial association with shipwrecks and harbours, their value as evidence for trade drops. Taking one step beyond the pronounced emphasis on trade in the archaeological discourse, this paper has discussed the secondary contexts of stray underwater finds, i.e. the formation processes that have affected their life in the dynamic zone of shallow waters, from antiquity to the recent past. Fishing with nets, a maritime activity with a very long history in the Mediterranean waters, can act as a repetitive 'scrambling' process that reshuffles stray finds on the seabed. The geophysical survey has not provided evidence for major coastal changes at *Louma*, which led to the conclusion that the pottery assemblage at the entrance of the cove may be the result of such an activity, although it is hard to determine if it happened in the remote or in the recent past. In either case, it seems that the pottery vessels were 'seafaring debris' from the periphery zone of the Salamis harbour, and as such, can add meaningfully to the archaeological record of the maritime landscape of the region.

Acknowledgments The pre-construction survey at Paralimni *Louma* was conducted after an invitation by the Department of Antiquities, which has undertaken the responsibility to raise funds and cover all the necessary costs, as well as to provide all necessary conservation treatment for the finds. Our collaboration was excellent and we are grateful to all personnel involved, and particularly to Eleni Loizidou the head of the Conservation Laboratory, as well as to Constantina Hadjivassili who assisted with the finds treatment. Special thanks are owed to Constantinos Nicolaou, maritime archaeologist and officer of the Cyprus Port and Marine police, Andonis Neophytou, maritime archaeologist and computer scientist, and Christos Patsalides, chief diver of the project, for their valuable contribution to fieldwork logistics, recording and safety. We also thank the two archaeology students, Christiana Chrisdoulou and Andonis Michael, for their assistance and we are indebted to the excellent Cypriot divers that participated in the project: Costas Mardacoftas, Yiorkos Hadgittofis, Andreas Kritiotis, Andreas Kazamias and Yiannis Tsangaris. We are also grateful to the anonymous reviewers for their insightful comments and suggestions.

References

Agourides, C. (1997). Greece. In J. E. Delgado (Ed.), *Encyclopaedia of underwater and maritime archaeology* (pp. 180–183). British Museum Press.

Andreou, G. M. (2018). Monitoring the impact of coastal erosion on archaeological sites: The Cyprus Ancient Shoreline Project. *Antiquity, 92*(361), 1–6.

Arbel, B. (2014). Maritime trade in Famagusta during the Venetian period (1474–1571). In M. J. K. Walsh, T. Kiss, & N. S. H. Coureas (Eds.), *The harbour of all this sea and realm: Crusader to Venetian famagusta* (pp. 91–103). Central European University Press.

Ausiayevich, M. (2019). *Surveying scattered pottery assemblages in shallow waters: The case of Nissia Coves, Paralimni, Cyprus.* MA thesis, University of Cyprus. https://honorfrostfoundation.org/wp-content/uploads/2019/10/Abstract_Magdalena.pdf

Autret, C., Yağcı, R., & Rauh, N. K. (2010). An LRA 1 amphora Kiln Site at Soli-Pompeiopolis. *ANMED Anadolu Akdenizi Arkeoloji Haberleri, 8*, 203–204.

Aznar, C. (2005). *Exchange networks in the southern Levant during the Iron Age II: A study of pottery origin and distribution.* Unpublished PhD thesis, Harvard University.

Barker, C. (2013). Rhodian amphorae from Cyprus: A summary of the evidence and the issues. In M. Lawall & J. Lund (Eds.), *The transport amphorae and trade of Cyprus* (pp. 101–110). University of Aarhus Press.

Bekker-Nielsen, T. (2010). Fishing in the Roman world. In T. Bekker-Nielsen & D. B. Casasola (Eds.), *Ancient nets and fishing gear: Proceedings of the international workshop on "Nets and fishing gear in classical antiquity: A first approach". Cádiz, November 15–17, 2007* (pp. 187–204). University of Cádiz Publications and Aarhus University Press.

Bekker-Nielsen, T., & Bernal Casasola, D. (Eds.). (2010). *Ancient nets and fishing gear. Proceedings of the international workshop on 'Nets and fishing gear in classical antiquity: A first approach', Cádiz, November 15–17, 2007.* University of Cádiz Publications and Aarhus University Press.

Benson, J. L. (1956). A tomb of the Early Classical period at Bamboula. *American Journal of Archaeology, 60*, 43–50.

Bettles, E. (2003). *Phoenician amphora production and distribution in the southern coastal Levant: A multi-disciplinary investigation into carinated-shoulder amphorae of the Persian period (539–332 BC).* Archaeopress.

Bezeczky, T. (2013). *The amphorae of Roman Ephesus. Forschungen in Ephesos 15/1.* Verlag der Österreichischen Akademie der Wissenschaften.

Bikai, P. M. (1987). *The phoenician pottery of Cyprus.* A.G. Leventis Foundation.

Blott, S. J., & Pye, K. (2001). GRADISTAT: A grain size distribution and statistics package for the analysis of unconsolidated sediments. *Earth Surface Processes and Landforms, 26*, 1237–1248. https://doi.org/10.1002/esp.261

Bonato, L. (2019). Chapter 10. The Harbor of Famagusta during the Ottoman period in French travelogues and consular archives. In M. J. K. Walsh (Ed.), *Famagusta maritima. Mariners, merchants, pilgrims and mercenaries* (Brill's studies in maritime history) (Vol. 7, pp. 218–238). Brill.

Bonifay, M. (2004). *Etudes sur la céramique romaine tardive d'Afrique.* Archaeopress.

Brunović, D., Miko, S., Hasan, O., Papatheodorou, G., Ilijanić, N., Miserocchi, S., Correggiari, A., & Geraga, M. (2020). Late Pleistocene and Holocene paleoenvironmental reconstruction of a drowned karst isolation basin (Lošinj Channel, NE Adriatic Sea). *Palaeogeography, Palaeoclimatology, Palaeoecology, 544*, 109587. https://doi.org/10.1016/j.palaeo.2020.109587

Burragato, F., di Nezza, M., Ferrazzoli, A. F., & Ricci, M. (2007). Late Roman 1 amphora types produced at Elaiussa Sebaste. In M. Bonifay & J.-C. Tréglia (Eds.), *LRCW2. Late Roman coarse wares, cooking wares and amphorae in the Mediterranean: Archaeology and archaeometry* (British archaeological reports international series 1662) (pp. 697–700). Archaeopress.

Calvet, Y. (1972). *Les timbres amphoriques (1965–1970). Salamine de Chypre III*. Editions E. De Boccard.

Calvet, Y. (1978). Timbres amphoriques de Salamine. *Report of the Department of Antiquities Cyprus*, 222–234.

Cannavò, A., Fourrier, S., & Rabot, A. (2018). *Kition-Bamboula VII: Fouilles dans les nécropoles de Kition (2012–2014)*. MOM Éditions.

Catling, H. W. (1972). An early Byzantine pottery factory at Dhiorios in Cyprus. *Levant, 4*, 1–82.

Davies, M. E. (2012). The problem of the missing harbour of Evagoras at Salamis, Cyprus: A review of the evidence and pointers to a solution. *International Journal of Nautical Archaeology, 41*(2), 362–371.

Demesticha, S. (2013). Amphora typologies, distribution, and trade patterns: The case of the Cypriot LR1s. In J. Lund & M. Lawall (Eds.), *The transport amphorae and trade of Cyprus* (pp. 169–178). Aarhus University Press.

Demesticha, S. (2014). Late Roman amphora typology in context. In N. PoulouPapadimitriou, E. Nodarou, & V. Kilikoglou (Eds.), *Late Roman amphorae and coarse ware 4 LRCW 4: Late Roman coarse wares, cooking wares and amphorae in the Mediterranean archaeology and achaeometry. The Mediterranean: A market without frontiers* (British archaeological reports international series 2616.I) (pp. 599–606). Archaeopress.

Department of Fisheries and Marine Research. (2012). *Initial assessment of the marine environment of Cyprus, part I – Characteristics. Implementation of Article 8 of the Marine Strategy Framework-Directive (2008/56/EC)*. Republic of Cyprus Ministry of Agriculture, Natural Resources, and the Environment.

Deshayes, J. (1963). *La necropole de Ktima*. Librairie Orientaliste Paul Geuthner.

Diamanti, C. (2010). *Local production and import of amphoras at Halasarna of Kos Island (5th–7th c.). Contribution to the research of the production and distribution of the Late Roman/Proto-Byzantine amphoras of the eastern Mediterranean*. National and Kapodistrian University of Athens.

Diedrichs, C. (1980). *Ceramiques hellenistiques, romaines et byzantines, Salamine de Chypre IX*. De Boccard.

Dixneuf, D. (2011). *Amphores Égyptiennes. Production, Typologie, Contenu et Diffusion (IIIe siècle avant J.-C.–IXe siècle après J.-C.)*. Centre d' Études Alexandrines.

Dobosz, A. (2013). Cyprus and Rhodes: Trade links during the Hellenistic period, in the light of transport amphora finds. In M. Lawall & J. Lund (Eds.), *The transport amphorae and trade of Cyprus* (pp. 111–122). University of Aarhus Press.

Dobosz, A. (2020). Hellenistic and Roman transport amphorae. In E. Papuci-Władyka (Ed.), *Paphos Agora Project (PAP). Volume 1. Interdisciplinary research of The Jagiellonian University in Nea Paphos, Unesco World Heritage Site (2011–2015)—First results* (pp. 323–362). Historia Iagellonica.

Du Plat Taylor, J. (1980). Excavations at Ayios Philon, the Ancient Carpasia. Part I: The Classical to Roman periods. *Report of the Department of Antiquities Cyprus*, 152–216.

Emmanouilidis, A., Katrantsiotis, C., Norström, E., Risberg, J., Kylander, M., Sheik, T. A., Iliopoulos, G., & Avramidis, P. (2018). Middle to late Holocene palaeoenvironmental study of Gialova Lagoon, SW Peloponnese, Greece. *Quaternary International, 476*, 46–62. https://doi.org/10.1016/j.quaint.2018.03.005

Empereur, J.-Y., & Hesnard, A. (1987). Les amphores hellénistiques. In P. Lévêque & J.-P. Morel (Eds.), *Céramiques hellénistiques et romaines II* (pp. 14–18). Les Belles Lettres.

Empereur, J.-Y., & Picon, M. (1989). Les régions de production d'amphores impériales en Méditerranée orientale. In *Amphores romaines et histoire économique: dix ans de recherche. Actes du colloque de Sienne (24–25 mai 1986). Collection de l'École Française de Rome 114* (pp. 223–248). Ecole Français de Rome.

Flemming, N. C. (1974). Report of preliminary underwater investigations at Salamis Cyprus. *Report of the Department of Antiquities of Cyprus*, 163–174.

Flourentzos, P. (2008). *The neolithic settlement of Paralimni*. Department of Antiquities, Cyprus.

Foley, B. P., & Ballard, R. D. (2004). Amphora Alleys I and II. In A. M. Mc Cann & J. P. Oleson (Eds.), *Deep-water shipwrecks off Skerki Bank: The 1997 survey* (Journal of Roman archaeology supplementary series, 58) (pp. 183–194). Portsmouth.

Folk, R. L. (1954). The distinction between grain size and mineral composition in sedimentary-rock nomenclature. *The Journal of Geology, 62*, 344–359. https://doi.org/10.1086/626171

Garzanti, E., Andò, S., & Scutellà, M. (2000). Actualistic ophiolite provenance: The Cyprus case. *The Journal of Geology, 108*, 199–218.

Georgiadou, A. (2017). Aspects of pottery production and circulation in the Early Iron Age Cypriot polities: Considering the evidence of the Salamis workshops. In V. Vlachou & A. Gadolou (Eds.), *Τέρψις. Studies in Mediterranean archaeology in Honour of Nota Kourou* (pp. 99–112). CReA-Patrimoine.

Georgiou, G. (2011). Ενα ταφικό σύνολο της Ελληνιστικής και Ρωμαϊκής περιόδου στην ακτή του Πρωταρά. In Α. Παπαφιλίππου (Ed.), *Το Παραλίμνι Ιστορία – πολιτισμός. Πρακτικά 2ου Συνεδρίου Μάρτιος 2011* (pp. 117–134). Κ. Επιφανίου.

Giangrande, C., Richards, G., Kennet, D., & Adams, J. (1987). Cyprus underwater survey, 1983–1984. A preliminary report. *Report of the Department of Antiquities Cyprus*, 185–197.

Gjerstad, E. (1948). *The Swedish Cyprus expedition. Volume IV.2*. Swedish Cyprus Expedition.

Gjerstad, E., Lindros, J., Sjoqvist, E., & Westholm, A. (1935). *The Swedish Cyprus expedition II. Finds and results of the excavations in Cyprus 1927–1931*. Swedish Cyprus Expedition.

Gjerstad, E., Lindros, J., Sjoqvist, E., & Westholm, A. (1937). *The Swedish Cyprus expedition III. Finds and results of the excavations in Cyprus 1927–1931*. Swedish Cyprus Expedition.

Gordon, J. M. (2019). Transforming culture on an Insula Portunalis: Port cities as central places in Early Roman Cyprus. *Land, 7*(4). https://doi.org/10.3390/land7040155

Green, J. (1970). *Cape Andreas expedition 1969*. The Research Laboratory for Archaeology.

Green, J. (1973). An underwater archaeological survey of Cape Andreas, Cyprus, 1969–70: A preliminary report. In D. J. Blackman (Ed.), *Marine archaeology* (pp. 141–178). Butterworths.

Hadjisavvas, S. (2012). *The Phoenician period necropolis of Kition. Volume I*. The Department of Antiquities, Cyprus.

Haenssler, E., Unkel, I., Dörfler, W., & Nadeau, M.-J. (2014). Driving mechanisms of Holocene lagoon development and barrier accretion in northern Elis, Peloponnese, inferred from the sedimentary record of the Kotychi Lagoon. *Quaternary Science Journal, 63*, 60–77. https://doi.org/10.3285/eg.63.1.04

Harpster, M. (2010). The 2008 Maritime Heritage Assessment Survey along the Karpaz Peninsula, Cyprus. *International Journal of Nautical Archaeology, 39*(2), 295–309. https://doi.org/10.1111/j.1095-9270.2009.00231.x

Houston, G. W. (1988). Ports in perspective: Some comparative materials on Roman merchant ships and ports. *American Journal of Archaeology, 92*(4), 553–564. https://doi.org/10.2307/505250

Iacovou, M. (2013). Historically elusive and internally fragile island polities: The intricacies of Cyprus's political geography in the Iron Age. *BASOR, 370*, 15–47.

Iacovou, M. (2018). From the Late Cypriot polities to the Iron Age "kingdoms": Understanding the political landscape of Cyprus from within. In A. Cannavo & L. Thely (Eds.), *Les royaumes de Chypre à l'épreuve de l'histoire: transitions et ruptures de la fin de l'âge du Bronze au début de l'époque hellénistique*. École Française d'Athènes. https://doi.org/10.4000/books.efa.2916

Ilves, K. (2011). Is there an archaeological potential for a sociology of landing sites? *Journal of Archaeology and Ancient History, 2*, 1–31.

Ionas, I. (2001). *Παραδοσιακά Επαγγέλματα της Κύπρου*. Cyprus Research Centre.

Jacoby, D. (2020). The economy of Frankish Famagusta, 1191–1373. In G. Grivaud, A. Nicolaou-Konnari, & C. Schabel (Eds.), *Famagusta, volume II. History and society. Mediterranean nexus 1110–1700. Conflict, influence and inspiration in the Mediterranean area* (Vol. 8, pp. 41–70). Brepols.

James, S. T., Blue, L., Rogers, A., & Score, V. (2021). From phantom town to maritime cultural landscape and beyond: Dreamer's Bay Roman-Byzantine 'port', the Akrotiri peninsula, Cyprus, and eastern Mediterranean maritime communications. *Levant, 53*(3), 337–360. https://doi.org/10.1080/00758914.2021.1887647

Johnston, A. W. (1981). Imported Greek storage amphorae. In V. Karageorghis, J. N. Coldstream, P. M. Bikai, A. W. Johnston, M. Robertson, & L. Jehasee (Eds.), *Excavations at Kition IV. The non-Cypriote pottery* (pp. 37–44). The Department of Antiquities, Cyprus.

Kaldeli, A. (2008). *Roman amphorae from Cyprus: Integrating trade and exchange in the Mediterranean.* Unpublished PhD thesis, University College London.

Kaldeli, A. (2013). 'Reading' the Hellenistic amphorae from Cyprus: Towards an understanding of economic aspects through the amphora stamps. In D. Michaelides (Ed.), *Epigraphy, numismatics, prosopography and history of ancient Cyprus: Papers in Honour of Ino Nicolaou* (pp. 307–322). Astroms Forlag.

Karageorghis, V. (1967). *Excavations in the Necropolis of Salamis I.* The Department of Antiquities, Cyprus.

Karageorghis, V. (1969). *Salamis: Recent discoveries in Cyprus; new aspects of archaeology.* McGraw-Hill.

Karageorghis, V. (1970). *Salamis IV: Excavations in the necropolis of Salamis II.* The Department of Antiquities, Cyprus.

Karageorghis, V. (1973/1974). *Excavations in the Necropolis of Salamis III.* The Department of Antiquities, Cyprus.

Karmon, Y. (1985). Geographical components in the study of ancient Mediterranean ports. In A. Raban (Ed.), *Proceedings of the 1st international workshop on ancient harbours. Caesarea Maritima 24–28.6.1983* (BAR international series 257) (pp. 1–6). Archaeopress.

Kassab Tezgör, D. (2009). *Les fouilles et le matériel de l'atelier amphorique de Demirci près de Sinope.* De Boccard.

Katrantsiotis, C., Kylander, M. E., Smittenberg, R., Yamoah, K. K. A., Hättestrand, M., Avramidis, P., Strandberg, N. A., & Norström, E. (2018). Eastern Mediterranean hydroclimate reconstruction over the last 3600 years based on sedimentary n-alkanes, their carbon and hydrogen isotope composition and XRF data from the Gialova Lagoon, SW Greece. *Quaternary Science Reviews, 194,* 77–93. https://doi.org/10.1016/j.quascirev.2018.07.008

Keay, S. (1984). *Late Roman amphorae in the Western Mediterranean, a typology and economic study: The Catalan evidence.* B.A.R.

Keith, M. E. (Ed.). (2016). *Site formation processes of submerged shipwrecks.* University Press of Florida.

Kingsley, S. A., & Raveh, K. (1996). *The Ancient Harbour and Anchorage at Dor, Israel: Results of the underwater surveys 1976–1991* (BAR international series 626). Archaeopress.

Kitchener, H. H. (1882). *A triconometrical survey of the Island of Cyprus.* The National Library of Scotland. https://maps.nls.uk/index.html

Lagroix, F., & Borradaile, G. J. (2000). Tectonics of the circum-Troodos sedimentary cover of Cyprus, from rock magnetic and structural observations. *Journal of Structural Geology, 22,* 453–469. https://doi.org/10.1016/S0191-8141(99)00168-6

Land and Survey Department, Republic of Cyprus, https://portal.dls.moi.gov.cy/. Accessed on 22 Jan 2022.

Lawall, M. (1995). *Transport amphoras and trademarks imports to Athens and economic diversity in the fifth century B.C.* University of Michigan, U.M.I. dissertation services.

Lawall, M. L. (1998). Ceramics and positivism revisited: Greek transport amphoras and history. In H. Parkins & C. Smith (Eds.), *Trade, traders and the Ancient City* (pp. 75–101). Routledge.

Lawall, M. L. (2004). Amphoras without Stamps: Chronologies and typologies from the Athenian Agora. In *ΣΤ' Επιστημονική Συνάντηση για την Ελληνιστική Κεραμική. Βόλος, 17–23 Απριλίου 2000* (pp. 445–454). Ταμείο Αρχαιολογικών Πόρων και Απαλλοτριώσεων.

Lawall, M. (2013). Two amphorae from the Swedish Cyprus expedition in the National Museum of Denmark: Late Archaic through Late Classical Cypriot trade. In M. Lawall & J. Lund (Eds.), *The transport amphorae and trade of Cyprus* (pp. 179–190). Aarhus University Press.

Lehmann, G. (1996). *Untesuchungen zur spaten Eisenzeit in Syrien und Libanon: Stratigraphie und Keramikformen zwischen ca. 720 bis 3000 v. Chr.* Ugarit-Verlag.

Leidwanger, J. (2013a). Amphorae and underwater survey: Making sense of Late Roman trade from scattered sherds and shipwrecks. In M. Lawall & J. Lund (Eds.), *The transport amphorae and trade of Cyprus* (pp. 180–190). Aarhus University Press.

Leidwanger, J. (2013b). Between local and long-distance: A Roman shipwreck at Fig Tree Bay off SE Cyprus. *Journal of Roman Archaeology, 26*, 191–208.

Leidwanger, J. (2013c). Opportunistic ports and spaces of exchange in Late Roman Cyprus. *Journal of Maritime Archaeology, 8*, 221–243.

Leidwanger, J. (2018). The Eastern Cyprus maritime survey: A report on the 2007–2009 field seasons. *Report of the Department of Antiquities Cyprus, New Series, 1*, 631–655.

Leidwanger, J. (2020). *Roman Seas. A maritime archaeology of Eastern Mediterranean economies*. Oxford University Press.

Leonard, J. R. (2005). *Roman Cyprus: Harbors, hinterlands, and "hidden powers". A dissertation submitted to the Faculty of the graduate School of the State University of new York at Buffalo, Department of Classics*. ProQuest Dissertations and Theses.

Lund, J. (2007). Transport amphorae as a possible source for the land use and economic history of the Akamas Peninsula, Western Cyprus. In M. Bonifay & J.-C. Tréglia (Eds.), *LRCW 2: Late Roman Coarse Wares, cooking wares and amphorae in the Mediterranean* (pp. 781–789). Archaeopress.

Lund, J. (2015). *A study on the circulation of ceramics in Cyprus from the 3rd century BC to the 3rd century AD*. Aarhus University Press.

Maarleveld, T. (2010). Fish and "Chips of knowledge": Some thoughts on the biases of the archaeological record. In T. Bekker-Nielsen & D. B. Casasola (Eds.), *Ancient nets and fishing gear: Proceedings of the international workshop on "Nets and fishing gear in classical antiquity: A first approach". Cádiz, November 15–17, 2007* (pp. 257–274). Universidad de Cádiz; Aarhus University Press.

Maarleveld, T., Guerin, U., & Egger, B. (2013). *Manual for activities directed at underwater cultural heritage guidelines to the annex of the UNESCO 2001 convention*. UNESCO.

Martin, D. W. (Ed.). (1998). *Sources for the history of Cyprus: English texts: Frankish and Turkish periods* (Vol. 5). Greece and Cyprus Research Center.

Marzano, A. (2013). *Harvesting the sea: The exploitation of maritime resources in the Roman Mediterranean (Oxford studies on the Roman economy)*. Oxford University Press.

Mavromichalou, K., & Michael, M. M. (2020). The tradition of fishery and fishing gear in the island of Cyprus (18th and 19th centuries AD). In *'Under the Mediterranean' The Honor Frost Foundation conference on Mediterranean maritime archaeology 20th–23rd October 2017* (Short report series). https://doi.org/10.33583/utm2020.06

Menzela, P., Schütta, C., Wranika, H., Paschena, M., & Drewsb, A. (2018). Towards a general prediction-model for the current-induced mobilisation of objects on the sea floor. *Ocean Engineering, 164*, 160–167.

Metcalf, D. M. (2009). *Byzantine Cyprus, 491–1191*. Cyprus Research Center.

Mitford, T. B. (1980). *Roman Cyprus*. Walter de Gruyter.

Muckelroy, K. (1978). *Maritime archaeology*. Cambridge University Press.

Mylona, D., & Nicholson, R. (Eds.). (2018). *The Bountiful Sea: Fish processing and consumption in Mediterranean antiquity. Proceedings of the international conference held at Oxford, 6–8 September 2017* (Journal of Maritime Archaeology Special Issue, 13.3). Springer.

Oleson, J. P., & Hohlfelder, R. L. (2011). Ancient harbors in the Mediterranean. In A. Catsambis, B. Ford, & D. L. Hamilton (Eds.), *The Oxford handbook of maritime archaeology* (pp. 809–833). Oxford University Press.

Papacostas, T. (2001). The economy of Late Antique Cyprus. In S. Kingsley & M. Decker (Eds.), *Economy and exchange in the east Mediterranean during Late Antiquity, Proceedings of a conference at Somerville College, Oxford 29 May 1999* (pp. 107–128). Oxbow Books.

Papageorghiou, A. (1993). Cities and countryside at the end of the Antiquity. In A. A. M. Bryer & G. S. Georghalides (Eds.), *"The Sweet land of Cyprus" papers given at the twenty-fifth jubelee Spring Symposium of Byzantine studies, Birmingham, March 1991* (pp. 27–51). Cyprus Research Centre.

Papanikola-Bakirtzis, D. (1996). *Μεσαιωνική εφυαλωμένη κεραμική της Κύπρου: τα εργαστήρια Πάφου και Λαπήθου.* A.G. Leventis Foundation.

Pettijohn, F. J. (1975). *Sedimentary rocks* (3rd ed.). Harper and Row.

Piéri, D. (2005). *Le commerce du vin oriental à l'époque Byzantine (Ve-VIIe siècles). Le témoignage des amphores en Gaule* (Vol. 174). Institut français du Proche-Orient.

Polidorou M, Saitis G, & Evelpidou N. (2021a). *Beachrock development as an indicator of paleogeographic evolution, the case of Akrotiri Peninsula, Cyprus.* Zeitschrift fur Geomorphologie 63 (1.3). https://doi.org/10.1127/zfg/2021/0677.

Polidorou, M., Evelpidou, N., Tsourou, T., Drinia, H., Salomon, F., & Blue, L. (2021b). Observations on palaeogeographical evolution of Akrotiri Salt Lake, Lemesos, Cyprus. *Geosciences, 11*, 321. https://doi.org/10.3390/GEOSCIENCES11080321

Raban, A. (1995). The heritage of ancient harbour engineering in Cyprus and the Levant. In V. Karageorghis & D. Michaelides (Eds.), *Proceedings of the international symposium Cyprus and the Sea. Nicosia 25–26 September 1993* (pp. 139–190). The University of Cyprus. Cyprus Ports Authority.

Reimer, P. J., & McCormac, F. G. (2002). Marine radiocarbon reservoir corrections for the Mediterranean and Aegean Seas. *Radiocarbon, 44*(1), 159–166. https://doi.org/10.1017/S0033822200064766

Reimer, P. J., Bard, E., Bayliss, A., Beck, J. W., Blackwell, P. G., Ramsey, C. B., Buck, C. E., Cheng, H., Edwards, R. L., Friedrich, M., Grootes, P. M., Guilderson, T. P., Haflidason, H., Hajdas, I., Hatté, C., Heaton, T. J., Hoffmann, D. L., Hogg, A. G., Hughen, K. A., Kaiser, K. F., Kromer, B., Manning, S. W., Niu, M., Reimer, R. W., Richards, D. A., Scott, E. M., Southon, J. R., Staff, R. A., Turney, C. S. M., & van der Plicht, J. (2013). IntCal13 and Marine13 radiocarbon age calibration curves 0–50,000 years cal BP. *Radiocarbon, 55*, 1869–1887. https://doi.org/10.2458/azu_js_rc.55.16947

Reynolds, P. (2005). Levantine amphorae from Cilicia to Gaza: A typology and analysis of regional production trends from the 1st to 7th centuries. In J. M. Esparraguera, J. B. Garrigos, & M. A. Ontiveros (Eds.), *LRCW I. Late Roman coarse wares, cooking wares and amphorae in the Mediterranean: Archaeology and archaeometry* (British archaeological reports international series 1340) (pp. 563–612). Archaeopress.

Riley, J. A. (1979). The coarse pottery from Berenice. In J. A. Lloyd (Ed.), *Excavations at Sidi Khrebish, Benghazi (Berenice) II* (pp. 91–467). Supplements to Libya Antiqua V.2.

Robinson, H. S. (1959). *The Athenian Agora V, Pottery of the Roman period: Chronology.* American School of Classical Studies at Athens.

Rothwell, R. G., & Croudace, I. (2015). Micro-XRF studies of sediment cores: A perspective on capability and application in the environmental sciences. In I. W. Croudace & G. Rothwell (Eds.), *Micro-XRF studies of sediment cores: Applications of a non-destructive tool for the environmental sciences* (pp. 1–21). Springer. https://doi.org/10.1007/978-94-017-9849-5_1

Safadi, C. (2016). Wind and wave modelling for the evaluation of the maritime accessibility and protection afforded by ancient harbours. *Journal of Archaeological Science: Reports, 5,* 348–360.

Sagona, A. G. (1982). Levantine storage jars of the 13th to 4th century BC. *Opuscula Atheniensia, 14,* 73–110.

Sailing Directions. (2017). *Sailing directions: Pub. 132: Eastern Mediterranean.* American Nautical Services.

Schiffer, M. (1987). *Formation processes in the archaeological record.* University of New Mexico Press.

Schiffer, M. (1972). Archaeological context and systemic context. *American Antiquity, 37,* 156–165.

Şenol, A. K., & Alkaç, E. (2017). The rediscovery of an LR1 workshop in Cilicia and the presence of LRA1 in Alexandria in the light of new evidence. In D. Dixneuf (Ed.), *LRCW 5: La céramique commune, la céramique culinaire et les amphores de l'Antiquité tardive en Méditerranée/Late Roman coarse wares, cooking wares and amphorae in the Mediterranean:*

Archaeology and archaeometry (2 vols.) Études Alexandrines, 42–43 (pp. 842–843). Centre d'Études Alexandrines.

Stern, E. J. (2012). *Akko I. The 1991–1998 excavations. The Crusader-period pottery. Parts 1–2, IAA reports, No 51/1*. Israel Antiquities Authority.

Stuiver, M., Reimer, P., Sept, R. R.-W. program. http://calib.org. A., 2017, U., 2017. CALIB 7.1.

Thieler, E. R., Himmelstoss, E. A., Zichichi, J. L., & Ergul, A. (2009). *The Digital Shoreline Analysis System (DSAS) Version 4.0 – An ArcGIS extension for calculating shoreline change* (Open-File Report). https://doi.org/10.3133/OFR20081278

Tozan, A. (2019). Chapter 11 the development of Famagusta harbor during the British Colonial Period (1878–1960). In M. J. K. Walsh (Ed.), *Famagusta maritima. Mariners, merchants, pilgrims and mercenaries* (Brill's studies in maritime history) (Vol. 7, pp. 239–263). Brill.

Tzochev, C. (2016). *Amphora Stamps from Thasos. The Athenian Agora, results of excavations conducted by the American School of Classical Studies at Athens 37*. American School of Classical Studies.

Waiman-Barak, P., Georgiadou, A., & Gilboa, A. (2021). Regional mineralogical and technological characterization of Cypriot Iron Age pottery: A view from Tel Dor. *Levant*. https://doi.org/10.1080/00758914.00752021.01972609

Ward, I., Larcombe, P., Ross, P. J., & Fandry, C. (2022). Applying geoarchaeological principles to marine archaeology: A reappraisal of the "first marine" and "in situ" lithic scatters in the Dampier Archipelago, NW Australia. *Geoarchaeology, 37*, 783–810.

Westerdahl, C. (2011). The maritime cultural landscape. In A. Catsambis, B. Ford, & D. L. Hamilton (Eds.), *The Oxford handbook of maritime archaeology* (pp. 733–762). Oxford University Press.

Williams, D. F. (1987). Roman amphorae from Kourion, Cyprus. *Report of the Department of Antiquities Cyprus*, 236–238.

Wriedt Sørensen, L., & Winther Jacobsen, K. (Eds.). (2006). *Panayia Ematousa I. A rural site in south-eastern Cyprus* (Monographs of the Danish Institute at Athens vol. 6.1). Aarhus University Press.

Yangaki, A. G. (2005). *La ceramique des IVe – VIIIe siecles ap. J.-C. d'Eleutherna: sa place en Crete et dans le bassin egeen*. Ekdoseis Panepistemiou Kretes.

Yon, M. (1999). Salamis and Kition in the 11th and 9th century BC: Cultural homogeneity of divergence? In M. Iacovou & D. Michaelides (Eds.), *Cyprus: The historicity of the geometric horizon* (pp. 17–33). University of Cyprus Press.

Zavagno, L. (2017). *Cyprus between late antiquity and the early Middle Ages (ca. 600–800): An island in transition*. Routledge.

Zomeni, Z. (2012). *Quaternary Marine terraces on Cyprus: Constraints on uplift and pedogenesis, and the geoarchaeology of Palaipafos*. PhD thesis, Oregon State University.

The Shell and the Skeleton: The Circumstances for the Transition in Shipbuilding Technologies in the Late-Antique Southern Levant

Gil Gambash [iD]

Abstract Current research on the transition from shell to skeleton in ancient Mediterranean ship construction concludes that due to the complex nature of the process no simple linear development may be assumed. Some of the earliest representations of the transition have now been traced along the coasts of Israel, dating to the Byzantine and early Muslim periods. By understanding the nature of the process and its timing, we are able to synchronize it with prominent phenomena characteristic of the region and period. This article aims to contextualize this significant technological shift, which rendered millennia-old building traditions irrelevant, and introduced a new method that soon became the preferred option in the Mediterranean and beyond. The article synthesizes insights from the fields of ancient technologies, maritime archaeology, environmental studies, and the history of the southern Levant, all soundly located at the heart of Tom Levy's lifelong research activity.

Keywords Shipbuilding · Technology · Transition · Late-antiquity · Shell-first · Frame-first · Environment

The actual moment of invention of new technologies in antiquity is rarely captured in our sources, and not necessarily for the immediately available reason of its absolute rarity, which certainly also existed. Where unseen to the eye, it would probably be more accurate to assume that most "inventions" were the product of long, gradual processes, which incorporated multiple parallel transitions from one moderate peak to another, rather than a single sudden exclamation of *eureka!* So much is certainly true for elaborate systems such as written scripts, but also for seemingly more straightforward technological developments, such as the introduction of hydraulic concrete to Roman architecture (Gazda, 2008).

G. Gambash (✉)
University of Haifa, Haifa, Israel
e-mail: ggambash@univ.haifa.ac.il

© The Author(s), under exclusive license to Springer Nature Switzerland AG 2023
E. Ben-Yosef, I. W. N. Jones (eds.), *"And in Length of Days Understanding" (Job 12:12): Essays on Archaeology in the Eastern Mediterranean and Beyond in Honor of Thomas E. Levy*, Interdisciplinary Contributions to Archaeology,
https://doi.org/10.1007/978-3-031-27330-8_65

In a practical sense, a hypothetic moment of invention should be less interesting to the social or economic historian, so long as it remains singular and isolated in time and space. Perhaps there have been many inventions out there in antiquity that never emerged beyond the immediate circles of their inventors; others may even have been invented more than once, separately and oblivious to each other. The value of an invention may not be fully appreciated before its impact on society is visible, and it is therefore – at least here in this article – the moment of a society's exposure to an invention, and its adoption of it, which holds the greater historiographic value, and may also be captured by everything that *eureka!* stands for, in the sense of *finding* – rather than inventing – the solution to a problem.

Next to "invention," employing the term "problem" in this discussion may in itself produce an undesirable bias in the consideration of innovation and its widespread adoption: may we assume that the replacement of old technologies with new ones in antiquity was usually generated through pressures, that it mostly came to solve clearly defined problems, and that it followed a solid societal rationale aiming for benefit and gain? Numerous variables must be factored into any attempt to answer such questions per any given process of innovation, and it would suffice to invoke the paralyzing effect of tradition on the one hand, and the whimsical impact of fashion on the other – both still very much valid in our own day – in order to introduce the caveat necessary for any such discussion.

The goal of this article is to consider possible alignment between relevant circumstances and the emergence of a new shipbuilding technology in the Late Antique southern Levant. In the sphere of commercial shipbuilding in antiquity, highly economical as it was bound to be, there would have been, perhaps, less room for ephemeral non-practical trends (Beresford, 2013: 107–172). But the tyrannical dominance of traditional knowledge ensured that the same technology which had produced the funeral ship of Pharaoh Khufu in the middle of the third millennium BCE was still without competition or even a mere alternative when the Byzantine empire emerged in the Eastern Mediterranean in the middle of the first millennium CE. This technology, known to specialists as "shell first," was based on producing the shell of the boat first, by means of attaching the strakes to each other through edge-joints. The latter could consist of various joineries, such as nails, sewn fastenings, or pegged and unpegged mortise and tenon joints; where added, a supportive transverse framework independent of the keel would follow the attachment of the strakes (Katvez, 1990).

In fact, until recently, the watershed which saw a completely new technology introduced to the domain of shipbuilding has been thought to have been captured by the eleventh-century shipwreck from Serçe Limani, in southern Anatolia, which boasted a structure defined by experts as "frame first" (Steffy, 1982, 2004). This technology consisted of producing a framework connected to the keel as a first step, followed by attaching the planks of the vessel to this framework, thus rendering edge joinery redundant. It is also considered to be more economical in material and labor, requiring less timber in order to produce more durable vessels (Steffy, 1994: 83–85).

Quite in agreement with the gradual approach to innovation and its adoption with which this article opened, the replacement of "shell first" with "frame first," though ultimately total and absolute, did not happen overnight, and the sources indicate a period of transition during which mortise and tenon connections gradually disappeared, making way for a skeletal structure. We are thus less interested here in the actual invention, which would have been but a first step in a longer process, shifting some of the integrity of the ship from shell to skeleton. More relevant for Mediterranean economy and connectivity would have been the culmination of the process and the universal absorption of the mature practice.

With the development of maritime archaeology and the significant expansion of the corpus of underwater finds, the shipwreck of Serçe Limani lost its premiership to a group of earlier vessels that contained a significantly low number of mortises and tenons. Relevant examples may be found in the Saint Gervais II shipwreck and in the shipwreck from Yassi Ada, both from the seventh century CE (Jezegou, 1989; Van Doorninck, 1982). While these shipwrecks suggest that frame-based technology was known in the Mediterranean around the time of the Islamic conquest, they have not been complemented to date by additional finds which would suggest that the new building system was adopted and employed systematically by the microregions and marine societies of Southern France or Anatolia.

Much more illuminating is the case of the southern Levant, and, more specifically, that of the Carmel coast and the area of Dor in it, well familiar to the honoree of this volume. An examination of ships and shipping in the southern Levant during the Byzantine and Early Islamic periods yields a small yet suggestive body of direct evidence. In a catalogue of ancient Mediterranean shipwrecks compiled in 1992, more than 1200 items were documented – of which some were excavated thoroughly while others were only superficially surveyed (Parker, 1992). By the early 1990s some 30 shipwrecks were recorded along the shores of the southern Levant.[1] The breakdown of this group may lead to several insights. Continuity in maritime activity in the region is one important aspect that may be brought to light by this general data, as well as some lacunae, perhaps the most glaring of which would be the scarcity of late Byzantine and early-Muslim shipwrecks (Gambash, 2015).

Continuous surveying, however, drew the attention of scholars to the area of Dor, particularly to the lagoon that lies south of the tell's southern bay, where several locations were marked as potentially hosting a shipwreck (Kingsley & Raveh, 1996). The systematic work which was undertaken in the 1990s by the Department of Maritime Civilizations and the Institute for Maritime Studies at the University of Haifa has thus far yielded seven shipwrecks, all dated, rather remarkably, to the Byzantine and Early Islamic period (Kahanov, 2010a, 2011).

Dor D is estimated to have been of medium size, some 15–20 m long. [14]Carbon analysis performed on the timber of the ship suggests a date around the middle of the fourth century CE; local late Byzantine pottery found in the area suggests a later

---

[1]The shipwrecks are documented in Parker (1992): nos. 1; 2; 3; 26; 27; 61; 136; 137; 138; 367; 494; 495; 503; 504; 505; 525; 540; 541; 612; 689; 690; 697; 700; 739; 740; 741; 809; 1069; 1078; 1115.

date, around the beginning of the seventh century. **Tantura A** was a small coaster, measuring some 12 m in length. It has been dated to the late fifth or early sixth century, based on ^{14}C analysis, as well as on potsherds found *in situ*. **Dor 2001/1** measured around 17 m and was able to carry some 35 tons of cargo, probably mostly along coastal routes. Analysis of the ceramics as well as ^{14}C tests performed on organic materials from the ship suggest a date around the early sixth century. **Dor 2006** appears to have been the largest vessel in this group, likely beyond 20 m long. Pottery and ^{14}C analysis have established a date within the fifth or sixth century. **Tantura F** is estimated to have measured 16 m in length, and to have served coastal purposes of either trade or fishing. Based on ^{14}C tests, as well as on the analysis of some 30 ceramic items found on board, it was attributed to the mid-seventh to late-eighth century. **Tantura E** was not preserved well enough to allow an estimation of its size. It was dated – by means of pottery analysis and ^{14}C tests – to the period of the seventh to ninth century. **Tantura B** is thought to have measured 18–23 m in length, and 5 m in width. Pottery and ^{14}C tests suggest a date around the early ninth century. In addition to this group, another shipwreck is currently being excavated in Ma'agan Michael, some 8 km to the south of the Dor lagoon. The vessel was possibly as large as Dor 2006, and is dated by its cargo to the seventh or eighth century. It has been dubbed the **Ma'agan Mikhael B** (Cvikel, 2020).

Previously, shipwrecks from the Byzantine period were discovered in Hof Hakarmel, Sdot Yam, Newe Yam, and Mikhmoret.[2] Generalizing on the entire group of the Late Antique shipwrecks of the southern Levant, we may say that their size ranged from small to medium, and their capacity may have reached a few dozen tons. Most of them could navigate in shallow waters, a fact which made natural anchorages a viable option for harboring and loading or unloading their cargo. This would have made the group particularly suitable for improvised coastal activity.

Most of the ships do not contain a clear indication regarding their cargo. They could have foundered empty; or the goods on board could have been carried by currents or perished in the run of time. Salvaging, however, was common enough in antiquity, and well-supported by particular legislation.[3] The closeness of the shipwrecks at issue to the shore makes the option of salvaging the one most likely to have taken place, though exceptions did occur, indicating, for example, trade in glass cullet between Egypt and the southern Levant (Natan et al., 2021).

This brief survey offers a picture of the vessels plying the waters of the southern Levant during Late Antiquity. While it demonstrates the expected dominance of the small vessels of *cabotage*, it includes at least two larger ships – Dor 2006 and Ma'agan Mikhael B – which would have been less manageable in shallow depths and narrow bays, and which may represent the part played by more organized channels of connectivity, operating bigger ships, sailing along fixed, pre-determined routes, and during a more rigidly defined sailing season, and preferring larger

---

[2] Parker (1992): Hof Hakarmel – no. 505; Sdot Yam – no. 1069; Newe Yam – no. 740; Mikhmoret – no. 697.

[3] The Rhodian Sea Law (*Nomos Rhodion Nautikos* e.g.,45–47) enumerates the reward payable to salvors who abide by the law. See also Ashburner (1909): cclxxxviii–ccxciii.

artificial harbors (Leidwanger, 2020). While none of the wrecks were found on the southern shores of Israel, the group in its entirety should be regarded as representative of the vessels that were servicing the coastal emporia of the entire coastline of the southern Levant. Some of them must have arrived at their final destination from Gaza or Asacalon, or were on their way there.

As we address our attention to the southeastern corner of the Mediterranean and its respective maritime heritage, it is important to keep in mind a couple of relevant truths. The shores of the southern Levant are unanimously considered to have been challenging to pre-modern seafarers. The reasons for this are varied, and include, among others, the dominant western vector of local winds, and the paucity of natural harbors along the coastline (Raban, 1995). This reality is captured by the description offered by Josephus of the coastline running between Jaffa and Dor (Joseph. *AJ* 15.331):

> Josephus. *Antiquitates Iudaicae.* 15.331:
> κεῖται μὲν γὰρ ἡ πόλις ἐν τῇ Φοινίκῃ κατὰ τὸν εἰς Αἴγυπτον παράπλουν Ἰόππης μεταξὺ καὶ Δώρων, πολισμάτια ταῦτ'' ἐστὶν παράλια δύσορμα διὰ τὰς κατὰ λίβα προσβολάς, αἳ ἀεὶ τὰς ἐκ τοῦ πόντου θῖνας ἐπὶ τὴν ἠόνα σύρουσαι καταγωγὴν οὐ διδόασιν, ἀλλ'' ἔστιν ἀναγκαῖον ἀποσαλεύειν τὰ πολλὰ τοὺς ἐμπόρους ἐπ'' ἀγκύρας.
>
> This city [i.e., Strato's Tower] is situated in Phoenicia, on the sailing route to Egypt, between Joppa and Dora, which are coastal towns with inappropriate anchorage, on account of the attacks of the winds upon them, which dragging the sand from the sea to the shore, do not allow the landing of ships, and the merchants are forced for the most part to anchor in the open sea.

Yet, this fact alone need not indicate that the degree of maritime activity in the area was significantly reduced in comparison to other stretches of Mediterranean shores. Our rapidly increasing knowledge of *cabotage* strongly suggests that wherever there existed a demand for goods of even the most basic nature, there could be found the merchantman overcoming all obstacles to answer it (Horden & Purcell, 2000: 365–400).

The fact that no Byzantine or early Muslim shipwreck has been discovered so far on the southern part of the Israeli coastline may also be ascribed to the fact that the area has not been studied as carefully as the north. Multiple finds retrieved from the southern shores corroborate the obvious, nonetheless: the south, with its chain of significant coastal emporia between Yavneh-Yam and Rhinocorura, was just as connected to Mediterranean trade as the north, and must have witnessed similar maritime traffic. Occasional discoveries of assemblages of artifacts such as anchors or amphorae may represent the sites of shipwrecks where hulls did not survive, though jettison as a result of sea- or ship-conditions always remains a valid option in such a case (Galili et al., 2015).

The shipwrecks of the Late-Antique southern Levant produce further evidence supporting the notion of an early emergence of frame-first technology (Kahanov et al., 2004; Kahanov, 2010b). Indeed, the presence in **Dor D** of mortise and tenon joints has led scholars to suggest that the vessel was shell based. But the absence of edge joints between planks in **Tantura A**, and the fact that planks were attached to the frame by iron nails, convinces scholars that the vessel was frame based. A closely studied section of **Dor 2001/1**, brought out of the water, has convinced scholars beyond doubt that the ship was built frame first. For **Dor 2006**, some presence of mortise and tenon joints between planks was recorded; however, it appears that also in this case the ship was constructed by means of frame-based techniques. An analysis of the building techniques of **Tantura F** suggests that this ship too was built frame first; and plank remains, butt-joints, and the absence of planking edge-fasteners suggest that **Tantura E,** too, was built frame first. In **Tantura B**, edge joints were absent and planks were attached to the frame by means of iron nails, leading scholars to the conclusion that the ship was built frame first. Finally, in **Ma'agan Mikhael B**, 28 fir planks were discovered attached to the frames by means of iron nails; no edge-joints have been revealed, suggesting that this larger vessel, too, was built frame first (Cvikel, 2020).

The most recent publication on the transition from shell to skeleton in ancient Mediterranean ship construction has laid out the fullest picture yet available for the attributes and timing of the said transition, and concluded that no simple linear development may be imagined, because of the complex nature of the process (Pomey et al., 2012). While the article has explained the technicalities and their chronology sufficiently, difficult questions of function and causality remain open and may receive initial answers through our growing understanding of the political, socio-economic, and environmental background against which the transition took place.

Varying degrees of attention have been dedicated in recent decades to the question of the circumstances in which the transition took place, the latest of which advocate, quite rightly, a holistic, multifaceted approach to the problem (Afane, 2016). Pomey and his colleagues argued in 2012 that "the transition was influenced by many factors, such as society, economics, geography, and environment; and probably varied from one region of the Mediterranean to another." They were well aware of the general tendency to explain the transition as a reflection of social and economic difficulties, such as those which are believed to have risen in the Byzantine era in the eastern Mediterranean, or after the Islamic conquest. They, therefore, called for a better definition of these factors and their technical, social and economic consequences, as well as for further consideration of environmental conditions, accepting that one of the possible influences was climate-change and its ecological effects on forest resources, and therefore on the supply of timber for shipyards.

To be sure, the ships discovered in the Dor lagoon were not necessarily built in or around the area of Dor. Discovering the place of construction of ancient shipwrecks is a challenging task, often resulting in frustration. Given the international character of seafaring, neither the inventory of finds, nor the ethnic identity of the crew, nor even the type of timber used for construction may supply definitive answers regarding the ship's place of production.[4] However, the remarkable technological consistency of the Dor shipwrecks may perhaps allow us to approach the

---

[4] The bibliography presented above for the shipwrecks of Dor includes discussions of provenance for each of the finds, but no definitive answers are supplied. See also the conclusions for the seventh-century shipwreck from Yassi Ada (G. F. Bass, 'Conclusions', in Bass and Van Doorninck, 1982: n. 60, 311–319).

problem of the provenance of these ships through the technology employed in building them, and the socio-economic circumstances that necessitated the adoption of this technology.

Particularly, a combination of alleged stressors – mostly environmental in nature – has led a dominant trend in Late-Antique historiography to define the period at issue as one of crisis and decline. Each of these stressors, as well as their cumulative effect, has been challenged by anti-catastrophalistic approaches, and the debate currently continues and is far from conclusion. Its results could potentially have significant bearing on the questions asked here about the adoption of a new economical technology, and it is therefore crucial to survey the key issues in brief. Relevant phenomena include the external stressors of pandemics and climatic fluctuations, local environmental changes, and the economic factors of supply and demand, production and consumption, both in Palestine and across the Mediterranean.

Written sources describe the effect of a serious pandemic breaking out in the year 541 among urban and rural communities in the eastern Mediterranean. Procopius reports that the daily number of deceased in Constantinople reached ca. 10,000 people, and that corpses had to be disposed of in mass graves and into the sea (*Wars* 2.22–2.33). John of Ephesus, who traveled through Syria and Palestine in 542, described abandoned villages whose inhabitants perished altogether (Sarris, 2011: 159). Mostly following those and similar written sources, the climax of the Justinianic plague is ascribed to the middle of the sixth century, but experts maintain that an epidemic of such scale would have remained present for much longer, including further outbreaks in later centuries.

The written sources find little support in material evidence. A survey of mass burials in the Mediterranean presents only a few cases in which a direct connection is established between burial and the victims of the pandemic (McCormick, 2016); more specifically to our area, extensive excavations in Byzantine Palestine and Jordan have not produced clear indication for the effects of plague on local populations. An increase registered in the number of death epitaphs dated to the 540 s is based on numbers too small for effective generalization – 20–30 per year (Benovitz, 2014). The effect of the plague has therefore been debated on these and other grounds (Mordechai & Eisenberg, 2019). To the extent that demographic pressures had been experienced in the southern Levant as a result of the plague, the demanding industry of shipbuilding, along with the many supplementary trades associated with it, could have benefitted from transitioning to a more economical, more durable technology.

Similarly, the debate about climate change during Late Antiquity, and its societal effects, is still very much in progress, fluctuating between locating our period within a long and significant cold period and ascribing to it common climatic variability (Büntgen et al., 2016; Harper, 2017; Haldon et al., 2018). Even this latter, most critical, approach towards late-antique temperature change admits widespread Northern Hemispheric cooling occurring between the mid-530 s and the 570 s. Interestingly, relevant south Levantine proxies do not indicate that temperatures in the area dropped significantly during this period (Vaiglova et al., 2020). However, like the pandemic, the consequences of such a regional climate change, brief as it might have been, could have affected societies – particularly fragile ones –indirectly, for example through their economy.

In addition to the possible climatic, environmental and epidemiologic effects on local societies, a major factor that triggered decline in the southern Levant was the impact of the economic changes which took place in the wider Mediterranean basin. The rise to prosperity of the Negev settlements aligns perfectly with the significant rise in the demand for wine in the western part of the Mediterranean (Lantos et al., 2020). The ceramic record of Italy, North Africa, Southern Gaul, and other areas suggests a sharp rise in demand for eastern goods, peaking towards the end of the fifth century. The same proxy shows a steady decline in eastern exports to the west during the first half of the sixth century, with African exports gradually taking over, while the absolute size of western markets dwindled (McCormick, 2001: 101). Another example of the decline of international trade in the Mediterranean may be found in the significantly smaller number of shipwrecks in the central and western Mediterranean during the sixth century, in comparison to their higher number in the fourth and fifth centuries (McCormick, 2012: 80–88).

While direct lines of causality are difficult to draw in relation to the shipbuilding industry, many areas in the southern Levant produce clear evidence for pressure and decline starting in the mid-sixth century. Some settlements and production centers were deserted and resettled again a few decades later (Avni et al., 2023). Others continued to diminish in activity and shrink in size until they vanished for good, the Negev settlements being the starkest and most somber example of this irreversible decline (Bar-Oz et al., 2019). Next to the demographic symptoms of the process, no doubt exacerbated also by war and conquest in the seventh century, signs of deforestation are also detectable in the area, again, with no clear link connecting them to a would-be climate change (Lucke et al., 2008; Hajar et al., 2009). Obviously, such pressures, if indeed significant, would have affected the shipbuilding industry, and could have encouraged it to adopt a technology more economical in wood consumption.

In his seminal work on wooden shipbuilding, J. R. Steffy suggested that the ancient shipbuilding industry would have leaned towards economical means of production in terms of time and resources (Steffy, 1994: 84). Of course, this insight would have signified different solutions in different periods, areas, and circumstances. If the stressors enumerated above indeed added up to produce a real economic challenge, it should at least be considered that the southern Levant seized upon an opportunity to upgrade a crucial technology, and began to adopt – faster and more widely than other regions – an alternative method of shipbuilding which had probably been available, or at least known, here and there beforehand, and offered the benefits of more economical production processes. The fact that the ships of the Late-Antique southern Levant were mostly small in size naturally strengthens the notion of maritime activity essentially local in nature.

Ascribing the transition in shipbuilding in the East to the particular circumstances of duress experienced in the region during Late Antiquity should nevertheless be approached with caution. Beyond the difficulties presented above regarding particular challenges during Late Antiquity, such as climate change and the plague, more issues problematize the discussion. The very terminology experts employ, to start with the basics, is still surprisingly inconsistent. The term "transition" is currently used both to mark the cultural shift as well as the technological one, while the two obviously do not overlap. When Pomey, Kahanov and Rieth say that "the transition was a process that lasted *c.*1000 years, mainly during the 1st millennium AD," they refer, as they explain later, to the full embrace by society of the frame-first technology. When another work, on the other hand, declares that with the shipwreck Dor 2001 – dated to the early sixth century – the transition was complete, it refers to the technological transformation that saw the disappearance of all mortise and tenon joints, and the earliest known example, for now, of a frame-first vessel in the eastern Mediterranean (Mor, 2001).

This differentiation should in fact reflect upon two parallel channels of analysis we are engaged in: one of innovation or even invention, the other of adoption. As suggested at the opening of this article, for the periods and technologies we are dealing with here it is not possible to spot the individual who shouted *eureka!* and, in our case, put a finger on the first carpenter who deviated from the old beaten track. What we *can* say is that here the West clearly holds precedence. Based on Celtic shipwrecks excavated in the British isles and the Atlantic coast of France, McGrail has dated primary skeletal developments to as early as the second century CE. And, in effect, this date may perhaps be pushed still earlier, to the first century BCE, if we pay careful attention to Julius Caesar's words:

> Caesar. *Bellum Civile.* 1.54:
> *Cum in his angustiis res esset [...] imperat militibus Caesar, ut naves faciant, cuius generis eum superioribus annis usus Britanniae docuerat. Carinae ac prima statumina ex levi materia fiebant; reliquum corpus navium viminibus contextum coriis integebatur.*
> As things were reduced to such a strait [...] Caesar ordered his men to build ships of the kind that his experience in Britain in previous years had taught him to make. The keels and the first ribs were made of light timber, the rest of the hull was wattled and covered with hides.

Our elaborate knowledge of networking and connectivity in the ancient Mediterranean suggests that a good idea dropped into the water of the Mediterranean on one location would surface in various others, whether connected to the point of origin or to one another. Going by the knowledge we own so far, this process took the frame-based shipbuilding technology long centuries to cross from the west of the Mediterranean to the east; but, if we wish to focus on adoption, it is the East, probably in the area of the southern Levant, that has shown the earliest signs of warming up towards the new technology.

It is not only the perfect example of Dor 2001 that is of interest here, but the fact that an overwhelming number of the shipwrecks discovered in the area and are dated to the immediately following centuries were built while employing distinct characteristics of the frame-first technology. What we may have here is a local example of adoption, or of advanced stages of cultural transition. As we approach the delicate task of assessing the background for this apparent local adoption of the new technology, several prevalent biases need to be noted and rectified.

The presence of Empire has been, so far, quite dominant in discussions of technological transitions, also in other spheres, such as harbor building. The further experts look into the problem the more they realize that the ancient empire, with its spontaneous and opportunistic routine, could hardly have developed a grand strategy or a master plan that would have allowed it to produce answers to market needs. The empire could bring Caesar to Gaul and Britain, where his engineers could have learned local traditions and benefitted from them; and the empire could produce significant demand in the market, for example for grain. But solutions would have come from the private sector. The first harbors to have employed hydraulic concrete were not built by the Roman empire; indeed, even the speculation that it was the empire that had commissioned the concrete harbor at Caesarea does not meet with the historical facts and should be abandoned (Gambash, 2013).

As we have seen, another theme that has instructed discussions on the transition is that of crisis and stress – be it economic, political, or environmental in nature (Steffy, 1994: 83–85). Also here we should be careful to define our so-called crisis precisely, before employing it as a possible motive for the adoption of new technologies, even if allegedly more efficient or economical. This is neither the time nor the place to elaborate on the work of numerous researchers who are engaged in the task of rejecting catastrophe, despite the optimistic nature of such an endeavor. It would suffice to mention theories that aim to eliminate the notion of destructiveness usually associated with the Muslim conquest of the Levant (Avni, 2014); or the debate over the actual implications of the "little ice-age" on late antique society in the Mediterranean and the Levant more specifically (Haldon et al., 2018). From the third century crisis to the Justinianic Plague, the impact of disasters, catastrophes, and more ordinary stresses is being modified, and with it should be modified our dependence on it for explanations for the transition (Mordechai & Eisenberg, 2019).

Towards conclusion, this last point should be pressed still further: perhaps we have been looking for too long only under the dim light of decline and duress. It is true, we often approach the frame-first technology as less demanding in resources, more efficient to produce, stronger, and more durable. Some of these notions require more work from our experimental archaeologists, and may be challenged in the future. Even if they were all true to the letter, we should still pause to ask: did societies produce or adopt more efficient innovations only during times of need? Is there not something to say for ancient prosperous societies that wanted to be still more prosperous, and produced an atmosphere that encouraged entrepreneurship and innovation?

Much of the evidence we are procuring from the field suggests nothing but prosperity in the Late-Antique southern Levant – particularly in the early Byzantine period (fourth–mid-sixth centuries). A case in point is the micro-region of the Negev area and the façade maritime that connected it to the Mediterranean – stretching from Gaza to Ascalon and beyond (Gambash et al., 2019). The paradigm of connectivity suggested by Horden and Purcell in their magisterial book *The Corrupting Sea* is clearly at work here, with local society engaging in wide diversification of produce, the redistribution of surpluses, and the importation – by maritime means – of required and luxury goods.

The wine produced in this micro-region dictated particular adaptation to the challenging arid climate. It nevertheless became famous all around the Mediterranean, transported by camels to Gaza, and from there by ships to Italy, Gaul, and Spain (Fuks et al., 2020). The marble demands of the micro-region, closely following Mediterranean fashions, were answered by shipments moving similarly in the opposite direction, dictating specific means to handle the heavy monolithic cargo. It is such a climate of ambition, entrepreneurship, and emulation, I suggest, that could also well have encouraged the adoption of a new shipbuilding technology.

References

Afane, E. (2016). *Histoire de l'architecture navale et des systèmes nautiques de la période byzantine en Méditerranée. Approche technique et environnementale*. PhD dissertation, Université Paris I Panthéon.

Ashburner, W. (Ed.). (1909). *The Rhodian sea-law*. Clarendon Press.

Avni, G. (2014). *The Byzantine – Islamic transition in Palestine – An archaeological approach*. Oxford University Press.

Avni, G., Bar-Oz, G., & Gambash, G. (2023). When the sweet gifts of Bacchus ended: Settlement abatement and the decline of wine production in Late-Antique southern Palestine. *Bulletin of the American Schools of (Oriental) Research*.

Bar-Oz, G., Weissbrod, L., Erickson-Gini, T., Tepper, Y., Malkinson, D., Benzaquen, M., Langgut, D., Dunseth, Z. C., Butler, D. H., Shahack-Gross, R., Roskin, J., Fuks, D., Weiss, E., Marom, N., Ktalav, I., Blevis, R., Zohar, I., Farhi, Y., Filatova, A., Goren-Rosin, Y., Xin, Y., & Boaretto, E. (2019). Ancient trash mounds unravel urban collapse a century before the end of Byzantine hegemony in the southern Levant. *Proceedings of the National Academy of Science USA, 116*, 8239–8248.

Benovitz, N. (2014). The Justinianic plague: Evidence from the dated Greek epitaphs of Byzantine Palestine and Arabia. *Journal of Roman Archaeology, 27*, 491–506.

Beresford, J. (2013). *The ancient sailing season*. Brill.

Büntgen, U., Myglan, V. S., Ljungqvist, F. C., McCormick, M., Di Cosmo, N., Sigl, M., Jungclaus, J., Wagner, S., Krusic, P. J., Esper, J., Kaplan, J. O., de Vaan, M. A. C., Luterbacher, J., Wacker, L., Tegel, W., & Kirdyanov, A. V. (2016). Cooling and societal change during the Late Antique Little Ice Age from 536 to around 660 AD. *Nature Geoscience, 9*, 231–236.

Cvikel, D. (2020). The Late-antique Ma'agan Mikhael B Shipwreck, Israel. *Near Eastern Archaeology, 83*(1), 30–37.

Fuks, D., Bar-Oz, G., Tepper, Y., Erickson-Gini, T., Langgut, D., Weissbrod, L., & Weiss, E. (2020). The rise and fall of viticulture in the Late Antique Negev Highlands reconstructed from archaeobotanical and ceramic data. *Proceedings of the National Academy of Science USA, 117*, 19780–19791.

Galili, E., Gorin-Rosen, Y., & Rosen, B. (2015). Mediterranean coasts – Cargoes of raw glass. *Hadashot Arkheologiyot, 127*, 1–15.

Gambash, G. (2013). Caesarea Maritima and the grand strategy of the Roman empire. *Skyllis, 13*(1), 53–58.

Gambash, G. (2015). Maritime activity in the ancient southern Levant – The case of Late Antique Dor. *ARAM, 27*, 61–74.

Gambash, G., Bar-Oz, G., Lev, E., & Jeremias, U. (2019). Bygone fish: Rediscovering the red-sea parrotfish as a delicacy of Byzantine Negev cuisine. *Near Eastern Archaeology, 82*(4), 216–225.

Gazda, E. K. (2008). Cosa's hydraulic concrete: Towards a revised chronology. *Memoirs of the American Academy in Rome, 6*, 265–290.

Hajar, L., Häidar-Boustani, M., Khater, C., & Cheddadi, R. (2009). Environmental changes in Lebanon during the Holocene: Man vs. climate impacts. *Journal of Arid Environments, 30*, 1–10.

Haldon, J., Elton, H., Huebner, S. R., Izdebski, A., Mordechai, L., & Newfield, T. P. (2018). Plagues, climate change, and the end of an empire: A response to Kyle Harper's. *The Fate of Rome, History Compass, 16*, e12508.

Harper, K. (2017). *The fate of Rome -climate, disease and the end of an empire*. Princeton University Press.

Horden, P., & Purcell, N. (2000). *The corrupting sea: A study of Mediterranean history*. Blackwell.

Jezegou, M. P. (1989). L'epave II de l'Anse Saint Gervais a Fos-sur-Mer (Bouches-du-Rhone): Un navire du haut moyen-age construit sur squelette. In H. Tzalas (Ed.), *Tropis I, first international symposium on ship construction in antiquity* (pp. 139–146). Organizing Committee, Hellenic Institute for the Preservation of Nautical Tradition.

Kahanov, Y. (2010a). "Ancient shipwrecks in the lagoon of Dor (Tantura) and their meaning" (Heb.). *Katedra, 134*, 6–24. Princeton University Press.

Kahanov, Y. (2010b). From shell to skeleton construction: Introduction. In P. Pomey (Ed.), *Transferts tchnologiques en architecture navale méditerranéenne de l'Antiquité aux temps modernes. Identité technique et identité culturelle* (pp. 77–85).

Kahanov, Y. (2011). Ship reconstruction, documentation and in-situ recording. In A. Catsambis, B. Ford, & D. L. Hamilton (Eds.), *The Oxford handbook of maritime archaeology* (pp. 169–181). Oxford University Press.

Kahanov, Y., Royal, J. G., & Hall, J. (2004). The Tantura wrecks and ancient Mediterranean shipbuilding. In F. M. Hocker & C. A. Ward (Eds.), *The philosophy of shipbuilding* (pp. 113–127). Texas A & M University Press.

Katvez, M. (1990). An analysis of the experimental voyages of the Kyrenia II. *Tropis, II*, 245–256.

Kingsley, S. A., & Raveh, K. (1996). *The ancient harbour and Anchorage at Dor, Israel*. Tempus Reparatum.

Lantos, S., Bar-Oz, G., & Gambash, G. (2020). Wine from the desert: Late-antique negev viniculture and the famous gaza wine. *Near Eastern Archaeology, 83*(1), 56–64.

Leidwanger, J. (2020). *Roman seas: A maritime archaeology of eastern Mediterranean economies*. Oxford University Press.

Lucke, B., Al-Saad, Z., Schmidt, M., Bäumler, R., Lorenz, S. O., Udluft, P., Heußner, K. U., & Walker, B. J. (2008). Soils and land use in the Decapolis region (northern Jordan). Implications for landscape development and the impact of climate change. *Zeitschrift des Deutschen Palästina-Vereins, 124*(2), 171–188.

McCormick, M. (2001). *Origins of the European economy – Communication and commerce AD 300–900*. Cambridge University Press.

McCormick, M. (2012). Movements and markets in the first millennium, information, containers and shipwrecks. In C. Morrison (Ed.), *Trade and markets in Byzantium* (pp. 51–99). Dumbarton Oaks Research Library and Collection.

McCormick, M. (2016). Tracking mass death during the fall of Rome's empire (II): A first inventory of mass graves. *Journal of Roman Archaeology, 29*, 1004–1046.

Mor, H. (2001). *Dor 2001/1 wreck: Evidence for the transition in shipbuilding construction*. PhD dissertation, University of Haifa.

Mordechai, L., & Eisenberg, M. (2019). Rejecting catastrophe: The case of the Justinianic plague. *Past and Present, 247*, 1–48.

Natan, E., Gorin-Rosen, Y., Benzonelli, A., & Cvikel, D. (2021). Maritime trade in early Islamic-period glass: New evidence from the Ma'agan Mikhael B shipwreck. *Journal of Archaeological Science: Reports, 37*, 1.

Parker, A. J. (1992). *Ancient shipwrecks of the Mediterranean and the Roman provinces*. Tempus Reparatum.

Pomey, P., Kahanov, Y., & Rieth, E. (2012). Transition from shell to skeleton in ancient Mediterranean ship construction: Analysis, problems, and future research. *International Journal of Nautical Archaeology, 41*(2), 235–314.

Raban, A. (1995). The heritage of ancient harbor engineering in Cyprus and the Levant. In V. Karageorghis & D. Michaelides (Eds.), *Proceedings of the international symposium cyprus and the sea, Nicosia*, pp. 139–141.

Sarris, P. (2011). *Empires of faith: The fall of Rome and the rise of Islam 500–700*. Oxford University Press.

Steffy, J. R. (1982). The reconstruction of the 11th century Serçe Liman vessel: A preliminary report. *International Journal of Nautical Archaeology, 11*, 13–34.

Steffy, J. R. (1994). *Wooden ship building and the interpretation of shipwrecks*. Texas A & M University Press.

Steffy, J. R. (2004). Construction and analysis of the vessel. In G. F. Bass, S. D. Matthews, & R. J. Steffy (Eds.), *Serçe Limani: An eleventh-century shipwreck, volume 1: The ship and its anchorage, crew, and passengers* (pp. 153–169). Texas A & M University Press.

Vaiglova, P., Hartman, G., Marom, N., Ayalon, E., Bar-Matthews, M., Zilberman, T., Yasur, G., Buckley, M., Bernstein, R., Tepper, I., Weissbrod, L., Erickson-Gini, T., & Bar-Oz, G. (2020). Climate stability and societal decline on the margins of the Byzantine empire in the Negev Desert. *Scientific Reports, 10*(1), 1–13.

Van Doorninck, F. H. (1982). The Hull remains. In G. F. Bass & F. H. Doorninck (Eds.), *Yassi Ada, a seventh-century Byzantine shipwreck* (Vol. I, pp. 32–64). Published with the Cooperation of the Institute of Nautical Archaeology by Texas A & M University Press.

By Boat or by Land – GIS Least-Cost Modeling of Indigenous Native American Transportation Choices in the San Francisco Bay Area

Brian F. Byrd and Paul Brandy

Abstract Archaeological applications of transportation cost studies have largely focused on walking and walking carrying loads across the landscape. We present a similar analysis using GIS least cost analysis of paddling small traditional watercraft. These boats, built of bundles of tule reeds readily available from the San Francisco Bay's ubiquitous marshes, share much in common with traditional reed boats used for riverine and seagoing travels in a wide range of settings throughout the world including ancient Mesopotamia, Egypt, the Indus Valley, and Lake Titicaca. Based on available information on Native American tule reed balsa watercraft of the region, published boat and metabolic metrics and crowd-sourced metabolic measurements we build a model to estimate metabolic cost of transport for individuals, pairs of rowers and loads. Additionally, we derive estimates of efficiency to compare least-cost water travel to land travel between a series of Native American ethnohistoric village locations in the San Francisco Bay area. Finally, we identify shortcomings of this method and discuss possible solutions. Overall, the results reveal that in typical weather conditions boat travel will be more energetically efficient and faster, particularly when goods are being transported.

Keywords North America · Archaeology · GIS · Native Americans · Transportation · Watercraft · California

1 Introduction

Archaeological applications of transportation cost studies have largely focused on walking and walking carrying loads across the landscape. We present a similar analysis using GIS least cost analysis that also includes consideration of paddling small

---

B. F. Byrd (✉) · P. Brandy
Far Western Anthropological Research Group, Davis, CA, USA
e-mail: brian@farwestern.com; paul@farwestern.com

© The Author(s), under exclusive license to Springer Nature Switzerland AG 2023
E. Ben-Yosef, I. W. N. Jones (eds.), *"And in Length of Days Understanding" (Job 12:12): Essays on Archaeology in the Eastern Mediterranean and Beyond in Honor of Thomas E. Levy*, Interdisciplinary Contributions to Archaeology,
https://doi.org/10.1007/978-3-031-27330-8_66

traditional watercraft. In doing so, this study assesses the nature of traditional travel routes and corridors and includes consideration of overland and water traveling options. The goal is to generate a series of expectations regarding how pre-contract overland and water travel using boats made of tule reeds by Native Americans within the San Francisco Bay area of the western coast of North America may have been structured. This can then provide a framework that can be used for future investigations of inter-community interaction.

We consider the following:

- Historical information regarding overland and water travel
- Modeling overland and water travel between key ethnohistoric locations
- Differences between modeled least-cost overland routes versus historical observations and maps regarding travel
- Consideration of the varied utility of and reliance on overland travel (especially east-west) versus water travel (especially north-south)

Our modeling of travel routes is a GIS-based exercise derived from least-cost analysis—individuals will move through the landscape in a manner that accumulates the least amount of cost. Various measures of cost include slope, speed, and metabolic cost (kilocalories). These can be used for a variety of analyses, including identifying a null model for determining the distribution of obsidian (King et al., 2011), likely travel corridors (Gustas & Supernant, 2017; Supernant, 2017), or the route with the least cost between two locations (Byrd et al., 2016; White & Barber, 2012). Least-cost analysis has been infrequently applied to boat travel. Gustas and Supernant (2017) explored potential maritime travel corridors and potential for site location in the Pacific Northwest, while Livingood (2012) compared overland travel and boat travel among the Mississippian mound people in the southern Appalachians. More recently, Fernandez (2021) argues that water should not be a barrier in least cost path analysis especially with respect to rivers, and Kaifu et al. (2021) are incorporating least cost path analysis into their exploration of boat travel and migration.

In this study we build a model to estimate metabolic cost of transport for individuals, pairs of rowers and loads based on available information on Native American tule reed balsa watercraft of the region, published boat and metabolic metrics and crowd-sourced metabolic measurements Additionally, we derive estimates of efficiency to compare least-cost water travel to land travel between a series of Native American ethnohistoric village locations in the San Francisco Bay area. Finally, we identify shortcomings of this method and discuss possible solutions.

2 Background

Watercraft built primarily of reeds are an integral aspect of indigenous boating traditions in a wide range of settings across the globe. This is no doubt due to the ubiquity of reeds, their buoyancy, and the degree of effort required for their construction compared to other more labor-intensive construction materials (Brindley,

1931). Reed-built watercraft include both rafts and boats propelled by bunts, paddles and sails that were traditionally used in riverine, marsh, lake, and open ocean settings. The tasks for which they were used were highly varied including subsistence practices such as fishing, travel, the transportation of goods, and long seagoing voyages of exploration. Based on archaeological evidence, reed-constructed vessels have considerable time depth, having been documented in such settings as ancient Mesopotamia, Egypt, Anatolia, and the Indus Valley (Bass, 1995; Bowen, 1956; Schwartz, 2002). For example, bitumen with reed impressions and barnacles from archaeological contexts demonstrates the importance of reed boats in trade between the Ubaid civilization of Mesopotamia and the eastern regions of Arabian Gulf more than 7000 years ago (Carter, 2002; Lawler, 2002).

In the Americas, boats constructed from bundles of reeds were used by indigenous populations in a wide range of settings (Brindley, 1931). Some of the best-documented include extremely large and elaborate reed boats (some of which could fit up to 60 people) in the Lake Titicaca environs of the South American highlands (Vranich et al., 2005), the more modest two-bundle reed boats used by the Paiute in the lakes of the North American Great Basin (Wheat, 1967), and the ubiquitous tule balsa boats of the greater San Francisco Bay area along western coast of North America (Heizer and Massey (1953).

Our study focusses on modeling tule boat use in the greater San Francisco Bay area, a setting with a temperate Mediterranean climate of typically wet winters and dry summers. Prior to urbanization, it was the largest estuary on the Pacific Coast with 2185 km^2 of tidal marshlands. This rich and diverse coastal setting was formed by the convergence of the Central Valley's Sacramento and San Joaquin rivers which drain 40% of the modern state of California.

At the start Spanish colonization of the area in the late 1700s, the San Francisco Bay area was densely inhabited, with an overall Native American population of around 15,000 – one of the highest population densities in North America (Byrd et al., 2018; Kroeber, 1939; Milliken, 1995; Milliken et al., 2009; Ubelaker, 1992). Moreover, the region was home to several Native American tribes, including the Coast Miwok in the northwest portion of the bay; the Ohlone in the southern and central portion of the bay; and the Bay Miwok, Plains Miwok, Patwin, and Delta Yokuts in the eastern San Francisco Bay area (Johnson, 1978; Kelly, 1978; Kroeber, 1925; Levy, 1978a, b; Wallace, 1978). Each of these indigenous groups lived in villages of several hundred individuals within one of almost 50 well-defined territorial communities, each of whom interacted and traded extensively with neighboring groups who often spoke different languages.

In the 1700s, Bay Area regional inter-territorial community interaction and alliance maintenance was highly structured and organized. These interactions were mediated by well-developed rules of political, social, and religious interaction led by community leaders (Bean & Lawton, 1973; Byrd et al., 2020; Gardner, 2013; Leventhal, 1993). The nature and extent of these interactions appear to have varied across the region, suggesting overlapping spheres of social interaction, earmarked by trade and exchange of finished goods, raw materials, mates, food resources, and other material attributes of iterative socio-political, economic, and symbolic interaction. Overall, these interaction spheres of west-central California highlight the varied nature of the social, political, and ceremonial mechanisms that facilitated interaction between and within territorial communities. Ritualized practices helped to bond distinctive territorial communities together into a rich tapestry of shared beliefs, practices, and obligations that helped to reinforce social order and promote regional cohesion within this densely populated area. Given this setting and the abundant ethnohistorical records and accounts of the indigenous inhabitants of the region that reveal the importance and ubiquity of tule boats, it is an ideal setting for a least-cost modeling of transportation choices.

3 Historical Travel Observations

This section discusses historical observations of indigenous overland travel and overview of tule balsa boats and their use at the of initial contact and then colonization by Europeans.

3.1 Overland Travel Routes

Travel corridors represented the conduits by which Native Americans interacted within the region and beyond, facilitating regional interaction, trade, ritual activity, and warfare. Ethnographic and ethnohistorical accounts reveal that a wide range of trade goods were moved throughout California and into Arizona and the Great Basin, along a series of established east-west and north-south travel routes (Davis, 1961; Heizer, 1978; Heizer & Treganza, 1944; Sample, 1950). Trail systems were the focal point of regional pre-contact travel, and key trails ran up and down the major valleys and through major mountain passes. Travel along river corridors and across the San Francisco Bay was also an important facet of this system.

Regular travel in west-central California region both created and negotiated a series of overlapping regional social and ideological interaction networks, as well as extensive movement of tangible trade goods including non-perishables such as obsidian, abalone pendants and shell beads (Byrd et al., 2017). For example, the Ohlone traded with adjacent groups, most notably the Yokuts and the Miwok (Barrett & Gifford, 1933: 251–252; Pilling 1950: 438). Some items were local, while others were extra-local and procured via down-the-line trading. For example, the Ohlone traded dried abalone and mussel coastal shellfish and salt to the Yokuts and received young dogs, obsidian, and pine nuts in return.

To further explore and model travel patterns, we focus on the northwestern portion of the San Francisco Bay area. Relatively few published ethnohistorical discussions focus directly on traditional land travel routes by the Coast Miwok and Pomo in the San Francisco Bay area of Marin County and southern Sonoma County (Goerke, 2007; Kelly, 1978; Slaymaker, 1974, 1982). For example, Davis's (1961) study of trade and major trail routes among Native Californian Tribes does not include any mapped routes in the area immediate north of the Bay; all those depicted are either north of Fort Bragg or to the east near Napa. Since there were certainly well-established and important travel corridors in northern near-bay area, these lacunae show that such routes were not systematically recorded by Euro-Americans, likely due to confusion by early explorers of their actual locations, as well as early disruption and displacement of local Native American populations.

Further north beyond the Russian River, Barrett (1908) presents considerable detail regarding individual trails between Pomo villages. For the Coast Miwok to the south, he discusses the redwood-forested areas from Mount Tamalpais northward, noting they were largely lacking major villages and only seasonally exploited: "These redwood-covered mountains are quite steep, and in aboriginal times were traversable only with difficulty except along a few trails" (Barrett 1908: 123, 127). In addition to river courses and low-lying topographic routes, ridge crests were occasionally used as travel corridors. For example, Barrett (1908: 244) notes that in the northern Pomo area:

> If a party wished to buy salt, they took the trail leading directly down Stony creek; but if they intended to steal it, they passed on northward along the crest of the range to the north side of St. John Mountain, where a trail led directly down to the salt-bed, thus removing the danger of passing any villages.

Kelly et al. (1991: 209–210) briefly discuss several important observations by Coast Miwok Native Tom Smith on travel and routes from Bodega Bay, regarding route choice and length of travel. For example, Smith noted that the trail from Bodega Bay to Sebastopol (perhaps referring to the Native village of *Lalahqa*) was "the same route as the present road." Presumably this refers to the Bodega Highway. Travel routes to more distant Healdsburg to the northeast went first to Sebastopol and then northward, passing by Santa Rosa, rather than traveling the longer route up the Russian River directly to Healdsburg. Both of these preferred routes take advantage of low-lying terrain. In contrast, Smith notes that travel from Bodega Bay to the village of *Tsüwütena* (north of the bay and much closer than the other two examples) involved going straight over the hill. Thus, distance appears to play a role in the choice of routes. Travel times also varied greatly—the trip from Bodega Bay to Sebastopol was "a two-day walk," while to Fort Ross (travelling along the coastal terrace), it was a one to one and a half day's walk.

Early historical maps of the region provide very little insight into the full nature and extent of early travel routes and trails. No Spanish-era maps are available, and review of maps for the Mexican land grants from 1834 to 1846 (see Goerke, 2007: Appendix J for overview) provide little insight due to the lack of resolution and detail along grant boundaries. We do, however, predict that the earliest travel routes were most likely reusing traditional overland corridors that linked Coast Miwok and southern Pomo villages. The most useful and comprehensive maps showing post-contact roads and routes are County maps produced much later in time—1866 for Sonoma County and 1873 for Marin County. By then, however, travel routes connected key Euro-American settlements dominated by routes designed for horse-driven vehicles, as well as railroad corridors that reached far afield. There is one Indian Rancheria depicted on an 1866 Sonoma County map, centered on the east side of Tomales Bay and lacking an associated trail. On the subsequent 1873 Marin County map, the rancheria is no longer present, the area is shown as owned by J. Miller, and the route of the planned North Pacific Coast Railroad runs along the bay edge through the prior Indian rancheria area.

3.2   Watercraft and Travel

In contrast to overland travel, Native American use of watercraft on San Francisco Bay and along the nearby outer coast was consistently noted by early European explorers and colonizers, and discussed by ethnographers. The earliest recorded European observation of a Native American boat in central California took place in June 1579, when Francis Drake's ship landed for repairs during his circumnavigation of the globe. Although the precise location is uncertain, many suspect they landed in Drakes Bay east of Point Reyes. As reported in the journal of Frances Fletcher, the ship's chaplain (published in 1628), the expedition was formally greeted on the second day of their arrival by a man in a "canoe." Subsequently, a Spanish landing in November 1595 (probably also at Drake's Bay) provides another early account of indigenous water craft. Heizer (1947: 256) notes that Sebastian Cermeño, the ship's pilot, wrote in 1595 "...many Indians appeared on the beach and soon one of them got into a small craft which they employ...." Heizer (1947: 256) also argues that both of these accounts represent observations of tule balsa boats rather than dugout canoes (which were commonly used in northern coastal California), in part because dugout canoes are always operated by more than one person, while a tule balsa can be operated by a single individual.

Subsequently, in the late eighteenth century, the Spanish provide more detailed observations that confirm the prevalence of tule balsas. For example, in 1775 Common Era (CE) during a detailed survey, the Spanish pilot Cañizeres reported upon an encounter in the northeast portion of San Pablo Bay where he observed four men in a tule balsa, each with a double-bladed paddle, traveling faster than a longboat (Galvin, 1971: 96). Similarly, Cook (1957) notes that the next year, Anza (diary pg. 140) observed five tule rafts cross the Carquinez strait in less than a quarter of an hour. The Spanish were much impressed by how these tule balsas were used to regularly travel across the bay even at its widest points, and noted their suitability for travel through marshes and in very shallow waters (Cook, 1957: 138, 141). Goerke (2007: 4, 42) also stresses how the Spanish relied upon, and highly valued, those Native Americans who were skilled at reading the tides and currents, employing them to carry letters of communication and to transport the Spanish around the bay in tule balsas, as well as to guide larger boats. One of those experienced boatmen was the well-known Coast Miwok *Huicmuse*, also known as Marino or Marin (Goerke, 2007: 52).

The Spanish also marveled at the well-built nature and versatility of the tule balsa. In 1776 CE, Pedro Font (as reported in his diary) stated:

> We saw there some launches very well made of tule, with their prows or points somewhat elevated. They had been anchored near the shore with some stones for anchors, and in the middle of the water some Indians were fishing with nets and that they anchored the launch with some very long slim poles [Font, 1931].

Maria Copa Frias and Tom Smith also noted that the Coast Miwok caught herring, perch, and sturgeon in nets between or from tule balsa boats in Tomales Bay, in shallow lagoons north of Novato, and elsewhere (Kelly et al., 1991: 143).

Two Spanish Mission Period images of tule balsas include multiple individuals traveling, and two people using the region's distinctive slim, pointed paddles (Fig. 1). Von Langsdorff's 1806 depiction of the San Francisco Presidio shows a tule balsa in the foreground with two passengers in the middle, and a covered basket in the stern (Von Langsdorff 1813). Choris' iconic image from an 1816 Russian sea voyage into San Francisco Bay has one passenger in the middle and two storage baskets in the stern (Choris, 1822).

A number of ethnohistoric studies have also focused on central California watercraft, discussing both their use and manufacture. Heizer and Massey (1953: 291) argued that tule balsas were used by Coast Miwok and Ohlone in the San Francisco Bay area and along the outer coast only up to Bodega Bay (based largely on early explorer accounts). In contrast, Kroeber (1922; reprinted in 1971) stated that the Pomo also had tule balsa and used them on the coast and on Clear Lake. Tom Smith stated that tules were not used on the ocean as they were too flimsy (Kelly et al., 1991: 210). In other contexts along the California coast, such as Baja, tule boat travel in outer coast and open water settings has been asserted (Des Lauriers, 2005: 346–347), and such use probably should not be precluded for the San Francisco Bay area.

Heizer and Massey (1953: 293) also quote Vancouver and Vancouver (1801) who in 1798 observed that boats were made of tules and dried grass (long broad leaf), some 10 feet long and three to four feet wide, with their maximum width in the middle. Barrett and Gifford (1933: 248–249) provide a complementary set of observations, stating that tule balsa boats were typically 15 feet long and three to four feet wide; they had a willow pole on each side as a gunwale, with eight willow ribs outside for rigidity (see also Kelly et al., 1991: 210). These descriptions share much in common with Fowler's (1990: 142–153) detailed discussion of tule technology and manufacturing in the Great Basin. The paddles used in the Bay Area were distinctive, however, being double-bladed (a characteristic not found farther north) with pointed ends (which also greatly differs in form from the double-bladed Chumash paddles; Heizer & Massey, 1953). Kelly et al. (1991: 524) also suggest there may have been some variation in form among the Coast Miwok, including single-bladed paddles (with rafts used on occasion), while Kroeber (1922) notes that in the Pomo area, tule balsa boats were often poled, but not in San Francisco Bay as the water is too deep.

Fig. 1 Tule Balsa use by Native Californians of the San Francisco Bay Area as depicted by (**a**) von Langsdorff's in 1806 and (**b**) Choris in 1816

In summary, several observations can be made regarding normative assessments of Coast Miwok boat travel. Travel was almost exclusively via tule balsa boats typically 10–15 feet long and four feet wide. They were powered by a two-bladed paddle with distinctive pointed ends. Typically, each boat had two to four paddlers situated in the front and back, with travelers often situated in the middle with transported goods in the stern. Tule boats were also fast, faster than late eighteenth-century longboats. These boats were used throughout San Francisco Bay, as well as in inlets and bays along the outer Pacific coastline; they were only infrequently used in open ocean contexts away from bays and inlets (if at all) due to the more rugged seas.

4   Approach to Reconstructing Travel Routes and Corridors

To better understand travel between major ethnohistoric villages and other key locations, we model likely overland and water travel routes by employing least cost paths. The base input for a GIS to calculate a least cost path is a cost surface. Each cell of a cost surface grid is an estimate of the effort required to cross that cell. If each cell were identical in a cost surface the tool would create Euclidean distance paths. Researchers have used various inputs to make the cost surface more accurately reflect ground conditions including terrain (van Leusen, 2002; Wood & Wood, 2006; Howey, 2007; Morgan, 2009; White & Surface-Evans, 2012) or travel time (Kantner, 2012). As with other studies we assume that archaeological site locations were often located in areas with relatively easy access and proximate to energetically low cost travel corridors (van Luesen, 2002; Wood & Wood, 2006; Byrd et al., 2016; Morgan, 2008). For this study we generated separate cost surfaces for time and metabolic cost for walking and paddling as follows:

1. Land Travel using metabolic cost based on Pandolf metabolic rate function (Pandolf et al., 1977).

   • Inputs are slope, weight of individual, load, travel speed.

2. Land Travel using travel time based on Tobler (1993) hiking function.

   • Input is slope.

3. Water Travel using metabolic cost of canoe travel derived from estimated online calculators for calories burned at specific rates of canoe travel.

   • Inputs include bay/ocean habitats as impedance (open ocean more difficult than shallow bay).

4. Water Travel using time derived from estimated online calculators for calories burned at specific rates of canoe travel.

   • Inputs include bay/ocean habitats as impedance (open ocean requires more time than the shallow bay).

These models are then used as baselines for several analyses, including the identification of "low cost corridors" which might have been frequently used, time and effort required for longer trips, and comparisons between land and water travel between near-shore villages.

The models presented below are simplistic. In general, there has been minimal prior research on metabolic rates for indigenous canoe travel, and we found none specific to tule balsas. Our models focus on the decision of a single, healthy individual to travel between two points when both boat and foot travel are options. To do this, we start with a few assumptions. First, our modeled individual cannot walk part way and switch to a canoe for a water crossing. Second, the individual does not need to build a balsa and no cost is incurred by having access to one. Third, the person must return along the same route. Finally, the only factor dictating the route for a person is the landscape. That is, there are no stops, no groups to avoid, and no need to redirect to find food or water.

4.1 Land Travel Model

To model energetic travel costs, the calories per second (cost) required to traverse each 10-x-10-meter elevation grid cell were calculated for the entire study area based on a formula for metabolic rate for walking on a slope (Pandolf et al., 1977):

$$M = 1.5 \bullet W + 2 \bullet (W + L)(L/W)^2 + n \bullet (W + L) \bullet \left[1.5 \bullet V^2 + 0.35 \bullet V \bullet G\right]$$

Where:

M – Metabolic rate
W – Subject weight
L – Load
V – Velocity
G – Slope
n – Terrain coefficient (an adjustment for differing ground cover [e.g., snow, mud])

For this model, we assume a 68-kilogram (150-pound) person carrying no load, and a terrain coefficient of 1 (i.e., no adjustments for vegetation, small water crossings). To estimate the velocity, we started with the hiker function (Tobler, 1993; Whitley & Hicks, 2003):

$$V = 6 \bullet e^{(-3.5 \cdot |G + 0.05|)}$$

Where:

V – Velocity
G – Slope

e – A real number derived from the exponential function of the slope of the tangent line, commonly defined as the base of the natural logarithm that is a mathematical constant—also called Euler's number.

However, since the Pandolf et al. (1977) model was designed to describe metabolic rate for a specific range of speeds, we set a lower limit on velocity. We used the velocity estimate to convert the metabolic rate from kilocalories per second to kilocalories per meter, which resulted in cost-surface with a continuous set of values ranging between about 0.10 kCal/meter and 0.53 kCal/meter. As calculated, the metabolic cost functions as a transformation of surface slope, where a linear increase in slope results in a much greater increase in metabolic cost.

4.2 Boat Travel Model

In general, boat travel is more difficult to model due to an increased number of variables affecting efficiency, including size and shape of the craft and hull, number of people paddling, cargo, currents, and wind. To estimate kilocalories, we relied on Ainsworth et al.'s (2011) published metabolic equivalent of task (METs) for different rates of canoe travel and published online calculators for converting METs to kcal for specific body weights. The estimates we used of effort and travel speed to derive kilocalories per second and kilocalories per meter are provided in Table 1. These measures are in line with anecdotal information on travel speed from Ames (2002).

To create a cost surface, we estimated the difference in effort based on bay habitats defined by San Francisco Estuary Institute (Table 2; Fig. 2) Specifically, we assumed that protected waterways would be the easiest to traverse, while open ocean would be the most difficult. Additionally, based on currents described at the Bay Area Sea Kayaker's website (https://www.bask.org/tides-and-currents/), we also weighted selected areas such as the Golden Gate and Raccoon Strait effectively increasing metabolic costs by 10% in these areas.

We used publicly available, crowd-sourced data to validate our model. Users on Garmin's Connect website (http://connect.garmin.com) can share their activities with other users. Their data are categorized by activity type, and include time, distance, calories, average pace, and often a KML (Keyhole Markup Language) of the route, which displays geographic data in an Earth browser. We were able to identify

Table 1 Estimates of rate of travel and kilocalories expended for canoe travel

Effort	Kcals/hour for 150-pound individual	Meters/second	Kcal/second	Kcal/meter
Light	204	1.78816	0.056667	0.031690
Moderate	476	2.68224	0.132222	0.049295
Vigorous	816	3.57632	0.226667	0.063380

Table 2 Bay and ocean habitats with associated effort

Effort	Habitat	Kcal/sec
Low	Filled bayland	0.0567
Low	Fully tidal	0.0567
Low	Fully tidal bayland	0.0567
Low	Muted tidal bayland	0.0567
Moderate	Fully tidal bayland	0.1322
Moderate	Shallow bay	0.1322
High	Deep bay	0.2270
Excluded	Aeolian land	–
Excluded	Fully tidal	–
Excluded	Hillslope	–

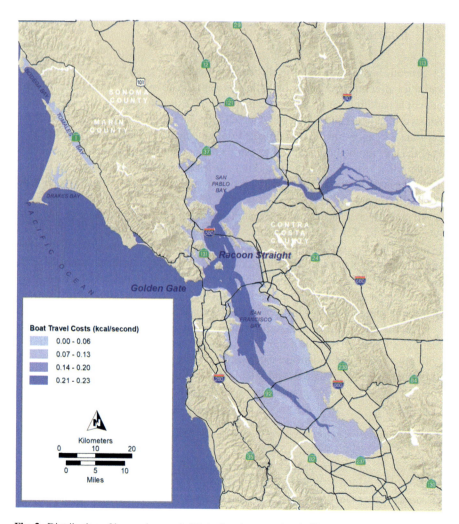

Fig. 2 Distribution of bay and ocean habitats showing associated effort

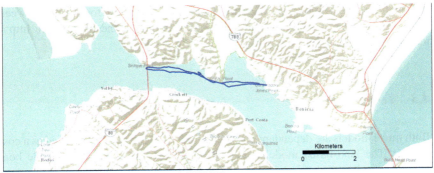

Credits: Sources: Esri, USGS, NOAA Sources: Esri, Garmin, USGS, NPS

Fig. 3 Example of downloaded Garmin connect modern paddling event at eastern entry into San Francisco Bay

Table 3 Example data recorded for a paddling event downloaded from Garmin connect

Time	Moving time (minutes)	Distance (miles)	Avg pace	Avg moving paces	Best pace	Avg HR	Max HR	Calories
32:02.4	28:05.0	6.23	0:14:46	0:14:08	0:08:01	166	185	551

55 paddling activities in various bay habitats which allowed us to compare the reported calories and time versus our model. Figure 3 and Table 3 show an example of one paddling event downloaded from the Garmin site. The figure shows the route of a paddler leaving Benicia, CA, rowing under the Carquinez Bridge then returning to Benicia. The table shows the time, distance and estimate of cost in kilocalories. We found that our estimates of metabolic rate were less than 100 kilocalories below the comparison group, and travel time was 25 min slower. Based on these results, we accepted our model as sufficient for this exercise. However, there are a few caveats: (1) we did not attempt to account for users' gender, weight, equipment (canoe, kayak or stand-up paddleboard), or fitness; (2) frequently the same individuals contributed more than one activity; (3) we cannot determine if the vessel has two people and only one is uploading data; and (4) we did not account for environmental conditions like weather and tides.

Finally, it should be noted that we assume people posting paddling activities to Garmin's website are both fit and experienced paddlers based on the number of posts individuals make and the relative exclusivity of Garmin watches designed for paddling.

The models for pedestrian and boat travel allowed us to construct comparable cost surfaces for both intra- and inter-model comparisons. Models were constructed with ArcGIS 10.4.1, cost distance was calculated with the Path Distance tool, and paths were created with the Cost Path tool. The Path Distance tool calculates the accumulative cost from a source to each cell in a raster. For land travel, we used elevation data as a horizontal factor input to accurately account for distance between cells at different elevations, and a vertical factor table to account for moving between cells of the same or similar values. For a description of the process see http://mapaspects.org/node/3744.

4.3 Travel Time

Both travel models are dependent on speed of travel which can also be used as a cost surface. The land-based model is dependent on the Tobler equation, while boat travel is based on our assignment of speeds for bay habitats.

4.4 Travel Corridors

Least-cost paths for land travel between 58 prominent ethnohistoric locations in the northern portion of San Francisco Bay were generated to identify corridors. These ethnohistoric locations—almost all village locations—are almost exclusively derived from maps provided by Collier and Thalman (1991) and McLendon and Oswalt (1978). The exact location of a path is dependent not just on the cost surface and barriers to travel, but also on the specific location of the beginning and ending points of a journey. As a result, the path from two similar places to the same destination likely will not use an identical path. Similarly, the modeled path from one location to another will not be the same if it is traversed in reverse (since the algorithm selects the next cell based on the lowest cost from the current cell). Therefore, to identify frequently used corridors we generated a density of paths based on a 180-meter search radius.

5 Analysis

To examine the efficiency of walking versus paddling in a tule balsa boat, we selected nine ethnohistoric locations at or near the shore margin in the northwest San Francisco Bay area. These included four along the outer Pacific coastline and five along the margins of bay itself. We then used our least-cost models to derive the shortest path from each village to every other village by foot and by canoe. The total kilocalories for each possible source and destination pair were used to determine the preferred transport method. This exercise assumed the tule balsa canoe was paddled by a single individual and there were no passengers or large amounts of cargo, and the walkers carried no weight. Finally, we modeled how costs change when additional paddlers join in.

5.1 Traditional Overland Travel Corridors

Figure 4 shows least-cost paths for overland travel between 58 prominent ethnohistoric locations in the northern Bay Area. These corridors were also ranked on a varied scale between high- and low-density routes based on the number of trips (from various locations) that would traverse the same route. A series of prominent high-density routes are visible and these are generally in contexts were the terrain is highly variable. Prominent examples include a key north-south route along the bay shore; the eastern margin of Marin; a path southeast to northwest across the uplands from the bay shore near Olompali to the Bodega Bay area; and along the Russian River. In general, fewer east-west paths cross over the rugged uplands of Marin County, and they are often separated from each other by considerable distance. In contrast, low density routes are widely dispersed across the low-lying Cotati/Petaluma Valley in the northeast. This demonstrates that without topographic variation or barriers, the most efficient route is simply to head in the direction of your destination.

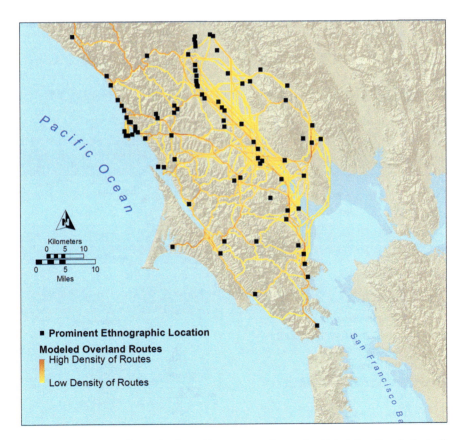

Fig. 4 Least-cost paths for overland travel between prominent ethnohistoric locations in the traditional lands of the Coast Miwok

5.2 Walking Versus Paddling

Our comparative modeling of select ethnohistoric locations indicates that there are different costs associated when a single individual travels by foot or by canoe. These trends are effectively illustrated in Fig. 5 where we present travel from one ethnohistoric location, *Chokecha* near the shore of San Francisco Bay (and the modern city of Novato) to a select number of other ethnohistoric locations. Of the 36 travel connections, walking would be preferred for 25 (69%), while canoeing would be preferred for 11 (31%; Table 4). The results demonstrate that for travel between locations situated near the shore of San Francisco Bay, travel by canoe is more efficient. Elsewhere—travel between locations along the Pacific coast and most coast-to-bay location travel—walking is more efficient.

In contrast to caloric modeling, where walking is much more efficient, when only considering time we find the opposite to be true. Boat travel is quicker than walking in 94% of the cases. The only village travel routes that indicate walking is

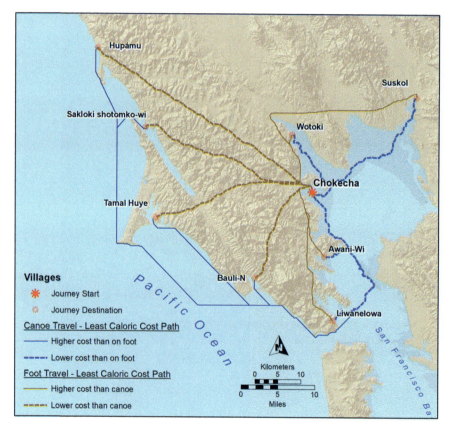

Fig. 5 Least-cost path ranking for overland versus water travel by an individual departing from Chokecha along San Francisco Bay

Table 4 Assessment of whether individual travel by Tule Balsa or walking used less calories

Ethnohistoric location (north to south)[a]	Hupámu	Suskol [a]	Sakloki shotomko-wi	Wotoki	Chokecha	Tamál Húye	Awani-Wi	Bauli-N	Liwanelowa
Hupámu	–	–	–	–	–	–	–	–	–
Suskol	Walk	–	–	–	–	–	–	–	–
Sakloki shotomko-wi	Walk	Walk	–	–	–	–	–	–	–
Wotoki	Walk	Canoe	Walk	–	–	–	–	–	–
Chokecha	Walk	Canoe	Walk	Canoe	–	–	–	–	–
Tamál Húye	Walk	Walk	Walk	Walk	Walk	–	–	–	–
Awani-Wi	Walk	Canoe	Walk	Canoe	Canoe	Walk	–	–	–
Bauli-N	Walk	Canoe	Walk	Walk	Walk	Walk	Walk	–	–
Liwanelowa	Walk	Canoe	Walk	Canoe	Canoe	Walk	Canoe	Walk	–

Notes: [a]All are Coast Miwok villages execpt *Susko*, a Patwin village (Johnson, 1978: Fig. 1)

faster than canoeing would be between Wotoki and Hupámu and Wotoki and Sakloki shotomko-wi (see Fig. 5).

Expanding this analysis to the entire San Francisco Bay Area we selected 10 prominent village locations distributed around the edge of the bay. Clearly, the bay is a major impediment to travel. For these village locations, no overland route is more efficient than water travel (Fig. 6). Additionally, the use of a boat allows an individual to make a day trip out of what might instead be a multiday trip while also avoiding travel through the territorial boundaries of other nearby communities, particularly if access had to be negotiated each time or if relationships were strained.

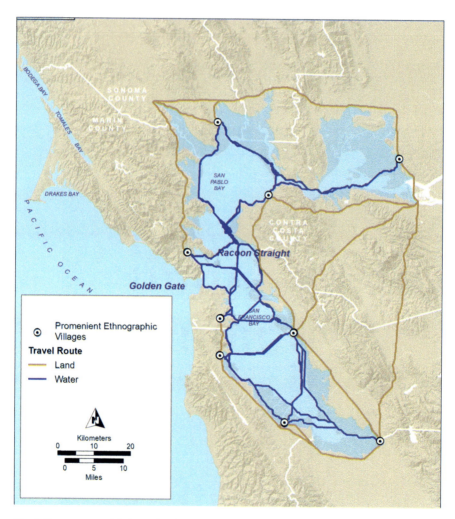

Fig. 6 Least-cost modeled travel paths for select ethnohistoric settlements around margin of San Francisco Bay

It has been noted that carrying cargo on a boat is much more efficient than transport on foot (Drennan, 1984). While hull designs behave differently, typically rowers estimate that speed is reduced by 1/6 of the percentage of cargo to mass. Therefore, a canoe being paddled by a 150-pound individual with 150 pounds of deadweight would only expect a 16% decrease in speed (see http://eodg.atm.ox.ac.uk/user/dudhia/rowing/physics/index.html). Using our walking and canoe models, we can compare the reduction of speed with increasing load while holding kilocalorie consumption constant (Fig. 7). While a balsa would expect a 16% reduction in speed with double the load, a person on foot in flat terrain would be 70% slower.

There are several implications of the effect of cargo on travel efficiency. First, if carrying a load, individuals should invariably prefer water transport if available. Second, it is expected that negative effect of increased number of people in the boat is minor if they are helping to paddle. For example, if two people travel in a boat taking turns paddling, they will expend the same number of calories with only a 16% increase in travel time as a single person. However, if two people set out walking they will expend twice the number of calories as a single person.

If we apply this logic and analysis to our calorie estimates calculated previously to the scenario where two people travel together, the results are dramatically different. In this situation, the majority (76%) of the trips in the northwest bay area would be more efficient by canoe, where previously only 31% of the trips were more efficient by canoe (Table 5). Specifically, we see that overland travel is now primarily only more efficient when going between villages north of Drakes Bay (*Hupámu*,

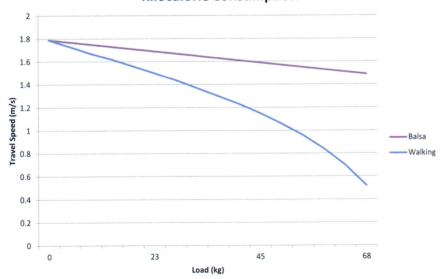

Fig. 7 Reduction in speed with increasing load and constant kilocalorie consumption

Table 5 Assessment of whether two individuals traveling together by Tule Balsa or walking used less calories

Ethnohistoric location (north to south)[a]	Hupámu	Suskol[a]	Sakloki shotomko-wi	Wotoki	Chokecha	TamalHuye	Awani-Wi	Bauli-N	Liwanelowa
Hupámu	–	–	–	–	–	–	–	–	–
Suskol[a]	Walk	–	–	–	–	–	–	–	–
Sakloki shotomko-wi	Canoe	Walk	–	–	–	–	–	–	–
Wotoki	Walk	Canoe	Walk	–	–	–	–	–	–
Chokecha	Walk	Canoe	Walk	Canoe	–	–	–	–	–
Tamál Húye	Canoe	Canoe	Canoe	Walk	Walk	–	–	–	–
Awani-Wi	Canoe	Canoe	Walk	Canoe	Canoe	Canoe	–	–	–
Bauli-N	Canoe	Canoe	Canoe	Canoe	Canoe	Canoe	Walk	–	–
Liwanelowa	Canoe	Canoe	Canoe	Canoe	Canoe	Canoe	Canoe	Canoe	–

Notes: [a]All are Coast Miwok villages excect *Susko*, a Patwin village (Johnson, 1978: Fig. 1)

Sakloki shotomko-wi, and *Tamál Húye*) on the Pacific Coast to San Francisco Bay villages from near Novato northward (*Chokecha, Suskol*, and *Wotoki*).

6 Study Limitations

The models and results presented here represent an initial assessment of travel routes and corridors and do have some limitations. For example, while foot travel modeling has been well-explored in the literature, boat travel has not. Much more work is needed to refine boat travel modeling. In particular, we've relied heavily on modern estimates of metabolic rates for canoe transport to build our model. We are lacking studies specific to metabolic rate, efficiency, and loads related to tule balsa. We are also assuming that paddling and pole propulsion have similar metabolic rates in the shallows. Additionally, environmental factors such as weather and currents have a greater impact on canoe travel than on overland travel. We have attempted to use habitat as a general proxy for current; however, daily wind and tide conditions likely influenced people's decisions regarding using boats or walking. Finally, how one travels by boat, particularly on longer excursions, should be explored further. Where the cost surface is unvarying, least-cost analyses will produce straight line paths. This may not reflect how people would travel, especially on longer trips in the ocean. Notably, it may have advantageous to stay close to shore for safety or to access resources.

7 Conclusion

Overall, the results reveal that in typical weather conditions boat travel will be more energetically efficient and faster, particularly when goods are being transported. Our models for boat and overland travel also corroborate anecdotes from early European colonial documentations. The prevalence of tule balsa clearly indicates their utility, and our modeling suggests they were also very efficient as a means of travel. Individuals travelling between communities on the northwest side of Bay Area would likely travel by boat within the protected bay. As more people join the excursion or the distances traveled around the bay increase, boat travel becomes more efficient, up to the limits of the boat. Similarly, an individual transporting cargo between two points would expend fewer calories using a boat than carrying their load overland.

Cost surface modeling is a powerful tool when considering how people moved across the landscape. We have demonstrated how to make this tool more useful by normalizing cost surfaces to a common unit for comparison purposes. Thus, determining how to calculate a cost surface in kilocalories per meter for both walking and boating allowed us to compare the two methods. Additionally, one could expand this analysis to estimate kilocalories for a mixed mode trip allowing water bodies on a walking trip to no longer be considered an impediment.

We have focused largely on decision-making tied to minimizing calories or time when comparing these models. Likely, however, many factors influenced people's decisions to use boats. First, what is being transported in addition to the paddler? We have shown that many kilocalories are saved by transporting heavy or bulky cargo in a boat rather than by foot. Also, people with decreased mobility or fitness could travel or be transported more efficiently via boat than overland. Elderly, children, or infirmed could participate in a journey, while providing little or no help paddling. In fact, such a person would only be required to generate enough work to overcome the 16% decrease in speed estimated for cargo for the group to break even metabolically.

Where one is travelling would also be an important decision. Water such as a bay or inlet could be viewed as a barrier to overland travel, making a boat an obvious choice. However, socio-political conditions may have also made boat travel an attractive transportation option. The path of an overland route, particularly when travelling from one side of the bay to the other, would have necessitated traveling through multiple territorial communities. If relationships between territorial communities were less than ideal at any point in time it may have been beneficial to avoid interactions and not have to negotiate permission for safe passage. Similarly, marshes and tidal flats may be difficult or impassable by foot, making boat travel a more desirable option.

Lastly, how quickly an individual needs to get to their destination may play a role. While not modeled specifically, there is a substantial energy efficiency gained by adding people to a boat to help paddle. It is also likely that if three or four people were paddling that boat, travel would become even more effective in terms of time and energy efficiency. No such efficiency, of course, is gained when traveling overland. Overall, the results have broad applicability as these boats, built of bundles of tule reeds readily available from the San Francisco Bay's ubiquitous marshes, share much in common with traditional reed boats used for riverine and seagoing travels in a wide range of settings throughout the world.

References

Ainsworth, B. E., Haskell, W. L., Herrmann, S. D., Meckes, Bassett, N., Jr., Tudor-Locke, D. R. C., Greer, J. L., Vezina, J., Whitt-Glover, M. C., & Leon, A. S. (2011). Compendium of physical activities: A second update of codes and MET values. *Medicine & Science in Sports & Exercise, 43*, 1575–1581.

Ames, K. (2002). Going by boat. In B. Fitzhugh & J. Habu (Eds.), *Beyond foraging and collecting* (pp. 19–52). Kluwer Academic/Plenum Publishers.

Barrett, S. A. (1908). The geography and dialects of the Miwok Indians. *University of California Publication in American Archaeology and Ethnology, 6*(2), 333–368. University Press.

Barrett, S. A., & Gifford, E. W. (1933). Miwok material culture: Indian life of the Yosemite region. *Bulletin of the Public Museum of the City of Milwaukee, 2*(4), 117–376.

Bass, G. F. (1995). Sea and river craft in the ancient Near East. In J. M. Sassoon (Ed.), *Civilizations of the ancient Near East Volume 3* (pp. 1421–1422). Scribner; Simon & Schuster and Prentice-Hall International.

Bean, L. J., & Lawton, H. W. (1973). Some explanations for the rise of cultural complexity in native California with comments on proto-agriculture and agriculture. In L. J. Bean & T. C. Blackburn (Eds.), *Native Californians: A theoretical retrospective* (pp. 19–48). Ballena Press.

Bowen, Richard LeBaron Jr. (1956). Boats of the Indus Civilization. *The Mariner's Mirror, 42*(4), 279–290.

Brindley, H. H. (1931). The sailing balsa of Lake Titicaca and other reed-bundle craft. *The Mariner's Mirror, 17*(1), 7–19.

Byrd, B. F., Garrard, A. N., & Brandy, P. (2016). Modeling foraging ranges and spatial organization of Late Pleistocene hunter-gatherers in the Southern Levant – A least-cost GIS approach. *Quaternary International, 396*, 62–78.

Byrd, B. F., Whitaker, A., Mikkelsen, P., & Rosenthal, J. (2017). *San Francisco Bay-Delta regional context and research design for Native American archaeological resources*. Caltrans District 4. Technical report submitted to Caltrans District 4. https://dot.ca.gov/-/media/dot-media/programs/environmental-analysis/documents/ser/sf-bay-delta-research-design-2017-a11y.pdf

Byrd, B. F., DeArmond, S., & Engbring, L. (2018). Re-visualizing indigenous persistence during colonization from the perspective of traditional settlements in the San Francisco Bay-Delta area. *Journal of California and Great Basin anthropology, 38*(2), 163–190.

Byrd, B. F., Engbring, L., Darcangelo, M., & Ruby, A. (2020). *Protohistoric village organization and territorial maintenance: The archaeology of Síi Túupentak (CA-ALA-565/H) in the San Francisco Bay Area*. Center for Archaeological Research at Davis Publication 20.

Carter, R. (2002). The Neolithic origins of seafaring in the Arabian Gulf. *Archaeology International, 6*, 44–47.

Choris, L. (1822). *Voyage pittoresque autour du monde, avec des portraits de sauvages d'Amérique. d'Asie, d'Afrique, et des îles du Grand Ocean; des paysages, des vues maritimes, et plusieurs objets d'histoire naturelle; accompagné de descriptions par m. le Baron Cuvier, et m. A. de Chamisso, et d'observations sur les crânes humains, par m. le Docteur Gall. Par m. Louis Choris, peintre.* Del'Imprimerie de Firmin Didot.

Collier, M., & Thalman, S. (1991). Interviews with Tom Smith and Maria Copa. In *Isabel Kelly's ethnographic notes on the Coast Miwok Indians of Marin and Southern Sonoma counties, California*. MAPOM Occasional Papers No. 6.

Cook, S. F. (1957). The aboriginal population of Alameda and Contra Costa counties, California. *University of California Anthropological Records, 16*(4), 4.

Davis, J. T. (1961). Trade routes and economic exchange among the Indians of California. *Reports of the University of California Archaeological Survey, 54*, 1–71.

Des Lauriers, M. R. (2005). The watercraft of Isla Cedros, Baja California: Variability and capabilities of indigenous seafaring technology along the Pacific Coast of North America. *American Antiquity, 70*(2), 342–360.

Drennan, R. D. (1984). Long-distance transport costs in pre-Hispanic Mesoamerica. *American Anthropologist, 86*(1), 105–112.

Fernandez, P. T. (2021). Mobility in ancient times: Combining land and water costs. *Digital Applications in Archaeology and Cultural Heritage, 22*, e00192.

Font, P. (1931). *Font's complete diary: A chronicle of the founding of San Francisco* (Translated by Herbert E. Bolton). University of California Press.

Fowler, C. S. (1990). *Tule technology Northern Paiute uses of marsh resources in Western Nevada. Folklife Studies 6*. Smithsonian Institution.

Galvin, J. (ed). (1971). *The first Spanish entry into San Francisco Bay, 1775*. John Howell Books.

Gardner, K. S. (2013). *Diet and identity among the ancestral Ohlone: Integrating stable isotope analysis and mortuary context at the Yukisma Mound (CA-SCL-38)*. Master's thesis, Department of Anthropology, California State University.

Goerke, B. (2007). *Chief Marin: Leader, rebel, and legend*. Heyday Books.

Gustas, R., & Supernant, K. (2017). Least cost path analysis of early maritime movement on the Pacific Northwest Coast. *Journal of Archaeological Science, 78*, 40–56.

Heizer, R. F. (1947). Francis Drake and the California Indians, 1579. *University of California Publications in American Archaeology and Ethnology, 42*(3), 251–302.

Heizer, R. F. (1978). *Handbook of north American Indians 8* (W. C. Sturtevant, General Editor). Smithsonian Institution.

Heizer, R. F., & Massey, W. C. (1953). Aboriginal navigation off the coasts of upper and lower California. *Bureau of American Ethnology Bulletin, 151*, 285–312.

Heizer, R. F., & Treganza, A. E. (1944). Mines and quarries of the Indians of California. *California Journal of Mines and Geology, 40*(3), 291–359.

Howey, M. C. L. (2007). Using multi-criteria cost surface analysis to explore past regional landscapes: A case study of ritual activity and social interaction in Michigan, AD 1200–1600. *Journal of Archaeological Science, 34*, 1830–1846.

Johnson, P. J. (1978). Patwin. In R. F. Heizer (Ed.), *California* (pp. 350–360). Handbook of North American Indians 8, William C. Sturtevant, general editor. Smithsonian Institution..

Kaifu, Y., Ishikawa, J., Muramatsu, Kokubugata, M., Goro, & Goto, A. (2021). Establishing the efficacy of reed-bundle rafts in the paleolithic colonization of the Ryukyu Islands. *Journal of Island and Coastal Archaeology, 10*, 1–14.

Kantner, J. (2012). Realism, reality, and routes: Evaluating cost-surface and cost-path algorithms. In D. A. White & S. L. Surface-Evans (Eds.), *Least cost analysis of social landscapes: Archaeological case studies* (pp. 225–238). University of Utah Press.

Kelly, I. T. (1978). Coastal Miwok. In R. F. Heizer (Ed.), *California* (pp. 414–425). Handbook of North American Indians 8, William C. Sturtevant general editor. Smithsonian Institution.

Kelly, I. T., Collier, M. E. T., Thalman, S. B., Smith, T., & Copa, M. (1991). *Interviews with Tom Smith and Maria Copa: Isabel Kelly's ethnographic notes on the Coast Miwok Indians of Marin and Southern Sonoma counties, California.* Miwok Archaeological Preserve of Marin.

King, J. H., Hildebrandt, W. R., & Rosenthal, J. S. (2011). Trans-Sierran movement of Bodie Hills obsidian. In R. Hughes (Ed.), *Perspectives on prehistoric trade and exchange in California and the Great Basin* (pp. 148–170). University of Utah Press.

Kroeber, A. L. (1922). Elements of culture in native California. *University of California Publications in American Archaeology and Ethnology, 13*(8), 259–328. Reprinted in 1972.

Kroeber, A. L. (1925). *Handbook of the Indians of California* (Bureau of American Ethnology Bulletin 78). Smithsonian Institution (Reprinted by Dover Publications, New York, 1976).

Kroeber, A. L. (1939). *Cultural and natural areas of native North America.* University of California Publications in American Archaeology and Ethnology.

Lawler, A. (2002). Report of oldest boat hints at early trade routes. *Science, 296*(5574), 1791–1792.

Leventhal, A. M. (1993). *A reinterpretation of some bay area shellmound sites: A view from the mortuary complex at CA-ALS-329, the Ryan Mound.* Unpublished Master's thesis, Department of Social Sciences, San Jose State University, San Jose, California.

Levy, R. S. (1978a). Costanoan. In R. F. Heizer (Ed.), *California* (pp. 485–495). Handbook of North American Indians. Smithsonian Institution.

Levy, R. S. (1978b). Eastern Miwok. In R. F. Heizer (Ed.), *California* (pp. 398–413). Handbook of North American Indians Volume 8. Smithsonian Institution.

Livingood, P. (2012). No crows made mounds: Do cost distance calculations of travel time improve our understanding of southern Appalachian polity size? In D. A. White & S. L. Surface-Evans (Eds.), *Least cost analysis of social landscapes: Archaeological case study.* University of Utah Press.

McLendon, S., & Oswalt, R. L. (1978). Pomo: Introduction. In R. F. Heizer (Ed.), *Handbook of North American Indians. California* (pp. 274–288). Handbook of North American Indians 8, William C. Sturtevant general editor, Smithsonian Institution.

Milliken, R. (1995). *A time of little choice: The disintegration of tribal culture in the San Francisco bay area 1769–1810* (Anthropological Papers 43). Ballena Press.

Milliken, R., Shoup, L. H., & Ortiz, B. R. (2009). Ohlone/Costanoan Indians of the San Francisco peninsula and their neighbors, yesterday and today. In *Prepared by archaeological and historical consultants*. Submitted to National Park Service Golden Gate National Recreation Area, San Francisco, California.

Morgan, C. (2008). Reconstructing prehistoric hunter-gatherer foraging radii: A case study from California's Southern Sierra Nevada. *Journal of Archaeological Science, 35*, 247–258.

Morgan, C. (2009). Optimal foraging patterns in the Sierra Nevada, Alta California. *California Archaeology, 1*, 205–226.

Pandolf, K. B., Givoni, B., & Goldman, R. F. (1977). Predicting energy expenditure with loads while standing or walking very slowly. *Applied Physiology, 43*, 577–581.

Pilling, A. R. (1950). The archaeological implications of an annual coastal visit for certain Yokuts groups. *American Anthropologist, 52*, 438–440.

Sample, L. L. (1950). *Trade and trails in aboriginal California* (p. 8). University of California Survey Reports 8.

Schwartz, M. (2002). Early evidence of reed boats from Southeast Anatolia. *Antiquity, 76*, 617–618.

Slaymaker, C. M. (1974). *Fidemo, the twilight and before: A study of coast Miwok political organization*. Master's thesis, Department of Anthropology, San Francisco State University, California.

Slaymaker, C. M. (1982). *A model for the study of Coast Miwok ethnogeography*. Ph. D. dissertation, Department of Anthropology, University of California.

Supernant, K. (2017). Modeling Métis mobility? Evaluating least cost paths and indigenous landscapes in the Canadian west. *Journal of Archaeological Science, 84*, 63–73.

Tobler, W. (1993). Three presentations on geographical analysis and modeling: Non-isotropic geographic modeling speculations on the geometry of geography global spatial analysis. *Technical report, National Center for Geographic Information and Analysis, 93*(1).

Ubelaker, D. H. (1992). North American Indian population size: Changing perspectives. In J. W. Verano & D. H. Ubelaker (Eds.), *Disease and demography in the Americas* (pp. 169–176). Smithsonian Institution Press.

Van Leusen, M. (2002). *Pattern to process: Methodological investigations into the formation and interpretation of spatial patterns in archaeological landscapes*. Rijksuniversiteit.

Vancouver, G., & Vancouver, J. (1801). *A voyage of discovery to the North Pacific Ocean, and round the world*. J. Stockdale. ISBN 0-665-18642-8.

Vranich, A., Harmon, P., & Knutson, C. (2005). Reed boats and experimental archaeology on Lake Titicaca. *Expedition, 47*(2), 20–27.

Von Langsdorff, G. H. (1813). Voyages and Travels In Various Parts Of The World During The Years 1803, 1804, 1805, 1806 And 1807. (Two Volume Set), London, H. Colburn.

Wallace, W. J. (1978). Northern Valley Yokuts. In R. F. Heizer (Ed.), *California* (pp. 462–470). Handbook of North American Indians Volume 8, William C. Sturtevant, general editor. Smithsonian Institution.

Wheat, M. M. (1967). *Survival arts of the primitive Paiutes*. University of Nevada Press.

White, D. A., & Barber, S. B. (2012). Geospatial modeling of pedestrian transportation networks: A case study from precolumbian Oaxaca, Mexico. *Journal of Archaeological Science, 39*(8), 2684–2696.

Whitley, T., & Hicks, L. (2003). A geographic information systems approach to understanding potential prehistoric and historic travel corridors. *Southeastern Archaeology, 22*(1), 77–91.

Wood, B. M., & Wood, Z. J. (2006). *Energetically optimal travel across Terrain: Visualizations and a new metric of geographic distance with, archaeological applications*. SPIE Proceedings, vol. 6060.

Part VI
Cyber-Archaeology and Archaeological Science: The Future of the Past

Inside the SunCAVE, UC San Diego, 2017 (https://chei.ucsd.edu/suncave/). Tom Levy examines 3D photographic data collected by his team at ancient Corinth, Greece. (Photo courtesy of Erik R. Jepsen)

From the Field to the Web: Towards an Integrative Approach in Data Processing from Excavations and Surveys into Quantitative Digital Archaeology – The Israeli Case Study

Gideon Avni, Avraham S. Tendler, and Liat Weinblum

Abstract In the past decade the Israel Antiquities Authority (IAA) moved from paper-based field documentation to digital tools aiming at processing all archeological data amassed during field and lab work. The data from hundreds of excavations conducted each year by the IAA is processed and stored under one national network of data processing and storing. These include field reports of excavations and surveys, digital documentation by plans and images, artifact documentation etc.

The main digital platform adopted at all IAA is DANA - Digital Archaeology and National Archive. This software has passed the stress test in the field and data for many hundreds of excavations is now available in digital format. The need to move towards a more integrative approach that includes also innovative solutions for post-excavation analysis and treatment in the lab, photogrammetric outputs, and the Digital database of 3D models of archaeological artifacts became indispensable and is well over-due.

The paper outlines new approaches and methods to meet the requirements of the experts involved in the post-excavations processes and present new tools to support the field archaeologists during the publication phase. In addition, we shall outline our suggestion for enabling interested scholars to query the IAA accumulated excavation, survey, artifacts and archival data in innovative ways. The advantages of the digitization process of the vast archaeological databases is presented by several case studies: Rescue excavations in a large site, the documentation of historical cities (Jerusalem and Ramla) and the documentation of a larger region in the Negev Highlands.

Keywords Archaeological surveys · Digital archaeology · DAAHL · DANA · GIS

G. Avni (✉) · A. S. Tendler · L. Weinblum
Israel Antiquities Authority, Jerusalem, Israel
e-mail: gideon@israntique.org.il; avrohomt@israntique.org.il; liat@israntique.org.il

© The Author(s), under exclusive license to Springer Nature Switzerland AG 2023
E. Ben-Yosef, I. W. Jones (eds.), *"And in Length of Days Understanding" (Job 12:12): Essays on Archaeology in the Eastern Mediterranean and Beyond in Honor of Thomas E. Levy*, Interdisciplinary Contributions to Archaeology,
https://doi.org/10.1007/978-3-031-27330-8_67

1 Introduction

One of the most significant advances in the implementation of digital technologies in archaeology was initiated by Tom Levy in the past two decades. As a pioneer in the use of advanced methodologies in documenting his excavations in Israel, Jordan and Greece, Tom Levy has expanded the framework of digital archaeology into a comprehensive view of larger regions in the Near East. The digital Archaeological Atlas of the Holy Land (DAAHL) provided extensive data on sites and regions of the southern Levant, enabling scholars the access to thousands of sites, and provided them with intensive archaeological data (Savage & Levy, 2014a). This large-scale project has created for the first time a network of archaeologically related database, based on spatial distribution and GIS infrastructures. The innovative network provided a vision for a wider Mediterranean database system (Savage & Levy, 2014b). The incorporation of data collecting from a single site with a large regional perspective of GIS based documentation of sites has proved to be one of the most efficient tools in cultural heritage management, particularly in the light of the wide destruction of archaeological sites in the Near East in the last decade (Levy et al., 2022).

This comprehensive initiative was formed *in tandem* with the development of a new approaches to systematic methodologies of digital documentation of archaeological sites in Israel, and shortly a fruitful cooperation was developed between the DAAHL and the Israeli systems of digital documentation. The major advantage for both parties lies in the fact that unlike many other countries, the overall data on surveyed and excavated sites in Israel is gathered under the auspices of one central agency – the Israel Antiquities Authority (IAA). This is particularly significant due to the fact that since the establishment of the IAA in 1990 Israel has experienced a dramatic raise in archaeological excavations, with salvage excavations related to modern construction and development activities taking the lead: while between 1948 and 1990 the number of rescue excavations averaged 30–50 per year, the foundation of the Israel Antiquities Authority as an independent government agency that combines the monitoring and safekeeping of the antiquity sites in Israel with academic activity in excavations, research and scientific publications, has increased this number to c. 300 excavations per year (Fig. 1).

This large volume has created both challenges and opportunities in the establishment of a unified system of documentation and data processing from all excavations throughout the country, into one centralized system. The vision behind the formation of a centralized database system is that it will provide a prime source of information and database. The use of archaeological data from thousands of excavations, covering the wide spectrum of human presence in the region, from the Lower Paleolithic to the Late Ottoman period, will provide new opportunities for research.

The reasons behind this accelerated archaeological activity lies in the fact that the northern and central regions of modern Israel, from the Galilee to the northern Negev, are regions which contain one of the most extensive concentrations of archaeological sites in the Near East. This area has witnessed a wave of modern construction in the last decades, aimed for the housing and transportation of a

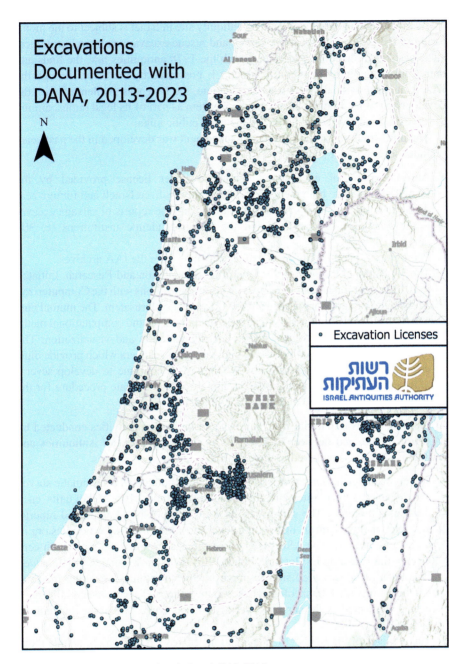

Fig. 1 Archaeological excavations in Israel 1990–2010

constantly increasing population of Israel, which have been raised from c. 1 million people in the early 1950s to more than 9 million in 2021, predicting c. 15 million in 2040.

As every development activity in an antiquity site in Israel is subject to the monitoring of the IAA, the inspection, survey and rescue excavations in archaeological sites was standardized. In accordance with the 1978 antiquities law, the finds and data from all antiquity sites in the country is possessed by the State, through the IAA as its professional agency. As an outcome, the IAA was challenged with the development of an efficient data collecting system as part of its legal duties, aiming to serve the academic community and the wide public alike.

The infrastructure for the IAA data management was developed in the past years includes several major sources:

- Annual reports of excavations conducted under license provided by the IAA. These include both the records of expeditions from Israeli and foreign academic institutions (c. 50 annual excavations) and the reports of salvage excavations, conducted by the IAA and the Israeli academic institutions (c. 300 per year).
- Photographs, plans of sites and artifact drawings from the IAA archives.
- The 3D National Laboratory for Digital Documentation and Research, initiated in 2013, is operating in parallel and with close connections with the Computerized Archaeology Laboratory at the Hebrew University of Jerusalem. The mutual purpose of the twin laboratories is to harness mathematical and computational methods to support archaeological research, documentation and visualization. The laboratory is equipped with modern, high precision scanners which provide digital models of archaeological finds. We apply and continue to develop several tools and algorithms which are used routinely as the ultimate procedure for the analysis, publication and digital storage of the finds.

In addition, archival material from surveys and inspection activities conducted by IAA from 1990, and between 1948–1990 by the Department of Antiquities and Museums (IDAM) is gathered in three on-line venues:

- The archaeological Survey of Israel (ASI), which conducted a systematic survey and documentation of sites, dividing Israel to a technical 10×10 km units, each defined as a "map". The survey results were first published as printed reports, and later included in an open-source website (https://survey.antiquities.org.il/index_Eng.html#/). The ASI, based on previous surveys in the nineteenth century by the Palestine Exploration Fund (PEF) (Wilson & Conder, 1890), added thousands of documented sites, a process which continues, updating the total number of recorded archaeological sites in the country. To date, over 34,000 have been documented by the survey, covering c. 15,000 km^2, 75% of the total area of Israel (Fig. 2).
- The archives of the British Mandate and the State of Israel which include thousands of files with valuable data from inspections and monitoring of archaeological sites and artifacts. (https://www.iaa-archives.org.il)

The main challenge of the developing IAA data collecting system is to integrate all these sources into one comprehensive system. The geographic location of a site or an artifact will form the prime identity, as all finds are retrieved from sites which

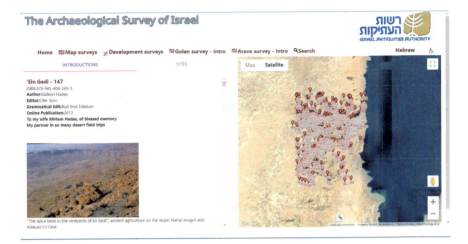

Fig. 2 Archaeological survey of Israel – map of Ein Gedi (Source: Website, texts and photos © Israel Antiquities Authority)

have a geographic identification. The collected data from an inspection activity, a survey, or an excavation includes written descriptions, technical details as lists of baskets and loci, pictures and drawings of the site and its finds, etc.

Yet, the major challenge of this new data collecting system is retrieving information from excavations into a unified system of documentation. Consequently, the IAA has implied since 2012 a unified system used in all excavations – the Digital Archaeology and National Archives (DANA) software (see the detailed description below).

2 Digital Archaeology in the IAA

Digital documentation and assimilation of computerized databases is currently used by the IAA in all its archaeological excavations by various methodologies. The current research intends to incorporate four digital methods in use into one fluent digital system which will be called Next Generation Archaeology (NGA). The four digital methods currently used are: (1) archaeological documentation system DANA, (2) photogrammetry, (3) three-dimensional documentation of objects, (4) GIS applications in archeology.

In the past two decades we are witnessing a revolution in archaeological field methodologies, with documentation shifting from manual to digital recording tools (Alperson-Afil, 2019; Birkenfeld & Garfinkel, 2020). While until the late twentieth century, archaeological data was recorded, tabulated, and plotted by hand, and the analysis of the archaeological information was restricted to manual and visual appraisal, the introduction of new technologies and techniques into the interpretative frameworks during the past decade have significantly increased the quality and volume of the archaeological data. The digital documentations of daily logs, field plans, photography, and artefact illustrations are now commonly practiced by many scholars and institutions, some of them are being further used in the process of finds analysis and publication.

2.1 Adopting Unified Documentation Systems: DANA and Photogrammetry

2.1.1 Dana

The Digital Archaeology and National Archives (DANA) software is a computerized documentation tool intended to streamline and facilitate the archaeological documentation process in a simplified administrative reporting workflow, including a seamless integration into the existing IT-framework. This system is currently being used in all the IAA salvage excavations (Figs. 3 and 4).

DANA was developed in the framework of a collaboration between the University of Bern in Switzerland and the IAA (Münger & Weinblum, 2022). This software is dynamic and was developed *in tandem* with the archeological fieldwork. It aims to be a suitable aid for the archaeologist, using the different methods and models listed below:

- Contexts: urban, rural or underwater contexts are manageable within the same framework.
- Excavation methods: classic, prehistoric (or a combination thereof), and underwater excavations are applicable without the need of sub-versions of the same system.

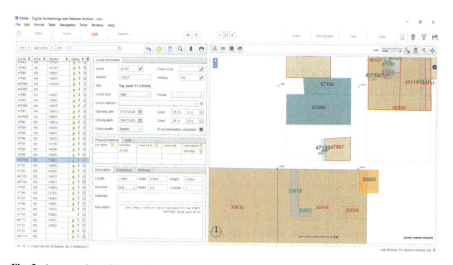

Fig. 3 A screenshot of locus list with verbal and schematic descriptions

From the Field to the Web: Towards an Integrative Approach in Data Processing... 1587

Fig. 4 A screenshot of the photo album. (Note baskets and wall numbers are marked on the photos)

- Ease of use and user friendliness: It is imperative to ensure the archaeologists working with the system could immediately adopt to the new technology without intensive training. Convenient and intuitive data selection from predefined data tables and the avoidance of redundant data entry characterizes the ease of use of the system.
- Use of a standardized 'archaeological language': The system uses a subset of terms from the institutional thesaurus.
- Web-independent, 'simple' technology: The stand-alone application needs to run on simple, cost-efficient PCs with basic computing power and to be independent of resources accessed via the WWW.
- Optimization of administrative processes: Efficiency of post-excavation processes is one of the top priorities of the system.
- Easy Data Export: The system allows data export to other file formats and data processing engines

2.1.2 Photogrammetry

Photogrammetry is the method of measuring the geometry of objects using a series of two-dimensional images. Over the past decade, photogrammetry has rapidly become a standard part of the archaeological documentation toolkit, allowing the production of photo-realistic three-dimensional digital models of finds, excavation areas, buildings and archaeological sites and landscape features (e.g. De Reu et al., 2014; Doneus et al., 2011; Fonstad et al., 2013; Howland et al., 2014; Kjellman, 2012; Magnani & Douglass, 2020; Westoby et al., 2012).

The recent accessibility and utility of photogrammetry as a method of archaeological documentation has come about due to parallel advances in the technological processing power of central and graphic processing units (CPUs and GPUs), the improvement of digital photography and the advent of affordable and reliable civilian drones with high quality digital cameras and the development of Structure from Motion (SfM) algorithms. These technological advances have made photogrammetry an accessible tool to the general public, requiring an understanding of photography and the use of one out of several already existing photogrammetric software platforms in order to produce digital three-dimensional models. These skills can be acquired by a wide range of personnel, students and researchers and do not require an academic or professional background in photography, graphic design, geodesy or other relevant fields (Jones & Church, 2020). However, it should be noted that in order to successfully carry out photogrammetric documentation in certain types of archaeological projects (e.g. large and multi-strata excavations and enclosed spaces such as buildings and caves), a high level of expertise is still required.

The application of photogrammetry in the IAA archaeological fieldwork includes two categories:

1. The documentation of archaeological excavations and cultural heritage sites. The use of photogrammetry as a primary or auxiliary tool for the documentation of excavations and cultural heritage sites is widely considered the best method for three-dimensional documentation for the purposes of archaeological field recording and cultural resource management (Fig. 5) (Cornelio, 2020; Douglass et al., 2015; Howland et al., 2014; Kjellman, 2012; Magnani et al., 2020; Prins, 2016; Quartermaine et al., 2014; Waagen, 2019).
2. Mapping and landscape documentation (Fig. 6). The use of UAVs (Unmanned Aerial Vehicles, or drones) for the photogrammetric documentation of landscapes with archaeological features is used to produce orthographic images and

Fig. 5 A photogrammetric model of an industrial area from the Byzantine period at Tel Yavne. (Credit: Alex Wiegmann, IAA)

From the Field to the Web: Towards an Integrative Approach in Data Processing... 1589

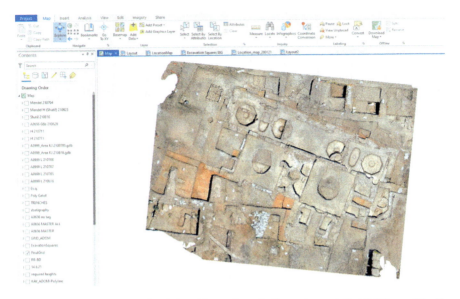

Fig. 6 An orthophoto map of an industrial area from the Byzantine period at Tel Yavne. (Credit: Alex Wiegmann, IAA)

maps, to document terrain topography and as a survey tool to identify archaeological remains. The photogrammetric models created through landscape documentation are frequently used as a basis for GIS (Geographic Information Systems) studies which integrate the topography and the geographical distribution of archaeological sites as documented in the photogrammetric models, with various other geographic information layers (Field et al., 2017; Muñoz-Nieto et al., 2014; Nikolakopoulos et al., 2017).

In recent years, the IAA has integrated photogrammetry as a primary tool for the documentation of archaeological excavations in a GIS-oriented work environment and has widely applied photogrammetry for the documentation of conservation projects and archaeological surveys (Wiegmann, 2016, 2020).

2.1.3 Three-Dimensional Documentation of Objects

In the last decade, the IAA shifted to 3D documentation of artifacts. The 3D documentation device was developed in-house. It enables to produce print-quality figures for the final publication of excavations replacing the traditional manual drawings of the artifacts. Today, every indicative artifact that needs to be published in a final report is scanned in 3D. The laboratory's team handles several different scanners, each one of them at different levels of resolution and accuracy. From the micro level of scanning small find such as coins and beads, and up to the scanning of a complete ceramic jar or a marble statue. At the National Laboratory for Digital Documentation and Research at the IAA we differentiate the post processing of these 3D models into two, based on the morphology of the artifacts (Figs. 7 and 8).

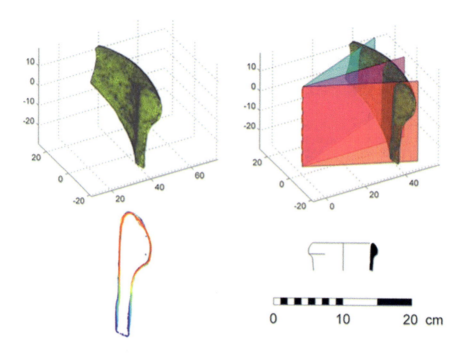

Fig. 7 A 3D model of a common pottery fragment (top-left), its computed rotation axis (top-right), the quality control based on overlapping profiles (bottom-left), and its final representation (bottom-right) for archaeological publication and further research

Fig. 8 Perpendicular views and cross-sections that represent the final publication output of two objects: lime-stone mold (left) and flint handaxe (right)

3 Between the Past and the Future: Implementation of Digital Archaeology in Excavation of Sites, Historic Cities and Regions

3.1 Excavated Sites – Modi'in Excavations – A Case Study for Unified Documentation Systems

Modi'in is a rapidly expanding modern city in the northern Judean foothills. The IAA has accompanied the development of the city from its initial founding in the early 1990s through every subsequent stage of development. During 2015–2016 the IAA directed a large-scale archaeological project at Horvat Ashun and its environs prior to the development of a new neighborhood in the city. The project consisted of a surface survey, trial excavation and salvage excavations in an area of 1700 dunam deemed Compound P that included: two ancient settlements—Horvat Ashun and Horvat Hamutzav—farmsteads with strata from the early Hellenistic period to the late Roman period; the outskirts of two additional settlements—Berfilya and Wadi Annabeh North/11; as well as hundreds of additional ancient remains in the surrounding landscape (Tendler, 2022; Tendler & Elisha, 2017) (Figs. 9 and 10). These remains include burial caves (Tendler et al., 2019); quarries; wine presses; agricultural terraces, plots and roads; lime-kilns and more. Remains of flint mining and quarrying and tool knapping from the Pre-Pottery Neolithic A period were also researched in several areas. The varying types of fieldwork, plethora of finds and

Fig. 9 Aerial photograph of Modi'in Kh, Ashuna

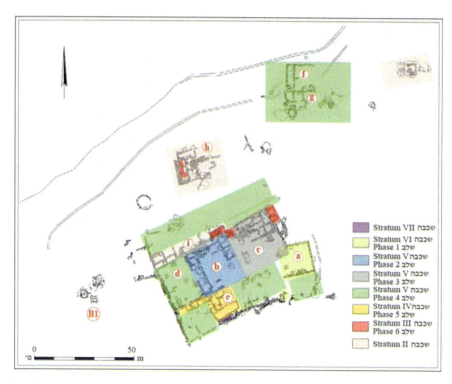

Fig. 10 Modi'in Kh. Ashuna excavation plan

numerous area supervisors presented a challenge in maintaining a uniform high level of documentation. This was accomplished by using the DANA system as described below.

All preparations for the excavation are done in a master file from which area files are exported and periodically imported. Every DANA file has eight main tabs: Sites, Areas, Loci, Baskets, Plans Photography, Diary, Units. Pertinent background information regarding the site, expedition, license, and collaborators is inserted in the Sites table A crucial preparatory stage executed in this tab is the creation of the excavation grid or grids depending on the type and size of the excavation. For example, in the excavation of the Modi'in P compound, areas within the ancient settlements used a standard grid of 5 × 5 meter squares, areas of landscape archaeology where unconnected agricultural installations were excavated used a grid of larger squares. Once the grid is created, geographically anchored by inserting the coordinates of the southwestern corner of the grid, and marked in the field, every subsequent submission of data: excavation areas, squares, features, loci, and baskets are georeferenced with precise coordinates.

The next tab used is the Areas tab where the excavation areas are designated. For each area the appropriate grid is chosen, and the area is marked on the grid using a polygon drawing tool. A bank of numbers for loci and baskets are allocated for each area.

At this stage area files can be exported for each area supervisor to work on independently. Periodically the excavation director can import the area files into the master file for review and backup.

The main tab used on the day-to-day basis is the Plans tab. The Plans tab is where every activity of the excavation is documented and where all the data originates. Each day a new page is opened showing the georeferenced excavation grid of the area and currently open loci. Here new loci are opened and automatically allocated available numbers from the area's bank. As soon as a locus is opened a locus type must be chosen, the options being: soil feature, wall, floor, installation, burial, and miscellaneous, each type has relevant subtypes. The locus must be drawn in the digital top-plan using available tools. Each drawing is automatically georeferenced. The stratigraphy and relationships of the locus are easily chosen from a drop-down list and the locus is described concisely. As finds are unearthed, baskets are opened and automatically allocated numbers from the bank. Basket types and subtypes are chosen using a drop-down menu. The location of the baskets can also be drawn in the digital top plan. Elevations are inserted for loci and baskets by pinpointing the location where the elevation was measured in the top plan. There are options for importing base layers, such as topographic maps or drafter's plans and the drawing the schematic top plan above the base layer. The daily diary can also be filled out within the Plans tab where the area supervisor can describe freely the developments in the excavation on that day.

The Photographs tab is also used on a daily basis, any graphic documentation—photographs, plans and sections from the excavation can be uploaded and tagged by loci or baskets and annotated.

The data from the Plans tab is drawn into the Loci and Baskets tabs where additional data regarding the loci and baskets can be filled in using guiding rubrics. Tagged photos, plans and sections are shown in their respective loci or baskets. Data from pottery reading can be submitted in a specific tab within the file alternatively a pottery file can be exported allowing the area supervisor and ceramicist to work simultaneously on separate computers. The Diary tab collects all the daily diary entries, any loci number entered is cross-referenced and can be searched for. As the excavation proceeds phases and units can be designated in the Units tab and loci are classified to units and phases.

The DANA system is useful in post excavation research to easily access information regarding the finds and their contexts. Excel worksheets can be exported for any type of find. They contain all the data collected up to that point and can be used as the basis for continued research.

3.2 Historic Cities: Jerusalem and Its Hinterland

The comprehensive archaeological research in Jerusalem, expressed in thousands of excavations conducted in and around the city from the 1850s to the present day provides the greatest challenge to the unified integration of archaeological and architectural sources. The knowledge of ancient Jerusalem is augmented by detailed archaeological and architectural surveys, which provided a huge database on the city's layout, its public buildings and monuments, streets, and residential areas. While early excavations focused on the study of major monuments, recent research yields reference to household archaeology, the urban necropolis, the agricultural hinterland, and the sophisticated water installations in and around the city. The exact number of archaeological excavations in Jerusalem since the beginning of modern research is debatable. The Israel Antiquities Authority archives contain some 1738 entries on excavations conducted in and around Jerusalem. The actual number, however, is probably far higher. Many "unofficial" or clandestine explorations were conducted in and within proximity to the city, mainly between the second half of the nineteenth century and the 1970s. Those, unfortunately, have not left any detailed written records. In addition, numerous occasional finds, which were not revealed during proper archaeological investigations, have been documented. It appears that the actual number of excavations conducted in and around the Old City of Jerusalem over the last 150 years comes much closer to 2350 single initiatives. The total area explored throughout those years is exceptional, with c. 30% of the ancient city excavated. Large-scale excavations were concentrated west and south of the Temple Mount – Haram al-Sharif, in the Jewish Quarter, and along the present-day city walls, (for summaries see NEAEHL V:1805-1839; Galor & Avni, 2011, Bieberstein & Bloedhorn, 1994; Küchler, 2007) and these were supplemented by hundreds of small-scale excavations and probes (Kloner, 2003). Particularly significant were the excavations south and west of the Temple Mount (Mazar, 1975; Ben Dov, 1985; Reich & Bilig, 2000; Baruch et al., 2018), in the Old City's Jewish Quarter (Avigad, 1983; Gutfeld, 2012), the City of David (Ben Ami & Tchekhanovets, 2020), and in the vast urban necropolis (Kloner & Zissu, 2007). In addition to excavations, hundreds of ancient buildings, most of them from Medieval and Early Modern times, have been surveyed and documented (Burgoyne, 1987. Hillenbrand, 2009; Auld et al., 2000), including the main religious monuments of Jerusalem – the Temple Mount – Haram al-Sharif (Grabar, 1996; Grabar & Kedar, 2009; Rosen Ayalon, 1989), and the Church of the Holy Sepulchre area (Corbo, 1981; Biddle, 1999; Vieweger & Gibson, 2016).

In addition to these major studies, hundreds of smaller scale rescue excavations have been conducted in and around Jerusalem in the past three decades and published in many venues. The preliminary reports of all excavations have been published in the IAA online journal *Excavations and Surveys in Israel* (http://www. hadashot-esi.org.il/default_eng.aspx), and the technical reports of all excavations are stored in the IAA archives (Matskevich & Weinblum, 2021).

Thus, Jerusalem and its surroundings provide a huge source of archaeological and architectural data, forming a major challenge in its representation on a GIS based database system. The incorporation of data from different sources: excavations, surveys, architectural surveys, archival data etc., which includes various sources of data, all used through one search engine, will provide a powerful research tool and will enable to address specific research questions in various fields.

For example, the accumulated data point toward an unprecedented urban expansion of the city in the Early Roman period (first century BC to 70 AD) and in Late Antiquity (between the fourth and the eighth centuries AD) (Bahat, 1996; Gafni et al., 2020; Tsafrir, 1999). New constructions expanded the urban area far beyond the city walls, especially to the north and east. This urban expansion persisted throughout most of the Early Islamic period and only in the tenth and eleventh centuries a considerable decline was noticed (Avni, 2014: 109–159 for a summary).

Yet, the situation in Jerusalem, as the main historical city that was explored in the region by hundreds of scholars and has very rich documentation from travelers and pilgrims' itineraries is very different from other ancient sites across the country, which were documented only sporadically, and archaeology provides the lion's share of available information. The data base gathered through excavations in Ramla provide a good example to the contribution of accumulative data from excavations to the documentation of the city.

3.3 Historic Cities: Early Islamic Ramla

The foundation of Ramla around 715 CE set the tone for a new concept in the urban architecture of Late Antique Palestine. While most large cities in the region were based on Hellenistic and Roman prototypes, Early Islamic Ramla was founded *ex nihilo* in an area surrounded by villages and farmsteads that formed the hinterland of Byzantine Lydda-Diospolis (Lod, Ludd). Unlike other historical cities, in which the ancient remains are visible in their present-day layout, the physical evidence of Early Islamic Ramla seems to have vanished into thin air. Except for two standing monuments, the White Mosque and Birkat al-ʿAnaziyya (the 'Pool of the Arches'), other remains of this large city are invisible, hidden under the buildings of the modern town. Thus, despite its leading position in Early Islamic Palestine, ancient Ramla remained *terra incognita* for archaeologists. Its invisibility is associated with the massive looting of building stones during the medieval and early modern periods. The ruins of the Early Islamic city provided an abundant supply of construction stones, which were taken to other sites in the coastal plain, leaving only the foundation trenches of walls as an indication of the building layouts. With this unfortunate situation, the study of ancient Ramla included at its first stage mainly the architectural analysis of its standing monuments, mainly the White Mosque and Birkat al-ʿAnaziyya (Kaplan, 1959; Rosen Ayalon, 1996; Luz, 1997 and see Petersen & Pringle, 2021 for an updated summary of the history and archaeology of Ramla).

This unpromising situation was dramatically changed in the 1990s, when, following an accelerated development in modern Ramla, scores of rescue excavations were conducted throughout and around the modern town. These revealed fragmentary remains of the hitherto invisible ancient city and provided substantial archaeological data for the reconstruction of its topographical layout and chronological sequence. The change in the archaeological exploration of Ramla is well represented by the number of excavations conducted in the last decades: only six between

1949 and 1990, and around 310 between 1990 and 2021, some of them extending over large areas and exposing continuous sequences of habitation. The main finds from the excavations relate to the Early Islamic city, between 715 and 1099.

The main problem in excavating Ramla is the poor state of preservation of architectural remains, due to massive looting of stones, and the randomly location of excavations, all connected to the modern development of the city. Thus, despite the large number of excavations, the reconstruction of architectural units poses considerable difficulties. The main features exposed in excavations are an exceptionally large number of industrial installations and water cisterns, which were embedded within the residential areas. The latter were better preserved, as they were dug into the ground, paved with stones and coated with plaster.

Under these circumstances, the need for a unified documentation system became crucial for an accurate reconstruction of the ancient urban layout. The introduction of DANA as a unified documentation system will enable the incorporation of the many small-scale excavations conducted in Ramla into one GIS based system which will enable of comparing excavations data from a defined areas which form the urban core and periphery of Early Islamic Ramla. This tool will enable a better reconstruction of the city's layout between the seventh and eleventh centuries.

3.4   Regional Data Bases: The Negev Highlands from Roman and Early Islamic Times

The formation of GIS archaeological databases of specific regions provide additional aspect of the integration of data from different sources. In this aspect, the Negev Highlands provide an excellent case study in a region that was comprehensively surveyed and excavated from the 1930s to the recent years. Following preliminary surveys in the early 1900s, the first steps of systematic excavations in the region were performed in when Shivta and Nessana were extensively excavated (Colt, 1962). Additional excavations were conducted at Shivta, `Avdat and Mamshit during the 1960s (Negev, 1986, 1988) (Mamshit); 1997 (Oboda). The next wave of excavations, conducted at Mamshit, Rehovot, `Avdat, and Nessana in the 1990s was only preliminarily published (Erickson-Gini, 2010; Tsafrir et al., 1988; Urman, 2004). These excavations exposed large segments of the settlements, concentrating on the public and religious buildings of churches and monasteries. In addition, the first systematic archaeological surveys in the Negev were conducted in the 1950s by Nelson Glueck and Emanuel Anati, who was sent by the Department of Antiquities to Explore the Negev under the request of the first Prime Minister of the State of Israel David Ben Gurion. (Anati, 1955; Glueck, 1959). The agricultural fields of the Negev Highlands were explored by an interdisciplinary team of Archaeologists and botanists, and their detailed studies provided an additional dimension to reconstructing the settlement picture and its chronological framework (Mayerson, 1960; Even Ari et al., 1982; Rubin, 1990; Avni et al., 2013). A new phase in the research of the Negev was initiated in 1979 with the Negev Emergency Survey, conducted for ten years following the Israeli-Egyptian peace treaty and the redeployment of the Israel army in the Negev. Approximately 1500 km^2. were systematically surveyed, revealing more than 10,000 sites from different periods. Hundreds of agricultural and pastoralist sites from Byzantine and Early Islamic times were discovered during the survey, creating the comprehensive picture of settlements hierarchy and diversity (Avni, 1996; Haiman, 1995). In addition to settlements, the Negev surveys documented the vast ancient agricultural systems in the Negev Highlands, which cover more than 30,000 hectares of cultivated plots dammed with stone-built terraces, alongside extensive channels designed for collecting run-off water from hillslopes and from occasional intensive floods in wadis (Even Ari et al. 1982; Rubin, 1990; Avni, 2014: 273–75 for a summary).

The data gathered in the excavations and surveys conducted in the Negev Highlands between the 1930s and the early 2000s provided a good basis for the current research, which is focused both on the impact of environmental questions on the Roman through Early Islamic settlements (e.g. Bar Oz et al., 2019; Tepper et al., 2020), on detailed excavations in the main sites (e.g. Tepper et al., 2018 in Shivta, Bucking and Erickson – Gini 2020 in Avdat, Schoene et al., 2019 in Elusa), and on comprehensive documentation of the large settlements and their agricultural hinterlands (Dahari & Sion, 2017 (Ruheibe), Sion & Israeli, 2021 (Mamshit), Sion & Rubin, 2020 (Sa'adon).

As in the excavation of a single site and in the incorporation of data from excavations in historic city, the comprehensive field work conducted in the Negev Highland in the past century requires the processing of these data through a unified data collecting system. The material from excavations and surveys, conducted by different expeditions and recorded in different systems, creates a challenge of different scale, calling for a unified search systems that will enable the incorporation of data from various sources which are not interconnected.

4 The Next Stage – Combining Digital Methods into a Unified Digital System

As stated above, the IAA has raised the flag of Digital Archaeology in its surveys and excavations, by ameliorating 'traditional' archaeological methods with state-of-the-art digital technologies and techniques. All traditional field registration (i.e. field diaries, basket and loci, pictures and graphic documentation, finds registration, archives, catalogues etc.), which have always been collected manually, are now recorded using the advanced DANA software; photogrammetry using aerial photography and remote sensing for creating 3D site models, top plans and sections, and orthophoto plans; 3D photo scanning of artefacts for illustrations and shape analyses;, and the implementation of advanced GIS-based analytical and statistical methods.

However, these different 'high-tech' technologies are operated and controlled on different platforms and are run by different experts within the IAA and as an outsourcing expertise. Processes and products are autonomous and are not interconnected. Moreover, we see very little involvement of the field archaeologists in the new processes. The next generation vision, which is currently in the course of implementation, aims to create a GIS-based platform, which will bring together these different technologies into a single, manageable, holistic system. This platform will collate, based on geographic space, all the different digital information available in a specific geographic location. It will enable the researcher not only to review the data at hand, but also to perform spatial and statistical analyses, and to create advanced displays of the results towards publication. This will maximize the benefits of each technology and technique, and will enable the creation of advanced, easy-to-access databases, for integrated analysis and research. Not less important, it will open up the boundaries between these technologies and the field archaeologist, providing access for researchers to the large database collected in archaeological excavations during the past century.

The next stage in the development of this national archaeological database system is the incorporation of the IAA data with other sources, such as the academic institutions in Israel and the National Library of Israel (NLI). A first step in combining digital databases is being done nowadays in the 'The Ronnie Ellenblum Jerusalem History Knowledge Center', a partnership between the Hebrew University of Jerusalem, the National Library of Israel, the Israel Antiquities Authority, and the Tower of David Museum of the History of Jerusalem (https://www.nli.org.il/he/at-your-service/who-we-are/projects/jerusalem-history-project). These institutions, all located in Jerusalem, provide a wide spectrum of various data sources. The center's vision is to unify the databases of all institutional partners and thus create a search environment that will enable users to find precise information, dependent on time and space. The center's products will eventually be available at two different levels: at the research level—the possibility of accessing different kinds of knowledge from multiple sources under one roof and in many cross-sections that answer specific research questions in the fields of history, archaeology, art, geography, social sciences, etc.—and at the popular level of the interested public: background material for educational activities, walking tours, 3D representations, etc.

With this long-term vision, the incorporation of the main sources of data collection on the archaeology, history and cultural heritage of Israel and the Holy land will be integrated into an overall big data search system at the national level. This will enable the 'trickle-down' process and the dissemination of Digital Humanities into the field of archaeology, creating a true 'Digital Archaeology' approach. Furthermore, it aims towards providing access to a large community of researchers and the wide public, in Israel and abroad, on a wide spectrum: from specifically designed research questions to the broad public interest in the cultural heritage of the Holy Land. Within this system, new opportunities will be provided for research and knowledge, serving the academic community and the wide public worldwide.

References

Alperson-Afil, N. (2019). Digitizing the undigitized: Converting traditional archaeological records into computerized, three-dimensional site reconstruction. *Journal of Geographic Information System, 11*(06), 747–765.

Anati, E. (1955). Ancient rock drawings in the Central Negev. *Palestine Exploration Quarterly, 1955*, 49–57.

Auld, S. R. Hillenbrand & Natshe, Y. (2000), *Ottoman Jerusalem, the living city 1517–1917*.

Avigad, N. (1983), *Discovering Jerusalem*.

Avni, G. (1996). *Nomads, farmers and town-dwellers: Pastoralist-Sedentist interaction in the Negev highlands, sixth-eighth centuries CE*. Israel Antiquities Authority.

Avni, G. (2014). *The byzantine Islamic transition, an archaeological approach*.

Avni, G., Porat, N., & Avni, Y. (2013). Byzantine–early Islamic agricultural systems in the Negev highlands: Stages of development as interpreted through OSL dating. *Journal of Field Archaeology, 38*, 332–346.

Bahat, D. (1996). The physical infrastructure. In J. Prawer & H. Ben-Shammai (Eds.), *The history of Jerusalem – The early Muslim period 638–1099* (pp. 38–100).

Bar-Oz, G., Weissbrod, L., Erickson-Gini, T., Tepper, Y., et al. (2019). Ancient trash mounds unravel urban collapse a century before the end of byzantine hegemony in the southern Levant. *Proceedings of the National Academy of Sciences*. www.pnas.org/cgi/doi/10.1073/pnas.1900233116

Baruch, Y., Reich, R., & Sandhaus, D. (2018). A decade of archaeological exploration on the Temple Mount. *Tel Aviv, 45*, 3–22.

Ben Ami, D. & Tchekhanovets, Y. (2020). *Excavations in the Tyropoeon Valley (Giv'ati parking lot) vol/ II: The byzantine and early Islamic periods*.

Ben Dov, M. (1985). *In the shadow of the temple – The discovery of ancient Jerusalem*.

Biddle, M. (1999). *The tomb of Christ*.

Bieberstein, K. & Bloedhorn, W. (1994). *Grundzüge der Baugeschichte vom Chalkolithikum bis zur Frühzeit der osmanischen Herrschaft*.

Birkenfeld, M., & Garfinkel, Y. (Eds.). (2020). *Digital archaeology: New research and advanced technologies. Collection of articles from a joint seminar day*. The Hebrew University of Jerusalem and the Israel Antiquities Authority.

Bucking, S., & Erickson-Gini, T. (2020). The Avdat in late antiquity project: Report on the 2012/2016 excavations of a cave and stone-built compound along the southern slope. *Journal of Eastern Mediterranean Archaeology and Heritage Studies, 8*, 22–57.

Burgoyne, M.H. (1987). *Mamluk Jerusalem, an architectural study*.

Colt, H. D. (1962). *Excavations at Nessana I*. British School of Archaeology in Jerusalem.

Corbo, V. (1981). *Il Santo Sepolcro de Gerusalemme*.

Corniello, L. (2020). Photogrammetric 3D information Systems for the management of models of cultural heritage. *The International Archives of Photogrammetry, Remote Sensing and Spatial Information Sciences, XLIV-4*(W1-2020), 11–18.

Dahari, & Sion. (2017). Ruheibe – Rehovot in the Negev as a model of a desert town. *Qadmoniot, 154*, 66–77. [Hebrew].

De Reu, J., De Smedt, P., Herremans, D., Van Meirvenne, M., Laloo, P., & De Clercq, W. (2014). On introducing an image-based 3d reconstruction method in archaeological excavation practice. *Journal of Archaeological Science, 41*, 251–262.

Doneus, M., Verhoeven, G., Fera, M., Briese, C., Kucera, M., & Neubauer, W. (2011). In A. Cepek (Ed.), *From deposit to point cloud: a study of low-cost computer vision approaches for the straightforward documentation of archaeological excavations* (pp. 81–88). 23rd International CIPA Symposium, 12–16 September 2011. Geoinformatics 6.

Douglass, M., Lin, S., & Chodoronek, M. (2015). The application of 3d photogrammetry for in-field documentation of archaeological features. *Advances in Archaeological Practice, 3*(2), 136–152.

Erickson-Gini, T. (2010). *Nabataean settlement and self organized economy in the Central Negev – Crisis and renewal*. BAR International Series 2054, Archaeopress.

Even, A., Shanan, M., & L. and Tadmor, N. (1982). *The Negev – The challenge of a desert*. Harvard University Press.

Field, S., Waite, M., & Wandsnider, L. A. (2017). The utility of UAVs for archaeological surface survey: A comparative study. *Journal of Archaeological Science: Reports, 13*, 577–582.

Fonstad, M. A., Dietrich, J. T., Courville, B. C., Jensen, J., & Carbonneau, P. (2013). Topographic structure from motion: A new development in photogrammetric measurement. *Earth Surface Processes and Landforms, 38*, 421–430.

Gafni, Y., Reich, R., & Schwartz, Y. (Eds.). (2020). *History of Jerusalem, the second temple period (332 BC – 70 CE)*. [Hebrew].

Galor, K. and G. Avni (eds.) (2011). *Unearthing Jerusalem – 150 years of archaeological research in the holy city* .

Glueck, N. (1959). *Rivers in the desert, an adventure in archaeology, exploration of the Negev*. Weidenfeld and Nicolson.

Grabar, O. (1996). *The shape of the holy – Early Islamic Jerusalem*

Grabar, O. & Kedar, B.Z. (2009). *Where heaven and earth meet: Jerusalem' sacred esplanade* (Jerusalem).

Gutfeld, O. (2012). *Jewish quarter excavations in the old city of Jerusalem Vol. V: The cardo (area X) and the Nea Church (Areas D and T)*. Final Report.

Haiman, M. (1995). Agriculture and nomad-state relations in the byzantine and early Islamic periods. *BASOR, 297*, 29–53.

Hillenbrand, H. & Auld, S. (2009). *Ayyubid Jerusalem – The holy city in context 1187–1250*.

Howland, M. D., Kuester, F., & Levy, T. E. (2014). Structure from motion: Twenty-first century field recording with 3d technology. *Near Eastern Archaeology, 77*(3), 187–191.

Jones, C. A., & Church, E. (2020). Photogrammetry is for everyone: Structure-from-motion software use experiences in archaeology. *Journal of Archaeological Science: Reports, 30*, 1–10.

Kaplan, J. (1959). Excavations at the White Mosque in Ramla. *'Atiqot, 2*, 106–115.

Kjellman, E. (2012). *From 2D to 3D: A photogrammetric revolution in archaeology? Master's dissertation*. University of Tromsø. At: https://munin.uit.no/handle/10037/4306. Accessed on 6 July 2021.

Kloner, A. (2003). Archaeological survey of Israel, survey of Jerusalem – The northwestern sector. *Introduction and Indices*.

Kloner, A. & Zissu, B. (2007). *The necropolis of Jerusalem in the second temple period*.

Küchler, M. (2007). *Jerusalem: Ein Handbuch der Studienreiseführer zur heiligen Stadt*.

Levy, T., Brady, L., Yoo, H. J., Liritzis, I., & Burton, M. (2022). From the field to the CAVE: A workflow for collecting, storing, and sharing archaeological data. In N. Lercari, W. Wendrich, B. W. Porter, M. M. Burton, & T. E. Levy (Eds.), *Preserving cultural heritage in the digital age – Sending out an S.O.S*. Equinox eBooks.

Luz, N. (1997). The construction of an Islamic city in Palestine: The case of Ummayad al-Ramla. *Jornal of the Royal Asiatic Society, 37*, 27–54.

Magnani, M., Douglass, M., Schroder, W., Reeves, J., & Braun, D. (2020). The digital revolution to come: Photogrammetry in archaeological practice. *American Antiquity, 85*(4), 737–760.

Matskevich, S., & Weinblum, L. (2021). Digital archaeological archiving in Israel. *Internet Archaeology, 58*. https://doi.org/10.11141/ia.58.10

Mayerson, P. (1960). *The ancient agricultural regime of Nessana and the Central Negev*. British School of Archaeology in Jerusalem.

Mazar, B. (1975). *The mountain of the Lord*.

Münger, S., & Weinblum, L. (2022). The archaeological documentation system Dana (digital archaeology and national archives): A view from the field. In Material, method, and meaning. Papers in eastern Mediterranean archaeology in honor of Ilan Sharon, U. Davidovich, S. Matskevich, N. Yahalom-Mack. Zaphon., 85–97

Muñoz-Nieto, A., Rodríguez-Gonzálvez, P., González-Aguilera, D., Fernández-Hernández, J., Gómez-Lahoz, J., Picón-Cabrera, J., Herrero-Pascual, J., & Hernández-López, D. (2014). UAV archaeological reconstruction: The case study of Chamartin Hillfort (Avila, Spain). *ISPRS Annals of the Photogrammetry, Remote Sensing and Spatial Information Sciences, II-5,* 259–265.

NEAEHL: *New Encyclopedia of Archaeological Excavations in the Holy Land,* vol 1–4 (Jerusalem, 1993); vol. 5 (Jerusalem).

Negev, A. (1986). *Nabatean archaeology today*. University Press.

Negev, A. (1988). *The architecture of Mampsis, final report II: The Late Roman and Byzantine Periods* (Qedem 27). Hebrew University, the Institute of Archaeology.

Negev, A. (1997). *The architecture of Oboda: Final report* (Qedem 36). Hebrew University, the Institute of Archaeology.

Nikolakopoulos, K. G., Soura, K., Koukouvelas, I. K., & Argyropoulos, N. G. (2017). UAV vs classical aerial photogrammetry for archaeological studies. *Journal of Archaeological Science: Reports, 14,* 758–773.

Petersen, A., & Pringle, D. (2021). *Ramla – City of Muslim Palestine 715–1917*. Archaeopress.

Prins, A. B. (2016). *3D modeling for archaeological documentation: Using the JVRP method to record archaeological excavations with millimeter-accuracy*. JVRP White Papers in Archaeological Technology. http://www.jezreelvalleyregionalproject.com/3d-modeling.html. Accessed on 18 Dec 2016

Quartermaine, J., Olson, B. R., & Killebrew, A. E. (2014). Image-based modeling approaches to 2d and 3d digital drafting in archaeology at Tel Akko and Qasrin two case studies. *Journal of Eastern Mediterranean Archaeology & Heritage Studies, 2*(2), 110–127.

Reich, R., & Billig, Y. (2000). Excavations near the Temple Mount and Robinson Arch, 1994–1996. In H. Geva (Ed.), *Ancient Jerusalem revealed* (pp. 340–352).

Rosen-Ayalon, M. (1989). *The early Islamic monuments of al-Haram al-Sharīf. An iconographic study* (Qedem 28). Hebrew University, the Institute of Archaeology.

Rosen-Ayalon, M. (1996). The first century of Ramla. *Arabica, 43,* 250–263.

Rubin, R. (1990). *The Negev as settled land – Urbanisation and settlement in the desert in the byzantine period*. Yad Ben Zvi [Hebrew].

Savage, S. H., & Levy, T. (2014a). The Mediterranean archaeological network – A cyberinfrastructure for archaeological heritage management. *Mediterranean Archaeology and Archaeometry, 14,* 135–141.

Savage, S. H., & Levy, T. (2014b). DAAHL – The digital archaeology atlas of the holy land: A model for Mediterranean and world archaeology. *Near Eastern Archaeology, 77,* 247–253.

Schone, C., Heinzelamn, M., Erickson-Gini, T., & Woznik, D. (2019). Elusa-urban development and economy of a city in the desert, in Achim Lichtenberger. In O. Tal & Z. Weiss (Eds.), *Judaea/Palaestina and Arabia: Cities and hinterlands in Roman and Byzantine Times. Panel 8.6* (Proceedings of the 19th International Congress of Classical Archaeology. Vol. 44. Cologne/Bonn, 22–26 May 2018) (pp. 141–154). University of Cologne.

Sion, O., & Israeli, S. (2021). Mamshit (Mampsis) – A new survey and discoveries in the city and its environs. In *Archaeological excavations and research studies in Southern Israel – Collected Papers 4* (pp. 65–79). Israel Antiquities Authority.

Sion, O., & Rubin, R. (2020). Ḥorvat Sa'adon and its environs: A large settlement, satellite settlements and agricultural systems in the Negev in antiquity. *Strata-Bulletin of the Anglo-Israel Archaeological Society, 38,* 125–177.

Tendler, A. S. (2022). Hellenistic hip baths in Hasmonean farmsteads. In G. D. Stiebel, D. Ben-Ami, A. Gorzalczany, Y. Tepper, & I. Koch (Eds.), *In Centrum I* (pp. 37–49). Tel Aviv.

Tendler, A. S., & Elisha, Y. (2017). Modi'in, Horbat Ashun. *Hadashot Arkheologiyot – Excavations and Surveys in Israel, 129.* http://www.hadashot-esi.org.il/Report_Detail_Eng.aspx?id=25350&mag_id=125

Tendler, A. S., Terem, S., & Eshed, V. (2019). Typical and atypical burial from the late Hellenistic-early Roman period at Horvat Ashun-Modi'in hills. In A. Tavger & Z. Amar (Eds.), *In the highland's depth 9* (pp. 14–40). Ariel.

Tepper, Y., Porat, N., & Bar Oz, G. (2020). Sustainable farming in the Roman-Byzantine period: Dating an advanced agriculture system near the site of Shivta. *Negev Desert, Israel, Journal of rid Environments*. https://doi.org/10.1016/j.jaridenv.2020.10413

Tsafrir, Y. (1999). The topography and archaeology of Jerusalem in the Byzantine period. In Y. Tsafrir & S. Safrai (Eds.), *The history of Jerusalem – The Roman and Byzantine periods (70–638 CE)* (pp. 281–352). [Hebrew].

Tsafrir, Y., & Holum, K. (1988). Rehovot in the Negev preliminary report 1986. *IEJ, 38*, 117–127.

Tsafrir, Y., Patrich, J., & Rosenthal-Heginbottom, R. (1988). *Excavations at Rehovot in the Negev I: The Northern Church* (Qedem 25). Hebrew University, Institute of Archaeology.

Urman, D. (2004). *Nessana I: Excavations and studies (Beer Sheva 17)*. Ben Gurion University Press.

Vieweger, D. & Gibson, S. (2016). *The archaeology and history of the Church of the redeemer and the Muristan in Jerusalem.*

Waagen, J. (2019). New technology and archaeological practice. Improving the primary archaeological recording process in excavation by means of UAS photogrammetry. *Journal of Archaeological Science, 101*, 11–20.

Westoby, M. J., Brasington, J., Glasser, N. F., Hambrey, M. J., & Reynolds, J. M. (2012). Structure-from-motion' photogrammetry: A low-cost, effective tool for geoscience applications. *Geomorphology, 179*, 300–314.

Wiegmann, A. (2016). *The application of photogrammetry in archaeology in the Jerusalem district.* Art & Archaeology 2016: 2nd International Conference, December 11–14, 2016, Jerusalem, Israel. At: https://art2016.isas.co.il/wp-content/uploads/sites/10/2017/03/Session-VIII-Digital-Imaging-and-Sites-3-Wiegmann.pdf. Accessed on 6 July 2021

Wiegmann, A. (2020). In M. Birkenfeld & Y. Garfinkel (Eds.), *Photogrammetric documentation at the salvage excavations of the Israel antiquities authority* (Digital Archaeology Conference, Hebrew University at Jerusalem, 16/5/2019) (pp. 17–28) (Hebrew).

Wilson, C. W., & Conder, C. R. (1890). *Palestine from the surveys conducted for the Committee of the Palestine Exploration Fund and other sources.* Palestine Exploration Fund.

Photogrammetric and GIS-Based Modeling of Rapid Sediment Erosion and Deposition on the Taskscape of Bronze Age Politiko-*Troullia*, Cyprus

Elizabeth Ridder (iD)**, Patricia L. Fall** (iD)**, and Steven E. Falconer** (iD)

Abstract A major strength of Tom Levy's archaeological research is its capacity to make us think about the archaeological past through a lens of creative non-traditional concepts. Accordingly, we explore Politiko-*Troullia*, Cyprus from an array of analytical perspectives that illuminate this locality amid its dynamic natural and social landscapes. We expand the definition of Politiko-*Troullia*'s Bronze Age community to encompass a broader stage for human behavior that stretched beyond the excavated settlement to include its surrounding terraced hillsides, which witnessed intense agrarian and metallurgical activities revealed by geographical modeling. We utilize drone aerial photography and artistic depiction to convey Politiko-*Troullia*'s setting in keeping with this expanded concept. Architectural shifts linked with Bayesian modeling of calibrated radiocarbon ages document community responses to local erosion, including downcutting of Kamaras Creek just after ~2000 cal BCE. Photogrammetric and GIS-based modeling allows us to conceptualize and quantify the erosion and deposition of archaeological and alluvial sediments at and around Politiko-*Troullia*. In general terms, these new insights help us explain the substantial and rapid sediment deposition in some parts of this settlement (>3 m,

---

Supplementary Information The online version contains supplementary material available at https://doi.org/10.1007/978-3-031-27330-8_68.

E. Ridder (✉)
Department of Liberal Studies, California State University San Marcos,
San Marcos, CA, USA
e-mail: eridder@csusm.edu

P. L. Fall
Department of Geography and Earth Sciences, University of North Carolina at Charlotte,
Charlotte, NC, USA
e-mail: pfall@uncc.edu

S. E. Falconer
Department of Anthropology, University of North Carolina at Charlotte, Charlotte, NC, USA
e-mail: sfalcon1@uncc.edu

© The Author(s), under exclusive license to Springer Nature Switzerland AG 2023
E. Ben-Yosef, I. W. N. Jones (eds.), *"And in Length of Days Understanding" (Job 12:12): Essays on Archaeology in the Eastern Mediterranean and Beyond in Honor of Thomas E. Levy*, Interdisciplinary Contributions to Archaeology,
https://doi.org/10.1007/978-3-031-27330-8_68

which is unusually deep for Cyprus). More specifically, our modeling quantifies the stages in Politiko-*Troullia*'s fast-paced record of founding, substantial architectural reconstructions, and abandonment, including a major architectural displacement about 2000 cal BCE. Our multi-faceted investigation of Politiko-*Troullia*'s natural and social landscape dynamics reflects the broadened analytical perspectives through which Tom Levy has enhanced scientifically-based archaeological exploration of our human heritage.

Keywords Taskscape · 14C chronology · Bayesian modeling · Photogrammetry · Erosion risk modeling · Politiko-*Troullia* · Cyprus

1 Introduction

Tom Levy's career is marked by his innovative application of emerging technologies to ask and answer an enhanced array of scientifically informed archaeological questions. In the course of these inquiries, he has challenged the traditional definition of archaeological "sites" and encouraged behavioral interpretation expanded in space, time, and most recently under the sea, in a manner bringing together landscape and society, deep history and tomorrow's technology (e.g., Ben-Yosef et al., 2019; Di Chiara et al., 2021; Levy, 1995; Levy & Jones, 2018; Milevski & Levy, 2016; Yasur-Landau et al., 2021). This paper applies this expanded analytical perspective to the locality of Politiko-*Troullia*, Cyprus to illuminate a broadened life history of this Bronze Age community as it was ensconced in dynamic local social, economic and natural landscapes. This study synthesizes our continuing exploration of the evidence from Politiko-*Troullia* through the use of field and laboratory analytical methods extending beyond time-honored survey and excavation. Integration of soil resistivity, Bayesian radiocarbon modeling, drone aerial photography, satellite imagery, and predictive modeling of agricultural terraces enable us to portray Politiko-*Troullia*, not just as an archaeological site, but in terms of an expanded, behaviorally more complex "taskscape." Tom's co-authored quantification of erosion at Khirbat Nuqayb al-Asaymir, Jordan (Howland et al., 2018) inspires the most recent facet of our investigations, in which we combine low-altitude drone photography and Structure from Motion photogrammetric image-based modeling to create spatially-referenced orthophotos and a digital elevation model to portray and quantify spatial and temporal variability in erosion and archaeological sedimentation as fundamentally important formative components of the Bronze Age landscape of Politiko-*Troullia*.

2 Study Area

Politiko-*Troullia* lies in the foothills of the Troodos Mountains at the interface of the fertile Mesaoria Plain to the north and copper-bearing pillow lavas to the southwest (Fig. 1), which provide readily accessible eroded exposures of the Troodos ophiolite containing some of the highest quality copper in the world. Village remains lie buried in alluvial and colluvial sediments on a terrace between the Pediaios River to the east and Kamaras Creek to the west (Fall et al., 2008). Perennial springs, today less than 1 km to the south of Politiko-*Troullia* (and presumably adjacent to *Troullia* West during the Bronze Age) provided a readily accessible water source for the village's inhabitants, with streamflow that eroded the banks of Kamaras Creek and the structures along the western edge of the village of *Troullia*. Thus, interpretation of this community must consider its situation on a geomorphologically dynamic landscape with access to both agricultural and mineral resources.

The local archaeological footprint includes material culture (potsherds, ground stone, and ceramic roof tiles) spread over about 20 ha across the fields of *Troullia* and the adjacent slopes of Politiko-*Koloiokremmos* (Fig. 2). Concentrated domestic refuse, accompanied by patterns of buried architecture revealed by soil resistivity, define the main component of Bronze Age village structures covering at least 2 ha on Politiko-*Troullia* (Falconer et al., 2005). Immediately to the south, widespread surface ceramics and ground stone artifacts associated with extensive agricultural terracing on the slopes of *Koloiokremmos* reflect intensive premodern management of the local landscape, including agricultural and copper ore processing (see Fig. 2; Fall et al., 2012; Galletti et al., 2013; Ridder et al., 2017). Spatial analysis of these

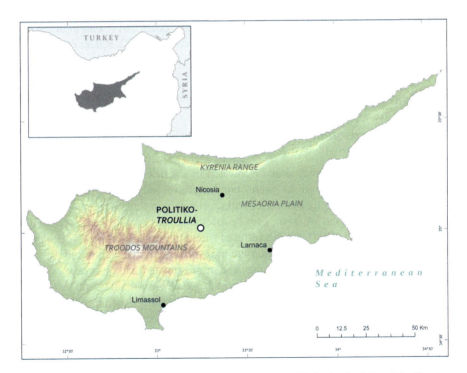

Fig. 1 Map of Cyprus showing the location of Politiko-*Troullia* in the foothills of the Troodos Mountains, along with an inset of Cyprus in the eastern Mediterranean

Fig. 2 (**a**) Map of Politiko-*Troullia* and *Koloiokremmos* overlain on a Quickbird satellite image with vegetation shown in false color (north to top of image). The local taskscape between the Pediaios River on the east and Kamaras Creek on the west is marked by the distribution of archaeological artifacts across the surface of Fields 1–4 (bounded with white lines) plus the area outlined in black, totaling roughly 20 ha. Excavation areas are depicted as yellow squares. (**b**) Drone aerial photograph looking southwest across agricultural terraces on Politiko-*Koloiokremmos* and the fields of Politiko-*Troullia* East, West and North in which the Bronze Age settlement is buried. The Troodos Mountains appear in the distance

agrarian features in conjunction with rich evidence of excavated seeds, charcoal and animal bones, document a mixed subsistence regime of grape and olive arboriculture, sheep/goat and cattle husbandry, plus hunting of wild deer and feral pigs on the verge of oak and pine woodlands (Falconer & Fall, 2013, 2014; Fall et al., 2015; Klinge & Fall, 2010; Metzger et al., 2021; Pilaar Birch et al., 2022; Ridder et al., 2017).

3 Field Investigations

3.1 Site Excavation

Politiko-*Troullia* was surveyed and excavated in a series of field seasons between 2004 and 2015. Excavations were conducted in varying configurations of 4 × 4 m units separated by one-meter balks, primarily in three portions of the site: *Troullia* East, North and West (see Fig. 2). Additional single units were excavated in Area L (near *Troullia* East) and in a series of soundings on Politiko-*Koloiokremmos*. All of these units were positioned on the basis of buried architecture indicated by exposed remains or subsurface sensing. The most extensive excavations at Politiko-*Troullia* involved a matrix of 4 × 4 m units in *Troullia* West (totaling 360 m^2), which were situated where soil resistivity revealed lengthy patterns of buried stone wall alignments (Falconer et al., 2005). The excavation squares of *Troullia* East (covering 142 m^2) were positioned over a particularly clear soil resistivity image of a subsurface cluster of structures. Excavations in *Troullia* North (81 m^2) were positioned near buried stone walls exposed by erosion along the site's edges. All sediments showing evidence of charred organic content were processed using manual, non-mechanized water flotation to recover carbonized seeds and charcoal (Fall et al., 2015; Klinge, 2013; Klinge & Fall, 2010). These remains provide crucial evidence of agricultural practices and local vegetation, as well as samples for AMS radiocarbon dating.

3.2 Landscape Survey

The interpretive context for the Bronze Age village of Politiko-*Troullia* may be expanded beyond a traditional archaeological "site" to encompass a roughly 20 ha extramural "taskscape." In keeping with its original definition (Ingold, 1993), we use this term to conceptualize an archaeological landscape defined by evidence for an array of social and economic activities. The north-facing slopes of Politiko-*Koloiokremmos* are traversed with numerous multi-course walls made from limestone blocks and igneous river cobbles (see Fig. 2). In order to assess this taskscape, a series of pedestrian surveys mapped the terrace system of *Koloiokremmos* and sampled the surface material culture in an array of collection circles with 2-meter radii over about 12 ha in Fields 1–4 on *Troullia* and *Koloiokremmos* (Fall et al., 2012). The resulting point data permit us to interpolate material culture densities between collection circles and thereby create continuous density surfaces over this terraced taskscape (Ridder et al., 2017). Expanding further, we developed a predictive model for modern and ancient terrace location based on environmental variables over a more extensive area covering about 25 km^2 surrounding *Troullia* and *Koloiokremmos* (Galletti et al., 2013).

The most detailed element in our landscape survey involved aerial photography of the landscapes of Politiko-*Troullia* and *Koloiokremmos* covering approximately 16 ha, which was taken with a DJI Phantom 3 unmanned aerial vehicle (UAV). The coordinates for an array of ground control points were utilized to geo-rectify and geo-reference these photographs, which were then aligned using Agisoft Metashape Professional 1.7 software (Agisoft, 2021). A high-resolution digital elevation model (DEM) created from these aerial photographs enables us to portray and quantify patterns of potential erosion and deposition that periodically remolded local *Troullia/Koloiokremmos* landforms, thereby enabling more comprehensive interpretation of the Politiko-*Troullia* taskscape.

3.3 Photogrammetry

UAV aerial image acquisition focused on the excavation areas in *Troullia* North and West and on *Koloiokremmos* in 2015, and over their surrounding taskscape in 2016. Nadir images were captured at 30 m above ground surface approximately every 30 s, resulting in ca. 65–70% overlap within and between flight lines. Images were corrected for lens distortion before use in Metashape. Ground control points were established by placing highly-visible black and white targets across the 20 ha task-scape, and target center coordinates were recorded with a Juniper Systems Archer 2. Ground control data were corrected to ca. 0.5 m using International GNSS Service ground tracking station data for Nicosia, Cyprus (Station ID: NICO00CYP) (Johnston et al., 2017).

4 Analytical Methods

4.1 Chronology

The occupational chronology for Politiko-*Troullia* is based on AMS ^{14}C ages for 25 excavated carbonized plant remains that have been calibrated using OxCal 4.4.4 (Bronk Ramsey, 2009a) and the IntCal20 atmospheric curve (Reimer et al., 2020; van der Plicht et al., 2020). The analytical tools in OxCal 4.4.4 were used for Bayesian modeling of the calibrated dates. Bayesian analysis permits probabilistic modeling of calibrated ^{14}C determinations using prior stratigraphic information, and can accommodate the non-normally distributed probabilities of calibrated ^{14}C ages (Bronk Ramsey, 2009a). Agreement values (A, A_{model}) may be used to assess the reliability of the individual calibrated ages in Bayesian models and the quality of overall models. Values of A calculate the overlap of the non-modeled distribution for each calibrated age with its Bayesian modeled distribution. Values of $A > 60$ approximate values of $p < 0.05$ for a χ^2 significance test (Manning, 2013: 496, fig. A5). We use values of $A_{model} > 60$ to identify statistically robust Bayesian models, and we treat calibrated ages with $A \leq 60$ as statistical outliers, which we exclude from our Bayesian modeling (Bronk Ramsey, 2009b). The radiocarbon ages from Politiko-*Troullia* were organized for modeling according to stratigraphic phases and in chronological order within phases, based on their uncalibrated AMS determinations. Our Bayesian analysis models 25 calibrated radiocarbon ages in six contiguous phases of occupation, beginning with Phase 5 and ending with Phase 1a. Our optimal model (producing the highest A_{model}) is structured primarily by the stratigraphy of Politiko-*Troullia* West and also incorporates ages from *Troullia* East and North in Phase 1b and a single age from *Troullia* North in Phase 2 (Falconer et al., 2022).

4.2 Point Cloud, 3-D Mesh and Orthophoto Construction

Aerial photos were loaded into Metashape in a single processing group and converted from the UAV geographic reference system (latitude/longitude) into the WGS 1984 UTM Zone 36N projected coordinate system. The Metashape photo quality tool identified poorly focused images, and any images with results below 0.5

were removed from the workspace. The remaining well-focused images were aligned using the imported photo camera location data and Metashape default settings. Images that could not be aligned were reset, and alignment was reattempted for these photos. Images that did not align a second time were removed from the workspace, resulting in 1328 images suitable for further processing. The default Metashape workflow was used to construct a dense point cloud, a 3-D mesh and a 1.5 cm resolution orthophoto. Ground control point coordinates were added to Metashape to align the coordinate markers to the target centers visible within the orthophoto. The resulting 3-D model's spatial error was reported as 5.5 m, which is the root mean square error between the ground control coordinates and their locations in the model. The Metashape animation tool was used to create a fly-through view of the 3-D model (see Supplementary Video 1). The dense point cloud and orthophoto were exported for further processing and visualization in ArcGIS Pro 2.9.

The points comprising the dense point cloud were classified as representing ground, and low, medium and high vegetation. Ground classification was completed in two iterations, with the first iteration using the default settings in the Classify LAS Ground tool. The second iteration detected ground surfaces using the aggressive classification setting and reusing the existing ground classification to capture surfaces in areas of steep topography. The classified ground points were converted into a 0.05 m resolution digital elevation model (DEM) using the binning average produced by natural neighbor interpolation. Vegetation categories were based on point height above ground surface: low vegetation ≤ 0.5 m, medium vegetation >0.5 to 5 m, high vegetation >5 m.

4.3 Erosion Risk Modeling

Long-term annual soil loss was quantified following methods outlined in Howland et al. (2018), with modified parameters to characterize Politiko-*Troullia*'s landscape. Soil loss is often calculated using the Revised Universal Soil Equation (RUSLE), a plot-scale empirical model first developed by Wischmeier and Smith (1978) to estimate rainfall-caused soil erosion risk for agricultural lands in the United States. The revised model incorporates methods to estimate the impacts of ground cover and farming practices, the influence of topography, and soil conservation strategies, such as terracing (Renard & Friemund, 1994; Renard et al., 1997). Our application modifies the approach in Howland et al. (2018) to investigate the factors that created the spatial patterning of deposition at Politiko-*Troullia*, in particular the unusually deep sedimentation (>3 m) in *Troullia* West. Although RUSLE cannot be utilized to estimate deposition locations or rates of deposition, it provides estimates of erosion risk (in terms of annual rates of erosion over time), which combined with surface hydrology analysis, can identify potential sediment sources and rainfall driven downslope pathways.

The RUSLE model is easy to implement in GIS environments and the required data can be implemented in raster format to illustrate variation of each variable across a site, rather than providing a summary value for each variable across the full plot. The flexibility of the RUSLE model permits the use of data of various spatial extents to characterize soil loss (Howland et al., 2018). RULSE is defined as:

$$A = R \times K \times LS \times C \times P \tag{1}$$

where A is mean annual soil loss in tonnes/hectare/year. R is the rainfall erosivity factor, which describes rainfall effects on soil erosion; K is the soil erodibility factor, which accounts for soil composition and texture, and a slope's resulting susceptibility to erosion; LS includes the slope length (L) and steepness (S) factors, which integrate the influence of local topography; C is the cover and management factor, which accounts for vegetation cover; and P is the support practice factor, which reflects the influence of soil conservation practices.

4.3.1 RUSLE Variable Specification

The rainfall erosivity factor (R) is one of the few variables requiring data that are often not available at the plot or finer scale because it is calculated from long-term records of storm energy and 30-min storm intensity (Renard et al., 1997). Various methods are used to address this common issue (see Benavidez et al., 2018 for a review). Renard and Freimund (1994: 299) describe an R factor equation for locations with mean annual precipitation less than 850 mm in which $R = 0.0483 \times P^{1.610}$. In this equation, P is annual precipitation, which we derived as a site-wide constant of 468 mm from WorldClim 1.4 30-arcsecond average annual precipitation for 1960–1990 (Hijmans et al., 2005). Use of this value for P results in an R factor of 37.2276 (unitless). The K factor, which measures soil erodibility, is based on soil loss on a 22.1 m × 1.83 m RUSLE plot with a slope of 9%. Wischmeier and Smith (1978) and Renard et al. (1997) derived an equation to approximate soil nomograph variables, which incorporates soil texture and structure, organic matter (%), and permeability. Because the percentages of very fine sand and organic matter are not available for Politiko-*Troullia*, we utilized a modified approximation (Sharpley & Williams, 1990: 26), which uses estimated percentages of sand, silt, clay, and organic carbon (OC).

$$K = \left[0.2 + 0.3 \exp\left(-0.0256 \times sand \times \left(1 - \frac{silt}{100} \right) \right) \times \left(\frac{silt}{clay + silt} \right)^{0.3} \right.$$
$$\left. \times \left(1 - \frac{0.25 \times OC}{OC + \exp(3.72 - 2.95OC)} \right) \times \left(1 - \frac{0.7 \times SN}{SN + \exp(-5.51 + 22.9SN)} \right) \right]$$

$$SN = 1 - \left(\frac{sand}{100}\right) \tag{2}$$

The 2007 field season (Fall et al., 2008) included a detailed geological assessment of the Politiko-*Troullia* locality, which defined the soils as poorly drained silt and clay parent materials. Subsequent excavation and field surveys led to the determination of *Troullia*'s soil composition as 29% clay, 53% silt, 18% sand, and 9.5% organic content, aligning with nearby 2009/2012 and 2015 Land Use and Coverage Area frame Survey (LUCAS) topsoil data (Jones et al., 2020; Tóth et al., 2013). The closest LUCAS survey points are in Politiko village (sample ID 31069), approximately 1.5 km north of Politiko-*Troullia*, and just south of the Tamassos Reservoir (sample ID 64301648), approximately 1.3 km south of *Troullia* (Table 1). Calculation of the K factor using Eq. 2 produced a site-wide value of 0.35895 (unitless). The LS factor was derived following the methodology in Howland et al. (2018) using the raster calculator, according to Eq. 3, which produced pixel-by-pixel estimates of the LS factor across the locality. To derive the LS factor variables, the 0.05 m resolution DEM was sink filled, whereby gaps in data and anomalous depressions are estimated from the surrounding pixels. The filled DEM was used to create a percent rise slope surface, using the surface parameters tool, with the adaptive neighborhood option selected. Flow direction was then determined for each pixel based on its steepest downslope neighbor. The final surface, indicating flow length, uses the flow direction raster to calculate flow path distances. Following Howland et al. (2018), the slope surface was reclassified into categories based on slope (Wischmeier & Smith, 1978), which represents the m-factor required in the calculation of the LS variable according to the following equation:

$$LS = \left(\frac{65.41 \times s^2}{s^2 + 10{,}000} + \frac{4.56 \times s}{\sqrt{s^2 + 10{,}000}} + 0.065\right)\left(\frac{l}{72.5}\right)^m \tag{3}$$

where s = slope, l = flow length, and m = slope category. The final two factors, C and P, relate to land cover and land use practices, respectively.

During the Bronze Age occupation of Politiko-*Troullia*, the hillslopes and terraces of *Koloiokremmos* were utilized for a variety of agrarian and social activities (Ridder et al., 2017), including crop cultivation that has continued to the present. Values of C are often determined using satellite imagery to derive the Normalized Difference Vegetation Index (NDVI) for each pixel in the study area, which

Table 1 Soil composition for Politiko-*Troullia*, and two nearby LUCAS Topsoil Survey sites. The soil composition is used to calculate the site-wide K factor

Location	Clay (%)	Silt (%)	Sand (%)	Organic content (%)
Politiko-*Troullia*	29	53	18	9.5
Politiko village	32	53	15	13.8
Tamassos Reservoir	25	53	22	5.3

establishes modern land cover that may differ from that of past landscapes. Analysis of excavated archaeobotanical evidence shows that the villagers of Politiko-*Troullia* cultivated wheat, barley, and olive, while pine and oak woodlands grew on nearby hillslopes (Fall et al., 2015; Klinge, 2013; Klinge & Fall, 2010). Hypothetical land cover surfaces can be derived based on this information and published *C* factors (see Benavidez et al., 2018) to investigate the various ways land cover influences water movement at *Troullia*. We used a *C* factor of 0.2, based on published *C* factors for various agricultural covers in Europe, including barley, spelt and wheat varieties (Panagos et al., 2015). The slope surface was used to derive a pixel-by-pixel *P* factor for bench terracing (David, 1988, as cited in Benavidez et al., 2018). Equation 4 summarizes the RUSLE equation for Politiko-*Troullia* and *Koloiokremmos*.

$$A = 37.2276 \times 0.86951 \times LS \times 0.2 \times P \tag{4}$$

Based on the methods above, mean annual soil loss was classified into soil erosion risk categories (based on Farhan et al., 2013 as cited in Howland et al., 2018) (Table 2).

4.4 Surface Hydrology Analysis

The hydrology toolset in ArcGIS Pro was used to identify courses of potential surface waterflow. The flow direction raster created to calculate *LS* was used as the input data for the flow accumulation tool, which calculates the number of cells that flow into each pixel in the surface. The resulting surface was then thresholded to select cells above a specific accumulation total. This threshold varied depending on the raster resolution and the topography from which the flow direction data were derived; it also attempts to differentiate channel flow from hillslope flow. Links between the remaining network of cells were constructed, and the stream order was classified using the Strahler method. The stream network was vectorized using the stream to feature tool, which retains the directionality of the stream network.

Table 2 Sediment loss risk categorization (Farhan et al., 2013 as cited in Howland et al., 2018)

Sediment loss risk (tonnes/ha/year)	
Minimal	0–5
Low	6–15
Moderate	16–25
Severe	26–50
Extreme	>50

5 Results and Discussion

5.1 Settlement Dynamics at Politiko-Troullia

The architecture excavated in *Troullia* West is comprised of six stratified phases of deposition measuring up to 3.30 m deep (Phases 5–1a, from earliest to latest) (Falconer & Fall, 2013, 2014; Falconer et al., 2012, 2014). The major architectural spaces in *Troullia* West feature two large rectangular open courtyards, which are bounded by a 2 m wide alley to the south (Fig. 3). The alley, which descended to the waters of Kamaras Creek, was filled with layer upon layer of household refuse consisting of well-trodden animal bones, burned seeds and charcoal, and small, presumably inadvertently deposited personal items (e.g., beads). The earliest phase in *Troullia* West (Phase 5) includes the lowermost sediments in the alley, which are stratified below the alley walls and represent the earliest archaeological sediments at Politiko-*Troullia*. In subsequent Phase 4, the courtyards were constructed with adjoining rooms on the west, all situated just upslope from Kamaras Creek. Some walls and doorways were modified slightly in Phase 3, while the architecture largely retained its alignments. The Phase 4 and 3 village also utilized a well dug in *Troullia* West just off Kamaras Creek that provided a more protected, less trash-afflicted means of obtaining drinking water (Fig. 4). Our excavations show that this well was accessed through either of two gates leading directly from the courtyards of *Troullia* West down spiraling stone steps to the water table, would have been linked with the streamflow of Kamaras Creek (see Fig. 4).

During Phases 2, 1b and 1a this entire complex, extending over about 250 m², was shifted upslope about 1 m to the east (Fig. 5). The latest evidence in *Troullia* West in Phase 1a includes a wine or olive oil processing area and a burned, possibly

Fig. 3 (**a**) Excavated architecture in Politiko-*Troullia* East, facing south-southeast. Roofed structures are separated by a cornering alley, with pit furnace and metallurgical workspace in background (in area with middle staff member). (**b**) View across two exterior courtyards and the walled alley in Politiko-*Troullia* West, facing south with lower slopes of Politiko-*Koloiokremmos* in background on left. Upper architecture belongs to Phases 2 and 1b. Lower walls on right belong to Phases 4 and 3. Note much deeper sedimentation in *Troullia* West. Ravine of incised Kamaras Creek streambed descending below the trees on the right has truncated the walls of Phases 4 and 3 along its edge

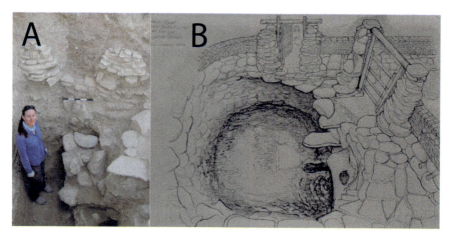

Fig. 4 (**a**) Photo of well in Politiko-*Troullia* West used during Phases 4 and 3; abandoned and capped in subsequent phases, facing north. Staff member stands at bottom of well; above her the northern door frame and threshold are shown in stratigraphic cross-section. (**b**) Artistic depiction of the well and its northern and eastern doorways, leading to stone steps that descended to the well water, based on excavated remains of Phases 4 and 3. (Artwork by Gary James)

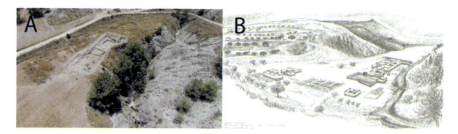

Fig. 5 (**a**) Drone aerial photo of Politiko-*Troullia* West, facing southeast, at the end of final excavations in 2015. Spring-fed Kamaras Creek, which flows from south (top of photo) to north (bottom of photo), has eroded through the alluvial sediments of Politiko-*Troullia* and has deeply incised its underlying limestone bedrock. (**b**) Artistic depiction of Politiko-*Troullia* in its later phases of occupation (Phases 2 and 1) after about 1980 cal BCE (artwork by Gary James). Structures of *Troullia* East on left, *Troullia* North in foreground, *Troullia* West farthest to right

offertory space. Our excavations revealed the eroded remains of the Phase 2-1a rooms along Kamaras Creek, with their cross walls exposed in section along the modern upper banks of the creek. As part of the architectural repositioning during these last three phases, the well in *Troullia* West was capped by a compacted limestone plaster, marking the end of its use. This stratified architectural sequence leads us to hypothesize that the occupational history of Politiko-*Troullia*, including its comprehensive relocation, and possibly its abandonment, was triggered by the alluvial and colluvial dynamics of its local environment.

Excavation of *Troullia* East revealed a compound buried in sediments 75 cm deep, occupied in a single stratigraphic phase (see Fig. 3). *Troullia* East features two apparently domestic rooms, which were surrounded by smaller outbuildings (Fall et al., 2008). An exterior workspace with a pit furnace, dense charcoal deposition, copper tongs, a limestone mold, copper slag and ore attest to a household scale metallurgical workshop (Falconer & Fall, 2013, 2014; Fall et al., 2008), in keeping with Politiko-*Troullia*'s proximity to local near-surface ore sources. Excavations in *Troullia* North similarly revealed remains that can be ascribed to a domestic compound, including a roughly square multi-room structure, with an external *terra cotta* oven and copper slag similar to that found in *Troullia* East. The structures in *Troullia* East and North were used during the latter portions of Politiko-*Troullia*'s occupational history.

Our Bayesian analysis (Fig. 6) models the occupation of Politiko-*Troullia* over about 200 years between the mid-twenty-first and mid-nineteenth centuries BCE, based on the modeled starting boundary for Phase 5 (1σ range: 2097–2021 cal BCE; median = 2056 cal BCE) and the ending boundary for Phase 1a (1σ range: 1882–1800 cal BCE; median = 1839 cal BCE) (Falconer et al., 2022). The intervals between modeled boundary medians suggest a series of about 20- to 30-year occupations in phases 5-1b. A longer occupation for Phase 1a is based on the two ages from a burned area in the uppermost stratum in *Troullia* West, which may mark a final event just prior to the abandonment of Politiko-*Troullia*. When analyzed separately, four AMS seed ages from *Troullia* East model over about a century or less between the starting boundary for this portion of the settlement (1σ range: 2053–1955 cal BCE; median = 2018 cal BCE) and its ending boundary (1σ range: 1994–1874 cal BCE; median = 1925 cal BCE).

A set of main inferences arise from the coordination of stratigraphic and chronological evidence for the occupation of Politiko-*Troullia*. Our initial assessment of the pottery wares and forms surveyed on *Troullia* West (Falconer et al., 2005) and excavated from *Troullia* East (Fall et al., 2008) suggested a relatively lengthy occupation from the Early through Middle Cypriot periods, and possibly into Late Cypriot. Our radiocarbon-based chronology now documents a shorter, roughly two-century occupation consisting of a series of relatively brief stratigraphic phases spanning the Early to Middle Cypriot transition. The major stratigraphic and chronological disjunction at Politiko-*Troullia* is marked by the shift from the more downslope positioning of architecture and the use of the village's well in the earlier phases (5–3) to the more upslope architecture and abandonment of the well in the later phases (2-1a). The boundary between Phases 3 and 2 produced by our Bayesian modeling estimates this transition slightly after 2000 cal BCE (1σ range: 1997–1962 cal BCE; median = 1981 cal BCE), which may correlate with climate changes hypothesized for the nearby Southern Levant (Soto-Berelov et al., 2015).

Fig. 6 Bayesian model of 25 AMS ages from Politiko-*Troullia*, Cyprus (A_{model} = 153.7). Light gray curves indicate single-sample calibration distributions; dark curves indicate modeled calibration distributions. Calibration and Bayesian modeling based on OxCal 4.4.4 (Bronk Ramsey, 2009a) using the IntCal20 atmospheric curve (Reimer et al., 2020; van der Plicht et al., 2020). Two ages (AA-94185, AA-104835) are excluded as statistical outliers based on A < 60

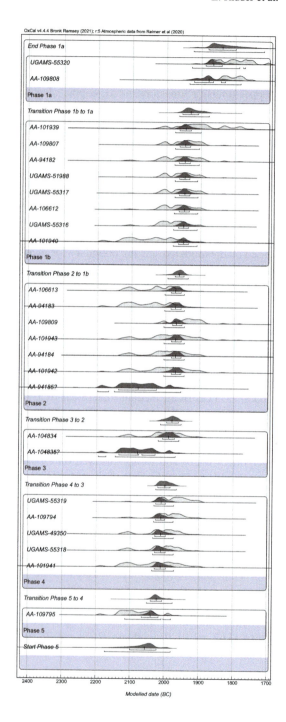

5.2 The Troullia/Koloiokremmos *Taskscape*

Extramural activities on the *Troullia/Koloiokremmos* taskscape are illuminated effectively by surface patterns of potsherds, gaming stones and ground stone artifacts. Pronounced surface concentrations of Prehistoric Bronze Age pottery (mostly Red Polished Ware sherds) coincided with the areas of buried architecture revealed by soil resistivity and subsequently excavated in *Troullia* West, East and North. Prehistoric Bronze Age sherds also form prominent concentrations on some of the lower terraces of *Koloiokremmos*, particularly on the easternmost terraces overlooking the Pediaios River (Fig. 7). Ground and gaming stones, which would have served as focal points for economic and social activities, are found in higher densities on the terraces on *Koloiokremmos* in Fields 3 and 4 than in the fields associated with the settlement of Politiko-*Troullia* (see Fig. 7).

Behavioral inferences derived from surface data often attribute artifact distributions across agricultural lands to refuse deposition and manuring of fields as a function of settlement distance, plowing, or immediate downslope erosion (Alcock & Cherry, 2004; Bintliff et al., 1999; Fall et al., 2012). However, patterns of deposition in our survey area do not diminish with increased distance from the village of Politiko-*Troullia*, and these factors do not explain the concentrations of both potsherds and ground stone fragments across both the steep upper slopes and relatively flat eastern expanses of Politiko-*Koloiokremmos*.

Ground stone classified as querns, basins and work surfaces (Swiny et al., 2003: 221–254) were used for initial processing of grains and olives (Hadjisavvas, 1992, 2003; Warnock, 2007: figs. 4.10, 4.11). Pecked basins indicate pounding and grinding of hard materials, as required in the initial stages of ore processing before smelting (Kassianidou, 2007). Gaming stones have been excavated within ritual, communal or living structures at other Bronze Age sites on Cyprus, leading to their interpretation as social locations (Crist et al., 2016; Frankel, 1993; Swiny, 1980).

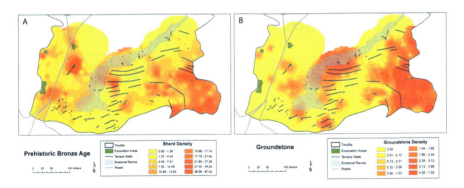

Fig. 7 (**a**) Bronze Age pottery sherd densities interpolated across Politiko-*Troullia* and *Koloiokremmos*. (**b**) Densities of ground stone fragments interpolated across Politiko-*Troullia* and *Koloiokremmos*. In both images darker red shading indicates higher densities against lower densities indicated by yellow shading

The greater abundance of gaming stones on the slopes of *Koloiokremmos* than in the spaces in and around *Troullia* reinforces the interpretation of terraces as settings for social interaction as well as economic tasks. Based on a variety of field and analytical methods, the distinct spatial distributions of surface archaeological evidence and differential patterns of erosion and sedimentation may be combined to interpret the creation of a multi-faceted *Troullia/Koloiokremmos* taskscape.

5.3 Aerial Photogrammetry

Integration of more than 1300 UAV aerial photos produced a detailed composite orthophoto of the *Troullia/Koloiokremmos* landscape that can be investigated from a variety of visual and analytical perspectives (Fig. 8). The relatively flat cultivated

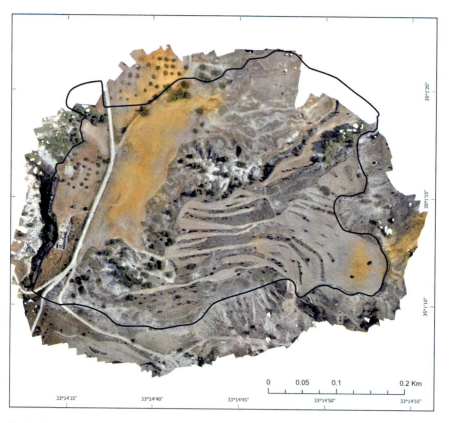

Fig. 8 Orthophoto showing fields of Politiko-*Troullia* shaded in brown below the terraced north-facing slopes of Politiko-*Koloiokremmos*. Note the excavations of *Troullia* West situated in deep sediments at the foot of a steep eroded hillside of *Koloiokremmos*, now covered with pine trees. Just below *Troullia* West lies the deeply-incised water course of Kamaras Creek, which has cut through the archaeological sediments and into the soft underlying limestone bedrock

fields of Politiko-*Troullia*, in which the Bronze Age village lies buried, stand out on the basis of low modern crop vegetation. Along *Troullia*'s western edge, Kamaras Creek is marked clearly by the high tree vegetation along the bottom of its deeply-incised stream course. Among obviously modern features, a road bisects Politiko-*Troullia*, but this imagery serves more powerfully as a tool for envisioning the agrarian and social landscape in which *Troullia*'s Bronze Age occupants subsisted and interacted. This extensive aerial photogrammetry highlights the abundance of arable land retained in a series of fields behind the terrace walls traversing *Koloiokremmos,* providing a clear depiction of the full extent of the local taskscape well beyond the more obvious potential horticultural fields and pastures immediately surrounding the village. Agricultural terracing likely was a major aspect of Bronze Age land management and local economy at Politiko-*Troullia* (Ridder et al., 2017), and at other ancient localities on Cyprus (Bevan & Conolly, 2011; Given & Knapp, 2003; Krahtopoulou & Frederick, 2008). While the terraced walls and fields preserved on *Koloiokremmos* capture a remarkable sense of ancient field systems, this agricultural system would have required considerable long-term maintenance and would been highly susceptible to the effects of changing climatic conditions, particularly significant changes in precipitation. Thus, this photogrammetry also is important as it conveys the variety of landforms that gave rise to pronounced variability in erosion and deposition that included the rapid deposition in *Troullia* West, the pronounced downcutting of Kamaras Creek, and the creation of the modern *Troullia/Koloiokremmos* landscape.

5.4 Erosion and Sedimentation Patterns

The overall erosion risk at Politiko-*Troullia* may be classified as moderate (16–25 tonnes/ha/year) while approximately 26% of the taskscape is classified as having severe (25–50 tonnes/ha/year) or extreme risk (>50 tonnes/ha/year) of sediment erosion (Fig. 9). These results are lower than anticipated based upon topography and soil texture composition. Our field-based estimates of sedimentation rates for *Troullia* East and West (Table 3) correlate well with predicted patterns of erosion and deposition. The slower deposition rate for *Troullia* East accords with the minimal erosion risk predicted for this portion of the site. The water network also flows away from *Troullia* East (Fig. 10), potentially contributing to its relatively shallow sediment layer. Conversely, the slopes of *Koloiokremmos* overlooking *Troullia* West are classified as having severe to extreme risk of sediment loss, and the water network flows directly down these slopes (interrupted today by the modern road), across *Troullia* West and into Kamaras Creek. When viewed in conjunction with patterns of erosion risk (Figs. 9 and 10), our hydrological analysis reveals water-driven sediment sources and sinks.

This approach illustrates spatial patterns of sediment erosion and deposition across Politiko-*Troullia* and *Koloiokremmos*, and may be used to interpret the irregular spatial distributions of potsherds and ground stone on the local taskscape (see

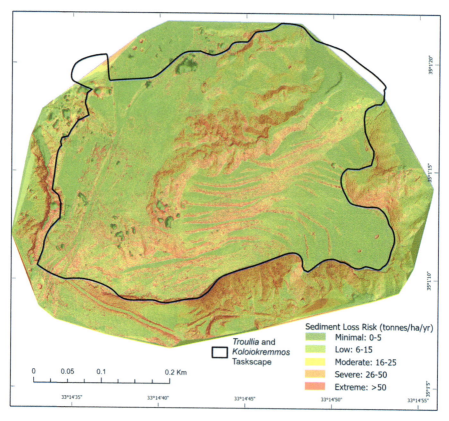

Fig. 9 Predicted risk of erosion across the *Troullia/Koloiokremmos* taskscape. Higher risk indicated by orange to red shading. Lower risk indicated by yellow-to-green shading. Note the particularly high erosion risk predicted along Kamaras Creek and on the west-facing slopes of Politiko-*Koloiokremmos* overlooking *Troullia* West. High erosion risk also is shown for the south-facing slopes of Koloiokremmos and for the ravines draining from the east slope of Politiko-*Troullia* down to the Pediaios River

Table 3 Sedimentation rates at Politiko-*Troullia*

Location	Depth	Time	Sedimentation rate
PT East	75 cm	92 years	0.82 cm/year
PT West	330 cm	215 years	1.53 cm/year

Fig. 7). Potsherds are concentrated along the flat areas of Field 2, near Politiko-*Troullia* East, and the eastern edge of *Koloiokremmos* (see Sect. 5.2), coinciding with areas of low sediment loss risk, as anticipated. The surface hydrology does not reveal potential source locations for potsherd origination. This supports previous conclusions that downslope erosion due to water is not a likely transport mechanism and reemphasizes the conceptualization of Politiko-*Troullia* and *Koloiokremmo*s as an interconnected taskscape, where cultural materials were purposefully placed or relocated and reutilized.

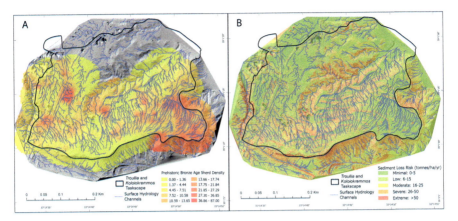

Fig. 10 (**a**) Predicted courses of water flow (indicated by blue lines) shown in conjunction with interpolated Prehistoric Bronze Age sherd densities across the *Troullia/Koloiokremmos* taskscape. Note the network of water flow courses leading from the western slopes of Koloiokremmos across *Troullia* West to the northward-flowing stream course of Kamaras Creek. Dense courses of water flow also lead from *Koloiokremmos* downslope to the Pediaios River. (**b**) Predicted courses of water flow and the predicted risk of erosion across the *Troullia/Koloiokremmos* taskscape overlain on same base image. (North to top of both images)

6 Conclusions

In keeping with contributions of Tom Levy to innovation in archaeological science, this multi-dimensional study applies a variety of analytical approaches to expand our conception and comprehension of the natural and social landscape dynamics that molded Bronze Age community life at Politiko-*Troullia*, Cyprus. Excavations across *Troullia* have revealed considerable variability in archaeological deposition, including rapid deposition of more than three meters of sediment over the course of only about two centuries of occupation. This phenomenon is accompanied by pronounced erosion along the settlement's western edge due to severe incision of adjacent Kamaras Creek. The stratigraphic and chronological record for *Troullia* documents a major disjunction involving repositioning of village architecture upslope away from the creek and the abandonment of the village's intramural well just after about 2000 cal BCE, which coincides with a modeled rainfall increase in the Southern Levant. We expand our assessment of the ancient landscape around Politiko-*Troullia* in terms of a "taskscape" incorporating the village at *Troullia* with evidence of agricultural landuse and social activities across the terraced hillsides of adjacent Politiko-*Koloiokremmos*. UAV aerial photogrammetry provides the structure for a detailed DEM of the local landscape, which we overlay with a vivid photographic depiction of the extent and geographical variability of the *Troullia/Koloiokremmos* taskscape. On this basis, we model patterns of sediment erosion and deposition to interpret the processes that molded the natural environment and settlement history of Politiko-*Troullia*.

Acknowledgments Fieldwork at Politiko-*Troullia* and *Koloiokremmos* was conducted under permit from the Department of Antiquities, Republic of Cyprus, in affiliation with the Cyprus American Archaeological Research Institute, Nicosia, and with the kind hospitality offered by our host community of Pera Orinis. Fieldwork and analysis were funded by National Science Foundation grants 0613760, 1031527, 1850259, 2114406, National Geographic Society grant 7820-05, and a Harris Endowment Grant from the American Society of Overseas Research.

References

Agisoft Metashape Professional (Version 1.7) (Software). (2021). Retrieved from https://www.agisoft.com/downloads/installer/

Alcock, S. E., & Cherry, J. F. (2004). *Side-by-side survey: Comparative regional studies in the Mediterranean world*. Oxbow Books.

Benavidez, R., Jackson, B., Maxwell, D., & Norton, K. (2018). A review of the (Revised) Universal Soil Loss Equation ((R)USLE): With a view to increasing its global applicability and improving soil loss estimates. *Hydrology and Earth System Sciences, 22*, 6059–6086. https://doi.org/10.5194/hess-22-6059-2018

Ben-Yosef, E., Liss, B., Yagel, O. A., Tirosh, O., Najjar, M., & Levy, T. E. (2019). Ancient technology and punctuated change: Detecting the emergence of the Edomite Kingdom in the Southern Levant. *PLoS One, 14*(9), e0221967. https://doi.org/10.1371/journal.pone.0221967

Bevan, A., & Conolly, J. (2011). Terraced fields and Mediterranean landscape structure: An analytical case study from Antikythera, Greece. *Ecological Modelling, 222*, 1303–1314.

Bintliff, J., Howard, P., & Snodgrass, A. (1999). The hidden landscape of prehistoric Greece. *Journal of Mediterranean Archaeology, 12*, 139–168.

Bronk Ramsey, C. (2009a). Bayesian analysis of radiocarbon dates. *Radiocarbon, 51*(1), 337–360.

Bronk Ramsey, C. (2009b). Dealing with outliers and offsets in radiocarbon dating. *Radiocarbon, 51*(3), 1023–1045.

Crist, W., De Voogt, A., & Dunn-Vaturi, A.-E. (2016). Facilitating interaction: Board games as social lubricants in the ancient Near East. *Oxford Journal of Archaeology, 35*, 179–196.

David, W. P. (1988). Soil and water conservation planning: Policy issues and recommendations. *Journal of Philippine Development, 15*, 47–84.

Di Chiara, A., Tauxe, L., Levy, T. E. L., Najjar, M., Florindo, F., & Ben-Yosef, E. (2021). The strength of the Earth's magnetic field from Pre-Pottery to Pottery Neolithic, Jordan. *Proceedings of the National Academy of Sciences, 118*(34), e2100995118. https://doi.org/10.1073/pnas.2100995118

Falconer, S. E., & Fall, P. L. (2013). Spatial patterns, households, and community behavior at Bronze Age Politiko-*Troullia*, Cyprus. *Journal of Field Archaeology, 38*(2), 101–119. https://doi.org/10.1179/0093469013Z.00000000041

Falconer, S. E., & Fall, P. L. (2014). The meaning of space and place in Middle Cypriot communities. In J. M. Webb (Ed.), *Structure, measurement and meaning. Studies on prehistoric Cyprus in Honour of David Frankel* (Studies in Mediterranean Archaeology) (Vol. 143, pp. 175–184).

Falconer, S. E., Fall, P. L., Davis, T. W., Horowitz, M. T., & Hunt, J. (2005). Initial archaeological investigations at Politiko-*Troullia*, 2004. *Report of the Department of Antiquities, Cyprus, 2005*, 69–85.

Falconer, S. E., Fall, P. L., Hunt, J., & Metzger, M. C. (2012). Agrarian settlement at Politiko-*Troullia. Report of the Department of Antiquities, Cyprus, 2010*, 183–198.

Falconer, S. E., Monahan, E. M., & Fall, P. L. (2014). A stone plank figure from Politiko-*Troullia* Cyprus: Potential implications for inferring Bronze Age communal behavior. *Bulletin of the Schools of Oriental Research, 371*, 3–16.

Falconer, S. E., Ridder, E., Pilaar Birch, S., & Fall, P. L. (2022). Prehistoric bronze age radiocarbon chronology at Politiko-*Troullia*, Cyprus. *Radiocarbon*, 1–23. https://doi.org/10.1017/RDC.2022.99

Fall, P. L., Falconer, S. E., Horowitz, M., Hunt, J., Metzger, M. C., & Ryter, D. (2008). Bronze Age settlement and landscape of Politiko-*Troullia*, 2005–2007. *Report of the Department of Antiquities, Cyprus, 2008*, 183–208.

Fall, P. L., Falconer, S. E., Galletti, C. G., Shirmang, T., Ridder, E., & Klinge, J. (2012). Long-term agrarian landscapes in the Troodos Foothills, Cyprus. *Journal of Archaeological Science, 39*, 2335–2347. https://doi.org/10.1016/j.jas.2012.02.010

Fall, P. L., Falconer, S. E., & Klinge, J. (2015). Bronze Age fuel use and its implications for agrarian landscapes in the eastern Mediterranean. *Journal of Archaeological Science Reports, 4*, 182–191. https://doi.org/10.1016/j.jasrep.2015.09.004

Farhan, Y., Zregat, D., & Farhan, I. (2013). Spatial estimation of soil erosion risk using RUSLE approach, RS, and GIS techniques: A case study of Kufranja watershed, Northern Jordan. *Journal of Water Resource and Protection, 5*, 1247–1261.

Frankel, D. (1993). Inter- and intra-site variability and social interaction in prehistoric Bronze Age Cyprus: Types, ranges and trends. *Bulletin of the American Schools of Oriental Research, 292*, 59–72.

Galletti, C. S., Ridder, E., Falconer, S. E., & Fall, P. L. (2013). Maxent modeling of ancient and modern agricultural terraces in the Troodos foothills, Cyprus. *Applied Geography, 39*, 46–56. https://doi.org/10.1016/j.apgeog.2012.11.020

Given, M., & Knapp, A. B. (2003). *The Sydney Cyprus survey project: Social approaches to regional archaeological survey*. The Cotsen Institute of Archaeology. University of California.

Hadjisavvas, S. (1992). *Olive oil processing in Cyprus from the Bronze Age to the Byzantine Period* (Studies in Mediterranean Archaeology XCIX). Paul Astroms Forlag.

Hadjisavvas, S. (2003). The production and diffusion of olive oil in the Mediterranean, ca. 1500–500 BC. In N. C. Stampolidis & V. Karageorghis (Eds.), *Interconnections in the Mediterranean, 16th–6th century BC* (pp. 117–123). University of Crete, Leventis Foundation.

Hijmans, R. J., Cameron, S. E., Parra, J. L., Jones, P. G., & Jarvis, A. (2005). Very high resolution interpolated climate surfaces for global land areas. *International Journal of Climatology, 25*, 1965–1978. https://doi.org/10.1002/joc.1276

Howland, M. D., Jones, I. W. N., Najjar, M., & Levy, T. E. (2018). Quantifying the effects of erosion on archaeological sites, low-altitude aerial photography, structure from motion, and GIS: A case study from southern Jordan. *Journal of Archaeological Science, 90*, 62–70. https://doi.org/10.1016/j.jas.2017.12.008

Ingold, T. (1993). The temporality of landscapes. *World Archaeology, 24*, 152–174.

Johnston, G., Riddell, A., & Hausler, G. (2017). The international GNSS service. In P. J. G. Teunissen & O. Montenbruck (Eds.), *Springer handbook of global navigation satellite systems* (1st ed., pp. 967–982). Springer. https://doi.org/10.1007/978-3-319-42928-1

Jones, A., Fernandez-Ugalde, O., & Scarpa, S. (2020). LUCAS (2015). *Topsoil survey. Presentation of dataset and results*, EUR 30332 EN. Publications Office of the European Union. ISBN:978-92-76-21080-1. https://doi.org/10.2760/616084JRC121325

Kassianidou, V. (2007). *Ground stone tools from Apliki Karamallos. Excavations at the Late Bronze Age mining settlement at Apliki Karamallos, Cyprus* (Studies in Mediterranean Archaeology 134). Paul Åstroms Forlag.

Klinge, J. (2013). *Assessment of environmental change in the near eastern Bronze Age.* Ph.D. Dissertation, Arizona State University. University Microfilms International.

Klinge, J., & Fall, P. L. (2010). A paleoethnobotanical analysis of Bronze Age land use and land cover in the eastern Mediterranean. *Journal of Archaeological Science, 37*, 2622–2629. https://doi.org/10.1016/j.jas.2010.05.022

Krahtopoulou, A., & Frederick, C. (2008). The stratigraphic implications of long-term terrace agriculture in dynamic landscapes: Polycyclic terraces from Kythera Island, Greece. *Geoarchaeology, 23*, 550–585.

Levy, T. E. (1995). *The archaeology of society in the Holy Land*. Facts on File.

Levy, T. E., & Jones, I. W. N. (2018). *Cyber-archaeology and grand narratives: Digital technology and deep-time perspectives on culture change in the Middle East* (One World Archaeology Series). Springer. https://doi.org/10.1007/978-3-319-65693-9

Manning, S. W. (2013). Cyprus at 2200 BC: Rethinking the chronology of the Cypriot Early Bronze Age. In A. B. Knapp, J. M. Webb, & A. McCarthy (Eds.), *J.R.B. Stewart. An archaeological legacy* (Studies in Mediterranean Archaeology) (Vol. CXXXIX, pp. 1–21). Åstroms Forlag.

Metzger, M. C., Ridder, E., Pilaar Birch, S. E., Falconer, S. E., & Fall, P. L. (2021). Animal exploitation at a Middle Bronze Age village on Cyprus. In J. Daujat, A. Hadjikoumis, R. Berthon, J. Chahoud, V. Kassianidou, & J.-D. Vigne (Eds.), *Archaeozoology of Southwest Asia and adjacent areas XIII* (Archaeobiology 3) (pp. 113–128). Lockwood Press. https://doi.org/10.2307/j.ctv2d7x51d.11

Milevski, I., & Levy, T. E. (2016). Introduction – Social theory and archaeology. In I. Milevski & T. E. Levy (Eds.), *Framing archaeology in the Near East – The application of social theory to fieldwork* (pp. 1–6). Equinox.

Panagos, P., Borrelli, P., Meusburger, K., Alewell, C., Lugato, E., & Montanarella, L. (2015). Estimating the soil erosion cover-management factor at the European scale. *Land Use Policy, 48*, 38–50. https://doi.org/10.1016/j.landusepol.2015.05.021

Pilaar Birch, S. E., Metzger, M. C., Ridder, E., Porson, S., Falconer, S. E., & Fall, P. L. (2022). Herd management and subsistence practices as inferred from isotopic analysis at Bronze Age Politiko-*Troullia*, Cyprus. *PLoS One, 17*(10), e0272757. https://doi.org/10.1371/journal.pone.0275757

Reimer, P. J., Austin, W. E. N., Bard, E., Bayliss, A., Blackwell, P. G., Bronk Ramsey, C., Butzin, M., Cheng, H., Edwards, R. L., Friedrich, M., Grootes, P. M., Guilderson, T. P., Hajdas, I., Heaton, T. J., Hogg, A. G., Hughen, K. A., Kromer, B., Manning, S. W., Muscheler, R., Palmer, J. G., Pearson, C., van der Plicht, J., Reimer, R. W., Richards, D. A., Scott, E. M., Southon, J. R., Turney, C. S. M., Wacker, L., Adolphi, F., Buntgen, U., Capano, M., Fahrni, S. M., Fogtmann-Schulz, A., Friedrich, R., Köhler, P., Kudsk, S., Miyake, F., Olsen, J., Reinig, Sakamoto, M., Sookdeo, A., & Talamo, S. (2020). The IntCal20 northern hemisphere radiocarbon age calibration curve (0–55 kBP). *Radiocarbon, 62*, 725–757. https://doi.org/10.1017/RDC.2020.41

Renard, K. G., & Friemund, J. R. (1994). Using monthly precipitation data to estimate the R-factor in the revised USLE. *Journal of Hydrology, 157*, 287–306.

Renard, K. G., Foster, G. R., Weessies, G. A., & McCool, D. K. (1997). Predicting soil erosion by water: A guide to conservation planning with the Revised Universal Soil Loss Equation (RUSLE). In D. C. Yoder (Ed.), *Agriculture handbook 703*. U.S. Department of Agriculture.

Ridder, E., Galletti, C. S., Fall, P. L., & Falconer, S. E. (2017). Economic and social activities on ancient Cypriot terraced landscapes. *Journal of Environmental Management, 202*(3), 514–523. https://doi.org/10.1016/j.jenvman.2016.12.037

Sharpley, A. N., & Williams, J. R. (Eds.). (1990). *EPIC – Erosion/productivity impact calculator: 1. Model documentation*. U.S. Department of Agriculture Technical Bulletin No. 1768.

Soto-Berelov, M., Fall, P. L., Falconer, S. E., & Ridder, E. (2015). Modeling vegetation dynamics in the Southern Levant through the Bronze Age. *Journal of Archaeological Science, 53*, 94–109. https://doi.org/10.1016/j.jas.2014.09.015

Swiny, S., (1980). *Bronze Age gaming stones from Cyprus*. Report of the Department of Antiquities, Cyprus, pp. 54–78.

Swiny, S., Rapp, G., & Herscher, E. (Eds.). (2003). *Sotira Kaminoudhia: An Early Bronze Age site in Cyprus* (CAARI Monograph Series, Vol. 4. ASOR Archaeological Reports Number 8). American Schools of Oriental Research.

Tóth, G., Jones, A., & Montanarella, L. (Eds.). (2013). *LUCAS Topsoil Survey. Methodology, data and results*. JRC technical reports. Publications Office of the European Union, EUR26102 – Scientific and Technical Research Series. ISSN:1831–9424 (online); ISBN:978-92-79-32542-7. https://doi.org/10.2788/97922

van der Plicht, J., Bronk Ramsey, C., Heaton, T. J., Scott, E. M., & Talamo, S. (2020). Recent developments in calibration for archaeological and environmental samples. *Radiocarbon, 62*, 1095–1117. https://doi.org/10.1017/RDC.2020.22

Warnock, P. (2007). *Identification of ancient olive oil processing methods based on olive remains*. British Archaeological Reports, International Series 1635.

Wischmeier, W. H., & Smith, D. D. (1978). *Predicting rainfall erosion losses – A guide to conservation planning*. U.S. Department of Agriculture, Agriculture Handbook No. 537.

Yasur-Landau, A., Shtienberg, G., Gambash, G., Spada, G., Melini, D., Arkin-Shalev, E., Tamberini, A., Reese, J., Levy, T. E., & Sivan, D. (2021). New relative sea level (RSL) indications from the Eastern Mediterranean: Middle Bronze Age to the Roman period (~3800–1800y BP) archaeological constructions at Dor, the Carmel coast, Israel. *PLoS One, 16*(6), e0251870. https://doi.org/10.1371/journal.pone.0251870

From Digital Recording to Advanced AI Applications in Archaeology and Cultural Heritage

George Pavlidis ⓘ

Abstract In the recent decades, the significance of digital technology applications in archaeology and cultural heritage has been widely recognized, and digital applications have already contributed to the recording, preservation, study and dissemination of cultural heritage. This bridging, or even merging, begins with digitization, and particularly in three or more dimensions, when the objects of study are tangible. Once digital, the artifacts become available for a wide range of studies and dissemination activities. Recent advances in computing infrastructures and algorithmic techniques, empowered a re-ignition of artificial intelligence approaches, paving the way for a more data-driven future. On one hand, there is rich data production through modern multi-dimensional digitization and digital data production; on the other hand, there are powerful tools to effectively study and disseminate this rich content, ranging from artifacts' analysis, to intelligent museums and personalized tourism. This chapter focuses on these two pillars towards a future of intelligent applications in archaeology and cultural heritage, by providing an account of modern state-of-the-art 3D digitization methods, as well as an account of AI applications, including deep and reinforcement learning, and automated recommendation systems for applications in the reality-virtuality continuum.

Keywords Computational archaeology · Digital humanities · Digital archaeology · Cyberarchaeology · Cultural heritage · Artificial intelligence · AI in archaeology · AI in cultural heritage · Digitization · Heritage science · Heritage analytics · Extended reality in cultural heritage · Predictive modeling in archaeology · Personalization in heritage applications · Cultural tourism

---

G. Pavlidis (✉)
Athena Research and Innovation Center in Information, Communication and Knowledge Technologies, Xanthi, Greece
e-mail: gpavlid@athenarc.gr

© The Author(s), under exclusive license to Springer Nature Switzerland AG 2023
E. Ben-Yosef, I. W. N. Jones (eds.), *"And in Length of Days Understanding" (Job 12:12): Essays on Archaeology in the Eastern Mediterranean and Beyond in Honor of Thomas E. Levy*, Interdisciplinary Contributions to Archaeology, https://doi.org/10.1007/978-3-031-27330-8_69

1 Introduction

Technology has become ubiquitous during the late twentieth century. Domains, in which only limited technology support was traditionally provided or envisioned, are now strongly assisted by applications of advanced technological innovations. Archaeology and cultural heritage is such a domain, which became technology-assisted and ultimately digital, within less than half of a century. The benefits for such a transition have been celebrated in a significant volume of published research in the recent decades. Modern-day archaeology and cultural heritage is already reaping the fruits of the everyday digital practice in recording, research, study and dissemination in multiple dimensions, including the off-site on-line access, the comparative study, the digital restoration and reconstruction, the advanced visualization, the digital data annotation, the automated information extraction, the geographical localization, the virtual context creation and study, the augmented study and dissemination, the physical reproduction at any scale. Apparently, it all begins with digitization, which enables the *life* of a digital replica, as a parallel to the *life* of the original, and it may be defined both for the tangible and the intangible.

Technically, digitization is more or less the process of recording quantized values of discrete-time and discrete-space measurements of physical quantities, typically termed as analog. Thus, it can be thought of as the conversion of analog quantities of the physical world into digital values in the digital domain, which are rounded values of the systematically sampled physical quantity. The representation of digital quantities is in binary form, which is a form that has been exploited in digital computing systems. Digitization in the domain of tangible cultural heritage is the digital recording of artifacts, cultural structures, monuments, historic manuscripts and any object that conveys information about history, tradition, language, art, religion, culture, also including science and technology. In cases in which digitization concerns the recording of the geometric structure and the spectral signature of three- dimensional (3D) physical objects, it is termed *3D digitization* (Tsirliganis et al., 2004; Pavlidis et al., 2007; Rakitina et al., 2008; Chamzas et al., 2008; Pavlidis & Royo, 2018). 3D digitization is one of the two main pillars for this chapter and it will be discussed in detail in the following sections.

Digitization enables numerous possibilities for digital applications that would exploit the wealth of the digitized content for various purposes. As high performance computing infrastructures and devices become all the more available, highly intelligent methods, tools, and applications emerge, capable of completing sophisticated tasks previously unattainable. As foundation theories for artificial intelligence (AI) were already present, the recent decades are definitely characterized by an increased AI penetration in technological innovations. Concepts about AI can be traced back in antiquity. Myths involving intelligent and conscious artificial beings have been saved including Talos of Crete, Pygmalion's Galatea, Hephaestus' Pandora, and later Heron's automatons, as also did the ideas of the philosophers who attempted to describe the process of human thinking by means of a mechanical manipulation of symbols, like in Aristotle's *Organon*. In modern times, the field of

AI research is widely considered to have been founded at the *Dartmouth Summer Research Project on Artificial Intelligence*, a workshop that took place in the summer of 1956, with the participation of some of those that took a leading role in advancing AI in the following years (Solomonoff, 1985; Moor, 2006; Kline, 2010; Kaplan & Haenlein, 2019). Now, at the age of *big data* and *artificial neural networks*, AI seems to gradually appear virtually everywhere. Its application has already been quite fruitful in diverse industries. The modern approach in AI is a kind of a brute force learning process from big data in high performance computing systems. Above this technology, one may meet, today, chatting and calling systems, recommenders, complex data analyzers, personal assistants, intelligent robots, self-driving vehicles, and more. The domain of archaeology and cultural heritage is not excluded from this advancement and specific intelligent and AI applications are already available and will be the second pillar of this chapter.

2 Digital Recording of Archaeology and Cultural Heritage

Two-dimensional (2D) digitization (originally *scanning*) is a rather simple process, traditionally based on optical recording of flat surfaces. Contrary to the simplicity of 2D digitization, creation of digital copies of real-world three-dimensional (3D) objects is challenging. The challenge escalates with the increasing geometric complexity. 3D digitization is typically applied to record the geometric and spectral characteristics of objects' surfaces, and thus results in the creation of 3D *shells* that are empty, as no information of the internal structure of the objects is captured. This is why it has been suggested that this form of 3D digitization results in 2.5D information. Real 3D information can only be attained by using tomography. Most of the currently available 3D digitization methods apply techniques for the modulation, manipulation, and detection of electromagnetic waves, such as the visible or infrared light, and this is why they are usually referenced as *optical documentation methods*. The original term *scanning* in 2D digitization, has also survived in the 3D domain and particular methods that follow the scanning paradigm are called *3D scanning methods*.

3D digitization consists of the measurement of the geometric structure and the spectral response of an object's surface, in a point-wise manner. As such, 3D digitization is characterized by its accuracy and density. *Accuracy* refers to how close the measurements are to the actual objective values, whereas density, or *resolution*, refers to how dense the sampling of measurements on the surface are. Another term, usually used erroneously, *precision*, refers to how dense repeated measurements of the same point can be (or quantity in general). Apparently, the ultimate goal for a successful 3D digitization in archaeology and cultural heritage would be to record structural and spectral information of tangible heritage with *the highest resolution and accuracy, using equipment of high precision*. A wide variety of methods and systems exist for the task and there are significant variations in the applications, the practice, the workflow and the outcomes. Depending on the mobility of the digitization system, it can be categorized as mobile, portable and immovable or fixed. Depending on the principle of operation and technology, there may be systems that depend on highly specialized and expensive equipment, and systems that depend mostly on algorithms and software solutions. In addition, based on the operation technology, some methods require longer on-site work, whereas other methods require extensive work in the laboratory.

Many of today's 3D digitization methods have been largely inefficient in the past, due to a lack in the required technology, including specialized measurement devices, high-performance computing facilities, and sufficient storage spaces. Evolution of those technologies led to a highly dynamic market for 3D digitization systems. Despite the rapid developments in the field, each method and system is based on particular assumptions and is subject to certain constraints, rendering the availability of an all-in-one, completely automated solution very challenging to reach. Nevertheless, 3D digitization has become common in a diverse set of applications and this is primarily due to advancements in 3D real-time computer vision and graphics methods and systems, enabling the ability to manage complex 3D geometries at low cost.

The wide range of heritage object types, sizes, materials and structures defines an application domain that is rather challenging for 3D digitization methods. Decades of research and development made 3D digitization a common practice in the field of archaeology and cultural heritage, bringing some very important benefits like:

- Effective preservation of the cultural wealth, which is constantly under threat by aging, natural and human-related factors.
- Efficient study, conservation and reconstruction tools for the experts, that enable a better understanding for the past.
- Pervasive cultural dissemination and education approaches, that enable heritage to be integrated with the Web.
- Effective diplomacy, tourism and regional economic and sustainable development in the globalized world.

In the scientific literature one may find a long list of various 3D digitization techniques, which may be divided in the categories shown in Fig. 1. The various technology solutions that have been proposed, adapt to particular challenges and take into account specific features of the heritage objects, such as the reflectance, the color diversity and the morphological-geometric complexity. Many commercially available systems are based on laser scanning, since this approach provides specifications for high accuracy and resolution, whereas other popular systems are based on photographic capturing under controlled or uncontrolled lighting conditions. In any case, the objective of any 3D digitization method is to measure the distance of the measuring device to the surface of the measured object, what is typically called the *depth*. The depth perception capabilities and limitations in humans (Cutting & Vishton, 1995) has been a strong motivation towards the development of the various technologies. The principles of operation of some of the most widely used methods are outlined in the following sections.

Laser scanning techniques
- Laser triangulation
- Time of flight scanning

Traditional techniques
- Traditional photogrammetry
- Traditional Topography
- Empirical techniques

Photographic techniques
- Shape from structured light
- Shape from silhouette
- Shape from stereo
- Shape from texture
- Shape from shadow
- Shape from shading
- Shape from photometry/Photometric stereo
- Structure from motion
- Depth from focus/defocus

Special techniques
- Digital holography
- Atomic force microscopy
- Stereo scanning electron microscopy
- Confocal microscopy
- White light scanning interferometry
- X-ray tomography

Fig. 1 3D digitization methods

The results of 3D digitization are typically points of the measured surfaces with spatial and color coordinates, in an arbitrary Cartesian coordinate system, forming what is known as a *point cloud*. Some digitization approaches readily provide correctly scaled 1:1 digital replicas, whereas some other cannot. The derived point cloud is an approximation of the measured surface *per se*, as it represents only some of the surface points with discontinuities and gaps and inherent measurement noise. Point clouds pass through a series of post-processing and filtering steps for the final delivery of a usable 3D digital replica (typically, a textured 3D model).

Primary concern in any digitization project is the size and freedom of movement of the digitization subjects. This is the main reason why heritage objects are distinguished into movable and immovable. Movable can be any relatively small, easily transportable object, which may be digitized either on-site or in a laboratory, using a variety of methods, such as laser or structured light scanning. This class of heritage objects includes statuettes, paintings, vases, pottery, utensils, jewelry, folk art (Pavlidis et al., 2007). On the other side, the class of immovable objects include large statues, structures and buildings, architectural ensembles, historical urban areas, archaeological sites, excavations. This class of objects may be digitized on-site only (Vlachos, 1998; Patias, 1999; Tziavos & Spatalas, 2004; Pavlidis et al., 2006, 2007; Daniil, 2009). Apart from size and mobility, the variety of materials and the morphological complexity of the heritage objects, are part of a wider set of features that challenge any 3D digitization method. It is expected that the quality of digitization is affected by the object itself and not the digitization method alone. For example, marble, a very frequently encountered material, has two important properties, translucence and uneven surface roughness, which result in increased measurement noise due to light diffusion, scattering, refraction and random reflection in its crystalline structure (Godin et al., 2001). Moreover, highly reflective or very dark objects are virtually impossible to measure, since most digitization methods rely on optical measurements. Last but not least, morphologically complex heritage objects are also highly challenging cases, as the detection of reflected light from their surfaces may be impeded due to the existence of cavities and holes. Apparently, there is a large number of heritage objects that pose significant challenges to the existing 3D digitization methods, rendering them virtually infeasible in some cases (Hawkins et al., 2001; Marbs, 2002; Pavlidis et al., 2007; Pavlidis & Royo, 2018).

2.1 Laser Triangulation

Laser beam triangulation (or simply laser triangulation) systems consist of a laser source, emitting usually in the visible spectrum, and an optical sensor to detect the laser light as it is reflected by the surface of the measured object. The principle of operation of laser triangulation is shown in Fig. 2. The relative location and orientation of the laser source and the detector are known, and the method is based on forming triangles with a known base, the baseline a, and two known angles θ, ψ. Triangulation is a technique known since the ancient times and it involves the fundamental geometric laws of sines and cosines. Calculating the distance b of a surface point from the digitization system is easy, using the law of sines as follows.

$$\frac{a}{\sin\phi} = \frac{b}{\sin\psi} \left[= \frac{c}{\sin\theta} \right] \Rightarrow b = a\frac{\sin\psi}{\sin(\pi-\theta-\psi)} \tag{1}$$

Figure 3 outlines how the unknown distance from point P_1 is transformed into a displacement of the detected laser beam on the 2D surface of the optical detector (typically, a photographic camera sensor) at position p_1, which results in the accurate calculation of the distance or depth. The figure shows the effect of a controlled change in the laser emitter angle, resulting in two different detected image points p_1 and p_2 for the two different surface points P_1 and P_2 correspondingly. The resolution of the measurement is related with the smallest possible angle change and the distance to the object, whereas the accuracy of the measurement is directly related to the accuracy in locating the focused beam on the image plane.

Lasers are ideal for such measurements due to their strict monochromatic nature and their concentrated power that is maintained over long distances. Most laser

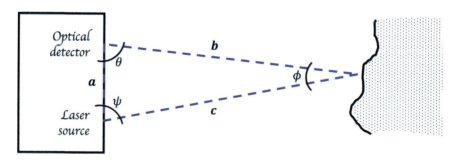

Fig. 2 Principle of operation of short-range laser beam triangulation systems

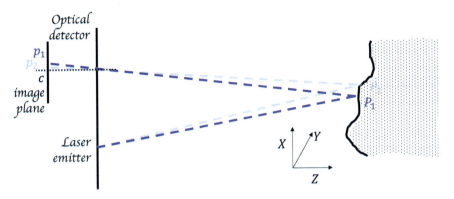

Fig. 3 Laser beam triangulation expressed as a displacement on the detector image plane

triangulation systems are based on point sources, but there is also a variety of different laser patterns that are used for 3D digitization. Although the laser beam is highly collimated, there is still a measurable beam divergence with the distance from the source. The beam divergence or spread, results in an increase in the beam diameter with distance, which leads in the detection of increasingly larger points that also increases the uncertainty of the measurements and ultimately affects the accuracy and the resolution of the scanning. As a result, laser triangulation is mostly useful for short distances, due to practical limitations of (a) the beam divergence with distance and (b) the limited resolution provided by the imaging sensor. The digitization accuracy and resolution are further limited by phenomena of diffraction and refraction. In fact, the thinner the laser beam, the higher the deviation created by these phenomena, notwithstanding the generally beneficial role of a thin beam (Beraldin et al., 2004). Furthermore, surface features also affect the performance of a laser triangulation system (Boehler & Marbs, 2002; Forest et al., 2004). Particularly, translucent surfaces tend to let light penetrate into the object's substrates and light diffuses and creates internal dispersion, resulting in multiple unwanted reflections (Cortelazzo & Marton, 1999).

The need for light-weight handheld, user-friendly, fast, accurate and low-cost solutions in laser triangulation was soon realized, and numerous solutions have been proposed since the end of the twentieth century. Although the handheld feature was not thought to be of utmost importance (Hébert, 2001) and, in some cases, it was required as a complementary feature (Levoy et al., 2000), fast and portable systems have been proposed like AutoScan (Borghese et al., 1998), the monocular range finder (Takatsuka et al., 1999), a real-time 3D model system based on object rotation (Rusinkiewicz et al., 2002), the ModelCamera (Popescu et al., 2003), a handheld system for heritage applications based on multiple view stereo (Pollefeys et al., 2003), and a similar approach that further tackles the issue of high computational complexity (Arnaoutoglou et al., 2006). Since those developments, many successful solutions have made their way to the market and are available for a number of applications.

2.2 Shape from Stereo

Shape from stereo is the method that extracts information about a scene structure from a pair of photos. It is analogous to binocular biological vision or *stereopsis*, and succeeds in finding the depth in scenes by exploiting the image content of a *stereo pair*, two slightly different photos. Stereo pairs consist of two largely overlapping images, in which the relative displacement between them is on a single axis that coincides with the axis of the *baseline*, the line joining the two image centers. This displacement is typically expressed as the *disparity* of the pair, and is closely related with the distances, or depth, in the scene. Practically, this is the same as triangulation, explained in previous texts. The simplified case is shown in Fig. 4, and the geometry makes it easy to derive the disparity and thus the depth in the viewed scene. The similarity of the triangles results in an estimate for the disparity and the depth as follows.

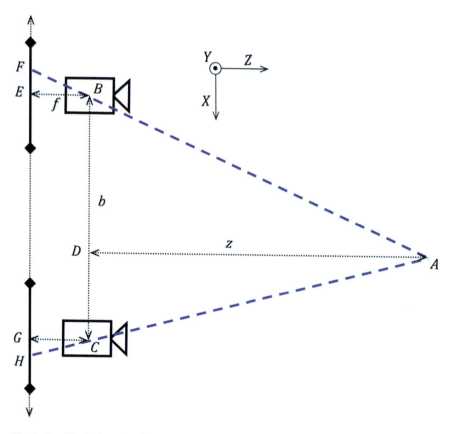

Fig. 4 Simplified binocular vision system

$$
\left.\begin{array}{l}
\dfrac{\text{EF}}{\text{BD}} = \dfrac{\text{BE}}{\text{AD}}, \quad \dfrac{\text{GH}}{\text{CD}} = \dfrac{\text{CG}}{\text{AD}} \\[2mm]
\text{BE} = \text{CG} \\[1mm]
d = \text{EF} + \text{GH}
\end{array}\right\} \Rightarrow d = \dfrac{bf}{z} \Rightarrow z = \dfrac{bf}{d}
$$

$$(2)$$

where d is the disparity, $b = \text{BC}$ is the baseline connecting the imaging devices, $f = \text{BE} = \text{CG}$ the focal length of the lenses (in the simply case, it is the same for both) and $z = \text{AD}$ the distance (depth) of the measured point A from the baseline. For all practical purposes, the numerator in the last expression can be disregarded since it is a constant and thus depth can be considered to be simply the scaled inverse of disparity.

The simplified case is a good approximation only if the imaging systems are exactly the same and their configuration is strictly parallel, facing towards the scene at a right angle. In more general cases, the imaging devices need to be calibrated. Calibration is the process which, in a way, leads to the simplified case. In calibration, image *rectification*[1] takes place (Loop & Zhang, 1999). A graphical representation of the rectification is shown in Fig. 5.

Recovery of depth of a point in the viewed scene requires the identification of the point in the two images of the stereo pair. This is equivalent to finding the same points in the two images, or finding *point correspondences*. The point correspondence problem can be found in a large number of computer vision applications that involve point matching and stereo vision, and an efficient solution is based on particular geometric constraints, the *epipolar constraints*. These constrains arise from the topology, and guide the search for point correspondences in a very fast manner. In addition to epipolar constraints, other constraints may be imposed to improve the depth estimates, such as the *similarity constraint* (correlation), the *uniqueness constraint* (single point-to-point correspondence), the *continuity* (disparity should be piecewise smooth), and the *ordering constraint* (particular ordering of the identified points). Nevertheless, the solution to the point correspondence problem is not trivial, as images are corrupted by noise, occlusions and lighting variations, thus the process should be guided by error minimization approaches (optimization).

Main advantage of shape from stereo is that it is easy to use and automate, and does not require specialized equipment or special conditions for data acquisition. On the other hand, the depth can be estimated only on point correspondences (leading to potentially sparse results), the estimated depth may contain erroneous data due to intense image noise, and to complete a 3D digital replica of an object would need a large number of stereo pairs, requiring, thus, a number of post-processing steps like alignment and consolidation of partial scans. More limitations include matching issues in areas around the boundaries of the objects, areas on the surface

---

[1] Rectification of images is the distortion of the images so that they correspond to imaging systems that are of parameters equivalent to the simplified case of Fig. 4.

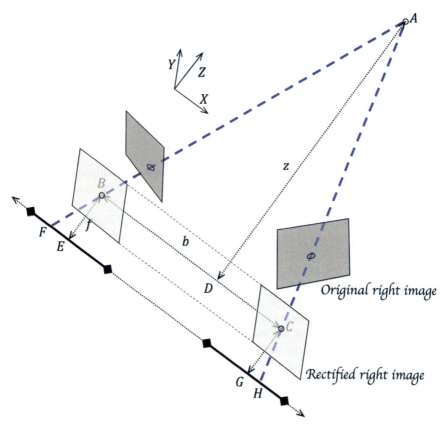

Fig. 5 Rectification of photos for stereo vision

of an object with strong light diffusion phenomena (non-Lambertian surfaces), occlusions on one of the imaging devices and the effects of the perspective projection on the viewed scenes (Bertozzi et al., 2002; Scharstein & Szeliski, 2002).

2.3 Shape from Structured Light

Quite similar to the case of laser triangulation, shape from structured light recovers depth using a projection of a light pattern. An imaging device captures the light pattern reflected from the surface of the measured object and uses the deformations of that pattern for the recovery of the depth, using triangulation. A fundamental difference to laser scanning is that, in this method, typical image projectors are used instead of laser sources. Figure 6 shows the principle of operation of shape from structured light, in which the pattern consists of three colored stripes projected onto a measured surface and imaged as a deformed pattern due to the surface geometry.

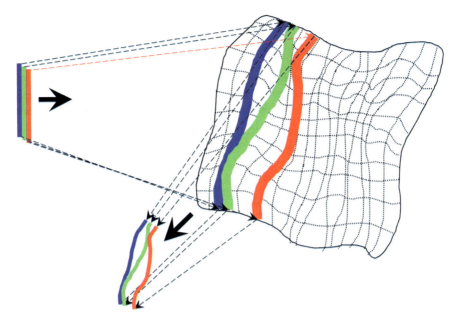

Fig. 6 Principle of operation of shape from structured light

Color coding of the stripes is used to enable the multiple line detection and depth recovery at each single shot. Color coding is not the only approach for such an encoding, and also intensity, shape and density variations have been proposed in the past.

The triangulation that would reveal the depth is pixel-wise and stripe-wise. The triangles are formed by the image projectors, the imaging sensors and the scanned objects, thus, as in other digitization methods, either the setup should be a priori known, or there should be a calibration process. By adopting the model of stereo vision (with the projector taking the place of an imaging device), the case is transformed into a stereo vision problem, thus the notion of disparity becomes relevant and the problem is largely simplified. As a result, (2) holds, and b becomes the baseline connecting the projector with the detector and f is the focal length of the detector lens. For a reference point at distance z_{ref} with a disparity d_{ref}, the distance at which an unknown point lies can be estimated using (2).

$$d - d_{ref} = \frac{bf}{z} - \frac{bf}{z_{ref}} \Rightarrow \cdots \Rightarrow z = \frac{1}{\frac{d - d_{ref}}{bf} + \frac{1}{z_{ref}}} \qquad (3)$$

The rate of change of depth with disparity can also be computed from (2).

$$\frac{\partial z}{\partial d} = -\frac{bf}{d^2} = -\frac{z^2}{bf}$$

(4)

This relation makes it possible to estimate the discrete depth resolution that the system may offer, as it is connected with the disparity and the image resolution of the camera. This estimate implies that the nominal resolution corresponds to a $\Delta d = 1$ disparity resolution, but methods have been proposed that achieve sub-pixel resolution (Scharstein & Szeliski, 2002; Szeliski, 2011).

$$\Delta z = \frac{z^2}{bf} \Delta d$$

(5)

Several structured light techniques have been proposed and made it to market (Salvi et al., 2004; Zanuttigh et al., 2016). Many approaches can be found in the literature using variations in the pattern encoding and setup. In general, shape from structured light requires data post-processing steps, including alignment, partial scans' consolidation, and texture blending (Wust & Capson, 1991; Chen et al., 1997; Horn & Kiryati, 1999; Rocchini et al., 2001). Spectral data of the objects' surfaces are derived from a set of additional images collected without using the patterns. The accuracy may be affected by the quality of the optics of the projection system, the focal length and the range of the projection system, the detector quality and the quality of the imaging optics, the permissible viewing angles and the characteristics of the measured surfaces (Horn & Kiryati, 1999; Rocchini et al., 2001).

2.4 Structure from Motion

Structure from motion (SFM) is the modern digital photogrammetry. Virtually a triangulation-based method, it operates on large sets of photos of a static rigid scene, captured from various viewpoints. In general, SFM uses photographic equipment (cameras) of unknown characteristics and settings. In essence, SFM simultaneous estimates the location of characteristic scene points (*structure*) and the pose of the camera (*motion*). SFM has been the subject of intense research and development during the recent decades and there is a significant volume of published work outranking any other topic in computer vision (Oliensis, 2000). The core of SFM is in solving the point correspondence problem in a multiple view setting, not just in a pair of images like in stereo vision. Overall, the process includes the detection of characteristic image points (features), the matching of image features across photos, the creation of tracks from matches and the solution of the SFM problem from the tracks. Tracks are the 3D coordinates of reconstructed points, accompanied with a list of the corresponding 2D coordinates in the photos, in which they are identified (Furukawa & Hernandez, 2015). The process has been automated and improved by using advanced feature extraction approaches, such as SIFT (Lowe, 1999) and SURF (Bay et al., 2006).

Originally, SFM resulted only sparse point clouds, reflecting the successful point correspondences. Thus, it was considered of limited practical value in archaeology and cultural heritage applications. Only after its integration with Multi-View Stereo (MVS) methods, SFM became comparable to other 3D high accuracy and resolution digitization methods. Nowadays, the original SFM is used to estimate the camera parameters and pose (intrinsic and extrinsic parameters) that initialize MVS, which subsequently results a dense point cloud. The hybrid SFM-MVS, the modern SFM, met a celebrated acceptance in various domains due to its highly successful performance, low cost and high quality digitization, when properly used. Currently, this modern SFM tends to replace other successful methods in archaeology and cultural heritage digitization, as studies shown extremely high quality results (Koutsoudis et al., 2014), at relatively low cost, ease of application by non-specialists, and further digitization automation capabilities.

An example 3D model of a standing stone from Jordan of around 40 cm height, created using SFM-MVS and 100 photos of 12 MPixels, is shown in Fig. 7. The figure illustrates the basic four steps in SFM-MVS. Top-left is the result of the first step, the classic SFM, showing the estimates of the camera pose for each photo, and the sparse point cloud consisting of around 100,000 identified and matched characteristic object points. Top-right is a close-up on the dense point cloud, consisting of

Fig. 7 3D reconstruction using SFM-MVS: (**a**) top-left is the camera pose for each photo and the sparse cloud; (**b**) top-right is the dense point cloud; (**c**) bottom-left is the polygonal mesh; (**d**) bottom-right is the final textured 3D model

around 8,300,000 points, which resulted from the second step, the MVS algorithm application. Bottom-left is the result of the polygonal mesh created from the dense point cloud amounting nearly 560,000 faces. The textured 3D model is shown on the bottom-right, which is the final result and output of the method.

Technically, SFM-MVS uses a set of computationally demanding and memory hungry algorithms, but is easy to apply, is basically software-dependent and can be applied to both indoor and outdoor digitization projects, as it is able to tackle changes in illumination and color intensity. Key point in SFM is the successful solution to point correspondences and, thus, the quality of the 3D reconstruction is related to intense morphological features and their accurate identification and matching. The method cannot be used for reflective and transparent surfaces, although some particular filters, like polarizers, might reduce some of the issues and enable at least a partial processing. Apparently, the method cannot be also used for homogeneous featureless surfaces, although several studies tried to address this issue, for example, by projecting noise patterns on the surfaces (Koutsoudis et al., 2015). Research has already focused on the issues of featureless and specular surfaces, the image pre-processing for SFM-MVS optimization and the selection of the proper acquisition setup (Baltsavias, 1991; Baltsavias et al., 1996; Mallick et al., 2005; Remondino et al., 2008; Guidi et al., 2014; MacDonald et al., 2014; Gaiani et al., 2016; Nikolov & Madsen, 2016; Ioannakis et al., 2017).

An example of a successful SFM application in a large scale cultural heritage digitization project that run during 2015–2017 is presented in Liritzis et al. (2016, 2017). The project involved the digitization of the archaeological site of Delphi, a UNESCO World Heritage Site, along with objects exhibited at the Delphi museum. For the terrestrial part of the expedition, 25,000 photos were captured in total, covering thirteen (13) subjects, including the theatre, the sphinx of Naxos, the charioteer, the column with the dancers, along with the base of the column, the omphalus, six of the statues from the pediment of the temple of Apollo, and the statue of the philosopher. The project resulted massive high resolution data for archival and digital safeguarding and also for impressive virtual reality applications and immersive visualizations.

3 AI in Archaeology and Cultural Heritage

Artificial intelligence (AI) can be defined as the intelligence exhibited by artificial, human-made, systems. In research and development, it has appeared at a cross-section of engineering, computer science, neuroscience and social science, focusing on understanding and, in some cases, mimicking biological intelligence in problem solving, adaptation and evolution. In essence, applied AI seeks for models of particular physical processes in order to develop a domain understanding and predict trends and future events. The relevant literature is increasingly becoming massive and one may easily find numerous, and not always converging, definitions (Nilsson, 1998; Poole et al., 2006; Luger, 2008; Goodfellow et al., 2016; Poole & Mackworth,

2017; Russell & Norvig, 2021). Nilsson (1998) defined intelligence as a complex set of skills that involves perception, reasoning, learning, communicating and acting in complex environments. AI evolved considerably during the twentieth century due to the leaps in engineering, computing and computer science. Nowadays, AI is being increasingly applied in a diverse range of applications. Archaeology and cultural heritage have already been assisted by AI applications to tackle various challenges, ranging from purely research problems to complex interpretation and dissemination tasks.

The tools of AI have a direct impact on sharing and representing information so as to encourage in-depth and up-to-date reflection on the concepts of historical trends, culture and identity. They allow the efficient spreading of the cultural meaning as an expression of relations, identities, and ultimately of collective memory. AI has been proposed for effective asset organization and knowledge representation, virtual and cyber archaeology, advanced visualization, asset analysis and interpretation, intelligent user interfaces and tools for the experts, personalized access, gamification and public dissemination[2] (Bordoni et al., 2013). The following sections serve as a brief account of recent innovations brought by AI applications in archaeology and cultural heritage.

3.1 AI in Advanced Digitization and Preservation

Digitization is a crucial advancement in archaeology and cultural heritage, and a required step for the unlocking of the potential of the digital data towards better interpretation, preservation and dissemination. As explained in the first half of this chapter, digitization of cultural heritage is, in most cases, a rather complex, time consuming and computationally demanding process, often with a high economic cost. The search for automation in digitization goes on for decades, targeting to alleviate some of the burden imposed by the various techniques. For example, it was as soon as 2012 that Khalfaoui et al. (2012) proposed the full automation of the digitization process using a purely robotic approach. The proposed method uses a turntable and a 3D scanning device attached to a robotic arm. The positioning of the scanning device is controlled by an algorithm that estimates the object bounding box, the turntable angle, and the required scanner poses (pairs of orientations and positions). Partial scan registration and integration is simplified by being based on a fixed coordinate system set by the scanning system and refined by applying the iterative closest point (ICP) algorithm (Chen & Medioni, 1992; Besl & McKay, 1992). The authors reported a full surface coverage in all their digitization tests and a significant improvement in scanning times between 2× and 5× with respect to

---

[2] An interesting account of relevant topics can be found in Arianna Traviglia's presentation *Artificial Intelligence applications to Cultural Heritage* given at the 9th Plenary session of the Steering Committee for Culture, Heritage and Landscape, Council of Europe, found at https://rm.coe.int/artifical-intelligence-applications-to-cultural-heritage-by-arianna-tr/1680a096b8

manual scanning. A more detailed analysis of this work was presented in Khalfaoui et al. (2013). In Menna et al. (2017), the ORION prototype system was presented, which is a low-cost all-in-one automated image-based 3D digitization solution, based on a micro controller and a turntable, capable of working with multiple cameras and projected patterns (to tackle the problem of featureless surfaces). The paper, apart from the classic tests, analyzes some interesting aspects which are not fully covered in other solutions, like the depth of field issue[3] in digitization. Another approach based on the turntable-robotic arm paradigm was presented recently in Tausch et al. (2020). This was a desktop photogrammetry approach, suitable for small artifacts, designed to be portable, easily deployable, and capable of using different camera lens combinations. The system plans the next camera pose based on the current (intermediate) reconstruction using an optimization loop, in which the digitization quality is maximized to a desired limit, while safety constraints are satisfied. Practically, the method applies a quick scan which is further refined in regions in which the resolution is lower. Recently, González-Merino et al. (2021) proposed a low-cost robotic system capable of automated laser scanning or photogrammetry, based on rotations of the digitized object, using a turntable, and of the scanning device on a semicircle on the dome above the object. Of course, there are, today, solutions based on multiple sensors, like camera or photogrammetry rig formations,[4] but those solutions are hardly economical, as the cost of the numerous high quality capturing devices is in most cases extremely high. Very recently commercial robotic solutions have been made available,[5] implementing and improving the ideas previously presented.

In the beginning of the twenty-first century, a series of publications (Tsirliganis et al., 2002, 2004; Arnaoutoglou et al., 2003) proposed a novel, innovative approach for the digital documentation of tangible heritage, adopting the GIS paradigm of multi-layered data on top of three dimensional geometries. The idea was to implement a geographical information system for artifacts, registering geometric, spectral, physical and chemical data on top of each point of an object's surface. The approach was a bridging of 3D digitization, computer graphics, archaeometry and Web technologies in a single light-weight, easy to use Web application for the experts. This idea was renewed some ten years later in Stratis et al. (2014), where the complete workflow was expanded by incorporating multispectral data, forming

---

[3] Depth of field (DoF) is the range of distances in front of a camera lens in which the camera captures sharp details. Everything outside the DoF is out of focus and increasingly blurry with the distance from that range. Although the impact of the DoF is beneficial in artistic photography, like in portrait photography, it is actually an issue in photogrammetry. In digitization projects, the objects' surfaces need to be sharply focused to provide usable image pixels for digital photogrammetry to be efficient. As heritage objects are usually rotationally symmetric or complex-shaped, having the whole object sharply focused is not trivial and needs special attention and settings in the capturing equipment.

[4] See for example the PI3DScan at https://www.pi3dscan.com or the ESPER LightCage at https://www.esperhq.com/product/lightcage-scanning-rig/

[5] See for example the ARAGO system at https://rigsters.com/arago, or the LION3DX system at https://bit.ly/31sUXBx

an 18-dimensional space, providing advanced visualizations and study capabilities.

Around 2008, major organizations have undertaken the task to address the climate change impact on cultural (particularly tangible) heritage (Sabbioni et al., 2008). Key topics were identified, including (a) understanding the vulnerability of materials to climate, (b) monitoring, modeling and projecting changes, (c) developing tools for cultural management in a changing climate and (d) preventing damage using long term strategies. *Preventive preservation* emerged as the naturally preferred approach to tackle the challenges in those key topics and strong research efforts have been made to lay stable foundations for preventive approaches. A decade later, a large-scale study on the adaptation of cultural heritage to climate change risks has been carried by Sesana et al. (2018), reporting on the conception and actions by heritage management institutions, the research and scientific community, the governmental institutions and the related authorities. The study listed and categorized the determining factors for implementing the required adaptation, while recognizing the requirements, the barriers, the opportunities and best practices towards that direction. It also highlighted a need for more research and practical solutions for the incorporation of climate change adaptation in the preservation and management of cultural heritage. This is also reflected in the recent report by the Climate Change and Heritage Working Group of ICOMOS (Change et al., 2019), where the required adaptation was categorized into three groups of actions based on the ambition and risk in relation to the *Paris Agreement*.[6] In this direction, many AI research and applications efforts now emphasize on the preventive aspects, to improve the resilience and longevity of tangible heritage. Two such cases are described in the following paragraphs.

The wealth of data resulting from modern heritage digitization campaigns consists a significant reference point on which to develop advanced applications for the monitoring and preservation of cultural heritage. On this front, Nousias et al. (2020), within the scope of the EU project WARMEST,[7] proposed an AI method to inspect and assess defects on 3D digitized monument surfaces that are, potentially, the result of aging, weathering and erosion, or deterioration, in general. The approach is based on deep learning (convolutional neural networks-CNN) and the extraction of saliency maps that highlight the most important features of a 3D model. The approach is capable of not only analyzing the surface structure but also providing adaptive geometry simplification and compression, which are also important operations in the context of easy visualization, access and sharing of the massive 3D data derived from digitization projects.

Advancing heritage digitization towards what is known as the advanced or extended digitization, is the alignment of multimodal information on massive areas for monitoring, risk modeling and disaster prevention. Such an attempt has been

---

[6] See the *Paris Agreement* page in the United Nations Climate Change page at https://unfccc.int/process-and-meetings/the-paris-agreement/the-paris-agreement

[7] WARMEST – Low altitude remote sensing for the monitoring of the state of cultural heritage sites: building an integrated model for maintenance, at https://warmestproject.eu

recently presented in Koutsoudis et al. (2021), within the scope of project ESTIA.[8] This work focused on the research and development of image-based recognition and segmentation on 3D digitized urban areas, by utilizing geometric and multi-spectral features. The authors present a new low-cost airborne eight-band multi-spectral capturing system for digital photogrammetry, which they used to complete the data acquisition and reconstruct the 3D model of the urban area under study. The 3D reconstruction resulted a massive 3D model that was then analyzed by a deep learning method in order to identify distinct types of building materials. Furthermore, the segmented 3D model was annotated by a specially developed massive 3D model annotator.

Cyber-archaeology, a term that appears in the relevant literature in Levy et al. (2012), brought to light another interesting approach to advanced digitization and cultural documentation. Although the term *cyber* was reduced in meaning to whatever relates to computers and networks, it was originally connected with notions of strategy, management, control and governance, as it originates in the term *cybernetics*, encoding the Greek κυβερνητική, the art of governance, of steering or control. Thus it is even more intriguing that Levy et al. (2012) coined the term for digitally assisted archaeology. Now, at the UC San Diego Center for Cyber-Archaeology and Sustainability site,[9] one may read

> Cyber-archaeology is the marriage of archaeology, computer science, engineering, and the natural sciences, and it offers 21st century solutions to safeguard the past for future generations.

Cyber-archaeology, practically, laid the foundations for a complete eco-system of data, tools and services for digital management, study and dissemination for archaeology and cultural heritage.

3.2 AI in Interpretation and Restoration

Digitized tangible heritage can be an invaluable dataset upon which to build advanced AI applications for the interpretation and restoration of the past. Image-based AI methods can be successfully employed to decipher ancient languages and decode epigraphic marks, in addition to restoring missing parts of texts. Representative cases of such methods are briefly presented in the following paragraphs.

As early as 2005, Terras and Robertson (2005) proposed a complex AI method to assist papyrologists in the interpretation of the Vindolanda writing tablets. The approach is based on a fusion of the contributions from a language and an image model, using the minimum description length as the proper model selection principle, under a reinforcement learning framework. In a recent project at the University

---

[8] ESTIA: Risk Management Platform in Cultural Heritage Areas, at https://www.estia-project.gr

[9] The UC San Diego Center for Cyber-Archaeology and Sustainability, at http://ccas.ucsd.edu

of Chicago, a group of researchers run a project to decipher cuneiform tablets using computer vision and AI.[10] This is a project with many analogies to the handwritten text recognition, where AI methods have been successful in the past, and there are good chances that this will also be a successful project. Preliminary results suggest an 83% success so far. Hamdany et al. (2021), proposed an image-based AI approach for the identification of Sumerian cuneiform symbols and their transliteration to English. They used a simple, shallow, neural network architecture and an augmented training dataset. They reported highly successful results.

On the front of the restoration of ancient texts using AI, research appears only in very recent publications. Assael et al. (2019) presented *PYTHIA*,[11] a text restoration model capable of recovering missing parts of texts using deep learning (bidirectional LSTM). The model was trained using the *PHI Greek Inscriptions*[12] and artificially created ground-truth data, and achieved high accuracy results around 75%. About the same time, Fetaya et al. (2020) proposed a method to restore Babylonian texts using recurrent neural networks, focusing primarily on the Late Babylonian dialect of Akkadian. In this approach, language is viewed as a series of discrete tokens and the goal is to fit a probabilistic model for token sequences. The authors reported that their system significantly outperformed the n-gram baseline approach. The data used in the development of this model are available as this is an open-access publication, and the system was open-sourced.[13]

3.3   AI in Heritage Analysis

What is particularly useful in cultural heritage in the digital domain is the potential of new insight provided by novel analysis approaches that are enabled. Either by geometric and spectral or by physical and chemical analysis, a wealth of tools are available, nowadays, for the analysis of digitized heritage. The following are just a brief account of the possibilities opened for intelligent applications for the experts.

In a series of publications Koutsoudis et al. (2008, 2009, 2010a, b) presented a research dedicated to shape analysis of 3D artifacts and content-based search and retrieval in 3D artifact databases. Shape understanding is particularly important and useful in ancient pottery studies. This research developed a novel descriptor for such artifacts and a mechanism for searching, comparing and retrieving digital replicas of heritage objects, also enabling query-by-sketch capabilities and content-based navigation in virtual environments.

---

[10] Check the project development at https://cdac.uchicago.edu/research/deciphering-cuneiform-with-artificial-intelligence

[11] PYTHIA was open-sourced and is online at https://github.com/sommerschield/ancient-text-restoration

[12] PHI can be found online at https://inscriptions.packhum.org

[13] The system has been named *Atrahasis* and is available online at https://github.com/DigitalPasts/Atrahasis

More advanced AI applications in heritage analysis appeared only recently, and in Ioannakis et al. (2018) another novel descriptor has been proposed for the classification of digital artifacts. The method estimates the 3D object's mesh extrema, computes the principal curvature, and encodes the data into a 2D image, termed the *CurvMap*, which is useful as an input to a deep learning method for object classification. In extensive tests, the CurvMap attained more than 90% classification accuracy when used with a convolutional neural network architecture.

Around the same time, Bogacz and Mara (2018) proposed a cuneiform tablet analysis method that is capable of spotting words and extracting text from 3D digitized artifacts. The researchers defined a 12-dimensional feature descriptor for the wedges (cuneiform signs) of the text, and formulated an intelligent method to identify and extract the wedges with high precision and recall values. By exploiting the new multi-dimensional feature the researchers were able to succeed also in the word spotting, by developing and using a keypoint based model, which eventually outperformed other methods by more than 10%.

On the material characterization front, Sevetlidis and Pavlidis (2018, 2019) developed and proposed hierarchical, tree-based methods for the effective Raman spectra identification, as an assisting tool in archaeometry. Raman spectroscopy has become increasingly significant in archaeometry, and is a method that exploits the monochromatic light interaction with the vibrations in molecules to provide information about vibrational, rotational or other low-frequency modes. The proposed approach, consisting of an extremely randomized trees classifier, was evaluated on the RRUFF dataset and outperformed even more complex approaches, like a deep learning state-of-the-art approach.

On the quest for easy-to-use tools for archaeological and cultural 3D data annotation, very recently, Arampatzakis et al. (2021) proposed a novel user-friendly archaeological and cultural objects' annotation tools that is based purely on computer graphics approaches and international interoperability standards. *Art3mis*, the proposed system, was designed to tackle all the major challenges in 3D annotation systems, and applies the direct-on-surface annotation approach based on ray-polygon intersection. The method supports multiple annotation per 3D object with a variety of tools in a WYSIWYG interaction model. Annotation tools are increasingly becoming significant in the deep learning era, as they provide the means for easy data labeling and the creation of ground-truth datasets which are necessary for the supervised training of AI models.

Recently, Davoudi et al. (2021) proposed an autoencoder-based architecture with sparse latent variables to tackle the ancient handwritten document layout analysis problem. The benefit of the approach is that it is unsupervised, thus, it does not require labeled data for the training. The researchers tested the representation learning accuracy of their model and it resulted a classification accuracy of around 97%. As regards the layout extraction performance, the authors provide comparative results that are of high accuracy, either outperforming other unsupervised learning methods, or being comparable to the state-of-the-art supervised learning approaches.

Artifact authentication is another challenging task, which was traditionally undertaken by selected experts. Nowadays, AI-based approaches can attain super-human performance in pattern recognition and style learning tasks, which may be considered as the foundations of authentication. There is mature technology for this task and commercial services are already available to assist the experts in the field.[14] This technology is primarily based on images and convolutional and generative adversarial neural networks. A stroke analysis in line drawings was presented in Elgammal et al. (2018), which targets the attribution problem of drawings of unknown artists. The method developed was reported to achieve a 70–90% accuracy in classifying individual strokes and above 80% in drawings, with a perfect 100% in detecting fakes. A research focused on learning art styles (a problem different than that of learning artists' styles) can be found in Mai et al. (2020). The researchers in this work focused on the psychological effects of the various art styles and the conceptualized differences between the Eastern and Western art and provide very insightful results. Apparently, inclusion of more data in the process, like the 3D geometry, archaeometry and multi-spectral data, is expected to yield improved authentication results.

3.4 AI in Predictive Modeling

A classic example of AI in predictive archaeological modeling can be found in Balla et al. (2012, 2013a, b), in which the goal was to create a model to predict the presence of burial sites for identification and management projects. The model exploited archaeological and geospatial information from a large bibliographic research on the particular case of the ancient Macedonian tombs in Northern Greece and was able to provide map-based predictions with color-coded probability visualization. The model used multi-dimensional data and employed parameter selection and tuning to relax the criteria imposed, and provide conservative or ambitious predictions. The fine-tuning of the parameters was extensively tested based on ground-truth data and various configurations have been proposed for different applications scenarios. It should be stressed that this was among the first and most complete cases of predictive modeling in archaeology that targeted excavation archaeology, as well as cultural management and urban development aspects.

3.5 AI in Virtual/Extended Reality Museums and Gamification

A domain in which AI is expected to deliver quite interesting results in that of virtual, augmented and extended reality (VR, AR, XR, let's call them *digital realities* for simplicity), along with that of gamification, either integrated or not with the digital realities. This is a complex domain with a large volume of published work in

---

[14] See for example the Art Recognition page at https://art-recognition.com

various application fields, with only limited contribution to archaeology and cultural heritage so far. Digital reality technologies and gamification can be an important tool for heritage experts, as it already is an established dissemination tool for the public.

Knabb et al. (2014) have clearly established how useful fully immersive VR can be in archaeological research by using a CAVE system for the study of an excavation (like the StarCAVE or the WAVE), including the total wealth of information provided by a digital excavation backend. This paper also demonstrated other VR solutions for advanced visualization of archaeological sites (like the TourCAVE). The same research group showcased another interesting solution for VR display of archaeological sites and artifacts to the public, the CAVEkiosk technology (Levy et al., 2020). These efforts are within the general scope of Cyber-archaeology set by this research group.

In the early years of the advanced virtual museums research, Koutsoudis et al. (2012) attempted an integration of formerly unconnected technologies, VR, gaming and content-based analysis. Specifically, this research presented a system that was based on the shape analysis of 3D museum exhibits and was able to provide a VR experience for a virtual museum in which content-based navigation was enabled. The concept of content-based navigation related to the navigation based on the similarity of an object of interest with other exhibits at the virtual museum. Game engine technology was the foundation of this solution, supporting state-of-the-art visualizations and real-time interactions.

Kiourt et al. (2017b) provided a systematic and mathematical analysis of concepts of realism in virtual environments for cultural heritage applications including aspects of exhibition and gamification. The authors analyzed the foundational technologies borrowed from computer graphics, and presented their effects using examples. In the direction of AI, the authors analyzed how concepts of intelligent virtual agents can be brought to VR museums. In addition, the authors integrated into the picture the digitization aspects, the game engine technology, the concepts of play, and how all ingredients connect with each other, forming the domain of serious games. Building on those concepts, the same research team focused on the virtual environments supported by multiple intelligent virtual agents in a framework for cultural applications (Kiourt et al., 2017a). The concept was to analyze the potential of multi-agent systems as autonomous social organizations capable of developing dynamic personalized virtual environments. The authors defined the structure of an enhanced VR experience as a three-dimensional process, constituting of content generation, knowledge modeling and gameplay, towards personal virtual museums.

Building on those theoretical studies, after a series of developments, Kiourt et al. (2016) proposed *Dynamus*, a fully dynamic virtual exhibition framework for the museum curators and the public. Dynamus is a complete WYSIWYG VR framework that enables the creation of Web powered exhibitions, offering linked open data functionalities and state-of-the-art game engine graphics and interaction. Dynamus was created to be open and free for access and use by all, and has already been tested in cultural and educational settings. The paper presents some insightful results by the user assessment in educational environments.

The serious games framework was also adopted in Kiourt et al. (2018), in which the researchers presented a set of rules, theory and best practices, for the development of virtual environments, content adaptation and interaction dynamics, for cultural heritage applications, and particularly virtual museums. The serious games framework, as the intersection of content, knowledge and play, was enhanced with user modeling to define the personalized VR. The paper included cases studied under this framework and provided insightful user-provided results.

3.6 AI in Personalized, Inclusive Cultural Tourism

Personalization of content and services is of significant importance in the big data era. As massive amounts of data are increasingly becoming available online, everyone is exposed to information overload to a point that the Web becomes an obstacle rather than a treasure. To tackle the overload of content and services, a successful remedy comes from what was traditionally known as adaptive technologies, now termed personalization. This encodes the attempt to model a user's preferences and potential needs and be able to narrow down the information provided to the most relevant. The field of AI that is associated with this task is that of *recommenders*. Recommenders are intelligent software engines that operate in a diverse range of applications, from music and movie recommendations, to tourism packages, friend connection proposals in social media, adaptive search results by search engines, and more.

Recommenders have already a history in archaeology and cultural heritage, primarily in the cultural tourism sector. Pavlidis (2019a) provided a detailed account of the developments in this sector, beginning with the early cultural recommenders at the end of the twentieth century. In addition, the paper presented the various alternative techniques upon which recommenders are being based, analyzing the benefits and limitations of each of the approaches, providing the mathematical foundation in each case. The paper concluded by identifying the way forward in this technology for applications in cultural heritage.

In a series of publications, Pavlidis (2018a, b, 2019b) laid out the foundations for a novel framework upon which to develop recommenders for cultural tourism, in which the task was set to minimize the visitor dissatisfaction, by potential distractions and obstacles, during a cultural visit in a museum, a historical or an archaeological site. In Pavlidis (2018a) the *Apollo* recommender was described based on this framework, which was a complete advanced personalization system for cultural tourism that was extensively tested in realistic simulated settings based on global data available on the Web. The approach adopted, which is a kind of a "defensive" approach termed *minimax*, as it seeks to minimize the dissatisfaction (and not maximize the satisfaction), resulted in having visitor dissatisfaction effectively controlled. At the same time, the evaluation of massive user preferences and dissatisfaction resulted in another interesting result, which related to preset visit scenarios, which museum curators can exploit to redesign their exhibitions.

Recently, Sidiropoulos et al. (2021) presented a complex mixed multi-agent environment, in which the intelligent agents perform actions based on historical context. In this study the agents were ancient warriors in a melee fight. In the framework of reinforcement learning, the agents were guided towards shaping their behaviors to achieve particular goals, and the presented results demonstrated how intelligent agents can learn new behaviors defined by algorithms and rules provided by the operators of the experiments. Behavior shaping of intelligent agents is at the fore-front of reinforcement learning and will lead to highly adaptive personal assistant technologies for archaeology and cultural applications both for the experts and the public.

Last but not least, Pistofidis et al. (2021) recently proposed an inclusive technological approach, that bridges 3D digitization, 3D printing, the Internet of Things (IoT) and AI to enable the interaction of visually impaired visitors with museum artifacts and exhibits.[15] The result was the creation of smart exhibits for haptic experiences, the printed replicas of actual digitized exhibits, which have been augmented with electronics and intelligence to become interactive. The interesting in this research is that the specifications were set by the target group by means of a pre-development research using printed prototype primitive objects.

4 Conclusion

In the recent decades, traditional Humanities have been transforming with the incorporation of computational approaches, giving shape to what is currently termed Digital Humanities, which ignited some controversy over the terminology. Pavlidis et al. (2018) made an account of the current challenges for Digital Humanities and identified a research agenda for the decades to come. In Markantonatou et al. (2020) the same researchers updated the original list of challenges in order to include socially relevant topics, by means of outlining the challenges where the Digital Humanities can make a social impact, somehow reversing the direction in which the challenges may be viewed.

In any case, with or without a philosophical foundation, digital technology has been widely applied in archaeology and cultural heritage in the recent decades, in a significant range of applications, contributing to the recording, preservation, study and dissemination of human civilization across the ages. This chapter focused on those two pillars that were identified as the foundation pillars upon which to base a future in archaeology and cultural heritage, the 3D digitization and the AI applications. In this context, 3D digitization was introduced and explained in terms of the most widely used methods and a set of topics in AI have been reviewed, including advanced digitization and preservation, interpretation and restoration, heritage analysis, predictive modeling, virtual/extended reality museums & gamification, and

---

[15] This research was conducted in the framework of project APTOS https://aptos.athenarc.gr

From Digital Recording to Advanced AI Applications in Archaeology and Cultural...   1651

personalized, inclusive cultural tourism. This cannot not be a conclusive list of topics and technologies, as the domain presented is highly dynamic, following the current exponential development in advanced digital technologies of the twenty-first century.

References

Arampatzakis, V., Sevetlidis, V., Arnaoutoglou, F., Kalogeras, A., Koulamas, C., Lalos, A., Kiourt, C., Ioannakis, G., Koutsoudis, A., & Pavlidis, G. (2021). Art3mis: Ray-based textual annotation on 3d cultural objects. In *CAA 2021*. Cyprus University of Technology.

Arnaoutoglou, F., Evagelidis, V., Pavlidis, G., Tsirliganis, N., & Chamzas, C. (2003). 3d-gis: New ways in digitization and visualization of cultural objects. *Workshop on the Digitization of Cultural Content, 27*, 28.

Arnaoutoglou, F., Koutsoudis, A., Pavlidis, G., Tsioukas, V., & Chamzas, C. (2006). Towards a versatile handheld 3D laser scanner. In *Proceedings of the 7th international symposium on virtual reality, archaeology and cultural heritage, Dresden, Germany* (p. 2527).

Assael, Y., Sommerschield, T., & Prag, J. (2019). Restoring ancient text using deep learning: A case study on Greek epigraphy. In *Proceedings of the 2019 conference on empirical methods in natural language processing and the 9th international joint conference on natural language processing (EMNLP-IJCNLP)*. Association for Computational Linguistics.

Balla, A., Pavlogeorgatos, G., Tsiafakis, D., & Pavlidis, G. (2012). Predicting Macedonian tombs' locations using GIS, predictive modeling and fuzzy logic. In *CAA 2012*. University of Southampton, CAA International.

Balla, A., Pavlogeorgatos, G., Tsiafakis, D., & Pavlidis, G. (2013a). Locating Macedonian tombs using predictive modelling. *Journal of Cultural Heritage, 14*(5), 403–410.

Balla, A., Pavlogeorgatos, G., Tsiafakis, D., & Pavlidis, G. (2013b). Modelling archaeological and geospatial information for burial site prediction, identification and management. *International Journal of Heritage in the Digital Era, 2*(4), 585–609.

Baltsavias, E. P. (1991). *Multiphoto geometrically constrained matching*. PhD thesis, ETH Zurich.

Baltsavias, E., Li, H., Mason, S., Stefanidis, A., & Sinning, M. (1996). Comparison of two digital photogrammetric systems with emphasis on DTM generation: Case study glacier measurement. *International Archives of Photogrammetry and Remote Sensing, 31*, 104–109.

Bay, H., Tuytelaars, T., & Van Gool, L. (2006). Surf: Speeded up robust features. In *European conference on computer vision* (pp. 404–417). Springer.

Beraldin, J.-A., Blais, F., Cournoyer, L., Godin, G., Rioux, M., & Taylor, J. (2004). Active 3D sensing for heritage applications. *Bar International Series, 1227*, 340–343.

Bertozzi, M., Broggi, A., Conte, G., & Fascioli, A. (2002). Stereo-vision system performance analysis. *Enabling Technologies for the PRASSI Autonomous Robot*, 68–73.

Besl, P. J., & McKay, N. D. (1992). Method for registration of 3-d shapes. In *Sensor Fusion IV: Control paradigms and data structures* (Vol. 1611, pp. 586–607). International Society for Optics and Photonics.

Boehler, W., & Marbs, A. (2002). 3D scanning instruments. *Proceedings of the CIPA WG, 6*, 9–18.

Bogacz, B., & Mara, H. (2018). From extraction to spotting for cuneiform script analysis. In *2018 13th IAPR international workshop on document analysis systems (DAS)* (pp. 199–204). IEEE.

Bordoni, L., Ardissono, L., Barceló, J. A., Chella, A., de Gemmis, M., Gena, C., Iaquinta, L., Lops, P., Mele, F., Musto, C., et al. (2013). The contribution of AI to enhance understanding of cultural heritage. *Intelligenza Artificiale, 7*(2), 101–112.

Borghese, N. A., Ferrigno, G., Baroni, G., Pedotti, A., Ferrari, S., & Savare, R. (1998). Autoscan: A flexible and portable 3D scanner. *IEEE Computer Graphics and Applications, 18*(3), 38–41.

Chamzas, C., Koutsoudis, A., Pavlidis, G., & Tsiafakis, D. (2008). Applying 3D digitisation technologies in the cultural heritage domain. In *Proceedings: International symposium on "Information and communication technologies in cultural heritage"* (p. 35). Earthlab.

Change, C., et al. (2019). *The future of our pasts: Engaging cultural heritage in climate action outline of climate change and cultural heritage.*

Chen, Y., & Medioni, G. (1992). Object modelling by registration of multiple range images. *Image and Vision Computing, 10*(3), 145–155.

Chen, C.-S., Hung, Y.-P., Chiang, C.-C., & Wu, J.-L. (1997). Range data acquisition using color structured lighting and stereo vision. *Image and Vision Computing, 15*(6), 445–456.

Cortelazzo, G. M., & Marton, F. (1999). About modeling cultural heritage objects with limited computers resources. In *Proceedings of international conference on Image analysis and processing* (pp. 848–853). IEEE.

Cutting, J. E., & Vishton, P. M. (1995). Perceiving layout and knowing distances: The integration, relative potency, and contextual use of different information about depth. In *Perception of space and motion* (pp. 69–117). Elsevier.

Daniil, M. (2009). *Topography – Topographic mapping of space.* Lecture notes. Democritus University of Thrace (in Greek).

Davoudi, H., Fiorucci, M., & Traviglia, A. (2021). Ancient document layout analysis: Autoencoders meet sparse coding. In *2020 25th international conference on pattern recognition (ICPR)* (pp. 5936–5942). IEEE.

Elgammal, A., Kang, Y., & Den Leeuw, M. (2018). Picasso, Matisse, or a fake? Automated analysis of drawings at the stroke level for attribution and authentication. In *Thirty-second AAAI conference on artificial intelligence.*

Fetaya, E., Lifshitz, Y., Aaron, E., & Gordin, S. (2020). Restoration of fragmentary Babylonian texts using recurrent neural networks. *Proceedings of the National Academy of Sciences, 117*(37), 22743–22751.

Forest, J., Salvi, J., Cabruja, E., & Pous, C. (2004). Laser stripe peak detector for 3D scanners. A FIR filter approach. In *Proceedings of the 17th international conference on pattern recognition. ICPR 2004* (Vol. 3, pp. 646–649). IEEE.

Furukawa, Y., & Hernandez, C. (2015). Multi-view stereo: A tutorial. *Foundations and Trends in Computer Graphics and Vision, 9*(1–2), 1–148.

Gaiani, M., Remondino, F., Apollonio, F., & Ballabeni, A. (2016). An advanced pre-processing pipeline to improve automated photogrammetric reconstructions of architectural scenes. *Remote Sensing, 8*(3), 178.

Godin, G., Rioux, M., Beraldin, J.-A., Levoy, M., Cournoyer, L., & Blais, F. (2001). An assessment of laser range measurement on marble surfaces. In *5th conference on optical 3D measurement techniques* (Vol. 3).

González-Merino, R., Sánchez-López, E., Romero, P. E., Rodero, J., & Hidalgo-Fernández, R. E. (2021). Low-cost prototype to automate the 3D digitization of pieces: An application example and comparison. *Sensors, 21*(8), 2580.

Goodfellow, I., Bengio, Y., & Courville, A. (2016). *Deep learning.* MIT Press. ISBN:978-0262035613.

Guidi, G., Gonizzi, S., & Micoli, L. (2014). Image pre-processing for optimizing automated photogrammetry performances. In *ISPRS technical commission V symposium* (Vol. 2, pp. 145–152). ISPRS.

Hamdany, A. H. S., Al-Nima, R. R. O., & Albak, L. H. (2021). Translating cuneiform symbols using artificial neural network. *Telkomnika, 19*(2), 438–443.

Hawkins, T., Cohen, J., & Debevec, P. (2001). A photometric approach to digitizing cultural artifacts. In *Proceedings of the 2001 conference on virtual reality, archeology, and cultural heritage* (pp. 333–342). ACM.

Hébert, P. (2001). A self-referenced hand-held range sensor. In *Proceedings third international conference on 3-D digital imaging and modeling* (pp. 5–12). IEEE.

Horn, E., & Kiryati, N. (1999). Toward optimal structured light patterns. *Image and Vision Computing, 17*(2), 87–97.

Ioannakis, G., Koutsoudis, A., Arnaoutoglou, F., Kiourt, C., & Chamzas, C. (2017). On structure-from-motion application challenges: Good practices. *International Journal of Computational Methods in Heritage Science (IJCMHS), 1*(2), 47–57.

Ioannakis, G., Arnaoutoglou, F., Koutsoudis, A., Pavlidis, G., & Chamzas, C. (2018). CurvMaps: A novel feature for 3D model classification. In *2018 international conference on intelligent systems (IS)* (pp. 242–248). IEEE.

Kaplan, A., & Haenlein, M. (2019). Siri, Siri, in my hand: Who's the fairest in the land? On the interpretations, illustrations, and implications of artificial intelligence. *Business Horizons, 62*(1), 15–25.

Khalfaoui, S., Aigueperse, A., Seulin, R., Fougerolle, Y., & Fofi, D. (2012). Fully automatic 3D digitization of unknown objects using progressive data bounding box. In *Three-dimensional image processing (3DIP) and applications II* (Vol. 8290, p. 829011). International Society for Optics and Photonics.

Khalfaoui, S., Seulin, R., Fougerolle, Y., & Fofi, D. (2013). An efficient method for fully automatic 3D digitization of unknown objects. *Computers in Industry, 64*(9), 1152–1160.

Kiourt, C., Koutsoudis, A., & Pavlidis, G. (2016). DynaMus: A fully dynamic 3D virtual museum framework. *Journal of Cultural Heritage, 22*, 984–991.

Kiourt, C., Pavlidis, G., Koutsoudis, A., & Kalles, D. (2017a). Multi-agents based virtual environments for cultural heritage. In 2017 *XXVI international conference on information, communication and automation technologies (ICAT)* (pp. 1–6). IEEE.

Kiourt, C., Pavlidis, G., Koutsoudis, A., & Kalles, D. (2017b). Realistic simulation of cultural heritage. *International Journal of Computational Methods in Heritage Science (IJCMHS), 1*(1), 10–40.

Kiourt, C., Koutsoudis, A., & Kalles, D. (2018). Enhanced virtual reality experience in personalised virtual museums. *International Journal of Computational Methods in Heritage Science (IJCMHS), 2*(1), 23–39.

Kline, R. (2010). Cybernetics, automata studies, and the Dartmouth conference on artificial intelligence. *IEEE Annals of the History of Computing, 33*(4), 5–16.

Knabb, K. A., Schulze, J. P., Kuester, F., DeFanti, T. A., & Levy, T. E. (2014). Scientific visualization, 3D immersive virtual reality environments, and archaeology in Jordan and the Near East. *Near Eastern Archaeology, 77*(3), 228–232.

Koutsoudis, A., Pavlidis, G., Arnaoutoglou, F., Tsiafakis, D., & Chamzas, C. (2008). A 3D pottery database for benchmarking content based retrieval mechanisms. In *Eurographics 2008 workshop on 3D object retrieval*, Chersonesos, Crete (Vol. 2).

Koutsoudis, A., Pavlidis, G., Arnaoutoglou, F., Tsiafakis, D., & Chamzas, C. (2009). Qp: A tool for generating 3D models of ancient Greek pottery. *Journal of Cultural Heritage, 10*(2), 281–295.

Koutsoudis, A., Pavlidis, G., & Chamzas, C. (2010a). Detecting shape similarities in 3D pottery repositories. In *2010 IEEE fourth international conference on semantic computing* (pp. 548–552). IEEE.

Koutsoudis, A., Pavlidis, G., Liami, V., Tsiafakis, D., & Chamzas, C. (2010b). 3D pottery content-based retrieval based on pose normalisation and segmentation. *Journal of Cultural Heritage, 11*(3), 329–338.

Koutsoudis, A., Makarona, C., & Pavlidis, G. (2012). Content-based navigation within virtual museums. *Journal of Advanced Computer Science and Technology, 1*(2), 73–81.

Koutsoudis, A., Vidmar, B., Ioannakis, G., Arnaoutoglou, F., Pavlidis, G., & Chamzas, C. (2014). Multi-image 3d reconstruction data evaluation. *Journal of Cultural Heritage, 15*(1), 73–79.

Koutsoudis, A., Ioannakis, G., Vidmar, B., Arnaoutoglou, F., & Chamzas, C. (2015). Using noise function-based patterns to enhance photogrammetric 3D reconstruction performance of featureless surfaces. *Journal of Cultural Heritage, 16*(5), 664–670.

Koutsoudis, A., Ioannakis, G., Pistofidis, P., Arnaoutoglou, F., Kazakis, N., Pavlidis, G., Chamzas, C., & Tsirliganis, N. (2021). Multispectral aerial imagery-based 3D digitisation, segmentation and annotation of large scale urban areas of significant cultural value. *Journal of Cultural Heritage, 49*, 1–9.

Levoy, M., Pulli, K., Curless, B., Rusinkiewicz, S., Koller, D., Pereira, L., Ginzton, M., Anderson, S., Davis, J., Ginsberg, J., et al. (2000). The digital Michelangelo project: 3D scanning of large statues. In *Proceedings of the 27th annual conference on Computer graphics and interactive techniques* (pp. 131–144).

Levy, T. E., Smith, N. G., Najjar, M., DeFanti, T. A., Kuester, F., & Lin, A. Y.-M. (2012). *Cyber-archaeology in the holy land.* California Institute for Telecommunications and Information Technology (Calit2), UC San Diego.

Levy, T. E., Smith, C., Agcaoili, K., Kannan, A., Goren, A., Schulze, J. P., & Yago, G. (2020). Chapter 7: At-risk world heritage and virtual reality visualization for cyber-archaeology: The Mar Saba test case. In M. Forte & H. Murteira (Eds.), *Digital cities: Between history and archaeology* (pp. 151–171). Oxford University Press. ISBN:9780190498900.

Liritzis, I., Pavlidis, G., Vosynakis, S., Koutsoudis, A., Volonakis, P., Petrochilos, N., Howland, M. D., Liss, B., & Levy, T. E. (2016). Delphi4delphi: First results of the digital archaeology initiative for ancient Delphi, Greece. *Antiquity, 90*(354).

Liritzis, I., Pavlidis, G., Vosinakis, S., Koutsoudis, A., Volonakis, P., Howland, M. D., Liss, B., & Levy, T. E. (2017). Delphi4delphi: Data acquisition of spatial cultural heritage data for ancient Delphi, Greece. In *Heritage and archaeology in the digital age* (pp. 151–165). Springer.

Loop, C., & Zhang, Z. (1999). Computing rectifying homographies for stereo vision. In *Proceedings of 1999 IEEE computer society conference on computer vision and pattern recognition (Cat. No PR00149)* (Vol. 1, pp. 125–131). IEEE.

Lowe, D. G. (1999). Object recognition from local scale-invariant features. In *The proceedings of the seventh IEEE international conference on Computer vision* (Vol. 2, pp. 1150–1157). IEEE.

Luger, G. F. (2008). *Artificial intelligence: Structures and strategies for complex problem solving* (6th ed.). Pearson Addison-Wesley. ISBN:978-0321545893.

MacDonald, L., Hindmarch, J., Robson, S., & Terras, M. (2014). Modelling the appearance of heritage metallic surfaces. *International Archives of the Photogrammetry, Remote Sensing & Spatial Information Sciences*, 45.

Mai, C. H., Nakatsu, R., Tosa, N., Kusumi, T., & Koyamada, K. (2020). Learning of art style using AI and its evaluation based on psychological experiments. In *International conference on entertainment computing* (pp. 308–316). Springer.

Mallick, S. P., Zickler, T. E., Kriegman, D. J., & Belhumeur, P. N. (2005). Beyond lambert: Reconstructing specular surfaces using color. In *2005 IEEE Computer society conference on Computer vision and pattern recognition (CVPR'05)* (Vol. 2, pp. 619–626). IEEE.

Marbs, A. (2002). Experiences with laser scanning at i3mainz. In *Proceedings of the CIPA WG6 international workshop on scanning for cultural heritage recording.* http://www.isprs.org/commission5/workshop

Markantonatou, S., Donig, S., Pavlidis, G., Gees, T., & Koumpis, A. (2020). Ten challenges for digital humanities and the way forward: Revisited from the social context. In *Applying innovative technologies in heritage science* (pp. 297–305). IGI Global.

Menna, F., Nocerino, E., Morabito, D., Farella, E., Perini, M., & Remondino, F. (2017). An open source low-cost automatic system for image-based 3D digitization. *The International Archives of Photogrammetry, Remote Sensing and Spatial Information Sciences, 42*, 155.

Moor, J. (2006). The Dartmouth college artificial intelligence conference: The next fifty years. *AI Magazine, 27*(4), 87–87.

Nikolov, I., & Madsen, C. (2016). Benchmarking close-range structure from motion 3D reconstruction software under varying capturing conditions. In *Euro-Mediterranean conference* (pp. 15–26). Springer.

Nilsson, N. J. (1998). *Artificial intelligence: A new synthesis.* Morgan Kaufmann. ISBN:978-1558604674.

Nousias, S., Arvanitis, G., Lalos, A. S., Pavlidis, G., Koulamas, C., Kalogeras, A., & Moustakas, K. (2020). A saliency aware CNN-based 3D model simplification and compression framework for remote inspection of heritage sites. *IEEE Access, 8*, 169982–170001.

Oliensis, J. (2000). A critique of structure-from-motion algorithms. *Computer Vision and Image Understanding, 80*(2), 172–214.

Patias, P. (1999). *Photogrammetric survey and documentation of architectural monuments and archaeological sites*. Lecture notes (in Greek). Lecture notes on the postgraduate program of studies entitled "Systems of cultural goods and management of the cultural heritage" of the University of Crete.

Pavlidis, G. (2018a). Apollo-a hybrid recommender for museums and cultural tourism. In *2018 international conference on intelligent systems (IS)* (pp. 94–101). IEEE.

Pavlidis, G. (2018b). Towards a novel user satisfaction modelling for museum visit recommender systems. In *International conference on VR technologies in cultural heritage* (pp. 60–75). Springer.

Pavlidis, G. (2019a). Recommender systems, cultural heritage applications, and the way forward. *Journal of Cultural Heritage, 35*, 183–196.

Pavlidis, G. (2019b). On the end-to-end development of a cultural tourism recommender. *International Journal of Computational Methods in Heritage Science (IJCMHS), 3*(2), 73–90.

Pavlidis, G., & Royo, S. (2018). 3D depth sensing. In *Digital techniques for documenting and preserving cultural heritage* (pp. 195–198). ARC, Amsterdam University Press.

Pavlidis, G., Tsirliganis, N., Tsiafakis, D., Arnaoutoglou, F., & Chamzas, C. (2006). 3D digitization of monuments: The case of Mani. In *3rd international conference of museology*, Mytilene, Greece.

Pavlidis, G., Koutsoudis, A., Arnaoutoglou, F., Tsioukas, V., & Chamzas, C. (2007). Methods for 3D digitization of cultural heritage. *Journal of Cultural Heritage, 8*(1), 93–98.

Pavlidis, G., Markantonatou, S., Donig, S., & Koumpis, A. (2018). Ten challenges for digital humanities and the way forward. *International Journal of Computational Methods in Heritage Science (IJCMHS), 2*(1), 1–7.

Pistofidis, P., Ioannakis, G., Arnaoutoglou, F., Michailidou, N., Karta, M., Kiourt, C., Pavlidis, G., Mouroutsos, S. G., Tsiafaki, D., & Koutsoudis, A. (2021). Composing smart museum exhibit specifications for the visually impaired. *Journal of Cultural Heritage, 52*, 1–10.

Pollefeys, M., Van Gool, L., Vergauwen, M., Cornelis, K., Verbiest, F., & Tops, J. (2003). 3D capture of archaeology and architecture with a hand-held camera. *International Archives of Photogrammetry Remote Sensing and Spatial Information Sciences, 34*(5/W12), 262–267.

Poole, D. L., & Mackworth, A. K. (2017). *Artificial intelligence: Foundations of computational agents* (2nd ed.). Cambridge University Press. ISBN:978-1107195394.

Poole, D., Mackworth, A., & Goebel, R. (2006). *Computational intelligence: A logical approach* (4th ed.). Oxford University. ISBN:978-0195685725.

Popescu, V., Sacks, E., & Bahmutov, G. (2003). The model camera: A hand-held device for interactive modeling. In *Proceedings of fourth international conference on 3-D digital imaging and modeling, 2003. 3DIM 2003* (pp. 285–292). IEEE.

Rakitina, E., Rakitin, I., Staleva, V., Arnaoutoglou, F., Koutsoudis, A., & Pavlidis, G. (2008). An overview of 3D laser scanning technology. In *Proceedings of the international scientific conference*, Citeseer.

Remondino, F., El-Hakim, S., Gruen, A., & Zhang, L. (2008). Development and performance analysis of image matching for detailed surface reconstruction of heritage objects. *IEEE Signal Processing Magazine, 25*(4), 55–65.

Rocchini, C., Cignoni, P., Montani, C., Pingi, P., and Scopigno, R. (2001). A low cost 3D scanner based on structured light. In *Computer graphics forum* (Vol. 20:3, pp. 299–308). Wiley Online Library.

Rusinkiewicz, S., Hall-Holt, O., & Levoy, M. (2002). Real-time 3D model acquisition. *ACM Transactions on Graphics (TOG), 21*(3), 438–446.

Russell, S., & Norvig, P. (2021). *Artificial intelligence: A modern approach* (4th ed.). Pearson, Global. ISBN:978-1292401133.

Sabbioni, C., Cassar, M., Brimblecombe, P., & Lefevre, R.-A. (2008). *Vulnerability of cultural heritage to climate change*. Technical report, EUR-OPA major hazards agreement, Council of Europe.

Salvi, J., Pages, J., & Batlle, J. (2004). Pattern codification strategies in structured light systems. *Pattern Recognition, 37*(4), 827–849.

Scharstein, D., & Szeliski, R. (2002). A taxonomy and evaluation of dense two-frame stereo correspondence algorithms. *International Journal of Computer Vision, 47*(1–3), 7–42.

Sesana, E., Gagnon, A. S., Bertolin, C., & Hughes, J. (2018). Adapting cultural heritage to climate change risks: Perspectives of cultural heritage experts in Europe. *Geosciences, 8*(8), 305.

Sevetlidis, V., & Pavlidis, G. (2018). Hierarchical classification for improved compound identification in Raman spectroscopy. In *3rd computer applications and quantitative methods in archaeology (CAA-GR) conference, 2018*.

Sevetlidis, V., & Pavlidis, G. (2019). Effective Raman spectra identification with tree-based methods. *Journal of Cultural Heritage, 37*, 121–128.

Sidiropoulos, G., Kiourt, C., Sevetlidis, V., & Pavlidis, G. (2021). Shaping the behavior of reinforcement learning agents. In *25th Pan-Hellenic conference on informatics*, Volos, Greece.

Solomonoff, R. J. (1985). The time scale of artificial intelligence: Reflections on social effects. *Human Systems Management, 5*(2), 149–153.

Stratis, J. A., Makarona, C., Lazidou, D., Sánchez, E. G., Koutsoudis, A., Pamplona, M., Pauswein, R., Pavlidis, G., Simon, S., & Tsirliganis, N. (2014). Enhancing the examination workflow for byzantine icons: Implementation of information technology tools in a traditional context. *Journal of Cultural Heritage, 15*(1), 85–91.

Szeliski, R. (2011). *Computer vision – Algorithms and applications*. Springer. ISBN:978-1-84882-934-3.

Takatsuka, M., West, G. A., Venkatesh, S., and Caelli, T. M. (1999). Low-cost interactive active monocular range finder. In *Proceedings of 1999 IEEE computer society conference on computer vision and pattern recognition (Cat. No PR00149)* (Vol. 1, pp. 444–449). IEEE.

Tausch, R., Domajnko, M., Ritz, M., Knuth, M., Santos, P., & Fellner, D. (2020). Towards 3D digitization in the glam (galleries, libraries, archives, and museums) sector: Lessons learned and future outlook. *IPSI BgD Transactions on Internet Research (TIR), 16*(1), 1–9.

Terras, M., & Robertson, P. (2005). Image and interpretation using artificial intelligence to read ancient roman texts. *Human IT, 7*(3), 1–56.

Tsirliganis, N., Pavlidis, G., Koutsoudis, A., Papadopoulou, D., Tsompanopoulos, A., Stavroglou, K., Loukou, Z., & Chamzas, C. (2002). Archiving 3D cultural objects with surface point-wise database information. In *Proceedings of first international symposium on 3D data processing visualization and transmission* (pp. 766–769). IEEE.

Tsirliganis, N., Pavlidis, G., Koutsoudis, A., Papadopoulou, D., Tsompanopoulos, A., Stavroglou, K., Loukou, Z., & Chamzas, C. (2004). Archiving cultural objects in the 21st century. *Journal of Cultural Heritage, 5*(4), 379–384.

Tziavos, I., & Spatalas, S. (2004). *Urban design applications and topographic surveys*. Lecture notes. Aristotle University of Thessaloniki (in Greek).

Vlachos, D. (1998). *Principles and methods of topographic recording*. Lecture notes (in Greek).

Wust, C., & Capson, D. W. (1991). Surface profile measurement using color fringe projection. *Machine Vision and Applications, 4*(3), 193–203.

Zanuttigh, P., Marin, G., Dal Mutto, C., Dominio, F., Minto, L., & Cortelazzo, G. M. (2016). Operating principles of structured light depth cameras. In *Time-of-flight and structured light depth cameras* (pp. 43–79). Springer.

New Approaches to Real-Time Rendering in Cyber-Archaeology

Neil G. Smith

Abstract Archaeology is an inherently destructive science. It necessitates that data in the field be adequately recorded and digitally stored in as accurate and comprehensive a record as possible. Once these datasets are recorded digitally, their spatio-temporal nature makes them ideal for advanced 3D visualization, allowing archaeologists to take advantage of modern visual analytics, modeling, and simulation. Thus, a core goal of Cyber-Archaeology is to develop digital immersive environments to enable archaeologists to visualize and analyze their archaeological sites in real-time. This paper presents an end-to-end pipeline that takes advantage of modern gaming engines to render in real-time the archaeological record. At each stage of the pipeline, novel approaches are introduced for capturing, processing, and analyzing archaeological sites. The site of Khirbat al-Iraq Shmaliyah (KIS) is used as a case study. It is one of the most well-preserved excavations in the region known as ancient Edom. It was scanned using LiDAR and SfM with millimeter accurate recordings of every *in situ* artifact. Through real-time rendering it was possible to become fully immersed in the archaeological site, navigate through it, and analyze the artifacts and stratigraphic layers.

Keywords Cyber archaeology · Real time rendering · Khirbat al-Iraq Shmaliyah · LiDAR

1 Introduction

Archaeology is an inherently destructive science. It necessitates that data in the field be adequately recorded and digitally stored in as accurate and comprehensive a record as possible. Moreover, once these datasets are recorded digitally, their

---

N. G. Smith (✉)
University of California, San Diego, La Jolla, CA, USA
e-mail: neil.smith@falconviz.com

© The Author(s), under exclusive license to Springer Nature Switzerland AG 2023
E. Ben-Yosef, I. W. N. Jones (eds.), *"And in Length of Days Understanding" (Job 12:12): Essays on Archaeology in the Eastern Mediterranean and Beyond in Honor of Thomas E. Levy*, Interdisciplinary Contributions to Archaeology,
https://doi.org/10.1007/978-3-031-27330-8_70

1657

spatio-temporal nature makes them ideal for advanced 3D visualization, allowing archaeologists to take advantage of modern visual analytics, modeling, and simulation. The archaeological record is not only preserved in a digital format, but the archaeologists' visual capacity is enhanced, enabling them to intuitively recognize deep patterns and structures, perceive changes and reoccurrences, and visualize massive cultural datasets at once. Thus, one of the core goals of the discipline of Cyber-Archaeology has been the development of digital immersive environments to enable archaeologists to visualize and analyze their archaeological sites in real time.

In order to digitally visualize the archaeological record, it must be 3D rendered. 3D rendering is the conversion of 3d wireframe models and 2D textured images into photorealistic 3D images. In the past, rendering a single photorealistic frame could take from seconds to even days. However, with new approaches developed for modern gaming engines, it is now possible to perform "real-time" rendering where the 3D images are calculated at a very high speed so that the scenes, which consist of multitudes of images, occur in real time and allow direct interaction and analysis by the user. In this paper, we utilize the Unreal Engine 4 (UE4).[1] UE4 is a AAA gaming engine that has been open-sourced to the research community. Recently, Epic Games branded the gaming engine as a "real-time 3D creation tool" and encouraged the scientific community along with the film industry to employ it not just for games but for simulation and film quality scene rendering. We use UE4 to render in real-time the archaeological record and to create a fully functioning 3D GIS. In addition, this paper presents an end-to-end pipeline for capturing, processing, visualizing and analyzing archaeological data recovered from field excavations.

As a demonstration of the pipeline, we use Khirbat al-Iraq Shmaliyah (KIS) as a case study (Smith et al., 2014). The archaeological site dating to the Iron II is one of the most well-preserved and intact excavations in the region known as ancient Edom. The site is reconstructed using Structure-from-Motion with millimeter accurate XYZ recordings of every special find and *in situ* artifact discovered during excavation (Fig. 1). Similarly, artifacts have also been 3d scanned and geo-referenced into their original found locations within the virtual archaeological excavation. Through real-time rendering the user is able to become fully immersed in the archaeological site, navigate through it, and analyze at 1:1 scale the artifacts and stratigraphic layers of the site.

2 Related Works

The development of novel computational methods in real-time rendering and digital immersive environments for archaeology originates from the seminal work over the last decade in Cyber-archaeology by Maurizio Forte, Thomas E. Levy and other scholars.

---

[1] https://www.unrealengine.com/

New Approaches to Real-Time Rendering in Cyber-Archaeology 1659

Fig. 1 Khirbat al-Iraq Shmaliyah excavations rendered inside UE4

In 2009, Maurizio Forte recast the meaning of Cyber-archaeology to refer to the simulation of the past (Forte, 2011). According to Forte, the goal of cyber-archaeology is to create a digital environment or virtual simulation that allows a space for multiple users to process information, increase the dynamics of learning, and lead to deeper understanding. A key element of Forte's cybernetic circle was the employment of virtual reality to immerse researchers within a virtual space where new forms of embodied cognitive discovery can be made. Since Forte's publication, many archaeologists have sought independently to create virtual and dynamic non-linear 3D environments (Berggren et al., 2015; Dell'Unto et al., 2016, 2017; Merlo, 2016; Poggi & Buono, 2018; Smith et al., 2013, 2015; van Riel, 2016).

Several scholars have utilized ESRI's ArcScene[©2] as a "3D GIS" to visualize archaeological excavations (Berggren et al., 2015; Dell'Unto et al., 2016, 2017; Merlo, 2016). In particular, the work of Dell'Unto et al. (2017) demonstrates the ability to take multiple LiDAR and photogrammetric captures of excavations and import them as aligned layers within ArcScene. Artifacts and loci can also be added as layers to be visualized in relation to the 3D meshes. Layers can be toggled on and off to visualize the excavation over time, which they call a '4D' GIS. The advantage of Dell'Unto et al. (2017)'s approach is that ArcScene is readily accessible to most archaeologists and supports many of the common formats of spatial data with which archaeologists are familiar. However, ArcScene is not an immersive rendering engine and it cannot load and render high poly-textured meshes. It is not a true 3D GIS environment that allows for object manipulation, segmentation or interaction. A significant amount of simplification and processing also must be conducted to import datasets into the viewer. Finally, ArcScene has a very limited set of analytical tools that are not geared toward three-dimensional studies.

Several works have emphasized the importance of volumetric representation of archaeological layers (Lieberwirth, 2008; Losier et al., 2007; Poggi & Buono, 2018; Nobles & Roosevelt, 2021). The most recent work by Nobles and Roosevelt (2021) improve upon these works by creating a pointcloud to volume mesh workflow. Their approach can create water-tight volumetric meshes representing the upper and lower

---

[2] https://desktop.arcgis.com/

surfaces of stratigraphic layers and is robust to outliers. They use Poisson Surface Reconstruction for final meshing of the upper and lower pointcloud surfaces. However, these approaches are only focused on the creation of the volumetric layers. Nobles and Roosevelt (2021) note in their work that visualization was not a core focus of the workflow and they could not find a true 3D GIS system for importing and visualizing their 3D volumes. They state: "were 3D GIS software available, we would be able to query by attribute or location, select, group, and order the context volumes along with other typical GIS and spatial database functions" (Nobles & Roosevelt, 2021: 609).

Most related to the work presented in this paper is ArtifactVis2 (Smith et al., 2013). During the 2013 Digital Heritage International Congress, Smith et al. (2013) presented ArtifactVis2 as a tool for real-time archaeological data in immersive 3D environments. ArtifactVis2 uses CalVR a framework built on top of OpenScene Graph[3] to render archaeological artifacts, polyhedral loci and 3D scanned models of archaeological sites. The goal was not only to be able to render the archaeological data but to interface it with conducting analyses and spatial queries using PostGIS.

ArtifactVis2 was also a computational solution to a major problem the researchers faced. They called the problem *data avalanche*, where the deluge of digital data being acquired in the field necessitated development of computational methods of curation, storage, and data retrieval (Petrovic et al., 2011). Jones and Levy (2018) subsequently acknowledged data avalanche as an early driving force in their adoption of cyber-archaeology as a new subfield. In contrast to Forte's focus on simulation, they more broadly defined cyber-archaeology as "the integration of the latest developments in computer science, engineering, science, and archaeology" (Jones & Levy, 2018: 28). However, still core to Cyber-archaeology practiced at UCSD by Jones, Levy, Smith and others is a recognition that the end goal is to build a cyber-infrastructure that enables collaborative and immersive research through linked regional archaeological databases and curated archaeological data.

Despite ArtifactVis2 being a true 3D GIS, its main drawback was that it required a computer engineer familiar with Linux to be able to compile it from source. Despite the interest of several archaeological research communities in ArtifactVis2, it was not easily adopted. Over the last decade significant changes have occurred within the VR community, especially with the open access of game engines such as Unity and UE4 and the development of budget-friendly VR head mounted displays. CalVR, OpenSceneGraph and other community-driven rendering engines have become obsolete as focus has shifted to development within game engines. In particular, Unity and UE4 have become the de-facto tools for student and graduate-led research in serious game development, VR and simulation. It is for these reasons we decided to port ArtifactVis2 to UE4 and develop a processing workflow that enables other archaeological projects to participate.

---

[3] http://www.openscenegraph.org/

3 Digital Recording Technologies at KIS

3.1 Context and Significance of Khirbat al-Iraq Shmaliyah for Digital Recording

In 2007 and 2010, Khirbat al-Iraq Shmaliyah (KIS) was excavated by the Lowlands 2 Highlands Edom Project (Smith et al., 2014). KIS is located just south of Showbak, Jordan along the plateau edge of the highlands. The site is situated on a naturally elevated mound surrounded by agriculturally rich fields on all sides. One of the goals of the L2HE project was to link the digital excavation and high-precision carbon dating being applied in the lowlands with the highlands, which at the time had not been excavated in over 20 years. A small probe was conducted at KIS in 2007 revealing three rooms with exceptional archaeological preservation. The ceramics and corroborating radiocarbon dates from the probe placed the site in the 8th–seventh centuries BCE, also known as the Iron IIB-C. The site is contemporary with many of the other sites excavated on the plateau and the late sites surveyed and excavated in the lowlands of Edom. In 2010, the L2HE project returned to conduct a more extensive excavation of the site expanding upon the initial probe in 2007. Similar to the discoveries made in 2007, the 2010 excavations exposed a complex public structure with similar rare preservation of hundreds of complete *in situ* vessels, artifacts, and processing centers. Excavations were conducted down to bedrock with many vessels found resting in place on the plaster surfaces 1–2 cm above bedrock. Many of the rooms were sealed from later wall collapse, preserving intact and partially broken vessels remaining on the surface of the rooms. A central courtyard was exposed with a monumental bench and a small four-course wall obscuring three *tannur* ovens on the other side. Several of the rooms contained massive pithoi that once stored grain.

KIS is one of the most well-preserved and intact excavations in the region, making it an ideal candidate for demonstrating the potential of 3D real-time rendering presented in this paper. In addition, the site's early adoption of digital field recording techniques, namely ArchField, has served as a primary dataset for continued development in cyber-archaeology over the last decade (Smith et al., 2014).

3.2 Archfield Digital Field Recording

During the 2007 and 2010 excavations at KIS, ArchField was used to conduct digital field recordings (cf. Smith & Levy, 2014). ArchField, at the time, was designed as a web-based version using the combination of HTML, PHP, and Javascript languages (Fig. 2). Data was stored either in a table for artifacts or for loci. Every *in situ* artifact was recorded using ArchField coupled with a Leica Total Station allowing for accurate 3D measurement. Loci were also delineated and recorded on a daily basis as the excavation progressed. A Nikon D80 camera was employed for both

Fig. 2 ArchField Google Maps version from 2010 excavations

seasons and used to take site photographs as the excavation progressed. During the opening of every new locus a 3D position was recorded and a set of images were captured with at least one image containing a scale bar and north arrow. In Fig. 2, the real-time top plan generated in the field is depicted. As one progresses through the excavation they are able to cycle through and re-load any top plan digitally from previous days of excavation. ArchField allowed the site registrar and supervisor to insure there was a controlled collection of the archaeological record.

Following the end of the 2010 season a month later, a LEICA C10 scanner was used to capture a LiDAR scan of the finished excavation. A series of ground control markers were made throughout the site on the top course of the architectural walls. These were measured using the total station to allow for proper alignment of the LiDAR scan. In addition, the first attempt at a terrestrial photometric capture of the entire site was conducted for comparison with the LiDAR scan (see discussion below).

4 Field to Real-Time Rendering Workflow

4.1 Images to Textured Static Meshes

In 2010, 1 month after the second season of excavations at KIS we conducted an experiment to see if we could reconstruct the entire site using just images after discovering a recently released open-source software called Bundler (Snavely et al., 2006). Six hundred and fifty six images were captured of the site with an attempt to capture the site with complete image overlap and from every angle. A Nikon D80 10 mp camera was used with automatic settings and fixed focal length. To our amazement, Bundler was able to reconstruct the site in its entirety. A fairly dense pointcloud (3.8 m points) of the site was generated. At the time this was one of the first sites SfM was used at this scale in archaeology. In comparison to the LiDAR scan of the site, it was very sparse but it was more complete since we could capture many of the areas that were occluded in the laser scan. Although many of the

Fig. 3 Original pointcloud of KIS versus the newly reconstructed pointcloud, and Textured Mesh

methodological practices of capturing SfM were not implemented at that time, we are still able today with much more advanced algorithms to produce an impressive model of the site. Using improved open-source algorithms and processing workflow we are able to generate not only a much denser pointcloud (24 m points) but a photo-realistic textured mesh (Fig. 3).

After applying our processing workflow and generating a much more complete and denser model of KIS than the original in 2010, we reviewed all the site photographs for the 2007 and 2010 excavations to determine if specific sets of images could also be reconstructed using our improved methodology. Structure-from-Motion was in its infancy at this time, so it was not part of the recording methodology in 2007 or 2010 to take overlapping images. However, the site photographer rarely took only a single photo but would purposely take several photos in case one was blurry or thought another angle may be helpful. Reviewing all the photographs of 2007 and 2010 excavations we found that we had at least 2–3 overlapping images for almost every *in situ* artifact or floor surface. In Fig. 4, we highlight several examples of *in situ* contexts reconstructed from only a small set of images.

Since 2010, we have been developing a processing workflow to convert images of our archaeological excavations to 3D texture models. The processing workflow is end-to-end covering image processing until importation into UE4. Much photogrammetric software has been developed over this period that is now a standard component of the archaeological toolbox. Agisoft Photoscan[4] is one of the most popular tools used by archaeologists on many projects; however, many have struggled to process large datasets using the software and the textured meshes are often over simplified. Reality Capture,[5] which can fully run on the GPU, can handle large datasets and processes an order of magnitude faster. However, it does not have an easy system for geo-referencing datasets and on complex sites it may lead to splitting the site into several models. This has led us to work on developing our own modification of open-source photogrammetry software to better meet the processing requirements of archaeological sites. We use Colmap for image matching, bundle adjustment, geo-referencing and generation of dense pointclouds and meshes (Schönberger & Frahm, 2016). For mesh texturing we use TexRecon which

---

[4] https://www.agisoft.com/
[5] https://www.capturingreality.com/

Fig. 4 *In situ* artifacts reconstructed using the processing workflow

produces pixel sharp textures on large scale meshes (Waechter et al., 2014). Finally, we modified OpenMVS[6] to produce high resolution orthophotos, digital surface models, and extremely dense pointclouds using the textured meshes from TexRecon. The final textured meshes are directly imported into UE4 as high poly static meshes for real-time rendering.

Structure-from-Motion is inherently a scale and orientation invariant, which means that the native reconstruction of images will not be scaled or oriented properly. Software such as Pix4D[7] or Photoscan use ground control points (GCP) and

---

[6] https://github.com/cdcseacave/openMVS

[7] https://www.pix4d.com/

their marked pixel position in the captured images to perform a similarity transformation (e.g., Helmert Transformation) to fit the reconstructed model as closely as possible to the GCP points. The added advantage of this approach is that it can be used to measure the accuracy of the reconstruction. Colmap does not natively support geo-referencing. However, Colmap's CPU based bundle adjustment algorithm uses Ceres which can support additional block adjustment problems such as fixed GCP points. Similar to proprietary software, we can take the GCP coordinates and their pixel coordinates in at least two images to perform a similarity transform. If the error is significant, we can also use the GCP coordinates to optimize the bundle adjustment of the reconstruction.

In order to efficiently create the static meshes in UE4, we carry out several other steps. Although, UE4 is able to render millions of triangles for each mesh we found limiting each model to under ca. 15 M triangles makes cleaning, importing of the model, data storage and rendering more efficient. After dense pointcloud reconstruction in Colmap, we use Screened Poisson Surface Reconstruction (SPSR) to generate the mesh (Kazhdan & Hoppe, 2013). The point clouds can range in size from 10 M to 1B points which would create extremely dense meshes that become unwieldly to use, especially if any cleaning or trimming is needed. However, by adjusting the depth value of SPSR it is possible to find a good balance of simplification without loss of detail, especially considering that often many of the points are redundant, spurious, or additional noise. The other advantage of SPSR as noted in other publications is that it attempts to create a water-tight mesh, thus filling holes in the reconstruction. We then apply Sven Forstmann's[8] fast quadric mesh collapse which can halve the number of faces with almost no visible loss in mesh detail. Finally, we load each mesh into Cloudcompare[9] to clean erroneous faces and vertices generated during the meshing.

TexRecon is an extremely fast and accurate algorithm for texturing the cleaned meshes. Although it can process meshes larger than 15 M triangles, the processing time increases exponentially and can consume more memory than available on our workstations. Unlike the textured mesh outputted by Reality Capture, TexRecon attempts to place the unwrapped textures in decreasingly smaller image sets starting from 8 K to 256. This generates hundreds of images for each mesh. However, UE4's mipmap-based loading of textures is very efficient and appears to benefit when a majority of the textures are lower resolution.

The aligned mesh is in meters and uses WGS84 UTM coordinates for global position. However, UE4's unit scale is in centimeters, which means during importation if we scale the mesh 100× it will be offset from the center more than 30 M units in game. This is addressed by creating a global offset that we subtract from the GCPs prior to geo-referencing. The global offset is also stored as a variable in UE4 to properly position the artifacts and voxel loci to the meshes.

---

[8] https://github.com/sp4cerat/Fast-Quadric-Mesh-Simplification

[9] https://www.danielgm.net/cc/

Having open-source access to the underlying code of each step of the processing workflow allows us to ensure that we can reconstruct even with only a limited set of images. For example, Fig. 4b, d were reconstructed from only 4 and 2 images, respectively. The original images were captured in 2007 during the initial probe conducted at the site. In both cases, the small set of images failed to initially reconstruct. By relaxing several key parameters in the error calculation of the bundle adjustment and conducting an early termination of the global alignment we were able to extract a fairly accurate camera pose, estimated focal length and orientation for the models. Since there are few images, we also use Domain Size Pooling and set the feature cut-off to 50 k, which outperforms SIFT and results in a much denser sparse pointcloud which is needed in this case where we have only 2–4 images. We use Colmap's PatchMatch algorithm for the depth estimation which performs well even with only a single second image. Finally, during fusion of the depth maps we accept every pixel which leads to a very dense pointcloud with only erroneous points on the fringes. Once the pointcloud is extracted, the remaining steps of the processing workflow can be performed as normal. Applying this method, we were able to reconstruct every image set captured in 2007 and 2010 that had at least two images. Since a majority of the captured images were taken very close to the artifacts or surfaces, we achieved higher detailed reconstructions for areas within the excavation compared to the entire site reconstruction (e.g., Fig. 4f). More importantly, the surfaces and *in situ* orientation of artifacts that had been destroyed through excavation and only recorded with a couple of images and possibly a single 3D position are now digitally preserved in full 3D.

As mentioned earlier, SfM reconstructions cannot determine scale, position or orientation, which is a problem to overcome if we want to properly situate the *in situ* artifacts in the context of the overall excavated KIS model in UE4. In this case, though, there are no GCP markers in the images or measurements made in 2007 or 2010 to derive this information. As can be seen in Fig. 4, most of the *in situ* reconstructions only reconstruct the foreground, making it impossible to find common features between the model and the site architecture. If this was not the case, we could use ICP or manually align one model to another using several common points. In order to overcome this problem, we created "virtual" GCPs that can be used at the initial stage of processing. We used the full KIS model captured in 2010 as the reference. The full KIS model used 7 GCPs recorded by a total station with an estimated accuracy of 2 mm. The GCPs were black X's marked with a sharpy but as the images were captured less than a meter away, they could be resolved to sub-pixel accuracy. After refinement of the model to the GCPs, the error measured to an accuracy of 3 mm in global position. Now that the entire model was accurately aligned, positioned and scaled we could use the outputted model as a reference for the individually scanned *in situ* artifacts and surfaces. Figure 5 shows how the virtual GCPs are found and marked in the images. We created virtual GCPs by marking distinctive features in the images that are on the stones of the architecture. This was conducted inside a GCP marking tool we created for use with Colmap. Then inside CloudCompare we loaded both the full KIS model pointcloud and its textured version to locate these same distinctive features. Since the model is textured with the

Fig. 5 Virtual GCPs in Cloudcompare on SQ A1 and in images

high-resolution images, we were able to clearly see the same distinctive colors and edges seen in the images. Using the point picking tool, we could select these features and get their 3D position, essentially creating an accurate "virtual" 3D GCP. A minimum of 4 virtual GCPs per reconstruction is needed to get a proper alignment and error estimation. The targeted alignment error is 5 mm; if we found the error to be higher, we checked the image markings and the point selection to make sure they were accurate and updated the alignment.

We conducted several tests in an effort to image match and bundle adjust the *in situ* artifact images with images of the same area in the final KIS model but there was either insufficient context of the architecture or the appearance and angle was too different for the SIFT algorithm to match properly similar features. We still believe this would be a faster and more accurate approach but would have required a greater number of images, better overlap, less angle diversity, and perhaps intermediate full site reconstructions rather than a capture taken a month after excavations. A real advantage of the virtual GCP technique is that we can use "human" detectable features of the architecture in the background of the image even though these cannot be properly matched by the SIFT algorithm and are not reconstructed in the final model. Overall, the use of virtual GCPs allows us to properly geo-reference any of our reconstructions, even from old excavation image capture methodologies. This approach can be applied to any archaeological excavation conducted in the last two decades that employed a digital camera, even if the intent was not to capture images for SfM reconstruction.

4.2 UE4 Rendering

Once the various reconstructions of the site, surfaces, and *in situ* artifacts are imported into UE4, they can be programmatically loaded into the main map. Since all the reconstructions are geo-located and share the same offset, they are all placed at the central origin. There does not appear to be a significant limitation in UE4 for rendering multiple high poly static meshes when a gaming or VR-ready pc is used. It can efficiently render more than 10 static meshes of 15 m polys at once at a steady 60fps.

At the opening of the program, the main program query widget tool queries the CouchDB database for a list of available models and loads their reference into a dropdown menu for the user to toggle on and off. As new models are added to the project they only need to be imported and saved in the project and their details entered into the database. In future work, we would like to store the models outside of the UE4 project and load them as procedural meshes. This approach would avoid having to recompile the project every time a new model is created for the project and allow a standalone version of the project to be shared with other archaeologists to add their own content.

There are still several limitations to the static meshes created for UE4 that can be resolved in the future. One of the reasons reconstructions from images look photorealistic is that they have baked into the textured meshes all the ambient light, shadows, reflections, and ambient occlusion of the real-world scene. However, UE4 relights the meshes, casting new shadows that conflict with the baked-in texture lighting. Although the textured mesh preserves at 1 mm resolution fine details of the scene, the underlying mesh faces and normals are at a much coarser resolution of 5 mm to 1 cm. The relighting inside UE4 exposes the coarser mesh detracting from the photo-realism achieved by the baked textures and overall darkens the appearance of the model. With an RTX Nvidia GPU, real-time raytracing can be used in UE4 but it cannot improve upon the static meshes because of the baked textured. Setting the textured meshes to be unlit partially solves the problem but gives a flatter appearance and does not allow other static meshes, artifacts or loci to cast ray-traced shadows and light onto the meshes. A possible solution is to estimate the global illumination of the mesh and then subtract all ambient light artifacts from the original texture. This is the approach used by the Megascans project[10] to produce the high-quality PBR materials and static meshes used by UE4. However, this is accomplished by capturing in the scene a color calibration chart, a 360 sphere of the environment and also a chrome reflection sphere to estimate the angle of the sun. All of this additional information is not available from the images captured during the excavation more than a decade ago. Finally, a significant amount of the lighting of excavations is a product of sub-surface scattering and micro-surface normals at <1–2 mm resolution. One possible approach is to extract the original image resolution surface normals or a BRDF of each original image and then use these instead of the color images for texturing the model. This could be done using TexRecon with modifications to the seam leveling algorithm.

4.3 Database Management and Visualization

In 2015, the original excavation data tables at KIS were converted from PostgreSQL to CouchDB (Smith et al., 2015). The main purpose for moving to CouchDB is the user-friendly setup and web-based accessibility it affords for other archaeologists. It allows syncing of data across databases, making sharing of client databases a straightforward process. It also allows for revision control to ensure that any changes made to a database are tracked. Although the data recorded by ArchField is tabular in form, it opens the possibility in the future to create more complex databases with nested information. In previous publications, we noted that NoSQL documents reflect more adequately the structure of data collection in field excavations (see Smith et al., 2015). CouchDB employs a REST API, allowing easy communication with UE4 through json-formatted http requests. An opensource plugin called VaRest allows UE4 to access CouchDB and many other RESTful API databases. Currently, a 3D Interactable UI Widget is used to send basic spatial query requests to the CouchDB database. It constructs simple "where" statements such as finding all radiocarbon samples within a square at a specific range of elevation (see Results section below for examples).

Storing and querying the artifact and loci data outside UE4 is advantageous since it does not require repackaging the project every time changes are made to the data. Once a query is made within UE4, a json document is returned from CouchDB with a list of all the resulting artifacts or loci. The json document is parsed and temporarily stored in a Struct variable. If the query is for artifacts, we use the 3D coordinates of its recorded position and its descriptor code to spawn a static mesh model inside UE4. We loop through the list of artifacts to display all the results. In previous versions of ArtifactVis, we created 3D models for each descriptor code. We imported these 3D models as static meshes and used a vector array as a lookup table to select

---

[10] https://quixel.com/megascans

the appropriate 3D model at runtime. Since UE4 can render thousands of high-poly meshes, we updated several of these models with photogrammetry-scanned archaeological artifacts. The loci were stored in a separate CouchDB table. They were queried similar to the artifacts but were constructed as voxels volumes (see Sect. 4.4). The opening and closing elevation of each locus was stored in the database. The elevations allowed the code to know how many voxels high the locus is. We also preprocess every locus in the database using the list of the polygon's vertices to create a 2D voxel grid, which we stored as a separate file outside of the CouchDB database and retrieved during the looping through of the loci query results.

4.4 Volumetric Voxel Loci

In order to create a volumetric locus, we first generated a two-dimensional voxel grid that covered the extent of the polygons (Fig. 6a). We added a buffer to ensure the polygon was fully enclosed within the grid. Currently, the voxel grid is set to a resolution of one cell per centimeter. Each cell was assigned an integer value of "1." indicating it is a cell to be rendered. Since all polygons are constructed in a clockwise direction, we can check whether each cell is inside or outside of the polygon by finding the sign of the determinant of the polygon vectors. If the cell was greater than zero (meaning outside the polygon boundary), we reassigned it a value of "0," indicating it would be "unrendered/empty." The generated grid was stored along with the top and bottom elevation of the locus. At runtime, the volumetric locus was rendered using the voxels generated by looping through the two-dimensional grid and along the z dimension using the provided top and bottom elevation. Voxel faces are only rendered if the adjacent cell is marked as "unrendered/empty." The added buffer of the original grid allows a fast check to be made to determine where to render the edge faces of the voxels. The voxel faces and vertices along with computed normals and vertex textures are combined to create a procedural mesh that UE4 can render. This approach is fast and allows changes to be made to loci in real-time. By storing the generated grid outside of UE4, we can switch to load a 2.5d surface to sample the voxels to better represent the complex three-dimensional structure of a stratigraphic layer.

The procedural mesh receives material for coloring the voxels. The current approach is to use the locus descriptor (e.g., Ash Fill) to select from a set of predefined materials the most appropriate material representation. An arbitrary color can be applied to the entire volumetric locus, a transparent color, or photo-realistic texture of gravel and other sediments. By using world aligned PBR textures as a material in UE4, the texturing appears seamless across an arbitrary number of voxels and does not show any patterning of the texture even at far viewing distances. UE4's Megascans collection of real-world allows for photo-realistic texturing.

Since the material texturing is a composite of multiple blended parameters and texture images, it could be extended in the future to create unique material instances using a set of details stored in the locus' data table such as color, texture, particle shape, compactness, inclusions, etc.

Once the procedural mesh is generated in game, any voxel can be removed (marked as empty) allowing one to dig into the locus to reveal archaeological finds. Alternatively, voxel layers can be removed to represent the locus elevation of a specific day of excavation.

By using the query system, we can load specific loci voxels within the whole site. More complex spatial queries can be conducted to not only select loci but also carve away portions of the loci for better visualization. The static mesh architecture is occluded by the volumetric loci. Allowing a better representation of the exposed excavation at a specific date of excavation or stratigraphic period.

In Fig. 6, we demonstrate the various approaches to rendering locus voxels in game. Here we isolate L.7083, which was opened to represent all finds collected around the most intact *tannur* (clay oven) found during the excavation. This volumetric locus contains the entire *tannur* from when it was opened to when it was closed at the end of the excavation. It can be visualized as a solid color (Fig. 6b), transparent (where can see the *tannur* and associated artifacts in 3D space) (Fig. 6c) or textured giving the appearance of the accumulated sediment that once surrounded the *tannur* (Fig. 6d).

Fig. 6 Voxelized Loci in the main courtyard highlighting the *tannur* with textured architecture

5 Results of KIS

5.1 *Rendering for Spatial Analysis*

In recent work by Nobles & Roosevelt (2021: 609) they claim that archaeologists "… lack a truly 3D GIS, one capable of working with multiple types of 3D geometry (e.g., polyhedrals, voxels) in projected 3D space." A major goal of this project is to address this claim and update the original 3D GIS system created in CalVR with ArtifactVis to run inside UE4 using the same database system. Here we present the results of the current 3D GIS and the advantages to previous attempts at creating such a system for archaeological data.

In Fig. 7, we demonstrate different types of spatial queries alluded to by Nobles and Roosevelt (2021). Determining the location and context of radiocarbon samples is an important step when selecting samples for [14] carbon dating. The ability to associate stratigraphic layers and their Z elevation to dated samples is very important. In a 2D GIS, a query of radiocarbon samples allows us to see where in the site the samples are located but cannot depict the elevation differences within the loci, rendering it hard to correlate them to stratigraphic profiles. In Fig. 7a, we conducted a 3D spatial query of the artifact database to show all RC samples located within a range of 10 cm off the final floor surfaces in all rooms excavated in 2010. The samples depicted in 3D were pomegranates, a common remain of the Iron Age that produces seeds with short life radiocarbon samples. Figure 7b shows a closeup of the courtyard complex where we render the voxel loci that contain these RC samples. Using these spatial queries within a 3D context allows the user to more clearly understand the relationship of the samples to their context and even take a virtual walk-through of the site to examine in greater detail the spatial location of the samples. In Fig. 7c, we show a spatial query of all recorded restorable vessels at the site. Many of the vessels appear in a 3D cluster in the northwestern room of the site. In Fig. 7d, we show a close-up view of this room and the 3D symbolic models used to represent the locations of the vessels. One can see these are all in the volumetric loci 7038 and 7055, the volumetric loci have been carved 60 cm down to expose the artifact positions, depicting the voxels of the loci above the recorded elevations of the restorable vessels in x-ray mode. In Fig. 7e, we show a spatial query of all hammerstones and pestles found across the site at all elevations. One can see that many of the stone tools are levigated in the fill of the excavation and not resting on the floor. In the southeast corner of the site, there is a stone-built trough where many of these stone tools appear to have been collected (Fig. 7f). This area was more exposed to the elements as it was an open courtyard that underwent a secondary erosional process resulting in the stone tools no longer being in their *in situ* position in comparison to the more closed rooms where we found less post-depositional disturbance.

In summary, Fig. 7 depicts a small subset of possible spatial queries that can be conducted within the 3D GIS system. We are still currently exploring the many different possible types of spatial analyses that can be made with the current system

New Approaches to Real-Time Rendering in Cyber-Archaeology

Fig. 7 Various spatial queries of artifacts and loci

and adding new filters and widgets to construct more complex queries from the spatial database. We expect many of the new tools needed to be implemented will emerge as archaeologists interact within the VR environment.

The spatial queries from a 3D GIS are very powerful but the applied methods discussed above allow new forms of spatial analysis previously unimagined. In earlier work in 3D GIS tools such as ArtifactVis, the visualization of architecture and surfaces could only represent the appearance of the site after completion of excavations. Although we could conduct spatial analyses and queries of the artifacts and loci, this information could only be displayed as points and polyhedrons. Many of the spatial insights that would have been made in the field are lost. For example, in Fig. 8 we show a comparison between the 2010 capture of the NE corner room of the site and the newly reconstructed model of how it looked in 2007 during excavations. Although we can depict the 3D position of the artifacts in the context of the 2010 model, they appear to be floating inside the locus and it is not clear that there is a distinctive organization of the different grinding tools. In comparison, the 2007 reconstruction allows us to see not only the position of the different grinding tools but their relation to the giant saddle quern installation. The saddle quern was set up as an installation with a small two-course partitioning wall between it and the smaller saddle quern on the east side of the room. The 2010 capture occurred 3 years after the excavation, after the rubber-stone still resting on the saddle quern and the smaller eastern saddle quern installation were removed. Between the two excavation periods, the large saddle quern had been disturbed and the partition wall was destroyed. The 2010 reconstruction fails to depict the rare preservation of the site. In contrast, the 2007 reconstruction allows us to see that there are two organized groups of grinding tools consisting of a pestle and hammerstone each. They are neatly aligned and placed as if the original inhabitants intended to return to use them the next day. South of the eastern saddle quern is a broken storage jar still *in situ* that may have been the initial vessel for storing flour collected from the grinding process. Figure 8 demonstrates the value reconstructed contexts bring to spatial analysis. By converting the original images to three-dimensional models "new processes of reasoning in spatial thinking" (Nobles & Roosevelt, 2021: 608) can be made that until now could only have been appreciated by the original excavators during excavation. These three-dimensional contexts aid in the process of spatial analysis, concepts of space and organization, reasoning and interpretation (see Huggett, 2015). Archaeologists can now virtually immerse themselves in 1:1 scale and physically walk into the grain processing room. They can examine the room's layout, making spatial inferences about the organization of grain processing at the site. Viewing the spatial organization of the northeast room allows one to see a level of grain production beyond the household level. Taken in its larger spatial context from the 2010 excavations one can step into the adjacent courtyard where three *tannurs* (typically used for bread making) were found *in situ* (see Fig. 6). The proximity of these two activity areas indicates an even higher level of organization in food production, perhaps even a *chaîne opératoire*. This type of participatory/experiential inter-site spatial analysis goes beyond 3D GIS spatial queries, allowing a new medium for archaeologists to achieve clearer lines of analysis and data exploration.

5.2 Time as the Fourth Dimension

Since multiple stages of the excavation have been converted into 3D models, we are able to explore time as a fourth dimension of analysis. Figure 9 depicts the far northwest room of the site (Sq. A1) at different time slices of the excavation. After 40 centimeters (two stone courses) of excavation, we began to find a soft sediment fill with collapsed large wall stones intermixed with restorable vessels and other special finds. As we excavated further, we found one layer after another of restorable vessels. The vessels were shattered and as we excavated deeper, we had to slowly remove the loose body sherds. Where possible we attempted to collect in groups associated sherds with each individual vessel, but at the pace of excavation, it was

Fig. 8 Comparison of 3D reconstruction from images captured in 2007 and 2010 in the Southeast grain processing room. (**a**) represents excavations in 2010; (**b**) from 2007 excavation; (**c**) 2010 and 2007 merged to show how the saddle quern was disturbed between excavation seasons

Fig. 9 Time as field excavation – time slices Sq A1

not possible to clearly see how each sherd connected. In Fig. 9a, one can see the upper surface captured as we began to expose the shattered vessels. The exposed vessels are not upright but rather turned over on their side. Figure 9b renders the excavation 3 days later, after 20 cm of fill, collapsed stones and pottery scatter had been removed. The turned-over multi-handled storage jar is still *in situ,* but the base of the other large vessel and other collapsed stones have been removed, exposing below it the upper rim and strap handle of a massive Krater. In Fig. 9c, we see the floor of the building exposed after three more days of excavation and another 40 cm lower. There are several complete and semi-intact vessels sitting upright on it. The base of the large krater is intact along with one-quarter of the upper vessel wall and its strap handle seen in Fig. 9b.

Since each time slice is globally aligned, we can maintain the same camera perspective to clearly see the transformation of the site over time. Note that there were only a couple of original images and these were taken from very different perspectives. The perspective shown in Fig. 9 is only possible within a 3D environment. The multiple aligned static meshes allow one to switch back and forth between the different periods of excavation and visually detect changes and similarities between the different periods of excavation. Viewing the data from a single perspective allows one to clearly see that the upper restorable vessels are different from the lower vessels of the excavation. The lower vessels are in their original position sitting upright on the floor, while the upper vessels are suspended in the fill, laying on their sides over the lower complete vessels. The upper vessels could not have taken their positions unless they had fallen from above. The collapse could have occurred from an earthquake, especially since there were many large stones in the fill that would not have easily dislodged from the wall under standard depositional processes. A similar scenario was found in other portions of the site. The analysis indicates that there must have been an upper story or large shelving over this area of the building. This is further supported by the evidence of the adjacent room containing pillars commonly used to support a second floor. The examination allows us to suggest that the entire north end of the building complex had a second floor that had collapsed. There is no indication of fire or ash or any form of conflict that would encourage the inhabitants to abandon the site, suggesting that they either left as a result of an earthquake or they left the site peacefully a couple decades thereafter. By using time as a fourth dimension, we can track changes in stratigraphy, deposition, and the strategies employed by the excavators to remove complex pottery scatters throughout the site. This method allows a new perspective in analysis of a building that cannot be reflected in just the 3D spatial recording of artifacts and loci boundaries.

5.3 Visualizing in VR and Collaborative Meta-Verse Infrastructure

One significant advantage to move ArtifactVis to the UE4 gaming engine is the interoperability with different immersive 3D environments. UE4 fully supports tiled 3D CAVE systems as used by ArtifactVis but also provides native support for many AR and VR head mounted displays. In Fig. 10, we show the use of an Oculus Quest 2[11] to visualize in VR the archaeological site and manipulate within its 3D scanned artifacts. UE4 supports several of the latest new features of the Quest 2 including its ability to track users' hands and display them in the gaming environment. This ability allows the user to directly interact with archaeological artifacts with their bare hands. Many of the artifacts excavated from KIS have been 3D scanned using a NextEngine scanner. Although we have a 3D position recorded for every artifact excavated, this position only allows us to know where the object was located, not its exact orientation *in situ*. In Fig. 10, we show one experimental setup where we use the reconstructed *in situ* position of a stone roller to accurately place the 3D scanned model in its original *in situ* orientation. We set the scanned model inside UE4 to simulate physics but with no gravitational force so that the user can pick it up and manipulate it; it will not, however, drop if the user lets go of the artifact. The hand

---

[11] https://www.oculus.com/quest-2/

Fig. 10 VR Hands interacting with a stone roller found *in situ* in Square A1

tracking creates two 3D handles that conform to the users' actual hand movement, allowing them to virtually manipulate the artifact as if they were holding it in their hand.

The ability to hold and examine in 1:1 scale all the minute details of an *in situ* artifact is one key scenario of how VR should be used to improve archaeological analysis. The user should be able to visualize and interact with the archaeological artifacts as they would have on site. VR has unfortunately been primarily for aesthetic purposes and experiencing the fleeting wow factor of immersion. The majority of archaeological analyses today are done either by in person examination of artifacts or through a two-dimensional screen. However, it is quite rare that archaeologists are located near where their artifacts are stored or have regular access to them even when living close by. In this post-pandemic climate where travel, labs and facilities can be closed down on short notice, it is becoming increasingly more difficult for archaeologists to study their data physically. Used properly, VR can transport an archaeologist back in time to the archaeological site and enable him to revisit over and over its depositional stages, cultural practices and material artifacts. Artifacts stored in another country can be virtually loaded into the immersive environment where they can be examined, measured, and organized as if in person. Moreover, VR environments do not have to be explored individually but allow for multiple users to log into the same session and collaboratively examine an archaeological site and its artifacts. These virtual environments allow us to breach physical distance and social barriers. Hence the reason VR is the key component in the push by many industries towards achieving the creation of a Meta-verse.

6 Discussion, Limitations and Future Work

We have argued that spatial analysis does not stop at queryable 3D GIS databases but can be explored in many other ways once data is accessible within a 3D environment. Representing loci as voxel based volumes enable us to go beyond just visualizing their opening, closing and stacking but allows us to arbitrarily carve away at the locus as one would remove fill during an excavation. We can step through time to compare and contrast stratigraphic layers and complex pottery scatters to make sense of them. Ultimately, analysis can be conducted using VR- and AR-based equipment enabling collaborative multi-user environments that transcend the physical limitations of traditional archaeological analysis.

We have briefly mentioned several limitations of our approach that could be overcome in the future. The ideal method of distribution of our project would be through Docker.[12] This will allow it to be run on any system and be self-contained, requiring no additional installations or work by the user. We can imbed both CouchDB and the compiled UE4 project and serve it up to the entire archaeological community. This would require storing as much content outside of the docker as possible such as the static meshes that are currently imported into UE4 and packaged within the project. Several adjustments to the code would also have to be made to make it more versatile for projects using very different database systems.

The processing workflow can produce photo-realistic static meshes for ingestion into UE4. However, due to the baked-in lighting of the reconstructions, the advances in real-time raytracing now possible within the engine do not add any visual improvement; in fact they detract from the visual appearance of the models. We hope that in future work we will see an open source approach to create PBR textures of the static meshes. We also found simplification of meshes to 15 M triangles allowed overall better performance not only in UE4 but also the various external tools used for cleaning and exporting the models. However, UE5 Nanite technology can handle meshes with hundreds of millions of triangles. The best solution may be to develop a cleaning and editing tool within UE5 since it is currently the only tool that can efficiently handle meshes of this magnitude.

There are also many user interaction tools and interfaces that are lacking within this current version. Other 3D spatial tools, such as 3D measuring and slicing devices should be implemented. One of the most valuable tools would be a selection and segmentation tool. This can be used to cut voxel loci, 3D surfaces, or *in situ* artifacts and generate new models that can be used for other analytical purposes. In this project, we demonstrated one artifact that was 3D scanned and placed back in its original orientation within the site. This can be done with all the artifacts scanned or captured *in situ* but would require better tools to make the cropping and placement faster. Finally, 3D equivalent GIS algorithms such as cluster analysis, discriminate analysis, and viewshed analysis should be integrated into the gaming engine.

---

[12] https://www.docker.com/

7 Conclusion

This paper presents an end-to-end pipeline that takes advantage of modern gaming engines to render in real-time the archaeological record. At each stage of the pipeline, novel approaches are introduced for capturing, processing, visualizing and analyzing archaeological sites. As a demonstration of the pipeline, we use Khirbat al-Iraq Shmaliyah (KIS) as a case study. Although the pristine condition of KIS has made it an ideal candidate for demonstrating how we can push the boundaries of 4D GIS environments, the processing workflow and tools discussed in the paper can be applied to any site excavated in the last two decades where digital tools have been partially implemented. Even with a limited set of images we have shown that informative discoveries can be made from reconstructions of excavation surfaces and *in situ* artifacts using photogrammetry. It is also possible with access to the original non-digital photographs of sites, top plans, and paper-based spreadsheets to generate the data needed to fully visualize pre-digital excavations. Conversely, we hope this work inspires future excavators to consider capturing digitally every stage of the excavation from top-soil to bedrock, putting into practice tools such as ArchField and daily if not hourly SfM captures of *in situ* artifacts and surfaces.

Acknowledgments I would like to thank first and foremost Thomas E. Levy for his guidance and direction over the years in developing what we today call Cyber-archaeology. It was in 1999 when we first went digital at Khirbat Hamra Ifdan and I have had the opportunity to ride along on this journey of new digital innovations in archaeology ever since. This project would not have been possible without the support of the many students, Jordanian Department of Antiquities and my family, who participated during the two seasons of excavation at Khirbat Al-Iraq. I would like to thank Tom DeFanti and the Qualcomm Institute, who set me on a new course of 3D development in archaeology, starting with ArtifactVis during my post-doctoral career.

References

Berggren, Å., Dell'Unto, N., Forte, M., Haddow, S., Hodder, I., Issavi, J., et al. (2015). Revisiting reflexive archaeology at Çatalhöyük: Integrating digital and 3D technologies at the trowel's edge. *Antiquity, 89*(344), 433–448.

Dell'Unto, N., Landeschi, G., Leander Touati, A.-M., Ferdani, D., Dellepiane, M., Callieri, M., & Lindgren, S. (2016). Experiencing ancient buildings from a 3D GIS perspective: A case drawn from the Swedish Pompeii project. *Journal of Archaeological Method and Theory, 23*, 73–94.

Dell'Unto, N., Landeschi, G., Apel, J., & Poggi, G. (2017). 4D recording at the trowel's edge: Using three-dimensional simulation platforms to support field interpretation. *Journal of Archaeological Science: Reports, 12*, 632–645.

Forte, M. (2011). Cyber-archaeology: Notes on the simulation of the past. *Virtual Archaeology Review, 2*(4), 7–18.

Huggett, J. (2015). A manifesto for an introspective digital archaeology. *Open Archaeology, 1*(1), 86–95.

Jones, I., & Levy, T. (2018). Cyber-archaeology and grand narratives: Where do we currently stand? In T. Levy & I. Jones (Eds.), *Cyber-archaeology and grand narratives. One world archaeology*. Springer. https://doi.org/10.1007/978-3-319-65693-9_1

Kazhdan, M., & Hoppe, H. (2013). Screened poisson surface reconstruction. *ACM Transactions on Graphics, 32*(3) Article 29 (June 2013), 13 pages.

Lieberwirth, U. (2008). 3D GIS voxel-based model building in archaeology. In A. Posluschny, K. Lambers, & I. Herzog (Eds.), *Layers of perception. Proceedings of the 35th international conference on computer applications and quantitative methods in archaeology (CAA), Berlin, Germany, April 2–6, 2007* (pp. 1–8). Dr. Rudolf Habelt GmbH.

Losier, L.-M., Pouliot, J., & Fortin, M. (2007). 3D geometrical modeling of excavation units at the archaeological site of Tell 'Acharneh (Syria). *Journal of Archaeological Science, 34*(2), 272–288.

Merlo, S. (2016). *Making visible: Three-dimensional GIS in archaeological excavation.* British Archaeological Reports.

Nobles, G., & Roosevelt, C. (2021). Filling the void in archaeological excavations: 2D point clouds to 3D volumes. *Open Archaeology, 7*(1), 589–614.

Petrovic, V., Gidding, A., Wypych, T., Kuester, F., DeFanti, T., & Levy, T. (2011). Dealing with archaeology's data avalanche. *Computer, 44*(7), 56–60.

Poggi, G., & Buono, M. (2018). Enhancing archaeological interpretation with volume calculations. An integrated method of 3D recording and modeling. In M. Matsumoto & E. Uleberg (Eds.), *CAA2016: Oceans of data proceedings of the 44th conference on computer applications and quantitative methods in archaeology* (pp. 457–470). Archaeopress.

Schönberger, J, & Frahm, J. (2016). Structure-from-motion revisited. In *2016 IEEE conference on Computer Vision and Pattern Recognition (CVPR)* (pp. 4104–4113).

Smith, N. G., & Levy, T. E. (2014). Archfield: A digital application for real-time acquisition and dissemination – From the field to the virtual museum. *Mediterranean Archaeology and Archaeometry, 14*(4), 65–74.

Smith, N. G., Knabb, K., DeFanti, C., Weber, P., Schulze, J. P., Prudhomme, A., Kuester, F., Levy, T. E., DeFanti, T. A. (2013). *ArtifactVis2: Managing real-time archaeological data in immersive 3D environments.* In Proceedings of Digital Heritage international congress (DigitalHeritage) 2013, October 28–November 1, 2013, pp. 363–370, ISBN 978-1-4799-3168-2.

Smith, N. G., Najjar, M., & Levy, T. E. (2014). New perspectives on the Iron Age Edom Steppe and highlands: Khirbat al-Malayqtah, Khirbat al-Kur, Khirbat al-Iraq Shmaliya, and Tawilan. In T. E. Levy, M. Najjar, & E. Ben-Yosef (Eds.), *New insights into the Iron Age archaeology of Edom, Southern Jordan* (pp. 247–296). The Cotsen Institute of Archaeology Press, UCLA.

Smith, N., Howland, M., Levy, T.. (2015). *Digital archaeology field recording in the 4th dimension: ArchField C++ a 4D GIS for digital field work.* In Proceedings of Digital Heritage international congress (DigitalHeritage) 2015, September 28–October 2, 2015.

Snavely, N., Seitz, H., & Szeliski, R. (2006). *Photo tourism: Exploring image collections in 3D.* In ACM transactions on graphics (Proceedings of SIGGRAPH 2006).

van Riel, S. (2016). *Exploring the use of 3D GIS as an analytical tool in archaeological excavation practice.* MA thesis. Lund University.

Waechter, M., Moehrle, N., & Goesele, M. (2014). Let there be color! Large-scale texturing of 3D reconstructions. *European Conference on Computer Vision, 8693*, 836–850.

Preservation of the Memory of Lost Cultural Heritage in Post-conflict Communities

Matthew Vincent ⓘ

Abstract In 2015, we witnessed the horrific destruction of the Mosul Museum and other sites by the so-called Islamic State. Rekrei is a crowd-sourcing platform that was initiated in response to this destruction in hopes of being able to preserve the memory of lost heritage. The platform provides a venue for anyone to contribute photos, help organize collections, or even download and process those photos photogrammetrically. Within the first months of launching the project, the volunteer community produced some impressive results, and the project even partnered with the Economist to produce a virtual museum experience retelling the story of the Mosul Museum, the destruction, and the hope for a future. Fast forward a few years to 2019 when Rekrei was invited to participate in the first public exhibition in the museum (and the city) after the occupation by Daesh. This paper looks at the role of Rekrei in preserving the memory of lost heritage from the Mosul Cultural Museum, and finally bringing that heritage back home to Mosul and the role that heritage plays in helping a community to recover in a post-conflict situation.

Keywords Cultural heritage · Mosul cultural museum · Rekrei

1 Introduction

When I first arrived at the University of California, San Diego to study with Tom Levy, he arranged for a tour of the various facilities that would be part of my research during my time at the university. The tour began with the more traditional areas that one might expect: a store room full of crates filled with dusty bags of samples brought back from the field for further research, labs occupied by students and their current research, the department library, and main meeting rooms. However, as the

---

M. Vincent (✉)
American Center of Research, Amman, Jordan
e-mail: matthew@rekrei.org

© The Author(s), under exclusive license to Springer Nature Switzerland AG 2023
E. Ben-Yosef, I. W. N. Jones (eds.), *"And in Length of Days Understanding" (Job 12:12): Essays on Archaeology in the Eastern Mediterranean and Beyond in Honor of Thomas E. Levy*, Interdisciplinary Contributions to Archaeology,
https://doi.org/10.1007/978-3-031-27330-8_71

tour progressed it certainly came to highlight one of Tom's passions: the applications of new technology to the field of archaeology. Toward the end of the tour, Tom walked me into the immersive visualization systems at Calit2 (for more information on these systems see: (Knabb et al., 2014; Liritzis et al., 2016; Vincent, DeFanti, et al., 2013a)). With the systems booted up and 3D glasses donned, we stepped into Khirbat Faynan, where I was able to visualize and experience the dig as if I were standing in the excavation myself. Next, we were whisked away to Egypt, where I was standing among the columns of the monuments at Luxor, only to then jump to Saudi Arabia to stand amongst Nabatean ruins at Mada'in Salih. Little did I know then what an impact 3D visualization would have on my work. I came to Tom primarily focused on and interested in databases for archaeology, yet years later, my work would take a direct turn toward the world of visualization and its role in archaeology.

During my time studying with Tom, I continued to think about how the visualization of these sites could make archaeology and cultural heritage more accessible to both researchers and the public. Standing in a room in San Diego, I was able to work through material from Jordan, Egypt, and Saudi Arabia all with relative ease. Tom's vision for the use of immersive visualization systems for cultural heritage formed the basis for my work later on, for which I owe him a debt of gratitude.

In this chapter, I will explore my work with Rekrei, a crowdsourcing platform for the preservation of the memory of lost cultural heritage. While Rekrei was founded initially as a response to the destruction of the Mosul Cultural Museum by the so-called Islamic State, its applications were clear and it soon expanded to become a global platform. Throughout my time working with Rekrei, I had plenty of opportunities to explore ideas of community and public engagement, and even to be involved in the first public exhibition at the Mosul Cultural Museum after the occupation of the city by the so-called Islamic state.

2 Rekrei: Beginnings

In early 2015, the so-called Islamic State released a video depicting the graphic destruction of the Mosul Cultural Museum. Of course, this is not the first time that the world has witnessed such blatant disregard for our global historical past. In 2001, the destruction of the Bamiyan Buddhas (Gruen et al., 2005; Grün et al., 2004) in Afghanistan represents another erasure of our global cultural past. One only has to continue leafing through the pages of history to find other examples of destruction. Sometimes the destruction is ideologically motivated, attempting to either replace a political or religious ideology for another. In other cases, the motivations could be cultural, erasing a cultural past to supplant a new one.

Having worked in Jordan since 2004, the destruction of the Mosul Cultural Museum was an event that felt much closer to home, which in turn, resulted in a much greater emotional impact. Fortunately, my time studying with Tom at UC San Diego had given me the necessary formation to work toward a response. Together with a fellow researcher with the Initial Training Network for Digital Cultural Heritage, Chance Coughenour, we decided to create a platform to preserve the memory of lost heritage. Initially, we focused entirely on the Mosul Cultural Museum, although subsequent events following the museum's demise demonstrated that the platform had much wider applications.

Initially, we were hesitant to launch the platform. We had no idea how such a project might be received by both the professional academic community as well as the wider public. The intention of the platform was never to claim preservation of lost heritage, but rather only to recover the memory of the heritage that had been destroyed. I will touch on this point later in this chapter, but it is absolutely imperative to highlight that digital documentation does not inherently mean preservation, and we absolutely must clarify this in our language as we talk about these new technologies and their possibilities for tools of preservation of the past.

It didn't take long for the platform to grow beyond the initial focus of the Mosul Cultural Museum. Shortly after the launch, Nepal suffered a severe earthquake which incurred significant death tolls and widespread destruction of cultural heritage. It was immediately clear that our platform had much wider applications than just the Mosul Cultural Museum. There was nothing unique about the Mosul Cultural Museum or the platform that would exclude it from other areas. It was at this point that Project Mosul shifted from the initial focus of a single museum to become a globally focused platform which we renamed to *Rekrei*, Esperanto for "recreate."

Shortly after the reorientation of the platform, the so-called Islamic State captured Palmyra. While the group assured the public that they would not harm any of the heritage, shortly after the occupation of the site, they destroyed several important monuments.[1] The following months only further reinforced the importance of not only preserving our existing cultural heritage through careful documentation but also preserving the memory of lost cultural heritage through crowdsourcing efforts such as Rekrei.

3   Rekrei: The Platform

It is worth taking a moment to describe the platform itself. Rekrei is a crowdsourcing platform, an idea that I will expand upon further below. But, summing up the idea, volunteers from around the world are the main drivers behind everything done on the platform. Even the platform itself can be influenced by anyone by contributing code that would improve the functionality. In essence, everything about Rekrei is meant to be open and able to be influenced by a wider community.

The basic workflow is as follows: a volunteer can identify a location where heritage has been lost (see Fig. 1). This can be anything, a natural disaster, vandalism,

---

[1] https://www.asor.org/chi/reports/special-reports/Update-on-the-Situation-in-Palmyra

Fig. 1 View of the Rekrei homepage with locations posted by volunteers

or loss as a result of political instability and war such as what we saw with Daesh. Once a place has been identified on the map, people can upload photographs to that location. Once photographs have been uploaded at a location, volunteers can organize them into relevant groups (see Fig. 2). For example, a tourist might have walked through Palmyra taking several photographs of different monuments. They might upload all those photographs to the platform, but they aren't useful as a group. It is only when they are organized into discrete groupings of the same monument that these photographs become useful for reconstruction. Once the photographs have been organized into relevant groups, people can download that entire group to then process it photogrammetrically with the software of their choice. Finally, once a digital reconstruction has been created, they can upload the reconstruction to Sketchfab and tag it with Rekrei to be automatically included in the 3D gallery. They can also specifically link the reconstruction to the location or group to help close the loop on the work already done (see Fig. 3).

It is important to note, at this juncture, that the photogrammetric models are rarely going to be complete with this sort of methodology. The availability of photographs for any given location or monument rarely represents complete coverage. When something is photographed with the intention of 3D reconstruction through photogrammetry, the object of reconstruction is generally photographed from many different angles, at regular intervals, and with calibrated equipment to be able to produce the highest quality 3D model possible. However, a tourist walking by a monument might snap a couple of shots from a few different angles. Perhaps they want to frame a monument in a particular way or capture a classic view that they saw from a brochure or film. Because of this, there might be many images of one

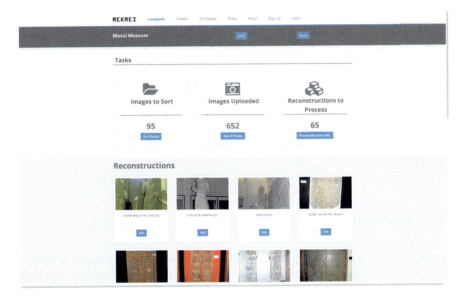

Fig. 2 Groups of images at a location

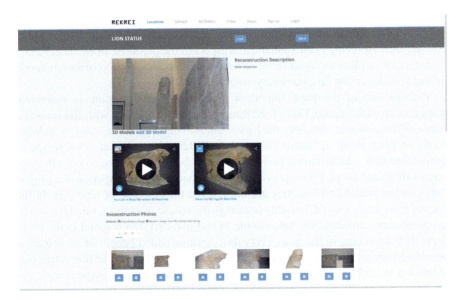

Fig. 3 A reconstruction with links to 3D models and the relevant images used to create it

facade of a monument, for example, while only a handful of images cover the rest of the monument. Therefore, the photogrammetric process might have no problem in modeling the areas with higher photographic coverage, but struggle to fill out areas with sparser photographic coverage.

For sites like the Mosul Cultural Museum, this was particularly problematic. There were very few available digital images taken before the museum was destroyed. While one could digitize analog photographs, the EXIF data is a crucial part of photogrammetry and unfortunately, these data are rarely preserved alongside analog photographs. However, with the advent of the digital camera, especially those available on mobile phones, we are almost inundated with photographs of sites around the world. So, while the Mosul Museum presented a significant challenge, other areas like Palmyra which had many more digital photographs available meant that it was possible to achieve greater coverage with the reconstructions.

4 Crowdsourcing

Crowdsourcing was originally coined by Von Ahn who presented the idea as dealing with tasks that computers were unable to handle by spreading them across a large group of humans. Since that point, it has grown to encompass all sorts of tasks that are better handled by a large group of humans rather than computers. In the current climate of excitement around machine learning and artificial intelligence, it seems almost to go against all of these sorts of advances. However, without a doubt, crowdsourcing still holds an important role in the realm of cultural heritage. In the case of Rekrei, crowdsourcing is the fundamental aspect of the platform. In essence, Rekrei is just a central place to organize the effort around the preservation of lost memory, where crowdsourcing takes on every aspect of the effort.

Perhaps one of the most important aspects of crowdsourcing is individual engagement with a cause. One of the things I heard consistently with Rekrei was a sense of frustration at watching the loss of cultural heritage and a sense of inability to do anything about it. Owens observed that often the motivation for a person to participate in a crowdsourced project stemmed from their desire to contribute to causes they care about. I have previously noted that active participation in a project helps an individual feel like they are influencing the outcome of a project. In the face of frustration with the inability to change the course of events around the world, crowdsourcing projects may help people to feel that they can respond to the problems they are seeing in the news every day. Another added benefit of participation in crowdsourcing projects is influencing others to join. Ridge noted that active participation in such projects encouraged participants to share their experiences, and therefore potentially encourage people to contribute as well.

Of course, one of the potential drawbacks to crowdsourcing is the lack of expertise. An anecdotal example is one contributor to Rekrei whom 3D reconstructed the lion relief from the Mosul Cultural Museum by duplicating the front side of the relief to make the lion appear as if it were a complete sculpture. On one hand, this is a normal assumption to make without knowing anything about Assyrian art. On the other hand, we can also say that it opens up interesting avenues for the remixing of past art and heritage into new pieces of expression today. Whatever the case might have been, it is an example of how someone who has an impressive understanding of 3D modeling and graphics might misunderstand the original piece and create something that is a further divergence from reality.

Whatever the case may be, one thing is clear: the success of Rekrei and other crowdsourcing projects must be attributed to the efforts of the volunteers. Without their work, very little could be achieved based on sheer numbers alone. Two people can only achieve so much, but when you have a large number of people contributing even a few minutes of their time here and there, there is a lot more that can be achieved.

5 Nichesourcing

We cannot talk about crowdsourcing without also addressing another concept, nichesourcing. This concept was first introduced by de Boer et al. in 2012 (De Boer et al., 2012). Perhaps the main contrast is that, while both crowdsourcing and nichesourcing leverage a virtual crowd of individuals to help with a series of tasks, crowdsourcing makes no presumption about the individuals' background nor the rigor of their work. The potential for mistakes due to lack of expertise is a clear risk in these cases, although there is always the hope that the sheer numbers of a crowd might help balance this out. Contrary to crowdsourcing, nichesourcing presumes a certain level of expertise or familiarity with the subject domain.

There is a time and place for either of these strategies to be employed. For example, one might opt for crowdsourcing to accomplish more work if domain knowledge is not required. In the case of Rekrei, uploading images or organizing them into related groupings might make perfect sense. When it comes to the actual reconstructions, some familiarity with the object or monument itself might help significantly. An individual with some familiarity might refine the parameters of a reconstruction to highlight particular aspects over others that might not be related to the actual object itself. Someone with intimate knowledge might even know what parts of a monument were previously reconstructed, and therefore not be as concerned with trying to capture that through photogrammetry.

One should be aware of the pros and cons of either one of these strategies when choosing to implement them in any given project. Neither one is superior to the other in all situations and cases, rather there is much to be considered when implementing either one. Ultimately, if domain knowledge and familiarity are imperative, nichesourcing is a clear choice, but one simply has to accept that the "crowd" will be significantly reduced. On the other hand, if numbers are of importance, and one can accept a variation in quality and results, crowdsourcing has great potential along the way.

I have previously suggested (Vincent, 2017) that a hybrid approach might be the ideal scenario in which experts take on some sort of mentorship role for the greater crowd. In such scenarios, the experts can be leveraged to spread their domain knowledge across many more participants to continue to leverage the greater number of participants, without sacrificing quality. Of course, such a scenario still puts the burden on the experts, and may not be ideal in all situations. It is a third possibility worth considering, especially in the cases where experts are willing to contribute their time in the form of mentorship versus asynchronous tasks that do not require the same level of commitment or dedication.

6 Open-Access

I have long advocated for open access to archaeology and cultural heritage (Bendicho et al., 2017; Vincent et al., 2013a, b, 2014a, b). Rekrei is an excellent example of this, as everything in the project is open-source, including the code for the platform itself. The only thing that is not made public are things like passwords and access credentials to the particular implementation that is Rekrei. However, anyone is free to copy the platform and create their own crowdsourcing platform using the Rekrei code. Likewise, every image uploaded to Rekrei is available to anyone in its raw form. The only processing the platform does is to generate thumbnails of these images for display on the web page.

In designing the project, we wanted to ensure that everything remained in the hands of the participants and that Rekrei was there just to facilitate the possibility for people to take an active role in preserving the memory of lost cultural heritage. Building on the power of engagement through crowdsourcing, open access only further bolsters this engagement by allowing people to take an active role not only through their participation but also through the possibility of shaping the project itself if they so wish.

Another aspect of the open-source approach is a certain amount of transparency and accountability for the work that is being done. For example, anyone can repeat a reconstruction of a group of photographs on the website, either improving on past reconstructions as software improves or new tools become available. This makes it possible for people to repeat reconstructions and verify or improve them as they wish.

Ultimately, open access must remain a cornerstone of Rekrei and other similar projects. Without open access, public participation is compromised, and it ends up being an imbalanced situation. Around the same time that Rekrei launched, other projects also launched focusing on the loss of cultural heritage. However, these projects did not maintain the same level of open access, and I would argue that this is a detriment to any such project. Perhaps a good comparison is a conversation, where a one-sided conversation would be seen as frustrating and useless. We expect that conversations should be dialogues and not monologues. Likewise, if we are advocating for crowdsourcing and public involvement, we must engage in a dialogue as well, making our projects equally open and accessible.

7 Preservation and Memory

One of the things I have continually emphasized with Rekrei is our focus on the preservation of the "memory" of lost heritage. With new technology comes the excitement that it could be the panacea for the challenges that we've faced in the past. The thought of being able to just push a button on a printer and replicate our past heritage is miraculous, to say the least. Unfortunately, these sorts of discourses are incredibly damaging to the preservation of the past. The excitement around the digitization of heritage puts far too much emphasis on a single aspect: the physicality. Without a doubt, 3D digital documentation of our heritage is incredible research that opens up many avenues of investigation. However, we must not ignore all the other aspects of our heritage. A photogrammetric capture of a monument, for example, might have a near-perfect geometric capture of the physical monument but ignores everything else about it.

This becomes even more worrisome when the dialogue brazenly declares that we have perfect copies of heritage and can simply recreate them at will. In 2016, the director of the Institute for Digital of Archaeology, Roger Michel, declared[2] that we could simply recreate anything that was destroyed by the so-called Islamic State. Such a declaration is incredibly worrying as it removes any need for us to preserve our heritage. After all, why should we invest our valuable resources in protecting anything that we can just recreate at will? This could even be taken to an extreme in the sense that commercial interests could outweigh the importance of protecting our cultural heritage since, after all, just printing out a copy would be fine.

For these reasons, Rekrei has carefully chosen to emphasize that it is about the preservation of the memory of lost heritage. There is no denying the incredible power of these new technologies to enable us to interact with the heritage that has been destroyed. For example, a dozen images from the Mosul Cultural Museum of the lion relief makes it possible for us to visualize the sculpture to a degree that it is nearly possible to read the cuneiform inscriptions. However, the original piece has been destroyed. Can the digital surrogate replace it? Absolutely not. Instead, it provides a way for us to continue to interact with it, memorialize it, and keep the memory of it alive without losing sight of the reality of its destruction.

It is right to celebrate the potential that new technologies give us. We should not, however, lose sight of the limitations of what these new technologies are capable of doing. We should not disrespect the heritage itself, passing it over in favor of digital copies of the heritage itself. Instead, we should continue to explore our ability to better preserve heritage through new technology without disregarding the heritage itself.

---

[2] https://www.theguardian.com/commentisfree/2016/mar/29/palmyra-message-isis-islamic-state-jihadis-orgy-destruction-heritage-restored

8 RecoVR

Several months after the launch of the Rekrei platform, The Economist proposed a collaboration to create a virtual reality experience to retell the story of the Mosul Cultural Museum, highlighting the ability to preserve the memory of lost heritage through the applications of new technologies. The initial edition of the virtual reality museum was released at the International Documentary Filmfestival Amsterdam (IDFA[3]) as an explorable world in which the visitor can direct their own experience (Fig. 4 depicts the first experience, with 3D models in the background and projections of the images used to create each of them on the wall). Feedback following this event suggested that a more directed experience would help focus the experience, thus guiding the virtual visitor through a narrative-based storyline. Finally, in May of 2016, The Economist released the completed virtual experience which ended up being a series of 3D 360-degree renders, accompanied by an audio soundtrack that guides the viewer through the experience (Fig. 5). These renders create the sense of an immersive visit to the museum, allowing the user to look anywhere they would like within that sphere, but by keeping all the attention into the single sphere, it maintains a connection to the storyline.

The initial version certainly gave the user the freedom to explore, but unfortunately also seemed to lack direction. The final version[4] guides users from start to finish. This ended up being a key element to make it possible to exhibit the museum in large public gatherings. It then became easy to set someone down, place a headset on them, and get them moving. Virtual reality is not yet a common enough experience that people can pick up and enter the world like they do any other app on their phones. Therefore, a more restricted version of the museum ended up being the ideal form of presenting the story. This, combined with the editorial audio soundtrack, meant that the VR museum experience became an experience where the user was guided through an experience that dealt with the loss of cultural heritage and then ultimately the preservation of its memory through the application of new technologies.

I believe that RecoVR can provide an interesting model for other projects. The initial work was far too open and did not result in a positive experience for the user. However, the final version meant that the virtual visitor to the museum could relax as they were guided through the experience, with the editorial track functioning as an audioguide, helping the user to comprehend everything that had happened, and what the potential future directions might look like. Furthermore, the final result being a series of 360-degree renders is simpler than creating an open-ended virtual world in a game engine, perhaps making it a much more accessible way to retell the story of our global heritage through virtual reality.

---

[3] https://www.idfa.nl/en/film/0f6fcdd2-684a-4301-ba13-4b4d81f01524/recovr-mosul-a-collective-reconstruction

[4] https://www.youtube.com/watch?v=0EazGA673fk

Fig. 4 The first edition of RecoVR Mosul at IDFA

Fig. 5 A screenshot of the final version of RecoVR Mosul, depicting a render of the Mosul Cultural Museum

9 Return to Mosul

Towards the end of 2018, Rekrei received an invitation to participate in an exhibition at the Mosul Cultural Museum. This was the first public exhibition in the museum since the occupation of the city by the so-called Islamic State, and furthermore, the first public exhibition since the invasion of Iraq in 2003. The exhibition was sponsored by Al-Ghad radio station, the resistance radio station that was set up during the occupation of the city and broadcasted into the city to help connect the otherwise disconnected citizens. Al-Ghad organized local Moslawi artists, the restoration of the Royal Hall (the original museum building), and all the other necessary logistics to make the exhibition possible.

The exhibition title, "Return to Mosul: Local Artistic Responses to Conflict, Reconciliation, and Recovery" highlights the spirit of the event and the theme of the art (see Fig. 6 for a view of the exhibition just before opening). The exhibition itself was an overwhelming success. During the week, people from all walks of life visited the exhibition. With each day, people relaxed that bit more, starting to shuffle off the weight of the years of occupation by Daesh.

Rekrei's presence was to help people reconnect with the heritage and the museum itself. The radio station helped with a translation of the RecoVR experience, which proved to be very successful with the public (Fig. 7). Likewise, three 3D printed

Fig. 6 A view inside the hall of the exhibition "Return to Mosul"

Preservation of the Memory of Lost Cultural Heritage in Post-conflict Communities

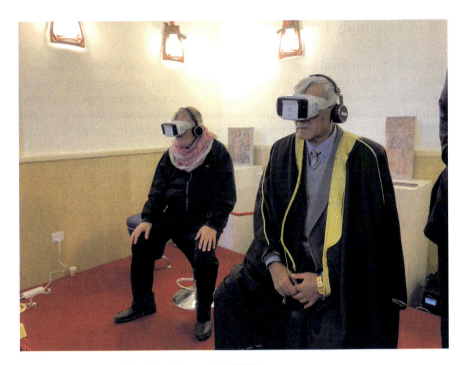

Fig. 7 Opening day and the first visitors to the VR Museum

pieces were exhibited to highlight some of the possibilities of these new technologies and the way that we can preserve the memory of lost heritage. Finally, we had a 3D printer running throughout the exhibition to demonstrate how a reconstructed model could move from virtual to physical.

Many people had never been able to visit the museum and the virtual museum experience was their first chance to step inside a building that was a major part of their city. For some, the experience was too much. Some people could not handle even the briefest reminders of the actual moments of destruction at the hands of Daesh. For others, it was a call to action, a hope that everyone would have a chance to experience the museum and understand the ways we can keep a hold of the heritage that had been destroyed.

The entire exhibition was finally released on the Google Arts and Culture platform[5] which both preserved the experience as well as made it possible for people around the world to visit the exhibition. This was rather important as it was nearly impossible for outsiders to get access to Mosul at this point, and for the Moslawi diaspora, it was a way for them to reconnect to their city without the challenges of traveling back for the exhibition.

---

[5] https://artsandculture.google.com/theme/return-to-mosul-an-exhibition-to-bring-the-city%E2%80%99s-people-back-together/oQLCZ_d_X8z2Kw?hl=en

10 Community Engagement

One of the fundamental principles of Rekrei has been people's contribution to the digital reconstruction of lost heritage, rather than one or two individuals doing all the work themselves. It is worth looking at the project as a nexus that concentrates and coordinates this work, while still emphasizing that the contributions to the platform are coming from the community who are giving of their time for the betterment of cultural heritage. The platform is simply a way to enable an individual to work virtually on any of the projects that inspire them. This could be uploading images, the organization and management of those images, 3D modeling, or even contributing to the development of the web platform itself. This opensource approach allows for many more voices to shape and influence the project, adding their voices, thoughts, and opinions towards the preservation of the memory of lost heritage.

One could say that the depiction of the destruction of heritage by Daesh was practically viral. The coverage they received was global and intense, to say the least. Who wasn't hyperaware of the loss of global heritage at the hands of such extremist groups? In the face of such losses, many felt helpless, unable to do anything to stop these losses. When Rekrei was initially launched, we never could have imagined the public response, and in large part, I suspect this was because it allowed people from any background to have a tangible response to the destruction they were seeing daily in the headlines around them.

With all the benefits that may come from crowdsourced photogrammetry, we should not ignore that the quality of these 3D reconstructions cannot compare to those of carefully calibrated and controlled acquisitions like those that we might expect in any archaeological project today. But, a platform like Rekrei with crowdsourcing at the heart of it all will naturally involve mixing many different sensors and will lack the complete coverage that we expect in reconstructions done by heritage professionals. Yet, the benefits are twofold. First, Rekrei focuses on the heritage that has been lost, there are no existing acquisitions or models. As such, these reconstructions are all that is left to the global community. Even with their imperfections, they are better than no reconstructions at all as long as there is an understanding of their imperfections. Second, they engage citizen scientists from around the world. People who might otherwise not have ever known about the heritage of any given region may find themselves connecting with regions and cultures, demystifying those and helping to create bridges across previously existing boundaries.

Ultimately, we have to weigh the benefits of community participation with the potential quality of professional acquisitions. Even if existing, standing heritage today, one could argue that there are real benefits to involving the wider community and not just limiting access to heritage professionals. Fortunately, as with all things open and crowdsourced, there are no limitations. There is no reason why we can't have both. They are not mutually exclusive. I would encourage projects to seek ways of involving the wider communities and stakeholders, while still engaging in the nichesourcing that can potentially result in high-quality results.

11 Heritage for Peace

As Horning and Breen note, most of the literature focusing on archaeology and cultural heritage in conflict and post-conflict zones deals with the heritage itself and less with the role it has in post-conflict restoration (Horning & Breen, 2017). Yet, there is already a precedent for cultural heritage as a tool for post-conflict resolution. One example is the Council of Europe's 2011 resolution entitled "The Role of Culture and Cultural Heritage in Conflict Prevention, Transformation, Resolution and Post-Conflict Action: the Council of Europe Approach." Yet, even as we think about the role of cultural heritage in post-conflict communities, Giblin (2013) rightly points out that they can be both painful and healing, depending on the context. For some of the viewers of the VR museum, the association of the heritage with Daesh was simply too strong of an association. For others, however, the VR museum was a way to reclaim the heritage that was destroyed, even if it was just through digital means.

The Return to Mosul exhibition highlighted the fact that cultural heritage, both past and present, are crucial for the rebuilding of the community. There is a nuance in how it is used, and what it can mean for each individual, but the space that was created through art and cultural heritage was a place that could be the beginnings of healing for a wounded community. In the middle of the rubble all around us, including the main building of the museum next door, art and cultural heritage certainly provided the space for people to hope for peace and restoration of the city.

12 Future Directions

It is important to look at the future possibilities for the project. While I have taken time to talk about the power of crowdsourcing and the importance of personal involvement, there is no question that there are very interesting applications for things like machine learning and artificial intelligence. One really clear possibility is the potential for grouping images together automatically, or even scraping images from elsewhere around the internet. For example. We already integrated Flickr with the platform, making it possible to see any open-access images at the same location as the location marked on the platform. Using machine learning, it would be possible to automatically scrape any images that were related and not already included at that location. Then, these images could be automatically assembled into relevant groups and piped into photogrammetric software.

While this would be an incredibly interesting technical exercise, it certainly seems like the spirit of the project has been one of looking for ways to preserve the memory of lost heritage, but through the active participation of individuals who wanted to dedicate their own time and energy to that preservation. Throughout this chapter, I've emphasized the importance of crowdsourcing for community engagement and dissemination of projects like Rekrei. Without a doubt, machine learning and artificial intelligence could certainly advance the project in very interesting ways, but would we see the same sort of active participation and interest if it was all being run through digital neural networks?

I would argue that the importance of the preservation of cultural heritage calls for the need to actively involve members of the public at all stages. There must be a blend of new technologies and human involvement. The moment that we no longer blend these two together, projects like Rekrei will cease to exist. Furthermore, involving the public in an archaeological project helps to demystify the process itself. Rather than distancing ourselves from the public, we should seek ways to involve them at any and every stage of our work.

To this end, I would argue that while there are technical directions that could be very interesting for projects like Rekrei to pursue, fundamentally, these projects are about the public engagement aspect and everything that can be gained from there. There has long been a public interest in archaeology, one only has to look at the variety of TV documentaries talking about pyramids or lost treasures, or even the great Hollywood blockbusters that have archaeology as a central plot. Therefore, it is best to continue to involve the public as much as possible, even while still seeking to find new ways of applying new technologies to our field. There very well may be ways of incorporating machine learning or artificial intelligence into Rekrei, but hopefully, those tools could be incorporated in such a way that continues to incorporate public participation.

13 Conclusion

Over a decade ago I first had the opportunity to work with Tom Levy. Without a doubt, my time spent with Tom set me on the path toward the work I have done and continue to do today. Tom's passion for integrating new technologies into traditional fieldwork is exemplified in his work. Tom has been a champion of exploring these new paths, and seeking ways of integrating them into the archaeological discipline without sacrificing the academic rigor of his fieldwork. Without a doubt, my work with Rekrei is rooted in the influence of Tom's guidance over the years.

Hopefully, Rekrei represents what can happen when we engage the public in cultural heritage projects, especially combined with new technologies. Rekrei, had it been just one or two people doing the work, would never have been able to achieve what it did. It is only through the active participation of so many people that Rekrei was able to make an impact in the preservation of our lost global cultural heritage.

Throughout this chapter, I've looked at the advantages of both crowdsourcing and nichesourcing. Without a doubt, crowdsourcing offers broad possibilities for public engagement and involvement in heritage projects. There is much to be said about the active participation of the general public in the preservation of our global cultural heritage, even if it is just the preservation of the memory of lost heritage. Likewise, there is great potential for expert crowds to be involved in such projects, potentially acting as mentors and guides to the wider public. A hybrid approach between crowdsourcing and nichesourcing can offer the greatest possibility for success in such projects.

Perhaps the most important thing to look at here is the optimism about what we can gain through the applications of new technologies in archaeology. If there is one thing I learned from Tom, it is that there is nothing to fear and it is well worth exploring the applications of new technology in archaeology. Tom was not seeking to replace traditional archaeology with new technology, but rather find ways to blend the two to find harmony between the two. New technology should be at the service of archaeology, and not the other way around.

I am forever grateful for the time I spent with Tom and the opportunities that grew out of our time together. Without him, Rekrei would never have existed. Thanks to Tom's enthusiasm for the applications of new technology in archaeology and his continued focus on the preservation of cultural heritage, I was able to build on what I learned during my time with him to find my path in heritage preservation and technological advancements in archaeology.

References

Bendicho, V. M. L.-M., Gutiérrez, M. F., Vincent, M. L., & León, A. G. (2017). Digital heritage and virtual archaeology: An approach through the framework of international recommendations. In *Mixed reality and gamification for cultural heritage* (pp. 3–26). Springer.

De Boer, V., Hildebrand, M., Aroyo, L., De Leenheer, P., Dijkshoorn, C., Tesfa, B., et al. (2012). Nichesourcing: Harnessing the power of crowds of experts. In *International conference on knowledge engineering and knowledge management* (pp. 16–20). Springer.

Giblin, J. D. (2013). Post-conflict heritage: Symbolic healing and cultural renewal. *International Journal of Heritage Studies, 20*(5), 500–518. https://doi.org/10.1080/13527258.2013.772912

Gruen, A., Remondino, F., & Zhang, L. (2005). The Bamiyan project: Multi-resolution image-based modeling. *Recording, Modeling and Visualization of Cultural Heritage, 415* (39208), 45–54.

Grün, A., Remondino, F., & Zhang, L. (2004). Photogrammetric reconstruction of the great Buddha of Bamiyan, Afghanistan. *The Photogrammetric Record, 19*(107), 177–199.

Horning, A., & Breen, C. (2017). In the aftermath of violence: Heritage and conflict transformation in Northern Ireland. In *Post-conflict archaeology and cultural heritage* (pp. 177–194). Routledge.

Knabb, K. A., Schulze, J. P., Kuester, F., DeFanti, T. A., & Levy, T. E. (2014). Scientific visualization, 3D immersive virtual reality environments, and archaeology in Jordan and the Near East. *Near Eastern Archaeology, 77*(3), 228–232.

Liritzis, I., Pavlidis, G., Vosynakis, S., Koutsoudis, A., Volonakis, P., Petrochilos, N., et al. (2016). Delphi4Delphi: First results of the digital archaeology initiative for ancient Delphi, Greece. *Antiquity, 90*(354), e4. https://doi.org/10.15184/aqy.2016.187

Vincent, M. L. (2017). In M. L. Vincent, M. Ioannides, & T. E. Levy (Eds.), *Crowdsourced data for cultural heritage* (pp. 79–91). Springer International Publishing. https://doi.org/10.1007/978-3-319-65370-9_5

Vincent, M. L., DeFanti, T., Schulze, J., Kuester, F., & Levy, T. E. (2013a). *Stereo panorama photography in archaeology: Bringing the past into the present through CAVEcams and immersive virtual environments* (pp. 455–455). 2013 Digital Heritage International Congress (DigitalHeritage). 28 Oct – 1 Nov. 2013.

Vincent, M. L., Kuester, F., & Levy, T. E. (2013b). *OpenDig: In-field data recording for archaeology and cultural heritage* (pp. 539–542). 2013 Digital Heritage International Congress (DigitalHeritage). IEEE.

Vincent, M. L., Kuester, F., & Levy, T. E. (2014a). OpenDig: Contextualizing the past from the field to the web. *Mediterranean Archaeology and Archaeometry, 14*(4), 109–116.

Vincent, M. L., Kuester, F., & Levy, T. E. (2014b). OpenDig: Digital field archeology, curation, publication, and dissemination. *Near Eastern Archaeology, 77*(3), 204–208.

Local Voices, Storytelling, and Virtual Reality: Fostering Community Archaeology and Preserving Cultural Heritage in a COVID Lockdown

Suzanne Richard and Douglas R. Clark

Abstract This paper discusses an innovative method in community archaeology to safeguard and preserve the cultural heritage of Madaba, Jordan – remotely. The community-engagement model utilized empowers local communities to play a major role in site preservation and cultural heritage awareness activities. In an era of COVID-19 lockdown, and the consequent travel restrictions, the authors teamed up with six international partners and twelve local stakeholders in a U.S. Department of State initiative to continue, remotely, our work of preserving and safeguarding the heritage of Madaba. That ambitious project, "The Madaba Digital Documentation and Tourism Project," is the focus of this article. Its success as a community archaeology project is a testament to new trends today that: eschew outdated colonially derived methods of community outreach in favor of a true collaboration that integrates local and historical voices in a more cohesive and comprehensive cultural narrative; and innovatively utilize technology/digital platforms to preserve a worldwide cultural heritage profoundly impacted by the COVID-19 pandemic.

Keywords Community archaeology · Virtual reality · Cultural heritage preservation · Storytelling · Madaba · Jordan · Covid 19 · MRAMP

S. Richard (✉)
Gannon University, Erie, PA, USA
e-mail: richard@gannon.edu

D. R. Clark
La Sierra University, Riverside, CA, USA
e-mail: dclark@lasierra.edu

© The Author(s), under exclusive license to Springer Nature Switzerland AG 2023
E. Ben-Yosef, I. W. N. Jones (eds.), *"And in Length of Days Understanding" (Job 12:12): Essays on Archaeology in the Eastern Mediterranean and Beyond in Honor of Thomas E. Levy*, Interdisciplinary Contributions to Archaeology,
https://doi.org/10.1007/978-3-031-27330-8_72

1 Introduction

1.1 COVID-19

On March 11, 2020, the World Health Organization (WHO, 2020a) "characterizes COVID-19 as a pandemic;" earlier, on January 30, 2020, a "Public Health Emergency of International Concern [was] declared" (WHO, 2020b). On March 13, 2020 "a national emergency was declared in the United States concerning the COVID-19 Outbreak." (CDC, 2020). The authors were in Jordan at the time considering flying out earlier given the rising concern of lockdown in the States and in Jordan (Richard departed on March 8, Clark on March 13). The severity of the situation is reflected in the widespread closure of schools (e.g., Gannon University closed on March 13) and the consequent conversion to the world of remote teaching/learning. Not only did the pandemic disrupt the lives of billions of people on the planet in manifold ways, including death, it profoundly impacted cities and countries that rely on tourism at their cultural heritage sites; ultimately the sites themselves, deserted and uncared for, were in imminent danger of neglect, deterioration, looting, and destruction. Cultural institutions (museums, the arts, music, performance, etc.) generally languished during this period. Such was the case in Jordan as well, where initially the entire country was forcibly shut down to any movement of its citizens; in time these restrictions were lessened, but only within regions of the country, before these too diminished as the COVID situation improved. Cultural institutions have only recently begun to make a comeback.

1.2 The Institutional Response

Concerned with isolation during COVID-19 and with people losing touch with cultural activities and heritage, a global initiative to "connect people with their humanity" set in motion a myriad of on-line, digital, and social media activities to promote culture and cultural heritage, from world heritage sites to creative cities (UNESCO, 2020a, b). Other institutions, concerned to protect cultural heritage, introduced videos on safeguarding heritage sites in the crisis (ICCROM, 2020). Likewise, the World Monuments Fund, which partners globally with 29 countries, was concerned about the safety of people engaged in heritage work and monitored sites closely to assess economic support at the sites and determine what role to play during COVID 19 (Montlaur, 2020a, b). In Jordan as well, considerable efforts may be noted to respond to the crisis, for example the USAID (United States Agency for International Development)/ACOR (American Center of Research)/SCHEP (Sustainable Cultural Heritage through Engagement of Local Communities Project) response continued support for SCHEP projects, maintained ties to stakeholders in the tourism industry, and sponsored numerous workshops and training courses (Al Adarbeh et al., 2020). The Madaba Digital project, in fact, likewise benefitted from outreach in large part by another institution: The U.S. Department of State Cultural Heritage Coordinating Committee (CHCC).

One could cite numerous scholarly responses to the cultural heritage crisis, most being attempts to counteract the inability of people to travel to heritage sites. Scholarly activities were varied, e.g., concerned to examine the on-line conversation about cultural heritage during COVID-19, some studied social media, such as Instagram and various hashtags discourse, also photos (Ginzarly & Srour, 2021). Digital platforms were widely utilized during COVID, with various technologies such as virtual reality, artificial intelligence, 3D modelling, even online 360 virtual reality (Ren & Cen, 2021). This article will concentrate on a virtual reality project that was not only produced remotely but that embodies the best of community archaeology practices.

2 MRAMP and the Genesis of the Digital Project

In September 2020, a grant (#SJ010019GR0089) from the U.S. Department of State's Ambassador Fund for Cultural Preservation (AFCP) and the Cultural Antiquities Task Force (CATF) inaugurated "The Madaba Digital Documentation and Tourist Project." The latter was an outgrowth of two other projects initiated to preserve, safeguard, and promote the cultural heritage of Madaba, Jordan (Fig. 1). The umbrella project (begun in 2015) is the USAID/SCHEP-sponsored Madaba Regional Archaeological Museum Project (MRAMP) in coordination with the Department of Antiquities of Jordan. This long-term American/Italian/Jordanian collaboration seeks to innovatively preserve the heritage of Madaba by building a museum within the Madaba Archaeological Park West, a museum that will preserve and envelop a complex of Jordanian traditional buildings from the late nineteenth century (Fig. 2). The envisioned Museum Complex includes the contiguous "Burnt Palace," Roman Cardo, and Martyrs Church and a repurposed early twentieth-century medical clinic in the park (Fig. 3). The project is founded in community archaeology with the goal to train and build capacity of the community to ensure sustainability that will positively impact local and international tourism as well as the local economy (for details on the MRAMP project, see Richard et al., 2016, 2019, 2020; D'Andrea et al., 2018, 2019–2020; Clark et al., 2017, 2018, 2020, 2022).

The second MRAMP project, funded by an AFCP/CATF grant (#SJ010020GR0058), out of which the "The Madaba Digital Documentation and Tourist Project" directly evolved, is titled "MRAMP Phase 4: Repurposing Current Museum and Preserving the Collection." The goal of this project was to repurpose the current museum in the Department of Antiquities Madaba regional offices and storerooms into a state-of-the-art storage facility, conservation lab, and research facility (initiated in September 2019; Fig. 4). The facility will support the planned regional archaeological museum for the Governorate of Madaba, which includes the region bounded by the Dead Sea to the west, the desert to the east, southern Amman in the north, and the Wadi Mujib in the south. The on-going work has enabled the

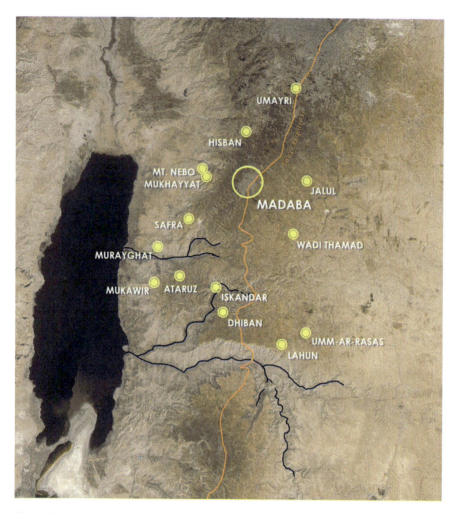

Fig. 1 Map of the MRAMP region showing the archaeological sites surrounding the city of Madaba

relocation of endangered artifacts from crowded, unsafe conditions to a renovated storage facility with a well-organized, inventoried, databased, and, ultimately, conserved artifact collection. Through training, capacity building, and the application of best practices in the preservation of cultural heritage, the project seeks to empower local stewardship as the best promise for the conservation and sustainability of the Museum Collection (Clark & Richard, 2021).

In March 2020, due to the considerable negative impact of the COVID-19 pandemic, along with Jordan closing its borders and the US restricting travel, the repurposing of the facility project fell into abeyance. This devastating situation improbably opened the doors to the "Madaba Digital Documentation and Tourism Project."

Fig. 2 Aerial photo of downtown Madaba showing the location of the Archaeological Park West and East in relation to St. George's Church and the King Hussein Mosque; 1. Traditional Jordanian buildings, 2. Burnt Palace, 3. Early twentieth century clinic, 4. Cardo, 5. Martyrs Church. (Photo (c) APAAME, Robert H. Bewley)

3 The Madaba Digital Documentation and Tourism Project

This project was a case study of an innovative approach to continue the community archaeology work of the authors to preserve and promote the cultural heritage of Madaba, Jordan, despite a COVID-19 lockdown (March 2020–July 2021). The impossibility of travel to Jordan to supervise and direct on-going projects was indeed a blow to long-term planning, budgets, and goals, not to say a void left in the local community in training, capacity building, employment. Particularly troubling were grant-funded projects with deadlines, put on hold like everything else due to the pandemic. With the MRAMP repurposing project on hold at the time, at the initiative of the U. S. Department of State CHCC, a new cultural heritage project was conceived that transformed and expanded MRAMP's vision and mission to safeguard Madaba's heritage: digitally document cultural heritage remotely. That perceptive view, along with an amazing convergence at the time of networking and contacts with specialists in the field of digital documentation, would ultimately pave the way to the project that is the topic of this paper: "The Madaba Digital Documentation and Tourism Project."

The resulting project was a collaborative endeavor of numerous entities that sought to document endangered antiquities sites for posterity through 3D mapping accomplished on the ground by a group trained (remotely) in photogrammetry; local tour guides would narrate tours of the sites, and members of the local

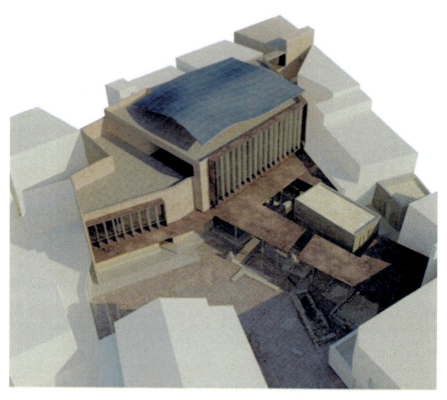

Fig. 3 An envisioned 3D rendering of the Museum complex in the Archaeological Park West (graphic elaboration by Valeria Gaspari for the Studio Strati © MRAMP)

community would share their memories and stories growing up amid the antiquities of Madaba. The community-engagement model benefitted from empowered local communities to play a major role in site preservation and cultural heritage awareness activities. This empowerment of the in-country staff led to their buy-in and ultimate ownership of, pride in, and dedication to the project. These new possibilities of remotely forging ahead with heritage preservation through reliance on the local community struck a chord with the authors and encouraged them to resume work on the AFCP/CATF Repurposing of the Current Museum project.

All of which served to cement a very basic principle—known before but not fully appreciated until then—that a bottom-up relationship is the essence of community archaeology, closely allied to promoting local ownership of a project. Recognizing this important principle, plus the unequivocal impossibility of being in Jordan in person, made it evident that any continued work on preservation of cultural heritage for both projects would almost solely have to rely on the local community. The Digital project, whose genesis occurred due to a worldwide COVID lockdown, which required totally new methodologies and research designs to maintain

Fig. 4 The regional offices of the department of antiquities, Jordan, location of the current Madaba Museum and the new storage facility

momentum with project objectives and expand project goals beyond original plans, led to a community archaeology engagement of local voices, storytelling, and virtual reality.

3.1 Collaboration and the Site

This ambitious undertaking included partners such as CyArk, a non-profit organization that digitally records significant cultural heritage (www.CyArk.org); the U.S. Embassy English Training Center; and StoryCenter, the founder of the digital storytelling movements (https://www.storycenter.org/). Other partners contributing to the project locally were both the national and regional offices of the Ministry of Tourism and Antiquities (MOTA), as well as the American University of Madaba (AUM), along with the Department of Antiquities of Jordan.

The site chosen for the project is the historic district of downtown Madaba, Jordan. A 3D capture focused on the Archaeological Park West, Archaeological Park East, St. George's Church, all along the Heritage Trail (Fig. 5). The above historic sites represent the sixth-century CE flowering of Madaba—the "city of mosaics." The Archaeological Park West includes the "Burnt Palace," the Martyrs Church, the nineteenth- century traditional Jordanian building complex and the western portion of the exposed Roman/Byzantine cardo linking the two parks. The Burnt Palace is an elite residence that includes marvelous mosaics, such as the Lion Attacking the Bull, exquisite geometric designs, a Tyche figure, and a pair of sandals marking the entrance for guests, a symbol of welcome and hospitality which MRAMP has adopted as its logo (Piccirillo, 1986; Fig. 6). The Martyrs Church, a well-preserved Byzantine Basilica, is known for its mosaic floor of both vegetal and figural designs, some defaced parts of which testify to the seventh-century CE iconoclastic phase (Piccirillo & Denton, 1996; on the mosaics of Jordan, see Piccirillo et al., 1993). The Archaeological Park East complex includes the Church of the Virgin Mary, the Church of the Prophet Elias, and the Hippolytus Hall. The mosaics in all are exquisite, for example, the well-preserved mosaic floor depicting the Greek Tragedy, Hippolytus, along with the famous Queen of Madaba mosaic (Fig. 7) (see further in Piccirillo & Denton, 1996). The Archaeological Parks border the Heritage Trail, a tourist-lined street that continues over to the Church of the Map—St. George's Greek Orthodox Church—that is one of the most often visited tourist attractions in Madaba. Its mosaic floor exhibits one of the earliest Holy Land maps, dated to the sixth century, which is unique in that it shows the geographical region extending from the Nile throughout the biblical lands on either side of the Jordan River (Fig. 8). All these sites, representing over two thousand years of the

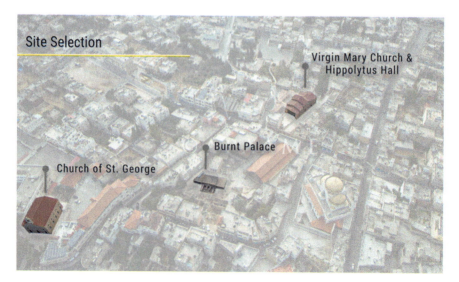

Fig. 5 The three sites of the project: Virgin Mary Church & Hippolytus Hall, Burnt Palace, and Church of St. George in 3D. (Courtesy CyArk and Kacey Hadick)

Local Voices, Storytelling, and Virtual Reality: Fostering Community Archaeology... 1709

Fig. 6 Logo of MRAMP: the welcoming sandals mosaic from the "Burnt Palace". (Photo (c) MRAMP)

history and heritage of Jordan, are the singular tourist attractions in downtown Madaba.

3.2 Methods and Materials

As a case study from which others could benefit, it would be worthwhile tracing the numerous steps essential to the planning and implementation stages. The programmatic plan of work included the following activities/objectives:

1. Identify local partners and trainees and send equipment to local team (MRAMP)
2. Provide remote training workshop on photogrammetry and data collection (CyArk/three data capture people)
3. Give remote English language training to six people (U.S. Department of State)
4. Provide remote training (six people) in narration and storytelling (StoryCenter)
5. Provide remote tour training and record audio/video content for experience (CyArk/trainees)
6. Finalize data capture using photogrammetry on the ground and with a drone (CyArk/drone company/trainees)
7. Process 3D data to create 3D model (CyArk)
8. Integrate audio into 3D model to create tour (CyArk)
9. Publish Experience

Fig. 7 The Queen of Madaba Mosaic depicted with turreted crown from the Hippolytus Hall. (Photo: D. R. Clark)

4 Data Capture, Tour Guides and Storytelling

4.1 Data Capture

The MRAMP team identified three data-capture team members (all from AUM), three tour guides (all from Madaba), and six storytellers (all members of the Madaba community). These twelve people did all the work on the ground (Fig. 9). Given the lockdown and difficulty contacting people in Jordan, the process to find candidates in three different activity areas was time-consuming and did take several months of seeking recommendations from colleagues, then contacting them through email, previewing resumes, and finally interviewing through Zoom. The MRAMP team was gratified to be able to train, build capacity, and employ people at a time when there was no tourism, no work, shops were closed, and generally people were hurting financially and otherwise from the pandemic. The photogrammetry equipment (camera, tripod, battery, software, etc.) was shipped to Jordan, where there were

Fig. 8 St. George's Greek Orthodox Church (the "Church of the Map") mosaic showing the Jerusalem panel in the middle of the earliest extant map of the Holy Land, dating to the sixth-century Byzantine Period. (Photo: G. Kochheiser)

Fig. 9 Participants included in One Place, Many Stories-Madaba, Jordan: Storytellers, Tour Guides, and the Data Capture Team. (Courtesy CyArk and Kacey Hadick)

delays (and costs) processing the equipment through customs, a factor which most archaeologists working in Jordan have experienced (Fig. 10). Thanks is due to the American Embassy in Amman and ACOR, who were both helpful in acquiring the equipment, the latter providing the logistical assistance in the absence of the authors and facilitating the downloading of the megafiles to transfer to CyArk.

2. Virtual Training via Online Workshop

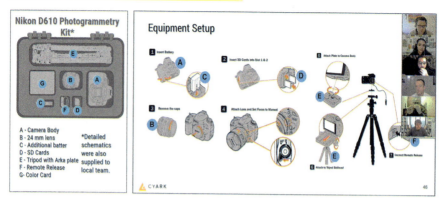

Fig. 10 Photogrammetry camera equipment and virtual training via online workshop. (Courtesy: CyArk and Kacey Hadick)

Fig. 11 American University of Madaba (AUM) participants and their photogrammetry work collecting data at the three sites of the project

Given time zone differences, Wi-Fi connectivity problems in Jordan, not to say the pandemic, it cannot be stressed enough that a project such as this is very demanding and challenging--but ultimately rewarding in the benefit accrued to the participants in the community and their sense of satisfaction and accomplishment by acquiring new technological skills and full partnership in the project. For the most part, the data capture team (Fig. 11 and see Fig. 8) had little if any previous background or experience with the technology. Over a two-week period, multiple remote training sessions occurred via Zoom despite time differences (for CyArk it was 3:00 AM PST). CyArk trained the three people in using the equipment including practice sessions with data capture of the designated antiquities locations in Madaba. Once trained, the data capture team over a 1–2-week period (all the while CyArk checking the data) were able to map the Burnt Palace in the Archaeological Park West, the Hippolytus Hall/Church of the Virgin in the Archaeological Park East, and St. George's Church (the church of the map).

With assistance from ACOR/SCHEP, a drone company was hired to provide drone coverage of the entire are, which CyArk was able to integrate with the terrestrial photogrammetric work mentioned above (Fig. 12). Ultimately, additional footage was necessary by the trainees in January 2021 to complete the capture required by CyArk, particularly considering the challenges of facilitating the drone flyovers (delayed due to permits, local regulations, and weather). Thus, in January 2021, the set date for completing the project, CyArk had all the data in hand. Over the next few months, they were able to complete the integration of the terrestrial photogrammetric work with the drone capture, develop the 3D model, and incorporate the audio/video from the tour guides and storytellers. As is clear from the above, support in country is especially crucial in a remotely led project such as ours. Not only did ACOR/SCHEP greatly facilitate interactions with the drone company, but ACOR willingly accepted responsibility for downloading the data cards and transferring the data to CyArk before January 31, 2021, as well as facilitating payment to the local partners in this endeavor.

4.2   Tour Guides and Storytelling

The challenge of a project like this is that it is necessary to synchronize the training and completion of the various project components to enable the significant video and audio work of CyArk. For example, while training and data capture were ongoing, training and coordination with StoryCenter, which set out as its mission to: "create spaces for listening to and sharing stories, to help build a just and healthy world…[to] provide individuals and organizations with skills and tools that support self-expression, creative practice, and community building" (https://www.storycenter.org/about), and the English Training Course occurred to enhance the English delivery of both the tour guides and the storytellers (all done remotely). Note in addition that several employees of MRAMP working in the current Museum also benefited from the English Training course. The narration and storytelling aspect of the project (working closely with the English Training Center) was successful in training and recording audio stories from the six participants (n). It involved multiple Zoom sessions, getting to know the participants, helping them with their stories, revising, translating, practicing, and finally recording. The tour guides, whose English was reasonably good, benefited from the Storytelling training as well, although they worked very closely with CyArk who trained them to record their narrative of the sites, and to edit same in both Arabic and English (and see Fig. 8).

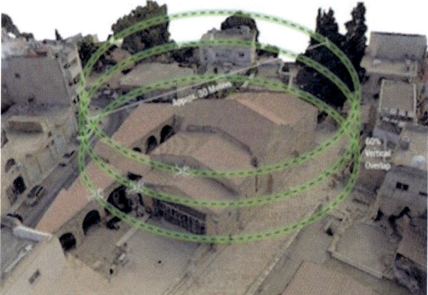

Fig. 12 The Virgin Mary Church & Hippolytus Hall showing routing for the drone fly-over

4.3 *Final Product: One Place, Many Stories – Madaba, Jordan*

The processing of 3D data by CyArk was on-going, requiring the integrating of the photogrammetric, drone, tour guide/storyteller audio into a 3D video and virtual interactive tour. Ultimately, CyArk, in partnership with Richard and Clark of MRAMP, provided social media packets to the partner institutions, launched the

4. Data Processing

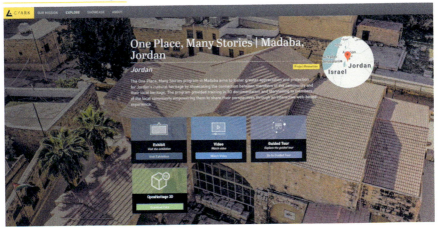

Fig. 13 One Place, May Stories – Madaba, Jordan video streaming on the CyArk website. (Courtesy CyArk and Kacey Hadick)

virtual tour on May 18, 2021 and published the project https://cyark.org/projects/madaba/overview (CyArk et al., 2021; Figs. 13 and 14). The 3D model and virtual tour is titled: *One Place, Many Stories – Madaba, Jordan*. The final product is an immersive audio and video 3D tour of the sites. Virtual tourists will be able to engage with the site through an interactive 3D model and learn directly from local experts through audio and video. CyArk promotes the publication of these experiences through its website, as well as promoting the publication through CyArk social media channels. All raw data from the project is disseminated via Open Heritage 3D to provide open access to the data. The program will support local communities today while generating awareness and understanding about cultural heritage to encourage future tourists when travel is again possible, and to make these locations accessible for those unable to travel at all. The virtual tour is also available on the MRAMP Museum Website platform as an extraordinary public relations vehicle to enhance the overall MRAMP project to build a museum in Madaba, Jordan (http://madabamuseum.org/en and http://madabamuseum.og/ar).

4.4 Madaba Mondays

As the 3D tour of Madaba, Jordan and accompanying audio tours and storytelling mark a new frontier for the Cultural Antiquities Task Force (CATF), it was decided to more widely publicize the project to the general public. Following the launch by CyArk of "One Place, Many Stories – Madaba, Jordan," the CATF, in collaboration with Public Affairs and Strategic Communications (PASC), proposed to launch a

Project Achievements

1. Develop capacity of local community members and students with new skills.
2. Oversee and coordinate 3D documentation of select areas of Madaba to provide a comprehensive point-in-time record.
3. Develop 3D online experience and supplementary multimedia to raise awareness for the Madaba region and support increased protection
4. Develop a template for future remote training to develop immersive media.

Fig. 14 Project achievements listed in the Madaba city-center project; logos of partners included. (Courtesy CyArk and Kacey Hadick)

series of hour-long pre-recorded YouTube conversations to be hosted by Paul Fischer of the Bureau of Educational and Cultural Affairs (ECA's) YouTube handle. "Madaba Mondays" launched on June 14, 2021, with a new episode coming every other Monday for a total of eight episodes. Each episode highlighted a particular feature of or partner in the project and brought to light different perspectives (Fig. 15). (https://www.youtube.com/watch?v=0hbMGBsE8zc).

4.5 Madaba: The Arab Tourism Capital of 2022

It was announced in mid-September across several Jordanian news outlets that Madaba, Jordan had been selected by the Arab Tourism Organization (ATO) as the Arab Tourism Capital for 2022 (see, for example: https://www.jordantimes.com/news/local/madaba-named-arab-tourism-capital-2022). This puts into sharp relief the important contributions of Madaba to our understanding of the past in central Jordan and should give a major boost to the local economy. This designation should also give impetus to the drive to preserve and protect the region's cultural heritage through digital channels in order to widen the global reach of awareness-raising and fundraising for the proposed new museum.

5. Project Launch

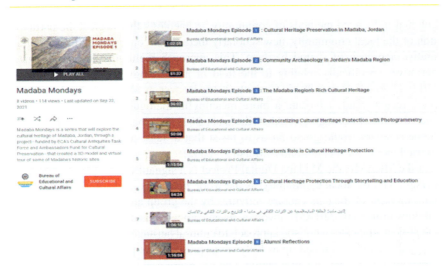

Fig. 15 Project launch of Madaba Mondays by the U.S. Department of State. (Courtesy of CyArk and Kacey Hadick)

5 Community Archaeology and Local Voices

The Madaba Digital Documentation and Tourism project embodies the MRAMP approach to heritage driven by a community archaeology approach that embraces the involvement of the local community as true collaborators. The overall MRAMP project uses a methodology for preserving, managing, and promoting cultural heritage resources in Jordan through a community-first approach. This precept has guided MRAMP to engage the local community as primary stakeholders, including policy makers (10 categories), business support organizations (2), academic research institutions (20), private and public organizations (14 entities), international organizations (7), businesses (dozens), and descendants of nineteenth-century immigrant families (dozens) who founded modern Madaba in the early 1880s (for details, see Harrison, 1996; Lesnes & Younker, 2013; Richard et al., 2019). MRAMP embodies a collaboration that highlights not a western interpretation of heritage but is founded on a concern for indigenous voices to be documented in a diverse life history of the local community's heritage in which they live. We believe that the multiple and diverse voices of the local community illuminated in "One Place, Many Voices – Madaba, Jordan" exemplify the importance and ethics of a shared heritage about the past, but at the same time highlight a mosaic of beliefs, sense of self, identity, and link with the past.

Such an understanding of a new dynamic in community engagement /archaeology was not always the case. Previously, collaboration in Community Archaeology generally meant consulting with and relegating the community to a relatively passive role in a project (Moser et al., 2002); it also included colonial-induced perspectives (see analysis by deVries, 2013 and Abu-Khafajah, 2014). Eschewing past colonial-influenced methods of community archaeology that neglect the participation of the local community, new scholarly theoretical constructs call for a collaborative approach of shared heritage. This approach highlights new, decolonized narratives specifically relating to the field of archaeology (Porter, 2010; Cesari, 2011; Lydon & Rizvi, 2016; Corbett, 2015; Boozer et al., 2020; Mickel, 2021). Such recent trends advocate a more meaningful dialogue that results in a truly shared cultural heritage (see Abu-Khafajah, 2011; Moshenska & Dhanjal, 2011). Some scholars would go so far as to insist that at least partial control should be exerted by the local community (Marshall, 2002).

Like MRAMP, the Madaba Digital Project is a signature example of a true partnership with the local community, as the work, decisions made on the ground, and thoroughness of the data capture activities by the group attest. Although the methodology utilized by MRAMP involves seven strategies (and see Moser et al., 2002), the project advocates a holistic approach to cultural heritage and community archaeology that can be summed up as follows: a) preserve the past, b) engage the local community in an active participation, and c) ensure a diversity of views in a truly shared heritage project. In this approach, which is the driving force behind sustainability, it is essential to promote cultural diversity (UNESCO, 2005, p. 8) and multiple voices that provides a link between past, present, and future communities. It is the intangible cultural heritage such as is epitomized in the stories by local voices that must be safeguarded (UNESCO Paris 2003, p. 2), as their very identity is intertwined with the past and this solidifies an indigenous ownership within the community of their own cultural heritage, a tradition that continues into future generations. The new community archaeology paradigm fosters an interaction with the past not possible previously.

We can see this interaction within a diverse group in the storytellers within the Digital Project whose stories allow us to understand their various interpretations of the past; one could also include the local tour guides who provide a historical narrative to the video, yet clearly from the vantage point of indigenous stakeholders intimately familiar with the sites and able to offer a perspective unique to the local culture. All of which speaks to the importance of engagement of the community to reach a shared heritage of diverse perspectives (see excellent examples of community engagement, for example, Akko in Israel (Killebrew et al., 2017), Umm al-Jimal in Jordan (deVries, 2013), Petra (Tuttle, 2013) and Quseir, Egypt (Moser, 2002), and see Abu-Khafajah (2011, 2014), and Kersel and Chesson (2013).

Indeed, MRAMP's museum project in the Archaeological Park West, where the descendants of the founders of modern Madaba still live in the vicinity of the late nineteenth -century houses of their ancestors, has engaged the descendant families to give an oral history of their memories growing up and the stories passed on by their ancestors. Thanks to the oral history, the lives of the ancient community can be grasped in a more meaningful way that keeps alive the native and local perspectives of the community, including details about everyday life in traditional Jordanian houses. One need not be amazed by the evident truth that community archaeology as a full partnership reaps great rewards, not just in the work accomplished to preserve heritage, but in the very satisfaction of the local community in their efforts and the unmistakable appreciation and feeling of ownership of their cultural heritage.

This article has elaborated on the particularistic approach of one project to remotely implement best-practices criteria in cultural heritage preservation in a COVID lockdown. The collaborative endeavor between MRAMP and the community has led to promoting local stewardship of cultural heritage – the gold standard objective of community archaeology projects. Clearly, the 3D model and tours streaming open access successfully meet the criterion to preserve the past while promoting the cultural heritage of downtown Madaba into the future. Along with Madaba's heritage and historical tradition in the three sites described by local tour guides, the project has a real story to tell about bonds between the local community and its past. The twelve members of the project epitomize a local community engaged and actively participating in its past/heritage. One valorizes a country's heritage and local traditions through linkages to memory and a community's history, so evident in the diverse storytelling of local people. Clearly, we have enhanced community engagement in training, capacity building, employment, and promoted development of skills transferable for future employment.

6 Preserving Cultural Heritage in a COVID-19 Lockdown

It is more than ironic that a horrendous global pandemic should engender such resilience in the arts and in cultural heritage. The silver lining in an enforced shutdown forced people to adapt, to be resilient, to think outside the box, to "pivot" for the arts to survive. The Madaba Digital Documentation and Tourism Project represents a pivot for the authors from in-person activities in Jordan to the realm of virtual reality to pursue the stated goals of MRAMP. In the end, despite the difficulties inherent in such a project, the very tangible results of a full partnership with the local community are a vital lesson learned in community archaeology. And it goes without saying that the educational value of the project raises awareness of cultural heritage among Jordanians and people around the world, and hopefully will encourage tourism to the country.

This project is especially important in documenting cultural heritage, given the recent Memorandum of Agreement between the U.S. and Jordan, signed in 2019. This Cultural Property Agreement not only bans the illegal transfer of cultural property into the U.S., but, significantly, it aims to encourage exchange between the two nations with the goal of increasing awareness of the Jordanian civilizational and cultural heritage. The Madaba Digital Documentation and Tourism Project epitomizes the aims of the MOU regarding the preservation, documentation, and dissemination of information on Jordan's cultural heritage. Anecdotally, the grantor of this project, the Department of State, has decided to use the Madaba project as a model for other AFCP projects. Called the Community Heritage Education Initiative, the plan is to document stories through community storytelling workshops with the help of StoryCenter, and to develop virtual tours with the help of CyArk.

Acknowledgments We jointly offer this contribution to Tom Levy's Festschrift with great enthusiasm and admiration for a good friend and colleague going back some years for all of us! A Festschrift is a great honor and for his many accomplishments and "state-of-the-art" scholarship in an enviable number of disciplines, Tom is certainly deserving of the accolades represented by this volume. With a shared colleagueship among the three of us in Jordan, in the fields of the Early Bronze Age and the Iron Age, and a shared passion for digging in the dirt, we offer a special contribution more aligned with Tom's keen interest in technology and heritage. We wish Tom the best in his ongoing research, hoping to still look forward to future scholarly contributions. With best regards, Suzanne and Doug.

References

Abu-Khafajah, S. (2011). Meaning-making process of cultural heritage in Jordan: The local communities, the contexts, and the archaeological sites in the citadel of Amman. In K. Okamura & A. Matsuda (Eds.), *New perspectives in global public archaeology* (pp. 183–195). Springer.

Abu-Khafajah, S. (2014). Community heritage at work in the post-colonial context of Jordan. In S. Thomas & J. Lea (Eds.), *Heritage matters public participation in archaeology* (pp. 149–159). The Boydell Press.

Al Adarbeh, N., Carter, S., Khiran, H., & Abu Aballi, S. (2020, July 15). *Jordan's tourism sector in the wake of COVID-19: Where do we go from here?* https://publications.acorjordan.org/insights/page/3/

Boozer, A. L., During, B. S., & Parker, B. J. (2020). *Archaeologies of empire: Local participants and Imperial trajectories*. University of New Mexico Press.

CDC. (2020). Available at https://www.cdc.gov/nchs/data/icd/Announcement-New-ICD-code-for-coronavirus-3-18-2020.pdf

Clark, D. R., & Richard, S. (2021). *Progress and next steps at current Madaba museum (AFCP/ CATF grant)*. Presentation at the Annual Meeting of the American Schools of Oriental Research, 22 November 2021.

Clark, D., Richard, S., Polcaro, A., D'Andrea, M., & Mahamid, B. (2017). *Lessons learned from a new collaborative archaeological adventure*. American Schools of Oriental Research Blog. Available at http://asorblog.org/2017/02/20/new-collaborative-archaeological-adventure

Clark, D. R., D'Andrea, M., Polcaro, A., Richard, S., & Mahamid, B. (2018). Madaba regional archaeological museum project. In J. D. M. Green, B. A. Porter, & C. P. Shelton (Eds.), *Archaeology in Jordan Newsletter: 2016 and 2017 seasons* (pp. 53–54). American Center of Oriental Research. https://www.acorjordan.org/wp-content/uploads/2018/12/AIJ-2016-2017-Hig-Res.pdf

Clark, D. R., D'Andrea, M., Polcaro, A., Richard, S., & Mahamid, B. (2020). The Madaba regional archaeological museum project. In P. P. Creasman, J. D. M. Green, & C. Shelton (Eds.), *Archaeology in Jordan 2, 2018–2019 seasons* (pp. 77–79). ACOR.

Clark, D. R., D'Andrea, M., Polcaro, A., Richard, S., & Mahamid, B. (2022). Community engagement in downtown Madaba: The Madaba regional archaeological museum project (MRAMP) 2016–2018. In *Studies in the history and archaeology of Jordan XIV* (Culture in Crisis: Flows of Peoples, Artifacts, and Ideas. Proceedings of the 14th International Conference on the History and Archaeology of Jordan, Florence, Italy, 21–25 January 2019) (pp. 785–802). Department of Antiquities.

Corbett, E. (2015). *Competitive archaeology in Jordan: Narrating identity from the Ottomans to the Hashemites*. University of Texas Press.

CyArk, Richard, S., & Clark, D. R. (2021). *One Place, Many Stories/Madaba, Jordan*. Available at https://cyark.org/projects/madaba/overview

D'Andrea, M., Polcaro, A., Clark, D. R., & Richard, S. (2018). "Museums without walls" and sustainable development in Jordan. Some thoughts from the Madaba regional archaeological museum project. *ARCHEOSTORIE, Journal of Public Archaeology, 2*, 29–46. https://doi.org/10.23821/2018_3a

D'Andrea, M., Polcaro, A., Richard, S., & Clark, D. R. (2019–2020). The new Madaba regional archaeological museum project (MRAMP). In *Studies in the history and archaeology of Jordan XIII* (pp. 475–487). Department of Antiquities, Jordan.

De Cesari, C. (2011). Controlling the past, owning the future: The political uses of archaeology in the Middle East, Ran Boytner, Lynn Schwartz Dodd & Bradley J. Parker, (Eds.). *Cambridge Archaeological Journal, 21*(3), 473–474. https://doi.org/10.1017/S0959774311000473

De Vries, B. (2013). Archaeology and community in Jordan and Greater Syria: Traditional patterns and new directions. *Near Eastern Archaeology, 76*(3), 132–141.

Ginzarly, M. & Srour, F. J. (2021). Cultural heritage through the lens of COVID-19. *Poetics*. www.elesevier.com/. https://doi.org/10.1016/j.poetic.2021.101622

Harrison, T. P. (1996). The history of Madaba. In P. M. Bikai & T. A. Dailey (Eds.), *Madaba: Cultural Heritage* (pp. 1–17). American Center for Oriental Research.

ICCROM. (2020). Available at https://www.iccrom.org/news/protecting-cultural-heritage-during-covid-19.

Kersel, M. M., & Chesson, M. S. (2013). Tomato season in the Ghor es-Safi: A lesson in community archaeology. *Near Eastern Archaeology, 76*(3), 158–164.

Killebrew, A. E., DePietro, D., Pangarkar, R., Peleg, S.-A., Scha, S., & Taylor, E. (2017). Archaeology, shared heritage, and community at Akko, Israel. *Journal of Eastern Mediterranean Archaeology and Heritage Studies, 5*(3–4), 365–392.

Lesnes, É., & Younker, R. W. (2013). *The shrine of the beheading of Saint John the Baptist and the origins of Madaba (Jordan)*. Latin Patriarchate of Jerusalem.

Lydon, J., & Rizvi, U. Z. (Eds.). (2016). *Handbook of postcolonial archaeology*. Routledge. https://doi.org/10.4324/9781315427690

Marshall, Y. (2002). What is community archaeology? *World Archaeology, 34*(2), 211–219.

Mickel, A. (2021). *Why those who shovel are silent: A history of local archaeological knowledge and labor*. University Press of Colorado.

Montlaur, B. D. (2020a). *The role we play now*. Retrieved from https://www.wmf.org/blog/role-we-play-now

Montlaur, B. D. (2020b). *Cultural heritage in the time of coronavirus*. Retrieved from https://www.wmf.org/blog/cultural-heritage-time-coronavirus

Moser, S., Glazier, D., Phillips, J. E., Nasser el-Nemr, L., Mousa, M. S., Aiesh, R. N., Richardson, S., Conner, A., & Seymour, M. (2002). Transforming archaeology through practice: Strategies for collaborative archaeology and the community archaeology project at Quseir, Egypt. *World Archaeology, 34*(2), 220–248.

Moshenska, G., & Dhanjal, S. (2011). *Community archaeology: Themes, methods and practices*. Oxbow.

Piccirillo, M. (1986). The burnt palace of Madaba. *Annual of the Department of Antiquities of Jordan, 30*, 333–339.

Piccirillo, M., & Denton, B. (1996). Archaeological remains. In M. Bikai & T. A. Dailey (Eds.), *Madaba Cultural Heritage* (pp. 25–45). American Center for Oriental Research.

Piccirillo, M., Bikai, P. M., & Dailey, T. A. (1993). *The mosaics of Jordan*. American Center for Oriental Research.

Porter, B. W. (2010). Near eastern archaeology: Imperial pasts, postcolonial present. In J. Lydon & U. Z. Rizvi (Eds.), *Handbook of postcolonial archaeology* (pp. 51–60). Routledge.

Ren, W., & Chen, X. (2021). *Evaluation of an online 360 virtual reality world heritage site during COVID-19*. Open Archaeology. https://doi.org/10.1515/opar-2020-0188

Richard, S., Clark, D., Polcaro, A., & D'Andrea, M. (2016). *A different Sort of community outreach in Jordan—Building a museum: The MRAMP Project (2016)*. American Schools of Oriental Research Blog. http://www.asor.org/blog/2016/09/14/different-sort-community-outreach-jordanbuilding-museum-mramp-project/. Accessed 8 May 2019

Richard, S., D'Andrea, M., Polcaro, A., & Clark, D. R. (2019). An innovative strategy to protect cultural heritage in Jordan: The Madaba regional archaeological museum project (MRAMP). *Journal of Eastern Mediterranean Archaeology and Heritage Studies, 7*(2), 221–250.

Richard, S., Polcaro, A., D'Andrea, M., & Clark, D. R. (2020). The Madaba regional archaeological museum project (MRAMP): A strategy to protect cultural heritage in Jordan. In A. Otto, M. Herles, & K. Kaniu (Eds.), *Proceedings of the 11th International Congress on the Archaeology of the Ancient Near East (11ICAANE), 03–07 April 2018, Ludwig-Maximillians Universität Munchen* (Vol. 1, pp. 361–376). Harrassowitz Verlag.

Tuttle, C. (2013). Preserving Petra sustainably (one step at a time): The Temple of the winged lions cultural resource management initiative as a step forward. *Journal of Eastern Mediterranean Archaeology and Heritage Studies, 1*(1), 1–23.

UNESCO. (2003). *UNESCO convention for the safeguarding of intangible heritage*. Downloadable at: http://unesdoc.unesco.org/images//0013/001325/132540e.pdf

UNESCO. (2005). *Convention on the protection and promotion of the diversity of cultural expressions*. Downloadable at: https://unesdoc.unesco.org/ark:/48223/pf0000142919

UNESCO. (2020a). *UNESCO supports culture and heritage during COVID-19 shutdown*. April 9. Available at: UNESCO https://en.unesco.org/news/unesco-supports-culture-and-heritage-during-covid-19-shutdown

UNESCO. (2020b). *UNESCO world heritage centre-world heritage list statistics*. UNESCO World Heritage Centre. Available at: https://whc.unesco.org/en/list/stat

WHO. (2020a). *WHO coronavirus disease (COVID-19) dashboard*. Available at: https://covid19.who.int/

WHO. (2020b). Available at: https://www.who.int/emergencies/diseases/novel-coronavirus-2019/interactive-timeline#!

"Cult and Copper": A VR Game Exploring the Intangible Heritage of Copper Smelting

Casondra Sobieralski 🄐

Abstract Cyberarchaeology trends encourage the creation of multi-sensory projects that leverage the affordances of multi-media and strive to create embodied experiences. Few projects dare, however, to speculate about intangible heritage. Thus this Media Studies paper describes the historical and design research, collaborative ideation, and collaborative prototyping processes used for creating "Cult and Copper" in order to encourage and inform similar cyberarchaelogy projects. A posthumanist, intra-active, Virtual Reality game, "Cult and Copper" suggests a relationship between Bronze Age copper smelting techniques and shamanism. Smelters seem to have held shaman status in the ancient Near East. Early smelting methods, which employed blowpipes to heat smelting furnaces, used deep and sustained breathing techniques. Today breathwork methods, such as those used in pranayama yoga, are associated with achieving altered states of consciousness. Hence this cyberarchaeology game probes, what if altered states manipulated by breath were one of the reasons shamanism and smelting were linked? In "Cult and Copper," players use their own breath, via a breath interface, to control a smelting fire. The game objectives are to both achieve a meditative state and to ensure a successful copper smelt such that copper is "born" of the furnace. The immersive game's unique interface design facilitates an experiential awareness of the physiological effects of deep, sustained breathing. The game design overall encourages players to ask questions about intangible heritage aspects of copper smelting and motivates further scholarly investigation.

Keywords Copper · Cyberarchaeology · Hathor · Interaction design · Serious games · Smelting · Timna

---

C. Sobieralski (✉)
University of California, Santa Cruz, Santa Cruz, CA, USA
e-mail: csobiera@ucsc.edu

© The Author(s), under exclusive license to Springer Nature Switzerland AG 2023
E. Ben-Yosef, I. W. N. Jones (eds.), *"And in Length of Days Understanding" (Job 12:12): Essays on Archaeology in the Eastern Mediterranean and Beyond in Honor of Thomas E. Levy*, Interdisciplinary Contributions to Archaeology,
https://doi.org/10.1007/978-3-031-27330-8_73

1 Introduction

Imagine it is dusk in the Negev desert, about 3300 BCE. The temperature is cooling to 104 °F (about 40 °C). The setting sun is casting a coral glow, hazy with dust, on the towering rust colored rock formations that surround you in a 360° panorama. Both the formations in the distance and the earth beneath you are rich with copper. You can feel the pulse of the landscape as you and four other smelters sit around a fire pit, about 2 ft wide, 15 inches high, and ringed with stone. Each of you takes long, deep breaths and exhales through a long blowpipe tipped with a clay nozzle. A woman playing a slow, steady, resonant frame drum guides your breathing rhythm. The rocky hills hypnotically reverberate the drum beat. Nestled in the flames is a small ceramic saucer surrounded by charcoal and acacia sticks. The saucer protects small nuggets of malachite, a copper carbonate ore with a greenish hue. You point the nozzle of a blowpipe to direct air towards the base layer of charcoal to create the most intense heat. Maintaining a fire temperature of about 2200 °F (1200 °C) is necessary to smelt pure copper out of this ore. A breeze aids your efforts to stoke the fire with air. The flames communicate to you as the copper starts to melt. It is easier to see their messages as night moves in. Green flames flickering like charmed snakes mean that the copper is turning molten. Hints of blue are also an auspicious sign, signifying that burning charcoal is bonding with the carbon in the ore, producing carbon dioxide gas and metal. As the copper melts, red slag (iron oxide) forms and rises to the top of the saucer. The copper sinks to the bottom. With wooden tongs you pick up the saucer to pour off the slag, a safe distance from skin. The slag runs in rivulets like snakes through the sand. Copper remains in the dish, coagulated into irregularly shaped pink-yellow clumps.[1] The copper is "born" of the furnace, under a constellation of stars representing a goddess of fertility and renewal, her arm reaching out in the shape of another undulating snake. An ibex, symbol of the copper smelter as shaman, watches over the group from a hilltop in the distance.[2]

"Cult and Copper" is a Media Studies project that explores intangible heritage aspects of copper smelting in the ancient Levant. As is established in Media Studies, the project uses a theory-praxis methodology, meaning theory and research inform critical making. The results of making in this case are designs and a playable prototype for a posthumanist, intra-active Virtual Reality game. The experiential, non-competitive game is intended for a museum setting and driven by a breath interface. The game is an exploration questioning whether sustained deep breathing might have been a factor in the apparent link between smelting and shamanism.

---

[1] This visualization represents a mix of factual information about smelting from experiments (Craddock, 2010, Fasnacht interviews 2021) and artistic imagination. For example, the detail about drumming is not historically verifiable, though plausible.

[2] For information on shamanic symbols associated with copper smelting, as suggested by Negev star lore (ibexes, snakes, birds), see Steiner (2016). Ibexes, snakes, and birds also appear on Chalcolithic pottery from the Negev, as exhibited in "Mind and Matter: The World of the First Copper Masters" (Sebbane, Eretz-Israel Museum, Tel Aviv 2019).

Designs for the game, including the interface design, are the result of research about Chalcolithic and Bronze Age copper production and its relation to cultic practices, current cyberarchaeology discourse, theories of immersion from the arts, and theories of human computer interaction (HCI) design. This text details said research process, plus design and collaborative processes, for "Cult and Copper" in order to inform and inspire other cyberarchaelogists as they develop their own projects.

Cyberarchaeology represents the maturation of approaches that apply computer technologies to heritage. Earlier techniques, which gained popularity in the 1990s/early 2000s, typically focused on improving computer graphics methods to create virtual 3D models of static temples, monuments, and artifacts. They privileged visuality over other means of perception and empirical data over story. The cyberarchaeologists who inform this project seek to go beyond 3D modeling to bring interpretation, meaning, and context to digital archaeology. Often they do so via embodied, experiential means that emphasize the multi-sensory affordances of multimedia.

This cyberarchaeology case study about ancient smelting evolved from an investigation as to why cultic evidence of Bronze Age love/sexuality goddesses exists at multiple copper production sites throughout the Levant. These goddesses included the Egyptian Hathor and the Canaanite Ba'alat, later called Astarte. Breath later became central to this design concept because Walter Fasnacht, an experimental archaeologist from University of Zurich, suggested that the early relationship between smelting and shamanism might have had something to do, in part, with hallucinatory states related to breath.[3] Fasnacht explained that prior to the invention of bellows for pumping air into furnaces, smelters used blowpipes. A smelt using blowpipes required a group of about four to six smelters to engage in deep, sustained breathing for about 2 h, assuming that they were starting with a furnace that was not already heated. In Fasnacht's years' worth of experiments, if a furnace is indeed "pre-heated," then a copper smelt with blowpipes takes about 20 min (Fasnacht, personal conversations via Zoom, December 23, 2020 & April 16, 2021). The potential relationship between breath and shamanism seems plausible in relation to meditative practices such as pranayama (breath focused) yoga and Holotropic breathwork which are associated with achieving altered states of consciousness, and even considering Lamaze breathing techniques for birthing.[4] Thus this cyberarchaeology project creates a virtual experience that allows participants to explore and speculate, through an experiential embodied approach, this aspect of intangible heritage surrounding cult and copper in the ancient Levant.

---

[3] Fasnacht noted that toxic smelting fumes and oxygen deprivation can also create hallucinatory states if novice smelters sit too close to the smelting crucible. Obviously, though, these variables are not safe to experiment with in a museum experience.

[4] For explanations on these various forms of breathwork, see: https://www.ncbi.nlm.nih.gov/pmc/articles/PMC3415184/ & https://www.yogajournal.com/practice/beginners/how-to/pranayama (pranayama), http://www.holotropic.com/holotropic-breathwork/about-holotropic-breathwork/ (Holotropic), https://www.ncbi.nlm.nih.gov/pmc/articles/PMC3209750/ (Lamaze)

The aim of the game is for a singular player to ensure a successful smelt by aptly regulating one's breath for about 10 min. Though that is half of the time of Fasnacht's smelts, asking museum visitors to invest 20 min is a high expectation. The immersive characteristics of the game, including the breath interface, are designed to at least partly evoke (the sensation of temperature, for example, is not realized in this prototype) a bodily sense of what it might have been like to be an ancient smelter using blowpipe technologies, under a night sky in the Timna desert, to heat a small crucible. Note, by the Late Bronze Age, bellows were in use. In order to keep with the theme of breath without temporally mis-matching technologies, then, the narrator of the game (an old man smelter-shaman) specifies that he is teaching the player "the old ways." Later iterations of the game could include "leveling up" to utilize an interface that mimics bellows so players could experientially learn how technologies evolved. Virtual Reality is the chosen medium for the game over Augmented Reality because VR is ideal for withdrawing from the ordinary world into an immersive cocoon. AR is best utilized for creating a virtual overlay onto an existing world. Thus AR lends itself well to site specific experiences and to facilitating more extroverted, socially engaged experiences, whereas VR enhances internal, meditative experiences.

2 Cyberarchaeology Design Research Questions for "Cult and Copper"

A primary design research question for this project was how to improve upon interaction for virtual heritage/cyberarchaeology design because in all of the historical VR pieces I playtested, interaction design was the weakest point of the storytelling. Subjectively, the interaction invariably broke my sense of immersion because it did not further the story or enhance any understanding of the past. In this VR game about cult and copper, player interaction via the breath interface instead co-creates the story and harkens the ancient past. Further, the breath interface adds an immersion strategy which game designer and yogini Carrie Heeter calls interoception. Interoception implies a sensory awareness of bodily systems (like breath or heartbeat), the environment that the body occupies, and the interplay between the two. Interoception, Heeter (2016) says, focuses on the present moment and is synonymous with embodied presence.

A secondary design research question was how to redefine interaction design as "intra-action" design in order to establish animism as a design metaphor. "Intra-action," as part of agential realism, is a term used by feminist physicist-philosopher Karen Barad. Barad (2007) defines intra-actions as being causal relationships between (social, cultural, technical) apparatuses of physical production and phenomena. To Barad, objects–with their individual boundaries and properties–are not primary ontological units. Rather, in agential realism the primary units of being are phenomena. In simplified terms, intra-action recognizes interdependent webs of ever-changing (dynamic) relational events, or entanglements. This fluid model dismantles the typical interaction design framework which assumes that independent entities (subjects) act upon other independent entities (objects). Designing intra-actively thereby flattens subject-object hierarchies, including human-animal, human-element, or human-tool hierarchies. The "Cult and Copper" VR game therefore grants agential roles to both human and non-human actors. This posthumanist design strategy explores: What non-human aspects of an archaeology story can have agency? How does their agency entangle with human agency? How does entangled intra-action enhance a sense of immersion?

Of course, Barad's concept of entangled agencies dovetails well with existing archaeological thought processes; archaeology has long examined relational aspects among people, technologies, social spaces, and even landscapes.[5] Applying Barad's concepts of intra-action to design for cyberarchaeology projects in particular, then, seems especially useful because this approach can help to illustrate such archaeological thought processes. Experimental media can perhaps convey concepts of relationality more effectively than the linear medium of text.

3   The Process of Preparatory Research for Cyberarchaeology Design

3.1   Content Research on the Topic: Cult and Copper

It is important to preface this section by noting that archaeological research for this project served to provide me with some understanding of the Bronze Age Levant as a worldbuilder; I am not a field archaeologist. Rather, stepping into these ancient worlds informed me as a designer so that I could select and represent a slice of that history in an immersive game. Of course, much of this exercise involved speculation and imagination, but archaeology claims precedents for this because the intangible aspects of the ancient past, including cultic and ritual practices, are often largely unknowable. However, "speculative" is not synonymous with "made-up." Speculation in the context of cyberarchaeology design is based on the best available evidence, recognizes that many holes that exist in current scholarship, and ideally distinguishes speculative elements through supporting text, paradata, or design cues.

Questioning the possible relationship between shamanism and smelting evolved from seeking to understand why Hathor and Astarte, two closely related goddesses of sexuality, were associated with copper and copper production. These two goddesses entangled in ancient Canaan and then made their way to the copper

---

[5] See Fisher (2014), an archaeologist specializing in the Bronze Age, for examples of what he calls "interanimations." He defines interanimations as the recursive relationships between people, place, and, one could certainly add, artifacts.

producing island of Cyprus via the Phoenicians. I first researched at Timna in modern Israel, where ancient copper miners utilized a sanctuary that they devoted to Hathor. I continued tracing threads through archaeology sites in Cyprus which evidenced a connection between goddess cults and copper. These sites included Kition (where Astarte temples were built next to copper production workshops) and Palaepaphos (a site that stood as a goddess cult center for 5000 years). Museum research–with guidance from museum curators–proved to be invaluable. Worldbuilding for this project is informed by artifacts and other resources from museums throughout Israel and Cyprus, the British Museum, and the Kelso Museum of Near Eastern Archaeology in Pennsylvania. I ultimately set the game in Timna, so for the purposes of this summary, decoding the relationship between cult and copper in that region is most pertinent.

Timna is a site in the Arabah Valley region of modern Israel's Negev desert (Fig. 1). From the end of the fourteenth century BCE into the middle of the twelfth century BCE (the Bronze Age), New Kingdom Egyptians mined copper in Timna under five pharaohs who collectively reigned from about 1280 BCE until 1145 BCE (Avner, 2014). Today Timna serves as a national park, and tourism primarily promotes the Egyptian portion of the area's history. This focus reflects interpretations originating in B. Rothenberg's excavations in the 1960s. Challenging many of Rothenberg's theories, more recent scholarship downplays Egyptian influence and calls more attention to the important technological and cultic contributions of local tribes (Avner, 2014). Contemporary archaeologists including Uzi Avner and Erez

Fig. 1 Landscape of Timna Park in the Negev Desert, Israel, near the Hathor sanctuary. (Photograph by Casondra Sobieralski, 2017)

Ben-Yosef have concluded that Timna mining and smelting technologies used during the time between Seti I and Rameses V were probably actually developed by these local tribes (Avner, 2014; Ben-Yosef et al., 2019). Egyptians, as occupiers of Canaan, oversaw the operations; but at that point in history, Egyptians probably were not developing the technologies (Avner, 2014). As a worldbuilder, I envisioned copper production at Timna as being collaborative, and expressing this collaboration became central to the game design by including both Canaanite and Egyptian characters and mythological iconographies.

The Egyptian miners at Timna maintained a shrine to their goddess Hathor (Fig. 2). Hathor's mythological role in Egypt was that of mother to the king and consort to the sun god Re. Hathor is popularly known for being a goddess of love, sensuality, and pleasure. She was associated with music, dance, celebrations, beer, sex, and motherhood. Stone inscriptions from the Sinai suggest that there, Hathor played an important role as the goddess of miners (Tanabe, 2017). The Hathor cult was celebrated differently at the copper mines of Timna and at the copper/turquoise mines of Serabit el-Khadim (in the Sinai) than at temples within Egypt; in these mining outposts, worshippers emphasized Hathor's role as "Goddess of the Mountain" (Ben-Dor Evian, personal communication, July 11, Ben-Dor Evian, 2018). This aspect of Hathor was added to her identity as Mistress of the Desert during the Old Kingdom when Egyptians merged her with aspects of mountain goddesses such as Meretseger, represented by a cobra (Morris, 2011). Hathor's mountain moniker explains in part why she was deemed a goddess of copper, malachite and turquoise, all minerals extracted from the hills. It is easy to imagine

Fig. 2 Remains of the Hathor sanctuary in Timna Park. (Photograph by Casondra Sobieralski, 2017)

miners of these minerals seeking a mountain goddess's protection as they toiled dangerously in the dark shafts of the Earth.

Avner, however, argues that at the Timna shrine to Hathor, the Egyptians added a naos to an existing local shrine. Avner interprets that Hathor was "not the owner of the house but a guest." He supports his assertion with architectural clues and by noting that "from the point of view of the gods in the masseboth and in the chapel, Hathor stands to the left of the local gods," indicating the less senior position [as per the conventions of Egyptian art]. The Egyptians would have sought the protection of the local gods as well as their own, and Hathor would have been welcome among the local tribes because she was similar to their beloved Ba'alat (Avner, 2014).

Rather than diminishing the role of the Egyptian goddess Hathor, though, the contradictions between the popular appeal of the park and more scholarly challenges make the story of the goddess and copper at Timna that much more fascinating in its complexity. Ancient Semitic and Egyptian mythologies mix at multiple Hathor temples located in Canaan, such as Serabit el-Khadim (Shalomi-Hen, 2016) and the temple of Ba'alat in Byblos (Diego Espinel, 2002). Through mechanisms of commerce, mining, and diplomacy, the iconography and adoration of Hathor and Ba'alat/Astarte started to intermingle in both ancient Syro-Palestine and in Egypt. Shalomi-Hen (2016) explains that Hathor was clearly the Egyptian deity most represented on local and imported objects in Late Bronze Age Canaan, which attests to her popularity. However, scholars are not sure to what degree Canaanites venerated Hathor as an Egyptian goddess versus to what degree she was assimilated into the local goddess. This recurring phenomenon of Hathor and a Canaanite goddess occupying the same sacred spaces lays a rich foundation for interpreting a world to design: who, then, was the actual copper goddess–Hathor, Astarte, or both? Or did the distinction between them become so blurred that it did not matter at the folk-level of religious practice among copper miners, smelters, and/or exporters?

Beyond Hathor being associated with minerals extracted from the Earth, reasons for connections between sexuality goddess cults and copper in the Levant seem to be multivalent. Research into authors including Mircea Eliade (a historian known for being a leading twentieth century interpreter of religious experience) elucidates that in many parts of the world, "smelting represents a sacred sexual union, a sacred marriage (cf. the mixture of 'male' and 'female' ores), and this union takes place in the furnaces" (Eliade, 1978). Avner writes that copper production, particularly smelting (Fig. 3) must be contextualized in terms of magic, alchemy, and shamanism. Avner notes that in Hebrew, the words "smith" and "create" use the same root word ["קנה"] and therefore being a smith is actually synonymous with being a magician, "creating a new substance, a metal from rock" (Avner, 2014). Smelters in the Arava Valley, as revealed by Ben-Yosef's osteoarchaeological studies of Early Iron Age smelters in Timna, seemingly held a high status (Ben-Yosef et al., 2017). This could suggest that they were perceived as keepers of esoteric knowledge.

Since little material evidence of intangible cultural heritage practices exists from the Levantine Bronze Age or from the preceding Chalcolithic (copper-stone) era, one means of speculating what spiritual beliefs surrounding copper might have been

Fig. 3 Remains of a smelting workshop with a smelting pit in Timna Park. (Photograph by Casondra Sobieralski, 2017)

is to look at ethnographic evidence of African smelting rituals for clues. For example, Africa historians Eugenia Herbert and Candice Gaucher created a documentary film case study about the Bassari people of Togo, who practiced smelting iron by traditional methods for 500 years, until industrial smelting processes outpaced their production. In this film, *Blooms of Bengali*, Bassari tribesmen use 1914 ethnographic footage combined with memories of tribal elders to create a reenactment of a traditional smelt. As researchers, Herbert and Gaucher especially sought to understand the gendered aspects of traditional smelting among this tribe so they could record this intangible cultural heritage before knowledge of it disappeared (Saltman et al., 1986).

The Bassari traditionally believed that smelting depended on a combination of technical skill and the assistance of spiritual forces invoked by rituals. From the ground up, over 5 days the furnace took the shape of a woman. The Bassari referred to the furnace's human parts: stomach, chest, head, nose, mouth. Tribesmen decorated the furnace with ash, adding leaves to represent abundance and fertility. They chanted (translated to English by the filmmakers), "Give birth to good iron, give birth to good furnace iron." The master smelter became a father. During a smelt, Bassari smelters were forbidden sexual relations with humans.[6] Smelters believed that such actions to be adultery against the furnace, which could cause a

---

[6] Bassari iron smelts lasted about 45 h, far longer than copper smelts, according to Saltman et al. (1986).

difficult labor or even "birth defects." While Bassari women were excluded from the smelt itself, they led preparatory offerings, and they traditionally supplied the charcoal that kept the furnace fire burning (Saltman et al., 1986).

How much Levantine customs and African customs mirrored or influenced one another is, again, speculative.[7] Thinking cross-culturally, however, it becomes easy to understand why goddesses of sexuality, fecundity, and sometimes motherhood *could* be associated with copper production, and not just with the ores mined from the fertile earth. In the Levant itself, prior to Hathor's worship at Timna, what little material evidence does exist of cultic practice related to copper production comes from the Ghassulian people. Ghassulians inhabited an area spanning the northern Negev through the Jordan Valley in the latter half of the fifth millennium BCE. Gošić and Gilead (2015) describe the Ghassulians as having the best documented Chalcolithic culture in the Southern Levant. Ghassulian tools are too thin/long to have been functional, and they lack wear patterns from use. These "tools" were also found in production sites and in burials rather than in domestic use contexts. Therefore, Gošić and Gilead (2015) deduce, "It is our contention that all of the Ghassulian copper artifacts were symbolically charged, as was the technology itself."

Symbols that occur in Ghassulian ceremonial artifacts also occur in rock art through the Negev. This rock art seems to record nomads' constellations in the sky. Thus petroglyph art and star lore of the Negev offer additional worldbuilding/design clues about relationships between smelting and spiritual practices in the region. Petroglyph scholar George F. Steiner (2016) writes that metallurgy practices impacted what nomads of the Negev desert represented in their rock carvings, such as ibexes, snakes, birds, and a goddess. Ibexes [also depicted on a Ghassulian copper staff and on Chalcolithic Negev pottery] were transmediators between day, night, and unseen realms, according to Steiner. They represented the shaman in disguise, and smelting itself. Snakes, inscribed on pottery as well as in petroglyphs, symbolized air. Rather than air just being a mechanical force that smelters pumped into the furnace to heat it, air was equated to "ruah," a Hebrew word meaning breath, life force, or spirit. Breath gave life to the furnace. Birds symbolized messengers between the realms, something akin to "proto-angels." Representations of a Semitic goddess, also mirroring a constellation, represented regeneration. Sometimes she was depicted with a snake arm. Negev petroglyphs depict a dome shape, like an upside down "u," with a dot in the middle. Steiner (2016) says this shape represents the pregnant furnace, with the dot signifying the gestating ore.[8]

---

[7] Determining whether a Near Eastern connection linking birthing and copper smelting influenced deeper Africa or vice-versa might perhaps be elucidated by extensive technology transfer tracing during the Bronze Age and beyond; presumably craft technologies and spiritual technologies would travel together.

[8] Interestingly, the ibex, snake, and bird themes also made their way to redware pottery in Cyprus. Exquisite examples are on exhibit at the Pierides Museum in Larnaca.

Research regarding the apparent contributions of both local tribes and Egyptians in Timna, Near Eastern goddess mythologies, and cultural perspectives on mystical beliefs about smelting informed the worldbuilding, visual design, scripting, interface design, and intra-action design of the "Cult and Copper" Virtual Reality game. The game designs include Canaanite and Egyptian characters working together. Iconographic and artifact allusions to Hathor and Astarte pervade. Since VR allows for a 360° experience, the Negev starlore inspired a skyscape from which intra-active animistic characters (snakes, ibexes, and Astarte) emerge to assist the player who performs as a novice smelter. When the copper is born, the player is rewarded with Hathor-inspired birthing festivities.

3.2 Establishing an Understanding of Cyberarchaeology Trends and Debates

In designing for cyberarchaeology, it is imperative to consider trends and debates within current discourse. A list of scholars influencing this "Cult and Copper" project including Eva Pietroni, Tara Jane Copplestone, Christopher Johanson, Diane Favro, Alice Watterson, Mauritzio Forte, Jeffrey Stuart, critical games scholar Erik Champion, and sensory archaeology proponent Jo Day. All offer considerations about how to effectively employ the affordances of multimedia to create multi-sensory digital archaeology experiences that move beyond mere documentation to instead create meaning and aid in new knowledge production. They seek to make the past seem more tangible, relevant, and "alive" to new audiences as well as to scholars. Many insist on the value of process in creating cyberarchaeology models, games, and simulations. They take stands on how to balance objectivity and subjectivity, i.e. empirical data with speculation and imagination. They question what methodologies can clarify to an audience what is known fact versus what is speculative interpretation. Such indications become especially challenging when attempting to represent intangible heritage as "Cult and Copper" does.

For example, Eva Pietroni (2016) laments that storytelling for virtual heritage is still weak compared to that of cinema and video games. Pietroni thinks that virtual museum storytelling should strive for emotional and cognitive impacts, embodied experiences, innovative interaction design, and smoother media integration. Pietroni is concerned that most virtual heritage environments are still not places for generating knowledge, and she points out that a phenomenological approach that heightens sensing and intuitive experience is still missing. She thus recommends that designers think about the affordances of virtual technologies in relation to perception and usability by integrating visualization, multi-layered models, metadata, story, and tools of interpretation (such in-world performative spaces). She suggests that digital heritage producers embrace non-linear narrative techniques, natural interaction interfaces, cinematography and theater techniques, augmented reality potentials, and soundscapes. "Cult and Copper" heeds many of Pietroni's recommendations.

Copplestone (2017) argues that the *process* of creating historical games can "disrupt normative practices," and encourage new ways of thinking that do not fit the traditional academic models. Favro (2012) also argues for the value in the process of creating these projects because they expand methods of investigation and they allow for simulated experiments within virtual environments. Watterson (2015) aligns with Copplestone and Johanson in arguing that the artistic/design process can change how archaeologists approach problems. Like Pietroni, Watterson cautions that early virtual archaeology projects were mostly about "techno-fetishism," not analytical advancement. As one suggested remedy, Watterson (2015) strongly advocates for engaging artists in archaeological interpretation because to her, archaeological visualization should be a convergence of evidence, interpretation, scientific data collection, and storytelling. Copplestone and Waterson legitimize the complementary role of artists, designers, and storytellers within cyberarchaeology discourse.

Erik Champion is interested in how to use digital media to convey history to an audience beyond "academic specialists," such as museum [or heritage site] visitors. Champion (2015), who researches historical games, questions how to make history seem more relevant to the public's lives. Museums, he says, make the process of historians opaque and tend to instill a "master narrative" with little room for visitor interpretation. To allow for such interpretation, Champion recommends that designers consider the relationship between historical simulation and interactivity in regard to: ritual knowledge, webs of cause and effect, and "what if" scenarios.

Forte (2016) strives for embodied, haptic/kinetic simulations, not just remote visual ones. He maintains that intersubjectivity, emotions, and sensations are vital to the hermeneutics of interpretation, part of how knowledge is acquired. Forte, too, cautions against "techno-festishism," which he defines as valuing the resolution of a computer rendering over determining how to achieve the strongest benefits of human-computer interaction. Aligned with the idea of embodiment, Stuart (2015), perhaps more than any of the aforementioned scholars, really stresses the importance of considering feeling in cyberarchaeology: "If we do not consider how digital representations actually feel to access, to use and re-use, and significantly how they feel to make one connected to the past emotionally as well as intellectually (i.e. their artistic auratic), then digital visualizations will continue to exist as as remote, disconnected, and sanitized entities…" In accord with Champion, he argues that researchers would miss the opportunity to reach an audience beyond academic specialists.

For any of their intended audiences, these cyberarchaeologists recognize that digital technologies afford more than just visuality; yet Western culture tends to privilege visuality, especially as an epistemological tool. Some cyberachaeologists have set out to challenge that. Day (2013) provokes archaeologists/designers to consider *all* of the sensory aspects of the past, including those of rituals, play, labor and craft processes (intangible heritage). In relation to "Cult and Copper," for example, one could ask what did an ancient smelter reaching into a hot furnace possibly hear, smell, and taste? When an ancient copper miner traversed the Negev desert, what did the geology sound like under his feet? How did the atmosphere and lighting shape perception? What animals did workers hear? Day prompts thinking phenomenologically about what other people might have experienced, and where our own cultural biases come in. In using our imaginations to ask questions about the past, Day (2013) poses, "What can archaeologists accomplish by using fiction, and what is given up in the process?" "Cult and Copper" asks players beyond a closed circle of academic specialists to co-create a fiction, but one based on a degree of plausibility, for the sake of expanding inquiry about ancient techno-practices.

3.2.1 The Balance Between "Truth" and Imaginative Interpretation in Experiential Cyberarchaeology

Questions about how to represent historical "truth" versus how to engage with a process of interpretation are critically debated within cyberarchaeology scholarship. Johanson (2009)–who explores the interrelationships among mapping, modeling, representation, and digital reconstruction in archaeology–critiques that early Virtual Reality efforts in archaeology that strove for large and "accurate" data models were merely aggregating knowledge in an encyclopedic manner. Johanson instead advocates for using historical models similarly to the way that models are used in science: to build abstractions, to test hypotheses, to explore inquiries and play with data abstractions. "Modeling is the creation of a useful fiction," he says (Johanson, 2009).

While Johanson, Favro, and Waterson all celebrate process, Watterson steps further out onto an artist-friendly limb by celebrating a significant role for imagination and creativity in virtual archeology. She argues that melding the apparent contradiction between subjectivity and objectivity can be a strength because creativity destabilizes established methods; art fosters "messy thinking." Thus Watterson says the field needs more artists:

> … the advantage of integrating artistic process into archaeology is not necessarily in an ability to collapse or reinvent conventional processes; instead, its power lies in the negotiation of a complimentary partnership between subjective and objective methods and perspectives, facilitating a practice-based methodology of thinking through doing (Watterson, 2015).

However, in order for this approach to communicate or foster knowledge, audiences need to understand nuances of interpretation, storytelling, and display. How does the public know where subjective, creative, editorial processes come into play even with a photograph (Watterson, 2015)? It thus falls on designers, with archaeologists, to ascertain how to demonstrate that digital visualizations are speculative interpretations because people's tendency is to cling to them as representations of "truth." Waterson's proposed solution is for archaeologists to use paradata to document the ambiguous and interpretive intellectual processes that go into digital projects, including mistakes made along the way. This practice of transparency might help to elucidate how digital archaeology creates new knowledge (Watterson, 2015). Since "Cult and Copper" is a prototype, I experimented with the feasibility of incorporating in-world paradata as part of game design (whereby clicking or hovering over an object reveals information about how speculative choices were made) versus using an accompanying web page for people who are interested in the paradata. In-world paradata has the advantage of being more readily accessible, but it compromises the sense of immersion if players read it as an interruption. I opted for supplementary paradata text to negate that interruption.

3.3 Considering Theories of Immersion and Presence from the Arts to Apply to Cyberarchaeology

In cyberarchaeology, a sense of immersion and presence can help to establish a sense of "being there." Champion (2015) argues that virtual archaeology can enhance that sense by employing kinetics, by repositioning the agency of spaces and objects, and by creating a sense of atmosphere and place that distinguishes one site from another. However, he urges designers to go a step further, to create a sense of cultural presence–the feeling of being *there and then*–by establishing a sense of how and why people valued things, and by conveying the interrelationship among rituals, artifacts, landscapes.

Champion is describing the art of worldbuilding, and Media Studies offers volumes of research on how to approach worldbuilding to establish a sense of immersion. John Bucher (2018), for example, asserts that environmental storytelling–building a story from its narrative space–is key. Henri Jenkins (2004) urges game designers to consider a sense of place, and to think of design as narrative architecture. Mark J.P. Wolf (2013) outlines methods to create a cognitive sense of place. He defines infrastructures and frameworks by which authors and audiences can conceptually organize immersive worlds into consistent wholes. He suggests narrative, maps (space), timelines (temporal anchors), nature, culture—including language, mythology, and philosophies—and genealogies of characters (social maps). Utilizing the distinct natural features of Timna automatically creates a ready-made narrative space for "Cult and Copper." Timna lends itself well to immersive VR representation because the landscape itself is already immersive. Hills and rock formations surround the visitor in every direction, the wind hewn geology itself is part of the story, and the visibility of the vast sky is unimpeded. The warm tones of the 360° landscape create a palette that evokes the heat of smelting. Whereas Cypriot sites of Bronze Age copper production, such as Kition, are surrounded by active contemporary towns creating disjointed layered temporalities, Timna is a vast national park with few visual or sonic distractions from other, competing "worlds." Timna offers a game stage to be documented rather than invented. Then weaving in Bronze Age Levantine artifacts, clothing and jewelry styles, mythologies, rituals, and craft processes creates a sense of cultural immersion and cognitive sense of place as Wolf advises.

Janet Murray and Marie-Laure Ryan are two other names that are familiar to Media/Games Studies and Literature scholars in relation to theories of immersion, but they might be less familiar names among archaeologists. Ryan (2015) introduces the term *metalepsis*, which describes the mental phenomenon one has as one feels the sense of becoming a character in the story one reads, watches, or enters. As a VR game, "Cult and Copper" allows a player to achieve this state from the start by entering the game as an in-world smelter via an avatar. Ryan (2015) also sees ritual and its techniques—gesture, performative speech, and/or manipulation of symbolic objects—as means of establishing immersion. "Cult and Copper" creates a ritualistic aura.

Murray (2017) cautions that immersion requires consistency and a regulation of the boundary between imaginary and real in order for that sense of immersion to be maintained. How is a participant cued as to when they are entering and exiting the fantasy space, which some in the gaming world call "the magic circle"? Here, archaeologists could well advise the media and literary theorists based on various approaches ancient cultures used to navigate crossing such boundaries. Designs for "Cult and Copper" cue players with a museum installation setting that is evocative of Timna to demarcate a "magic circle" space. The installation design includes a "sandbox" inspired by the Phoenician exhibit[9] at University of Haifa's Hecht Museum[10] and wall art suggesting the Timna landscape.

Heeter's advocacy for the use of interoception in games of course adds a dimension to discourse about immersion. Her methods of facilitating embodied presence in virtual experiences are informed by her meditation practices (Heeter, 2016). "Cult and Copper" strives towards Heeter's recommendations by using breath as an interface to affect a smelting fire. It also does so by choosing to employ the introverted, meditative qualities of VR over the social affordances of AR.

Thus in regard to strategizing immersion, cyberarchaeologists need not reinvent the wheel, so to speak. By including a variety approaches to immersion borrowed from Literature and Media/Games Studies as described here, but also from Architecture, Theatre Design, and Sound Studies, cyberarchaeology designers can more effectively induce a sense "being in" another place in time. Likewise, the unique expertises of archaeologists can surely inform Media Studies' immersion strategies because archaeologists are especially well skilled at inferring site-level stories, considering the roles of artifacts in stories, and using maps and timelines to better understand time periods.

3.3.1 Interaction Design as an Underrecognized Component of Immersion: Archaeology, HCI Design Theory, and Intra-action

Since creating better harmonization between immersion and interaction in historical VR pieces was a design goal of this project, Human Computer Interaction (HCI) research also became important. The aforementioned term intra-action, which

---

[9] https://www.youtube.com/watch?v=VuJaFQYqlTw&t=1s
[10] https://mushecht.haifa.ac.il/index.php?lang=en

Barad defines as mutually entangled/relational agencies, is used by two contemporary HCI designers, Lucy Suchman and Josh McVeigh-Schultz. Thus Suchman and McVeigh-Schultz offered inspiration to this project.

Suchman (2007) approaches HCI–and intra-actions among humans and technologies more broadly–from anthropological and feminist perspectives. She is interested in breaking down subject-object binaries and encourages the reader to think of technologies as artifacts and active co-agents. She is an advocate of situated action, meaning that human machine interaction should be an embodied, responsive process. McVeigh-Schultz engages in what he calls "tangible imaginaries and fictive practices." McVeigh-Schultz explains:

> Tangible imaginaries can include prototypes from a range of techniques including: speculative design, discursive design, imaginary media, critical making, world-building, situation design, and—of course my own topic of—speculative ritual design. In each case, the prototype includes a tangible element, something you can hold, experience, or understand as having qualities of an artifact or experience. And in each case there is a mediation between a structure (whether social rule set or system of technical affordances), on the one hand, and a vision of some kind of inhabited world or context of experience on the other (McVeigh-Schultz, 2016).

McVeigh-Schultz (2016) also posits that animism as a design metaphor can open up practices of myth-making about, and through, objects. "Cult and Copper," which is what McVeigh-Schultz would consider to be a speculative ritual design prototype, explores entangled agencies of the human and copper. It looks at the flames of the smelting fire as agent and medium because the color of the flames communicate the state of the ore to a smelter as the ore transforms from solid to liquid. The flames then serve as one animistic design element, but so, too, do snakes from the flames and a transmediating ibex into which the old man smelter-shaman (narrator) can shape-shift. These animistic qualities of the game serve to break subject-object binaries which Suchman describes as a femininist intra-action design strategy.

3.4 Collaborative Design Ideation via "Bronze Age Productions"

The archaeological research phase of the project–spanning from Timna to Cyprus–revealed that the Levantine Bronze Age was not one world. Far from it, the Bronze Age was a dizzying array of intersecting worlds allowing for an overwhelming number of possibilities for intra-actions. Thus, in the midst of a global pandemic that barred researchers from fieldwork and in-person collaborations, I became the director and producer of "Bronze Age Productions" (BAP) to experiment with possibilities. BAP was a Zoom-based, international improvisational theater troupe comprised of archaeologists, digital heritage enthusiasts, game designers, and performers. This series of improvisation theater games served as a means of collaborative design ideation; performance served as a method to collectively think through some of the many possibilities for intra-actions among human and non-human characters within a Bronze Age copper context, and to narrow a specific setting for the game.

We held three improv jams between August 2020 and January 2021. Each was based on the classic participatory improvisational theater game Freeze Tag. In this game, the audience (in our case, other players) suggests characters and a situation for two players to improvise. Then at any time that an additional player feels inspired to do so—which usually happens when the action between the two original characters starts to lag—he or she can shout, "Freeze" to stop the scene, replace one of the existing performers, assume a new character, and invent a new scene. In our BAP version of Freeze, however, the character set and situations were limited to the Bronze Age copper production sites at which I was researching. In accordance with design goals, I directed actors to consider both human and non-human agents as potential characters.[11]

Bronze Age Productions performers improvised scenes in copper mines, at Hathor's Timna sanctuary, at Astarte's Kition temple, et cetera. Some characters enacted in the first two jams included Hathor, Astarte, a priestess, a sacred barber of Astarte, a Timna mountain, the wind, copper ore melting in a smelting furnace, birds, snakes, the Earth herself, copper miners, musicians, and sacred artifacts. Informed by the first two jams, for the third I narrowed choices for scenes and characters to those specific to the process of copper smelting. Additional intra-active characters became mining tools, the smelting furnace, an ingot as a fetus being born of a furnace, the air and fire that are part of the smelting process, and a child miner speaking on behalf of a (fictional) children's "mining union." Fasnacht (BAP jam 2021) assumed the role of a narrator, in the form of speaking copper ore, to teach the actors about the smelting process so that they could enact it. He narrated that blow pipes were used before bellows to heat the fire, that the smelters read the colors of the flames, and that the flames turned green when the ore reached a liquid state. He educated about the risks that oxygen deprivation from the consuming flames posed to smelters, and how noxious fumes became a threat if a furnace cools too quickly and cracks near the bottom.

Cyberarchaeologists cited including Watterson, Copplestone and Johanson defend the importance of the design process as a means of generating new knowledge, perhaps sometimes more than the finished product does. Improvisational theater via BAP functioned best as an epistemological engine when we hit up against ignorance in acting out a scene. For example, in our second improv, a character made a reference to starting a job at Astarte's temple in "2 weeks." Then

---

[11] To prepare Bronze Age Productions participants, I provided players with curated folders of research photos I had taken at museums and at archaeological sites. These photos included artifacts, ruins of temples, sanctuaries, and copper workshops, tourist information placards with texts, images and timelines. I created a folder of "fake Zoom backgrounds" to use as "set design," and I demonstrated how to create a fake background effect as one of the theatrical affordances of Zoom. I also provided participants with drafts of my written research if they requested more information about Hathor, Astarte, Timna, or other elements they would be enacting. (Generally the participants who were not archaeologists requested such information to garner more background knowledge.)

she paused in thought for a moment: "How is time measured in this culture?" The group agreed that was an important question. Luckily, an archaeologist on our team had insight. Without this creative process, though, we probably never would have considered such aspects of intangible heritage. More importantly, in realizing one cultural presupposition–how time is marked–we became critically aware of the need to question what else we project from our own cultural experience.

The knowledge imparted and the ideas collaboratively generated by BAP jams established the clarity I needed to conceptualize more specifically the sort of intra-active project I wanted to design, one about the shamanic aspects of copper smelting vis-a-vis breath. These performance games also clarified that Timna should provide the setting for the Virtual Reality game. Having performers who were not archaeologists showed that Bronze Age Cyprus, with its hybridized styles, is difficult for nonspecialists to parse as a "world." Timna makes for more consistent worldbuilding in that the landscape and stylistics are easier to identify and perform with.

3.5 Establishing How to Use Breath as an Interface

In April 2021, BAP met for a fourth time to playtest how to sustain breathing, collectively, for the duration of time needed to complete a smelt. As preparation I worked with professional breathwork coaches to learn different breathwork techniques. While contemporary people cannot know exactly how ancients breathed, some methods with which I experimented seemed completely implausible for smelting work because over a long session, they resulted in headaches, dizziness, muscle cramps, and/or they used a quick, forceful exhale that seemed conducive to extinguishing, rather than sustaining, a fire. Bonnie Coberly of San Francisco Breathwork taught me a comfortable technique that she described as a "two-part pranayama."[12] It entails breathing deeply into the belly, inhaling a bit more into the upper chest, and letting the exhale fall out. For playtesting this method, people used props like wrapping paper tubes to simulate exhaling through a three-foot blowpipe. Doing so guided the exhale much differently than using no prop. Most of the group found the technique to be profoundly relaxing. I experienced the breathwork as creating a space for meditative imaginings, intuitive insights.

One main takeaway from the breathwork playtesting was, there is no one breathing pace that feels comfortable to all, and it is not adequate to choose a median point. Among BAP playtesters–some of whom were runners and singers and some of whom were not physically active–what felt comfortable to one person felt straining to another. This was a vital realization from a design perspective, including for physical safety considerations. Playtesting informed that the breath interface

---

[12] https://www.sanfranciscobreathwork.com/resources

design for "Cult and Copper" would need to offer at least three breath speeds for players, just as a treadmill at the gymnasium necessarily allows speed choice.

A second important result of playtesting the breathwork technique was that people unanimously expressed the need for a rhythm, like drumming, to guide them. Fragments of sistra and menat necklaces–rhythm instruments sacred to Hathor– were found at Timna; these are part of a permanent exhibit at the Eretz-Israel Museum in Tel Aviv. My research did not reveal any evidence of drums at Timna. However, Dendara temple in Egypt, which is a Hathor temple, includes a hallway with reliefs depicting 32 priestesses dressed as Hathor playing frame drums. The hall ends in what archaeologists interpret to be a birthing chamber. The architectural decoration seems to suggest that priestesses used rhythm to guide women through labor contractions and through the dangerous journey of birth (Redmond, 1997). Drums could also, then, tie to the idea of smelting being a birthing process. Using the specific aural aesthetic and mythic connotations of a frame drum, instead of using rhythm instruments that were factually specific to Timna, became a design decision. This is an example of choice that required a paradata notation. Since Hathor was a goddess associated with music and dance as well as with copper, sexuality, and motherhood, this playtest raised questions for further research: might the natural pairing of copper smelting with rhythm be yet another reason that Hathor was associated with copper? What did smelting sessions sound like? And if rhythm musicians attended smelts, did people dance, too?

4   Prototyping and Playtesting

4.1   Forging a Collaboration with UCSC Serious Games Program to Build a Prototype

In 2019, University of California, Santa Cruz started a Serious Games program within the Engineering department. With the assistance of the program's co-director, Magy Seif El-Nasr, I assembled a design team of Serious Games graduate students who were interested in cultural heritage games. "Timna Studios" included Technical Director and Programmer Amber Sargeant, 3D Modeler Wenbo Xie, 2D and Sound Designer Yichen Yao, and Producer Yuanzhu Wu. Industry mentor Steven Goodale, whose resume includes having been the Creative Director and Lead Systems Designer on the "Tomb Raider" series, oversaw their work.

To guide worldbuilding, I provided the game designers with the 360-degree video, photographic, and audio assets that I gathered from museum research and field documentation at Timna. For reference, I shared video footage of experimental smelting from the Central Timna Valley archaeology team (led by Ben-Yosef in 2020) and documentary film footage of an experimental smelt led by Fasnacht. I created a 22 page design document, e.g. a game script synthesizing my 3 years of research for the game. The design document includes worldbuilding reference images and "stage directions," such as how the "magic circle" of the VR game space (as an installation) should be demarcated within a museum setting. The script also provides instructional text for the museum attendant overseeing the game space.

The game designers additionally requested a one-page, bullet-point design document outlining the smelting process, the key objects that would be needed for it (such as the furnace, blowpipes, ore, charcoal), and what additional objects/characters (human and non-human) were included in the script. This served as a "quick reference guide" for the scope of the game build. The team requested a list of the game's goals. I separated design goals from game play goals and defined both. I specified design goals as: (1) to improve upon immersion strategies relative to other history games; (2) to develop a breath interface to give players an embodied, experiential sense of blowpipe technology; and (3) to redefine interaction design as intra-action design (i.e. to break subject-object binaries and instead establish "animistic" relationality). Game goals for players are: (1) to ensure a successful copper smelt using simulated blowpipe technologies; (2) to achieve a meditative state; and (3) to generate questions about intangible heritage related to Bronze Age copper smelting.

4.2 The Design Document

Though full sophistication of the design document (long version) is not yet realized in this initial prototype, the script specifies that upon entering the game world, the player can choose a Canaanite or Egyptian avatar, and that character can be male, female, or non-binary.[13] In the design document, players also choose characters representing in-world smelters. These additional smelters indicate historicity in that it took four to six people with blowpipes to keep the fire going; but these characters also allow for a mechanism by which the player can take a break if needed. Long periods of deep breathing take endurance and practice. Rather than have people quit if they cannot maintain their breath for long, the game encourages players to respect their body wisdom and rest if necessary. The design document specifies that an in-world smelter can "take over" until the player is ready to resume. Such instructions are narrated by an old man smelter-shaman, who guides the player as to how to regulate the crucible temperature with breath and charcoal, and how to read the colors of flames. Other human characters in the document include an old woman who crushes ore (a process called benefaction), and a drummer to keep rhythm as per breathwork playtesting results.

---

[13] Offering the choice of a non-binary character is in part to foster equity and inclusion, in harmony with University of California, Santa Cruz's long tradition of being a welcoming place to all expressions of gender identity; however, it is also a historically relevant nod to Astarte's dual-gender nature as expressed in Cypriot art (MacLauchlan, 2002) and to the one dual-gendered Astarte figurine discovered in Transjordan, not far from Timna (Sugimoto, 2014).

The design document reads like a play, but one with limited branching structure where the player has choices about how to balance breath and additional charcoal to regulate the fire temperature. As the fire heats, snakes dance in the flames in trance-like fashion to act as intermediaries that aid communication between the fire and the player. As the ore starts to melt, an ibex from a constellation rides across the sky with the goddess, a "family-friendly" (given the museum context) allusion to the sexual union taking place in the crucible. The ibex descends from the sky to merge with the shaman at some points, showing the relationship between the two. On the ground, the ibex can also move closer/farther from the player as she gets closer to/farther from the ideal fire temperature. Birds serve to deliver data upon request, such as how many liters of breath per minute the player is producing, and how much time has elapsed at different stages of the smelt. At the end of the smelt, when the copper is born, the player is rewarded with a Hathoric birthing celebration. This celebration is a simplified version of the celebrations that were held for new mothers in ancient Egypt: Bes (the Egyptian dwarf god who protected newborns and mothers) dances and plays a frame drum while the smelter is presented with a Hathor mirror. Note, in the built/playable prototype thus far, the only characters are: the player, an old man smelter/narrator, a drummer represented by sound only, the fire, the copper ore, an ibex, snakes morphed from slag, an intra-active Hathor mirror, and a dancing blue figure representing Bes.

4.3 Prototype Design Results

The Serious Games graduate students were afforded two, ten-week academic quarters–Fall 2021 and Winter 2022–to build a playable Virtual Reality prototype of my "Cult and Copper" design document. They began Fall quarter by spending 2 weeks on concept design and pre-production, which included meetings with me to verify their understanding of my design documents and goals, and to set realistic expectations. The production team created user experience mock-ups requiring my feedback. The production team determined the "core flow" (primary sequence) of the game to be: ore selection followed by breathing results in the birth of copper. They defined the "core loop" (primary game mechanics) to be: breath influences temperature influences the behavior (including color shifts) of the flames. Therefore, breath, fire temperature, and flames would be the three "core" foci for the player.

With these core concepts articulated, the team focused on "minimum prototype" design and development over weeks three through six. That means they developed the core experience of the game, the copper smelt. The player's avatar hand grasps pieces of ore and pieces of charcoal, places them in a crucible saucer, and places the saucer in the fire. The player then uses slow, sustained breath to control the heat of the flames. I scripted the game to be played sitting for safety, in case the player experienced lightheadedness from breathing too quickly/slowly. However, early playtesting revealed that playing while sitting also reduced the general dizziness that is often experienced in VR.

Fig. 4 Establishing shot within "Cult and Copper" VR world, after dusk has turned to night, Phase I prototype. Negev starlore informed the constellations in the sky in Phase II of prototyping. (Gameplay video still by Timna Studios, 2021)

The "minimum prototyping" for this core experience involved coordinating several components. From my media assets and script, the 3D modeler (Xie) created the Virtual Reality environment, including an immersive landscape to evoke Timna, and 3D game objects such as the fire pit, flames, smoke, and drifting embers; bits of copper ore and charcoal; the copper crucible; three-foot blowpipes (to which I asked him to add "clay" nozzles for better historicity) (Fig. 4). For this stage, the programmer (Sargeant) worked out the mechanics of picking up in-world objects with the handheld VR controller (Figs. 5 and 6). This took some trial, error, and playtesting because initially the player's in-world "hand" grabbed right through objects and gravity behaved such that charcoal floated away.

Sargeant also built and playtested iterations of the breath interface, which originally used an Ardunio microcontroller to interpret data from a temperature sensor called a thermistor. In the first iteration, the player held the breath interface in one hand and the VR controller in the other. To make managing the breath interface easier, in a second iteration the Sargeant optimized the design such that the Arduino-driven device attached to the VR controller. This design modification allowed the player to hold just one device instead of two.

The 2D artist (Yao) developed a breath meter graphic (Fig. 7). This meter guides the player as to when to inhale/exhale, and it indicates the changing temperature of the fire as the player adds oxygen via breath. Yao also researched and implemented ambient sound design for the crackling fire.

Weeks seven through ten marked the "iteration phase" of the project. This involved polishing the minimum prototype and inventing a VR tutorial at the beginning of the game. The tutorial, set in a mock Timna visitor center, instructs the

"Cult and Copper": A VR Game Exploring the Intangible Heritage of Copper Smelting

Fig. 5 The "Cult and Copper" player's avatar uses the VR controller to select pieces of copper ore in Phase I prototype. (Gameplay video still by Timna Studios, 2021)

Fig. 6 The "Cult and Copper" player's avatar uses the VR controller to place their selected pieces of copper ore into the smelting saucer, or "crucible," in Phase I prototype. (Gameplay video still by Timna Studios, 2021)

player as to how to use the VR controller to activate elements of the game. For this narration, I recorded, and Yao implemented, a male "old miner" voiceover.[14]

Over Winter 2022, the production team further refined all visual, sonic and mechanical aspects of the game. They created game "illusions" from the script. Illusions include aspects of the game that go beyond the core game experience, such as the snakes hypnotically appearing from the flames and the ibex descending from its constellation in the sky. The Hathoric birthing celebration, which marks the

---

[14] Dr. Stephen Martin, a physicist who did not previously know he could act so well, performed "the old miner" voice.

Fig. 7 With the copper crucible in the fire, the "Cult and Copper" player's avatar uses their breath to add oxygen to the fire. The original breath interface, driven by an Arduino micro-controller that converted analogue sensor data to digital data, calculated the rate at which the fire temperature rose. This image is an example of where I as the researcher needed to collaborate iteratively with the game builders because the image suggests that copper flames turn green–an indication that the copper has reached a liquid state–as the fire temperature reaches 1150-degrees Fahrenheit. However, this transformation happens at about 1200-degrees Celsius. So Prototype II corrected Fahrenheit to Celsius as per my production notes. (Gameplay video still by Timna Studios, 2021)

successful "birth" of the copper from the crucible, is also classified as an illusion (Figs. 8, 9 and 10).[15]

Also in Winter 2022, Sargeant made improvements to the breath interface. The thermistor worked but was inconsistent; it tended to be either too sensitive or not sensitive enough. She replaced the temperature sensor with a wind (pressure) sensor as an experiment to see if that produced more consistent results for smoother interpretation and display of breath-generated data. Yao integrated a separate, meditative Hathor frame drum rhythm to help regulate breathing.[16]

However, at the start of this prototyping stage, we hit an unexpected obstacle: the San Francisco Bay Area (our location) faced a covid-19 surge because of the highly transmissible omicron variant. Even individuals vaccinated and boosted against the original covid-19 virus were susceptible to infection with omicron. Team Timna decided there was no way to safely playtest the breath interface anymore because we had to remove our hygiene masks and blow on it, which would disperse respiratory aerosols that could carry the virus. As a safer alternative, Sargeant with her faculty mentors designed a "simulated" breath interface. The in-world breath meter still functions the same way, guiding the player as to when to inhale and when to exhale. Now, though, the player indicates each inhalation by pressing, and each

---

[15] The frame drum recording for this celebration was generously performed and recorded specifically for this "Cult and Copper" game by Heather Kelley of the Entertainment Technology Center at Carnegie Mellon University.

[16] This frame drum rhythm was also performed and contributed by Kelley.

"Cult and Copper": A VR Game Exploring the Intangible Heritage of Copper Smelting 1747

Fig. 8 Added in Phase II of the prototype, an ibex as a game illusion guides the smelter-shaman. (Gameplay video still by Timna Studios, 2022)

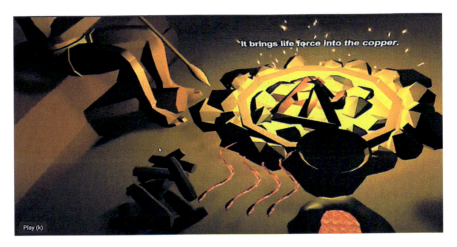

Fig. 9 Added in Phase II of the prototype, slag turns into snakes in a game illusion. The snakes represent breath that brings divine life force to the copper smelt. (Gameplay video still by Timna Studios, 2022)

exhalation by releasing, a trigger on the VR controller. While omicron unexpectedly thwarted my original interface ideal, our solution did have advantages in addition to better safety. First, by canceling the need for special hardware to operate "Cult and Copper," the game can be disseminated more easily; it can still be used in a museum setting, but players can also enjoy it at home. Second, as per the results of my breathwork playtesting with Bronze Age Productions performers, this third iteration of the interface allows the player to steer individualized, comfortable breathing rhythms. (This surpassed my hope for incorporating three distinct breathing rhythms.)

Fig. 10 Added in Phase II of the prototype, an intra-active Hathor mirror serves as another game illusion. Such mirrors were bestowed upon new mothers during Ancient Egyptian birthing celebrations. This one appears in the crucible after the copper is successfully "born" from it. (Gameplay video still by Timna Studios, 2022)

4.4 Playtesting Results

Team Timna playtested incremental aspects of game development with other people in the Serious Games program. After completing stage two prototyping, playtesting also served to determine how the target audience–museum goers with interests related to the game–engaged with the game in a museum setting. Does the game promote the intended state of deep relaxation, as measured by qualitative assessment? (We were not equipped to measure pulse rate or cortisol levels, though this would have been ideal.) How long do players engage with the game? What game content communicates successfully, and what is confusing? What do players take away from the game in terms of new knowledge and new questions to investigate? Does the game suggest an "esoteric secret?" Playtesting methods used direct observation of game play, plus short questionnaires designed to assess responses to specific elements of design and mechanics.

The Egyptian and Rosicrucian Museum in San Jose, California agreed to host a playtesting session with museum members in February 2022. Playtesting results from six participants revealed that people engaged with the game for 10–12 min. Two-thirds of players reported feeling more relaxed, kind, and/or creative after the game; this was our qualitative measure of how "meditative" the game was. The Serious Games students also collected eye tracking data from within the game world to test players' focus on/distraction from the central smelting fire; they took this as an additional measure of how meditative the game was. Their presumption was that if a player's focus was not fixed on the smelting fire, she was anxious or distracted. I suggest, however, that this empirical approach was perhaps ultimately as open to subjective interpretation as qualitative questions because perhaps some players (including me) found visual explorations of the virtual environment to be relaxing/ meditative. In fact, players in the museum, just as players in the Serious Games studio, commented on how calming the virtual Timna environment itself was. This eye tracking approach also did not take into account neurotype differences (such as autism or attention deficit hyperactivity disorder) that might create different focus/ distraction patterns. All players found the drum rhythm and the guided breathing within the game to be favorable to relaxation.

In terms of what was confusing within the game, some players thought that the language used for game instruction was at times unclear. We modified the voice narration and in-world instructional text in accordance with their collective feedback. Players had mixed levels of understanding regarding the role of the old man shaman-smelter. Half said that they felt guided and supported by his 3D character (as was my intention); half said that they perceived his form to be that of a companion smelter and thought that the narrator's guiding voice was a separate character "off-camera."

Players attested that they learned something about the intangible heritage of Bronze Age smelting from the game; each felt inspired to learn more. They successfully interpreted at least some intended part of the "esoteric secret" that the game reveals; they all recognized that in the Bronze Age Levant smelting was somehow related to transformation and to birthing. Player Three interpreted that the link between smelting and shamanism had to do with "bringing out the fire within" and raising spiritual energy. Player Four reported learning that smelting had to do with breath and that it was perhaps a spiritual, not just an industrial, activity. She wanted to know more about the connection of goddesses to smelting and whether women were involved in the process. She interpreted the "esoteric secret" to be that the power of breath can change states of matter and consciousness, and that "higher states of consciousness allowed connection to the goddess." Player Five found the relationship among folkloric, alchemical, and metallurgical traditions at the forge to be "intriguing," and realized that the spiritual aspects of metallurgy practice are forgotten in materials science today. Player Six learned that smelting was done in community over an open fire at night. For him, the storytelling approach of the game provoked contemplation about the oral transmission of traditions. He interpreted the esoteric secret of the game to be that smelting was blessed by Hathor. Thus playtesting revealed that the game was remarkably successful in meeting my game play goals of conveying knowledge, and provoking further speculation/ questions, about intangible heritage.

5 Conclusions

The "Cult and Copper" Virtual Reality game designs that resulted from my historical and theoretical research conducted from 2017 through 2020, my collaborative ideation with Bronze Age Productions, and my technical collaboration with the University of California, Santa Cruz Serious Games program, did indeed meet project design goals. The game improves upon immersion strategies used in existing history VR games. It does so in part by employing worldbuilding advice offered by Jenkins, Wolf, and Champion. Worldbuilding techniques such as utilizing Timna's distinctive landscape, Levantine Bronze Age artifacts, and ancient mythologies from the region work together to create a coherent, consistent sense of being in a particular time and place, i.e. being *there and then* as encouraged by Champion (2015).

The game realizes the design goal of redefining interaction design as relational intra-action design. Snakes, ibexes, copper, fire, air, slag, blowpipes, and rhythm all have roles in the game, which affords them posthumanist agencies that challenge anthropocentrism. The strategy of using intra-active agents to drive the story enhances immersion by creating a magical, animistic world that is separate from ordinary reality.

The built prototype for "Cult and Copper" originally met my interface design specifications absolutely. The programmer was able to successfully realize a custom breath interface to evoke an embodied sense of what it might have been like to be an ancient smelter using blowpipe technologies to heat a small crucible. This created the sense of interoception–bodily awareness–that Heeter says is necessary for creating a sense of presence (Heeter, 2016). The subsequent covid-19 virus surge necessitated reworking the interface goals, but the "simulated" breath interface, in which the player indicates their breathing pattern via the VR controller, still keeps the important goals of embodiment and interoception central.

This project generally met my game play goals, both among our Serious Games student playtesters and among museum playtesters. Both groups found the game to be meditative via the facilitation of conscious breathing. The nighttime atmosphere around the fire pit, with the sound of the cracking flames and the trance-inducing pace of drifting embers, evoked responses of relaxation as well. Museum members, representing the target audience for the game, demonstrated that the game does successfully educate about copper smelting in the ancient Negev desert. They were inspired to ask further questions, postulate their own speculations, about the associated intangible heritage. The culmination of the game–the Hathoric birthing celebration with music and dance that occurs when the copper is birthed from the fire–allowed playtesters to feel a sense of reward. At least as importantly, however, it suggested to them why sexuality goddesses might have been associated with copper smelting. Thus playtesters earned not just a party, but an esoteric secret.

Acknowledgments Many thanks to a long list of contributors to this collaborative project including Timna Studios (Amber Sargeant, Wenbo Xie, Yichen Yao, and Yuanzhou Wu), Steven Goodale, Dr. Magy Seif El-Nasr, and Dr. Edward Melcer, all from the Serious Games Program at University of California, Santa Cruz; Bronze Age Productions participants (including Walter Fasnacht of Zurich University/Almyras Excavation in Cyprus; Dr. Daniela DeAngeli of University of Bath; UC Berkeley Anthropology Professor Emeritus Ruth Tringham; Despoina Sampatakou of University of York; game designer Dr. Anamaria Ciucanu; former Jim Henson Muppet artist Luise Shafritz; performer/gamer Kathryn Kane, and others); Heather Kelley from the Carnegie Mellon University Entertainment Technology department for her Hathor frame drum recordings and advice; Dr. Stephen Martin for his voice performance as a miner; and Andrew Sobieralski for his engineering research on low-cost, DIY, open source code spirometers to guide our breath interface development. Thank you to my advisors at UC Santa Cruz, Dr. Susana Ruiz, Dr. Elaine Sullivan, and Dr. Anna Friz. I also express much gratitude to Dr. Erez Ben-Yosef from Tel Aviv University for welcoming me to observe his 2017 excavation in Timna, for inspiring my imagination, for pointing me to research resources, and for patiently enduring years of related email questions. Thank you to Dr. Adina Paytan for jump-starting this endeavor by including me on her 2017 research trip to Israel via the International Research Experience for Students in Coastal Zone Research (IRES) program. IRES is a National Science Foundation (NSF) funded program. Other funding for this project came from SSRC-Mellon Foundation, the UC Santa Cruz Film & Digital Media department, and Florence French.

References

Avner, U. (2014). Egyptian Timna reconsidered. In J. M. Tebes (Ed.), *Unearthing the wilderness: Studies on the history and archaeology of the Negev and Edom in the Iron Age* (pp. 103–162). Peeters.

Barad, K. M. (2007). *Meeting the universe halfway: Quantum physics and the entanglement of matter and meaning.* Duke University Press.

Ben-Dor Evian, S. (2018, July 11, Israel Museum, Jerusalem). *Personal communication.*

Ben-Yosef, E., Langgut, D., & Sapir-Hen, L. (2017). Beyond smelting: New insights on Iron Age (10th C. Bce) metalworkers community from excavations at a gatehouse and associated Livestock Pens in Timna, Israel. *Journal of Archaeological Science: Reports, 11*, 411–426. https://doi.org/10.1016/j.jasrep.2016.12.010

Ben-Yosef, E., Liss, B., Yagel, O. A., Tirosh, O., Najjar, M., & Levy, T. E. (2019). Ancient technology and punctuated change: Detecting the emergence of the Edomite Kingdom in the Southern Levant. *PLoS ONE, 14*(9). https://doi.org/10.1371/journal.pone.0221967

Bucher, J. K. (2018). *Storytelling for virtual reality: Methods and principles for crafting immersive narratives.* Routledge, Taylor & Francis Group.

Champion, E. (2015). *Critical gaming: Interactive history and virtual heritage.* Ashgate Publishing Limited.

Copplestone, T. J. (2017). Designing and developing a playful past in video games. In A. A. A. Mol, C. E. Ariese-Vandemeulebroucke, K. H. J. Boom, & A. Politopoulos (Eds.), *The interactive past: Archaeology, heritage & video games* (pp. 85–98). Sidestone Press.

Craddock, P. T. (2010). *Early metal mining and production.* Archetype Publications Ltd. (First published by Edinburgh University Press Ltd., 1995).

Day, J. (2013). Introduction. In J. Day (Ed.), *Making senses of the past: Toward a sensory archaeology* (pp. 1–31). Center for Archaeological Investigations, Southern Illinois University Carbondale and Southern Illinois University Press.

Diego Espinel, A. (2002). The role of the temple of Ba'alat Gebal as intermediary between Egypt and Byblos during the Old Kingdom. *Studien Zur Altägyptischen Kultur, 30*, 103–119.

Eliade, M. (1978). *The forge and the crucible* (2nd ed.). University of Chicago Press.

Fasnacht, F. (2020, December 23, & 2021, April 16). Online interviews via Zoom.

Favro, D. (2012). Se Non è Vero, è Ben Trovato (If not true, it is well conceived): Digital immersive reconstructions of historical environments. *Journal of the Society of Architectural Historians, 71*(3), 273–277. https://doi.org/10.1525/jsah.2012.71.3.273

Fisher, K. D. (2014). Investigating monumental social space in late Bronze Age cyprus, an integrative approach. In E. Paliou, U. Lieberwirth, & S. Polla (Eds.), *Spatial analysis and social spaces: Interdisciplinary approaches to the interpretation of prehistoric and historic built environments* (pp. 202–242). De Gruyter.

Forte, M. (2016). Cyber archaeology: 3D sensing and digital embodiment. In M. Forte & S. Campana (Eds.), *Digital methods and remote sensing in archaeology: Archaeology in the age of sensing* (pp. 271–289). Springer.

Gošić, M., & Gilead, I. (2015). Unveiling hidden rituals: Ghassulian metallurgy of the Southern Levant in light of the ethnographical record. *Bar International Series, 2753*(25), 25–38.

Heeter, C. (2016, November). A meditation on meditation and embodied presence. *Presence: Teleoperators & Virtual Environments, 25*(2), 175–183. https://doi.org/10.1162/PRES_a_00256

Jenkins, H. (2004). Game design as narrative architecture. In N. Wardrip-Fruin & P. Harrigan (Eds.), *First person: New media as story, performance, and game* (pp. 119–129). MIT Press.

Johanson, C. (2009). Visualizing history: Modeling in the eternal city. *Visual Resources, 25*(4), 403–418.

MacLauchlan, B. (2002). The ungendering of aphrodite. In D. Bolger & N. J. Serwint (Eds.), *Engendering aphrodite: Women and society in ancient Cyprus* (Vol. 3, 7, pp. 365–378). American Schools of Oriental Research.

McVeigh-Schultz, J. (2016). *Designing speculative rituals: Tangible imaginaries and fictive practices from the (Inter)personal to the political.* Doctoral dissertation, University of Southern California.

Morris, E. F. (2011). Paddle dolls and performance. *Journal of the American Research Center in Egypt, 47*, 71–103.

Murray, J. H. (2017). *Hamlet on the Holodeck: The future of narrative in cyberspace* [Updated edition]. The MIT Press.

Pietroni, E. (2016). From remote to embodied sensing: New perspectives for virtual museums and archaeological landscape communication. In M. Forte & S. Campana (Eds.), *Digital methods and remote sensing in archaeology: Archaeology in the age of sensing* (pp. 437–474). Springer.

Redmond, L. (1997). *When the drummers were women: A spiritual history of rhythm.* Three Rivers Press.

Ryan, M.-L. (2015). *Narrative as virtual reality 2: Revisiting immersion and interactivity in literature and electronic media.* Johns Hopkins University Press.

Saltman, C., Herbert, E. W., & Gaucher, C. (Directors). (1986). *The blooms of Banjeli: Technology and gender in African Ironmaking* [Documentary Film]. Documentary Educational Resources (DER).

Sebbane, M. (2019). *Mind and matter: The World of the first copper master* [Exhibition catalogue]. Eretz Israel Museum. https://www.eretzmuseum.org.il/e/398/

Shalomi-Hen, R. (2016). The Goddess Hathor. In D. Ben-Tor (Ed.), *Pharaoh in Canaan, The untold story* (pp. 148–161). The Israel Museum.

Steiner, G. F. (June 2016). The goddess and the copper snake: Metallurgy, star-lore and ritual in the rock art of the Southern Levant. *Expression Quarterly Journal of Atelier Editions in Cooperation with UISSP-CISNEP (International Scientific Commission on the Intellectual and Spiritual Expressions of Non-Literate Peoples), 12*, 73–95.

Stuart, J. (May 2015). Challenging heritage visualisation: Beauty, aura and democratisation, Open Archaeology 1(1), 144–152. https://doi.org/10.1515/opar-2015-0008

Suchman, L. A. (2007). *Human-machine reconfigurations: Plans and situated actions.* Cambridge University Press.

Sugimoto, D. T. (2014). The Judean pillar figurines and the "Queen of Heaven". In D. T. Sugimoto (Ed.), *Transformation of a goddess: Ishtar–Astarte–Aphrodite, Orbis Biblicus Et Orientalis* (pp. 141–165). (Fribourg)). Academic Press.

Tanabe, R. H. (2017, August 4). *New world encyclopedia.* Retrieved August 26, 2021, from https://www.newworldencyclopedia.org/p/index.php?title=Hathor&oldid=1006124

Watterson, A. (April 2015). Beyond digital dwelling: Re-thinking interpretive visualisation in archaeology. Open Archaeology 1(1), 119–130. https://doi.org/10.1515/opar-2015-0006

Wolf, M. J. P. (2013). *Building imaginary worlds: The theory and history of subcreation.* Routledge.

Uncertainties in Archaeointensity Research: Implications for the Levantine Archaeomagnetic Curve

Lisa Tauxe, Ron Shaar, Brendan Cych, and Erez Ben-Yosef ⓘ

Abstract Archaeomagnetism is the study of the magnetic properties of archaeological artifacts, in particular the magnetic field vectors trapped in objects when fired. The data collected serve multiple communities, from geophysicists who model past variations of the magnetic field through time to archaeologists who use such field models to provide chronological constraints for the archaeological artifacts themselves. In addition to age constraints, archaeomagnetic data can answer questions such as "Was an object fired?", or "Can these two objects be the same age?". Accomplishing these divergent goals requires active collaboration between geophysicists and archaeologists to the benefit of both groups. Professor Tom Levy has fostered such active collaborations for decades, mentoring graduate students and post-docs with expertise in archaeology and facilitating access to rare archaeological artifacts from Jordan by the geophysical community and collaborating on joint archaeological/archaeomagnetic expeditions to Cyprus. In this paper we will describe the principles and practice archaeomagnetism, in particular, archaeointen-

---

The original version of the chapter has been revised. A correction to this chapter can be found at
https://doi.org/10.1007/978-3-031-27330-8_83

L. Tauxe (✉)
Scripps Institution of Oceanography, La Jolla, CA, USA
e-mail: ltauxe@ucsd.edu

R. Shaar
The Institute of Earth Sciences, The Hebrew University of Jerusalem, Jerusalem, Israel
e-mail: ron.shaar@mail.huji.ac.il

B. Cych
Scripps Institution of Oceanography, La Jolla, CA, USA

Department of Earth Ocean and Ecological Sciences, University of Liverpool,
Liverpool, UK
e-mail: bcych@ucsd.edu

E. Ben-Yosef
Department of Archaeology and Ancient Near Eastern Cultures, Tel Aviv University,
Tel Aviv, Israel
e-mail: ebenyose@tauex.tau.ac.il

© The Author(s), under exclusive license to Springer Nature
Switzerland AG 2023, corrected publication 2023
E. Ben-Yosef, I. W. N. Jones (eds.), *"And in Length of Days Understanding" (Job
12:12): Essays on Archaeology in the Eastern Mediterranean and Beyond in
Honor of Thomas E. Levy*, Interdisciplinary Contributions to Archaeology,
https://doi.org/10.1007/978-3-031-27330-8_74

sity which uses the strength of the Earth's magnetic field in the past. We review the development of the Levantine Archaeointensity curve, present its current state and illustrate its uses to archaeology with examples from current research in the Levant.

Keywords Archaeomagnetism · Paleomagnetism · Dating techniques · Secular variations · Levantine Iron Age geomagnetic Anomaly (LIAA) · Archeaointensity

1 Introduction

Archaeomagnetism relies on the measurement of magnetic properties of archaeological artifacts to provide insights into questions of importance to both archaeologists and geophysicists. It provides one of the prime approaches to understanding the history of the Earth's magnetic field as many artifacts are heated during manufacture and can retain a record of the field at the time of firing. For unoriented archaeological materials (such as pottery fragments, etc.), we can only obtain field strength and not its direction, but archaeointensity is still a powerful tool. Because the field is quite dynamic, when the history at a given location is well determined it can be used to help establish chronologies for archaeological artifacts themselves. These histories are compiled as geomagnetic field models which allow predictions of ancient field vectors as a function of location and time which in turn can provide age constraints for archaeological materials. And even when detailed time series are not available, it is possible to determine whether two artifacts could have been fired in the same time window or not by comparing the strength of the field recorded in the objects. All of these benefits rely on the accuracy and precision of both the intensity and age estimates made for artifacts.

The field of archaeointensity is one of the oldest fields in geophysics (Gallet, 2021). It relies on the fundamental property of materials that contain magnetic grains, that they acquire (block) a remanent magnetization when they are cooled from above the Curie Temperature in the presence of a magnetic field. This so-called thermal remanent magnetization (TRM) is a quasi-linear function of the field in which the object cooled, so, in theory, retains a record of the ancient magnetic field strength, when calibrated against a TRM acquired in a known magnetic field. There are multiple sources of bias and uncertainty in these experiments, such as a change in the ability to acquire TRM (alteration), or a failure of the requirement that magnetization is lost (unblocked) at the same temperature as it was frozen in (blocked), or several generations of magnetization resulting from subsequent reheating of the object. Experiments generally build in checks that attempt to detect such changes and there are many approaches to data selection that have evolved over the years. Dating of the archaeological fragments used in archaeointensity studies rely on a variety of approaches such as radiocarbon dating or archaeological context and has its own set of uncertainties.

The payoff of archaeomagnetic effort comes when geomagnetists attempt to compile the field vectors as a function of space and time as sets of field models. These are lists of coefficients which can then be used to compute a model field vector for any place and date. Recent versions of these global field models are the SHAWQ2k and

SHAWQIA models of Campuzano et al. (2019) and Osete et al. (2020) respectively. The most recent longer term field models, extending back 10,000 years, are those published by Constable et al. (2016) or even 100,000 years (Panovska & Constable, 2012). Field models are necessarily smoothed as construction of such models attempt to take into account uncertainties in both the field vector and age. In this paper we will discuss these twin issues as they relate to the development of the history of geomagnetic field variations in the Levant. We conclude with the current status of a regional field model, known as the Levantine Archaeomagnetic Curve or LAC.

2 Archaeomagnetic Intensity Research in the Levant

Work on developing what is now called the Levantine Archaeomagnetic Curve (LAC, Shaar et al., 2022) began with the efforts of Genevey et al. (2003) who constructed an 8000 year record of magnetic field intensity changes using pottery and brick fragments from Syria in the Northern Levant. They chose materials dated by archaeological context and used a modification of the traditional Thellier-Thellier method in which the NRM remaining is directly measured by heating and cooling to room temperature in a null field, followed by acquisition of a partial TRM (pTRM) step cooled in a laboratory field. Additional in-field cooling steps are inserted at lower temperatures to detect changes in the ability of the samples to acquire a pTRM by using so-called pTRM check steps (Coe et al., 1978).

The initial work of Genevey et al. (2003) was followed by Gallet and Le Goff (2006) and Gallet et al. (2006) who used a different technique. They measured the magnetization of specimens at increasingly high temperature (instead of at room temperature) up to the Curie Temperature, both in a null field and controlled fields, a method known as the Triaxe method. The combined Syrian data provided a glimpse at field behavior over the last eight thousand years in the Northern Levant.

Work in the Southern Levant began with Ben-Yosef et al. (2008) who analyzed samples taken from copper mining slag from Israel and Jordan. They used a modified experiment from the Coe-Thellier one of Genevey et al. (2003) (which cools first in zero-field then in-field, ZI) by also performing an infield cooling step followed by zero-field (IZ). The two sequences alternate with increasing temperature and is known as the IZZI method (Yu et al., 2004).

The combined pre-2008 results from the Northern and Southern Levant are shown in Fig. 1. Because field strength varies with location around the globe, it is the frequent practice to convert local field strengths (measured in μT) to a single location (e.g., Paris). Here we adopt the practice favored by geophysicists to convert the estimated intensity to an equivalent strength of a magnetic dipole aligned with the spin axis at the Earth's center that would give rise to the observed field strength, known as a virtual axial dipole moment or VADM in units of Am^2 or ZAm^2 (Z, or Zeta is 10^{21}). For reference, the strength of the present axial dipole moment is about 76 ZAm^2. Also shown are field strengths predicted for the region from the field model available at the time, CALS7K (Korte & Constable, 2005). While the contemporaneous data from Northern and Southern Levant agree fairly well with each other, and in fact are complementary, with age ranges missing data in one area being

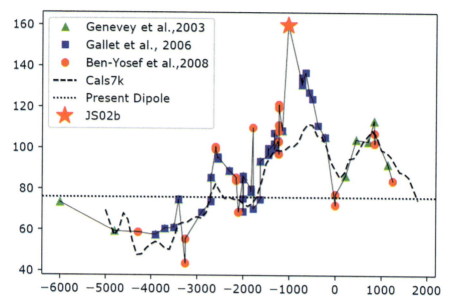

Fig. 1 Original version of the Levantine Archaeomagnetic Curve. Northern Levantine data (Syria) are from Genevey et al. (2003, green triangles), Gallet et al. (2006, blue squares), including those from Gallet and Le Goff (2006). Data from the Southern Levant (Israel and Jordan) are those with reliable ages from Ben-Yosef et al. (2008, red dots). Also shown are the predicted values from the CALS7K field model of Korte and Constable (2005) and the strength of the present dipole field. The star is the data point from JS02b from Ben-Yosef et al. (2008) which had an unexpectedly high VADM not observed in the Syrian data

filled in by the other. The data agree with the model predictions, as the model was based in part on the Northern Syrian data of Genevey et al. (2003). However, the data sets depart significantly from the model particularly around 3000 BCE. The largest departure between model and data was found at Khirbat al Jariya (JS02b) from the study of Ben-Yosef et al. (2008), with an age of about 1030 ± 110 BCE and a VADM of about 160 ZAm^2, or about twice the present field (2020) value (dotted line in the figure).

Our collaboration with Professor Levy was focused on whether the unexpectedly high field value discovered by Ben-Yosef et al. (2008) (star in Fig. 1) was reproducible. We now call VADM values in excess of 160 ZAm^2 a geomagnetic 'spike' and the slags of Khirbat al Jariya were the first evidence of such a phenomenon in the Levant. Professor Levy was the lead archaeologist on excavations in Jordan of the copper mining slag mounds in Khirbet en Najas (KEN), near to the Khirbat al Jariya location of JS02b. Our association with him allowed us to gain access to a thick section of slag as it was being excavated. The KEN archaeointensity research, summarized in Ben Yosef et al. (2009), relied on the excellent radiocarbon age control of Levy et al. (2008) and we were able to confirm the brief period of exceptionally high geomagnetic field strength in the early Iron Age found by Ben-Yosef et al. (2008), who placed it in the late tenth century BCE.

The work at KEN was followed by a parallel study that found similarly high field values at about the same age in copper mining slag deposits excavated at Timna-30, in the Arava Valley of Southern Israel (Shaar et al., 2011). In an attempt to replicate these unexpected results in different, more conventional materials, Shaar et al. (2016) used well-dated pottery and cooking ovens from two contemporaneous mounds in Israel: Tel Hazor and Tel Megiddo. Again, the high field values were found, along with an even higher 'spike' at around 740 BCE. Ben-Yosef et al. (2017) confirmed this seventh century Levantine spike in well dated royal Judean stamped jar handles with age estimates between 750 and 701 BCE. The work in Tel Megiddo continues to today with Shaar et al. (2020) and Shaar et al. (2022).

Since the discovery of the tenth century BCE 'Levantine spike' (sometimes referred to as the Levantine Iron Age Anomaly, LIAA), other studies have discovered similarly high values in neighboring regions using different experimental approaches. From East to West, Cai et al. (2017) found spike VADMs (166 ZAm^2) in Zhejiang Province of China dated at 1300 ± 300 BCE. Ertepinar et al. (2012) found VADM values of around 180 ZAm^2 in furnaces from the Arslantepe mound (in Malatya province of Turkey) dated at 1050 ± 150 BCE. Di Chiara et al. (2014) found VADMs of 164 ± 21 ZAm^2 in the Azores with an age estimate of 593 ± 236 BCE. But, while efforts to find similar features in Europe did document rapid field changes with one major pulse of high field strength in the sixth century in Germany (540–660 BCE), the maximum value of $\sim 148 \pm 10$ ZAm^2 is just shy of the spike threshold and occurred slightly later than the Levantine spikes. Similar studies in Spain (Gómez-Paccard et al., 2016; Osete et al., 2020) also did not find a reliable case for the extremely high values observed in the Levant, although there was one data point with apparently good experimental characteristics that was eliminated because it was deemed 'too high' (200 ZAm^2). Nor were high values found in western Africa (Mitra et al., 2013) for the same time intervals. These observations have led some to suggest a highly non-dipolar field as the cause of the Levantine spike.

Observations of spikes are accompanied by apparently rapid growth and decay of the field and were met with considerable skepticism by the geomagnetic community. Livermore et al. (2014) pointed out that such apparently rapid rates of change with such high peak values were difficult to generate with commonly accepted behavior of the core-surface flow. In an attempt to alleviate the problem, Livermore et al. (2021) suggested that if samples are averaged over multiple fragments from the same archaeological contexts, the spikes disappear. The question then arises as to how contemporaneous archaeological units are and whether averaging of multiple fragments could suffer from what we will call the 'old house effect', similar to bias introduced into radiocarbon based chronologies by dating 'old wood'. The problem is that single archaeological contexts can contain materials spanning decades if not centuries.

There are, therefore, two entirely different sources of uncertainty in archaeointensity studies: those inherent to the experimental estimation of field strength (the y-axis) and those associated with assigning age (the x-axis), including the old house effect, differences in archaeological (context) ages, etc. We consider both of these issues in the following.

3 Uncertainties in Estimating Ancient Field Strength

3.1 Brief Note on Terminology

There are differences in the use of many words between paleomagnetic and archaeological communities. Here we will use the paleomagnetic conventions. A 'specimen' is what gets measured. Multiple specimens are generally made from a 'sample', which is what gets taken in the field. A 'sample' therefore is a fragment of ceramic, slag, or other coherent piece collected at the excavation such as a bricks from a burnt structure. A 'site' is a group of specimens (or sometimes sample averages) that are assumed to be the same age and can therefore be averaged together. A site can be a single fragment, for example, if the archaeological unit spans many years, or could be composed of many samples, if for example in the case of a burnt structure, the samples (bricks) can be considered contemporaneous in their last firing. The concept of 'site' is therefore vague and open to interpretation, but crucial in the construction of archaeointensity curves.

3.2 Instrumental Noise

One source of uncertainty in estimating ancient field strength comes from instrumental noise. Paterson et al. (2014) explored the many sources of instrumental noise, particularly in Thellier-type experiments like the Coe-Thellier or the IZZI method used in many of the studies contributing to the LAC. Repeated temperature steps (zero and infield cooling) require that the same temperature be reached for each step and temperature reproducibility and thermal gradients in some ovens can be significant. The rate at which the specimen is allowed to cool in the oven must also be consistent. The laboratory field applied during infield cooling must be the same for each step and specimens must be placed in the field in exactly the same way for each of the subsequent steps. Measurement of the magnetization also can be difficult, particularly in weakly magnetized specimens and here again, placement of the specimen into holders must be done with great care to insure reproducible measurement of the magnetic vector. Paterson et al. (2014) considered each of these sources of noise (and more) using sophisticated Monte Carlo modeling and estimated that intensity estimates can be expected to vary by 6–7%. Therefore, a measurement of a 'spike' value of 160 ZAm^2 can be expected to have an uncertainty of some 10–11 ZAm^2 from just instrumental noise alone. They also stated that IZZI and Coe protocols had the same noise distributions.

3.3 Experimental Protocol

Paterson et al. (2014) only considered Thellier-type experiments, including Coe and IZZI methods but the instrumental noise in the Triaxe experiments has not been considered in such great detail and the uncertainty remains uncertain. However, Shaar et al. (2020) compared the Triaxe method (as practiced in the Thellier paleomagnetic laboratory in Paris) with the IZZI method (as practiced in the lab at the Hebrew University of Jerusalem, Israel, HUJI) in a blind test. They found that both methods yielded consistent results. Moreover, the HUJI IZZI method has also been compared with the same method as practiced in the Scripps Paleomagnetic Laboratory and also found to produce consistent results. Therefore, at least in the three laboratories involved in the data considered so far, different labs and experimental protocols are not a significant source of uncertainty or bias.

3.4 Non-ideal Materials

There are a number of assumptions in all forms of paleointensity experiments. These were laid out in detail by Thellier and Thellier (1959). The method relies first and foremost on Néel theory (Néel, 1949). In this theory, magnetic grains are assumed to have only two 'easy' axes along which the magnetic moment lies in the absence of an applied external field. These grains are called 'uni-axial'. Each grain is uniformly magnetized, (single-domain, or SD) and each has a temperature (the blocking temperature, T_b) above which the rate of changing between the two easy directions is high, say, 100 s, and below which is slow, say, the age of the Earth. As an assemblage of such particles cools from the Curie temperature in the presence of an applied field, the magnetic moments in the grains flip rapidly between the two states but have a slight preference for the direction closest to the applied field. As each grain cools through its blocking temperature, the moment gets 'stuck' in whatever direction it was in. So, when cooled to room temperature, the assemblage has a net moment that is proportional to and parallel to the external field. On heating from room temperature up to the 'unblocking' temperature T_{ub}, the magnetic memory is lost. If the proportionality constant can be determined through re-heating and cooling in a known field, the ancient field strength can be estimated.

The rate at which a sample cools from high temperature to room temperature affects the maximum value of the TRM acquired (e.g., Halgedahl et al., 1980; Nagy et al., 2021). Anisotropic distribution of magnetic easy axes can result in additional uncertainty in the resulting intensity estimates (e.g., Aitken et al., 1981). And the built-in assumption is that the TRM is a linear function of the applied field may not always be true (e.g., Selkin et al., 2007).

For paleointensity estimates to be valid, the following must be true:

1. The specimen's natural remanent magnetization (NRM) must be a TRM.
2. The capacity for a specimen to acquire pTRM in the laboratory must not change during laboratory reheating.
3. The blocking temperature must be the same as the unblocking temperature.
4. The TRM acquired by cooling from the Curie Temperature to room temperature must be the same as that acquired by step-wise acquisition of pTRMs up to the Curie Temperature.
5. Effects of anisotropy, cooling rate and non-linear TRM must be calculated precisely and compensated for.

There are a number of tests built in to the Thellier type experiments in order to check whether the assumptions of the method have been met. The first requirement, that the magnetization be a TRM, is usually established from the archaeological context. That said, there are ways to improve the chances that is true. For example, comparing the remanent to induced magnetization, a procedure first described by Königsberger (1938) in the context of magnetic anomalies, can help distinguish between magnetizations of sedimentary or lightning strikes as the former gives very low ratios while the latter gives very high ratios. A recent example of this practice for archaeological specimens is that of Di Chiara et al. (2021). The second requirement is tested in the Coe and IZZI Thellier variants through the use of the pTRM check step, which must demonstrate reproducibility of a pTRM at a given temperature step, after heating to higher temperatures. The third and fourth requirements are supported if the Arai plots comparing NRM remaining against pTRM acquired are linear (see Fig. 2a for example). Non-linear plots result from the failure of the $T_b = T_{ub}$ requirements and these have been associated with bias in the estimated intensity (Krása et al., 2003; Tauxe et al., 2021; Nagy et al., 2022). Assessing the effects of cooling rate, anisotropy and non-linear TRM acquisition corrections are all included in the experiments considered here.

3.5 Selection Criteria and Data Analysis

Given that checks have been built into the archaeointensity experiment to verify that the basic requirements of the method have been met, there have been many attempts at quantifying what constitutes a reliable estimate. There are therefore abundant parameters to test if the NRM represents a single, well defined magnetization, to test the reproducibility of pTRMs, the equivalence of blocking and unblocking temperatures and so on. Paterson et al. (2014) compiled these and we rely on that source in the following for definitions.

Clearly the criteria and threshold values by which intensity experiments were judged changed over the years. Some of the criteria have similar functions. For example, FRAC replaced $f_{V\,DS}$ and SCAT replaced DRATS and MD% and also screens for curvature. Some experimental details are not included in the table. For

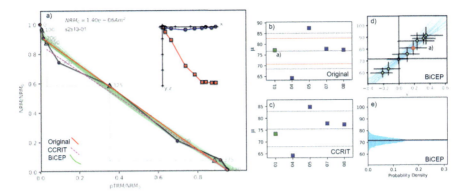

Fig. 2 Examples of the different approaches to data analysis used in this paper. (**a**) Arai plot (Nagata et al., 1963) of data from one specimen (s2a13-01) from site s2a13. Blue (red) dots are the ZI (IZ) steps. Triangles are pTRM check steps. Red line is the best-fit line chosen by the original criteria (76.4 μT). Dashed magenta line is that chosen by CCRIT criteria (72.9 μT). Light green curves are fits from the BiCEP method. Inset: Zijderveld diagram (Zijderveld, 1967). Blue dots (red squares) are the x,y (x,z) projections. Note that x has been rotated to the NRM direction. (**b**) Specimen estimates for the site using the original criteria. Labelled estimate is for specimen shown in (**a**). Dashed lines are the allowed site level 1σ confidence bounds (black) and site level estimate (red). (**c**) Same as (**b**) but for the CCRIT selection criteria. (**d**) BiCEP intensity estimates plotted against estimates of specimen curvature $\vec{k}$ and the Monte Carlo estimates for slopes relating the two. (**e**) Probability density for intensity estimates for the site

example, all of the studies incorporated some corrections for the effect of anisotropy on the intensity estimate and all but Ben-Yosef et al. (2008) tested for the non-linearity of TRM with applied field. GAP-MAX and $\vec{k'}$ were not included in any of the studies, but at least the latter is now considered quite useful (Tauxe et al., 2021). The CCRIT criteria were suggested by Cromwell et al. (2015) and tested on historical lava flows in Hawaii, whose magnetic fields during cooling were well constrained. They found excellent agreement between the estimated values and the historical fields using CCRIT. Also, Yamamoto et al. (2022) found that the CCRIT criteria led to intensity estimates in good agreement with the applied field (1σ = 4.5 μT) in artificial remanences allowed to age for two years in controlled fields.

Given the plethora of parameters used and their changing threshold values, it is interesting to compare the effect of different strategies on the outcome. Here we have used the program Thellier GUI (Shaar & Tauxe, 2013), part of the PmagPy package (Tauxe et al., 2016) which uses tables of selection criteria to find specimen interpretations that satisfy the specified threshold values. There may be more than one interpretation that 'passes' and there are different strategies for treating these. In the STDEV-OPT mode, the interpretations are chosen that minimize the site level standard deviation. In the 'extended error bar' approach of, e.g., Shaar et al. (2016), uncertainties are estimated using the minimum and maximum values of the specimen results that passed the selection criteria. Most of the studies considered here predated the availability of Thellier GUI and the experimental data were interpreted 'by-hand', a less reproducible approach.

Recently, a new data analysis method was introduced which minimizes the use of selection criteria and their necessarily binary threshold values. Following the suggestion of Tauxe et al. (2021) that results from curved Arai plots tend to be biased, Cych et al. (2021) developed a Bayesian approach, BiCEP, that considers all of the measurements from specimens at a site, accounts for possible bias stemming from Arai plot curvature and estimates intensity with 95% credibility intervals. The BiCEP credibility intervals are not unlike the 'extended error bars' calculated by the method used by Shaar et al. (2016).

Examples of the different approaches considered here are shown in Fig. 2. The original interpretations adopted by Shaar et al. (2011) used the selection criteria listed in Table 1 for the specimen level and Table 2 for the site (fragment) level (here s2s13). The original criteria resulted in the best-fit line shown as a solid red line with an intensity of 76.4 μT. This interpretation fails the curvature criterion in CCRIT with a value of 0.180, but CCRIT allowed the interpretation shown as a dashed magenta line, with an intensity of 72.9 μT. All of the chosen intensities for the original criteria (those that minimized site level scatter) are shown in Fig. 2b and those that the CCRIT criteria chose in Fig. 2c. But the original criteria failed at the site level because the standard deviation exceeded the allowed limits, while the CCRIT

Table 1 Specimen level selection criteria used in Thellier type LAC studies. Criterion: β: standard error of the slope of the best fit line. DANG: Deviation Angle. f_{VDS}: fraction of the vector difference sum of NRM used in calculation. MAD: unanchored maximum deviation angle of the best-fit direction. MD%: maximum difference between pTRM tail check steps and original measurement. N_{pTRM}: number of pTRM check steps. q: quality criterion. aniso_alt: Anisotropy alteration check. N_{meas}: number of temperature steps used in the slope calculation. FRAC: fraction of remanence. GAP-MAX: maximum gap between successive temperature steps. $|\vec{k}'|$. absolute value of the curvature criterion. SCAT: if TRUE, all measurements on the Arai diagram plot within the uncertainty of the best-fit line. BY08: Ben-Yosef et al. (2008, strict criteria); BY09: Ben Yosef et al. (2009); S11: Shaar et al. (2011); LAC.v.1.0: Shaar et al. (2016); CCRIT: Criteria of Cromwell et al. (2015)

Criterion	Operation	BY08	BY09	S11	S16 (LACv.1.0)	BY17	CCRIT
β	$\leq$	0.08	0.1	0.055	0.1	0.1	0.1
DRATS	$\leq$	18	20	10			
DANG	$\leq$	7	10	6	10	10	10
f_{VDS}	$\geq$	0.5	0.7	0.8			
MAD	$\leq$	5	10	6	5	5	5
MD%	$\leq$	5	15				
N_{pTRM}	$\geq$	2	2	2	2	2	
q	$\geq$	1.0	1.0				
N_{steps}	$\geq$				4	4	4
FRAC	$\geq$				0.79	0.79	0.78
GAP-MAX	$\leq$				0.5	0.5	0.6
$|\vec{k}'|$	$\leq$						0.164
SCAT	Boolean				True	True	True

Table 2 Site level selection criteria used in Thellier type LAC studies. B_σ (μT): standard deviation of the site level intensity values. B_σ (%): standard deviation of the site intensity values expressed as a percentage of the intensity estimate. N_{spec}: number of specimens used in the site level average

Criterion	Operation	BY08	BY09	S11	LAC.v.1.0	S17	CCRIT
B_σ (μT)	$\leq$	5	5		3	3	4
B_σ (%)	$\leq$	10		6	8	8	10
N_{spec}	$\geq$	3	2	3	3	3	3

site level criteria did yield an acceptable mean of 75.5 ± 7.5 (9.9%) μT owing to the more generous bounds for $\sigma_\%$.

BiCEP (Cych et al., 2021) operates completely differently from the binary selection criteria (accept/reject) approach. It considers all the specimens at a site level, except for those that have no component that goes to the origin (curved Zijderveld diagrams or ones that bypass the origin) or alter during the experiment. BiCEP uses a Monte Carlo Markov Chain and Bayesian statistical approach to find fits for curvature at the specimen level (light green lines in Fig. 2a) which can be translated into intensity estimates with uncertainties in both intensity and curvature (Fig. 2d). Then, by assuming that there is a relationship between curvature and bias in the intensity estimate, best-fit lines through the data points in Fig. 2d give bias-corrected intensity estimates, plotted in the probability density graph shown in Fig. 2e. These give the intensity estimate and credibility (confidence) intervals at the site level. We only consider sites with five or more specimens for analysis with BiCEP. Using all the data without editing or selecting for single components in those specimens that display curved or kinked Zijderveld diagrams gave an estimate of 69–80 μT, which translates to a 1σ error of ~3 μT. Using only the components that trend to the origin (see Fig. 3) we get an answer of 66–77 μT, which is slightly lower, but quite similar within the confidence bounds.

In Fig. 4 we explore the effect of various selection criteria on the evolution of the LAC. The four studies considered here are those of Ben Yosef et al. (2009), Shaar et al. (2011), Shaar et al. (2016), and Ben-Yosef et al. (2017). The original interpretations are shown in Fig. 4a, c, e, and g and the interpretations from the CCRIT and BiCEP approaches are in Fig. 4b, d, f and h.

The most permissive set of selection criteria were those employed by Ben Yosef et al. (2009), resulting in the largest difference between the original (in Fig. 4a) and the re-analyzed interpretations in Fig. 4b). These are plotted against age as estimated in the original study. There are two sites with spike level intensities, but the very high value of 250 ZAm^2 had only two specimens and therefore failed the CCRIT site level criteria.

Starting with the study of Shaar et al. (2011), the criteria were tightened at both the specimen and site levels (see Tables 1 and 2). As a consequence, the comparison between the original interpretations (Fig. 4c) with those selected by the CCRIT and BiCEP criteria (Fig. 4d) are quite similar, with multiple periods of spike level intensities. The same is true for all subsequent studies. That of Shaar et al. (2016) is shown in Fig. 4e,f and that from Ben-Yosef et al. (2017) in Fig. 4g,h.

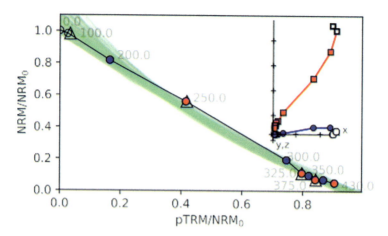

Fig. 3 Example of a multi-component specimen (s2s13-08) from site s2s13. Arai plot same as in Fig. 2a and inset is Zijderveld diagram. White symbols were excluded from the BiCEP analysis

We conclude from the re-analysis exercise that the criteria used in the LACv1.0 of Shaar et al. (2016), Ben-Yosef et al. (2017), CCRIT (Cromwell et al., 2015) (see Tables 1 and 2) give similar results and uncertainty estimates. BiCEP can have the additional advantage of providing estimates for sites that fail because of curved Arai plots for specimens, but in general the site means and uncertainty bounds are similar. Therefore in following we will use the re-analysis of Shaar et al. (2022) in the construction of the current version of the Levantine Archaeomagnetic curve.

4 Uncertainties in Chronology

To be able to build a model of ancient magnetic field behavior, the age of the data points that constrain it must be well determined. Ages in archaeomagnetism come from either the archaeological context or from radiocarbon dating of associated organic materials. We focused our early attention on slag mounds in part because of the abundant potential for radiocarbon dates from the charcoal and even seeds left in them. But radiocarbon is not without problems. Radiocarbon is produced in the atmosphere by bombardment of nitrogen atoms by neutrons in cosmic rays to create the radioactive ^{14}C isotope. This then decays over time back to ^{12}C. The ratio of the two carbon isotopes allows us to estimate the age of the source material. If the cosmic ray flux were constant, this would be a straightforward measurement, but the flux is not constant. It is modulated by the strength of the Earth's magnetic field and the translation from the isotopic ratio to age has 'wiggles' and 'plateaus' resulting in either large age uncertainties or even biomodel distributions. Stillinger et al. (2015) discussed difficulties inherent to radiocarbon dating in the Syrian chronologies which arise from variations in radiocarbon production.

Uncertainties in Archaeointensity Research: Implications for the Levantine... 1765

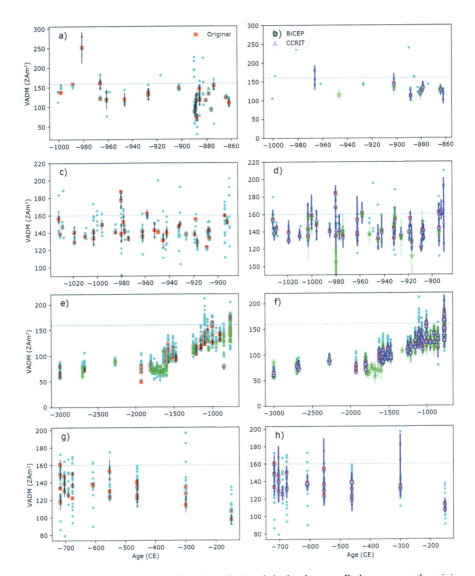

Fig. 4 Specimen level interpretations (cyan dots) and site level means. Red squares are the original estimates and their extended error bars. Blue triangles are those interpretations that pass specimen and site level criteria of Cromwell et al. (2015) (CCRIT). Green stars are BiCEP site level intensities with their Bayesian minimum/maximum intensities (**a**) Data of Ben Yosef et al. (2009) with the original interpretations. (**b**) Same as (**a**) but re-analyzed using CCRIT and BiCEP approaches. (**c**) Same as (**a**) but with data of Shaar et al. (2011); (**d**) Same as (**c**) but re-analyzed using CCRIT and BiCEP approaches. (**e**) Same as (**a**) but with data of Shaar et al. (2016). (**f**) Same as (**e**) but re-analyzed using CCRIT and BiCEP approaches. (**g**) Same as (**a**) but with data of Ben-Yosef et al. (2017). (**h**) Same as (**g**) but re-analyzed using CCRIT and BiCEP

A second difficulty in radiocarbon dating is the age of the organic material itself. When a tree grows, its carbon isotopic ratio is in equilibrium with the atmosphere and when it dies that ratio is fixed. But the age obtained from it will be the age of the tree when it died and not the age it was burned giving rise to the 'old wood effect'. So, if an old tree was burned in a hearth, the date obtained for the burning will be 'too old'. In our efforts, we targeted young wood (twigs) and seeds to avoid this complication. However, many archaeological contexts were dated with different means and the archaeological contexts for different regions may be quite different. This issue was discussed in detail by Shaar et al. (2020) when aligning the Northern and Southern Levantine data sets.

One other issue we must address is the problem of what constitutes an archaeomagnetic 'site', the group of specimens that are averaged as they are assumed to be the same age. Here we have the problem we call the 'old house effect'. Every item in a single archaeological stratum might not actually be the same age. That is why in the foregoing we have averaged specimens from the same fragment and indeed there are many cases in which different fragments (samples) from the same archaeological context give significantly different results. However, in order to construct a regional field model, it is necessary to average out short term fluctuations or experimental 'noise' and avoid over-weighting of horizons with many fragments. While it might be preferable to account for this difficulty with a resampling scheme such that each horizon is weighted equally and the variability reflected in the uncertainty bounds of the curve, the current version of the Levantine Archaeointensity Curve (LACv.1.0) averages the results by context prior to constructing the curve as described in the following.

5 Uncertainties in Regional Model Construction

5.1 The Concept of a Site

In the above sections we outlined the main sources of uncertainties in archaeointensity (i.e. y-axis) and age (i.e., x-axis). In Sect. 3, we concluded that by using a set of modern (post-2010) criteria (e.g. CCRIT, LAC.v.1.0, etc.) and an automatic algorithm-based interpretation technique (e.g. auto-interpreter or BiCEP) the results are similar at the sample (fragment) level. The questions of if and how samples should be averaged at the higher hierarchy—site—should be considered by taking into account the two sources of uncertainty. We consider these questions from a perspective of geomagnetic modeling, recalling that one of the ultimate goals of the LAC is delivering a continuous curve for archaeomagnetic dating. Constructing a geomagnetic curve using the samples' data seems at first to be the most appropriate and straightforward choice because archaeointensity uncertainty at the sample level can be modeled fairly well. Moreover, multiple samples that cover the same age interval provide the time-variability of the field during that time interval, addressing the "old house effect". Nevertheless, there are two main limitations. The first is oversampling and unequal weights: archaeological contexts represented with more samples are given much more weight in the curve model than contexts with fewer samples. The second problem is consideration of data, which were analyzed using methods that cannot be analyzed using the BiCEP or Thellier GUI. We demonstrate this in Fig. 5a that shows in blue symbols samples analyzed with Thellier GUI using LAC.v.1.0 criteria. Other data from Syria, obtained almost exclusively using the Triaxe method are shown in orange. One can see that the two subsets apparently complement each other in a nearly ideal fashion, demonstrating the necessity of using them both for the curve modeling. Yet, these two datasets are essentially different: not only were they produced using different laboratory methods, the Thellier-IZZI data used at least three specimens per sample, while most of the Syrian sites include only one or two specimens per sample. Thus, the archaeointensity error estimations are done in different ways.

Following Gallet et al. (2006), Shaar et al. (2020) adopted a strategy of averaging samples within a 'group' or 'site' (Fig. 5b–c), where a group/site is a collection of samples from the same archaeological context, e.g., locus, archaeological level, slag layer, a structure, etc. There are a number of advantages in averaging samples per group/site: The archaeointensity uncertainty is similar in all data points, and it is simply the standard deviation of the mean; each context is now represented by a single data point, eliminating the problem of oversampling densely sampled contexts; each group/site includes a "built-in" control group, so outlier samples, or extremely scattered groups/sites can be excluded and rejected from further analysis of the curve. The averaging by group/sites "normalizes" the results from Syria and Southern Levant, so now each data point represents the same quantity. The main disadvantages are the "old house" effect discussed above and that the uncertainty of the samples is not propagated to the sites' mean. We note that our current research is focusing on addressing these problems and we hope to more rigorously resolve these issues in our future work.

6 The Levantine Archaeomagnetic Curve (LAC)

Nearly two decades after the first modern archaeomagnetic intensity study of Genevey et al. (2003), a continuously growing amount of data has accumulated to the point where a Levantine curve could be generated. Yet, as discussed above the published datasets were obtained by several laboratories that applied different methods with various sets selection criteria. This leads to a difficulty in rigorously assessing of the total uncertainty of the data—an essential prerequisite in geomagnetic modeling. Shaar et al. (2020) addressed this problem for the time interval between Early Bronze Age (EB) IVB to Late Bronze Age (LB) I (twenty-third to fifteen centuries BCE) and concluded that unless the complete measurement data are uploaded to the MagIC database (https://www.earthref.org/MagIC), there is no practical way to quantify archaeointensity errors. The data, which were available in

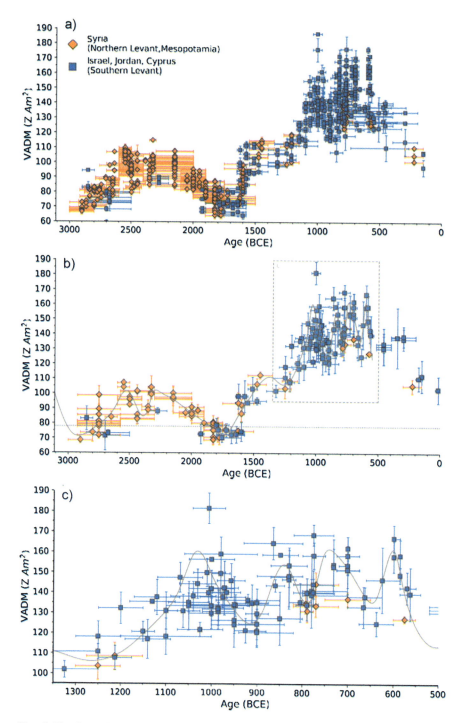

Fig. 5 The Levantine archaeomagnetic intensity curve (LAC.v.1.0) (Shaar et al., 2022). (**a**) Compilation of fragments passing acceptance criteria. (**b–c**) Compilation of sites as averaged here, passing acceptance criteria. The AH-RJMCMC Bayesian curve is shown in gray. (**c**) Interval of the LAC with four geomagnetic spikes

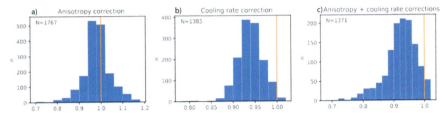

Fig. 6 Histograms of corrections on the data in the LAC. (**a**) Anisotropy corrections. (**b**) Cooling rate corrections. (**c**) Combined anisotropy and cooling rate corrections

MagIC, were re-analyzed using the Thellier_GUI tool and a set of criteria that includes, in addition to the ones in Tables 1 and 2, additional criteria about the anisotropy and cooling rate corrections. The latter was found to be important because these corrections can change the final results by a factor of up to 20% (Fig. 6). Shaar et al. (2020) also concluded that samples' data from Syria, that are not in the MagIC database and obtained using the Triaxe method (Le Goff & Gallet, 2004; Gallet & Le Goff, 2006) and the Coe method with the criteria of Genevey et al. (2003) can be considered as reliable and comparable to the IZZI data described here because these two methods were tested against each other and against the IZZI method. Following Shaar et al. (2020), Shaar et al. (2022) re-calculated all the Thellier-IZZI data published to date using the LAC.v.1.0 criteria (Ben Yosef et al., 2009; Ben-Yosef et al., 2017; Shaar et al., 2011, 2015, 2016, 2020, 2022; Vaknin et al., 2020, 2022) and compiled all the relevant Triaxe and the Coe-method data (Genevey et al., 2003; Gallet and Le Goff, 2006; Gallet et al., 2008, 2014; Gallet and Butterlin, 2015; Gallet et al., 2020; Livermore et al., 2021). This so-called LAC compilation includes to date 343 Thellier-IZZI samples and 383 Thellier-Coe/Triaxe samples (Fig. 5a), averaged by sites/groups (Fig. 5b–c).

The final step in constructing the LAC is calculating a continuous curve. Following Gallet et al. (2020), Shaar et al. (2020, 2022) applied the AH-RJMCMC (Age-hyperparameter reverse-jump Monte Carlo Markov Chain) algorithm of Livermore et al. (2018). The details behind this Bayesian approach are beyond the scope of this review paper, but we would like to highlight some of its properties. The algorithm is based on piece-wise linear extrapolation between vertices, drawn in a random-walk like perturbation within a space permitted by a likelihood function, which is calculated directly from the errors of the LAC data points. The AH-RJMCMC does not assume any prior assumption regarding the amplitude and frequency of field changes, and in this sense it is "objective". The LAC (compilation and curve) is defined as an in-progress project. Shaar et al. (2022) presented the first version, i.e. LAC.v.1.0, and after each new archaeointensity publication, LAC will be updated with the new data. LAC.v.1.0 provides quantitative robust description of at least four spikes (Fig. 5c), demonstrates that although the averaging scheme by sites/groups is theoretically expected to smooth high-frequency changes, in practice, dense and adequate sampling strategy such as, for example, Vaknin et al. (2022), leads to a curve that enhances the details of fast geomagnetic changes. It also resolves previous debates regarding the reliability of spikes (Livermore et al., 2021).

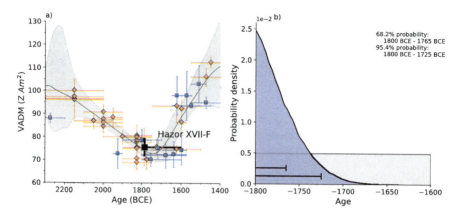

Fig. 7 Example of archaeomagnetic dating (after Shaar et al., 2020). (**a**) LAC.v.1.0 with stratum Hazor XVII-F (lower level in Hazor Middle Bronze strata) highlighted in black. Prior ages are between 1800 to 1600 BCE, reflecting age uncertainty in archaeological dating. (**b**) Archaeomagnetic dating showing the prior age as gray uniform distribution and the posterior ages in blue. The available archaeomagnetic data (mainly from Mari and Ebla) suggest an earlier age to the beginning of Hazor Middle Bronze settlement

As a concluding remark, we would like to highlight the application of the Levantine Archaeomagnetic Curve and the future generations of this curve for archaeomagnetic dating. One of the outputs of the Bayesian model is an age posterior distribution for each of the data points in the LAC compilation. Figure 7 demonstrates the concept of archaeomagnetic dating using LAC. Additional examples can be found in Vaknin et al. (2022) and in Chapter 34 in this book.

The archaeomagnetic journey we took with Prof. Levy, starting with the work on the slag mounds in Jordan, Israel, and Cyprus is still continuing to day, with new generation of students in archaeomagnetism that follow the footsteps of our colleague, teacher, and collaborator.

Acknowledgments This work was supported in part by BSF Grant 2018305 to LT and EB-Y.

References

Aitken, M., Alcock, P., Bussel, G., & Shaw, C. (1981). Archaeomagnetic determination of the past geomagnetic intensity using ancient ceramics: allowance for anisotropy. *Archaeometry*, *23*, 53–64.

Ben-Yosef, E., Millman, M., Shaar, R., Tauxe, L., & Lipschits, O. (2017). Six centuries of geomagnetic intensity variations recorded by royal Judean stamped jar handles. *Proceedings of the National Academy of Sciences, 114*, 2160. https://doi.org/10.1073/pnas.1615797114

Ben Yosef, E., Tauxe, L., Levy, T., Shaar, R., Ron, H., & Najjar, M. (2009). Archaeomagnetic intensity spike recorded in high resolution slag deposit from historical biblical archaeology site in southern Jordan. *Earth and Planetary Science Letters, 287*, 529–539.

Ben-Yosef, E., Tauxe, L., Ron, H., Agnon, A., Avner, U., Najjar, M., & Levy, T. (2008). A new approach for geomagnetic archeointensity research: insights on ancient metallurgy in the southern levant. *Journal of Archaeological Science, 35* , 2863–2879.

Cai, S., Jin, G., Tauxe, L., Deng, C., Qin, H., Pan, Y., & Zhu, R. (2017). Archaeointensity results spanning the past 6 kiloyears from eastern China and implications for extreme behaviors of the geomagnetic field. *Proceedings of the National Academy of Sciences, 114*, 39–44. https://doi.org/10.1073/pnas.1616976114

Campuzano, S., Gómez-Paccard, M., Pavón-Carrasco, F., & Osete, M. (2019). Emergence and evolution of the south Atlantic anomaly revealed by the new paleomagnetic reconstruction shawq2k. *Earth and Planetary Science Letters, 512* , 17–26. https://doi.org/10.1016/j.epsl.2019.01.050

Coe, R. S., Grommé, S., & Mankinen, E. A. (1978). Geomagnetic paleointensities from radiocarbon-dated lava flows on Hawaii and the question of the pacific nondipole low. *Journal of Geophysical Research: Solid Earth, 83*, 1740–1756.

Constable, C., Korte, M., & Panovska, S. (2016). Persistent high paleosecular variation activity in southern hemisphere for at least 10,000 years. *Earth and Planetary Science Letters, 453*, 78–86.

Cromwell, G., Tauxe, L., Staudigel, H., & Ron, H. (2015). Paleointensity estimates from historic and modern Hawaiian lava flows using basaltic volcanic glass as a primary source material. *Physics of the Earth and Planetary Interiors, 241* , 44–56. https://doi.org/10.1016/j.pepi.2014.12.007

Cych, B., Morzfeld, M., & Tauxe, L. (2021). Bias corrected estimation of paleointensity (BiCEP): An improved methodology for obtaining paleointensity estimates. *Geochemistry Geophysics Geosystems* , 22, e2021GC009755. https://doi.org/10.1002/2021GC009755

Di Chiara, A., Tauxe, L., Levy, T., Najjar, M., Florindo, F., & Ben-Yosef, E. (2021). The strength of the Earth's magnetic field from Pre-pottery to Pottery Neolithic, Jordan. *Proceedings of the National Academy of Sciences, 118*, e2100995118. https://doi.org/10.1073/pnas.2100995118

Di Chiara, A., Tauxe, L., & Speranza, F. (2014). Paleointensity determination from São Miguel (Azores Archipelago) over the last 3 ka. *Physics of the Earth and Planetary Interiors, 234*, 1–13.

Ertepinar, P., Langereis, C., Biggin, A., Frangipane, M., Matney, T., Ökse, T., & Engin, A. (2012). Archaeomagnetic study of five mounds from upper mesopotamia between 2500 and 700 be: Further evidence for an extremely strong geomagnetic field ca. 3000 years ago. *Earth and Planetary Science Letters, 357–358*, 84–98. https://doi.org/10.1016/j.epsl.2012.08.039

Gallet, Y. (2021). The dawn of archeomagnetic dating. *Comptes Rendus Géoschiece, 353*, 285–296. https://doi.org/10.5802/crgeos.73

Gallet, Y., & Butterlin, P. (2015). Archaeological and geomagnetic implications of new archaeomagnetic intensity data from the early bronze high terrace "massif rouge" at Mari (Tell Hariri, Syria). *Archaeometry, 57*, 263–276. Retrieved from <Go to ISI>://WOS:000357017400016

Gallet, Y., D'Andrea, M., Genevey, A., Pinnock, F., Le Goff, M., & Matthiae, P. (2014). Archaeomagnetism at Ebla (Tell Mardikh, Syria). New data on geomagnetic field intensity variations in the near east during the bronze age. *Journal of Archaeological Science, 42*, 295–304.

Gallet, Y., Fortin, M., Fournier, A., Le Goff, M., & Livermore, P. (2020). Analysis of geomagnetic field intensity variations in mesopotamia during the third millennium bc with archeological implications [Journal Article]. *Earth and Planetary Science Letters, 537* . Retrieved from <Go to ISI>://WOS:000525394700010. ARTN 116183. https://doi.org/10.1016/j.epsl.2020.116183

Gallet, Y., Genevey, A., Le Goff, M., Fluteau, F., & Ali Eshraghi, S. (2006). Possible impact of the Earth's magnetic field on the history of ancient civilizations. *Earth and Planetary Science Letters, 246*, 17–26.

Gallet, Y., & Le Goff, M. (2006). High-temperature archeointensity measurements from mesopotamia. *Earth and Planetary Science Letters, 241*, 159–173.

Gallet, Y., Le Goff, M., Genevey, A., Margueron, J., & Matthiae, P. (2008). Geomagnetic field intensity behavior in the Middle East between similar to 3000 BC and similar to 1500 BC. *Geophysical Research Letters, 35*(2). Retrieved from <Go to ISI>:// WOS:000252751700001. https://doi.org/10.1029/2007gl031991

Genevey, A., Gallet, Y., & Margueron, J. (2003). Eight thousand years of geomagnetic field intensity variations in the eastern Mediterranean. *Journal of Geophysical Research: Solid Earth, 108*. https://doi.org/10.1029/2001JB001612

Gómez-Paccard, M., Osete, M., Chauvin, A., Pavón-Carrasco, F., Pérez-Asensio, M., Jiménez, P., & Lanos, P. (2016). New constraints on the most significant paleointensity change in Western Europe over the last two millennia. A non-dipolar origin? *Earth and Planetary Science Letters, 454*, 55–64. https://doi.org/10.1016/j.epsl.2016.08.024

Halgedahl, S., Day, R., & Fuller, M. (1980). The effect of cooling rate on the intensity of weak-field TRM in single-domain magnetite. *Journal of Geophysical Research: Solid Earth, 85 ,* 3690–3698.

Hervé, G., Fasbinder, J., Gilder, S., Metzner-Nebelsick, C., Gallet, Y., Genevey, A., et al. (2017). Fast geomagnetic field intensity variations between 1400 and 400 BCE: New archaeointensity data from Germany. *Physics of the Earth and Planet Interiors, 270*, 143–156. https://doi.org/10.1016/j.pepi.2017.07.002

Koenigsberger, J. (1938). Natural residual magnetism of eruptive rocks, pt I, pt II. *Terrestrial Magnetism and Atmospheric Electricity, 43*, 119–127;299–320.

Korte, M., & Constable, C. (2005). Continuous geomagnetic field models for the past 7 millennia: 2. cals7k. *Geochemistry, Geophysics, Geosystems, 6*, Q02H16. https://doi.org/10.1029/2004GC000801

Krása, D., Heunemann, C., Leonhardt, R., & Petersen, N. (2003). Experimental procedure to detect multidomain remanence during Thellier-Thellier experiments. *Physics and Chemistry of the Earth, Parts A/B/C, 28 ,* 681–687. https://doi.org/10.1016/S1474-7065(03)00122-0

Le Goff, M., & Gallet, Y. (2004). A new three-axis vibrating sample magnetometer for continuous high-temperature magnetization measurements: applications to paleo- and archeo-intensity determinations. *Earth and Planetary Science Letters, 229*(1–2), 31–43.

Levy, T., Higham, T., Bronk-Ramsey, C., Smith, N., Ben-Yosef, E., Robinson, M., et al. (2008). High precision radiocarbon dating and historical biblical archaeology in southern Jordan. *Proceedings of the National Academy of Science, 105*, 16460–16465. https://doi.org/10.1073/pnas.0804950105

Livermore, P., Fournier, A., & Gallet, Y. (2014). Core-flow constraints on extreme archeomagnetic intensity changes. *Earth and Planetary Science Letters, 387*, 145–156. https://doi.org/10.1016/j.epsl.2013.11.020

Livermore, P., Gallet, Y., & Fournier, A. (2021). Archeomagnetic intensity variations during the era of geomagnetic spikes. *Physics of the Earth and Planetary Interiors, 312*, 106657. https://doi.org/10.1016/j.pepi.2021.106657

Livermore, P. W., Fournier, A., Gallet, Y., & Bodin, T. (2018). Transdimensional inference of archeomagnetic intensity change. *Geophysical Journal International, 215*(3), 2008–2034. Retrieved from <Go to ISI>://WOS:000456615200037. https://doi.org/10.1093/gji/ggy383

Mitra, R., Tauxe, L., & McIntosh, S. (2013). Two thousand years of archeointensity from West Africa. *Earth and Planetary Science Letters, 364*, 123–133.

Nagata, T., Arai, Y., & Momose, K. (1963). Secular variation of the geomagnetic total force during the last 5000 years. *Journal of Geophysical Research: Solid Earth, 68*, 5277–5282.

Nagy, L., Williams, W., & Tauxe, L. (2021). Estimating the effect of cooling rate on the acquisition of magnetic remanence. *Journal of Geophysical Research: Solid Earth, 48*, e2021GL095284. https://doi.org/10.1029/2021GL095284

Nagy, L., Williams, W., Tauxe, L., & Muxworthy, A. (2022). Chasing tails: Insights from micromagnetic modeling for thermomagnetic recording in non-uniform magnetic structures. *Geophysical Research Letters, 49*, e2022GL101032.

Néel, L. (1949). Théorie du trainage magnétique des ferromagneétiques en grains fines avec applications aux terres cuites. *Annales de Géophysique, 5* , 99–136.

Osete, M., Molina-Cardín, A., Campuzano, S. A., Aguilella-Arzo, G., Barrachina-Ibañez, A., Falomir-Granell, F., Oliver Foix, A., Gómez-Paccard, M., et al. (2020). Two archaeomagnetic intensity maxima and rapid directional variation rates during the early iron age observed at iberian coordinates. implications on the evolution of the levantine iron age anomaly. *Earth and Planetary Science Letters, 533*, 116047. https://doi.org/10.1016/j.epsl.2019.116047

Paterson, G., Biggin, A., Yammamoto, Y., & Pan, Y. (2012). Towards the robust selection of Thellier-type paleointensity data: The influence of experimental noise. *Geochemistry Geophysics Geosystems, 13*(5). https://doi.org/10.1029/2012GC004046

Paterson, G., Tauxe, L., Biggin, A., Shaar, R., & Jonestrask, L. (2014). On improving the selection of Thellier-type paleointensity data. *Geochemistry Geophysics Geosystems, 15*(4), 1180. https://doi.org/10.1002/2013GC005135

Selkin, P., Gee, J. S., & Tauxe, L. (2007). Nonlinear thermoremanence acquisition and implications for paleointensity data. *Earth and Planetary Science Letters, 256*, 81–89.

Shaar, R., Bechar, S., Finkelstein, I., Gallet, Y., Martine, M., Ebert, Y., et al. (2020). Synchronizing geomagnetic field intensity records in the Levant between the 23rd and 15th centuries BCE: chronological and methodological implications. *Geochemistry Geophysics Geosystems, 21*, e2020GC009251. https://doi.org/10.1029/2020GC009251

Shaar, R., Ben Yosef, E., Ron, H., Tauxe, L., Agnon, A., & Kessel, R. (2011). Geomagnetic field intensity: How high can it get? How fast can it change? Constraints from iron-age copper-slag. *Earth and Planetary Science Letters, 301*, 297–306. https://doi.org/10.1016/j.epsl.2010.11.013

Shaar, R., Gallet, Y., Vaknin, Y., Gonen, L., Martin, M., Adams, M.J., & Finkelstein, I. (2022). Archaeomagnetism in Levant and Mesopotamia reveals the largest changes in the geomagnetic field. *Journal of Geophysics, 127*, e2022JB02492. https://doi.org/10.1029/2022JB024962

Shaar, R., & Tauxe, L. (2013). Thellier GUI: An integrated tool for analyzing paleointensity data from Thellier-type experiments. *Geochemistry, Geophysics, Geosystems, 14*, 677–692. https://doi.org/10.1002/ggge.20062

Shaar, R., Tauxe, L., Ben-Yosef, E., Kassianidou, V., Lorentzen, B., Feinberg, J. M., & Levy, T. (2015). Decadal-scale variations in geomagnetic field intensity from ancient Cypriot slag mounds. *Geochemistry, Geophysics, Geosystems, 16*. https://doi.org/10.1002/2014GC005455

Shaar, R., Tauxe, L., Ron, H., Ebert, Y., Zuckerman, S., Finkelstein, I., & Agnon, A. (2016). Large geomagnetic field anomalies revealed in bronze to iron age archeomagnetic data from Tel Megiddo and Tel Hazor, Israel. *Earth and Planetary Science Letters, 442*, 173–185. https://doi.org/10.1016/j.epsl.2016.02.038

Stillinger, J., M.D. nad Feinberg, & Frahm, E. (2015). Refining the archaeomagnetic dating curve for the Near East: new intensity data from Bronze Age ceramics at Tell Mozan, Syria. *Journal of Archaeological Science, 53*, 345–355. https://doi.org/10.1016/j.jas.2014.10.025

Tauxe, L., Santos, C., Cych, B., Zhao, X., Roberts, A., Nagy, L., & Williams, W. (2021). Understanding non-ideal paleointensity recording in igneous rocks: Insights from aging experiments on lava samples and the causes and consequences of 'fragile' curvature in Arai plots. *Geochemistry, Geophysics, Geosystems, 22*, e2020GC009423. https://doi.org/10.1029/2020GC009423

Tauxe, L., Shaar, R., Jonestrask, L., Swanson-Hysell, N., Minnett, R., Koppers, A. A. P., et al. (2016). Pmagpy: Software package for paleomagnetic data analysis and a bridge to the magnetics information consortium (magic) database. *Geochemistry, Geophysics, Geosystems, 17*. https://doi.org/10.1002/2016GC006307

Thellier, E., & Thellier, O. (1959). Sur l'intensité du champ magnétique terrestre dans le passé historique et géologique. *Annales de Géophysique, 15*, 285–378.

Vaknin, Y., Shaar, R., Gadot, Y., Shalev, Y., Lipschits, O., & Ben-Yosef, E. (2020). The Earth's magnetic field in Jerusalem during the babylonian destruction: A unique reference for field behavior and an anchor for archaeomagnetic dating. *Plos One, 15*(8). Retrieved from <Go to ISI>://WOS:000561029000017. ARTN e0237029. https://doi.org/10.1371/journal.pone.0237029

Vaknin, Y., Shaar, R., Lipschits, O., Mazar, A., Maeir, A., Garfinkel, Y., et al. (2022). Reconstructing biblical military campaigns using geomagnetic field data. *Proceedings of the National Academy of Sciences, 119*(44), e2209117119.

Yamamoto, Y., Tauxe, L., Ahn, H., & Santos, C. (2022). Absolute paleointensity experiments on aged thermoremanent magnetization: assessment of reliability of the Tsunakawa-Shaw and other methods with implications for 'fragile' curvature. *Geochemistry, Geophysics, Geosystems*, in review.

Yu, Y., Tauxe, L., & Genevey, A. (2004). Toward an optimal geomagnetic field intensity determination technique. *Geochemistry, Geophysics, Geosystems, 5*(2), Q02H07. https://doi.org/10.1029/2003GC000630

Zijderveld, J. D. A. (1967). *A.C. demagnetization of rocks: Analysis of results*. Chapman and Hall.

Part VII
Anthropological Archaeology in the Southern Levant and Beyond

Tom and Alina Levy in the Swamimalai hereditary bronze workshop in southern India (2007), with members of the Sthapathy family. (Photo courtesy of Tom Levy)

More than Antiquity: How Archaeologists See

Raphael Greenberg

Abstract I attempt to characterize the shared foundations of archaeology, in light of the significant fragmentation of the discipline, the expansion of its chronological reach from deep antiquity to the present and of its scale and resolution from micro to macro, and the urgent call for its decolonization. I briefly explore the intersections of archaeological practice with the archaeosphere, temporality, memory, and archive, and locate the inflection point of personal values in the interface between archaeological epistemology—how archaeologists see and interpret the world—and praxis—how they go about creating the archaeological record.

Keywords Archaeological epistemology · Archaeosphere · Temporality · Archive · Memory · Forgetting

1 Introduction

If we follow the standard histories of Levantine archaeology, the generation of archaeologists who came of age in the late 1970s—a generation to which both the author and this volume's honoree belong—has seen the field transformed by several "paradigm shifts," moving from a focus on biblical culture history, to one on field method and data accumulation, to more explicit concerns with social evolution, and then to a close alliance with sciences and big data. The chapters of P.R.S. Moorey's *A Century of Biblical Archaeology* (Moorey, 1992) take us from "New Nations, New Methods" (after WWII), to "The Passing of the Old Order" (in the early 1980s), and finally to "The Growing Impact of Natural and Social Sciences" (early 1990s).

The original version of the chapter has been revised. A correction to this chapter can be found at https://doi.org/10.1007/978-3-031-27330-8_83

See = Apprehend, discern, grasp, understand, realize, know, form an opinion.

R. Greenberg (✉)
Tel Aviv University, Tel Aviv, Israel
e-mail: grafi@tauex.tau.ac.il

© The Author(s), under exclusive license to Springer Nature
Switzerland AG 2023, corrected publication 2023
E. Ben-Yosef, I. W. N. Jones (eds.), *"And in Length of Days Understanding" (Job 12:12): Essays on Archaeology in the Eastern Mediterranean and Beyond in Honor of Thomas E. Levy*, Interdisciplinary Contributions to Archaeology, https://doi.org/10.1007/978-3-031-27330-8_75

Eric Cline's popular introduction to Biblical Archaeology identifies a series of transformations, including a "precise method of stratigraphical excavation", the adoption of elements of archaeology as "a 'hard' science" in the later decades of the twentieth century, and, finally, the use of "advanced detection techniques," which are poised to revolutionize archaeological practice in the new millennium (Cline, 2009, Part I). Tom Levy (2018), sees microarchaeology, mathematic modelling, and the informatics that inform "cyber-archaeology" as the key to the control of time and space that will make Levantine archaeology a key player in global archaeology. These resumes of the field are all predisposed to a positivistic, evolutionary reading of the discipline and tend to downplay the complicated relationships between archaeological praxis and varying types of colonialisms, nationalisms and economic regimes that have shaped the field in their image. Significant recent initiatives to decolonize the archaeology of the Levant have led, among other things, to the revision of archaeological histories (e.g. Corbett, 2015; Greenberg & Hamilakis, 2022; Mickel, 2021) and to the renaming of major institutions like the American Schools of Oriental Research (now the American Society of Overseas Research), and the Oriental Institutes at Cambridge and Chicago.

Beyond the transformations that the discipline has experienced, many of us have led a nomadic existence within archaeology, moving from region to region, site to site, period to period, and from one institution to another. A few of us have crossed the traditional temporal boundaries of archaeology in the Levant, engaging with community-based archaeology and democratization, and wading deep into archaeology in and of the contemporary world. We have seen our discipline become seemingly fragmented and highly specialized and, insofar as conferences are still attended, we have experienced them either as mega-events that are broken up into many specialized sub-sections, or as highly selective seminars attended by scholars of like interests. It may thus be a fair question to ask: What, if anything, holds archaeology together, over time and space? Is there something that still might be considered the core of a shared discipline?

In honoring an archaeologist who has embraced innovation and new perspectives from the days of his late 1970s fieldwork in the Negev desert and right up to his recent commitment to "transdisciplinary" cyber-archaeology, I would like to attempt an identification of the ways of seeing (discerning, understanding) the world that appear to be shared across the many bifurcations of our discipline and the scales at which it is practiced. Through dialogue with recent attempts to redefine "the archaeological" (Nativ, 2017), and by means of a review of several fundamental concepts such as *temporality*, with its corollaries of duration and decay, *memory* and the related binaries of inclusion and exclusion, erasure and preservation, *archive* and the archaeological record itself, I will try to characterize an archaeological epistemology and a creative praxis that is not so much about the past, as it is about defining a vision of the present for the future: we archaeologists, as a group, still see things differently from others.

Finding this common denominator is especially urgent in view of the twenty-first century decolonial project: It is imperative to understand what will remain of archaeology once it is finally detached from the modernist colonial and imperial mindsets in which it was engendered, and to reimagine its appeal. As I will attempt to show, an archaeological epistemology can be imagined in which morality and politics, beyond the commitment to confronting what others might prefer to hide and preserving that which they wish to demolish, appear to play a minor role. But putting such an epistemology into practice, through the creation and interpretation of archaeological archives, requires us to acknowledge and give scope to the values that motivate us.

2 What Archaeologists Share

2.1 An Archaeological Universe

Elaborated by Edgeworth (2016) and by Nativ and Lucas (2020), the concept of "archaeosphere" offers a catholic definition of what it is that archaeologists study: everything that has been, is, or will be created or altered by humans, primarily (but not necessarily) on planet Earth. This would extend from stones shifted to accommodate a fire in the Early Paleolithic to microplastics impacting a desert island in the Pacific Ocean, and to anything in between. In other words, the material products of human agency. If that sounds like a lot, let's keep in mind that this is the reservoir of things given to archaeological study, not what each individual archaeologist might be required to address. It points to nearly unconstrained potential in terms of time-frames—from deep prehistory to the present (which is the past of the immediate future)—and resolution of study, which can range from the molecular to the molar, or from the singular actant (e.g., an individual's DNA) to the behavioral patterns of a populations of millions. This inclusive definition allows the coexistence within archaeology of disparate specializations, fields of interest, institutional and economic frameworks and methodologies that may often be incompatible: micro- and macro-archaeologies; contract archaeology and indigenous heritage initiatives; tourism infrastructure projects and forensic investigations of sites of mass murder or incarceration.

As a corollary of this definition, the objects of archaeological study are not to be confused with "antiquities". They may very well be ancient, but since the production of "stuff" (and its archaeological incarnation, junk)[1] has accelerated greatly in recent decades, the proportion of materials in the archaeosphere produced in the last 100 years outweighs everything that came before it in millions of years of human existence, and there is no other field exclusively devoted to its study, that is, to the study not only of the products of human culture but of their materialization as refuse and as residue. The potential of archaeology is, therefore, boundless, nor is it limited to the activities of the "one percent," in highly technologized, well-funded and prestigious elite research centers. On the contrary, a broadly conceived

---

[1] Or "kipple", to cite Philip K. Dick's unforgettable term.

archaeosphere opens up to a potentially democratized field of study and practice that can expand well beyond the traditional centers.

Defining the archaeosphere, while necessary to the delineation of the scope of archaeological epistemologies, is not yet sufficient to characterize them; the next section discusses the peculiar lens through which archaeologists view the objects of their desire: the lens of time, abandonment and decay.

2.2 An Acute Sense of Temporality

All archaeological objects—whether visible on the surface, curated in collections, or exhumed by excavation—exist in the present: what is absent cannot be studied. That said, archaeologists are carefully attuned to—not to say obsessed by—temporality (or temporalities), entropy and decay, the ghosts of what has gone missing, and the palimpsests forged by the co-presence of things and traces of different times (e.g., Bailey, 2008; Hamilakis, 2017; Lucas, 2005; Olivier, 2011). When we look at a landscape or townscape, an abandoned lot or a pattern of fields and fences, we see it as it is now but also as it once might have been. Every assemblage that we approach is composed of objects, structures, and larger features that carry with them their individual histories of creation, use, abandonment and decomposition; each carries its own temporality—the pace and duration of its "biography". Each assemblage reflects a fleeting coming-together of these disparate temporalities—a coming together that we might imagine as a fortuitous convergence in time and space.

A classic exposition of such a temporal co-incidence is Laurent Olivier's description of the sixth century BCE Hochdorf tomb in southwest Germany (Olivier, 1999), where an assemblage of personal effects and material representations of social and cultural affinities and status serve almost as a snapshot of momentary associations and superimposed intentions. These are deftly woven by Olivier into a narrative of overlapping cycles, durations, and life-histories. Thus, the tomb group itself is composed of materials (some physically preserved, others disintegrated and represented only by gaps, voids, and imprints) prepared ahead of inhumation, objects associated with the burial ceremony, and those introduced into the tomb after inhumation, but before it was sealed. Then, within each of these groups, there are "old" objects (such as those that were used, worn or wielded by the deceased) and "new" objects, produced or acquired for the ceremony. Moreover, the construction of the tomb and the disposition of the body and associated artifacts could be placed in their cultural temporality, some associated with long-standing funerary traditions of central Europe and others with recently adopted Mediterranean banqueting practices. By adopting a perspectival view of time– each object has a different "pace", governed by its materiality, by its place in a stylistic tradition, or by the accidents of its ownership and use—archaeologists unpack the assemblage as given to them (i.e., everything in the tomb, on a single plane, at the time of its discovery) and rearrange it in its multiple dimensions.

The same concerns, though in an utterly different setting and scale, can be seen in an exercise in contemporary archaeology conducted by Tel Aviv University students and myself in a 2021 seminar: Together, we examined the temporality evident in the buildings, pedestrian paths and streets, and topography of the Tel Aviv University campus, superimposed, as it is, over the wadi-beds, fields, orchards and house-plots of the Palestinian village of al-Shaykh Muwannis, depopulated in 1948 and then reoccupied as the peripheral Tel-Aviv neighborhood of "Sheikh Munis." What interested us, as archaeologists, were not so much the occasional surviving buildings or facades from the earlier settlements, but the way the earlier—now ostensibly invisible—elements of the village and its topography continue to make themselves present in building orientations, in the location of streets and campus gateways, or in the aesthetics of landscaping. While nowhere acknowledged on the campus itself, these palimpsests—faint traces of earlier lives and values that often have no clear function or demonstrable expression in the present—are there to be observed; once pointed out by archaeologists, they can no longer be ignored (Figs. 1 and 2). In addition to this superposition, we also examined the juxtaposition of campus buildings of different ages, noting how their relative size and the sequence of their construction reflects changes in the values espoused by the university itself, from a now-forgotten focus on the humanities and natural sciences to one on technology, computational science, and entrepreneurship.

Unlike historians, archaeologists work primarily with material objects, and unlike the students of materiality in the social sciences, or architects who structure our built environment, we always begin from the present and work our way back, looking primarily at things that have stopped functioning and unraveling the precise sequence (the stratigraphy and chronology) of their temporal relations. This focus on things and places that have lost or left their systemic context, the living framework that gave them their meaning when they were first formed, takes us to the next characterization of the archaeological project.

2.3 A Commitment to Memory-Work

Archaeologists work against the grain of modernity, countering its many projects of forgetting, which include the forgetting embedded in capitalist development, consumption and production; the forgetting embedded in nation-building; and the forgetting embedded in projects of ethnic homogenization and purification. Before modernity, archaeology as currently practiced did not exist: there certainly were appreciations of the past and of its remnants, speculations on the role of ancient objects and ruined buildings, value attached to things that embodied extended temporalities and that were often incorporated in contemporary buildings and objects. But these were not encoded in an independent *discipline*, whose existence is owed, paradoxically, to the "modern constitution" (Latour, 1993), where things and places must be specifically designated as antique or ancient if they are to be separated from the present and possibly spared destruction. As originally conceived, therefore,

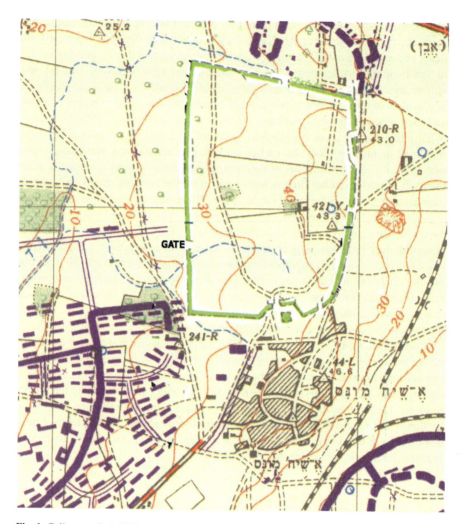

Fig. 1 Palimpsest I: A 1961 map detail of the (then) future site of the Tel Aviv University campus, with new Israeli construction over-printed in purple on the previous topography and the depopulated-repopulated village of Al-Shaykh Muwannis (hatched). The green outline of the campus, which tracks parts of the old topography and plot divisions, has been superimposed by the author

archaeology was constituted by moderns to save modernity from a self-annihilation inflicted by the devouring of its own past.

But it is not only the buried and distant past, designated by antiquities laws, that needs to be recovered. Connerton (1989, 2009) notes many forms of forgetting that are peculiar to modernity: the forgetting of labor, both in industrial products and in romanticized conceptions of landscape, the forgetting of nature, the forgetting of place (and its sensations) and of itineraries (memory routes), the forgetting of pre-national identities (a forgetting and social homogenization that Ernest Renan

Fig. 2 Palimpsest II: The Tel Aviv University campus under construction, 1970s, from the north, with remnants of earlier structures and topography still visible beneath it. At top left, the site of the future Faculty of Engineering is marked on the village buildings, tracking their orientation, which is oblique to that of the main campus. (Photo courtesy of the Tel Aviv University archives)

described as a prerequisite for the emergence of a nation), and of social obligations (the dominance of terminal transactions). How are these relevant to archaeology? These are precisely the aspects of memory that archaeologists activate when they study the entanglement of human and non-human agents (the "natural" environment), the ecology of food production, the chaîne opèratoire of material production, the web of social obligations of which economic and social relations are constructed, or the multiple meanings and temporalities of places and landmarks.

Similar consideration may be offered to the forms of forgetting that Gonzalez-Ruibal (2019) attributes to "supermodernity": ruination, disaggregation, forms of abjection that are rendered invisible through intentional concealment (sewage, garbage, marginalization, eviction, places of mass incarceration, enslavement, murder and genocide). The archaeological practice of "revealing" (excavating, recovering, recording) is uniquely placed to counter the losses of memory that are constantly incurred in our world, creating evidence "that no witness could have observed" (Gonzalez-Ruibal, 2019: 21). We literally wallow in ruins and garbage, seek out abandoned places, forensically examine theatres of conflict and death in the deep, historic or recent past.

Lastly, there is what Nativ and Lucas (2020) call "engage[ment] in future-making practices": Because the materials of archaeology are all in the multitemporal present, the memories that we activate are in the present as well, relying on an active transformation of the past; it is memory-work that constructs the narratives and assemblages that receive the moniker of "heritage." Here there intrudes the delicate question of selectivity: Whose memory? Whose heritage? Who is included and who is excluded? How do we avoid becoming the means to implement new forms of intentional forgetting and purification? These are matters, underdetermined by the discipline itself, that need to be addressed by each archaeologist on their own.

2.4 Labor: Creating the Archive

The basis of all archaeological knowledge is labor and the act of retrieval and recording. If nothing else, archaeologists are willing workers: they will go to extraordinary lengths to physically inhabit—and often, indeed, to possess or be possessed by—the places that they survey or excavate (Butler, 2020), to extract the objects of study, to record them and often to convey them to storage. These are practices that demand funding and organizational skills, as well as an aptitude for real-world interactions. In the past, these lengths were subsumed in colonial and imperial projects, with archaeologists—primarily white males—embarking on voyages of "discovery" at the edges of civilization or accompanying military expeditions and depositing their spoils in the vaults of imperial museums or state and institutional collections. This invasive, domineering, extractive, and masculinized topography of research is slowly disappearing, and frontiers are no longer defined solely by their distance from the metropole or by the dangers attendant on reaching them (although this is still one of the chief selling points of archaeology as a consumer product). We now recognize that the previously inaccessible (or simply unaccessed) may be much nearer to home, whether residing in new technologies of recovery or in the study of places, periods and cultures that were previously ignored or deemed unworthy of interest.

Regardless of the locus of their activity and of the techniques they use to recover, visualize or otherwise sense and experience the objects of study, archaeologists construct formalized collections of evidence, physical and virtual, that comprise the "archaeological record." These include masses of objects and data whose accumulation is determined by contemporary norms of "good practice" as well as by whatever is deemed relevant to a broad range of questions that might be put to the evidence, often extending beyond the immediate competences of the excavation team and including materials and records that have no apparent significance. Because recording and storage capabilities are increasing exponentially, the databases and collections have taken on characteristics of archives, what Aleida Assman (2008: 102) has called "the basis of what can be said in the future about the present when it will have become the past." In Assman's formulation (2008: 103), the archive, in contrast to the canon, contains masses of "passive" or "inert" knowledge. "It is stored and potentially available, but it is not interpreted. This would exceed the competence of the archivist." This calls to mind the classic, "Indiana Jones" vision of the untapped archive of the State, the endless storage spaces of archaeological material that are "located on the border between forgetting and remembering... in a state of latency, in a space of intermediary storage."

But the creation of archives is not a question of mere chance, mere passivity. Derrida (1995: 20) speaks of the "archontic dimension", derived from the etymology of the Greek word *arkhe*, which refers to authority, as well as to beginnings. The archaeological record, this hybrid of things and representations, is no passive repository of facts. It is "institutive and conservative" (Derrida, 1995: 12), as much an event in itself as it is a record of one, because every entry made in the archive is "an instance of identification, interpretation and classification" (Derrida, 1995: 38). To align these two divergent concepts of the archive, we might say that while the archival impulse may extend well beyond the realm of prior intentions—casting its net across masses of information that remain uninterpreted (in Assman's formulation)—the very structure of the archive and the terms used to organize it are, following Derrida, stamped with the seal of the archiving authority and filtered through the archival present. Archaeology, as an archive-making discipline, differs from "passive" archival bureaucracies due to its intense and focused activity. While the virtual, or potential "archaeological record" (i.e., the contents of the as yet uninvestigated segment of the archaeosphere to which the investigator has applied themselves) might be a passive repository of archaeological objects, the *actual* record—what has been archived by the excavator on the basis of their work, the methods employed, and the affordances of the materials at hand—is a different animal: it is of the present, and composed in a large part of things and representations that have been deemed, at some level, as worthy.[2] Moreover, as Derrida states, it grows by dint of the re-inscription of its contents in new texts (such as archaeological reports and papers): "By incorporating the knowledge which is deployed in reference to it, the archive augments itself,... It opens out of the future (Derrida, 1995: 45).

It is, therefore, in our archival labor that we create value, and it is in that labor that our values (what we view as meaningful, noteworthy, etc.) find their immediate expression.

3 Working for Tomorrow

> The question of the archive is not, we repeat, a question of the past.... It is a question of the future, the question of the future itself, the question of a response, of a promise and of a responsibility for tomorrow. (Derrida, 1995: 27)
>
> It is the task of ... the academic researcher or the artist to examine the contents of the archive and to reclaim the information by framing it within a new context. (Assmann, 2008: 103)

---

[2] Here I diverge from Derrida's—and Freud's—concept of the archaeologist as someone who simply reveals the naked truth: "the very success of the dig must sign the effacement of the archivist: the origin then speaks by itself. The *arkhe* appears in the nude, without archive." (Derrida, 1995: 58).

In these brief remarks, I have tried to describe the ways of seeing and understanding that archaeologists have in common with one another. While they are bound to no particular period in time, they do address only things that have a sensorial existence (in contrast to planners, architects, engineers, or storytellers), particularly those things that are hidden, obscured or forgotten. These things are so widely distributed in the "archaeosphere" that the means to address and recover them can vary enormously: some can be seen only from a great distance, others only at extreme magnification. Some require unusual effort, others are hiding in plain sight. In all cases, it is the archaeological gaze that seeks them out and reveals them. This is the part of our work that often has the greatest popular appeal, where archaeologists assume the role of magicians, inverted prestidigitators who make the invisible visible; but that is merely the surface of our work.

Archaeologists study assemblages, that is, intentions, concepts, processes, and means—each on a different temporal trajectory—that have been articulated in materiality at a particular place and time. They therefore deal not only with chronological time, but with a multiplicity of durations that diverge and converge along the temporal axis. Because they uncover suppressed or buried things, whether through physical labor or by employing non-invasive techniques, archaeologists work against the grain of modern forgetting; they are a drag on the industrial, technological and bureaucratic project of eliminating the physical past as well as on the near-universal exhortations to consume more and improve our lives, and thus often find themselves in conflict with those who want to "get on with it." Their work may thus appear to be homologous with nostalgia, or with a conservative wish to prevent any change, but in practice it is more likely to undermine the repression of collective memories, the erasure of uncomfortable truths, or the construction of simulacra of the past—virtual or actual historical theme-parks, exhibits, entertainments or curricula—designed to serve those in power: In other words, while archeologists act in the public domain, they are not there to serve or to please. Their work always harbors a subversive potential.

Archaeologists are the creators of archives, and are often those who interpret those archives. This duality, attempting to create an impassive or indifferent collation of things and observations—a material unconscious—and then endowing it with significance through the description of assemblages and juxtapositions as they are given to us in the present, brings archaeology into proximity with art. Doug Bailey (2017: 17) advocates for a disruptive process that repurposes archaeological objects to pose provocative questions in our world "Once separated from its past, the artifact or monument becomes available for the archaeologist, or the artist, or the art/archaeologist to use as if it were a raw material to be deployed in the creation of a new work, perhaps archaeological, but more forcefully in a new context, a new place, and a new set of debates that rest in the world in which we live and work." By dint of being awarded license, by the state or the public, to dig into the earth or otherwise pry beneath the surface of the world around us, we have acquired the power to affect people's imaginations. I would add that with that power to provoke comes responsibility.

In recent decades—and more pointedly in the wake of the political, economic, climatic and pandemic crises of the past few years—it has become increasingly clear that the unilateral actions and enduring structural inequities of colonial and imperial archaeologies must be confronted. Beyond the plight of looted artifacts and human remains in museums of the West, the call to decolonize the discipline itself has gained traction in the academic centers of Europe and the Americas and the archaeology of the Levant and the "Ancient Near East" is due for a reckoning. Reflecting on what is left when old habits and privileges are rooted out is an important step toward reimagining our roles and reconstituting the field to which many of us have devoted the better part of our lives (Greenberg, 2021). It is no easy thing to relinquish the power that we have become accustomed to wield, but if the swiftly mutating landscape of archaeological method, theory and practice in our lifetime has taught us anything, it is not to fear change. The expansion of archaeology to new places, times and people is an opportunity to enlarge our discursive field and find new intellectual partners, within academia and outside it; partners who are intrigued not so much by antiquity, but by how archaeologists see.

Acknowledgments The content of this paper grew out of conversations with the Tel Aviv University students who participated in my 2021 seminar "Archaeology of the Contemporary" and with colleagues, primarily Assaf Nativ and Yannis Hamilakis; none bear responsibility for the result.

References

Assmann, A. (2008). Canon and archive. In A. Erll & A. Nünning (Eds.), *Cultural memory studies: An international and interdisciplinary handbook* (pp. 97–107). De Gruyter. https://doi.org/10.1515/9783110207262

Bailey, G. (2008). Time perspectivism: Origins and consequences. In S. Holdaway & L. Wandsnider (Eds.), *Time in archaeology: Time perspectivism revisited* (pp. 13–30). University of Utah Press.

Bailey, D. (2017). Disarticulate—repurpose—disrupt: Art/Archaeology. *Cambridge Archaeological Journal, 27*(4), 691–701.

Butler, B. (2020). Jericho syndromes: 'Digging up Jericho' as ritual dramas of possession. In R. T. Sparks, B. Finlayson, B. Wagemakers, & J. M. Briffa (Eds.), *Digging up Jericho: Past, present and future* (pp. 47–68). Archaeopress.

Cline, E. H. (2009). *Biblical archaeology: A very short introduction.* Oxford University Press. ProQuest Ebook Central. https://ebookcentral.proquest.com/lib/tau/detail.action?docID=472230

Connerton, P. (1989). *How societies remember.* Cambridge University Press.

Connerton, P. (2009). *How modernity forgets.* Cambridge University Press.

Corbett, E. D. (2015). *Competitive archaeology in Jordan: Narrating identity from the Ottomans to the Hashemites.* University of Texas Press.

Derrida, J. (1995). Archive fever: A Freudian impression (Trans. E. Prenowitz). *Diacritics, 25*(2), 9–63.

Edgeworth, M. (2016). Grounded objects: Archaeology and speculative realism. *Archaeological Dialogues, 23*, 93–113. https://doi.org/10.1017/S138020381600012X

Gonzalez-Ruibal, A. (2019). *An archaeology of the contemporary era.* Routledge.

Greenberg, R. (2021). What would a decolonized archaeology of Israel-Palestine look like? In O. Bartov (Ed.), *Israel-Palestine: Lands and peoples* (pp. 315–328). Berghahn.

Greenberg, R., & Hamilakis, Y. (2022). *Archaeology, nation, and race: Confronting the past, decolonizing the future in Greece and Israel*. Cambridge University Press.

Hamilakis, Y. (2017). Sensorial assemblages: Affect, memory, and temporality in assemblage thinking. *Cambridge Archaeological Journal, 27*(1), 169–182.

Latour, B. (1993). *We have never been modern* (C. Porter, Trans.). Harvard University Press.

Levy, T. E. (2018). Foreword. In A. Yasur-Landau, E. Cline, & Y. Rowan (Eds.), *The social archaeology of the Levant* (pp. xvii–xxviii). Cambridge University Press.

Lucas, G. (2005). *The archaeology of time*. Routledge.

Mickel, A. (2021). *Why those who shovel are silent: A history of local archaeological knowledge and labor*. University Press of Colorado.

Moorey, P. R. S. (1992). *A century of biblical archaeology*. Westminster John Knox Press.

Nativ, A. (2017). No compensation needed: On archaeology and the archaeological. *Journal of Archaeological Method and Theory, 24*, 659–675.

Nativ, A., & Lucas, G. (2020). Archaeology without antiquity. *Antiquity, 376*, 852–863.

Olivier, L. (1999). The Hochdorf 'princely' grave and the question of the nature of archaeological funerary assemblages. In T. Murray (Ed.), *Time and archaeology* (pp. 109–138). Routledge.

Olivier, L. (2011). *The dark abyss of time* (A. Greenspan, Trans.). Altamira.

Pragmatism in Archaeology: The End of Theory?

William G. Dever

Abstract This paper will survey the uses of theory in the archaeology of the southern Levant since the late nineteenth century BCE, but particularly since the 1970s. It will argue that the application of theory generally has been sporadic, naïve, and of little consequence. It will also show that in worldwide archaeology, there is a growing disillusionment with abstract theory, and that the interest now is on pragmatism, what actually works. Finally, some case-studies will illustrate how pragmatism might be relevant to reaching what should have been the goals of Levantine archaeology, conceived as history, all along.

Keywords Theory · Pragmatism · Levantine archaeology · Goals of archaeology and history

I am delighted to contribute to a *Festschrift* honoring Tom Levy. He took his first course in archaeology with me in the Fall of 1975, when I first came to the University of Arizona. And he had begun his first fieldwork at Gezer already in 1971.

Since then, I have followed Tom's career closely. I helped to promote his becoming Associate Director of both our American research centers in Jerusalem. I wrote the letters that supported his appointment and promotion at UC San Diego. All along, Tom has been diligent in keeping me appraised of his work as he became a leader in our field. Tom's published volume of symposia he organized in 1995, 2005, and 2010 are landmark works, securing his legacy.

Since Tom was the first to broach the idea of "neopragmatism" in our branch of archaeology in 2010, it is to that topic that I return here. But Tom had already introduced the topic of theory generally as early as 1995 (1995: 2–8, with Augustin F.C. Holl).

W. G. Dever (✉)
Lycoming College, Williamsport, PA, USA
e-mail: gaber@lycoming.edu

© The Author(s), under exclusive license to Springer Nature Switzerland AG 2023
E. Ben-Yosef, I. W. N. Jones (eds.), *"And in Length of Days Understanding" (Job 12:12): Essays on Archaeology in the Eastern Mediterranean and Beyond in Honor of Thomas E. Levy*, Interdisciplinary Contributions to Archaeology,
https://doi.org/10.1007/978-3-031-27330-8_76

1789

1 The Rise of Theory

Archaeological theory, in anything like a deliberate sense, began in 1969 with David Clarke's *Analytical Archaeology*, which precipitated the "New Archaeology" of the subsequent decade. There followed a series of theories, all of them significantly borrowed belatedly from other disciplines. The list is impressive and instructive as well. (Bintliff 2006; cf. Sabloff & Willey, 1980).

Historical archaeology (19th, early 20th century)
Cultural history (positivism, 19th, early 20th century)
Ethno-archaeology (early-mid 20th century)
Structuralism, semiotics (1950–)
Marxism (1950–)
Anthropological archaeology (1965–)
Ecology (1965–)
Modern historical archaeology (1965–)
New Archaeology (processualism) (1970–)
Settlement archaeology (1970–)
Post-structuralism (1975–)
Hermeneutics, phenomenology (1975–)
Agency (1980–)
Cultural resource management (1980–)
Critical theory (1980–)
General systems theory (1980–)
Postmodernism (1980–)
Feminism (1980–)
Structuralism (1980–)
Post-processualism (1985–)
Cognitive archaeology (1985–)
Post-colonialism (1990–)
Landscape archaeology (1990–)
Contextual archaeology (1990–)
Industrial archaeology (1990–)
The *Annales* school (1990–)
Household archaeology (1990–)
Chaos theory (complexity, 1990–)
Globalization (2000–)
Agency (ANT, 2010–)
Connectivity (2015–)
Neo-pragmatism (2015–)

After some 40 years of experimenting with various theories, some of them extreme, none of them particularly helpful, archaeologists began to tire of "theory" all together. The bellwether was Preucel & Mrozowski's 2010 edited volume *Contemporary Archaeology in Theory: The New Pragmatism* (Preucel & Mrozowski,

2010). The same year, in our own discipline, one should note the essays of Tom Levy, *Historical Biblical Archaeology and the Future: The New Pragmatism*. Then in 2011 there appeared the provocative survey of opinions in Bintliff and Pearce's *The Death of Archaeological Theory?* Some of the European contributors asked the question lingering in the minds of many. Had many of the American archaeological theorists ever carried out excavations at a site? Some leading theorists, like my colleague at Arizona, Michael Schiffer, had not, nor had Norman Yoffee (but see Yoffee & Sherrat, 1995). Other theorists, however, like Lewis Binford, had done fieldwork. In any case, the emphasis on epistemology was welcome. But there were very few projects that demonstrated the utility of any particular theory.

Archaeology in Israel was scarcely affected by any of this "loss of innocence," as the new awareness of theory was sometimes called. Israelis, always pragmatic, simply ignored the discussion. "Theory" was dismissed as useless speculation, not legitimate interpretation. The concept of hermeneutics was apparently beyond comprehension (Mazar, 1988; Bunimovitz, 1995; Kletter, 2006; Dever, 1980, 2020).

Both Israelis and Americans made great progress from 1970 to the present, especially in field methods and in multi-disciplinary teamwork, borrowing some of the methods, if not the theory of the sciences. But the 40-year revolution in world archaeological and anthropological theory came and went with scarcely a notice.

2 Beyond Theory?

I began to write about how theory might influence our discipline in 1980, but with little response (see now Dever, 2017). As a distinguished collogue once said to me: "We're only interested in the facts." Another declared: "Dever! You were once an archaeologist, but now you've become a philosopher." Israel Finkelstein, who once dismissed me as "the prophet of the New Archaeology," did employ some aspects of the *Annales* historical school, but that was it.

American archaeologists working in Israel did pioneer from the beginning in method—that is, field excavating and recording techniques—but they rarely adapted or even discussed *theory*. The late Larry Stager often spoke of the French *Annales* school, but he wrote no real long-time history. Glenn Rose, not a trained archaeologist, touted theory at his excavations at Tell el-Hesi; but that was a dismal test-case (as the Israelis duly noted).

The only Levantine archaeologist who pursued theory in any detail was David Schloen. His published Harvard dissertation, *The House of the Father as Fact and Symbol: Patrimonialism in Ugarit and the Ancient Near East* (2001), analyzed more than 30 philosophical theories from a number of disciplines, focusing on the "house of the father" as a metaphor, a symbol. But when he came to studying *actual* Israelite houses known from archaeology, his approach was almost entirely conventional. The only theory he seemed to favor was that of Paul Ricoeur, which is a literary theory, applicable only to texts.

The disillusionment with theory in American archaeology and anthropology emerged deliberately only recently. But the malaise had earlier roots in a series of works in philosophy and literary criticism—particularly in a growing rejection of postmodernism, which aggrandized theory over facts ("there are no facts, only interpretations").

Already in 1992, Steven Knapp and Walter Benn Michaels had published a critique of theory in literary criticism, summarized and critiqued in 1985 in a work edited by W.J.T. Mitchell, entitled *Against Theory: Literary Studies in the New Pragmatism*. They argued not just that theory was largely useless, but that it should be discarded. They advocated instead what they called the "new pragmatism." As they put it in effect, "When confronted with a text, *read it*" (Mitchell, 1985: 21). Don't obfuscate with esoteric theories about language and discourse. A text *means* what it *says*.

The distinguished British literary critic Terry Eagleton published his own reevaluation in 2004 in *After Theory*. Numerous other early twenty-first century works echoed the feeling that "theory" had been largely a distraction. Back to basics (Birns, 2010; Osborne, 2000).

In a related revival of pragmatism, a number of leading philosophers pointed out that pragmatism had a long tradition as a genuinely native, American philosophy, one that was enjoying a revival as early as the 1970s. Richard Bernstein's 1971 work, entitled *Praxis and Action: Contemporary Philosophies of Human Activity*, hailed what he called the "pragmatic turn" (contra the prevailing "literary turn" of postmodernism).

In subsequent works like *Beyond Objectivity and Relativism: Science, Hermeneutics, and Praxis* (1983); *The Pragmatic Turn* (2010); and *Pragmatic Naturalism: John Dewey's Living Legacy* (2020) Bernstein went back to John Dewey, Charles Saunders Peirce, and William James, to define "neo-pragmatism" as it developed after the early 1980s. He explained pragmatism as "naturalism" or "realism," concluding:

> During the past few decades, the philosophical scene has begun to change dramatically. There is a resurgence of pragmatic theories in philosophy throughout the world, and a growing interest in the works of classic pragmatists (Bernstein, 2010: 13)

James (1843–1916) and Peirce (1839–1914) had been the founders of pragmatism, a uniquely American philosophy, or more precisely a way of thinking. The essence was that "truth" was not to be determined by philosophical speculation, much less by objective verification, but rather by concrete experience, existential facts, and plans for action. The meaning of truth or ideas must be determined by their "practical consequences," their usefulness, their workability.

James' lasting contribution was to recommend "leave the classroom and cloister and start living and acting in the world"—the *real* world. He defended himself against the obvious charge of relativism by insisting that "When... we give up the doctrine of objective certitude, we do not thereby give up the quest of hope or truth itself" (summarized in Bernstein, 2010; 51–69).

Pragmatism, although distinctly American in its origin, had some twentieth century European counterparts. Philosophers like Edmund Husserl and Martin Heidegger had pioneered as early as the 1930s in a movement called phenomenology, which stressed how subjective appearances, rather than "objectivity," shape our experience. As both put it, "back to the facts themselves." Stressing that the "facts" were independent of any theory, facts as perceptions. Heidegger, one of the most influential twentieth century philosophers, declared "Let truth happen."

Similarly, the subsequent existential movement of Sarte and others in the post-War years highlighted the sheer contingency of all human life. But the rediscovery of James and Pierce, along with Dewey, was due largely to protracted discussions between Richard Rorty and Harvard's Hilary Putnam in the 1970s and 1980s. Putnam did not care for the term "pragmatism," preferring instead "internal realism." Rorty, on the other hand, became perhaps the most famous (and notorious) neo-pragmatist. As far as he was concerned, we must "accept our inheritance from, and our conversation with, our fellow-humans as our only source for guidance." What we have is "truth without any foundations." The best that philosophers can do is to foster community, to express some hope for the world (cf. Preucel & Mrozowski, 2010: 30).

3   Pragmatism as "What Works"

As attractive as neopragmatism has become, one problem has been acknowledged almost from the beginning: relativism. If truth is determined only by a consensus of what "works" best in a given situation, isn't one interpretation as good as any other in actual practice? And doesn't this amount to sheer expediency, without any moral justification? In short, what does "working" *mean*?

Already in the 1930s, pragmatism's forerunner in Europe, phenomenology, engaged these issues. Far from ignoring epistemology and hermeneutics, philosophers like Husserl and Heidegger had emphasized their importance, especially the latter, as in Heidegger's famous "hermeneutical circle."

Hermeneutics was also an essential element of a later movement, the Frankfurt school, known as "critical theory." It addressed a wide range of moral concerns in social, cultural, and political spheres. In no sense did pragmatism devolve into nihilism: it provided a welcome alternative to postmodernism's rejection of any truth or values. But the emphasis shifted from abstract theory to practice, from objective proof to existential reality.

Pragmatism proceeds not so much as philosophy, but as a set of "operating principles" that could guide archaeological practice, could help to illuminate material culture data and their interpretation. Pragmatism in archaeology, by definition, would be:

Specific	About "things," not theories
Existential	Factoring in subjectivity
Phenomenological	Starting with appearances
Eclectic, experimental	Open to new interpretations
Credible	According with common sense
Universal	Appealing to essentials
Functional	Illuminating
Relevant	Has "moral currency."

Fundamental to a discussion of "what works" is the distinction between two types of knowledge, as in Aristotle: *epistēmē,* intellectual knowledge and theoretical knowledge, the moral ability to cope with experience. Thus we must ask ourselves as archaeologists whether we want to corroborate some Grand Theory, some disembodied "truth," *or* produce some useful knowledge of the past and wisdom for acting in the future in the real world.

This leads us to the question of what we *want* to "work," what kind of truth we hope to attain. Since Ian Hodder's 1986 work *Reading the Past: Current Approaches to Interpretation in Archaeology* (one of the few real theoretical advances) we have seen how "reading" texts and artifacts is similar hermeneutically. Their vocabulary, grammar, syntax, and interpretation are comparable. Thus the truth—the "meaning"—of texts lies in what they *say,* because of the author's intent. The truth of an artifact—its "meaning"—lies in what it does, because of the maker's and user's intent.

As pragmatists Knapp and Michaels said (above) when confronted with an archeological artifact, "reconstruct its use." Look, listen, imagine, learn. There is no larger, objective truth, at least none available to us. Theory, in the form of typology and chronology, are important, but best left until later. They are epiphenomena. The essential is function. How did this artifact *work* in its particular social and cultural context? The utility of pragmatism will depend on our asking: What do we *want* to work?

4 Some Case-Studies

Let us now turn to how a pragmatic approach to archaeological interpretation might work with particular artifacts, in this case the ubiquitous analysis of pottery. As an example, let us suppose that we have a typical eighth century BCE Judahite cooking pot. What do we hope to learn from it, and how do we propose to go about the quest?

Like a text, with Hodder, can be read, a cooking pot is also to be read, not used to confirm a general theory about typology, cuisine, or cultural identity. It is to be read as a vessel for cooking, to reveal the intent of its maker and users—the practical embodiment of an idea.

This is not a "Marxist" cooking pot, about class conflict. It is not a "postmodern" cooking pot about power and politics, to be deconstructed. It is not even necessarily about gender. It is about food, about the universal and timeless human phenomenon of hunger and satiety. (If that dismisses me as an essentialist, so be it).

Initially, we need to confront the phenomenon itself, apart from notions of its "type" (our modern category) or even its date. What are its essential qualities? What traits are not present? How does it compare with other examples of cooking pots, other categories of vessels? How is it made? How else could it have been made? How was it actually used? How efficiently? How long?

Few of these questions have been asked. For instance, Gloria London is almost alone pioneering in ceramic production. She has lived for extended periods of time in the Philippines and Cyprus, working with native potters, making pottery itself. That is why her published work on cooking pots is masterful (London, 2016). But who else has done such research (although we do have studies of diet)? (MacDonald, 2008; Schafer-Elliott, 2012). Why not replicate our eighth century Judahite cooking pot and *cook in it?* As the British say, "the proof of the pudding is in the eating."

In a pragmatic view, the "proof" of the cooking pot lies in what it *did* for its users—and can in principle do for *us.* That is the "truth"—not an objective, universal, philosophical, or metaphysical truth. Nor is its truth a confirmation of our typologies, however useful they may be at a later date. It is an *empirical* truth, revealed through open-mindedness, intuition, creative imagination, and experimentation. It is the result of common sense—once ridiculed but now refurbished as "self-referential knowledge." That is pragmatism.

5 The Real Goal of Archaeology

With this approach to artifacts, we would be closer to what should always have been the goal of our inquiry: "What was it *really* like to live there and then?" (cf. Dever, 2012). To see how far we are from that goal, pick up a recent final report volume, admirably full of artifactual data, replete with statistical tables, accompanied by technical reports from specialists in many disciplines. Do you gain any sense of the actual lives of *people* in the remote past? Or read an analysis of cultural assimilation based on pottery that never mentions *people.* Did the pots assimilate?

Archaeologists are essentially cultural materialists, although not in the Marxist sense. We deal with *things* as the best reflection of culture, often even more significant than texts (not directly accessible to us in any case). We can write history, our own history, from things, even if necessary without texts.

In my recent book *Beyond the Texts: An Archaeological Portrait of Ancient Israel and Judah* (2017), I draw on the insights of several scientific specialists in material culture studies. At conferences at the Smithsonian in Washington, one scholar declared that "the things humankind makes and uses at any particular time and place are probably the truest representations we have of the values and meanings, and meanings within a society." Another stated that artifacts are unique in being "the only class of historical events that occur in the past but survive into the present. They can be re-experienced: they are authentic, primary historical material available for first-hand study" (Lubar & Kingery, 1993: ix).

Biblical scholars tend, of course, to prioritize texts, and many ignore archaeology simply because they are oblivious to artifacts as potential historical sources. They should remember the wise words of a leading recent biblicist, Norman Gottwald in his magisterial study of early Israel:

> Only as the full *materiality* of ancient Israel is more securely grasped will we be able to make proper sense of its *spirituality* (his italics) (Gottwald, 1979: xxv).

Archaeology is quotidian, all about an everyday, *real-life* context of the biblical text—not an abstract, ideological context, dependent on other texts. Again, that is pragmatism, not theory.

If theory ever becomes regnant again, we should recall that the term "theory" derives from the Greek *theōrein*, "to look at, observe." Theory is only the *means* to an end, not the end. It is valuable only as an insight—one among many.

Some years ago, on a symposium-sponsored trip in Denmark, I visited a field school where graduate students in archaeology were required to spend a full year replicating life in the Danish Iron Age. They had to be entirely self-supporting, building their own houses with local materials; planting, harvesting, and grinding their own grains; growing all their own foods; finding their own fuel; making all their tools, even forging their own iron implements; devising health strategies. After many months' time, the students looked pretty desperate to me; but they would never forget the real-life lessons they learned. They had relived the past, not simply imagined it. Unlike most archaeologists working in Israel, I have had experience similar to that of the Danish students. I lived for some 6 months in Arab villages in the West Bank in the 1960–1970s, before any modernization. When I write about an Iron Age village somewhere in Judah in the eighth century BCE, I can not only see it, I can feel it, smell it, taste it. As a result of these experiences, I can perceive the reality of life for many people in antiquity as it really was. No more romantic illusions.

Why shouldn't we have such a field school? We know enough about Iron Age technology to recreate it. One area where we have been pragmatic is in interpreting Iron Age houses, reconstructing daily life in considerable detail (Albertz et al., 2014). Isolating would-be archaeologists in a real-life situation, reconstructing life in ancient Israel, would revolutionize our discipline. Such a pragmatic, experimental approach would give us *much* more credence as culture critics (for that is what we are). And it might eliminate ivory-tower theoreticians.

Our branch of archaeology has a long history, with many significant advances. But we are still a long way from answering the most relevant question. What was it *really like* for most people, most of the time, to *live* in ancient Israel? And what can *we* learn from their experience? It is time to try pragmatism, which would work better, would teach us more lessons from the past.

6 What "Meaning" Means

When we ask about the "truth" of a text or a thing, we are asking about *meaning*. Our English verb "to mean" comes from an Old English verb "to say." Thus a text means what its authors say, presuming that they are not ambivalent and are competent writers. We can call that the "original" meaning, expressing the authors' intent.

Even though that meaning should be obvious to a perceptive reader, one may attribute other readings or meaning to the text—"secondary" meanings. That seems to be human nature: external things constitute phenomena—appearances. And appearances can be deceptive. In short, our comprehension of reality is always partial, often changing, always provisional. From the dawn of human consciousness, philosophers have struggled with that dilemma. Thus we should be cautious about using the word "proof."

That is true of archaeology in particular. But the original intent or meaning of an artifact is usually less clear than with a text. That explains why archaeological interpretations often vary considerably, to the dismay of non-specialists. It is also why a pragmatic approach is the most productive. Secondary meanings are not only legitimate, they are inevitable. Simply put, there are multiple ways of viewing the past, as most archaeologists have come to acknowledge.

If the meaning of an artifact is reached through a pragmatic approach, that meaning is experimental; it must be evaluated on the basis of what it *does* for us, what we can learn from it to cope with our own reality in this world. That is what phenomenologists like Heidegger mean by *Dasein*, "living-in-the-world" *as though* we had the truth. That is the best that we mortals can do.

7 What We Learn

In the light of this philosophical digression, let us return to our essential question: what can we learn from our archaeological investigations? If we learn nothing, archaeology is not only a waste of time and money, it is immoral, a wanton destruction of cultural heritage.

Once we abandon arrogant and destructive positivist approaches to the acquisition of archaeological knowledge, the way is open to better interpretations. First, we can learn something about materiality, about the physical as well as the metaphysical level on which we all live. Without things, used as agents, we cannot survive. We shape objects; but then they shape us. Much of how we turn out as individuals has to do with how we manage things. They are an indisputable clue to our identity, to what we think counts.

Second, archaeology can teach us about mortality; all things perish (so we contemplate their ruin), and so do we. That fact should teach us modesty. We may look at our reconstructed past and explain how superior we moderns are. But in the end, *sic transit gloria.* We archaeologists, who spend our lives examining the ruins of failed civilizations, should know that. Technology cannot save us.

Third archaeology can teach us about the sheer contingency of human life. The particular culture that we bring to light may be different, if not unique. But *why?* As good historians, we may offer partial explanations; but the ultimate truth eludes us.

Finally, archaeology can teach us empathy and tolerance, because we humans are all one and always have been since the origin of our species some 70,000 years ago. In trying to understand our remote ancestors, we may come to understand ourselves and the actual circumstance of our fellows.

8   Conclusion

These above are all generalizations, perhaps moralisms. But what *specifically* can we learn from the archaeology of Israel and the southern Levant? Have we learned anything pragmatic, anything useful?

Not much, it seems. The Middle East is on a familiar collision course, as always. And we observers in the West have forgotten what moral and ethical values that may once have obtained briefly. Nevertheless, we must persevere.

We archaeologists possess some of the few clues to wisdom that are available. If we shirk our responsibility, history will not forgive us. We do not know everything, or perhaps anything for certain. But we know enough to make a difference. Pragmatism is *doing* the Truth as far as we know it.

References

Albertz, R., et al. (Eds.). (2014). *Family and household religion: Toward a synthesis of old testament studies, archaeology, epigraphy, and cultural studies.* Eisenbrauns.

Baert, P. (1998). *Social theory in the twentieth century.* New York University.

Bernstein, R. J. (1971). *Praxis and action.* University of Pennsylvania Press.

Bernstein, R. J. (1983). *Beyond objectivism and relativism: Science, hermeneutics and praxis.* University of Pennsylvania Press.

Bernstein, R. J. (2010). *The pragmatic turn.* Polity.

Bernstein, R. J. (2020). *Pragmatic naturalism: John Dewey's living legacy.* Graduate Faculty Philosophical Journal.

Bintliff, J. (2006). *A companion to archaeology.* Blackwell Publishing.

Bintliff, J., & Pearce, M. (Eds.). (2011). *The death of archaeological theory?* Oxford Books.

Birns, N. (2010). *Theory after theory: An intellectual history of literary theory from 1950 to the early 21st century.* Broadview Press.

Bunimovitz, S. (1995). How mute stones speak: Interpreting what we dig up. *BAR, 21*(2), 58–67, 96.

Clarke, D. L. (1968). *Analytic archaeology.* Methuen.

Dever, W. G. (1980). Archaeological method in Israel: A continuing revolution. *BA, 43,* 41–48.

Dever, W. G. (1981). The impact of the 'new archaeology' on Syro-Palestinian archaeology. *BASOR, 242,* 15–29.

Dever, W. G. (2012). *The lives of ordinary people in ancient Israel: Where archaeology and the bible intersect*. Eerdmans.

Dever, W. G. (2017). *Beyond the texts: An archaeological portrait of ancient Israel and Judah*. SBL Press.

Dever, W. G. (2020). *My nine lives: Sixty years in Israeli and biblical archaeology*. SBL Press.

Eagleton, T. (2004). *After theory*. Penguin Press.

Gottwald, N. K. (1979). *The tribes of Yahweh: A sociology of the religion of liberated Israel* (1250-1050 BCE). Orbis.

Hodder, I. (1986). *Reading the past: Current approaches to interpretation in archaeology*. Cambridge University Press.

Kletter, R. (2006). *Just past? The making of Israeli archaeology*. Equinox.

Levy, T. E. (Ed.). (2010). *Historical biblical archaeology and the future: The new pragmatism*. Equinox.

Levy, T. E., & Holl, A. F. C. (1995). Social change and the archaeology of the Holy Land. In T. E. Levy (Ed.), *The archaeology of Society in the Holy Land* (pp. 2–8). Leicester University Press.

London, G. (2016). *Ancient cookware from the Levant: An Ethnoarchaeological perspective*. Equinox.

Lubar, S., & Kingery, D. (Eds.). (1993). *History from things: Essays on material culture*. Smithsonian Institute Press.

Mazar, A. (1988). Israeli Archaeologists. In J. F. Prinkard, G. L. Mattingly, & J. M. Miller (Eds.), *Benchmarks in time and culture: An introduction to Palestinian archaeology* (pp. 109–128). Scholar Press.

Mitchell, W. J. T. (Ed.). (1985). *Against theory: Literary studies and the new pragmatism*. University of Chicago Press.

Osborne, P. (2000). *Philosophy in cultural theory*. Routledge.

Preucel, R. W., & Mrozowski, S. A. (Eds.). (2010). *Contemporary archaeology in theory: The new pragmatism*. Wiley-Blackwell.

Sabloff, J. A., & Willey, G. R. (1980). *A history of American archaeology* (Rev ed.). Freeman.

Schloen, D. (2001). *The house of the father as fact and symbol: Patrimonialism in Ugarit and the Middle East* (SAHL 2). Eisenbrauns.

Shafer-Elliott, C. (2012). *Food in Ancient Judah: Domestic cooking in the time of the Hebrew Bible*. Acumen.

Yoffee, N., & Sharrett, A. (1995). *Archaeological theory—Who sets the agenda?* Cambridge University Press.

Polycentrism and the Rise of Secondary States in the Eastern Mediterranean: Aspects of a Southern Levantine Cultural Paradigm

Øystein S. LaBianca

Abstract This chapter will situate the rise of secondary states during the first millennium B.C. in the Southern Levant within an anthropological archaeology/global history context. Attention will be focused on the region's long-standing resistance to centralizing forces that would impose upon it, or its sub-regions, a top-down, hierarchical system of governance. While such processes have been set in motion on numerous occasions over the past four millennia, almost always by the agency of foreign powers to the north, south, east, and west; they have not typically succeeded in establishing and sustaining over long periods the sort of top-down, centralized systems of governance as happened to a much greater extent in ancient Egypt and Mesopotamia. A consequence of this is that the apparatus of centralized governance—bureaucracy, writing, monumentality, and so forth—arrived in the region barely 3000 years ago, compared with their emergence more than 5000 years ago in the pristine states of Mesopotamia and Egypt. Once in evidence in the Southern Levant—fully so by the first half of the first millennium B.C.—their scale in terms of political power and monumentality was much smaller and far less durable. The chapter will introduce several theoretical notions as an aid to explaining the trajectory of state formation in the Southern Levant. These include cultural production; the perspective and approach of global history; recent research on the agency of invisible people; aspects of an unfolding Levantine cultural paradigm; the endemic polycentrism hypothesis; the nature and agency of tribes; the emergence of secondary states; and finally, the tribal kingdom hypothesis. The chapter concludes with a discussion of the implications of these theoretical proposals for the current discourse on the origins and nature of state-level polities in the Southern Levant.

Keywords Polycentrism · Secondary states · Iron Age · Southren Levant · State formation · Cultural production · Global history · Tribal kingdoms

---

Ø. S. LaBianca (✉)
Andrews University, Berrien Springs, MI, USA
e-mail: labianca@andrews.edu

© The Author(s), under exclusive license to Springer Nature Switzerland AG 2023
E. Ben-Yosef, I. W. N. Jones (eds.), *"And in Length of Days Understanding" (Job 12:12): Essays on Archaeology in the Eastern Mediterranean and Beyond in Honor of Thomas E. Levy*, Interdisciplinary Contributions to Archaeology,
https://doi.org/10.1007/978-3-031-27330-8_77

1 Introduction

Anthropological archaeologists, and more recently, global historians, investigate long-term patterns of cultural production and change and the underlying drivers that produce these. Cultural production is what happens as members of a given local community or society go about living their daily lives, adapt to opportunities and threats, and organize themselves to achieve desired ends. A more technical definition of the cultural production concept would be "social processes involved in the generation and circulation of cultural forms, practices, values and shared understandings" (Chandler & Munday, 2011). In this chapter my goal is to offer an anthropological archaeology/global history perspective on the nature and rise of secondary states in the Southern Levant region of the Eastern Mediterranean. I shall argue that cultural production in the region unfolds in accordance with certain analytically distinguishable, long-term, temporal patterns or cultural paradigms whose shaping influence help account for the origin and nature of state-level polities during the first millennium B.C. in the region. But before proceeding with this task, the larger context of this inquiry must first be introduced, namely, the perspective and approach of global history.

2 Global History

The dawn of our global age has necessitated a new approach to history writing, namely global history. Global history draws its inspiration from our planet as seen from space—a pale blue dot (Sagan, 1990) on which all of humanity's history has unfolded—along with the history of all other living things and that of the planet itself, our common earth home. As a lens for studying and narrating the past, global history has several advantages. The first is its two-fold focus on the history of globalization and on a closely related topic, namely the accumulative impact of human cultural production on the environment and other living things (Maurell, 2011; Schäfer, 2003, 2004; Sommer, 2014; Steffen et al., 2007). This emphasis on the history of human-environment interactions represents not only a timely response to the current crisis of a planet on the verge of climate catastrophe, it also constitutes a long overdue and much-needed initiative to crystallize a way forward for a history of humanity on a planet-wide canvas. Global history is thus less about the history of powerful individuals or the rise and fall of particular kingdoms, empires or civilizations; instead, its aim is to uncover and narrate the story of gradually accelerating connectivity between different human communities (Belich et al., 2016; Crossley, 2008). To this end, global historians are as interested in the world's oceans, seas, and rivers as they are in studying events on its terrestrial continents (Horden & Purcell, 2006). As for its concern with humans as our planet's most prolific and consequential eco-system engineers, the aim is to deepen understanding of the long-term processes that have led to the environmental affordance of our Earth home being altered, threatening our planet's future as a habitable place for our kind and other living things (Schäfer, 2004; Steffen et al., 2007). Although global history aspires to an integrated view of the planet's past, its practitioners tend to fall into two types: those tracing particular human activities on a planet-wide canvas (Brooke, 2014) and those who take deep dives into a particular geographical region or microregion (Abulafia, 2011; Sommer, 2014). In both instances, the focus gravitates toward uncovering the bottom-up contributions of the planet's invisible masses to this journey rather than concentrating on the top-down actions of its powerful elites.

A final advantage of the global history approach is that it aspires to overcome many biases implicit in much received history writing—biases arising from Eurocentric, orientalist, nationalist, and denominational mindsets and orientations (Belich et al., 2016; Crossley, 2008; Geyer & Bright, 1995). Also, to the extent that such history writing favors particular civilizational, imperial, or national cultural heritages, it has contributed to what David Lowenthal has famously observed with regard to the raison d'être of heritage—"confining possession to some while excluding others" (Lowenthal, 1998). In this regard, the perspective of global history is promising (at least one can hope it is) as a way forward for a more inclusive approach to a yet to be fully crystallized pan-human past—opening for greater global consciousness and awareness where more exclusivist mindsets and orientations have previously prevailed (den Dekker, 2016).

Although we are still a long way off from when archaeologists and historians will agree about the extent of the Levantine contribution to the causation of globalization, a few examples about which I believe there is general agreement deserve highlighting. Surely the story of the Natufians—an indigenous Levantine people—would belong in such a narrative (Bar-Yosef, 1998; Bar-Yosef & Valla, 1991). They are among the earliest people to begin experimentation with cultivating cereals and raising sheep and goals, and they paved the way for one of the most consequential events in human history, namely the Neolithic Revolution. Though not the only location where settled farming began, the Southern Levant played a key role in the dissemination of this new way of life to other world regions. The region is also where four other globally consequential developments occurred, namely development of transhumant pastoralism (Levy, 1983; Arbuckle & Hammer, 2019); origination of mining and metallurgy (Ben-Yosef, 2018; Golden, 2016; Greenfield, 2016); beginnings of terrace construction and orchard farming (Gibson & Lewis, 2017); and the rise of the first cities and city states (Düring, 2014). These components were all in place by the fifth millennium B.C. By the end of the following millennium, two additional components came into place that would have a profound and lasting impact on the Southern Levant. First was the rise of early empires along the irrigated banks of the Tigris-Euphrates rivers in Mesopotamia, the Nile in Egypt, and the Indus and its tributaries in Pakistan (Sinopoli, 1995). Second was the emergence of the Bronze Age World System (Frank et al., 1993; Kardulias, 1996), which established a web of connections of communication and trade between these various early empires and civilizations that would, in the end, take on a life of its own, regardless of the fate of one or the other of its imperial components. Thus, the key pieces came into place that would be crucial to the crystallization of a distinctive Levantine Cultural Paradigm (more about this below).

3   The Agency of Invisible Peoples

As already indicated, one of the important advantages of the global history approach is its concern with illuminating the contributions of our planet's invisible masses–the silent majority of long ago (and today) whose achievements have been either neglected and/or deliberately overlooked by much traditional historical research. A seminal publication in this regard is Eric Wolf's *Europe and the People without History* (1982), which is widely credited with having launched research on this topic. The volume offers a history of the invisible masses who since 1400 AD participated as slaves and low-paid laborers in the colonial project of producing cash crops for export to Europe. The volume inspired renewed consideration of the agency of invisible actors by anthropologists, archaeologists, and historians. In *Agency in Archaeology* (Dobres & Robb, 2000), archaeologists are challenged to move beyond looking at broad structural or environmental change and instead to consider the impact of actions by less visible individuals and groups. To this end the concept of agency is crucial because it creates space for recognizing the role and impact of individual human choices and intentions in shaping cultural production and change. Finally, in the edited volume, *Globalization in Prehistory* (Boivin & Frachetti, 2018), a dozen case studies are collected showing how "people without history" had significant agency in the unfolding history of early globalizations. They did so in two ways: their "local knowledge" of medicinal botany and forest products provided the hidden foundations for worldwide European colonial expansion; and their prowess as masters of both maritime and desert transportation laid the foundations for global trade networks. Most of this occurred before the invention of urban centers, states, or empires. The volume thus contests the urban, statist, and imperial bias of much received scholarship on the deep-time history of globalization.

The most recent contribution to this line of research is David Graeber and David Wengrow's *The Dawn of Everything: A New History of Humanity* (2021). Theirs is not only a call for renewed consideration of the agency of invisible peoples, they appeal for reconsideration of the very premises underlying "the standard world-historical narrative." By this they mean the oft-repeated stages view of human societal evolution. Pivotal moments along this trajectory were the agricultural and urban revolutions that are invariably linked—according to the standard view—to the rise of systems of hierarchy and inequality. Their objection to this narrative is that it is not supported by recent archaeological discoveries and that it offers a very pessimistic view of human nature at a time when we desperately need to be able to imagine other possible ways of being human. According to Graeber and Wengrow, this standard view oversimplifies the beginnings of agriculture and village life and underestimates the extent of agency and creativity of humans at the dawn of civilization. In support of this view, they marshal archaeological and ethnographic evidence from all around the world to make their case against oversimplification as seen in the standard narrative.

4   Aspects of a Levantine Cultural Paradigm

A good starting point for a discussion of cultural paradigms is the seminal study of the long-term history of the Mediterranean region by global historians Peregrine Horden and Nicholas Purcell, *The Corrupting Sea* (2000). Their study traces long-term cultural and economic conditions and exchanges in and around the Mediterranean Sea going back to Hellenistic-Roman times. The premise of their work is that, contrary to much received understanding, the Mediterranean region is a fragmented one—a world whose environmental affordances and risks vary greatly. The key to understanding it is to venture beyond the imperial gaze—to examine the diversity of livelihood strategies in the region while at the same time tracking the connections that have nourished and sustained them. In this way "the connectivity that overcomes fragmentation" will come into view.

If in *The Corrupting Sea* we may discern a glimpse of a Mediterranean cultural paradigm, is it also possible to distinguish a cultural paradigm for one of its most storied sub-regions, the Southern Levant, herewith defined as the region of today's Israel, Jordan, and the Palestinian Authority territories? What sets this paradigm apart is the extent to which it is anchored in a bottom-up nature of social order in which the tribal element plays a central role. But first, and as an aid to this task, the following definition of the paradigm concept as utilized in this context is proposed: "*Cultural paradigms are the bundle of artifacts, ideologies, institutions, habits and practices that facilitate identity formation and path-dependent, accumulative cultural production and adaptation to changing environmental and socio-political conditions over the long-term by the population of a particular world region*" (LaBianca & Hudon, 2022). Particularly noteworthy is this definitions' inclusion of the words "path-dependent," "accumulative," and "long-term." The point here is that cultural paradigms represent an unfolding constant (oxymoron intended) that both enfolds and transcends the agency role of particular rulers, social, or religious movements, states, empires, or civilizations. They represent, as it were, the guardrails that shape the accumulative unfolding of various cultural products, institutions, and practices in a given region over multiple centuries and millennia. It is this deep-time dimension of the cultural paradigm notion that makes it an apt heuristic construct for uncovering and describing accumulative cultural production over time in particular world regions—in our case, the Southern Levant.

In our recent volume, *Levantine Entanglements, Cultural Productions, Long-Term Changes and Globalizations in the Eastern Mediterranean* (2021b), Terje Stordalen and I discuss four examples of paradigms that play a major role in the cultural production of the Southern Levant. Here I propose to bundle these as constituent aspects of a single Levantine Cultural Paradigm. At the most fundamental level is *endemic polycentrism,* which refers to how social and political order in the region has consistently trended toward multiple, interacting centers of power rather than the opposite, namely a single top-down center of power. This situation, in turn, created a space for the development of a bottom-up basis for social power, legitimacy, and authority derived from having a recognized role with the curation, teaching, and recitation of a collection of superb texts. Stordalen's term for this is *canonical ecology.* The many affordances of this latter configuration in terms of empowering local authority, resilience, and transferability enabled its spread throughout much of the ancient world and beyond. And this, in turn, created the conditions that led to various notions of the *holy land trope* whereby the region where these superb texts originated became the raison d'être for artistic expression, performative arts, spiritual longings, and pilgrimages by men and women from every continent. Together, these three constituent aspects account for the fourth aspect of this paradigm, which as is suggested by the title of our volume, is *worldwide entanglements.* By this we have in mind the myriad of ways that certain Southern Levantine cultural products have and continue to inspire and inform, and are thus involved or entangled with, cultural productions the world over. As each of these aspects of the Levantine Cultural Paradigm have been introduced and discussed in *Levantine Entanglements* (2021c), the remainder of this chapter will examine in greater detail the consequences of endemic polycentrism for the rise of secondary states in the Southern Levant during the late first millennium B.C.

5   The Endemic Polycentrism Hypothesis

In a seminal article in *Annals of the Association of American Geographers* (1939) the political geographer Richard Hartshorne takes up the question of what makes a state and what makes a nation? To answer this question Hartshorne introduces the concepts of centrifugal versus centripetal forces. While the former tends to negate the formation of states, the latter does the opposite. Examples he gives of forces that negate state formation include "regions that are more or less separated from each other by physical or human barriers; regions that in greater or lesser degree diverge in their relations with outside states; and regions that differ among themselves in character of population, economic interests, and political attitudes" (Hartshorne, 1939). By contrast, for a state to form and flourish it needs to "establish centripetal forces that will bind together the regions of that state, in spite of centrifugal forces that are always present … The basic centripetal force must be some concept or idea justifying the existence of this particular state incorporating these particular regions; the state must have a raison d'être—reason for existing" (Hartshorne, 1939; see also Meir, 1988).

Hartshorne's concepts of centrifugal vs. centripetal have great relevance for understanding the rise of state-level polities in the Eastern Mediterranean. In *The Mind of Egypt* (2003), Jan Assman seeks to understand the ups and downs of centralized power during the pharaonic era, ca. 3000–200 B.C. The extent to which particular pharaohs and dynasties managed to impose centralized control over the land of Egypt varied significantly. During periods when such power was ascendant (due to centripetal processes), great monumental works could be completed, such as the building of enormous pyramids and temples. When centralized power flamed out (due to centrifugal processes), work on such grand building projects typically suffered as well. The terms that Assman uses to describe these ups and downs in pharaonic power are unicentric and polycentric respectively. Egypt's pharaonic past could thus be characterized as involving shifts back and forth along a continuum with unicentrism on one end and polycentrism on the other.

When the two—Egypt and the Levant—are compared in light of Hartshorne's opposing forces, the contrast is rather stark. During pharaonic times, the vast majority of Egypt's population lived in agricultural villages along the two banks of the Nile. While a wide range of options existed in terms of ways of farming these lands, the annual flooding cycle of the Nile River was a huge risk factor. Its waters were thus both a great blessing and a constant source of uncertainty. To the extent that the political, economic, and cultural programs of the various pharaohs were understood by these farmers to be a means for managing such risks and benefitting their livelihood pursuits, the state had a raison d'être. Where such rationale flailed, the centralized polity also floundered. Hence the alternating sequence of unicentric and polycentric social order throughout the pharaonic era of Egypt.

The situation in the Southern Levant was very different. Here a varied canvas of different types of highland and lowland environments existed, each with its own risk regime. Unlike Egypt, where the flooding of the Nile prevailed as a ubiquitous risk factor, Levantine farmers faced no such overriding risk regime. Instead they faced a wide range of risks, depending on the affordances of their particular local environment. Furthermore, as farming villages became established in the region, many ended up in rather isolated locations, which in turn favored local self-sufficiency as a means to survival and managing risks. The continuous influx of Bedouin tribes, which has been part of the Levantine experience since prehistoric times, also kept injecting into the region sentiments favoring communal level self-reliance. In these ways the conditions for managing risks in the Levant favored centrifugal practices and institutions that tended to negate centralization and state formation. The opposite was the case in Egypt where conditions were much more favorable to the sorts of centripetal forces that are required to form and sustain state-level polities.

The difference in scale between the temples and pyramids of pharaonic Egypt when compared with what has survived from the same time periods in the Southern Levant is striking. Compare, for example, the difference in scale between the Megiddo triple temple (Adams et al., 2014) and the Pyramid of Abusir (Fig. 1). Both are dated to about the same period, the former to the Intermediate Bronze Age (ca. 2000–2500 B.C.) and the latter to Old Kingdom Dynasty V (ca. 2686–2181 B.C.). While the base of the Abusir pyramid is estimated to have been about 105 m × 105 m, the base of the triple temple at Megiddo is estimated at roughly 20 m × 20 m. The difference in scale is at least five-fold. Add to this that monuments on the scale of the triple temples of Megiddo are very rare in Southern Levant until the first millennium B.C., and the extent to which these two regions differ becomes even more

Fig. 1 Abusir pyramid, Egypt and Triple Temple, Megiddo. (**a**) Abusir pyramid, Egypt. (Image credit: Chanel Wheeler, CC BY-SA 2.0, https://creativecommons.org/licenses/by-sa/2.0, via Wikimedia Commons (image enlarged)). (**b**) Triple Temple, Megiddo. (Image credit: Matthew J. Adams, July 2008, ASOR Photo Collections (image enlarged))

apparent. Indeed, it is really not until the Roman period that monuments at the scale of Egyptian temples and pyramids become part of the landscape in the Southern Levant.

The reason for this stark difference is, of course, that centripetal forces took off much earlier in Egypt and were far more powerful there than in the Levant. While state-level polities were in place in Egypt by 3000 B.C., it took 2000 years before the first state-level polities emerged in the Southern Levant, and these were fledgling ones at best. Furthermore, while the state level entities that arose in Egypt established enormous bureaucracies to support them, this was not the case in the Levant. As will be discussed further on, what emerged here were fledgling tribal kingdoms. These were a type of secondary state in which tribal loyalties and sentiments remained in force and in which the sort of bureaucratic institutions that developed and sustained the state apparatus in Egypt never really emerged.

The difference between the two regions when it comes to the use of writing follows from this observation. In Egypt the invention and use of hieroglyphs was primarily in the service of the pharaoh and the state and thus goes back to the emergence of state-level society in Egypt in the third millennium B.C. When writing eventually does emerge in the Southern Levant, it coincides roughly with the rise of the secondary states of Ammon, Israel, Moab, and Edom at the beginning of the first millennium B.C. And in this case, the scripts that came into use were far more eclectic in origin and form, reflecting the fact that their use was not primarily in the service of the state but that of non-state actors such as prophets, poets, and priestly chroniclers (Stordalen, 2021). This begins to explain why evidences of writing are far rarer in the Southern Levant than in Egypt (Fig. 2).

Fig. 2 Two types of social order. (a) Pharaonic Egypt social order. Centripetal forces have favored mono-centrism and hierarchy, force and bureaucracy, and less local level agency. (Image credit: Reptail82, CC BY-SA 4.0, https://creativecommons.org/licenses/by-sa/4.0, via Wikimedia Commons). (b) Southern Levantine social order. Inside a shig tent of the Majali bedouins at an encampment near Karak, Transjordan, ca. 1943. Centrifugal forces have favored polycentrism and heterarchy, trust and honor, and greater local level agency. (Image credit: Frank Hurley, *Inside a shig tent of the Majali bedouins at an encampment near Karak, Transjordan, ca. 1943*, National Library of Australia, nla.obj-151359365)

Another related contrast between the two regions is that of social stratification—the extent to which each society ranked various individuals and groups according to their perceived social value and function. In Egypt, such ranking was extensive, with hierarchy being more the norm, while in the Southern Levant heterarchy was more prevalent. Heterarchy is a more flexible type of social order in which individuals and groups can be ranked in a number of different ways, and in which there can be multiple centers of authority, depending on the circumstances.

This is an important distinction because of the extent to which individuals and communities experience a sense of agency and freedom of action under the two systems. Generally, people living under a bottom-up, heterarchical type of order experience a greater sense of agency or motivation to imagine and follow through on ideas than is typically the case under a top-down hierarchical type of order. Heterarchical orders also rely to a far greater extent on trust and honor as a way for its members to achieve consensus and deal with conflict. As might be expected, the latter also provides the opportunity for both positive and negative deviance from the established order.

To sum up what we have said so far about the endemic polycentrism hypothesis: it posits the existence of a distinctive Southern Levantine cultural paradigm in which centrifugal forces have tended to overpower centripetal ones, thus bending the region toward polycentrism and heterarchical social structure (see Fig. 3). The extent to which this paradigm operated in any particular time or place is a matter for empirical investigation and will depend to a considerable extent on its environmental affordances and prevailing conditions with regard to access to markets and major trade routes. As a general rule, the more extreme the environmental affordances and the greater the risks involved in accessing markets and major trade routes, the stronger the downward pull toward local self-sufficiency and resistance to outside interference (see Fig. 4).

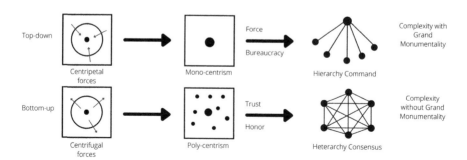

Fig. 3 Two contrasting models of agency and social order in the ANE

Polycentrism and the Rise of Secondary States in the Eastern Mediterranean: Aspects... 1811

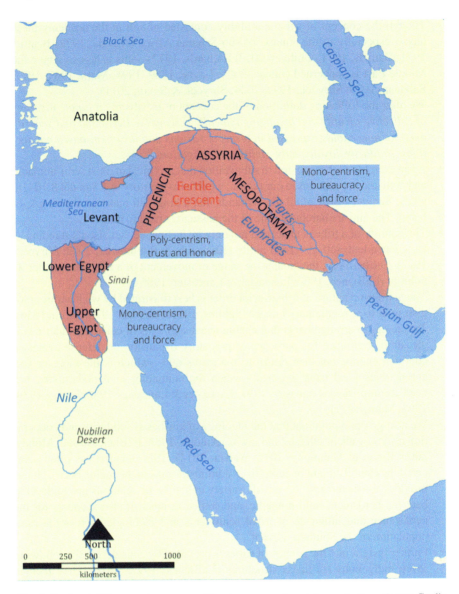

Fig. 4 Regional differences in patterns of local agency and social organization. (Image Credit: Image by Nafsadh – Map of fertile cresent.png, CC BY-SA 4.0, https://commons.wikimedia.org/w/index.php?curid=15272124. Some text added)

6 The Agency of Tribes

In a forthcoming book chapter (2022) LaBianca and Hudon discuss in some detail the topic of agency of semi-nomadic and nomadic tribes. Here I briefly summarize the points made about this topic in that chapter:

- Though the concept of tribe is a highly contested notion in the academy these days—especially in the context of sub-Saharan Africa (Atanda, 1972; Beattie, 1971; Daniels, 1971; Gulliver, 2013; Richards, 1972)—this is less so where the Middle East is concerned (James, 2006; Layne, 1989, 1994; Marx, 1967, 1977; Salzman, 1979; Shryock, 1997, 2004; Shryock & Smail, 2011).
- We offer the following definition of the concept of tribalism: *"a supple ideology of collective identity and belonging typically serving the livelihood and security needs of households expressed in terms of various notions of kin-based connections, solidarity, loyalty, duty, rights and obligations."*
- As an example of the aversion to subjugation that is typical of most semi-nomadic and nomadic populations in our region, we refer to the story in 1 Samuel 8:10–18, where Samuel warns of all the demands that a king will make on the people of Israel. The anti-monarchical tone of the passage is hard to miss.
- The nobility of a tribe is measured not only by its lineage, but also its standing as an independent, self-governed polity (Khawalde & Rabinowitz, 2002; Shryock, 1997). Furthermore, the greater the range of movement of a tribe, the greater its nobility (LaBianca, 1990; Lancaster & Lancaster, 1986).
- The bottom-up nature of tribal social order is best illustrated by what anthropologists refer to as segmentary lineage (Sahlins, 1961; Salzman, 1978; Smith, 1956). This refers to arrangements that enable tribal segments to coalesce under a single, unified alliance for purposes of predatory expansion or defense against a common enemy, but then return to the status quo—which is the more or less autonomous local tribal segment—when the animating joint undertaking has been accomplished (Lancaster, 1997; Lancaster & Lancaster, 1986; Layne, 1989, 1994; Marx, 1977).
- We next go on to point out that the ideology of kin-based solidarity and cooperation also prevails in villages and towns (Antoun, 1968; LaBianca, 1990; Mundy, 2000; Rjoub & Mahmoud, 2012; Walker, 2014). This situation has often hampered the establishment of centralized administrations in the region even as it has provided fertile territory for a wide variety of symbiotic relationships to develop between herdsmen, semi-nomadic, and settled farmers. It also accounts for the persistence and influence of tribal sentiments and ideologies across the rural population of the Southern Levant.
- Further insight into the agency of tribes is provided by considering the following seven indigenous hardiness structures (LaBianca, 1997, 2007). They include *local level water management* or the practice of relying on natural springs, man-made cisterns, and hillside terracing for water to meet household and farming needs. *Fluid shared commons* involving pastures and croplands being held in common by different families as members of a particular tribal segment or village. *Argo-pastoralism* or the practice of combining crop cultivation with animal husbandry and being able to shift back and forth between these as risk and opportunity dictates. *Residential flexibility* by means of which families can shift the location of their production activities from houses to caves or tents, depending on what is efficient for their particular mode of production. *Hospitality* as a means of transmitting vital information within a tribal community and between

members of a tribe and outsiders. *Honor and shame* whereby tribes have been able to police themselves without relying on a paid constabulary or a codified system of civil and/or criminal law. And finally, and as already extensively discussed, *tribalism*—the flexible polity involving strong, in-group loyalty based on variously fluid notions of identity, common lineal descent, and cooperation.

- Four salient characteristics of the Southern Levantine lands help account for the inextinguishable nature of tribal sentiments and ideologies in the region: First are its natural endowments—especially its great elevational and topographical variability—which have made parts of the region difficult to dominate by foreign invaders. Second is the region's geographic position astride an intercontinental land bridge linking the continents of Africa, Europe, and Asia. Third is the region's proximity to the Arabian steppe. This steppe has served not only as the desert headquarters of long-distance caravan trade, but also as a wellspring of Bedouin culture and aspirations. And fourth is the Mediterranean Sea, which connects the Southern Levant to ports of call around the Mediterranean and beyond. Coastal cities, such as Tyre, Sidon, Ashkelon, and Caesarea, are harbors through which trade goods could be channeled from inland cities and towns to distant ports of call and vice versa.
- The fate of efforts to build centripetal and hierarchical polities in the Southern Levant is reflected in its archaeological record. When compared to the birthplaces of pristine civilizations such as Egypt and Mesopotamia, the Southern Levant is notable for its far less impressive archaeological traces of centralized government power.
- Remains of monumental buildings, archives yielding inscriptions, or statues containing royal propaganda begin to appear in the region nearly two millennia after their appearance in Egypt and Mesopotamia (Herr, 1999; Lipschits, 2004; Tyson, 2014).

7 The Tribal Kingdom Hypothesis

Initiatives by biblical scholars during the decades of 1960–1980 drawing on the social sciences as an aid to reconstructing the rise of state-level polities in ancient Israel and its neighbors, Ammon, Moab, and Edom were highly influenced by the standard world historical narrative mentioned earlier. The inspiration for much of this line of research by biblical scholars was Elman Service's seminal stages model of linear progression from band, to tribe, to chiefdom, to state (Fig. 5). For example, in his *Formation of the State in Ancient Israel* (1985) Frick portrays Israel's path to statehood as an evolution from a segmentary society in the tribal period of the twelfth and eleventh centuries B.C. to a chiefdom at the time of Saul, and then to a state under David and Solomon. Many other biblical scholars have gone down the same road, making this the de-facto standard model of evolution of the state for nearly three decades in biblical scholarship.

Fig. 5 Elman Service model of evolution of the state

In a contribution to the volume *The Archaeology of Society in the Holy Land*, LaBianca and Younker (1995) took exception to the use of the social evolution model as applied to the situation in Ammon, Moab, and Edom. Instead, they made the case for the persistence of kin-based (tribal) sentiments and practices through every stage of the Service model. According to their model, the state-level polities that arose in ancient Israel and Jordan during the Iron Age were "tribal kingdoms." That is to say, these were state-level polities in which tribal sentiments and practices continued unabated. The article also posits a close link between the environmental affordance of the homelands of the Ammonites, Moabites, and Edomites, thus accounting for the temporal sequence of the rise of these tribal kingdoms: first the Ammonites, then the Moabites, and lastly, the Edomites. Some salient features of these tribal kings can be seen in Fig. 6 (LaBianca, 1999).

Recent research on the rise of state-level polities in the Southern Levant has, for the most part, built on the tribal kingdom model (Bienkowski & van der Steen, 2001; Hawkins, 2013; Petter, 2018; Thomas, 2021). This research seeks to answer the question: what were the factors that gave rise to these kingdoms? To this question, some emphasize external forces, examples of which would be the hegemonic order hypothesis (Routledge, 2000, 2004, 2013) and Neo-Assyrian hypothesis (Burnett, 2016; Finkelstein & Lipschits, 2011). Others emphasize agency at the local level (Porter, 2013; Stordalen & LaBianca, 2021a). Thanks to these and other related studies, a body of theory is now available to guide future research into questions about the role of tribes and tribalism in the evolution of centralized states in the Iron Age Southern Levant. Archaeology can contribute by helping to generate data to test these various theories regarding the nature of and agency behind state formation in the Iron Age Southern Levant (Fig. 7).

8 Discussion

How, then, can the various theoretical notions introduced in this chapter help advance the search for solutions to questions about the origins and nature of state formation in the Eastern Mediterranean—concepts such as cultural production,

Salient features of tribal kingdoms

1. Tribal structure intimately tied to how food was procured.
2. Co-existence of land-tied and range-tied agricultural regimes.
3. Tribal affiliations based on generative genealogies.
4. Pre-monarchical tribal structures were not extinguished.
5. Emergence of supra-tribal polities did not produce dimorphic social structures.
6. Tribal hinterlands were administered from fortified towns.
7. Most people lived in the rural hinterlands beyond the towns.
8. Political landscape characterized by heterarchical social structure.
9. Political landscape characterized by fluid and overlapping territorial units.
10. Each polity maintained its own militia.

Fig. 6 Salient features of tribal kingdoms

global history, agency, invisible people, cultural paradigms, endemic polycentrism, and tribal kingdoms?

Theories are the lenses we use to help detect and make sense of raw data and observations generated through our fieldwork, laboratory, or library research endeavors. We all use such lenses when we do our research whether we are aware of it or not. Where we may differ is in the extent to which we make a priority of making our lenses or theories explicit—open for all to see. For those of us who identify as anthropological archaeologists, as I do, we make it a priority to make known the theories we use. Thus, my aim with this chapter has been to make the case for several lenses that I have found helpful to the task of interpreting archaeological and

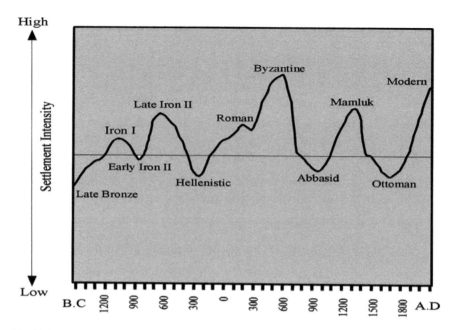

Fig. 7 Cycles of intensification and abatement

other data that has potential bearing on the questions about social order and state formation during the Iron Age in the Southern Levant.

To begin with, then, the concept of cultural production. Where I find this lens helpful to the task at hand is that it directs attention to the drivers (social processes) that generate and produce shared understandings and cultural forms. In other words, it enables us to interrogate behind-the-scenes elements—in our case here, notions such as agency, endemic polycentrism, and cultural paradigms as a means to explain the trajectory of state formation in ancient Ammon, Israel, Moab, and Edom. Most important of all, perhaps, the notion of cultural production offers a way out of slavish empiricism—the privileging of information and knowledge derived by sensory means over all other forms of information and knowledge—definitely a long-standing and consequential practice in much recent biblical archaeology.

The global history lens matters to the task at hand for several reasons. First is the emphasis on interregional connectivity as a key driver of cultural change and exchange throughout history. A related gain is its focus on long-term processes, such as globalization, as they have unfolded on both a global canvas and within particular world regions, such as the Eastern Mediterranean. A final benefit is its point of departure for studying the past—not the past for its own sake, but the past as a window on long-term processes that have relevance for understanding present and future trends. The global history perspective is thus not only of relevance to students of history, it has relevance also for policy makers and others seeking information to inform discussions about a way forward for humanity in our current day and age.

The agency lens is also important for several reasons. Most importantly, perhaps, because it brings into focus the interactive nature of cultural production—how individual actors help create cultural forms and how pre-existing cultural forms shape the actions of individual actors. And as I have emphasized above, the agency lens also enables consideration of the contributions of invisible people to cultural production. In so doing, it presents a direct challenge to much received understanding based on archaeological research, precisely because it raises questions about the extent to which received narratives of a particular past have accounted for the agency and achievements of actors whose contributions may be wholly or partially inaccessible to archaeological methods.

This brings us to the notion of cultural paradigms. In our case, the idea of a characteristic Southern Levantine Cultural Paradigm is here offered as a heuristic for guiding future research on cultural production in this particular region, especially where research into the unfolding history of social order and state formation is concerned. Though there are no doubt many more aspects to this paradigm that could be added to the four posited in our recent publication, *Levantine Entanglements* (Stordalen & LaBianca, 2021c)—endemic polycentrism, canonical ecology, holy land, and worldwide entanglement—these four suffice as a proof of concept and lay open for discussion and criticism this notion as an aid to future research on social organization in our region.

With specific regard to the notion of endemic polycentrism, its merit as a lens on the unfolding story of social order and state formation in the Southern Levantine lands is that it challenges both the notion of stages of social evolution—band-tribe-chiefdom-state—and default assumptions about gradual centralization and hierarchy. Instead, it enables the investigation of alternating drivers of social order—centrifugal versus centripetal—and the notion of transient state-level organization unfolding within a landscape of predominantly heterarchical and polycentric modes of social organization.

Perhaps the most important reason why these various lenses matter is, as already indicated, that they fundamentally challenge received understandings and narratives about how cultural production and change unfolded in our region. A case in point is the tribal kingdom hypothesis, which contests received notions about stages of social evolution and encourages reconsideration of the enduring contribution of actors (nomadic and semi-nomadic tribesmen) whose visibility in the archaeological record is often nearly or altogether absent. A closely related example is the ongoing discussion of complexity without monumentality. This is a long-overdue topic with regard to archaeology in our region and we have Erez Ben Yosef and his mentor, Thomas Levy, to thank for bringing it up for critical consideration in our community of scholars. I hope the above theoretical ruminations will add further weight to their call for new thinking on the received narratives.

References

Abulafia, D. (2011). 4. Mediterranean history as global history. *History and Theory, 50*(2), 220–228.

Adams, M. J., Finkelstein, I., & Ussishkin, D. (2014). The great temple of Early Bronze I Megiddo. *American Journal of Archaeology, 118*(2), 285–305. https://doi.org/10.3764/aja.118.2.0285

Antoun, R. T. (1968). On the modesty of women in Arab Muslim villages: A study in the accommodation of traditions. *American Anthropologist, 70*(4), 671–697.

Arbuckle, B., & Hammer, E. (2019). The rise of pastoralism in the ancient Near East. *Journal of Archaeological Research, 27*, 391–449. https://doi.org/10.1007/s10814-018-9124-8

Assmann, J. (2003). *The mind of Egypt: History and meaning in the time of the pharaohs*. Harvard University Press.

Atanda, J. A. (1972). Review of tradition and transition in East Africa: Studies of the tribal element in the modern era, by P. H. Gulliver. *Economic Development and Cultural Change, 21*(1), 200–202.

Bar-Yosef, O. (1998). The Natufian culture in the Levant, threshold to the origins of agriculture. *Evolutionary Anthropology: Issues, News, and Reviews, 6*(5), 159–177.

Bar-Yosef, O., & Valla, F. R. (1991). *The Natufian culture in the Levant* (International monographs in prehistory). Berghahn Books.

Beattie, J. (1971). Review of tradition and transition in East Africa: Studies of the tribal element in the modern era, by P. H. Gulliver. *Bulletin of the School of Oriental and African Studies, 34*(1), 190–192.

Belich, J., Darwin, J., Frenz, M., & Wickham, C. (2016). *The prospect of global history*. Oxford University Press.

Ben-Yosef, E. (Ed.). (2018). *Mining for ancient copper: Essays in memory of Beno Rothenberg*. The Institute of Archaeology of Tel Aviv University/Eisenbrauns.

Bienkowski, P., & van der Steen, E. (2001). Tribes, trade, and towns: A new framework for the late Iron Age in southern Jordan and the Negev. *Bulletin of the American Schools of Oriental Research, 323*, 21–47. https://doi.org/10.2307/1357590

Boivin, N., & Frachetti, M. D. (2018). *Globalization in prehistory: Contact, exchange, and the "people without history."*. Cambridge University Press.

Brooke, J. L. (2014). *Climate change and the course of global history: A rough journey*. Cambridge University Press.

Burnett, J. S. (2016). Transjordan: The Ammonites, Moabites, and Edomites. In B. T. Arnold & B. A. Strawn (Eds.), *The World around the Old Testament: The people and places of the ancient Near East* (pp. 309–353). Baker Academic.

Chandler, D., & Munday, R. (2011). *A dictionary of media and communication*. OUP Oxford.

Crossley, P. K. (2008). *What is global history*. Polity.

Daniels, R. E. (1971). Review of tradition and transition in East Africa: Studies of the tribal element in the modern era, by P. H. Gulliver. *American Anthropologist, 73*(2), 378–380.

den Dekker, W. (2016). *Global mindset and cross-cultural behavior: Improving leadership effectiveness*. Springer.

Dobres, M. A., & Robb, J. E. (2000). *Agency in archaeology*. Routledge.

Düring, B. S. (2014). Urbanism in the ancient Near East. In C. Smith (Ed.), *Encyclopedia of global archaeology* (pp. 7568–7572). Springer. https://doi.org/10.1007/978-1-4419-0465-2_2300

Finkelstein, I., & Lipschits, O. (2011). The genesis of Moab: A proposal. *Levant, 43*(2), 139–152.

Frank, A. G., Algaze, G., Barceló, J. A., Chase-Dunn, C., Edens, C., Friedman, J., Gilman, A., Gosden, C., Harding, A. F., & Joffe, A. H. (1993). Bronze Age world system cycles [and comments and reply]. *Current Anthropology, 34*(4), 383–429.

Frick, F. S. (1985). *The formation of the state in ancient Israel: A survey of models and theories*. Almond.

Geyer, M., & Bright, C. (1995). World history in a global age. *The American Historical Review, 100*(4), 1034–1060.

Gibson, S., & Lewis, R. (2017). The Origins of terracing in the southern Levant and patch cultivation/box fields. *Journal of Landscape Ecology, 10*(3), 256–265. https://doi.org/10.1515/jlecol-2017-0037

Golden, J. M. (2016). *Dawn of the Metal Age: Technology and society during the Levantine Chalcolithic*. Routledge.

Graeber, D., & Wengrow, D. (2021). *The dawn of everything: A new history of humanity*. Farrar, Straus and Giroux.

Greenfield, H. (2016). Metallurgy in the Near East. In H. Selin (Ed.), *Encyclopaedia of the history of science, technology, and medicine in non-western cultures* (pp. 3171–3180). https://doi.org/10.1007/978-94-007-7747-7_8819

Gulliver, P. H. (2013). *Tradition and transition in East Africa: Studies of the tribal factor in the modern era*. Routledge.

Hartshorne, R. (1939). The nature of geography: A critical survey of current thought in the light of the past. *Annals of the Association of American Geographers, 29*(3), 173–412.

Hawkins, R. K. (2013). *How Israel became a people*. Abingdon Press.

Herr, L. G. (1999). The Ammonites in the Late Iron Age and Persian period. In B. MacDonald & R. W. Younker (Eds.), *Ancient Ammon* (pp. 219–237). Brill.

Horden, P., & Purcell, N. (2000). *The corrupting sea: A study of Mediterranean history*. Wiley.

Horden, P., & Purcell, N. (2006). The Mediterranean and "the New Thalassology". *The American Historical Review, 111*(3), 722–740. https://doi.org/10.1086/ahr.111.3.722

James, P. (2006). *Globalism, nationalism, tribalism: Bringing theory back in*. Pine Forge Press.

Kardulias, N. (1996). Multiple levels in the Aegean Bronze Age world-system. *Journal of World-Systems Research, 2*(1), 378–408. https://doi.org/10.5195/jwsr.1996.93

Khawalde, S., & Rabinowitz, D. (2002). Race from the bottom of the tribe that never was: Segmentary narratives amongst the Ghawarna of Galilee. *Journal of Anthropological Research, 58*(2), 225–243.

LaBianca, O. S. (1990). *Hesban 1 sedentarization and nomadization: Food system cycles at Hesban and vicinity in Transjordan*. Andrews University Press.

LaBianca, O. (1997). Indigenous hardiness structures and state formation in Jordan: Towards a history of Jordan's resident Arab population. In M. Sabour & K. S. Vikør (Eds.), *Ethnic encounters and cultural change* (pp. 143–157). Nordic Society for Middle Eastern Studies.

LaBianca, O. S. (1999). Salient features of iron age tribal kingdoms. In *Ancient Ammon*, Leiden: Brill 17:19.

LaBianca, O. (2007). Great and little traditions: A framework for studying cultural interaction through the ages in Jordan. *Studies in the History and Archaeology of Jordan, 9*, 275–289.

LaBianca, O. S., & Hudon, J. P. (2022). Tribal kingdoms and the tribal element in southern Levantine Iron Age polities. In K. Keimer & G. Pierce (Eds.), *The ancient Israelite world*. Routledge.

LaBianca, O. S., & Younker, R. W. (1995). The kingdoms of Ammon, Moab and Edom: The archaeology of society in Late Bronze/Iron Age Transjordan (ca. 1400–500 BCE). In T. E. Levy (Ed.), *The archaeology of society in the Holy Land* (pp. 399–415). Leicester University Press.

Lancaster, W. (1997). *The Rwala Bedouin today*. Waveland Press Inc.

Lancaster, W., & Lancaster, F. (1986). The concept of territory among the Rwala Bedouin. *Nomadic Peoples, 20*, 41–48.

Layne, L. L. (1989). The dialogics of tribal self-representation in Jordan. *American Ethnologist, 16*(1), 24–39. https://doi.org/10.1525/ae.1989.16.1.02a00020

Layne, L. L. (1994). *Home and homeland: The dialogics of tribal and national identities in Jordan*. Princeton University Press.

Levy, T. E. (1983). The emergence of specialized pastoralism in the southern Levant. *World Archaeology, 15*(1), 15–36.

Lipschits, O. (2004). Ammon in transition from vassal kingdom to Babylonian province. *Bulletin of the American Schools of Oriental Research, 335*, 37–52.

Lowenthal, D. (1998). *The heritage crusade and the spoils of history*. Cambridge University Press.

Marx, E. (1967). *Bedouin of the Negev*. Manchester University Press.

Marx, E. (1977). The tribe as a unit of subsistence: Nomadic pastoralism in the Middle East. *American Anthropologist, 79*(2), 343–363.

Maurell, C. (2011). A history of global history. *Analele Universității din Oradea, Relații Internationale și Studii Europene, TOM 3*, 38–48.

Meir, A. (1988). Nomads and the state: The spatial dynamics of centrifugal and centripetal forces among the Israeli Negev Bedouin. *Political Geography Quarterly, 7*(3), 251–270. https://doi.org/10.1016/0260-9827(88)90015-8

Mundy, M. (2000). Village authority and the legal order of property (the Southern Hawran, 1876–1922). In R. Owen (Ed.), *New perspectives on property and land in the Middle East* (pp. 63–92). Harvard University Press.

Petter, T. D. (2018). Tribes and nomads in the Iron Age Levant. In J. S. Greer, J. W. Hilber, & J. H. Walton (Eds.), *Behind the scenes of the Old Testament: Cultural, social, and historical contexts* (pp. 391–395). Baker Academic.

Porter, B. W. (2013). *Complex communities: The archaeology of Early Iron Age west-Central Jordan*. University of Arizona Press.

Richards, A. I. (1972). Review of tradition and transition in East Africa: Studies of the tribal element in the Modern Era, by P. H. Gulliver. *Africa, 42*(3), 244–245. https://doi.org/10.2307/1159165

Rjoub, A., & Mahmoud, A. (2012). The emergence of agro-pastoral villages in Jordan Hamamet al-Olaimat village as a case study. *Journal of Human Ecology, 38*(3), 231–243.

Routledge, B. (2000). The politics of Mesha: Segmented identities and state formation in Iron Age Moab. *Journal of the Economic and Social History of the Orient, 43*(3), 221–256. https://doi.org/10.1163/156852000511295

Routledge, B. (2004). *Moab in the Iron Age: Hegemony, polity, archaeology*. University of Pennsylvania Press.

Routledge, B. (2013). *Archaeology and state theory: Subjects and objects of power*. A & C Black.

Sagan, C. (1990). *Pale blue dot*. Random House.

Sahlins, M. D. (1961). The segmentary lineage: An organization of predatory expansion. *American Anthropologist, 63*(2), 322–345. https://doi.org/10.1525/aa.1961.63.2.02a00050

Salzman, P. C. (1978). Does complementary opposition exist? *American Anthropologist, 80*(1), 53–70. https://doi.org/10.1525/aa.1978.80.1.02a00040

Salzman, P. C. (1979). Tribal organization and subsistence: A response to Emanuel Marx. *American Anthropologist, 81*(1), 121–124.

Schäfer, W. (2003). The new global history: Toward a narrative for Pangaea two. *EWE, 14*, 75–88.

Schäfer, W. (2004). Global history and the present time. In P. Lyth & H. Trischler (Eds.), *Wiring Prometheus: Globalisation, history and technology* (pp. 103–125). Aarhus University Press.

Shryock, A. (1997). *Nationalism and the genealogical imagination: Oral history and textual authority in tribal Jordan*. University of California Press.

Shryock, A. (2004). The new Jordanian hospitality: House, host, and guest in the culture of public display. *Comparative Studies in Society and History, 46*(1), 35–62.

Shryock, A., & Smail, D. L. (2011). *Deep history: The architecture of past and present*. University of California Press.

Sinopoli, C. M. (1995). The archaeology of empires: A view from South Asia. *Bulletin of the American Schools of Oriental Research, 299/300*, 3–11. https://doi.org/10.2307/1357342

Smith, M. G. (1956). On segmentary lineage systems. *The Journal of the Royal Anthropological Institute of Great Britain and Ireland, 86*(2), 39–80. https://doi.org/10.2307/2843992

Sommer, M. (2014). OIKOYMENH: Longue durée perspectives on ancient Mediterranean 'globality'. In M. Pitts & M. J. Versluys (Eds.), *Globalisation and the Roman world: World history, connectivity and material culture* (pp. 175–197). Cambridge.

Steffen, W., Crutzen, P. J., & McNeill, J. R. (2007). The Anthropocene: Are humans now overwhelming the great forces of nature. *Ambio: A Journal of the Human Environment, 36*(8), 614–621.

Stordalen, T. (2021). The production of authority in the levantine scriptural ecologies. In T. Stordalen & O. S. LaBianca (Eds.), *Levantine entanglements: Cultural productions, long-term changes and globalizations in the Eastern Mediterranean*. Equinox Publishing Limited.

Stordalen, T., & LaBianca, Ø. S. (2021a). The production of authority in the Levantine scriptural ecologies: An example of accumulative cultural production. In T. Stordalen & O. S. LaBianca (Eds.), *Levantine entanglements: Cultural productions, long-term changes and globalizations in the Eastern Mediterranean* (pp. 322–372). Equinox.

Stordalen, T., & LaBianca, Ø. S. (2021b). A new format for writing the history of the Levant: Introduction to the volume. In T. Stordalen & O. S. LaBianca (Eds.), *Levantine entanglements: Cultural productions, long-term changes and globalizations in the Eastern Mediterranean* (pp. 1–17). Equinox.

Stordalen, T., & LaBianca, O. S. (Eds.). (2021c). *Levantine entanglements: Cultural productions, long-term changes and globalizations in the Eastern Mediterranean*. Equinox.

Thomas, Z. (2021). On the archaeology of 10th century BCE Israel and the idea of the 'state'. *Palestine Exploration Quarterly, 153*(3), 244–275. https://doi.org/10.1080/0031032 8.2021.1886488

Tyson, C. W. (2014). *The ammonites: Elites, empires, and sociopolitical change (1000–500 BCE)*. Bloomsbury Publishing.

Walker, B. (2014). Planned villages and rural resilience on the Mamluk frontier: A preliminary report on the 2013 excavation season at Tall Hisban. In S. Conermann (Ed.), *History and society during the Mamluk period (1250–1517)* (pp. 157–192). Bonn University Press.

Wolf, E. (1982). *Europe and the people without history*. University of California Press.

Markets, Barter, and the Origins of Money: How Archaic States and Empires Organized Their Economies

Geoffrey E. Braswell

Abstract We take it for granted that the values of material things are determined by the forces of supply and demand, and that exchanges are made using mutually agreed upon proxies for value called money. How did money come to be? Can economies function without it? Do factors other than supply and demand determine value in such systems? How is exchange organized in pre-industrial economies? Does money come before the state or only as a tool of it? In this chapter, I examine the theoretical underpinnings of non-modern economies and look at specific examples from the Middle East, Mesoamerica, Europe, and beyond.

Keywords Money · Economic history · Exchange · Ancient Maya · Egypt · Cryptocurrencies · Barter · Archaic states · Banking · Coinage · Weights and measures · Cacao money

Thomas Evan Levy, his students, and colleagues have conducted ground-breaking research on ancient copper production in the region of Wadi Faynan, Jordan. Their work has carefully documented the *chaîne opératoire* of mining, smelting, and casting, and has contributed greatly to our understanding of the organization of production, long-distance trade, chronology, and sociopolitical structure in the Middle East (Beherec et al., 2016; Ben-Yosef et al., 2010; Jones et al., 2012; Levy et al., 2002). Copper production was conducted in Faynan over a time span of roughly 8000 years, from early experimentation with metals through the recycling of slag during the Mamluk era. For this reason, this great body of work allows us to study regional ancient economy from a diachronic perspective that considers evental history, medium-term conjunctures of important change, and even the great patterns of the *longue durée* (Ben-Yosef et al., 2019). When asked to contribute to this volume, I considered paying homage to Tom and his team by describing some of my own

G. E. Braswell (✉)
University of California, San Diego, La Jolla, CA, USA
e-mail: pusilha@gmail.com

© The Author(s), under exclusive license to Springer Nature Switzerland AG 2023
E. Ben-Yosef, I. W. N. Jones (eds.), *"And in Length of Days Understanding" (Job 12:12): Essays on Archaeology in the Eastern Mediterranean and Beyond in Honor of Thomas E. Levy*, Interdisciplinary Contributions to Archaeology,
https://doi.org/10.1007/978-3-031-27330-8_78

1823

research on obsidian extraction, production, and long-distance exchange in the Maya region of Central America, that is, to present a complementary synthesis of research on stone-age technology and economy for a different corner of the world (Braswell & Glascock, 2002; Golitko et al., 2012). Nonetheless, this task proved impossible for a short contribution and my results could only pale in comparison to the work conducted in Faynan. Moreover, it seemed that a more general chapter would be of use to the readers of this volume. For these reasons, and because of my growing interest in the different ways objects are valued and exchanged, I have shifted to a more theoretical topic.

My chapter describes the gradual development over millennia of something we worry about every day, yet whose existence we take for granted: money. For most of our time as a species, money did not exist. Yet throughout the 200,000 years of our prehistory and history, we have engaged in exchange. To do so means that we must have some way to determine the value of the objects, actions, and ideas—the goods and services—that we give away and receive in return. From the very start, our ancestors must have had a way to determine value. One way to do so is to compare with an object of agreed upon value. The commodity theory of money, argued by Aristotle (1984: 1255b–1256b), states that money is little more than a physical commodity of intrinsic worth that can function as a standard that all can understand, as a measure of value, as a medium of exchange, and as a system for storing wealth. This theory is still advocated by some today (e.g., Parkin, 2018), even though it cannot explain inflation (e.g., Keynes, 1936). In Depression era America, a silver coin weighing an ounce would purchase 20 cups of coffee. In 1979, it could buy 35 cups. Today the same amount of silver will purchase just five cups of joe. If silver or gold of a certain weight and purity has an established intrinsic value, why does its purchasing power change over time?

In addition to having a way to determine the value of what they traded, our earliest ancestors must also have understood that return on an exchange need not be instantaneous. This is a key aspect of what only fairly recently has become money; fundamentally it is a series of promises and the memory of those promises. Money, therefore, can be thought of as the abstract way that we measure personal and social relationships in terms of debt and credit (Macleod, 1889; Mauss, 2016 [1925]; Ingham, 2004). The notion that money is a social construction rather than a physical entity is called the credit theory of money.

Most discussions of the short history of money (e.g., Ferguson, 2008; Weatherford, 1997) take an evolutionary approach that begins with objects thought to have intrinsic worth.[1] This notion of money is often portrayed as gradually transformed into a social

---

[1] The philosophical notion of intrinsic value is beyond the scope of this chapter. I recognize that the value of, say, gold is determined by the beholders and therefore is ultimately extrinsic to the metal itself. Moreover, the industrial utility of gold contributes only a small fraction of its value, which is historically related to its use in jewelry, gift-giving, and displaying wealth. That is, the value of gold is almost entirely socially ascribed rather than related to truly intrinsic factors. I use the word 'intrinsic' simply to mean that some materials are viewed nearly universally as valuable or precious in their own right, regardless of their form and utilitarian potential. Put another way, widespread extrinsic recognition of value *is* intrinsic value.

construct of credit and debt. Thus, discussions of the development of money seek to blend the two principal theories into a sequential evolutionary narrative. In doing so, three fundamental stages are described. First, money had intrinsic value. We call this "commodity money." The value of money came from the utilitarian or precious nature of the material from which it was made. A second stage is seen to be "representative money," where something that has no value itself, such as a slip of paper, represents a claim to some commodity. Finally, there is "abstract money," the purest form of all. Abstract money does not represent any concrete commodity, but instead symbolizes an intangible and complex series of credits, debts, promises, previous transactions and those foreseen for the future, and a sense of worth that is defined in the minds of its users rather than by reference to any specific class of material object.

Although often explicitly described as distinct stages of evolution, it is important to stress that all three kinds of money can co-exist, and indeed still do in the form of gold coins, paper bills, and cryptocurrencies. None have been out-competed or have gone extinct in an evolutionary sense, and each has its use. Gold coins and ingots, for example, will always be highly prized as a way to store wealth, yet have limited use as a medium of exchange except for specialized or illicit purchases. Moreover, there is substantial debate concerning how, why, and within what sort of economic or political framework these distinct forms came to exist. Rather than view the development of different forms of money from a strictly unilinear evolutionary perspective, it is therefore better to consider them as following distinct historical trajectories related to their strengths and weaknesses as media of exchange, standards, tools to measure value, and stores of wealth. Critically, we should never forget that money represents relationships among people, and between individuals and institutions. In fact, these social relationships were central to trade long before commodities came to serve as standards or media of exchange and before the emergence of the state (Polanyi, 2001 [1944]). The notions of credit and debt being central to exchange must be as old as human memory itself. Abstract money often transactionalizes, conceals, and distances these relationships, but is still a proxy for them.

In rejecting an explicitly evolutionary framework, I do not deny that history follows a certain temporal order. In this chapter, I present an archaeological history of how exchange occurred in the past, beginning in the present and troweling downwards and backwards in time so as to avoid the implication that one form of money necessarily evolved into another. I use as a conceit examples of how a common person could interact in a market place to buy himself or herself a meal, or how a more prosperous merchant might transfer funds and conduct larger trades. I begin with abstract money because today we all use it, even if we rarely think about what it is.

1 Cryptocurrencies: The Newest Abstract Money

Most of us rarely contemplate the existential qualities of money. This is probably a good thing because money in the modern world—for the most part—is not real. Instead, it is the representation of a complex set of promises and expectations that are exchanged and that can be stored. But currency as a physical thing has no value greater than the paper it is printed on. In fact, in our world money is rapidly ceasing to be a physical thing at all, even though it has emergent manifestations and we measure all goods and services in monetary terms.

Today, we all conduct many exchanges on the internet, mostly using electronic bank transfers or credit. But perhaps the purest form of money ever invented is the most abstract: so-called virtual or cryptocurrencies. Virtual currencies do not rely on banks (more on them below), but on something called a blockchain. Fundamentally, a blockchain is a financial ledger distributed in parts across a network. It is a record of the history of all transactions ever made using a particular medium of exchange, but everyone has access to only a part of that record. Put another way, the promises and expectations and history represented by a cryptocurrency are preserved in the blockchain, and that is what makes it money with value. Privacy keeps holders of cryptocurrency from seeing the entirety of the chain beyond their own transactions, but we all know how little privacy matters. Some view cryptocurrencies as a way to avoid government scrutiny, but this is only temporary. Totalitarian governments love the idea of cryptocurrency, as long as they control it and have access to all the codes that unlock the details of the complete blockchain, and hence the history of each and every transaction. I predict that in the very near future, governments will issue their own cryptocurrencies and every single financial transaction that we make will be known and centrally recorded.

Because cryptocurrencies are not backed by the full faith and credit of any government, they are particularly subject to fraud and other risks. A woman named Ruja Ignatova (Fig. 1) invented a cryptocurrency called OneCoin and made more

Fig. 1 Ruja Ignatova, the Bulgarian swindler who founded OneCoin. Her victims will never receive complete reimbursement for the 4.6 billion dollars she, her family, and associates stole. The lessons: interpersonal trust is still central to interaction, and without a proper blockchain, ledger, or public memory, exchanges can be manipulated by criminals

than four billion dollars selling it, mostly in the United Kingdom (Marson, 2020). But do not buy OneCoin because it does not have a blockchain. That means there is no history of the amount or kinds of promises that have been made that are at the core of what money is. Instead, the promises are only what Ignatova chose to tell people, which apparently was neither detailed nor truthful. Without a record of such promises and their history—or a government that by fiat determines value—money becomes a Ponzi scheme where its value is unknown. Although a single OneCoin once traded for as much as $25–$40 based on false promises, today it has a legal negative value equal to the amount that was stolen through fraud in its promotion. In this way, a fictitious blockchain has been transformed into a well-documented record of deceitful transactions, and what was once sold as a form of credit has been transformed into a debt.

El Salvador has tried to establish Bitcoin as a co-standard and measure of value, but for the most part cryptocurrencies have yet to serve either purpose. Moreover, all cryptocurrencies still share more in common with speculative commodities than with functional media for legal exchange. That is, most exchanges involving cryptocurrencies are about their buying and selling, typically using dollars as a standard, measure, and medium. It is still quite difficult to use cryptocurrencies in daily life, even to purchase an electric car. Nonetheless and as our first example of how exchanges occur, it is possible for an urban professional in Seattle, San Francisco, or New York to enter a specific chain café and pay for an overpriced soy latte with an electronic transfer of cryptocurrency. The fees of doing so may surpass the cost of the coffee.

Is cryptocurrency money that is universally valued and considered a standard, or is it just a gimmick? As we shall see, one theory holds that it takes the threat of state sanctions to give abstract money any value at all. To date, not even El Salvador has been able to impose a cryptocurrency as the single mandated standard, measure, medium, or store of wealth. In my opinion, any nation that does so without also controlling the ability to create and destroy money will be giving away important facets of its sovereignty that are existentially critical to being a state.

2 Abstract and Representative Money: The Wealth of Modern Nations

Abstract money is modern, and its invention was just as revolutionary as agriculture or writing or the wheel. We can pinpoint when and where abstract money began to develop in the western world: Italy during the Renaissance (Ferguson, 2008: 39–45) and in seventeenth century England (Wennerlind, 2011). Until 1640 C.E., the wealthy merchants of England stored their gold and silver with the Royal Mint. But King Charles I took the gold and silver that the government was storing from the merchants as a forced loan. Merchants did not appreciate being alienated from their wealth, and so they began to store their precious metals with the private goldsmiths

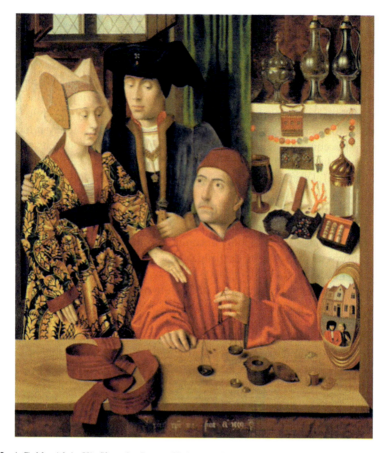

Fig. 2 *A Goldsmith in His Shop*, by Petrus Christus (1449). This painting depicts a Flemish goldsmith about 200 years before the age of the goldsmith bankers

of London (Fig. 2). Within two years of Charles' actions, the English Civil War began, and within nine years he was executed for treason.

2.1 The Goldsmith Bankers

Almost overnight, English goldsmiths became much more than jewelers and craftsmen. The goldsmiths who were storing precious metals for merchants began to do things with them, including lending. But the merchant owners wanted a share, so the goldsmiths started paying them interest. In the past, a depositor might have to pay someone to keep his gold safe, but no longer. The goldsmith bankers—building on earlier inventions of the Knights Templar and the Medici Bank—also created the modern accounting practices that provided the ledger of transactions that eventually inspired the blockchain, and gave patrons deposit slips that could, in turn, be exchanged with other merchants. This meant that gold itself did not have to change hands in a major transaction. Certificates of deposit acted like primitive bank notes. In the USA, representative money of this sort was printed until 1964. Silver certificates, which look like dollar bills printed with a blue stamp, could be taken to a bank for one dollar's worth—an ounce—of silver. In practice, though, no one turned them in for silver unless they needed pocket change for small purchases. Instead, silver and gold certificates circulated like regular paper bills.

The goldsmith bankers of England did a second very important thing: they wrote letters to their compatriots in distant cities promising them repayment if the receiver would disburse gold or silver to a named bearer. This allowed merchants to travel around the world with slips of paper rather than heavy sacks of gold. Most importantly, it provided safety. Thus, we can imagine an eighteenth-century merchant travelling from London to Paris with letters of credit that he could use to access the funds needed for his business. For centuries earlier, there were other methods of performing this same long-distance task, but they were sold as an expensive service. The Knights Templar became fabulously wealthy assisting early crusaders transport funds to and from the Holy Land using letters of credit, and once even served as a pawn shop for the crown jewels of England (Barber, 1994).

Key to this is that the money that was transferred on slips of paper was not always backed by nation states or the Catholic church, that is, by governmental agencies. One of the most important forms of money during the Renaissance was the *écu de marc*, a private currency invented in Lyon, the city that still is the banking capital of France (Wee, 1967). A seventeenth-century merchant from Antwerp might travel to Milan to sell his fine textiles, stop in a bank there and trade the local coins he earned (or, in the case of a large transaction, a letter of credit for funds in a local currency) for a bill of exchange valued in *écus*, and trade that piece of paper either in Lyon or his home city for currency usable there. An important aspect of the *écu de marc* is that bankers buying and selling this private currency would get together annually, compare their ledgers (i.e., pieces of a distributed record, like those in a blockchain), and reconcile accounts.

A third important development was that the goldsmith bankers were granted royal charters to mint coins using the precious metals in their possession (Desan, 2014). This implies at least two critical things. First, money can only be truly made by the state or by its representatives. Second, given the crises of the time, the state did not have enough gold or silver on hand to create and circulate the medium in which it desired to collect taxes. It is the demand for the specific form in which taxes must be paid that gives money value and makes states wealthy. These are critical aspects of what is called chartalism (more on this below).

A final and key development of the goldsmith bankers was the system of fractional-reserve banking. Until the era of the goldsmiths, bankers were creditors rather than debtors. That is, they were owed money when a loan was made. But in the seventeenth century, the Stockholms Banco became the first lending bank (*Lanebank*) in the world to deliberately lend out considerably more money than it held in reserve as metals (Ferguson, 2008). This was a single bank, and so a demand from depositors for all their wealth would have been disastrous. In a similar manner and at about the same time, many British goldsmith bankers became heavily indebted by lending much more money on paper than they had on deposit. By grouping together, however, these crafty goldsmiths were able to share risk by each maintaining a fraction of their assets in real holdings. If a run on one bank occurred, it could rely on the others to pool their liquid assets together and loan them until the crisis abated. In sum, this was a distributed insurance scheme. Fractional-reserve banking, where one lends out much more than one's actual liquid reserves, is how all major banks work today. The great benefit and curse of fractional-reserve banking is that allows credit to be created out of nothing.[2] By the end of the seventeenth century, much more "gold" was circulating in the form of loans than all the bankers could possibly get their hands on. Put another way, all that keeps money afloat is a belief in promises, accounting practices tracking those promises, and the hope that a collapse will be small and less than the total value of all reserves within the system.

On the plus side, fractional-reserve banking allows wealth to be created out of thin air (Fig. 3). There are politicians and other fools in the USA who advocate a return to the gold or silver standard, but this simply is not possible.[3] The value of all the precious metals in the world is nothing compared to the quantity of dollars

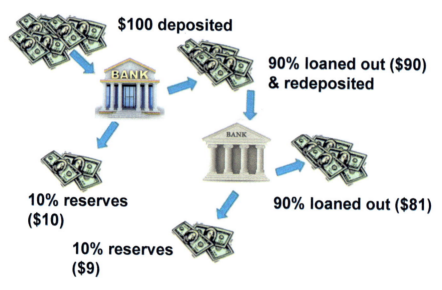

Fig. 3 How fractional-reserve bank creates debt and credit, and therefore wealth, out of thin air. In this case, an initial deposit of $100 becomes $271 backed by only $19 in reserves. Nonetheless, this is not the creation of new money, because the records of debits and credits balance

---

[2] I write 'credit,' rather than 'money' deliberately. This is because fractional reserve banks maintain books that are always balanced; the amount lent by a bank is the amount owed to it, so there is no money created. From a chartalist perspective, only states and their proxies can create money.

[3] Of the first category, consider Paul (2009). For a classic critique of fractional-reserve banking that is beloved by conservative extremists, see Hayek (1967).

created by the state that now circulate in the form of promises. Our economies today are much larger than anything that can be represented by precious commodities. This is why I call the invention of money revolutionary, and also why I write that money is not real.

The system of corporate banking quickly spread throughout Europe and beyond. Eventually, governments got in on the act in order to produce wealth in the form of credit for a particular cause. In the USA, the government opened banks during our Civil War of the 1860s, and a monetary system where federal banks were allowed to print a massive amount of bills compared to their real holdings in silver and gold began after that war (Champ, 2007). Abstract money, whose value is neither seemingly intrinsic like a gold coin, nor representative like a bill that can be exchanged for silver, is quite new. In the USA, we did not completely shed the pretenses of intrinsic and representative monies until 1964 when we ceased minting silver coins, and until 15 August 1971 when Richard Nixon ended by fiat the trade of dollars for gold at the fixed price of $38 per ounce. A year later, the Dow Jones Industrial Average closed at 1000 points for the first time, and today—even with COVID and a major European war—it is worth 35 times that amount. Converting from metals to fully abstract money made this possible. Why? Because we do not actually have enough gold or silver to cover all our debts and never will. Instead, we create wealth out of promises.

3 Commodity Monies and Ancient Trade

3.1 Coins in Classical Antiquity and the Middle Ages

How was trade conducted before goldsmith bankers invented the convoluted system of lending, borrowing, accounting, and risk-sharing that we call representative and abstract money? The next stop in our historical journey is the coin. For centuries people relied on coins made of precious metals. Coins were supposed to be of standard size and purity, although often they were not. Gold, silver, and even copper are not especially utilitarian metals in that on their own they cannot be used to make durable tools, but they are recognized as having intrinsic value. The intrinsic value of precious metals can used to measure the value of goods and services, and this is the basis of coinage. Thus, a highly valuable commodity is used to measure and judge all others. Coins are convenient because the metals that make them are relatively scarce, they require a fair bit of labor to create, and have a content guaranteed by their makers. A little gold goes a long way, and you do not need to bring a wheelbarrel full with you to the market. Moreover, for reasons of scarcity, metals can be controlled and hence they appeal to kings and nations as a medium of exchange, especially for receiving taxes. No one can make gold—although alchemists tried— and the chance of an individual finding a lot is minimal.

Coins minted by governments also carried the promise that they were made of metal of a given purity and weigh a certain amount, and so they can be used as a standard for exchange. In contrast, the coins of untrusted kings and privately cast ingots are of less or unknown value. We see in stamped coins the beginning of a system based on promises in the preference of one form over another. Thus, a farmer living outside Roman Pompeii in the years following the Punic Wars could go to the forum with one or two bronze coins called *assēs* and buy himself a meal at a thermopolium. When the food vendor had 16 *assēs*, he could convert them into a silver *denarius* of known purity and weight backed by the full faith—and more importantly, power—of the Roman Republic. For me, it is this power that creates money, and so there are very good political and economic reasons why coins are often decorated with images of rulers or other symbols of state.

Coins are not very old (Haselgrove & Krmnicek, 2012). The earliest known examples come from the Temple of Artemis at Ephesus, and date to the eighth century BCE. These valuable medallions or tokens stamped were left as offerings to the goddess, and did not circulate for other purposes, so they cannot be considered to be currency (Fig. 4a). From 610 to 560 BCE, the king of Lydia made coins stamped with a royal lion out of electrum, an alloy of gold and silver (Fig. 4b). He was succeeded by his son Croesus, who minted the first gold and silver coins (Weatherford, 1997).[4] His wealth was so fabled that we still say "rich as Croesus," but that wealth did not save him from Cyrus the Persian, who conquered Lydia in 546 BCE. Croesus' coins were the first to be used widely as a standard medium of exchange, but coins did not really catch on until the Classical Age of Greece in the fifth and fourth centuries BCE. As an example, in 300 BCE, a farmer in Sicily could go to the agora in Syracuse, pay for his lunch with a silver *stater* minted in the city under the auspices

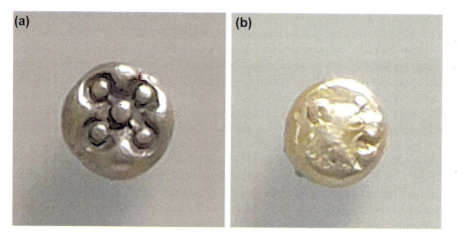

Fig. 4 Early coins of Lydia: (**a**) token from the Temple of Artemis representing the paw of a lion; (**b**) electrum coin with image of a lion. (Photographs by the author)

---

[4]Zhao et al. (2021) argue that the minting of coins may be decades older in China.

of Agathokles, and expect a fair bit of change. But this still was not very long ago. What did people do before coins?

3.2 The Bronze and Iron Ages: Commodities and Standardized Measures

During the Bronze and early Iron Age, commonly used media of exchange were valued for their intrinsic and often utilitarian value. Like coins, these artifacts can be thought of as commodities against which the value of other goods and services could be measured. Throughout this period, Faynan copper was used to make ingots of various standard sizes and purity against which the value of other objects and labor could be measured. Faynan ingots were objects of trade because of their utilitarian potential, but also were a form of commodity money used to purchase imported pottery, textiles, food, and precious goods that bolstered elite status. Although we do not know for sure, it is highly probable that the value of other commodities was sometimes measured in terms of Faynan ingots.

A copper or bronze ingot contains a known amount of metal, and hence can serve as a medium of exchange and measure of value, but without assay it is less useful as a standard than a coin minted by a trustworthy ruler or city. An ingot also stores wealth in a transportable but somewhat bulky form. Ingots, therefore, fulfill the functions of money, albeit not as well as minted coins issued by the state. One form that particularly interests me are large, copper and tin ingots shaped like animal skins stretched for drying. So-called ox-hide ingots (Fig. 5) dating to the Late

Fig. 5 Copper commodity money in the form of an ox-hide ingot found in Sardinia. The copper in these Bronze Age ingots came from Cyprus, which likely was the place of manufacture. (Photograph by the author)

Bronze Age are well known in the Mediterranean, and most copper examples seem to have been made from ore mined on Cyprus (Stos-Gale et al., 1997; the source of the tin remains uncertain). These were valued for the amount of copper or tin used to make them, but also may represent an earlier medium of exchange or perhaps were valued in terms of a known number of ox hides (for example, 100 skins). This makes me wonder if the story of Jason and the Golden Fleece has its root in an understanding of measuring value in terms of "hides" made of different materials.

Although they are not themselves directly utilitarian, ingots can be transformed into tools, and metals often were cast in the form of axes of standardized mass and purity. So-called axe monies were common around the world and are known from Europe (Kuijpers & Popa, 2021), Mesoamerica, and the Andean region (Hosler et al., 1990). In fact, axe monies called *grzywna* (a unit of both mass and exchange) continued to be used alongside coins in Poland as late as the Middle Ages (Bochnak, 2016). In Zhou dynasty China, bronze was shaped into standardized spades or shovels of a given size and weight (Zhao et al., 2021). These two forms explicitly tie value to agricultural production, just as ox-hide ingots are tied to pastoralism. But these are not the only examples of money being related to and derived from notions of food production.

One of the earliest exchange media was called the *šiqlu* or *siqlu*, from which the Israeli New Shekel gets its name. The šiqlu was first developed in ancient Mesopotamia and represented a particular weight, about 8.4 g (Hafford, 2012), of wheat. The development of a system of weights and measures, and the structures to administer them, are critical to all economies that operate on a standard, even one based on a plant product like wheat. An accountant-priest in Mesopotamia could measure the wheat he controlled in šiqlu, and then describe an exchange in terms of what was received by the temple for that wheat, or describe an exchange of other materials by their equivalents in wheat šiqlu. Wheat is a particularly bad material for a standard because anyone can grow it and a lot of wheat might be needed for a transaction. It is possible, but difficult, for a government to limit the amount of wheat in circulation. Moreover, wheat is regularly consumed and can go bad—even explode. It is therefore a poor long-term store of wealth, and thus, lacks the desired durability of currency. Finally, there are years when wheat is common and others when it is scarce. Its value can fluctuate wildly, and therefore can be a poor measure of the value of other commodities. All of these problems beg the question: was the šiqlu really just a quantity of wheat, or was it a more abstract state-mandated standard and measure of wealth? That is, although the šiqlu was tied to a commodity, was it fundamentally an invention and tool of state control? We know it was a unit of taxation, which implies that it was at least used and perhaps created by the state.

3.3 The Egyptian Economy

The ancient Egyptians had several media of exchange and ways of measuring value before the eventual adoption of coins, and these too relied on weights and measures. During the Old Kingdom and First Intermediate period (c. 2686–2025 BCE), the values of large transactions were described in terms of weights of metals, but these almost never were the items actually traded. Instead, grain (which lost value quickly) and especially cloth (which held it longer) seem to have been more common media of exchange. Copper, grain, and cloth continued in importance throughout the Middle Kingdom and Second Intermediate periods (2025–1550 BCE; Muhs, 2016: 37, 76). By New Kingdom times (1550–1069 BCE), exchanges were made of objects whose value was generally expressed in terms of weights of metals, and there is some indication that *seniu* or *shati*—metal rings—emerged as media of exchange and the storage of wealth (Muhs, 2016: 114). By the Third Intermediate (1069–664 BCE), values of exchanges were almost always described in terms of weights of silver, and it is possible but unproven that silver became the actual medium of exchange. This pattern continued in the Saïte and Persian periods (664–332 BCE), even after the Greeks introduced the notion of coins (Muhs, 2016: 160–61, 190–191). The storage of wealth in ancient Egypt follows a similar pattern, moving away from perishable commodities such as wheat and barley, to cloth and metals, and eventually to hoards of weighed silver and coins.

We know about prices of various goods such as incense that were used in mortuary cults dating to the Old Kingdom from the Abusir papyri (Willems, 2012). There are temple records and even model tallies dating to the Middle Kingdom, and we have particularly good records from Deir el-Medina about how workmen who worked in the Valley of Kings were paid during the New Kingdom. Also recorded are commodity values for that time, and how these were affected by low harvests during a period of climate crisis.

The most basic aspects of Egyptian economy were bread and beer, which formed the way laborers were paid throughout the millennia. Bakeries and breweries were state controlled, and most often adjacent to one another in ancient Egypt because they required the same ingredients—grain, water, and yeast. Most importantly, they used standard quantities of grain in a system called *pfs*, or "baking value." This allowed a known number of loaves of a given size to be baked with the same amount of ingredients. There are ceramic tallies or markers in the shape of a standard bread loaf that date to the Middle Kingdom. These would have been used to measure the payment—typically 10 loaves per day—of a workman. Similarly, beer jars were standardized in size. A minimum salary for a workman also would contain up to two jars of beer per day during this period. Together, the bread and beer of a minimum salary was thought to provide what was needed to support a single man—but just barely. Of course, more valued workers would earn multiples of these daily rations. The highest salaries were about fifty times the basic wage. On such a wage a person could feed his family and his household helpers. It is hard to imagine that these high wages were paid in actual bread and beer. Instead, it must have been granted in tokens or ostraca (i.e., representative money) that could be traded in the market and used for barter. Importantly, these tokens could be saved or loaned or traded to others. Thus, they provided a way not only to measure wealth, but also to store it and trade it.

During Dynasty XIX and XX of the New Kingdom, known as the Ramesside period, workers constructing the tombs in the Valley of the Kings lived in Deir el-Medina (Fig. 6), a special village or compact town that segregated them on the West Bank of the Nile across from Thebes (Janssens, 1976). Workers here were given housing, charcoal for cooking, cloth, foodstuffs including bread, beer, and meat, and, importantly, the tools for their trades, such as stone cutting. Many of these materials could be bartered.

There are good records of the prices of commodities and inflation during this period. Most such prices are discussed in terms of equivalents in mass or volume of other goods. Egyptian scribes at the end of the New Kingdom refer to four units of commodity pricing. The most common was the *dbn*, a unit for the weight of metals of about 91 g (Petrie, 1883). There were debens of copper or bronze, of silver, and of gold, and each sort had different values. A deben was divided into ten *qdt* (qedet or kite) and the lowest denomination in practice seems to be 5 kites of copper, or about 45.5 grams. Personal records of transactions seem to refer only to copper deben, but official papyri commonly discuss deben of silver as the values of larger quantities of commodities. Problematical is that the value of distinct metals themselves were not constant. A deben weight of silver fluctuated between 96 and 104 deben of copper in Dynasties XVIII and XIX before plunging to 60 deben of copper during Dynasty XX (Černy, 1954).

Fig. 6 Deir el-Medina, Egypt. (Photograph by the author)

Two other units were the *hin* (used to measure oil, equivalent to about half a liter or a pint) and the *khar* (*ẖ3r*, or sack), a unit of volume for grain of about 76.6 liters or 20.2 gallons. It seems that a *hin* of sesame oil was thought to be worth about one copper deben. Baskets were commonly made in khar or fractional khar sizes, and their costs were expressed in terms of their volume, which could be translated into deben as units of value.

A more theoretical unit was the *seniu* or *shati*, meaning "ring" of silver. Before the New Kingdom, these were rarely exchanged in actual transactions, but instead were largely used as a measure of value and as a calculating tool in ledgers. For example, Stela Cairo JdE 42787 describes a house that was sold for 10 shati but actually paid for with a bed worth four shati and two pieces of cloth worth three shati each (Menu, 1998). Thus, the shati was a theoretical measuring tool that could be used to value quantities of goods measured in deben, khar, and hin in comparable terms. Put another way, it was fundamentally an early form of abstract money used to simplify state and private transactions. Key to the utility of the shati as an abstract unit rather than as actual commodity money is the understanding that while the weight and volume units were constant, relative values of goods fluctuated. Thus, different documents describe a shati (as a unit of value) as purchasing anything from five to nearly nine deben of copper.

This complex system required specialization. In the late New Kingdom, accountants kept track of inflation for various goods quantified by count, weight, or volume, and then calculated equivalencies between them using shati. During Dynasty XIX, a khar of wheat was worth one deben of copper, but during Dynasty XX it gradually rose as high as eight deben, before sinking again to just one deben (Černy, 1934). The shati served as a mechanism to measure and keep track of such fluctuations in the relative values of commodities.

We can imagine a New Kingdom merchant arriving at a market and selling his load of mixed goods. He might calculate their total value in terms of shati, but trade for them in terms of the two units of volume, in terms of weights of metals, or even in terms of daily rations. Key to success was a knowledge of inflation and value across the kingdom, and an ability to calculate. To trade was to speculate, and successful merchants needed up-to-date pricing information. Commoners were allowed to engage in direct barter, or trade among themselves using daily rations, or make large purchases of household goods in terms of copper weight or other items valued in shati. A New Kingdom commoner therefore could go to the market on the outskirts of Thebes and purchase a donkey for about seven deben of copper, or a mixed lot of goods evaluated at around one shati, not that different from what his ancestor paid in the Middle Kingdom. He might also trade a few daily rations of bread (in either food form or tokens) for meat or vegetables.

Another important dimension to Egyptian finance was the grain bank, which began early in the history of Egypt and became more elaborate in Ptolemaic times. These began as local sites where yearly taxes in grain were collected from communities. Simple farmers could also store their excess at the bank. Written slips were used to transfer ownership of wheat or barley in payment for goods or service. That is, wheat stored at the bank could be used as commodity money for resolving debts, and, because it was constantly shipped onward and replenished, shares belonging to an individual would not spoil. Grain banks also could lend seed at an interest rate set at 50% at the next harvest (Muhs, 2016: 232).

In the Ptolemaic period, or after about 300 BCE, a central grain bank was established in Alexandria. This was a place for centralized record keeping and played some of the roles of a modern central bank. Specifically, the director of the bank could determine the amount of seed that was stored and released in a given year. If a year had a bumper crop and devaluation was likely, the director of the central grain bank could release less seed in the form of loans as a way to mitigate the surplus. On the other hand, if a bad crop occurred, he could release more seed on loan to correct for inflation. Today, we call this a strategic reserve, and Ptolemaic Egypt developed a rather sophisticated way to prevent the economic upheavals typical of earlier eras such as Dynasty XX.

3.4 Cacao: Money That Grows on Trees

Other civilizations around the world developed ways of creating standardized and accepted value for certain commodities. The ancient Aztecs, for example, sometimes described value in terms of feather quills filled with gold dust. Most famously of all, cacao beans were used as standards of predetermined value to measure exchange in Mesoamerica. Cacao, of course, is not all of equal quality, and the Aztecs rated the value of beans into four ranked categories (Baron, 2018: 212). The smallest and lower quality beans were typically used to make a frothy beverage consumed by elites.

In sixteenth century Nicaragua, a slave could be purchased for 100 cacao beans and the services of a prostitute could be rented for five (Coe & Coe, 2013: 58–59). The values of other goods and services in cacao beans also are known. Nonetheless, the most frequent physical use of cacao as commodity money was in the form of tribute to elite rulers and conquering states. Mesoamerican cultures used a base-20 numerical system, and a standard unit of tribute was 20^3 or 8000 cacao beans (Fig. 7). Both the number 8000 and the special sack used to present that many beans as tribute was called *xiquipilli* by the Aztecs (Karttunen, 1992: 326) and *pik* by the Maya.

The most important aspect of cacao was that it, like the Egyptian shati, served as a translation tool that allowed different goods or services to be compared in value. That is, cacao beans served as a representative commodity to measure value. We often assume that in societies that lack money, exchanges are conducted as barter. But without money or a representative commodity that functions as a measure like money, barter is extremely difficult. Barter exchanges, therefore, became more common *after* the development of money or commodities with widespread and accepted value against which exchanges could be measured and compared. We should not view barter as an evolutionary stage before the development of money or such commodities, even though that is how it is commonly portrayed.

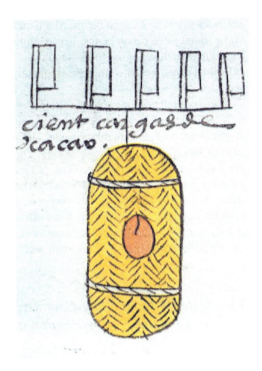

Fig. 7 Cacao: Image from the *Codex Mendoza* of Aztec tribute showing 5 × 20 = 100 *xiquipilli* of 8000 cacao beans each

Imagine a Maya man goes to the market place in the Classic Maya city of Calakmul. He has a small seashell in his bag, two axes he made from local stone, and an old obsidian spearpoint. His *xa'an* (wife) has told him to come home with a basket of corn, some tomatoes, and maybe a jade bead. How does he negotiate a trade? The answer, of course, is that he barters. But what if a vendor at the market does not want to trade her food for an axe because she already has one? Or if there is no demand for a shell or obsidian? In other words, suppose there are differences in the *levels of need* of two people who wish to trade. This is a central conundrum in all economic systems where exchange is conducted without an agreed-upon currency or representative commodity that can be used to measure value, and can make a barter transaction impossible. It implies that value is situational and unpredictable. Such systems cannot support surplus because no one agrees upon its value. In English, we use the expression "a hill of beans" to mean worthless, because it can be worthless unless you have a trading partner who happens to need a whole hill made of beans.

This is where a commodity like cacao (beans again), with a recognized value established by the state, can be used to measure and determine the value of a stone axe for someone who already has a toolshed full of axes at home. Yet another stone axe may have little or no utilitarian value, but it can serve to store a small but known amount of wealth that later may be exchanged long after today's ripe tomatoes have rotted. At our Maya market, a vendor agrees that a stone axe she does not need is worth eight cacao beans, and is content to handover tomatoes and a basket of corn worth a total of five cacao beans. She then evens-up the exchange by passing our Maya friend three cacao beans. It was more in these two manners—as measuring and equalizing/leveling-up tools—and not as the principal medium of exchange that individual cacao beans were most frequently employed at the Mesoamerican market place.

There is another factor that may help motivate an exchange for an axe that is not truly needed: all direct dyadic exchanges involve building social networks that are in and of themselves valuable. A seller and a buyer both have an impetus, however large or small, to see that a trade occurs. This allows us to imagine barter exchange in a world lacking a state-defined unit of measure for value. If our Maya man enters a market place and cannot find someone who wants what he has to offer in immediate exchange, he can surely find someone who will extend credit and "gift" him what he needs for the time being. Such gifting with the expectation of delayed reciprocity is at the core of the social aspects of exchange and the construction of prestige (Mauss, 2016 [1925]), as we shall see.

3.5 States Without Fully-Commercialized Markets: Control of the Means of Distribution and Destruction

Even with an agreed upon standard for comparison, a medium to conduct exchange, and a measuring tool in which value can be expressed, how was the worth of a good or service determined in archaic states?

Contemporary neoclassical economists believe that value is set by the forces of supply and demand. Moreover, those with a Marxist bent discuss control of the means of production as central to the creation of wealth and the maintenance of power. I disagree somewhat with both perspectives. Neither completely captures the reality or complexity of archaic economies. In particular, it is much easier for an archaic state without modern communication and transportation systems to control the means of distribution than of production itself. It is easier for a king to determine and limit how trade occurs than it is to control each and every production node, because there are many fewer merchants than there are farmers.[5] This is what I mean by control of the means of distribution. In Egypt, grain banks and treasuries were controlled by the state or important temples, so the king and his representatives could indirectly oversee the most significant exchanges. Moreover, many archaic states are predatory. They extract surplus as tribute or through rapine. That is, if surplus is not turned over by a community or subject territory, it can be invaded and put to the torch and sword. This is what I mean by control of the means of destruction. The Huns, Tatars, Mongols, Persians, Assyrians, Egyptians, Inka, and Aztecs all understood this principle very well. We have ancient codices that list Aztec trib-

---

[5] Moreover, as the English goldsmiths and bankers of Lyon would learn, the principal way wealth is generated is exchange, not production. Lending is a form of exchange.

ute from subdued provinces (Berdan & Anawalt, 1992). In addition to cacao beans, the empire was most commonly paid in food stuff, raw cotton, plain and decorated cloth, and fancy military uniforms decorated with exotic feathers. Tribute lists show illustrations of these goods and contain information concerning the quantity and frequency that were due to the empire. To not pay tribute carried the risk of military destruction. For me, therefore, Marx missed the point: distribution and destruction are much easier and more important to control than production. To go further, control of the means of distribution and destruction can be used to define the state. Of course, the easiest way to control distribution is to mandate the use of a state-created currency whose value is maintained by the demand for its use created by the threat of sanctions. But let us consider other ways to control exchange.

It is important at this point to introduce terms defined by Carol Smith (1976). A *fully-commercialized market system* is one where the laws of supply and demand determine both wholesale and retail prices of goods. This requires a communication system that allows the rapid and free circulation of information concerning current values. A *partially-commercialized market system* is one where either wholesale or retail prices are fixed by other factors. Colonial or dendritic systems rely on controlling the wholesale price and extracting profit through retailing on a supply-and-demand open market. A fixed and artificially low price paid to rural producers greatly increases retail profit. Think of the exploitation of sugar plantations in the Caribbean by the British, or the relations between the USA and so-called banana republics. Colonial systems, therefore, can be quite large—what Wallerstein (2004) calls "world-systems"—and depend on the development of underdevelopment in the colonies through a monopolistic buyer who sets exploitive purchase prices.

A second kind of partially-commercialized economy, called the *administered market*, tends to be quite small, only the size of a kingdom or city-state where trade can be monitored in a small number of market places. In an administered market system, states control retailing. They can determine, who, what, where, and for how much goods are traded. Moreover, they can tax exchange by collecting surplus directly from merchants who enter a marketplace with a certain amount of goods and leave it with less. I imagine that Maya markets, which often were located in the very center of cities not far from the palace, were controlled in this manner. Thus, a Maya merchant might enter with 20 obsidian cores for making stone tools, and leave with only ten. A tax of 10% could be extracted by taking a core from those that remained unsold. This core could be used by the royal palace for its own utilitarian needs, or saved for later exchange in the market place, or gifted as a means of creating a social bond and obligations. Unlike cacao beans, the obsidian core would not go bad.

3.6 Determining Value Without Resorting to Supply and Demand Explanations

In market economies that are not fully commercialized, value may be determined in a number of ways. First, either retail or wholesale prices can be fixed as I described. But a proportional tax on an obsidian transaction, mentioned above, does not rely on fixing prices let alone on determining value. Indigenous markets in the New World today are physically structured in a way that may seem illogical from the perspective of competition. All the sellers of vegetables gather together in the same part of the market place. All the sellers of corn sit together in a different spot. All the sellers of clothes are in yet another corner of the market space. If you want to buy a cooking pot, you have to wade through all the tin mongers to get your goods and you may haggle with several before you make your purchase. One important reason that all the sellers of a certain class of goods stay together is the determination of value. A modern Maya woman selling maize is not attune to the Chicago Mercantile Exchange; she does not have up-to-the-minute price information. But by sticking close together in a marketplace, all the vendors of a certain good know what price is being offered and accepted that day (Fig. 8). Proximity provides communication. It also presents a way for our ancient Maya farmer to trade his axe for corn. Because there are multiple women trading corn in the same area of a market, he maximizes his chance of finding an exchange partner who either needs an axe in trade for food, or—more likely—one who knows she can eventually trade an axe in her home community. Moreover, the values of both the axe and the food, as measured in cacao beans, are public knowledge because of the proximity of many vendors.

Fig. 8 Produce sellers at a modern Maya market of highland Guatemala

One way that prices in market systems that are not fully commercialized may be determined is according to what David Ricardo (2004 [1817]: 5–30) proposed as the labor theory of value. This does not require money as a standard or a particular commodity like cacao as a measure of value. Most neoclassical economists hate this notion because it rejects the principles of supply and demand. Nonetheless, it is useful for understanding non-western economies.

Let us say it takes our Maya farmer an hour to gather good stone to make an axe and 12 more hours to grind it down. The amount of total work is more or less known and agreed upon, so the axe—made of a material that has no intrinsic value in itself—may be traded for other materials that require about the same amount of time to produce. When purchasing a stone axe, a buyer in turn considers the value of the labor that he will save by having one. If you go to a Maya market today and haggle for a *po'ot* or *huipil* as the woven blouses made by women are called, you undoubtedly will be told how many days it took to weave it. The labor invested in production is part of the understanding of the transaction, as is the savings in labor a purchaser will have by not weaving one herself. Regardless of the standard or medium used to conduct the exchange, a price is arrived at by understanding the amount of labor expended in production and the labor saved through the purchase.

Stanish and Coben (2013: 426–429; see also Stanish, 2010) make an important point. Exchanges in many markets involve behaviors that can be difficult to describe using formalist economic terms. A very big part of exchange is prestige and the construction of social networks. An ancient Maya merchant may have judged success not in terms of the total surplus that he or she extracted, but by the size of the social network and the strength of the relationships forged through exchanges. In other words, a merchant may gain status not solely through western notions of the accumulation of capital, but also in terms of social bonds—especially those forged through debts owed to her and favors that accrue yet may never be repaid. Although these concerns are by no means excluded from consideration by formalist economic anthropologists and are often formulized by them, such scholars view social values in terms of the maximization of utility within the context of scarcity and demand. Formalist (like functional) analyses, therefore, always lead to the inevitable and unprovable tautology that all behavior is "rational" from a western perspective if only framed in the proper narrative. For many anthropologists, this approach to culture seems artificial, forced, and beside the point, much like an evaluation of Mozart's music from the perspective of wave mechanics.

For social and cultural reasons, a seller in the market may not seek to extract the most advantageous trade from her customer. Instead, she may seek to provide a fair price not only to maximize profit over time, but more importantly to repeat the social-status building aspects of interaction, build a friendship to mitigate against future risks, because it is demanded by a cultural categorical imperative offering no reward, or even for reasons that may elude completely our western sense of rational maximization. We say "whoever dies with the most friends wins" and that is a principle that often can be applied to non-western economic systems where exchange is conducted directly between producers and consumers rather than indirectly through intermediaries using money. Moreover, rather than being *Homo economicus*, we are

Homo reciprocans (Bowles & Gintis, 2002), and often act in ways that display an inclination towards social cooperation rather than rational cost benefit to ourselves. In sum, social relations and values merge with economic ones in complex ways, what Polanyi (2001 [1944]) called the "embedded" nature of economy, and these ways are not always easily or convincingly expressed in terms of rational maximization, despite the efforts of formalist anthropological economists.

3.7 Status-Endowing Artifacts, Fungibility, and Alienation

Archaeologists argue that items that endow status are especially important to archaic states and acephalous political systems. Status-endowing objects may be made of rare or exotic materials but the intrinsic value of the material does not play a major role in determining value. Such artifacts are not fungible, meaning they are not interchangeable as a class. My son is a painter, and the materials and time used to create one of his paintings are roughly equivalent to those used by van Gogh: the paints and canvas of each cost about $50 and, let us say, the labor is worth $300 dollars (Fig. 9). Despite the equivalence of both intrinsic and labor value, a van Gogh and a Braswell are not fungible.[6]

For the ancient Maya, jade is an example of a non-fungible good (Andrieu et al., 2014). We know that carved objects made of jade were highly valued by Maya elite, so much so that they were not always alienable and often were subject to sumptuary laws. By these, I mean that some pieces could not be traded and that there were rules concerning who could and who could not possess a particularly important jade object. Nonetheless, jade as a raw material had little value in its own right. Many commoners owned jade beads, and we know from research around the jade sources that the communities there were quite modest and not at all wealthy (Taube et al., 2011). These villages extracted jade and made simple pieces, but they did not produce iconographic representations or write hieroglyphs on jade. Thus, the jade they extracted had little value until it was worked by craftsmen with specialized skills

---

[6]A recent invention is the non-fungible token or NFT. These are traded on the same blockchains as a particular cryptocurrency. While there are multiple bitcoins (up to a theoretical maximum of 21 billion), each bitcoin is worth the same as any other (i.e., is fungible); this is not the case for NFTs. That they most often are metadata associated with digital art is beside the point; an NFT can be anything virtual that is unique and generates value through exchange. What is confounding for many is that in the case of digital art, an image may be found for free on the internet and can be replicated infinitely. In the case of a van Gogh, prints and posters copies of it may be made, but these are not the same as the original. This raises the question of what "original" means in the case of a digital file. The dissemination of prints and posters may lead to an increase in the value of a work of art by creating demand for the original, but this is not necessarily the case for an NFT that is indistinguishable from all of its copies. Moreover, possession of an NFT is rarely traded with its copyright. Thus, while an owner of a painting uniquely possesses the work and often owns legal rights to its reproduction, the owner of an NFT most often owns and trades the metadata of a file without controlling rights to the image.

Markets, Barter, and the Origins of Money: How Archaic States and Empires Organized... 1845

Fig. 9 Non-fungible paintings with approximately the same intrinsic value (i.e., cost of materials): (**a**) Self Portrait by Vincent van Gogh; (**b**) classroom study by Aaron L. Braswell

and esoteric knowledge. Research at the Maya cities of Aguateca and elsewhere demonstrates that such craftspeople often were members of the royal family itself (Inomata, 2001). Instead of intrinsic or even a labor valuation of their creation, such artifacts were treasured because of their religious content, the specialized knowledge and status of the artisans who made them, and, especially, the status of the person who gave the objects to their owners.

A jade pectoral from Nim li Punit provides an example (Braswell, 2017, 2019; Prager & Braswell, 2016). It carries on its front the T-shaped hieroglyph *ik*, which means "wind," "breath," and "life" (Fig. 10). At the time it was carved, the basic form and idea of a jade wind-jewel had been around for more than 1200 years. We can trace such wind jewels to the Olmec, who created stylized *Strombus* (conch) shells out of jade. When we put our ear to a conch shell, we say we hear the ocean. The people of Mesoamerica heard the wind. The Maya wind jewel had a religious function. It was worn by rulers during the performance of the very important scattering ritual. The king was the summoner of the winds that brought the rainclouds of the monsoon season. He would then scatter balls of incense or perhaps even maize seed into a fire as an offering to the gods and as the first symbolic planting of the agricultural year. The kings of Nim li Punit wore this jewel and performed this ritual for 150 years; we know this because of images and texts on dated monuments. The pectoral was completely inalienable from the rulers because of its magical and religious properties, like the crown worn by Queen Elizabeth.

The reverse side of the jewel provides evidence of its value beyond the ritual realm. It contains an abbreviated family history of its first wearer, describing a king whose origins were foreign. Most likely, this piece was a gift from the powerful king of Caracol, one that helped legitimize the reign of the king roughly 20 years after he was first installed. The wind jewel, therefore, had great political value in that it symbolized this connection with a powerful and distant polity. It is likely that the Nim li Punit wind jewel also was viewed as a living if supernatural being.

Fig. 10 The Wind Jewel of Nim li Punit, Belize: (above) front with T-shaped glyph *ik* meaning wind or breath; (below) reverse showing hieroglyphic text. (Photographs by the Toledo Regional Archaeological Project)

One-hundred-fifty years after its creation, the wind jewel was laid to rest in a cenotaph or false grave. It was placed on top of another ritual object, and together they were laid out and given offerings as if they were the body of a king. The burial of the wind jewel corresponds roughly with the end of the Nim li Punit dynasty, and I cannot help but think its interment symbolizes the end of the kingdom.

Such status-endowing goods that are non-fungible and subject to sumptuary laws limiting their distribution play pivotal roles in political economies. When they do change hands, they not only build status, but also can symbolize the formation of alliances, conquest or domination, or other political relations. They also may be viewed as pivotal to ritual, maintaining the wellbeing of a people, or even recreating cosmic order. Finally, when they are displayed in public or if they do change hands, it is within a cultural context that often promotes other exchanges.

4 Money Without States or States Without Money?

Thus far, my chapter may give the impression that I argue that more complex forms of money were derived naturally from the earlier adoption of commodities used to measure value, as a direct medium of exchange, or both. From this perspective, money—even if only in the form of a mutually agreed upon commodity used for calculation and equivalency purposes—was a logical step that made exchange easier for people who did not want to cart around sacks of stone axes and shells whose daily value was unknown and unagreed upon before reaching the marketplace where a trading partner who needed them might not be found. But can the origin of money truly be found in the needs of exchange partners? Put another way, did commodity money evolve to meet the needs of bartering or for some other reason? Related to this is the chicken-and-egg question: Which came first, money in any form or the state?

If money developed to assist individuals in barter, then it almost certainly predates the emergence of the state. If, on the other hand, money was invented for the purpose of taxation and tribute, then it accompanied the emergence of centralized political authority that controlled the means of distribution and destruction. My perspective is that it is difficult to imagine how any commodity just happened to be mutually agreed upon as a measure or standard without: (1) the state desiring to control distribution; (2) the imposition of taxes or tribute in specific desired and quantified materials; and (3) the threat of state-sponsored sanctions mandating the use of a standard to measure value and to be used as a medium of exchange.

This latter heterodox position, that money was invented for the use of states, was named "chartalism" by Georg Friedrich Knapp (1924) in his book *The State Theory of Money* (for extensive critical comments, see Weber, 2019). My brief discussion of the chartalist theory that commodity monies and other forms did not evolve spontaneously out of the needs of bartering partners is borrowed liberally and shamelessly from a recent work by Robert Rosenswig (2022). Following the chartalists, Rosenswig argues that money was developed as a calculating and accounting device of the state. Rulers imposed their unit of account as the standard form in which they would accept payment of fees, fines, taxes, and tribute. Such state money retained its value and was used in other non-state transactions because rulers regularly and periodically demanded payment, and thus having state money on hand (in whatever form) guaranteed a way to avoid sanctions. For this reason and the fear of reprisals, state-imposed money became standards of payment, measures of value, stores of wealth, and widely accepted media of exchange.[7] Key is that they served to calculate equivalencies in transactions and served accounting purposes, even in the absence of physical money. Thus, the value of goods and services might come to be expressed in a state-recognized commodity like cacao beans, even if they were not used in an actual transaction.

Moreover, state-sponsored money need not even exist. The Egyptian shati was much more a theoretical accounting device that allowed different materials to be compared and debts and credits to be resolved than an actual coin. In medieval England, the only physical coin was the penny. In that society with very little literacy, accounts of debts were kept on tally sticks representing the abstract units of pounds and shillings, money that had no physical manifestation other than nicks on rods of hazelwood (Rosenswig, 2021). Such sticks were devised as accounting tools for the taxes, fees, and fines imposed by the kingdom, but they also could be traded in their own right and used to resolve debts. In such a manner, the pound and shilling—which existed without physical form—came to be mandated as the official standard, measure, medium, and store for wealth in England.

These records of debts and credit evince the context in which money developed: the archaic state. Therefore, for Rosenswig (2021, 2022), appearance of tally sticks in England, Qin China, and among the ancient Maya, as well as the invention of accounting devices like the Andean *quipu*, provide important archaeological and empirical evidence for the chartalist position that the primary purpose of money from the start was its use as a state-mandated accounting device. Although intrinsically valuable commodities could be chosen to represent wealth, money itself had no intrinsic value and has always been a bookkeeping device like the écu de marc. The purpose of taxation, therefore, was not so much to stockpile huge amounts of commodities such as cacao beans or other even gold, but to create dependency and the even greater demand that generates wealth. With the Alexandria grain bank, a secondary purpose was to mitigate against inflation, like our own central bank.

Thus, money was not created in less-complex societies as a tool to make barter more efficient or even possible. It was invented by the state. If we are to understand how exchange was conducted before the relatively recent origin of the state some five thousand years ago, that is, throughout most of our history as a species, we need to consider modes other than market exchange. These include redistribution (i.e., polyadic exchange)—virtually the definition of chiefdoms—and reciprocal forms of dyadic exchange that do not entail the use of money or reference to commodities

---

[7]Recognizing the importance of sanctions and the threat of state-sponsored violence, cryptocurrencies will not serve all the functions of money until they are either created by states themselves or adopted by them as a required standard. Moreover, since a state through its policies determines how much money is in existence, cryptocurrencies based on mining or other principles of independence will always be commodities of a sort rather than tools under the control of the state. This may seem like a welcome limit to governmental power, but it also means that a state cannot control inflation, influence employment rates, or otherwise create the capital it may periodically need to defend and assist its people in times of need.

with an accepted value. Karl Polanyi (2001 [1944]) viewed economies that relied on reciprocity or redistribution as the principal modes of exchange as "embedded" within broader social relations and systems, but it must be stressed that such modes of exchange—like different forms of money—persist and are embedded in even the most modern economic systems. Key to such exchange is status. I argue that all exchanges potentially endow at least a modicum of status upon the participants in the form of recreating, building, or extending social networks. Moreover, seemingly simple exchanges of quotidian goods are often themselves linked to or embedded within more politically and socially charged exchanges of status-endowing goods. Finally, quite a lot of exchange takes place within the contexts of ritual that creates and recreates the world like the Maya wind jewel did. In sum, trade is one form of action that produces a social system and its structures. Exchange relationships with or without money are needed as a way to shape and reshape the practices of people, and, in turn, for agents to change structure in the way described by Anthony Giddens (1984).

5 Exchange Without Money or Markets: The Non-fungible Tokens of the Kula Ring

Accepting that archaeological data support the chartalist position, how is trade conducted in less-complex societies: those that lack partially commercialized economic systems with permanent market spaces, and those that do not even use redistribution as a mode of exchange? I end with a classic anthropological example from the Trobriand Islands of Melanesia.

First described by Bronisław Malinowski (1921), the Kula Ring was a complex trade system involving status-endowing goods, but not limited to them. Within the Massim Archipelago of today's Solomon Islands, thousands of sailors—whom Malinowski called the "argonauts of the western Pacific" (Malinowski, 2013 [1922])—traveled hundreds of miles to engage in the exchange of what appear to be simple shell trinkets (Fig. 11). Specifically, white shell armbands called *mwali* were traded in a counter-clockwise direction around the archipelago, while red shell necklaces called *veigun* or *soulava* were traded in a clockwise direction. Any series of exchanges began with the symbolic gift of one type of artifact and ended with the gift of the other. The most valued items in this network were the oldest, and most had long stories concerning their previous owners that could be recounted as they were gifted and slowly worked their way in a circle around the archipelago. Value of these completely non-fungible artifacts was related through such provenance stories, which everyone would come to know. Competition among trade partners would ensure that an exchange was fair, although the final shell item generally would be valued more highly than the first that instigated the exchange. This assured a debt that someday would need to be repaid, and that the last owner would become part of the provenance story of the artifact and therefore gain status. Key to understanding

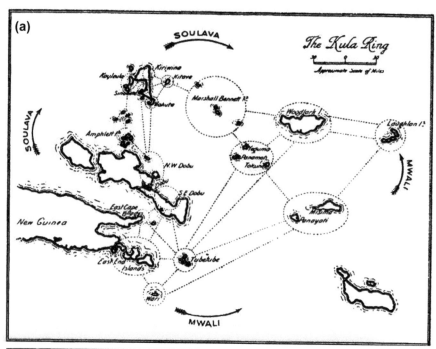

Fig. 11 The Kula Ring of the Trobriand Islands, as described by Branisław Malinowski (1921, [1922]): (**a**) conceptual map of the clockwise flow of *soulava* shells and counter-clockwise flow of *mwali* armbands (Malinowski, 2013: Map V); (**b**) ritual and social performance of a kula (*gimwali*) exchange, note the public presentation of items on a platform to the right. (Malinowski, 2013: Frontispiece)

the kula is that an item could not be possessed forever; for a holder to maintain prestige, a mwali or soulava had to be traded away at a later time so that his name and generosity would be recorded in the narrative associated with the shell. In this respect, a kula ornament is a non-fungible token (see footnote 6) whose value is the status achieved through receiving, displaying, and—especially—exchanging the item.

Finally, the accounting practice that kept track of the debt was the collective memory of the large community that gathered to witness the exchange of kula objects. We should *not* think of this memory as a contemporary ancestor of the blockchain, but instead as a functional relative and alternative to it. Public exchanges conducted in an agreed upon ritual framework provide a powerful tool for record keeping, even within complex societies such as our own. A public handshake, and the risk of loss of prestige implied by violating it, still can be as important as an encoded electronic record of a transaction.

The kula ring was about much more than the mutual exchange of status-endowing items. Dozens or even hundreds of people would participate in any trading event, and they, too, would engage in exchange, especially for food and other everyday items. My point is that status-endowing ceremonial exchange seldom is practiced alone. It also fosters and makes possible purely economic exchange. It is important to note that the kula ring involved many groups that often regarded each other as enemies. Without status-endowing ceremonial exchange, potential trade partners might have been met with violence.

Imagine for one last time our simple trader. He has been sent out by his mother and sisters to get clay for making pottery, a material that can be found on only two of the islands in the Massim Archipelago. He has in his boat a small pig and a totally unknown soulava necklace that he himself made. He lands with the larger party run by his tribal big man who has a famous soulava to trade. After it is presented to a local big man and the history of the soulava is recounted, our friend and all who have traveled with him are guaranteed safety and are free to engage in trade. He might initiate his own trade by first presenting his own necklace to a new partner, and then offer to trade the pig for clay. Such a trade is evened out by his partner adding a few large yams and concluded by presenting a mwali armband of slightly more social value.

After a large feast, our friend returns safely to his island, gives his family the clay and yams, and proudly wears his new shell armband. He has earned a new trading partner to whom he owes in return a debt, he has increased the size of his social network and his status by trading for a kula armband, he participated in a long-distance sea voyage with his neighbors, he has accomplished his simple economic goals, and he has a story to tell. All of this was purchased without reference to a commodity of recognized value against which his goods could be measured, let alone with state-created money. And for our friend, the memory of this trade, the status associated with it, and the knowledge that there will be more in the future all provide more satisfaction than a purely monetary exchange at Walmart or a faceless purchase on Amazon ever could. They help build his world.

Acknowledgments Many of the thoughts here were stimulated by the work of others. Chief of among these is Charles Stanish, who presented his ideas on the spatial organization of contemporary indigenous markets and the labor theory of value some years ago at an archaeology colloquium at UCSD. In January 2020, shortly before COVID-19 suspended travel, my friend and colleague Ivan Šprajc provided me the opportunity to present an early version of this paper at the ZRC SAZU, Ljubljana, Slovenia. I thank him for a wonderful experience that tided me over the epidemic. I also thank Mariusz Ziółkowski and Michał Gilewski for the chance to present a slightly updated version of this work at a seminar at the Institute of Archaeology, University of Warsaw. This event was followed by hours of perspicacious questions that I hope I have addressed. Many of the gracious yet more critical—and therefore most helpful—ones came from Rob Rosenswig. Further conversations with him, as well as his kind offer to share with me and allow me to cite yet unpublished articles, have significantly improved this work. Finally, I thank Tom Levy for his years of patient colleagueship and encouragement to broaden my horizons beyond Mesoamerica.

References

Andrieu, C., Rodas, E., & Luin, L. (2014). The values of Classic Maya jade: A reanalysis of Cancuen's jade workshop. *Ancient Mesoamerica, 25*(1), 141–164.

Aristotle. (1984). Politics. In J. Barnes (Ed.), *The complete works of Aristotle*. Princeton University Press.

Barber, M. (1994). *The new knighthood: A history of the order of the temple*. Cambridge University Press.

Baron, J. P. (2018). Making money in Mesoamerica: Currency production and procurement in the Classic Maya financial system. *Economic Anthropology, 5*(2), 210–223.

Beherec, M. A., Levy, T. E., Tirosh, O., Najjar, M., Knabb, K. A., & Erel, Y. (2016). Iron Age nomads and their relation to copper smelting in Faynan (Jordan): Trace metal and Pb and Sr isotopic measurements from the Wadi Fidan 40 cemetery. *Journal of Archaeological Science, 65*(1), 70–83.

Ben-Yosef, E., Levy, T. E., Higham, T., Najjar, M., & Tauxe, L. (2010). The beginning of Iron Age copper production in the Southern Levant: New evidence from Khirbat al-Jariya, Faynan, Jordan. *Antiquity, 84*(325), 724–746.

Ben-Yosef, E., Liss, B., Yagel, O. A., Tirosh, O., Najjar, M., & Levy, T. E. (2019). Ancient technology and punctuated change: Detecting the emergence of the Edomite Kingdom in the Southern Levant. *PLoS One, 14*(9), e0221967.

Berdan, F. F., & Anawalt, P. R. (1992). *The Codex Mendoza*. University of California Press.

Bochnak, A. (2016). Early medieval axe-like iron bar in the collection of the numismatic cabinet, national museum in Krakow. *Notae Numismaticae. Zapiski numizmatyczne, 11*, 261–279.

Bowles, S., & Gintis, H. (2002). Homo reciprocans. *Nature, 415*(6868), 125–127.

Braswell, G. E. (2017). Recent discoveries in the Classic Maya Palace Complex of Nim li Punit, Belize. *Journal of Field Archaeology, 42*(2), 69–81.

Braswell, G. E. (2019). From vertices to Actants: Two approaches to network analysis in Maya archaeology. In T. Kerig, C. Mader, K. Ragkou, M. Reinfeld, & T. Zachar (Eds.), *Social network analysis in economic archaeology—Perspectives from the New World* (pp. 51–66). Verlag Dr. Rudolf Habelt.

Braswell, G. E., & Glascock, M. D. (2002). The emergence of market economies in the ancient Maya world: Obsidian exchange in terminal Classic Yucatan, Mexico. In M. D. Glascock (Ed.), *Geochemical evidence for long-distance exchange* (pp. 33–52). Greenwood Publishing Group.

Champ, B. A. (2007). *The national banking system: A brief history* (FRB of Cleveland Working Paper 07:23). Retrieved January 7, 2022, from https://doi.org/10.2139/ssrn.1171222

Coe, S. D., & Coe, M. D. (2013). *The true history of chocolate* (4th ed.). Thames & Hudson.

Černy, J. (1934). Fluctuations in grain prices during the twentieth Egyptian dynasty. *Archiv Orientální, 6*, 173–178.

Černy, J. (1954). Prices and wages in Egypt in the Ramesside period. *Cahiers d'histoire mondiale, 1*, 904–906.

Desan, C. (2014). *Making money: Coin, currency, and the coming of capitalism.* Oxford University Press.

Ferguson, N. (2008). *The ascent of money: A financial history of the world.* Penguin Books.

Flinders Petrie, W. M. (1883). On new examples of Egyptian weights and measures. *The Archaeological Journal, 40*, 419–427.

Giddens, A. (1984). *Elements of the theory of structuration.* Routledge.

Golitko, M., Meierhoff, J., Feinman, G. M., & Williams, P. R. (2012). Complexities of collapse: The evidence of Maya obsidian as revealed by social network graphical analysis. *Antiquity, 86*(332), 507–523.

Hafford, W. B. (2012). Weighing in Mesopotamia: The balance pan weights from Ur. *Akkadica, 133*, 21–65.

Haselgrove, C., & Krmnicek, S. (2012). The archaeology of money. *Annual Review of Anthropology, 41*, 235–250.

Hayek, F. (1967 [1931]). *Prices and production* (2nd ed.). Augustus M. Kelly.

Hosler, D., Lechtman, H., & Holm, O. (1990). *Axe-monies and their relatives* (Studies in pre-Columbian art & archaeology, 30). Dumbarton Oaks Research Library and Collection.

Ingham, G. (2004). *The nature of money.* Polity Press.

Inomata, T. (2001). The power and ideology of artistic creation: Elite craft specialists in Classic Maya Society. *Current Anthropology, 42*(3), 321–349.

Janssen, J. J. (1976). The economic system of a single village. *Rain, 15*, 17–19.

Jones, I. W., Levy, T. E., & Najjar, M. (2012). Khirbat Nuqayb al-Asaymir and Middle Islamic Metallurgy in Faynan: Surveys of Wadi al-Ghuwayb and Wadi al-Jariya in Faynan, Southern Jordan. *Bulletin of the American Schools of Oriental Research, 368*(1), 67–102.

Karttunen, F. (1992). *An analytical dictionary of Nahuatl.* University of Oklahoma Press.

Keynes, J. M. (1936). *The general theory of employment, interest and money.* Palgrave.

Knapp, G. F. (1924). *The state theory of money* (H. M. Lucas & J. Bonar, Trans.). Macmillan (Original work published 1905).

Kuijpers, M. H., & Popa, C. N. (2021). The origins of money: Calculation of similarity indexes demonstrates the earliest development of commodity money in prehistoric Central Europe. *PLoS One, 16*(1), e0240462.

Levy, T. E., Adams, R. B., Hauptmann, A., Prange, M., Schmitt-Strecker, S., & Najjar, M. (2002). Early Bronze Age metallurgy: A newly discovered copper manufactory in Southern Jordan. *Antiquity, 76*(292), 425–437.

Macleod, H. D. (1889). *The theory of credit.* Longmans, Green, and Co.

Malinowski, B. (1921). The primitive economics of the Trobriand Islanders. *The Economic Journal, 31*(121), 1–16.

Malinowski, B. (2013 [1922]). *Argonauts of the Western Pacific: An account of native enterprise and adventure in the archipelagoes of Melanesian new guinea.* Routledge.

Marson, J. (2020). OneCoin took in billions. Then its leader vanished. *Wall Street Journal*, August 27, 2020. Retrieved January 8, 2022, from www.wsj.com

Mauss, M. (2016 [1925]). *The gift.* Hau Books.

Menu, B. (1998). Le système économique de l'Egypte pharonique. *Mediterranées, 17*, 71–91.

Muhs, B. (2016). *The ancient Egyptian economy: 3000–30 BCE.* Cambridge University Press.

Parkin, M. (2018). *Economics* (13th ed.). Pearson Addison-Wesley.

Paul, R. (2009). *End the Fed.* Grand Central Publishing.

Polanyi, K. (2001 [1944]). *The great transformation.* Beacon Press.

Prager, C. M., & Braswell, G. E. (2016). Maya politics and ritual: An important new hieroglyphic text on a Carved Jade from Belize. *Ancient Mesoamerica, 27*(2), 267–278.

Ricardo, D. (2004 [1817]). *On the principles of political economy and taxation.* Dover.

Rosenswig, R. M. (2021) *Ancient tally sticks reveal the nature of modern money.* Ms. In possession of the author.

Rosenswig, R. M. (2022). Money, currency, and heterodox macroeconomics for archaeology. *Current Anthropology*. In press.

Smith, C. A. (1976). *Economic systems. Regional analysis* (Vol. 1). Academic.

Stanish, C. (2010). Labor taxes, market systems, and urbanization in the Prehispanic Andes: A comparative perspective. In C. P. Garraty & B. L. Stark (Eds.), *Archaeological approaches to market exchange in ancient societies* (pp. 185–205). University Press of Colorado.

Stanish, C., & Coben, L. S. (2013). Barter markets in the pre-Hispanic Andes. In K. G. Hirth & J. Pillsbury (Eds.), *Merchants, markets, and exchange in the pre-Columbian world* (pp. 421–436). Dumbarton Oaks Research Library and Collection.

Stos-Gale, Z. A., Maliotis, G., Gale, N. H., & Annetts, N. (1997). Lead isotope characteristics of the Cyprus copper ore deposits applied to provenance studies of copper oxhide ingots. *Archaeometry, 39*(1), 83–123.

Taube, K. A., Hruby, Z. X., & Romero, L. A. (2011). Archaeological reconnaissance in the Upper Rio El Tambor, Guatemala. In Z. X. Hruby, G. E. Braswell, & O. Chinchilla Mazariegos (Eds.), *The technology of Maya civilization: Political economy and beyond in lithic studies* (pp. 143–150). Equinox Publishing.

Wallerstein, I. (2004). *World-systems analysis*. Duke University Press.

Weatherford, J. (1997). *The history of money*. Three Rivers Press.

Weber, M. (2019). *Economy and society* (K. Tribe, Trans.). Harvard University Press (Original work published 1921).

Wee, H. V. D. (1967). Anvers et les innovations de la technique financière aux XVIe et XVIIe siècles. *Annales. Histoire, Sciences Sociales, 22*(5), 1067–1089.

Wennerlind, C. (2011). *Casualties of credit: The English financial revolution, 1620–1720*. Harvard University Press.

Willems, H. (2012). An archaeological note on the economic value of incense in the old kingdom. *Göttinger Miszellen: Beiträge zur Ägyptologischen Diskussion, 233*, 95–97.

Zhao, H., Gao, X., Jiang, Y., Lin, Y., Zhu, J., Ding, S., Deng, L., & Zhang, J. (2021). Radiocarbon-dating an early minting site: The emergence of standardised coinage in China. *Antiquity, 95*(383), 1161–1178.

Making Peoples: The Nabatean Settlement of the Dhiban Plateau and Beyond

Chang-ho Ji

Abstract The archaeological research in Ataruz and Dhiban Plateau regions has provided prolific data that focuses on the Nabatean settlements and history in central Jordan. This paper summarizes and combines the results of excavations and surveys in the regions. The Nabatean debut for the Dhiban Plateau occurred late in the Hellenistic period, but a phase of reduction or intraregional relocation followed, caused by the Hasmonean infiltration into the region. The first century CE marked the zenith of Nabatean settlement in the Dhiban Plateau. During the era, the region was encircled by summer shelters and storage facilities built by nomadic tribes along the plateau rim. Towns were mainly in the region's center and along the major trade roads. Besides caravan trade and religious pilgrimage, Nabateans assiduously engaged in agriculture in small wadis and tributaries flowing into Wadi Mujib and Wadi Walla. This settlement history does not fit the Ataruz region; the Nabateans appear never to have set their dominion in the Ataruz region. The paper also compares the Dhiban Plateau with the Madaba Plains and Kerak Plateau to understand its Nabatean history and settlement in a broader regional context.

Keywords Nabateans · Dhiban Plateau · Road system · Hasmonean · Herodian · Late Hellenistic · Early Roman · Caravansary · Qasr buildings · Central Jordan

According to Zenon papyri and other sources, by the mid third century BCE, Nabateans already resided in the neighborhood of the Hauran in Syria and were merchants of aromatics with Ptolemaic agents in central Jordan (Graf, 1997). In approximately 100 BCE, the conquest of Gaza by Alexander Jannaeus blocked Nabatean access to the Mediterranean coast. This event put a halt to Nabatean trade via the Petra-Gaza road and forced them to advance northwards along the roads in Transjordan. Towards the end of the first century BCE, Nabateans established

---

C. Ji (✉)
La Sierra University, Riverside, CA, USA
e-mail: cji@lasierra.edu

© The Author(s), under exclusive license to Springer Nature Switzerland AG 2023
E. Ben-Yosef, I. W. N. Jones (eds.), *"And in Length of Days Understanding" (Job 12:12): Essays on Archaeology in the Eastern Mediterranean and Beyond in Honor of Thomas E. Levy*, Interdisciplinary Contributions to Archaeology,
https://doi.org/10.1007/978-3-031-27330-8_79

1855

caravansaries, commercial centers, and settlement in central and northern Jordan, whereas in the less populous Hauran, they were able to solidly control the whole region (Negev, 1976). This expansion to the north roughly corresponds to the Middle Nabatean period, during which the Nabatean kingdom flourished and reached its zenith (cf. Hammond, 1973; Negev, 1969, 1976).

This historical view has received some archaeological credence as Nabatean pottery was uncovered at Amman and Jerash, and the Hauran region has yielded Nabatean inscriptions (Ji, 2009b). The Nabatean period in central Jordan, however, still awaits integrative studies regarding overall Nabatean history and archaeology despite some studies recently published through different venues (Al-Fuqaha, 2018; Ji, 2009a, b). This also holds for the Dhiban Plateau, even though the region has been the target of multiple archaeological expeditions for several decades. This paper brings together available evidence on Nabateans in the region and its vicinity and presents some interim conclusions for future research and discussion.

1 Nabatean Sites

1.1 Excavated Sites

There is evidence of Nabatean activity at Dhiban. Tushingham (1972) distinguishes two periods of Nabatean settlement at this site. The first period began early in the first century CE and came to an end about the middle of the same century. Dhiban recovered late in the first century CE but was abandoned again in 106 CE. The discovered Nabatean evidence includes a Nabatean temple on the southern end of the mound and a staircase, a retaining wall, a city gate, an aqueduct, and several other architectural remains (Tushingham, 1972; Winnett & Reed, 1964). The artifact corpus comprises coins of Aretas IV (9 BCE – 40 CE) and Rabbel II (70–106 CE), and many Nabatean eggshell wares. Of the published Nabatean painted sherds, all samples seemingly belong to the late corpus dated to the first century CE with one exception attributable to the late second – early first centuries BCE (Ji, 2020). A Nabatean funerary inscription from Dhiban is also dated to the first or second century CE (Al-Salameen & Al-Rawahneh, 2017).

Lehun is home to a small Nabatean temple (Homes-Fredericq, 2010). It is square in shape with an altar on the east side. The pottery from the temple dates back to the first century CE. Apart from the temple, there are no excavated houses or walled settlements of the Nabatean period. The excavators concluded that Lehun was a small stop-off market village of some religious importance where nomads and merchants passed by to worship at the sanctuary while they conducted the sale and purchase of provisions, livestock, and other commodities in the vicinity.

At Aroer, three seasons of excavations have revealed Hellenistic and Nabatean remains from the end of the third century BCE to the beginning of the second century CE (Olavarri, 1965). In the Hellenistic period, the inhabitants rebuilt part of the

Making Peoples: The Nabatean Settlement of the Dhiban Plateau and Beyond

Iron II fortress as houses and shelters. Remains of two farms were also noted. The evidence points to the seminomadic character of the Hellenistic inhabitants (Olavarri, 1993). Differently, Aroer was quite densely populated during the first century CE before it came to a violent end at the turn to the second century CE. The absence of monumental edifices and fortification walls suggests that Aroer had lost its former strategic importance during the Nabatean period.

Nabateans who inhabited Mudayna ath-Thamad in the first century CE built buildings and reservoirs at the foot of the site and in its vicinity (Daviau & Foley, 2007). The pottery from the site points to the first and second centuries CE for the construction and use of the buildings. A Roman coin found in the debris proposes the third century CE as the final date of the settlement, but no evidence earlier than the first century CE was found in association with the Nabatean buildings.

1.2 Major Survey Sites

The Dhiban Plateau Survey Project began in 1996 and completed its principal field-work in 2000 (Ji & 'Attiyat, 1997; Ji & Lee, 1998, 2000; see also Glueck, 1934, 1939). The research continues as part of the ongoing Ataruz Regional Project in the form of special visits to critical sites for updates and further data collection. As illustrated in Fig. 1, there are sites other than those excavated that contain evidence assignable to the Nabatean and early Roman periods. This section proceeds from the southeastern sector of the Dhiban Plateau to the northeast and then covers the sites west to Dhiban and the modern King's Highway.

For the southeast, Saliya (Dhiban Plateau Survey Site 3; hereafter DS) is an extensive site overlooking Wadi Saliya from the north. At the center is a large building that seems to be Nabatean; it stands on top of the seemingly Iron Age fortress (Glueck, 1934, p. 35). More ruins, stone heaps, and sherds are visible at the site. East of the central building is an artificial depression (*ca.* 30 × 40 m), a possible ancient installation for water reservation. Ramah (DS-23) is close to Saliya, located on a natural hill spreading over 150 × 150 m. Despite modern structures and graves on the site, evidence of architectural remains is distinguishable at Ramah, especially on the summit and the northern slope. The summit contains a rectangular tower or altar. Centered on the north part are some impressive wall lines and corners of a large building complex, although its overall plan is difficult to determine.

Musaytiba (DS-153) is an important Nabatean site *ca.* 6.5 km southeast of Umm ar-Rasas. Its most notable feature is a large square building on the west side of the site. Roughly 70 m northeast of this building is a rectangular water reservoir with steps inside of it leading down from its northwest corner. The reservoir, measuring 13 × 24 m, was dug 6.3 m deep into bedrock. The inner walls and steps of the reservoir were plastered with clay cement and contained large numbers of pottery sherds. There is another water reservoir about 150 m east of the first reservoir. This one is currently in use, and its inner walls are cemented using modern cement. East of the square building is a single small structure connected with a stone heap and

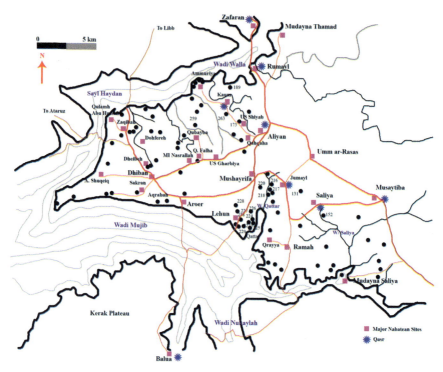

Fig. 1 Nabatean road system & Late Hellenistic-Early Roman sites in the Dhiban Plateau

additional walls. Some 100 m south of this building is a completely ruined building. Wall lines represent a rectangular building with a cluster of inner chambers. Additional wall lines are traceable on the west and south side of this building.

Qrayya (DS-149) is a village site on a ridge overlooking Wadi Qattar. It has a large building compound, a round structure, and at least six dwelling caves. The building is spread over an area of 50 × 50 m. Its southern quadrant is comprised of six rooms; the north quadrant also includes many small chambers. East of this building are rectangular houses and a large animal enclosure. Centered on the west quadrant of the complex are two circular structures. At Jumaiyil (DS-4), numerous buildings and wall lines encompass an area of about 150 × 200 m. The most distinctive edifice, which is 8.5 × 8.5 m, is at the site's highest point. Nearby is a large rectangular building with interior walls. Many wall lines and stone heaps are visible on the western and northern sides. Besides, the site includes an ancient reservoir that measures 3 m deep and *ca.* 7 × 10 m in area. Mushayrifa (DS-254) is positioned *ca.* 4 km northeast of Lehun. The main ruin pertains to a well-built villa-like building of 24 × 30 m. It currently stands 4 m high. At least seven interior wall lines are discernable in addition to three exterior walls. Approximately 100 m southwest are the foundation walls of a building that is sized 14 × 20 m. A third main feature also represents a large building with multiple inner chambers.

Next, I take on the northeastern section of the Dhiban Plateau. Aliyan (DS-6) is a conspicuous site covering an area of more than 150 × 200 m. A massive building stands at the acropolis. Additional structures are recognizable to the north; there are many caves and building remains on the northern and western terraces. At the southwestern edge of the site, wall lines visible at ground level mark three sides of a large edifice measuring 25 m by 40 m. The main feature at Kaum (DS-172) is also a rectangular edifice that occupies the acropolis of this site. The collapsed remains of a residential building with multiple chambers are northeast of this building. Another house composed of eight to ten rooms is visible on the western side. Kaum contains many additional wall lines, structures, cisterns, and caves. Ammuriya (DS-186) is marked by ruined block houses and enclosure walls, some of which are still in use for animals. The foundation wall lines on the flat top of the site denote a large building, which seems to be a fort connected with three to four structures. There are more buildings west of the acropolis, extending over 25 × 30 m.

Situated 1 km to the west of Aliyan, Umm Shujayrat al-Shiyab (DS-162) includes ancient wall lines that can be traced only partially today. A characteristic feature of this site is a partitioned rectangular structure (*ca.* 6 × 20 m) at the site's highest point. Evidence of another building is noted west of the acropolis, which includes three to four rooms. Qahqaha (DS-166) is another Nabatean site, located *ca.* 2 km northeast of Umm Shujayrat al-Gharbiya. This site stretches over an area of 120 m by 140 m. In the middle of the site are two buildings solidly built with limestone blocks. The heaviest concentration of building ruins is on the southeastern side, although only several wall lines can be traced with any degree of certainty. In addition, Qariyat Falha (DS-293) is a modern village on top of a large ancient town. Only a small part of ancient buildings is traceable under modern houses.

Umm Shujayrat al-Garbiya (DS-214) is midway between Qahqaha and Qariyat Falha. Ancient foundation walls are still clearly visible under the Ottoman building ruins. A large building, *ca.* 35 × 35 m, comprised of partition walls and small chambers, is observable on the site's north side. On the south side is another building, *ca.* 12 × 25 m, made of finely dressed blocks. Directly west of this compound are another large building and foundation walls. In addition, Qubayba (DS-283) is a potential Nabatean site that contains four building remains, one of which is a large rectangular house. On the south side of the site is a square animal enclosure, *ca.* 31 × 31 m, associated with a couple of small edifices.

Glueck (1939) visited Maqad bin Nasrallah (DS-296) and described, "practically all vestiges of the ruins which once marked the place have disappeared. The ancient occupation of the site is, however, testified to by a small quantity of Nabatean sherds of all kinds found there, including several pieces of sigillata" (p. 116). Presently, only one building that can be traced with confidence suggests the site's antiquity. It is a well-built, rectangular building divided into two rooms by a compartment wall. Dheibeh (DS-344) is a small Nabatean settlement dotted with many caves, cisterns, and modern houses. The survey team identified one ancient wall line that remained 6 m long and three courses wide.

Turning to the western region, Rujm Sakran (DS-2) is a medium-sized Nabataean-Roman site with a large building complex comprised of two rectangular buildings with several internal divisions. Dohfereh (DS-334) is *ca.* 3.5 km north of Dhiban. In the middle of the modern village, an ancient wall line stretches about 7 m in the northwest-southeast direction. About 20 m northeast of this wall line is the ruin of a circular structure. Further, a square structure was noted near the southeastern edge of the site.

Zaqibah (DS-374) is characterized by two large buildings separated by a possible courtyard. The southern complex includes nine rectangular rooms and one possible inner courtyard. The northern one is about 35 × 35 m and contains more than 15 compartment walls. Both structures were well constructed with semi-dressed limestone blocks and appear to have been public buildings. There is an additional rectangular edifice *ca.* 25 m northeast of the northern complex. Located on the western edge of the Dhiban Plateau is 'Ayn Shuqayq (DS-398). The building remains cover 150 × 200 m, indicating it was a considerable settlement in antiquity. Fortification walls can be traced 70–80 m on the northern and western sides of the site. Inside the fortification are wall lines and three building complexes.

Lastly, Qulamh Abu Hussein (Rujm Qala'ma; DS-397) is situated at the northernmost spur of the Sahl Mastah stretch, surrounded almost entirely by a loop in Sayl Haydan. The ruins represent two fortresses, one built on top of the earlier one. The walls of the later fortress currently stand more than ten courses high, illustrating a solid and impressive fortification system. It was built in the northwest-southeast direction according to a rectangular plan measuring 25 × 60 m. On the eastern section of the fortress was a round watchtower with a potential stairway leading up to the top of the structure. This later fortress sits on an earlier one that was 50 × 100 m in size. Although the later fortress completely covered up two-thirds of this earlier fortress, its northwestern part remains intact, including at least two structures built adjacent to the northern fortification wall.

2 Settlement Chronology

From the above review of the excavation results, we learn that the Nabatean settlements at Lehun and Mudayna ath-Thamad were contemporaneous, both in the first century CE. There is evidence for a gap in occupation in the Hellenistic period at both sites. For Dhiban, there are Nabatean painted sherds assignable to the first century BCE, but no architecture from that era was identified. Likewise, a modest settlement appeared at Aroer during the Hellenistic period, even though we lack evidence to define it as Nabatean. Nabateans later resided at Aroer in the first century CE. Put otherwise, the finds from Dhiban and possibly Aroer suggest the Nabatean presence in the Dhiban Plateau late in the Hellenistic period. Yet, effective Nabatean colonization of the entire region transpired only in the first century CE.

A picture from archaeological surveys is alike in large part. Given the surveys, the intensification of Hellenistic settlement began late in the period, following an occupation gap during the Persian-early Hellenistic period (Ji & Lee, 2007). The surveys identified about 80 sites with late Hellenistic sherds. This intensification continued into the early Roman period. Pottery of the Roman period is present at 65 of the 78 Hellenistic sites. That is, 81% of the Hellenistic sites were reused during the Roman period. This figure corresponds to almost 60% of the entire Roman sites. Similarly, about one-third of the Hellenistic sites contain fragments of Nabatean painted ware, comprising roughly 90% of 27 sites with Nabatean painted sherds.

Nabatean painted wares help to elucidate the matter further. A preliminary study of the corpus from the 1996–2000 Dhiban Plateau Survey Project was published about 10 years ago (Ji, 2009a); since then, the research team revisited some of the essential Nabatean sites as part of the ongoing Ataruz Regional Project. According to the updated data, of the 421 surveyed sites on the Dhiban Plateau proper, 27 sites contain Nabatean painted sherds, which corresponds to 6% of the total survey sites. The sherds total 89, indicating that the 27 sites hold roughly three to four Nabatean painted sherds on average. Mudayna as-Saliya and Qulamh Abu Hussein yielded 28 and 29 painted sherds, respectively, the numbers far exceeding those from other Nabatean sites.

Next, Schmid's division (2007a, b) of Phases I-III breaks the painted sherds into three groups. As shown in Fig. 2, all three types are represented in the Dhiban Plateau. As per the data, 77% of the samples pertain to Phase III with Phase II next at 15%. Eleven sherds are linked with Phase I, constituting 8% of the entire sample. Phase III is best represented in the Dhiban Plateau. Phase I and II samples are more

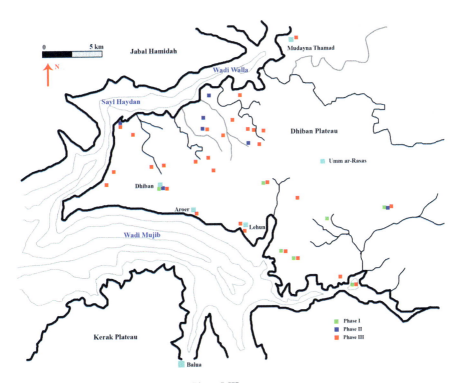

Fig. 2 Nabatean Painted Ware sites by Phase I-III

or less similar in frequency, even though they are much less commonplace than the Phase III assemblage. As attested by Schmid, Phase I vessels denote the earliest Nabatean painted ceramic group assigned to late second century BCE and the first half of the first century BCE. Phase II pots align with the second half of the first century BCE to the first quarter of the first century CE. Phase III runs from then on to roughly 100 CE. Schmid suggests that the Phase II–III transition took place during the reign of Aretas IV and that Phase III came to an end when the Nabatean kingdom was annexed to the Roman empire.

The presence of Phase I Nabatean painted potsherds points to the early first century BCE, or the transition from the second to the first century BCE, for the debut of the Nabatean settlement in the Dhiban Plateau. Phase I and II samples come from nine and seven sites, respectively. This fact postulates that Nabateans continued to stay in the region through the second half of the first century BCE, even though their settlement might have experienced a modest reduction in geographical range. The Dhiban Plateau then witnessed a dramatic increase of Nabatean settlement in the first century CE; Phase III samples appear at 23 sites, which make up more than 75% of the entire painted-ware sites in the Dhiban Plateau.

3 Road System

In the Dhiban Plateau, as in the Iron Age, major Nabatean sites are often located near the head of the inland wadis and tributaries, whereas the majority of small structure sites or seasonal remains are noticeably pronounced along the rim of the plateau (see Ji & Lee, 2003 for the Iron Age settlements). Notice that wadis near the towns seem not related to the wealth of water since most of these wadis are entirely dried up during the dry months. Most of the Nabatean settlements had multiple cisterns dug into bedrock, which were the primary source of water rather than wadis for the Nabatean towns. Accordingly, the wealth in water cannot explain the location of major Nabatean settlements. Then, what factors would account for the location of large Nabatean settlements?

The courses of major roads often regulate the location of cities and villages in Palestine. Thus, "it has been a long recognized principle that a chain of ancient settlements from a particular period preserves a line of communication from that period" (Dorsey, 1991, p. 53). In a similar vein, I would suppose that trade routes and local roads were closely linked with the locations of the Nabatean settlements in the Dhiban Plateau. This section attempts to reconstruct the courses of the Nabatean roads by connecting the locations of the major settlements with Nabatean evidence (Fig. 1).

In the Nabatean period, there seem to have been three longitudinal arteries that ran north and south through the Dhiban Plateau, connecting Petra, the Kerak Plateau, and the Madaba Plains. Also, two main lateral roads were used to link towns and villages east-west within the region. These five highways constituted one large regional road system that circled the Dhiban Plateau, except for the Sahl Subhiya region in the west, and the northern promontories northwest of Aliyan, and the Wadi Thamad basin in the northeast, all of which were linked with the main network through local branches that veered from Dhiban and Aliyan.

For the longitudinal arteries, the eastern road ran north-south through the easily traveled flat dry land along the border between the Arabian Desert and the pasture land east of the Dhiban Plateau. It led from the Desert Highway to Musaytiba, passing Umm ar-Rasas, afterward went over the upper stream of Wadi Walla, and wound to Madaba via Nitil. The eastern route was strategically pivotal, given its short distance, easy topography, and the ancient ruins and caravansaries along the desert route, facilitating the direct economic and military exchanges possible between Petra in the south and Amman and the Madaba Plains in the north. The Nabatean ruins at Musaytiba testify to the use of this eastern route during the period. The route between Musaytiba and the Desert Highway was one of the two southeastern roads of the Dhiban Plateau. The other road was the Saliya-Ramah-Wadi Mujib-Kerak Plateau route, the easternmost road that directly connected the Dhiban Plateau and Kerak Plateau (Kloner & Ben-David, 2003). The course of both roads can be supported by the Nabatean ruins at Saliya, Mudayna Saliya, and Ramah. From Musaytiba, the eastern highway proceeded 6.5 km west to Umm ar-Rasas, the course of which is employed by the modern road to Umm ar-Rasas from the modern Amman-Aqaba Highway. From Umm ar-Rasas, the road would have turned north and then northwest to reach Aliyan and due north again to Za'faran and Nitil.

The western route originated at Aroer, passed Dhiban on its way to Zaqibah, descended to and crossed the middle stream of Wadi Walla, and climbed the northern bank of the valley to Libb, and went on to Madaba. It should have operated as the main highway between Dhiban and the Nabatean towns in the Kerak Plateau, such as Balua, ar-Rabbah, and Kerak (Graf, 1992; Ninow, 2009). Further, this route required the least journey time and cost for the travel from the western Dhiban Plateau to the Madaba Plains. The western district of the Dhiban Plateau has better soil quality than the other parts of the region. It was the region's breadbasket in antiquity. This was also the case for the northern Kerak Plateau (cf. Miller, 1991). Hence, the western route, critical to the lives of local Nabateans, was used for local commodity exchanges of grains and agricultural products, apart from its utility for the international caravans laden with spices and other valuable commodities from Petra and the Arabian Desert.

The central route would have provided an alternative path for travelers to journey from the Kerak Plateau to the eastern Dhiban Plateau and the Madaba and Amman regions. This longitudinal route led from Balua to Lehun by way of the ford of the Arnon River near the modern-day bridge and dam in Wadi Mujib. That this route was in use during the Nabatean period is substantiated by the Nabatean remains discovered at Balua and Lehun. From Lehun, the Nabatean road changed direction slightly northeast toward Aliyan where the road joined the eastern road from Umm ar-Rasas. This section of the route is marked by the Nabatean and early Roman sites at Mushayrifa and Rujm Salim.

This central road roughly corresponds to the geographic boundary separating the Dhiban Plateau into the farming area in the west and the pasture land on the east, a region suitable for grazing sheep, goats, and camels. In this sense, the proposal that Lehun was a trading post of some significance where livestock and grains were stored and traded is persuasive (Homes-Fredericq, 2010). The Nabatean temple was built to offer a space for the merchants and travelers on this road to worship before or after they crossed the valleys of Wadi Mujib and Wadi Nukaylah. That Lehun lacks buildings of the Nabatean period other than the temple supposes that Mushayrifa, about 4 km northeast as the crow flies, was the main destination for any travelers who needed water, food, and accommodation for long-distance travel or trade. Further, Mushayrifa was a junction of the central longitudinal route and the vital lateral thoroughfare that connected Dhiban, Aroer, Ramah, and Saliya, the point of divergence for traffic from the south, wishing to continue either to Madaba and Amman or to Dhiban and Saliya.

Apart from the longitudinal highways, in all likelihood, two important lateral roads were in use during the Nabatean period. One was the road above that meets the central longitudinal road at Mushayrifa. This southern route was approximately 25 km long, running parallel to the south rim of the Dhiban Plateau. It connected several Nabatean towns, such as Musaytiba, Saliya, Ramah, Mushayrifa, Aroer, and Dhiban. While the southern route worked for those who wished to reach Dhiban from the Kerak Plateau and the southeastern sector of the Dhiban Plateau, we have evidence that another artery provided access to the western region for those traveling south from Amman and the eastern Madaba Plains. Along this northern lateral route, many Nabatean towns and villages flourished across the northern section of the Dhiban Plateau. They are Aliyan, Qahqaha, Umm Shujayrat Garbiya, Qariyat Falha, Maqad bin Nasrallah, and Dheibeh. Aliyan was perhaps a significant travel hub strategically located at the junction where three major routes merge into one road before crossing the upper stream of Wadi Walla into the southeastern corner of the Madaba Plains.

From the line of Nabatean sites encircling the heartland of the Dhiban Plateau, it appears that one local road branched from Dhiban and proceeded west to 'Ayn Shuqayq. The presence of another local branch connecting Aliyan with Kaum and Ammuriya can be suggested. The Kaum-Ammuriya region corresponds to the northernmost terrain of the Dhiban Plateau, comprised of some remote and narrow promontories that jut out into Wadi Walla. In addition, north of Aliyan, another branch undoubtedly veered toward the northeast to connect the Wadi Thamad basin to the Dhiban Plateau. The road fragments that Daviau and Foley (2007) identified in association with the Nabatean settlements in the region may bear witness to the existence of this branch road system during that time. For reference, probably, the Iron Age road from Dhiban to Ataruz was not in much use or practically abandoned due to the political and military tensions between the Nabatean and Hasmonean-Herodian kingdoms (cf. Ji, 2019; see below).

In summary, the Dhiban Plateau was equipped with a sophisticated road system during the Nabatean period, stitching agricultural villages to places of commerce and trade in the region. Nabateans were skilled traders engaged in international commerce of myrrh, frankincense, and other incense. Their trade routes stretched from Petra to Gaza across the Negev and to Damascus along the western fringe of the Arabian Desert. The roads that Nabateans established in the Dhiban Plateau would be considered a regional system connected to the Petra-Damascus road, which was at the top of the Nabatean trade system in the early Roman period. Four places stand out concerning their importance to the Nabatean road system: Dhiban, Aliyan, Mushayrifa, and Musaytiba. Multiple roads met at each of these sites. They would have been the central points for trade across the region, providing market-places for interregional commerce during the Nabatean period. A major Nabatean temple at Dhiban makes sense in this perspective. It offered a place of rest and prayer for the merchants and travelers in their caravans on the complex and long journey across central Jordan.

4 Pastoral and Burial Sites

During the Nabatean period, the Dhiban Plateau was potentially encircled, by and large, by small buildings and circular stone structures found in isolation or in groups around the region, except for the east. Within the region, the most frequent appearance of such sites occurs in the southeastern sector. The Qattar basin area is a case in point. The area includes many small sites comprised of remote rectangular (DS-218, 224, 226, 229) or circular (DS-220, 227, 228, 230, 238) stone structures. These sites are associated with flints and Nabatean or late Hellenistic-early Roman potsherds. One example is DS-228, a site situated on a low hill to the southeast of Lehun. The wall lines indicate a circular structure with one inner wall, *ca.* 5 m in diameter. About 800 m southeast of DS-228 is DS-229, a rectilinear structure constructed of small boulders and cobbles, measuring 3 × 7 m. This site contains evidence of modern Bedouin camps, which may posit that the area was used as a seasonal camping ground in ancient times.

This observation also applies to the northern part of the Dhiban Plateau. DS-173 is comprised of a couple of wall lines spread over a gentle slope. It likely represents a Nabataean structure, granted that the sherds collected at this site were almost exclusively Nabatean and early Roman. DS-189 concerns a circular structure situated north of Ammuriya. The round structure, *ca.* 7 m in diameter, revealed Nabatean and early Roman sherds. Further to the west, DS-259 is comprised of two buildings that occupy an area of 13 × 21 m. The western structure was potentially used for animals, and the eastern one was a small house connected with another animal enclosure. Besides four Nabatean painted ware, this site contains many sherds dated to early Roman. At DS-263, near the edge of a natural bedrock and rocky ridge south of Wadi Nafkha, are the ruins of two structures. One structure is rectilinear, *ca.* 7 × 10 m; the other is circular, situated 10 m south of the first one.

It is doubtful that all these sites can be referred to as watchtowers or military installations since they are almost absent in the eastern desert fringe. There are too many of them within a short distance from each other along the plateau's rim. A chance is also slim for their being prehistoric burial sites given the presence of Nabatean and early Roman pottery sherds on the surface (cf. Avner, 1984; Haiman,

1989; see below for Nabatean burials). At the same time, it is hard to conceive that they were related to agricultural settlements (cf. Younker, 1989). Most structures under consideration were built in the locales with no immediate relation to agriculture. Another essential observation is that they are almost totally missing in the central part of the region. What is the cause behind a concentration of small Nabatean or early Roman sites along the rim of the Dhiban plateau?

I would associate these sites mainly with pastoral nomadism. Unlike those who lived in towns and dug cisterns for water, the Nabatean herders who lived in tents were more dependent upon the natural distribution of water. In consequence, their camp sites may have clustered along the plateau edge near Wadi Mujib and Wadi Walla. Here they could take advantage of the water in the valleys and the pasture on the slopes, and at the same time, enjoy the cool wind blowing up from the valley. This suggestion is tenable because water resources are sparse in the central plain region even during the good years. In the dry season, the only water available in the Dhiban Plateau is from springs and streams in Wadi Mujib and Wadi Walla, and grazing was virtually confined to the slope and bottom of these wadis. Nabatean herders should have been obligated to set up camps near the plateau rim to compensate for the scarcity of water resources. In the process, Nabatean tent dwellers built round or rectangular structures to shelter themselves from wind and rain and store their belongings when they moved to other areas for grazing.

On the other hand, some circular stone lines found along the plateau rim could be used for burials. DS-217, for example, probably served as a burial ground during the Nabatean period. It is located on a gentle hill overlooking Wadi Qattar, one peppered with many small stone rings spread over the area of 30 × 50 m. The stones are loosely arranged in an oval or ellipse form rather than completely circular. They are undressed, small in size, and occasionally set upright with some space between them. The survey team found the stone rings with Hellenistic to Roman pottery sherds scattered on the surface. DS-224 is another example. A small rectangular building is located at this site, one built on top of the saddle between two small knolls. Some potential ancient graves marked by stone lines are clustered over the hill north of this building. The survey team collected several possible Nabatean and early Roman pottery sherds there.

These burial sites remind us of the "Qumran type" Nabatean graves at Khirbat Qazone in Lisan Peninsula. The site has over 3500 shaft tombs, each containing a single burial with no evidence of re-internment (Politis, 1998), a practice different from the Petra region. Nabateans in the Dhiban Plateau possibly adopted similar direct burial customs to those in the Ghor region, as demonstrated by the Nabatean tomb discovered in the ruin of Iron I settlements at Lehun (Homes-Fredericq, 2010). Nabateans practiced both direct and secondary burial customs in the Negev, although the second custom was more commonplace than the first (Negev, 1971, 1986). With the settlement in the sedentary centers far away from Petra, contacts with other peoples in the neighboring areas might have brought the influence of local traditions on the burial customs of the Nabateans in the Dhiban Plateau.

5 Agricultural Remains

While Nabateans never reached the point of complex urban development with fortified settlements in the Dhiban Plateau (Ji, 2020), there is strong evidence that many Nabateans invested significant time, resources, and energy in agriculture and water management. A considerable number of ancient dams, agricultural plots, and reservoirs were documented over the Dhiban Plateau, with four heavy areas of concentrations in the regions of Jumayil, Saliya, Dhiban, and Mudayna ath-Thamad. One of the most prominent facets of Nabatean civilization was its achievement in hydraulic engineering and the cultivation of semiarid regions (Graf, 1983). Nabateans were perhaps responsible for the intricate systems of dams, cisterns, and reservoirs in the Dhiban Plateau.

The Nabatean involvement in water management for agriculture purposes is well attested to in the Wadi Thamad basin at the northeastern corner of the Dhiban Plateau (Daviau & Foley, 2007; Ladurner, 2013). The settlement encompasses several agricultural sites located on the perimeter of a broad valley bottom, such as Northern al-Mudayna (WT-1), Toga (WT-6), WT-12, al-Wahir (WT-14), and WT-48. They were associated with a variety of water collection and transportation systems. WT-14 had three dams and a carved bedrock water channel that carried runoff water into a large cistern. A similar water installation system was noted at Toga and WT-48. The most sophisticated system exists at the Nabatean settlement at Mudayna ath-Thamad. The rainwater was collected from nearby hills and carried to small settling tanks through water channels. Daviau and Foley (2007) suggested these settlements were built and used in the Nabatean period; fragments of Nabatean painted ware, terra sigillata, and other early Roman vessels were scattered at or around the survey sites.

A similar land use and water management mode is frequently noted across the Dhiban Plateau proper, usually not far from major Nabatean settlements. DS-152 is a showcase for a large farming compound in the Saliya region. Here, as given in Fig. 3, ancient water catchment installations spread over an area of 0.5 × 1 km, along the stream of Wadi Manshala. The position of cisterns and dams leaves no doubt that they were constructed with a plan. Sixteen dams and 15 cisterns were located at this site. The cisterns vary in depth from 3 m to 5 m. Dams average 5 m to 6 m long and 80 cm thick. Another example lies in DS-139, comprised of an ancient dam and a watchtower-like structure. The dam extends 25 m across a small wadi that flows into Wadi Saliya. It is five to ten courses thick (*ca.* 1.2 m) and remains up to 1 m high.

Figure 4 illustrates DS-131, *ca.* 1.5 km southeast of Jumayil, which includes terrace dams and enclosure walls built along the tributary of Wadi Hinu Saliya. The enclosure walls were erected of two to three rows of medium to large boulders, 80 cm wide. It extends over 400 m north-south and is two to three courses high. Associated with this enclosure wall are nine dams built of small to medium stones across the wadi and its tributaries. The length of the dams ranges from 60 m to 100 m; they are about 1.8 m thick and remain standing up to 60 cm high.

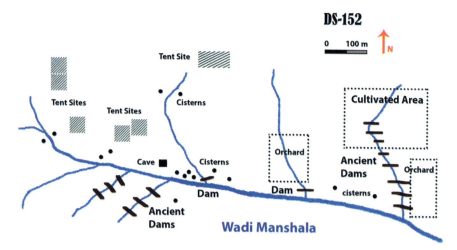

Fig. 3 DS-152 agricultural and water catchment

Equally germane, the surveys identified a Nabatean farming community in the Wadi Qattar region, the aforementioned drainage basin between Ramah and Lehun on the southeastern sector of the Dhiban Plateau. Rujm Qattar (DS-222) is a prominent ruin in this area, a farmstead site including at least four buildings and one modern animal pen built on top of ancient remains. The site commands clear visibility over many small sites in the vicinity, suggesting that it was the center of the Nabatean agricultural complex in the region. The main structure is a square building that sizes *ca.* 25 × 25 m. To the south of this building are circular structures solidly constructed using semi-hewn stone blocks. About 200 m northeast of the square building is a rectilinear residential house with its entrance on the east side of the building. North of this site is DS-225 with rectangular building ruins, circular structures, and animal pens. At the head of Wadi Qattar is another agricultural site (DS-216), containing two building ruins and one animal enclosure. The walls and associated sherd scatter cover an area *ca.* 90 × 100 m. The region also comprises ancient dams and water catchment installations. DS-223, for instance, is characterized by a dam across Wadi Qattar, *ca.* 200 m north Rujm Qattar. The dam was about 30 m across and 3 m thick. The eastern half of the dam remains intact and stands 15–17 courses high.

Most of these water catchment sites would be accredited to the Nabateans based on the presence of Nabatean and early Roman sherds on the surface. Besides, the building technique of these dams and terraces is similar to those in the region of Petra and southern Jordan (cf. Dentzer & Zayadine, 1992). Of course, specific difficulties arise when one attempts to date a site based on survey data since chronological verification cannot be reached from a few pottery sherds found on the surface (Worschech, 1992). Nevertheless, there is circumstantial evidence for the date of the first century CE for these agricultural sites. According to the evidence from Petra and the Negev, the transition from the late first century to early second century CE

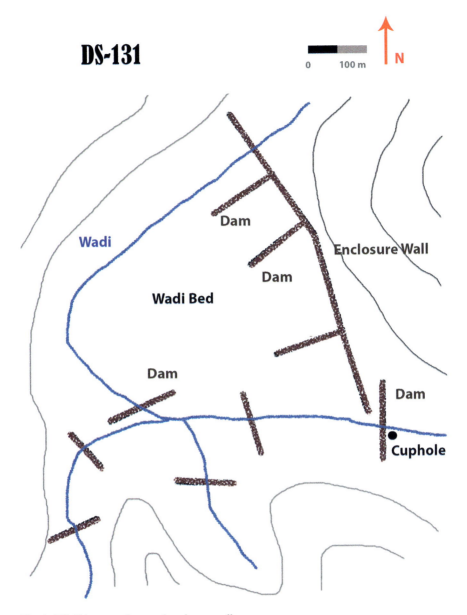

Fig. 4 DS-131 terrace dams and enclosure walls

was a period of extensive agricultural activities in Nabatean history (Dentzer & Zayadine, 1992; Negev, 1969). The elevation of Nabatean investment in land use for agricultural purposes began under the auspices of Aretas IV. Agriculture became the top contributor to the Nabatean economy in the mid and late first century CE, when Rabel II promoted the development of sedentarized agricultural communities around his kingdom (Bowersock, 1983; Graf, 1992). In the Dhiban Plateau, when they were not discovered with Nabatean painted potsherds, the hydraulic sites included distinctive, egg-shell-thin sherds that are usually assigned to the middle Nabatean kingdom period. Given this rough chronological congruity between the reigns of Aretas IV and Rabbel II and the ceramic evidence from these sites, it may be gleaned that the Dhiban Plateau experienced an agricultural boom in the first century CE, which lasted into the early second century CE.

6 Qasr Buildings

6.1 Distribution and Chronology

The Dhiban Plateau includes another notable architectural feature that I suspect has a Nabatean connection. These are rectangular platform-style buildings that dot the northern and eastern sections of the Dhiban Plateau. Local people call them "Qasrs." Six were documented in the Dhiban Plateau: Saliya, Jumayl, Musaytiba, Aliyan, Kaum, and Rumayl. Similar qasr architectures exist at Za'faran in the north and Balua in the Kerak Plateau.

At the center of Musaytiba is a roughly square building measuring approximately 20×21 m (Fig. 5). The external walls are solidly constructed with roughly cut blocks of limestone and still stand 3.3 m high. Glueck (1934) described it as "a raised platform of masonry" with "two flights of broad steps, one each on the northern and southern sides, leading to the top of the platform" (p. 40). The stairs that Glueck described appear to have been largely obliterated by the modern settlers, yet the stone tumbles on the northern and southern sides still bear some evidence of the stairs. Glueck closely investigated this structure and discovered inner vaulted chambers, which led to the suggestion that it was a Nabatean cultic platform.

Another qasr edifice is located at Saliya, which is estimated at 16×20 m in dimension and currently reaches a height of 2.3 m in places (Fig. 6). This structure, unlike Qasr Musaytiba, was built as a vertical extension of an earlier fort-like building that was constructed solidly of medium to large stone blocks. The survey team noticed several interior rooms and multiple wall lines inside the qasr, including two square rooms (ca. 5×5 m) at the edifice's northwest and southwest corners. Akin to Qasr Saliya in size is the central edifice at Rumayl (DS-11), an Iron Age fortress site situated ca. 4.5 km north of Aliyan (Ji & 'Attiyat, 1997). The qasr building itself measures roughly 15×20 m. Its walls are about 1.5 m thick and remain standing 6 m high. The corners are laid in the header and stretcher system. This qasr appears to have been built upon an earlier tower or building; occasional traces of this earlier edifice are still discernable. Equally imposing is the qasr at the site of Kaum, which is solidly constructed with roughly hewn limestone blocks. It is ca. 19×22 m in dimension, presently standing 3.5 m high.

Making Peoples: The Nabatean Settlement of the Dhiban Plateau and Beyond 1871

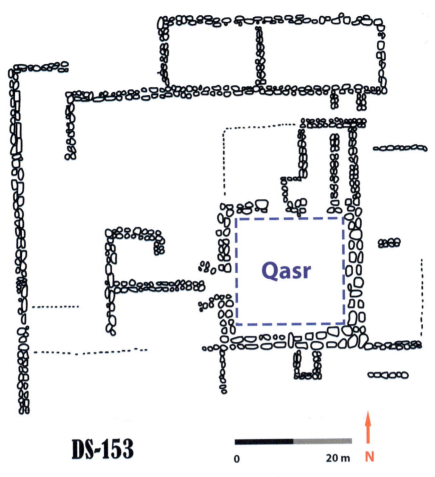

Fig. 5 Qasr Musaytiba and adjacent buildings (site sketch, 1997)

The qasr ruin at the acropolis of Aliyan is the most massive of its kind in size. Qasr Aliyan is oriented north-south and measures roughly 25 × 40 m. Inside the qasr are several visible wall lines. On the contrary, the tower-like qasr at Jumayl is the smallest of its type in dimension, measuring 8.5 × 8.5 m. Its exterior walls are about 1.4 m thick. Despite its small size, Qasr Jumayl is impressive as it sits at the site's highest point. The edifice is filled with tumbled stones, and thus it is difficult to identify interior walls without cleaning the surface. Evidence shows that Qasr Jumayl was also built on top of an earlier round structure.

The dating of the qasr buildings involves us in a certain amount of guesswork until excavations take place at the buildings. Speculation, however, leads me to hone in on the Nabatean period. At most sites, the qasrs were added as "superstructures" on top of the earlier edifices used as their "foundations." I may attribute the earlier structures to Iron Age because the lower building under Qasr Rumayl is seemingly

Fig. 6 Qasr Saliya (looking southwest)

architecturally connected with the site's circular-shaped Iron Age fortress ruin. The Rumayl fortress is dated to Iron Age in light of the dominant Iron I–II potsherds on the site. The Rumayl survey also yielded a small number of sherds that can be dated to the early Roman period. Combined, Qasr Rumayl is likely to be an Early-Roman upward extension of an existing structure that was part of the Iron Age fortress. A similar picture emerges at other qasr sites. As noted, the Saliya and Jumayl qasrs were built upon earlier buildings suspected to be Iron Age. Both sites were inhabited in the Iron Age when they operated and thrived as the urban centers of the southwestern Dhiban Plateau. This also holds valid for Kaum and possibly Aliyan. Qasr Musaytiba is the only case without the evidence of earlier structures as it was built directly above the ground. The evidence from Musaytiba, other than a couple of Iron Age sherds on the surface, strongly indicates the Nabatean period for constructing the qasr building.

At this point, it is imperative to refer to Qasr Za'faran and Qasr Balua located north and south of the Dhiban Plateau along the major longitudinal trade route. Qasr Za'faran is situated *ca.* 4.5 km north of Rumayl as the crow flies (Fig. 7). The archaeological work at Za'faran was carried out by Glueck (1934, p. 30), who defined the site as first settled in the Iron Age and revived again by the Nabateans early in the Roman period. The original dating of Za'faran was re-confirmed when Parker (1976) and Ferguson (2009) surveyed, who discovered Iron Age and Nabatean sherds from the site. In sum, Za'faran's settlement history looks analogous to those of the qasr sites in the Dhiban Plateau.

Fig. 7 Qasr Za'faran (looking west)

As for Za'faran, a qasr structure is the defining feature of the site of Balua. Qasr Balua is constructed of massive basalt and limestone blocks and currently stands up to 6 m high in places. The ongoing excavations in the qasr area have produced first century CE Nabatean sherds and Roman glasses (Vincent, 2017). They were associated with the early Roman pavement around the qasr. Under the pavement were the earth layer and a cobble floor. The pottery from this layer dates to Iron IIB, suggesting that the building was initially in use or constructed during the Iron Age (Bramlett, 2017a; Tyson, 2019). The excavations unearthed Late Bronze and some Iron II pottery at the bottom of the qasr wall. This layer consists of destruction debris, which may posit Iron II as a *terminus ante quem* for the construction of Qasr Balua (Bramlett, 2017b).

6.2 Functions of the Qasrs

What was the function of the qasr buildings? The original Iron II structures were founded possibly for military and public purposes. The fortress at Rujm Ataruz sheds light on this matter (Ji, 2016). The Rujm Ataruz fortress, *ca.* 17.5 × 18 m, was constructed as a military outpost in the ninth century BCE by the residents of Khirbat Ataruz. It was continually used for the same purposes through the eighth–seventh centuries BCE. The fortress' northern part was utilized as a look-out podium or watchtower, whereas the southern side was used for residence and domestic activities. Rujm Ataruz is remindful of the qasr-foundation edifices in terms of date, size, and building shape. The qasrs might have had the same defensive functions as for the Iron Age buildings granted that they were all constructed in a solid manner using moderate to massive boulders. They usually stand at the acropolis or the most vulnerable section of the settlements in terms of topography. They could be strongholds that provided their users with security and an advantage in defending the towns during wars.

Next, Nabateans worshiped the sun, put up altars to it in their towns and homes, made libations regularly upon them, and burnt frankincense or other substances (Hammond, 1973). The discovery of a Nabatean altar at Balua aligns with this reference to Nabatean house or town altars. Tyson and Ninow (2019) noted three phases of altar construction. In the second phase, the initial square structure (ca. 3 × 3 m) was enlarged by two meters on the eastern and northern sides. A stairway was added on the north side during the third phase. The altar is dated to the first century CE and was built closely (*ca.* 15 m) to Qasr Balua. This relatedness suggests some cultic functions were attached to the qasr building. There could be rooms or spaces inside the qasrs for private worship, pouring of libations, incense burning, and other religious rituals. Differently, the rooftop of the qasrs could provide an open space for larger public gatherings or religious ceremonies. In Hebrew text, we note the occasional association of the rooftop with worship to deities in ancient times (e.g., Psalms 95:1).

This point of view may find further support in the staircase towers that are commonly found at Nabatean settlements in the Negev and southern Jordan. The staircase towers made their appearance in the Nabatean realm toward the end of the first century BCE and reached their full development in the first half of the second century CE (Negev, 1973). Nabateans first adapted this architectural tradition to their religious and public needs, and it was only at the end of the following century that it was used in private edifices. The staircase towers are found in the Negev in linkage with forts, caravansaries, and other installations tied with the caravan traffic.

Qasr Musaytiba is in line with the Nabatean staircase tower as it was equipped with a staircase leading up to the rooftop. Nabateans constructed temples and shrines throughout their kingdom and territories, known as "high places" because they are usually open-air structures placed atop nearby hills or mountains. The qasr buildings were built as square or rectangular platforms with a flat surface at the rooftop. They could operate as high places for Nabateans who traveled across the deserts and flatlands in central Jordan. Standing on a flat surface of the eastern Dhiban Plateau, the qasrs should have been the salient landmarks for travelers as they were easily seen and recognized from a distance, enabling them to establish their location. They perhaps gave them feelings of safety, security, direction, hope, and even possibly religious piety. Moreover, the qasrs might cause them to think of the temples or the cultic paraphernalia inside the sanctuaries granted their geometric resemblance. The square or rectangular form was central to Nabatean religious imagination, as tipped by a *betyl* (stone pillar) or the podiums inside Qasr al-Bint and the Winged-Lions temple (Hammond, 2003; Larche & Zayadine, 2003).

A third possibility lies in caravansaries or wayside inns. In Palestine, the connection between traveling and caravansaries goes back to the pre-Iron Age periods (Dorsey, 1991). In the time of the incense trade prosperity when Nabatean merchandising was flourishing and the power of the central monarchy at Petra climaxed, many trade routes were built and used throughout Jordan (Graf, 1992; Schmid, 2004). Likewise, places in the Dhiban Plateau would have been designed to provide overnight housing to travelers and merchants. Some readers may have already noticed that the qasr buildings are all lined up along the major trade routes in the east of the Dhiban Plateau. The eastern highway led from Saliya and ran to Rumayl through Musaytiba and Aliyan; Kaum was also connected with the route through a local branch road. Za'faran and Balua were on this longitudinal highway as well. Similarly, Jumayl is situated on the southern lateral thoroughfare to Dhiban, which starts from Saliya. As trade routes developed and the Nabatean population grew in the Dhiban Plateau and the Madaba Plains, caravansaries must have become more of a necessity. I would assume the qasrs are the remains of Nabatean hostels and guest houses, whose construction intensified in the first century CE of political and social stability under the Roman empire.

Qasrs in the Dhiban Plateau average 492 square meters in size, after the small one at Jumayl is excluded. The buildings thus can be illustrated as a square 22 meters on each side on average. Comparing these figures with a couple of well-known Islamic caravansaries in eastern Jordan is informative. Qasr Kharana is a square building with 35 meters on each side (Petersen, 2002, p. 139). It is roughly 2.5 times larger than the qasr buildings in the Dhiban Plateau. Qasr Mushash is another example for reference (Bart et al., 2016). The size of its main structure measures 676 square meters; the four sides each measure 26 m long. The qasrs in the Dhiban Plateau are about 40% to 60% smaller than the Islamic caravansaries. Qasr Kharana has 60 rooms on two levels arranged around a central courtyard; in the middle of Qasr Mushash is a central courtyard surrounded by 13 rooms. Typically, Islamic desert caravansaries were located outside the nearest towns or villages and surrounded by immense walls for protective purposes. The interior was a sizeable ground-floor courtyard ringed with storerooms and stables for camels, donkeys, and horses. Rooms for lodgers were located on the second floor. The qasrs in the Dhiban Plateau appear to be one-story buildings, and there is no evidence for the interior central courtyard or stable for donkeys and camels. Imaginably, the animals were kept outside using the enclosed animal pens adjacent to the qasr buildings.

How many rooms could be installed inside the qasr buildings? Let me turn to Boz al-Mushelle for insight. It is a wayside village located on a late Hellenistic-early Roman ancient road, *ca.* 3 km northwest from Ataruz (Ji, 2019; Strobel, 1990). At the acropolis is a rectangular building measuring 12 × 23 m. Inside this 276 square meter building is one longitudinal hallway flanked by two rows of three to four small rooms. The Boz al-Mushelle building is comparable to the qasrs at Rumayl and Saliya, whereas it is smaller than those at Kaum, Musaytiba, and Aliyan. Therefore, the qasr buildings could be easily furnished with 8–30 rooms, while Qasr Jumayl was perhaps a one-room inn or a space with 2–4 interior compartments.

These modest-size buildings might be a good fit for the caravans through the region. Nabatean caravans through the Dhiban Plateau could have been smaller, sometimes with only several mules and camels, compared to the large to massive caravans along the roads connected with major trade routes like the Silk Road between China and the Islamic empires.

Most typically, ancient caravansaries were built at regular intervals so that travelers and merchants did not have to spend the night exposed to the dangers of the road and desert. The distance between the qasr buildings under discussion is estimated to be 9 km on average. The calculation reflects a straight line distance between the two locations based on their latitudes and longitudes, which should differ from the actual travel distance during the Nabatean period. Caravanserais were ideally positioned within a day's journey of each other. This resulted in a caravanserai every 30–40 km in the Middle East. In the Dhiban Plateau, however, the qasrs are located related to each other at much shorter intervals.

Two reasons are conceivable for this qualification. First, the qasrs in the Dhiban Plateau were located within the town or village precincts, which differs from the Islamic desert castles found outside the towns and villages. In the latter case, constructing a caravansary in a remote area facilitated the development of new cities and towns in the vicinity. The Dhiban Plateau was seemingly the opposite case. The qasrs were built in the existing villages or simultaneously with the emergence of new settlements. Accordingly, they had to be rather small to fit the hosting villages or new towns, which might have increased the necessity of multiple caravansaries in short distances along the routes. Second, the caravans through the Dhiban Plateau were supposedly heading for Madaba, Amman, and Jerash. Perhaps there was a great demand for multiple caravansaries because of the heavy traffic to the popular destinations. As in the modern hospitality industry, the clustering could be beneficial to the local economy during the Nabatean period as it engendered local competitiveness and infrastructure innovations (cf. Rodgriguez-Victoria et al., 2017).

Lastly, two small structures at Ramah and Mudayna as-Saliya are worthy of a short note. At Mudayna as-Saliya, amid the buildings near the acropolis, a single structure (ca. 4.3 × 4.7 m) was built with dressed stones on three sides. It was approached from the south side, possibly by one or two steps. This structure stands alone and remains more or less intact. It appears to be an altar used for religious purposes, reminiscent of the Nabatean altar at Balua (Tyson & Ninow, 2019). Both structures are somewhat alike in size and shape, being furnished with a stairway on one side. On the other hand, Ramah contains a square-like structure that measures 3.6 × 4.3 m. It currently stands about 1.4 m high above the ground. Given the pottery around the building, it is plausible to associate it with Nabateans and the first century CE. The structure gives the impression of being religious, perhaps an altar or small tower-like edifice mentioned above.

As noted, Nabateans were religious, and major Nabatean sites have often yielded evidence of religious architecture (Healey, 2001). The Dhiban Plateau did not differ from other Nabatean regions. They appear to have had the tradition of erecting small wayside shrines or cultic installations by a pathway or at crossroads. Ramah was at the head of the road down to Wadi Mujib; Mudayna as-Saliya was close to a route from the desert to the Dhiban Plateau. Similarly, the Nabatean temple at Lehun was built by a travel route, near the point where the road descends to the middle section of Wadi Mujib. The Nabatean town of Dhiban had a large-scale temple. At Dhiban, no evidence of structures of the early first century CE, except for the temple, has been found. Therefore, there is ambiguity about the exact nature of the Nabatean Dhiban town, but it was probably a religious or pilgrimage site at the junction of multiple roads. The Dhiban Plateau is devoid of religious monuments or extravagant images and tombs carved out of the rock faces. But various religious structures, ranging from simple altars to more elaborate temples, are found at multiple sites in the Dhiban Plateau. It is reasonable to be sure that the Nabatean settlement of the region was religiously rich and diverse.

7 Comparison to Neighboring Regions

The following section compares the Dhiban Plateau with its neighboring regions to grasp its Nabatean settlement history in a broader regional context. To begin with the north, the Ataruz region presents a different picture from the Dhiban Plateau. Nabatean evidence, including painted sherds, is scarce, if not absent, in the Libb-Machaerus region. The Ataruz region was visited by Glueck (1939, 1970), who reported the ubiquity of Nabatean potsherds at Mukawer and Ataruz. The results put forward a thesis for the Nabatean hold of the Libb-Machaerus region during the early Roman period. Despite three decades of excavations, however, Ataruz and Machaerus have failed to yield any attestation to the Nabatean settlement at the sites (Ji, 2011, 2012; Ji & Bates, 2014; Ji & Schade, 2021; Voros, 2013, 2015, 2019). Similarly, east to Ataruz is Libb, a prominent ruin appearing several times in Glueck's report (1939). I visited Libb in the summer of 2001. While the ancient remains suffered from modern development, I could salvage about 400 diagnostic sherds from the site (Ji, 2009b). Notwithstanding the presence of Roman sherds, there was no distinctive painted pottery convincingly attributable to the Nabateans. My visitation was preceded by Elder's (Elder, 2001), who carried out mapping and exhaustive pottery sampling at the site for two seasons of fieldwork. He collected more than 9000 sherds, half of them dated to Roman-Byzantine. Only two sherds were identified as Nabatean.

To be fair, it is worthwhile to speak of two minor caveats against the above observation. First, Machaerus have yielded eight Nabatean painted sherds, mostly recovered from a *mikveh* of the first century CE (Voros, 2015, fig. 291). They all seem to belong to the Phase III painted ware group. Second, in the past, a local person brought me a low-resolution photo of one coin that he claimed to have found at the base of Khirbat Ataruz. The picture showed on its obverse bearing the profile of jugate busts, possibly the images suggestive of Aretas IV and Shaqilath, his second wife, on a Nabatean coin from 16–40 CE (cf. Meshorer, 1975, pl. 7:112–114). There was no way at that time to determine whether or not the claim was authentic. Should it be genuine, the coin is the first sort of material evidence connecting Ataruz with the Nabatean kingdom.

If found in quantity or controlled research contexts, coins and pottery specimens can help determine certain place or settlement's dates and ethnic identity. A challenge arises when they come from a random sample in small quantity. This might be the Nabatean case for the Ataruz region. The coins and potsherds mentioned above could result from trade or private travels rather than Nabatean occupation of the area. Nabatean merchants and travelers should have occasionally visited the Ataruz region with painted vessels and other valuable goods. Their pottery was a popular commodity for its fine quality and design (Schmid, 2004). Nabatean coins would be understood in like manner.

On the other hand, the case of the Madaba Plains was well-covered previously, so I have nothing much to add here except for some updates (Ji, 2009b). Harrison and his team (Harrison et al., 2003) carried out excavations at the site of Madaba. It can be established that Nabateans inhabited Madaba in the early Roman period. Their settlement reportedly started between 63–15 BCE, which continued until the Nabatean annexation to the Roman empire around 106 CE (Ferguson, 2010). In contrast, the western region of the Madaba Plains is deficient in Nabatean evidence. Despite the decades of excavations, there is no data for the Nabatean presence at Mukhayyat, Nebo, Hesban, and 'Umayri, suggesting that Nabatean settlement did not spread from Madaba to the west and northwest (Foran et al., 2018; Ji, 2009b). Contrastingly, Jalul was perhaps in use during the period granted the existence of Nabatean pottery on the surface (Ji, 2009b). Four sites in the 5 km radius of Jalul were also reported to have Nabatean potsherds. The appearance of Nabatean pottery at Nitil, Khirbat al-Qerieyat, Khirbat al-Melih, Khirbat ad-Deleilat al-Gharbiyya, and Khirbat ad-Deleilat al-Sherqiyya indicates that Nabateans populated the southern and southeastern areas of the Madaba Plains (Al-Fuqaha, 2018, pp. 56–59).

Unlike the Ataruz region, the story of the Nabatean settlement in the Dhiban Plateau may work for the Kerak Plateau. There was a Nabatean settlement at Balua, with its qasr building at the northern center of the site. The pottery from the qasr and its associated altar date Nabatean Balua to the first century CE. (Tyson & Ninow, 2019). Faris was a dense Nabatean rural village during the first century CE (McQuitty et al., 2020). Dhat Ras is famous for its well-preserved Nabatean temple (Eddinger, 2004). The temple sits on a rectangular podium constructed with ashlar limestone blocks. A surface survey of the temple area revealed a number of Nabatean and Roman sherds, which support the assignment of the temple to the first century CE (Zayadine, 1970). Also, ar-Rabba accommodated a Nabatean temple and water reservoir. The temple is measured *ca.* 24 × 30 m and dated to the first century CE, even though it has not been systematically excavated yet (Gysens & Marino, 1996). Nabatean inscriptions from the Kerak Plateau are mainly dated to the late years of Aretas IV reign (Al-Salameen & Shdaifat, 2017; Zayadine, 1970).

A similar account emerges from Brown's (Brown, 1991) publication of the pottery from the Kerak Plateau survey. The final report illustrates two dozen Nabatean wares, including two plain egg-shell ware bowls with an inverted or elongated rim (nos. 312 and 313), forms that occurred in abundance during the late first century

BCE and the first century CE. The other sherds in the same assemblage are also attributable to the first century CE. The report includes one Nabatean painted vessel (no. 331) that belongs to the Phase III group. Brown (1991, p. 211) states that this form is ubiquitous in the Kerak Plateau and appears on the interiors of the Nabatean egg-shell bowl with a carinated and inverted rim. In addition, Worschech (1992) surveyed the northwestern section of the Kerak Plateau. Nabatean sherds are seemingly widespread in the area, but further subdivision into early and late is not feasible due to limited information.

Ayer (2006) studied 1221 Nabatean and Roman potsherds from the Kerak Plateau Survey Project and the 1995–2001 Kerak Resource Survey Project. The sherds pertain to 108 sites in the southern Kerak Plateau. The analysis identified a relatively small quantity of Nabatean painted and plain wares, respectively, from eight and 13 locations. The assemblage also included five sherds of eastern sigillata and one Nabatean cream ware. All published Nabatean painted specimens are classified as Phase III. As a matter of interest, all Nabatean painted samples came from the sites along the Desert Highway, except for one specimen. The results bespeak that the Kerak Plateau was under the Nabatean jurisdiction in the first century CE. The settlers chose the east side of the region for inhabitation, which points to their involvement in caravan trade along the eastern desert fringe.

The preceding discussion firmly puts Nabateans on the first century CE Kerak Plateau map. The issue of the first century BCE or earlier remains, however. Indeed, there is yet no confirmatory corroboration for earlier Nabatean settlement in the Kerak Plateau. Even so, I may attend to a couple of details from the survey reports, which can temporarily move up the Nabatean debut to the first century BCE.

Ad-Dayr is appropriate to be considered first. According to Worschech (1986), earlier Nabatean evidence may exist there, a prominent ancient ruin west of the modern city of Qasr. Ad-Dayr includes ceramic and architectural evidence for the late Hellenistic and early Roman periods. Worschech (1986) published some pottery samples from the site in a preliminary mode, including four Nabatean painted bowl and cup fragments. Most of the samples, including three painted sherds, are assignable to the early Roman period. However, one specimen has a decoration of red paint, consisting of a simple line having the alternate right and left turns (Worschech, 1986, abb. 6:7). It can be the vestiges of decoration lines, straight or wavy, that commonly appear on the inside of the Nabatean bowls from the early first century BCE (cf. Ji, 2009a, fig. 2:4–6; Schmid, 2007a, fig. 1:5, 2007b, fig. 10:18–19). Also curious is one published bowl in the Kerak Plateau survey report (Brown, 1991, no. 333). It is painted with small roundish or gourd-like marks that run concentrically around the vessel's rim. Its up-turned rim may indicate the early first century CE for the chronology (Brown, 1991, p. 212). Similar decorations, however, are often associated with Phase II painted wares from the late first century BCE (cf. Schmid, 2007b, figs. 9 and 10:21).

Taken together, in all likelihood, Nabateans advanced to Madaba late in the first century BCE. Their settlement carried on through the beginning of the second CE. The evidence from Jalul, Nitil, Za'faran, and their vicinities postulates that the land to the south and southeast of Madaba was also under Nabatean control. Less is known about the Kerak Plateau. Yet, it is certain that Nabateans settled there no later than the early first century CE and flourished through the century. It is more challenging to define when they came on the scene, but it could be the first century BCE when other Nabateans entered the Dhiban Plateau in the north. Their emergence in the Madaba Plains thus seems to be about 50–75 years behind, mid or late in the first century BCE, compared to settlement in the Dhiban Plateau and the Kerak Plateau. It might have been only after or around the same time with the Nabatean take-over of the northern rim of the Dhiban Plateau. The time frame of the Nabatean debut across the Dhiban Plateau and its neighboring regions is consistent with Graf's (1992) observation that their settlements also "burst into existence overnight" (p. 254) into prominence in southern Edom during the first century BCE.

However, this archaeological reconstruction of the Nabatean settlement history in the Dhiban Plateau and its neighboring areas is not relevant to the region between Machaerus and Libb. Nabateans seem never to have set their dominion in the region northwest to the Dhiban Plateau. What can explain this radical gap between the Ataruz region and the other parts of central Jordan? In order to account for the source, it is necessary to review the historical context.

8 Historical Consideration

The Ataruz region formed the southern part of Jewish Paraea during the late Hellenistic and early Roman periods. Machaerus was at the heart of south Paraea. Alexander Jannaeus built a fortress at Machaerus in about 90 BC to safeguard the kingdom's southeastern border. King Herod rebuilt it in 30 BC, a fortress passed to his son Herod Antipas (4 BC – 39 CE). A detailed analysis of existing data from the Ataruz region shows that Sayl Haydan, the northern tributary of Wadi Mujib, was a *de facto* border between Jewish Paraea and Arabian Nabataea during the periods (Ji, 2009b, 2020). The Hasmonean-Herodian rulers fortified the site of Tall ar-Raya in the valley to protect the Ataruz region and to establish their rule in the Sayl Haydan area. The Nabateans were the main rival of the Hasmoneans, and wars and battles were frequent between them during the late second – early first centuries BCE.

The sparsity of Nabatean evidence in the Ataruz region is explainable in this context. The hilly area of Ataruz lay inside the Hasmonean-Herodian territory for most of the late Hellenistic and early Roman periods, except maybe for the late first century CE, when the region came under direct Roman control. The sporadic appearance of Nabatean coins and vessels in the Ataruz region might associate with their brief incursion into the area during this period, if not as the results of occasional trade and private crossings over the border.

Similarly, the Nabatean-Hasmonean rivalry can shed light on the peculiar geographical gap between the Phase I–II Nabatean painted ware distributions in the Dhiban Plateau. Phase I sherds are found at Musaytiba, Ramah, Qrayya, Mudayna as-Saliya, Mushayrifa, Dhiban, Musaytiba, and DS-152 and DS-410. DS-152 would be thought part of the Saliya site, granted its proximity to the site of Saliya. As

Making Peoples: The Nabatean Settlement of the Dhiban Plateau and Beyond

depicted in Fig. 2, all these Phase I sites are grouped in the southeastern section of the Dhiban Plateau, except for Dhiban and DS-410. The latter is a small house ruin *ca.* 4 km southwest of Dhiban. This pattern differs from the distribution of Phase II painted vessels. Phase II samples come from Qulamh Abu Hussein, Dhiban, Ammuriya, Musaytiba, and DS-167, 259, and 263. The last three sites are all pertinent to the ruins of rectangular buildings in the Ammuriya-Qubayba region. Notably, 13 of the 21 Phase II sherds relate to Qulamh Abu Hussein, albeit three samples are from Dhiban. Incongruously, Phase III settlements are widely spread over the entire Dhiban Plateau, being situated at every sector of the region, even though they are most common in the southeastern sector. However, Phase II sites, other than Dhiban and Musaytiba, all assemble along the northern rim of the Dhiban Plateau. Formerly, they were perceived to muster mainly in the northeastern section of the Dhiban Plateau (Ji, 2009a). It would now extend to the west covering the entire northern rim because of the new findings from Dhiban and Qulamh Abu Hussein. The Phase III pattern is assuredly a throwback to the Nabatean control of the entire region in the first century CE. The pattern for Phase I vessels may attest to the southeastern part being the place of first arrival of the Nabateans in the late second – early first centuries BCE.

A question remains as to why Phase II Nabatean painted wares disappeared from the southeastern region while it later clusters along the northern edge of the Dhiban Plateau. By inference, this alteration may have to do with the Hasmonean colonization of Mudayna as-Saliya early in the first century BCE, a military stronghold site near the head of Wadi Mujib. According to Josephus (*Ant.* 13.15.4), Alexander Jannaeus took down the Moabite cities of Madaba, Libb, and several other unidentifiable towns in the region (Avi-Yonah, 2002, pp. 70–71). Possibly, Mudayna as-Saliya (Fig. 8) was one of these Moabite cities subdued by the king. Recent studies postulate that Alexander Jannaeus fortified Mudayna as-Saliya to control the Desert Highway (Ji, 2020; Ji & Ben-David, 2020), which emerged as the alternative for the incense trade after his conquest of Gaza in 100 BC. Perhaps, this development displaced the early Nabatean settlers across the eastern Dhiban Plateau to the region's northern edge. Another scenario is also conceivable. The Hasmonean military operation effectively drove the Nabateans to the desert and the south, engendering a short hiatus of Nabatean settlement between the Phase I and II periods. We are told once again by Josephus (*Ant.* 14.1.4) that after the death of Alexander Jannaeus, the Hasmoneans surrendered the territory of Moab to Aretas III during the civil war of Hyrcanus II and Aristobulus II. This concession would have led to the return of Nabateans to the Dhiban Plateau in the mid-late first century BCE, and they settled mainly along the border to protect the region from the Herodian kingdom. Presumably, this settlement project was not optional but should have been an urgent requirement for the Nabateans. King Herod was expanding his territory to the southeast, forcing a way into Wadi Mujib, as demonstrated by a couple of Herodian forts erected in the middle of Wadi Mujib and Sayl Haydan around this period (Strobel, 1997). This state of political affairs seems to have materialized into the congregation of Phase II Nabatean painted ware along the northern rim of the Dhiban Plateau.

Fig. 8 Mudayna as-Saliya (looking west)

Finally, before concluding the paper, I elaborate briefly on the Nabatean military operation in the Dhiban Plateau. According to textual evidence, Abd-Maliku, son of Obaishu, a Nabatean strategos, and his son La'muru, strategos, lived at Umm ar-Rasas in the year of 41 CE (Graf, 1994; Piccirillo, 1993). Nabatean strategoi were in charge of the districts' civil and military administration, and their residence was usually associated with cavalry units. Nabateans spent their lives on camelback, herding, and trading. Further, they heavily engaged in incense trade and commerce, which should have required a strong military power to protect their caravans and trade routes (Wenning, 2007). These lifestyles and economic needs transferred to warfare. Nabateans put horsemanship to good use during wars, and their battle tactics primarily hinged on their agile and durable horses and camels. We must note that military horsemen normally required the assistance of grooms and servants, and cavalry units made significant demands for horse-breeding and pasturage on the Nabatean kingdom. The combination of these facts indicates that the administrative center at Umm ar-Rasas should have necessitated the creation of strings of corrals, horse-breeding facilities, and military guard posts around the Dhiban Plateau, in which cavalry was an instrumental part.

However, the archaeological evidence from Umm ar-Rasas is fragmentary concerning the Nabatean period (Piccirillo, 1988). Fortunately, two potential candidates for such facilities were noted during the Dhiban Plateau survey. They are Musaytiba and Aqrabah (Ji & 'Attiyat, 1997; Ji & Lee, 1998). At Musaytiba, adjacent to the qasr building, is a large structure comprised of wall lines and many large chambers. In the middle of this structure are prominent open places enclosed by walls, which cover an area of at last 30 × 35 m. Aqrabah is located on a low hill about 3 km southeast of Dhiban, offering a commanding view over Wadi Mujib. It is an extensive archaeological ruin covering an area of no less than 100 m by 170 m. Remains of the main building (34 × 42 m), possibly Nabatean, are still visible on the east side of this site. There are several thick wall-lines west of this building, and some of them, constructed of large cut stones, extend almost 50 m in a roughly east-west direction.

Put otherwise, the large rectangular structures of Musaytiba and Aqrabah can be animal corrals built for military purposes in the Nabatean period. Both sites contain Nabatean and early Roman sherds and are positioned on major trade routes. The builders constructed them solidly with well-dressed limestone blocks according to overall building plans. They were not mostly for private use. Future excavations of the sites may throw light on Nabatean military operations and architectures that still largely remain terra incognita in the field of Nabatean archaeology.

9 Conclusion

In light of the data, the Nabatean migration to the Dhiban Plateau probably began late in the second century BCE or early in the first century BCE. Still, a phase of short settlement gap or intraregional relocation to the north followed, caused by the Hasmonean intrusion into the southeastern region. The Dhiban Plateau witnessed a high intensification of Nabatean settlements in the first century CE. During this era, the region was more or less encircled by seasonal shelters or storage facilities built by nomadic tribes along the plateau rim. Towns were mainly in the region's center, along the trade roads, or near small tributaries flowing into Wadi Mujib and Wadi Walla. Besides caravan trade and religious pilgrimage, Nabatean settlers intensely engaged in agriculture in these tributaries. Possibly, the military and administrative centers at Musaytiba and Umm ar-Rasas protected the region and the trade along the roads that connected Petra and the Madaba Plains.

This settlement history for the Dhiban Plateau is overall compatible with the archaeological records from the Madaba Plains and the Kerak Plateau. Based on the evidence from the Negev, southern Jordan, and the Hauran, it has been assumed that in the first century BCE, Nabateans began to establish their commercial, administrative, and military centers along the trade routes in central Jordan. This view would find empirical support from the present study. The same historical disposition is found irrelevant to the Ataruz region, however. Nabateans seem to have failed to establish their control there, even late in the first century CE when the area was under direct Roman rule. The hilly region of Ataruz remained in the hands of the Hasmonean-Herodian kingdoms for most of the late Hellenistic and early Roman periods.

References

Al-Fuqaha, M. M. H. (2018). *The Nabatean settlement in central and northern Jordan*. Unpublished doctoral dissertation, University of Bochum.

Al-Salameen, Z., & Al-Rawahneh, M. R. (2017). A new Nabataean inscription from Dhiban, with a brief account on Dhiban during the Nabataean period. *Arabian Archaeology and Epigraphy, 28*(2), 246–253. https://doi.org/10.1111/aae.12097

Al-Salameen, Z., & Shdaifat, Y. (2017). A new Nabatean inscription from the Moab plateau. *Arabian Epigraphic Notes, 3*(3), 1–10.

Avi-Yonah, M. (2002). *The holy land: A historical geography from the Persian to the Arab conquest, 536 B.C. to A.D. 640*. Carta.

Avner, U. (1984). Ancient cult sites in the Negev and Sinai deserts. *Tel Aviv, 11*(2), 115–131. https://doi.org/10.1179/tav.1984.1984.2.115

Ayer, M. K. (2006). *Nabatean and Roman survey pottery from the Kerak Plateau, Jordan.* Published MA thesis, University of Tennessee-Knoxville.

Bart, K., McPhillips, S., & Wordsworth, P. D. (2016). Water management in desert regions: Early Islamic Qasr Mushash. In S. McPhillips & P. D. Wordsworth (Eds.), *Landscapes of the Islamic world archaeology, history, and ethnography* (pp. 50–68). University of Pennsylvania Press.

Bowersock, G. W. (1983). *Roman Arabia*. Harvard University Press.

Bramlett, K. (2017a). Results of week 2. *BRAP Beat, 1*(2), 1–5.

Bramlett, K. (2017b). Results of week 3. *BRAP Beat, 1*(3), 1–6.

Brown, R. M. (1991). Ceramics from the Kerak Plateau. In J. M. Miller (Ed.), *Archaeological survey of the Kerak Plateau* (pp. 169–279). Scholars Press.

Daviau, P. M. M., & Foley, C. M. (2007). Nabatean water management systems in the Wadi ath-Thamad. *Studies in the History and Archaeology in Jordan, 9*, 357–365.

Dentzer, J.-M., & Zayadine, F. (1992). L'escape urbain de Petra. *Studies in the History and Archaeology of Jordan, 4*, 233–252.

Dorsey, D. A. (1991). *The road and highways of ancient Israel*. Johns Hopkins University.

Eddinger, T. W. (2004). A Nabatean/Roman temple at Dhat Ras, Jordan. *Near Eastern Archaeology, 67*, 14–15.

Elder, D. (2001, August). *Libb surface survey*. Unpublished paper. Retrieved on December 29, 2021 from http://sites.utoronto.ca/tmap/prelim_2001.html#Libb

Ferguson, J. (2009). Rediscovering az-Za'faran and az-Zuna: The Wadi Thamad Project regional survey. In P. Bienkowski (Ed.), *Studies on Iron Age Moab and neighbouring areas in honor of Michele Daviau* (pp. 227–243). Peeters.

Ferguson, J. (2010). Pottery, chronology and cultural succession at Tall Madaba in the late Hellenistic and early Roman periods. *Studies in the History and Archaeology of Jordan, 11*, 431–445.

Foran, D., Dolan, A., & Edwards, S. (2018). The second season of excavation of the Khirbat al-Mukhayyat Archaeological Project. *Liber Annuus, 66*, 301–3019.

Glueck, N. (1934). *Explorations in eastern Palestine II*. American Schools of Oriental Research.

Glueck, N. (1939). *Exploration in eastern Palestine III*. American Schools of Oriental Research.

Glueck, N. (1970). *The other side of the Jordan*. American Schools of Oriental Research.

Graf, D. F. (1983). The Nabataeans and the Hisma: In the steps of Glueck and beyond. In C. L. Meyers & M. O'Connor (Eds.), *The word of the lord shall go forth: Essays in honor of David Noel Freedman* (pp. 647–664). Eisenbrauns.

Graf, D. F. (1992). Nabataean settlements and Roman occupation in Arabia Petraea. *Studies in the History and Archaeology of Jordan, 4*, 253–260.

Graf, D. F. (1994). The Nabataean army and the cohortes ulpiae petraeorum. In E. Dabrowa (Ed.), *The Roman and Byzantine army in the East* (pp. 265–311). Jagiellonski University.

Graf, D. F. (1997). Nabateans. In E. M. Meyers (Ed.), *The Oxford encyclopedia of archaeology in the Near East* (pp. 82–85). Oxford University.

Making Peoples: The Nabatean Settlement of the Dhiban Plateau and Beyond

Gysens, J. G., & Marino, L. (1996). Étude du temple antique de Qasr ar-Rabba dans le Moab: Rapport sommaire d'une première campagne de relevés (1996). *Annual of the Department of Antiquities of Jordan, 41*, 189–193.

Haiman, M. (1989). Preliminary report of the western Negev highlands emergency survey. *Israel Exploration Journal, 39*(3/4), 173–191.

Hammond, P. C. (1973). *The Nabateans: Their history, culture, and archaeology.* Lund.

Hammond, P. C. (2003). The temple of winged lions. In G. Markoe (Ed.), *Petra rediscovered* (pp. 223–229). The Cincinnati Art Museum.

Harrison, T., Foran, D., Graham, A., Griffith, T., Barlow, C., & Ferguson, J. (2003). The Tall Madaba Archaeological Project: Preliminary report of the 1998–2000 field seasons. *Annual of the Department of Antiquities of Jordan, 47*, 129–148.

Healey, J. (2001). *The religion of the Nabataeans.* Brill.

Homes-Fredericq, D. (2010, November 24). *Excavation results.* Lehun Belgian Excavations in Jordan. Retrieved on December 23, 2021 from http://www.lehun-excavations.be/index.html

Ji, C. (2009a). The Nabatean painted pottery in the Dhiban Plateau, Jordan: Statistical modeling and its implication for the Nabatean settlement. *Leidan Journal of Pottery Studies, 25*, 119–140.

Ji, C. (2009b). Drawing the borderline: The Nabatean, Hasmonean and Herodian kingdoms in Central Jordan. *Studies in the History and Archaeology in Jordan, 10*, 617–632.

Ji, C. (2011). Khirbat 'Ataruz: An interim overview of the 10 years of archaeological architectural findings. *Annual of the Department of Antiquities of Jordan, 55*, 561–579.

Ji, C. (2012). The early Iron Age II temple at Hirbet 'Atarus and its architecture and selected cultic objects. In J. Kamlah (Ed.), *Temple building and temple cult: Architecture and cultic paraphernalia of temples in the Levant (2.-I. mill. B.C.E.)* (pp. 203–222). Harrassowitz.

Ji, C. (2016). One tale, two 'Ataruz: Investigating Rujm 'Ataruz and its association with Khirbat 'Ataruz. *Studies in the History and Archaeology of Jordan, 12*, 211–222.

Ji, C. (2019). The ancient road in Wadi Zarqa-Main, north of Khirbat Ataruz. *Studies in the History and Archaeology in Jordan, 13*, 143–157.

Ji, C. (2020). A late Hellenistic-early Roman fortress at Khirbat Mudayna as-Saliya, Central Jordan. *Palestine Exploration Quarterly, 152*(3), 207–233. https://doi.org/10.1080/0031032 8.2020.1759297

Ji, C., & 'Attiyat, T. (1997). The reconnaissance survey of the Dhiban Plateau, 1996. *Annual of the Department of Antiquities in Jordan, 41*, 115–128.

Ji, C., & Bates, R. D. (2014). Khirbat 'Ataruz 2011–2012: A preliminary report. *Andrews University Seminary Studies, 52*(1), 47–91.

Ji, C., & Ben-David, C. (2020). The siege wall at Mudayna as-Saliya in Central Jordan. In M. Eisenberg & R. Khamisy (Eds.), *The art of siege warfare and military architecture from the classical world to the Middle Ages* (pp. 81–90). Oxbow.

Ji, C., & Lee, J. K. (1998). Preliminary report on the survey of the Dhiban Plateau, 1997. *Annual of the Department of Antiquities of Jordan, 42*, 549–571.

Ji, C., & Lee, J. K. (2000). A preliminary report on the Dhiban Plateau Survey Project, 1999: The Versacare expedition. *Annual of the Department of Antiquities of Jordan, 44*, 493–506.

Ji, C., & Lee, J. K. (2003). Iron Age in the Dhiban Plateau. In F. Ninow (Ed.), *Wort und stein: Studien zur theologie und archaeologies festschrift fur Udo Worschech* (pp. 105–132). Peter Lang.

Ji, C., & Lee, J. K. (2007). The Hellenistic period in the Dhiban Plateau: A quantitative analysis. *Studies in the History and Archaeology of Jordan, 9*, 233–240.

Ji, C., & Schade, A. (2021). Excavating a monumental stepped stone structure at Khirbat Ataruz: The 2016–2017 season of fieldwork in Field G. *Andrews University Seminary Studies, 58*(2), 227–256.

Kloner, A., & Ben-David, C. (2003). Mesillot on the Arnon: An Iron Age (pre-Roman) road in Moab. *Bulletin of the American Schools of Oriental Research, 330*, 65–81.

Ladurner, M. (2013). Nabataean agricultural settlements in Central Jordan: Preliminary report on the example from the Wadi Thamad region. *Studies in the History and Archaeology of Jordan, 11*, 613–623.

Larche, F., & Zayadine, F. (2003). The Qasr al-Bint of Petra. In G. Markoe (Ed.), *Petra rediscovered* (pp. 199–213). The Cincinnati Art Museum.

McQuitty, A., Parton, H., & Petersen, A. (2020). *Khirbat Faris: Rural settlement, contiguity and change in southern Jordan: The Nabatean to modern periods (1st century BC to 20th century AD)*. Archaeopress.

Meshorer, Y. (1975). *Nabatean coins*. Hebrew University of Jerusalem.

Miller, J. M. (1991). *Archaeological survey of the Kerak Plateau*. Scholars Press.

Negev, A. (1969). The chronology of the middle Nabatean period. *Palestine Exploration Quarterly, 101*(1), 5–14.

Negev, A. (1971). The Nabatean necropolis of Mampsis (Kurnub). *Israel Exploration Journal, 21*(2/3), 110–129.

Negev, A. (1973). The staircase-tower in Nabatean architecture. *Revue Biblique, 80*(3), 364–383.

Negev, A. (1976). The early beginning of the Nabataean realm. *Palestine Exploration Quarterly, 108*(3), 125–133.

Negev, A. (1986). *Nabatean archaeology today*. New York University.

Ninow, F. (2009). Crossroads and sites at the northern edge of the central Moabite plateau. *Studies in the History and Archaeology of Jordan, 10*, 663–640.

Olavarri, E. (1965). Sondages a 'Aro'er sur l'Arnon. *Revue Biblique, 72*(1), 77–94.

Olavarri, E. (1993). Aroer (in Moab). In E. Stern (Ed.), *The new encyclopedia of archaeological excavations in the Holy Land* (pp. 92–93). Israel Exploration Society.

Parker, S. T. (1976). Archaeological survey of the limes Arabicus: Preliminary report. *Annual of the Department of Antiquities of Jordan, 21*, 19–31.

Petersen, A. (2002). *Dictionary of Islamic architecture*. Routledge.

Piccirillo, M. (1988). The mosaics at Um er-Rasas in Jordan. *Biblical Archaeologist, 51*, 208–213.

Piccirillo, M. (1993). Umm er-Rasas. In E. Stern (Ed.), *The new encyclopedia of archaeological excavations in the Holy Land* (pp. 1490–1493). Israel Exploration Society.

Politis, K. D. (1998). Rescue excavations in the Nabatean cemetery at Khirbat Qazone 1996–7. *Annual of the Department of Antiquities, 42*, 611–614.

Rodgriguez-Victoria, O., Puig, F., & Gonzalez-Loureiro, M. (2017). Clustering, innovation and hotel competitiveness: Evidence from the Colombia destination. *International Journal of Contemporary Hospitality Management, 29*(11), 2785–2806.

Schmid, S. G. (2004). The distribution of Nabatean pottery and the organization of Nabataean long distance trade. *Studies in the History and Archaeology of Jordan, 8*, 415–426.

Schmid, S. G. (2007a). Nabatean pottery. In K. D. Politis (Ed.), *The world of the Nabateans, Volume 2 for the international conference the world of the Herod and the Nabateans held at the British Museum, 17–19 April 2001* (pp. 309–326). Franz Steiner.

Schmid, S. G. (2007b). Nabatean find ware from Petra. *Studies in the History and Archeology in Jordan, 5*, 637–647.

Strobel, A. (1990). Ez-Zara – Mukawer survey. *The Near East in Antiquity, 1*, 81–85.

Strobel, A. (1997). Ancient roads in the Roman district of south Parea: Routes of communication in the eastern area of the Dead Sea. *Studies in the History and Archaeology of Jordan, 6*, 271–280.

Tushingham, A. D. (1972). *The excavations at Dibon (Dhiban) in Moab*. American Schools of Oriental Research.

Tyson, C. W. (2019). The qasr. *BRAP Beat, 2*(2), 1–2.

Tyson, C. W., & Ninow, F. (2019). A basalt volute capital fragment from el-Balu, Jordan. *Zeitschrift des Deutschen Palastina-Vereins, 135*(2), 158–167.

Vincent, M. (2017). Introduction to the project and team. *BRAP Beat, 1*(1), 1–5.

Voros, G. (2013). *Machaerus I: History, archaeology and architecture of the fortified Herodian royal palace and city overlooking the Dead Sea in Transjordan: Final report of the excavations and surveys 1807–2012*. Edizioni Terra Santa.

Voros, G. (2015). *Machaerus II: The Hungarian archaeological mission in the light of the American-Baptist and Italian Franciscan excavations and surveys: Final reports 1968–2014*. Edizioni Terra Santa.

Voros, G. (2019). *Machaerus III: The golden jubilee of the archaeological excavations. Final report on the Herodian chapel (1968–2018)*. Edizioni Terra Santa.

Wenning, R. (2007). The Nabateans in history. In K. D. Politis (Ed.), *The world of the Nabateans, Volume 2 for the international conference the world of the Herod and the Nabateans held at the British Museum, 17–19 April 2001* (pp. 25–44). Franz Steiner.

Winnett, F. V., & Reed, W. L. (1964). *The excavations at Dibon (Dhiban) in Moab*. American Schools of Oriental Research.

Worschech, U. (1986). Dimon und Horonaim. *Biblische Notizen, 31*, 70–95.

Worschech, U. (1992). Ancient settlement patterns in the northwest Ard al-Karak. *Studies in the History and Archaeology of Jordan, 4*, 83–87.

Younker, R. W. (1989). Towers in the region surrounding Tell el-'Umeiri. In L. G. Herr et al. (Eds.), *Madaba Plains Project 1* (pp. 195–198). Andrews University.

Zayadine, F. (1970). Une tombe nabateenne pres de dhat-ras (jordanie). *Syria, 47*(1/2), 117–135.

The Hexagram Graves: Symbols and Identity in Ottoman Jaffa

Yoav Arbel

Abstract Two coffins decorated with hexagrams were discovered in 2016 during excavations in a late Ottoman Muslim cemetery in Jaffa. The hexagrams are of the type known as Star of David, an image strongly associated with Judaism. The symbols presumably indicate an unlikely situation in which some of Jaffa's Jews may have been buried in a Muslim graveyard during times of rising tensions and budding violence between the two communities. Broader analysis suggests a more complex picture, casting doubt on this axiomatic religious identification. This study reviews the discovery against the backgrounds of Jewish and Muslim funerary customs, the historical circumstances of the period and the peculiar association of the hexagram form within Judaism. It focuses on Jaffa in the twilight of Ottoman rule, but also reflects the potential contribution of historical archaeology to the investigation of society, faith and symbolism beyond specific sites, artifacts and periods.

Keywords Hexagram · Jaffa · Ottoman Empire · Burials

1 Introduction

In 1916, Jaffa's Ottoman authorities forbade the further use of the city's main Muslim cemetery, which was leveled shortly afterwards. The declared intention of this blunt step was to defuse a source of epidemics, but urban planning must have been a major motive, for once the directive was implemented, a major obstruction was removed in adjoining Manshiya, Jaffa's new northern neighborhood to the city center (Yinnon, 2001: 234; Kark, 1990: 299).

Jaffa's northern Muslim cemetery is first noted on a 1799 map by Pierre Jacotin, an engineer who served under Napoleon during his Syrian campaign, and later

---

Y. Arbel (✉)
Israel Antiquities Authority, Jerusalem, Israel
e-mail: yoar07@gmail.com

© The Author(s), under exclusive license to Springer Nature Switzerland AG 2023
E. Ben-Yosef, I. W. N. Jones (eds.), *"And in Length of Days Understanding" (Job 12:12): Essays on Archaeology in the Eastern Mediterranean and Beyond in Honor of Thomas E. Levy*, Interdisciplinary Contributions to Archaeology,
https://doi.org/10.1007/978-3-031-27330-8_80

appears on maps and photographs from the nineteenth and early twentieth centuries (Shacham, 2011: Figs. 13.5, 13.13, 13.15, 13.18, 13.21–22). By its final days it had expanded from the southern limits of Manshiya to the fringes of the new government center at the Clock Tower Square, established in the closing decade of the nineteenth century.

Archaeological excavations in grounds that were formerly parts of the cemetery have proven that while most tombstones were uprooted, many of the subsoil burials remained undisturbed. Hundreds were discovered under the *Qishle*—a late nineteenth century Ottoman military compound (Arbel, 2021b: 45–53; Nagar, 2021; Edrey & Gross, forthcoming), and Ratosh Street (Sion & Rapuano, 2017), northeast of the Clock Tower Square. Additional graves were found in smaller excavations (Arbel, 2017a: 103–107). Numerous burials must have been destroyed during construction and infrastructure work in the decades prior to regulated archaeological supervision or remained sealed under modern streets and buildings.

The most recent salvage projects within the cemetery's grounds took place in 2016, 2018 2020 and 2021 on plots next to Elisabeth Bergner Street, in the northern outskirts of modern Jaffa (Fig. 1).[1] Two of the graves excavated in 2016 contained coffins decorated with hexagrams, a six-pointed star closely associated to Judaism. This paper investigates the circumstances that might have led to the use of symbols identified with Judaism in a Muslim graveyard, at the turn of the twentieth century—a time of intensifying antagonism between Jaffa's Muslim and Jewish residents.

2 The Site

Over 110 graves were unearthed in 2016 (Fig. 2). The bases of 30 grave markers were preserved; the others were completely dismantled during the destruction of the cemetery. A single inscribed tombstone survived. The epitaph, incised on a marble tablet, dates it to 1243 AH (=1828 CE). The name of the deceased was eroded, but the town of Chāwdir, present day Çavdarhisar (Aizanoi) in western Turkey, is mentioned as his or her place of origin. The marker had been inserted in secondary use into the frame of a later burial cist,[2] a situation which, under normal circumstances, could only happen if the person it commemorated had no surviving family members. At least two generations would have to have separated the tombstone's primary and secondary utilization. Furthermore, graves contained more than one deceased; others were disturbed to accommodate new burials between them and in

---

[1] The 2016–2020 excavations were directed by the author on behalf of the Israel Antiquities Authority (IAA). A final report is at an editing stage. For a preliminary report of the 2016 excavation see Arbel, 2017b. The 2021 excavation was conducted by O. Gutfeld of Israel Archaeological Services and will be published separately.

[2] For other Ottoman-period gravestones from Jaffa see Sharon, 2016: 71–72, 103–105, 121–122; Buchennino, 2011.

The Hexagram Graves: Symbols and Identity in Ottoman Jaffa

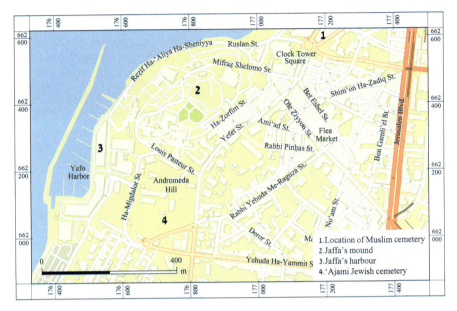

Fig. 1 General map of Jaffa and location of the site. (Map by I. Bendersky and Y. Gumenny, Israel Antiquities Authority)

a few cases older remains were pushed aside so the recently dead could be deposited in their place.

The burials, all of which were in a roughly east-west orientation, consisted of simple pits or stone-framed cists covered with sandstone slabs. Depth ranged between 0.60 and 1.60 m. Fourteen of the cist graves had gabled roofing, consisting of two opposing sets of stone slabs (average size: 45 × 45 cm) laid at ca. 40° angle. Such graves demanded additional labor and funds and are likely to have belonged to people of means. In all other graves, the slabs were laid out horizontally over the cist frames.

The remains of 149 individuals were discerned, some without clear grave context.[3] Preservation varied between scattered bones and full articulation. Gender could be designated for 39 adults, of which 21 were males and 18 females, a normal ratio in a civilian population. Among those whose age could be determined only 11 lived past their 40th year and 41 died before the age of 10. The generally low longevity was to a great extent due to the poor hygienic conditions and recurrent epidemics prevalent in Ottoman Jaffa.

Approximately 80 of the dead were sufficiently preserved for their burial position to be noted. All were laid with their heads at the western end of the grave and most were on their right side facing south toward Mecca, corresponding to standard

---

[3] Once exposed, analyzed in the field for gender, age and pathologies, the human remains were reinterred in the site, outside the area planned for development. All remains were treated in this way, other than a few burials appropriated by Muslim protesters during the project's second stage.

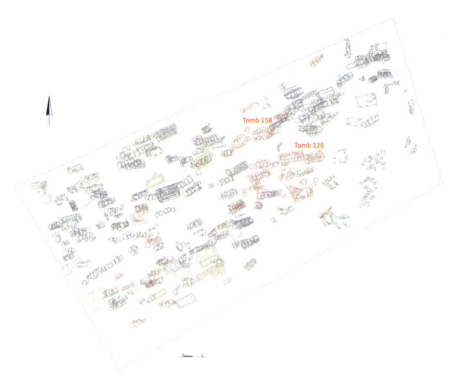

Fig. 2 General plan of the graves and location of the two hexagram graves. (Plan by M. Kahan, Israel Antiquities Authority)

Muslim burial custom (Canaan, 1927: 25; Noor, 2017: 34–35; Halevy, 2007: 188–189). In only seven graves the deceased lay on their backs. In one case, the face was turned southwards. The remaining six skeletons were insufficiently preserved for determination. There were no adjoined grave artifacts other than common jewelry worn in life, mostly bracelets and beads made of glass or copper. Pottery, glass sherds and metal objects found above the burials may have originated in disturbed graves but seem more likely to have been lost by visitors to the cemetery or by post-cemetery passersby or residents of the area. Similar characteristics were noted in other recorded or excavated Muslim graveyards from the Ottoman period (Macalister & Masterman, 1905: 349–350; Guz-Zilberstein & Raveh, 1988–1989: 25; Eakins, 1993: 64, Pl.110; Toombs, 1985: 106–108, Pl. 82; Taxel, 2007: 22). They reflect the basic Muslim funerary tradition in the Holy Land during that time.

2.1 The "Hexagrams Graves"

Thirteen of the gabled tombs contained rudimentary, partly collapsed wooden caskets. Each casket held the fragmentary bones of one individual, in some cases along with bits of cotton shroud and glass bracelets. These were the only coffins found so far in sites associated with the northern Muslim cemetery.[4] They were made of European timber, mostly fir (*Abies* sp.), of northern Mediterranean or other European sources, and Norway spruce (*Picea abies*). The boards show marks of electric sawing—a technology dating no earlier than the late nineteenth century. Industrial iron nails joined the boards. Strips of cotton fastened with metal tacks and interlaced with copper alloy wire in various patterns decorated the coffins. Oxidization of the copper tainted the wire and the originally white fabric into a greenish-blue shade.[5] The decorative strips of fabric on two of the coffins (in Loci 129, 158; see Fig. 2) were fashioned as hexagrams (Figs. 3 and 4), the shape popularly known as "Star of David" (Hebrew: *Magen David* – Shield of David). There were two equal-sized images (each arm 15 cm long) in full or partial preservation on each coffin. There were no other ornaments on any of the coffins.

3 Discussion

The hexagram is the most common symbolic identifier of Judaism, by both Jews and others. Far more than an informative sign or aesthetic adornment it is a shared religious symbol that stands above ideological divisions, much like the Cross in Christianity. How can the presence of the hexagram in an unequivocally Muslim graveyard be explained? Were members of Jaffa's Jewish community buried in a Muslim graveyard, and if so, why? If the dead were Muslims, why would hexagrams be attached to their coffins?

Lacking inscribed tombstones or other identifiers of the deceased, we must turn to circumstantial clues and inferences rooted in the realities and understandings prevalent in Jaffa at the turn of the twentieth century. First, let us examine the intuitive option, following which the hexagram, as an intrinsic ethno-religious Jewish symbol highlighted by no other faith, identifies the dead as Jewish, thus their burial in the non-Jewish graveyard resulted from unusual circumstances. Next, the ostensibly less likely Muslim alternative will be discussed.

---

[4] The remains of a late Ottoman wooden casket with bits of fabric affixed with nails were discovered at Andromeda Hill, to the south of Jaffa. This sole comparative artifact from Jaffa probably originated in one of the Christian cemeteries located there. I wish to thank Dr. Rina Avner of the Israel Antiquities Authority, the site's excavator, for this information.

[5] I thank Dr. Brita Lorenzen of Cornell University, who identified the wood, Avner Hillman of the Israel Antiquities Authority, who analyzed the boards and nails, and Dr. Naama Sukenik of the Israel Antiquities Authority, who studied the fabric. The results of their efforts will be further presented and discussed in the forthcoming final report of the excavation.

Fig. 3 Hexagrams on coffin fragments at discovery. (Photograph by Assaf Peretz, Israel Antiquities Authority)

3.1 Analysis of the Jewish Option

Jews returned to live in Jaffa during the eighteenth century, after an absence of nearly four hundred years (Ram, 1996: 18–22). The community was small and probably short-lived, for sources from the early nineteenth century, a time when

The Hexagram Graves: Symbols and Identity in Ottoman Jaffa

Fig. 4 Hexagram on coffin fragment at discovery (Photograph by Assaf Peretz, Israel Antiquities Authority)

Jaffa housed between 1500 and 3000 Muslims and Christians, fail to mention it. Reliable testimonies date its permanent reestablishment to 1820; by 1899, the number of Jews in the community reached ca. 5000 souls (after sources cited in Kark, 1990: 146–151).

Prior to the last two decades of the nineteenth century, relations with Jaffa's Muslim's were usually peaceful, an outcome of stable demographic and social balances and also of the basic proximity between the tenets of the two religions. The theological resemblances were recognized and highlighted by the renowned medieval scholar Rabbi Moshe ben Maimon (Maimonides), who went as far as legitimizing Jewish prayers in Muslim mosques (Kraemer, 2008: 311; Seeskin, 2005: 17). Recent religious scholars, such as Israeli rabbis Ovadia Yosef (1920–2013) and David Haim Halevy (1924–1998) (Amar, 1996: 160) expressed comparable thoughts—contemporary Middle Eastern politics notwithstanding. It should also be noted that unlike many of the ideologically-motivated European Jewish immigrants of the late nineteenth and early twentieth centuries, who strived for exclusive communities, keeping minimal contacts with Gentiles, the pragmatic Sepharadi community in the Holy Land, to which the Jews of Jaffa belonged, maintained regular commercial and personal contacts with their Muslim neighbors (Hart, 2014: 51–53, 163–164). Realities during life remained relevant at its conclusion. Oral traditions testify that in Jaffa of the early nineteenth century Jewish graves could be found in a plot "conjoined with the graves of the Arabs" (Ram, 1996: 351). Conversely, in the circumstances of the turn of the twentieth century, religious-ideological similarities would not suffice to support a Jewish identity for the hexagram graves. In fact, several key factors cast doubts on such identification.

3.1.1 The Religious Perspective

Throughout the history of Judaism, burial in consecrated Jewish cemeteries has not been a mere recommendation, but a fundamental, strictly observed principle. The official website of the Orthodox *Chabad* movement offers a representative example, categorically stating that every effort must be made to ensure that Jews would be buried in a Jewish cemetery, among fellow members of the faith.[6] As evidenced by countless burial grounds, Jews living in the Roman period or at present, in the Land of Israel or abroad, equally upheld this rule whenever possible. Well-known exceptions are the graves of Jewish soldiers in British and American military cemeteries from both world wars, as well as in German military cemeteries from World War I. The Jewish dead were buried amidst comrades from other religions, based on the principle of common remembrance for common sacrifice. The only testimonies of their ethno-religious origins are Stars of David that replace crosses on the markers (Fig. 5).[7] The military option is irrelevant for the Jaffa cemetery, a civilian burial ground with no exclusive military plots, and will or consent by Jewish families in Jaffa to bury their relatives there would suggest religious laxity supported by no available data, and for which there was no actual necessity.

An incident recorded by Y.E. Sheloush (1870–1934), a Jaffa-born Sepharadi trader and community leader, illustrates the rigor with which the principle was regarded. During World War I, the Ottoman authorities expelled the entire Jewish population from Jaffa. Sheloush and his family temporarily settled at Kafr Jammal, an Arab-Muslim village 50 km to the north of the city. While there, his mother passed away. Having no license to transport the body to a cemetery in the nearest Jewish colony, local dignitaries offered the family a place in the village graveyard. Sheloush, however, insisted on purchasing a burial plot near the house the family was staying in, explaining to his kind hosts that Jews cannot bury their dead in "a strange land" (land not owned by Jews) (Sheloush, 1931). Burial in a Muslim graveyard was not an option for the Sheloush family, despite the irregular and stressful circumstances, and many years of amity with Arabs both in Jaffa and in the village.

The aforementioned testimonies to a joint burial ground in Jaffa relate to the peculiar situation in the early nineteenth century, predating the hexagram graves by some eight or nine decades, when local Ottoman authorities barred Jews from purchasing land for a cemetery. Bodies had to be transported across the country to Jewish cemeteries in Jerusalem or Hebron (Ram, 1996: 351), a demanding and hazardous journey that during most of the year would be carried out in climate detrimental to the dignity of the deceased. Burial in a plot adjoined to a Muslim cemetery

---

[6]*The Basics: The tahara, funeral and burial.* http://www.chabad.org/library/article_cdo/aid/282548/jewish/The-Basics.htm (accessed 2 September 2021).

[7]Israeli rabbis and religious officials conform to the implementation of this ironclad regulation in British military cemeteries in the country, although they would never voluntarily endorse it. An unusual appeal by rabbinical officials in the city of Haifa to transfer four Jewish graves from local British military cemeteries sparked protests in the secular Israeli media and public and the proposal was never carried out (Shefi, 2011).

The Hexagram Graves: Symbols and Identity in Ottoman Jaffa

Fig. 5 Graves of Christian and Jewish casualties in a burial plot at the British military cemetery in Ramla. (Photograph by the author)

would not have been an ideal solution, but with no available options it would have been accepted. The establishment of the Jewish cemetery to the south of the city in 1840 (near the grounds of the future 'Ajami quarter) solved the problem (Fig. 6).[8] Since then, there was no religious justification for Jewish burials in cemeteries of other faiths, and no textual or oral testimony suggests that such burials had ever taken place.

3.1.2 Political Tensions

In a petition to the sultan from 1891, 500 Arab dignitaries from Jerusalem and Jaffa demanded to stop Jewish immigration and ban real estate purchases by Jews. Mutual hostilities intensified in the first decade of the twentieth century, with the eruption of violent, occasionally lethal clashes. Relations temporarily improved in the wake of the Young Turks revolution and the establishment of a constitutional government in Istanbul in 1908 but deteriorated again due to conflicting interests between the

---

[8] Secondary testimonies to the existence of a Jewish cemetery in 1825, allegedly based on documents from Jaffa's Muslim courts (Hart, 2014: 24) found no support in any other sources consulted for this article.

Fig. 6 General view of the Jewish cemetery at the 'Ajami quarter, Jaffa. (Photograph by the author)

Arab and Jewish nascent national movements (Hart, 2014: 38–44, 55–58; Ram, 1996: 255–225). It is unlikely that Jews would have insisted on burial in a Muslim cemetery during such turbulent times and when a Jewish graveyard was available. Consent by local Muslims is likewise improbable. Based on *hadith*, Islamic scholars explicitly instruct that Muslims are "not be buried beside non-Muslims, nor non-Muslims beside Muslims. Each should have their own separate graveyard" (Philips, 2008: 76). Religious moderation that may have been possible in remote villages such as Kafr Jammal or in the conditions of Jaffa in the early nineteenth century was not plausible in the much larger, populous and significant city of the early 1900s, even less so in times of rising tensions.

3.1.3 Epidemic Stress

Visitors and residents alike reported deplorable sanitary conditions in nineteenth and early twentieth century Jaffa, which were the probable cause of various endemic diseases (Kark, 1990: 211–214; Büssow, 2011: 255). The authorities did little to protect the population, other than subjecting newcomers to a period of medically-supervised quarantine on their ships or in an isolated station to the south of the city. During the 1890s, a waste disposal network was finally installed in some parts. In other parts, cesspits drained waste from adjacent homes (Kark, 1990: 216; Goren,

2016: 104–105); Arbel, 2010; Jakoel & Marcus, 2017: 52–58). Yet these solutions benefitted only those living next to Jaffa's central or newer streets. They had little effect on people living in the hundreds of crowded dwellings along the serpentine alleys and culs-de-sac.

Between the last decade of the nineteenth century and 1910, the time sphere of the hexagram graves, Jaffa was rife with lethal bouts of influenza (1893, 1910), cholera (1902, 1904, 1910) and other intestinal afflictions (1897–1899). The link between corpses and disease supplied the Ottoman authorities with a pretext for closing down the old cemeteries of all Jaffa's religious groups, once outside the city limits yet by then surrounded by the expanding new neighborhoods. Their more pressing intention was apparently to fill the urban gaps between these neighborhoods and the city core. The ban on new burials was published in 1916. One may propose that the burial of Jewish epidemic victims in the northern Muslim cemetery in the relative insulation of coffins was an emergency step taken after the old Jewish graveyard was closed down. The Stars of David could be explained as a religious gesture toward community members who were denied by circumstances a ritually proper resting place among their Jewish brethren.

There are, however, two main flaws in this epidemiological explanation. The first is the similar distance between the Jewish and Muslim cemeteries to the city core; as the potential health hazard was equal, there would be no point in forbidding the burial of epidemic victims in the first while allowing it in the the second. Other than that, there was no need to bury Jewish epidemic victims in a Muslim graveyard, because a new Jewish cemetery was inaugurated to the north of Jaffa in 1902 (presently at central Tel Aviv's Trumpeldor Street, near the seashore). This was over a decade before the government ban on the old cemeteries. The new site was needed because space in Jaffa's old graveyard was becoming scarce, a cholera outbreak was claiming many lives and the community wished to avoid committal in the common plot improvised by the local authorities for the hasty disposal of all epidemic victims. The location of Shmuel Gershenson's tomb, the first Jewish cholera victim to be buried in the new graveyard, is unknown, but the tombs of other victims of that outbreak are still evident at the site. The epitaph on the gravestone of "Nishka, daughter of Rabbi Baruch Bramberg, who passed away in the spring of her days…in the distressful year (5)663 (= November 12, 1902)" reflects the agony of those days (Fig. 7). Burials in the old cemetery in Jaffa resumed for a short time once the epidemic ebbed, but in 1920 it was officially closed. It should be noted that unlike the northern Muslim cemetery and most Christian graveyards that were destroyed and built over, the main part of the Jewish cemetery is preserved.

3.1.4 The Use of Coffins

Burial in sarcophagi and ossuaries was common among Jews in antiquity—including residents of Jaffa (Rahmani, 1994; Jakoel, 2017: 278–282). In recent centuries, however, custom in the Holy Land (elsewhere Jews follow the law of the land) dictates that bodies be laid directly on the burial pit's ground. The pit should be covered

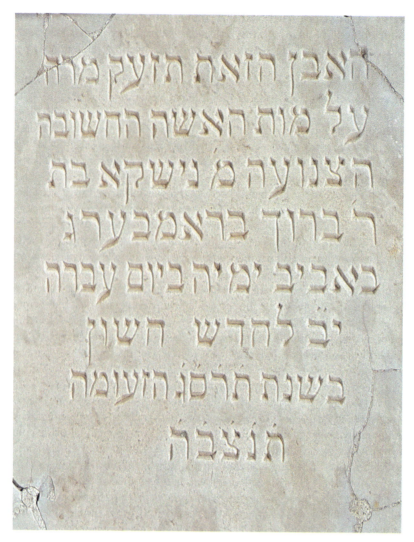

Fig. 7 Grave of cholera victim (1902) at Trumpeldor Street cemetery. (Photograph by the author)

and framed with slabs, but its floor must remain exposed. The custom intends to fulfill God's decree in Genesis 3:18: "for dust thou art, and unto dust shalt thou return." According to the *Shulchan Aruch*, a comprehensive Jewish legal code dating to the mid-sixteenth century, while burial in coffins does not plainly transgress halachic directives, "it is [more] appropriate to bury him in the earth proper."[9] In a book dedicated to halachic aspects of death and burial, Rabbi Yechiel Michel Tucazinsky (1947: 58–59) applies the negative view on burial in caskets not only to

---

[9] *Yoreh De'ah*, Siman 362, 1.

burial in the Land of Israel but even to coffins in which foreign Jews are imported for burial. Bodies must be removed from such caskets for the funeral and "it is the custom to break [the coffins] up and leave [their] fragments on the covering of the dead inside the grave." Incidentally, in all Jaffa examples, the coffin parts were found within the burial cist—not over the sealing slabs. They appear to have contained the bodies at burial, later falling apart. In modern Israel, a mostly secular state where religious institutions nonetheless hold considerable sway, the Orthodox burial society (*Hevra Kadisha*) is responsible for most of the Jewish burials. Loyal to the custom, it allows burial in coffins only for military casualties (and some state funerals). In such cases, holes are drilled in the bottom of the casket to allow contact between the body and the natural soil. Coffins can also be used in secular funerals taking place in private cemeteries that are not under *Hevra Kadisha* regulation. Such alternative arrangements did not exist at the turn of the twentieth century.

3.2 The Hexagram as a Recent Jewish Convert

For over a century, Judaism has been identified with the Star of David more than with any other image. It surpassed even the seven-branched candelabrum, a symbol directly associated with the Jerusalem Temple and commonly depicted in Jewish contexts since antiquity—including tombs. Symbols may be replaced or assume new meanings, but the hexagram has risen to its present prominence strikingly fast. Gershom Scholem, eminent scholar of Jewish Kabbalah and mysticism, showed the hexagram to be the latest in a sequence of Jewish symbols, but also one of trifling ideological and historical substance:

> It does not express any "idea," it does not arouse ancient associations rooted in our experiences, and it is not a shorthand representation of an entire spiritual reality, understood immediately by the observer. It does not remind us of anything in Biblical or in rabbinic Judaism. Indeed, until the middle of the 19th century, it did not occur to any scholar or Cabalist to inquire into the secret of its Jewish meaning, and it is not mentioned in the books of the devout or in all of Hasidic literature… Its occasional appearance as a decoration gives it no claim to be a "Jewish" symbol; and even as a simple decoration it is only rarely found among our antiquities (Scholem, 2008: 25; originally published on September 1, 1949).

Let us examine the last claim. Meaningful religious symbols feature in synagogue imagery. As noted by Israeli archaeologist Michael Avi-Yonah (1981: 281), an authority on Jewish art in antiquity, such imagery represents "the evolution of Jewish symbolism." Indeed, the candelabrum (*menorah*), the palm frond (*lulav*), the ram's horn (*shofar*) and the citron (*etrog*) often appear on mosaic floors, architectural elements and (rarely surviving) wall paintings in excavated synagogues from the Roman and Byzantine periods in Israel and Syria (Levine, 2005; Kraeling, 1956). Variations of these biblically-rooted and ritually-loaded elements continued to adorn synagogues through the generations and across geographic locations and cultural distinctions. Conversely, hexagrams are virtually missing in architectural contexts of antiquity. Where the form does appear, as at the synagogue of Capernaum (third–fifth centuries CE), it is in a purely decorative role (Tzaferis, 1989). Stars of David fail to appear on nine out of 11 detailed models of pre-nineteenth century synagogues from various cities in Europe, North Africa and North America, displayed in Tel Aviv's Museum of the Jewish People. The two exceptions show it on glass panes and iron gates. As such materials are highly susceptible to damage and rust, the elements may well post-date the original construction phases in the seventeenth and eighteenth centuries. The symbolic substance of the "Star of David" is clearly more recent, a product of long evolution.

During the seventeenth century, the hexagram was a symbol of the Jewish community of Prague (Eder, 1987: 6) and other communities in central Europe gradually adopted the image. Ritual objects from the eighteenth century show the hexagram infrequently. Its popularity grew during the nineteenth century, when it was often depicted in religious contexts alongside more traditional symbols (Scholem, 2008: 46–54). By the late part of that century, the hexagram had also gained new political-Zionist meaning that culminated in its depiction at the center of the flag of the State of Israel. A banner showing horizontal blue stripes over a white background with a Star of David in its center was first designed in 1885, for commemorations held at the Jewish settlement of Rishon LeZion, 14 km southeast of Jaffa,[10] and a similar flag was flown in 1891 during festivities at the adjacent colony of Nes Ziona. An almost identical flag was displayed at the First Zionist Congress in Basel in 1897. Nonetheless, the candelabrum, not the hexagram, showed on the community flag carried by Jewish participants in local festivities in Jerusalem as late as 1908 (Lemire, 2013). The ideological link between Judaism and the hexagram was apparently crystallizing during that period but had not ripened yet among many of the native and immigrant Jews in the Holy Land.

Jaffa's contemporaneous funerary scene reflects that liminal stage in the Jewish-hexagram bond. Records of the *Hevra Kadisha*, count ca. 2000 graves in Jaffa's Jewish cemetery during its eight decades of operation, but only ca. 800 tombstones can presently be found there; most of them have epitaphs in varying degrees of clarity. Road paving over the cemetery's margins and effects of time and weather may explain the discrepancy. In a count by this author covering the full extent of the cemetery only 35 gravestones showing the hexagram were noted—a total of 4.2% of the overall number of visible graves. Six of the gravestones mark tombs from 1894 to 1900; nine are dated between 1900 and 1909 and 17 between 1910 and 1916. On three of the markers the dates are illegible. In comparison, out of 500 gravestones in the western part of the Trumpeldor Street cemetery, all dated between its foundation in 1902 and the early 1930s, 105 markers include the form—over 20%. These figures may attest to the gradual recognition of the symbol but should be viewed with caution. The inherent relation of the Cross to death and salvation explicates its frequency in Christian cemeteries of most denominations. The

---

[10]The flag is discussed in a letter from August of that year by Israel Belkind, one of its makers (published in the monthly *Me-Yamim Rishonim*, Vol. 1, 1934) and a replica is displayed in the Rishon LeZion Museum. A similar flag is said to have been flown by members of the Jewish community of Boston, Massachusetts, during a Columbus Day parade in 1892 (Moskowitz, 2016).

hexagram's role as an identifier of Judaism is far more recent; its meaning is less palpable, and it holds no associations to Jewish theological notions of demise and the afterlife.

3.3 Analysis of the Muslim Option

Jaffa's resettlement in the seventeenth century was a direct consequence of pressure by European powers on the Ottoman government to allow their sponsored churches to construct monastic institutions and pilgrim hosting facilities. Nevertheless, most of the farmers, traders and other pilgrim service providers who moved to the recovering town were Muslims. The still active mosque by the harbor (*Masjad el-Baher*) was built during those years. Muslims remained the dominant majority in Jaffa for the following three centuries, a heterogeneous community comprised of migrants from elsewhere in the land as well as Egyptians, Maghrebis, Bedouins and others (Arbel, 2021a). The Muslim community outlived significant setbacks, such as the destructive conquests and brief occupations by the Egyptian officer Abu Dahab (1776) and Napoleon Bonaparte (1799) as well as internal strife resulting from the Ottoman political power play in the aftermath of Napoleon's withdrawal and during the Egyptian occupation of 1831–1840. In the period to which the hexagram graves belong, Jaffa's Muslim population numbered ca. 25.000, alongside 9000 Christians and up to 7000 Jews (Kark, 1990: 151). From the mid- or late-eighteenth century, the cemetery (later named el-Isaf) was its chief burial ground.

3.3.1   Hexagrams in Muslim Settings

Associations between the hexagram and Islamic art and architecture predate its late election as the prime symbol of Judaism. The form adorns sites as diverse as mosques from the sixteenth or seventeenth centuries such as Jamali Kamali in Delhi, India, Mir Sultan Ibrahim in Thatta, Pakistan and Arasta in Kosovo, as well as the khan's palace in Bakhchisaray, Crimea, and the mausolea of two Mamluk sultans in Cairo (Stierlin & Stierlin, 1997: 74, 135). It also appears on Muslim amulets, coins and book-binders (Ettinghausen & Grabar, 1987: 333).

Turning to the Holy Land, a hexagram appears at the twelfth century *minbar* of the Al-Aqsa mosque in Jerusalem, along with other star-forms of possible astrological significance (Auld, 2005: 47). Hexagrams are among the geometrical forms carved on a Mamluk or early Ottoman tombstone in the Mamilla cemetery in central Jerusalem (Fig. 8) and on the early sixteenth century Ottoman ramparts of Jerusalem. Closer to our times, 13 hexagrams were sketched among images of banners and crescents on the plastered wall in the mausoleum of Sheikh Yassin, in a village that stood near Jerusalem until 1948 (Canaan, 1827: 41). The form is also engraved on the entrance lintel to the early nineteenth century governor's bathhouse in Jaffa

Fig. 8 An hexagram on Mamluk or Early Ottoman grave in Mamilla, Jerusalem. (Photograph by the author)

(Fig. 9). Still, no prior record exists of its use on coffins—an artifact which in itself is irregular in Muslim funerary culture.

3.3.2 Coffins in Islamic Funerary Practice

According to Ermette Pierotti (1864: 242), an Italian engineer who worked in the Holy Land in the mid-nineteenth century and witnessed several Muslim funerals, the shrouded corpse is "laid upon a bier or in an open coffin in which a pitcher of water, some loaves, and a few coins are placed." This is a rare notice of coffins in Muslim burials, for their use defies common custom (Halevy, 2007: 188). It is also not clear whether the bodies were buried in the coffin or just carried in it to the grave, as the analogous mentioning of a coffin and a bier suggests. Still, coffin-free burial is not a strict regulation. Certain conditions would allow the use of coffins, such as soft soil that could expose the body to animal burrowing, or an explicit requirement by non-Muslim governments under which Muslims live, as is the case in Europe and many countries elsewhere (Hulmes, 2008: 137; Ekpo & Is'haq, 2016: 62; Norcliff, 1999: 156). The first exception does not apply to the relatively firm ground of Jaffa's cemetery and the second is irrelevant, bearing in mind that as Muslims, Ottoman rulers never made such a requirement. Yet two other factors should be considered.

The Hexagram Graves: Symbols and Identity in Ottoman Jaffa

Fig. 9 Hexagrams on lintel of entrance to nineteenth c. bathhouse, Jaffa. (Photograph by the author)

First, although common graves for hasty burial were prepared during epidemics, wealthy and influential families may have secured exemptions from such unbecoming disposal of their dead relatives, provided that the infected bodies be sealed in the insulation of coffins. Second, Islamic tenets also allow concessions if bodies were seriously affected by heavy trauma or prolonged exposure. As public sentiments precluded forensic examinations of the Jaffa remains, the option of trauma could not be tested. Yet seven out of the thirteen coffins contained only fragmentary bones while skeletons were fairly intact in dozens of cist and pit graves. In four others the facing direction of the bodies could not be determined. Of particular importance are the two remaining coffins (Loci 443, 507), which held skeletons in full Muslim posture, proving Muslim burials in this cemetery in this way, despite the deviation from standard funerary rules.

3.3.3 Objects in the Graves

The presence of items of jewelry in the hexagram graves counters Islamic funerary principles that uphold the equality of believers in death, and thus forbid grave goods or any other accompanying objects at burial other than shrouds. Yet in fact, jewelry is quite commonly found in Muslim cemeteries, particularly of the later centuries, and was also discovered in many other tombs in Jaffa (Fig. 10). Witness accounts (Pierotti, 1864: 242; Rogers, 1865: 165) and ethnographic studies (Walker, 2001: 58) offer additional testimonies to this discrepancy between precept and practice. Lawrence Oliphant (1887: 330) reports the deposit of jewelry over graves as tributes to the dead, yet numerous bracelets and anklets remained on the actual bodies of their wearers within the graves. Jewelry is commonly found in the graves of females of various ages, sometimes along with cosmetic items such as combs, soap bars and paint sticks (Taha, 2018: 146).

Jewelry made of copper, silver and rarely gold was discovered in tombs, but most of the assemblages in Jaffa and elsewhere consist of polychromatic, translucent and opaque bracelets and beads made of glass. They can probably be traced to the reputable workshops of Hebron, where a glass industry flourished for centuries and sold its wares throughout the Levant (de Vincenz, 2017: 126). The industry and its jewelry products impressed foreign travelers, who mentioned or described it in their records (Rogers, 1865: 44, 48, 291, 402; Wittman, 1803: 217, 374; Burton, 1875: 68; Warren, 1876: 517; Burckhardt, 1831: 233). Ulrich Seetzen (1854: 49) counted 12 bracelet workshops in Hebron, and 10 others that specialized in beads. From Pierotti's sardonic comment (1864: 146) that women would only wear glass jewels "until their husbands have the good fortune to provide them with better," we learn that they were popular for affordability as well as charm. Explanations for their presence in the graves despite the religious prohibition range between alleged apotropaic powers (Simpson, 1995: 246), a wish to avoid the inevitable physical contact with the corpse while removing the jewels (Walker, 2001: 58), or, as a member of the Islamic endowments institution (*Waqf*) disclosed to this author, in consideration of family members who did not wish to part their female relatives from the adornments they had prized in life.

Fig. 10 Copper and glass bracelets in one of the broken coffins. (Photograph by Assaf Peretz, Israel Antiquities Authority)

4 Conclusions: Who Was Buried in the Hexagram Graves?

In attempting to identify the deceased in the hexagram coffins we must evade the lure of anachronism. The unambiguous identification of the hexagram with Judaism as it crystallized during the late nineteenth and early twentieth century cannot be ignored. However, it must not be considered irrefutable proof of the Jewish ethnicity of the deceased, for the coffins date to an interim period in the peculiar history of the form. The more informed among Jaffa's Muslims may have been acquainted with the rising religious and political-ideological status of the hexagram among the Jews but broader awareness only spread and sharpened with the growing tension between Zionism and the Arab national movement, and the subsequent escalation in violence. The distancing of Muslims from what was rapidly becoming the chief symbol of their foes was inexorable, but by the turn of the twentieth century this was an on-going development that had yet to ripen into its conclusion.

Additional points must also be weighed:

- The coffins were found in the heart of a Muslim cemetery, not in its margins, and their affiliated tombs were surrounded by unquestionably Muslim burials.
- Their gabled roofing resembled other gabled tombs found throughout the site, in which the position of the dead was unquestionably Muslim.
- The accompanying objects found with the remains are typical of the Muslim burials of that period, and a product of the relative pliability with which many Muslims treated the orthodox ban on the custom.
- The fragmentary condition of the remains in these graves fall into the categories that make the use of coffins permissible in Islam.

In fact, had the caskets been otherwise adorned, a Jewish link would never have been pondered. The presence of this form compels the consideration of such a link, but when doing so, we should bear in mind that while all Stars of David are hexagrams, not all hexagrams are Stars of David. The religious and ethnic identities of those buried in the hexagram graves remain elusive, and the body of evidence presented in this paper cannot categorically prove or dismiss either the Muslim or the Jewish options. Nevertheless, advantage should be given to the indisputable Muslim context within which the tombs were found and to the lack of reason for Jews to bury their dead there when Jewish cemeteries were readily available. Obscure circumstances had led the relatives of the dead to bury them in such highly irregular decorated coffins. Once the decision to do so was made, there would have been no grounds to repel an aesthetic geometric image of probable symbolic value—one that Muslims have integrated for centuries in religious, secular and funerary structures, objects and locations. It would soon be identified with a rival faith but not just yet. Thus, when all is considered, it is highly likely that Muslims were laid to rest in the hexagram graves, as in all other graves of this historical cemetery.

References

Amar, Z. (1996). The worship of trees near tombs of saints in Jewish and Muslim tradition. In E. Shiler (Ed.), *Religion, cult and tombs of Muslim saints in the Land of Israel* (pp. 155–162). Ariel 118–119. (Hebrew).

Arbel, Y. (2010). Yafo, Ha-Zorfim Street. *Hadashot Arkhaeologiyot—Excavations and Surveys in Israel.* http://www.hadashot-esi.org.il/report_detail_eng.aspx?id=1474&mag_id=117

Arbel, Y. (2017a). Post-Medieval Muslim burials in Jaffa: Archaeological evidence and historical perspective. *Journal of Islamic Archaeology, 4*(1), 87–112.

Arbel, Y. (2017b). Yafo, Elisabeth Bergner Street. *Hadashot Arkhaeologiyot—Excavations and Surveys in Israel 129.* http://www.hadashot-esi.org.il/report_detail_eng.aspx?id=25312&mag_id=125

Arbel, Y. (2021a). New archaeological indicators for Muslim immigrants in late *Ottoman* Jaffa. *ARAM, 33*(1 & 2), 239–258.

Arbel, Y. (2021b). Stratigraphy. In Y. Arbel (Ed.), *Excavations at the Ottoman military compound (Qishle) in Jaffa, 2007, 2009* (The history and archaeology of Jaffa) (Vol. IV, pp. 15–58). Zaphon.

Auld, S. (2005). The *minbar* of Al-Aqsa form and function. In R. Hillenbrand (Ed.), *Image and meaning in Islamic art* (pp. 42–60). Al Tajir Trust.

Avi-Yonah, M. (1981). *Art in ancient Palestine.* The Magness Press.

Buchennino, A. (2011). Tel Aviv, Manshiya. *Hadashot Arkhaeologiyot—Excavations and Surveys in Israel 123.* http://www.hadashot-esi.org.il/Report_Detail_Eng.aspx?id=1660&mag_id=118

Burckhardt, J. L. (1831). *Notes on the Bedouins and Wahábys: Collected during his travels in the East* (Vol. I). H. Colburn and R. Bentley.

Burton, I. (1875). *The inner life of Syria, Palestine, and the Holy Land* (Vol. 2). H.S. King.

Büssow, J. (2011). *Hamidian Palestine: Politics and society in the District of Jerusalem 1872–1908.* Brill.

Canaan, T. (1927). *Mohammedan saints and sanctuaries in Palestine.* Luzac.

Eakins, J. K. (1993). *Tell El-Hesi: The Muslim cemetery in Fields V and VI/IX (Stratum II).* Eisenbrauns.

Eder, A. (1987). *Der Davidstern: Seine Bedeutung in der geschichte und im Verlauf der Erlösung.* Ot Chen.

Edrey, M., & Gross, B. (Forthcoming). The stratigraphy of the eastern area of the Qishleh Compound. In Z. Herzog, M. Edrey, & B. Gross (Eds.), *Excavations at Jaffa: The mound and its surrounding area.* Salvage Excavation Reports.

Ekpo, C. G., & Is'haq, A. B. (2016). Islam and the environment: Implications of Islamic funeral practice on environmental sustainability. *Journal of Research & Method in Education, 6*(1), 58–63.

Ettinghausen, R., & Grabar, O. (1987). *The art and architecture of Islam: 650–1250.* Yale University Press.

Goren, T. (2016). *Rise and fall: The urban development of Jaffa and its place in Jewish-Arab Strife in Palestine 1917–1947.* Yad Izhak Ben-Zvi. (Hebrew).

Guz-Zilberstein, B. & Raveh, K. (1988–1989). Dor: Site K-60. Excavations and Surveys in Israel, 7–8, 50–51.

Halevy, L. (2007). *Muhammad's grave: Death rites and the making of Islamic society.* Columbia University Press.

Hart, R. (2014). *So close, so far away: Jewish and Arab relations in Jaffa and Tel Aviv, 1881–1930.* Resling. (Hebrew).

Hulmes, E. D. A. (2008). Death and burial (*Mawt, Dafn, Jinaza*). In I. R. Netton (Ed.), *Encyclopedia of Islamic civilization and religion* (p. 137). Routledge.

Jakoel, E. (2017). The postal compound excavations in Jaffa, 2009–2011: Final report. In A. A. Burke, K. S. Burke, & M. Peilstöcker (Eds.), *The history and archaeology of Jaffa* (Vol. II, pp. 273–300). Cotsen Institute of Archaeology Press.

The Hexagram Graves: Symbols and Identity in Ottoman Jaffa

Jakoel, E., & Marcus, J. (2017). The northeastern fringes of Yafo (Jaffa) in light of the excavations at the Jerusalem Boulevard and its vicinity. *'Atiqot, 88*, 43–70.

Kark, R. (1990). *Jaffa, a city in evolution 1799–1917*. Yad Izhak Ben-Zvi Press.

Kraeling, C. H. (1956). The synagogue. In A. R. Bellinger (Ed.), *The excavations at Dura Europus, Final report VIII, Pt. I* (pp. 54–62). Yale University Press.

Kraemer, J. L. (2008). *Maimonides: The life and world of one of civilization's greatest minds*. Doubleday.

Lemire, V. (2013). *Jerusalem 1900—La ville sainte à l'âge des possible*. Points-Histoire.

Levine, L. I. (2005). *The Ancient Synagogue: The first thousand years*. Yale University Press.

Macalister, R. A. S., & Masterman, E. W. G. (1905). Occasional papers on the modern inhabitants of Palestine. *Palestine Exploration Fund Quarterly Statement, 37*(4), 343–356.

Moskowitz, E. (2016, December 14). An unlikely Boston connection to Israel's flag. *The Boston Globe*. https://www.bostonglobe.com/metro/2016/12/14/unlikely-boston-connection-israel-flag/zrqaupafnx9cai0meslapk/story.html

Nagar, Y. (2021). Reconstructing the population history of Jaffa: Human remains from the Qishle. In Y. Arbel (Ed.), *Excavations at the Ottoman military compound (Qishle) in Jaffa, 2007, 2009* (The history and archaeology of Jaffa) (Vol. IV, pp. 349–364). Zaphon.

Noor, I. (2017). *A practical guide to funeral rites in Islam*. Islamic Academy of Coventry.

Norcliff, D. (1999). *Islam: Faith and practice*. Sussex Academic Press.

Oliphant, L. (1887). *Haifa; or life in modern Palestine*. William Blackwood and Sons.

Philips, A. B. (2008). *Funeral rites in Islam*. Retrieved June 26, 2021, from https://www.noor-book.com/en/ebook-Funeral-Rites-In-Islam%2D%2Dpdf

Pierotti, E. (1864). *Customs and traditions of Palestine*. Deighton, Bell and Co.

Rahmani, L. Y. (1994). *A catalogue of Jewish ossuaries in the collections of the State of Israel*. The Israel Antiquities Authority and the Israel Academy of Sciences.

Ram, H. (1996). *The Jewish community in Jaffa; from Sepharadic community to Zionist center*. Carmel Publishing. (Hebrew).

Rogers, M. E. (1865). *Domestic life in Palestine*. Poe & Hitchcock.

Scholem, G. (2008). *The Star of David: History of a symbol*. Translated and edited by G. Hasan-Rokem. Mishkan Le-Omanut (Hebrew).

Seeskin, K. (2005). *The Cambridge companion to Maimonides*. Cambridge University Press.

Seetzen, U. J. (1854). *Reisen durch Syrien, Palästina, Phönizien, die Transjordan Länder, Arabia Petraea und Unter-Aegypten*. G. Reimer.

Shacham, T. (2011). Jaffa in historical maps (1799-1948). In M. Peilstöcker & A. A. Burke (Eds.), *The history and archaeology of Jaffa* (Vol. I, pp. 137–174). Cotsen Institute of Archaeology Press.

Sharon, M. (2016). *Corpus Inscriptionum Arabicarum Palaestinae VI*. Brill.

Shefi, Y. (2011, May 24). Leave the dead in their graves. *Ha'aretz*.

Sheloush, Y. E. (1931). *Reminiscences of my life, 1870–1930* (chapter 22). Retrieved June 26, 2021, from https://benyehuda.org/read/9421#ch1263 (Hebrew).

Simpson, S. (1995). Death and burial in the Late Islamic Near East: Some insights from archaeology and ethnography. In S. Campbell & A. Green (Eds.), *The archaeology of death in the ancient Near East* (pp. 240–251). Oxbow Books.

Sion, O., & Rapuano, Y. (2017). Yafo: Razi'el and Ratosh Streets. *Hadashot Arkhaeologiyot—Excavations and Surveys in Israel* 129. http://www.hadashot-esi.org.il/Report_Detail_Eng.aspx?id=25311

Stierlin, H., & Stierlin, A. (1997). *Splendours of an Islamic world*. I.B. Tauris.

Taha, H. (2018). Ethnography of death in Palestine. *Journal of Historical Archaeology and Anthropological Sciences, 3*(1), 143–148. https://doi.org/10.15406/jhaas.2018.03.00076

Taxel, I. (2007). Stratigraphy and architecture. In R. Gophna, I. Taxel, & A. Feldstein (Eds.), *Kafr 'Ana, a rural settlement in the Lod Valley* (pp. 9–32). Salvage Excavation Reports 4.

Toombs, L. E. (1985). *Tell el-Hesi, modern military trenching and Muslim cemetery in Field I, Strata I-II*. Wilfrid Laurier University Press.

Tucazinsky, Y. M. (1947). *Gesher ha-hayyim (The bridge of life): A treatise on life viewed as a bridge between past and future*. Etz Hayim. (Hebrew).

Tzaferis, V. (1989). *Excavations at Capernaum 1978–1982*. The Pennsylvania State University Press.

de Vincenz, A. (2017). Ottoman pottery and glass bracelets from Yafo (Jaffa), Jerusalem Boulevard and its vicinity. *'Atiqot, 88*, 115–129.

Walker, B. J. (2001). The Late Ottoman cemetery in Field L, Tall Hisban. *Bulletin of the American Schools of Oriental Research, 322*, 47–65.

Warren, C. (1876). *Underground Jerusalem*. Richard Bentley.

Wittman, W. (1803). *Travels in Turkey, Asia-Minor, Syria, and across the desert into Egypt during the years 1799, 1800, and 1801*. Richard Phillips.

Yinnon, Y. (2001). *Around the clock tower*. Yad Izhak Ben-Zvi Press. (Hebrew).

"Napoleon's Hill" and the 1799 Siege of Acre/Akko, Israel

Ann E. Killebrew and Jane C. Skinner

Abstract Napoleon's famous 1799 defeat at the walls of Ottoman Acre marked a turning point in the French campaign to control the Middle East, an event that lives on in the memory of the citizens of modern Akko. Visitors to the UNESCO World Heritage Site of Acre, Israel, can follow a walking route exploring several locations that played a key role in Bonaparte's 1799 siege of the city. In this contribution, we recreate Napoleon's unsuccessful siege of Acre to examine the role of Tel Akko ("Napoleon's Hill") in his defeat. Based on maps dating to the period of the 1799 siege and contemporary eyewitness accounts, we examine the claim that there is no evidence Napoleon ever set foot on Tel Akko. We also employ Esri StoryMaps to present an in-depth investigation and contextualization of Bonaparte's defeat by British and Ottoman forces, an event which Napoleon, on his deathbed, lamented as the obstacle that prevented his dream of recreating Alexander the Great's empire.

Keywords Akko · Acre · Napoleon · al-Jazzar · Ottoman

1 The Legend of "Napoleon's Hill"

Ottoman-period Acre (Akko/Akka) has gone down in history as the city that withstood Napoleon Bonaparte's 1799 siege during his ambitious, but ultimately unsuccessful, campaign to conquer Egypt, Syria, and the Holy Land. More than 200 years later, Napoleon's defeat remains a source of local pride and touristic interest. To

---

A. E. Killebrew (✉)
Department of Classics and Ancient Mediterranean Studies, Jewish Studies, and Anthropology, The Pennsylvania State University, University Park, PA, USA
e-mail: aek11@psu.edu

J. C. Skinner
Jewish Studies, The Pennsylvania State University, University Park, PA, USA
e-mail: jcs5138@psu.edu

© The Author(s), under exclusive license to Springer Nature Switzerland AG 2023
E. Ben-Yosef, I. W. N. Jones (eds.), *"And in Length of Days Understanding" (Job 12:12): Essays on Archaeology in the Eastern Mediterranean and Beyond in Honor of Thomas E. Levy*, Interdisciplinary Contributions to Archaeology,
https://doi.org/10.1007/978-3-031-27330-8_81

commemorate this event, visitors to the UNESCO World Heritage Site, the Old City of Acre, today can follow a walking route that marks several locations associated with Napoleon's siege (https://www.akko.org.il/en/route/מסלול-נפוליאון).

Tourists can also visit "Napoleon's Hill," an archaeological site located to the east of Old Acre and the modern town of Akko. This name, which appears frequently in British Mandate archival records when referring to Tel Akko (Archive of the Department of Antiquities of Mandatory Palestine [1919–1948]: https://www.iaa-archives.org.il/search.aspx?loc_id=15762&type_id=; also known by its Arabic name, Tell el-Fukhar, and referred to by its Crusader names, Turon or Richard Coeur de Lion's Mount), suggests that the mound played a role in Napoleon's attempt to conquer Acre. Today, its association with the 1799 siege is commemorated by two signs and a statue. One sign appears at the main entrance to the tell (Fig. 1). A second sign at the northern base of the mound provides a detailed text that claims Napoleon was likely never there (Fig. 2). However, the most visible monument to Napoleon is a huge metal statue of him on a horse, inspired by the iconic painting by Jacques-Louis David of Bonaparte crossing the Alps, that crowns the apex of the tell (Fig. 3). This landmark is visible for miles. Unfortunately, due to the hill's association with Napoleon, most residents and tourists who visit Tel Akko, today a municipal park, are unaware that the mound was a major Canaanite and Phoenician city before settlement moved westward to its current location. This is confirmed by

Fig. 1 Sign at the entrance to the Tel Akko municipal park. (Courtesy of the Tel Akko Total Archaeology Project, photograph by Ann E. Killebrew)

Fig. 2 Large information sign at the base of Tel Akko. (Yuval Y, CC BY-SA 3.0)

large-scale excavations directed on the tell by M. Dothan (1973–1989) and by A. E. Killebrew and M. Artzy (2010–2019) that reveal human occupation spanning the Early Bronze through Hellenistic periods (ca. 3000–100 BCE; see Artzy & Beeri, 2010; Dothan, 1976, 1993; Killebrew et al., 2023 for summaries of the excavation results).

Though Tel Akko boasts a rich history, is Napoleon part of its past? Did Napoleon ever set foot on Tel Akko? What role did the mound play during Napoleon's siege

Fig. 3 Statue of Napoleon on the top of Tel Akko and Jacques-Louis David's portrait of *Napoleon Crossing the Alps*. (Photo courtesy of the Tel Akko Total Archaeology Project, photograph by Ann E. Killebrew; Portrait Jacques-Louis David, public domain)

Fig. 4 Scan this QR code or visit https://bit.ly/NapoleonAcre to view the StoryMap that accompanies this paper

of Acre in 1799? In what follows, we explore these questions, beginning with a brief historical overview of the three individuals who led the French, British, and Ottoman forces involved in the siege. This is followed by a review of contemporary primary sources and an analysis of the movements of Napoleon and his army during the siege to determine what, if any, role Tel Akko played in the unsuccessful French attempt to conquer Acre. To supplement and further illustrate the issues covered in this text, we utilize Esri's ArcGIS StoryMap application at https://bit.ly/NapoleonAcre (Fig. 4). We dedicate this article to Tom Levy, whose groundbreaking work in the use of GIS, advanced 3D imagery, and ArcGIS StoryMap in archaeological research has been an inspiration for our work at Tel Akko (see, e.g., Howland et al., 2020; Levy et al., 2010; Smith & Levy, 2014).

2 Historical Context

2.1 Regional Context

Following the fall of Crusader Acre to Mamluk forces in 1291, this harbor town and other major coastal cities were razed to the ground to prevent any future Christian invasions from the sea. Acre remained largely abandoned for over four centuries and, according to travelers' accounts, its ruins served as a fishing village (Philipp, 2001, pp. 1–8). Its resettlement and development in the eighteenth century coincided with the beginning of the Industrial Revolution and increasing European demand for high-quality cotton from the foothills of the Galilee and southern Lebanon. French merchants initially dominated trade in cotton but were quickly challenged by other European nations. By the mid-eighteenth century, Zahir al-Umar of the Zaydani Bedouin clan centralized control of the very lucrative export of cotton. He rebuilt Acre and established it as the capital and commercial center of his Galilean autonomous domain (Silberman, 1989, pp. 228–243 for a discussion of the role of cotton in eighteenth-century Galilee and Phillip 2001 for a detailed analysis of Acre between 1730 and 1831). Development continued under his successor, Ahmad al-Jazzar, who expanded Acre's influence and undertook ambitious building projects. This is the backdrop for the fateful meeting at Acre of three individuals, Napoleon Bonaparte, William Sidney Smith, and Ahmad al-Jazzar, that sets the stage for Napoleon's historic defeat in 1799 (Fig. 5).

2.2 Napoleon Bonaparte (1769–1821)

Napoleon Bonaparte first rose to prominence during the French Revolution (1789–1799). In 1798, he embarked on a military and scientific expedition to Ottoman-controlled Egypt and Syria. The original goal of this campaign was to control and block the route of commerce between the British and their colonies to the east (Bourrienne, 1891, p. 127; Barrow, 1848, p. 233). Initially, Bonaparte and his army succeeded in gaining control of Egypt as well as coastal cities such as Gaza and Jaffa. However, his failed attempt to conquer Acre forced Napoleon to turn back south, ending his campaign in Syria. Bonaparte and his decimated forces returned to Egypt to assert French influence and combat the looming local and British threats there. He partially restored his military reputation by defeating the British and Ottoman forces during the 1799 Battle of Aboukir, an encounter that marked his last military action in Egypt. Following his return to France in October of 1799, he served as First Consul (1799–1804) and later as emperor (1804–1814 and 1815). In these roles, Napoleon transformed France into an imperial power. Prior to his death in exile on St. Helena, Napoleon continued to reflect on his loss at Acre as a low point in his career that prevented him from realizing his true destiny.

2.3 William Sidney Smith (1764–1840)

Sir Sidney Smith was a British naval officer who Napoleon described, when referring to his defeat at Acre, as the man who "made me miss my destiny" (Alison, 1835, pp. 16, 465, 478; Thiers, 1836, p. 299). He joined the British Royal Navy before the age of 13. In his early career, he fought in the American and French Revolutions. He initially faced Napoleon at the Siege of Toulon, which marked the beginning of a rivalry between the two men that would continue throughout their

Fig. 5 Portraits of the three leaders of the 1799 Siege of Acre: William Sidney Smith, Napoleon Bonaparte, and Ahmad al-Jazzar. (Reproduced from John Eckstein, National Portrait Gallery, London, public domain; Watson, 1854, p. 110; Thomas Aldridge, CC BY-SA 4.0)

careers. Sidney Smith was captured by the French and imprisoned for 2 years (1796–1798) in Paris at the Temple Prison. He sought Bonaparte's help for his release to no avail. He was later rescued by Antoine Le Picard de Phélippeaux, a French officer who subsequently played a pivotal role in Napoleon's defeat at Acre. In the fall of 1798, Smith was dispatched to the Mediterranean and served in two roles, as a commodore and a co-Minister Plenipotentiary to the Ottoman court of Constantinople. After Napoleon's capture of al-Arish and Jaffa, Smith sailed to Acre to assist Ottoman and local forces under the command of Ahmad al-Jazzar. His capture of the French siege artillery and naval blockade of the city from the sea played a key role in Napoleon's defeat. By the time of his death in 1840, Smith had been knighted three times: by Sweden in 1790, by Portugal in 1811, and later by Great Britain in 1838.

2.4 Ahmad al-Jazzar (1720s/1730s–1804)

Al-Jazzar was born in Stolac, Bosnia, and is best known as the Acre-based Ottoman governor of the Eyalet (province) of Sidon whom withstood Napoleon. He ruled for 29 years. There are several competing and often contradictory biographies of his life by Arab and European authors. After fleeing Bosnia to Constantinople under murky circumstances, he worked as a barber. In 1756, he arrived in Egypt, where he embarked on a successful military career. He became known as al-Jazzar (the butcher) after his slaughter of 70 Bedouin in revenge for the killing of his patron, the Mamluk Abdullah Bey. In 1768 he left Egypt and drifted between Syria, Anatolia, and Egypt. During this time, he briefly served as the garrison commander of Beirut protecting Ottoman interests. Following the 1775 Ottoman defeat and the death of the Bedouin leader, Zahir al-Umar, al-Jazzar was appointed governor of the province of Sidon in 1776/1777 with its capital at Acre. His definitive defeat of Napoleon, which marked the turning point in the French campaign against the Ottoman Empire, transformed al-Jazzar into a "defender of the faith" and hero in Muslim public opinion. He was also known as an indefatigable builder. Al-Jazzar's numerous building projects are some of the most important historic sites in Acre today, notably the Khan al-Umdan (Fig. 6) and the Al-Jazzar Mosque. Al-Jazzar is buried in a modest domed structure next to the mosque (Figs. 7 and 8; for a summary of al-Jazzar's building projects, see Dichter, 2000, pp. 72–73, 85, 108–109, 194, 202, 210, 216, 230–231).

3 The 1799 Siege of Acre

In our attempt to reconstruct Napoleon's movements and interaction with Tel Akko during the 1799 siege, we prioritize contemporary written sources and maps created during the siege or shortly thereafter that describe or depict the location

Fig. 6 Aerial view of Khan al-Umdan. (Zeev Stein, from Pikiwiki Israel, CC BY 2.5)

Fig. 7 The Al-Jazzar Mosque and the small structure to the right containing al-Jazzar's tomb. (Roaa Amer Zatari, CC BY-SA 4.0)

Fig. 8 Al-Jazzar's tomb in the mosque complex. (Photo courtesy of Amani Abu-Hamid)

of troops, siege works, and munitions. Some of the most complete first-hand accounts are by Sir William Sidney Smith (Barrow, 1848) and Napoleon Bonaparte (his military journal [Bonaparte, 1800] and later direct conversations on St. Helena in Gourgaud, 1903; Montholon, 1847; O'Meara, 1827). These are supplemented by the memoirs of these men written during their lifetimes or by men who knew them personally (e.g., Smith's memoirs in Howard, 1839; Bonaparte's in

Bourrienne, 1891). Other key primary resources are letters written by officers who participated in the siege (Bernoyer, 1976; Berthier, 1799; Doguereau, 1904 [English translation: Brindle, 2002]; Richardot, 1839). Archaeological excavations have occasionally uncovered evidence of the siege that corroborate the written accounts (Berman et al., 1997). Lastly, there are several excellent later secondary sources that create narrative accounts of Napoleon's 1799 siege of Acre based on a compilation and interpretation of the primary sources (e.g., Alison, 1835; La Jonquière, 1907; Thiers, 1836). Unfortunately, no contemporary written account of the siege exists from the perspective of al-Jazzar. However, letters from men at the siege, like Sidney Smith and Bernoyer, comment on the strengths of the pasha (Bernoyer, 1976, p. 161; Barrow, 1848, pp. 287, 295). Modern historians have also recognized his great personal courage, military acumen, and political savvy during the siege as major factors in Bonaparte's defeat at Acre (see, e.g., Cohen, 2002).

Most literature describing the 1799 siege divides the events into three phases (see, e.g., contemporary accounts: Montholon, 1847, pp. 277–286; Barrow, 1848, pp. 270–319; modern accounts: Schur, 1999, pp. 80–150). The early stage represents the excavation of the trenches and the initial assaults on the walls. The second phase coincides with Napoleon's Galilee campaign, where he carried out a series of successful battles, most notably at Mount Tabor. During this time, the French troops stationed at Acre continued to bombard fortifications and attempted to detonate mines below the northeast tower. The third and final phase commenced upon Napoleon's triumphant return from the Battle of Mount Tabor and the arrival of reinforcements at the end of April. It includes several unsuccessful assaults that culminated in the failed final push to capture Acre on May 10 leading to Napoleon's retreat to Egypt on May 21.

3.1 Preparing for the Siege

Napoleon rallied approximately 13,000 troops from Cairo for his campaign into Syria (numbers vary between accounts: Bonaparte, 1800, p. 10 [12,895]; Bourrienne, 1891, p. 185 [12,000]; Howard, 1839, p. 154 [13,000]; Barrow, 1848, p. 262 [12,000–13,000]). In response, Commodore Sidney Smith sailed from Constantinople with two large warships to provide military support to al-Jazzar from the sea. According to Smith's letters, his ships arrived on March 16, 2 days before Napoleon (Barrow, 1848, p. 264; Howard, 1839, p. 163 [3 days earlier, on March 15]). He dispatched Colonel Phélippeaux—chief engineer, classmate of Napoleon, and Sidney Smith's close friend—into the walled city to assist al-Jazzar with the fortifications (Barrow, 1848, p. 266). Smith then sailed south in hopes of intercepting Napoleon's army, and he was able to capture most of the French siege artillery, which was being sent by boat along the coast (Bonaparte, 1800, pp. 25–26; Howard, 1839, p. 167; Barrow, 1848, pp. 267–269).

3.2 Early Stage (March 20–April 1; Fig. 9)

When Napoleon reached Acre, his army was in a weakened condition. Bonaparte's siege artillery had been captured by the British near Haifa, and his army was suffering from the plague (Berthier, 1799, pp. 84–85; Bourrienne, 1891, p. 199; Montholon, 1847, p. 286; Barrow, 1848, p. 305). Additionally, Napoleon's massacre of 3500–3800 of al-Jazzar's soldiers at Jaffa triggered outrage among local populations in Palestine and the international community alike (Alison, 1835, pp. 462–465; Bourrienne, 1891, p. 198; Howard, 1839, pp. 188, 212; Barrow, 1848, pp. 264–265, 271, 307).

Based on contemporary accounts, Bonaparte nevertheless was confident that he would be able to take Acre as quickly and easily as he had captured Jaffa (Bourrienne, 1891, pp. 200–207; Montholon, 1847, p. 279). The French forces set up camp on the kurkar ridge to the east of the city walls as indicated on contemporary maps depicting the siege (see Fig. 9, Sidney Smith's map of the early stage of the siege, and Figs. 11 and 13 that depict later stages of the siege; see also the discussion below and Fig. 13). The quartermaster set up headquarters at the point where al-Jazzar's aqueduct met the kurkar ridge approximately 2 km from the walls of Acre (see maps in Figs. 11 and 13; Bonaparte, 1800, pp. 26–27; Howard, 1839, p. 165). The French

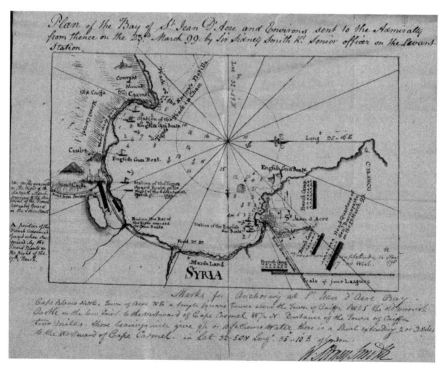

Fig. 9 Map by Sidney Smith documenting the initial stage of the siege from a naval perspective. (Sidney Smith, 1799, from Greenwich Royal Museums, public domain)

"Napoleon's Hill" and the 1799 Siege of Acre/Akko, Israel

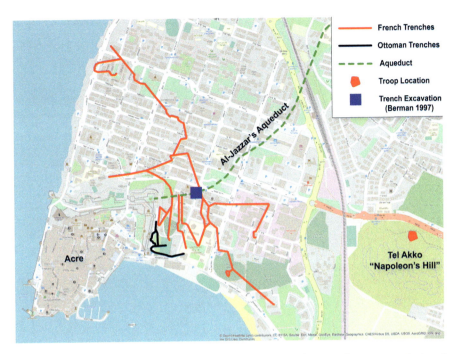

Fig. 10 The 1799 French and Turkish siege works, 1991 excavation area, Ottoman aqueduct, and the location of French forces on Tel Akko based on contemporary maps superimposed on a street map of modern Akko. (Courtesy of the Tel Akko Total Archaeology Project, graphics by Jane C. Skinner)

determined that the best place to dig trenches and set mines would be around the large tower in the northeast corner of the city (Fig. 10; Bonaparte, 1800, p. 27; Howard, 1839, pp. 169–170).

In response, the British fleet barraged the French troops and provided supplies to besieged Acre from their ships surrounding the city. The English also placed an 18-pounder gun on the Tower of Flies in the Acre harbor (Light House in Figs. 11 and 15, Phare in Fig. 13; Barrow, 1848, p. 285; Howard, 1839, p. 176). Al-Jazzar, with the assistance of the French royalist and engineer Phélippeaux reinforced Acre's city walls.

By the end of March, the French trenches outside of Acre's fortifications were finished. These trenches are indicated on numerous maps dating from the time of the siege (Figs. 11 and 13). Archaeological salvage excavations in 1991 prior to the construction of the courthouse in the modern city of Akko uncovered the remains of four French soldiers in one of the siege trenches (Fig. 10). They were identified by buttons that were common on French uniforms (Berman et al., 1997).

The first breach was made on March 26. However, as the initial breach was high, ladders were necessary to reach the opening (Bonaparte, 1800, pp. 28–29; Montholon, 1847, p. 279; Barrow, 1848, pp. 272, 274). Every time the French tried to mount the breach, al-Jazzar's troops bombarded the infantry (Bonaparte, 1800, p. 30).

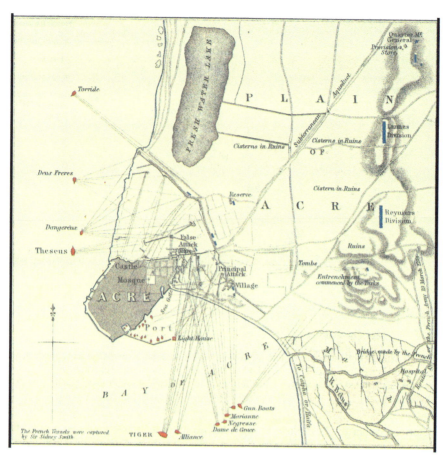

Fig. 11 Map illustrating the interlude phase of the siege when most of the French army was at the battle of Mt. Tabor. (Alison, 1848, Plate 19, public domain)

3.3 Battle of Mount Tabor and Siege Interlude (April 1–27; Fig. 11)

In April, reports reached Napoleon that a large number of Ottoman forces were on their way from Damascus to assist al-Jazzar in Acre (Bonaparte, 1800, pp. 31, 35). To avoid being surrounded and overrun in Acre, Bonaparte sent Generals Kléber and Junot with their divisions eastward. After a series of smaller skirmishes at Loubi, Sed Jarra, and Nazareth, the French army, now joined by Napoleon, defeated Ottoman reinforcements at the Battle of Mount Tabor, resulting in the Ottoman retreat to Damascus.

Back in Acre, the primary actions on both sides of the breach were centered on defending or undermining the northeast tower and walls (Montholon, 1847, pp. 281–282; Barrow, 1848, p. 277). The British and Ottoman allied forces made

Fig. 12 General Caffarelli's tomb. (Avishai Teicher, public domain)

strides to increase their fortifications, taking advantage of the absence of most of the French troops including the commander in chief. Both the French and British lost important military leaders during this period. On April 27, the French General Caffarelli succumbed to his wounds incurred in the trenches (Bourrienne, 1891, pp. 281–282; Montholon, 1847, p. 282). His burial was discovered by B. Dichter (2000, pp. 245–246) in 1975 based on the description in La Jonquière's account (La Jonquière, 1907, p. 457; see Fig. 12). Al-Jazzar's forces also suffered a strategic loss when Colonel Phélippeaux died of heat stroke on May 1 (Barrow, 1848, pp. 282, 297).

3.4 Final Stage of the 1799 Siege (April 28–May 20; Figs. 13 and 14)

On April 28, French hopes of capturing Acre rose with the arrival of artillery to replace that captured by Sidney Smith (Bonaparte, 1800, pp. 45–46). For about 10 days, the French assaulted the walls of Acre (Barrow, 1848, p. 294). The French temporarily captured the northeast tower on May 1 but were unable to hold it. By the fourth, they were running out of gunpowder (Bonaparte, 1800, p. 47; Bourrienne, 1891, p. 202). An Ottoman fleet arrived from Rhodes on May 7. Seeing his window of opportunity closing, Napoleon ordered another attack on the

Fig. 13 Map of the final stage of the siege showing the French army adjacent to the kurkar ridge. (Bibliothèque nationale de France, département Cartes et plans, GE D-17239, public domain)

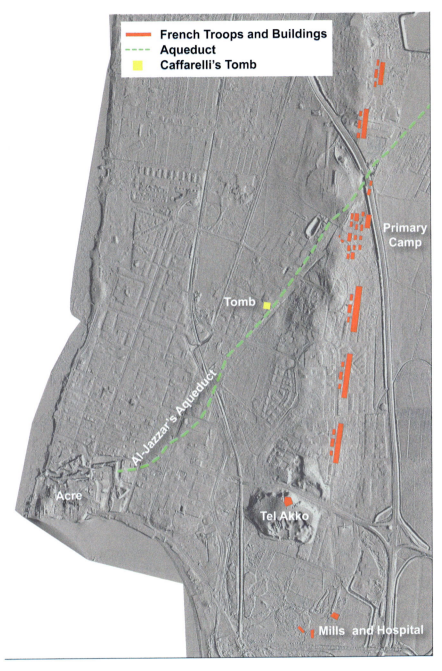

Fig. 14 Position of Napoleon's troops at the end of the siege digitized on a digital terrain model. (Courtesy of the Tel Akko Total Archaeology Project, graphics by Jane C. Skinner)

PLAN OF THE SIEGE OF ACRE.

1. Corride. 2. Deux Frères. 3. Dangereux. 4. Theseus. 5. Castle. 6. Sea Gate. 7. Port. 8. English. 9. Light House. 10, 11, 12. Gun-boats. 13. Marianne. 14. Negress. 15. Dame de France. 16. Alliance. 17. Tiger. 18. Bay of Acre. 19. Mediterranean. 20. Cultivated Valley. 21, 22. Ruined Cisterns. 23. Subterranean Aqueduct. 24. Old Turkish Entrenchment. 25. French Hospital. 26. River Belus. 27. Road to Caifia. 28. French Army—Head Quarters. 29. Lanbes. 30. Regniex. 31. Freshwater Lake. 32. French Reserve. 33. Village. 34. French Camp 35, 36. Parallels.

Fig. 15 Isometric plan of the siege and the hinterland around Akko. (Reproduced from Smith & Howitt, 1857, p. 174, public domain)

breach (Bernoyer, 1976, p. 161; Bonaparte, 1800, p. 49; Barrow, 1848, p. 285). On May 8, the French successfully entered the city (Bonaparte, 1800, p. 50). In response, Sidney Smith and his men came ashore and defended the breach, forcing the French out of the city. According to Sidney Smith, al-Jazzar himself pulled them off the breach to prevent any harm to his "British friends" (Barrow, 1848, pp. 286–287, 295).

May 10 marked Napoleon's final serious attempt to conquer Acre (Bonaparte, 1800, pp. 51–52). The French initially succeeded in entering Acre through the breach and rushed into al-Jazzar's gardens. Their success was short-lived. Ottoman reinforcements met them with knives and scimitars, which proved more effective in killing French soldiers at close range than single-shot rifles (Alison, 1835, pp. 475–476; Barrow, 1848, p. 289). Napoleon and his secretary, as well as Sidney Smith, write that Bonaparte himself led the efforts from the battlefront (Bonaparte, 1800, pp. 251–252; Bourrienne, 1891, p. 203; Barrow, 1848, p. 306).

On May 20 the siege was raised, and though the French failed in their attempts to conquer Acre, Napoleon reported to his army that the undertaking was a success (Bonaparte, 1800, pp. 53, 57–59). To lighten the load of his retreating army, Napoleon ordered that the remaining artillery be used to destroy al-Jazzar's palace inside the city walls. Additionally, cannons were buried or thrown into the sea

(Bonaparte, 1800, p. 57; Barrow, 1848, p. 308). The French army retreated slowly, one division at a time (Bonaparte, 1800, pp. 59–60) with the wounded and ill leaving first, often traveling at night (Bourrienne, 1891, p. 209). When Napoleon reflected on this siege later in life, he blamed Sir Sidney Smith for his failure to capture Acre and ruining his dream of recreating the eastern empire of Alexander the Great (Alison, 1835, pp. 16, 465, 478; Bourrienne, 1891, p. 200; O'Meara, 1827, p. 209; Thiers, 1836, p. 299).

4 The Role of "Napoleon's Hill"/Tel Akko in the 1799 Siege of Acre

When we initially began our research on Bonaparte's relationship to Tel Akko, we doubted that the mound played any significant role in the siege. As pointed out above, this commonly held view even appears on signage at the base of Tel Akko (Fig. 2). However, reading through primary sources, it became evident that Napoleon frequented the tell, and the mound did perform an important function during the siege.

First, a map depicting the position of French forces during the siege indicates a French presence on Tel Akko, shown in blue (Fig. 11). The same map illustrates guns shooting from the tell and the mound being shot at from the bay. Based on the map in Fig. 13, we have superimposed the position of French forces over a digital terrain model created from LiDAR data (Fig. 14). This highlights the strategic advantage of the kurkar ridge that reaches its highest elevation in the south at Tel Akko with a clear view of Acre. The French could also best observe the movements of the British fleet and al-Jazzar's troops from the vantage point of the tell.

Contemporary accounts also mention French activities on Tel Akko, including the presence of Bonaparte. General Jean-Pierre Doguereau's journal describes visiting Tel Akko on his arrival during the early stages of the siege and notes that al-Jazzar's forces had started to dig trenches.

Doguereau, 1904, pp. 198–199:

Translated text:

> We passed with the cavalry and the guides, and we stopped on the height that dominates the town, at 700 or 800 toises [1400–1600 meters]; it is there that Djezzar had begun a work of fortification of his genius, which I have spoken of previously.
>
> ("Nous passâmes avec la cavalerie et les guides et nous nous arrêtâmes sur la hauteur qui domine la ville, à 700 ou 800 toises; c'est là que Djezzar avait commencé un ouvrage de fortification de son génie, dont j'ai déjà parlé.")

These trenches are indicated on several maps as "Entrenchment commenced by the Turks" (Figs. 11 and 15). Other maps show the French troops next to the tell, which suggests that they had full control over the area, including the tell itself (Fig. 9).

In a letter written on May 9 to his superior officer, Sidney Smith reports that Napoleon met with his officers on Richard Coeur de Lion's hill (Tel Akko) to discuss the assault (Barrow, 1848, p. 288–289 [same letter quoted in Howard, 1839, p. 180; La Jonquière, 1907, p. 484]):

> The groups of generals and aides-de-camp, which the shells from the 68-pounders had frequently dispersed, were now reassembled on Richard Coeur-de-Lion's mount. Buonaparte was distinguishable in the centre of the semi-circle; his gesticulation indicated a renewal of attack...

As the evidence shows, control of Tel Akko, the highest and most prominent feature in the Akko environs, with a clear view of the bay, harbor, and city, was an important strategic asset from which Bonaparte could conduct his siege and land attack (Figs. 14 and 15). In addition to its strategic importance, the mound was in the area under French control, between their encampments to the north and their flour mills and the military hospital to the south (Figs. 11, 13, 14, and 15). Most importantly, both contemporary eyewitness accounts and representations of a French presence on the mound depicted on maps support the claim that Tel Akko rightly deserves the title "Napoleon's Hill."

References

Alison, A. (1835). *History of Europe from the commencement of the French Revolution in M.DCC. LXXXIX. To the restoration of the Bourbons in M.DCC.XV* (Vol. 3, 2nd ed.). Blackwood.

Alison, A. (1848). *Atlas to Alison's history of Europe.* Blackwood.

Artzy, M., & Beeri, R. (2010). Tel Akko. In A. E. Killebrew & V. Raz-Romeo (Eds.), *One thousand nights and days: Akko through the ages* (Catalogue No. 31) (pp. 15*–24*). Hecht Museum.

Barrow, J. (1848). *The life and correspondence of Admiral Sir William Sidney Smith, G.C.B* (Vol. 1). 2 vols. Bentley.

Berman, A., Zias, J., & Schick, T. (1997). A siege-trench of Bonaparte's army in areas TB and TC. *'Atiqot 31. 'Akko (Acre): Excavation reports and historical studies* (pp. 91–103). Israel Antiquities Authority.

Bernoyer, F. (1976). *Avec Bonaparte en Égypte et en Syrie 1798–1800: Dix-neuf lettres inédites de François Bernoyer ... retrouvées, transcrites et presentées par Christian Tortel.* Paillart.

Berthier, A. (1799). *Relation des campagnes du Général Bonaparte en Égypte et en Syrie.* Didot.

Bonaparte, N. (1800). *Military journal of General Buonaparte; being a concise narrative of his expedition from Egypt into Syria, in Asia Minor: Giving a succinct account of the various marches, battles, skirmishes, and sieges, including that of St. John D'Acre, from the time he left Cairo, until his return there. Together with an account of the memorable battle of Aboukir, and recapture of the fortress. The whole taken from the original and official documents* (Trans. from the French). Warner & Hanna.

Bourrienne, L. A. F. de (1891). *Memoirs of Napoleon Bonaparte* (Vol. 1) (R. W. Phipps, Ed.). Scribner.

Brindle, R. (2002). *Guns in the desert: General Jean-Pierre Doguereau's journal of Napoleon's Egyptian expedition* (R. Brindle, Trans.). Praeger.

Cohen, A. (2002). Napoleon and Jezzar: A local perspective. In A. Shmuelevitz (Ed.), *Napoleon and the French in Egypt and the Holy Land, 1798–1801: Articles presented at the 2nd international congress of Napoleonic studies, Israel, 4–11 July 1999* (pp. 79–86). Isis Press.

Dichter, B. (2000). *Akko sites from the Turkish period* (A. Carmel & Z. Baumwoll, Eds.). University of Haifa.

Doguereau, J.-P. (1904). *Journal de l'expédition d'Égypte, publié d'après le manuscrit original, avec une introduction et des notes, par C. de La Jonquière, chef d'escadron d'artillerie breveté. Avec un portrait et une carte.* Perrin.

Dothan, M. (1976). Akko: Interim excavation report first season, 1973/74. *Bulletin of the American Schools of Oriental Research, 224*, 1–48.

Dothan, M. (1993). Tel Acco. In *New encyclopedia of archaeological excavations of the Holy Land 1* (pp. 17–23). Israel Exploration Society.

Gourgaud, G. (1903). *Talks of Napoleon at St. Helena with General Baron Gourgaud together with the journal kept by Gourgaud on their journey from Waterloo to St. Helena* (E. W. Latimer, Trans.). McClurg.

Howard, E. (1839). *Memoirs of Admiral Sir Sidney Smith, K.C.B., & c. by the author of "Rattlin the Reefer," & c* (Vol. 1). R. Bentley.

Howland, M. D., Liss, B., Levy, T. E., & Najjar, M. (2020). Integrating digital datasets into public engagement through ArcGIS StoryMaps. *Advances in Archaeological Practice, 8*(4), 351–360. https://doi.org/10.1017/aap.2020.14

Killebrew, A. E., Skinner, J. C., & Artzy, M. (2023). Tel Akko – 2010–2019 excavations. In *Hadashot Arkheologiyot: Excavations and surveys in Israel*, 135. https://hadashot-esi.org.il/report_detail_eng.aspx?id=26307&mag_id=135

La Jonquière, C. de (1907). *L'expédition d'Égypte 1798–1801* (Vol. 4). H. Charles-Lavauzelle.

Levy, T. E., Petrovic, V., Wypych, T., Gidding, A., Knabb, K., Hernandez, D., et al. (2010). On-site digital archaeology 3.0 and cyber-archaeology: Into the future of the past—New developments, delivery and the creation of a data avalanche. In M. Forte (Ed.), *Cyber-archaeology* (pp. 135–153). Archaeopress.

Montholon, C.-T. c. d. (1847). *History of the captivity of Napoleon Bonaparte* (Vol. 2). H. Colburn.

O'Meara, B. E. (1827). *Napoleon in exile: Or, a voice from St. Helena: Being the opinions & reflections of Napoleon on the most important events of his life and government, in his own words* (Vol. 1). Jones.

Philipp, T. (2001). *Acre: The rise and fall of a Palestinian city, 1730–1831.* Columbia University Press.

Richardot, C. (1839). *Relation de la Campagne de Surie, spécialement des sièges de Jaffa et de Saint-Jean-d'Acre, par un officier d'artillerie de l'armee d'orient.* J. Corréard.

Schur, N. (1999). *Napoleon in the Holy Land.* Greenhill Books.

Silberman, N. (1989). *Between past and present: Archaeology, ideology, and nationalism in the modern Middle East.* Holt.

Smith, J. F., & Howitt, W. (1857). *Cassell's illustrated history of England* (Vol. 6). Cassell, Petter, and Galpin.

Smith, N. G., & Levy, T. E. (2014). ArchField in Jordan: Real-time GIS data recording for archaeological excavations. *Near Eastern Archaeology, 77*(3), 166–170.

Thiers, A. (1836). *Histoire de la Révolution française* (Vol. 10, 5th ed.). Furne.

Watson, H. C. (1854). *The camp-fires of Napoleon: Comprising the most brilliant achievements of the emperor and his marshals.* Porter & Coates.

The Curious Case of Albright at Megiddo (aka "A Mysterious Affair at Armageddon")

Eric H. Cline

> *the attempt to exclude me from the site of Megiddo... very nearly broke up the Megiddo expedition.*
>
> W.F. Albright, 15 June 1926.
>
> *"Is there any point to which you would wish to draw my attention?"*
> *"To the curious incident of the dog in the night-time."*
> *"The dog did nothing in the night-time."*
> *"That was the curious incident," remarked Sherlock Holmes.*
> Inspector Gregory and Sherlock Holmes in "Silver Blaze" (The Memoirs of Sherlock Holmes, 346–47, Doubleday 1893).

Abstract Even after extensive research in the archives of the Oriental Institute (OI), the Israel Antiquities Authority (IAA), and the Rockefeller Foundation for my book *Digging Up Armageddon* (2020), a number of minor mysteries remained unresolved. Among them is the question of exactly what happened at Megiddo in mid-October 1925, when William F. Albright visited the site. Now, as a result of further research in two additional archives, the mystery has been partially solved, although questions still remain.

Keywords Megiddo · William F. Albright · James Henry Breasted · Clarence S. Fisher · Daniel Higgins · Daniel D. Luckenbill · William F. Badè

E. H. Cline (✉)
George Washington University, Washington, DC, USA
e-mail: ehcline@email.gwu.edu

© The Author(s), under exclusive license to Springer Nature Switzerland AG 2023
E. Ben-Yosef, I. W. N. Jones (eds.), *"And in Length of Days Understanding" (Job 12:12): Essays on Archaeology in the Eastern Mediterranean and Beyond in Honor of Thomas E. Levy*, Interdisciplinary Contributions to Archaeology, https://doi.org/10.1007/978-3-031-27330-8_82

1 Introduction and Background to the Mystery

By the Fall of 1925, James Henry Breasted, Director of the newly founded Oriental Institute at the University of Chicago, had finally succeeded in getting both the necessary permissions from the British Mandate Department of Antiquities in Palestine and scraping together enough funding (courtesy of John D. Rockefeller, Jr.) to send an archaeological expedition to excavate at Megiddo, aka biblical Armageddon. He was interested in digging at the site not least because of its biblical associations, reportedly including Solomonic building activities (according to 1 Kings 9: 15), but also because of Thutmose III's great battle in the area ca. 1479 BCE, the details of which were recorded on the wall of a temple in Luxor, Egypt.[1]

The expedition was part of a larger push by Breasted to get his fledgling Institute off the ground and to make as big a splash as possible by excavating simultaneously in several countries, including Egypt, Turkey, and Iraq, as well as British Mandate Palestine where Megiddo was located. He was strongly supported in his efforts by his colleague and confidante at the Oriental Institute, Daniel D. Luckenbill, whom Breasted affectionately addressed as "D.D." in all of his communications. Luckenbill was a distinguished professor of Assyriology and one of Breasted's closest friends; he also strongly supported the idea of digging at Megiddo and actively helped Breasted to choose the members of the first expedition team sent to the site.

That first OI team consisted of four men. Clarence Fisher, recently fired from the University of Pennsylvania Museum and Beth Shean excavations, and who had also previously excavated in Egypt and at the site of Samaria near Megiddo, was tapped to serve as Field Director; he was about 49 years old at the time. His nephew, also named Clarence Fisher but who went by the name Stanley, was the group's accountant and chauffeur; he was 26 years old at the time. Daniel Higgins, who was from the Geology department at the University of Chicago, and who was stalwartly

---

[1] I would like to thank at the outset a number of people without whom this paper could not have been written; these include the following: at the Oriental Institute of the University of Chicago: Anne Flannery (Head of Museum Archives); at the American Philosophical Society in Philadelphia: David Gary (Associate Director of Collections), Charles Greifenstein (Associate Librarian & Curator of Manuscripts), Valerie-Ann Lutz (Head of Manuscripts Processing), and Joe DiLullo (Reference Staff); at the Badè Museum of Biblical Archaeology, Pacific School of Religion: Aaron Brody (Director), Melissa Cradic (Curator), and Sam Pfister and Tara Lewandowski (Collections Managers). I would also like to thank them for permission to cite and quote at length from the various letters and other materials below. I would also like to thank Peter Feinman, Norma Franklin, Rachel Hallote, and Jeff Zorn, all of whom commented and gave valuable advice on earlier drafts of this paper, and Ian Jones and Erez Ben-Yosef for inviting me to contribute to this volume in honor of Tom Levy. It should also be noted that portions of the current article utilize material originally published in my book (Cline, 2020) and are reproduced here with permission; full references for that material is not repeated here again, for the most part, but can be found in the book. Note that the material at the Oriental Institute of the University of Chicago is all in the Museum Archives, abbreviated below as "the OI Museum Archives."

championed by Luckenbill,[2] was hired as the group's surveyor and cartographer; he was about 5 years younger than Fisher. Finally, Edward DeLoach, a young man who had taken surveying classes with Higgins while he was an undergraduate at the university, was to serve as Higgins' assistant; he was 24 years old at the time. Of them all, only Fisher had any actual excavation experience, and only Fisher and Higgins had been outside the United States before.

They expected that four additional Americans would join them 6 months later, but only one of them actually made it to the dig. That was John Payne Kellogg, who was 28 years old at that point. He had been studying with Luckenbill at the Oriental Institute, after graduating from Yale in 1921. However, he wished to gain experience in the field as well as learn the ancient languages and history in the classroom, so he contracted with Breasted to join the Megiddo expedition after the Winter quarter had ended at the university. Unbeknownst to the others, Kellogg became Breasted's informant during his 6 months at the site, from mid-May through October 1926, surreptitiously reporting directly to him on everything from their emotions to the discoveries made by the team.

The four initial men, plus Higgins' wife and two daughters (who elected to live in Beirut rather than at the dig site), made their way as passengers on two separate passenger ships. Fisher and his nephew Stanley were on one ship; Higgins and his family plus DeLoach were on the other. The two Fishers arrived at Megiddo by mid-September 1925, having stopped enroute in Cairo, Jerusalem, and Haifa to get supplies and arrange for the workmen. Higgins and DeLoach got there before the end of the month, after getting Higgins' family settled in Beirut.

In the weeks that followed, the four intrepid members of the team began their initial work at the site, aided by a number of Quftis (Egyptian workmen well versed in the ways of archaeology) and local villagers. They started by surveying the mound, as planned, as well as beginning the construction of a dig house in which they could live and work during the coming years (note that portions of the house are still present at the site today, as part of the Welcome Center).

After no more than a few weeks, having negotiated with local landowners and signed a lease for the right to excavate on the eastern half of the mound, Fisher decided that it was time to begin trial excavations. Higgins immediately intervened, however, claiming that he had been told by those back in Chicago—i.e., Breasted and Luckenbill—that they were only to survey and construct the house during these first weeks, and begin excavating later, perhaps not until the Spring.[3]

That was the first argument between the two men, but by no means the last. Things got so bad that the two couldn't even agree on a time to eat breakfast. Matters eventually came to a head just 1 week after the digging started several months later,

---

[2] See, e.g., letters from Luckenbill to Breasted dated 4 February and 15 May 1925 (both in the OI Museum Archives: Directors Correspondence Box 053, Folder 043).

[3] Cable from Fisher to Breasted dated 8 October 1925 and cabled reply from Breasted to Fisher dated 12 October 1925; letters from Higgins to Breasted and to Luckenbill, both dated 14 October 1925; letter from Breasted to Fisher dated 21 October 1925 (all in the OI Museum Archives: Directors Correspondence Box 053, Folder 038).

in mid-April 1926, when Fisher sent a cable to Breasted, resigning his position (although Breasted refused to accept it).

Higgins was eventually fired in mid-June, for a variety of sins, all of which were spelled out in detail in two letters sent by Breasted to Higgins. One was sent at the end of May 1926; the other, which was Higgins' termination letter, was dispatched just 2 weeks later.[4] The "sins" listed by Breasted included causing a number of different problems with Fisher; a total lack of the tact and graciousness that Breasted considered to be essential on a field excavation, as well as a further lack of loyalty and obedience; and a variety of other specific grievances.

However, at the time, all such problems still lay in the future; here we are concerned with something that happened much sooner, but which was not listed in the termination letter for some reason.

2 The "Affair d'Albright"

It was in mid-October 1925, probably not more than 2 weeks after the team had begun work, that William Foxwell Albright came to visit Megiddo. At the time, Albright was the Director of the American School in Jerusalem (as it was known then), which had been established by the American Schools of Oriental Research (ASOR). He and Professor Raymond Dougherty, who was the Annual Professor at the School in 1925–1926, were touring the region before embarking on a trip to explore sites in Mesopotamia. Their journey was apparently being undertaken on behalf of their sister organization, the newly formed Baghdad School of the American Schools of Oriental Research, which has been described as "an offshoot of the School in Jerusalem" and for which Dougherty was also serving as the Annual Professor that year.[5]

However, according to the 1975 biography of Albright written by Leona G. Running and David Noel Freedman, "There was a misunderstanding at Megiddo and Albright was forbidden access to the mound." As they state, "the 'ban' on Albright's presence on the mound of Megiddo…puzzled and bothered him," so he wrote to Luckenbill, telling him what had happened. However, Luckenbill—thinking that Albright was still in Mesopotamia—didn't answer for nearly 6 months. In the meantime, Fisher, who apparently was not at the site during Albright's attempted visit, tried to smooth things over, telling Albright that he was always welcome at Megiddo and that he "would always be proud to show Albright his excavations." Without giving any further details, Running and Freedman (1975: 130–31) reported that the incident "nearly shattered the expedition."

---

[4] Letters from Breasted to Higgins dated 29 May and 16 June 1926 (in the OI Museum Archives: Directors Correspondence Box 058, Folder 019); see previously the full discussion in Cline, 2020: 35–43.

[5] On the Baghdad School, see the information at www.bu.edu/asor/overseas/baghistory.html

During the research for my book, *Digging Up Armageddon*, I could find no other information about this incident in any other sources, however carefully I searched. Nor could I locate the primary material that Running and Freedman seemed to have consulted in order to write their account, including the letters exchanged between Luckenbill and Albright pertaining to this specific episode. They implied that these letters were at Johns Hopkins University, but even if that were once the case, it is no longer.

Within the archives of the Oriental Institute, though, I did find a letter sent by Kellogg to Breasted in mid-July 1926,[6] just after Higgins had been fired. In it, Kellogg told Breasted that Higgins had, at some point, created "quite a mess" between Luckenbill and Albright. I surmised that this was a reference to the incident at Megiddo involving Albright, and that it had been Higgins who had denied Albright access to the mound, which was the hypothesis that I published in my book (Cline, 2020: 41–42).

I also found a few letters exchanged between Breasted and Luckenbill in which their own personal animosity towards Albright is apparent. The first one is a letter from Luckenbill to Breasted, sent in June 1925, when Luckenbill had initially been dispatched to Philadelphia to offer the position of Field Director to Clarence Fisher. The second is Breasted's reply to Luckenbill, sent in early July.

Luckenbill's letter, in which he was describing his initial meeting with Fisher, includes the following: "There was one point on which I said [to Fisher] you would need to be assured. That the Oriental Institute was not ready to have any supervision of its work by Dr. Albright. I made it clear that we could not be expected to do much cooperating with him." He then continued, "Fisher then assured me that it was not the intent of his scheme to have the American Schools Field Director in on his job. He also told me that it was not at all certain that Albright would return as director after his furlough."[7]

This met with Breasted's approval. In his reply to Luckenbill, he wrote: "I was very glad to have your letter of June 23rd, which reached me this morning with full information about your dealings with Fisher. You did a wise thing in going to Philadelphia, and I am very glad you have settled the matter so satisfactorily. I'm [e]specially glad that you told Fisher clearly our position with regard to Albright. We should not be in need of any of his assistance."[8]

However, the lack of additional material meant that I could not corroborate what Running and Freedman had reported or why they had said that Albright hadn't been allowed up on the mound. Nor was it obvious what exactly had transpired during Albright's visit or whether Higgins was acting under specific orders from someone else, such as Luckenbill or Breasted.

---

[6] Letter from Kellogg to Breasted dated 17 July 1926 (in the OI Museum Archives: Directors Correspondence Box 058, Folder 022).

[7] Letter from Luckenbill to Breasted dated 23 June 1925 (in the OI Museum Archives: Directors Correspondence Box 053, Folder 043).

[8] Letter from Breasted to Luckenbill dated 6 July 1925 (in the OI Museum Archives: Directors Correspondence Box 053, Folder 043).

Surely, I thought, there had to be additional information somewhere which could shed light on this mystery and perhaps bring some resolution. As it turned out, there was. It came about in two stages, as follows.

3 New Information

First, in February 2020, just weeks before my book was due to appear, Sam Pfister and Melissa Cradic, two former students of mine, called my attention to a letter in the archives of the Badè Museum of Biblical Archaeology, in California. I had previously been in touch several times with Aaron Brody, the Director of the Museum, while I was conducting my initial research for the book, but had been primarily asking about letters between Breasted and William F. Badè, who had excavated Tell en-Nasbeh, not far from Jerusalem. As it turned out, I should have been asking about letters between Badè and Albright, not Breasted.

This particular letter was sent by Albright to Badè from Virginia Beach on 26 November 1926 (Fig. 1).[9] It reads in part as follows, complete with crossed-out words:

> Dear Dean Badè:
> Since the 29th of October, a few days after landing, I have been busy lecturing, but now have a few days at home for Thanksgiving. … In Chicago, where I lectured at McCormick, Garrett and the university, I had a very good time, meeting a great many friends. Professor Breasted and the other members of the Oriental institute were extremely kind, doing all in their power to make up for a certain episode in which friend Higgins figured about fourteen months ago. Higgins is out of a job, it seems, and is decidedly persona non grata in Chicago. It is a pity in some ways; he is an energetic fellow, gifted in some ways, though tact and judgment are not among his qualifications.

So, this was an independent verification, from none other than Albright himself, which specifically fingers Higgins as being involved in the incident at Megiddo. That meant that my initial hypothesis was correct, but even so, the letter did not shed any additional light on *what* happened nor *why* it happened.

Second, at just about the same time that I was alerted to the existence of the above letter, I also found out that during his lifetime, and for much of his academic career, Albright was an active member of the American Philosophical Society, which has its headquarters in Philadelphia. He served on several committees, including the Research Committee in particular, according to their website. A few years after he passed away in 1971, his family members apparently decided to bequeath some twenty-five boxes of material, which include both personal and

---

[9] Letter from Albright to Badè misdated 26 November 1927 (courtesy of the Bade Museum, Pacific School of Religion). The "1927" is written in pencil and is most likely an error introduced by a later archivist, or perhaps by Chester McCown, who was the Director at the time, for the letter must be from 26 November 1926 rather than 1927, if the reference to the incident having been approximately 14 months earlier is to be accurate (it was actually closer to thirteenth months earlier, but we won't quibble). Explanation courtesy of email sent from Pfister to Cline on 28 February 2020.

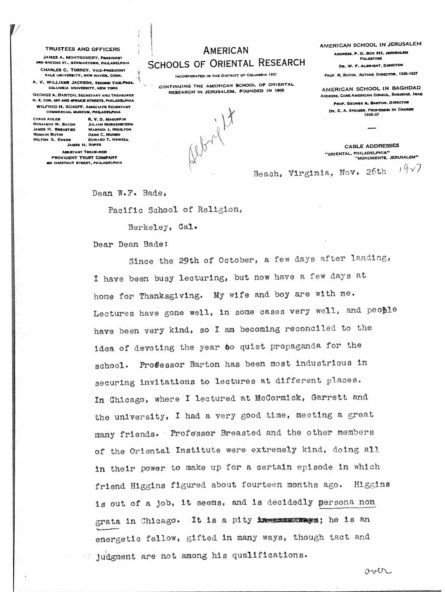

Fig. 1 Letter from Albright to Badè from 26 November 1926. (Courtesy of the Badè Museum, Pacific School of Religion)

professional correspondence as well as drafts of his talks and publications, to the APS, where they were accessioned in 1979. I was able to visit and see this material in early March 2020, at almost the exact same time as my book appeared (and just a few days before the APS temporarily closed down because of the COVID-19 pandemic).

The boxes of material turned out to be a gold mine, particularly one labelled "Box 2: Correspondence, 1920–1935," which has 600 items in it. Here, as it turned out, were most of the letters exchanged between Albright and Luckenbill that I had been unable to locate previously in the archives at the Oriental Institute or at Johns Hopkins. There were other letters as well, sent between Albright and other Chicago people, including Breasted and Fisher, as well as other archaeologists, such as Badè. Obviously, Albright had kept copies of much of his outgoing correspondence in addition to that which was incoming. It was clear to me that I had finally located the material that Running and Freedman had consulted for their biography, regardless of where it had been when they first saw it.

What appears to be almost the full story, except for one tantalizingly missing piece, was contained in the letters, so we can now spell it out in the participants' own words. It begins with a letter sent from Albright to Fisher on 11 October 1925. "Professor Dougherty and I leave Thursday morning [Oct 15] on our trip to Mesopotamia," Albright said. "We shall spend a day or two in Palestine, about a week or two in Syria, and go down the Euphrates River to Babylonia, where Professor Dougherty is staying until next Spring. We hope to visit Megiddo on our way, but just when I cannot say, since the mode of travel is not yet certain. We shall not be able to stay overnight, in any case, though we are taking camp bed with us."[10]

This dovetails with a cable that had been sent 10 days earlier, on 1 October, from Higgins to Luckenbill, which read "REPORT ALLRIGHT (sic) LEAVES SOON MOSUL AND SURVEY SITES LOWER MESOPOTAMIA—HIGGINS." He followed it up with a letter to Luckenbill dated 14 October, which reads in part: "You have received long since the cable I sent you about Albright's going to Mesopotamia soon to make a reconnaissance of the sites of the lower part of the region between the rivers. This is just what you and I were planning on, and it seems that he is stealing a march on you and Breasted. Fisher let this information slip inadvertently. He obviously keeps other information as to what is going on out here from me for fear of its getting back to you."[11]

The next relevant letter in the APS archive, which may well be the most important of the extant materials in this story, was sent Tuesday, 20 October, from Fisher to Albright. He posted it to Jerusalem, where it would either be forwarded or await Albright's return from his travels in Mesopotamia. It was clearly written after the incident because it reads: "I have written to Prof. Montgomery about affairs here in connection with your visit. Mr. Higgins said he had orders, and refused to accede to them, and upon your arrival last week was proud and happy to show you all we had. This attitude I will always have. This whole matter I leave with the Committee and am willing to resign my position here to take up the School work, if such a course

---

[10] Letter from Albright to Fisher dated 11 October 1925 (in the APS archives: Albright material, Box 2; see also Running & Freedman, 1975: 130).

[11] Cable from Higgins to Luckenbill dated 1 October 1925 and letter from Higgins to Luckenbill dated 14 October 1925 (both in the OI Museum Archives: Directors Correspondence Box 053, Folder 041).

is necessary. I have made a fight for clean and open archaeology and mean to continue it."[12]

The letter confirms that Fisher was not present when Albright arrived at Megiddo, even though he had had advance notice (albeit without a specific date). Higgins is also specifically named as the person who had interacted with Albright: "Mr. Higgins said he had orders," said Fisher, "and refused to accede to them." So there is now yet more independent confirmation of the events, indicating once again that it was Higgins who was at the center of the controversial actions.

However, Fisher does not specify what were the orders that Higgins said he had been given, or who had given them. Nor is it clear what he meant by "refused to accede to them." It certainly sounds as if Higgins did not actually follow the orders he had been given, which Fisher seems to further imply by saying that Higgins "was proud and happy to show you all we had." The mystery had perhaps only deepened in some ways, but fortunately there was more material still to consult.

Six days later, on 26 October, Breasted wrote to Higgins, apparently in reply to the cable and letter that Higgins had sent to Luckenbill earlier that month, reporting on Albright's intended trip to Mesopotamia. Breasted seemed less concerned than the others, suggesting that there was plenty of material (i.e., sites to excavate) for everyone: "Dear Higgins, Your cablegram of the 1st October regarding Albright's departure for Mosul has been received, and, after giving the matter mature consideration and waiting to see what results might follow the disturbance in French territory, I do not see that we can do anything at present but hope for improvement. It is highly unlikely under the present circumstances that Albright will be making the trip. However, if he does I do not see that we can do anything about it. In my judgement there will be work enough for everybody. Meantime we can have a talk about it when I see you at Megiddo."[13]

In point of fact, Breasted and the OI subsequently sent an archaeological expedition to the site of Khorsabad in Iraq, where they excavated from 1928 to 1935. The Baghdad School was already involved with excavations at the site of Nuzi as early as April 1925, well before Albright's visit to Megiddo and thence to Mesopotamia, as well as at Yorghan Tepe from 1927 to 31, Tepe Gawra in 1927 and again from 1931 to 1938, and Tepe Billa from 1930 to 1937.[14] There was indeed "work enough for everybody," as Breasted had said.

Almost exactly 2 months later, on 18 December 1925, writing in a very shaky hand from Beirut where he was recovering from malaria, Higgins reported to Breasted that "Albright is here today, passing thru on his return from Baghdad…"[15]

---

[12] Letter from Fisher to Albright dated 20 October 1925 (in the APS archives: Albright material, Box 2).

[13] Letter from Breasted to Higgins dated 26 October 1925 (in the OI Museum Archives: Directors Correspondence Box 053, Folder 041).

[14] See again the information at www.bu.edu/asor/overseas/baghistory.html

[15] Letter from Higgins to Breasted dated 18 December 1925 (in the OI Museum Archives: Directors Correspondence Box 053, Folder 041).

Just a week afterward, Albright sent a letter to Fisher, on the day after Christmas, 26 December, which confirmed this latter meeting. In it he wrote,

> After two months in Mesopotamia and northern Syria, I returned to Jerusalem Dec. 18th, by train. … Since leaving Beirut, I have learned nothing further about that puzzling attitude of the University of Chicago, as I know only what Dr. Higgins told me at Tell el-Mutesellim [i.e., Megiddo], when I was there, and later at Beirut, as well as what I found in your letter of Oct 20th after I got home. While in Beirut I wrote Professor Luckenbill, telling him that Mr. Higgins had suggested to me that I had better get in touch with him as soon as possible, and stating that I would naturally follow my usual course of treating everything learned at excavations as confidential until the site was published.[16]

From this we now know that Higgins had actually met and spoken with Albright in Beirut on 18 December, while the latter was passing through enroute back to Jerusalem. What we don't know is what was said at that additional meeting between Higgins and Albright, but Albright then continued on in his letter to say, "I am hoping to see Professor Breasted, in order to talk over things with him; perhaps I should have written him and not Luckenbill, but Higgins mentioned Luckenbill and hinted that Breasted had nothing to do with it, so far as he knew. I am going to be extremely careful, since I don't know just what the situation is, and I should be very unhappy if incautious action should cause you trouble."

It is unclear what "the situation" might have been and what "incautious action" by Albright might unintentionally cause trouble for the Megiddo people, but we shall return to this in a moment. In the meantime, there are additional clues contained in this long letter, for Albright then continued on:

> Many thanks for your kind letter of Oct. 20th, which I have mentioned above. No letters were forwarded to me, so I saw it only a few days ago. I hope it will be possible to see you soon, to talk things over... If you are coming to Jerusalem again, I shall wait for you; otherwise I can meet you at Haifa or at Tell el-Mutesellim, in case the apparent ban on my presence there has been lifted—I say 'apparent' because I really don't feel that I have adequate reason for saying that there is a ban, since I haven't a word of anything in writing. I wrote Luckenbill from Beirut about Oct. 18th, and ought to hear soon, if the letter reached him. It is a little late, but I can't think that he will refuse to reply, so will write again in a week or two, on the chance that something happened to the letter—unless I see Professor Breasted before then. I am rather keen on having the mystery cleared up. In any case, you can rely upon my discretion and loyalty (Very sincerely yours, W.F. Albright).

So, we now know for certain that whatever had happened seems to have involved Luckenbill, rather than Breasted, but we still don't know how or what actually transpired, especially since the letter that Albright says he sent to Luckenbill from Beirut on 18 October—to which Luckenbill took fully 6 months to respond—cannot be located at the moment. It is not to be found in the archives of either the Oriental Institute or the American Philosophical Society.

---

[16] Letter from Albright to Fisher dated 26 December 1925 (in the APS archives: Albright material, Box 2).

4 Ruminations

However, in that same letter of 26 December, Albright also then introduces an apparently irrelevant aside—which actually turns out to be quite relevant after all, as we shall see. On the back side of the paper, i.e., page two of the letter (which was so illegible that I was unable to read it at the time, and which only yielded to the gentle ministrations of the APS curators and sent to me several weeks later), Albright said:

> I also promised in addition that I would not examine or copy any epigraphic documents which should turn up—without explicit permission or request from the University of Chicago authorities. This is naturally the crucial point for them and I consider it quite reasonable, since University of Chicago has all the necessary epigraphers and philologists. I also asked for an early reply, so that no misunderstanding could arise meanwhile. For all I know, I have put my foot into it—some things seem to require promptness, when we are separated by so many thousands of miles.

What was Albright talking about? Why would the Megiddo staff, or rather Higgins in particular, make Albright, of all people, promise that he would not examine or copy any epigraphic documents which should turn up? They had only just arrived at the site themselves a few weeks earlier, and hadn't yet begun digging, so what could have prompted this? What had they found?

I believe it is conceivable that they had already found the famous Sheshonq inscription by the time of Albright's visit, though they would not have been able to read it yet—that would have to wait until Breasted's visit in March 1926, when he read the hieroglyphics inscribed on the fragment. We know, from a letter that Higgins later sent to Luckenbill,[17] that the fragment had been found at least by early November 1925, when the Egyptian workmen were bringing down loose rocks and stones they had scavenged from Schumacher's backdirt piles, in order to use them during the construction of the dig house (see also full discussion, with references, in Cline, 2020: 28–30). Perhaps it had already been found 2 weeks earlier, by the time of Albright's visit in mid-October? There is no other reason for them to have impressed upon Albright the importance that he "not examine or copy any epigraphic documents which should turn up—without explicit permission or request from the University of Chicago authorities," for, as stated, they hadn't yet even begun digging, and would not do so for another 6 months.

Appealing as this hypothesis might be, it would have been very easy for the Chicago team to have hidden the fragment so that Albright couldn't accidentally see it, so such a scenario seems unlikely to be the reason underlying the promise that they had extracted from him. However, as Peter Feinman pointed out to me, we should note that in the October 1926 issue of *BASOR*, published just a few months after the official announcement by Breasted of the discovery of the Sheshonq inscription,

---

[17]Letter from Higgins to Luckenbill dated 19 May 1926 (in the OI Museum Archives: Directors Correspondence Box 058, Folder 019).

Albright was at pains to give credit where credit was due, and to note that he was most certainly not prematurely revealing a discovery made by the Chicago archaeologists, writing: "The discovery at Megiddo of a fragment of a stela of Shishak, recently announced by Professor Breasted..." (Albright, 1926b: 5). In fact, in a rough draft of their biographical manuscript, Running and Freedman say "[note how careful Albright was to state that this item concerning Megiddo had been officially announced by an authorized person from Chicago University!]" (Running & Freedman, n.d., 610; see also Running & Freedman, 1975: 148).[18]

Despite all of the material in Box 2 of the Albright material at the APS archives, there was one letter that was not there: the letter that Albright sent to Luckenbill from Beirut on 18 October, immediately after the incident, as just mentioned. Presumably he was not able to make a copy of it for his records, since he was on the road, which may be why it is not among his papers at the APS. It should, though, be in the OI archives, among Luckenbill's papers, but it is not. Perhaps it is lost forever or perhaps we shall locate it during a future deep dive into one of the various archives. We can only hope so, for it is in this letter, of all others, that we might expect the events that took place on that day to be laid out in full, by Albright himself.

In the meantime, what we do have is Luckenbill's response to that letter from Albright, i.e., the one that he wrote almost exactly 6 months later, on 19 April 1926. In this letter, Luckenbill began by writing (somewhat deviously): "I hope I may be forgiven for putting off answering your letter for so long. At the time I received it, I took for granted you would be off in Mespot [sic] for some time and there was no need of [illegible word] [eve]rything at once. You know what happens when this is done."[19] He then continued on, in a new paragraph:

> I am still at a loss to know just how what I said could have come to mean what it seems to have meant. Indeed I do not know just what was said, but I do remember that we here in Chicago were thoroughly put out by a letter that was being sent out in the name of the American schools in which there was a long list of publications, (to be) headed by the Yale expedition's publication of the Harran expedition, a few more Yale vols [and] some others, and down the line, in tenth place, or thereabouts, the University of Chicago's account of the Megiddo expedition. This prospectus was sent without a word to us. Are you surprised that we, who had the funds for excavation, were somewhat surprised, to put it mildly, to find ourselves suddenly gathered into the fold? ... We made it plain to Fisher that we were not in any hurry to climb on the new bandwagon.

After a few additional words about the recent death of a mutual colleague, Albert Clay, who was a professor of Assyriology at Yale and the founding curator of the Yale Babylonian Collection, Luckenbill then ended his letter by saying, "I assure you, Dr. Albright, that I have the highest regard for you and your work. We may not

---

[18] I am indebted to Peter Feinman for pointing this out to me and for sending me the relevant page(s) from Running and Freedman's rough draft, which is in his possession (pers. comm., 6 September 2021).

[19] Letter from Luckenbill to Albright dated 19 April 1926 (in the APS archives: Albright material, Box 2).

always come out at the same place, but anyone who works as you do, has my best wishes."

While we may now be getting closer to a possible motive for Higgins' actions, beyond perhaps not wishing Albright to say anything about the Sheshonq fragment, if indeed he had seen it, we still don't know what orders or instructions from Luckenbill Higgins might have thought he was acting upon. Was he simply passing along a message or was it something more than that? Moreover, what was this "letter that was being sent out in the name of the American schools in which there was a long list of publications" and the "prospectus that was sent without a word to us"?

Before we get to that, however, there is yet one more relevant document to discuss from the archives at the OI and another from Box 2 at the APS. Luckenbill had apparently written to Higgins on the very same day that he wrote to Albright, on 19 April 1926. For some reason that letter is also now missing, so we don't know what was said in it, but we do have the reply from Higgins to Luckenbill, which was sent a month later, on 19 May 1926. In Higgins' letter, he began by writing: "Your letter of the 19th April is to hand, and right glad I am to have the same. I was beginning to wonder if you had forgotten me altogether. ..." He then said,

> The Albright matter is very quiet. He and I are on the best of terms personally, altho [sic] I did follow out your instructions in what to tell him—which made Fisher very angry. Albright is anxious to meet you and to have a talk with you when he is home this next year. I have tried to impress upon him that you are a straight, reasonable fellow and a good sport. He thinks that you and Breasted have been misinformed adversely about him by certain enemies of his, notably Gordon. If you and he could have a little visit over lunch at the club, all would be well, I am certain.[20]

So, from this we now have yet more confirmation that Higgins was the one involved in whatever had happened with Albright at Megiddo, but it is also clear that he might not have been completely out of line in so doing, if he were simply following Luckenbill's instructions regarding what to tell Albright. As for "Gordon," whom Albright thought might have been misinforming Luckenbill and Breasted, this is most likely a reference to George B. Gordon, who was the Director of the University Museum at the University of Pennsylvania. He had been responsible for firing Fisher from both the University Museum and from the excavations at Beth Shean, which ironically freed up Fisher to join the Megiddo expedition. However, why Gordon should have been spreading misinformation about Albright to Breasted and Luckenbill is not clear ... and it is conceivable (though unlikely) that a completely different "Gordon" could be meant.

One month later, on 15 June 1926 (which was, ironically, just 1 day before Breasted fired Higgins on 16 June), Albright replied to Luckenbill's 19 April letter. In it, he refers specifically to the offensive "list of publications," writing as follows:

> Dear Professor Luckenbill:
> Returning from our excavations at Tell Beit Mirsim, at the close of our first season, I find your letter of April 19th awaiting me. Many thanks. The matter has turned out just as I

---

[20] Letter from Higgins to Luckenbill dated 19 May 1926 (in the OI Museum Archives: Directors Correspondence Box 058, Folder 019).

thought. Naturally, as soon as I saw a certain list of publications, I worried what the reaction elsewhere to this list would be. It did not appear particularly tactful to me—but I had and have nothing to do with these plans, so will bend my efforts in the direction of peace.

Albright then moved on to the other topic that was causing distress. "So far as I am concerned," he wrote, "I long ago reached the very definite conclusion that the attempt to exclude me from the site of Megiddo did not come from either Professor Breasted or you, but was due to some misunderstanding and blundering which I have since succeeded in explaining to my own satisfaction. I only regret that it very nearly broke up the Megiddo expedition, as I learned later. Things seem to be much better now, as far as I can judge."

He ended on a conciliatory note, writing "My own relation to the members of the Megiddo staff is wholly in the direction of peace. Both the Field Director and the Assistant Field Director are men of great ability in their respective lines, with whom I have had the pleasantest relations. If want of tact and occasional misunderstanding disturbed me greatly, I would not be in Jerusalem now."[21]

This seems to have ended the "Albright affair" amicably, for there are no more letters in any of the archives that deal with the situation, even though it is now clear that Albright was either simply incorrect, or gracious enough, to absolve Luckenbill and Breasted of any blame in the matter.

5 Possible Motives

If we are to continue searching for a potential motive, it may be that Albright's trip to Mesopotamia to survey potential sites for excavation is a red herring; it is a barking dog rather than the more important dog that didn't bark, as Sherlock Holmes might have said. Instead of Albright's trip, what may have so thoroughly "put out" Breasted and Luckenbill and triggered everything is a letter that had been sent months earlier, before any of the members of the first Megiddo expedition team had even been chosen. Currently in the archives at the Oriental Institute, it is a letter which was sent to Breasted on 11 June 1925 by George A. Barton, the Secretary and Treasurer of the American Schools of Oriental Research (ASOR), along with a four-page attachment; it might be relevant to note that, at the time, Barton was also serving as the first Director of the Baghdad School.[22]

It begins with a generic opening ("Dear Sir"), rather than being addressed specifically to Breasted, as might have been more proper. It is concerned with a proposal to establish a Biblical Research Foundation in connection with the work of ASOR, and to raise two million dollars to support the foundation. Accompanying

---

[21] Letter from Albright to Luckenbill dated 15 June 1926 (in the APS archives: Albright material, Box 2; see also Running & Freedman, 1975: 131).

[22] Letter from Barton to Breasted dated 11 June 1925 (in the OI Museum Archives: Directors Correspondence Box 053, Folder 003).

the letter is a four-page "Preliminary Prospectus of the Biblical Research Foundation," which includes "A list of the possible first ten volumes of the series to be issued under this program." That list is found on the fourth and final page; it is this list, along with the fact that Barton had sent the letter out of the blue, that seems to be the unexpected smoking gun here and which apparently was the genesis of all the problems.

A suggested volume on the Megiddo inscriptions by the University of Chicago did indeed languish in the tenth and final spot on this list, as Luckenbill said to Albright in his letter of 19 April 1926, but he neglected to mention that there was also another one listed for them, on the actual archaeology of the excavations at Megiddo, which was in the sixth spot. Regardless, the perceived insult was obvious, because ahead of Chicago on the list were volumes by Yale, Princeton, and Harvard on their archaeological excavations, while a volume on the University of Pennsylvania's excavations at Beisan was in the seventh position.

In all, on this list of ten proposed volumes, there were three for Yale (nos. 1, 4, and 9); two for Chicago (nos. 6 and 10); one for Princeton (no. 2); one for Harvard (no. 5); and one for Penn (no. 7); plus two volumes to be written by Fisher on the Corpus of Palestinian Antiquities. On the surface it is, quite frankly, somewhat unclear as to why Breasted and Luckenbill were so outraged, because Chicago was being allotted more volumes than anyone but Yale, and they were the only non-Ivy League school on the list. The problem, I believe, really lies in the fact that Breasted had not been previously consulted about any of this, but there may have also been additional forces at play, including his antagonism towards Albright specifically and an ambivalence towards ASOR as a whole at that point.

Along those lines, Breasted was particularly incensed by the letter from Barton because, as he told Luckenbill, it was "written on stationary bearing the names of the Directors of American Schools of Oriental Research including three from Yale University, a situation which, in itself, has always seem to me quite enough to show that the people who built up this board do not want any cooperation from us. As soon, however, as it comes to matters of money, they write us."[23] Therein, I think, lies part of the problem, for although it is never said out loud, at least in any of the correspondence to this date, Breasted had not been tapped to serve as one of the academic brain trust in charge at ASOR, for it was dominated by scholars from East Coast schools. This was a point which surely rankled him.

Breasted finally replied to Barton on 9 July 1925. He was polite to a fault, though he refers to Barton's letter as having a date of 25 June rather than 11 June, so he either got a second letter in the interim or he got his dates wrong; I would suspect it is the latter, given what he says. In his answer, he said that he found the proposed Biblical Research Foundation of much interest and that he was in favor of the proposal for cooperation, "in so far as it can be made practically feasible."[24]

---

[23] Letter from Breasted to Luckenbill dated 6 July 1925 (in the OI Museum Archives: Directors Correspondence Box 053, Folder 043).

[24] Letter from Breasted to Barton dated 9 July 1925 (in the OI Museum Archives: Directors Correspondence Box 053, Folder 003).

1948   E. H. Cline

However, he also said that it would be necessary to consult with their own Board of Trustees at the University before committing to such a policy of cooperation and, in any event, that they would not take part in the proposed publication series, in which their volumes were listed in the sixth and tenth positions, as we have seen above. His reasoning was that the OI was already committed to publishing a series of volumes on their various excavations and that two of the volumes had already appeared. They could not simply suspend the series at this point. Moreover, the OI, he said, was gaining its own identity at long last and he did not want that affected by "a seeming absorption into a general scheme."

By way of reply, on 12 August 1925, Barton told Breasted that he appreciated his attitude toward the proposed plan. He also agreed that the suggestion they had made to adopt "a uniform format for the publications of the different universities is clearly impractical," for, as Breasted had pointed out, "each university already has its own." He ended by indicating that they would be "grateful for further criticisms and suggestions."[25]

And, a few months later, on the last day of December in 1925, Barton wrote again to Breasted, with the good news that Breasted had been elected a Trustee of ASOR, for an initial term of 3 years.[26] I presume that they had realized their error in the interim, and that Breasted would not play ball, or commit his Institute to any such proposed project, or anything else for that matter, unless he were given a position on the ASOR Board, so they acted promptly, if belatedly, to rectify the situation. Breasted thereafter served as a Trustee of ASOR from 1926 until his death in 1935 (Abt, 2011: 335). I do not know, however, what subsequently became of Barton's proposed plan for cooperation, especially if they had abandoned plans for the publication series.

6   A Final Plot Twist

I now believe that the letters that were flying back and forth in June and July 1925, between Barton and Breasted (re the proposal) and between Breasted and Luckenbill (re their antagonism toward Albright), and well before any team members had even left for Megiddo, provide some of the background and context that underlies this entire situation. However, it seems unlikely that the proposal from Barton was also the cause of their antagonism towards Albright, for he is nowhere mentioned in that proposal.

Why there was such personal animosity is still unclear, especially since Breasted was apparently one of Albright's role models (Feinman, 2004: 18, 131–33, 143 n. 68). It is not clear whether Breasted ever knew that, however, and it would seem that

---

[25] Letter from Barton to Breasted dated 12 August 1925 (in the OI Museum Archives: Directors Correspondence Box 053, Folder 003).

[26] Letter from Barton to Breasted dated 31 December 1925 (in the OI Museum Archives: Directors Correspondence Box 053, Folder 003).

Albright's admiration of Breasted was certainly not reciprocated. Albright's trip to Mesopotamia cannot be the source for Breasted and Luckenbill's initial antagonism, however, since that still lay several months in the future at that point. It could simply be that, for them, Albright personified ASOR, an organization that Breasted does not seem to have been enthusiastic about until he was selected to be on its Board. Obviously, though, more work needs to be done regarding this aspect as to why there does not appear to have been mutual respect between the parties at this point.

Still, if we were playing the board game "Clue" and laying out our final hypotheses regarding the mystery of the "Affair d'Albright," at this point we would be able to identify the culprit, the location, and approximately what happened. We would now be able to say for certain that it was Higgins who did it, at the site of Megiddo, based on instructions given to him by Luckenbill (at least according to Higgins himself).

In fingering Higgins beyond a reasonable doubt, we have been able to corroborate the identification that I first proposed in my book. We have also added in a goodly amount of additional and relevant material which fleshes out the picture of what was really going on behind the scenes during the early days of biblical archaeology.

However, there is one final plot twist, which presents an additional, and possibly insurmountable, problem. In September 2021, at the same time that he called my attention to the October 1926 issue of *BASOR*, Peter Feinman also remarked upon the earlier February 1926 issue. In there, Albright had published an account of the journey that he and Dougherty had just taken to Mesopotamia, in which he states explicitly that they had visited Megiddo on 17 October. Most importantly, and in direct contradiction to what his biographers would later write, he says specifically that they had in fact been taken up on top of the mound at Megiddo. He writes as follows:

> Early in the forenoon of the following day [17 Oct] we spent a short time at Megiddo, where the University of Chicago has just started excavations under the direction of Dr. Clarence S. Fisher, who is ably assisted by Mr. Higgins. We were most kindly shown the beginnings of a work which is to continue for many years. ... As we stood on its summit and looked over the wide Plain of Esdraelon we could not refrain from picturing to ourselves the stirring events which took place in its vicinity (Albright, 1926a: 2).[27]

So, now we have a mystery above and beyond everything else that we have already discussed. Is it possible that Albright would say publicly, and in print for all of his colleagues to see, that he had stood on top of the mound of Megiddo on 17 October, if he hadn't actually done so and was at the very same time complaining privately to Luckenbill and others that he had been denied access? Is it conceivable that he would say one thing in public and quite another thing in private? Or was he, in fact, allowed access to the mound, as he said in *BASOR*? If that is the case, then why did Running and Freedman say that Albright was denied access, if he hadn't been?

---

[27] I am indebted to Peter Feinman for pointing out this article to me (pers. comm., 6 September 2021).

Furthermore, if he hadn't been denied access, then why did Albright subsequently say privately, in his letter to Luckenbill on 15 June 1926, that "the attempt to exclude me from the site of Megiddo...very nearly broke up the Megiddo expedition, as I learned later," which Running and Freedman then paraphrased in their book (i.e., that the attempt to exclude him had "nearly shattered the expedition")? What happened in the aftermath of his visit? Did Fisher and Higgins have a huge fight about it when Fisher got back to camp? That seems likely to have been the case, since Higgins says that Fisher was very angry after learning about whatever was said to Albright during the visit.[28]

So, what are we to conclude? Is there, in fact, no story here after all; no "Mysterious Affair at Armageddon" or "Curious Case of Albright at Megiddo," but instead simply a misinterpretation by his biographers of what actually happened? Did Albright, like the grand old Duke of York in the English nursery rhyme, march up to the top of the hill and then back down again? Or should we suggest a compromise and say that he only went halfway up and was neither up nor down? Note also, however, that Albright said in his private letter(s) that the attempt was to exclude him from the site, by which he may have meant the whole site, including the expedition headquarters, not just to stop him from climbing the mound. In that case, it may have had much more to do with not wanting him to see anything that they might have discovered, such as the Sheshonq inscription, if indeed they had already happened upon it by that time, rather than not wanting him to climb the hill.

At the moment, I have no answers to these final questions, or a solution to this final plot twist, though I strongly suspect that Albright's biographers simply misinterpreted what had happened and that Higgins had indeed taken Albright to the top of the mound at Megiddo, as well as around the dig house and everywhere else, rather than denying him access to anything. I see no reason why Albright would have said one thing publicly and another thing privately, especially if his printed word could have been so easily refuted by those at Megiddo if it were contrary to what had actually transpired.

Thus, my current take on the matter is as follows: Whatever the motivation for the instructions that Luckenbill gave to Higgins regarding Albright and his visit to Megiddo, the orders clearly came from Chicago, despite Luckenbill's protestations to the contrary and Albright's willingness to absolve Luckenbill of responsibility. We must remember what Higgins said in his letter to Luckenbill on 19 May 1926: "I did follow out your instructions in what to tell him [Albright]—which made Fisher very angry." But we must also remember what Fisher said in his letter to Albright on 20 October 1925: "Mr. Higgins said he had orders, and refused to accede to them, and upon your arrival last week was proud and happy to show you all we had." So, I would suggest that Higgins gave the verbal message (whatever it may have been) to Albright, as he later reported to Luckenbill, but then did not obey the rest of the orders that he had been given ("refused to accede," as Fisher said) and

---

[28] Letter from Higgins to Luckenbill dated 19 May 1926 (in the OI Museum Archives: Directors Correspondence Box 058, Folder 019).

instead showed Albright around the site, including taking him up to the top of the mound. This may therefore have all been a bit of a "tempest in a teapot," as the saying goes, but it is also part of the background story which ultimately ended with Higgins being fired in June 1926.

This is a hypothesis that can be tested if and/or when we eventually locate the letter that Albright sent to Luckenbill from Beirut the day after the incident, on 18 October 1925, and read his own words about what actually took place. I can only hope that the missing letter, and perhaps other relevant materials as well, will eventually come to light in one of the relevant archives, for inquiring minds need to resolve what did or did not happen at Megiddo during the "Affair d'Albright."

Author's Note This contribution is dedicated in admiration to Tom Levy, with great respect for his unflagging energy and dedication to asking and answering probing and difficult questions worthy of Sherlock Holmes, and for his interest in a wide variety of topics, including the history of biblical archaeology and the stories of those who have dug before us in the southern Levant. I hope that he will be interested in the mystery surrounding this incident, especially given his own long association (1982-present) with the W.F. Albright Institute of Archaeological Research in Jerusalem (aka the original "American School in Jerusalem" which Albright was directing at the time of this incident).

References

Abt, J. (2011). *American egyptologist: The life of James Henry breasted and the creation of his oriental institute*. University of Chicago Press.

Albright, W. F. (1926a). From Jerusalem to Baghdad Down the Euphrates. *BASOR, 21*, 1–21.

Albright, W. F. (1926b). The excavations at tell Beit Mirsim. *BASOR, 23*, 2–14.

Cline, E. H. (2020). *Digging up Armageddon: The search for the lost city of Solomon*. Princeton University Press.

Feinman, P. D. (2004). *William Foxwell Albright and the origins of biblical archaeology*. Andrews University Press.

Running, L. G., & Freedman, D. N. (n.d.). Rough draft manuscript of *William Foxwell Albright: A twentieth-century genius*. Currently in the possession of Peter Feinman.

Running, L. G., & Freedman, D. N. (1975). *William Foxwell Albright: A twentieth-century genius*. Two Continents Press.

Correction to: "And in Length of Days Understanding" (Job 12:12)

Erez Ben-Yosef and Ian W. N. Jones

Correction to:
E. Ben-Yosef, I. W. N. Jones (eds.), *"And in Length of Days Understanding" (Job 12:12): Essays on Archaeology in the Eastern Mediterranean and Beyond in Honor of Thomas E. Levy,* **Interdisciplinary Contributions to Archaeology, https://doi.org/10.1007/978-3-031-27330-8**

The book has been corrected with the following changes made in Chapters 36, 74, and 75:

- The name "Jane Brown" has been corrected to "Judith Brown" in the caption of Figure 22 in Chapter 36 "The Buqeiʿa Plateau of the Judean Desert in the Southern Levant During the Seventh to Early Sixth Centuries BCE: Iron Age Run-off Farmland or a Pastoralist Rangeland?".
- The text "Additional examples can be found in Chapter xxx in this book by Vaknin et al. (2022)." has been changed to "Additional examples can be found in Vaknin et al. (2022) and in Chapter 34 in this book." in Chapter 74 "Uncertainties in Archaeointensity Research: Implications for the Levantine Archaeomagnetic Curve".
- The word "See =" has been added before the text "Apprehend, discern, grasp, understand, realize, know, form an opinion." and in the title of Chapter 75 "More than Antiquity: How Archaeologists".

The updated original version for these chapters can be found at
https://doi.org/10.1007/978-3-031-27330-8_36
https://doi.org/10.1007/978-3-031-27330-8_74
https://doi.org/10.1007/978-3-031-27330-8_75

© The Author(s), under exclusive license to Springer Nature Switzerland AG 2023
E. Ben-Yosef, I. W. N. Jones (eds.), *"And in Length of Days Understanding" (Job 12:12): Essays on Archaeology in the Eastern Mediterranean and Beyond in Honor of Thomas E. Levy,* Interdisciplinary Contributions to Archaeology,
https://doi.org/10.1007/978-3-031-27330-8_83

Index

A

Abel, F.-M., 945
Abigail, 546
Abu Sinan, 221, 222, 225, 229, 231, 232, 239, 240
Abusir, 1057–1066, 1807, 1808, 1835
Adits, 1308, 1430
Administration, 488, 498, 514, 718, 719, 791, 808, 820, 995, 1007, 1018, 1020, 1040, 1211, 1392, 1399, 1408, 1440, 1526, 1812, 1882
ADNA, 116, 458, 580
Aegean, 541, 558, 574, 578, 628, 691, 701, 1186, 1189, 1191, 1193, 1204, 1215, 1288, 1289, 1293, 1294, 1298, 1308, 1313–1315, 1324, 1327, 1328, 1336, 1381, 1382, 1400, 1469–1487, 1519–1521
Aerial photography, 1108, 1111, 1115, 1118, 1597, 1604, 1607
Africa, 12, 74, 414, 473, 494, 497, 557, 575, 576, 580, 699, 1059, 1076, 1080, 1259, 1306, 1500, 1546, 1731, 1757, 1813, 1902
Agamim, 129, 298, 302–306, 309–311
Age profiles, 70, 76, 89, 90, 164, 271
Agriculture, 10, 16, 21, 45, 59, 61, 76, 116, 118, 127, 129, 136, 187, 268, 285, 414, 430, 474, 481, 492, 641, 683, 687, 712, 717, 840, 842, 888, 948, 1804, 1827, 1866, 1883
Ahiram, 542
Ahmose, 1050

Ajloun, 1452, 1453
Akko, 1204, 1494, 1718, 1911–1930
Al-Hajar Mountains, 1403
Alloys, 1346, 1364, 1375, 1377, 1396, 1408, 1422, 1426, 1427, 1431, 1435–1436
Al-Muʿarradja, 1210, 1217
Alois Musil, 1158
Altiplano, 1420, 1421, 1427, 1432–1436
Amarna Letters, 517, 702, 1203–1205, 1347, 1381
Amasis I, 1060
Amasis II, 1060
Ambassador-Fund/Cultural Antiquities Task Force, 1703
Amber, 574, 579, 1313
American Center of Oriental Research (ACOR), 1150, 1702, 1711, 1713
American University of Madaba (AUM), 1707, 1712
Amman, 426, 620, 945, 947, 988, 1703, 1711, 1856, 1863, 1864, 1876
Amman Airport Structure, 1204, 1213
Amman Citadel, 1213
Ammon, 513, 620, 873, 908, 912, 915, 947, 954, 1406, 1809, 1813, 1814, 1816
Ammonite, 620, 622, 902, 908, 950, 952, 954, 1161, 1400, 1814
Amphoriskos, 610, 613, 908–910
Ancient Therme, 1471, 1472, 1486
Ancón, 1434, 1440
Andahuaylas, 1433
Andes, 1419–1441

© The Editor(s) (if applicable) and The Author(s), under exclusive license to Springer Nature Switzerland AG 2023
E. Ben-Yosef, I. W. N. Jones (eds.), *"And in Length of Days Understanding" (Job 12:12): Essays on Archaeology in the Eastern Mediterranean and Beyond in Honor of Thomas E. Levy*, Interdisciplinary Contributions to Archaeology,
https://doi.org/10.1007/978-3-031-27330-8

1953

1954 Index

Animal, 10, 59–77, 84, 118–120, 148, 208, 236, 268, 301, 352, 455, 645, 698, 814, 846, 933, 1050, 1058, 1147, 1231, 1331, 1363, 1404, 1424, 1510, 1606, 1735, 1785, 1812, 1833, 1858, 1904
Animal husbandry, 120, 136, 237, 268, 285, 891, 1331, 1812
Animal remains, 24, 103, 455, 464, 650, 664, 668, 669
Anthropological archaeology, 1802
Anthropomorphic ossuaries, 127, 236
Anubis, 635, 1021, 1027–1029, 1033, 1034, 1061
Apion, 1034, 1038
Apis, 1060, 1061
Apries, 1060
Arabah, 200, 381, 429, 538, 541, 544, 545, 574, 697, 698, 1123, 1141, 1146, 1157, 1162, 1171–1173, 1181–1194, 1201–1221, 1228, 1231, 1234, 1238, 1240, 1248, 1392, 1402, 1450, 1728
Arabah Hand Made Ware (AHMW), 1215, 1216
Arad, 45, 64, 403–404, 577, 697, 761, 1087, 1093–1095, 1100, 1228, 1240
Araʿir, 1210
Aram, 726, 790
Archaeological gaze, 1786
Archaeological Park East, St. George's Church, 1708, 1713
Archaeological Park West, 1703, 1705, 1708, 1713, 1718
Archaeological practice, 559, 1778, 1783, 1793
Archaeological technology, 40, 50, 477, 772
Archaeological theory, 474, 476, 480, 489, 502
Archaeology, 4, 14, 115, 174, 192, 208, 224, 380, 440, 472, 537, 556, 574, 619, 641, 683, 724, 754, 788, 812, 840, 901, 924, 948, 1058, 1090, 1108, 1138, 1175, 1187, 1202, 1255, 1368, 1392, 1450, 1508, 1541, 1582, 1628, 1657, 1684, 1703, 1725, 1777, 1789, 1802, 1856, 1912, 1934
Archaeometallurgy, 1304–1306, 1450
Archaic, 488, 515, 988, 989, 1001, 1006, 1060, 1432, 1470, 1472, 1475, 1479, 1823–1852
Ard el-Samra, 223, 225, 233, 237
Argentina, 1420, 1430, 1432, 1440
Armour, 582
Aroer, 579, 1856, 1863, 1864
Ar-Rumayl, 901

Arsenic, 285, 306, 308, 1190, 1337, 1339, 1340, 1343–1345, 1432, 1435, 1437, 1439
Artifact collection, 1704
Asherat, 223, 225, 229, 232
Ash-Shorabat, 1209
Ashurbanipal, 1059
Asia, 10, 12, 15, 16, 46, 497, 557, 563, 577, 583, 1027, 1029, 1035, 1037, 1040, 1393, 1400, 1408, 1476, 1813
Assemblages, 21, 22, 24, 26, 28, 30, 40, 62, 64, 70, 71, 76, 85, 87, 101, 115, 137, 174, 177, 186, 206, 209, 214, 223, 271, 300, 307, 327, 353, 378, 430–431, 446, 449, 545, 627, 671, 759, 777, 788, 901, 1096, 1149, 1294, 1296, 1298, 1405, 1430, 1508, 1519, 1527, 1543, 1784, 1786, 1906
Assur Balu, 915
Assyria, 726, 915, 1059, 1402
Astarte, 1725, 1727, 1728, 1730, 1733, 1739
Atacama, 1426, 1428–1430, 1434, 1435, 1440
Atacamite, 1428
Atarus, 947

B

Baluʿa, 923–940, 1210
Baqah, 1204
Barqa el-Hetiye, 1094
Barrel flask, 908
Barzillai, 546–550
Basalt, 136, 148, 149, 157, 159, 162, 168, 179, 183, 187, 231, 235, 236, 239, 240, 246–248, 253–255, 257, 260, 302, 306–308, 311, 324, 336, 351, 353, 395, 424, 438, 614, 741, 789, 868, 928–930, 938–940, 1213, 1215–1219, 1428, 1873
Basalt chalices, 236, 239, 240
Bata, 1021, 1025, 1027–1030, 1033, 1034, 1037
Batan Grande, 1430, 1441
Beersheba-Arad Valley, 1205
Be'er Sheva, 74, 84, 85, 179, 209, 269–272, 282–285, 641, 694, 696, 1121, 1228, 1232, 1236, 1240, 1245, 1248
Beer Sheva basin, 694, 697, 1213
Beersheba sites, 282–285
Be'er Ẓonam, 223, 225, 232
Benjamin Plateau, 772, 777–779, 1001
Beno Rothenberg, 1159
Ben-Shlomo, D., 355, 390, 575, 602, 603, 607, 609, 621, 635, 775, 779
Besor-Grar complex, 269–272, 282–285

Index

1955

Beth Shean, 174, 187, 444, 622, 631, 779, 787–808, 1041, 1189, 1191, 1204, 1934
Beth Shemesh, 578, 711, 759, 772, 1451
Bezer of Reuben, 945, 946
Bifacial celt, 299
Bioanthropology, 271, 286
Bitumen, 134, 301, 311, 579, 894, 1555
Black-on-Red (BoR), 545, 775, 916, 917
Blow furnaces, 1431
Bokchoris, 1035, 1036
Bone mass, 275
Bones, 19, 20, 22, 26, 74, 75, 85, 87–90, 97–99, 103, 129, 130, 132, 136, 164–168, 193, 202, 271–276, 281, 346, 353, 455, 456, 459, 462–465, 645, 649, 650, 652, 653, 655, 660, 662, 664, 669, 733, 776, 814, 860, 867, 933, 1039, 1097, 1099, 1276, 1280–1283, 1606, 1613, 1891, 1893, 1905
Bostra, 946
Bottle, 915–917
Bowl, 209, 229, 230, 299, 301, 304, 346, 348, 350, 356, 433, 645, 691, 735, 847, 911, 932, 934, 954, 1261–1263, 1265, 1268, 1290, 1294, 1295, 1449, 1456, 1460–1463, 1879
Bozra, 946
Bozrah/Bosor of Gilead, 945
Bozrah of Edom, 945, 946
Bozrah of Moab, 945
Breath interface, 1726, 1740, 1742, 1744, 1750
Bronze, 644, 684, 815, 1076, 1162, 1193, 1292–1294, 1296, 1298, 1316, 1332, 1339, 1360–1370, 1379, 1405, 1426, 1435, 1439, 1452, 1481, 1486, 1832, 1834
Bronze Age, 14, 16, 28, 31, 46, 52, 61, 75, 102, 118, 129, 133, 136, 176, 246, 255, 284, 325, 391, 414, 428, 455, 456, 479, 492–494, 501, 506–512, 514, 536, 567, 577, 629, 701, 712, 733, 754, 815, 951, 1038, 1069–1082, 1087–1102, 1158, 1182, 1187, 1202–1205, 1231–1232, 1237–1239, 1258, 1303–1318, 1323–1347, 1397, 1402, 1481, 1495, 1501, 1604, 1617, 1726, 1738–1740, 1834
Bronze objects, 456, 545, 1186, 1315, 1334, 1364, 1369, 1471, 1484
Bubasteion, 1061
Buildings, 120, 121, 127, 133, 149, 153, 158, 162, 227, 302, 309, 311, 314, 343, 390,
476, 482, 483, 507, 619, 647, 690–693, 696, 703, 713, 719, 734, 737, 739–742, 760–762, 777, 789, 806, 808, 851, 902, 951, 1158, 1264, 1308, 1405, 1440, 1475, 1588, 1594, 1631, 1703, 1781, 1857, 1865, 1870–1876
Bun ingot, 1324, 1330, 1331, 1346
Burials, 116, 117, 122–137, 213, 234–236, 240, 271–273, 299, 344, 356, 378, 428, 431, 455, 466, 478, 543, 626–628, 635, 739, 1017, 1058, 1062, 1071, 1234, 1426, 1433, 1435, 1473, 1545, 1732, 1866, 1890, 1891, 1899, 1904
Burnish, 232, 613, 915, 933
Burnt Palace, 1703, 1705, 1708, 1709, 1713
Busayra, 538, 911
Busra ash-Sham, 946
Busrana, 946
Butchering, 83–109, 168, 658, 661, 1097
B[w]trt, 956, 957
Byblos, 22, 542–543, 994, 1039, 1730

C

Caleb, 1161, 1162
Callejon Larrache, 1426
Caloric modeling, 1568
Cambyses II, 1060
Camera equipment, 1712
Canaanite blade, 303, 306
Capacity building, 105, 1704, 1719
Cape Gelidonya, 1324, 1328, 1330
Caprine, 14–17, 20, 24–26, 60, 64, 67, 70–72, 75–77, 163–165, 281–284
Carabaya, 1432
Caravans, 893, 990, 1203, 1207, 1235, 1243, 1430, 1863, 1865, 1876
Caries, 275, 277, 279
Casa Parroquial, 1426
Casemate walls, 603, 605–607, 609, 611, 614, 618, 620, 621, 714, 717, 718, 737, 740, 773, 864, 926
Casma and Supe, 1420
Casserite, 1439
Casting, 538, 1091, 1094, 1095, 1097, 1207, 1237, 1310, 1326, 1330, 1340, 1344, 1364–1370, 1375, 1377, 1433, 1435, 1437, 1450, 1668, 1724, 1785, 1823
Cave Archaeology, 47, 115, 116, 127, 129, 135, 205–214, 240, 258, 301, 849, 881, 1170, 1430, 1591, 1858
Cave of the Treasure, 47, 205–214

Index

Cemeteries, 127, 129, 136, 137, 234–235, 268, 273, 312, 314, 378, 381, 411–440, 457, 478, 544, 627–629, 1331, 1471, 1481, 1486, 1896, 1899, 1902, 1905
Centers of Pottery Production, 238, 359–383, 1217, 1476, 1482
Central hill country, 500, 779, 1215, 1216
Cerro Rico de Potosí, 1435
Cerro Songoy, 1430
Chaeremon, 1034, 1048
Chalcocite, 1428
Chalcolithic, 16, 28, 31, 39–53, 59–77, 83–109, 127–129, 135, 136, 173–187, 191–202, 219–240, 245–262, 267–286, 295–314, 323–338, 343–357, 1227–1250
Chalcolithic Cult, 135, 187, 1732
Chalcopyrite, 1428
Chancay, 1438
Chan Chan, 1430
Chavín, 1431, 1436
Chicken, 578
Chile, 1419, 1425–1427, 1430, 1433, 1434, 1440
Chimú, 1422, 1431, 1437–1440
China, 493, 580, 583, 1757, 1834, 1848, 1876
Chipped stone tools, 85, 94, 99, 102, 103
Chiripa, 1434
Chongoyape, 1436
Chotuna, 1441
Chronicler, 712, 1160, 1165, 1171, 1424, 1809
Chrysocolla, 1428, 1434, 1440
Church of the Prophet Elias, 1708
Church of the Virgin Mary, 1708, 1714
Churn, 61, 76, 209, 223, 239, 250, 260, 299, 300, 302, 310, 314, 327, 337, 348, 866
Cisjordan, 559, 952, 1008, 1203, 1204, 1216
Citron, 578, 1901
Clark, D.R., 1702–1704, 1714
Clark, J.A., 494
Clark, J.E., 311, 1134
Classical, 474, 556–560, 566, 568, 971, 1470, 1472, 1473, 1479, 1495, 1519, 1831
Cleveland, 1158, 1172
Climate, 11–15, 25, 29, 30, 43, 51, 52, 64, 76, 147, 192, 269, 306, 537–538, 661, 684, 687, 844, 888, 1135, 1141, 1207, 1210, 1400, 1500, 1545, 1555, 1615, 1643, 1678, 1688, 1802, 1835, 1896
Climate change, 25, 29, 30, 52, 1400, 1544–1546, 1643
Coastal changes, 1530
Coastal Plain, 136, 174, 178, 220, 225, 236, 302, 377, 444, 503, 690, 694, 696–700,

704, 729, 748, 966, 1171, 1202, 1205, 1215, 1216, 1221, 1595
Collaborative approach, 1718
Collaborative design ideation, 1738–1740
Colombia, 1419, 1435, 1437, 1438, 1456
Colonial perspectives, 1718
Commercial networks, 652
Connective tissue, 582
Connectivity, 20, 440, 447, 574–586, 771–781, 844, 891, 1065, 1092, 1314, 1407, 1494, 1541, 1542, 1547, 1548, 1712, 1802, 1805, 1816
Consumer-producer spectrum, 1134, 1317, 1843
Cooking pot, 364, 430, 443–450, 579, 613, 645, 738, 760, 775, 860, 861, 866, 873, 937, 951–953, 983, 1040, 1217, 1220, 1519, 1529, 1794, 1795, 1842
Copiapó, 1425, 1440
Copper, 74, 84, 211, 236, 255, 302, 308, 458, 538, 698, 704, 1071, 1081, 1087–1102, 1108, 1116, 1122, 1135, 1155–1176, 1181–1194, 1201–1221, 1227–1250, 1304–1309, 1311–1313, 1316, 1324–1346, 1382, 1391–1408, 1419–1441, 1450, 1483, 1605, 1723–1751, 1757, 1831, 1833, 1836, 1837, 1893
Copper production, 337, 364, 509, 510, 538, 544, 808, 1088, 1091–1101, 1108–1110, 1125, 1135–1151, 1173, 1183, 1184, 1191, 1193, 1202, 1205–1208, 1212, 1220, 1228, 1236, 1239, 1259, 1263, 1304, 1316, 1331, 1346, 1367, 1392–1394, 1397, 1402, 1407, 1725, 1727–1730, 1732, 1739, 1823
Copper slag, 1071, 1116, 1137, 1167, 1174, 1239, 1329, 1396, 1434, 1615
Cornet, 209, 213, 231, 238–240, 250, 260, 299, 302–305, 310, 311, 314, 327, 337
Cornwall, 464
Covellite, 1428
Cow, 63, 578
Craftsmen ehelle cemetery, 465, 466
Craft Specialization, 132, 137, 180, 285, 324
Cribra orbitalia, 275, 276, 281, 284
Crops, 11, 15, 51, 52, 70, 202, 269, 271, 281, 284, 285, 661, 682, 727, 874, 890, 1024, 1147, 1804
Crucibles, 85, 1091, 1311, 1326, 1346, 1422, 1431, 1440, 1470, 1482
Cultural diversity, 1718
Cultural Heritage Coordinating Committee (CHCC), 1703, 1705

Index

Cultural preservation, 1119, 1630, 1643, 1698, 1704, 1706
Cultural Property Agreement, 1719
Cup, 249, 381, 433, 644, 666, 667, 673, 716, 907, 908, 1001, 1150, 1477, 1879
Cupisnique, 1433
Cuprite, 1397, 1428, 1434
Curamba, 1440
Cusco, 1430, 1440
Cuzco, 1424, 1425, 1433, 1437
CyArk, 1707–1709, 1711–1717, 1721
Cyberarchaeology, 1725–1738
Cypriot pottery, 545, 628, 629, 703, 775, 789, 908, 917–919, 1072, 1076, 1079, 1081, 1190, 1193, 1204, 1304–1306, 1308, 1309, 1311–1316, 1326, 1332, 1345, 1379, 1521, 1615
Cypro-minoan, 1328
Cyprus, 510, 578, 644, 701, 915, 1036, 1069–1082, 1186, 1303–1318, 1326–1330, 1337, 1343, 1345–1347, 1360, 1381, 1509, 1519, 1529, 1603–1621, 1732, 1740, 1795, 1834

D

Dadan, 1169
Daidan, 1169
Damascus, 448, 765, 790, 940, 1864, 1924
Dana, 1119, 1169, 1182, 1585–1587, 1593, 1596, 1597
Data collection/capture, 1108, 1598, 1669, 1709–1713, 1734, 1857
David, A., 85
David, C.B., 1246
David, R., 1077
David, W.P.1, 1612
Decolonization, 1718, 1778, 1787
Dedan, 1169
Deforestation, 1307, 1546
Dental disease, 269, 272, 275, 278, 286, 577, 649, 653, 660, 1077
Dental hypoplasia, 275, 281
Department of Antiquities of Jordan, 429, 1703, 1707
Desert Highway, 948, 1207, 1863, 1879, 1881
Dhiban, 957, 1856, 1860, 1863, 1877, 1881
Dhiban plateau, 901, 920, 1855–1883
Diaguita, 1427, 1440
Dibon, 504, 901, 913, 918, 956
Diet, 51, 76, 164, 269, 278, 281, 285, 286, 465, 652, 870, 872, 1134, 1795

Digital documentation, 1582, 1584, 1589, 1642, 1685, 1691, 1703–1710, 1717, 1719
Digital platforms, 1108, 1703
Disease load, 271, 275, 277, 281, 286
Diverse perspectives, 1718
Diversity of views, 1718
Divided Monarchy, 811
Djoser, 1058, 1061–1063, 1065
Domestic Mode of Production (DMP), 133, 359, 363
Donkey, 61, 71, 74–77, 132, 136, 268, 949, 1004, 1100, 1101, 1241, 1243–1244, 1331, 1450, 1837, 1875
Dor, 272–279, 281, 669, 1493–1503, 1541–1544, 1547
Dor, Tantura, 1495, 1496, 1542
Dos Cabezas, 1426
Drone, 153, 156–158, 615, 618, 886, 889, 1517, 1604, 1614, 1709, 1713, 1714
Dugouts, 1475, 1480

E

Early Bronze IV, 453–466
Early Iron Age (EIA), 472, 476, 478, 479, 484, 501, 509, 510, 517, 535–551, 558, 577–579, 582, 584, 626, 636, 639–674, 691, 703, 713, 715, 735, 759, 813, 951–952, 1039, 1041, 1108, 1110, 1123–1125, 1135, 1138, 1183, 1201–1221, 1242, 1314, 1381, 1396, 1397, 1399–1404, 1406, 1461, 1470, 1730, 1756, 1833
Ecclesiastical History, 1169
Economy, 10, 15, 22, 24, 25, 29, 52, 59–77, 120, 136, 163–166, 267–269, 271, 281, 284, 285, 296, 302, 308, 313, 324, 474, 510, 548, 551, 575, 639–674, 712, 719, 775, 820, 841, 869–874, 892, 974, 994, 1010, 1134, 1259, 1305, 1308, 1313, 1356, 1384, 1392, 1396, 1400, 1407, 1429, 1440, 1470, 1486, 1541, 1546, 1619, 1703, 1716, 1823–1851, 1869, 1876
Ecuador, 1420, 1434, 1435, 1437, 1438
Edom, 476, 506, 509–512, 516, 517, 519, 537, 538, 546, 562, 911–913, 919, 920, 945, 946, 978, 1000, 1108, 1110, 1135, 1138, 1141, 1155, 1157–1159, 1161, 1162, 1168, 1169, 1174, 1175, 1182, 1202, 1209, 1228, 1242, 1256, 1404, 1406, 1658, 1661, 1809, 1813, 1814, 1816, 1880
Eggshell pottery, 1477–1479, 1487

Egypt, 45, 60, 164, 430, 488, 542, 558, 578, 636, 690, 726, 817, 981, 1014, 1053, 1058, 1071, 1093, 1193, 1203, 1228, 1257, 1306, 1327, 1361, 1402, 1521, 1542, 1555, 1718, 1729, 1803, 1835, 1911, 1934
1880s, 1717
Ein-Gedi, 61, 199, 207, 262, 305, 1279, 1290, 1585
Ein Yahav, 1095, 1096, 1238
Elam, 580, 582
Electrum, 1429, 1832
Elephantine stela, 1030, 1031
Eliba'al, 542, 543, 550
Elite (elite culture), 52, 120, 133, 137, 300, 314, 391, 406, 457, 458, 464–466, 478, 480, 482, 485, 490, 492, 494, 503, 536, 541–551, 565, 577, 578, 584, 586, 704, 727, 733, 746, 774, 779, 780, 820, 939, 996, 1020, 1022, 1058, 1064–1066, 1094, 1124, 1126, 1138, 1147, 1183, 1277, 1306, 1315, 1392, 1393, 1399, 1402, 1405–1408, 1424, 1426, 1431, 1440, 1708, 1779, 1803, 1833, 1838, 1844
El-Medeiyineh. *see* Khirbat al-Mudayna
Engaging community, 1697, 1778
En Gedi, 205–214, 343, 353, 1261
English Training Center, 1707, 1713
Enkomi, 1304, 1315–1317, 1325, 1329, 1355–1384
Environment, 4, 5, 8, 10–14, 19–22, 24, 27–31, 44, 60, 64, 75, 116, 120, 269, 281, 283–285, 306, 308, 352, 472, 478, 479, 481, 489, 495–497, 601, 659, 687, 702, 803, 871, 888, 979, 981, 983, 994, 997, 1101, 1126, 1134, 1135, 1149, 1221, 1304, 1307, 1308, 1405, 1422, 1432, 1496, 1497, 1500–1503, 1510, 1512, 1518, 1544, 1589, 1598, 1610, 1614, 1621, 1641, 1645, 1648–1650, 1658–1660, 1669, 1673, 1676–1680, 1726, 1733, 1734, 1744, 1749, 1781, 1783, 1802, 1807
Environmental variations, 659, 1610
Esarhaddon, 1059
Ethnic distinctions, 455, 464
Eurasia, 574–576, 579, 581, 583
Eusebius Pamphilias of Caesarea, 1168
Ex 2:10, 1052, 1053
Exotica, 585
Explorations in Eastern, 1156, 1159, 1160, 1167, 1169

Export of copper, 1306
Ezion-geber, 1159, 1172, 1173

F
Famagusta Bay, 1507–1530
Fauna, 13–15, 20, 22–24, 64–75, 83–109, 122, 164, 237–238, 578, 639–674, 712, 1483, 1501
Faunal analysis, 164, 649–650
Faynan, 8, 12, 19, 31, 74, 509, 538, 544–546, 562, 788, 808, 1092–1096, 1100, 1101, 1107–1126, 1134–1141, 1146–1150, 1161, 1169, 1170, 1173, 1176, 1181–1194, 1202, 1214, 1220, 1221, 1228, 1232, 1234–1240, 1242, 1243, 1255–1268, 1308, 1395, 1404, 1450, 1684, 1823, 1824, 1833
Faynan, Phaeno, 1169
Finkelstein I., 220, 444, 477, 561, 567, 585, 661, 682, 712, 725, 754, 772, 812, 892, 940, 983, 1038, 1093, 1110, 1205, 1227, 1404, 1451, 1791, 1814
Fish, 87, 89, 465, 578, 581, 651, 652, 665, 667, 668, 670, 776, 1072, 1080, 1081, 1527–1529
Flint, 14, 17, 20, 22, 28, 30, 31, 120, 136, 158, 174, 177, 178, 182, 184, 186, 223, 233–234, 238, 239, 246, 248, 249, 253, 254, 257–260, 299, 301, 302, 305–308, 311, 323–337, 602, 614, 868, 872, 1218, 1590, 1591, 1865
Food processing, 103, 120, 1099, 1144
Food production, 52, 1134, 1674, 1783, 1834
Fragmentation, 86, 329, 585, 659, 1805
Frank, F., 1158, 1245
FTIR, 1462

G
Gad, 864, 948–950, 953, 988, 1001, 1002
Galena, 1428, 1429, 1431, 1440
Galilean pottery, 239
Geographic Information Systems (GIS), 114, 1107–1126, 1234, 1264, 1512, 1517, 1553–1574, 1582, 1585, 1589, 1594, 1596–1598, 1603–1621, 1642, 1658–1660, 1672–1674, 1679, 1680, 1915
Gezer, 444, 514, 723–748, 773, 962–967, 974, 993, 994, 1007, 1008, 1019, 1023, 1040, 1204, 1789

Index 1959

Ghassulian, 61, 62, 64–67, 69–76, 118, 120, 121, 127–129, 135–137, 174, 179, 187, 199, 206–214, 219–240, 268, 269, 271, 296–313, 1732

Gibbor ḥayil, 548

Gilat, 66, 71, 72, 74, 75, 128, 193, 195, 199, 201, 202, 210, 214, 236, 255, 262, 269, 272–283, 300, 305, 307, 343, 353

Gilding, 1436, 1438, 1439

GIS Least-Cost Modeling, 1553–1574

Glass, 85, 579, 581, 869, 1072, 1078–1081, 1088, 1092–1094, 1323, 1324, 1470, 1501, 1542, 1684, 1873, 1892, 1893, 1902, 1906

Glaze, 917, 1075, 1520–1522

Globalization, 582, 1790, 1802–1804, 1816

Goat, 15, 17, 18, 20, 22, 24, 27, 60–64, 71, 72, 74, 76, 87, 89, 90, 92–98, 101, 102, 120, 164, 165, 237, 238, 282, 283, 346, 464, 546, 649, 652, 653, 657, 659–669, 671–673, 690, 704, 841, 844, 858, 860, 869–871, 879, 888, 891, 893, 1039, 1311, 1606, 1864

Gold, 130, 456, 458, 464, 817, 820, 985, 1031, 1072–1076, 1080, 1081, 1296, 1311, 1365, 1393, 1394, 1398, 1421–1441, 1481, 1482, 1486, 1719, 1824, 1825, 1827–1832, 1836, 1838, 1848, 1906, 1940

Gold alloys, 1431, 1437–1439

Gordon, C.H., 1157

Gossans, 1308, 1429

Grar, 210, 257, 262, 269–272, 282–285, 300, 305, 307, 641, 661

Graves, 115, 117, 121–124, 130, 132, 134, 193, 201, 272, 356, 378, 446, 454–459, 463–466, 478, 629, 858, 864, 868, 1266, 1480, 1484, 1486, 1545, 1846, 1857, 1866, 1889–1907

Greece, 429, 510, 545, 579, 582, 698, 808, 814, 988, 1288, 1293, 1294, 1298, 1313, 1471, 1476, 1481, 1483, 1582, 1647, 1832

Ground stone, 99, 102, 174, 177, 179, 183, 184, 186, 187, 268, 301, 302, 307, 325, 327, 336, 614, 933, 1088, 1097, 1310–1312, 1402, 1475, 1605, 1617, 1619

H

Hadad, 546

Hagrites, 949

Hala Sultan Teke, 578

Hala Sultan Tekke, 1069–1082, 1304, 1317, 1329

Hammerstone, 162, 301, 1095, 1096, 1433, 1434, 1672, 1674

Hamrat Ifdan Sounding A (RHI-A), 1214

Hanigalbat, 1203

Hathor, 1184, 1187, 1384, 1725, 1727–1730, 1732, 1733, 1739, 1741, 1743, 1746, 1748, 1749

Haurān, 945, 946

Hazor, 444, 507, 514, 579, 581, 773, 774, 780, 997, 1019, 1184, 1185, 1190, 1191, 1193, 1345, 1346, 1451, 1453, 1522, 1757, 1770

Health status, 267–286

Hebrew Bible, 201, 472, 477, 480, 488, 501, 502, 504, 506, 510, 512–514, 519, 536, 540, 545–549, 556, 567, 814, 816, 818, 947, 948, 1042, 1052

Hebron, 546, 696, 718, 757, 892, 1161, 1163, 1171, 1187, 1896, 1906

Hejaz, 510, 1204, 1212, 1213, 1215

Hematite, 246–248, 255, 260, 306, 308, 1422, 1428, 1433, 1455

Heraclitus law, 1057–1066

Heritage Trail, 1708

Hesban, 944, 951–954, 1210, 1219, 1878

Hillel ben Garis, 1170

Hippolytus Hall, 1708, 1710, 1713, 1714

Ḥisban, 902, 912

Historicity of the Bible, 567

Honeybee, 578, 581

Horemheb, 1023, 1079, 1081

Huaca Menor, 1426

Huajje, 1434

Huantajaya, 1430, 1440

Huayrachina (wayra), 1431

Hula decoration, 232, 238, 240

Hydrology, 1109, 1120–1126, 1609, 1612, 1620

Hymn to the King in his Chariot, 1027–1030, 1033

I

Iberia, 479, 581, 1289, 1293, 1294

I Chronicles, 1160–1165, 1170–1172, 1174, 1175

Image-based modeling, 1107–1126, 1604

Imhotep, 1060, 1061, 1063

Immigrant families, 1717

Inca, 1420, 1422–1427, 1429, 1430, 1434–1436, 1439–1441

Incensario, 1425
Inclusions, 4, 129, 177, 231, 332, 437, 563, 635, 666, 905, 908, 925, 934, 1036, 1213–1215, 1217–1219, 1312, 1383, 1397, 1433, 1454, 1647, 1671, 1742, 1778, 1805
India, 492, 559, 578, 581, 1076, 1450, 1451
Indian Ocean, 580, 585
Indigenous transportation, 1553–1574
Indigenous voices, 1717
Infectious diseases, 284, 286
Ingot, 1093, 1095, 1099, 1101, 1182, 1186, 1187, 1190, 1192, 1193, 1238, 1304, 1306, 1310, 1313–1317, 1323–1347, 1355–1384, 1397, 1407, 1455, 1739, 1825, 1832–1834
Inscriptions, 492, 494, 502, 504, 506, 507, 536, 539–544, 549, 550, 579, 820, 821, 868, 881, 939, 947, 949, 953, 954, 956, 957, 992, 1015, 1019, 1022–1024, 1029, 1031, 1075, 1158, 1176, 1243, 1244, 1247, 1248, 1262, 1263, 1369, 1380, 1473, 1645, 1691, 1729, 1785, 1813, 1856, 1878, 1943, 1947, 1950
Intangible, 119, 518, 519, 563, 774, 1628, 1718, 1723–1750, 1825
Interaction design, 1726, 1727, 1733, 1737–1738, 1742, 1750
Interaction spheres, 536, 541, 550, 584, 1094, 1306, 1314, 1556
Interoception, 1726, 1737, 1750
Interregional connections, 187, 1208
Intra-action, 1726, 1727, 1733, 1737–1738, 1742, 1750
Intramural burial, 629
Ir, 1155–1176, 1216, 1218, 1219
Iron, 245, 248, 261, 282, 440, 510, 538, 543, 545, 577–579, 581, 582, 584, 601–603, 605, 607, 608, 610, 611, 614, 615, 618–623, 628, 629, 635, 668, 671–673, 681–705, 711–719, 754–766, 775, 778, 788, 789, 794, 806, 808, 815, 829, 830, 901, 915, 926, 927, 929–940, 951–955, 964–966, 971, 977–1010, 1039, 1041, 1161, 1172, 1175, 1184, 1185, 1191–1193, 1203, 1205–1212, 1214–1217, 1220, 1221, 1241, 1342, 1395, 1397, 1407, 1408, 1429, 1430, 1432, 1439, 1449–1464, 1471, 1481, 1483, 1484, 1486, 1497, 1499, 1501, 1543, 1544, 1658, 1661, 1724, 1731, 1796, 1857, 1866, 1872, 1873, 1893, 1902

Iron Age, 61, 149, 174, 199, 201, 224, 245, 426, 472, 536, 558, 574, 602, 625, 641, 681, 713, 725, 754, 775, 788, 812, 840, 902, 924, 944, 962, 992, 1037, 1108, 1134, 1155, 1183, 1202, 1228, 1256, 1276, 1288, 1298, 1314, 1364, 1392, 1451, 1470, 1495, 1519, 1672, 1730, 1756, 1796, 1814, 1833, 1857
Iron Age I, 501, 503, 504, 506–509, 511, 516, 625–636, 666, 725, 732, 734, 735, 744, 746, 759, 774, 777, 791, 945, 974, 1038–1041, 1054, 1147, 1185, 1204
Iron Age II, 577, 775, 840–842, 847, 849, 859, 866, 868, 870, 900–902, 928, 945, 951, 965, 969, 972, 1207, 1241
Iron Age archaeology, 510, 688–694, 815, 860, 1155, 1452
Iron Age paleobotany, 1135
Iron bar, 1458
Iron bloom, 1461
Iron production, 1451–1453, 1455, 1456, 1460–1462
Irsw, 1031–1033
Islamic conquest, 565, 1541, 1544
Island Southeast Asia, 583
Isotope analysis, 164, 545, 690, 1092, 1100, 1186–1188, 1266, 1292, 1304, 1327–1329, 1331, 1334, 1337, 1338, 1340, 1394, 1454, 1456
Israel Stele, 1014, 1015, 1024, 1036, 1040
Italy, 479, 578, 1074, 1546, 1549, 1827
Iufaa, 1061, 1064, 1066

J

Jahaz, 944, 946, 947, 957
Jalul, 902, 910, 943–958, 1210, 1878, 1879
Jehu, 544, 996
Jemeil, 919
Jequetepeque, 1426
Jeremiah, 517, 945, 993, 1169, 1175
Jericho, 45, 47, 49, 62, 64, 70, 76, 123, 129–131, 268, 325, 366, 368, 393, 401, 403, 439, 446, 448, 453–466, 602, 621, 622, 843, 846, 870, 874, 892, 1161
Jericho tombs O1, P12, P20 and P22, 455, 463, 465
Jerobpam II, 772, 780
Jerusalem, 85, 87, 103, 174, 257, 261, 344, 365, 380, 382, 501–503, 507, 508, 513, 514, 517, 540, 578, 579, 581, 635, 649, 718, 753–766, 771–781, 817, 846, 847, 892–894, 927, 963, 981, 986, 987, 989, 1048, 1160, 1204, 1247, 1259,

Index

1261–1263, 1265, 1266, 1268, 1279, 1291, 1584, 1593–1595, 1598, 1711, 1759, 1789, 1896, 1897, 1901–1904, 1935, 1936, 1938, 1940, 1942, 1946, 1951

Jiskairumoko, 1421, 1432

Jordan, 3, 8, 40, 59, 147, 174, 192, 209, 220, 256, 324, 360, 399, 411, 444, 455, 478, 537, 561, 578, 601, 694, 808, 851, 901, 924, 945, 986, 1040, 1108, 1134, 1155, 1182, 1202, 1231, 1256, 1308, 1393, 1451, 1545, 1582, 1604, 1639, 1661, 1684, 1702, 1732, 1755, 1805, 1823, 1855

Jordan Valley, 40, 43–45, 48–51, 59, 66, 159, 174, 179, 184, 187, 209, 220, 232, 233, 256, 324, 325, 337, 360, 361, 366, 426, 444, 446–449, 455, 466, 516, 538, 543, 544, 550, 578, 601–603, 620, 622, 623, 808, 851, 870–872, 920, 986, 1002, 1041, 1204, 1207, 1732

Josephus, 818, 820, 832, 946, 981, 1032, 1052, 1543, 1881

Józef Milik, 1167

Judah, 500, 501, 507, 513, 514, 517, 539, 546, 579, 620–622, 628, 662, 682, 687, 696, 697, 704, 711, 712, 719, 759, 761, 765, 771, 772, 775–781, 788, 816, 817, 844, 892–894, 912, 988, 998, 1039, 1157, 1161–1163, 1165, 1174, 1175, 1453, 1795, 1796

Judean Antiquities, 818, 820, 832

Jug, 228, 419, 420, 422, 432, 434, 436, 437, 613, 614, 777, 779, 856, 903–908, 912, 951, 1310, 1339, 1479, 1522

Juglet, 368, 378, 381, 430, 432, 436, 439, 614, 735, 738, 739, 901, 905, 908, 915–919

Justinianic plague, 1545, 1548

K

Kabri, 221, 222, 225, 366, 577, 578, 581

Kadesh Barnea, 912, 1205, 1228, 1232, 1238, 1240–1244

Kafr Ana, 1165, 1167

Kafr Juna, 1165, 1167

Kahanov, Y., 1541, 1543, 1547

Kanesh, 1203

Karabournaki, 1469–1487

Karak plateau, 901, 920, 924, 1217

Karduniash, 1203

Kathleen Kenyon, 455

Kaukab Springs, 222, 223, 225, 227–229, 231–233, 237, 238

Kedemoth, 945, 946

Kenaz, 1162, 1163, 1171

Kenites, 990, 995, 1000, 1009, 1160–1162, 1175

Kenizzites, 1160–1162

Kerak Plateau, 927, 1041, 1209, 1210, 1217, 1218, 1862–1864, 1870, 1878–1880, 1883

Kha-em-ter, 1014, 1020, 1021, 1027, 1030

Khirbat al-Jariya (KAJ), 1118, 1122, 1124, 1126, 1133–1151, 1183, 1214, 1215, 1756

Khirbat al-Mudayna, 900, 901

Khirbat al-Mudayna al-ʿAliya (KMA), 1146–1149, 1210, 1211, 1217, 1218

Khirbat al-Mudayna al-Muʿammariyya, 1210

Khirbat al-Mudayna ʿala al-Mujib, 1210

Khirbat Dubab, 1209

Khirbat en-Nahas (KEN), 527–538, 544, 545, 550, 551, 812, 912, 1108–1120, 1122, 1124, 1135, 1137, 1138, 1148, 1150, 1155–1160, 1163, 1167–1170, 1172–1176, 1182, 1214, 1404

Khirbat es-Samra, 840, 841, 843, 846, 847, 850, 863, 868–874, 877, 1168, 1174

Khirbat Hamra Ifdan, 1091, 1093–1099, 1101, 1124, 1182, 1237, 1336, 1347

Khirbat Khatuniyeh, 915

Khirbat Safra, 1210

Kiln, 361, 364, 731, 794–796, 801, 802, 841, 873, 892, 920, 1310, 1431, 1433, 1470, 1479, 1591

Kilwa, 899

Kingdom/kingship, 133, 456, 488, 494, 495, 499–502, 504–507, 510–519, 538, 539, 542, 543, 546–551, 563, 567, 579, 620–622, 626, 629, 631, 636, 688, 700–704, 711, 712, 719, 724, 754, 759, 765, 772–774, 777, 778, 780, 781, 788, 806, 808, 815, 817–820, 829, 831, 832, 893, 894, 902, 924, 979, 995, 1015, 1021, 1029, 1050, 1051, 1054, 1058, 1060–1062, 1065, 1110, 1135, 1161, 1171, 1184, 1207, 1210–1212, 1365, 1404, 1453, 1487, 1728, 1729, 1802, 1807, 1809, 1813–1815, 1817, 1835–1837, 1846, 1848, 1856, 1862, 1864, 1870, 1874, 1878, 1880, 1881, 1883

King Hazael, 790

King's highway, 946, 1207, 1220, 1857

Kinrot, 577, 581, 669

Kissufim, 194, 195, 250, 273

Kotosh, 1436

Krater, 229, 230, 232, 236, 238, 239, 248–250, 260, 346, 348, 374, 613, 614, 735, 742, 868, 903–910, 912, 934, 937, 953, 1262, 1265, 1481, 1676
Kuntur Wasi, 1436
Kuseife, 298, 301–302, 305
KV 10, 1015

L
Lahun, 901, 1210, 1217, 1218
Lake Taypi Chaka, 1434
Lake Titicaca, 1425, 1555
Lamp, 455, 456, 735, 778, 779, 860, 866, 873, 880, 881, 912–914, 1097, 1479
Land and Water Travel Routes, 1561
Late Bronze Age, 456, 465, 474, 479, 501, 506–508, 510–512, 514, 517, 536, 578, 579, 644, 701, 704, 705, 729, 732–734, 754, 763, 815, 927, 951, 965, 1030, 1038–1041, 1050, 1076–1078, 1147, 1165, 1184, 1185, 1202–1205, 1209, 1210, 1220, 1278, 1304, 1312, 1314, 1323–1325, 1327–1332, 1336, 1343, 1345–1347, 1356, 1383, 1384, 1397, 1400, 1470, 1471, 1481, 1495, 1502, 1726, 1730, 1767
Late Period, 1015, 1057–1066, 1422
La Tolita-Tumaca, 1438
Lead, 1181–1194, 1275–1283, 1287–1299
Lead isotope analysis (LIA), 545, 1092, 1100, 1186–1188, 1288, 1289, 1291, 1304, 1313, 1327–1329, 1331, 1334, 1337, 1338, 1340, 1394, 1453, 1454, 1757
Lebanon, 50, 220, 324, 510, 560, 564, 1025–1028, 1037, 1215, 1916
Levitical cities, 945, 946, 948–949, 1003
Libb, 901, 1863, 1877, 1880, 1881
Life history, 271, 1091, 1604, 1717, 1780
Lipéz, 1429
Lithics, 21–23, 85, 99, 102, 179, 238, 268, 286, 324, 325, 650, 815, 1090, 1093, 1422, 1528
Lithology, 1495, 1498
Local community, 214, 718, 719, 773, 1308, 1702, 1705, 1706, 1715, 1717–1719, 1802
Local storytellers and tour guides, 1710–1717
Local voices, 1701–1720
Lod, 962, 966–967, 1165, 1167, 1171, 1174, 1595
Lod Valley, 66, 1167

Longevity, 51, 269, 271, 273, 286, 903, 1471, 1643, 1891
Lost wax, 211, 212, 1364, 1367, 1437, 1438, 1451
Low-altitude aerial photography, 1115, 1118
Luwian, 579, 703
Lysimachos, 1034

M
Ma'agan Mikhael, 1542, 1544
Madaba, 446, 901, 908, 913, 924, 943–950, 953, 957, 1204, 1210, 1216, 1217, 1219, 1220, 1702–1719, 1862–1864, 1875, 1876, 1878–1881, 1883
Madaba Mondays YouTube, 1715–1717
Madaba Plateau, 1210, 1216, 1217, 1219, 1220
Mafraq, 899
Malachite, 14, 1183, 1428, 1434, 1724, 1729
Malnutrition, 275, 286
Mamluk-Ottoman period, 611
Manetho, 1014, 1032, 1034–1036, 1038, 1048
Mantaro Valley, 1427, 1436
Map, 8, 25, 41, 47, 85, 103, 114, 174, 175, 196, 213, 221, 222, 226, 245–247, 270, 326, 361, 362, 392, 454, 573, 575, 576, 583, 642, 682–686, 695, 713, 771, 772, 775, 843–869, 876, 878, 881, 884, 886, 947, 962, 993, 1070, 1089, 1090, 1098, 1107–1126, 1139, 1159, 1163, 1165, 1168, 1170, 1206–1208, 1229–1231, 1233, 1237–1241, 1245–1249, 1257, 1258, 1260, 1305, 1327, 1330, 1398, 1452, 1494, 1495, 1502, 1509, 1512, 1517, 1519, 1527, 1554, 1557, 1558, 1566, 1584, 1585, 1589, 1593, 1605, 1606, 1643, 1647, 1662, 1666, 1668, 1686, 1704, 1708, 1711, 1713, 1736, 1737, 1782, 1811, 1850, 1879, 1889–1891, 1918, 1922–1924, 1926, 1929, 1930
Mapping, 488, 615, 1111, 1115–1120, 1175, 1395, 1512, 1588, 1705, 1735, 1877
Mari, 494, 495, 499, 516, 702, 1026, 1203, 1345, 1770
Maritime, 583, 1205, 1288, 1304, 1313, 1314, 1317, 1486, 1494, 1497, 1508, 1526–1530, 1541, 1543, 1546, 1548, 1554, 1804
Maritime silk road, 584
Marj Rabba, 66, 71, 72, 74, 75, 193, 197, 202, 222, 223, 225, 228–233, 237, 238

Index

Martyrs Church, 1703, 1705, 1708
Mean sea level (msl), 1498, 1502
Media archaeology, 1737
Meditation games, 1737
Mediterranean, 11, 43, 64, 147, 157, 177, 192,
    220, 257, 278, 298, 366, 474, 537, 557,
    574, 670, 684, 776, 893, 915, 974, 981,
    1059, 1071, 1141, 1187, 1238, 1288,
    1304, 1327, 1356, 1397, 1494, 1517,
    1540, 1555, 1582, 1605, 1780, 1802,
    1834, 1855, 1893, 1918
Mediterranean imports, 1204
Megiddo, 136, 174, 183, 250, 346, 365, 371,
    448, 514, 577, 581, 668, 726–727, 729,
    737, 742, 746, 759, 762, 773, 774, 778,
    780, 791, 811–833, 983, 994–999,
    1001, 1003, 1005, 1025, 1130, 1141,
    1184, 1185, 1191, 1278, 1451, 1453,
    1757, 1807, 1808, 1933–1951
Memorandum of Agreement, 1719
Memory-work, 1781–1784
Menasseh Hills survey, 601
Menekhibnekau, 1061, 1064, 1065
Mephaath, 946, 947
Mercury, 1429, 1438
Mesha, 504, 539, 696, 702, 940, 945,
    947–950, 953, 957, 1001, 1211, 1212
Mesha inscription, 945, 947–950, 953, 957,
    1211, 1212
Mesha stele, 539
Mesopotamia, 17, 26, 48, 49, 75, 356, 492,
    495, 512, 515, 525, 541, 564, 567, 581,
    701, 729, 822, 915, 1402, 1403, 1555,
    1803, 1813, 1834, 1936, 1940–1942,
    1946, 1949, 5961
Messuwy, 1020
Metal, 84, 130, 209, 236, 262, 285, 307, 439,
    455, 510, 574, 614, 698, 728, 872,
    1072, 1088, 1135, 1159, 1183, 1207,
    1237, 1276, 1288, 1304, 1323, 1360,
    1392, 1421, 1450, 1470, 1512, 1724,
    1823, 1892, 1912
Metallurgy, 84, 85, 102, 118, 120, 205, 206,
    210, 212, 214, 296, 297, 299, 306, 310,
    312, 324, 336, 815, 1088, 1158, 1161,
    1162, 1175, 1255, 1304, 1306–1316,
    1331, 1356, 1381–1384, 1391–1408,
    1419–1441, 1450, 1732, 1749, 1803
Metal residue, 1483
Metal technology, 455, 1393
Metal tools, 85, 614
Metalworking, 285, 307, 1095, 1135, 1147,
    1159, 1161, 1168, 1172, 1182, 1310,

    1312, 1315, 1340, 1345, 1370, 1382,
    1384, 1419, 1421, 1426, 1427, 1432,
    1433, 1435–1437, 1440, 1470, 1476,
    1481, 1482, 1485–1487
Methone, 1470, 1481, 1486
Mezad Aluf, 272–274
Midbar, 844, 945–947
Middle Bronze Age (MB), 246, 249, 259, 444,
    446–448, 455, 456, 494, 567, 577, 578,
    580, 615, 628, 754, 951, 965, 1037,
    1039, 1075, 1278, 1309, 1331,
    1339–1346, 1494, 1497, 1499, 1501
Mid-Holocene, 12, 13
Mina Perdida, 1433
Mina Primavera, 1433
Miniature, 346, 349, 354, 355, 368, 735, 909,
    911, 915, 916, 918, 919, 1304, 1316,
    1326, 1361, 1366, 1375, 1379, 1482
Minimalist-maximalist debate, 539
Ministry of Tourism and Antiquities
    (MOTA), 1707
Moab, 504, 511, 512, 539, 873, 902, 908, 917,
    920, 924, 925, 940, 945–948, 950, 953,
    956, 957, 1009, 1041, 1125, 1157,
    1158, 1201–1221, 1406, 1809, 1813,
    1814, 1816, 1881
Moche, 1425, 1426, 1429, 1431, 1436, 1439
Modes of Pottery Production, 360, 361,
    363, 368
Monkey, 580, 582
Monochrome pottery, 1479, 1480
Morococha, 1434
Mosaics, 10, 582, 585, 955, 1708–1711,
    1717, 1901
Mould, 100, 1310, 1324, 1326, 1329,
    1331–1333, 1336, 1337, 1339–1342,
    1344, 1346, 1347, 1365
Mšy, 1048–1054
Mt. Illimani, 1434, 1435
Mudayna Thamad, 900–905, 908, 912,
    915, 917–920
Mugharet el-Wardeh, 1452–1455, 1460
Muisca, 1437
Mujib, 947, 949, 1210
Multi-sensory archaeology, 1733
Museum exhibit design, 1648
Museum storeroom, 1703

N
Nabal, 546–550
Nahal Beersheva, 269, 282–284
Nahal Besor, 697, 1121

Nahal Mishmar, 205–213, 255, 281, 314, 1450, 1451
Nahariya, 577, 581
Nahash, 998, 1155–1176
Naipes, 1423, 1424, 1426
Namir Road, 305, 337
Nazca, 1427, 1440
Near East, 44, 45, 49, 52, 61, 74, 84, 285, 297, 355, 356, 391, 474, 479, 488, 491–495, 497–499, 510, 512, 513, 558, 563, 565, 574, 580–585, 724, 823, 871, 1242, 1305, 1345, 1361, 1363, 1383, 1582, 1787
Near Eastern goddess cults, 1728
Near Eastern mythology, 1733
Nebo, 908, 912, 913, 918, 919, 1060, 1878
Necho I, 1059
Necropolis, 199, 212, 428, 1016, 1060, 1061, 1486, 1523, 1594
Negev, 45, 59, 84, 195, 209, 220, 261, 268, 296, 447, 500, 545, 574, 621, 626, 661, 694, 823, 870, 1025, 1092, 1125, 1156, 1187, 1203, 1227, 1308, 1402, 1453, 1546, 1582, 1724, 1778, 1856
Negev desert, 45, 84, 269, 887, 1092, 1453, 1724, 1728, 1732, 1734, 1750, 1778
Negev Highlands, 510, 545, 621, 694, 697–699, 870, 883, 892, 1093, 1095, 1096, 1099, 1100, 1187, 1216, 1227–1250, 1596–1597
Nehemiah, 446, 955, 1160, 1165–1167, 1171, 1172, 1174
Nehushtan, 1161
Nickel, 1394, 1435–1437
Nile fish, 1081
Nimshi, 544, 996–998
19th century, 1901
Nineveh, 915
Nomads, 297, 472–474, 477–479, 481, 493, 495, 498, 499, 506–511, 516, 517, 544, 561, 697, 698, 891–893, 957, 1004, 1009, 1122, 1149, 1212, 1402, 1406, 1732, 1856
North Aegean, 1289, 1469–1487, 1519
North American Archaeology, 541
Northern Europe, 579
Northern Negev, 60, 75, 84, 209, 220, 233, 261, 262, 267–286, 296–298, 306, 309, 500, 515, 545, 574, 661, 697, 879, 1094, 1215, 1216, 1221, 1582, 1732
Nova Trajana Bostra, 946

O

Oman, 1392–1396, 1398–1401, 1407, 1408
Omride Dynasty, 806, 808, 811, 815, 832
One Place-Many Stories, 1711, 1714–1715
Ono, 1165, 1167, 1174
Onomasticon, 1169
Open pit, 1430
Ophiolite, 1394–1396, 1398, 1604
Ophrah, 985, 986, 1001, 1008, 1163, 1165, 1171
Optically stimulated luminescence (OSL), 1499
Oracle of the Lamb, 1033, 1035
Ore deposit, 1092, 1187, 1304, 1306, 1307, 1311, 1326–1330, 1339, 1341, 1343, 1345, 1428, 1429, 1453, 1458–1460
Organic Residue Analysis, 966
Osiris, 1061, 1365
Osmium isotopes composition (Os-IC), 1454, 1457, 1459, 1463
Osorkon I, 543
Ossuary, 197, 236, 303
Osteoporosis, 276, 281
Ostrich eggs, 439, 580, 1072, 1081
Overland, 700, 940, 1004, 1328, 1554, 1556–1558, 1561, 1567, 1571, 1573, 1574
Oxhide ingot, 1190, 1193, 1306, 1313, 1314, 1324–1331, 1346, 1347, 1361, 1363, 1381–1383

P

Padihor, 1061
Paleobotanical sampling, 1135, 1146, 1148–1150, 1221
Paleobotany, 1135
Paleopathology, 286
Palestine, 60, 273, 284, 286, 455, 560, 685, 845, 850, 862, 900, 912, 927, 1023, 1040, 1157, 1160, 1169, 1172, 1241, 1595, 1862, 1875, 1922, 1934
Palpa, 1433
Pandemic, 1545, 1678, 1702, 1704, 1712, 1738, 1787, 1939
Parallel evolution, 327, 353–356, 558, 907, 908, 910, 911, 913
Partnership, 996, 1598, 1712, 1714, 1718
Pastoralism, 10, 15–17, 21–27, 29–31, 64, 76, 84, 165, 268, 474, 492, 841, 892, 1402, 1803, 1834

Index 1965

PChassinat III, 1013, 1034, 1036
Pella, 40, 993, 1010, 1094, 1204
Peqi'in, 195, 225, 227, 240, 255, 273, 275, 277, 278, 281
Peqi'in Cave, 222, 227, 229, 231, 234–236, 337, 353
Peqi'in Ben Shemen, 195, 273
Perforated disks, 233, 234, 240
Periodicity, 507
Periostitis, 275, 281
Persian Gulf, 580, 583, 1393
Peru, 1420–1422, 1425, 1426, 1430, 1431, 1433–1438
Petrography, 350–352, 775, 1217, 1237, 1518
Pharaoh Shoshenq I, 690, 818
PHarris I, 1027, 1029, 1031–1033
Philistia, 578, 584, 625–636, 640, 661, 669, 682, 704, 775
Phoenicia, 510, 566, 584, 775, 808, 913, 916, 981, 997, 1244, 1289, 1400, 1523, 1728, 1737, 1912
Photogrammetry, 1108, 1110, 1111, 1113, 1585, 1587–1589, 1619, 1621, 1638, 1642, 1680, 1686, 1689, 1705, 1710
Piccirillo, 908, 1708, 1882
Pigs, 60, 64, 70, 75, 270, 283, 578, 661, 672
Pine Valley, 1027, 1028, 1030
Pitheones, 1475
Pit smelting, 1453
Placer, 1429, 1430, 1432
Plano-convex ingot, 1192, 1345
Plants, 13, 19, 21, 51, 118, 124, 163, 282, 510, 578, 878, 1159, 1424, 1439
Policy makers, 1717, 1816
Political economy, 994, 1392, 1396
Pomey, 1544, 1547
Pools of Heshbon, 944
Posthumanist design, 1727
Potter's Oracle, 1033, 1036
Pottery, 23, 40, 49, 51, 60–62, 64–70, 115, 120, 127, 136, 174–179, 182, 186, 208, 222, 228–233, 239, 246, 249–253, 257–260, 300, 304, 327, 344, 359–383, 394, 412, 440, 446–449, 456–458, 544, 574, 609, 611, 626–628, 634, 645, 690, 712, 746, 766, 774–775, 789, 826, 847, 873, 901, 927, 934, 1079, 1212–1220, 1310, 1339, 1440, 1477–1481, 1487, 1519–1525, 1542, 1677, 1755, 1833, 1877
Pottery and patterns of trade and social intercourse, 28, 383, 1220
Pottery trade and cultural diffusion, 383, 1487

Pranayama, 1725, 1740
Precious Stones, 1072, 1079, 1081
Prehistoric Bronze Age, 628, 1345, 1346, 1617, 1621
Preserving past, 1691, 1718
Prestige objects, 260, 261, 550, 574, 575
Primary burial, 122–124, 127, 135, 137, 199, 202, 271, 273
Primary stakeholders, 1717
Production, 17, 26, 40, 44, 52, 61, 71, 74, 85, 98, 115, 117, 120, 132, 136, 212, 238, 268, 283, 301, 306–314, 334, 337, 359–383, 391, 449, 509, 544, 661, 703, 716, 775, 840, 915, 1030, 1081, 1090–1102, 1110, 1120, 1173, 1193, 1212, 1275–1283, 1288, 1304, 1310, 1331, 1381, 1393, 1402, 1422, 1435, 1451, 1462, 1476, 1546, 1587, 1726, 1731, 1743, 1804, 1834
Psamtek, 1059
Petrography, 350–352, 775, 1217, 1237, 1518
Ptolemaios I, 1035
Ptolemaios VIII, 1035, 1036
Pucara, 1434
Punanave, 1422
Punon, 1161, 1169, 1256
Purple-dyed textiles, 1071, 1074, 1081
Putushio, 1434
Pyrotechnology, 364, 382

Q
Qasile, 577, 640, 642, 671–673, 966, 969
Qasr Saliyeh, 918
Qasr Shamamuk, 915
Qasr Za'faran I, 919, 1872, 1873
Qatna, 1026, 1203
Qeya, 1431
Queen of Madaba, 1708, 1710
Quimbaletes, 1430
Qurayyah Painted Ware (QPW), 545, 1204, 1212, 1242

R
Ramaditas, 1434
Ramallah, 1165
Rameses II, 1016, 1023, 1025, 1030, 1033, 1041, 1050
Ramses III, 1024, 1031–1033
Rechabites, 517, 1175
Recycling of metal, 337, 1075, 1283, 1298, 1305, 1306

Red Sea, 13, 414, 578, 580, 776, 1053, 1173, 1232, 1243
Red slip, 231, 232, 238, 239, 436, 613, 902, 912, 919, 932–934, 1217, 1259, 1260
Rehov, 543–546, 550, 578, 788, 791–807, 996–998, 1002, 1004, 1189, 1451, 1453
Remote English language training, 1709
Remote tour training, 1709
Remote training, 1709, 1712
Repoussé, 1425, 1426, 1436, 1437
Richard, A.I., 1812
Richard, M.P., 286
Richard, S., 446, 447, 466, 563, 1702, 1704, 1717
Rieth, T.M., 583
Roman Cardo, 1703
Rome-Roy, 1022
Rujim el-'Atik, 1167, 1168, 1174
Rujm, 1124, 1214, 1241, 1859, 1860, 1863, 1868, 1873, 1874
Rupert L. Chapman III, 1169
Rural/village social-complexity, 466

S

Saba', 1203
Sahab, 627, 902, 1204, 1210
Sahem tombs, 1204
Sailing, 583, 1317, 1495, 1501, 1503, 1526, 1528, 1542, 1543
Saint Gervais, 1541
Salango, 1434
Saliya, 919, 1857, 1863, 1864, 1867, 1870, 1872, 1875, 1880
Samaria, 41, 366, 377, 756, 771–781, 829, 892, 913, 972, 979, 981, 1001–1004, 1934
Sampling bias, 1147, 1148
San Francisco Bay Area, 1553–1574, 1746
Saqqara, 631, 1058, 1060, 1061, 1063–1065
Sardinia, 581, 1189, 1192, 1277, 1280, 1282, 1289, 1306, 1313, 1314, 1324, 1327, 1833
Sá-tu-na, 1025
Saul, 545–550, 702, 949, 952, 983, 985, 986, 989, 998, 1008, 1010, 1813
Scanning electron microscopy, 42, 86, 1138
Scribes, 494, 501, 515, 539, 540, 542, 543, 1017, 1022, 1024, 1025, 1027, 1030, 1035, 1836
Secondary burial, 123, 124, 127, 129, 130, 135–137, 202, 234, 235, 239, 258, 262, 268, 272–274, 1866

Secondary products, 17, 24, 25, 52, 60–62, 70, 71, 74–77, 118, 120, 268, 283, 285, 296, 297, 870, 1331
Second Jewish Revolt, 1169–1171
Sedentism, 283, 284, 473, 474, 482, 490, 491, 498, 499, 511, 1122, 1406
Sediment cores, 1422, 1495, 1496, 1512, 1513
Seismic profiles, 1495, 1496
Serçe Limani, 1540, 1541
Serious games, 1648, 1649, 1660, 1741–1743, 1748–1750
Sethnakht, 1022, 1030–1033
Sethos II, 1014–1022, 1031, 1033
Settlement, 8, 51, 59, 84, 115, 174, 193, 212, 220, 247, 268, 295, 325, 344, 361, 390, 414, 446, 454, 476, 539, 610, 631, 640, 682, 713, 726, 754, 772, 815, 840, 901, 924, 943, 965, 980, 1014, 1070, 1087, 1121, 1138, 1160, 1182, 1202, 1227, 1256, 1306, 1329, 1393, 1440, 1460, 1470, 1494, 1527, 1546, 1557, 1591, 1606, 1770, 1781, 1856, 1902, 1912
Shaft furnace, 1455–1460, 1463
Shaft tombs, 431, 1057–1066, 1866
Shallow underwater sites, 1508
Shared heritage, 660, 1717, 1718
Shasu, 507, 508, 510, 957, 1204, 1209, 1210
Sheep, 15, 17, 18, 22, 24, 25, 27, 60–64, 74, 76, 87, 89, 90, 92, 93, 95–98, 101, 102, 120, 164, 165, 237, 238, 282, 283, 302, 346, 464, 546, 649, 652, 653, 657–669, 671–673, 690, 704, 841, 844, 858, 860, 866, 869–871, 878, 888, 891, 893, 949, 1039, 1311, 1510, 1606, 1803, 1864
Shells, 51, 124, 209, 306–308, 439, 580, 582, 969, 971, 972, 974, 1080, 1238, 1422, 1425, 1497–1499, 1501, 1539–1549, 1556, 1629, 1839, 1845, 1847, 1849–1851, 1870, 1878, 1879, 1930
Shephelah, 174, 178, 245, 246, 249, 250, 257–260, 444, 447, 545, 690, 694, 696–698, 704, 711–719, 729, 765, 777, 780, 1157, 1163, 1168, 1170, 1174, 1213, 1215, 1221, 1454
Shipping, 1173, 1304, 1317, 1541
Shipwreck, 583, 1076, 1205, 1298, 1324, 1325, 1327–1329, 1331, 1347, 1508, 1527–1530, 1540–1544, 1546, 1547
Shiqmim, 61, 66, 71, 72, 74, 75, 83–109, 127, 193–195, 262, 269, 272–283, 285, 300, 305, 306, 353
Shoshenq I, 543, 545, 791, 806–808, 811–833
Shoshenq's Campaign, 713, 819–821, 832

Index

Sicán, 1422, 1425, 1437
Sickle blade, 177–179, 182, 184, 186, 187, 233, 238–240, 270, 282, 299, 302, 307, 310, 324, 872
Sidon, 1001, 1025, 1193, 1204, 1813, 1918
Sihon, 944, 946
Silk road, 584, 1876
Silver, 458, 545, 574, 579, 581, 820, 1031, 1072, 1075, 1081, 1192, 1276, 1287–1299, 1312, 1393, 1394, 1396, 1422–1431, 1434–1441, 1454, 1481, 1719, 1824, 1827, 1829–1832, 1835–1837, 1906
Simon Bar Kohkba, 1169
Sinai, 200, 201, 477, 506, 564, 988, 1039, 1040, 1079, 1092, 1094–1096, 1183, 1188, 1189, 1203, 1205, 1228, 1229, 1232–1236, 1238–1240, 1243, 1244, 1392, 1393, 1395, 1729
6th century CE, 1256, 1263, 1708
Skeletal pathology, 275, 281
Skeletons, 62, 93, 102, 115, 116, 122, 127, 132, 456, 635, 669, 725, 733, 747, 1539–1549, 1892, 1905
Skilled potters, 360, 364, 374, 380–382
Slag, 85, 545, 698, 1071, 1095, 1108, 1110–1114, 1116, 1118–1120, 1134, 1137, 1138, 1140, 1158, 1167, 1168, 1174, 1182, 1213–1216, 1239, 1241, 1256, 1304, 1311, 1312, 1329, 1331, 1339–1341, 1345–1347, 1392, 1396, 1397, 1399–1401, 1407, 1408, 1422, 1431, 1433, 1434, 1440, 1452–1463, 1481, 1483, 1615, 1724, 1743, 1747, 1750, 1755–1758, 1764, 1767, 1770, 1823
Slice marks, 86, 87, 92, 98–102
Smelter, 1158, 1159, 1173, 1397, 1407, 1430, 1440, 1455, 1457, 1459, 1461, 1463, 1724–1726, 1730–1734, 1737–1739, 1742, 1743, 1747, 1749, 1750
Smelting, 268, 270, 509, 510, 698, 701, 1088, 1091–1097, 1099–1101, 1108–1110, 1122–1124, 1134, 1135, 1137, 1138, 1149, 1155, 1157, 1159, 1160, 1168, 1171, 1173, 1183, 1184, 1186, 1193, 1237, 1304, 1306–1312, 1316, 1329, 1331, 1339–1341, 1343–1346, 1392, 1393, 1396, 1397, 1399, 1407, 1422, 1428, 1429, 1431, 1433–1436, 1439, 1440, 1449–1464, 1723–1750, 1823
Snacking behavior, 1135, 1149

Solomon, 500–503, 513–518, 537, 540, 545, 585, 735, 745, 755, 773, 788, 815–818, 820, 822, 827, 829, 831, 832, 944, 981, 983, 997, 1157, 1159, 1162, 1172, 1173, 1813, 1849
Sorojche, 1429
South Arabia, 47, 559, 699, 701
South Coast Peru, 1420, 1440
Southeast Asia, 577–579, 583–585
Southern Levant, 24, 40, 59, 85, 113, 165, 177, 201, 205, 220, 259, 267, 295, 323, 343, 360, 390, 444, 472, 536, 556, 574, 602, 635, 644, 681, 724, 771, 795, 812, 839, 917, 940, 1072, 1087, 1108, 1155, 1183, 1202, 1255, 1277, 1289, 1324, 1392, 1450, 1540, 1582, 1615, 1732, 1755, 1798, 1802, 1951
Spain, 559, 579, 581, 1549, 1757
Spatial analysis, 349, 350, 1605, 1672–1674, 1679
Spatial and temporal reconstruction, 793
Spatial distribution, 301, 309, 351, 445, 448, 664–668, 1118, 1450, 1582, 1618, 1619
Spheres of interaction, 541, 582, 583, 585, 586, 1383
Spices, 585, 704, 1244, 1314, 1863
State complexity, 538, 539
Stature, 280–281
Storejar, 732, 903, 904
Storerooms, 644, 645, 648, 664, 666, 667, 734, 735, 912, 1475, 1703, 1875
StoryCenter, 1707, 1709, 1713, 1720
Strategies, 16, 19, 51–53, 59, 60, 62, 71, 118, 120, 163, 164, 282, 283, 314, 474, 483, 652, 660, 661, 672, 892, 996, 1053, 1099, 1101, 1102, 1108, 1313, 1363, 1370, 1463, 1464, 1548, 1609, 1643, 1644, 1677, 1689, 1718, 1726, 1727, 1737, 1738, 1742, 1750, 1761, 1767, 1769, 1796, 1805
Subsistence, 15, 16, 19, 21, 28, 51, 75, 118, 120, 133, 147–168, 272, 283, 296, 302, 324, 430, 473, 474, 477, 479–481, 492, 496, 510, 515, 539, 690, 691, 694, 701, 892, 1101, 1146, 1147, 1209–1211, 1220, 1221, 1305, 1308, 1316, 1555, 1606
Subsistence base, 473, 479, 492, 539, 701, 1146, 1316
Subterranean, 116, 193, 201, 268, 299, 307, 1062, 1159, 1402, 1470, 1475–1477

Sustainability, 269, 888, 890, 1644, 1703, 1704, 1718
Sustainable Cultural Heritage through Engagement of Local Communities Project (SCHEP), 1702, 1703, 1713
Suḫu, 1203
Swamimalai, 1775
Symposion, 1480
Sympotic vessels, 1479
Syria, 60, 77, 164, 324, 356, 444, 447, 448, 495, 512, 515, 550, 560, 564, 567, 578–581, 801, 913, 915, 917, 946, 1018, 1035, 1262, 1521, 1545, 1755, 1756, 1767, 1769, 1855, 1901, 1911, 1916, 1918, 1921, 1940, 1942

T
Tablet, 303, 763, 1004, 1040, 1108, 1330, 1435, 1644–1646, 1890
Tabular scraper, 103, 201, 270, 299, 307, 324
Taharqo, 1059
Tale of Two Brothers, 1020, 1022, 1024, 1025, 1027–1030, 1033–1034, 1036, 1037
Tall Abu Kharaz, 1204
Tall al-Magass, 1093
Tall al-ʿUmayri, 924, 953, 1146–1148, 1219
Tall es-Saʔidiyeh, 1204
Tall Hujayrat al-Ghuzlan, 1093
Tall Jawa, 902, 908, 910, 912, 915, 917, 1210, 1219, 1220
Tantamani, 1059
Tap Slag, 1460
Taquia, 1431
Tarapacá Vieja, 1440
Taybeh, 1163, 1165
Tayma, 1203, 1212, 1244
Technology, 20, 59, 84, 120, 224, 268, 307, 324, 443, 455, 482, 574, 635, 644, 702, 1058, 1088, 1108, 1220, 1290, 1304, 1356, 1393, 1419, 1453, 1471, 1539, 1559, 1582, 1604, 1628, 1661, 1684, 1703, 1725, 1781, 1796, 1824, 1893
Teeth, 124, 236, 271, 275, 277–281, 283, 308, 465, 466, 649, 652, 657, 658, 666, 699, 1275–1283
Tel ʿAmal, 544
Tel Dan, 65, 67, 68, 70, 513, 539, 826, 830, 1019, 1185, 1191, 1207
Tel Dan stele, 772
Teleilat Ghassul, 40, 66, 71, 72, 75, 127, 256, 306, 310, 353

Tel Erani, 368, 393, 402–403, 405, 407, 577
Tell Atchana, 453–466
Tell Deir ʿAlla, 1041, 1204
Tell El-Khalifieh, 1157, 1159, 1173
Tell es-Safi/Gath, 91, 258, 448, 543, 625, 626, 640, 661, 662, 668, 718, 777, 780, 1452–1454, 1460–1462
Tel Masos, 538, 696–697, 1205, 1240
Tel Nami, 578, 1494
Tel Rehov, 543–546, 550, 551, 578, 759, 773, 788–803, 805–808, 833, 1185, 1189, 1451, 1453
Tel Sheva, 298–301, 305, 306, 311
Terqa, 580, 581
Tewosret, 1016, 1018, 1031
Textiles, 61, 74, 76, 120, 163, 268, 510, 579–582, 712, 714, 716, 717, 719, 934, 1071, 1074, 1081, 1339, 1425, 1440, 1470, 1829, 1833
The Other Side of the Jordan, 1157–1160, 1167, 1173
Thera, 580, 582
Thermaic Gulf, 1470, 1471, 1477, 1479, 1481, 1486, 1487
Thessaloniki, 1471–1473
3D model, 1590, 1631, 1633, 1639, 1640, 1643, 1644, 1670, 1686, 1709, 1713, 1715, 1719
3D modelling, 1703
Timber, 578, 581, 1141, 1470, 1472, 1540, 1541, 1544, 1547, 1893
Timna, 509, 510, 545, 640, 690, 694, 698, 699, 701, 704, 808, 1092–1095, 1135, 1142, 1147, 1149, 1159, 1173, 1175, 1181–1194, 1202, 1205
Timnian, 200, 311, 1093, 1237
Tin, 574, 579, 581, 1294, 1305, 1306, 1324, 1327–1328, 1330, 1334, 1364, 1369, 1370, 1432, 1435, 1436, 1439, 1833, 1834, 1842
Tiwanaku, 1422, 1425, 1426, 1431, 1434–1437, 1440
Tocochimbo, 1431
Tour guides, 1705, 1710–1719
Tourism, 1630, 1649–1651, 1702–1710, 1716, 1717, 1719, 1728, 1779
Tourism Capital of 2022, 1716
Tpn/tbn, 956
Trade, 28, 44, 60, 268, 306, 366, 414, 492, 541, 574, 670, 692, 719, 772, 808, 872, 903, 940, 1001, 1071, 1088, 1123, 1134, 1175, 1193, 1202, 1228, 1283,

Index

1288, 1304, 1324, 1396, 1434, 1470, 1508, 1542, 1555, 1803, 1823, 1855, 1896, 1916

Trade routes, 414, 544, 579, 692, 699, 701, 1205–1208, 1212, 1215–1221, 1236–1245, 1248, 1250, 1314, 1404, 1810, 1862, 1864, 1872, 1875, 1876, 1882, 1883

Traditional Jordanian buildings, 1705, 1708

Training, 70, 77, 841, 844, 862, 1587, 1645, 1646, 1685, 1704, 1705, 1707, 1709, 1712, 1713, 1719

Training courses, 1702, 1713

Transgression, 1496, 1502

Transjordan, 123, 446, 506–508, 516, 560, 808, 873, 900, 908, 944, 946–949, 951–953, 957, 1010, 1040, 1041, 1156, 1157, 1173, 1203–1205, 1207, 1209–1213, 1216, 1220, 1221, 1742, 1809, 1855

Tripod, 545, 908, 913, 953, 1379, 1710

Troodos, 1304, 1308, 1309, 1311, 1329, 1346, 1395, 1510, 1604–1606

Trujillo, 1426, 1430

Tulán, 1426, 1433

Tule reed balsa watercraft, 1554

Tumbaga, 1422, 1425, 1426, 1435, 1436, 1439

Tumi knife, 1437

Tupu pin, 1426

Tuthmosis III, 1071, 1075

Tuyère, 1310–1312, 1346, 1399, 1432, 1457, 1460–1462

Tyche mosaic, 1708

Type II diabetes, 459, 462, 465

Tyre, 911, 1162, 1813

U

Udjahorresnet, 1061, 1062, 1065

Uluburun, 1076, 1324, 1325, 1328, 1329, 1331, 1347

ʿUmayri, 1204, 1210

Underwater Pottery Assemblages, 1508

UNESCO, 1640, 1702, 1718, 1912

United Monarchy, 476, 484, 497, 500–519, 537, 791, 815, 822, 829, 831, 832, 1157

United States Agency for International Development (USAID), 1702, 1703

Unmanned aerial vehicle (UAV), 1588, 1607, 1608, 1618, 1621

Uqdat al-Bakrah, 1408

U.S. Department of State, 1703, 1705, 1709, 1717

V

Valley, 40, 59, 159, 174, 200, 209, 220, 245, 298, 324, 360, 390, 414, 444, 455, 538, 564, 578, 601, 671, 695, 714, 729, 755, 772, 788, 813, 842, 920, 986, 1015, 1076, 1092, 1135, 1157, 1184, 1202, 1229, 1402, 1420, 1450, 1555, 1728, 1757, 1835, 1863

Valorize, 1719

Van De Velde, C.W.M., 1170

Village, 15, 52, 53, 59, 63, 76, 103–106, 119, 120, 125, 127, 129, 133–137, 165, 193, 220, 257, 258, 261, 262, 268, 272, 284, 295–314, 383, 455, 466, 476, 498, 503, 602, 640, 658, 682, 684–687, 694, 700, 759, 762, 944, 955–957, 981, 1002, 1015–1017, 1165, 1170–1172, 1174, 1209, 1306, 1308, 1309, 1311, 1331, 1399, 1404, 1405, 1425, 1433, 1434, 1454, 1545–1555, 1557, 1561, 1562, 1566, 1568–1573, 1595, 1605, 1607, 1611, 1613, 1615, 1617, 1619, 1621, 1781–1793, 1796, 1804, 1807, 1812, 1836, 1844, 1856, 1858–1860, 1862, 1864, 1875, 1876, 1878, 1896, 1898, 1903, 1915

Violin figurines, 236, 237, 239, 240

Virtual reality, 1640, 1659, 1692, 1701–1720, 1724, 1726, 1733, 1735, 1740, 1743, 1744, 1749

Virtual tourists, 1715

V-shaped bowl, 223, 229–231, 285, 299, 300, 302–304, 307, 310, 314, 343–357, 432

W

Wadi al-Hasa, 426, 428, 1207, 1209, 1217

Wadi al-Mujib, 1207, 1210

Wadi al-Nukhayla, 1210

Wadi al-Raki, 1397, 1399

Wadi Araba, 12, 17, 22, 25, 26, 426, 1095

Wadi Arabah, 1123, 1125, 1141, 1146, 1157, 1160, 1162, 1165, 1167, 1171–1174, 1182, 1202, 1228, 1229, 1231, 1232, 1234, 1235, 1240, 1241, 1243, 1245, 1248, 1392

Wadi el-Makkukh, 273

Wadi Faynan, 8, 19, 31, 509, 1123, 1124, 1146–1149, 1173, 1182, 1256, 1264, 1823

Wadi feinan, 3, 4, 47, 447, 698, 1237

Wadi Fidan 4, 1093, 1182

Wadi Mujib, 901, 924, 940, 956, 1217, 1703, 1863, 1864, 1866, 1876, 1877, 1880, 1881, 1883

Wadi Murabba'at (Nahal Darga), 1170

Wadi Thamad, 901, 1863, 1864, 1867

Wanka, 1436

Wari, 1422, 1435, 1440

War Kabud, 915

Water reservoir, 619, 860, 944, 1857, 1878

Waywaka, 1433

Wellhausen paradigm, 817

Wood, 40–42, 44–47, 49, 334, 369, 690, 829, 1141, 1147, 1308, 1361, 1455, 1546, 1757, 1766, 1893

Workshops, 233, 268, 307, 311, 360, 361, 364, 371, 374, 383, 580, 712, 778, 902, 905, 908, 917, 920, 1071, 1073, 1076, 1081, 1095, 1097, 1101, 1160, 1173, 1182, 1237, 1307, 1310, 1312, 1315, 1329, 1331, 1365, 1382, 1408, 1422, 1434, 1461, 1470, 1471, 1473, 1475–1487, 1615, 1629, 1702, 1709, 1712, 1720, 1728, 1731, 1739, 1906

World Health Organization (WHO), 269, 1702

World heritage sites, 22, 1640, 1702, 1912

WT-13, 901, 908, 913, 917, 918

Y

Yassi Ada, 1541, 1544

Yavneh, 577, 581, 644, 1543

Yehimilk, 542

Yiron, 221, 231

Yoel Elitzur, 1169

Yposkapta, 1475

Yurza, 1204

Z

Zarqa Ma, 901

Zawiye, 915

Zebu cow, 578

Zooarchaeology, 103

Zoom, 947, 1259, 1710, 1712, 1713, 1725, 1738, 1739

Zoomorphic ossuaries, 236, 238

Zoonoses, 284